PENGUIN BOOKS

GRANT

Ron Chernow is the prizewinning author of six previous books and the recipient of the 2015 National Humanities Medal. His first book, *The House of Morgan*, won the National Book Award; *Washington: A Life* won the Pulitzer Prize for Biography; and *Alexander Hamilton*—the inspiration for the Broadway musical—won the American History Book Prize. A past president of PEN America, Chernow has been the recipient of eight honorary doctorates. He resides in Brooklyn, New York.

ronchernow.com

Praise for Ron Chernow's *Grant*

"This is a good time for Ron Chernow's fine biography of Ulysses S. Grant to appear. . . . As history, it is remarkable, full of fascinating details sure to make it interesting both to those with the most cursory knowledge of Grant's life and to those who have read his memoirs or any of several previous biographies. . . . For all its scholarly and literary strengths, this book's greatest service is to remind us of Grant's significant achievements at the end of the war and after, which have too long been overlooked and are too important today to be left in the dark. . . . As Americans continue the struggle to defend justice and equality in our tumultuous and divisive era, we need to know what Grant did when our country's very existence hung in the balance. If we still believe in forming a more perfect union, his steady and courageous example is more valuable than ever."
—Bill Clinton, *The New York Times Book Review*

"Marvelous . . . Chernow's biography gives us a deep look into this complicated but straightforward man, and into a troubled time in our history that still echoes today."
—Thomas E. Ricks, *Foreign Policy*

"Chernow rewards the reader with considerable life-and-times background, clear-eyed perspective, sympathy that stops short of sycophancy, and gritty and intimate details."
—*The Boston Globe*

"*Grant* is vast and panoramic in ways that history buffs will love. Books of its caliber by writers of Chernow's stature are rare, and this one qualifies as a major event. . . . Chernow is clearly out to find undiscovered nobility in his story, and he succeeds; he also finds uncannily prescient tragedy. There are ways in which Grant's times eerily resemble our own. . . . Indispensable."
—*The New York Times*

"Ron Chernow . . . has written an expansive new life of Grant. It is a work of striking anecdotes, skillful pacing, and poignant judgments."
—David W. Blight, *The New York Review of Books*

"Ron Chernow's monumental biography of the eighteenth president is essential to understanding our race-conscious nation today." —*Bloomberg*

"Chernow's Grant is as relevant a modern figure as his Hamilton. His Grant is a reminder that the very best American leaders can be, and should be, self-made, hard-working, modest for themselves and ambitious for their nation, future looking, tolerant, and with a heart for the poor. . . . Chernow turns the life of yet another . . . misunderstood figure from U.S. currency into narrative gold." —*Slate*

"Ron Chernow's biography reminds our twenty-first-century selves of the distinction between character and personality." —*National Review*

"Chernow's special gift is to present a complete and compelling picture of his subjects. His biographies do not offer up marble deities on a pedestal; he gives us flesh-and-blood human beings and helps us understand what made them tick. Just as he did with George Washington and Alexander Hamilton, Chernow brings Ulysses S. Grant to life. At the end of the book, the reader feels as if he knows the man. . . . A magnificent book . . . This is richly rewarding and compelling reading."
—*The Christian Science Monitor*

"In 1948, a survey of historians ranked Ulysses S. Grant as the second-worst American president. . . . But recent surveys have been kinder. Grant now lands in the middle, thanks to his extraordinarily progressive work on race relations. . . . Ron Chernow's 1,100-page biography may crown Grant's restoration. . . . Mr. Chernow argues persuasively that Grant has been badly misunderstood." —*The Economist*

"Chernow writes definitive biography of Ulysses S. Grant . . . [An] essential read . . . Restores Grant to the pantheon of great Americans." —*Newsday*

"Grant's true story needed desperately to be told. Thanks to a great historian, it has."
—Chris Matthews, *Parade Magazine*

"Reading Ron Chernow's new biography, a truly mammoth examination of the life of Ulysses S. Grant, one is struck by the humanity—both the pitiful frailty and the incredible strength—of its subject." —*Philadelphia Inquirer*

"Masterful and often poignant . . . Chernow's gracefully written biography, which promises to be the definitive work on Grant for years to come, is fully equal to the man's remarkable story." —*Minneapolis Star Tribune*

"Reading this compelling book, it's hard to imagine that we'll continue to define Grant by these scandals rather than all he accomplished in winning the war and doing his best to make peace, on inclusive terms that would be fair to all."

—*Milwaukee Journal Sentinel*

"Chernow's new book is the latest and most far-reaching assessment [of Grant]. He is an indefatigable researcher with a wonderfully readable narrative style. He is able to convey with clarity the complex details of military campaigns and political developments."

—Eric Foner, *The Times Literary Supplement* (London)

"What's most compelling about *Grant* is the author's search for the keys to Grant's personality. If Mr. Chernow can't completely solve the riddle of the Sphinx-like Ulysses, he does succeed in giving us as complete a portrait of him as we're likely to see for a long time."

—*Pittsburgh Post-Gazette*

"Ron Chernow is the leading biographer of our era. . . . His latest biography, *Grant*, presents a clear and meticulously researched narrative of one of America's greatest military leaders and presidents."

—*Global Atlanta*

"Ron Chernow has written acclaimed biographies of George Washington and Alexander Hamilton. . . . His latest book, *Grant*, cements his reputation as America's preeminent historical biographer. Upon finishing the book, the reader will feel privileged to have spent time with one of America's true heroes whose virtues far surpassed his faults."

—*Lincoln Journal Star*

"Once I began *Grant*, I had trouble putting it down each evening. If the point of a great historical book is to have a reader totally rethink their predisposed biases about an event or subject, *Grant* clearly falls into that category."

—*The Lowell Sun*

"Throughout his rich, lively, and well-paced narrative, Chernow develops a case against the 'pernicious stereotypes' that have dogged Grant's reputation. . . . Grant could not have wished for a better or more winning advocate."

—*Literary Review* (London)

"*Grant* is an impressively researched and elegantly written tome about one of our country's most important figures."

—*Cincinnati City Beat*

"The recent explosion in Grant scholarship has shed new light on and created new appreciation for our eighteenth president. . . . Of the books on Grant written in the past few decades, Chernow's *Grant* is the best and comes closest to presenting a full picture of a man historians have found difficult to decipher."

—*The Federalist*

"Destined to be a classic biography, the author's details of battles in which General Grant was involved are worthy of inclusion in any military history of the Civil War. . . . What is intriguing are Chernow's descriptions of every major character involved in Grant's life. . . . This biography confirms again Ron Chernow's masterful talent."   —Frank J. Williams, *Civil War Book Review*

"Chernow's new book, *Grant*, is deft at navigating tricky currents. It is a stirring defense of an underrated general and unfairly maligned president. Its great contribution to the popular understanding of the Civil War and its aftermath is to expose the roots of the longstanding bias against Grant."   —*The New Republic*

"A magisterial biography."   —*San Francisco Chronicle*

"Chernow has done it again with a landmark work on the much-maligned Ulysses S. Grant. Like his earlier biographies of Washington and Alexander Hamilton, it is deeply researched, eminently balanced, and fair. . . . Chernow gives us a military genius who understood the full scope of the war . . . and a sometimes inept president who . . . made his highest priority the protection of the lives and rights of freed slaves."   —*The American Scholar*

"Ron Chernow's new biography, *Grant*, is Extra Large. . . . Not one of those pages is boring. He is a compelling storyteller . . . he adds rich detail and brings to vivid life the reticent, unprepossessing, but resolute man whom Walt Whitman called 'nothing heroic . . . and yet the greatest hero.'"
—Geoffrey C. Ward, *The Wall Street Journal*

"Chernow's book about Grant is without a doubt one of the most powerful and insightful biographies I've ever read."   —*The Charlotte Observer*

"Chernow's defense of Grant's military ability is persuasive. One of the great strengths of his biography is his serious attention to Grant's postwar career. Chernow believes Grant's presidency has been ignored or unfairly treated by historians, and makes a strong case that President Grant played an integral role in defending the civil rights of the freed people. He has now provided us with a compelling explanation of why Grant was indeed the first soldier of the Civil War."
—*History News Network*

"*Grant* is a 1,000-page tome that reads more like Tolstoy than a scholarly work."
—*Pittsburgh City Paper*

ALSO BY RON CHERNOW

Washington: A Life

Alexander Hamilton

Titan: The Life of John D. Rockefeller, Sr.

*The Death of the Banker: The Decline and Fall of the
Great Financial Dynasties and the Triumph of the Small Investor*

*The Warburgs: The Twentieth-Century Odyssey of
a Remarkable Jewish Family*

*The House of Morgan: An American Banking
Dynasty and the Rise of Modern Finance*

GRANT

RON CHERNOW

PENGUIN BOOKS

PENGUIN BOOKS

An imprint of Penguin Random House LLC
375 Hudson Street
New York, New York 10014
penguinrandomhouse.com

First published in the United States of America by Penguin Press,
an imprint of Penguin Random House LLC, 2017
Published in Penguin Books 2018

Maps by Jeffrey L. Ward
Illustration credits appear on pages 1033–1034.

ISBN 9780143110637 (paperback)

THE LIBRARY OF CONGRESS HAS CATALOGED THE HARDCOVER EDITION AS FOLLOWS:
Names: Chernow, Ron, author.
Title: Grant / Ron Chernow.
Description: New York : Penguin Press, 2017.
Identifiers: LCCN 2017025263 (print) | LCCN 2017027493 (ebook) | ISBN 9780525521952 (ebook)
| ISBN 9781594204876 (hardback)
Subjects: LCSH: Grant, Ulysses S. (Ulysses Simpson), 1822–1885. | Presidents—United States—
Biography. | Generals—United States—Biography. | United States. Army—Biography . |
BISAC: BIOGRAPHY & AUTOBIOGRAPHY / Presidents & Heads of State. | HISTORY /
United States / Civil War Period (1850–1877). | BIOGRAPHY & AUTOBIOGRAPHY / Military.
Classification: LCC E672 (ebook) | LCC E672 .C47 2017 (print) | DDC 973.8/2092 [B]—dc23
LC record available at https://lccn.loc.gov/2017025263

Printed in the United States of America
7 9 10 8

BOOK DESIGN BY LUCIA BERNARD

To my loyal readers,
who have soldiered on through my lengthy sagas

What a man he is! what a history! what an illustration—his life—of the capacities of that American individuality common to us all. Cynical critics are wondering "what the people can see in Grant" to make such a hubbub about. They aver . . . that he has hardly the average of our day's literary and scholastic culture, and absolutely no pronounc'd genius or conventional eminence of any sort. Correct: but he proves how an average western farmer, mechanic, boatman, carried by tides of circumstances, perhaps caprices, into a position of incredible military or civil responsibilities . . . may steer his way fitly and steadily through them all, carrying the country and himself with credit year after year—command over a million armed men—fight more than fifty pitch'd battles—rule for eight years a land larger than all the kingdoms of Europe combined—and then, retiring, quietly (with a cigar in his mouth) make the promenade of the whole world, through its courts and coteries, and kings and czars and mikados . . . as phlegmatically as he ever walk'd the portico of a Missouri hotel after dinner . . . Seems to me it transcends Plutarch. How those old Greeks, indeed, would have seized on him! A mere plain man—no art, no poetry . . . A common trader, money-maker, tanner, farmer of Illinois— general for the republic . . . in the war of attempted secession—President following, (a task of peace, more difficult than the war itself)—nothing heroic, as the authorities put it—and yet the greatest hero. The gods, the destinies, seem to have concentrated upon him.

WALT WHITMAN, *Specimen Days*

CONTENTS

PART THREE: A LIFE OF PEACE

PART FOUR: A LIFE OF REFLECTION

AUTHOR'S NOTE

Since Ulysses S. Grant's spelling could border on the eccentric, I have taken the liberty of correcting that and his punctuation and capitalization throughout the book for the sake of smoother reading and easier comprehension. I have done the same with private letters of other figures in the book, except in those cases where I think that defective writing tells a significant tale about the author.

The Sphinx Talks

EVEN AS OTHER CIVIL WAR generals rushed to publish their memoirs, flaunting their conquests and cashing in on their celebrity, Ulysses S. Grant refused to trumpet his accomplishments in print. The son of an incorrigible small-town braggart, the unassuming general and two-time president harbored a lifelong aversion to boasting. He was content to march to his grave in dignified silence, letting his extraordinary wartime record speak for itself.

Then, at the close of 1883, fate dealt him a series of progressively more savage blows that shattered this high-minded resolve. Returning to his Manhattan town house on Christmas Eve, Grant, sixty-one, pivoted to hand the driver a holiday tip when he slipped on the icy pavement and crashed to the ground, tearing a thigh muscle and possibly fracturing his hip. Until then a robust man, he crumpled over in excruciating pain and was hoisted up the steps by servants. Through anxious winter weeks, he remained bedridden or hobbled about on crutches. Before long, his discomfort intensified with the agonizing onset of pleurisy, coupled with severe rheumatism that crept up his legs, making it difficult for him to negotiate the familiar rooms.

Still worse lay in store. Several years earlier, Grant had entered into a promising partnership, christened Grant & Ward, with twenty-nine-year-old Ferdinand Ward, touted as the "Young Napoleon of Finance." Thanks to his colleague's financial wizardry, Grant seemed to coast on a tide of easy riches, fancying himself a newly minted millionaire. Then, one morning in early May

1884, he awoke to discover that Ward had manufactured the profits from thin air, the whole scheme was a colossal fraud, and he was ruined along with friends and family members who had entrusted their life savings to the firm. Abruptly Grant was thrust back into his early years of hardship at lonely frontier garrisons, on his unprofitable farm in St. Louis, and at his father's leather goods emporium in Galena, Illinois—places where he was branded an economic failure. Now, to scrape by and pay household bills, he had to endure the degradation of accepting money sent by total strangers as acts of charity.

At this point, Grant was seized by more than a desperate need to earn ready cash: he had to cast off the stigma of failure and reclaim his stature before the public and posterity. As his longtime friend William Tecumseh Sherman observed, he had "lost everything, and more in reputation."[1] To a friend, Grant confided, "I could bear all the pecuniary loss if that was all, but that I could be so long deceived by a man who I had such opportunity to know is humiliating."[2] So Grant proved receptive when editors of the prestigious *Century Magazine* solicited a series of articles about his foremost Civil War victories. "I consented for the money it gave me," Grant admitted, "for at that moment I was living upon borrowed money."[3]

That June, at his rambling seaside cottage in Long Branch, New Jersey, Grant experienced a strange sensation that foreshadowed another grave problem. His wife, Julia, served him "a plate of delicious peaches on the table," but as he swallowed one, he stopped and winced. "Oh my," he said, "I think something has stung me from that peach." He sprang from his chair, strode the porch in distress, then rinsed out his throat, to no avail. "He was in great pain and said water hurt like fire," Julia recalled.[4] Throughout the summer, Grant, who had once smoked twenty cigars a day, was vexed by a baffling sore throat that never faded. Although Julia begged him to see a physician, he procrastinated for months; this man who was so intrepid on the battlefield seemed to dread the looming diagnosis. When at last he consulted his Manhattan doctor in October, he received grim tidings: a mass on his throat and tongue was "epithelial" in character—code language for cancer. To worsen matters, he was afflicted by painful neuralgia and had three large teeth extracted. All the while, he limped about from the Christmas Eve mishap.

Terrified that if he died he would leave Julia destitute, Grant agreed to pen his memoirs and relive his glory days of battle. As seen in his wartime orders, he had patented a lean, supple writing style, and a crisp narrative now flowed in polished sentences, honed by the habits of a lifetime. Words poured from this supposedly taciturn man, showing how much thought and pent-up feeling lay beneath his tightly buttoned facade. He wrote in an overstuffed leather arm-chair, his outstretched legs swaddled by blankets, resting on a facing chair. He wore a wool cap over thick brown hair now streaked with gray, a shawl draped over his shoulders, and a muffler around his neck concealing a tumor the size of a baseball.

Seldom, if ever, has a literary masterpiece been composed under such horrific circumstances. Whenever he swallowed anything, Grant was stricken with pain and had to resort to opiates that clouded his brain. As a result, he endured ex-tended periods of thirst and hunger as he labored over his manuscript. The tor-ment of the inflamed throat never ceased. When the pain grew too great, his black valet, Harrison Terrell, sprayed his throat with "cocaine water," temporar-ily numbing the area, or applied hot compresses to his head. Despite his fear of morphine addiction, Grant could not dispense entirely with such powerful med-ication. "I suffer pain all the time, except when asleep," he told his doctor.[5] Al-though bolstered by analgesics, Grant experienced only partial relief, informing a reporter that "when the suffering was so intense . . . he only wished for the one great relief to all human pain."[6]

Summoning his last reserves of strength, through a stupendous act of will-power, Grant toiled four to six hours a day, adding more time on sleepless nights. For family and friends his obsessive labor was wondrous to behold: the soldier so famously reticent that someone quipped he "could be silent in several languages" pumped out 336,000 words of superb prose in a year.[7] By May 1885, just two months before his death, Grant was forced to dictate, and, when his voice failed, he scribbled messages on thin strips of paper. Always cool in a crisis, Grant ex-hibited the prodigious stamina and granite resolve of his wartime effort.

Nobody was more thunderstruck than Samuel Clemens, aka Mark Twain, who had recently formed a publishing house with his nephew-in-law Charles Webster. To snare Grant's memoirs, sure to be a literary sensation, Twain boosted the royalty promised by the *Century*'s publishers and won the rights. Twain had never seen a writer with Grant's gritty determination. When this man "under sentence of death with that cancer" produced an astonishing ten thousand words in one day, Twain exclaimed, "It kills me these days to write half of that."[8] He was agog when Grant dictated at one sitting a nine-thousand-word portrait of Lee's surrender at Appomattox "never pausing, never hesitating for a word, never repeating—and in the written-out copy he made hardly a correction."[9] Twain, who considered the final product a masterwork, scoffed at scuttlebutt he had ghostwritten it. "There is no higher literature than these modest, simple memoirs," he insisted. "Their style is flawless . . . no man can improve upon it."[10]

For Twain, the revelation of Grant's character was as startling as his storytelling. Eager to spare his family, Grant was every inch the stoic gentleman. Only at night, when he was asleep, did his face grimace with pain. "The sick-room brought out the points of General Grant's character," Twain wrote. "His exceeding gentleness, kindness, forbearance, lovingness, charity. . . . He *was* the most lovable great child in the world."[11] For one observer, it was wrenching to watch Grant "with a bandage about his aching head, and a horrible and mortal disease clutching his throat." He felt "a great ache when I look at him who had saved us all when we were bankrupt in treasure and in leaders, and see him thus beset by woes and wants."[12] In a magnificent finale, Grant finished the manuscript on July 16, 1885, one week before his death in upstate New York. He had steeled himself to stay alive until the last sentence was done and he could surrender his pen.

The triumph of the *Personal Memoirs of U.S. Grant,* which sold a record-breaking three hundred thousand copies in two-volume sets, was vintage Grant. Repeatedly he had bounced back from adversity, his career marked by surprising comebacks and stunning reversals. He had endured many scenes, constantly growing and changing in the process. Like Twain, Walt Whitman was mesmerized by Grant and grouped him with George Washington, Abraham Lincoln, and Ralph Waldo Emerson in the quartet of greatest Americans. "In all Homer and Shakespeare there is no fortune or personality really more picturesque or rapidly changing, more full of heroism, pathos, contrast," he wrote.[13] The plain unadorned Grant had nothing stylish about him, leading sophisticated people to underrate his talents. He was a nondescript face in the crowd, the common man from the heartland raised to a higher power, who proved a simple westerner could lead a mighty army to victory and occupy the presidential chair with distinction.

Dismissed as a philistine, a boor, a drunk, and an incompetent, Grant has been subjected to pernicious stereotypes that grossly impede our understanding of the man. As a contemporary newspaper sniffed, Grant was "an ignorant soldier, coarse in his taste and blunt in his perceptions, fond of money and material enjoyment and of low company."[14] In fact, Grant was a sensitive, complex, and misunderstood man with a shrewd mind, a wry wit, a rich fund of anecdotes, wide knowledge, and penetrating insights. Many acquaintances remembered the "silent" Grant as the most engaging raconteur they ever met. His weather-beaten appearance during the war, when he wore simple military dress, often caked with mud, could be misleading, for an inner fineness and delicacy lay beneath the rough-hewn exterior. At the same time, Grant could be surprisingly naive and artless in business and politics.

The caricature of Grant as a filthy "butcher" is ironic for a man who couldn't stomach the sight of blood, studiously refrained from romanticizing warfare, and shied away from a military career. "I never went into a battle willingly or with enthusiasm," he remarked. "I was always glad when a battle was over."[15] Invariably he deprecated war. "It is at all times a sad and cruel business. I hate war with all my heart, and nothing but imperative duty could induce me to engage in its work or witness its horrors."[16] Grant never grew vainglorious from military fame, never gloated over enemy defeats, never engaged in victory celebrations. He has been derided as a plodding, dim-witted commander who enjoyed superior manpower and matériel and whose crude idea of strategy was to launch large, brutal assaults upon the enemy. In fact, close students of the war have shown that the percentage of casualties in Grant's armies was often lower than those of many Confederate generals. If Grant never shrank from sending masses of soldiers into bloody battles, it had nothing to do with a heartless disregard for human life and everything to do with bringing the war to a speedy conclusion.

The relentless focus on Grant's last battles against Robert E. Lee in Virginia has obscured his stellar record of winning battles in the western war long before taking charge of Union forces in early 1864. After that, he did not simply direct the Army of the Potomac, but masterminded the coordinated movements of all federal forces. A far-seeing general, he adopted a comprehensive policy for all theaters of war, treating them as an interrelated whole. However brilliant Lee was as a tactician, Grant surpassed him in grand strategy, crafting the plan that defeated the Confederacy. The military historian John Keegan paid homage to Grant as "the towering military genius of the Civil War" and noted the modernity of his methods as he mobilized railroads and telegraphs to set his armies in motion.[17] Grant, he concluded, "was the greatest general of the war, one who would have excelled at any time in any army."[18]

Many Grant biographies dwell at length on the Civil War, then quickly skip over his presidency as an embarrassing coda to wartime heroism. He is portrayed as a rube in Washington, way out of his league. But Grant was an adept politician, the only president to serve two full consecutive terms between Andrew Jackson and Woodrow Wilson. Writing in 1888, British historian James Bryce assigned him to the "front rank" of presidents with Washington, Jefferson, and Lincoln.[19] After that his reputation tumbled, his presidency degraded to an unfair cartoon of an inept executive presiding over a scandal-ridden administration. Recent biographies have begun to rehabilitate Grant in a long overdue reappraisal. While scandals unquestionably sullied his presidency, they eclipsed a far more notable achievement—safeguarding the civil rights of African Americans. Even eminent historians have gotten wrong—sometimes badly wrong—Grant's relationship with the black community. Typical is the view of C. Vann Woodward: "Grant had shown little interest during the war in emancipation as a late-developing war aim and little but hostility toward the more radical war aim of the few for black franchise and racial equality."[20]

In truth, Grant was instrumental in helping the Union vanquish the Confederacy *and* in realizing the wartime ideals enshrined in the Thirteenth, Fourteenth, and Fifteenth Amendments. The Civil War and Reconstruction formed two acts of a single historical drama to gain freedom and justice for black Americans, and Grant was the major personality who united those two periods. He was the single most important figure behind Reconstruction, and his historical reputation has risen sharply with a revisionist view of that period as a glorious experiment in equal rights for all American citizens instead of a shameful fiasco.

What has been critically absent from Grant biographies is a systematic account of his relations with the four million slaves, whom he helped to liberate, feed, house, employ, and arm during the war, then shielded from harm when they became American citizens. Frederick Douglass paired Grant with Lincoln as the two people who had done most to secure African American advances: "May we not justly say . . . that the liberty which Mr. Lincoln declared with his pen General Grant made effectual with his sword—by his skill in leading the Union armies to final victory?"[21] For the admiring Douglass, Grant was "the vigilant, firm, impartial, and wise protector of my race."[22] More recently the historian Sean Wilentz has ratified this verdict: "The evidence clearly shows that [Grant] created the most auspicious record on racial equality and civil rights of any president from Lincoln to Lyndon B. Johnson."[23]

The imperishable story of Grant's presidency was his campaign to crush the

Ku Klux Klan. Through the Klan, white supremacists tried to overturn the Civil War's outcome and restore the status quo ante. No southern sheriff would arrest the hooded night riders who terrorized black citizens and no southern jury would convict them. Grant had to cope with a complete collapse of evenhanded law enforcement in the erstwhile Confederate states. In 1870 he oversaw creation of the Justice Department, its first duty to bring thousands of anti-Klan indictments. By 1872 the monster had been slain, although its spirit resurfaced as the nation retreated from Reconstruction's lofty aims. Grant presided over the Fifteenth Amendment, which gave blacks the right to vote, and landmark civil rights legislation, including the 1875 act outlawing racial discrimination in public accommodations. His pursuit of justice for southern blacks was at times imperfect, but his noble desire to protect them never wavered.

Perhaps the most explosively persistent myth about Grant is that he was a "drunkard," with all that implies about self-indulgence and moral laxity. Modern science has shown that alcoholism is a "chronic disease," not a "personal failing as it has been viewed by many."[24] Because Grant's drinking has been scrutinized in purely moralistic terms, his admirers have felt the need to defend him from the charge as vigorously as detractors have rushed to pin it on him. The drinking issue, both real and imaginary, so permeated Grant's career that a thoroughgoing account is needed to settle the matter. This biography will contend that Grant was an alcoholic with an astonishingly consistent pattern of drinking, recognized by friend and foe alike: a solitary binge drinker who would not touch a drop of alcohol, then succumb at three- or four-month intervals, usually on the road. As a rule, he underwent a radical personality change and could not stop himself once he started to imbibe. Alcohol was not a recreation selfishly indulged, but a forbidden impulse against which he struggled for most of his life. He joined a temperance lodge in early adulthood and lent the movement open support in later years. While drinking almost never interfered with his official duties, it haunted his career and trailed him everywhere, an infuriating, ever-present ghost he could not shake. It influenced how people perceived him and deserves close attention. As with so many problems in his life, Grant managed to attain mastery over alcohol in the long haul, a feat as impressive as any of his wartime victories.

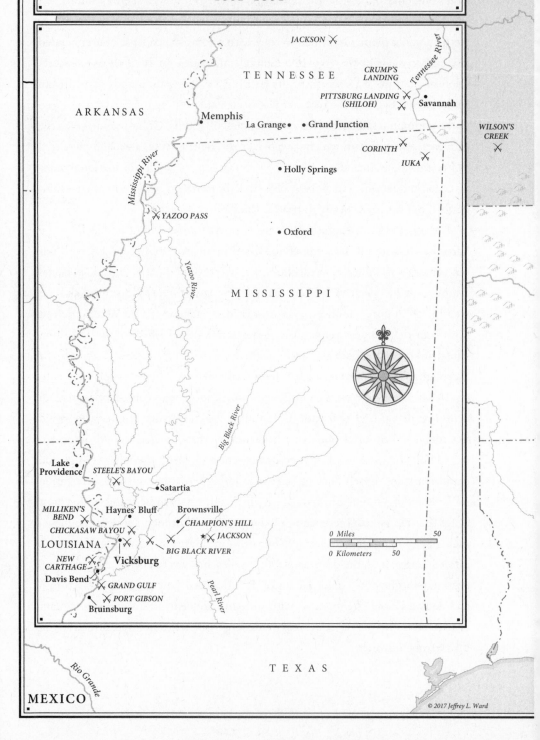

GRANT'S WESTERN THEATER OF WAR
1861–1864

JACKSON ✕

TENNESSEE

CRUMP'S LANDING

Tennessee River

PITTSBURG LANDING (SHILOH) ✕

Savannah

ARKANSAS

Memphis

La Grange • • Grand Junction

WILSON'S CREEK ✕

CORINTH ✕

IUKA ✕

Mississippi River

• Holly Springs

✕ YAZOO PASS

• Oxford

Yazoo River

MISSISSIPPI

Big Black River

Lake Providence •

STEELE'S BAYOU

✕

• Satartia

MILLIKEN'S BEND

Haynes' Bluff •

Brownsville

• CHAMPION'S HILL

CHICKASAW BAYOU ✕

★✕ JACKSON

LOUISIANA

BIG BLACK RIVER

NEW CARTHAGE

Vicksburg

Davis Bend

✕ GRAND GULF

✕ PORT GISSON

Pearl River

Bruinsburg

0 Miles 50

0 Kilometers 50

TEXAS

Rio Grande

MEXICO

© 2017 Jeffrey L. Ward

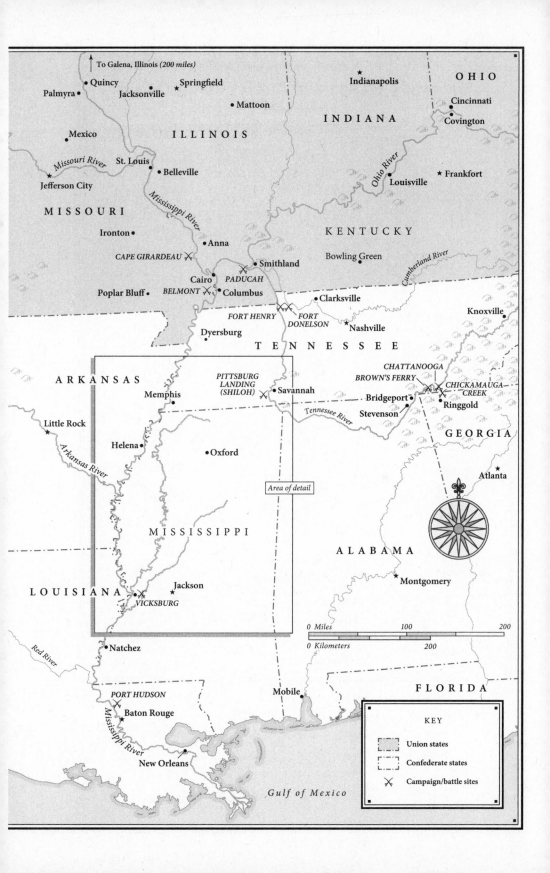

To Galena, Illinois *(200 miles)*

Quincy
Palmyra
Jacksonville
Springfield
Mattoon
Indianapolis
OHIO
Cincinnati
Covington

Mexico
Missouri River
St. Louis
Belleville
ILLINOIS
INDIANA
Ohio River
Louisville
★ Frankfort

Jefferson City
Mississippi River

MISSOURI
Ironton
Anna
Cairo
KENTUCKY
Bowling Green
Cumberland River
Knoxville

CAPE GIRARDEAU ✕
Smithland
PADUCAH
Poplar Bluff
BELMONT ✕ Columbus
Clarksville
Nashville

FORT HENRY ✕✕ *FORT DONELSON*
Dyersburg
T E N N E S S E E

ARKANSAS
PITTSBURG LANDING (SHILOH) ✕ Savannah
CHATTANOOGA
BROWN'S FERRY ✕ *CHICKAMAUGA CREEK*
Memphis
Bridgeport Ringgold
Stevenson
Tennessee River

Little Rock
Helena
Oxford
GEORGIA
Arkansas River

Atlanta
Area of detail

MISSISSIPPI
ALABAMA

LOUISIANA
Jackson
✕ *VICKSBURG*
Montgomery

0 Miles		100		200
0 Kilometers			200	

Natchez
Red River

PORT HUDSON
Baton Rouge
Mobile
F L O R I D A

Mississippi River

New Orleans

Gulf of Mexico

KEY

⬚ Union states
⬚ Confederate states
✕ Campaign/battle sites

GRANT'S EASTERN THEATER OF WAR
1864–1865

PENNSYLVANIA

Indianapolis ★

INDIANA

WEST VIRGINIA
(statehood 1863)

Harpers Ferry
Charles Town •
Winchester •

Frederick •
Monocacy •

Potomac River

MARYLAND

Louisville • *Ohio River*

Baltimore •

CEDAR CREEK ✕

FISHER'S HILL ✕

Shenandoah River

FORT STEVENS
✕

Washington, D.C. •

Bowling
Green
•

Shenandoah Valley

Rapidan River

✕ *BRANDY STATION*
• Culpeper

★ Nashville
Franklin •

THE WILDERNESS
SPOTSYLVANIA ✕

Fredericksburg •

Guiney's
Station •

Charlottesville •

North Anna R.

Mattaponi R.

Rappahannock R.

Potomac River

Chesapeake Bay

VIRGINIA

James River

Hanovertown •

YELLOW TAVERN ✕   *COLD HARBOR* ✕

Richmond ★

FORT HARRISON

Chickahominy R.

ALABAMA

FORT DARLING/
Drewry's Bluff ✕

✕ *MALVERN*
HILL

York R.

Montgomery •

APPOMATTOX
COURT HOUSE ✕

Lynchburg •

Amelia Court House •

Bermuda Hundred

• Jetersville

Farmville •
SAYLER'S CREEK ✕

THE CRATER ✕

City Point

James River

HATCHER'S RUN ✕

FORT STEDMAN

Petersburg

FIVE FORKS ✕

FORTRESS MONROE/
Old Point Comfort —

To Danville ←

Hampton Roads

0 Miles   20   40

0 Kilometers   40

Mobile •
✕

TEXAS

LOUISIANA

Mississippi River

Baton Rouge ★

MOBILE BAY

New Orleans •

Gulf of
Mexico

Pittsburgh • **PENNSYLVANIA** Philadelphia •

NEW JERSEY

★ Columbus **MARYLAND**

Potomac River

OHIO Washington, D.C. ★ ★ Dover

DELAWARE

• Cincinnati

James River

★ Charleston Richmond ★

WEST VIRGINIA (statehood 1863)

Frankfort ★ **VIRGINIA**

Area of detail

KENTUCKY

★ Raleigh
Goldsboro •

TENNESSEE **NORTH CAROLINA**
New Bern •

Fayetteville • *Cape Fear River*

Chattanooga

• Dalton Wilmington •
✕ *FORT FISHER*

Camden •
Columbia ★
★ Atlanta

SOUTH CAROLINA

GEORGIA

Charleston •

Atlantic Ocean

Savannah •

✕ *SEA ISLANDS*

0 *Miles* 100 200

0 *Kilometers* 200

★ Tallahassee

FLORIDA

KEY

Union states

Confederate states

✕ Campaign/battle sites

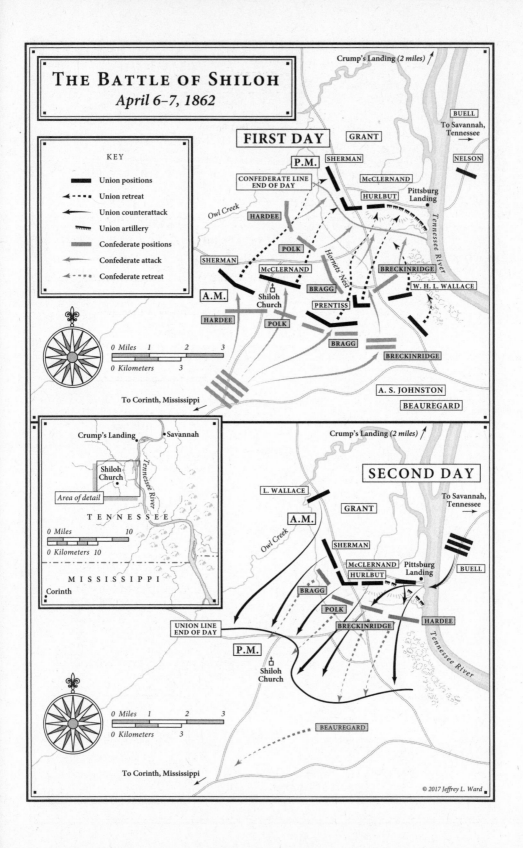

THE BATTLE OF SHILOH
April 6–7, 1862

Crump's Landing (2 miles)

FIRST DAY

BUELL
To Savannah, Tennessee

GRANT

NELSON

P.M.   SHERMAN

CONFEDERATE LINE
END OF DAY

McCLERNAND

HURLBUT   Pittsburg Landing

KEY

Owl Creek

— Union positions

HARDEE

---▶ Union retreat

◀— Union counterattack

ᴠᴠᴠ Union artillery

▬ Confederate positions

◀— Confederate attack

◀--- Confederate retreat

POLK

SHERMAN

McCLERNAND

BRECKINRIDGE

W. H. L. WALLACE

A.M.

BRAGG

Shiloh Church

HARDEE

POLK   PRENTISS

BRAGG

0 Miles   1   2   3

0 Kilometers   3

BRECKINRIDGE

To Corinth, Mississippi

A. S. JOHNSTON

BEAUREGARD

Crump's Landing   •Savannah

Crump's Landing (2 miles)

Shiloh Church

SECOND DAY

Area of detail

Tennessee River

L. WALLACE

To Savannah, Tennessee

TENNESSEE

GRANT

A.M.

0 Miles   10

0 Kilometers 10

SHERMAN

MISSISSIPPI

McCLERNAND   Pittsburg Landing

Corinth

HURLBUT

BUELL

BRAGG

POLK

HARDEE

BRECKINRIDGE

UNION LINE
END OF DAY

Tennessee River

P.M.

Shiloh Church

BEAUREGARD

0 Miles   1   2   3

0 Kilometers   3

To Corinth, Mississippi

© 2017 Jeffrey L. Ward

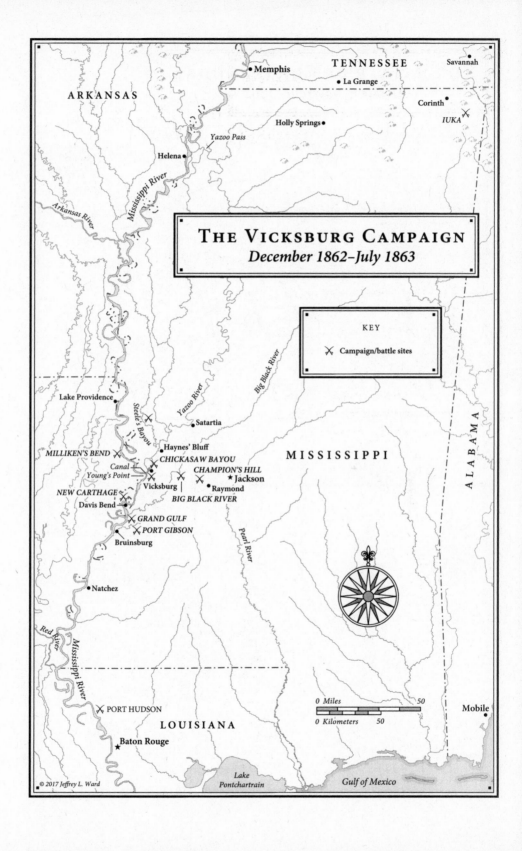

THE VICKSBURG CAMPAIGN
December 1862–July 1863

KEY

✕ Campaign/battle sites

TENNESSEE

• Memphis
• La Grange
Savannah

ARKANSAS

Holly Springs •
Corinth •
✕ *IUKA*

Yazoo Pass

Helena •

Arkansas River

Mississippi River

Big Black River

Lake Providence •

Steele's Bayou

Yazoo River

• Satartia

Haynes' Bluff
MILLIKEN'S BEND ✕

MISSISSIPPI

CHICKASAW BAYOU
Canal
Young's Point —
CHAMPION'S HILL
Vicksburg │
★ Jackson
• Raymond
NEW CARTHAGE ✕
Davis Bend •
BIG BLACK RIVER

✕ *GRAND GULF*
✕ *PORT GIBSON*
• Bruinsburg

Pearl River

• Natchez

ALABAMA

Red River

Mississippi River

✕ PORT HUDSON

0 Miles   50

0 Kilometers   50

LOUISIANA

Mobile

★ Baton Rouge

Lake Pontchartrain

Gulf of Mexico

© 2017 Jeffrey L. Ward

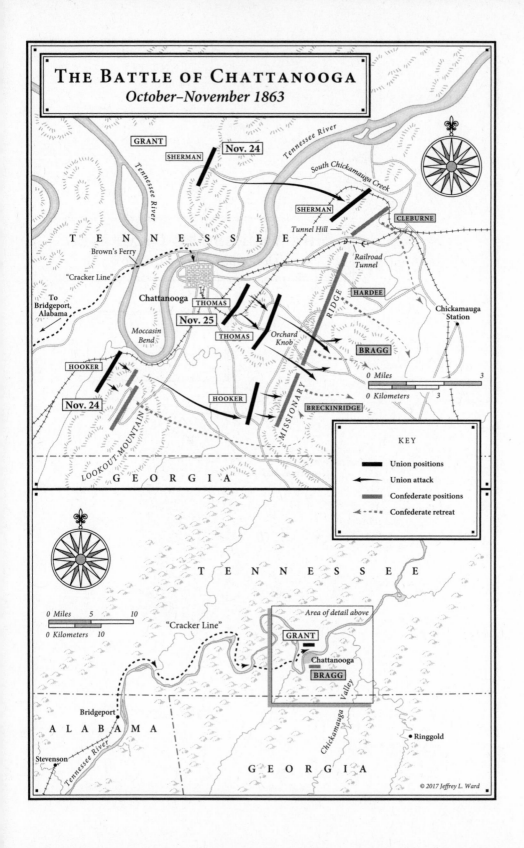

THE BATTLE OF CHATTANOOGA
October–November 1863

GRANT

SHERMAN

Nov. 24

Tennessee River

South Chickamauga Creek

SHERMAN

CLEBURNE

Tunnel Hill

TENNESSEE

Brown's Ferry

Railroad Tunnel

"Cracker Line"

HARDEE

To Bridgeport, Alabama

Chattanooga

THOMAS

Nov. 25

THOMAS

Chickamauga Station

Moccasin Bend

Orchard Knob

RIDGE

BRAGG

HOOKER

0 Miles 3

0 Kilometers 3

Nov. 24

HOOKER

MISSIONARY

BRECKINRIDGE

LOOKOUT MOUNTAIN

GEORGIA

KEY

▬ Union positions

← Union attack

▬ Confederate positions

◄┅┅ Confederate retreat

TENNESSEE

0 Miles 5 10

0 Kilometers 10

"Cracker Line"

Area of detail above

GRANT

Chattanooga

BRAGG

Chickamauga Valley

Bridgeport

ALABAMA

Ringgold

Stevenson

Tennessee River

GEORGIA

© 2017 Jeffrey L. Ward

PART ONE

///

A Life of Struggle

CHAPTER ONE

Country Bumpkin

O N APRIL 27, 1822, Ulysses S. Grant was born in Point Pleasant, Ohio, tucked away in the rural southwestern corner of the state near Cincinnati. The tiny, boxy house, constructed of wood and painted white, stood a short stroll from the Ohio River with Kentucky clearly visible on the far shore. Under its slanting roof the residence was humble, consisting of a single open room with a fireplace. Point Pleasant was little more than a nondescript cluster of makeshift cabins overlooking bustling river traffic.

Delivered by a stern-faced, bearded abolitionist, Dr. John Rogers, the plump baby weighed in at ten and three-quarters pounds, with reddish-brown hair and blue-gray eyes. For many weeks, his father, Jesse Root Grant, and mother, Hannah Simpson Grant, conferred with relatives to find a suitable name for the hefty infant. The choices bandied about suggest a literate clan with high expectations for the child. Hannah opted for Albert to honor Thomas Jefferson's treasury secretary, Albert Gallatin, while her father opted for Hiram as a "handsome" biblical name. Hannah's stepmother evinced "enthusiastic admiration for the ancient commander, Ulysses," recalled Jesse Grant, and urged "that the babe should be named Ulysses."[1] Some accounts claim the matter was settled by plucking names from a hat. Whatever the case, the family agreed on Hiram Ulysses Grant, which translated into the unfortunate initials H.U.G. The boy would show a decided preference for Ulysses and gradually discard Hiram, especially when other boys "teased him about his initials."[2] But this didn't halt the taunts since Grant was known as "Ulyss" or "Lyss," soon bastardized by malicious schoolmates

into "Useless Grant." The name Ulysses *S.* Grant was the product of a later bureaucratic error that stuck.

Jesse Grant worked as a foreman at the tannery just up the hill. At six feet
tall, he was a large, imposing man, always considerably taller than his son, with
broad shoulders and a florid complexion, who wore his silk hat low over large
golden spectacles. He was a bumptious type common in small towns on the
American frontier, a self-assertive windbag and congenital striver, brimming
with schemes and bright ideas. Voluble and opinionated, he delighted in verbal
combat. With his brusque manner and sharp-elbowed style, he went through
life brawling with people in business and politics. Smart and enterprising, he
kept a sharp eye on the main chance—one neighbor sneered he would "follow a
dollar to hell"—and his business success and self-promotion tended to gall more
modest people.[3]

Jesse proudly traced his ancestry to two early Puritan settlers, Matthew and
Priscilla Grant, who emigrated from Dorset County in England and arrived in
Dorchester, Massachusetts, in 1630. "My family is American," Ulysses later declared proudly, "and has been for generations, in all its branches, direct and collateral."[4] Before long, Matthew and his son Samuel, traveling south to Connecticut,
helped settle the town of Windsor on the Connecticut River. While Matthew
served as town clerk and surveyor, his male descendants were strongly drawn to
arms. One of them, Noah Grant, fought and died in the French and Indian War
along with his brother Solomon. As a confirmed abolitionist, Jesse Root Grant
delighted in showing off an original muster roll made out by Captain Noah Grant
in 1755 that bore the words, "Prince, *negro*" and "Jupiter, *negro*" as company members.[5] Far more controversial was the military record of Jesse's own father, another
Noah Grant. In his *Memoirs,* Ulysses credited this Noah Grant with having fought
in the Revolutionary War from Bunker Hill to the fall of Yorktown.[6] Unfortunately, no biographer has been able to unearth documentary evidence to substantiate this wartime service.

What seems certain is that Noah Grant's life went sadly awry. During the
war, he married and fathered two children before becoming a widower. Then,
afterward, he moved to western Pennsylvania, just east of Pittsburgh, where he
married Rachel Kelly, a capable housewife who bore him several children, including Jesse; they ultimately moved to Deerfield, Ohio. When Rachel died in
1805, Noah was saddled with seven children from two marriages. His father
was born rich and died poor, Jesse maintained, because the "long period of

soldiering spoilt him for all financial business"—ironically, the charge Jesse later leveled at his eldest son.[7] After his wife's death, Noah took to drink, depleting an ample inheritance. In Jesse's words, his father "lost something of his self-control, and acquired the fondness for stimulants," a fact worth flagging because of the hereditary component in alcoholism.[8] As a result, Jesse Root Grant had to support himself from age eleven, while the younger children were farmed out to relatives and neighbors. Jesse developed a robust streak of independence, defining himself in contrast to his shiftless, alcoholic father and showing a chronic zeal for self-improvement.

After working as a farmhand for three years, Jesse performed chores for an Ohio Supreme Court judge, George Tod, whose family showed unusual kindness to the talkative young man. Finding Jesse illiterate, Mrs. Tod tutored him, taught him to read, and even paid for the only five months of schooling he ever enjoyed. For someone largely self-taught, Jesse was remarkably articulate, but he smarted from a sense of his deficient education and crammed in four weeks of English grammar lessons right after his marriage. So graciously had the Tods treated him that Jesse forever regarded them "with all the reverence he could have felt if they had been parents instead of benefactors," Ulysses noted.[9] Mrs. Tod encouraged Jesse's ambitions, fostered his love of reading, and urged him to cultivate a marketable trade.

Determined to master tanning—a lucrative business at a time when people needed bridles and saddles—Jesse apprenticed with his older half brother Peter, who owned a tannery in Maysville, Kentucky. One is struck by how quickly the headstrong Jesse Grant latched on to his calling; he was never one to squander time or dither over decisions. Quite courageously, Peter Grant headed the local abolitionist society, denouncing slavery as "the blot which stains our government."[10] During his Maysville stay, Jesse beheld the corrupting effects of slavery and later chided his Kentucky and Virginia relatives for depending "too much on slave labor to be trained in self-reliance."[11] The depth of his antislavery convictions prompted him to leave Kentucky when his apprenticeship expired. "I would not own slaves and I would not live where there were slaves and not own them."[12] His next job came in an Ohio tannery owned by Owen Brown, father of militant abolitionist John Brown. Jesse resided in the Brown household and came to admire John's "purity of character" and "physical courage," but later faulted him for being "a fanatic and extremist in whatever he advocated."[13] After hanging out the shingle for his own tannery in Ravenna, Ohio, Jesse contracted a debilitating "fever and ague" that forced him to discontinue business briefly before going to work at the Point Pleasant tannery.

Full of vim and drive, Jesse searched for a worthy partner and found her in the pious, frugal Hannah Simpson, who was almost five years his junior when they married in June 1821. She had grown up outside Philadelphia, the third child of John Simpson, a farmer who had uprooted his family and moved to southwest Ohio two years earlier. The Simpsons owned a substantial amount of land and some neighbors saw Hannah as marrying down. "At the time of our marriage, Mrs. Grant was an unpretending country girl; handsome, but not vain," Jesse wrote, boasting that the Methodist Episcopal Church had "never had a more devoted and consistent member."[14] As if intent upon monopolizing all future marital discussions, Jesse had tracked down a bride as thrifty with words as he was loquacious; he never stopped talking while Hannah never started. An early photo shows the bearded Jesse bristling with irrepressible energy, his big fists resting on his thighs, while the self-effacing Hannah sits small and strangely placid beside him, a quiet woman withdrawn behind her spectacles and content to be so. Slim and erect, she was quietly refined and never called attention to herself, displaying an unbending sense of duty toward God, family, and country. Blessed with grit, she possessed all the domestic talents, from milking cows to baking cookies, required of a small-town bride.

It seems crystal-clear that Ulysses S. Grant modeled himself after his mutely subdued mother, avoiding his father's bombast and internalizing her humility and self-control. The unflappable Hannah spoke in a low voice, never swore, and remained calm and sweet-tempered. She was kind and solicitous toward neighborhood children. One of Ulysses's friends remembered her as a woman of "deep feeling but not demonstrative," her reserve so resolute that she seldom joked and never laughed.[15] Ulysses later praised her as "the best woman he had ever known; unselfish, devoted to her family, thoroughly good, conscientious, intelligent, of a quiet and amiable disposition, never meddling with other persons' affairs, genuinely pious without any cant, with a strong sense of right and justice."[16] He attributed his good sense and moral compass to her beneficent influence. Molded by her always dignified presence, Ulysses grew up with a deep, abiding respect for women and never treated them lightly or flirtatiously.

Unlike her husband, Hannah doled out praise sparingly and recoiled from anything that faintly smacked of bragging. Even when her son grew famous, a journalist noted, "she not only refrained from boasting of him, but oftentimes blushed like a girl, and left the room when his praises were sounded in her ears; for it seemed akin to hearing self-praise."[17] Hating mean-spirited gossip, she regarded others charitably and shrank from spiteful comments. One day, when women in her church group groused about a drunken husband in the congregation, Hannah chimed in: "Well, Mr. A. was a good fiddler, anyhow."[18] Hannah's tendency to trust people was a lesson that her innocent son Ulysses would learn almost too well.

Despite her sterling traits, something was missing in Hannah Grant, a maternal warmth whose absence Ulysses felt keenly. "I never saw my mother cry," he claimed.[19] Deeply repressed, Hannah never bared her emotions or discussed them with her children. As she later told a reporter proudly, "We are not a demonstrative family."[20] The Grants never showed affection openly and a curious distance always separated Ulysses S. Grant and his mother. In his *Memoirs,* he gave a full-blooded portrait of Jesse Grant's willful nature but, when it came to Hannah, he mentioned her maiden name but failed to endow her with a fully rounded personality. Jesse bursts from the page, while Hannah recedes and vanishes. However infuriating Ulysses found his father, he cared deeply about his opinion. With the emotionally arid Hannah, an enigmatic silence lingered and they had a constrained relationship in later years. This strange family background made Ulysses S. Grant a man who could seem emotionally blocked, although he freely poured forth his bottled-up feelings with his wife and children later on.

When Jesse Grant planted his family in Point Pleasant, he thought the small village had a major future, but for a man of his vaulting hopes, it proved a hopelessly sleepy backwater. In August 1823, he purchased a corner lot in Georgetown, Ohio, the new county seat of adjoining Brown County, and built a two-story brick house—brick connoting wealth and standing—near the courthouse square. Jesse kept adding to the edifice during Ulysses's boyhood since he and Hannah needed to accommodate their growing brood, soon adding Samuel Simpson (called Simpson) in 1825; Clara Rachel in 1828; Virginia Paine (Jennie) in 1832; Orvil Lynch in 1835; and Mary Frances in 1839. (One notes how neatly this self-disciplined couple spaced their offspring.) A natural joiner, Jesse served as senior warden at Georgetown's new Masonic lodge while he and Hannah participated actively in the Methodist church across from their residence, often inviting visiting ministers to stay with them.

A small but up-and-coming place of corn and potato farmers, Georgetown was an ideal spot for Jesse to situate his own tannery, which he placed across the street from his home. Nearby White Oak Creek furnished plentiful water while abundant tanbark came from adjoining forests. Jesse was reputed to be a tough but fair-minded boss, a "hard-working man," who "brooked no laziness," said a relative."[21] One resident recalled Jesse as "very shrewd in money transactions, but scrupulously honest. He was what might be called a Yankee gentleman with plenty of old-school gentility and home-bred culture."[22] The tannery, however, was a malodorous place that stank from lampblack and grease used to dress hides, and Ulysses, whose upstairs bedroom window stared out on the business, was revolted by the stench that regularly wafted across the street—a revulsion that lasted a lifetime.

The boy grew up in a household that percolated with political commentary. With politics his first love, Jesse contributed to a lively newspaper called *The Castigator* that made its local debut in 1826. He relished controversy, publishing pungent polemical essays on a variety of topics. His literary style leaned heavily on sarcasm, and his bruising diatribes earned him a host of enemies. When disputing one opponent, he gave this self-description in a piece he signed PLUTO: "Now sir, I am a *little dog,* and generally disposed to be peaceable, but when a BIG DOG snarls at me, I will at least show my teeth."[23]

The paper's editor was David Ammen, a passionate abolitionist. Slavery was an incendiary topic in the town by virtue of its geography. Ohio had been the first state carved out of the old Northwest Territory, where slavery was banned by ordinance in 1787. At the same time, Georgetown stood just ten miles from the Ohio River, where runaway slaves from Kentucky made a spirited dash for freedom, often with slave catchers in hot pursuit. So commonplace was slavery in Kentucky that bondsmen constituted one-fifth of its prewar population. Many southern Ohio residents, originally from Kentucky and Virginia, sympathized with slave owners. It took real gumption for Jesse Grant and David Ammen to stand up to proslavery sentiment in this solidly Democratic town. Reared in this borderland area, with the town split harshly over slavery, Ulysses S. Grant was exposed as a boy to both sides of the controversy, perhaps breeding a spirit of tolerance later evident at Appomattox.

Both Jesse and Hannah Grant began as rabidly partisan Democrats who supported Andrew Jackson. Jesse took to the pages of *The Castigator* to defend Jackson's veto of the charter for the Second Bank of the United States, a symbol of concentrated financial power, suggesting that only those with "the hateful taint of aristocracy" disputed the move.[24] The Democratic persuasion ran so deep in Georgetown that it continued unabated during the Civil War. As Ulysses later observed, "There was probably no time during the rebellion when, if the opportunity could have been afforded, it would not have voted for Jefferson Davis for President of the United States, over Mr. Lincoln."[25] For all that, the small town would enrich the Union cause with no fewer than four generals.

Propelled by a thrusting ambition, Jesse was a persistent if frustrated politician, a perennial candidate who was "made secretary of almost every public meeting which I attended where clerical services were required."[26] In 1830 he ran unsuccessfully for Georgetown mayor, lost a bid for the state legislature two years later, then failed in his effort to become a justice of the peace. Although the hot-blooded Jesse lacked the winning charms of a candidate, he ascended to town mayor in the late 1830s. In the 1832 elections, he abandoned the Democratic Party, switching his earlier position on the bank issue and suddenly favoring its renewed charter. This sparked a heated clash with his friend Thomas Hamer, a lawyer who ran for Congress on an orthodox Jacksonian platform. A self-made man born to poor Irish parents, with a thick thatch of reddish hair, Hamer had educated himself with borrowed books and risen to become speaker of the state legislature. In a blistering attack, Jesse wrote that Hamer cared "not who sinks so as he swims . . . he is alike faithless in his political principles, and his personal attachments."[27] Jesse's apostasy brought their friendship to an abrupt close. Hamer's flourishing career as the leading figure in county politics would hamper Jesse's future chances in that realm.

Before long, Jesse popped up at conventions for the new Whig Party, a political tradition that Ulysses absorbed as a boy. Jesse revered Henry Clay, who led the Whigs from 1834 to 1846, endorsing his American System of internal improvements, high tariffs, and a national bank—an orientation later reflected in his son's presidency. The Whigs denounced what they saw as the overweening executive power of "King" Andrew Jackson, selecting the "Whig" name to liken their struggle to that against King George III. Abraham Lincoln ventured into politics as an ardent Whig, characterizing the party as one founded to depose that "'detestable, ignorant, reckless, vain and malignant tyrant,' Andrew Jackson."[28] By 1831, when William Lloyd Garrison initiated publication of *The Liberator*, Jesse had embraced the antislavery position of some northern Whigs, even though this strained relations with many conservative townspeople and family members in Kentucky.

The Whig ideology featured a strong moralistic component that doubtless resonated in the straitlaced, church-going Grant household. To strengthen the country's moral fiber, many Whigs wanted to expand the school system and favored Sabbath observance. They inveighed against the menace of alcohol, which was both a national problem—by 1830 each American drank, on average, seven gallons of pure alcohol per year—as well as a local scourge in Brown County, which had two dozen distilleries and many grape-growing sections. When the journalist Albert Richardson visited Georgetown for a biography of Grant published in 1898, he reeled at the prevalence of alcohol abuse: "To be temperate in Brown [County] means to be intoxicated only two or three times a year."[29] While Jesse Root Grant has gone down in history books as a headstrong temperance advocate, there are scattered suggestions that he might have wrestled early on with his own drinking demons. One person remembered him as "a low, drunken common fellow—who loves his whiskey above all else."[30] A second said he "was a Kentuckian in his liking for whiskey," while a third said Jesse "would take a drink but never pay for it."[31] Since Jesse's own father was ruined by drink, it would not have been surprising if he had championed the temperance movement as a way to conquer his own powerful temptations. Rumors of his drinking did not recur later on, suggesting that, if he had a problem, he had conquered it.

At first glance, there seemed something forgettable and colorless about Ulysses S. Grant in his youth. He had nothing wayward or rambunctious in his nature and seldom wandered off into skylarking mischief with other boys. Like his mother, he was self-contained, as if he had trained his face to mask emotion and keep his inner life secret. Also like Hannah, he was uncommonly eventempered. When he was only two, Jesse dared a neighbor to fire a pistol near his son, sure he would take it in stride. Instead of erupting in tears, the child seemed to revel in the loud noise. "Fick it again!" he cried. "Fick it again!"[32] The incident set a lifelong pattern of Grant appearing impervious to physical danger.

In respect to the boy's appearance, Jesse rendered a mixed verdict, contending that Ulysses "was our most beautiful child; but I thought he did not grow up as handsome as our other boys."[33] If his stoop-shouldered gait was inelegant, it bespoke a firm sense of purpose. "He was always a steady, serious sort of boy who took everything in earnest; even when he played he made a business of it," Hannah recalled.[34] One cousin remembered a "short, stout boy" who never talked much and stayed at home a great deal, "but he had more determination than any boy I ever saw."[35] Often, amid gangs of rowdy youths, he stood apart, as if lost in thought. "He was more like a grown person than a boy," declared one school chum.[36] As befit this seriousness, Grant gravitated to older boys, always speaking in a clear, melodious voice that later reminded the novelist William Dean Howells of "the soft, rounded, Ohio River accent" he had heard from his "steamboating uncles."[37]

Though never a smooth boy, skilled in social graces—he could be awkward and flustered in large groups—Ulysses exhibited a strict Methodist propriety. No dancing, card playing, or cursing was tolerated in the proper Grant household. "It has been a principle of mine never to swear at any time in my life," Ulysses attested in future years.[38] Even as a raw country boy, he allowed himself no oath stronger than "Thunder and Lightning!" Once, when quarreling with an acquaintance, he was provoked to say "Darn." During the Civil War, Grant recounted this episode to someone who recalled him saying "that the very sound of the word to his ears bothered him, so that for an entire week it continued to literally haunt him."[39] He spent a lifetime avoiding the coarse jokes and bawdy anecdotes that were commonplace in the military. "He revered women and thought such stories demeaned the female sex," said a cousin. "I have seen him freeze up a man instantly with a look when a vulgar story was told in his presence."[40]

As part of their Methodist austerity, the Grants frowned upon liquor consumption and not until age eleven did Ulysses steal his first forbidden taste of alcohol. Since cholera cases had appeared in town, local authorities dispatched Jesse to Maysville, Kentucky, to obtain a sweet blackberry cordial that purportedly contained medicinal qualities. When the cholera threat abated, Jesse stowed the liqueur in his cellar. When his parents went off to church, Ulysses and his friends sneaked downstairs on several occasions and gulped large quantities of the sugary spirits.[41]

Impeccably polite and usually (but not always) neatly dressed, Ulysses reflected Hannah's prim parenting. He preferred innocent pastimes, such as swimming, playing marbles, or ice-skating. While he delighted in fishing barefoot in summer, seated by a brook near the tannery, he seldom hunted and derived no pleasure from the casual butchering of animals. "He was unusually sensitive to pain," said a friend, "and his aversion to taking any form of life was so great that he would not hunt."[42] Such a tame boy inevitably became the butt of mockery, and Grant grew sensitive to public humiliation. Never one to initiate a fight, he refused to back down when bullied. He was roused to fury if sadistic boys tormented an innocent child or a defenseless horse, and smaller boys embraced him as their steadfast protector. On one occasion, Grant saw a big, oafish boy named Slifer picking on a much smaller boy. "Grant stepped forward, rolled up his sleeves, and told Slifer that he shouldn't fight that little fellow; that if there was any fighting to be done he could fight him," said a cousin.[43] Grant never deviated from this philosophy, which he later applied to his eldest son. "I do not want him to feel afraid to *pitch in* when boys impose on him but he had better avoid boys who are inclined to quarrel."[44]

In the absence of free public schools, Jesse sent his son to a small brick subscription school, perched on a nearby ridge, with boys and girls seated on long wooden benches and segregated in adjoining classrooms. Ulysses remembered John D. White, the village schoolmaster, as a "kind-hearted" and "respected" man, who nonetheless lashed with beechwood switches any boys who dared to misbehave.[45] Grant already stood out for his terse expression and unruffled nature. Another teacher, Isaac Lynch, praised his "quiet demeanor, studious attention to his books, and remarkably good behavior."[46] With his bashful nature, Grant found public speaking "unbearable" and only submitted to this torture "by the greatest exertion."[47] Though a conscientious student, he excelled solely in mathematics. Drawn to history and politics, he read *The Life of George Washington* and avidly followed the newspapers. Jesse Grant promoted literacy at home, amassing a library of thirty volumes. Regretting his own lack of education, he wanted to drum learning into his children's heads. Ulysses conveyed a vivid sense of his father's insatiable thirst for knowledge. As a boy, he had "read every book he could borrow in the neighborhood where he lived. This scarcity gave him the early habit of studying everything he read, so that when he got through with a book, he knew everything in it."[48]

Jesse Grant committed the common error of willful fathers who try to stimulate their sons and overpower them instead. He doted on his eldest boy, smothering him with attention and attempting to live vicariously through him. Reluctant to assert himself against his bossy father, Ulysses quietly resented the pressure to succeed, and Jesse was perplexed that his son "never seemed inclined to put himself forward at all; and was modest, retiring, and reticent."[49] Instead of accepting this, Jesse prodded the boy mercilessly at every turn. When he took Ulysses on a trip to eastern Ohio, a telling scene unfolded, recounted by a friend. "At this time Ulysses though young could read very well, of this his father was naturally very proud, and when they arrived at their destination, to his little son's dismay, he brought out a school reader, and telling his friends of how beautifully Ulysses could read, proceeded to open his book and requested him to read something, but Ulysses declined absolutely and stuck to it, to his father's chagrin and disappointment."[50]

From this clash between grandstanding father and stubbornly private son, Ulysses developed a deeply entrenched modesty, "a particular aversion to egotists and braggarts," said a later colleague.[51] He wanted people to discover his strengths, not have them advertised. Reluctant to flout his father openly, he developed a strategy of passive resistance, retreating behind a facade of silent obstinacy. He only stood up to his father indirectly, holding back his emotions, as if fearing their violent release. Torn between an intrusive father and a painfully retiring mother, he kept a world of buried feelings locked up inside. Even at the end of his life, one of his physicians delivered this judgment on his emotional makeup: "He is the most suppressive man I ever knew. He is not devoid of emotional nature, but his emotions from early life have been diverted from their natural channels of expression . . . What has been called imperturbability in him is simply introversion of his feelings."[52]

The major outlet for Grant's suppressed emotions was his rapturous love of horses. Hannah noted this special affinity: "Horses seem to understand Ulysses."[53] Somewhat clumsy in his gait, the boy was surprisingly graceful on horseback. Riding horses was an ideal way to escape from the social complexities of home into a world where he enjoyed complete freedom and didn't have to kowtow to others. He liked to ride without a saddle or stirrups, sitting astride a blanket on the horse's back, and he was so expert at handling horses that he began riding at age five. He became known for breaking in wild horses for local farmers, a sight that drew admiring spectators to the village square. He tamed even the most refractory horses through a fine sensitivity to their nature rather than by his physical prowess. "If people knew how much more they could get out of a horse by gentleness than by harshness," Grant once observed, "they would save a great deal of trouble both to the horse and the man."[54]

For all his ingrained caution, the boy proved a daredevil on a horse, riding at top speed by age five while standing one-legged on its back. He would plant one foot on a sheepskin lashed to the animal, then maintain his balance by grasping the reins. Even when he was older and used a saddle, he had a startling way of putting his left foot in the stirrup, grabbing the horse's mane with his left hand, then swinging his body nimbly over the horse in a single lithe, fluid motion. Perhaps no story better demonstrates his mastery of horses than Jesse's tale of when a circus came to town:

Once when [Ulysses] was a boy, a show came along in which there was a mischievous pony, trained to go round the ring like lightning, and he was expected to throw any boy that attempted to ride him. "Will any boy come forward and ride this pony?" shouted the ring-master. Ulysses stepped forward, and mounted the pony. The performance began. Round and round and round the ring went the pony, faster and faster, making the greatest effort to dismount the rider. But Ulysses sat as steady as if he had grown to the pony's back. Presently out came a large monkey and sprang up behind Ulysses. The people set up a great shout of laughter, and on the pony ran; but it all produced no effect on the rider. Then the ring-master made the monkey jump on to Ulysses' shoulders, standing with his feet on his shoulders, and with his hands holding on to his hair. At this there was another and a still louder shout, but not a muscle of Ulysses' face moved. There was not a tremor of his nerves. A few more rounds and the ring-master gave it up; he had come across a boy that the pony and the monkey both could not dismount.[55]

When it came to horses, Ulysses was quite enterprising in dreaming up moneymaking ventures. By age eight, he drove a team of two and hauled enormous logs for his father's business. On one occasion, he managed single-handedly to load giant timbers that ordinarily required a crew of eight. Jesse boasted about this episode, but a Simpson cousin noted that an aggrieved Ulysses returned from the encounter with tears in his eyes, convinced "his father had imposed upon him and had not treated him with justice."[56] Two years later the boy was allowed to own his own horses and had enough self-possession to transport adult passengers to Cincinnati, a distance of 40 miles; on one occasion, his livery service extended as far afield as Toledo, 250 miles distant. Another time, when he drove two young women back from Kentucky, they had to ford a creek swollen with rainwater and Grant refused to be deterred. Without giving the women any warning, the twelve-year-old and his team plunged into the stream and "the first thing they knew the horses were swimming and the water went up to their own waists," recalled Jesse. The ladies screamed in terror. "In the midst of the excitement, Ulysses, who was on a forward seat, looked back to the ladies, and with an air perfectly undisturbed, merely said: '*Don't speak—I will take you through safe.*'"[57] He deposited the two shaken women, soggy but safe, back in Georgetown.

Money was a black art that Grant never learned to master, and he spent years trying to live down derision elicited by his bargaining for a colt at age eight. Jesse had offered a farmer named Ralston $20 for the animal; Ralston held out for $25. Jesse sent his son to haggle with Ralston, instructing him to make a $20 opening bid, followed by $22.50 if necessary, and then settle for $25 if he must. Utterly incapable of guile, Ulysses bungled the bargaining. "When I got to Mr. Ralston's house, I said to him: 'Papa says I may offer you twenty dollars for the colt, but if you won't take that, I am to offer twenty-two and a half, and if you won't take that, to give you twenty-five.'"[58] The story circulated widely to the merriment of village youth. Grant later commented, "It cost me more heartburning than almost any transaction in life."[59] He was so traumatized by the mockery that it remained evergreen in his memory. "Boys enjoy the misery of their companions," Grant concluded, ". . . and in later life I have found that all adults are not free from the peculiarity."[60] The trusting naïveté displayed in the Ralston episode would haunt the adult Grant no less than the boy.

Unlike many great historical figures, Grant brooded on no vast dreams, harbored no spacious vision for his future, and would have settled for a contented, small-town life. Something solitary about farming pleased him, and he was happiest when riding, plowing crops, sawing wood, or milking cows. The one business for which he was clearly unsuited was his father's tannery, which emitted a potent stench that clung to its workers. For a young man who adored animals and identified with their suffering, it was a sickening way for his father to earn a living.

Inside the dreaded beam room, Jesse soaked hides in vats in a lye solution before they were removed and stripped of hairs by knives. The floor grew slimy with blood and animal fat as giant rats swarmed through the mess. One day, short of help, Jesse commandeered Ulysses for the beam room, and he was revolted by the experience. "Father, this tanning is not the kind of work I like," Ulysses explained. "I'll work at it though, if you wish me to, until I am one-and-twenty; but you may depend upon it, I'll never work a day at it after that."[61] To his credit, instead of pushing his son, Jesse inquired what he would like to do. The boy cited three pretty pedestrian possibilities: become a farmer, become a trader, or get an education. The depth of his disgust with tanning expressed itself in his lifelong insistence on eating meat burned to a crisp and free of blood. He refused to swallow meat that swam in its own juices, an abhorrence that extended to mutton, poultry, and game. "I never could eat anything that goes on two legs," he admitted.[62]

By the time Grant reached early adolescence, his father had prospered in business and diversified his interests. Appointed an agent for the Columbus Insurance Company in 1835, he peddled fire insurance and also won a contract to build the local jail. Flush with cash, he packed Ulysses off the next autumn to an excellent private academy, Maysville Seminary, in Maysville, Kentucky, a two-story brick school on the banks of the Ohio River. Grant boarded with the widow of his rich uncle Peter, who had thrived in tanning, salt, and river shipping. At fourteen Ulysses was now "a stumpy, freckle-faced, big-headed country lad."[63] Aside from math, he remained an indifferent student. In the debating society, however, he displayed a keen interest in current affairs, especially the annexation of Texas, and argued for the proposition that intemperance represented a more severe threat than war. After school, on warm days, he and his classmates cobbled together rafts from logs and leapt from them into the Ohio River, often swimming across and gathering fruit and mulberries on the Kentucky bank. "He was always very liberal and generous in sharing anything he had with other boys, as apples, cakes, etc," said a companion. "He was an exception as a boy for *truth, honesty and fairness.*"[64]

This idyllic period ended the next spring when the 1837 financial panic forced Jesse to economize and bring his son back to Georgetown for a year before sending him to the Presbyterian Academy in nearby Ripley, Ohio. The school was run by the Reverend John Rankin, a famous antislavery cleric who had emerged as an early conductor on the Underground Railroad, attaining legendary status among abolitionists. In the window of his house, set on a bluff high above the Ohio River, Rankin would kindle lamps to guide to freedom fugitive slaves from Kentucky. William Lloyd Garrison and Henry Ward Beecher credited Rankin with exceptional influence in stamping out slavery, while Harriet Beecher Stowe collected material from him for *Uncle Tom's Cabin.* Rankin, who said that slavery "hangs like the mantle of night over our republic and shrouds its rising glories," served as minister of a nearby Presbyterian church, where Ulysses Grant heard him preach many times.[65] That Jesse shipped his son to Rankin's school suggests a possible attempt to imbue him early on with abolitionist ideals.

Grant's classmates there remembered a stocky boy with a rustic air who seemed slow in speech, sluggish in movement, and careless in appearance. He was affable and well-liked, if not especially sociable, and seldom showed up at parties. He studied algebra, Latin, and math and was inquisitive in class, though never much of a talker. That he failed to dazzle classmates with his intelligence was shown by the reaction of one to later news that Grant had been accepted at West Point: "Well, if that numbskull could pass, I know I could."[66]

By late 1838, Jesse had lost faith that his son could chart his own future and took his destiny in hand with brisk efficiency. Since the stalled economy had put a crimp in his business, he could not educate Ulysses further without withdrawing much-needed capital. It dawned on him that if the boy attended West Point, he would be schooled at government expense. At the time, many cadets avoided military careers, using the academy as a high-class vocational school specializing in math and civil engineering. Not bothering to consult Ulysses, Jesse wrote to the Ohio senator Thomas Morris, an impassioned opponent of slavery, about a possible place at West Point for his son. The senator informed him that a vacancy existed in Jesse's district. By an extraordinary coincidence, G. Bartlett Bailey, son of Grant's near neighbor, Dr. George Bailey, had been discharged from the academy for misbehavior and/or failing exams, which his shame-ridden parents had kept secret by forbidding their son to return home, banishing him to a private military school. Ulysses thought Mrs. Bailey disclosed the secret to his mother, perhaps prompting Jesse's letter to Senator Morris.

When he received the encouraging reply around Christmas, Jesse turned to his son and announced, "Ulysses, I believe you are going to receive the appointment." "What appointment?" Ulysses asked. "To West Point; I have applied for it." "But I won't go," replied Ulysses. Jesse insisted he would go *and I thought so too, if he did,* as Ulysses recalled his cowed reaction to this paternal edict. The young man had little confidence he could meet the entrance requirements. "I did not believe I possessed them, and could not bear the idea of failing."[67] It was a classic encounter between the domineering Jesse, exerting his will, and Ulysses, who lacked the strength to stand up and defy him and sheepishly consented.

The matter required a delicate next step. Jesse needed to write to his local congressman, Thomas Hamer, who had to nominate his son for West Point. There was time pressure involved: Hamer was a lame duck whose term ended March 4. Far more worrisome was that Jesse Grant and Thomas Hamer, quondam friends, had not spoken since they parted company over Jacksonian politics, when Jesse accused him of "gross deceit."[68] Ulysses later said both men, regretting the breach, wanted a rapprochement. Jesse addressed a businesslike letter to Hamer, making no allusion to past unpleasantness. It reached Hamer the night of March 3 and, instead of being vindictive, he graciously agreed to submit Grant's name. In his haste, he listed the applicant as Ulysses S. Grant. The confusion came about either because Hamer confused Ulysses with his younger brother Simpson or because he assumed Ulysses was his first name and he had taken Hannah's maiden name for his middle name. (Grant himself blamed Senator Morris for the long-lived error.) The mistaken name, which persisted at West Point and beyond, was the bane of the young man's life and seemed symbolic of his almost comic passivity under Jesse's heavy-handed tutelage. As Grant later confessed to his wife in frank exasperation, "You know I have an 'S' in my name and don't know what it stand[s] for."[69]

The young Grant was right to fret about whether he would pass the exams administered once he arrived at West Point, for many would-be cadets had graduated from college or taken preparatory courses especially designed for the academy. He was not reconciled to going. "I did not want to go to West Point," he maintained. "My appointment was an accident, and my father had to use his authority to make me go."[70] The astonishing news that Grant, the country bumpkin, was heading off to West Point elicited condescending smirks around Georgetown. One Grant peer remembered that "none of us boys, high or low, rich or poor, could clearly imagine how Uncle Sam's schoolmasters were going to transform our somewhat *outré*-looking comrade into our *beau idéal* of dandyism—a West Pointer."[71]

CHAPTER TWO

The Darling Young Lieutenant

ON MAY 15, 1839, Ulysses S. Grant bade his family a stiffly formal farewell and left behind the small, provincial world he had inhabited. At seventeen, he was tiny for his age, weighing a mere 117 pounds and standing five feet two inches tall; at West Point he would reach his full height of five feet eight inches. It was typical of Hannah that she extracted from him a promise he would never resort to profane language at West Point. One senses that Grant was starved for outright maternal affection, for when he crossed the street to say good-bye to the Baileys, Mrs. Bailey and her daughters stood bathed in tears. Grant was taken aback by the emotional display, which struck him as a revelation. "Why you *must* be sorry I am going," he said with dawning wonder. "They didn't cry at our house."[1] Grant lugged a suitcase imprinted with brass tacks of his initials. To avert teasing, he had rearranged H.U.G. into the far more palatable U.H.G, the shifting initials emblematic of his confused sense of identity.

The boy nursed a certain wanderlust, the first hint of some broader vision of life, and was eager to set eyes on Philadelphia and New York. Nevertheless, he experienced such foreboding about West Point that he daydreamed about a travel accident that would abort the whole trip. "When these places were visited I would have been glad to have had a steamboat or railroad collision . . . by which I might have received a temporary injury sufficient to make me ineligible, for a time, to enter the Academy," he wrote with dry humor. "Nothing of the kind occurred, and I had to face the music."[2] He traveled by steamer to

Pittsburgh, then switched to a canal boat for Harrisburg. From there he clambered aboard a train bound for Philadelphia and was thrilled as it accelerated to a maximum velocity of eighteen miles per hour.

During five days in Philadelphia, he boarded with his mother's relatives and roamed its streets with rapt attention, visiting the theater and touring Girard College. He looked like a hayseed from the heartland, "a rather awkward country lad, wearing plain clothes and large, coarse shoes as broad at the toes as at the widest part of the soles," in the amused memory of one female cousin.[3] In New York, Grant experienced a fateful encounter with a foppish young man from Missouri named Fred Dent, who stayed at the same hotel. As westerners, the two teenagers struck up an instant camaraderie, and, when they discovered they were both headed for the military academy, traveled up the Hudson River together.

Upon arrival at West Point, Grant registered under the name U. H. Grant, inscribing his name as Ulysses Hiram Grant in the adjutant's office. He then discovered, despite his unavailing protests, that he had been nominated for West Point under "Ulysses S. Grant" and perhaps began to suspect that fate had pasted this label permanently on him. As soon as fellow cadets, including William Tecumseh Sherman, spotted the name "U. S. Grant" on the bulletin board, they made great sport of it and promptly branded the newcomer Uncle Sam Grant, or "Sam" Grant for short. Henceforth, he would be known as Sam Grant among the cadets. By the end of four years at West Point, he had capitulated to the tyranny of the clerical error and adopted Ulysses S. Grant as his new moniker for life.

Grant was surprised that he breezed through the entrance exams, especially since one out of four candidates flunked. The tests included a physical to see whether candidates had dental or skeletal defects as well as tests of penmanship and spelling. Once they passed, Grant and other new "plebes" had their heads shaved nearly bald and spent the next few months in "summer encampment," sleeping in tents and drilling in an open area called the Plain before taking up barracks residence in September. Grant never forgot his initial glimpse that summer of General Winfield Scott, who came to review the cadets. A gigantic, stately man, standing six feet five inches tall, he was all aglow in a profusion of medals and gold lace. "I thought him the finest specimen of manhood my eyes had ever beheld . . . I could never resemble him in appearance, but I believe I did have a presentiment . . . that some day I should occupy his place on review."[4] For this shambling young man, short on ambition, it was an uncharacteristic mental leap into a shining military future.

On September 14, 1839, Grant signed his enlistment papers, which required him to serve in the Army of the United States for eight years. This was no idle act, and Grant would abide devoutly by this pledge. When the Civil War broke out, he repeatedly reminded people that he had vowed to serve his country in exchange for being educated in warfare, reinforcing a fervent indignation that Robert E. Lee and other Confederate generals who attended West Point had violated their sworn oaths.

The new cadet, blue-eyed and clean-shaven with a rubicund complexion, was quite handsome, bearing scant resemblance to the later general of the stubbly beard and weathered face. He was enchanted by West Point's natural beauty, writing home about its bucolic wonders and sighing over the "beautiful river with its bosom studded with hundreds of snow[-white] sails."[5] When he visited a house once occupied by Benedict Arnold, his fiery reaction foreshadowed things to come as he patriotically denounced Arnold as "that *base* and *heartless* traitor to his country and his God."[6] Notwithstanding his reluctance to go to the academy, he quickly accepted its sound practicality on the economic grounds touted by his father. "The fact is if a man graduates here he [is] safe for life."[7]

When he surveyed his freshly uniformed self in the mirror, he laughed at the spic-and-span figure suddenly staring back at him. "My pants sit as tight to my skin as the bark to a tree," he told a friend, "and if I do not walk *military,* that is if I bend over quickly or run, they are very apt to crack with a report as loud as a pistol. My coat must always be buttoned up tight to the chin."[8] This snappy appearance did not last long, however, and Grant soon received demerits for careless deportment, untied shoelaces, and lateness for drills. He was so diminutive that when he donned a pair of overalls and went down to the riding hall, his spurs and huge clanking cavalry sword seemed to dwarf his boyish frame.

In Ohio, Grant had been the butt of taunts by town toughs, whereas the cadets discerned sterling qualities beneath his quiet, stolid manner. The academy counted 250 cadets in all, so that everyone mostly knew everyone else, and fellow cadets commended Grant's honesty, candor, and generosity. Perhaps the highest accolade came from a tall, rangy cadet, James Longstreet, who hailed from the Deep South and later won renown as the man Robert E. Lee dubbed "my old warhorse."[9] With his doughty independence and integrity, he retained warm memories of Grant at West Point, citing his "girlish modesty; a hesitancy in presenting his own claims; a taciturnity born of his modesty; but a thoroughness in the accomplishment of whatever task was assigned him."[10] For three years, Grant roomed with Fred Dent, who also singled out Grant as "the clearest headed young man I ever saw . . . He always wanted to do what was right, and we all had great respect for him. He was a singed cat—a great deal better than he looked."[11] Grant also shared rooms with Rufus Ingalls, later distinguished as quartermaster general of the U.S. Army. Although Grant experimented with tobacco, which was forbidden, he did not acquire a smoking habit and only occasionally partook of liquor.

By stripping them of all luxuries and housing them in barracks of extreme simplicity, West Point introduced cadets to a rigorous military life. With two cadets squeezed into each cramped room, they had to fetch water from a downstairs pump, scrub floors, make their beds, and fold their sheets. At 5 a.m., they were roused from sleep by rumbling drums and marched off to the dining hall. Grant mostly obeyed institutional rules, with a few significant lapses. William B. Franklin recalled that cadets could not cook in their rooms, but often sneaked in meat and potatoes. One night Grant was "roasting a chicken in his room when an officer rapped." Grant stood rigidly at attention as the officer alluded to a telltale cooking odor. "'I've noticed it,' replied Grant, and the officer retired, thoroughly impressed by the innocent look on the cadet's face."[12] As in Georgetown, Grant refused to be hazed when a strapping cadet named Jack Lindsay kept shoving him from the squad as they drilled on the parade ground. When Lindsay pushed him once too often, Grant retaliated by knocking down the larger boy, flattening him with a punch. In time, Grant, despite his short stature, developed a reputation for a fearless sense of fair play and was regularly approached by other cadets to mediate their disputes.

The West Point curriculum was long on math, engineering, geography, and history. Though it presented courses on artillery, fortifications, and cavalry maneuvers, Grant later laughed at the primitive tactics, based on musket and flintlock weapons. In his first year, the course work emphasized French for a straightforward reason: the French were the foremost military theorists of the day. The reigning figure in military strategy was Antoine-Henri Jomini, a Swiss-born officer who had fought by Napoleon's side. Jomini's ideas came filtered through the mind of the academy's most charismatic teacher, Dennis Hart Mahan, who transformed the study of Napoleon into a worshipful cult. He adapted French theory to American frontier conditions, teaching lessons about flexible supply bases, the rapid movement of troops, and concentration of forces that Grant would faithfully apply throughout the Civil War. Mahan remembered Grant fondly: "Grant's mental machine is of the powerful low-pressure class . . . which pushes steadily forward and drives all obstacles before it."[13] It has often been said that Grant was ignorant of military history, but in later years he could recapitulate in minute detail the campaigns of Napoleon, Frederick the Great, and Julius Caesar, as the journalist John Russell Young discovered to his astonishment when he interviewed Grant in 1879.[14]

The stereotype of Grant as a flop at West Point is misleading. His performance was lackluster, not awful, and he proved modestly successful in selected areas. "I had no occasion for any aids in mathematics," he said. "The subject was so easy to me as to come almost by intuition."[15] In a world of competitive young men, Grant could come across as a laggard. "In his studies he was lazy and careless," said Rufus Ingalls. "Instead of studying a lesson, he would merely read it over once or twice; but he was so quick in his perceptions that he usually made very fair recitations even with so little preparation."[16] The academy suffered such a heavy attrition rate that, a year after Grant entered, his class was whittled down from eighty-two to forty-nine members. Although many of his letters speak fondly of the academy, he displayed small interest in military matters and portrayed his West Point stay as a trial to be endured. The furthest he allowed his fantasies to range ahead was to imagine himself an assistant math professor at the academy, followed by a college professorship. Only the specter of his father's disapproval kept him firmly stationed on the Hudson. "If I could have escaped West Point without bringing myself into disgrace at home, I would have done so," he reminisced. "I remember about the time I entered the academy there were debates in Congress over a proposal to abolish West Point. I . . . read the Congress reports with eagerness . . . hoping to hear that the school had been abolished, and that I could go home to my father without being in disgrace."[17]

Already possessing a literary bent, Grant often escaped into the world of fiction, devouring novels by Sir Walter Scott, Washington Irving, and James Fenimore Cooper and serving as president of the literary society. Shy, closemouthed, he did not dance and came up short with the ladies, especially compared with the polished young southern boys with their ingratiating manners. Perhaps most surprising was the talent he exhibited in a drawing course given by a popular instructor, Robert Walter Weir, who had studied painting in Italy and specialized in landscapes and historical subjects. With cartography in its infancy, West

Point emphasized drawing so that future officers could sketch rough maps and record a battlefield's topography. The clarity and acuity of Grant's vision—his uncanny ability to visualize chaotic fighting amid the fog of war—would account in no small measure for his military triumphs. Grant executed fanciful Italian scenes and tender genre studies of Native Americans and, in one droll, delightful painting, showed a horse with its head drooping into a feed bag, a picture notable for its palpable affection for the creature.

Grant also thrived in horseback riding and was lucky that the academy introduced equestrian classes during his tenure. Cadets training to be cavalry officers were expected to leap over hurdles, their sabers flailing in the air. Everybody noted the perfect harmony that united man and animal when Grant sat erect in the saddle. "In horsemanship . . . he was noted as the most proficient in the Academy," said Longstreet. "In fact, rider and horse held together like the fabled centaur."[18] As in Georgetown, knots of cadets would gather and stare with hypnotic admiration as Grant subdued unruly horses, and one said appreciatively, "It was as good as any circus to see Grant ride."[19] In scaling hurdles he exceeded all rivals, and when cadets competed in jumps, attendants would hike up the bar a full foot higher to spotlight Grant's star turn.

During the Civil War, Grant attributed some of his success to a thorough knowledge of Confederate officers, stored up at West Point and in the Mexican War. Indeed, a goodly portion of the dramatis personae of the Civil War trooped through his academy life. He was mesmerized, if a bit appalled, by a zealous Christian cadet from a poor family in rural western Virginia, Thomas J. Jackson. "At West Point he came into the school at an older age than average, and began with a low grade. But he had so much courage and energy, worked so hard, and governed his life by a discipline so stern that he steadily worked his way along and rose far above others who had more advantages."[20] Grant remembered Jackson's bouts of hypochondria, his belief in possession by demonic spirits, his tireless bent for self-improvement. Grant never directly faced Stonewall Jackson during the Civil War, when he fought like a man possessed, his eyes said to be fiercely lit by inner fires.

Among the older cadets, which included John Pope and Simon Bolivar Buckner, Grant was especially drawn to William Tecumseh Sherman, who was as witty and energetic as Grant was constrained in manner. He was "generous to everybody," Grant recalled, and "one of the most popular boys at the Academy."[21] Grant's critique of another older cadet, George H. Thomas, later hero of

Chickamauga, prefigured his impatience with Thomas's lumbering style of command. "At West Point, when he was commanding cadets in cavalry drill, he would never go beyond a slow trot. Just as soon as the line began to move, and gain a little speed, Thomas would give the order, 'Slow trot.' The boys used to call him 'Slow Trot' Thomas."[22] Among younger cadets the most impressive was the precocious George B. McClellan, who entered West Point at fifteen after two years at the University of Pennsylvania. By a strange juxtaposition of fate, his class included George E. Pickett of Gettysburg fame.

After two years of study, West Point rewarded cadets with a two-month furlough, and Grant celebrated this interlude as a long-awaited reprieve from his New York exile. "This I enjoyed beyond any other period of my life," he stated, with understandable hyperbole.[23] By now Jesse had followed his usual practice of trading up to ever-richer towns, moving from Georgetown to Bethel, a mere twelve miles away, but a distinct step upward in socioeconomic status. He and Hannah had moved into an imposing brick house recently owned by Senator Thomas Morris, and noxious fumes no longer floated in from a nearby tannery. Jesse had formed a partnership agreement with E. A. Collins under which Jesse would expand their Bethel tannery while Collins hawked its products in the Mississippi River town of Galena, Illinois, forging a connection that was to prove consequential for Ulysses. Jesse planned to groom his two younger sons, Simpson and Orvil, to take over his tanning business, a prospect pointedly spurned by Ulysses.

As restless as ever, Jesse donated his time to a dizzying array of causes, sitting on the board of the Methodist church and joining the local Masonic lodge. Still a stalwart Whig, he had campaigned heartily in 1840 for William Henry Harrison, whose slogan in the presidential race was "Tippecanoe and Tyler, too." (Harrison had been the hero of the battle of Tippecanoe and John Tyler was his running mate.) Inspired by this slogan, Jesse took part in a campaign parade in which he pulled an oar in a gargantuan canoe mounted on wheels that was pulled down the town's main street. Many locals were offended by Jesse's ostentatious air of prosperity, his insufferable boasting about Ulysses, and his outspoken politics. "He was an uncompromising anti-slavery Whig, a strong temperance advocate, the richest man in town, owned a piano, wore gold-bowed spectacles, and sent his children to college," explained one townsman.[24] Yet the hard-driving Jesse was enterprising enough to be elected mayor of Bethel within a decade.

Encased in his starchy uniform, his frame well toned by parade ground drills, the Ulysses S. Grant who returned to Bethel by stagecoach had the upright carriage of a cadet instead of his familiar boyhood slouch. Training had made him lean and muscular. When he encountered his mother, she didn't shower him with tears or hugs, but inspected him closely instead. "Ulysses, you have grown much straighter," she commented, and he shot back, "Yes, that was the first thing they taught me."[25] The improvement proved only temporary. In the agrarian isolation of a small Ohio town before the railroad boom, Ulysses whirled in like some visitor from a faraway world who imparted strange lore of distant places. On Bethel's streets, he was often surrounded by flocks of locals who listened, mouth agape, to his stock of West Point tales, relieved to find him free of his father's vanity.

In the emotional desert of the Grant household, Ulysses was ripe for romance and found his first love interest in a young woman named Kate Lowe, who lived in nearby Batavia. He rode over frequently to see her and experienced the early transports of desire. Before returning to West Point, Grant, in courting mode, even sent the damsel rhymed couplets to testify to his affection: "Kindly then remember me / I'll also often think of thee, / Nor forget the Soldier story / Gone to gain the field of glory."[26]

Back at West Point in the fall, Grant was briefly accorded the honor of being named a sergeant who exercised leadership in one of four companies formed for military exercises. Instead of being galvanized into superior performance, Grant preferred to languish. As he confessed, "The promotion was too much for me."[27] As he accumulated demerits—in May 1842, he was confined to quarters for two weeks for speaking disrespectfully to a superior officer—he was stripped of his sergeant stripes and reverted to a private for his last year. Time hung heavy on his hands. "The last two years wore away more rapidly than the first two, but they still seemed about five times as long as Ohio years, to me."[28] As so often in Grant's career, his mental depression acquired a physical correlative. During his last six months at West Point, he was gripped by a "desperate cough" that slimmed him down to 117 pounds—the same weight recorded during his entrance exam, even though he had gained six inches in height.[29] Two of Jesse Grant's brothers had died of consumption, perhaps adding an extra element of concern to Grant's condition.

Despite his infirmity, Grant rode regularly and astounded people with his equestrian theatrics, routinely clearing a bar set at five feet by the riding master, the Prussian sergeant Henry Hershberger. The most fearsome horse in the academy stables was York, an intractable animal dreaded by most cadets. When one classmate warned Grant, "That horse will kill you some day," he coolly responded, "Well, I can't die but once."[30] The pinnacle of Grant's horsemanship came at graduation time, when the senior class performed mounted exercises before a vast throng of spectators. A young onlooker named James B. Fry never forgot Grant's bravura performance at the close:

> When the regular services were completed, the class, still mounted, was formed in line through the center of the hall, the riding-master placed the leaping-bar higher than a man's head, and called out *"Cadet Grant!"* A clean-faced, slender, blue-eyed young fellow, weighing about 120 pounds, dashed from the ranks on a powerfully built chestnut-sorrel horse and galloped down the opposite side of the hall. As he turned at the farther end and came into the straight stretch across which the bar was placed, the horse increased his pace, and, measuring his strides for the great leap before him, bounded into the air and cleared the bar, carrying his rider as if man and beast had been welded together. The spectators were breathless. *"Very well done, sir!"* growled "old Hershberger," the riding-master, and the class was dismissed and disappeared; but "Cadet Grant" remained a living image in my memory.[31]

Grant established an academy record that stood for decades, and the story's afterlife was no less remarkable. On his deathbed, when Fry called upon him, Grant could retrieve every detail of the memorable episode. "'Yes,' he whispered, 'I remember that very well. York was a wonderful horse. I could feel him gathering under me for the effort as he approached the bar. Have you heard anything lately of Hershberger?'"[32]

When Grant graduated in June 1843, his rank was middling, not miserable: twenty-first in a class of thirty-nine. If one includes the many cadets who had already dropped out, Grant nearly stood in the top quarter of candidates who set out on the four-year marathon. The results were highly creditable in light of Grant's lackadaisical work ethic and the fact that some students entered with college preparatory work under their belts. Ironically, Grant scored best in subjects that might someday be of service in civilian life (math, engineering, and

geology) and fared poorly in strictly military subjects (artillery and infantry tactics), confirming his disinclination for military service. Because of Grant's strong
performance in math, Professor Albert E. Church soon encouraged him to return to the academy as an assistant professor, and Grant cherished this lowly as-
piration. Although the feeling was far from universal, several cadets recognized
Grant's uncommon strength of character. Shortly before graduation, classmate
James A. Hardie prophesied, "Well, sir, if a great emergency arises in this country during our life-time, Sam Grant will be the man to meet it."[33]

Looking back on his life, Grant declared that his happiest day was his last as
president—with the possible exception of graduation day at West Point.[34] For all
that, he retained enduring respect for the academy and an affection for those
who had survived its exacting ordeals. "He preferred West Point men as soldiers," wrote a later staff officer, "he loved them as friends . . . he thought higher
even of Sherman and Sheridan because they were graduates of the Academy."[35]

As he contemplated the military career to which he was now committed for
several years, Grant coveted a cavalry assignment—an illustrious branch of
service—and was crestfallen at being rejected. He had to settle for a commission
as brevet second lieutenant attached to the Fourth Infantry Regiment, based at
Jefferson Barracks, just south of St. Louis, Missouri. Grant spent a last summer
in Ohio and ordered an infantry uniform from a local tailor. Evidently proud of
his uniform and hoping it would impress the young ladies, he sported it on a trip
to Cincinnati. "While I was riding along a street of that city, imagining that
everyone was looking at me . . . a little urchin, bareheaded, barefooted, with
dirty and ragged pants held up by a single gallows . . . and a shirt that had not
seen a wash-tub for weeks, turned to me and cried: 'Soldier! will you work? No,
sir—ee; I'll sell my shirt first!!'" That Grant recalled this chance encounter with
a nameless mocking waif underscores his uncommon sensitivity to ridicule.

At the same time he could not escape the barbs of small-town envy that had
so bedeviled him before in Bethel. Because he wore a fancy uniform, some people scorned him as uppity. "The stable-man was rather dissipated, but possessed
of some humor," Grant wrote. "On my return I found him parading the streets,
and attending in the stable, bare-footed, but in a pair of sky-blue nankeen
pantaloons—just the color of my uniform trousers—with a strip of white cotton
sheeting sewed down the outside seams in imitation of mine. The joke was a
huge one in the mind of many of the people, and was much enjoyed by them;
but I did not appreciate it so highly."[36] According to one resident, Grant had

fallen victim to shafts meant to land elsewhere: "Such incivilities were really aired less at the genial unoffending Lieutenant than at his offending father who was known to be very proud of him."[37]

In being assigned to Jefferson Barracks, Grant found himself posted to the largest military outpost in the United States, manned by two infantry regiments. As it had since the Lewis and Clark expedition, nearby St. Louis served as gateway to western expansion, the army post throwing a protective shield around white settlers threatened by Indian raids on the Great Plains. Graced with gray limestone buildings, an enormous parade ground, and white picket fences on softly rolling hills, Jefferson Barracks was a prized posting and port of call for a succession of future generals. More than two hundred Civil War generals passed through its expansive grounds. The commanding officer was Colonel Stephen Kearny, whom Grant valued as a model professional in the way he adhered to high standards without shackling soldiers with onerous rules.

The young Grant, twenty-one, who reported to Jefferson Barracks on September 30, 1843, misunderstood the nature of his special gifts. Ruddy and fresh-faced, he continued to train for a math professorship, plowing through mathematical studies as well as "many valuable historical works, besides an occasional novel."[38] He even contacted Professor Church, the West Point math instructor, to solicit a job as an assistant professor. Always attentive to his military status, he chafed at being shipped off to the infantry and made a futile request to be transferred to the dragoons, or mounted troops, who stood on a higher echelon.

While Colonel Kearny expected his men to snap to attention at drills and roll calls, he showed a more relaxed attitude toward social activities beyond the base. Officers were constantly drafted for parties and cotillions in St. Louis, which made Jefferson Barracks a good place to shop for a wife. James Longstreet, also sent to Jefferson Barracks, extolled the "hospitable city" and remembered wistfully that "the graceful step of its charming belles became a joy forever."[39] Grant hoped to see his West Point roommate, Fred Dent, who had grown up on a slave plantation known as White Haven that lay only five miles from the army base. When Fred was dispatched farther west into Indian country, he encouraged Grant to visit his family anyway; in the company of Longstreet, who was related to Fred's mother, Grant made a courtesy call there that autumn. Fred had smoothed the way with glowing letters to his eldest sister, Julia. "He said, I want you to know him," Julia remembered. "He is pure gold. I have never known him to use a profane or vulgar word . . . he is a splendid fellow."[40]

The Ulysses S. Grant who galloped up to White Haven was something of a pretty boy, his face not yet careworn from drink, depression, and business failure. His skin was smooth and unclouded, his features attractively regular, and he cut a fine figure in a blue uniform with gold buttons running down the front. Although Julia Dent was then at boarding school in St. Louis, her younger sisters swooned over the second lieutenant. Emma Dent, age six, thought him "the handsomest person I had ever seen in my life" and left a detailed account of her first impressions. "He was very youthful looking, even for his age, which was just twenty-one. His cheeks were round and plump and rosy; his hair was fine and brown, very thick and wavy. His eyes were a clear blue, and always full of light." His figure was "so slender, well formed, and graceful that it was like that of a young prince to my eye."[41] Nellie Dent, fifteen, equally smitten, began to indulge in romantic hopes. Warmly received by the Dent parents and with these adoring sisters panting after him, Grant began to canter out to White Haven with some regularity.

Enchanted by the family, Grant sometimes lingered there too long, returning late for meals at Jefferson Barracks. He possessed an easygoing side that never quite conformed to the strict dictates of army discipline. Captain Robert C. Buchanan, overseer of the Fourth Infantry mess, was a martinet of the old school who took sadistic delight in harassing recent West Point graduates, fining them bottles of wine for tardiness. Three times in ten days he levied this penalty upon Grant, who bristled at the unwonted reprimand. "Grant, you are late, as usual; another bottle of wine, sir." "Mr. President," Grant replied, "I have been fined three bottles of wine within the last ten days and if I am fined again I shall be obliged to repudiate." "Mr. Grant, young people should be seen, not heard."[42] This exchange is noteworthy, for a decade later Buchanan would reemerge as a major nemesis in Grant's career, with highly destructive consequences.

At this point, Grant had no notion that St. Louis might form the backdrop of pivotal moments in his life. The city already ranked as a major port, its crowded wharves swarming with river captains, traders, fur trappers, miners, and merchants who supplied pioneer families. French and English were still spoken on its streets, reflecting its colonial roots. As a border state that permitted slavery, Missouri threw into dramatic relief the tensions roiling the country prior to the Civil War. From his growing liaison with the Dents, Ulysses S. Grant would be forced to straddle two incompatible worlds: the enterprising free labor economy of the North and the regressive world of southern slavery. An influx of liberal German immigrants had introduced into St. Louis a sizable community of small farmers with an abolitionist bent, sharpening tensions with large planters over slavery.

Poised on a hill, amid a grove of lofty trees, the main house at White Haven was tan-colored, with dark-brown edges, giant stone chimneys at both ends, and a two-story verandah in front. It boasted a barn, a lime kiln, an ice house, a chicken house, and other amenities. The Dents had moved out from St. Louis, making this their primary residence to escape pollution and disease prevalent downtown; with prices still affordable, they had amassed 850 acres of deeply rolling woodland. The Dent daughters always viewed White Haven through the softening haze of nostalgia. "Our home was then really the showplace of the county, having very fine orchards of peaches, apples, apricots, nectarines, plums, cherries, grapes, and all of the then rare small fruits," wrote Julia.[43] And Emma: "The farm of White Haven was even prettier than its name, for the pebbly, shining Gravois [Creek] ran right through it, and there were beautiful groves growing all over it."[44] The breathless prose thinly disguised the brutal reality that the Dents owned thirteen slaves—the figure would rise to thirty within a decade— who grew the cash crops of wheat, oats, corn, and potatoes that formed the basis of the family wealth.

Not until February did Grant meet Julia Dent, four years his junior, who had just wound up seven years at a tony finishing school in St. Louis. Elegance, taste, and refinement always qualified as magical words in Julia's lexicon. Never a highly motivated student, she was nonetheless a voracious reader and well educated by the standards of her day. She loved the *Iliad* and the *Odyssey* and anything that savored of mythology and history. Her literary tastes ran the gamut from Samuel Johnson to Lord Byron to Victor Hugo. Perhaps with the benefit of hindsight, she claimed she had told her classmates of her wish to find "a *soldier,* a gallant, brave, dashing soldier."[45] She had spent the St. Louis winter with her parents' friends, the O'Fallons, who had introduced her into local society, where she was courted by a steady procession of eligible young officers from Jefferson Barracks.

Both as a young girl and as a mature woman, Julia had a penchant for viewing the world through rose-colored spectacles. Late in life, when writing her memoirs, she depicted her girlhood in the flowery prose of a romance novel, allowing no shadows to tinge her past. The daughter of "noble, brave, true and loving" parents, she had been born after four boys and was thus "a veritable queen in our household," a spoiled pet.[46] "The first, ripest, mellowest of apples, peaches, and pears were mine, as also the brightest of flowers, all of which I owed to my brothers."[47] She presented her childhood as the picturesque saga of a southern belle pampered by adoring slaves. The "dear old black uncles always brought to me pet rabbits, squirrels, and all the prettiest birds' eggs they found . . . Besides, we always had a dusky train of from eight to ten little colored girls of all hues, and these little colored girls were allowed to accompany us if they were very neat."[48] In Julia's view, the Dent slaves were all "very happy. At least they were in mamma's time, though the young ones became somewhat demoralized about the beginning of the Rebellion, when all the comforts of slavery passed away forever."[49] It is not surprising that Julia Dent grew up seeing her girlhood in these storybook terms. It is surprising that when she wrote her memoirs as an elderly woman, the Civil War and Reconstruction had done so little to temper these retrograde views.

When Julia returned to White Haven that February, she had heard flattering descriptions of Grant from her mother and knew her sister Nellie already angled for his affection. Grant was about to ride off after a visit when he turned and saw Julia. The beardless lieutenant, young and inexperienced, made an immediate impression on Julia Dent. According to Emma, Grant told her "it was a case of love at first sight . . . that he had never had but the one love affair, but the one sweetheart in his life. Not even the boyish amours that usually precede a young man's real passion had ever been his."[50] But it took time for Grant to fathom the depth of his attachment to Julia, and she was also slow to acknowledge the growing amorous nature of their mutual attraction.

Grant repaired to White Haven up to four times weekly to the point that he and Julia grew inseparable. He loved her spunk, gumption, and resolutely upbeat personality. Whether strolling by Gravois Creek or taking long rides down country lanes, they were totally comfortable with each other and fell into easy conversation. Grant delighted in teasing her affectionately, often playing practical jokes and showing a whimsical wit. When Julia's pet canary died, Grant crafted a tiny coffin for the bird, painted it yellow, then coaxed eight young officers into attending a mock funeral. Even though Grant did not dance, he and Julia became fixtures at military balls. When Grant failed to show up at one, another officer inquired of Julia: "Where is that small man with the large epaulets?"[51]

By Julia's own admission, she never counted as a stunning beauty. "It is needless to mention what everyone knows, that Dame Nature was most chary of her gifts to me, no single special talent did she bestow, and of personal charms she was simply miserly."[52] As a young girl, she worshipped an elusive beauty that she could never quite possess. "I used to cry when I was a little girl because I was so ugly," she confided to a friend. "'Never mind, Julia,' my dear mother would say, 'you can be my good little girl.' I used to wish I could ever once be called her 'pretty little girl.'"[53] On some level, Julia seemed as famished for love as Grant.

Julia's most glaring defect was a congenital lazy eye, a so-called strabismus, which meant that one eye turned inward. (One story claims that she suffered a childhood eye injury when an oar struck her in a boating accident.) This problem shadowed her life and surgeons repeatedly urged her to repair it. "I had never had the courage to consent," she said. Her vision would worsen with the years, making it difficult to concentrate for sustained periods when reading or writing. Ulysses or a companion often read aloud to her. Julia was so self-conscious about the wayward eye that, even in the White House, she preferred to pose for photographs in profile.

Although Julia stood just five feet two inches tall and grew stout and homely with the years, she was a dainty adolescent with many attractive features. "I can only remember my abundance of soft brown hair, a fair complexion, and every one told me my feet and hands were fairy-like."[54] There was something captivating about her personality, with a zest, a warmth, and an animation that must have been balm to Grant's soul after his parched Methodist upbringing with its legacy of stifled feelings. However plain others found her, for Grant she stood forth as the perfection of womanhood. From his reaction to Julia, one can see how much he secretly yearned for open displays of affection and needed the emotional outlet she so abundantly provided.

For Julia, Grant descended like some heavenly apparition in uniform. "I thought he was a Knight from one of the romances that I used to read . . . He entirely enchanted me . . . He was handsome, kind, honest, brave, he was scarcely real to a little girl like myself."[55] She loved his graceful form in the saddle, his sly humor and facetious quips, his shyly boyish manner. Julia sensed a decency about Grant that set him apart from other young soldiers. She was the first to discover that the supposedly silent lieutenant was a riveting raconteur, always ready with a rich treasury of anecdotes. But to her dismay, when others stopped by, Grant tended to clam up. "I finally said, 'Ulys! I told these people you were a fascinating and wonderful conversationalist. I think they have gone away disappointed. Why can't you be as interesting to them as you are to me?'"[56]

Julia was destined to be the bedrock of Grant's life, and he was a hero in her eyes long before he became a national hero. They formed the deep bond craved by bashful men who need the unconditional devotion of one loving, loyal woman. In the face of whatever doubts beset Grant, Julia offered implicit faith in his ability to succeed—a faith that endured even amid catastrophic failure. She was the first to divine the special qualities that lay behind his modest exterior. From early on, she believed in him more than he believed in himself and was more ambitious for him as well. She bolstered his confidence, soothed his wounds, and pierced through his shyness until he learned to count on her constant strength. Whatever her feminine charms, she had a core of steel, a will so fixed that family members nicknamed her "the boss."[57] In future years, Grant would seem adrift when Julia was not around.

As the cosseted eldest daughter, Julia grew up with an idealized picture of her father, Colonel Frederick F. Dent, who pumped her full of expectations that squared with his preferred self-image as a patrician planter. The colonel title was purely honorific. "He was one of the most prominent citizens of the State," Julia said, insisting he had been "the kindest of masters to his slaves, who all adored him."[58] She went so far as to say that he "was most kind and indulgent to his people [i.e., slaves], too much so perhaps."[59] Clad in a long black coat, Colonel Dent often sat on the front porch, puffing his pipe and flipping through newspapers. A photo of him presents a fiery, pugnacious man, who directly confronts the camera. He has a bulbous nose, bushy eyebrows, wispy gray hair, and a sour, unfriendly expression; his hooded eyes stare back warily at the viewer. He was ferociously reactionary, loved to curse, and was unapologetic about the slave-holding South. Dr. William Taussig, a local mayor, remembered him as a hot-tempered character who feuded with neighbors and brooked no opposition. "He was a gentleman of considerable energy, masterful in his ways, of persistent combativeness, of the grim, set purpose peculiar to the Southerners of the old generation and was, where foiled, inclined to be vindictive."[60] "Old man Dent was a man without tact or respect for anybody," a Grant friend recalled. "He was a fat old man, [who] drank a good deal."[61] Colonel Dent could be cordial until the talk turned to politics and then he grew dogmatic. Endowed with the entrenched prejudices of the planter class, he was fond of saying commerce had been ruined by Yankees who came west and "reduced business to a system."

Although he identified with southern gentry, Frederick Dent was a Maryland native who made his earliest money performing road surveys and trading fur on the eastern seaboard. He married the beautiful young Ellen Bray Wrenshall, who was born in England, grew up in Pittsburgh, and was educated in Philadelphia. Around 1816 they struck out for the frontier and moved to St. Louis. Julia cherished the family legend of how they had lashed logs together to form a flotilla of three rafts, with little wooden cabins set on each raft, then floated from Pittsburgh down to Illinois before completing the final stretch by carriage.

Ellen Dent had all the sweetness and none of the vinegar in her husband's dyspeptic nature. Pretty, demure, with a kindly nature and delicate health, she remained homesick for the refined life she had left back East. "She was a small, slender woman with rather serious gray eyes, a smiling mouth, and a gentle voice," wrote daughter Emma. "I remember that she wore snowy caps and dainty kerchiefs on her head, as I have occasionally seen very old-fashioned old ladies do since."[62] Ellen Dent read aloud to her children, encouraged them to play music, and fostered the stimulating cultural atmosphere of the household.

It is a striking feature of Grant's early life that women spied his hidden potential and forecast great things for him, whereas men counted his gentleness against him and overlooked his virtues. Ellen Dent immediately took a fancy to Grant, charmed by his unspoiled nature and quiet demeanor and his common sense in political discussions with the Colonel, a Jacksonian Democrat. Often, after Grant returned to Jefferson Barracks, she declared, "That young man will be heard from some day . . . He will make his mark."[63] As with Julia, Ellen's premonitions only grew more pronounced with time. "She prophesied that he would rise to the highest seat in the government," Julia wrote.[64]

Unfortunately, Colonel Dent governed his daughter's fate with an iron fist and made no bones that he opposed her marriage to the young officer. With Grant he feared Julia would relinquish the style of life to which he had accustomed her. "Old man Dent was opposed to him, when he found he was courting his daughter, and did everything he could to prevent the match," recalled Mary Robinson, one of the Dent slaves.[65] The problem was not one of personality—Colonel Dent found Grant pleasant enough—but hardheaded money concerns. He took a dim view of army life and the economic austerity that accompanied it. "My father knew how arduous, pinched and restless was army life and how it provided few of the home comforts and opportunities for the care which a woman in delicate health might require," explained Emma."[66] On the other hand, Julia was a young woman of rare determination and Grant a young man soon renowned for his tenacity.

Grant hardly needed another despotic father figure in his life, but that is exactly what he got. It did not help matters that the abolitionist Grants came to detest the slave-owning Dents and vice versa, leaving Julia and Ulysses caught in a cross fire that lasted for decades. It could only have damaged Grant to be at the mercy of both an adoring but overbearing father and a hypercritical future father-in-law who thwarted his desire to marry for several years. Trapped between these two men, the young officer was condemned to experience a prolonged adolescence in which he could never fully assert himself without getting slapped down.

That spring, Grant learned his infantry was being shipped to Louisiana. For Ulysses and Julia, the looming separation revealed the degree to which their emotions had been knotted together. Seizing the initiative, he decided to propose to her and ventured out to White Haven on a stormy night that tested his youthful mettle. When he reached Gravois Creek—which ordinarily lacked enough water "to run a coffee mill," Grant joked—he encountered a churning, foaming river swollen by torrential rain. Throughout his life, he had a superstitious dread of turning back—a perfect metaphor for his bullheaded determination—and dove into the overflowing creek on horseback, turning up soaked at White Haven. "We all enjoyed heartily the sight of his ridiculous figure with his clothes flopping like wet rags around his limbs," said Emma. Julia's brother John, who was taller than Grant, gave him dry clothes that only made him look more laughable.[67] Aware of his comical appearance, Grant blushed furiously.

During a weeklong stay at White Haven, Grant waited for a private moment with Julia and found it when, driving her by buggy to a St. Louis wedding, they paused on a bridge over a ravine. "On this ride, he declared his love and told me that without me life would be insupportable," Julia recorded. "I was surprised at his telling me this, for although I was just eighteen, I was very young for my age and very shy indeed. When he spoke of marriage, I simply told him I thought it would be charming to be engaged, but to be married—no! I would rather be engaged."[68] Her reluctance upset Grant, but he realized he must tread carefully and exercise patience with this sheltered girl, especially when she pleaded with him not to tell her father about their engagement. Before leaving for Louisiana, he invited Julia to wear his class ring. "Oh, no," she objected, "mamma would not approve of my accepting a gift from a gentleman."[69] In the end she wore the ring. Unaware of this secret engagement, Ellen Dent hoped the relationship would prosper. Colonel Dent hoped that with Grant packed off at a considerable distance, Julia's emotions would cool off, she would come to her senses, and she would enter into a suitable match with a more affluent man.

//////////////////////

CHAPTER THREE

Rough and Ready

W HEN ULYSSES S. GRANT joined his regiment in May 1844 at a place called "Camp Salubrity," outside of Natchitoches in western Louisiana, his life suddenly meshed with a watershed moment in American history. A month earlier, President John Tyler, a Virginia slaveholder, had presented the Senate with a treaty to annex the independent Republic of Texas. Because Texas had legalized slavery, the treaty spurred impassioned debates between North and South, flaring into a national referendum over the westward spread of slavery. Speaking in upstate New York, William Seward articulated the Whig contention that Texas annexation would provoke an "unjust war" with Mexico "to extend the slave-trade and the slave-piracy."[1]

Grant's regiment camped near the Texas border as part of the Army of Observation. Its ostensible purpose was to deter American filibusters into Texas, but the unspoken agenda was to warn Mexico, which regarded the breakaway republic as renegade Mexican territory, against meddling in the proposed annexation. In his *Memoirs,* Grant blasted the Texas scheme as an imperialist adventure, pure and simple, designed to add slave states to the Union. "For myself, I was bitterly opposed to the measure, and to this day regard the war, which resulted, as one of the most unjust ever waged by a stronger against a weaker nation."[2] He always said he never forgave himself for going into the Mexican War.[3] If Grant thought this way at the time—and some contrary evidence exists—he certainly was not outspoken about it. However wicked the war, he "had not moral courage enough to resign" and felt an overriding duty to serve the flag.[4]

Grant kept Julia apprised of his journey up the Red River to Natchitoches, describing pesky clouds of mosquitoes, knots of raffish gamblers, and low shores teeming with alligators. Camp Salubrity took its name from a high, sandy ridge favored with pure spring water, pine woods, and elevated air free of bugs. Ever since West Point, Grant had fought a nagging cough, which he feared might be consumption, but the wholesome atmosphere and daily exercise banished any remnants of this, restoring him to full vigor. Grant seemed cheerful enough about the rough army life. "As for lodgings I have a small tent that the rain runs through as it would a sieve . . . and as to a floor we have no such a luxury yet," he told his Georgetown friend Mrs. Bailey.[5]

Grant posted frequent letters to Julia, converting drumheads into desks and tenderly pressing flowers between leaves. Colonel Dent hovered in his mind, a baleful presence. "Julia can we hope that your pa will be induced to change his opinion of an army life?" Grant wondered. "I think he is mistaken about the army life being such an unpleasant one."[6] Although Julia eagerly awaited his letters and pored over them repeatedly, she never replied with the speed Grant wished, leaving him dangling on tenterhooks. At one point, he counted only eleven letters from her in a twenty-month period. One wonders whether, to test Grant's fidelity or undermine their relationship, Colonel Dent forbade Julia from writing more often. Another possibility is that her chronic eye problem converted even simple letter writing into an onerous task. We do know that Colonel Dent kept Julia busily distracted with St. Louis parties where she would be exposed to hordes of handsome young bachelors.

In November, with potent backing from slaveholding states, James K. Polk, a Tennessee Democrat, who had made Texas and Oregon annexation the centerpiece of his campaign, scored a narrow victory in the presidential race over Whig Henry Clay. Like other Whigs, Jesse Root Grant feared admission of Texas might further entrench slavery and strengthen the Democratic majority in Congress. Colonel Dent was equally hell-bent on absorbing Texas into the Union. Emboldened by the Democratic victory, the lame-duck Tyler administration lobbied hard for a joint congressional resolution to annex Texas, which passed on February 26, 1845. Once outgoing President Tyler signed it, Mexico severed diplomatic relations with the United States and mobilized for war.

Before the outbreak of open hostilities, Grant wangled a twenty-day leave to return to St. Louis, hoping to secure Colonel Dent's permission to marry his daughter. The surprise visit startled the Dents: Grant materialized on a dappled gray horse and bounded earnestly up the verandah steps, looking tanned and fit after his southern sojourn. Since Colonel Dent was about to leave on a trip, Grant rode with him to St. Louis the next morning, hoping to spring his momentous question. Julia's father reiterated that his delicate daughter could never withstand the rigors of an itinerant army life. Showing some flexibility, Grant informed the Colonel that he now had an offer of a math professorship at a college in Hillsboro, Ohio. Unappeased, Colonel Dent issued a startling counteroffer: "Mr. Grant, if it were Nelly you wanted now, I'd say 'yes.'" "But I don't want Nelly," rejoined Grant. "I want Julia."[7] He extracted a promise that he and Julia could correspond and, if they were still intent on marriage a year or two hence, the Colonel would relent. Emma Dent's postmortem of this pact has the ring of truth: "When Julia wanted a thing of my father she usually got it."[8] When he returned to Camp Salubrity in early May, still gnashing his teeth over Colonel Dent's prickly behavior, Grant nonetheless wrote brightly to Julia, "I shall always look back to my short visit to Mo. as the most pleasant part of my life."[9]

Relations between the United States and Mexico had deteriorated in his absence. The flashpoint of controversy was whether the Nueces River formed the southern border of Texas, as Mexico believed, or the Rio Grande, 130 miles farther south, as the Polk administration insisted. The Polk interpretation would conveniently double the size of the newly adopted state. The president planned to stage a confrontation that would enable him to declare war against Mexico, and Grant claimed to see through this ploy—at least in retrospect. "We were sent to provoke a fight, but it was essential that Mexico should commence it."[10] To this end, Polk ordered General Zachary Taylor to march the Army of Observation, including Grant's regiment, into the disputed zone near the Rio Grande. As a first step, Taylor shifted the army to a staging area near New Orleans. While Grant was there, his commanding officer, William Whistler, was hauled up on charges of drunkenness and disorderly conduct. Grant sat beside him in the courtroom, giving him time to contemplate the damage public inebriation could inflict upon a military career. As it happened, soldiers soon arrived from Grant's company and whisked Whistler away before he was tried.

By the Fourth of July, Texas had voted for American annexation, heightening the likelihood of war. At this point, Grant took a young man's view of the conflict, finding it a boyish lark despite many annoyances. To cater to his personal needs, he had taken as his servant a black boy who spoke English, Spanish, and French. Writing to Julia, Grant dwelt more on his chances for promotion than the tense political standoff, finding soldiering "a very pleasant occupation," marred only by the inconvenience it posed "in the way of our gaining the unconditional consent of your parents to what *we,* or at least I, believe is for our happiness."[11] He told her she had little inkling of the moral authority she exerted over him and that whenever he felt tempted to do anything amiss, he thought of her and refrained from doing so. "I am more or less governed by what I think is your will."[12] Treasuring her judgment, bowing to her desires, Grant had begun to internalize Julia's values when exercising self-control.

By September 1845, Grant's infantry regiment was relocated to Corpus Christi, Texas, the spot where the Nueces River empties into the Gulf of Mexico. A tiny Mexican seaside village with assorted adobe houses and fewer than a hundred people, it was now overrun by several thousand soldiers, the bulk of the American army commanded by Taylor. "We are so numerous here now," Grant reassured Julia, "that we are in no fear of an attack upon our present ground."[13] Responsive to the scenery, Grant galloped across open plains and was entranced by the pristine Texas setting, with its herds of wild horses, Indian wigwams, and mesquite shrubs. Far from being openly outraged by the war, he reported to Julia, "the most numerous class of Mexicans are much better pleased with our form of government than their own" and "would be willing to see us push our claims beyond the Rio Grande if we would promise not to molest them in their homes and possessions."[14]

Grant had plenty of opportunity to study Taylor and ape the uncouth manners of Old Rough and Ready. The owner of a Louisiana plantation, with more than two hundred slaves, Taylor shunned fancy military dress, sometimes donning a linen duster with a wide-brimmed planter's hat. He preferred to ride a mule or an ordinary nag and frequently roamed alone on the battlefield, taking personal stock of the enemy. When resting on a march, he did so in unorthodox fashion, letting both legs hang over the same side of the horse as he munched an apple. For all that, he was widely respected for his "blunt, honest, and stern character," in the words of William Tecumseh Sherman.[15] With his leathery face and tousled hair, he was frank, down-to-earth, and a fine storyteller. As a Whig, he privately denounced annexation as "injudicious in policy and wicked in fact."[16] In describing Taylor, Grant provided a perfect description of his own economical writing style: "Taylor was not a conversationalist, but on paper he could put his meaning so plainly that there could be no mistaking it. He knew how to express what he wanted to say in the fewest well-chosen words."[17] During the Civil War, General George Gordon Meade thought he knew where Grant's style had originated. "He puts me in mind of old Taylor, and sometimes I fancy he models himself on old Zac."[18] Grant confirmed this hunch: "There was no man living who I admired and respected more highly" than Taylor.[19]

At Corpus Christi, Grant caught Taylor's eye when he was deputized to lead a team of men assigned to scrape away oyster beds obstructing the passage of ships. Grant grew so exasperated when his men would not follow orders that he jumped into waist-high water to demonstrate his preferred method. While some nearby officers mocked Grant's take-charge style of leadership, Taylor promptly endorsed it: "I wish I had more officers like Grant, who would stand ready to set a personal example when needed."[20] Through such quick-witted actions, Grant soon earned promotion from brevet second lieutenant to full second lieutenant.

Already an acknowledged virtuoso on horseback, Grant specialized in breaking untamed horses that Mexicans rounded up from the countryside to sell. James Longstreet described one especially dramatic incident when Grant had a refractory horse "blindfolded, bridled, and saddled," then rode it for three hours to subdue it.[21] The man who performed such robust feats had a surprisingly sedate personality. He liked to laugh, joke, play cards, and smoke a pipe, but mostly kept to himself. "He was always a very mild-spoken man, he spoke like a lady almost," recalled J. D. Elderkin, a drum major. "He was about as nice a man as you ever saw . . . He had a very heavy beard all through Mexico and his whiskers were of a reddish-brown color . . . His general character was of a quiet, inoffensive man. He spoke but few words to anybody but he loved to ride on horseback."[22]

All that fall, Grant fantasized that war would be averted and a diplomatic solution found. He wanted desperately to marry, bridled at his interminable engagement to Julia, and reiterated his willingness to resign from the army. Oddly enough, Julia pleaded with him not to resign, even though he offered to do so for her sake. Meanwhile, with every letter, the relentless Jesse Grant badgered Ulysses to quit the army and alerted him that the offer of a math professorship in Hillsboro, Ohio, would stand until spring. Once resigned that his son would not leave the service, Jesse took matters into his own inimitable hands and secretly, but futilely, lobbied Thomas Hamer to have Ulysses transferred to a new regiment of mounted riflemen.[23]

The extended stay in Corpus Christi, a hotbed of smuggling, generated worries that idle soldiers would be corrupted by the lax atmosphere. The town's civilian population had burgeoned to one thousand and was not of the most savory sort, the place reviled by one officer as "the most murderous, thieving, gambling, cut-throat, God-forsaken hole" in Texas.[24] Commanding officers thought performing plays might stave off debauchery among the soldiers. By January, Corpus Christi boasted two new theaters, including one holding eight hundred people and playing to packed houses nightly, with officers usually handling both male and female roles. After suitable costumes were obtained from New Orleans, the decision was made to stage *Othello*. The first choice for Desdemona was James Longstreet, who stood six feet tall and would have towered over Othello, so the prudish Grant was drafted instead. This seems an unlikely choice until we recall that Emma Dent thought him "pretty as a doll," while Longstreet alluded to his "girlish modesty."[25] As it turned out, Theodoric Porter, playing Othello, couldn't work up enough body heat around Grant. "Porter said it was bad enough to play the part with a woman in the cast," said Longstreet, "and he could not pump up any sentiment with Grant dressed up as Desdemona."[26] To put Porter out of his misery, Grant was cashiered and a professional actress imported from New Orleans.

Not long after this rare thespian interlude, Grant's regiment was ordered to the north side of the Rio Grande, moving into the heart of disputed territory as President Polk resolved to bring the crisis to a head. "Texas had no claim beyond the Nueces River," Grant later noted, "and yet we pushed on to the Rio Grande and crossed it. I am always ashamed of my country when I think of that invasion."[27] To trek south across dry, uninhabited prairie, broken by salt ponds, Taylor split his army into four columns that marched up to thirty miles a day. Riding a mustang, Grant marveled at the huge herds of wild horses that sometimes blanketed the plain as far as the eye could see. At the Little Colorado River, the Fourth Infantry waded across in water up to their necks with wagons and mules tugged across with ropes. Upon arriving at the Rio Grande, the Americans gazed across the narrow waterway at the heavily armed Mexican city of Matamoros, which had a small fort and artillery mounted on sandbag breastworks. Grant's letters to Julia lost their youthful ardor and grew somber. The proximity of two armies, he wrote, would spark a confrontation that could only be resolved "by treaty or the sword."[28]

On April 12, 1846, General Pedro de Ampudia warned Taylor that unless he withdrew American forces to the Nueces River within twenty-four hours, a state of war would ensue. A man of crisp decision, his spine stiffened by Polk's truculence, Taylor declined to budge. "Gen. Taylor made a courteous but decided reply," Grant informed Julia, "to the amount that we would not leave but by force."[29] Two weeks later, Mexican troops ambushed American soldiers north of the Rio Grande, slaughtering or wounding sixteen of them. At once Taylor apprised Washington that hostilities had commenced. President Polk now seized upon the casus belli he had long craved, and with the country inflamed by patriotic fervor, Congress voted for war with Mexico by overwhelming margins. Imbued with a sense of honor, Grant believed it would be unconscionable to leave the army at such a moment fraught with danger, and he jettisoned forever his cramped dream of becoming a math teacher. The war now under way would be known as "Mr. Polk's War."

On the morning of May 8, Zachary Taylor and his three-thousand-man army came face-to-face with a much larger Mexican force at a wooded prairie named Palo Alto due to its tall trees. Grant was impressed by the serried ranks of Mexican spears and bayonets glinting in the strong sunlight. Deep in enemy territory, he identified with his commanding general and sympathized with his terrible burden: "I thought what a fearful responsibility General Taylor must feel, commanding such a host and so far away from friends."[30] The battle of Palo Alto developed into an artillery contest. Once oxen-drawn cannon were in place, Taylor barked: "Canister and grape, Major Ringgold. Canister and grape."[31] Firing comparatively primitive weapons, the Mexicans could only return solid shot, while Taylor had howitzers that hurled explosive shells across immense distances and tore apart Mexican lines.

Even though the Mexicans were outmatched, they gave Grant his first unforgettable taste of the horrors of combat. When the first barrage of Mexican cannonballs bounced toward American lines, soldiers sidestepped them easily. Then a cannonball streaked through the air near Grant, missing him but shattering the skull of an enlisted man, spattering his blood and brains on surrounding soldiers. The sudden blast inflicted a disfiguring wound on a Captain Page in Grant's regiment. "The under jaw is gone to the wind pipe and the tongue hangs down upon the throat," Grant wrote. "He will never be able to speak or to eat."[32]

During his maiden battle, Grant discovered something curious about his own metabolism: he was tranquil in warfare, as if temporarily anesthetized, preternaturally cool under fire. The night of the Palo Alto battle he fell into a deep, dreamless slumber on the battlefield. The next day, as he surveyed the terrain, he was powerfully affected by the carnage around him, including sixty American casualties. He told Julia it was a "terrible sight" to see the ground "strewed with the bodies of dead men and horses."[33] To the youthful Grant, "the engagement assumed a magnitude in my eyes which was positively startling." Years later, hardened by the unspeakable casualties he had seen in the Civil War, he mused, "Now, such an affair would scarcely be deemed important enough to report to headquarters."[34] The Mexicans sustained several hundred casualties at Palo Alto, a victory that subsequently helped to catapult Zachary Taylor into the White House.

The next day, the Mexicans, bolstered by fresh troops, formed a long, thin line behind a pond called Resaca de la Palma. Unlike that of Palo Alto, the topography was rough and swampy, covered with tangled chaparral, rendering artillery useless and bringing infantry into play. When Taylor sent two senior captains from Grant's company on a scouting mission, Grant was temporarily placed in charge of a company for the first time. "He was wonderfully cool and quick in battle," said J. D. Elderkin. "Nothing ever 'rattled' him."[35] He proved intrepid leading men through holes in thickets until enemy fire had whittled away the chaparral in a chaotic free-for-all. "We could not see the enemy, so I ordered my men to lie down," Grant wrote, "an order that did not have to be enforced."[36] In a clearing between two ponds, Grant had his men storm the Mexican lines. When they returned with a wounded American officer, Grant realized he had retraced ground already gained. As he observed, "This left no doubt in my mind but that the battle of Resaca de la Palma would have been won . . . if I had not been there."[37] The Mexican retreat devolved into a panicky rout as fleeing soldiers plunged pell-mell into the Rio Grande. As the Army of Observation metamorphosed into the Army of Invasion, Zachary Taylor led his triumphant troops into Matamoros on May 18. "I think you will find that history will count the victory just achieved one of the greatest on record," Grant told Julia.[38] He derived cynical amusement from "reading of the deeds of heroism attributed to officers and soldiers, none of which we ever saw."[39]

During two rain-soaked months stuck in Matamoros, Grant had plenty of time to ponder his three-year engagement to Julia. He sent her wildflowers handpicked from the Rio Grande banks and tried to figure out ways to speed up their marriage. Once the war was over, he told her, he might resign and work in his father's leather goods store in Galena, Illinois. "My father is very anxious to have me do so."[40] He also grew into a perceptive student of Mexico. He already thought Mexican soldiers courageous, but badly supervised by inept generals. In commenting on the American occupation, he betrayed a populist streak and profound sense of social justice, telling Julia: "Some of the volunteers and about all the Texans seem to think it perfectly right to impose upon the people of a conquered City . . . and even to murder them where the act can be covered by the dark. And how much they seem to enjoy acts of violence too!"[41] It was his first lesson on the need to be magnanimous in victory and not lord it over a conquered people. He saw how freely rich Mexicans exploited their downtrodden brethren. "The better class are very proud and tyrannize over the lower and much more numerous class as much as a hard master does over his negroes, and they submit to it quite as humbly."[42] This last comment shows that Grant, early in his career, fully comprehended the barbarity of slavery.

Only twenty-four, Grant guessed correctly that Taylor would transfer his army west to Monterrey, giving him a commanding position in northeastern Mexico, coupled with access to the main road to Mexico City. When they reached Camargo, Colonel John Garland tapped Grant as acting assistant quartermaster of his regiment and he balked at what struck him as a banal administrative post. "I respectfully protest against being assigned to a duty which removes me from sharing in the dangers and honors of service with my company at the front."[43] Since Grant had gained a reputation for competence, Garland turned him down flat. The appointment was actually a godsend for Grant, turning him into a compleat soldier, adept at every facet of army life, especially logistics. With the exception of ammunition and weaponry, the quartermaster supplied everything needed to clothe and transport an army, including uniforms, shoes, canteens, blankets, tents, cooking utensils, horses, forage, and mules. Here Grant would learn not battlefield theatrics but the essential nuts and bolts of an army—the mundane stuff that makes for a well-oiled military machine. This provided invaluable training for the Civil War when Grant would need to sustain gigantic armies in the field, distant from northern supply depots. As quartermaster, Grant could have ducked battles altogether, but he fought in them all and never chose to shirk combat. Showing an understated proficiency, he seemed in his element. "When you spoke to him about anything under the sun," said J. D. Elderkin, "he would have an answer in a moment and never hesitate at all."[44]

Just how well Grant grasped large-scale strategy became manifest when he received an unexpected visit from Thomas Hamer, the Ohio congressman who had sponsored him at West Point and was now a brigadier general of volunteers. One day the two men rode into the countryside, pausing on the brow of a hill, and pretended to be generals with two armies contending on the plain below. Hamer lost their imaginary encounter and was astounded by the cunning moves Grant executed to defeat him. Afterward he scratched off a prophetic letter: "I have found in Lieutenant Grant a most remarkable and valuable young soldier." He added that Grant was "too young for command, but his capacity for future military usefulness is undoubted."[45] Such was Grant's respect for Hamer that when the latter died of illness in early December, Grant not only mourned the loss of a friend but believed the country had lost a future president.

As Taylor marched his army west to Monterrey, a dreary tramp in heavy rain over washed-out roads, Grant's talents as quartermaster shone. By the time troops arrived at their encampment each night, Grant had wood prepared for campfires and herds of cattle ready to be butchered for fresh meat. War had already surrendered its charm for him, and he was frustrated by the slow pace of events, complaining to Julia that "wherever there are battles a great many must suffer, and for the sake of the little glory gained I do not care to see it."[46]

When Taylor's army arrived outside Monterrey, Grant perceived that the Mexicans held a strong position with superior numbers. The town had thick stone walls and was sheltered by mountains on three sides. Outside the city, in a defensive structure dubbed the Black Fort, the Mexicans had erected a citadel that could strafe approaching soldiers from almost any direction. General Ampudia and his men could also fire cannon mounted on surrounding parapets at troops entering the central plaza. Grant was supposed to remain with camp equipment at a place called Walnut Spring, when he heard at daylight a furious volley of intensifying fire. "My curiosity got the better of my judgment, and I mounted a horse and rode to the front to see what was going on."[47] When the order came to charge, Grant duly accompanied the Fourth Infantry into battle. The artillery and musket blasts belching from the Black Fort raked the advancing regiment, killing or wounding one-third of them in minutes. Grant could have dodged combat with a clear conscience, but he deliberately exposed himself to fire. He blamed the steep loss of life on Colonel Garland, who could easily have withdrawn his men beyond the lethal range of the Black Fort guns.

During the retreat, in a gallant gesture, Grant loaned his horse to the regiment's exhausted adjutant, Lieutenant Charles Hoskins, who was subsequently killed. In a measure of Grant's humanity he crept out alone onto the battlefield that night to identify the body. Another lieutenant recalled spotting a shadowy figure bending over a wounded man, "giving him water from a canteen and wiping his face with a moistened handkerchief."[48] The merciful man was Grant, who temporarily became the new regimental adjutant. Before the Monterrey fighting ended, Grant suffered the loss of West Point classmate Robert Hazlitt. "We have been intimate friends and rather confidential ones," Grant told his brother, "and no one but his relations can feel more harshly his loss than myself."[49]

Grant's supreme moment of valor arose during fierce fighting on September 23. That afternoon, his regiment bored deep into the city under a hail of deadly fire. The enterprise grew hazardous whenever they reached intersections where they were exposed to musket balls and grapeshot fired by Mexican infantry posted on low rooftops. "It was as if bushels of hickory nuts were hurled at us," said one soldier.[50] At one point, his ammunition dangerously depleted, Colonel Garland needed to send someone for fresh supplies. The risk was so huge that he requested volunteers rather than simply dispatching someone. Grant stepped forward to tender his services and here his agility with a horse named Nellie appeared to stunning effect. With daredevil dexterity, he wound one foot around the saddle, draped an arm over the neck of the horse, and rode off at full gallop, using the horse to shield his entire body. The Mexicans got only brief, intermittent glimpses of his hidden, low-slung figure as he streaked by at high velocity. "It was only at street crossings that my horse was under fire, but these I crossed at such a flying rate that generally I was past and under cover of the next block of houses before the enemy fired. I got out safely without a scratch."[51] At one point, Grant coaxed his horse into scaling an earthen wall four feet high. He would regale listeners with his derring-do for years.

Right before dawn the next day, Ampudia sent a messenger under a white flag to Taylor, requesting an armistice. Taylor gave remarkably lenient terms that seem to foreshadow the generous terms bestowed by Grant at Appomattox. Paroled soldiers would be allowed to retain their muskets and horses as the army retreated to a spot sixty miles south during an eight-week cease-fire. Characteristically Grant experienced no schadenfreude as he observed Mexican troops surrender, only infinite pathos for their miserable plight. "My pity was aroused by the sight of the Mexican garrison of Monterrey marching out of town as prisoners . . . Many of the prisoners were cavalry, armed with lances, and mounted on miserable little half-starved horses that did not look as if they could carry their riders out of town."[52] Grant praised Taylor's "humane policy," but President Polk was furious with the generous surrender terms that failed to divest the Mexicans of their weapons.[53] Among other things, he scented a political rival in Taylor, who was lionized by the press and presented as a potential presidential candidate for the 1848 election.

As the American army tarried near Monterrey, Grant savored his time there and was beguiled by Mexico—an attraction that lasted a lifetime, feeding a love of foreign travel. "The climate is excellent, the soil rich, and the scenery beautiful," he informed Julia.[54] The only thing disturbing his peace of mind was a typically inconsiderate act by his gauche father, who had, without permission, taken one of his letters and published it in a newspaper. Grant was doubtless irked by this behavior both as an invasion of privacy and as a boorish attempt at self-promotion by Jesse. Grant vowed to Julia that "I intend to be careful not to give them any news worth publishing."[55] In the meantime, he purchased food from local farmers, established a bakery for his regiment, and stood out for his energy and unobtrusive manner. While he did not entirely abstain from drinking, no accusations of alcohol abuse surfaced during this period. "He was at that time a temperate, sober man, free from the drink habit," said Chilton White, who knew Grant at Monterrey. "I have seen him at times when I thought he felt the exhilarating effects of intoxicants, but he was at all times a level headed man."[56]

THE MEXICAN WAR did more than just educate Grant in strategy and tactics, it also tutored him in the manifold ways wars are shot through with political calculations. "The Mexican war was a political war," he would observe, "and the administration conducting it desired to make party capital out of it."[57] Monterrey's fall made Zachary Taylor the darling of the Whig press. When this was followed by Whig victories in the November elections, giving the opposition party control of both houses of Congress, President Polk grew leery of Taylor as a Whig rival for president. In a Machiavellian maneuver, he decided to divest Taylor of most of his troops and replace him with Winfield Scott, a Whig lacking Taylor's brand of popular charisma.

In high-handed fashion, Polk dispatched Scott to Texas without notifying Taylor of what was afoot. When Scott arrived in Point Isabel after Christmas, he informed Taylor by letter that he had taken over the Army of Invasion and was radically revamping the war strategy. Instead of pushing south from Monterrey, he planned to take Taylor's regular troops, land them at Veracruz farther down the Mexican coast, then guide them inland to take Mexico City—the historic

trail charted by Hernán Cortés. "Providence may defeat me," bellowed the grandiloquent Scott, "but I do not believe the Mexicans can."[58] Taylor was relegated
to a sideshow of the main event. "It was no doubt supposed that Scott's ambition
would lead him to slaughter Taylor or destroy his chances for the Presidency,"
recalled Grant, "and yet it was hoped that he would not make sufficient capital
himself to secure the prize."[59]

Grant was with Taylor when he received the shocking news of his demotion
and never forgot his hero's befuddled reaction. "Taylor was apt to be a little
absent-minded when absorbed in any perplexing problem, and the morning he
received the discouraging news he sat down to breakfast in a brown study,
poured out a cup of coffee, and instead of putting in the sugar, he reached out
and got hold of the mustard-pot, and stirred half a dozen spoonfuls of its contents into the coffee. He didn't realize what he had done till he took a mouthful,
and then he broke out in a towering rage."[60] This early experience made Grant
tend to view war as a hard-luck saga of talented, professional soldiers betrayed by
political opportunists plotting back in Washington.

Between the founding era of the Republic and the Civil War, no figure embodied the American military more splendidly than Winfield Scott, who was
promoted to brevet major general by the War of 1812. Straddling two eras, he
would serve under presidents as far apart as James Madison and Abraham Lincoln. Mocked as "Old Fuss and Feathers" behind his back, he had never seen a
parade ground he didn't long to tread or a uniform he didn't wish to wear. With
his enormous height, wavy hair, and ample flesh, he loved to flash medals, flaunt
plumed hats, and preen before mirrors, a vanity that made him susceptible to
flattery. Grant noted how Scott sent word ahead to commanders of the precise
hour he planned to arrive. "This was done so that all the army might be under
arms to salute their chief as he passed. On these occasions he wore his dress
uniform, cocked hat, aiguilletes, sabre and spurs."[61] Such vainglory was so alien
to Grant that it is sometimes hard to say whether he modeled himself after
Zachary Taylor or in opposition to Winfield Scott.

For all that, Grant credited Scott with a brilliantly resourceful mind and
strategic daring. To travel from Veracruz to the capital, an army of twelve thousand would quit a secure supply base, traverse 250 miles of mountainous terrain,
then face a much larger and well-fortified enemy in a populous capital. To do
this, Scott assembled a first-rate team of bright junior officers, including Pierre
G. T. Beauregard and George B. McClellan and a rising star on the engineering

staff, Robert E. Lee. Throw in a host of other officers who later reappeared in the Civil War—Joseph Johnston, John Pemberton, James Longstreet, Winfield Scott Hancock, Albert Sidney Johnston, Joseph Hooker, George Thomas, Braxton Bragg, and George Gordon Meade—and the Mexican War seemed a dress rehearsal for the later conflict. With a retentive memory for faces and events, Grant accumulated a detailed inventory of knowledge about these varied men that he drew on later.

Winfield Scott's advent turned everything topsy-turvy. By early February 1847, Grant's regiment was reassigned to a division commanded by Brigadier General William J. Worth and braced to board a ship at the Rio Grande for passage to the island of Lobos north of Veracruz. By the end of the month, Grant was writing to Julia from the *North Carolina,* a ship laden with four hundred soldiers that pitched so crazily in heavy seas that Grant feared it would capsize. The weather was blazing hot, and the discomfort for passengers exacerbated by a boat designed to haul cargo instead of humans. Jesse Grant prodded his son to leave Mexico, and Ulysses himself was eager to be done with the war, especially after a nearly two-year absence from Julia. "If we have to fight," he told Julia, "I would like to see it all done at once."[62] Around this time, Zachary Taylor foiled Polk's plan to emasculate him, scoring a resounding victory at Buena Vista— success that ensured him the Whig nomination in 1848, propelling him into the White House.

On March 9, Scott disembarked his army on the Veracruz beaches in what he boasted was "the largest amphibious invasion yet attempted in history."[63] The men took flatboats then waded ashore, breasting high breakers and brandishing their rifles above the surf. "The Mexicans were very kind to us, however," Grant wrote drily, "and threw no obstacles in the way of our landing except an occasional shot from their nearest fort."[64] Instead of storming the walled city, Scott opted for a siege and, once big guns were installed, pounded the place mercilessly, with Robert E. Lee and George McClellan engaged in placing batteries. Grant and Pierre Beauregard reconnoitered enemy fortifications, and Grant also studied American siege lines. On March 29, nearly reduced to starvation in a shattered city, the Mexicans officially capitulated, yielding five thousand prisoners. Like Taylor at Monterrey, Scott allowed Mexican soldiers to depart with their dignity intact. Instead of taking them as prisoners, he permitted them to be paroled and keep their sidearms and horses, providing another humane precedent for Grant later on. In narrating events for Julia, he dispensed with false bravado. "I am doing the duties of Commissary and Quarter Master," he wrote, and only needed to have "the Pork and Beans rolled about."[65]

The campaign's most perilous phase commenced as Scott cut loose from his coastal base and ventured into the hinterlands. In London, the Duke of Wellington stared aghast at this high-stakes strategy, which flouted all military prudence. "Scott is lost . . . he cannot fall back upon his base," he declared.[66] Grant watched intently as this strategy unfolded and would imitate it during his Vicksburg Campaign. Passing through scenic but treacherous countryside, the army forded rivers, filed through narrow mountain passes, and crossed deep ravines in the Sierra Madre. The strategy of living off the land placed inordinate pressure on quartermasters. Some soldiers shed superfluous baggage in the wilting heat, and Grant, now a permanent quartermaster, had to make up their deficiencies. The long march meant he could no longer communicate with his parents, who grew alarmed by his silence. "During this time his mother's hair turned white from her anxiety about him," Jesse Grant recollected.[67] Grant's sister Mary similarly remembered Hannah Grant "with a look of concern supplanting the pleasant expression her face usually wore," while Jesse avidly tracked his son's doings in the pages of the Army Register.[68]

When his army reached a spot called Cerro Gordo, Scott seemed to hit an insuperable obstacle. The main road zigzagged around a mountainside, often running between sheer walls of rock, with Mexican artillery posted on their crests. Seeing the futility of a frontal assault, Scott dispatched Robert E. Lee on a secret mission to discover ways to circumvent Antonio López de Santa Anna's fortified position. Lee detected a mountain trail that bypassed the Mexicans and widened it to make way for troops. This enabled the Americans to circle around their foes in a surreptitious flanking maneuver, attacking them from the rear. In writing home, Grant likened this intricate maneuver to Napoleon crossing the Alps. The Mexicans soon surrendered, suffering more than a thousand casualties with thousands more taken prisoner. The battle taught Grant indelible lessons about military leadership: the need for supreme audacity and the vital importance of speed, momentum, and the element of surprise. Scott praised Lee unstintingly, promoting him to brevet major.

Grant was now operating on two levels of reality. One side of him monitored the war minutely with a sharp eye for arresting details. "As soon as Santa Anna saw that the day was lost he made his escape with a portion of his army," he wrote to Julia, "but he was pursued so closely that his carriage, a splendid affair, was taken and in it was his cork leg and some Thirty thousand dollars in gold."[69] At the same time, he fell under Mexico's enchantment—they had arrived at the high plateau, eight thousand feet above sea level—and was mesmerized by the sublime peaks. "Around us are mountains covered with eternal snow," Grant wrote, calling the town of Jalapa, with its orange groves and gardens, "the most beautiful place I ever saw in my life" and saying he would gladly make it his home if Julia agreed to join him there.[70] At more melancholy moments, he regretted that he had not taken his father's advice, resigned from the army, and headed into business.

After the decisive Cerro Gordo victory, Scott's army resumed its triumphant progress along the National Highway toward Mexico City, and Grant's division secured the roadway. Scott was forced to halt for months because of expiring one-month enlistments. As he awaited reinforcements, Santa Anna had a chance to strengthen Mexico City's defenses. The approach to the city presented fiendish difficulties because thin causeways on level ground made approaching troops easy targets for Mexican artillery. Encamped at Puebla, staying near the central plaza, Grant showed deepening insight into the fighting. He had a growing appetite for leadership and reaped a rich harvest of ideas for later use. After poring over maps and quizzing Mexican scouts, Grant grew convinced that Scott should swing his army around to the north of Mexico City. On the southern side, the army would flounder "through morass and ditches" whereas it would proceed to the north on solid, elevated ground.[71] At first Grant hesitated to criticize his superiors, thinking such conduct "contrary to military ethics," then he tried without success to relay his message up through the ranks.[72] When Robert E. Lee stumbled upon a southern route, Scott heeded his advice instead.

By August, with dysentery rife at Puebla, Scott again elected to break loose from his supply lines and march on Mexico City, pioneering a new style of warfare. "We had to throw away the scabbard," he explained, "and to advance naked blade in hand."[73] In striking at Contreras, San Jerónimo, and Churubusco, he shattered Mexico City's outer defenses in bloody fighting. He sacrificed more than a thousand men, but Mexican casualties rose four times higher, robbing Santa Anna of a full one-third of his army. Lee was again singled out for bravery and bumped up to brevet lieutenant colonel. Even in retrospect, Grant could find no fault with the meticulous steps Scott had executed. He was also struck by the cheers lavished upon the general, and, writing home, tried on for size the feelings of the victorious commander. "I wondered what must be the emotions of General Scott, thus surrounded by the plaudits of his army. The ovation was genuine, and from the hearts of his men."[74]

With Scott's army poised to strike at Mexico City's gates, President Polk had his emissary, Nicholas P. Trist, attempt on September 2 to negotiate a peace treaty by which Mexico would relinquish Texas to the Rio Grande and transfer New Mexico and California to the United States for a negotiated sum. The Mexicans rebuffed this insulting offer and a brief armistice ended two days later. On September 8, Scott launched an attack against Molino del Rey—the King's Mill, in English—which was incorrectly thought to be deserted. An entire Mexican division opened up withering fire from the mill. After American artillery reciprocated, bombarding its stone walls with bullets and cannonballs, four American companies charged forward. Grant raced to the mill only to discover his ex-roommate, Fred Dent, lying wounded and spouting blood from his thigh. Grant "refreshed him from his canteen and dragged him to a place of safety close under the wall," Julia wrote.[75]

For a young man, Grant was remarkably clearheaded and self-possessed in combat. "At the Battle of Molino del Rey," said Longstreet, "I had occasion to notice [Grant's] superb courage and coolness under fire."[76] Grant discerned that several armed Mexicans still stood atop the building. After backing up a cart to the wall, he sprang onto the roof only to find that an American had single-handedly captured the Mexicans. "They still had their arms, while the soldier before mentioned was walking as sentry, guarding the prisoners he had *sur-rounded*, all by himself."[77] Quite typically, Grant incorporated this mock-heroic tale into his *Memoirs* even though it cast him in a slightly comic-opera light.

At Molino del Rey, Grant exhibited bravery and compassion, tending so many wounded Americans on the battlefield that one fellow soldier portrayed him as "a ministering angel" with "a kind heart."[78] The night after the battle, he came upon young Virginia lieutenant George Pickett shivering in the cold. When Grant asked why he trembled, Pickett replied, "I shall fr-fr-freeze to d-death." "Oh no you won't," said Grant, who found a piece of roasted red chili pepper, blew away the ashes, then handed it to the West Point graduate. "Here, Pickett, you eat that and it will be as good as a stove inside of you."[79] When Winfield Scott was asked in future years whether he remembered Grant from Mexico, he noted that he "attained special distinction at Molino del Rey"—a distinction that earned Grant the honorary grade of brevet first lieutenant.[80] Grant learned the importance of following up promptly on victory and chided Scott for not pursuing the fleeing enemy once the mill was taken. Though an American victory, Molino del Rey carried a fearful price tag of almost eight hundred American casualties.

On the morning of September 12, American heavy artillery battered the fortress at Chapultepec, once a royal residence, now a military school. When it fell the next morning, Grant and his men sprang forward under an aqueduct toward the gate of San Cosme, sprinting from arch to arch to evade Mexican bullets. With about a dozen volunteers, joined with soldiers from another company, Grant cleared Mexican snipers from parapets and rooftops, enabling the American column to pass. Then he spotted a church steeple a hundred feet high that might allow an unobstructed shot at the back of San Cosme gate. In narrating this maneuver in his *Memoirs,* Grant gave an amusing description of the scene at the church: "When I knocked for admission a priest came to the door, who, while extremely polite, declined to admit us. With the little Spanish then at my command, I explained to him that he might save property by opening the door . . . and besides, I intended to go in whether he consented or not. He began to see his duty in the same light that I did, and opened the door, though he did not look as if it gave him special pleasure to do so." Grant and his men hoisted a dismantled howitzer into the belfry, assembled it, then trained it on Mexicans behind the gate, creating "great confusion."[81]

Elated, General Worth sent Lieutenant John Pemberton (who would someday surrender Vicksburg) to summon Grant. The appreciative general told Grant he wished to deliver a second howitzer to the belfry. Grant's reaction showed his canny nature. "I could not tell the General that there was not room enough in the steeple for another gun, because he probably would have looked upon such a statement as a contradiction from a second lieutenant. I took the captain with me, but did not use his gun."[82] Thanks to Grant's shrewdly commandeering the church, Worth's men overran the San Cosme gate, leaving Mexico City defenseless before them. Toward the end of this eventful day, Grant learned that a close friend, Lieutenant Calvin Benjamin, had received a mortal wound. He found him lying on a cot in the street and wiped away dirt that begrimed the dying man's face—a poignant moment that revealed strong emotion beneath Grant's impassive facade. For his assault on the San Cosme gate, Grant attained the honorary rank of brevet captain for "gallant and meritorious conduct in the battle of *Chapultepec.*"[83] This temporary promotion would allow him to wear the bars and perform the duties of a captain. Irvin McDowell, later a

Union general, termed Grant in Mexico "the best horseman and the bravest fellow in the army."[84] Promoted to brevet colonel, Robert E. Lee received a rare accolade from Winfield Scott, who extolled him as "the very best soldier that I ever saw in the field."[85]

Bedecked in military finery, Winfield Scott strode into the National Palace of Mexico City on September 14—the storied Halls of Montezuma. Veteran military observers agreed with the Duke of Wellington that Scott now stood forth as "the greatest living soldier."[86] Local residents deserted the streets, lending them an eerie silence. As a parting shot, Santa Anna emptied the prisons of inmates, and one of them, posted atop a roof, shot Grant's friend Lieutenant Sidney Smith of the Fourth Infantry. Grant never forgot the ghoulish sequel. Smith "retained his natural color, his respiration, pulse and temperature were almost normal, he was cheerful and he had no idea of dying. He even laughed and joked about it and said that after he got well he should never be careless again. Suddenly his complexion changed to that of a corpse and in a few hours he was dead."[87] Based on seniority, Grant was promoted to first lieutenant by this sudden death. Had it not been for this fatality, Grant realized, he would have remained a second lieutenant "after having been in all the engagements possible for any one man and in a regiment that lost more officers during the war than it ever had present at any one engagement," he wrote with a distinct trace of bitterness.[88]

Grant was thrilled by Scott's panache and military acumen, especially since he believed President Polk, by holding back troops, had tried to undercut a feared political adversary. "Since my last letter to you," he told Julia, "four of the hardest fought battles that the world ever witnessed have taken place, and the most astonishing victories have crowned the American arms. But dearly have they paid for it! The loss of officers and men killed and wounded is frightful."[89] Baked by the tropical sun, worn out by years of war, Grant had a red beard that hung four inches long and he thought he had aged ten years in appearance. Yet despite the heavy toll from combat and disease—13,283 Americans had died, nearly a fifth of all soldiers who fought—Grant was still in some ways a callow young man, seeing an exotic new country for the first time and gushing to Julia that "Mexico [City] is one of the most beautiful cities in the world . . . No country was ever so blessed by nature."[90]

The Mexican government having fled, American troops lingered as an occupation army while politicians hammered out a peace agreement. Winfield

Scott, after fiercely prosecuting the war, proved generous in victory. At first Grant witnessed brutal reprisals by Mexicans against their peers who had cooperated with the Americans, including women who had their heads shaved for fraternizing with United States officers. But in time Grant saw how a wise, charitable policy toward a conquered civilian population restored peaceful conditions with impressive speed. "Lawlessness was soon suppressed," Grant wrote, "and the City of Mexico settled down into a quiet, law-abiding place."[91] Other accounts of the American occupation depicted atrocities raging on both sides.

The Fourth Infantry camped in the small village of Tacubaya, four miles outside of Mexico City. Although Grant still had quartermaster duties and dealt with a clothing shortage in his regiment, he had free time to ride to the city daily and play cards with future president Franklin Pierce. Besieged by beggars, Grant deplored the gross inequality of Mexican society and instinctively sided with the oppressed. "With a soil and climate scarcely equaled in the world," he protested, Mexico "has more poor and starving subjects who are willing and able to work than any country in the world. The rich keep down the poor with a hardness of heart that is incredible."[92] Whatever his criticisms of their society, Grant never regarded the Mexicans as racial inferiors.

Because bullfighting was the national sport, Grant attended one fight purely for the experience and was sickened by it. "I could not see how human beings could enjoy the sufferings of beasts, and often of men, as they seemed to do on these occasions."[93] In his *Memoirs,* he included a vivid description of a bullfight that gains its power from Grant's patent identification with the dying bull after it is pierced with spears. "The flag drops and covers the eyes of the animal so that he is at a loss what to do; it is jerked from him and the torment is renewed. When the animal is worked into an uncontrollable frenzy, the horsemen withdraw, and the matadores—literally murderers—enter, armed with knives having blades twelve or eighteen inches long, and sharp."[94]

For Grant, the most fascinating moment in Mexico came when he joined with Simon Bolivar Buckner and other officers in a hair-raising ascent of the enormous volcanic mountain of Popocatépetl. Their mules negotiated trails that skirted yawning chasms, flanked by sheer vertical walls of rock. The next day, buffeted by heavy snow and wind, they were forced to turn back a thousand feet below the crater. Nine officers suffered severe snow blindness and had to be led back down the mountain on horseback. After returning, the group visited the Valley of Cuernavaca and explored a mammoth cave festooned with singular rock formations that hypnotized Grant. "We had with us torches and rockets and the effect of them in that place of total darkness was beautiful."[95]

It is consistent with Grant's later drinking patterns that he abstained from alcohol during combat periods, when he was actively engaged and shouldered responsibility. "I never saw Grant under the influence of liquor at all," said one soldier. "I know he did drink a little, but that was pretty good whisky he had."[96] Another person noted he "never drank to excess nor indulged in the other profligacy so common in that country of loose morals."[97] But idleness, boredom, and the loneliness of occupation mixed a toxic brew of emotions that slowly led him into temptation and people noticed an abrupt change. One Ohio soldier wrote home in May 1848 that Grant was "altered very much: he is a short thick man with a beard reaching half way down his waist and I fear he drinks too much but don't you say a word on that subject."[98] A more damning recollection came from his friend Richard Dawson, who said Grant "got to drinking heavily during or after the war." Right after his return from Mexico, he encountered Grant and said he "was in bad shape from the effects of drinking, and suffering from *mania a potu* [delirium tremens] and some other troubles of the campaign."[99]

Despite such lapses, Grant had compiled an extremely commendable record during the Mexican War, which had turned him into a seasoned officer, steeped in battlefield wisdom and logistical finesse. And then there were useful contacts with dozens of soldiers later elevated to general in the Civil War. Even though Robert E. Lee had rendered meritorious service, Grant had studied him close-up and knew he was not endowed with supernatural abilities: "I had known him personally, and knew that he was mortal; and it was just as well that I felt this."[100]

The war culminated with the Treaty of Guadalupe Hidalgo, a huge bonanza for the United States. It expanded American territory by nearly a quarter, forcing Mexico to shed half its territory. The United States gained Texas with the crucial Rio Grande boundary as well as New Mexico and California—territories encompassing the current states of California, Nevada, and Utah, most of Arizona and New Mexico, and part of Colorado. In exchange, the United States relinquished claims to Baja California, assumed $3.5 million in Mexican debts owed to American citizens, and handed over $15 million.

As the war's rabid opponents—Senator Charles Sumner, Henry David Thoreau, and Ralph Waldo Emerson among them—had predicted, the victory carved out a vast territory up for grabs between slave owners and abolitionists, possibly tipping the tenuous balance between North and South. In August

1846, Congressman David Wilmot of Pennsylvania had introduced a measure to outlaw slavery in territory acquired from Mexico, putting slavery front and center in American politics. As one congressman stated, "It would really seem there is no other subject claiming the deliberations of this House but negro slavery."[101] While southern legislators quashed the Wilmot Proviso, it stimulated debate that showed just how extraordinarily divisive slavery had grown. Grant insisted the Civil War was "largely the outgrowth of the Mexican war. Nations, like individuals, are punished for their transgressions."[102] As a Whig opponent of slavery, Abraham Lincoln supported the Wilmot Proviso and denounced President Polk's war in thunderous terms: "He is deeply conscious of being in the wrong . . . he feels the blood of this war, like the blood of Abel, is crying to Heaven against him."[103]

/////////////////////////////

CHAPTER FOUR

The Son of Temperance

R IGHT BEFORE HE LEFT MEXICO, in June 1848, Grant suffered a small mishap that would plague him for several years. As quartermaster, he was responsible for the care of regimental funds, which he kept tightly guarded in a trunk. After his own chest was broken into, he took the seemingly prudent step of depositing the $1,000 in his care in the locked trunk of Captain John H. Gore. When that trunk was purloined from Gore's tent, Grant faced a board of inquiry, which exonerated him of any wrongdoing. It would be some time, however, before he straightened out the situation with authorities in Washington, and, until that happened, he was legally responsible for replacing the lost thousand dollars—an anxious situation for him.

On July 16, after having been camped for one week on a sandy beach under a tropical sun, Grant and his regiment were relieved to quit Veracruz and the yellow fever rampant there. They sailed on transport ships to East Pascagoula, Mississippi, where they were supposed to spend the summer at Camp Jefferson Davis. By this point, Grant, twenty-six, had been engaged to Julia Dent for four years, but had seen her only once three years earlier, a separation that tormented him. In May, having received no mail from Julia for two months, he lashed out in a missive: "I believe you are carrying on a flirtation with someone, as you threaten of doing."[1] Either then or later, the line was blotted out, but it testifies to the grave toll the years apart had taken.

Obtaining a leave of absence, Grant made a beeline for St. Louis, where the Dents spent the summer in the city. Everyone saw, at a glance, that Grant had matured and appeared more worldly and cosmopolitan. Although he had shaved off his beard, restoring his clean-shaven image, he had shed his boyish softness. "When he came back from Mexico he had put on perhaps 20 pounds of muscle, tanned, ready for the battles of life," said Julia.[2] Emma Dent, now twelve, found Grant more reserved, but applauded the changes wrought in her rugged, sinewy hero. "His face was more bronzed from the exposure to the sun, and he wore his captain's double-barred shoulder straps with a little more dignity than he had worn the old ones, perhaps."[3] The last known photograph of Grant before the Civil War, taken a year later, shows a handsome, dashing young man with something sad and downcast in his expression. His eyes seem crossed, as if turned inward in sorrowful contemplation.

The four-year engagement had confirmed the steadfast attachment between Ulysses S. Grant and Julia Dent. One Dent acquaintance remembered the young couple sitting on the steps of the St. Louis house, holding hands and gazing soulfully at each other. "I remember Grant as a quiet kind of a man who volunteered but little conversation until some topic coming within his experience was referred to, when he would warm up and talk with great interest."[4] By this time, Colonel Dent had encountered financial setbacks and was embroiled in a costly lawsuit, which may explain why he consented to the marriage, even though Grant had decided to stay in the army with a meager $1,000 annual salary. After waiting so long to marry, Grant pressed Julia for a hasty wedding and they set a date for August 22 in St. Louis.

Grant traveled to see his parents in Bethel, Ohio. Across America, small towns embraced Mexican War veterans with patriotic adulation, and Grant drew rapt attention wherever he went. The war had charged his imagination and reminiscing about it became a favorite pastime for the duration of his life. He could be a compelling raconteur with a penetrating power to visualize battles and conjure them up in graphic detail. "How clear-headed Sam Grant is in describing a battle!" a later listener exulted. "He seems to have the whole thing in his head."[5] Adding to public curiosity was that Grant had brought back from Mexico a bright boy named Gregorio, who was only twelve or thirteen and did not speak a word of English; Grant conversed with him in Spanish. An expert with a lasso, the youth instructed Grant in his full repertoire of tricks. "They practiced on my sheep and cows and horses," said Grant's uncle. "Ulysses got so he was quite handy with the lasso himself."[6]

During Grant's Bethel stay, Jesse and Hannah Grant must have made plain their displeasure with the slave-owning Dents and explained their refusal to attend the wedding. Savage stories about the Dents circulated in the Grant family, typified by the caustic later commentary of Ulysses's sister-in-law. "I never met Julia's father but I heard he was a cross, lazy man, a surly Democrat and a Rebel. They said he was asleep all day except to wake up to eat and argue . . . Jesse Grant . . . grew to know Mr. Dent from Missouri and had no kind words for him or any other Dent. He said they were a lazy, self-satisfied lot, slave owners and worse. He could not believe Ulysses could treat the Rebel father Dent so kindly."[7] The extended Grant family registered its disapproval of the Dent clan by boycotting the St. Louis wedding.

The Dents reciprocated the antipathy. Julia's cousin Louisa Boggs said of the marriage: "[Grant] was a northern man married to a southern, slave owning family. Colonel Dent openly despised him. All the family said 'poor Julia' when they spoke of Mrs. Grant. So you can see why everybody thought Captain Grant a poor match for Miss Dent."[8] A victim of this interfamily feud, Grant was plunged into his own private civil war, uncomfortably suspended between the easygoing, hedonistic Dents and his thrifty, tightfisted family of die-hard abolitionists.

On August 22, 1848, Ulysses S. Grant and Julia Boggs Dent got married in the small brick downtown house that the Dents occupied at Fourth and Cerre Streets. A simple ceremony, illuminated by candlelight, the wedding took place on a sultry night in an overheated parlor, with a banquet table laden with fruit, ices, and wedding cake set up in a back room. Described in a local paper as "a lady of refinement and elegant manners," Julia swept down the staircase in a white silk dress with a white tulle veil.[9] Always flustered in large crowds on formal occasions, Grant fidgeted nervously all night. "He wore his regimentals and some people thought it would have been better had he dressed in civilian's clothes," noted Louisa Boggs. "They said he seemed very awkward and embarrassed and his long sword nearly tripped him up on several occasions!"[10] Emma Dent depicted the young soldier more charitably. "Captain Grant was as cool under the fire of the clergyman's questions as he had been under the batteries of the Mexican artillery."[11] James Longstreet served as best man and two groomsmen, Cadmus M. Wilcox and Bernard Pratte, were to join him in the Confederate army; all three later surrendered to Grant at Appomattox.

The day after the wedding, Ulysses and Julia Grant left for Bethel so she could meet her new in-laws. A sheltered young woman who had never left

St. Louis or even traveled on a boat, Julia relished the dreamlike sensation of a steamboat gliding smoothly down the Mississippi then up the Ohio River to Louisville, where they stopped to visit Grant's rich cousin, James Hewitt, who entertained them in his opulent home. Grant dropped modest hints that he might resign from the army should an advantageous business opportunity arise, but his cousin turned a deaf ear and Grant stayed in the military. Julia resented that Hewitt left her new husband empty-handed, and she possessed a long memory for such slights: "I always remembered this, and did not forget it when my Lieutenant was General-in-Chief nor when he was President of the United States."[12]

For the most part, Julia did not dwell on such unpleasantness and recorded a sweetly sanitized version of her first brush with Grant's family. When their boat reached Cincinnati, she recalled, "there stood my dear husband's little brother Orvil with his flaxen curls and blue eyes—as pretty a boy as I ever saw. He had come all the way down to meet us, saying he could not wait for us."[13] Similarly, she remembered Jesse Grant being cordial toward her and Hannah even more welcoming. "Mrs. Grant . . . was then a handsome woman, a little below medium height, with soft brown eyes, glossy brown hair, and her cheek was like a rose in the snow. She too gave me an affectionate welcome, and I must say right here she was the most self-sacrificing, the sweetest, kindest woman I ever met, except my own dear mother."[14] In fact, although Jesse and Hannah Grant treated Julia with all due civility, they could not detach her from their scathing critique of the Dents and harbored secret reservations about her boasting, superstitions, and overt displays of affection for their son.

In November, Grant had to report for duty in Detroit, now home of the Fourth Infantry, and he shepherded Julia back to St. Louis for what he assumed would be a final visit before they launched a new life on an army base. Instead Colonel Dent tried one last time to drive a sharp wedge between his daughter and son-in-law. Having led a narrow, overprotected life, Julia grew distraught at the thought of parting from her father. "I could not . . . think of it without bursting into a flood of tears and weeping and sobbing as if my heart would break."[15] After four years of daydreaming about married life, Grant was distressed by this belated attack of nerves. Colonel Dent intervened with a proposal so cruelly preposterous that Grant must have felt hurt. "Grant, I can arrange it all for you. You join your regiment and leave Julia with us. You can get a leave of absence once or twice a year and run on here and spend a week or two with us. I always knew [Julia] could not live in the army."[16] Grant had now been pushed to the breaking point. His Mexican War exploits had enhanced his self-confidence, and he slipped his arm around Julia, whispering, "Would you like this, Julia? Would you like to remain with your father and let me go alone?" "No, no, no, Ulys. I could not, would not, think of that for a moment." Grant asserted himself. "Then dry your tears and do not weep again. It makes me unhappy."[17] At that moment, Grant declared his independence and liberated Julia from her father's manipulative wiles, showing Colonel Dent that he was not a timid young man to be trifled with forever.

On November 7, 1848, General Zachary Taylor emerged victorious in the presidential race, despite a glaring lack of experience in public office. Editor Horace Greeley, among others, writhed with indignation at his proslavery platform: "We scorn it; we spit upon it; we trample it under our feet!"[18] Nevertheless, Taylor showed no patience with mounting talk of southern secession. "If they attempted to carry out their schemes," he warned a senator, "they should be dealt with by law as they deserved and executed."[19] On Election Day, Grant was in Kentucky and couldn't vote, but he said he would have voted for Taylor. Taylor's presidential tenure proved remarkably short-lived. In 1850, after attending July Fourth orations on a torrid day, he consumed an enormous quantity of possibly tainted cherries and iced milk and died mysteriously five days later.

When Grant and his bride arrived in Detroit on November 17, he came in for a rude awakening. During his four-month leave of absence, Lieutenant Henry D. Wallen had replaced Grant, who never formally gave up his regimental quartermaster position. Now that he returned, Wallen refused to cede the Detroit position and Grant was reassigned to the bleak outpost of Madison Barracks at Sackets Harbor, New York, on the eastern shore of Lake Ontario, near the Canadian border. Still more infuriating was that Wallen's own company had been deployed to Sackets Harbor, and he should have departed with them. Sackets Harbor was a frigid, desolate garrison and with winter approaching Grant must have wondered how the sheltered Julia would survive in this inhospitable place. Indignant, he filed an official complaint with the commanding officer in Detroit, who forwarded it to General John E. Wool with the comment that "Lieutenant Grant has unquestionably been hardly and wrongly done by."[20] In the meantime, Grant had no choice but to obey orders and take Julia along, even though cold weather had sealed off traffic on Lake Ontario, forcing them into a prolonged overland journey.

Once installed at Sackets Harbor, Grant was dismayed that soldiers in this inclement climate lacked proper clothing and bedding for the winter. Rather than watch men shiver as they awaited supplies from New York or Philadelphia, he showed his usual initiative by buying up supplies on his own. Now a veteran quartermaster, he was soon busily fixing leaky roofs, repairing dilapidated fences, and refurbishing decaying houses.

The winter stay at Sackets Harbor was much happier than he and Julia had anticipated, and they formed numerous friendships in the tight-knit military community. For the first time, Julia, with scant domestic experience, learned to manage a household without assistance from slaves. She took pride in their small, well-furnished home with its bright carpet, china dishes adorned with floral patterns, and silver cutlery that came as a wedding gift from the Grants. Whenever Ulysses had surplus cash to spend, he journeyed to nearby Watertown and bought finery for Julia at a dry goods store operated by Jesse and Henry Seligman, Bavarian Jewish brothers who became lifetime friends and later emerged as wealthy bankers and substantial donors to Grant's presidential campaigns. Everyone found Grant modest and retiring, an altogether likable fellow. "His only dissipation was in owning a fast horse," said a regimental colleague. "He always liked to have a fine nag, and he paid high prices to get one."[21] Grant enjoyed playing chess and checkers, attending parties with Julia, and worshipping with her at the Methodist church.

On March 2, 1849, after four months marooned at Sackets Harbor, Grant learned he had won his appeal and was being sent back to Detroit, where he resumed his job as regimental quartermaster. By all accounts, he was popular with the soldiers, who appreciated his lack of superior airs. Known for impartial honesty and a judicial temperament, he often arbitrated disputes among soldiers, as in Mexico. Still the peacetime army did not showcase his talents and he often seemed mildly bored, as if he needed a bigger challenge to mobilize his energy. According to one officer, Grant struggled with incessant paperwork—never his strong suit—but when it came to "drill, the manual of arms, fighting," he had no equal in handling the regiment.[22] One fellow officer noticed that Grant had both an active, dynamic side to his personality and a curiously passive one, comparing him to "a trained athlete, who leans listless and indifferent against the wall, but who wakes to wonders when the call is made upon him."[23] This split personality was one reason why people could find Ulysses S. Grant quite ordinary one moment and extraordinary the next.

However humdrum his duties, he enjoyed his stay in Detroit, which had a population of about twenty-five thousand and was a raw, unpaved western town with pastures still lying behind many houses. He and Julia moved into a narrow frame house on Fort Street, set off by a white picket fence, in a neighborhood of poor, working families. The house had an arbor covered with wild grapevines and the newlyweds found it an inviting abode. For a time, Gregorio served as valet, bringing food to the table and answering the door, but when he was lured away by higher wages, the Grants felt betrayed by his departure.

Whether playing cards or reading at night, Ulysses and Julia Grant seemed a cozy, companionable pair. More literate than people supposed, Grant perused romances of Sir Walter Scott and historical novels by Edward Bulwer-Lytton. "He would read to me novels, newspapers, books and such," Julia wrote. "We would discuss what he would read, it was something we looked forward to."[24] In time, Julia recognized how spoiled she had been as a young bride, how unwilling to compromise. When she was difficult or petulant, Grant, instead of chiding her, subjected her to the silent treatment. "The most he would ever say is, 'Julia, I'm amazed at you.' That was cutting me to the quick and it would sting like a lash, he said it so calmly."[25] This understated form of rebuke worked: Julia would apologize and beg his forgiveness, which he always offered.

Like many young couples, the Grants flung themselves into an incessant round of parties, dances, and dinners, and Julia took pride in throwing "a fancy dress ball," a novelty for Detroit and a throwback to her St. Louis girlhood. Local preachers found the concept much too pagan for their tastes. "We had kings, knights, troubadours, and every other character pretty and gay," remembered Julia, who dressed up as a tambourine girl.[26] Grant seemed older and more serious than other young officers, and, undoubtedly feeling a little silly and self-conscious about showing up in a costume, wore his uniform instead. He loitered on the fringes of gatherings, standing with hands clasped behind his back, an impassive spectator who opened up with selected people. When called on to propose a toast at one dinner, Grant grew tongue-tied. "I can face the music," he confessed blushingly, "but I cannot make a speech."[27] People noticed how Julia overcame his habitual reserve, lightened his somber moods, and fleshed out his life. In the view of one officer, Grant "came out of his shell in her presence. They were two people who hitched well together, they fit like hand to glove."[28]

Where Grant clearly shed his inhibitions was in racing horses down Fort Street, when the passionate daring of his nature appeared to advantage. With the town offering few pastimes, Grant electrified the large gatherings who turned out to watch as he whizzed by in his buggy, outstripping competitors and even driving on the River Rouge when it froze. "He was the best horseman I ever saw," said Colonel James E. Pitman. "He could fly on a horse, faster than a slicked bullet."[29] One impression superseded all others: that Grant was "just power and will and resolution," said a resident.[30]

By early fall 1849, Julia was pregnant and decided to return to St. Louis to have the baby. On May 30, 1850, she gave birth to their first child, named Frederick Dent Grant in honor of the Colonel—which could not have thrilled her husband. Two weeks later, Grant applied for permission to travel to St. Louis for "urgent family reasons" and brought Julia and baby Fred back to Detroit.[31] From the outset, he was a more relaxed and playful parent than Jesse Grant, free of the persistent badgering and demanding expectations that had so disconcerted him in his own father. Julia was a conscientious, hardworking mother, and one friend remembered her supervising the small household "with a great lump of a baby in her arms."[32]

Julia's prolonged absence during the winter of 1849–50, coupled with a dearth of challenging work, proved a formula for trouble for Grant. Heavy drinking was commonplace in frontier garrisons, making it difficult for Grant, stranded in freezing Detroit, to abstain. The problem was neither the amount nor the frequency with which he drank, but the dramatic behavioral changes induced. He and Julia kept a pew in a Methodist church led by Dr. George Taylor, and perhaps realizing his newfound responsibilities as a father, Grant sought counsel from his pastor about his drinking. "I think that Dr. Taylor helped Grant a great deal," said Colonel Pitman. "It was said that he had a long talk with Grant at that time and told him that he could not safely use liquor in any form and Grant acknowledged this and took the pledge and thereafter used no liquor at all in Detroit."[33] This episode makes clear that Grant, from an early age, acknowledged that he had a chronic drinking problem, was never cavalier about it, and was determined to resolve it. This overly controlled young man now wrestled with a disease that caused a total loss of control, which must have made it more tormenting and pestered his Methodist conscience.

Even as a young man, Grant was infused with a strong sense of justice. No less than as a boy, he could be proud, a bit moody, and hypersensitive, refusing to be bullied. Colonel Pitman stated that Grant "would whip a man who crossed him or who sold him short cords of wood or who was in any way derogatory towards

him."[34] During the winter of 1850–51, Grant slipped on the ice and injured his
leg in front of the house of Zachariah Chandler, a big, imposing man soon to be
Detroit's mayor. Grant had the courage to file a complaint against Chandler,
claiming he violated a city ordinance demanding that residents keep their sidewalks free of snow and ice. During the trial, Chandler taunted Grant: "If you
soldiers would keep sober, perhaps you would not fall on people's pavements and
hurt your legs."[35] One wonders whether Chandler hinted obliquely at rumors of
drinking by Grant. Although the jury found Chandler guilty, he was fined a
laughable six cents, perhaps suggesting the court agreed with Chandler's insinuation that excessive alcohol consumption had accounted for the fall.

It is unclear how closely Grant followed current affairs as the national debate
over slavery broadened and intensified. Through the Compromise of 1850, California was admitted as a free state while other territories wrested from Mexico
were left free to adopt slavery or not. In exchange, the North appeased the South
by submitting to a strict new fugitive slave law that made many northerners feel
like accomplices in the hated institution of their southern brethren.

In June 1851, the Fourth Infantry was transferred to Sackets Harbor and
Grant at first welcomed returning to a place where he and Julia had launched
many satisfying friendships. It occurred at a time when Julia had taken the baby
to visit the Grants in Bethel and then enjoyed an extended stay with her family
in St. Louis. Little Fred had been very sick in Detroit, likely accounting for Julia's desire to take him somewhere with superior medical care. Almost as soon as
she and the baby were gone, Grant keenly missed them. "You don't know how
anxious I am to see him," he wrote to Julia. "I never dreamed that I should miss
the little rascal so much."[36] Grant had quickly grown domesticated, a doting
father at loose ends without his family. As had happened during the Mexican War,
he was a faithful correspondent, whereas Julia's letters turned up sporadically,
arousing his already palpable anxiety. "Your not writing keeps me in constant
suspense lest poor little Freddy may be sick again," he informed her after arriving
at Sackets Harbor. "Has he improved much since he left? . . . I feel a constant
dread lest I shall hear bad news."[37]

In his frequent letters, Grant tried hard to sound cheerful and sang the
praises of Sackets Harbor with its cool, salubrious climate and excellent fishing,
sailing, riding, and picnics. Yet he admitted the town was "as dull a little hole as
you ever saw," and his letters thinly veil a creeping depression dampening his
spirits.[38] Again and again he complained that Julia did not write often enough,

beseeched her to come sooner to Sackets Harbor, and referred to her reluctance to leave St. Louis. He may have dreaded that she was ensnared again in the predatory talons of Colonel Dent and appeared pathetically eager for scraps of news about his baby boy. "Do you think he recollects me?" he asked Julia. "Has he any more teeth? You don't tell me anything about him."[39] Even though he renewed ties with old acquaintances, the distant outpost did not seem nearly as sociable without Julia. One wonders whether her infrequent letters resulted from her eye problem or whether she silently punished her husband for subjecting her to a cheerless existence at remote army bases. Deprived of the foundation of her love, Grant seemed solitary, adrift, afflicted with excess nervous energy. The underlying pathos of his life grew painfully apparent. As one officer observed, Grant "was regarded as a restless, energetic man, who must have occupation, and plenty of it, for his own good."[40]

Loneliness, ennui, frustration, inactivity—such unsettled feelings always conspired to drive Grant to drink. Luckily, he recognized his alcoholism just as the temperance movement gathered strength, and he embraced this new faith with fervor. "I heard John B. Gough lecture in Detroit the other night," he told a Sackets Harbor friend, "and I have become convinced that there is no safety from ruin by drink except from abstaining from liquor altogether."[41] The full-bearded John Bartholomew Gough was a reformed drinker and failed actor who delivered temperance speeches that mingled folksy humor with spellbinding theatricality to convert wavering listeners. He was a charismatic spokesman for the Washingtonian movement, which was inaugurated in a Baltimore barroom in 1840 and urged adherents to sign pledges of abstinence. It has been estimated that the indefatigable Gough gave more than ten thousand speeches, reaching more than nine million grateful people.[42] He was fond of recounting how he had lost his wife and child from drink, a theme that would have resonated powerfully with Grant.

At Sackets Harbor, Grant helped to organize the Rising Sun Division, Lodge No. 210, of the Sons of Temperance and took the pledge not to "make, buy, sell, or use, as a beverage, any Spiritous or Malt Liquors, Wine, or Cider."[43] Despite some local hostility, he advertised his involvement by wearing the lodge's white sash and red-white-and-blue ribbon in his lapel. He talked freely about his problem with his friend Walter Camp, who recalled that Grant "gave hearty encouragement to the order in the village by his presence. He marched once in the procession, wearing the regalia of the lodge. I heard him refuse to join in a drinking bout once . . . It took courage in those days to wear the white apron of the Sons of Temperance, but Lieutenant Grant was prepared to show his character."[44] Stubbornly protective of her husband's reputation, Julia Grant always refused to admit publicly to his drinking problem, but her early biographer Ishbel Ross notes, "Grant attended the weekly meetings with Julia's hearty approval. She hung his parchment proudly in their home."[45]

In September 1851, Grant insisted that Julia and the baby come to Sackets Harbor, and she arrived to discover that Grant had charmingly, if rather clumsily, fitted out their small quarters. "I remember a fine center table and two large fine chairs that were so high that when I sat in them my feet were quite a foot from the floor," the diminutive Julia noted. "This mistake was overcome by his having two pretty little stools made for my feet to rest upon when I sat in those chairs of state."[46] The remainder of their Sackets Harbor stay passed pleasantly enough with diversions ranging from bowling to sleigh rides across the frozen expanse of Lake Ontario, bundled under buffalo robes. They played whist and checkers and attended church.

The Sackets Harbor idyll ended in May 1852 when the Fourth Infantry was ordered to the West Coast, triggering a slow-motion crisis in Grant's life. The Gold Rush had drawn a stampede of settlers to California that demanded a strengthened military presence. At first, Julia indulged in quaint fantasies of a joint trip and pictured going "through the Caribbean Sea, parting its slashing, phosphorescent waves and sailing under the Southern Cross."[47] But she was now seven months pregnant with their second child, and Grant realized she could not brave the extreme perils of travel from New York to San Francisco. "You know how loath I am to leave you," he told her, "but crossing Panama is an undertaking for one in robust health; and then my salary is so small, how could you and my little boy have even the common necessaries of life out there."[48] In the end, Julia sadly acquiesced. She and two-year-old Fred went to stay with the Grants and then the Dents, forcing Ulysses to hazard the journey alone. For four grueling years, they had endured separation during the Mexican War and ever since had struggled to forge a stable family life. Now Grant was again being deprived of the one thing indispensable for his emotional health and well-being. Eventually, he hoped, Julia and Fred would be able to join him, but he had no assurance of that as he journeyed to Governors Island in New York to prepare his regiment for the taxing journey to Panama, across the isthmus, then up the West Coast to San Francisco.

Before sailing, Grant squeezed in a three-day trip to Washington to settle the matter of the stolen $1,000 in regimental funds that had hovered over him since leaving Mexico. By an unfortunate coincidence, the renowned Whig leader Henry Clay died just before Grant checked into the fashionable Willard Hotel, and he found government offices shut down and the whole town draped in mourning. A southern city still dependent upon slavery, Washington was a dusty, unpaved place with open drainage canals and army cattle browsing around the unfinished Washington Monument. "I was very much disappointed in the appearance of things about Washington," Grant confided to Julia. "The place seems small and scattering and the character of the buildings poor."[49] While Grant knew almost a dozen members of Congress from the Mexican War, he grew frustrated in tracking down a solution to his problem. It required a congressional act to resolve the matter, and the Military Committee of the House of Representatives would not meet until after he departed Washington. Thus, no action was taken on his petition. For such a proud, honorable man, the stigma of the missing funds must have still rankled.

AT GOVERNORS ISLAND in New York Harbor, Grant and his regiment endured sweltering weeks of countless drills and roll calls until they attained the requisite number of troops to travel. It was an arduous task to transport an entire infantry regiment and its cumbersome equipment to the West Coast and much of the onus fell on the capable quartermaster. One soldier retained a distinct memory of Grant, "a thin, quiet, reticent man, full of kindly and generous feelings for those about him, giving close and strict attention to his duties."[50] Knowing the rainy season had descended on Panama, with cholera everywhere, Grant already had queasy feelings about the journey and was eager to sail before conditions worsened there. Major Charles S. Tripler, the regimental surgeon, warned the War Department that it would be "murder" to move men through a zone rife with cholera, but he was blandly reassured by army brass that the epidemic would be "quickly over."[51] In the end, his anxiety proved more than justified.

From the outset, the ill-fated trip was an irremediable fiasco. People headed for the California Gold Rush packed the ships bound for Panama—traveling across the continent by wagon train was deemed too dangerous—and only at the last instant did the War Department book places aboard the steamer *Ohio*. By that point, the ship had secured its full complement of civilian passengers.

The Fourth Infantry added 730 people—650 soldiers, 60 wives, and 20 children—so that a vessel built for 330 passengers groaned under a burden of nearly 1,100. The journey on the side-wheeler had a voyage-of-the-damned quality, its three open decks constantly crammed with people milling about to escape stifling conditions belowdecks.

Despite remarkably fine weather and the diversion of fishing, card playing, and whale watching, Grant and other passengers fell hopelessly seasick on the lurching voyage. As the ship edged toward Panama, he scribbled a last letter to Julia: "I write this on deck, standing up, because in the cabin it is so insufferably hot that no one can stay there." Julia was about to give birth to their second child. The first son having been named after Colonel Dent, Grant insisted upon balancing the family ledger. "If it is a girl name it what you like," he wrote, "but if a boy name it after me."[52] Indeed, one week later, on July 22, 1852, Julia gave birth to Ulysses S. Grant Jr. Born in Bethel, Ohio, where Julia had stayed with her in-laws, the boy for the rest of his life sported the nickname "Buck" bestowed by White Haven slaves to honor the Buckeye State. "Mother always told us her greatest regret was not accompanying [Father] to the west," Buck said later, "but in her delicate condition the doctors forbade it."[53] Grant retained vague hopes that Julia would join him that winter, though he would not set eyes on her or the two boys for a couple of miserable years.

On the boat, Grant tolerated the crusty supervision of his commanding officer, Lieutenant Colonel Benjamin L. E. Bonneville, a flamboyant character partial to white beaver hats. He liked to stride the deck, cane in hand, provoking so many quarrels among his men that Grant often had to adjudicate. Bonneville had tried and failed to replace Grant as quartermaster and the latter smarted under the affront. Grant became an "incessant smoker," who seldom went to bed before 3 a.m., observed a passenger, and "during every day and an early part of each night . . . I would see him pacing the deck and smoking, silent and solitary."[54] The ceaseless smoking betrayed an inner restlessness, doubtless an amalgam of missing Julia and enduring the crushing pressures of the overcrowded ship.

The situation was ripe for a resort to alcohol, and Grant was innocently abetted by the ship's captain, James Findlay Schenck, who was profoundly impressed by him. Grant "seemed to me to be a man of an uncommon order of intelligence. He had a good education, and what his mind took hold of it grasped strongly and thoroughly digested."[55] Schenck, with no inkling of his drinking history, recalled Grant's "excellent taste for good liquors. I had given him the liberty of the sideboard in my cabin, and urged him frequently never to be backward in using it as though it were his own, and he never was. Every night after I had turned in, I would hear him once or twice, sometimes more, open the door quietly and walk softly over the floor so as not to disturb me; then I would hear the clink of the glass and a gurgle, and he would walk softly back."[56] These late-night raids on Schenck's liquor cabinet fit Grant's later pattern of private, late-night indulgence in alcohol. It seemed as if with Julia's absence the discipline of the temperance movement and the ringing exhortations of John Bartholomew Gough crumbled during a tumultuous week at sea.

When the ship arrived at the port of Aspinwall, the steaming town, drenched with torrential rains, stood "eight or ten inches under water," Grant wrote, "and foot passengers passed from place to place on raised footwalks."[57] According to Schenck, Grant remained "sleeplessly active" in rescuing his charges from the submerged city.[58] A new railroad lay under construction across the isthmus, and terrifying reports contended that forty of one hundred workers had perished from cholera. The Fourth Infantry took this incomplete railroad as far as the Chagres River, where they boarded long, flat-bottomed boats pushed along by scantily clad locals wielding long poles. When they reached the upstream town of Cruces, the soldiers marched the remaining distance, but their families were supposed to mount mules to carry them across the mountain trails. Here disaster struck. The steamship company had signed an agreement with a contractor who failed to deliver a single animal, the Gold Rush passengers having wooed them away with higher prices. Still worse, no agent of the steamship company even greeted the party. As Grant wrote, "There was not a mule, either for pack or saddle, in the place."[59]

With his split metabolism, Grant came alive in emergencies, drawing upon a fund of strength that often lay dormant in more tranquil times. Taking the initiative as quartermaster, he dismissed the original contractor and entered into an agreement with one who demanded extortionate prices. While Grant wrestled with this intractable problem, "cholera had broken out, and men were dying every hour."[60] Since Bonneville left him with the most vulnerable passengers, Grant stayed behind for a week with 150 sick soldiers, women, children, and regimental baggage until adequate transportation was arranged. Cholera was a swift and lethal disease that could carry off its victims within hours. One woman under Grant's care, Delia Sheffield, claimed it was "a common sight to see strong men . . . taken with cramps and die in a short time." In Grant she saw not only a streak of humanity but true nobility in his solicitude for his wards. "Captain Grant . . . and the surgeons did everything in their power to check the spread of the disease, and to alleviate the sufferings of the stricken ones. Too much praise cannot be given them for their tireless energy and great presence of mind during this outbreak of cholera."[61]

When Grant and his entourage finally moved out, the women rode mules, led by native guides, while men walked and carried parcels; several nuns had to be hoisted in hammocks. Drum major J. D. Elderkin never forgot how Grant saved his wife by giving him a $20 gold piece to hire a mule, while also furnishing her with a coat to shield her from malarial flies. As they wound over narrow, twisting hillside paths, Grant tended this strange cavalcade, making sure they didn't drink water from contaminated springs and urging them to drink wine sparingly instead. In spite of these precautions, many members died from cholera and had to be hastily buried by the wayside.

When they at last reached Panama City on the Gulf of Panama—then a backward village of adobe houses with thatched roofs—the cholera epidemic was not yet contained. For the most virulent cases, the coolheaded Grant converted an old relic of a ship into a temporary hospital and bravely tended many patients himself. "He was like a ministering angel to us all," said Elderkin, "a man of iron, so far as endurance went, seldom sleeping, and then only two or three hours at a time."[62] Altogether Grant estimated that one-third of the people under his care died at Cruces or Panama City as well as one-seventh of the Fourth Infantry group that had left New York Harbor. As the hellish story surfaced, it provoked fierce condemnation of War Department negligence, an indictment Grant endorsed, telling Julia darkly "there is a great accountability somewhere for the loss which we have sustained."[63]

To Julia, Grant emphasized the wisdom of having omitted her from the trip. "My dearest you never could have crossed the Isthmus at this season . . . The horrors of the road, in the rainy season, are beyond description."[64] He felt vindicated in not having allowed their firstborn son, Fred, to come along. "Had you come he no doubt would now be in his grave."[65] Grant stated that all twenty children who made the passage died either from the rigors of the overland journey or from diseases contracted along the way. For Grant, with his special fondness for children, this part of the saga must have been particularly haunting.

During the ghastly crossing, Grant had undergone a trial as harrowing as anything he experienced during the Mexican War. The nightmarish odyssey was seared into his memory, and he would unburden himself of the story many times in his life. Perhaps some of this obsession arose from lingering guilt about those he could not save, but there must also have been extraordinary pride in his courage and fortitude. Perhaps no episode before the Civil War so exposed his superlative leadership gifts. From the Panama ordeal sprang his later vision of a canal between the oceans that would do away forever with lengthy, hazardous journeys across the isthmus. Not surprisingly, Grant would always prefer Nicaragua as the site for such a project.

By early August, the exhausted remnants of the Fourth Infantry embarked on the steamer *Golden Gate,* bound for California. For a month, the soldiers stayed in Benicia Barracks, northeast of San Francisco, until they had recuperated from the Panama crossing and were reinforced by the arrival of additional troops who had been ailing when the steamer sailed. San Francisco was then aflame with Gold Rush fever, and Grant was entranced by its roaring, brawling atmosphere, where men "wore their pantaloons in their boots, and carried about with them an arsenal of bowie-knives and pistols."[66] He was susceptible to get-rich-quick schemes in a city jammed with hucksters of every stripe. "There is no reason why an active energetic person should not make a fortune every year," he told Julia. "I feel that I could quit the Army to-day and in one year go home with enough to make us comfortable . . . all our life."[67] It appears patent that Grant entertained such pipe dreams because he could not afford to bring his family to the West Coast. "No person can know the attachment that exists between parent and child until they have been separated for some time," he told Julia. "I am almost crazy sometimes to see Fred."[68]

Grant kept busy during his Benicia stay. The soldiers improvised a theater, with log boxes constructed for officers, and Grant attended regularly. He visited two of Julia's brothers, who had cashed in on the Gold Rush by running a hotel and ferry service on the Stanislaus River, but his favorite diversion was card playing. San Francisco was chock-full of gambling houses and Grant, mesmerized by games of chance, immediately went ashore with a friend and won money for dinner at the faro table. Always a probing observer of human nature, Grant was touched by the plight of well-to-do young men who had flocked to San Francisco, lured by dreams of riches, only to slave away as carpenters or masons. "Many of the real scenes in early California life exceed in strangeness and interest any of the mere products of the brain of the novelist," he declared.[69]

On September 14, the Fourth Infantry left for its new home at Columbia

Barracks, on the Columbia River, in Oregon Territory, across the water from the small settlement of Portland. (The barracks was renamed Fort Vancouver in July 1853 and the land became part of Washington Territory.) The ship that transported the regiment up the coast, the *Columbia,* had a turbulent voyage, encountering three days of gale-force winds that made Grant and other passengers seasick. Right before arriving at Columbia Barracks, Grant had a vivid dream, telling Julia "that I got home and found you, Fred. and a beautiful little girl, all asleep. Fred. woke up and we had a long conversation and he spoke as plainly as one of ten years old."[70] Grant still did not know the sex of the baby he presumed had been born in late July and imagined it as a girl. The letter reveals the extent of his anxiety about a prolonged separation from his family.

An army outpost since 1849, Columbia Barracks was set in a beautiful wilderness sparsely populated by Indian tribes and frontier settlers. When the weather was clear, it disclosed glistening vistas of snow-covered Mount Hood shimmering in the distance. But when it rained, the fort could seem lonely and godforsaken; when it snowed, the river grew icy. By December, snow stood ten inches thick on the ground and the mercury often dipped below freezing. "It either rains or snows here all the time at this place so I scarcely ever get a mile from home, and half the time do not go out of the house during the day," Grant reported to Julia.[71] For someone prone to depression, the everlasting rain and snow, combined with enforced confinement, were sure to prey on his mind. Grant began to suffer cramps in his legs and feet in the damp, frigid climate, a possible symptom of alcoholic neuropathy.[72] "He was quiet and kept his room a good deal," said one officer. He "was not a man who showed his griefs with his friends. He suffered alone."[73]

Originally an important trading post for the Hudson's Bay Company, Columbia Barracks still had the wooden stockade and three-story guard tower from that era. Grant was lucky to live in a building known as the Quartermaster's Ranch, where he resided with his old West Point roommate Rufus Ingalls and two other officers. With porches on three sides, the two-story building stood on a slope above the Columbia River and Grant thought it the finest house in the territory. Made in New England, it had been dismantled and shipped around Cape Horn to the West Coast. At first, Grant was subordinate to Captain Thomas Lee Brent, but when the latter was transferred in May, Grant assumed total responsibility as regimental quartermaster, superintending all buildings, a blacksmith shop, a tin shop, a saddler's shop, a carpentry shop, and two hundred mules.

As if touched with Gold Rush mania, Grant rashly entered into a business venture that caused him no end of grief. In Sackets Harbor, he and Julia had befriended a prominent family, the Camps, who were ruined by a railway invest-ment. To rescue Elijah Camp, Grant paid for him to accompany the regiment to Columbia Barracks, where Camp opened a sutler's store and Grant, with pay saved up from the Panama journey, supplied the needed $1,500 in capital. The con artist and the scoundrel always found a ready target in U. S. Grant. While the business boomed, Camp balked when Grant asked for a profit statement and "began to groan and whine and say there was no money in his trade at all," Julia said.[74] Perhaps detecting Grant's gullibility, Camp complained that he would feel better owning the business outright. Grant, always good-natured to a fault, agreed to withdraw his $1,500, apparently taking $700 in cash and $800 in personal notes from Camp. "I was very foolish for taking it," Grant admitted to Julia, "because my share of the profits would not have been less than three thou-sand per year."[75] Still not satisfied, Camp began to assert he couldn't sleep at night, worrying that the notes Grant held might fall into the wrong hands. The obliging Grant then burned the notes by candlelight in front of Camp. Camp sold gunpowder in the shop, and when some of it accidentally blew up the store, he decided to return to Sackets Harbor. He refused to pay Grant the $800 he owed him, even though he had earned ten times that amount.

That November, Grant's old card-playing partner from the Mexican War, Franklin Pierce, won the presidency on the Democratic ticket, defeating Gen-eral Winfield Scott, who carried only four states for the Whigs. This lopsided defeat threatened the Whigs' survival and would soon lead to formation of the Republican Party. As Charles Sumner told William Seward, "Now is the time for a new organization. Out of the chaos the party of freedom must arise."[76]

Forlorn in the frosty northern woods, Grant must have felt quite distant from national politics. He wore a long beard, grew stout, and agonized over his separa-tion from Julia. Their psychological distance seemed even greater than the geo-graphical. As the Columbia River froze and blocked mail steamers, it took two months for her letters to reach him, and his morose return messages make for pitiable reading. "Just think," he wrote in October, "our youngest is at this mo-ment probably over three months of age, and yet I have never heard a word from it, or you, in that time."[77] Not until December 3, 1852—more than four months after his birth—did Grant learn that Julia had brought Ulysses Jr. into the world. Simultaneously he received confirmation from his sister Virginia and brother

Orvil, and he bubbled over with relieved excitement: "It made tears almost start in my eyes, with joy, to hear so much about them by one mail," he confided.[78]

Despite long absences from Julia, Grant's life was miraculously free from allegations of womanizing. He would show up for dances, watch couples wordlessly for a while, then retire to the privacy of his room. "He did not run after the women as some of the officers did," said Elderkin. "When he was in Oregon in 1852, his wife was in the eastern states, and he never ran after anyone."[79] Everyone noticed how he pined for his wife. "Often, of a winter's night, when we were seated around the fire," wrote Delia Sheffield, "he would tell me of his wife and children and how he missed them."[80] One morning, Grant dropped by the cottage of the artillery sergeant Theodore J. Eckerson, who recalled Grant showing him a letter from Julia where she "had laid baby Fred's hand on the paper and traced with a pencil to show the size of it. He folded the letter and left without speaking a word; but his form shook and his eyes grew moist."[81] All the while, Grant struggled with gnawing suspicions that Colonel Dent wished to sabotage his marriage and steal away his children. As he wrote to Julia in July 1853, with a noticeable touch of anger, "How can your pa & ma think that they are going to keep Fred. & Ulys always with them?"[82]

The only rumor of philandering that ever trailed Grant concerned a Native American woman, named either Moumerto or Maria, who later claimed she gave birth to a daughter fathered by Grant. Grant's fellow soldiers tended to discount the story, which remains vague and wholly unsubstantiated.[83] What is certain is that Grant showed striking sympathy for Indians whom his regiment had come to police. "It is really my opinion that the whole race would be harmless and peaceable if they were not put upon by the whites," he told Julia.[84] He saw firsthand the fraud and abuse practiced upon Native Americans by corrupt white agents who swindled them on goods, not to mention the devastating effects of smallpox and measles communicated by white settlers.

Army pay was paltry in these years. One officer pointed out that "laborers and mechanics could in one week earn a captain's pay . . . even the highest officers . . . were compelled to practice the most rigid economies."[85] Many officers, like Grant, couldn't afford to bring their families to the western outpost. The Gold Rush inflated prices to stratospheric levels, sharpening the pinch for Grant, who feared military life would condemn him to a nomadic existence at frontier garrisons without his family. Under the circumstances, he told Julia in May 1853 that if he could "get together a few thousand dollars," he might quit the army and rejoin her.[86] At the very least, he could then send for her and the boys. The speculative atmosphere bred by the gold miners must have buttressed the idea that one business bonanza—one big killing—might free him from this lonely exile.

After leasing one hundred acres near the Columbia River, Grant and three other officers began to plant potatoes, oats, onions, and corn, the diligent Grant doing all the plowing and furrowing himself. His hands grew rough and callused from hard labor and he developed a slight stoop from bending in the field. "Passing this field one day, in the early spring, I saw Captain Grant, with his trousers tucked in his boots, sowing oats broadcast from a sheet tied about his neck and shoulders," remembered Delia Sheffield.[87] By the spring, his efforts had yielded a bumper crop. Then in June, the sudden melting of snow from the Cascades caused the Columbia River to overflow, drowning the oats, onions, and corn, and half the potato crop. The rising water also wrecked timber that Grant had neatly stacked for sale to steamboat captains. To aggravate matters, the price of potatoes plummeted and the four partners had to pay someone to cart away a rotting, worthless crop.

After the farming venture backfired, Grant and a partner bought up chickens and shipped them to San Francisco, only to have most perish en route. Then Grant and Rufus Ingalls learned that ice sold for exorbitant prices in San Francisco. To capitalize on this, they packed one hundred tons aboard a sailing vessel only to have headwinds detain the ship and melt the ice; by the time it arrived in San Francisco, other boats packed with ice had preceded it, leading to a price skid. To top things off, Grant and another officer tried to start a social club and billiard room at the Union Hotel only to have the hired manager abscond with their funds.

Why did Grant's speculative schemes invariably go awry? Partly the explanation lies in his desperate desire to bring Julia and the boys to Fort Vancouver. He aimed to make a windfall and exploit sudden rises in price instead of engaging in sure, steady work. It was also the triumph of hope over experience: he never learned from earlier mishaps that commodities are perishable items with wildly fluctuating prices. He was also congenitally naive in business. Sincere himself, he could never imagine how deviously other people could behave. "Neither Grant nor myself had the slightest suggestion of business talent," said partner Henry D. Wallen. "He was the perfect soul of honor and truth, and believed everyone else as artless as himself."[88]

As in many frontier garrisons, soldiers dealt with boredom and loneliness by escaping into an alcoholic stupor. Second Lieutenant George Crook claimed officers were drunk daily "and most until the wee hours of the morning. I never had seen such gambling and carousing before or since."[89] Grant drank less often than other officers but went on "sprees" consistent with his lifelong tendency to engage in sporadic binge drinking. "He would perhaps go on two or three sprees a year," said Lieutenant Henry C. Hodges, "but was always open to reason, and when spoken to on the subject, would own up and promise to stop drinking, which he did."[90] The problem was not the frequency with which Grant drank but the extreme behavioral changes induced. Officer Robert Macfeely observed: "Liquor seemed a virulent poison to him, and yet he had a fierce desire for it. One glass would show on him," his speech became slurred, "and two or three would make him stupid."[91] Alcohol loosened up Grant's tightly buttoned personality, giving him a broader, often jovial emotional range; the description of being "stupidly" or "foolishly" drunk would recur with striking regularity in future years. Rumor mills hummed busily in the small, insular peacetime army before the Civil War, and when Grant made a public spectacle of himself, those who glimpsed him in this silly, sloppy state never forgot the sight.

Drinking may have been a needed release from the nervous tension he accumulated during the long abstinence between episodes. Brought up in a strict Methodist household, Grant was moralistic enough to reprimand others who succumbed to alcoholic temptation. Delia Sheffield recalls the time the skipper of a small boat got drunk and disturbed the audience during a private theatrical. "Captain Grant walked to where he was sitting, and taking him firmly by the collar, marched him out of the hall. He had a true soldier's love of order."[92] But Grant's drinking lapses would be costly and ultimately ruinous to his reputation. Robert Macfeely says that one day Grant was riding a pony that slipped and fell on top of him on a muddy road, leaving him bruised and disheveled and giving rise to reports that he was drunk. Brevet Major Benjamin Alvord "preferred charges against him. Grant protested that he had not been drinking then, but Alvord sent in charges against him and Grant pledged himself not to drink any more."[93] Alvord would forward this pledge to the commanding officer of Grant's next posting, with calamitous results.

One other consequential encounter returned to hurt Grant a decade later. One of his quartermaster duties was to supply pack animals and other provisions for parties surveying a railroad route through the Cascade mountains for what became the Northern Pacific Railway. In July 1853, one such survey was led by the twenty-six-year-old brevet captain George B. McClellan. Unlike Grant, McClellan had graduated near the top of his West Point class and showed little patience for slipshod performance. While his expedition was being outfitted at Fort Vancouver, said Henry C. Hodges, "Grant got on one of his little sprees, which annoyed and offended McClellan exceedingly, and in my opinion he never quite forgave Grant for it."[94] Though suffering from a severe cold, Grant delivered two hundred horses and other supplies on time, but he had made a powerful enemy who would associate him with this alcoholic binge.

By now Grant was despondent and almost frantic to be reunited with Julia. "Mrs. Sheffield, I have the dearest little wife in the world," he exclaimed. "I want to resign from the Army and live with my family!"[95] Then on August 5, 1853, Captain William W. S. Bliss died and the resulting vacancy led to Grant's promotion to full captain. Secretary of War Jefferson Davis ordered him to report to Company F of the Fourth Infantry at Fort Humboldt, California. Grant had known that, if promoted, he would likely go there, having told Julia a few months earlier, "Col. Buchanan is there at present, I believe, establishing the post."[96] Lieutenant Colonel Robert C. Buchanan was all too familiar to Grant as the strict disciplinarian who used to fine him wine bottles at Jefferson Barracks for his frequent late returns from White Haven. The memory of this bogeyman could only have depressed his mood as he got ready to leave Fort Vancouver for the wilds of northern California.

CHAPTER FIVE

Payday

O N JANUARY 5, 1854, Ulysses S. Grant, after sailing 250 miles up the coast from San Francisco on a "long and tedious voyage," arrived at Fort Humboldt, a scenic but abysmally secluded destination.[1] The fort commanded a hundred-foot bluff with spacious views of Humboldt Bay and the sea beyond, and was hemmed in by deep stands of towering sequoia and other redwood trees, steeped in perpetual shadow. Since one could only reach San Francisco by water, mail trickled in on an irregular basis. The largest nearby town was Eureka, a modest hamlet with a handful of sawmills and approximately five hundred people. The officers' quarters and furnishings were rough-hewn from giant logs cut from nearby forests. Aside from recreational drinking and dancing, the only available pastimes were fishing and hunting elk, deer, and black bears, activities that awakened little interest in Grant.

The claustrophobic setting exacerbated his solitude, making him feel fearfully cut off from the outer world and tipping him over the edge psychologically. "Imagine a place closed in by the sea having thrown up two tongues of land, closed in a bay that can be entered only with certain winds," he told Julia.[2] Only a month after his arrival, he lapsed into self-pity. "You do not know how forsaken I feel here!"[3] A pall smothered his often sparkling prose, which lost its humor, buoyancy, and charm. "I got one letter from you since I have been here but it was some three months old," he complained, speculating that little Ulysses Jr. must be talking by now.[4] His laments betray the earmarks of acute depression, including lethargy and indifference to his environment: "I do nothing here but sit in my room and read and occasionally take a short ride on one of the public horses."[5] He had applied for orders to travel to Washington to settle his Mexican War account and remained despondent over unaccountable delays. "The state of suspense that I am in is scarcely bearable," he declared.[6]

Grant watched despair etch deep lines in his face. When he had a troublesome tooth extracted, his face swelled up until it was "as round as an apple," and, as he stared at himself in the mirror, he reflected gloomily: "I think I could pass readily for a person of forty five."[7] He came down with chills and fever that February and had to be treated for "severe attacks."[8] His colleagues readily intuited his profound yearning for his family and the turmoil engendered by their absence. One day, when he lost a ring that Julia had given him at their engagement, he was beside himself. "The intrepid soldier, who preserved his coolness in the bloodiest battles, was completely unstrung," recalled a local businessman. "The next morning half of the command was turned out and the parade ground was 'panned' until the ring was found."[9]

With relatively little work to do, Grant found himself at loose ends. He roved around the post, wearing a battered straw hat and puffing on a pipe or cigar. Taking excellent care of his company, he planted a garden to furnish them with fresh vegetables and arranged with a local hunter to serve fresh elk meat, but such work yielded little comfort. "He was an ordinary looking man with firmly set mouth and deep, searching eyes that seemed to take me in at a glance and then turned indifferently away," said a local rancher.[10] Because local Indians posed no real threat, all the drills and discipline performed at the post seemed pointless and irksome.

Hypersensitive to taunts, Grant had been singled out as a target by bullies since boyhood. As he already knew, the commanding officer at Fort Humboldt, Robert C. Buchanan, was a martinet who had graduated from West Point in 1830, serving with distinction in the Mexican War. For his admirers, Buchanan was a consummate professional with elegant manners. One associate remembered "a man of refined habits, a courtly gentleman . . . Fine physique and of commanding presence, respected and admired, a thorough officer in all duties or obligations to his government or military standard of excellence."[11] But a darker side often governed Robert Buchanan, who enjoyed meting out punishment to those who did not share his punctilious regard for military etiquette. As A. P. Marble, Grant's body servant, put it, "Colonel Buchanan was an efficient officer but strict in petty details to the verge of absurdity."[12] George Crook, who served under the ornery Buchanan before Grant arrived, left a chilling portrait of his despotism: "Our Commander seemed particularly elated at his own importance . . . He seemed to take delight in wounding the feelings of those under him, and succeeded pretty generally in making himself unpopular amongst the citizens as well as the army."[13]

Grant and Buchanan were bound to clash. Grant could be slovenly in dress and careless in his habits and was sure to grate on a spic-and-span officer. He was nettled by this blustering new boss who insisted upon tight procedures at a remote outpost, where such caviling seemed misplaced. Buchanan had already been alerted by Benjamin Alvord to Grant's drinking problem and pledge of abstinence, a handy weapon to brandish over his new captain.

Unfortunately for Grant, alcohol was ubiquitous at Fort Humboldt. Once morning drills ended, officers resorted to whiskey and poker to pass the time. "Commissary whisky of the vilest kind was to be had in unlimited quantities and all partook more or less," said a military wife.[14] To deal with his private sadness and mitigate the pain of migraine headaches, Grant got into the habit of drinking more frequently, often stopping for alcoholic refreshment at a local saloon or a general store run by James T. Ryan. Buchanan's adjutant, Lewis Cass Hunt, said Grant "used to go on long sprees till his whole nature would rebel and then he would be sick."[15] Echoing comments made elsewhere, a beef contractor named W. I. Reed claimed Grant drank less often than other officers, but with more harmful consequences for "with his peculiar organization a little did the fatal [work] of a great deal . . . he had very poor brains for drinking."[16]

In his *Memoirs,* Grant was adamant that he left the army voluntarily that spring from a wish to be reunited with his family. "I saw no chance of supporting them on the Pacific coast out of my pay as an army officer. I concluded, therefore, to resign."[17] This became the standard version favored by Julia, the Grant family, and several biographers, and little doubt exists that Grant meditated seriously retirement from the army. "I sometimes get so anxious to see you, and our little boys, that I am almost tempted to resign and trust to Providence, and my own exertions, for a living where I can have you and them with me," he told Julia in early March 1854. Then in the next breath, he backtracked from this impractical wish. "Whenever I get to thinking upon the subject however *poverty, poverty,* begins to stare me in the face and then I think what would I do if you and our little ones should want for the necessaries of life."[18] Grant said he was so depressed he hadn't strayed more than one hundred yards from his quarters for two weeks. "But you never complain of being lonesome so I infer that you are quite contented." Then he related a dream that seemed laced with fear, jealousy, and barely disguised anger. "I thought you were at a party when I arrived and before paying any attention to my arrival you said you must go, you were engaged for that dance."[19] It was not the first time Grant betrayed jealousy or accused Julia of being indifferent to his desperate plight.

While Grant laid down the preferred version of his resignation in his *Memoirs,* where he never breathed a syllable about his drinking problem to posterity, he was more candid in later private conversations, telling Civil War chaplain John Eaton that "the vice of intemperance had not a little to do with my decision to resign."[20] To General Augustus Chetlain he admitted that "when I have nothing to do I get blue and depressed, I have a natural craving for a drink, when I was on the coast I got in a depressed condition and got to drinking."[21]

Overwhelming evidence suggests that Grant resigned from an alcohol problem. Lewis Cass Hunt told several people how Buchanan sent him to reprimand Grant after one drinking episode. As Colonel Granville O. Haller heard the tale, Hunt told Grant that Colonel Buchanan would "withdraw the drinking charge if Grant didn't offend again—he had Grant write out his resignation, omitting the date." There was an "explicit understanding that if Grant forgot his pledge, Buchanan would forward his resignation and save Grant the odium of being cashiered by a General court martial."[22] The journalist Benjamin Perley Poore later confirmed that Buchanan had warned Grant, "You had better resign or reform," to which Grant responded, "I will resign if I don't reform."[23]

One Sunday morning, Grant showed up at his company's pay table under the influence of drink. Bristling at this display, Buchanan told Hunt to buckle on his sword and lay down the law to Grant, warning that if he did not resign, he would face a court-martial. According to Colonel Thomas M. Anderson, who heard the story from Hunt, "Grant put his face down in his hand for a long time and then commenced writing something . . . Grant said that he did not want his wife to know that he had ever been tried . . . Grant then signed his resignation and he gave it to the commanding officer."[24] Some of Grant's friends, convinced he would have been acquitted, pleaded with him to stand trial. Henry C. Hodges said the regiment deemed Buchanan's action "unnecessarily harsh and severe."[25] Rufus Ingalls, Grant's old roommate at West Point and Fort Vancouver, believed that since Grant had not been incapacitated by drink, he would have been exonerated, but he confirmed that Grant refused to stand trial because "he would not

for all the world have his wife know that he had been tried on such a charge."[26]
The idea that Grant feared Julia's wrath makes one wonder whether she had
extracted a strict promise from him to refrain from drinking altogether.

During the Civil War, Thomas M. Anderson discussed Grant's resignation
with Robert Buchanan, then his commander in the Army of the Potomac. "I was
very intimate with Col. Buchanan & had my first information as to the Humboldt episode . . . from him . . . I remember absolutely that Col. Buchanan told
me distinctly that he had condoned a similar offense in Grant before he fired, or
as he said *permitted* his resignation as a favor." From discussions with Lewis Cass
Hunt, Anderson, later commander at Fort Vancouver, added that Hunt had
warned Grant not to show up intoxicated at the pay table and had even volunteered to go in his place, but Grant had refused.[27]

On April 11, 1854, Grant received his formal commission as full captain.
Having achieved this rank, he tendered his resignation to Colonel Buchanan
while confirming his commission in a simultaneous letter to the War Department. His resignation may have stemmed from a convergence of factors. Grant
knew Buchanan was conducting a vendetta against him and did not want to
endure a humiliating trial. He may also have reflected that he was profoundly
unhappy with army life, could not afford to bring his family out West, and was
dying a slow death in the service. Hence, Grant may have seen a redeeming side
to his resignation, even though it had been wrung from him against his will.

The story of Grant's resignation echoed down the years into the Civil War.
In the small peacetime army, libels and scandals traveled swiftly among officers,
whose rotations at far-flung outposts guaranteed wide currency for gossip. In
such a situation, soldiers had to guard their reputations or missteps could dog
them for years. Starting in April 1854, Grant's bibulous nature became a part of
army folklore and, rightly or wrongly, he was never again entirely free from
charges of being a "drunkard." "The reason for Grant's resignation in 1854 . . .
was known," General Michael R. Morgan subsequently commented. "Grant's
case was unusual at the time and was discussed by the Army."[28] During the Civil
War, both sides knew what had unfolded at Fort Humboldt. As the Union
general James H. Wilson wrote: "It is a part of the history of the times that
[Grant] had fallen for a season into the evil ways of military men serving on the
remote frontier and that his return to civil life was commonly believed to have
been a choice between resignation and a court-martial."[29] The grapevine even

reached deep into the Confederacy, where diarist Mary Chesnut would allude to Grant's earlier downfall in the Far West. "Put out of the army for habitual drunkenness."[30]

Grant did not notify his censorious father of his resignation, an omission suggesting deep fear or shame. A perturbed Jesse Grant learned about it after Jefferson Davis accepted the resignation on June 2, and then he tried to prevail upon his local congressman, Andrew Ellison, to get the decision reversed. When that failed, he sent a humane letter to Jefferson Davis, entreating him to withdraw his acceptance of the resignation. He thought Ulysses had been conditioned by the army and could never readjust to civilian life. He penned prophetic words: "I think after spending so much time to qualify himself for the Army, & spending so many years in the service, he will be poorly qualified for the pursuits of private life." He requested a six-month leave for his son, who "has not seen his family for over two years, & has a son nearly two years old he has never seen. I suppose in his great anxiety to see his family he has been induced to quit the service."[31] Unfortunately, Davis considered the matter settled, and his reply delicately evaded the true reason behind the resignation. He observed that since Ulysses had "assigned no reasons why he desired to quit the service, and the motives which influenced him are not known to the Department," he would let the decision stand.[32] Grant's failure to specify a reason for departing from the army strengthens the suspicion that drinking lay at its root.

Fiercely protective of her husband's reputation, Julia's "indignation was intense as stories spread in army circles and were whispered in St. Louis" about Ulysses's resignation, wrote Julia's biographer Ishbel Ross.[33] Her sister Emma was no less irate at the notion that alcohol had undone Grant's army career: "It is not true that the Captain's personal habits at that time led him into such difficulties that he was asked to resign."[34] Julia spent a lifetime reflexively denying such problems and glossing over the purgatorial months at Fort Humboldt. "He was happy in the fight and the din of battle, but restless in the barracks," she later explained to a reporter. "He resigned from the army, and took a plantation in Missouri, and went to farming."[35] Grant was no less breezily dismissive to the press: "When I resigned from the army and went to a farm I was happy."[36] Grant stood on firmer ground in later arguing that his army departure was providential. "If I had stayed in the army I would have been still a Captain on frontier duty at the outbreak of the war and would thus have been deprived of the right to offer my services voluntarily to the country."[37] Indeed, his momentary disgrace can be seen in retrospect as his salvation, preserving him for a starring role in the Civil War instead of stranding him at a post in the hinterland.

The nearly two years of hardships on the West Coast had engraved a worried expression on Grant's face, giving sad depths to his eyes. He tried to sound sanguine as he prepared to leave Fort Humboldt: "Whoever hears of me in ten years will hear of a well-to-do old Missouri farmer," he told his comrades.[38] He was still beset by ailments, including migraine headaches and fever, and Colonel Buchanan reported to the Pacific Department Headquarters on May 1, "Captain Grant is too unwell to travel just yet . . . but will proceed to San Francisco by the first steamer."[39] Having turned thirty-two, Grant retained enough self-confidence to know that his life to date did not reflect the wealth of talent stored up inside him. Dr. Jonathan Clark had treated his ailments at Fort Humboldt. In bidding him farewell, Grant spoke these parting words: "Well, doctor, I am out. But I will tell you something and you mark my words: my day will come, they will hear from me yet."[40] Despite his grim stint at Fort Humboldt, Grant had fallen in love with the natural beauty of northern California and grown so attached to the place that he had visions of making it his permanent home in future years.

On May 7, 1854, Grant boarded the steamer *Arispe,* heaped with timber and gold dust, bound for San Francisco. A few days earlier, he had written Julia an evasive letter that was short, cryptic, and devoid of his usual effusive affection. He chided her again for not writing, made no mention of his resignation, and simply announced that he had taken a leave of absence. "After receiving this you may discontinue writing because before I could get a reply I shall be on my way home. You might write directing to the City of New York."[41] It was a weirdly elliptical message that testifies to Grant's confusion as to how he should break the shocking news to Julia.

The San Francisco that Grant encountered was no longer the rip-roaring, wide-open town he first saw. "Gambling houses had disappeared from public view," he wrote. "The city had become staid and orderly."[42] Short of funds, he went to his friend Captain Thomas H. Stevens Jr., an officer who had begun a banking business. Grant had left $1,750 with Stevens in January and expected to collect that amount. Stevens offered 2 percent monthly interest and a more sophisticated investor might have realized no legitimate banker paid such exorbitant rates. "I can't pay you now," Stevens insisted, "but if you will wait a couple of weeks I will pay you in time for you to take the next steamer."[43] The obliging Grant agreed. Julia narrated the sequel: "At the end of the two weeks, the captain returned to find that Stevens had conveniently gone out of town and the captain was again cheated."[44] Once more the credulous Grant had been duped by a trickster in what had become a striking pattern. Clearly other people thought him something of a simpleton who could be defrauded with impunity. Not until 1863, amid the Civil War, did Julia send Stevens a blunt letter and finally receive belated payment.

While waiting for Stevens to pay, Grant visited Julia's brother Lewis on the Stanislaus River only to return and find Stevens had vanished. With his life spiraling out of control, Grant grew desperate in his hunt for money. As he walked the streets, consumed with anxiety, he bumped into J. D. Elderkin, who was stunned by Grant's seedy appearance. "I was almost ashamed to speak to him on the street, he looked so bad. I felt very sorry for him—poor fellow."[45]

Thanks to the Elijah Camp fiasco, the perfidious T. H. Stevens, and the abortive farming ventures, Grant had squandered money he could ill afford to lose. The chief quartermaster on the West Coast, Robert Allen, an old friend of Grant's, learned he was holed up in a cheap miner's hotel called "What Cheer House." He found Grant in a spartan garret room furnished with a cot, a pine table, and a chair. "Why, Grant, what are you doing here?" Allen asked. "Nothing," Grant replied. "I've resigned from the army. I'm out of money, and I have no means of getting home."[46] Allen promised to help Grant and encouraged him to stop by his office.

Grant could only book passage to New York if he presented a certificate at the quartermaster's office that entitled him to a $40 per diem payment the government owed him. Office clerk Richard L. Ogden remembered Grant shuffling into his work space late one afternoon, bearing the certificate. When Ogden announced it was improperly drawn up and he had no cash on hand, Grant's "countenance fell, and a look of utter despair came over it." Grant asked if he could sleep on a threadbare old lounge chair there, explaining "I have not a cent to my name." The good-hearted Ogden offered him a dollar for lodgings. "I am greatly obliged," Grant said, "but, with your permission, I will use the dollar for my dinner and breakfast and the lounge will save me the dollar." The next morning, Ogden not only cashed Grant's certificate but escorted him to the office of the Pacific Mail Steamship. Since the quartermaster gave ample business to the steamship line, Ogden cajoled the manager into awarding Grant something "tantamount to a free pass to New York." This was a godsend for Grant, who received a stateroom far more luxurious than anything he had imagined and would still have $15 when he arrived in New York.[47]

On June 1, 1854, Grant boarded a passenger ship owned by Commodore Cornelius Vanderbilt, the *Sierra Nevada,* that would carry him down to Nicaragua. In Washington, Congress had just passed the Kansas-Nebraska Act, which repealed the Missouri Compromise of 1820 and opened the possibility that settlers could create new slave states in the vast territories of Kansas and Nebraska, igniting explosive controversy. Southern Whigs joined with Democrats to enact the bill, leading Horace Greeley to predict that "the passage of this Nebraska bill will arouse and consolidate the most gigantic, determined and overwhelming party for freedom that the world ever saw."[48] That new party would be the Republican Party. These seminal events would profoundly affect the fortunes of Ulysses S. Grant, who likely knew little of what was happening.

When his boat reached the west coast of Nicaragua on June 13, Grant wrote to Thomas H. Stevens that the place was "as hot as the final resting place of the wicked." He referred to Stevens's scandalous behavior in exceedingly mild terms. "I was sorry not to see you before starting. I was anxious to see if some money could not be raised." He said he was owed $500 from Humboldt Bay, which would be sent directly to Stevens. "I wish you would send me a N[ew] York check for $500.00 as soon as you can."[49] There is no evidence the money was ever paid. Within a few days, Grant had crossed Lake Nicaragua and embarked on the steamer *Prometheus,* which carried him with more than five hundred other passengers to New York, where they landed on June 25.

Fresh miseries awaited Grant on the eastern seaboard. At Governors Island, he was received in kindly fashion by old army friends who loaned him money. He then set out for Sackets Harbor to collect the $800 Elijah Camp still owed him, riding much of the way on horseback. However dubious he may have been about succeeding—he had already told Julia his fear that the faithless former sutler was "slightly deranged"—it was his only chance to land some money before facing the inquiring stares of the Grants and the Dents, and he sent a letter ahead to notify Camp he was coming.[50] One version of events claims Elijah Camp went off sailing on Lake Ontario when Grant arrived, having been alerted by Grant's letter. What we know for certain is that Grant failed to extract a single penny.

When he had last resided at Sackets Harbor, a man named Walter Camp (no relation to Elijah) had counseled him about his drinking problem, applauding his courage in joining the Sons of Temperance. Now with Grant back in town, Camp passed him on horseback and was shocked to see him drunk. "Evidently under the influence of his Enemy" was how Camp phrased it. "His temperance principles were well known to me while stationed here and I was pained to see him overcome by what he had told me, years before, that he had such a desire for stimulants that his only safety was in letting them entirely alone."[51] From the way Camp told the story, it is apparent he did not stop to greet Grant, but only sorrowfully observed his fallen state. At this point, the lessons of the Sons of Temperance must have seemed a distant, slightly unreal memory to Grant, who returned to New York City bruised by Elijah Camp's betrayal.

Luckily for Grant, he sought out his old West Point chum Simon Bolivar Buckner, who was on commissary duty in New York. Having checked into the Astor House, Grant needed help to pay the hotel tab. According to Buckner, Grant apprised him that "his money was all gone and he had been unable to get anything to do and had no means to reach home. He asked for a loan in order to repay his bills at the hotel and reach his father."[52] Buckner introduced Grant to the hotel proprietor and declared he would vouch for his expenses. It is perhaps not surprising that Grant then appealed to his father for money instead of Colonel Dent, who would have gloated over his misery, but it must have irked him to have to be bailed out by his family.

From his home in Covington, Kentucky, Jesse responded by dispatching his middle son, Simpson, to New York to fetch Ulysses and settle the hotel bill. It seems rather odd that Jesse chose to send an escort instead of simply arranging credit for Ulysses. One possible solution to this mystery lies in a letter written by Frederick Law Olmsted, the renowned designer of Central Park and other urban parks, to his wife at the end of the Civil War. Olmsted had just spent an evening with Major Ralph W. Kirkham, who recalled that during the summer of 1854 he and Winfield Scott Hancock were stationed at Jefferson Barracks in St. Louis "when a letter was received from Buckner telling them that he had found Grant in New York. Grant had resigned, arrived at New York, got drunk, got into a row and been locked up by the police. Buckner relieved him and supplied him with means to go to his father in Missouri [sic]."[53] The story, if true, may suggest why Grant, who was so desperately homesick and eager to see his wife and children, dallied in Manhattan until late summer and why his brother came to retrieve him. A careful search of the sketchy New York court records for the period fails to provide any confirmation of the story.

When Ulysses and Simpson arrived in Covington, Jesse and Hannah Grant must have sensed that their eldest son had slipped off the rails. They were surely disturbed by his altered appearance and the suspicion, or knowledge, that he had succumbed to his drinking demons. Hannah professed pleasure that her son had left the army—she told a cousin she "was sorry Ulysses ever had anything to do with this army business"—while Jesse asserted that his son had made a costly mistake and wasn't shy about saying so.[54] He liked to spout a new insight: "West Point spoiled one of my boys for business."[55] By now Ulysses could only envision his life in limited terms, the wings of his ambition having been thoroughly clipped by experience. He stayed with his parents for a week, likely to look presentable when his wife and children set eyes on him.

For Julia Grant and her eldest son, Fred, the moment of Ulysses's return to White Haven was dreamlike and long enshrined in family lore. Four-year-old Fred, who had his father's broad, open face, was playing on the porch when a bearded man in a buggy drove up the drive. "Just as he was throwing the laprobe over the dashboard a colored woman ran out of the house and said: 'It's Mr. Grant.' And so it was," recalled Fred, "but I didn't know him. It is very likely he didn't know me."[56] With both arms Grant scooped up Fred and Buck, the curly little blond brother with blue eyes whom he had never seen before. For Julia, it was a moment of inexpressible happiness. "I waited for a long time, never knowing when he would come back," she later wrote. "It was like a dream when he drove up the turnstile."[57] Grant turned to Julia and said, "You know I had to wait in New York until I heard from you."[58] The biographer William McFeely has suggested that the marriage between Ulysses and Julia Grant may have been on the verge of a severe rupture when he left the army, and it is not impossible that he had nervously awaited some reassurance from her before he returned.[59]

Where Grant would live and how he would support himself became urgent matters, and he whisked his family off to Covington to settle them. For Ulysses and Julia Grant, the sting of that terrible trip never faded. Even Julia, ever the Pollyanna, remarked frankly afterward: "There are no pleasant memories of that visit."[60] Jesse Grant, now sixty, hoped to withdraw from supervision of his leather business and pass daily control to his three sons. Ulysses responded readily to his suggestion that he join Simpson in running the store in Galena, Illinois. Then Jesse added an absolutely outrageous condition that floored his son and daughter-in-law: he wanted Julia and the two boys to stay with him and Hannah in Covington to benefit from the local schools; both Grant parents viewed Julia as a spendthrift and wished to rein in her expenses. If Julia did not like that idea, they suggested she go back and live with the Dents in Missouri while her husband toiled in Galena. It was a proposal of breathtaking cruelty, all the more so because Ulysses had so long awaited reunion with his family. As Julia wrote, "Captain Grant positively and indignantly refused his father's offer."[61] One can only wonder whether his son's drinking problem made Jesse Grant issue such a heartless proposition. One further wonders whether Jesse was openly mocking Colonel Dent, who had long suggested that Julia and the children live with him while Ulysses languished at faraway military posts.

The contretemps with his father left Grant with the unappealing alternative of relying on the largesse of his father-in-law. Colonel Dent had given Julia sixty acres of White Haven land as a wedding gift, but with a catch: he did not transfer legal title to her. Colonel Dent "did this out of regard for his favorite daughter," said Louisa Boggs. "He had a very poor opinion of his son-in-law."[62] Grant decided to try his hand at farming this land. He lacked money to stock his farm and Jesse later boasted he had supplied the funds for tools, seed, and horses. To take land from his father-in-law was a terrible comedown for Grant, who had to swallow the Colonel's barely concealed scorn. Grant's friend George W. Fishback, a St. Louis journalist, sympathized with his plight: "It must have been a terrible mortification to [Grant] to be set apart on that little tract of farm land, given to his wife by her father." Colonel Dent contributed "little or nothing" to support Grant, and preferred to comment "with ridicule and bitterness upon his unpromising son-in-law."[63]

At first Ulysses and Julia Grant shared the main house at White Haven, but by spring 1855 an opportune moment arose to flee Colonel Dent's baleful eye. Julia's brother Lewis, who remained in California, allowed them to use his house "Wish-ton-wish"—an Indian term meaning whip-poor-will—that stood shaded by majestic oaks about a mile from the Colonel's quarters. This large, rambling house, which Julia lauded as "a beautiful English villa," had front and back porches, pitched roofs, and dormer windows, and was commodious enough to absorb the latest addition to Grant's family, a little girl named Ellen (in honor of Julia's mother), who was born on July 4 and was always known as Nellie.[64]

Rolling up his sleeves, Grant cleared the sixty acres for farming, pulling up tree stumps and planting corn and grinding wheat at the nearby gristmill of Henry Clay Wright. Grant "was a small, thin man then, with a close-cropped, brown beard," recalled Wright. "He had no overcoat, I remember, and he wore tall boots, quite unlike any others in the neighborhood . . . He had a way of keeping people at arm's length."[65] Eager to prove his worth, Grant soon added oats, Irish potatoes, sweet potatoes, melons, beets, cucumbers, and cabbages, working with a resolve that won plaudits even from his skeptical father. "During all this time he worked like a slave," admitted Jesse Grant. "No man ever worked harder."[66]

In this grueling labor, Grant was industrious and resourceful, selling timber props for tunnels of nearby coal mines. In the winter, donning dingy old army overalls, he loaded wagons to sell cords of wood on St. Louis street corners—surely another blow to his pride. Invariably he strolled beside the loaded wagons rather than ride, even though this entailed a ten-mile hike. "The horses," he quipped, "have enough to draw without carrying a lazy rider."[67] Dr. William Taussig, mayor of Carondelet, remembered how Grant lingered on a log before a blacksmith's shop—"a serious, dignified looking man, with slouched hat, high boots, and trousers tucked in, smoking a clay pipe and waiting for his horses to be shod."[68] Taussig perceived that Grant's "seemingly indolent and apathetic" manner fooled people into overlooking his true powers "hidden under the surface of this silent, phlegmatic man."[69]

Perhaps to show independence, Grant decided to craft a house with his bare hands. Julia was reluctant to leave Wish-ton-wish, which "suited me in every way," but she recognized her husband's preference for a place closer to the land he farmed.[70] At Colonel Dent's urging, Grant constructed a warm log house that required felling trees, stripping bark, shaping logs, carting cellar stones, and splitting shingles. "I worked very hard, never losing a day because of bad weather, and accomplished the object in a moderate way," Grant wrote.[71] In its final phase, the building evolved into a communal project, finished with neighborly goodwill. When the logs were ready to be installed, Grant sent out invitations for a "raising" and enthusiastic friends demonstrated the respect Grant had earned in the community. One man stood at each corner as they lifted logs into place in two days, with Grant completing the roof and interior by himself.

From the outside, the house seemed rough and crude with uneven timbers and an eccentric wood pattern emblazoned across the front. It was a handmade house, hewn by a willing amateur. This rustic dwelling, with two stories, had a hall running down the middle, flanked by stone chimneys on either side. Showing his puckish humor, or perhaps mocking the fancy names of White Haven and Wish-ton-wish, Grant anointed his log cabin Hardscrabble, a name reflecting his troubles. Whatever pride he took in this residence, it violated Julia's sense of gentility. "It was so crude and so homely that I did not like it at all, but I did not say so," said Julia. "I got out all my pretty covers, baskets, books, etc., and tried to make it look home-like and comfortable, but this was hard to do."[72] When she nearly yielded to depression, Julia decided instead to will herself to be happy.

Even during this trying period, Grant displayed a steady temper. Once his arduous days in the field ended, he retreated with gratitude to Hardscrabble. After long years confined on army posts, he prized his domesticity and his simple home became a haven, where he was completely relaxed and happy. When Grant later became famous and reporters portrayed this as a difficult time, Julia scoffed at such negative talk, sprinkling stardust over the period. "We always had enough for us and our little children," she insisted. "We were always happy even when circumstances around us weren't going as planned."[73] She had little patience with those who recollected her husband as "dejected, low-spirited, badly dressed, and even slovenly . . . they did not know *my* Captain Grant, for he was always perfection, both in manner and person, a cheerful, self-reliant gentleman."[74] Partly Julia's sanguine view arose from joy that her family had finally come together, a novelty that trumped any hardship. She often pointed out that this was the first place she and Ulysses ever called home. But there was also a make-believe side to Julia Grant, who had a penchant for romanticizing whatever suffering she and her husband had endured. Her devout creed was never to admit failure and to gaze unashamedly on the bright side of things.

Her incurable optimism proved correct when it came to the special destiny reserved for her husband. Although he never thirsted for fame, Julia, tugged by restless ambition for him, spied greatness lurking in his future. Dent slave Mary Robinson recalled Julia sitting on a rocking chair and speaking to relatives about her financial distress. "But we will not always be in this condition," she announced, disclosing that the previous night she had dreamed Ulysses was elected president. "The rest all laughed and looked upon it as a capital joke."[75] Although Julia's sisters teased her about these exalted prophecies, she never surrendered faith in her husband's worth and, beset by repeated failure, he needed that unwavering affirmation. Everyone who knew the Grants commented on the power Julia exercised over her husband.

Julia doted on Ulysses, who beamed as he soaked in her bottomless adoration. She fussed over his unkempt hair, whiskers, and clothing. "Your father is perfection," she instructed her children. "I just want to make sure others see this too."[76] For Julia, he was simply a superman, capable of wondrous feats. She remembered how he lifted a two-hundred-pound beam; how he could draw almost anything; how he made paper boats for the children; how he rode fifty miles in a day without breaking a sweat. Even as president, she maintained, he could perform twenty-five or thirty chin-ups without exertion, and he always shared her pride in his strength. The Grants delighted in holding hands and kept their love affair fresh. "He was the tenderest and sweetest of husbands," Julia declared.[77] When Ulysses teased her, she interpreted this dry mirth as shot through with deep love. She was fond of dresses with enormous bows tied in back, and Ulysses liked to slip behind her and unravel the knot. "Ulys!" she would cry in mock anger. "You must leave my bows alone!"[78] The couple seldom quarreled, but when they did, Grant withdrew in silence. When he returned, they immediately made up and embraced.

Nothing bothered Julia more than insinuations that her husband was an illiterate yahoo. To save her eyes, he read aloud to her for hours each evening, and they plowed through hundreds of books. Mary Robinson confirmed that Grant was unusually bookish. "Most of his leisure time he spent in reading. He was one of the greatest readers I ever saw."[79] Grant retained special affection for Dickens, especially *The Pickwick Papers, Dombey and Son, Little Dorrit,* and *Oliver Twist.* "He rarely laughed aloud," said his son Fred, "but his eyes would twinkle over a good bit of wit, and occasionally, when very much pleased, he would utter a gentle laugh, which held the essence of mirth."[80]

While the Grants faulted Julia as a free-spending southern woman, it was Ulysses who had trouble managing money and Julia who took charge of family finances. By now it was clear that Grant was an easy victim for spongers, even when he could scarcely spare the money. As Hannah Grant observed, "Ulysses would cheerfully give his last garment to a needy friend."[81] Whenever Julia wanted some bauble or piece of jewelry, he would buy it for her, whether they could afford it or not. The children found money safer in their mother's hands.

Ulysses and Julia Grant were loving parents, incorporating their children into social activities. Whether attending a dance, a quilting bee, or church, they showed up with at least one child propped on each saddle. Grant had two congenital weaknesses, children and horses, and was gentle with both. "I have never known a man who had such nice ways about him in that respect as my father," said Fred.[82] Grant could be jovially indulgent, glorying in the mischievous antics of his boys, whom he dubbed "little rascals" or "little dogs." He derived special pleasure from roughhousing with them, getting down on all fours to wrestle. Entering into their world, he kneaded pellets of bread and flung them at his children during meals. He playfully encouraged Nellie, born on July 4, to imagine the annual fireworks were staged in her honor. He tried to instill courage in his children, putting them on horses and urging them to swim at early ages, and he thought it important that they hold their own with neighborhood ruffians: "It teaches a boy how to take care of himself."[83] The household showed all the open affection that had been absent in Grant's own boyhood home.

With none of the disciplinarian in his nature, Grant tolerated the rowdy behavior of his sons, sometimes to the dismay of straitlaced friends. He gave his children moral instruction—"Lying is the foundation of all crimes and follies" was a favorite maxim—but never resorted to corporal punishment or raised his voice.[84] When the children got out of hand, it fell to Julia to restore order, and she could be quite definite in her views. If the children balked, Ulysses told them, "You must not quarrel with mama. She knows what is best for you, and you must always obey her."[85] The children were sensitive enough to their father's moods that a sharp look sufficed to correct unruly behavior. Grant rarely showed anger, preferring to bury his hurts. "He ignored most slights," said Buck, "even if he felt them keenly."[86]

At first glance, it seems remarkable that the drinking issue did not detract from the Grants' happy marriage, but he seldom drank with his family around. "During all the time I knew Grant, between his return from California in 1854 to the fall of Vicksburg, I never saw him intoxicated," wrote Emma Dent.[87] Whatever the grinding misery of these Missouri years, they were mostly a triumph for Grant's sobriety, which surely owed much to Julia's steadfast, loving concern. Anchored in the bosom of his family, free from loneliness, Grant was able to conquer his craving for drink.

During these years, Grant shrank from the booze-soaked society of army friends. He often ran into fellow officers from Jefferson Barracks, who discovered the new Grant practiced abstinence. Don Carlos Buell, then a captain, averred that Grant "drank nothing but water," and Major Joseph J. Reynolds agreed: "He will go into the bar with you, but he will not touch anything."[88] When one old West Point classmate invited Grant to the Planter's House hotel bar, Grant avowed his new sobriety: "I will go and look at you; but I never drink anything myself."[89] The one dissenting voice from this portrait of Grant's abstinence was Jesse A. Jones, who years later recounted that his relative, Edward

Gray, a civil engineer, often said he "had carried Grant home on his back drunk from St. Louis, Mo. to Grant's home on his farm."[90] Such reports of Grant imbibing in St. Louis are conspicuous by their absence, however, and he appeased his always powerful oral cravings by smoking pipes and cigars. "In those days I often heard doctors tell him his incessant smoking would kill him," said Mary Robinson. "At that time he chewed tobacco excessively also."[91]

Though sober, Grant projected a defeated air on the St. Louis streets, a man with the life beaten out of him. His injured pride cast a deep gloom over him. The depression visible in his expressionless face, seamy clothes, and absence of mirth were discernible to those around him. His need to sell firewood on the streets, huddled in a faded blue army coat, broadcast his decline to the world. "Great God, Grant, what are you doing?" exclaimed an officer who had last seen him in Mexico. "I am solving the problem of poverty," Grant explained.[92] His reliance on Colonel Dent's charity must have grated. When one officer encountered Grant striding outside the Planter's House, he inquired what he was now doing, and Grant retorted that he was "farming on a piece of land belonging to Mrs. Grant, some ten miles out in the country."[93]

Grant was dignified in his downcast state, exhibiting a rigid sense of honor and virtue. James Longstreet was playing cards at the Planter's House when Grant walked in, and he was shocked to see how far down the social ladder his old friend had tumbled. Grant was "poorly dressed . . . and really in needy circumstances."[94] The next day, Grant accosted him and pressed a five-dollar gold piece into his palm to repay a debt now fifteen years old. "You must take it," Grant said, even after Longstreet refused. "I cannot live with anything in my possession that is not mine."[95] To allow Grant to save face, Longstreet reluctantly accepted the money. The two men would next meet at Appomattox Court House, when Longstreet was Robert E. Lee's chief commander.

A sad letter in Grant's papers suggests that even his father kept a wary distance from him. Right after Christmas 1856, Grant was shocked to see inscribed in the register of the Planter's House "J. R. Grant, Ky." He checked with the hotel clerk that it was indeed his father's signature. "I made sure it was you and that I should find you when I got home," Grant wrote to his father. "Was it you?"[96] We don't know what Jesse Grant replied or why he might have been dodging his eldest son in this manner.

On January 14, 1857, Julia's mother, Ellen Wrenshall Dent, died and a lonesome Colonel Dent asked his daughter and son-in-law to move back into the main house with him. This delighted Julia, who had detested the cramped simplicity of Hardscrabble, but it must have mortified her husband, who had just told his father he hoped to support himself on his farm income before too long and begged him for a $500 loan at a steep 10 percent interest rate. "Ulysses," Jesse supposedly said, "when you are ready to come North I will give you a start, but so long as you make your home among a tribe of slaveholders I will do nothing."[97] Luckily for Grant, within a year Colonel Dent rented White Haven to him and moved into St. Louis, leaving his son-in-law with 200 acres of plowed farmland and 250 woodland acres.

One Sunday afternoon, shortly before Ellen Dent's demise, Colonel Dent and Captain Grant sat smoking on the porch, differing over the hotly debated question of admitting new slave states to the Union. Proslavery sentiment was widespread in St. Louis, with auctions still conducted on the courthouse steps and slave plantations dotting the countryside. Ellen Dent was impressed by how thoughtfully her son-in-law dissected the situation. Afterward, she told her daughters, "Remember what I say. That little man will fill the highest place in this government. His light is now hid under a bushel, but circumstances will occur, and at no distant day, when his worth and wisdom will be shown and appreciated."[98]

In time, Grant emerged as a staunch critic of slavery. As he stated in his *Memoirs,* "Southern slave-owners believed that . . . the ownership of slaves conferred a sort of patent of nobility . . . They convinced themselves, first, of the divine origin of the institution and, next, that that particular institution was not safe in the hands of any body of legislators but themselves."[99] At this period, however, Grant, like many northern whites, felt more ambivalent, opposing slavery in theory yet also fearing that outright abolitionism might lead to bloody sectional conflict. Julia still clung to a paternalistic attitude toward slavery, associating it fondly with her girlhood and the southern traditions represented by her father.

In November 1856, Grant cast his first vote in a presidential election. After selling a load of firewood, he was galloping by a St. Louis polling station when he decided to stop, lash his horse to a tree, and vote. The Whig Party had collapsed after the brouhaha over the Kansas-Nebraska Act, leading to the rise of the antislavery Republicans, who nominated John C. Frémont as their first presidential candidate, while the nativist American Party—the Know-Nothings—opted for ex-president Millard Fillmore. To his later embarrassment, Grant voted for Democrat James Buchanan of Pennsylvania, a seasoned diplomat and former secretary of state, who hoped to avert civil war by appeasing the South. Grant knew little about Buchanan, but a good deal about Frémont, the famous "Pathfinder" who had explored the Far West and whom Grant deplored as a shameless self-promoter. "The reason I voted for Buchanan was that I knew Frémont. That was the only vote I ever cast. If I had ever had any political sympathies they would have been with the Whigs. I was raised in that school."[100] In future years, Grant liked to joke that his "first attempt in politics had been a great failure."[101] Even though Abraham Lincoln delivered more than a hundred speeches for the Republican ticket, Buchanan carried Illinois and the election.

It seems unlikely that Grant, having grown up in a household saturated with abolitionist politics, was as ignorant about Buchanan's views as he claimed. As everybody observed, he was an assiduous newspaper reader. "While Grant lived quietly on his farm from 1854 to 1858," noted a friend, "no man was better informed than he on every phase of the controversy."[102] In his *Memoirs,* Grant dropped any pretense that he had solely voted *against* Frémont and not *for* Buchanan: "It was evident to my mind that the election of a Republican President in 1856 meant the secession of all the Slave States, and rebellion."[103]

Southern fervor, already tinged with violence, threatened the tenuous balance between North and South. In May 1856, Congressman Preston Brooks of South Carolina thrashed and nearly killed Senator Charles Sumner of Massachusetts after the latter made a scalding antislavery speech, "The Crime Against Kansas." Many incendiary political events unfolded not far from where Grant lived. A few days after the Sumner beating, in "Bleeding Kansas," John Brown and his sons brutally executed five men who endorsed slavery. Abolitionist settlers there, known as Free-Soilers, had to fend off incursions from proslavery forces from Missouri, who employed bullets and fraudulent ballots to secure their goals. In the end, two separate legislatures vied for power in the state.

Then, in March 1857, Chief Justice Roger B. Taney handed down the infamous Dred Scott decision. Scott was a Missouri slave taken to the free state of Illinois and the free Wisconsin Territory who then sued for freedom on this basis after his master died. The court denied Scott's right to sue on the grounds that he was a Negro, an inferior being, and therefore not a citizen. To worsen matters, Taney said Congress lacked power to ban slavery from the territories, annulling the Missouri Compromise. Taney's verdict made the whole country complicit in the horror of slavery. Bemoaning the decision, the New York editor William Cullen Bryant wrote, "Wherever our flag floats, it is the flag of slavery," a comment that typified northern outrage.[104] Although we have no contemporary observations by Grant on the case, he enjoyed a direct connection to it. After the decision, Dred Scott and his wife were purchased by Taylor Blow, who supported Scott's lawsuit and then freed the couple. Blow, a close friend of Grant's, would recommend him for a county job two years later.

Through marriage into the Dent family, Grant was thrust into a vexing situation vis-à-vis the passionate slavery controversy. Colonel Dent had given Julia the use of four slaves—Dan, Julia, John, and Eliza—all teenagers. "They were born at the old farm and were excellent," wrote Julia, "though so young."[105] Colonel Dent never transferred to Julia legal title to these slaves for the simple reason that, under Missouri law, his hated son-in-law would become their owner. Having grown up in an ardent abolitionist household, Grant made it known, according to Mary Robinson, that "he wanted to give his wife's slaves their freedom as soon as possible."[106] Emma Dent, who thought Grant still conflicted about slavery, commented tartly, "I do not think that Grant was such a rank abolitionist that Julia's slaves had to be forced upon him."[107] At the same time, she conceded Grant's opposition "to human slavery as an institution."[108] Most people sensed that Grant opposed slavery and, when a neighbor doubted the loyalty of a Dent slave, Grant shot back: "I don't know why a black skin may not cover a true heart as well as a white one."[109] Henry Clay Wright, who milled Grant's grain, detected his dissatisfaction with slavery: "We were all slaveholding farmers in that day, and Grant's wife had a couple of slaves, and yet we felt that he was not exactly one of us."[110] Legend claims that Grant halted the whipping of a slave by a local farmer.

Since Julia's four slaves were young, they remained house servants. For field work, Grant hired two black men and employed a Dent slave named William Jones to help raise corn, potatoes, oats, wheat, and clover. He exhibited no false pride in working alongside these men, something that would have been beneath the dignity of his purse-proud father-in-law. It was not in Grant's nature to coerce people and his just treatment of black men said much about his egalitarian feelings. As Julia's cousin recalled, "He was no hand to manage negroes. He couldn't force them to do anything. Mrs. Grant would say aren't you going to whip Jule for doing that? And he would only smile and say, 'No I guess not.'"[111] One slave, Uncle Jason, confirmed that Grant "was the kindest man he ever worked for."[112] Grant hired free black workers and paid them a decent wage, which bothered slave-owning neighbors.

Every time Ulysses S. Grant appeared to touch rock bottom, his fortunes sank even further. Despite his initial lack of knowledge about farming, he had gamely tried to succeed until his hands grew coarse, he visibly aged, and he developed a permanent stoop. "The work was done . . . principally with his own hands, notwithstanding the fact that many of his neighbors owned slaves and considered manual labor beneath a gentleman," observed an acquaintance.[113] As early as February 1857, Grant warned his father that it was pointless to persist in farming without a fresh cash infusion. To survive, he continued to hawk firewood on the St. Louis streets and the time thus spent destroyed any chance of prospering as a farmer: "I regard every load of wood taken, when the services of both myself and team are required on the farm, is a direct loss of more than the value of the load."[114]

By that summer he bewailed that his wheat crop yielded only seventy-five bushels instead of the four or five hundred he had projected, although he still bravely held out hope for his potato, sweet potato, melon, and cabbage crops. Then the 1857 economic depression provoked widespread bank failures, massive unemployment, and precipitous declines in commodity prices, dashing any chance of an economic rebound for Grant. As his life steadily unraveled, he pawned his gold watch and chain for $20 on December 23, 1857, to purchase Christmas presents for his children—perhaps the symbolic nadir of his life. Then, on February 6, he and Julia had a fourth mouth to feed with the birth of a third son, named Jesse after his grandfather. That Grant named a son after his fallible father shows how he still loomed very large in his life.

Perhaps in response to stress, Grant developed crippling headaches as frequently as once a month. "Oh, do not ask me to speak," he would moan to Julia. "I have a dreadful headache."[115] Julia would seat him in an armchair, dim the lights, then bathe his feet in mustard solution. Ever since childhood Grant had been afflicted with "fever and ague," whose signs were severe chills and sweats. In 1858 this malady recurred along with malaria, likely contracted while crossing Panama or Nicaragua and with similar symptoms. In Galena, his brother Simpson was slowly wasting away from tuberculosis, and Grant must have feared he was drifting in that direction. His various illnesses hung on for months, even as a cold spring played havoc with his crops, and he curtailed drastically the time devoted to farming. Julia and the slaves also fell sick until White Haven resembled a small hospital ward. Most upsetting was that Fred came down with typhoid fever and Grant worried he might not survive. Although Fred pulled through, the time had come for him and Buck to get proper schooling, which would further hamper the straitened family finances. Until this point, Grant had schooled the two older boys at home, teaching them arithmetic, reading, and spelling.

With his son cast into this abject state, Jesse Grant showed up and made a vigorous pitch for him to move his family to Covington, Kentucky, and join his business. Where he once boasted of his son's prowess, he now openly disparaged him. When an old Georgetown neighbor ran into him, Jesse said "he would have to take U. S. and his family home and make him over again, as he had no business qualifications whatever—had failed in everything—all his other boys were good business men."[116] With extreme reluctance, Ulysses agreed to wind up the farm and relocate to Kentucky, a plan scotched when his sisters protested. Julia had "bitterly opposed" the plan and celebrated its demise. "I was joyous at the thought of not going to Kentucky, for the Captain's family, with the exception of his mother, did not like me . . . They considered me unpardonably extravagant, and I considered them inexcusably the other way and may, unintentionally, have shown my feelings."[117] According to Julia Boggs, even Hannah Grant had quietly soured on her daughter-in-law. "Old Mrs. Grant was a woman who did her own house work, and she couldn't think well of a daughter-in-law who employed slaves, though she said very little about it."[118]

Notwithstanding his medical and monetary travails, Grant watched with mounting dread the political turmoil convulsing the country. From August 21 through October 15, Abraham Lincoln and Stephen A. Douglas, rivals for the U.S. Senate in Illinois, squared off in a series of debates that focused on slavery and Grant followed the newspaper coverage. Like Grant, Lincoln was plain in dress and traveled from one debate to the next on ordinary passenger trains. Grant admitted he was "by no means a 'Lincoln man' in that contest; but I recognized then his great ability."[119] He thought it "a nice question to say who got the best of the argument" in the debates.[120] Even though Lincoln lost the election, the debates elevated him to a figure of national stature, while Republicans scored stunning triumphs in New York, Pennsylvania, and Indiana that fall.

After four frustrating years, by autumn 1858 Grant's farming ambitions had foundered forever and he auctioned off his stock, crops, and farming equipment. This capped a four-year period of failure so excruciating that Grant skipped over it altogether in his *Memoirs*. He now paced the St. Louis streets, searching for work, obscure and invisible to the many people he passed, a bleak, defeated little man with a mysterious aura of solitude. "He walked about like any citizen," said one woman, "but people made way for him, and he walked through the crowd as though solitary."[121] Grant could never escape the shadow of his father and father-in-law and it was now Colonel Dent who turned to his relative Harry Boggs for help. In early 1859 Boggs agreed to join Grant in a real estate partnership titled Boggs and Grant in which Grant would serve as a glorified clerk. Grant still knew many army officers at Jefferson Barracks and Colonel Dent thought that despite his son-in-law's abysmal ignorance of real estate, he might woo them as clients. While eager for her husband to find work, Julia suspected he lacked professional aggression and would overly sympathize with debtors. "I cannot imagine how my dear husband ever thought of going into such a business, as he never could collect a penny that was owed to him."[122]

Boggs and Grant operated from the Pine Street law offices of McClellan, Hillyer & Moody, its stated mission to buy and sell real estate, collect rents, and negotiate loans. At the outset Grant was hopeful about the firm, but when a dozen similar real estate partnerships sprang up downtown, the glut doomed its prospects. Julia was prescient that her husband was not cut out for collecting rent. If he dunned an old army comrade, he ended up lighting a cigar and whiling away the afternoon with reminiscences. Grant also lacked administrative skills and kept untidy records. "Mr. Boggs went east on business, leaving the Captain in charge, and when he returned he found everything upside down," recalled Louisa Boggs. "The books were in confusion, the wrong people had been let into houses and the owners were much concerned."[123] Still debilitated by fever and ague, Grant sometimes had to be helped to the streetcar by one of the McClellan, Hillyer & Moody lawyers.

Grant was so broke he could not afford to stay in a hotel or boardinghouse, much less bring his wife and four children to St. Louis. Harry and Louisa Boggs offered him a bare room in their house on South Fifteenth Street, where he turned into a melancholy presence. His austere room had only a bed, a bowl, and a pitcher set on an adjoining chair; since this wretched back room was unheated, he sat with his hosts in the evening, warming himself by their living room fire. "He would smile at times, but I never heard him laugh aloud," said Louisa Boggs. "He was a sad man . . . he seemed almost in despair."[124] Grant seemed to be staring into an abyss. "I don't think he saw a light ahead—not a particle. I don't think he had any ambition further than to educate and take care of his family."[125] Every Saturday Grant trudged twelve miles to White Haven, spent an evening with his family, then retraced his steps on Sunday. The Boggses, well aware of Grant's drinking history, stayed vigilant about the problem. "It was his one weakness," said Louisa Boggs. "His worst temptation was in meeting some old army friend."[126] Luckily, Harry Boggs was a strict temperance man and Grant never drank around him.

As secession gathered strength, Grant discovered a deep-seated patriotism that he may not have known existed before. St. Louis had many residents with southern sympathies and it was dangerous to declare pro-Union sentiments too openly. It seemed as if the "irrepressible conflict," of which Senator William Seward warned, would soon arrive.[127] Profane and blustering, Harry Boggs liked to rant about "black Republicans" and Grant must have found this talk insufferable. "He was Northern," said Louisa Boggs, "while Mr. Boggs and I were both Southern in sentiment."[128] As he monitored current affairs, Grant was upset by what he read in the press and enjoyed talking with William S. Hillyer, a young Republican lawyer from Kentucky with whom he shared office space. His friend John W. Emerson remembered Grant at the office "sitting alone at his desk with his hand holding a newspaper hanging listlessly by his side, with every evidence of deep thought, suggesting sadness."[129] Grant underwent a slow-dawning political awakening: "When I was in St. Louis the year before Lincoln's election, it made my blood run cold to hear friends of mine, Southern men—as many of my friends were—deliberately discuss the dissolution of the Union as though it were a tariff bill. I could not endure it."[130] Grant's views, simple but clear, were fiercely held.

Grant never said anything to indicate that he saw war coming or might play a prominent part. On the other hand, the attorneys he worked with discerned the evident zest with which he analyzed battles then raging in Italy. He would study newspaper maps and exclaim, "This movement was a mistake. If I commanded the army, I would do thus and so."[131] The attorneys listened with suppressed smirks, as if Grant's words betrayed a pathetic streak of self-delusion in this thwarted man.

By early March, Grant brought his family to a house on Seventh and Lynch Streets that proved too expensive. He then swapped Hardscrabble for a snug, plain two-story house at Ninth and Barton Streets on the edge of town. Since Hardscrabble was worth more than the St. Louis town house, Grant received a $3,000 note but was swindled yet again and had to initiate a lawsuit that dragged on for years. His new house was quite modest, with a porch on one side and a low upper story, but he was at least reunited with his family.[132] Fred and Buck began to attend school regularly and family life, if threadbare, regained some

semblance of normality. Grant delighted in the idiosyncracies of his four children, treating the sturdy Fred like a young man; exercising care with the smart
but delicate Buck; being tender with his beloved Nellie; and rejoicing in the
antics of mischievous Jesse.

By this point, the Grants could no longer mask the depressed state of their
finances. One day, a business friend of Grant's suggested to his wife that she
drop by and pay a courtesy call on Julia. The woman did so and returned to her
husband in high dudgeon. "Why did you send me there? The house is shabbily
furnished, and they must be very poor."[133] For Julia, who grew up in pampered
comfort, the fall in status contradicted her favored self-image. On one occasion,
a lady friend asked Julia to accompany her on a shopping trip downtown. "I can't
do it," Julia protested. "I have no shoes fit to wear on the street."[134]

Through it all, Julia maintained her custom of keeping slaves and had two
slaves help with the children. In March 1859, she was scheduled to take the family to visit Jesse and Hannah Grant in Kentucky and wanted to take along one
slave to care for the children. Upon reflection, she worried what would happen
as she passed through Illinois, Indiana, and Ohio. While the Dred Scott decision had endorsed a master's right to take slaves into free states, Julia was afraid
that in passing through free states "she might have some trouble," Grant explained to his father in citing the reason for Julia canceling her trip.[135]

That Grant was progressively more troubled by the immorality of slavery
became patently clear that spring. He had acquired from Colonel Dent the mulatto slave named William Jones who had worked on Dent's farm and was now
thirty-five years old. It was the only time Grant ever owned a slave and Jones
may have come as a gift. Then, on March 29, 1859, Grant appeared at circuit
court in St. Louis to file papers that declared "I do hereby manumit, emancipate
& set free said William from slavery forever."[136] Still struggling financially,
Grant could have earned a considerable sum had he chosen to sell Jones rather
than liberate him. Instead he made good on his pledge to set free Dent slaves
when it came within his power. In the inflamed political atmosphere in St. Louis,
this bold step planted Grant firmly on the side of those critical of the South's
"peculiar institution."

By summer 1859 the partnership of Boggs and Grant teetered in a rocky
condition. Grant did not have the stomach for collecting rents and hated how
Boggs violated the privacy of clients and retailed gossip behind their backs.
Worse still, the flagging business could scarcely support one partner but

definitely not two. Louisa Boggs, a schoolteacher, pressed her husband to wind up the business and go into something more lucrative, and the Boggs and Grant partnership was formally dissolved.

Once again the job outlook for Grant appeared ominous, and he applied for a position as county engineer: he would superintend local roads and receive a $1,500 annual salary. He submitted to the five-member Board of County Commissioners an impressive array of thirty-five supporting letters, including one from Taylor Blow, who had backed Dred Scott. Joseph J. Reynolds, who knew Grant at West Point, wrote that he had "always maintained a high standing, and graduated with great credit, especially in mathematics and engineering."[137] Throughout his life, Grant shrank from applying pressure to obtain positions and now conducted himself in gentlemanly fashion, refusing to lobby the commissioners. Both he and Julia were still superstitious, so he consulted a French fortune-teller, who forecast his defeat. "I will come within an ace of being elected, but I will be beaten," he reported to Julia. "In a short time we will leave the city and I will engage for a time in a mercantile business. Something will happen very soon and then I will begin to rise in the world."[138]

The selection process for county engineer turned out to be highly politicized, and Grant fell on the wrong side of the political divide. Three of the five commissioners were Free-Soil Republicans, the remaining two Democrats, and Grant was voted down because of his association with Colonel Dent. As a Republican member, Dr. William Taussig, admitted: "The Dents, at least the old gentleman, were known to be pro-slavery Democrats and . . . outspoken rebels. Grant lived with them, and though nothing was known of his political views, the shadow of their disloyalty necessarily fell on him."[139] With a potential war looming, the commissioners stressed Union loyalty and Grant understood the bias against him. "You may judge from the result of the action of the County Commissioners that I am strongly identified with the Democratic party!" he wrote to his father. Aside from voting for Buchanan, he had adhered mostly to Whig tradition and had approached candidates pragmatically. The sensitive Grant reeled from his defeat for county engineer and later referred to the "agony" this caused him.[140] Julia long remembered with "some bitterness" her husband's defeat "by that most unjust majority."[141]

Grant knew the winner was a German immigrant at a time when St. Louis had a large German population. "My opponent had the advantage of birth over me (he was a citizen by adoption) and carried off the prize," Grant wrote.[142] In breaking the news to Julia, he grumbled, "The *Germans* are loyal to each other."[143] To another local resident, he protested that "no American can get anything in this town" and complained that almost all county jobs were held by immigrants.[144] In this woeful mood, Grant flirted briefly with the Know-Nothing Party, which inveighed against immigration and the Catholic Church. As foreign laborers flocked to build railroads, native-born Protestant workers resisted their competition and banded together in the mysterious Order of the Star-Spangled Banner. To safeguard their secrecy, they were instructed to reply to outside questions: "I know nothing."[145] Grant's attraction to this movement was short-lived: "There was a lodge near my new home, and I was invited to join it. I accepted the invitation; was initiated; attended a meeting just one week later, and never went to another afterwards."[146] In time, Grant renounced such secret societies and any groups that opposed freedom of worship. He also came to view his loss of the county engineer job as a blessing, for had he gotten it, he would have been ensconced in a comfortable position at the outbreak of the Civil War and might never have joined the military.

While Grant recuperated from his disappointment, John Brown and a group of abolitionist zealots raided the federal armory at Harpers Ferry, Virginia, hoping to seize weapons and foment a slave rebellion in the South. After barricading themselves inside the fire engine house, they were surrounded and seized by a marine contingent led by Robert E. Lee. The unrepentant Brown, charged with murder and treason, was marched off to the gallows, but he left behind an apocalyptic prophecy that "the crimes of this guilty land" would "never be purged away" except with blood.[147] For the South, Brown's raid gave flesh to their worst nightmares and deepened the widening gulf with the North, where many embraced him as a martyr. Grant had grown up hearing stories about Brown from Jesse Grant. Nevertheless, he denounced categorically the abortive raid on Harpers Ferry: "It was certainly the act of an insane man to attempt the invasion of the South, and the overthrow of slavery, with less than twenty men."[148]

As a consolation prize for losing the county engineer position, Grant got a job as a clerk in the custom house, but when the collector died within a month and was replaced by a new person, he prowled the streets again, searching for work. Those who now encountered him never forgot his hopeless, downcast air. "He greeted me kindly but seemed to be in a very distressed and disconsolate condition," said George W. Fishback. "I had never before seen him so much depressed. He was shabbily dressed, his beard unshaven, his face anxious and the whole exterior of the man denoting a profound discouragement at the result of his experiment to maintain himself in St. Louis."[149] Grant flailed about for a job and devised a quixotic plan to launch a hardware business in Colorado—a far-fetched idea that Jesse Grant refused to finance.

As the impecunious Grant soldiered on, it became clear that only his father could provide an escape route from his misery. When Julia suggested that he go to see Jesse, he adamantly resisted. Julia then reminded him that his father "had always been not only willing but anxious to serve him (in his own way, to be sure) . . . After a little hesitation at leaving me with the children and servants, he decided to start the next day."[150] Grant must have known his father would try to lure him back north, a position now more appealing than it had been two years earlier. As Fishback surmised, Grant "no doubt foresaw the threatened Civil War and felt that as an old defender of the Flag he had better take his chances among his people in the Northern States."[151]

Within a week, Julia claimed, her husband began sending her from Kentucky "long and cheerful letters,"[152] but the documentary record suggests a far more pessimistic picture. As soon as he reached Covington, Ulysses wrote her that he had arrived "with a headache and feeling bad generally . . . My head is nearly bursting with pain."[153] Simpson Grant, then staying with Jesse and Hannah, was waging a losing struggle against tuberculosis, which forced him to keep going south in search of a cure. Although growing deaf in one ear and suffering from failing eyesight, Jesse Grant remained robust at sixty-six, serving as Covington's postmaster.

Having prospered as a merchant, Jesse was now worth $100,000—equivalent to nearly $3 million today—and employed about fifty people. When he reached sixty in 1854, he had begun to withdraw from active management of his business interests. His holdings included several tanneries near Portsmouth, Ohio, and leather goods stores in Wisconsin, Iowa, and Galena, Illinois. Ulysses came to Covington at a fortuitous juncture. The ailing Simpson had managed the Galena store and was more capable than his younger brother, Orvil, who assisted him. Simpson's health and the prospect that the erratic young Orvil would end up running the Galena business must have alarmed Jesse Grant. When it came to a job for Ulysses, he deferred to Simpson, who agreed to send his older brother "to the Galena store to stay until something else might turn up in his favor, and told him he must confine his wants within $800 a year," Jesse recalled.[154]

As it turned out, Ulysses left behind such a long trail of debts in St. Louis that he would draw out $1,500 the first year, money he returned to the store after he went into the Union army. Always honorable about debts, Grant reassured creditors he would eventually repay every dollar. To be forced to serve as a clerk in his father's store at age thirty-eight, in a decidedly junior position to his two younger brothers, was a demeaning situation that Grant could only have regarded with rueful laughter. He had spent futile years trying to become a successful breadwinner, free of the twin tyrants who had lorded over him, his father and Colonel Dent. Now he had to shed his pride and capitulate to his father's will. As he told a friend in St. Louis, "because he loved his family so much," he had decided that "we'll all go to Galena and starve to death together."[155] So gathering up his family and modest belongings, he set off for Illinois bearing a heavy load of blighted hopes.

PART TWO

A Life of War

CHAPTER SIX

The Store Clerk

I N APRIL 1860, Ulysses S. Grant, cloaked in his old blue army cape, arrived in Galena aboard the Mississippi steamer *Itasca*. Clasping in each hand chairs that had served the family as deck seats, Grant, along with Julia and the four children, stepped ashore into what they hoped would be a new, more secure life. As Julia recalled, "The atmosphere was so cool and dry, the sun shone so brightly, that it gave us the impression of a smiling welcome."[1] However inviting the atmosphere, nothing could distract from the unpleasant truth that Grant had been a failure, battered by life at every turn. Everything indicated he would someday die a forgotten and thoroughly forgettable American, leaving no trace in historical annals.

Hidden away in the northwest corner of Illinois, across the Mississippi from Iowa, Galena was an affluent town filled with lead miners, lumberjacks, and riverboat roustabouts. A profitable hub for regional commerce, it had boomed along with nearby lead mines, but its prosperity had started to fade a few years earlier when the Illinois Central Railroad chose Dubuque as its western terminus. "It used to be a great business center," Elizabeth Cady Stanton wrote elegiacally some years later, "but since the railroad and Dubuque put their heads together to plot against its welfare, its glory has departed."[2]

After spending a few days with Simpson and Orvil, the newcomers established their residence in a snug brick house on a high bluff that afforded excellent vistas of the Galena River and the business district below. Set on the aptly named High Street, the modest house had shuttered windows and a pitched

roof. Grant imagined that Galena, with its good schools and churches, might be a
fine place to raise children and would provide him with some long elusive financial
stability.³ Julia seemed jittery away from Missouri, so Grant assisted her in decorating the house, trying to set her homesick mind at ease. When she broke open
a box and found a cracked antique mirror from White Haven, an heirloom associated with her father, she sobbed uncontrollably. "The Captain, in place of
being impatient with me, tried to soothe me, saying, 'It is broken, and tears will
not mend it now,'" she remembered appreciatively.⁴

Every day Grant descended to the downtown business center via a long, steep
wooden staircase, negotiating hundreds of steps that bottomed out right by the
leather goods store. He moved with his typical no-nonsense stride, eyes straight
ahead, purposeful but aloof. "At this period Grant was a square shouldered spare
built man with a very perceptible stoop caused as he said by the Mexican campaign followed by hard work on the St. Louis farm," said a new colleague.⁵ His
confidence, if damaged, had not been snuffed out and he retained an underlying
self-esteem despite the vagaries of recent years. Fred Grant described his father's
mental state in 1860: "He was a sensitive and retiring man, but behind his modesty was a fair estimate of his own worth. He tolerated no disrespect and was
most determined."⁶

At a bend in the meandering Main Street, Jesse's leather goods store was a
handsome establishment, housed in a prime four-story brick building and dealing in everything from fancy saddles to boot leather. As befit employment in a
family firm, Ulysses performed multiple functions, serving customers, buying
and selling hides, handling paperwork, and collecting bills. Melancthon T.
Burke, a relative who worked with him, said Grant's brawn served him well in
heaving hides that sometimes weighed more than 250 pounds. He would hop up
on the carts of farmers who came to town and bid on their cargo of carcasses,
which were then shipped to one of Jesse's tanneries. "Grant was of great physical
strength and I have seen him many times lift a hide that no ordinary man could
manage," Burke said. "After tossing and weighing the hides, he would calmly
walk over and wash his hands. Then he would resume his common position of
reclining in a chair, feet on the counter."⁷ Orvil's wife recalled Grant hefting
hides effortlessly on his shoulder, then hurling them down a chute to a basement
storage area. He tossed them "with a fling of his arm, whereas Orvil could not,
nor could Simpson when he was in the business."⁸

Grant displayed small business aptitude and sometimes acted as if the work were so much meaningless drudgery. "He was restless I think," Julia speculated. "It wasn't congenial to do the work required of him."[9] Periodically he climbed into a buggy and traveled around collecting debts, but confessed to having "no 'faculty for dunning people.'"[10] In the store, where he sat puffing on his customary clay pipe, Grant struck some folks as haphazard or apathetic. John E. Smith, who owned a nearby jewelry shop, observed that Grant refused to function as an ordinary sales clerk, asking customers to wait until the "real" clerk returned. If the customer was in a hurry, Grant "would go behind the counter very reluctantly, and drag down whatever was wanted; but [he] hardly ever knew the price of it, and, in nine cases out of ten, he charged either too much or too little."[11] With his guileless nature, he was easily hoodwinked by customers who suggested lower prices. Jesse Grant credited his son for working with gusto, although he also thought he did not bother to ingratiate himself with customers. When Ulysses later grew famous, townspeople stood on the sidewalk and peered into the leather shop window, trying to figure out exactly which Grant had turned into the victorious general.

Perhaps too insistently, Grant professed contentment with his job, denying he felt degraded. "In my new employment I have become pretty conversant, and am much pleased with it," he wrote. "I hope to be a partner soon, and am sanguine that a competency at least can be made out of the business."[12] For the rest of his life, he expressed pride in his Galena accomplishments. Through advances from the firm and gifts from Colonel Dent, Grant slowly regained solvency, paying off residual debts in St. Louis. His niggardly salary of $600 per annum, soon boosted by Jesse to $800, barely supported his family. If he never declined into shabby desperation, he had to practice extreme frugality. One town resident recalled a Sunday morning when he encountered Grant bundled in his old military coat. "People wonder why I wear the coat, fact is I had this coat; it's a good coat, and I thought I'd better wear it out," Grant said.[13]

His brother Simpson had managed the store and built up the business until consumption forced him to retire, making Grant's advent timely. "We all looked up to him as an older man and a soldier," said Burke. "He knew much more than we in matters of the world, and we recognized it."[14] By all accounts, Simpson was cut from the same cloth as Ulysses. Thin, quiet, and handsome, he was a gentleman of sterling integrity and sound business sense. He went to live with Ulysses and Julia on the bluff, and on sunny days, people saw him sitting outside, trying to regain his health. Tuberculosis was then an untreatable disease, a gradual, remorseless killer.

Because of Simpson's illness, Orvil, thirteen years younger than Ulysses, ran the Galena store. With his broad, square face, he bore a conspicuous resemblance to his eldest brother. Orvil's wife, Mary, said Ulysses "was a bit shorter than Orvil, more muscular, a sturdily built man. They had the same sandy blonde beard, the Captain's hair was blonder and tawny, Orvil's hair was reddish."[15] In due time, Orvil would prove a corrupt and irresponsible rascal and already showed signs of a wayward disposition. His reputation was of "an uncongenial soul, quite Grant's opposite, more like old Jesse, an uninhibited sharper, and rather arrogant and conceited as well, disliked by Galenians heartily," said one townsman.[16] To work under Orvil must have mortified his scrupulous eldest brother. Since the lowly job lay far beneath Grant's talents, many Galena friends suspected he was simply marking time and awaiting a better opportunity.

In future years, Orvil's wife, a sharp-tongued, envious woman, took wicked pleasure in entertaining newspapermen with scurrilous gossip about Ulysses and Julia Grant. She snickered at Ulysses as a henpecked husband, helplessly under his wife's thumb. "She decided for him what he would wear. Even in later years if he wanted to wear a blue coat, she would say he looked better in a black coat and with no word of protest, the black coat would be donned."[17] Like other Grants, she deplored Julia's boasting and superstition and cringed at her public displays of affection with her husband, complaining that "no two people of that age ever deported themselves quite like that pair."[18] She accused Julia of showing a ghastly temper with servants, while Grant behaved more graciously, tipping generously. Because Orvil and Jesse Grant disapproved of Julia, Ulysses's wrath flared whenever they carped about her.

Orvil's wife saved her most poisonous barbs for Grant's indulgence toward his children, especially the rapscallion Jesse. "He and the Captain would spend time rolling around on the floorboards, kicking, wrestling and paying no mind to the dust or trouble they stirred up."[19] Other friends admired the Grants' tolerant attitude toward their offspring, who darted in and out of the kitchen with abandon, their home a favorite haunt of neighborhood children. As an adult, Jesse looked back fondly on his daily tussles with his father. When Grant mounted the long wooden stairs at day's end, Jesse confronted him in mock defiance: "Mister, do you want to fight?" Grant countered: "I am a man of peace; but I will not be hectored by a person of your size."[20] In their subsequent wrestling match, he would allow Jesse to emerge triumphant. Despite his permissive nature, Grant wanted respectability for his children, and Fred complained he couldn't go barefoot like other boys and had to wear a waistcoat buttoned down to his trousers.

In general, Grant lived a quiet, unobtrusive life, attending the Methodist church, smoking his clay pipe, and reading aloud to Julia every evening as she sewed. Although he and Julia were well respected in Galena, they didn't venture out much and stuck to a small circle of friends. Their constricted social life safeguarded Grant from the temptation of drink in a town with forty saloons. Most people who knew Grant agreed he did not touch a drop of liquor during his time in Galena. Burke said he even abstained from hard cider, but he also knew alcoholism was endemic in the Grant clan. "The family couldn't drink. They all were so constituted that to drink was fatal."[21] The only time Grant ever strayed was when he was away from Julia and collecting overdue bills in his buggy in Iowa and Wisconsin, where he "usually followed the evening meal with a drink of whiskey," according to one source.[22]

The one significant tale of Grant drinking in Galena came from a full-blooded Seneca Iroquois sachem, Ely S. Parker, who grew up on an Indian reservation in upstate New York and was a chief of the Six Nations. Trained as a civil engineer, he was a man of giant girth with jet-black hair, penetrating eyes, and exceptional strength who styled himself a "savage Jack Falstaff of 200 [pound] weight."[23] After working on the Erie Canal and Great Lakes lighthouses, he was assigned by the Treasury Department to build a new limestone building in Galena for the post office and custom house. Parker frequented the Grant leather goods store and something about the "diffident and reticent" Grant seized his attention. "Selling goods from behind a counter did not seem to be his forte, for if he was near the front door when a customer entered, he did not hesitate to make a pretty rapid retreat to the counting-room."[24] Over time, Grant lost his shyness with Parker, showing a "warm and sympathetic nature" and forming a strong bond with him.[25]

An early Parker biographer repeated a barroom story about Grant's drinking that supposedly originated in a letter written by Parker himself.[26] Parker told how he had been passing a Galena tavern when his attention was arrested by a loud scuffle inside and he heard Grant's voice. He rushed in to Grant's defense, he claimed, and the two men warded off the attackers together. The story does not gibe with Grant's drinking history for several reasons. He was not a brawling type, much less a drunken one. He was also a solitary drinker who shied away from bars and public exposure. It is also hard to imagine that, if such an incident occurred, it never drifted back to Grant family members.

A riveting storyteller, Grant loved to regale people with anecdotes of his Mexican War exploits. One person enthralled by these tales was his neighbor John Rawlins, a young lawyer who did work for the leather goods store, which evolved into a small hotbed of political debate, with Grant doing much of the talking. "Grant's unusual conversational powers easily made him the prominent figure among those who frequented the leather store for . . . discussing politics and the turmoil in the southern states," maintained Melancthon Burke.[27] The issue of whether to extend slavery into the new territories had precipitated a final showdown over its future. Grant's acquaintances noticed a shift in his thinking, not all the way to the Republican side, but with newfound sympathy for the antislavery viewpoint. Augustus Chetlain, a Republican grocer, said Grant became a Free-Soil Democrat before the end of Buchanan's administration.[28]

The major party conventions that year testified to the extreme fragmentation of American politics. When Democrats gathered in Charleston, South Carolina, in April, Stephen Douglas led the balloting but could not secure the two-thirds vote needed for nomination. Breaking away and reconvening in Baltimore, the Douglas men nominated their champion, who campaigned on a pledge of allowing new territories to decide their own future on slavery, thus "burying Northern Abolitionism and Southern Disunionism in a common grave."[29] Although Douglas presented himself as a candidate of regional compromise, the middle ground was fast disappearing. Many southerners were spoiling for a fight that would harden the battles lines. In a self-destructive act that helped to elect a Republican, southern Democrats created a new Democratic Party, nominating Vice President John C. Breckinridge of Kentucky to head their ticket.

In May, Republicans met in Chicago at a huge, barnlike wooden structure known as the Wigwam where Abraham Lincoln emerged as the presidential standard-bearer. While his opposition to extending slavery was well known, he ducked many controversial issues. A comparative unknown, a dark horse who could juggle conflicting constituencies, he became the nominee less because he appealed to the most people than because he offended the fewest. Instead of trying to cultivate friends, he sought to avoid making enemies, refraining from utterances designed to soothe or antagonize the South. Even though Lincoln attempted to appeal to former Whigs, many ended up voting for John Bell of Tennessee, who had been nominated by the Constitutional Union Party a week earlier.

Among those who fervently greeted Lincoln's nomination was Jesse Grant. "When I return home, I will take Springfield in my rout[e], & make the acquaintance of Mr. Lincoln," he wrote in late May. "And I am going to work for the success of the ticket."[30] Both Simpson and Orvil Grant cast votes for Lincoln as well.

Stymied as a newcomer by Illinois residency requirements, Ulysses was ineligible to vote for president in 1860. "I was really glad of this at the time," he wrote sheepishly in his *Memoirs,* "for my pledges would have compelled me to vote for Stephen A. Douglas, who had no possible chance of election."[31] In fact, Grant was torn by indecision that mirrored his predicament as the son of an abolitionist and the son-in-law of a slave owner. After attending a Douglas speech in Dubuque, he was asked to appraise the candidate. "He is a very able, at least a very smart man," answered Grant, "but I can't say I like his ideas. If I had the legal right to vote I should be more undecided than ever."[32] A letter he wrote in early August shows his defection from the Democrats, though he could not bring himself to sign up with the Republicans: "The fact is I think the Democratic party want a little purifying and nothing will do it so effectually as a defeat. The only thing is I don't like to see a Republican beat the party."[33] When the race boiled down to Lincoln versus Breckinridge, Grant wrote that "he wanted . . . to see Mr. Lincoln elected."[34] Grant did not foresee how momentous the November election would be, nor how profoundly it would transform his entire existence.

As political emotions mounted, Galena's streets were often illuminated at night by torchlight processions snaking through town. The Republican marching club was known as the Galena Wide Awakes—Orvil Grant was a member— and as they tramped along, clad in dark oilcloth capes and caps, their martial air portended war. Grant rebuffed an effort, spearheaded by John Rawlins, to help the Douglas Democrats learn how to drill, but one night, after spotting the erratic marching of the Galena Wide Awakes, led by Augustus Chetlain, he discreetly offered tips on military style behind closed doors.

As the election approached, Grant drifted closer to positions articulated by Lincoln, a process observed by Melancthon Burke, who accompanied Grant to a speech given by the Illinois abolitionist congressman Owen Lovejoy: "On the way home from the Lovejoy speech he discussed the situation seriously and with deep concern stating that the election of Lincoln was a political necessity if majority rule was to be maintained."[35] However much he feared the supposed extremism of some Republicans—an exaggerated fear Burke attributed to Grant's long residence among Missouri slave owners—Grant realized that Unionism and abolitionism had become intertwined issues. "As long as slavery was confined to the states where it belonged I wouldn't interfere with it," he told Burke, "but if it is to be used as an instrument to disrupt the government I hope every slave will rise against his master."[36]

Grant's conversion to Republicanism was probably retarded by Julia's firm adherence to her Democratic roots. One night, while she and the children gazed down from the bluff on a Wide Awake torchlight procession, she imagined she beheld "a great, fiery serpent" that "would crush in its folds the beloved party of my father, of Jefferson, of General Jackson, of Douglas, and of Thomas Benton."[37] Colonel Dent had attempted to dissuade her from going to Galena, warning, "You know you cannot do without servants."[38] Afraid of bringing her slaves into the free state of Illinois, she left them behind with her father and relied instead on a competent maid named Maggie Cavinaugh. While Julia would soon find her husband enlisted in the Union cause, her own attitude toward slavery remained far more ambivalent.

On November 6, 1860, Abraham Lincoln was elected president in a vote full of troubling omens. Besides winning less than 40 percent of the popular vote, he did not win a single vote in the Deep South, where his name failed to appear on the ballot; he carried every northern state, except for New Jersey, where he managed a split with Douglas. Almost universally underrated, Lincoln was deemed a mediocrity at best, a coarse bumpkin from the backwoods. Grant's fortuitous move to Illinois on the eve of the election had monumental consequences, conveniently situating him in the president's home state and overtly pro-Union northern Illinois. It also placed him in the district of Congressman Elihu B. Washburne, an emphatic Lincoln supporter. Had Grant remained in Missouri, riven by internal strife, he would never have enjoyed the same chance for rapid advancement in the coming war.

Although Galena voted for Stephen Douglas by a narrow margin, local Wide Awakes burst into festivities on election night, complete with trumpets, fireworks, and cannon fired from the bluff. Down at the Grant store, Orvil hosted a little party where he distributed oysters and beer. Rampant speculation arose that Lincoln's election would bring southern secession, touching off a militant mood among townspeople who had never set foot on a battlefield. Grant's friend William R. Rowley, a clerk at the circuit court—Grant had met him when he went to the courthouse to install leather for a desk chair—declared, "There's a great deal of bluster about these Southerners; but I don't think there's much fight in them." Grant's dour correction was prescient. "Rowley, you are mistaken. There *is* a good deal of bluster—that's the result of their education—but if they ever get at it, they will make a strong fight."[39] It started to dawn on Grant that his West Point education and Mexican War experience had readied him for further service to his country, and he talked to John Rawlins "of his military education, his debt therefore to the country, and . . . the capacities of the North to raise troops."[40]

For many southerners, Lincoln's election threatened to halt the spread of slavery into new territories, stifling their homegrown institution and dangerously eroding their national power. Fire-breathing secessionists exploited the interregnum between the election and inauguration to stoke rabid fears. Thinking the move suicidal, Grant believed the South would stop short of the "awful leap" of secession.[41] Then, on December 20, 1860, delegates in Charleston, South Carolina, voted to secede from the Union. The decision was taken in an exuberant holiday atmosphere and with no sense that this would prove the catalyst for the bloodiest war in American history. The step was especially fateful, for three federal forts that stood in the harbor now lay in foreign territory. The feckless President Buchanan, who opposed secession, thought the federal government powerless to stop it, and in his last annual message blamed the "incessant and violent agitation of the slavery question throughout the North for the past quarter of a century."[42]

If Grant had dithered on how best to deal with slavery, secession clarified his thinking on preserving the Union, turning him into an outright militant. He conceded that the Constitution might have allowed one of the original thirteen states to secede, but such a right "was never possessed at all by Florida or the states west of the Mississippi, all of which were purchased by the treasury of the entire nation. Texas and the territory brought into the Union in consequence of annexation, were purchased with both blood and treasure."[43]

Every night, Grant read the newspaper aloud to Julia, who thought, somewhat illogically, that states had a right to leave the Union, but that the national government had a duty to prevent it—a blatant contradiction that amused her husband. Grant grew irate when Buchanan, whom he denounced as "the present granny of an executive," allowed Secretary of War John B. Floyd, a southerner, to redistribute arms from northern arsenals to southern forts in expectation of civil war.[44] Riding his buggy through Wisconsin, Minnesota, and Iowa that winter,

Grant engaged local townspeople in heated discussions, predicting the North would defeat the South in any war in ninety days—a mistaken optimism he maintained through the early period of conflict. Suddenly Grant was fired by a mission, a clear sense of purpose, something that had been lacking in the 1850s. He was now wide awake, his pulse quickened by an overriding sense of duty. A young Methodist clergyman named John Heyl Vincent met Grant on a frosty morning in Dubuque as they warmed themselves before a hotel stove. "Standing by the fire, in his old blue army overcoat, his hands clasped behind him, he reminded me then of the familiar picture of Napoleon," recalled Vincent. The grasp shown by Grant "of national questions, his knowledge of men and measures, his . . . ambition and earnestness, both surprised and interested me."[45]

In January 1861, a crescendo of state secessions occurred as Mississippi, Florida, Alabama, Georgia, and Louisiana departed from the Union, seizing control of federal forts and arsenals and widening the rift with the North. Then in February, joined by Texas, delegates from the seceded states met in Montgomery, Alabama, and consecrated the new Confederate States of America, drafting Jefferson Davis as interim president. He made a triumphant journey from his Mississippi plantation to Montgomery, greeted by jubilant crowds at every stop. Secessionists presented themselves as the true heirs to the American Revolution, adopting most of the U.S. Constitution as their own, albeit with special provisions to strengthen states' rights and protect slavery. On February 18, Davis took the oath of office in a mimicry of Washington, D.C., inaugurations, resting his hand on a Bible and uttering "So help me God!" Saying the time for compromise had vanished, he warned those who opposed the Confederacy that they would "smell Southern powder and feel Southern steel if coercion is persisted in."[46] A true believer, Davis would oversee the Confederacy with a fanatical zeal that never wavered.

Grant had a notably fierce reaction to events in Montgomery. When informed of what had happened, he shook an angry fist and exclaimed, "Davis and the whole gang ought to be hung!"[47] For once, Grant and his father thought perfectly in tandem. Living in northern Kentucky, Jesse found himself surrounded by plenty of Confederate apologists, even outright secessionists. In his own mind he was clear about what course he would follow if Kentucky seceded: "If our Union is to be severed, & Ky goes with the southern Confederacy, I shall follow the 'stars & stripes' of my country," he told former Ohio governor Salmon P. Chase.[48]

With the Stars and Bars fluttering over the Confederate capitol, Abraham

Lincoln traveled from Springfield, Illinois, to Washington, pausing in many towns to give mostly bland, extemporaneous speeches, marked by an unadorned eloquence that skirted the combustible issue of how to safeguard federal forts in southern hands. Avoiding hot-blooded rhetoric, he nonetheless refused to rule out the use of force or trim his view that nothing "can ever bring me willingly to consent to the destruction of this Union."[49] Lincoln had fooled himself into believing that the South was bluffing and that Unionist sentiment there would prevail. Then, on February 21, William Seward received word of a plot to murder Lincoln as he changed trains in Baltimore the next day. Traveling incognito, Lincoln changed his hat, switched to a special train from Harrisburg, and slipped unnoticed through Baltimore and into Washington on the morning of February 23, where he was greeted at the station by his old friend Congressman Elihu B. Washburne of Galena. When Lincoln was inaugurated on March 4, he and President Buchanan rode in an open barouche down Pennsylvania Avenue, beneath the watchful gaze of sharpshooters posted on rooftops lining the route. At the swearing-in ceremony, Lincoln invoked the "mystic chords of memory" that bound Americans, even as tense riflemen peered from every window in the Capitol that faced the platform where the new president spoke.[50]

AT 4:30 A.M. ON APRIL 12, 1861, the elegant Pierre Gustave Toutant Beauregard—a freshly minted brigadier general in the provisional Confederate army, with dyed black hair, a thick mustache above a chin beard, and a firm, determined gaze—gave orders to shell Fort Sumter amid rejoicing from Charleston citizens, who crowded nearby rooftops as if rooting for a sporting event. Gunners were cheered as they delivered a sustained pounding of several thousand shots before the federal garrison surrendered to overwhelming Confederate force. In the confrontation over the fort, Lincoln had seized the moral high ground and avoided firing the first shot of the Civil War, lest he lend credence to southern charges of being a despot and thereby forfeit the loyalty of border states.

Despite pro-Union sentiment thinly scattered through the South, many southern officers felt that loyalty to their states outweighed attachment to the federal government. The decision of Robert E. Lee, who rebuffed an offer to command the U.S. Army and rushed to Virginia's defense, was typical of southern officers who opposed secession but stuck with their native states. As Grant recounted, "The Southern feeling in the army among high officers was so strong that when the war broke out the army dissolved."[51] This meant that the South, which accounted for about a third of prewar army officers, would seek to offset northern superiority in manpower with superior generalship. If the North could manufacture everything from railway cars to clothing, the South would even the score with sheer gallantry.

Both sides underestimated the duration and savagery of the warfare ahead, nourishing pleasing fantasies of a massive blow that would knock out the enemy. The U.S. Army was shockingly understaffed, leaving gaping holes in the national defense. Many regular army men had been fighting Indians or protecting western settlers, and only four thousand served east of the Mississippi River. Right after Fort Sumter, Lincoln issued a proclamation to recruit seventy-five thousand state militiamen for ninety days. His northern detractors now saw that this shambling, awkward, loose-limbed man would be a strong, decisive leader, although the move also ratified southern views of him as a would-be tyrant.

Buoyed by a tremendous upsurge of patriotic feeling—Walt Whitman said the news of Fort Sumter's surrender "ran through the Land, as if by electric nerves"[52]—energetic northern men stampeded to local recruiting stations to sign up for the fight. The news from Charleston, along with Lincoln's military call-up, had the effect of broadening the Confederacy, until this point composed of cotton states. It was soon joined by Virginia, Arkansas, North Carolina, and Tennessee, presenting a far more formidable combination. Four slave-owning border states—Delaware, Maryland, Kentucky, and Missouri—stayed in the Union fold.

Soon to turn thirty-nine, Grant lingered in the shadowy wings of history, ready to fight. Emboldened by the cause, he cast off the lethargy and depression that had enwrapped him like a tight cloak. When Ely Parker encountered him, he asked if Grant planned to enter the conflict. "He replied that he honored his country, and that having received his education at the expense of the Government, it was entitled to his services."[53] The Civil War was about to rescue Grant from a dismal record of antebellum business failures. Even his posture became more erect, more military. "I saw new energies in Grant," said Rawlins. "He dropped a stoop shouldered way of walking, and set his hat forward on his forehead in a careless fashion."[54] Many major figures in history could have succeeded in almost any environment, whereas Grant could only thrive in a narrower set of circumstances. He not only had military skills and experience, but believed wholeheartedly in the Union case. As he reminisced, "I wanted to leave the country if disunion was accomplished . . . I only wanted to fight for the Union."[55]

Once again sectional warfare riled his family. "I was not for war," Julia admitted, noting that Galena was equally divided between those who favored and opposed it.[56] "I was Southern by all rights, born and reared in a Southern state" and "a slaveholder at the beginning of the war, and a very pronounced Democrat." When she tried to nudge her husband toward the Douglas Democrats, he shot back, "I took a solemn oath to support the government and the administration, and that is now Republican."[57] But Julia, a practical woman, recognized the vast potential for wartime glory for her husband and faithfully followed his path, saying Ulysses "could no more resist the sound of a fife or a drum or a chance to fire a gun than a woman can resist bonnets."[58]

After Fort Sumter, ebullient crowds surged into Galena's streets, flags hung everywhere, and small boys donned military caps. The Wide Awakes grabbed muskets for drills and rummaged through military manuals. It was inevitable that Grant, trained at West Point, would step into the huge vacuum of military leadership laid open to seasoned officers. Once Lincoln's call for volunteers reached Galena, posters announced a courthouse meeting that evening. Entering a packed hall that tingled with excitement, Grant sat down unobtrusively in the rear. The Democratic mayor Robert Brand presided and promptly infuriated the audience. "I am in favor of any honorable compromise," he stated. Incensed, Congressman Washburne delivered a stinging rebuttal: "I never will submit to the idea that in this crisis, when war is upon us and when our flag is assailed by traitors and conspirators, the government should be thus dealt with."[59] Denouncing the "wicked and unjustifiable war unleashed in South Carolina," he introduced a well-received resolution to create two military companies in Galena.[60] The audience applauded as Washburne sat down, followed by loud chants that reverberated through the room: "Rawlins! Rawlins!"[61]

At this summons, Grant's young, bearded lawyer friend, fated to play an outsize part in his life, mounted the platform. At five feet eight inches in height, wiry and muscular, the thirty-year-old Rawlins had tousled hair that tumbled over a high forehead, penetrating black eyes, and pale skin. Of an emotional, bombastic nature, he tended to speechify at a moment's notice. Possessed of a fiery nature, he would have made a superb, charismatic preacher. A patriot of spotless purity, he had voted for Stephen Douglas and been such a die-hard Democrat that friends had warned that, if he attended the town meeting, he might damage the party. "I don't know any thing about party now," he objected. "All I know is, traitors have fired on our flag."[62]

In a rich baritone voice, his eyes smoldering, Rawlins let loose a stemwinder of a speech that lasted forty-five minutes. His voice throbbing with emotion, he thundered, "I have been a Democrat all my life; but this is no longer a question of politics. It is simply country or no country. I have favored every honorable compromise; but the day for compromise is passed." Electrified, the crowd rose, stamped their boots, emitted lusty cheers. "If you are ready to die for your country, enlist," Rawlins had told friends. "I for one am."[63] As the audience drifted from the hall, William Rowley commented to Grant, "It was a fine meeting after all." To which Grant replied with quiet assurance, "Yes, we're about ready to *do* something now."[64] Grant said he had listened with "rapt attention" to Rawlins's speech, which wiped away any residual doubts about pitching into the war effort. Rawlins, in turn, was filled with a powerful conviction that Grant, with his military background, would advance rapidly in the impending conflict. Strolling home with Orvil, Grant fell into a reflective mood. "I think I ought to go into the service," he said. "I think so too," rejoined Orvil. "Go, if you like, and I will stay at home and attend to the store."[65] The time had come for Grant to wash his hands of the retail job he detested, and he never again set foot in the hated leather goods store.

Two days later a larger crowd convened at the courthouse to raise the first company of Galena volunteers. Before the meeting, Washburne huddled with Augustus Chetlain and they agreed on Grant as the optimal person to chair the gathering. He had fought in Mexico and his former Democratic tendencies might lend a useful bipartisan veneer to the evening. That decision first propelled Grant into the public spotlight. When a motion was made to have "Captain U.S. Grant for chairman," one person protested that he had a slave-owning wife from St. Louis, but the rest of the crowd shouted its approval. A bit nervously, Grant edged toward the platform, then drew to a full stop before it. "Go up, Captain!" the audience hollered. "Platform! Platform!" Still a bit jittery, Grant climbed to the podium, wearing his old blue army coat and a dented black hat. His light-brown beard was full and closely cropped. "With much embarrassment and some prompting," he spoke for the first time at a public gathering: "Fellow-citizens: This meeting is called to organize a company of volunteers to serve the State of Illinois."[66] The company would be named, after the county, the Jo Daviess Guards.

Washburne and Rawlins stirred the crowd with resounding speeches before Grant gave a tutorial in military life: how many men were in a company, how many in a regiment, and what their duties would be. All the old lore stored in his head sprang to fresh life. Characteristically, he delivered a sober speech for grown-ups, stripping away romantic flourishes from military rhetoric, and honestly foretold the grim sacrifices ahead. "The army is not a picnicking party," he emphasized. "Nor is it an excursion. You will have hard fare. You may be obliged to sleep on the ground after long marches in the rain and snow. Many of the orders of your superiors will seem to you unjust, and yet they must be borne."[67] When people posed questions, Grant showed his encyclopedic knowledge of warfare, prompting twenty-two young men to enroll that night, joined by another eighteen by noon the next day. Within a week, this company—the first in northwest Illinois outside of Chicago—was fully recruited.

Though the town clamored to have Grant as its captain, he rejected such a post as beneath his experience and knew he needed to aim much higher. Augustus Chetlain stepped up as captain instead. The self-confidence that had eluded Grant in civilian life now revived in this well-trod military setting. As he explained to Chetlain, "I have been graduated at West Point, I have been a Captain in the regular army and I should have a Colonelcy or a proper staff appointment—nothing else would be proper."[68] Nonetheless, Grant happily drilled and provided pointers for the Jo Daviess Guards.

The most remarkable proof of his sudden transformation was the forthright letter he now wrote to Colonel Dent. Old pent-up anger boiled to the surface. He did not mince words about the political situation, warning that "now is the time, particularly in the border Slave states, for men to prove their love of country. I know it is hard for men to apparently work with the Republican party but now all party distinctions should be lost sight of and every true patriot be for maintaining the integrity of the glorious old *Stars & Stripes,* the Constitution and the Union." Prophesying slavery's "doom," he predicted the North would "refuse for all time to give it protection unless the South shall return soon to their allegiance."[69] He envisioned a war that would destroy the South's export markets for cotton and render worthless slaves working in the cotton fields. Colonel Dent didn't heed the warning and remained an unreconstructed rebel throughout the war.

Much harder for Grant was to break away from his father's domination. On April 21, he wrote to him about his intention to leave the leather goods store in Orvil's hands and join the army. "What I ask now is your approval in the course I am taking, or advice in the matter." He stressed that political differences between them, the cause of earlier friction, had now ended. Having abandoned irrevocably the Dents, he drifted back for good into the Grant camp. "Whatever may have been my political opinions before I have but one sentiment now. That is we have a Government, and laws and a flag and they must all be sustained. There are but two parties now, Traitors & Patriots and I want hereafter to be ranked with the latter."[70]

To issue spirited pleas for volunteers, Grant, Rawlins, and Rowley traveled to schools and courthouses in nearby towns. After one meeting, Rowley remarked naively to Grant, "I guess the seventy-five thousand troops the President has called for will stop all the row." Grant, who knew southern officers intimately, was not convinced. "I think this is a bigger thing than you suppose. Those fellows mean fight, and Uncle Sam has a heavy job on his hands."[71] He lectured several optimistic friends that the South had "most of the equipment and ammunition and nearly all the regular army now in their possession."[72]

Back in Galena, Grant took the inexperienced local company, many of them farm boys, clerks, and mechanics, and broke them down into squads, teaching them to march on the broad lawn of Elihu Washburne's house as they hoisted pine laths instead of real guns. Grant's core competency from his old army days remained perfectly intact as he fell back into the familiar grooves of military habits. However much he may have preferred that his talents lay elsewhere, he came startlingly alive within the daily, sometimes hourly, challenges of a military world.

By April 24, Galena's soldiers wore brand-new uniforms with blue frock coats and gray pants. The next day, they were ready to travel to the state capital in Springfield, where they would be assigned to a regiment called the Eleventh Illinois Volunteer Infantry. As the Jo Daviess Guards marched to the train station, serenaded by brass bands and rewarded with a beautiful silk flag sewn by town ladies, they basked in a huge outpouring of patriotic ardor. Amid the delirium, few noticed a small, inconspicuous man in civilian dress with a slouch hat and a small carpetbag, also bound for Springfield. He distanced himself from the green troops, calling no attention to himself. Grant "seemed oblivious to all that was passing around him," said Chetlain, "and was apparently the least of all that vast throng."[73] En route to the train depot, Grant bumped into Rawlins. "Rawlins," he cried, "if I see anything that will suit you, I'll send you word." "Do captain!" the young lawyer replied.[74] Rawlins was soon sidetracked from the war effort, however, by word from his wife, Emily, staying with her family in

Goshen, New York, that she suffered from consumption; Rawlins would shortly leave to join her. As her husband left Galena, Julia Grant felt apprehension for his safety mingled with rising exaltation for his prospects. When pastor John Heyl Vincent dropped by to transmit his hope that Ulysses "might be preserved from all harm and restored to his family," Julia fairly burst out with a new fantasy: "Dear me! I hope he will get to be a major-general or something big!"[75]

On his way to Springfield, Grant was heartened by the throngs who poured onto platforms and lined tracks at every town, so "the whole population seemed to be out to greet the troops."[76] Not since the American Revolution, he thought, had the citizenry yielded to such patriotic elation. He tagged along with the Galena company because Washburne had promised an introduction to Governor Richard Yates, who might give him a regimental command. Grant encountered a state capital abuzz with war fever: thousands of volunteers flooded the town while the harried governor was buttonholed by supplicants at every turn. Grant thought the South should tremble at mass mobilization in the North, telling his sister Mary that "the conduct of eastern Virginia has been so abominable through the whole contest that there would be a great deal of disappointment here if matters should be settled before she is thoroughly punished."[77]

Since Washburne had served longer than any other House Republican, Grant had enlisted the allegiance of a champion with extraordinary clout in Washington. The relationship had begun inauspiciously. The previous October Grant had met Washburne in the offices of the *Galena Gazette* when the two men squared off over politics. As Melancthon Burke remembered, they "soon engaged in an earnest discussion . . . Grant had preconceived a dislike for Washburne and regarded him as an ultra extremist especially on the question of slavery. Grant at that time was radically opposed to slavery as an institution, but . . . did not believe it was good policy to interfere with slavery in the existing slave states."[78] Perhaps suspecting their careers would soon dovetail—Grant was Galena's most experienced military man—Washburne developed a close, almost proprietary feeling about him. As Lincoln subsequently noted, Washburne had "always claimed Grant as his right of discovery."[79]

A big, rawboned man with a thick nose, tufted gray eyebrows, and long gray hair that swept over his collar, Washburne had the bluff, backslapping manner and hearty laugh of a western politician. Energetic, restless, and impatient, he struck many people as brusque but honest. One of eleven children born to a Maine storekeeper, he had enjoyed little formal schooling and worked as a farmhand and a printer's devil as an adolescent. Largely self-taught, he had been introduced to Shakespeare and Dickens at public libraries, finally gaining admission to Harvard Law School. He became one of three Washburne sons elected to the U.S. Congress from different states, rising to become chairman of several influential committees, including Appropriations, Commerce, and Military Affairs. As young lawyers, he and Lincoln had argued cases before the Illinois Supreme Court and remained so close that Washburne had written a campaign biography for him the year before.

Unluckily for Grant, Washburne seemed on less than cordial terms with Yates. A Kentucky-born lawyer and former Whig who had served in the state legislature and Congress, Yates found his political leverage dramatically enhanced by his long-standing relationship with Lincoln. In 1854 Lincoln had virtually managed Yates's congressional campaign, and Yates returned the favor during Lincoln's presidential bid, functioning as a key Illinois operative. However conservative in other respects, Yates didn't restrain his views on slavery: "The earliest impressions of my boyhood," he stated bluntly, "were that the institution of slavery was a grievous wrong."[80] As Illinois's new governor, he dreaded that neighboring Missouri might defect to the Confederacy, blocking the flow of Illinois farm products down the Mississippi River.

Charged with assembling volunteer companies and appointing their officers, northern governors such as Yates came to wield enormous power. An entire army was being created overnight with coveted military titles handed out wholesale. After days spent waiting to see Yates, Grant received a brush-off. "I'm sorry to say, captain, there is nothing for you now to do," said Yates. "Call again." Augustus Chetlain thought Grant's appearance worked against him, as if the years of hardship had seeped visibly into his pores. Grant's "dress was seedy—he had only one suit and that he had worn all winter—his short pipe, his grizzled beard and old slouch hat did not make him look like a promising candidate for a colonel."[81] Indeed, an unimpressed aide informed Governor Yates that Grant's "features did not indicate any high grade of intellectuality. He was very indifferently dressed, and did not at all look like a military man."[82] Grant's drinking history may also have come back to haunt him at an inopportune moment. One colleague in the adjutant general's office regarded Grant as "a dead-beat military man—a discharged officer in the regular army," making one wonder whether his difficulties obtaining a command stemmed partly from his long-rumored history at Fort Humboldt, now part of army folklore.[83]

Lacking Napoleonic ambitions, Grant did not envisage himself at the helm of vast armies and merely aspired to head a regiment or cavalry brigade. As always, he studiously avoided jockeying for position. Reared with Methodist modesty, he could never admit nakedly to the true depth of his ambition. In this way, he was strictly Hannah Grant's son, not Jesse's. Ethical and honorable, he wanted to receive jobs based squarely on his merits, a faith he held so unalterably he called it "one of my superstitions."[84] Refusing to grovel, he considered it unseemly to profit from favoritism. It irked him to watch others maneuver for position, and he was "sickened at the political wire pulling for all these commissions and would not engage in it," he wrote.[85] Chummy with few politicians, Grant labored at an extreme disadvantage in securing a commission. "I was a carpetbagger and knew but few of them."[86]

Once the Galena company was mustered into service, Grant despaired of a command and was on the verge of taking a night train home when he ran into Governor Yates after dinner in his hotel. Yates addressed him as "Captain," said he had heard of his impending departure, and requested that he stay and check with his office the next morning. Grant happily complied. At a follow-up meeting the next day, Yates invited Grant to join the adjutant general's staff where, he predicted, his army experience would prove of inestimable value.

For several weeks, a disheartened Grant toiled at tedious administrative tasks, filling out reports and submitting requisitions for supplies. As a former quartermaster, he was well drilled in military bureaucracy. With no systems in place to handle such matters or even printed forms, Grant took blank sheets and drew lines across them. This paperwork must have felt like another degradation, another slap in the face, more suitable for an aide-de-camp than a veteran officer. Chetlain was shocked at the primitive cranny to which Grant was consigned, an anteroom of the adjutant's office. "He was seated at an old table with but three legs, which was shoved into a corner in order to stand. He had his hat on, and his pipe in his mouth, and was writing busily. As I spoke he looked up, with an expression of disgust on his face, and said, 'I'm going to quit. This is no work for a man of my experience. Any boy could do this. I'm going home.'"[87] Nonetheless, Grant's consummate professionalism stood out clearly amid the pervasive amateurism.

While confined to this back office, the despondent Grant was suddenly sprung from his solitary drudgery by an unexpected break. At West Point and in the Mexican War, he had befriended Captain John Pope. From a well-to-do

family, Pope enjoyed the privileged network of connections Grant lacked and
was in charge of Camp Yates, a mustering site on the outskirts of Springfield.
When Pope stormed off in high dudgeon after being denied appointment as a
brigadier general of Illinois volunteers, Yates elevated Grant to "mustering officer and aide" and he became the camp's temporary commandant for four days.
In that brief interval, Grant instilled discipline in the new soldiers with an air of
military precision. No longer chained to a desk, he seemed rejuvenated in the
field. Doubtless harking back to his West Coast days, he confided to Chetlain
that "when I have nothing to do I get blue and depressed."[88]

Impressed by the ongoing rush of new recruits, Grant again thought the
South might be cowed by this show of northern power. He worried about "negro
revolts," he told Julia, whose family may well have influenced such thinking.
"Such would be deeply deplorable and I have no doubt but a Northern army
would hasten South to suppress anything of the kind."[89] The initial war objective, however, was preserving the Union, not eliminating slavery. Grant's thinking would evolve quite rapidly on the slavery issue as the war progressed.

Goaded by Washburne, Governor Yates came to realize that Grant's talents
demanded greater leeway. When the Illinois legislature authorized him to raise
ten additional regiments, he assigned Grant to oversee the process of mustering
them in at Mattoon, Belleville, and Anna. Grant spent a day in Mattoon, then
went on to Belleville, which was not yet ready to stock a full regiment. Since
Belleville lay just east of St. Louis, he decided to visit Colonel Dent and debate
with him what to do about Julia and the four children while the war lasted.

CHAPTER SEVEN

The Quiet Man

W HEN GRANT CONFERRED with his father-in-law at White Haven, Colonel Dent made no apologies about his political beliefs or
fiery devotion to the Confederacy. The Dent household was already in an uproar about the war. Julia's brother John angled to be a colonel in
the Confederate army, while Aunt Fanny was adamantly pro-Union. Grant and
his father-in-law held hot-tempered political discussions, lasting well into the
night, with the enslaved Mary Robinson eavesdropping on them: "Dent was opposed to Lincoln, and tried to induce Grant not to fight with the Union army.
He wanted him to cast his destiny with the South."[1] When Dent declared that
he wanted Julia and the children to spend the war with him, Grant surely heard
disquieting echoes of earlier years. In frustration, Grant reported to Julia that
"your father professes to be a Union man yet condemns every measure for the
preservation of the Union. He says he is ruined and I fear it is too true."[2] During
the first year of the war, many White Haven slaves would escape, giving Grant
the upper hand with his defiant father-in-law, who suddenly lost the economic
foundations of his wealth. The conflict also endowed Grant with the moral
fervor to confront him over the treasonous nature of secession, which he
thought would prove suicidal for its adherents.

The Colonel never yielded an inch on secession. When he saw Grant was
obstinate, he told him to enter the Union army and "rise as high as you can, but
if your troops ever come to this side of the river I will shoot them."[3] It wasn't just
Union soldiers Colonel Dent ached to shoot. "After Capt. Grant took up the

Northern side," said Louisa Boggs, "Col. Dent swore with a big oath that if his worthless son-in-law ever came on his land he would shoot him as he would a rabbit."[4] Perhaps no state was more savagely divided by internecine warfare than Missouri.

While in St. Louis, Grant witnessed epochal events as the city divided into two armed camps of northern and southern sympathizers. Its federal arsenal contained the largest cache of weapons—sixty thousand muskets, ninety thousand pounds of gunpowder—of any slaveholding state. Unionists feared that the southern-leaning governor, Claiborne Fox Jackson, would direct his pro-secession militia units, waiting at Camp Jackson on the edge of the city, to grab the arsenal with its rich bounty of munitions. Jackson was a particular hero of Julia Grant's, who had found it exhilarating when he "called for 20,000 troops to protect my native state."[5]

Because of decisive action by Captain Nathaniel Lyon and Representative Francis P. Blair Jr., pro-Union regiments sprang up and covered the arsenal grounds with their white tents. Trailed by frenzied Unionists, they surrounded Camp Jackson and forced its surrender. Confederate flags were lowered blocks from where Grant had recently languished in the real estate business, and he credited Lyon and Blair for quick thinking in saving a major arsenal from Confederate hands. "If St. Louis had been captured by the rebels," Grant later reflected, "it would have made a vast difference in our war . . . Instead of a campaign before Vicksburg, it would have been a campaign before St. Louis."[6] Grant long remembered rejoicing as he "saw Blair and Lyon bring their prisoners into town."[7]

Back in Illinois, Grant mustered troops at Mattoon, southeast of Springfield, for the Twenty-First Illinois Infantry, his brief stay leaving a profound imprint on new recruits. They discerned that Grant "knew his business, for everything he did was done without hesitation," said Lieutenant Joseph Vance. "He was a little bit stooped at the time, and wore a cheap suit of clothes and a soft black hat," but anyone "who looked beyond that recognized that he was a professional soldier."[8] The soldiers expressed gratitude for this competent, if transient, visitor, bestowing upon him his first wartime accolade by renaming their encampment "Camp Grant."

When he finished inducting troops, Grant returned to Springfield and resumed his lonely vigil for a permanent job. He was so broke that he sometimes skipped dinners to husband his limited funds. One editor who accosted Grant at a hotel found him looking "fagged out, lonesome, poor, and dejected." "What are you doing here, Captain?" he asked. "Nothing—waiting," Grant replied sulkily.[9] He considered anything less than a colonel's rank insufficient, but Governor Yates offered no such appointment, and he grew convinced that politicians had rigged the process. His friend Davis White claimed that Yates penalized Grant because he assumed Grant was a Democrat. "This is a Republican war and our friends must have the offices," Yates told him. "Why, Governor," retorted White, "you can't fight this war out with all Republicans; Grant is a Democrat but a military educated man."[10]

Dejected, Grant trooped back to Galena, where the local newspaper took up his cause, rewarding him with his first press notice: "We are now in want of just such soldiers as he is, and we hope the government will invite him to higher command. He is the very soul of honor, and no man breathes who has a more patriotic heart."[11] Experiencing a sense of duty "paramount to any other duty I ever owed," Grant yearned to throw himself into the war effort at a suitable level, yet it seemed as if this supreme chance of his life was slipping from his eagerly outstretched grasp.[12]

In late May 1861, when the Confederate Congress voted to move its capital to Richmond, Grant realized that the war's principal battles would be fought on Virginia soil, producing terrible insecurity in the Lincoln administration about Washington's safety. At this point, it seemed unlikely that Grant might figure significantly in the war, and he later admitted that the zenith of his ambition was command of a cavalry brigade. He did not remain entirely passive in awaiting recognition. Swallowing his pride and contrary to his belief of never pushing himself forward, he composed a letter to the adjutant general of the army in Washington, soliciting a position: "I would say that in view of my present age, and length of service, I feel myself competent to command a regiment, if the President, in his judgment, should see fit to entrust one to me."[13] It seemed a modest enough request, given the pressing search for experienced officers, but already bruised by rejection, Grant felt he might be aiming too high. He could have saved himself the paperwork: he never received any acknowledgment from Washington, much less the job he sought.

Having mustered in the last regiments authorized by the Illinois legislature, Grant visited his parents in Covington and took advantage of his time there to lobby the wunderkind Major General George McClellan, whose headquarters lay across the Ohio River in Cincinnati. The two men, who had overlapped briefly at West Point, had met during the Mexican War, then again in the Pacific Northwest, when Grant was unfortunately drinking. Retaining considerable respect for McClellan's talents—he had graduated second in his class at West Point—Grant was eager to serve under the younger man, even as a major or lieutenant colonel. For two consecutive days, he cooled his heels for two hours in the waiting area of McClellan's headquarters and was pointedly snubbed. Both times he was informed the general had gone out. McClellan never acknowledged Grant's presence, giving him a foretaste of the arrogance that would so infuriate Abraham Lincoln and Secretary of War Edwin Stanton. At his wit's end, Grant went off to Columbus, Ohio, hoping to wring from Governor William Dennison, a boyhood friend, a contract to bake bread for soldiers. He no longer pretended that he could passively await recognition of his intrinsic worth.

Then, on June 16, 1861, Grant received a telegram from Governor Yates, appointing him colonel of the 7th Congressional District Regiment, shortly renamed the Twenty-First Illinois, the same outfit he had drilled into shape at Mattoon. No sooner had he digested this long-awaited news and wired acceptance to Yates than he received an offer to command an Ohio regiment, which he declined. Grant's life had changed abruptly, irrevocably, and rather miraculously. Julia was overjoyed at this sudden turn of fortune, perhaps because she had no sense of just how long and ghastly the war would be. "Strange to say, I felt no regret at his going and even suggested that our eldest son, just then eleven years old, should accompany him . . . I considered it a pleasant summer outing for both of them."[14]

Grant replaced Colonel Simon S. Goode, a flamboyant, blustering character—he liked to stuff two revolvers in his belt—with hardly an iota of military experience. A high-spirited, uproarious character, Goode drank to excess and his obliging men followed suit. As his soldiers rebelled against bad food by pillaging local farms and burned down a guardhouse crawling with vermin, discipline crumbled in his disorganized regiment. As Private Joseph H. Wham explained, "We had too much self-respect to serve under a drunken, incompetent colonel."[15] Alarming reports of near-mutiny filtered back to Governor Yates, who summoned the regiment to Springfield and met with its commissioned officers, a majority of whom requested Goode's replacement by Grant. As Wham said, "There was not a murmur at his being thus promoted over the heads of the ten captains and two field officers who outranked him."[16] It says much about Grant that his professionalism was so palpable to even the most callow soldiers.

Grant rode off on a horse trolley to the fairground near Springfield where the Twenty-First Illinois was encamped. Outfitted in civilian garb—a light-colored shirt, elbow-patched coat, and dented plug hat—he bore no insignia of rank as he sauntered around the grounds. As so often with Grant, people badly underestimated him, and his small size and slatternly appearance brought out sadistic impulses in some men. A few soldiers began to razz their new colonel, hissing in derision, "Well, I'll be damned. Is *that* our colonel?" One man said mockingly, "He don't look as if he knew enough to find cows if you gave him the hay."[17] Grant threw the man a glance that suggested he meant business. One soldier crept up behind him and started to shadowbox tauntingly until another shoved him hard against Grant, who remained imperturbable and offered no reproach. He knew that, to project authority, he had to transcend petty anger.

As he scouted the terrain, Grant noticed that Goode had created a police force of eighty guards, heavily armed with clubs, to prevent men from sneaking off. Grant knew the difference between being strict and punitive, and sat down in the adjutant's tent to draft an order abolishing these camp guards. The same order announced three daily drills, warning that those who missed them would be subject to confinement. If the men regarded Grant as overly harsh at first, they soon grew to admire his fairness, competence, and aplomb. He never threw temper tantrums, never engaged in theatrics, and performed his duties in a placid, levelheaded manner.

Once he took command, a remarkable change overcame Grant, mirrored in his letters. He now sounded energized, alert, and self-confident, as if shaken from a long slumber. Working with clockwork precision, he briskly issued orders. In his understated style, he was fearless and exacting. When several officers, attempting to flout Grant, showed up for dress parade without the requisite coats, he simply stated, "Dismiss the men to quarters."[18] Then he turned on his heels and departed. Such tomfoolery never recurred. Grant responded to infractions with cool, unwavering rigor. He fumed when a rough old rascal named Mexico showed up at a drill with a hangover. When Grant posted him to the guardhouse, Mexico swore, "I'll have an ounce of your blood."[19] Grant had him promptly gagged. A few hours later, he assembled the regiment and silently tore off Mexico's gag. Instead of retaliating, the tamed Mexico slunk off in humbled silence. Within days, Grant had smoothly shaped order from chaos.

In plain blue coat and black felt hat without marks of rank, he showed an egalitarian spirit that the volunteers appreciated. In ten days, he boosted regimental numbers from 630 to a full complement of 1,000. All the while, he found time to study William J. Hardee's manual of tactics and reports written by George McClellan as a Crimean War observer. Short of cash, Grant turned to his father and Orvil for a loan to enable him to buy a horse and a dress uniform appropriate to his new rank. Both men spurned his request in a last humiliation meted out by his family. Grant was forced to borrow from a Galena bank, with Jesse Grant's former business partner E. A. Collins endorsing the note. Before too long, Grant purchased a fine, yellow saddle horse named Jack that was to be one of his stable of mounts during the next four years.

Hounded from the army seven years earlier due to drinking, Grant reentered the service beneath a cloud and policed his men with unswerving zeal whenever he discovered evidence of alcohol abuse. How he dealt with drinking infractions reveals much about how he regarded his own alcohol problem. He limited field officers to one pint of liquor for the war's duration. "He allowed no whiskey in the camp," said Lieutenant Vance. "I've seen him personally inspect the canteens, and spill the liquor on the ground, and yet for all that he was so strict a disciplinarian, he was never angry or vindictive."[20] Grant smashed liquor barrels and warned grocers not to peddle alcohol to his men. "He refused to drink brandy when cold or wet," said one soldier. "'I do not use it,' he said."[21] Clearly Grant did not view alcohol consumption kindly.

By June 19, Grant's soldiers were urged to switch over from short-term militia service to three-year stints in the federal service. Two Illinois congressmen, John A. McClernand and John Logan, arrived and delivered florid speeches, exhorting the men to make the change. Throughout the speeches, Grant hovered discreetly in the background until Logan shoved him to the fore. To thunderous cheers, Logan said, "Allow me to present to you your new colonel, U.S. Grant." The bashful Grant stepped forward. "Cries of 'Grant, Grant; Colonel Grant!' arose and so did the Colonel slowly and with quiet dignity," said Wham.[22] Every man strained to hear what their laconic colonel would say, and he pronounced exactly five words: "Men, go to your quarters."[23] In a resounding affirmation of his leadership, virtually the entire regiment agreed to submit to three-year federal service. "We knew we had the best commander," boasted one soldier, "and the best regiment in the State."[24]

Its first assignment was to travel to Quincy, Illinois, near the state's western border. Wanting his men to be tough and hardy, Grant made a daring decision: instead of transporting them by train, he would march them halfway across the

state, "preferring to train them in a friendly country."[25] On June 3, when the
march got under way, whole towns turned out to applaud the soldiers. Women
fluttered handkerchiefs and tossed bouquets. From the outset, Grant knew he
had to earn the allegiance of the populace and punished those who pinched hens
and roosters from local gardens. He brought along his eldest son, Fred, who
profited from his father's popularity. "The Soldiers and officers call him Colonel
and he seems to be quite a favorite," Grant informed Julia.[26] He expressed delight with the regiment's progress, telling them after one week that they compared favorably with "veteran troops in point of soldierly bearing, general good
order, and cheerful execution of commands."[27] Grant was back in his element,
as proficient in war as he had been ineffectual in business. The incessant activity
was clearly therapeutic for a man whose foremost enemy had been unwanted
idleness. "I don't believe there is a more orderly set of troops now in the volunteer
service," Grant wrote proudly to Julia. "I have been very strict with them and the
men seem to like it."[28]

Grant struck up an intimate friendship with the regimental chaplain, James
L. Crane, whom he asked to deliver blessings at meals. Crane marveled at Grant's
cool, unruffled temperament, his candor among trusted friends, and his charitable nature: "He has no desire to rise by the fall of others; no glorying over another's abasement; no exulting over another's tears."[29] Invigorated by the cause,
Grant evinced no symptoms of the depression that had dogged him in recent
years. "He is always cheerful; no toil, cold, heat, hunger, fatigue, or want of
money depresses him." Crane had a chance to probe Grant's political views.
While Grant still lacked patience with extreme abolitionists, he loathed slavery
with all his soul. "He believed slavery to be an anomaly in a free government like
ours; that its tendency was subversive of the best interests of the master and the
enslaved . . . that it resulted in denying the slave the rights of his moral nature."
At this juncture, Grant knew the war's sole purpose was to preserve the Union
and suppress the rebellion, but he already perceived that its inexorable logic
would carry more profound repercussions in its wake. "He often remarked . . .
that he believed slavery would die with this rebellion, and that it might become
necessary for the government to suppress it as a stroke of military policy."[30]

Crane noticed that Grant abstained completely from alcohol, refusing all
wine and brandy and "usually remarking that he never indulged in anything
stronger than coffee and tobacco."[31] With his men, Grant remained extremely
vigilant against alcoholic temptation. On July 4, while the regiment stayed at the

Jacksonville fairgrounds, Grant stood at the gate, personally examining canteens for illicit whiskey. When he found a local vendor purveying jugs of whiskey from a wagon, he had them confiscated, forcing the seller to scramble away. At Exeter the next day, Grant again emptied canteens in the dust. When all else failed, he had intoxicated soldiers lashed to baggage wagons or tree trunks until they sobered up. When the regiment reached Quincy and the old soldier known as Mexico got roaring drunk, Grant berated him with unwonted severity: "You are a trifling, dirty old dog, and of no account on this earth. You get across the river and never let me see you again."[32]

At Quincy, Grant received orders from Brigadier General John Pope to proceed to Palmyra, just across the Mississippi River in Missouri, to rescue an Illinois regiment pinned down by rebels on a railway line. Grant, who had never been in command before and now faced the ultimate test of battle, was seized with trepidation. "Before we were prepared to cross the Mississippi River at Quincy my anxiety was relieved; for the men of the besieged regiment came straggling into town," Grant wrote. "I am inclined to think both sides got frightened and ran away."[33] An atypical male, Grant never hesitated to admit human fears. It is perhaps no accident that at this stressful moment he suffered migraine headaches, nor that he decided to send young Fred home for his safety.

After several days at Palmyra, the next objective for Grant's regiment was to apprehend General Thomas A. Harris, who commanded a force of twelve hundred mounted secessionists in northern Missouri. So far, Confederates in the region constituted a ghostly but destructive presence, tearing up railroad tracks and pouncing on small pockets of Union troops. Harris was rumored to be in the small town of Florida, some twenty-five miles south. With rising dread, Grant led six companies through a deserted landscape. They approached a hill where they expected to find Harris and his men lurking at a creek bottom on the other side. In an oft-quoted passage of his *Memoirs,* Grant described his first whiff of fright as his heart "kept getting higher and higher until it felt to me as though it was in my throat. I would have given anything then to have been back in Illinois, but I had not the moral courage to halt." To his relieved astonishment, Grant discovered that Harris and his men had absconded in response to his approach. "My heart resumed its place. It occurred to me at once that Harris had been as much afraid of me as I had been of him."[34] This anticlimactic moment was formative for Grant, who never forgot the nugget of practical wisdom learned. He would emerge as a master of the psychology of war, intuitive about enemy weakness. Henceforth he would project himself into opponents' minds and comprehend their fears and anxieties instead of blowing them up into all-powerful bugaboos, giving him courage when others quailed. Around this time, Mark Twain belonged to a small, irregular Confederate company and later claimed for comic effect that he had been pursued by Grant's troops. As he said facetiously, "I did not know that this was the future General Grant or I would have turned and attacked him. I supposed it was just some ordinary Colonel of no particular consequence, so I let him go."[35] In fact, Twain had been in the vicinity weeks earlier.

On July 20, Grant's regiment set off by train southward for Mexico, a town in Missouri. The next day, a sweltering Sunday in the East, Union troops staged the war's first major confrontation, assaulting Confederate forces at Manassas, Virginia, west of Washington. General Winfield Scott, who oversaw the northern war effort, was too old, creaky, and overweight to lead armies into battle, so the task fell to the tall, bearded General Irvin McDowell, a West Pointer who had served in the Mexican War. A student of military strategy, McDowell had enrolled at a French military college, but he had never commanded troops in the field. The battle of Bull Run (First Manassas) drew a vast flock of enraptured spectators from the federal capital, including six senators and at least ten congressmen, not to mention fashionable ladies hoping to enjoy some bloodshed as a holiday outing and history lesson. What had looked like certain victory degenerated into a panicky rout of Union forces, who streamed back into the capital in a dreary, drenching rain.

President Lincoln and his cabinet were shocked by the unexpected vigor of southern resistance and a shaken Elihu Washburne wrote home that he had never seen "a more sober set of men."[36] Bull Run dashed the confidence of armchair generals who had predicted the North would coast to easy victory, breeding a corresponding euphoria in southern towns. It also exposed for the first—but not the last—time the shortcomings of Union generals in the eastern theater. It always irritated Grant that the competent McDowell was stigmatized for his loss. "You will remember people called him a drunkard and a traitor," Grant later said. "Well, he never drank a drop of liquor in his life, and a more loyal man never lived."[37] In the days after Bull Run, the president signed two bills to enlist a million new volunteers as the scale of the conflict exploded dramatically and the nation lurched toward total war.

When his regiment reached Mexico, Grant found himself in Missouri territory infested with secessionists, and as he gauged the depth of the irrational emotions driving secession, he feared guerrilla warfare would spiral out of control. "I hope from the bottom of my heart I may be mistaken," he told Julia, "but since the defeat of our troops at Manassas things look more gloomy here."[38] Thanks to a decision by General Pope, Grant now commanded three infantry regiments and a section of artillery. Attuned to the war's political imperatives, he again worked hard to prevent his troops from alienating local residents by pilfering food and drink.

While in Mexico, Grant grappled for the first time with a runaway slave who appeared in camp and asked for the commanding colonel. As Chaplain Crane recalled, the man—frightened, exhausted, breathing heavily—explained that he had been treated atrociously by his master. "Kin yo help me, cunnel?" he asked Grant. "Can't help you, sir, we are not here to look after negroes, but after rebels," Grant rejoined. "You must take care of yourself." Crestfallen, the man hung his head and sighed dejectedly. "Lawd, I's afeerd massa 'll be onto me!"[39] Although Grant did not help the man, Chaplain Crane gave him bread, meat, and money and steered him to an escape route across the Mississippi. When the slave's master and his sidekick appeared in camp two hours later and inquired about the fugitive's whereabouts, Grant not only shielded the runaway, but demanded that the two men divulge their feelings about the rebellion. When they evaded his question, Grant detained them in camp until they agreed to take an oath of allegiance, giving their former slave more time to escape.

In early August, Crane handed Grant a copy of the *Daily Missouri Democrat* and remarked, "I see that you are made brigadier-general." Taken unawares, Grant sat down to study the news item from Washington, which said his name had been sent to the Senate for the post. "Well, sir, I had no suspicion of it," he said. "It never came from any request of mine." Grant guessed correctly that the appointment derived from Washburne's amicable relations with Lincoln. Crane was amazed by Grant's unflappable response as "he very leisurely rose up and pulled his black felt hat a little nearer his eyes . . . and walked away about his business with as much apparent unconcern as if some one had merely told him that his new suit of clothes was finished."[40] For Grant it was a dreamlike transformation: the man who had recently toiled as a store clerk, who had felt cursed by fate, who had lobbied wearily for appointment as a colonel, had been unexpectedly bumped up to brigadier general in charge of four regiments, or about four thousand men, without having fought a single battle. And in the end he required political pull to do so. After years of wandering, Grant had popped up in the right congressional district in the right state. Lincoln had the power to appoint brigadier generals of volunteers, and the Illinois caucus enjoyed such sway that six Illinois brigadiers were selected, two more than any other state. "This is certainly very complimentary to me," Grant told his father, "particularly as I have never asked a friend to intercede in my behalf."[41] Back home in Galena, Julia trumpeted the news everywhere. She was unapologetically ambitious for her husband, perhaps expressing what he secretly felt but dared not say. As Orvil's wife noted with chagrin, "Julia boastfully told the townsfolk that her Ulyss had become a Brigadier and she had always known his mettle."[42]

AFTER YEARS OF SEEING his life maddeningly stalled, Grant began to experience gigantic leaps in power. On August 8, the new brigadier general took command of the military district of Ironton, a railway terminus seventy miles south of St. Louis, then threatened by Confederate troops under General William J. Hardee. Here Grant made his headquarters in a small rustic farmhouse, hard by a lovely spring, amid mountain scenery that he found bracing. He still lacked a sword, a sash, or a uniform befitting his new rank, but he had always led by the force of personality, not by gold braid and ribbons. Under a spreading oak tree, he set out a pine table and surveyed maps, marking them with a red pencil. Significantly, he ordered a new set of maps with an expanded overview of the region. Already a grand strategy began to germinate in his mind of how to exploit the broad waterways that provided entry into the heart of Confederate territory.

Although he had brought along the Twenty-First Illinois, Grant had new regiments under his supervision in Ironton and labored to whip these amateurs into a band of crack troops. "The loud laugh and bluster, the swagger of loafing squads, were hushed," said one soldier approvingly. "Instead you heard the bugle calls, the roll of drums, the sharp commands of officers to the drilling and marching and wheeling battalions."[43] Since alcohol abuse was widespread among local troops, Grant shut down saloons in Ironton and the railroad station at Pilot Knob.

On August 10, at the battle of Wilson's Creek, Confederate forces handed a stunning defeat to the Union army in southwest Missouri, killing General Nathaniel Lyon—the first Union general to succumb in battle. While Grant still hoped the Confederacy might be conquered by the following spring, Wilson's

Creek made him wonder. As he admitted to his sister, the rebels were so persistent "that there is no telling when they may be subdued."[44] Grant viewed himself as relegated to a backwater of the war and itched to be farther east. "I should like to be sent to Western Virginia but my lot seems to be cast in this part of the world."[45] He had not yet fully grasped the vast strategic opportunities and chances to sparkle afforded by the western theater.

Just as Grant cherished his newfound worth as a general, General John C. Frémont, commanding the Western Department, replaced him at Ironton with Brigadier General Benjamin M. Prentiss. Without warning, Prentiss showed up on a train bearing orders to take command. Even though both men held the same rank, Grant was technically senior by virtue of his old army rank, but he felt powerless to halt the move. Rudely jolted, he took a midnight train to St. Louis to see Frémont, accompanied by Colonel John M. Thayer, who watched Grant brood silently. "Why he was thus summarily displaced by another he could not divine," said Thayer. "He felt severely the humiliation of being thus recalled from his command, for which there was no apparent justification; and he was thoroughly cast down and dejected by the wholly unexpected change in his military position."[46] For a man with Grant's checkered history, the unjust reprimand could only have aroused unpleasant memories.

Popularly celebrated as "Pathfinder of the West," Frémont had helped to map the Rocky Mountains. A self-dramatizing figure with a fatal penchant for fancy uniforms, he had served as one of California's first senators and the first presidential nominee of the new Republican Party in 1856. Touched with an imperious streak, he operated from a three-story mansion where he strutted about with monarchical airs. He had converted his headquarters into a private fiefdom, with a Praetorian Guard of foreign mercenaries clad in pretentious uniforms, many stalked by rumors of corruption. The great man vouchsafed only a brief audience to Grant and seemed to ramble on in mumbo jumbo. "Fremont had as much state as a sovereign," Grant recollected. "He sat in a room in full uniform, with his maps before him. When you went in, he would point out one line or another in a mysterious manner, never asking you to take a seat."[47] When Thayer encountered a subdued Grant afterward, he "did not exhibit an angry spirit, did not utter a harsh word, but his feelings seemed to be deeply wounded."[48]

Before leaving St. Louis, Grant paid a call on his former real estate partner, the conservative Harry Boggs. Two years earlier, Grant had lodged in a drab, poorly furnished room in the Boggs home. Now he came clothed with the immense prestige of a brigadier general. "[Boggs] cursed and went on like a Madman," Grant wrote to Julia. "Told me that I would never be welcome in his house; that the people of Illinois were a poor miserable set of Black Republicans." In a strange role reversal, Grant felt sorry for the insignificant Harry Boggs, upon whom he had once so sorely depended. "Harry is such a pitiful insignificant fellow that I could not get mad at him and told him so."[49]

Although Grant longed to be transferred farther east, Frémont assigned him to take command in Jefferson City, the state capital, deep in the Missouri heartland, a town menaced by marauding raiders and a Confederate force under General Sterling Price. When he arrived, Grant found the countryside "in a state of ferment" and injected discipline into a large body of troops in extreme disarray.[50] The soldiers had been "recruited for different periods and on different conditions; some were enlisted for six months, some for a year, some without any condition as to where they were to serve, others were not to be sent out of the State."[51] Grant also grappled with severe shortages of ammunition, weapons, blankets, tents, and clothing. Fortunately, after a week, a bantam colonel with a bushy beard and melancholy eyes, implausibly named Jefferson C. Davis, came to relieve him of his command. "The orders directed that I should report at department headquarters at St. Louis without delay, to receive important special instructions."[52] Within an hour, Grant hopped a train bound for St. Louis.

It was unclear whether he was being promoted or demoted. When he arrived at headquarters, Frémont let him stew in the corridor for several hours. Major Justus McKinstry, who had known Grant in prewar army days, greeted him before proceeding to a staff meeting where Frémont and his officers debated which general could best counter Confederate activity on the Mississippi River. McKinstry argued robustly for Grant, citing his Mexican War gallantry, but was hooted down by others, who alluded to Grant's 1854 resignation, prompted by a drinking problem. Once embedded in a responsible position, McKinstry claimed, Grant would not revert to the bottle. After an emotional argument, Frémont chose Grant, later writing that "General Grant was a man of unassuming character, not given to self-elation, of dogged persistence, and of iron will."[53] When Grant was ushered into the meeting, he learned that he would preside over the District of Southeast Missouri, encompassing territory south of St. Louis and in southern Illinois. There is a competing story as to how Grant got this highly consequential promotion. Postmaster General Montgomery Blair averred that Lincoln received a gentle nudge from Elihu Washburne, then directed the secretary of war to "send an order to General Frémont to put Grant in command of the District of Southeast Missouri."[54]

Whatever the case, Grant was ordered to proceed to Cape Girardeau on the Mississippi River, in southeast Missouri, across the river from Illinois, where he would be poised to operate against Kentucky and Tennessee. Writing to Julia, Grant sounded decidedly hopeful about his newly conferred powers: "I wish I could be kept with one Brigade steadily. But I suppose it is a compliment to be selected so often for what is supposed to be important service."[55] Lifting his mood was his improved financial picture: he would receive a handsome annual salary of $4,000 with only $40 in monthly expenses.

Soon after meeting Grant, the Pathfinder perpetrated a breathtaking act of hubris that confirmed talk of his imperial rule. Without consulting Lincoln, Frémont declared martial law in Missouri, ordered the death penalty for captured Confederate guerrillas, and enunciated his own emancipation proclamation: he would free rebel slaves who took up arms for the Union. Lincoln was aghast. Aside from bridling at the blatant insubordination, he feared the defection of Democrats and border states and asked Frémont to modify his measure. The headstrong Frémont refused, even dispatching his wife, Jessie, to reason with Lincoln. She got an icy reception and her presence only worsened her husband's predicament, although he was not formally relieved until early November. Lincoln's decision to cashier Frémont served as a cautionary tale for Grant, who noted, "The generals who insisted upon writing emancipation proclamations . . . all came to grief as surely as those who believed that the main object of the war was to protect rebel property, and keep the negroes at work on the plantations while their masters were off in the rebellion."[56] With few exceptions, Grant would qualify as a model general who accepted military subservience to civilian leadership.

When he took the steamer to Cape Girardeau, he met a journalist from the *New York Herald* who left a brief verbal sketch of his appearance: "He is about forty-five years of age, not more than five feet eight inches in height, and of ordinary frame, with a slight tendency to corpulency. The expression of his face is pleasant, and a smile is almost continually playing around his eyes."[57] Not often was Grant conjured up in this cheerful vein, and it was clear that Frémont's orders had, at least temporarily, bucked up his flagging morale.

Before going to his new headquarters, Grant undertook a mission to chase down Brigadier General M. Jeff Thompson, whose Confederate partisans harassed federal forces in the swamps of southeast Missouri. The operation was impeded by a personal clash. Grant had a rendezvous with Brigadier General Benjamin M. Prentiss—the same general who supplanted him at Ironton—but Prentiss recoiled from taking orders from Grant. In his *Memoirs,* Grant attributed the contretemps to a seniority dispute. Prentiss "was very much aggrieved at being placed under another brigadier-general, particularly as he believed himself to be the senior."[58] But Prentiss, who rushed off to complain to Frémont, may have been moved by baser motives. When the journalist Albert D. Richardson ran into him, Prentiss explained why he had left: "I will not serve under a drunkard."[59] Later on, Grant came to value Prentiss as an able, selfless commander and regretted the earlier history of friction.

Grant decided to make his headquarters at Cairo, at the southern tip of Illinois, a vital intersection where the Ohio River flowed into the Mississippi. It arose as the perfect hub for massive operations by water that would penetrate the Deep South. Frémont's master plan was to dominate the Mississippi from Cairo to New Orleans, bisecting the Confederacy, and to control the Cumberland and Tennessee Rivers, natural gateways to Tennessee, Alabama, and Mississippi. No longer was Grant consigned to a lesser stage in the war and now acted in one of its main theaters.

Upon arriving in Cairo, he donned civilian garb as he awaited his brigadier general uniform from New York. At first, the resident commander, Colonel Richard J. Oglesby, did not catch Grant's name or realize that the small, forgettable man in mufti had been sent to succeed him. Then Grant scrawled his orders on a sheet of paper and handed it to the bemused colonel, who "put on an expression of surprise that looked a little as if he would like to have someone identify me. But he surrendered the office without question."[60] For his headquarters, Grant set up shop on the second floor of a bank building, where he sat behind a counter, sucking on a meerschaum pipe, as if he were an everyday bank teller. Dr. John H. Brinton, an army surgeon, at first dismissed Grant as "a very ordinary sort of man," then noticed his unusual concentration, his capacity to make rapid-fire decisions under extreme pressure. Grant got things done without the pomp and frippery of a Frémont. "He did not as a rule speak a great deal . . . did nothing carelessly, but worked slowly, every now and then stopping and taking his pipe out of his mouth."[61] Periodically, as if deep in thought, Grant paused and stared out the window at a fleet of gunboats anchored in the river—a fleet that opened up a wealth of strategic initiatives with the dense network of navigable waterways nearby.

Flooded in many places, Cairo was a hellish place with an infestation of small creatures attracted by standing pools of water. Soldiers were bitten by ubiquitous mosquitoes, dead horses and mules floated downriver, and swarms of rats scurried along muddy streets. Frémont had labeled Cairo "the most unhealthy post within my command" and the pestilential atmosphere bred malaria and dysentery.[62] Without a staff to delegate tasks, Grant felt overwhelmed by clerical duties and complained to Julia that his hand had grown cramped from all the letters he drafted. He was obliged to feed, house, and train new regiments who arrived incessantly by train, and he often worked alone until midnight. Burdened with the responsibilities of commissary and quartermaster as well as brigadier general, he conducted an unending battle against mercenary contractors who sought to swindle the government.

Despite his exemplary sense of duty, Grant proved almost laughably inefficient when it came to filing paperwork, much as in his hapless real estate days. He had an absentminded habit of stuffing letters into his pockets and neglecting them. Indeed, one journalist claimed that "the camp story was but slightly exaggerated which asserted that half his general orders were blowing about in the sand and dirt of the streets of Cairo."[63] He urgently needed aides to rescue him from his own disorganized nature. Grant made plain that he did not want as staff officers "these gay, swelling, pompous adventurers," but young men "who had some conscience."[64] From his former regiment, he plucked Clark B. Lagow, thirty-two, and William S. Hillyer, thirty, the young lawyer with whom he had debated politics at the real estate office in St. Louis. Showing a weakness for nepotism that later caused him no end of trouble, he appointed his brother-in-law, Dr. Alexander Sharp, as brigade surgeon.

Grant needed a commanding personality to manage his office and ride herd over his staff and from the outset selected John Rawlins for a special place in his entourage. Rawlins was the pallid young lawyer with the full dark beard, saturnine aura, and enormous dark eyes who had bowled over Grant with his impassioned oratory at the Galena recruiting meeting. On August 30, Rawlins was appointed assistant adjutant general with the rank of captain, effectively making him Grant's chief of staff. With no military background, he was startled that Grant gave him such a high appointment.

All through August, Rawlins sat by the bedside of his wife, Emily, as she lay dying of tuberculosis in Goshen, New York. While there, he spotted an item in the *New York Tribune* about Grant's appointment as brigadier general and little realized its enormous meaning for him. On August 30, Emily died, leaving the thirty-year-old Rawlins a young widower with three small children. He was tortured by her loss and distraught over his children's fate: "The God of Heaven only knows what will become of our three little children."[65] He mourned his wife fervently for years, evoking her in saintly terms: "Few of earth's daughters were so lovely; none in Heaven stands nearer the throne."[66] Once he arranged for his children's care, he hastened to join Grant's staff, reaching Cairo on September 14. A photo of Rawlins taken that October betrays the deep ravages of grief: he holds a sword in his hand, but no martial triumph illuminates his eyes, which are sad and haunted with widely dilated pupils. He seems to be peering into a troubled future.

Born in East Galena, Rawlins was the second of nine children in a poor family. His mother, a pious Christian woman of Scotch-Irish heritage, taught him hymns that he often recited at bedtime during the war. His Kentucky-born father was a farmer who burned charcoal to sell to local lead mines. For three years his father tested his luck in California's gold fields, forcing the adolescent John to care for his family and charcoal business. When the young man entered Galena politics, he carried the nickname "the Coal Boy of Jo Daviess County."[67] Some dispute exists as to whether Rawlins's father was a full-blown alcoholic—"He hit the bottle liberally, wasn't a drunkard at all, but drank freely," a nephew testified—but his drinking was excessive enough to convert Rawlins into a fierce temperance advocate.[68] His friend James H. Wilson later wrote, "It is certain that from his earliest manhood John A. Rawlins exhibited an earnest and uncompromising hatred for strong drink, and during his military life waged constant warfare against its use in the army. His dislike of it amounted to a deep and abiding abhorrence, and . . . he was often heard to declare that he would rather see a friend of his take a glass of poison than a glass of whiskey."[69] Because of his father's fondness for alcohol and irresponsible nature, Rawlins received a spotty education and always regretted his deficient schooling. Yet he was smart and determined enough to pass the bar after a one-year apprenticeship with a local lawyer and soon became a city alderman and auditor.

Rawlins's family history with alcohol abuse gave him a special purchase on Grant's drinking troubles, making it an all-consuming preoccupation. Before joining his staff, he extracted a pledge from Grant that he would not touch a drop of liquor until the war ended, and he would monitor this vow with Old Testament fervor, carrying on a lonely, one-man crusade to keep Grant sober.

That Grant agreed to this deal shows his strong willingness to confront his drinking problem. The mission perfectly suited Rawlins's zealous nature. With Grant's consent, he laid down draconian rules to curb drinking, forbidding the open use of liquor at headquarters. In general orders that announced Rawlins's appointment, Grant berated men who "visit together the lowest drinking and dancing saloons; quarrel, curse, drink and carouse . . . Such conduct is totally subversive of good order and Military Discipline and must be discontinued."[70] With Rawlins on the premises, even senior officers drank secretly in their tents. Any staff member who furnished Grant with alcohol faced the fervid wrath of Rawlins and likely dismissal. Rawlins fretted over Grant, agonizing over suspected lapses from the straight path of abstinence. He had no compunctions about chastising Grant for lapses, and his unflagging vigilance was remarkable in its forthright passion and candor.

Rawlins's papers reveal another dimension to the story. He feared his own susceptibility to alcohol, so that in saving Grant from temptation, he was perhaps saving himself as well. One year after joining Grant's staff, he signed a pledge not to drink, along with Clark B. Lagow and William S. Hillyer: "This pledge signed by me shall never be broken. Teach my boy its great value, tell him his father never was a drunkard, but [he] signed this that he might exert a proper influence over those with whom and under whom he served his country."[71]

Grant never discussed publicly his drinking pact with Rawlins, but he must have taken it to heart since Rawlins became his right-hand man and alter ego during the war. He allowed Rawlins to be the moralistic scourge and resident conscience of his staff. Later in the war, Grant wrote that Rawlins "comes the nearest being indispensable to me of any officer in the service."[72] In entering the army and assuming tremendous responsibilities, Grant must have feared he would be hurled back into the hard-drinking world of officers from which he fled in 1854, endangering the hard-earned sobriety of his St. Louis and Galena years. A general could not afford even occasional bouts of dissipation. In the army Grant would also lack the firm, restraining hand of his wife. Prolonged absence from Julia could easily set him up for a major relapse into the periodic degradation of his West Coast years. With some notable exceptions, Rawlins largely succeeded in his role as self-appointed watchdog. In later years, Grant's Galena physician, Dr. Edward Kittoe, paid tribute to "Grant's repeated efforts to overcome the desire for strong drink while he was in the army, and of his final victory through his own persistency and advice so freely given him by Rawlins."[73]

The ever-watchful Rawlins enjoyed special license to be frank and even scold Grant. "It was no novel thing to hear the zealous subordinate administer to his superior a stiff verbal castigation because of some act that met the former's stern disapproval," said the cipher operator Samuel Beckwith. "And Grant never resented any reprimand bestowed by Rawlins."[74] Rawlins spoke to him with a freedom that flabbergasted onlookers. Only he could slap Grant on the back or engage in familiar banter. Grant shrank from profanity, yet he tolerated with amusement the barrage of oaths that constantly poured from Rawlins's mouth.

Because of the purity of his motives, Rawlins became Grant's closest friend. "Gen. Grant was a man who made friends very slowly," noted a journalist. "While he had a great many acquaintances, I think he had a very limited circle of friends—I mean men whom he trusted or whose advice he accepted."[75] Only Rawlins could penetrate the zone of privacy that Grant drew subtly about himself. With his single-minded devotion, Rawlins could confront him with uncomfortable truths and fiercely contest his judgment, spouting opinions in a stentorian voice. With his thoroughgoing skepticism and mistrust of people, he was the ideal foil to Grant's excessively trusting nature. Rawlins "was always getting excited about something that had been done to Grant," recalled Lieutenant Frank Parker. When someone showed disrespect for Grant, "he would prance around and say, 'General, I would not stand such things' to which Grant would say, 'Oh, Rawlins! what's the use in getting excited over a little thing like that; it doesn't hurt me and it may make the other fellow feel a little good.'"[76]

Perhaps because it contrasted vividly with his listless manner at the Galena store, Rawlins never forgot his initial glimpse of Grant at Cairo: "He had an office in a great bank there, and I was amazed at the quiet, prompt way in which he handled the multitude of letters, requisitions, and papers, sitting behind the cashier's window-hole, with a waste basket under him, and orderlies to dispatch business as he did."[77] Fresh from personal calamity, Rawlins threw himself into a whirl of military activity. Before long, he worked day and night, tidying up Grant's office, creating files, and instituting sound working procedures. Long politically active—Grant thought him the most influential young man in northern Illinois—Rawlins also assisted Grant in perfecting his relations with Washington. When Washburne boasted to Secretary of the Treasury Salmon P. Chase that Grant in Cairo was "doing wonders in bringing order out of chaos," Rawlins surely deserved much of the credit.[78]

Such was the influence of John Rawlins over Grant that some observers would later exaggerate or misinterpret the nature of his power, attributing to him the military acumen that properly belonged to Grant. He had excellent common sense and swiftly grasped many basic principles of warfare, especially the need to concentrate forces instead of spreading them too thinly. And he became a formidable warrior in his own right, personally signing off on every letter and plan of campaign that came from Grant's command and never hesitating to differ with him. Nevertheless, Rawlins had no military background and lacked Grant's general knowledge of warfare. He could never have done what Grant did. While Grant developed tremendous respect for Rawlins's fearless judgment, it was Grant who originated the plans, Grant who improvised in the heat of battle, and Grant who possessed the more sophisticated strategic sense.

CHAPTER EIGHT

Twin Forts

F ROM THE OUTBREAK OF THE WAR, Abraham Lincoln recognized the pivotal role of Kentucky, a centrally located buffer state between North and South. "I hope to have God on my side," he admonished colleagues, "but I must have Kentucky."[1] Another time he reflected, "I think to lose Kentucky is nearly the same as to lose the whole game."[2] With Kentucky, Confederates would be camped on the Ohio River, positioned to strike the North. And with Kentucky gone, Maryland and Missouri might follow suit, weighting the scales to southern victory.

Although nominally on the Union side, Kentucky turned into a state of wavering loyalty, bitterly riven in its tendencies. Much as in neighboring Missouri, homegrown secessionists flocked to State Guard regiments organized by Governor Beriah Magoffin, while Unionists manned their Home Guard counterparts. Despite his southern inclinations, Magoffin warned both the Union and the Confederacy that any violation of Kentucky's neutrality would push his state into the opposing camp. Despite covert support to Kentucky Unionists, Lincoln carefully upheld the pose of neutrality, forbidding Union commanders from invading the state.

The Confederacy blundered by invading Kentucky first, the interloper being a man of the cloth, Major General Leonidas Polk. Tall with silvery hair, a broad face, and sideburns, Polk had attended West Point only to renounce his military career and become an Episcopal bishop in Louisiana. When the war started, his West Point friend Jefferson Davis lured the Fighting Bishop back into military

uniform. When Polk dispatched Brigadier General Gideon J. Pillow to seize
Columbus on the Mississippi River, in Kentucky's southwest corner, he was immediately upbraided by superiors and told to withdraw, but he had correctly
guessed that Grant planned to advance on the town, which marked the intersection of a key railroad with the Mississippi River. After Confederate forces threw
a chain across the river to obstruct navigation and installed 140 guns on its steep
bluffs, Columbus for a time constituted a more important Confederate fortress on
the Mississippi than Vicksburg itself. If taking Columbus seemed a masterstroke
from a military standpoint, it counted as a colossal political error. It destroyed any
pretense of Kentucky neutrality, incited the state legislature to a more belligerent
Unionism, and opened the way for Union forces to march into the state under a
banner of liberation.

Now free to enter Kentucky, with an irresistible opportunity to make his
mark, Grant eyed a prize much greater than Columbus: Paducah. On September 5, a Union spy imparted crucial information: Confederate forces were preparing to move on Paducah, which stood about forty-five miles northeast of
Cairo. Speed meant everything. The town lay at the juncture of the Ohio and
Tennessee Rivers, making it the perfect springboard for securing Confederate
territory. No less important, it stood near the confluence of the Ohio and Cumberland Rivers and was thus the linchpin for river traffic in the whole area. The
seizure of Paducah would also sever Confederate supply lines and isolate the
high fortifications at Columbus. Before moving on the town, Grant telegraphed
Frémont twice that he intended to launch the operation at 6:30 p.m. The deadline expired without any response from Frémont. In a high state of nervous tension, Grant delayed his start until 10 p.m. "I can wait no longer," he said at last.
"I will go if it costs me my commission!"[3] Although Grant had anticipated Frémont's wish, he acted solely on his own initiative. For a man long crippled by
doubt and stalled in his life, it was a step of breathtaking audacity, displaying
a more forceful, direct, and aggressive Grant. He herded two well-equipped
regiments and an artillery battery aboard steamers and headed up the Ohio
River, escorted by two gunboats. If this mission failed, responsibility fell on his
shoulders alone.

As he approached Paducah, he beheld a town awash with Confederate
flags in anticipation of the arrival of Confederate troops, but the quick-witted
Grant beat them to the punch and the town fell without a shot. The political
dimension of the operation proved far trickier since Grant needed to reassure a

civilian population traumatized by his advent of his peaceful intentions: "I never after saw such consternation depicted on the faces of the people. Men, women and children came out of their doors looking pale and frightened at the presence of the invader."[4]

To pacify them, Grant issued a proclamation boldly written in the first person. He cleverly assumed that he was addressing loyal people and made common cause with them:

> I have come among you, not as an enemy, but as your friend and fellow-citizen, not to injure or annoy you, but to respect the rights, and to defend and enforce the rights of all loyal citizens. An enemy, in rebellion against our common government, has taken possession of, and planted its guns upon the soil of Kentucky and fired upon our flag . . . He is moving upon your city. I am here to defend you against this enemy and to assert and maintain the authority and sovereignty of your Government and mine.[5]

For the first time, Grant demonstrated his fine political tact and a command of the English language that would assist his success. He only stayed in Paducah for a day, leaving behind strict instructions that occupying soldiers should refrain from plunder and respect the rights of residents. When Lincoln set eyes on Grant's proclamation, he was impressed. "The modesty and brevity of that address shows that the officer issuing it understands the situation and is a proper man to command there at this time."[6] Elihu Washburne touted Grant for major general, reporting to him from Washington that his Paducah actions "had attracted the attention of the President and met with his approval."[7] The combined movements of Polk at Columbus and Grant at Paducah led the Kentucky legislature to demand the expulsion of Confederate forces from the state.

Grant was buoyed by his sudden triumph. "You have seen my move upon Paducah Ky!" he wrote to Julia. "It was of much greater importance than is probably generally known."[8] It was not in Grant's nature to boast, but the reversal in his fortunes was so startling he could scarcely resist. "I suppose you have seen from the papers that I have quite an extensive and important command. It is third in importance in the country and Gen. Frémont seems desirous of retaining me in it."[9] Exuberantly confident, he asked Julia to send their son Fred to join him for the campaign. Not long after the town surrendered, Julia went to

Paducah and had a conversation that shows her speedy conversion into an ardent Unionist. She told a female resident, "It is dreadful; why, this mania for secession seems to be epidemic throughout the South." To which the woman retorted: "Mania! Mania! Madam! Epidemic! Madam! Why the whole South has gone *ravin'* mad!"[10]

After Paducah, Grant yearned to move on Columbus, but he could not obtain Frémont's approval or even elicit a reply. By November 1, he would have twenty thousand well-trained men and was eager to use them, but he had to endure a lull in the fighting. He was still frightfully busy with paperwork at Cairo, even if now helped by Rawlins and a competent staff, and he stayed up until two every morning responding to mail. On September 13, he received word that his brother Simpson had died of tuberculosis near St. Paul, Minnesota, and he was profoundly saddened. The body was shipped to his own house in Galena before the burial, which was attended by Jesse Grant and his daughters. Ulysses was too busy to join them and Jesse sent him Simpson's watch as a keepsake. "I want to preserve it to the last day of my life," Grant told Julia, "and want my children to do the same thing, in remembrance of poor Simp. who carried it in his lifetime."[11]

In late October, General Frémont took the field in Missouri against Major General Sterling Price, the former governor of the state. Grant rushed troops to help him and sent three thousand men under Colonel Oglesby to pursue M. Jeff Thompson as well. On November 5, he received word that the Confederate garrison at Columbus intended to divert troops to Price. Thus, to protect Union forces in Missouri, Grant decided to undertake an operation against Belmont, a small, muddy Missouri town with a steamboat landing that was controlled by the enemy and stood directly across the Mississippi from Columbus. Unlike other Union generals, who freely invented excuses for inaction, the restless Grant always scanned the horizon for reasons to fight. "There is but very little doubt . . . that we can hold this place," he told Julia from Cairo. "What I want is to advance."[12] At first, he was only supposed to make a "demonstration" against Belmont and Columbus—that is, harass and distract the Confederates. Then, after learning on November 6 about Frémont's dismissal, he took advantage of the momentary confusion to initiate more decisive action. After his hard knocks during the prewar period, one might have expected him to be pessimistic, cautious, and self-doubting. Instead he was becoming the most self-confident of Union commanders, perhaps needing to wipe away the stigma of earlier failures in civilian life—failures that had implanted in him a high level of motivation that no other general could quite match.

Now swinging into action, Grant poured five regiments (about three thousand men) onto four transports, accompanied by two wooden gunboats, and moved to within six miles of Columbus. The transports were so overloaded that Grant had to sleep on a deck chair on the ship. Then, at two in the morning on November 7, Grant learned that rebel troops were being ferried across the Mississippi from Columbus to Belmont—troops that might operate against Colonel Oglesby in his hot pursuit of Thompson in Missouri. (The report proved inaccurate.) When setting out from Cairo, Grant had no idea that he was about to blaze into aggressive action. But keenly attuned to the psychology of his men, he feared they had grown dangerously restive in the fetid, unhealthy atmosphere of Cairo and knew a battle would revitalize their energy.

Not long after dawn, Grant and his men sailed down the Mississippi and disembarked a few miles upstream from Belmont, on the river's west side. "The early autumnal morning was delightful," wrote Dr. Brinton. "The air fresh and invigorating, without being cold."[13] Since it would be impossible to hold terrain with Confederate guns frowning down on them across the river, Grant expected to make a lightning strike and asked his soldiers to carry a mere two days' rations in their haversacks. This was the first time Grant presided over a full army in combat, and many of his untested men were newcomers to battle. He marched them toward Belmont, guided them through clearings and dense forests, then formed them into clear lines. Once General Polk got wind of Grant's move, he swiftly parried the advance, moving five regiments to hold off the Union incursion.

Around 9 a.m., when they met enemy regiments under General Pillow, Grant's units reacted with tremendous esprit de corps. They obeyed his orders "with great alacrity," he said, "the men all showing great courage."[14] Union soldiers clambered over brush and fallen timber, chasing Confederates through the thick woods in a furiously contested fight. Buoyed by high spirits, the youthful soldiers began to fire indiscriminately at the rebels. "Stop the men," Grant yelled on horseback at Rawlins, "they are wasting ammunition."[15] Even leather-lunged Rawlins couldn't make himself heard above the din, so Grant galloped close to officers, leaned down, and hollered in their ears, "Don't fire till you see somebody, and then take good aim."[16] He didn't yet trust his subordinates or know their skills and had to perform many tasks he later delegated to others. Grant's horse was shot from under him and he swapped it for another. Swept up in the whirlwind of battle, he stayed coolheaded and composed, manifesting a fierce tenacity. He also showed he was fully prepared to share risks with his men and inspire them by his presence.

When they encountered a long line of felled trees with sharpened points—a so-called abatis—Union forces smashed through these defenses, throwing the startled rebels back against the riverbank. After four hours of torrid fighting, the rebel withdrawal broke down into a disorderly rout. Suddenly, to their astonishment, Grant's men possessed the Confederate camp, strewn with food, baggage, and artillery. This unexpected conquest was too tempting for novice soldiers and discipline collapsed on the spot. Flushed with victory, transported by powerful emotions, the men began to plunder the site for trophies, sent up cheers, declaimed premature speeches, and generally acted as if the battle had ended. Grant could not stop them from crowing over their feat, his sound strategy undone by this amateur behavior. In stopping to exult and loot the camp, his men failed to pursue the Confederates, who flocked to the riverbank and regrouped.

Soon rebels began to creep back toward the camp, this time strongly reinforced from Columbus. "I saw . . . two steamers coming from the Columbus side towards the west shore, above us, black—or gray—with soldiers from boiler-deck to roof," said Grant.[17] Faced with this ominous sight, he futilely tried to get his men to shoot at the steamers. When this failed, he ordered the camp set ablaze. No longer worried about hitting their own soldiers, Confederate cannoneers, firing from the Columbus heights, rained down shells on Grant's troops, who went from rejoicing to sheer terror as they thought themselves surrounded. They had snatched defeat from the jaws of victory. Grant stemmed the panic, recalling, "When I announced that we had cut our way in and could cut our way out just as well, it seemed a new revelation to officers and soldiers."[18] Averting disaster, he reversed the psychology of the moment, leading his men to carve out an avenue of escape and battle their way back to safety aboard their steamboat transports. Extricated from danger, petrified Union soldiers rushed pell-mell onto the waiting boats. As one mate remembered, "They rushed across [to] the other side of the boat till she listed over so that one wheel went whirling around uselessly in the air."[19]

After supervising the embarkation of wounded soldiers, Grant scouted the area on horseback, checking on guards he had posted to prevent attacks on the transports. To his surprise, the guards had fled. As he crossed a cornfield, he came within view of General Polk, who advised his riflemen, "There is a Yankee; you may try your marksmanship on him if you wish."[20] Luckily for Grant, nobody fired. The boats were about to push off when one captain, his boat's smokestack blasted with bullets, spied Grant on the steep riverbank, waiting to come aboard. For a moment it was unclear how he could do this since the boat had cut its lines and floated slightly offshore. "My horse put his fore feet over the bank without hesitation or urging," Grant wrote, "and with his hind feet well under him, slid down the bank and trotted aboard the boat, twelve or fifteen feet away, over a single gang plank."[21] It was an exquisite display of horsemanship by Grant, who characteristically credited the horse.

Grant lay down on a sofa in the captain's stateroom when he was startled by a fusillade of rebel musketry. As he went to inspect the situation, a bullet flew through the room and struck the sofa where he had just been. It was the harrowing conclusion of a day of heavy fighting. On the trip back to Cairo, the officers dined and engaged in animated discussion, while Grant, with customary sangfroid, officiated in silence at the head of the table. "We thought he was hardhearted, cold and indifferent," noted one soldier, "but it was only the difference between a real soldier and amateur soldiers."[22]

Deriving considerable pride from his troops' behavior at Belmont, Grant praised them the next day, saying he had "been in all the battles fought in Mexico, by Genls. Scott and Taylor, save *Buena-Vista,* and never saw one more hotly contested, or where troops behaved with more gallantry."[23] He had broken up the enemy camp at Belmont and unleashed the animal spirits of his men, imbuing them with lasting confidence. Indeed, Belmont damaged the mystique that Confederate soldiers were always fearless and fought to the bitter end.

After the battle, Leonidas Polk proudly informed Jefferson Davis of the "complete rout" of Union forces, transmitting an erroneous report that "General Grant is reportedly killed."[24] From a purely statistical standpoint, the bloody battle was a narrow Union victory against overwhelming Confederate numbers. Grant suffered 80 killed, 322 wounded, and 54 missing versus 105 killed, 419 wounded, and 117 missing for the rebels. Grant and Rawlins believed they had averted Confederate mischief in Missouri. "Belmont is entirely abandoned by the enemy," Rawlins wrote, "and thus the Southeastern portion of Missouri is without a rebel army."[25] As days passed and Grant heard that Memphis was plunged into mourning, its largest hotel converted into a hospital for Belmont casualties, his sense of the magnitude of his victory grew. He collected his first positive notices in the national press, *The New York Times* saluting Belmont as "in high degree creditable to all our troops concerned in it, and the success of the brilliant movement is due to Gen. Grant."[26]

On a personal level, Belmont was Grant's baptism of fire. He had shown a boldness bordering on impetuosity and a preternatural coolness under fire. He had improvised new solutions when the original battle plan went awry—a key mark of military leadership. Belmont probably removed any doubts about himself that he had carried over from civilian life. It certainly advanced his standing in Washington, where Washburne kept Lincoln minutely apprised of his achievements. On November 20, Grant informed Washburne that the Confederate loss at Belmont "proves to be greater and the effect upon the southern mind more saddening." Washburne rushed this commentary into Lincoln's hands, saying, "I want you to take a moment's time to read this letter of Genl Grant."[27] Speculation was rife that Grant would be promoted to major general. When a relative told Julia Grant that her husband should be content with a brigadier general's rank, she grew indignant. "There is no danger of his reaching a position above his capacity," she insisted. "He is equal to a much higher one than this, and will certainly win it if he lives."[28]

Grant's modest Belmont victory was not an unalloyed success. Perhaps thinking of that battle, he later observed, "In the beginning [of the war] we all did things more rashly than later."[29] He had exceeded his instructions and carried out a costly raid that neither seized territory nor captured an army. One northern officer jeered that Belmont was "called a victory, but if such be victory God save us from defeat."[30] Military historians have faulted Grant for not providing sufficient guards for transports; for failing to block the arrival of Confederate reinforcements from Columbus; and for not incorporating the two gunboats into his overall strategy. Belmont also previewed one of Grant's few salient weaknesses. Intent on his own offensive strategy, he often failed to anticipate countermoves from opposing generals, leaving him vulnerable to dramatic surprises, and Belmont was not the last time he was blindsided by the enemy.

On the same day as the Belmont battle, Julia Grant beheld in her bedroom a grave apparition of her husband that shook her to the roots. As she recounted, "I only saw his head and shoulders, about as high as if he were on horseback."[31] The wraith stared down at her in earnest reproach. Both Julia and Ulysses Grant were still avowed believers in dreams and portents. Reacting to this vision, Julia gathered up the children and left that evening for Cairo, where Grant met her at the train station. "I told him of my seeing him on the day of the battle. He asked at what hour, and when I told him, he said: 'That is singular. Just about that time I was on horseback and in great peril, and I thought of you and the children, and what would become of you if I were lost.'"[32] Julia was less than smitten with the town—"I remember how high and angry the river was and how desolate Cairo seemed"—nor was she satisfied by their house, which resembled a "great barracks."[33] She also didn't warm to the lengthy beard, cut square at the bottom, that her husband now sported, and she had him trim it closer, giving him a somewhat neater look for the rest of the war.

Grant had finally reached a plateau high enough to suit the social vanity of Julia and her family. Earlier, when Grant was sent to Mexico or posted to the western frontier, Julia and her father had criticized the military life. Now Julia's heart beat faster at waving flags and the rhythmic tread of troops on parade grounds. She was overcome by the abrupt elevation of her husband's status. "How proud I was . . . hearing the bands play 'Hail to the Chief' as *my* General rode down the columns inspecting! . . . nothing could be more interesting, more thrilling, than to see these columns of brave men in motion."[34] For the rest of the war, Julia Grant, the slave owner's daughter, would be heart and soul for the Union army.

With no major battle in the offing, Grant showed commendable zeal in ferreting out corruption and disloyalty he saw spreading around him. He believed the lower Mississippi River was crawling with steamship employees working for the Confederacy and wanted to shut down river traffic south of nearby Cape Girardeau. "There is not a sufficiency of Union sentiment left in this portion of the state to save Sodom," he declared.[35] As part of his anticorruption campaign, he ordered the arrest of the district quartermaster and his chief clerk, informing Washington that "I also had all the books and papers of the department seized and locked up in the safe and the key kept in custody of a member of my staff."[36]

A schemer all his life, Jesse Root Grant could not comprehend his son's ethical purity. Now that Ulysses could be useful to him, he professed to find new virtues in him. "I know that Ulyss was never worth anything in business," he told an associate; "it's because he's all soldier, Ulyss is."[37] First Jesse sought to exploit his son's standing to obtain a position for a friend, sending Ulysses into a rage. "I do not want to be importuned for places," he protested. "I have none to give and want to be placed under no obligation to anyone."[38] Next his father sought help in landing a Union army contract to furnish harnesses. "I cannot

take an active part in securing contracts," Grant lectured his father. "It is necessary both to my efficiency for the public good and my own reputation that I
should keep clear of Government contracts."[39] As Grant cracked down on illicit
trade between northern merchants and southern suppliers, his father lobbied for
a commercial pass for yet another friend. "It is entirely out of the question to pass
persons South," he told him in exasperation. "We have many Union Men sacrificing their lives now from exposure, as well as battle . . . and it is necessary for
the security of the thousands still exposed that all communication should be cut
off between the two sections."[40] Jesse Grant never quite grasped that his incorruptible son refused to be a party to his self-interested schemes.

ON NOVEMBER 19, 1861, Major General Henry W. Halleck succeeded Frémont as commander of the renamed Department of the Missouri, which also
encompassed western Kentucky and Arkansas. Frémont had fallen victim to
corruption allegations as well as Lincoln's emphatic displeasure with his ill-
timed emancipation proclamation. The rest of the western command, including
Tennessee and the rest of Kentucky, would now fall to the Department of the
Ohio under the command of Don Carlos Buell. In Washington, the military
boy wonder, thirty-four-year-old George B. McClellan, had superseded the aging Winfield Scott to become field commander of the Army of the Potomac and
the youngest general in chief in American history. The conservative McClellan
stressed to Halleck that the war was being fought solely to preserve the
Union and had nothing to do with freeing slaves. As a result, Halleck banned
fugitive slaves from Union camps under his command and Grant duly obeyed.

Halleck was a pudgy, odd-looking fellow with a high forehead, balding pate,
heavy eye pouches, and bulging, slightly crossed eyeballs. Because of his gog-
gle eye, he often seemed to stare over the shoulder of interlocutors. A brusque,
crotchety loner, he often offended people with his peevish remarks. He gave off a
strangely uncouth air. One journalist portrayed him as a "short countrified
person . . . who picked his teeth walking up and down the halls at Willard's
[Hotel], and argued through a white, bilious eye and a huge mouth."[41] Lincoln's
secretary John Hay mocked Halleck's uniform as "a little white at the seams, and
seedy at the button-holes," and said he had "a stooped and downward glance."[42]

Halleck had worked as a corporation lawyer and mining expert in San Francisco before the war. Even those who disliked him admired his erudition. By the

Civil War, he had left behind a rich trove of writing on warfare and international law. His textbook *Elements of Military Art and Science* was virtually required reading at West Point, and he had also translated from French into English a four-volume biography of Napoleon. So daunting was his knowledge of military lore that when he was later dubbed "Old Brains," the nickname stuck.

Unluckily for Grant, Halleck was strictly an armchair, by-the-book general. Steeped in the theory of war, he lacked Grant's visceral instinct for fighting. Halleck was a soldier in his brain, whereas Grant was a soldier in his marrow. By nature a spectator, Halleck was the sort of military bureaucrat who preferred to keep a safe distance from the battlefield. He severely punished army infractions and kept a tight rein on subordinates. He carped at generals in a way that offended rather than motivated them. At first taken with him, Lincoln came to view Halleck as a paper-pusher who ducked tough decisions in the field. Hay later encapsulated Halleck's conduct by saying he "hates responsibility; hates to give orders," while Secretary of the Navy Gideon Welles groused that he "suggests nothing, is good for nothing."[43] Such insights still lay in the future, however, and for the moment Halleck was riding high, winning the admiration of Grant, Sherman, and other generals.

The overworked Grant worried that Halleck would ditch him in favor of a personal favorite. "I am somewhat troubled lest I lose my command here," he confided to his father, "though I believe my administration has given general satisfaction not only to those over me but to all concerned."[44] While proud of his men's hard-earned discipline, he found himself bogged down in minutiae. He was short on transportation, grumbled about inferior uniforms, and protested the dated flintlock muskets he received. "Eight Companies are entirely without arms of any description," he complained.[45] Grant persisted in his crusade against profiteering, annulling overpriced contracts that added up to 30 percent to prices paid by the government. Instead of sweetheart deals, he favored open, competitive bidding.

Grant's honesty won him a host of business enemies who sought revenge by any means. One disaffected contractor was Captain William J. Kountz, hired by the government to buy, charter, and operate boats for transporting troops on the Ohio River. Thirty-one Cairo boatmen protested his appointment, claiming "a more unpopular man with all classes of boatmen, could not have been se-lected."[46] Grant suspected irregularities in Kountz's handling of this business, and after a violent argument, he and Rawlins tossed the quarrelsome captain

from the room. On January 14, 1862, Grant ordered Kountz's arrest for "disobe-
dience of orders and disrespect to his superior officer."[47]

After fourteen days stewing in the brig, the venomous Kountz retaliated
against Grant with blistering charges about his allegedly drunken behavior. After Belmont, Grant had met his Confederate counterparts aboard a steamer,
under a flag of truce, to work out burial arrangements for dead soldiers and
prisoner exchanges. During one such meeting, Kountz declared, Grant became
"by the use of intoxicating liquors . . . beastly drunk."[48] Writing to Washington,
Kountz laid down sensational charges. He accused Grant of "drinking with traitors and enemies to the Federal Government, while under a Flag of Truce"; of
"occupying the cook's room on a Government Steamer while under a Flag of
Truce, and vomiting all over the floor"; and of "getting drunk at the St Charles
Hotel and losing his sword and uniform." He further accused Grant of visiting
a drunken "Harlot" at her private hotel room; drunkenly attending a "Negro
Ball" with aides; and getting "so drunk that he had to go up stairs on all fours,
conduct not becoming a man."[49] Kountz demanded an investigation, if not a
court-martial, of Grant. Grant was never investigated and thought it best not to
dignify such vitriol with a response. One Grant colleague scoffed at the allegations: "I saw [Grant] after he came back from Belmont, he was sober as a judge."[50]

It is tempting to write off Kountz's allegations as the baseless ravings of a vindictive man. While there is clearly a large element of grotesque exaggeration in his
statements, they loosely conform to a pattern of wartime drinking charges against
Grant. These sporadic episodes often occurred in the aftermath of large battles
when Grant could afford to relax and take short side trips and when neither Rawlins nor Julia was present. The Kountz charges find echoes in a letter by William
Bross of the *Chicago Tribune,* a passionate Lincoln supporter, to Secretary of War
Simon Cameron. On December 30, 1861, two weeks *before* Kountz's arrest, Bross
wrote "that Gen. U.S. Grant commanding at Cairo is an inebriate . . . The inclosed anonymous letter would not deserve a moment's attention, were [there] not
facts abundant from other sources that what the letter writer says is true."[51] The
anonymous writer accused Grant of "being perfectly inebriate under a flag of
truce with rebels."[52] The writer also detected grumbling in Cairo about Julia
Grant bringing a slave into camp: "Until we can secure pure men in habits and
men without secesh [secessionist] wives with their own little slaves to wait upon
them, which is a fact here in this camp with Mrs. Grant, our country is lost."[53]

Bross's warning landed on the president's desk. On January 4, Lincoln penned atop it: "Bross would not knowingly misrepresent. Gen. Grant was appointed chiefly on the recommendation of Hon. E. B. Washburne—Perhaps we should consult him."[54] The war secretary forwarded the letter to Washburne, who needed no prompting in the matter. He had just received a message from Benjamin H. Campbell of Galena, who had heard similar reports of Grant drinking on a recent trip to St. Louis. "I am sorry to hear from good authority that Gnl [*sic*] Grant is drinking very hard, had you not better write to Rawlins to know the fact."[55] Washburne dashed off a concerned letter to Rawlins, inquiring about "liquor drinking in high places."[56]

In reply, Rawlins stated in an outraged tone that he was "astounded at the contents" of Washburne's note. "I would say unequivocally and emphatically that the statement, that 'Genl. Grant is drinking very hard' is utterly untrue and could have originated only in malice. When I came to Cairo, Genl Grant was as he is today, a strictly total abstinence man, and I have been informed by those who knew him well, that such has been his habit for the last five or six years."[57] He noted Grant's extraordinary productivity as a commander—he even wrote his own reports—and said an intemperate man could never accomplish this. Rawlins provided a detailed account of every drop of liquor Grant had touched. Because of stomach trouble, a physician had prescribed two glasses of ale or beer daily, but Grant had never exceeded that amount. Rawlins also mentioned that Grant drank with visiting friends at the St. Charles Hotel—a detail mentioned by Kountz—"*but in no instance* did he drink enough to manifest it, to any one who did not see him drink." Grant had also enjoyed half a glass of champagne with a visiting railroad president, but right after that "he voluntarily stated he should not during the continuance of the war again taste liquor of any kind."[58]

Rawlins concluded his message with a melodramatic flourish:

> No one can feel a greater interest in General Grant than I do; I regard his interest as my interest . . . I love him [as] a father, I respect him because I have studied him well, and the more I know him the more I respect & love him. Knowing the truth, I am willing to trust my hopes of the future upon his bravery & temperate habits . . . I say to you frankly and I pledge you my word for it, that should General Grant at any time become a [*sic*] intemperate man or an habitual drunkard, I will notify you immediately, will ask to be removed from duty on his staff (kind as he has been to me) or resign my commission.[59]

Already Rawlins functioned as Grant's protector as well as watchdog. Before sending the reply to Washburne, he showed it to Grant, who perused it closely. "Yes, that's right; exactly right," he told Rawlins. "Send it by all means."[60] A month later, William Rowley waded into the controversy, asserting to Washburne that anyone who accused Grant of becoming dissipated was "either misinformed or else he lies. [Grant] is the same cool, energetic and unassuming man that you supposed him to be."[61]

In general, Julia Grant avoided any mention of her husband's drinking, although she noted the confrontation between Grant and Captain Kountz in her memoirs: "Of course, Captain Kountz was very angry and at once proclaimed broadcast that General Grant and his staff were all drunk."[62] Despite the varied drinking anecdotes about Grant, they possess one common denominator: Julia Grant was absent when they supposedly happened. Late in life, Grant told Mrs. Leland Stanford how Julia had cured him of drinking. Once, when they were traveling together, a friend had sent him a small keg of fine whiskey, which he stood on a washstand. As Mrs. Stanford related the tale: "That night the General was awakened by a noise, and found that Mrs. Grant was up. Asked what the gurgling noise was, she told him that she had drawn the stopper and was letting the whiskey run down the drainpipe to prevent him from drinking it. He declared this cured him of the habit."[63]

On December 23, 1861, Grant notified his troops that he now headed the new District of Cairo, which would encompass southern Illinois, some southern Missouri counties, and western Kentucky. Though he was swamped with paperwork, his real passion lay in planning future battles. His troops were now fully outfitted, and he marveled at the size of the army under his aegis. "I have now a larger force than General Scott ever commanded prior to our present difficulties," he told his sister. "I do hope it will be my good fortune to retain so important a command for at least one battle."[64] His command now extended to the mouths of the Tennessee and Cumberland Rivers in northwest Tennessee, two large tributaries of the Ohio River that would enable him to infiltrate the Confederacy. To exploit this required close coordination with the navy and Grant would benefit from the steadfast cooperation of Flag Officer Andrew Hull Foote, who supervised the gunboat flotilla.

Born in New Haven, Connecticut, Foote had dark hair, a piercing eye, a clean-shaven upper lip, and a full beard. He was a faithful member of the Congregational Church whose piety spilled over into his political views. He hated slavery and had patrolled the African coast years earlier as part of a navy campaign against the slave trade. On Sunday mornings he offered sermons on his ships. No less than Grant, he detested swearing. The puritanical Foote was forever on the warpath against drinking, having years earlier extracted temperance pledges from men on his ships. With his blunt, salty manner, he was the perfect navy counterpart to Grant, sharing his aggressive instincts and preferring to take the war to the enemy. In the absence of smooth institutional arrangements between the army and the navy early in the war, Foote and Grant managed to forge a harmonious working relationship.

In the fall of 1861, Foote dispatched a reconnaissance mission to ascertain Confederate defenses along the Tennessee and Cumberland Rivers. Despite potent Union sentiment in its eastern portion, Tennessee had seceded in June. The Confederate general Albert Sidney Johnston had to defend a long east-west line that stretched from Missouri to Bowling Green, Kentucky, to the Cumberland Gap. The two parallel rivers represented the soft underbelly of his defensive shield. As a result, the Confederacy hastily constructed Fort Henry on the east bank of the Tennessee and Fort Donelson on the west bank of the Cumberland, twin fortresses a dozen miles apart. The capture of one fort might quickly topple the other, and Johnston fretted about their exposed condition, inadequate manpower, and unfinished state. Though he sensed a catastrophe in the making, he felt powerless to stop it in time, despite a multitude of rushed warnings to subordinates.

Johnston worried for good reasons. Control of Fort Henry would create a river pathway for Union forces, laying bare a broad swath of rebel territory as far south as Muscle Shoals, Alabama. Control of Fort Donelson would render Nashville vulnerable to Union forces. After General Charles F. Smith made a demonstration against Fort Henry, he returned to Grant on January 22 with a hopeful verdict for an assault: "I think two iron clad gun-boats would make short work of Ft. Henry."[65] Grant required little convincing: "Well, if it can be taken," he declared, "it should be without delay."[66]

Contemplating his next action, Grant chafed at Halleck's hidebound style. On January 6, he had requested permission to travel to St. Louis to see Halleck and present plans for the conquest of Forts Henry and Donelson, but not until January 23 did he secure permission for a four-day visit. Halleck had an "abrupt, brusque style," according to William Tecumseh Sherman, and lost no time treating Grant in patronizing fashion, making clear who stood higher in the military hierarchy.[67] Short-tempered, impatient, he shook Grant's hand coldly, resumed his seat, and told Grant to "state briefly the nature of the business connected with your command which brought you to headquarters." Unfurling a map, Grant showed how twenty-five thousand men, backed up by gunboats, could grab the two riverside forts. Halleck, having none of this, rudely interrupted him: "Is there anything connected with the good of your command you wish to discuss?" When Grant returned to his map, Halleck brushed him aside. "All of this, General Grant, relates to the business of the General commanding the department. When he wishes to consult you on that subject he will notify you."[68] Having pulled rank, Halleck stormed from the room while Grant stood nursing his wounds. "I was cut short as if my plan was preposterous," he wrote. "I returned to Cairo very much crestfallen."[69]

In his *Memoirs,* Sherman gave Halleck credit for having already mapped out the general move against the Tennessee forts a month earlier, but Grant insisted he was first to spot the precise point of Confederate vulnerability: "My mind was made up from the time I went to Cairo—before Halleck assumed command of the Dept.—where that point was."[70] However impeccable in preparation, Halleck was slow and lumbering in execution and did not appreciate the rapid tempo, daring decisions, and assertive nature of his gifted subordinate. He also fancied himself the authority on grand strategy, condescending to Grant as a lowly upstart. Historian John F. Marszalek suspects that Halleck viewed Grant through the lens of his troubled past in the antebellum army. "Halleck knew all about Grant's reputation for having had a prewar drinking problem in California, and unfounded rumors had reached Washington that Grant had recently fallen off the wagon. Grant's unkempt appearance did not help either."[71]

While Grant was in St. Louis, he stopped by White Haven, a plantation now depleted by runaway slaves, for a turkey dinner with Colonel Dent, who was in a more hospitable mood than previously. As they ate, Grant narrated for him the Belmont battle. A large contingent of Confederate sympathizers lurked in St. Louis and had formed an organization to funnel aid to rebels. One member had suggested kidnapping Grant and hauling him farther south as a valuable prisoner. It was testimony to Grant's popularity during his St. Louis years that the leaders rejected the idea.

Back in Cairo, Grant conferred with Foote, who concurred in his plan to take Fort Henry. The two men decided to renew their entreaty for a bold move to Halleck, and Grant sent off a startling one-line telegram that exuded supreme confidence: "To Major General Halleck: With Permission I will take Fort McHenry on the Tennessee and hold & establish a large camp there."[72] Grant's words were effective because of their extreme economy. On the same day, Foote sent a telegram to Halleck contending that troops, escorted by four ironclad gunboats, could seize the fort. Grant believed a prompt attack stood an excellent chance of success and that delay would permit the Confederates to shore up the fort's shoddy defenses.

To the surprise of Grant and Foote—Rawlins even banged his fist in spontaneous celebration—Halleck endorsed the campaign on January 30: "Fort Henry should be taken & held at all hazards."[73] The letter contained the principal reason for Halleck's sudden about-face: he had received startling intelligence from Washington that P. G. T. Beauregard, accompanied by fifteen regiments, was marching from Manassas to Kentucky to strengthen the lengthy defensive line that Halleck, Grant, and Foote wished to pierce. The intelligence proved mistaken—Beauregard was heading there alone, not with troops—but the error proved fruitful for Grant.

In addition to news about Beauregard, Halleck may also have felt pressure from Lincoln, who was annoyed by jockeying for position between Halleck and Buell and the resulting inaction. "Delay is ruining us," Lincoln warned both generals. "It is indispensable for me to have something definite."[74] After receiving a dispatch from Halleck making excuses for his lethargy, Lincoln poured out his frustration to Quartermaster General Montgomery Meigs. "General, what shall I do? The people are impatient . . . The bottom is out of the tub. What shall I do?"[75] Lincoln read the riot act to his generals, ordering that "Land and Naval forces" ought to move "against the insurgent forces" by Washington's Birthday on February 22.[76] Among the forces specified for action were the "Army and Flotilla at Cairo."[77] The new war secretary, Edwin Stanton, also hungered for action and had become disillusioned with the do-nothing McClellan, whose grandiosity concealed deep insecurity. Stanton wrote internally that "as soon as I can get the machinery of office going, the rats cleared out, and the rat holes stopped, we shall *move. This army has got to fight or run away; . . . the champagne and oysters on the Potomac must be stopped.*"[78]

Brimming with confidence, Grant prepared to take Fort Henry, employing fifteen thousand men and nine gunboats under Flag Officer Foote. He proceeded with a secrecy that became a trademark of his operations, confiding in the fewest number of people. Even Grant's commanders were kept in the dark until the last moment. "I am quietly making preparations for a move," he alerted Halleck, "without as yet having created a suspicion even that a move is to be made."[79] Striving to perfect a new style of swiftly mobile warfare, he planned to have the whole army travel lightly and elected to dispense with cumbersome baggage trains as well as cavalry for the high command.

In general, Grant operated free from immediate oversight by Halleck, but the latter planted a spy with a mission to function as his eyes and ears. Halleck appointed Lieutenant Colonel James Birdseye McPherson of Ohio, thirty-three, as the expedition's chief engineer, and he arrived with Halleck's instructions to Grant. After graduating first in his West Point class, McPherson had overseen fortifications on Alcatraz Island off San Francisco. If Halleck had intended to keep watch on Grant's rumored drinking, the plan soon boomeranged, for the bearded young McPherson quickly shifted loyalty to his new boss. Smart and handsome, he had an unusually keen grasp of military affairs and a farsighted look of shrewdness in his eyes. He also had a pleasing way with people, and Grant soon viewed him as one of the finest gentlemen he had ever encountered. From the outset, Grant predicted McPherson "would make one of the most brilliant officers in the service" and came to regard him as a virtual member of his family.[80]

When he boarded his flagship at Cairo on February 2 to commence the Fort Henry campaign, the ordinarily imperturbable Grant seemed edgy, eager to overrun the fort before it was reinforced. Timing was always critical in his missions. Fearing that Halleck, at the last moment, might revoke his orders, he kept stealing backward glimpses at the wharf as his boat departed, as if a message might suddenly detain him. When Cairo disappeared behind him, Grant was so relieved that he cuffed Rawlins on the shoulder—Grant seldom behaved with such genial familiarity—and exclaimed, "Now we seem to be safe, beyond recall . . . We will succeed, Rawlins; we must succeed."[81]

On the rainy morning of February 3, 1862, Grant set off up the Tennessee River from Paducah, Kentucky, toward Fort Henry, leading a fearsome flotilla of four ironclad and three wooden gunboats that protected twenty-three regiments of Illinois, Indiana, and Iowa volunteers, who stood packed on transports. The new ironclads, designed by James B. Eads, rode low in the water, presenting a spectacle never seen before. They had thick armor plates welded to the bow and tilted sides to deflect flank shots. These humpbacked monsters were surprisingly nimble, with thirteen guns apiece mounted on top. They proceeded with extreme precaution down a perilous river swimming with mines called "torpedoes" or "infernal machines," which could blow even ironclads to smithereens. These devices bobbed unseen below the surface, each packed with seventy-five pounds of powder, and Foote's sailors delicately swept up and defused eight of them before they exploded. Luckily the swollen river put the boats beyond the reach of many submerged mines tethered to the river bottom in fixed positions.

Always curious about new technology, Grant asked the ship's armorer to bring him a defused mine plucked from the river. When the man obliged, the device started to give off a threatening hiss at which point several bystanders threw themselves flat on the deck or dove into the water. Grant and Foote bolted helter-skelter up the ship's ladder. When they reached the top, both felt a trifle foolish and Foote inquired with a smile, "General, why this haste?" "That the navy may not get ahead of us," Grant replied drolly.[82] By then the menacing hiss had ceased.

By next morning, Grant had landed an entire division under Brigadier General John A. McClernand at a spot three miles below Fort Henry. Grant's force was so large that once the transports were emptied, he sent them steaming back to Paducah to bring forward the remaining troops under General Smith. He wanted to place his men at a staging area that offered quick access to Fort Henry yet lay beyond the reach of its seventeen powerful guns. For surprised Confederates at Fort Henry, smoke curling from the boats alerted them to the abrupt approach of danger. "Far as the eye could see," one wrote, "the course of the river could be traced by the dense volumes of smoke issuing from the flotilla."[83] Brigadier General Lloyd Tilghman, the Confederate commander, hunkered down inside the fort instead of trying to disrupt Grant's landing.

To figure out the range of Fort Henry's guns, Grant didn't leave matters to a team of officers, but showed personal bravery and involvement. He boarded the gunboat *Essex,* joined by two other gunboats, and the three ships crept slowly toward Fort Henry until they drew fire, establishing the precise trajectory of rebel weapons. "One shot passed very near where Captain [William] Porter and I were standing, struck the deck near the stern, penetrated and passed through the cabin and so out into the river," Grant wrote.[84] Afterward, aboard the steamer *Uncle Sam,* Grant sent Julia a letter that gave a fine snapshot of his excited, self-assured state of mind. "The enemy are well fortified and have a strong force," he informed her. "I do not want to boast but I have a confident feeling of success. You will soon hear if my presentiment is realized."[85]

Fort Henry's location represented a colossal miscalculation by the Confederates, for its natural features gave the advantage to attacking forces. When the river was swollen with rain, as now, buoyant enemy ships actually gazed *down* on its earthworks. As one Confederate captain put it, "We had a more dangerous force to contend with than the Federals—namely the river itself."[86] Portions of the fort's low, outlying grounds were submerged in two-foot puddles. It had been a harebrained scheme to place a fort in this unsafe spot. Tilghman's men had to defend a five-sided structure with antiquated weaponry that included hunting rifles brought by soldiers from their farms and flintlock muskets reminiscent of bygone wars. Many of the fort's heavy guns had to be retired because they blew up in preliminary tests or lacked suitable ammunition.

Grant's strategy for seizing Fort Henry was simple but effective. Foote and his gunboats would first pummel the Confederates at close quarters. On the high ground opposite Fort Henry stood another thinly manned Confederate work called Fort Heiman. Grant would have General Smith and two brigades sneak up behind Heiman and occupy it. At the same time, General McClernand and an infantry division would envelop Fort Henry from behind, bottling up its defenders and preventing them from scampering to safety at nearby Fort Donelson.

Perhaps nothing highlighted Grant's meteoric rise more than the fact that one of his main commanders, General Charles F. Smith, had been Commandant of Cadets when Grant attended West Point, having instructed him in infantry tactics. A stately figure with blue eyes and a handlebar mustache, Smith was a gentlemanly soldier and Grant remained awed by his regal presence. He held Smith in such reverence that he found it hard to act as his superior. "It does not seem quite right for me to give General Smith orders," Grant admitted.[87] "General, I am now a subordinate," Smith said graciously. "I know a soldier's duty. Pray, feel no awkwardness whatever about our new relations."[88] Instead of resenting that he had to answer to Grant, Smith reciprocated the high regard of his former cadet, fondly remembering him from academy days "for his modesty, superior horsemanship, and proficiency in mathematics."[89] He scoffed at stories about Grant's drinking as fables. "The public are all astray about Genl *Grant:* his habits (drink) are unexceptionable."[90]

On the night of February 5, 1862, Grant was stirred by the beautiful sight of Union campfires flickering on both sides of the Tennessee River. He issued orders for the attack against Fort Henry at 11 a.m. the next day, even though he was not absolutely certain that all his infantry would arrive in time. As always, Grant rated speed and timing as more important than having every soldier in perfect position. That he expected his army to roll over the enemy swiftly was apparent from his field order: "The troops will move with two days rations of bread and meat in their haversacks."[91] That night, heavy rains soaked the soldiers, many of whom slept outdoors without tents to shelter them.

By the next day, rainy weather had transformed footpaths into bogs, impeding an infantry advance. At around 11 a.m., four ironclads began the journey toward Fort Henry, while three timberclads hung in the rear. Grant began to write orders so expeditiously that his hand ached. The orders were terse, hard-hitting. All seven of Foote's ships unleashed maximum firepower on the rebels, who responded with deafening fire, scoring eighty hits on Union ships and inflicting special damage on Foote's ironclad flagship. Undeterred, Foote kept the remaining three ironclads roaring ahead, firing with prodigious ferocity. By the time they approached within three hundred yards of Fort Henry, they had created such havoc inside the fort that Tilghman ran up a white flag. It had taken Foote's fleet little more than an hour to snuff out Confederate batteries, and Tilghman surrendered with his staff and ninety other men. Once inside the fort, the Union men stared in amazement at the horrifying damage they had wrought, with "mangled bodies, arms and legs and brains scattered all around," said a junior officer from Illinois.[92] Foote's boats had prevailed over the fort's primitive artillery while Grant's infantry still lagged in the rear, mired in mud and threading their way through dense forests. One infantryman probably spoke for many in saying that they "really felt sore at the sailors for their taking of the fort before we had a chance to help them."[93]

The sailors had performed the lion's share of the work and by the time Grant arrived at 3 p.m., the Union flag had already fluttered above the fort for almost an hour. It was a stunning victory for new naval technology, mobilized by an old infantryman, U. S. Grant.[94] Tilghman told Grant he had evacuated almost his entire garrison—some 2,500 of a total of 2,600—to Fort Donelson, leaving a skeletal crew of 100 men to stave off Union forces and allow time for these soldiers to escape. Other accounts claim that rebel defenders yielded to panic under fire, fleeing of their own accord. Setting his style for the rest of the war, Grant was mild-mannered in victory, although when he met Confederate officers, they felt the steely core beneath the surface. Captain Jesse Taylor, who greeted Grant on behalf of Tilghman, appraised him as "a modest, amiable, kind-hearted but resolute man."[95] Grant magnanimously invited the Confederate officers to join his staff for meals aboard the steamer he had tapped as his headquarters.

Taking Fort Henry was a spectacular breakthrough. "Fort Henry is ours," Halleck telegraphed to McClellan. "The flag of the Union is re-established on the soil of Tennessee. It will never be removed."[96] The North reacted ecstatically, the news feeding unreasonable hopes that the war might be wrapped up in short order. "A few more events such as the capture of Fort Henry," the *New York Tribune* predicted, "and the war will be substantially at an end."[97] Fort Henry served as a tonic to Lincoln's flagging spirits. As naval officer Henry Wise reported to Foote from Washington, "We all went wild over your success . . . Uncle Abe was joyful, and said everything of the navy boys and spoke of you—in his plain, sensible appreciation of merit and skill."[98] Spirits sagged correspondingly in Confederate circles. Albert Sidney Johnston was dismayed by the severe damage done to his defensive line, informing his Richmond superiors that Fort Donelson was "not long tenable."[99] After debating whether to withdraw altogether, Johnston made a fatal, halfhearted decision, sending only twelve thousand men to Fort Donelson to withstand Grant's advance.

Once Grant made short work of Fort Henry, he was ready to do the same for nearby Fort Donelson. On February 10, he gathered officers aboard his steamer for a rare council of war. In general, Grant avoided such meetings, believing the fewer people privy to a secret, the better its safety, but this time he made an exception. "The question for consideration, gentlemen, is whether we shall march against Fort Donelson or wait for reinforcements," Grant announced. "I should like to have your views."[100] As each officer spoke, Grant puffed meditatively on a meerschaum pipe while Rawlins stared hard, sizing up each speaker. For anybody who knew Grant's nature, it was certain that he would opt for immediate action instead of tarrying to await reinforcements. If he allowed his fellow officers to air their views, in the end he consulted his own intuitions. True to form, Grant concluded by telling his officers to be ready to move at a moment's notice, a position they unanimously endorsed.

In the flush of victory, Halleck still meditated what the Confederates might do to Grant, rather than what Grant might do to them. He chose to regard Grant as a rival and a threat rather than as a valued extension of his own power and secretly connived to replace Grant with another general. "Hold on to Fort Henry at all hazards," he notified Grant. "Impress slaves of secessionists in vicinity to work on fortifications."[101] It was a perfect example of the timid, static thinking favored by a desk-bound general beset by fears. With perhaps a touch of sarcasm, Grant told Halleck that "there are no Negroes in this part of the Count[ry] to work on Fortifications."[102] Never one to look back, his self-confidence growing daily, Grant had little time for Halleck's instinctive caution. His style as a commander—scrappy, mobile, opportunistic—was maturing. With his sights set on Fort Donelson, he wanted to maintain the winning tempo of his campaign, to "keep the ball moving as lively as possible," as he phrased it.[103] He had developed a bracing self-reliance as a commander and had learned, if necessary, to operate on his own. "General Halleck did not approve or disapprove of my going to Fort Donelson," Grant later wrote. "He said nothing whatever to me on the subject."[104]

CHAPTER NINE

////////////////////////////////

Dynamo

ESPITE HIS IMPLACABLE WILL, Grant stood under no illusions
that Fort Donelson on the Cumberland River would succumb as easily
as its sister fort on the Tennessee. The Cumberland commanded river
traffic to nearby Nashville, a regional entrepôt for many agricultural and manufacturing goods, boosting dramatically the fort's strategic value. "Fort Donelson
is a very strong point naturally and an immense deal of labor has been added to
strengthen it," Grant told his brother Orvil.[1] Unlike Fort Henry, Donelson stood
on high, dry ground, towering more than a hundred feet above the river in spots.
While the term "fort" conjures up a fortress, Fort Donelson consisted more of an
extensive series of earthworks. It bristled with heavy guns staggered at different
elevations and deeply planted in niches scooped from the bluff, enjoying unobstructed views of gunboats rounding a distant bend. It had miles of ramifying
trenches and its seventeen thousand men were well equipped with arms and provisions. Finally, its rolling topography was punctuated by streams, gullies, and
ravines that seemed to make it impregnable.

For days after Fort Henry's fall, Grant was detained by a downpour that
churned roads into mud, slowing the passage of wagons and artillery. He also
awaited the arrival of the all-important gunboats, which had to travel a circuitous 150-mile water route while his infantry only needed to traverse 12 overland
miles. Once again, Grant demanded firsthand knowledge of the terrain, scouting it himself. On February 7, he organized a cavalry reconnaissance group that
approached within a mile of Fort Donelson's defensive perimeter. He profited

from prewar knowledge of Confederate commander Gideon J. Pillow and "judged that with any force, no matter how small, I could march up to within gunshot of any intrenchments he was given to hold . . . I knew that [John B.] Floyd was in command, but he was no soldier, and I judged that he would yield to Pillow's pretensions."[2] On his personal survey, Grant discovered two roads by which his troops could approach the fort safely.

Amid his preparations, Grant wrote a revealing letter to his sister Mary that attests to his burgeoning confidence and dreamlike rise in the world: "You have no conception of the amount of labor I have to perform. An army of men all helpless looking to the commanding officer for every supply. Your plain brother however has, as yet, had no reason to feel himself unequal to the task and fully believes that he will carry on a successful campaign against our rebel enemy."[3]

Once again Grant hatched battle plans of immaculate simplicity. His infantry would pin down the Confederates while Foote's trusty gunboats strafed their cannon at close range. On February 11, Foote sent Grant the message he longed to hear: "I shall be ready to start tomorrow evening with two Boats."[4] The next day, boasting an army fifteen thousand strong, Grant set out for Fort Donelson in balmy, nearly summery, weather. "River, land, and sky fairly shimmered with warmth," one Union general said.[5] As skies cleared and ridge roads turned dry, Grant's men marched east with unfettered good spirits, singing lustily. When the horse of surgeon John Brinton darted impetuously ahead of him, Grant joked aloud, "Doctor, I believe I command this army, and I think I'll go first."[6] In unseasonably warm weather, some men stripped off their overcoats and chucked them by the wayside along with blankets.

To Halleck's dismay, instead of strengthening Fort Henry as a base to which he could scramble back in safety, the audacious Grant had broken loose and wagered everything on conquering Fort Donelson. He again showed a glandular optimism that his boss could scarcely fathom. Reflecting his gathering confidence, he wired Halleck: "I hope to send you a despatch from Fort Donelson tomorrow."[7] The next day, as he besieged the fort and awaited gunboats, Grant sounded less jaunty than when he pounced on Fort Henry. A small shadow of doubt suddenly tempered his words. Writing to Julia on February 13, he reported that at least a dozen of his soldiers had been killed and 120 wounded that day in skirmishes. "We have a large force to contend against but I expect to accomplish their subjugation. Do not look for it for three days yet however."[8] Until more gunboats and troop transports came along, he was outnumbered by rebel

soldiers inside the fort. That night, to his relief, Foote steamed into the Cumberland with four ironclads and two wooden gunboats while transports brought
needed reinforcements. To bolster his forces, Grant summoned 2,500 men left
behind at Fort Henry.

Those improvident soldiers who had cavalierly dumped coats and blankets
by the roadside regretted their decisions on the night of February 13, 1862. The
mercury plummeted to twelve degrees as the area was pelted by snow. Grant,
nursing a cold, slept in a feather bed in a modest log farmhouse, but his soldiers,
within range of enemy muskets and lacking sufficient tents, lay down in the cold
with weapons tightly clutched at their sides. To worsen matters, Grant had to
forbid campfires that might draw enemy fire. "At midnight I noticed some of the
men who had blankets lying on the ground completely covered with snow and
you would think they were dead if it was not for their breath like little puffs of
steam," said an Illinois officer.[9] The men of the Twelfth Iowa, to avoid frostbite,
ran around in endless circles.

On the afternoon of February 14, Flag Officer Foote, barking orders into a
megaphone, came up the Cumberland with his entire gunboat fleet: four black
ironclads surged ahead, trailed by two wooden ships. Grant took up position
along the shore with a clear view of the naval attack as the Confederates girded
for withering fire from the river. "Parson, for God sake pray!" Confederate cavalry commander Nathan Bedford Forrest beseeched a staff officer who was a
minister in civilian life. "Nothing but God Almighty can save that fort."[10]

Foote was far more sober about his prospects, knowing that the downward
angle of fire from the high batteries at Fort Donelson could inflict massive damage on his ironclads. He compounded the problem by sailing too close to the
fort, making the plunging fire still more destructive. With ear-piercing sounds,
the garrison's big guns crashed through the gunboat armor—"as lightning tears
the bark from a tree," said one captain—and raked smokestacks with deadly
fire, demolishing pilothouses.[11] In the meantime, Foote's gunners widely over-
shot their marks. So many shells sprayed down on the Union fleet that every
ironclad took at least forty hits, producing fifty-four Union casualties. Even
Foote, inside the pilothouse of his flagship *St. Louis,* received solid shot in the
ankle and thought he had never withstood such a punishing bombardment. As
Grant watched, the badly battered fleet began to drift back down the river after
ninety minutes of tempestuous conflict. Confederate soldiers sent up huge
cheers while their leaders hastened to telegraph news of victory to Richmond.

At Fort Henry, gunboats had wrapped things up before the hapless soldiers even arrived. At Fort Donelson, the situation was reversed with the army now bearing the burden. As a rule, Grant did not like soldiers to build fortifications, which he thought sapped their fighting spirit, but he now contemplated a prolonged siege. "I retired this night not knowing but that I would have to intrench my position, and bring up tents for the men or build huts under the cover of the hills."[12] That night soldiers again suffered cruelly from a snowstorm that blanketed their camps, producing a bizarre incident: when rough winds flung icicles from tree branches, the Confederates mistook this for an attack and started firing madly.

That night, the three main Confederate generals huddled inside Fort Donelson. Grant had strong opinions about all three. John B. Floyd of Virginia was the war secretary under James Buchanan who had transferred arms from the North to southern arsenals to prepare the South for war—a notorious action Grant deemed treasonous. He thought Gideon J. Pillow proud and conceited. He still felt warmly toward his old West Point classmate Simon Bolivar Buckner, who had rescued him financially in Manhattan in 1854. Buckner was now third in command at the fort, though he was "much the most capable soldier."[13] Later explaining why he dared to confront a larger Confederate force at the fort, Grant said: "Of course there was a risk in attacking Donelson as I did, but I knew the men who commanded it. I knew some of them in Mexico. Knowledge of that kind goes far toward determining a movement like this."[14] The comment again speaks to Grant's command of the psychology of battle.

Despite the wreckage of Union gunboats that afternoon, the three generals recognized their desperate plight. Foote still dominated the river, Grant hemmed in the fort on the land side, and they would be squeezed to death in a vise as the siege was perfected. Things would deteriorate as more Union troops descended, tightening the stranglehold. In a high-stakes decision, Pillow and Buckner agreed to hazard a surprise attack on the Union right the next morning, slashing a hole through it, then trying to make a run for safety in Nashville.

At about 2 a.m. on February 15, Foote, still incapacitated by his ankle injury, urgently requested a meeting with Grant aboard the savaged *St. Louis*. At dawn Grant rode to the river through a bleak landscape of frozen turf and advised his three commanders—McClernand, Smith, and Lew Wallace—to refrain from aggressive action in his absence. During his conference with Grant, Foote said he wanted to take all his wounded ships back to Cairo for repairs, but Grant prevailed upon him to take only two and keep the rest at Fort Donelson for a few more days. Around noon, Grant returned to shore and was immediately met by his aide William Hillyer, who looked "white with fear," recalled Grant.[15] Following their plan, the Confederates had furiously broken from the fort, pounded the Union right under McClernand, inflicted heavy losses, and provoked a full-blown Union retreat. Because the wind had blown in the wrong direction, Grant had missed the extraordinary racket of the conflict, which sounded "as if a million men were beating empty barrels with iron hammers," in Lew Wallace's image.[16] Always better at plotting his own moves than at anticipating enemy reactions—he could sense weakness better than strength—Grant had been caught by surprise, but now assumed personal charge of the situation.

Biting on the stub of a cigar Foote had given him, Grant spurred his horse for seven miles over icy terrain and found McClernand and Wallace in a clearing. When Grant arrived, Wallace recollected, his face "already congested with cold, reddened perceptibly and his lower jaw set upon the other. Without a word, he looked at McClernand."[17] Grant found dazed, demoralized men milling about aimlessly. McClernand's men had fought gallantly until their ammunition ran out, but had suffered from an absence of effective leadership. Taking a dig at Grant, McClernand snarled, "This army wants a head," to which Grant shot back, "It seems so."[18] Grant worked off his upset by crumpling paper balls in his palm. Then he delivered a calm but forceful line that reflected his determination. "Gentlemen, the position on the right must be retaken."[19] Wallace admired how Grant conducted himself. "In battle, as in camp, he went about quietly, speaking in a conversational tone; yet he appeared to see everything that went on, and was always intent on business."[20]

Grant devised an ingenious way to gauge enemy intentions. Since rebel soldiers had barreled out of Fort Donelson carrying haversacks, he inspected the gear of captured soldiers and saw that they carried three days' cooked rations. Some officers interpreted this as proof that the Confederates meant to stand and fight. Grant begged to differ, deducing correctly that "they mean to cut their way out," but "they have no idea of staying here to fight us."[21] Typically for Grant, he focused on enemy defects, not on his own. Unlike other Union generals who magnified rebel power to imaginary proportions, Grant's knowledge of his foes demystified them. Perhaps from his own background of failure, he was always attuned to the mentality of defeat. "Some of our men are pretty badly demoralized," he told a staff officer, "but the enemy must be more so, for he has attempted to force his way out but has fallen back; the one who attacks first now will be victorious, and the enemy will have to be in a hurry if he gets ahead of me."[22] Once again Grant showed a predilection for taking the offensive. Coordinating all facets of battle, he ordered his stricken gunboats to throw shells at the fort at long range, giving at least moral support to his men on the ground. He also rallied McClernand's men. "Fill your cartridge-boxes, quick, and get into line; the enemy is trying to escape and he must not be permitted to do so." In Grant's memory, "This acted like a charm."[23]

Grant read the enemy perfectly. He saw that Pillow had not only intended to break out and escape but failed to capitalize on the momentary confusion of McClernand's division. This convinced Grant the other side was disoriented and vulnerable. After seeing the casualties his exhausted men suffered, Pillow concluded that a breakout to Nashville was too risky. Over Buckner's anguished protest, he ordered his men to retreat to the fort's defenses, throwing away the morning's dearly won victory. Realizing this, Grant redoubled his efforts to counterattack. Assuming that Confederate strength on the Union right meant corresponding weakness on the Union left—an insight he exploited repeatedly in later battles—he ordered General Smith to attack the Confederates on that side, predicting he would encounter only "a very thin line to contend with."[24] During the afternoon, galloping across the battlefield, Grant recouped the positions yielded to Confederates that morning. Smith performed with special brilliance, overrunning a ridge that formed part of the enemy stockade.

For Grant it had been a day of bloody triumph. As usual, he didn't whoop with delight over enemy losses. At dusk, riding back to headquarters through fields littered with frozen corpses, he came upon a wounded Union lieutenant sprawled next to a Confederate private. Grant dismounted, got a flask of brandy, and impartially gave a swig to each man. He immediately had Rawlins summon stretcher bearers, but was dismayed when they removed the Union officer and overlooked the Confederate private. "Take this Confederate, too," he said. "Take them both together; the war is over between them."[25] Grant seemed sickened by the carnage. "Let's get away from this dreadful place," he told an officer. "I suppose this work is part of the devil that is left in us all." As Grant watched a parade of bandaged warriors trudging by, one aide heard him softly recite verse from Robert Burns: "Man's inhumanity to man / makes countless thousands mourn."[26] It was uncommon for Grant to quote poetry, especially upon the battlefield.

Eager for a certifiable victory, Lincoln followed events at Fort Donelson with mounting apprehension. "Our success or failure at Donelson is vastly important; and I beg you to put your soul in the effort," he urged Halleck.[27] Without fanfare or prompting from Lincoln, Grant was taking the decisive measures the president wanted, while George McClellan procrastinated with his large, well-accoutred army in the East.

On the night of February 15, with things looking bleak, Confederate commanders sorted through their shrinking options. While Floyd and Pillow, the ranking officers, vowed never to surrender, the Union army now blocked any escape route to Nashville. Buckner, the third-ranking officer, thought it the height of folly to try to smash through Union lines and predicted that three-quarters of their men would perish in such a suicidal mission and that no general "had the right to make such a sacrifice of human life."[28] Because Floyd feared being captured and tried for treason, he and Pillow decided to flee that night and enacted a curious transfer of power. "I turn the command over, sir," Floyd told Pillow. "I pass it," Pillow told Buckner. "I assume it," Buckner said.[29] Contrary to chivalric traditions beloved by the South, Floyd and Pillow were selfishly abandoning their men, while Buckner, instilled with a deep sense of soldierly honor, refused to desert them. Floyd and Pillow fled by water to Nashville while Nathan Bedford Forrest and his cavalry slipped out by an unguarded stream. It therefore fell to Buckner to surrender and he showed exceptional courage in doing so, knowing he would be reviled throughout the South for surrendering an entire Confederate army for the first time.

In the early hours of February 16, under a flag of truce, a Confederate emissary delivered Buckner's letter to General Smith, who took it to the farmhouse where Grant lay on a mattress on the floor. Smith handed him the letter, saying, "There's something for you to read General." Buckner requested a formal armistice with commissioners appointed to negotiate terms of surrender. "What answer shall I send to this, General?" Grant inquired of Smith, who answered categorically: "No terms to the damned Rebels!"[30] With that, Grant sat down at the kitchen table and composed a classic statement in American military history. In lapidary prose, he wrote: "Sir; Yours of this date proposing Armistice, and appointment of commissioners, to settle terms of capitulation is just received. No terms except an unconditional and immediate surrender can be accepted. I propose to move immediately upon your works."[31] When finished, Rawlins said, Grant raised his eyes to his old West Point instructor, gave him the letter, and said drily, "General, I guess this will do." Smith agreed. "It could not be better."[32]

Buckner was taken aback by Grant's harsh terms, which struck him as ungentlemanly, and he reluctantly replied that "the overwhelming force under your command, compel me . . . to accept the ungenerous and unchivalrous terms which you propose."[33] A modern general, Grant retired outmoded forms of chivalry, showing that gentility had given way to a stark new brand of modern warfare. He did not soften his words in deference to past friendship with Buckner and delivered a powerful military message instead. In conventional warfare, Buckner would have been entitled to the preliminary armistice and negotiation of surrender he requested, but Grant believed the South had conducted an illegal rebellion and wasn't entitled to enjoy the niceties of military etiquette.

Shortly after dawn, Grant rode across a snowy landscape, past rebel lines that sprouted white flags, to meet Buckner at the Dover Hotel. This low frame building, with an unpainted double row of porches, lay right by the Cumberland River, where it provided a stopping place for travelers. The meeting between Grant and Buckner surely had a fairy-tale quality. The last time Buckner, with his broad swarthy face and handlebar mustache, had seen Grant in 1854 the latter was sad and broke after departing in disgrace from the army. Now Grant was the victorious Union general at the zenith of his career to date. Despite their stiff exchange of messages, Grant and Buckner turned warmly companionable in person, as befit old friends.

After their greetings, Grant asked why Pillow had fled. "Well, he thought you would rather have hold of him than any other man in the Southern Confederacy." "Oh no," Grant smirked. "If I had got him I'd let him go again; he will do us more good commanding you fellows."[34] Grant and Buckner, both veterans who remembered Pillow from Mexico, shared a good laugh at this caustic remark. Grant liked to tell stories of how Pillow once dug a ditch on the wrong side of his breastworks or described himself as "cut down by grape shot" when a bullet grazed his foot.[35] During this friendly banter, Buckner said that if he had been in command, Grant would not have approached Fort Donelson so readily. "I told him that if he had been in command I should not have tried in the way I did," Grant recalled.[36] In his personal dealings with Buckner, Grant showed the gratitude missing from their official communications. "After I became his prisoner Grant tendered me the use of his purse," recalled Buckner. "I did not accept it, of course, but it showed his generosity and his appreciation of my aid to him years before, which was really very little."[37]

Grant had captured an army of at least thirteen thousand men, a record on the

North American continent. He showed mercy toward the conquered force, giving them food and letting them keep their sidearms. Avoiding any show of celebration, he refused to shame defeated soldiers and vetoed any ceremony in which they marched out of Fort Donelson and stacked their arms. "Why should we go through with vain forms and mortify and injure the spirit of brave men, who, after all, are our own countrymen," he asked.[38] In treating the sick and wounded, he made no distinction between federal and Confederate troops and prevented the indignity of having souvenir hunters scavenge trophies from the battlefield.

In the wake of Fort Donelson, Grant's behavior toward fugitive slaves signaled a shift. Aligned with new national policy, he rebuffed attempts by masters to seek runaway slaves in his camps, although he still prohibited slaves from finding sanctuary with his army. On the other hand, he refused to return two hundred slaves captured at Fort Donelson who had worked on Confederate fortifications and enlisted them instead as "contraband" of war to cook, handle horses, and perform other jobs. "We want laborers, let the negroes work for us," he announced to Buckner.[39] This momentous first step looked forward to the recruitment of former slaves as full-fledged Union soldiers.

Grant comprehended the historic nature of his victory. With Julia, he struck a jubilant tone. "Dear Wife I am most happy to write you from this very strongly fortified place, now in my possession, after the greatest victory of the season. Some 12 or 15 thousand prisoners have fallen into our possession to say nothing of 5 to 7 thousand that escaped in the darkness of the night last night. This is the largest capture I believe ever made on the continent."[40] To Congressman Washburne, he portrayed Fort Donelson as "a battle that would figure well with many of those fought in Europe where large standing armies are maintained."[41]

Without major victories elsewhere that winter, the North's attention became fixated on the splendid triumph at Fort Donelson, curbing a defeatist psychology that had begun to take hold. Sherman said that in America's "hour of its peril," Grant had "marched triumphant into Fort Donelson. After that none of us felt the least doubt as to the future of our country."[42] Governor Yates described the pandemonium that broke out in Illinois as thousands gathered "on the roads and at the stations, with shouting and with flags."[43] Church bells chimed, grown men embraced, people burst into patriotic songs. The celebration in Chicago lasted a full day. As the *Chicago Tribune* reported, "Chicago reeled mad with joy . . . Such events happen but once in a lifetime, and we who passed through the scenes of yesterday lived a generation in a day."[44]

This first major Union victory bestowed instant fame on Grant, who became the war's first certified hero. Rocketed to stardom—*The New York Times* affirmed that Grant's *"prestige* is second now to that of no general in our army"— he leapt to the front pages of newspapers across America.[45] In homage to his message to Buckner, Grant was endearingly dubbed "Unconditional Surrender Grant," a nickname that tallied nicely with his initials. With the public famished for details about him, one reporter obliged by saying that Grant's face had three characteristic expressions: "deep thought, extreme determination, and great simplicity and calmness."[46] He was such a fresh celebrity that when the *New-York Illustrated News* ran a photo of him, it mistakenly showed a beef contractor from Illinois named William Grant. The U. S. Grant legend began taking shape as papers identified him as someone who personified the American heartland, a folksy character partial to homespun speech. "I was so brought up," Grant explained, "and if I try fine phrases I shall only appear silly."[47] He was a superior version of the ordinary American and the public loved it. As a general, he epitomized the fighting soldier, bashful and self-effacing, who went about his grim business without any self-aggrandizement.

Amid this Grant mania, many newspaper readers noted that in reports of the final day's fighting at Fort Donelson, Grant was holding a cigar—the one he received from Foote. Until that point, Grant had been primarily a pipe smoker. Now admirers flooded him with "boxes of the choicest brands" of cigars "from everywhere in the North. As many as ten thousand were soon received."[48] Before long, Grant smoked eighteen to twenty cigars a day and they became an inescapable part of his persona. While many people characterized him as even-tempered, the compulsive smoking bespoke a deeper tension bottled up inside him. "Smoking seemed to be a necessity to General Grant's organism," said Ely Parker, who "noticed that he smoked the hardest when in deep thought, or engaged in writing an important document."[49] The gift of so many cigars bred an ultimately fatal addiction.

One person unimpressed by Grant's victory was his father-in-law. Not long after the Confederate capitulation, Dr. William Taussig was out driving with Grant's friend John Fenton Long when they ran into Colonel Dent at a crossroads. Long made the mistake of alluding to the famous victory at Fort Donelson, and Colonel Dent erupted in anger. "Don't talk to me about this Federal son-in-law of mine. There shall always be a plate on my table for Julia, but none for him."[50]

Within a week of Fort Donelson's downfall, Grant heard from his young favorite, Colonel James B. McPherson, who was in St. Louis and described Halleck's joyous reaction to the news. "Genl. Halleck is exceedingly gratified and says you could not have done better—Immediately on the receipt of the news he telegraphed to the President to nominate you for a *Major General.*" Then referring to drinking allegations against Grant, McPherson added, "You will not be troubled any more by *Kountz.*"[51] In the wake of Fort Donelson, rumors about Grant's drinking subsided, and his friend J. Russell Jones wrote sarcastically to Washburne, "Grant made a pretty fair fight for a Drunken man."[52] Sherman saw Fort Donelson as proof that Grant had mended his ways from prewar army days, telling his brother that "Grant's victory was most extraordinary and brilliant— he was a plain unostentatious man, and a few years ago was of bad habits, but he certainly has done a brilliant act."[53]

Stanton rushed over to Lincoln bearing Grant's nomination as Major General of Volunteers, catapulting him ahead of every western general except Halleck. The president signed the order at once and commended the western spirit of Grant's army, pointing out that "if the Southerners think that man for man they are better than our Illinois men, or western men generally, they will discover themselves in a grievous mistake."[54] The comment previewed the special affinity between Grant and Lincoln as the war progressed. Those in the know in Washington were amused by efforts by McClellan partisans to present him as the mastermind of Fort Donelson. Stanton observed tartly that the image of a heroic McClellan, ensconced at the telegraph office in the capital, "organizing victory, and by sublime military combinations capturing Fort Donelson *six hours after* Grant and Smith had taken it," made for "a picture worthy of *Punch.*"[55]

After being promoted to major general, Grant thought back on all the doubts about his military ability conveyed to him by his busybody father and clearly felt vindicated by his performance. "Is father afraid yet that I will not be able to sustain myself?" he asked Julia sardonically, saying Jesse had "expressed apprehensions on that point when I was made a Brigadier."[56] Grant had now proved himself beyond a shadow of a doubt and would never again have to truckle to his father or father-in-law.

BY SEVERING THE EXTENDED DEFENSIVE LINE that Albert Sidney Johnston had constructed from Bowling Green to the Mississippi River, Grant's conquests at Forts Henry and Donelson carved open huge chunks of Confederate territory, enabling the North to command Kentucky, western and central Tennessee, and portions of the Mississippi Valley, while driving a wedge into Alabama and the Deep South. "'Secesh' is now about on its last legs in Tennessee," Grant informed Julia.[57] In an analysis published in Vienna, Karl Marx predicted accurately that the loss of so much territory in Kentucky and Tennessee would threaten the Confederacy's integrity.[58] The South now had to abandon its key fortress on the Mississippi at Columbus. As a result of his defeats at the twin forts, Johnston was knocked off his high pedestal in the South and subjected to scathing denunciations. Nonetheless, Jefferson Davis remained loyal to him in the teeth of a clamor to cashier him.

Grant's military philosophy called for following up on victories before the enemy had time to recuperate. He blamed Halleck's inertia and internal squabbling in the Union army for squandering a major opportunity to exploit the Fort Donelson victory. Had he been able to join his forty-five thousand men with thirty-five thousand under Don Carlos Buell, the united force could have damaged the Confederate army. As Grant later wrote, "If one general who would have taken the responsibility had been in command of all the troops west of the Alleghenies, he could have marched to Chattanooga, Corinth, Memphis and Vicksburg with the troops we then had . . . Providence ruled differently. Time was given the enemy to collect armies and fortify his new positions."[59]

Commanding the new District of West Tennessee and still basking in Fort Donelson's afterglow, Grant headed east along the Cumberland River to take the town of Clarksville, the first time the Union army had regained seceded territory in the larger Department of the Missouri. Union soldiers were cheered by the black populace, while whites largely deserted the town. As Grant's ascendant star brought new personal scrutiny, the drinking issue inevitably resurfaced. In the Virginia theater of war, Stephen M. Weld heard from his commander, General Fitz-John Porter, that Grant was "a man of great energy and a laborious worker, but the general says that he cannot be depended upon. He is just as likely to be drunk in the gutter as to be sober."[60] Such scurrilous rumors circulated freely in western Tennessee as well. As Grant's army approached Clarksville, rumors cropped up that a drunken Grant could not contain his rowdy troops, and a local committee of safety, anticipating his arrival, poured large quantities of whiskey on the ground.[61]

With his army controlling the Cumberland, Grant thought taking the next stop, Nashville, "would be an easy conquest," and Halleck backed his plan enthusiastically.[62] Even in Clarksville, Grant heard reports that the statehouse in Nashville had been abandoned, its legislators hurrying off to Memphis. After Fort Donelson's downfall, Nashville residents were affected by southern propaganda that portrayed the Yankee soldiers as vulgar brutes; now these same vandals were marching straight to their defenseless town. Even as General Buell approached Nashville from the north, Grant sent William "Bull" Nelson—a brash six-foot-five general weighing three hundred pounds—to beat him there, and Buell was bitter at being denied the glory of conquering the first Confederate capital. Federal authorities recognized Andrew Johnson as the new military governor of Tennessee.

On February 27, Grant entered Nashville and held an uneasy meeting with the aggrieved Buell. Like Grant, Buell was a West Point graduate and highly decorated Mexican War veteran whose taste for combat had been tempered by years in the adjutant general's department. Buell feared the Confederates would soon try to recapture Nashville. Grant thought they were fleeing the area as fast as they could, and he wanted to resume the offensive. He was soon proved right: Confederate troops beat a hasty retreat south to the important railroad center at Corinth in northern Mississippi. Once again, Grant rightly anticipated enemy intentions, reading fear and flight where the bullheaded Buell descried aggression. Nonetheless, in Buell Grant had made a powerful enemy who stood in the good graces of George McClellan.

While Grant suffered from a severe cold and headache that sapped his energy, the balding, jowly Halleck was working steadily to undermine him in brazen disregard of Grant's new heroic stature. Fancying himself Fort Donelson's hero, Halleck tried to capitalize on Grant's victory by seeking power from Washington to command all western armies. He gave credit to Foote and Smith and attempted to deny it to Grant. He resented that, in the recent crop of new major generals, Grant would outrank both Buell and John Pope and be second in authority to him in the western theater. Halleck also faulted Grant for being a slipshod general who did not heed proper bureaucratic forms. Halleck had been reprimanded by McClellan for sending insufficient information about his forces and he passed on the blame to Grant. He ordered him to provide daily reports on the number and disposition of his forces and was outraged by a sudden, mysterious halt to these updates. Instead of waiting for Grant to explain this hiatus, Halleck devised a malevolent interpretation: willful neglect. Even as Grant hungered to advance against Confederate forces, Halleck summoned up an absurd fantasy of him complacently leaning back and coasting on his laurels. As he told McClellan:

> I have had no communication with General Grant for more than a week. He left his command without my authority and went to Nashville . . . It is hard to censure a successful general immediately after a victory, but I think he richly deserves it. I can get no returns, no reports, no information of any kind from him. Satisfied with his victory, he sits down and enjoys it without any regard to the future.[63]

Privy to prewar gossip about Grant's alcohol abuse, he wrote again to McClellan and, with thinly veiled innuendo, depicted Grant as a drunkard. "A rumor has just reached me that since the taking of Fort Donelson General Grant has resumed his former bad habits. If so, it will account for his neglect of my often-repeated orders. I . . . have placed General Smith in command of the expedition up the Tennessee. I think Smith will restore order and discipline."[64]

McClellan's draconian response to his first telegram must have shocked even Halleck:

> Your dispatch of last evening received. The future success of our cause demands that proceedings such as Grant's should at once be checked. Generals must observe discipline as well as private soldiers. Do not hesitate to arrest him at once if the good of [the] service requires it, & place CF Smith in command.[65]

Both Halleck and McClellan, having been upstaged by Grant, were determined to knock him down. Their grossly unfair and shocking treatment of him bespeaks settled malice instead of sound military judgment. Neither man bothered to give Grant the benefit of the doubt or await his explanation.

There was no truth about Grant drinking during the preceding weeks. On March 20, Colonel Joseph D. Webster of Grant's staff wrote home of this charge: "It is a vile slander, out of whole cloth. During all my acquaintance with him I have never seen him drinking anything intoxicating but once, & then he put a little brandy into some medication to disguise the taste."[66] Halleck may have been deflecting attention from his own persistent problems with alcohol. Later on, Assistant Secretary of War Charles A. Dana told Rawlins, "The testimony of those best informed says that Halleck's mind has been seriously impaired by the excessive use of liquor and that as [a] general thing it is regularly muddled after dinner every day."[67] The surgeon John Brinton remembered Halleck as "fond of good living, and of good wine . . . After dining, he was often sleepy."[68] The diarist George Templeton Strong walked away with this impression of Halleck: "His silly talk was conclusive as to his incapacity, unless he was a little flustered with wine."[69] Halleck was to die of chronic heart and liver disease.

Grant had been innocent of insubordination and had faithfully filed daily reports of his troop strength. Hence, he reacted with "utter amazement" when he received the following dispatch from Halleck on March 4: "You will place Maj. Genl C.F. Smith in command of expedition, & remain yourself at Fort Henry. Why do you not obey my orders to report strength & positions of your command?"[70] Grant reassured Halleck about his daily reports, to no avail, and, in despair, asked to be relieved from command. "I have done my very best to obey orders . . . If my course is not satisfactory remove me at once."[71] Halleck made plain that in dealing with McClellan, he had been embarrassed by a shortage of information; Grant would pay the price. With tears in his eyes, a perplexed and deflated Grant showed Halleck's dispatch to a fellow officer. "I don't know what they intend to do with me . . . What command have I now?"[72]

After Fort Donelson Grant started to appreciate what he meant to the Union war effort. "I began to see how important was the work that Providence devolved upon me."[73] It was a rare allusion to a religious meaning of his work. Yet at this moment, implausibly, he was "virtually in arrest and without a command."[74] The staggering reversal of fortune was profoundly hurtful to a man who had recently escaped such misery in his life. It later turned out the telegraph operator at Cairo, who forwarded telegrams to Halleck in St. Louis, was a rebel spy and had not transmitted Grant's dispatches. Not until March 3 did Grant receive Halleck's dispatch of February 16, asking for daily reports of his combat readiness.

Isolated at Fort Henry with a small garrison, Grant was crushed by the abrupt loss of faith in him. He could never seem to savor good fortune without fresh troubles appearing. Lacking in guile, he was stunned to encounter it in those who specialized in it. Halleck treated him in the patronizing manner he had known in the 1850s when he did not yet possess the supreme confidence, born of repeated success, to resist it. The dispiriting sequel to Fort Donelson must have made him feel he would never shake off the ill luck that had bedeviled him in antebellum years. It was as if the dark, powerful undertow of the past always tugged him backward, forcing him to relive ancient misery.

During this impasse, Grant was heartened by a rousing message of support from John A. McClernand and his staff that put his strange purgatory in perspective: "You have slain more of the enemy, taken more prisoners and trophies, lost more men in battle and regained more territory to the Union than any other leader."[75] Grant spent his confinement aboard the flagship *Tigress,* which lay anchored in the Tennessee River off Fort Henry. One friend who visited him saw how despondent the outcast commander was. "No one was on board but a watchman and Grant; not a damned soul beside. He was the most disconsolate looking man you ever saw and he was mad too. Grant said, 'This is no time for red tape; this is a time for war. Halleck has arrested me for a breach of red tape.'"[76]

Another man who would repeatedly rescue Grant from the doldrums was William Tecumseh Sherman. During the Fort Donelson siege, Sherman had been assigned to forward supplies to Grant from Smithland, at the mouth of the Cumberland River. Grant had been favorably impressed by the way Sherman, his senior in rank, rushed him whatever he needed.

The bond between the two men was to become the war's most consequential military friendship. About six feet tall, weighing less than 150 pounds, the lanky Sherman had close-cropped reddish hair, a stubble beard, and a leathery, pocked face that perfectly expressed his hard-bitten nature. He was a restless, jittery character, who carried more nervous energy than his lean body could contain, his sharp eyes flashing with emotion. With surplus verve, he paced, smoked, stroked his beard, and fiddled with his coat buttons. Like Grant, he was a compulsive smoker plagued by stress-induced headaches. He had an overly active mind that always simmered with strong opinions, and sarcastic asides poured forth in rapid utterance. He dabbled in watercolors, attended the theater, and quoted liberally from Shakespeare and Dickens. Passionate in his hatreds, he directed withering scorn at the world's follies. In his stern morality, he saw a purity in soldiers that civilians could never match. Whether people liked or detested him, they found Sherman a fascinating figure, a human dynamo who never rested.

For all his rough-hewn character, Sherman came from a refined background, born into a well-to-do family in Lancaster, Ohio. His father, who named him after the Shawnee chief Tecumseh, was a state Supreme Court justice. He died when William was nine, and the boy was taken into the home of Thomas Ewing, a U.S. senator who saw to it that he entered West Point. Sherman ended up marrying Ewing's daughter Ellen, by which point Thomas Ewing was interior secretary. The wedding sparkled with political luminaries: Daniel Webster, Henry Clay, Thomas Hart Benton, and President Zachary Taylor attended.

After graduating from West Point and serving in the army, Sherman resigned in 1853 to become a banker in the freewheeling San Francisco that so mesmerized Grant. His exposure there to crooked politicians and corrupt journalists left him with a lasting distaste for both professions. Sherman steered his bank ably through the 1857 panic, but suffered heavy personal losses. Beleaguered by asthma and insomnia, he wound up his bank. In 1859 he became head of a new military college in Louisiana, the Louisiana State Seminary of Learning and Military Academy, which opened soon after Lincoln's election. Although Sherman loved southern culture, he deplored secession as a treasonous act and threatened to resign if Louisiana seceded. One professor remembered that when Sherman read of Louisiana's secession proclamation in a local newspaper, "he cried like a child, exclaiming, 'My God, you Southern people don't know what you are doing! . . . There can be no *peaceable secession*. Secession means war.'"[77] Sherman foresaw that northern determination and technical superiority would annihilate the South and he felt duty-bound to resign a position he adored.

Becoming president of a horse-drawn trolley line in St. Louis, he enjoyed a ringside seat for the virulent conflict there between Confederate and Union sympathizers. In May 1861, he was appointed an infantry colonel and by July led a brigade at Bull Run. No less than Grant, Sherman was prone to depression and viewed northern missteps with consternation. In October 1861, he believed that while Frémont and McClellan were lavishly funded and supplied with men, Kentucky remained a low priority and was starved by Washington. When he confidentially told war secretary Cameron that two hundred thousand troops would be needed to suppress the rebellion in Kentucky, it leaked to the press and Sherman was branded "insane." Relieved from duty on November 13, 1861, he tumbled into a deep depression, even flirting with suicidal thoughts. He was still being stigmatized as thoroughly unhinged when he was assigned to serve under Halleck, who gave him a second chance. This providential move brought Sherman into direct contact with Grant.

Both Grant and Sherman were damaged souls who would redeem tarnished reputations in the brutal crucible of war. They were both haunted men, tough and manly on the outside, but hypersensitive to criticism, and they sustained each other at troubled moments. Even though Sherman was more prolix and irascible than Grant, their letters display generosity, trust, and mutual admiration. As one of Grant's officers wrote, "In all the annals of history no correspondence between men in high station furnishes a nobler example of genuine, disinterested personal friendship and exalted loyalty to a great cause."[78]

Sherman spent decades pondering the mystery of Grant's personality. "He is a strange character," he wrote. "Nothing like it is portrayed by Plutarch or the many who have striven to portray the great men of ancient or modern times."[79] While never as talkative as Sherman, Grant opened up to him and even confided in him about his drinking problem. "We all knew at the time that Genl. Grant would occasionally drink too much," said Sherman. "He always encouraged me to talk to him frankly of this and other things and I always noticed that he could with an hour's sleep wake up perfectly sober and bright, and when anything was pending he was invariably abstinent of drink."[80] With facetious overstatement, Sherman once remarked, "He stood by me when I was crazy and I stood by him when he was drunk, and now, sir, we stand by each other always."[81]

Perhaps the strongest link between the two men resulted from a shared outlook about how to wage war. They both exhibited a bold fighting spirit, preferred to take unexpected actions that flustered the enemy, and hated to be on the defensive. Each complemented the other's work. Not surprisingly, the literate Sherman was better read in military texts. "I am a damned sight smarter man than Grant; I know a great deal more about war, military history, strategy, and grand tactics than he does."[82] But whereas Sherman dwelled on what the enemy might do, Grant was often more fearless and flexible in carrying out his own plans. As Sherman admitted, Grant "knows, he *divines,* when the supreme hour has come in a campaign of battle, and always boldly seizes it."[83] In an unsurpassed tribute, Sherman said, "Grant is the greatest soldier of our time if not all time."[84] Grant was no less enamored of Sherman's dauntless skill. "Sherman is not only a great soldier, but a great man," he later affirmed. "He is one of the very great men in our country's history."[85] But such accolades lay far in the future.

By mid-March, Grant had emerged from the limbo to which Halleck had consigned him. Either Grant or Rawlins, or the two together, had sent Washburne copies of the correspondence between Grant and Halleck, and Washburne promptly brought them to the attention of the White House. Fuming over chronic stalling by George McClellan, Lincoln could not afford to sacrifice a general who took the initiative and had won an unbroken string of major victories in the West. The president was astute in reading Halleck and sized up the situation. In consequence, Stanton had Lorenzo Thomas, adjutant general of the army, dispatch a sharply worded order to Halleck, asking him to back up his charges against Grant. He indicated that he wrote at the direction of Lincoln and Stanton, showing that Grant now had friends in high places and could not be browbeaten.

Two other developments changed Halleck's mind about Grant. On March 11, Lincoln removed McClellan as general in chief, reducing his authority to just the Army of the Potomac. This meant Halleck no longer had the cover of a superior general patently hostile to Grant. At the same time, Lincoln brought together the armies in Tennessee and the Mississippi Valley under Halleck's command, making him head of a new Department of the Mississippi with the authority over western armies he craved. For the moment, Halleck's envious instincts were appeased by success. As a result, he replied to Lorenzo Thomas in a sweetly reasonable tone, stating that Grant had never been insubordinate and that all "irregularities have now been remedied."[86] Without admitting to having instigated the trouble, Halleck informed Grant: "Instead of relieving you, I wish you, as soon as your new army is in the field, to assume immediate command, & lead it onto new victories."[87] Unlike his suspicious staff, Grant had been blind to Halleck's machinations. He was still a newcomer to bureaucratic games, never having occupied a significant organizational position before the war. He naively assumed that Halleck had been his champion and did not learn the truth about his duplicitous drinking insinuations to McClellan until after the war. For the moment, still unaware of the true situation, Grant told Julia that he regarded Halleck as "one of the greatest men of the age and there are not two men in the United States who I would prefer serving under to McClellan & Halleck. They would be my own choice for the positions they fill if left to me to make."[88]

CHAPTER TEN

A Glittering Lie

W**ITH THE FALL OF FORTS HENRY** and Donelson, the next logical step for the Union army was to sail up the Tennessee River and take Corinth in northern Mississippi, near the Tennessee border. The town served as a crossroads for two major railroads that connected the Mississippi River with the Atlantic Ocean, and its capture would pave the way for vanquishing Memphis, Vicksburg, and broad swaths of the Deep South.[1] "What you are to look out for I cannot tell you but . . . your husband will never disgrace you nor leave a defeated field," Grant assured Julia. "We have such an inside track of the enemy that by following up our success we can go anywhere."[2] Now fully restored to action, he scented "a big fight" in the offing. "I have already been in so many [battles] that it begins to feel like home to me."[3] In northeast Mississippi, Albert Sidney Johnston was consolidating a giant force of fifty to sixty thousand troops. To counter this, Henry Halleck fashioned a strategy that would merge Grant's army with that of Don Carlos Buell in a race to see which army could first attain critical strength and assault the other.

On March 17, 1862, Grant resumed his command in Savannah, Tennessee, and awaited the arrival of Buell's forces from Nashville. His old West Point commandant, General Charles F. Smith, had preceded him, locating his headquarters in a roomy brick mansion atop a bluff, owned by Union sympathizer William H. Cherry. Although Halleck had assigned credit for the Fort Donelson victory to Smith and plotted to advance him ahead of Grant, Smith knew nothing of his wiles and retained an abiding respect for his former pupil. He was a big enough man that he did not care to be promoted over Grant's head through any injustice. "General Smith was delighted to see me and was unhesitating in his denunciation of the treatment I had received," wrote Grant, who was protective of Smith.[4] When the seasoned commander was accused of drinking during the Fort Donelson campaign, "Grant did not hesitate to resort to the most arbitrary measures to prevent the spread of such reports," wrote an officer, declaring such stories a lie.[5] In a freakish accident, Smith had scraped his leg while stepping into a boat and it became dangerously swollen and infected. When Grant arrived, the older man had been confined to an upstairs bedroom and limped about, unable to mount a horse or slide on a boot.

Grant had begun to move his men into position at an old steamboat stop on the Tennessee River known as Pittsburg Landing that lay twenty miles from Corinth and stood near a tiny Methodist meetinghouse, crafted from rough-hewn logs, called Shiloh. (An Old Testament name meaning "place of peace," Shiloh was the place of Jewish worship before the First Temple.) The other staging area for the proposed thrust into Mississippi was Crump's Landing. Grant was powerfully attached to his Army of the Tennessee, which he now thought capable of wonders. It was created in his own image: sturdy, earthy, and gritty with men who reciprocated his affection. Colonel Walter Gresham of Indiana wrote admiringly of Grant: "The grasp General Grant then exhibited in the teeth of the incompetency of Halleck and the inefficiency in the War Department stamped him, at least in the eyes of his subordinates, as a man of force and genius."[6]

To keep his men tough and nimble, Grant again made a fateful decision *not* to have them grab spades and dig entrenchments. He did not expect to stay long in the area, hoping to march south when Buell arrived. Colonel James B. McPherson defended Grant's decision, citing the many creeks and ravines that wound through the thick woods and meadows, providing natural defenses. Early in the war, generals tended to resort to fortifications infrequently; as casualty counts soared to horrifying levels, they turned more to earthworks. Each day, as new soldiers disembarked from steamers in cold, damp weather, they were hastily assembled into companies and regiments. Under such circumstances, Grant argued, "the troops with me, officers and men, needed discipline and drill more than they did experience with the pick, shovel and axe."[7]

Characteristically viewing the campaign as offensive in nature, Grant remained so wedded to this muscular approach that he suffered from a certain tunnel vision, blinding him to threats launched by the other side. In fine spirit after weeks of poor health, he saw the battle shaping up as one that would allow federal troops to strike a decisive blow and maybe squash the rebellion for good. He was encouraged by local men enlisting in the Union army and derived false comfort from reports of low enemy morale divulged by Confederate deserters. As he breezily told Halleck, "The temper of the rebel troops is such that there is but little doubt but that Corinth will fall much more easily than Donelson did."[8]

At the forthcoming battle, Grant would confront Confederate commanders who matched his aggressive spirit. Late at night on April 2, Pierre G. T. Beauregard sent word to Albert Sidney Johnston: "Now is the moment to advance, and strike the enemy at Pittsburg Landing."[9] Aware that Grant would shortly be reinforced by Buell, the Confederates decided to pound him hard before this union occurred. Despite skirmishes with the enemy on April 3, Grant still thought he enjoyed the luxury of waiting for Buell before assuming the initiative. "Soon I hope to be permitted to move from here and when I do there will probably be the greatest battle fought of the War," he predicted to Julia. "I do not feel that there is the slightest doubt about the result."[10] Only a fine line separated immense self-confidence from egregious complacency and Grant had probably crossed it here.

On April 4, Grant spent the day upstream at Pittsburg Landing, and, despite telltale clashes between Union pickets and the enemy, he missed warning signals and did not foresee the juggernaut about to overtake his army. When he received intelligence that Confederates might attack General Lew Wallace at Crump's Landing, he opted to reinforce him, telling Sherman that "I look for nothing of the kind, but it is best to be prepared."[11] That night, caught in a downpour marked by flashes of lightning, Grant rode back to the steamer that returned him to Savannah. As he rode through the woods at a slow trot, he mistakenly trusted the skill of his horse. As he wrote, "My horse's feet slipped from under him, and he fell [on his side] with my leg under his body. The extreme softness of the ground, from the excessive rain of the few preceding days, no doubt saved me from a severe injury and protracted lameness. As it was, my ankle was very much injured, so much so that my boot had to be cut off. For two or three days after I was unable to walk except with crutches."[12]

The charge of being blindsided at Shiloh would long be a sore point with Grant. Ordinarily the soul of honesty, he sought to rewrite history, claiming to have known a major battle was imminent. Unfortunately, his April 5 correspondence makes crystal-clear that he had no intimation of a massive attack in the offing. He dismissed raids on Union outposts as the work of reconnaissance forces, insisting, "I have scarcely the faintest idea of an attack, (general one), being made upon us but will be prepared should such a thing take place."[13] He still planned to march on Corinth, convinced he would find the bulk of the rebel army there, and gave his personal guarantee to his old Ohio friend Jacob Ammen that "there will be no fight at Pittsburg Landing."[14] Perhaps remembering the public reaction to his previous worries in Kentucky, Sherman discounted predictions of any impending threat. "I have no doubt that nothing will occur today more than some picket firing," he told Grant. "The enemy is saucy, but got the worst of it yesterday, and will not press our pickets far . . . I do not apprehend anything like an attack on our position."[15]

That day Union soldiers seemed a carefree bunch, as if relaxing in a rural idyll. One Iowa soldier admired the numberless tents stretching through a "delightful Tennessee forest" and thought the scene resembled "a gigantic picnic."[16] Trigger-happy novices shot off muskets in the woods and were entertained that night by regimental bands. Those musicians had no idea that their tunes, drifting through darkened woods, could be heard by unseen rebel pickets. The Confederate army, more than forty thousand strong and encamped just two miles away, picked up the drums of Sherman's division.

On the night of April 5, the two Confederate chieftains, Albert Sidney Johnston and Pierre G. T. Beauregard, huddled and planned a dawn attack. A tall, upright Texan, born in Kentucky, Johnston had a handlebar mustache, glowering eyes, and lank hair that fell flat against his skull. He saw a chance to redeem an exalted reputation badly blemished by Fort Donelson and was ready to stake everything on this colossal gamble. Early in the war, he had been considered the South's premier military man, veneration later transferred to Robert E. Lee. Jefferson Davis puffed him up to godlike proportions, touting him as "the greatest soldier, the ablest man, civil or military, Confederate or Federal, then living."[17] Johnston had a knack for inspiring his men with high-flown rhetoric, and he swore the next day he would water his horse either in the Tennessee River or in hell. Beauregard, an elegant Creole with a French accent and dyed hair who admired Napoleon, was still feted as the hero of Bull Run. He had a thin face with a small beard that stood like an exclamation point at his chin. When he expressed last-minute reservations to Johnston, saying delays might have robbed them of the element of surprise, Johnston waved away this fainthearted caution. "I would fight them if they were a million," he promised.[18]

The Union side had intimations of trouble in the predawn hours. General Benjamin Prentiss sent out a night patrol that stumbled upon advanced rebel skirmishers and, thanks to this accidental encounter, he lined up his division, bracing for an attack. Based on this clash, John Rawlins hotly insisted that "this battle was not, in a military sense, a surprise to us . . . it is sufficient to say that we did not expect to be attacked in force that morning . . . we had sufficient notice, before the shock came, to be under arms and ready to meet it."[19] Grant was even more categorical that all five of his divisions had been drawn up in line of battle, ready to face the enemy. "There was no surprise about it, except perhaps to the newspaper correspondents. We had been skirmishing for two days before we were attacked."[20]

Many soldiers narrated a different tale. At six on Sunday morning, April 6, rebel soldiers burst from the woods near Shiloh church, whooping with demonic fury. Clad in Confederate gray or butternut brown, they surged forward in three neatly formed lines, hollering with raw gusto as their bands beat out "Dixie." Not until 8 a.m. as the sun rose on a "clear, bright and beautiful" day and he spotted the sunlit glimmer of muskets in the woods did William Tecumseh Sherman fathom the magnitude of the assault.[21] When the orderly beside him dropped dead from a Confederate shot and he himself was grazed in the hand, he exclaimed, "My God, we're attacked!"[22] Although he failed to foresee the hordes now hurtling from the woods, Sherman rose to the occasion in spectacular fashion and prepared his entire division to meet the enemy.

Perhaps no moment in the Civil War has generated such fierce debate about what happened. Some newspaper correspondents argued that sleeping Union soldiers were bayoneted in their tents and killed over breakfast coffee. Many such reports were grossly exaggerated, some even fabricated. William Rowley insisted that "I do not believe in truth a *single man* was killed by a bayonet during the two days' fight."[23] But allegations of a lack of preparedness were commonplace among soldiers no less than journalists. Second Lieutenant Patrick White of Chicago said rebel "bullets came whistling through our tents." He testified to "men shot in their beds and regiments preparing for dress parade on the eve of this great battle."[24] The inexperienced troops, he contended, "ran like sheep," tossing away their guns and flocking to the safety of the Tennessee River landing. From firsthand experience, White could never accept the sanitized versions presented by Grant and Sherman: "Some of our great Generals have denied that the battle of Shiloh was a surprise. I claim no one no matter how exalted or

high his position in life, has the right to deny an actual fact."[25] Despite his punctilious regard for accuracy, Grant shaded the truth, making it seem as if he had
been far more prepared than he was.

That morning, Grant was enjoying an early breakfast at the Cherry mansion
when he detected the distant boom of cannon. "Holding, untasted, a cup of coffee, he paused in conversation to listen a moment at the report of another cannon," said Mrs. Cherry. "He hastily arose, saying to his staff officers, 'Gentlemen,
the ball is in motion; let's be off.'"[26] In short order, Grant and his staff hurried
to the wharf and boarded his flagship *Tigress,* which then steamed to Pittsburg
Landing. It seemed reminiscent of the situation at Fort Donelson, when Grant
had been conferring with Flag Officer Foote at the time the battle erupted.

Much like Grant's men at Belmont, rebel soldiers who stormed into abandoned Union camps stopped to plunder booty and botched their advantage.
They were amazed by the material comforts available to Union soldiers compared with their own impoverished lot. Hungry Confederates paused to feast on
rich stores of food and coffee and snatch away superior bedding. Some even inspected personal letters that offered a glimpse into the emotional state of their
opponents.

Speeding upriver to Pittsburg Landing, Grant passed a dispatch boat coming
downstream that corroborated dark tidings of a blood-drenched spectacle ahead.
As he approached the landing, the racket of muskets and cannon grew deafening. Around 9 a.m., Grant disembarked, found the divisions of McClernand
and Prentiss engaged in heated battle, and took charge of the situation with
tremendous energy. Still hobbling from his injury, he was hoisted onto his horse,
his crutch lashed under his saddle. Johnston and Beauregard had hurled their six
divisions into the fray, sending many callow Union troops reeling back in headlong flight. As many as half of the bluecoats had never seen combat before, some
having been handed weapons for the first time only days earlier. "We met hundreds of cowardly renegades fleeing to the river and reporting their regiments
cut to pieces," recalled William Hillyer. "We tried in vain to rally and return
them to the front."[27] Thousands of fearful men, many wounded, stood quaking
beneath the bluff at Pittsburg Landing. Grant did his best to restore some semblance of order, organizing two Iowa regiments into a line to halt the flow of
deserters to the river, but the line buckled under the onslaught of panic-stricken
men. As Grant reported to Washburne, "I have never had a single regiment

disgrace itself in battle yet except some new ones at Shiloh that never loaded a musket before that battle."[28]

The bucolic setting, with its gently rolling woods and scattered meadows, soon became a charnel house as the conflict devolved into the war's most harrowing battle. Bodies of soldiers piled up in heaps as "Death, with fifty thousand mowers, stalked over the field," wrote Hillyer.[29] The sky grew dark with acrid smoke and the dense flight of bullets, producing a continuous patter like the rapid fall of lethal raindrops. The combined din of artillery and musketry reverberated endlessly. Despite his injury, Grant soon rode all over the battlefield, heedless of danger even "in the midst of a shower of cannon and musket balls," said Hillyer.[30] Dogged, unshaken, never doubting the final outcome, Grant puffed coolly on his cigar, issuing orders "as though he was simply reviewing the troops."[31] When John Rawlins came up from Pittsburg Landing, searching for Grant, he told a fellow officer, "We'll find him where the firing is heaviest"— which turned out to be the case.[32] A bullet that smashed the scabbard of his sword left Grant completely unfazed. Heavily outnumbered, facing more than forty thousand Confederate soldiers versus thirty-three thousand in his own army, he was gratified by his men's valor under exceptionally terrifying circumstances.

Shiloh was a free-for-all of death in which brute force trumped tactical subtleties. "It was a case of Southern dash against Northern pluck and endurance," Grant wrote.[33] By 10 a.m., he caught up with Sherman, who protected a pivotal position on the Union right that guarded the landing. Falling back at first, Sherman now made an obstinate stand against unrelenting assaults, showing magnificent courage. As if made of indestructible stuff, he stood caked with dust, his bloody hand bandaged, his arm in a sling from a bullet to his shoulder; before the day ended another bullet slashed harmlessly through his hat and three horses were shot from under him. Grant was simply amazed at Sherman's adroit handling of his green soldiers. There, "in the midst of death and slaughter," Sherman contended, the friendship between the two men solidified.[34] Grant anointed Sherman "the hero of Shiloh. He really commanded two divisions—his own and McClernand's—and proved himself to be a consummate soldier."[35] In perhaps his loftiest tribute, Grant said he scarcely needed to give Sherman any advice. For Sherman, Shiloh was the moment in which he recaptured the reputation he had squandered earlier in the war amid journalistic charges of insanity. If war was a grim and dirty business for Grant, Sherman seemed to be invigorated by it, as if it restored him to his natural habitat.

Among the generals who did not cover themselves with glory was Lew Wallace, a short, pale man with a dark beard, flowing mustache, and smoldering gaze that betokened a latent romanticism. He had worked as a lawyer in Indiana and served in the state legislature; in after years he would distinguish himself as the author of *Ben-Hur*. As the battle unfolded at Shiloh, Grant sent word to Wallace at around 11 a.m. to bring his veteran division from Crump's Landing to Pittsburg Landing along a road by the Tennessee River. Since the distance to be covered was no more than six miles, Grant expected these critical reinforcements to arrive by noon or 1 p.m., shoring up forces on his right who had withstood blistering fire. After an agonizing wait, Wallace never arrived. He marched his men on a long, circuitous route *away* from Pittsburg Landing and failed to join the main army until nightfall, when the day's fighting had ended.

A furious Grant thought him insubordinate and believed that by circling around with his army, Wallace had hoped to land on the enemy's rear and emerge with heroic splendor. Like Grant, Rawlins was indignant, arguing that there was no excuse for a division commander to "march and countermarch all day within sound of a furious battle, less than five miles away, without getting into it."[36] Enraged at such accusations, Wallace spent the rest of his life reliving that day and trying to wipe away the Shiloh stigma from his name. He claimed he had been told by Captain Algernon Baxter to "effect a junction *with the right of the army*" and had strictly followed orders.[37] For years, Wallace would ply Grant with argumentative letters, hoping to persuade him he had acted honorably. Grant thought Lew Wallace typical of politically well-connected generals who had risen to excessively high positions. This problem bedeviled the North, where there were deep divisions in the electorate, forcing Lincoln to curry favor with opposition politicians by plucking generals from their ranks. Whatever the truth of what happened, there is little doubt that the timely arrival of Wallace's division might have allowed Grant to reverse the tide of battle and even switch into an offensive mode on Shiloh's first day.

No less than Grant, Albert Sidney Johnston was a vigorous, inspirational presence to his men, standing up in his stirrups and waving his hat over his head as he led them into battle. At around 2 p.m. he rode to the front to galvanize his flagging troops when a bullet struck him near the right knee. At first he felt nothing. But when his aides sliced open his boot, they found it soaked with

blood, the bullet having slashed an artery. Grant believed that Johnston's bravery, his refusal to abandon his men and seek immediate treatment in the rear, led
to his rapid death from bleeding. The highest-ranked general killed in the war,
he was succeeded by Beauregard. However much he had admired Johnston's
grace under fire, Grant regarded him as an overrated general, "vacillating and
undecided in his actions."[38] By midafternoon, with Johnston gone, Grant sensed
enemy strength ebbing away. When Colonel Augustus Chetlain ran into him
near the landing, he was startled by Grant's composure. "The enemy has done
all he can do today, and tomorrow morning with the fresh troops we shall have,
we will finish him up," Grant predicted.[39] As always, Grant understood the seesaw psychology of so many Civil War battles.

Amid the chaos of that awful day, a nucleus of strength under General Prentiss crystallized at the heart of the federal line, staving off a decisive rebel victory.
His 4,500 troops dug in along a woodland path known to history as the Sunken
Road. For six hours, fortified by blazing artillery, Confederate officers launched
wave after wave of soldiers against this stubborn pocket of resistance, the fighting so frenzied the spot was christened the Hornets' Nest by rebel soldiers. Moving in the background, a ubiquitous Grant coaxed cowering regiments back into
the sanguinary fray, telling them, "Now boys pitch in."[40] Against a foe several
times more numerous, Prentiss's men held out until forced to surrender at
5:30 p.m., by which point their numbers had been shaved in half. Their stout
defensive shield had bought priceless time for Grant, enabling him to mass artillery on the crest of a hill and cobble together a new infantry line in the rear.

Even with dead bodies heaped up around him, Grant retained his equanimity and unwavering faith in victory. When General Buell suddenly materialized
on the scene and glimpsed the crush of terrified stragglers at the landing, he
asked Grant about his plans for retreat. The thought having never entered his
mind, Grant replied coolly, "I haven't despaired of whipping them yet!"[41] He had
the gift of believing in his men and simply refused to concede that things looked
so gloomy. At around 5 p.m., right after a scout reported to Grant, the man's
head was blown off, spattering him with blood. Grant didn't flinch, staring
fixedly ahead. "Not beaten yet by a damn sight," he mumbled, going about his
business.[42] One journalist said Grant glanced at the sinking sun and observed
evenly, "They can't break our lines tonight. Tomorrow we shall attack with fresh
troops, and of course will drive them."[43] Here was Grant's matchless strength: he
did not crumble in adversity, which only hardened his determination, and knew

that setbacks often contained the seeds of their own reversals. The most dangerous situations brought out his indomitable will. He now kept up his spirits despite a ghastly toll of seven thousand Union soldiers killed or wounded and up
to three thousand captured that day.

By nightfall, Beauregard rushed off a premature telegram to Richmond: "After a severe battle of ten hours, thanks be to the Almighty, [we] gained a complete victory, driving the enemy from every position."[44] Far from seeing disaster,
Grant thought his men had performed creditably against overwhelming odds
and hailed the day's fighting "as one of the best resistances ever made."[45] For
Grant, it was the *first* day of Shiloh, not the second, that represented the real
triumph, especially since half his men had never withstood battle before. On
that stormy first night, two thousand corpses lay strewn across a reeking battlefield that stretched for twelve square miles. In this nightmarish landscape, thousands of wounded men lay writhing and moaning in drenching rain, their
contorted figures lit by sporadic lightning. The ground was slick with blood and
carpeted with torn limbs and decapitated heads. Wild pigs rooted among putre-
fying bodies, their snorts audible to the dying soldiers. Meanwhile, Union gunboats, anchored in the Tennessee River, showered Confederate positions with
shells, adding to an unearthly cacophony. Many soldiers died of exposure that
night while the living found no shelter as they slept in puddles. "This night of
horrors will haunt me to my grave," swore a Confederate soldier.[46]

Grant was never one to mourn the dead openly or describe the grotesque
butchery about him; such thoughts remained locked up inside him. But beneath
his self-protective silence, he was far from insensible to suffering. He had planned
to spend the night sleeping under an oak tree, on a bed of hay, a few hundred
yards from the river. All day long, distracted by battle, he had ignored his injured leg, but once he dismounted and stood on it, he felt excruciating pain and
had to limp about on crutches. His leg was so bruised and swollen that surgeons
had to cut off his boot, and the throbbing, aching limb, along with the steady
rain, made sleep impossible.

Sometime after midnight, he hobbled off to seek shelter in a log house converted into a field hospital. To ward off gangrene, Civil War surgeons often
amputated on the spot and stacks of arms and legs had accumulated inside.
These begrimed doctors, ignorant of the germ theory of infection, stood in
clothes splashed with blood, pus, and filth. Many operations were performed
without anesthesia, relying on whiskey instead. The stoical Grant was staggered

by his glimpse of all the amputees. "The sight was more unendurable than encountering the enemy's fire, and I returned to my tree in the rain."[47] During battles, some emotional narcotic anesthetized Grant, while in the aftermath individual cases affected him powerfully. It is telling that Grant, seemingly immune to mass carnage, found unbearable the close-up horror of the makeshift hospital, which reduced things to a human scale. This was the same Grant who was repelled by bloody meat and had been revolted by the slimy tannery as a boy. As his son Fred noted, "In battle I have seen him turn hurriedly from the sight of blood, and look pale and distressed when others were injured."[48]

Wrapped in his greatcoat, Grant returned to the haven of the nearby oak tree with its spreading canopy of branches. Sherman found him standing there, streaming with rain, hat pulled low over his face, collar upturned, holding a lantern and chewing a cigar. "Well, Grant, we've had the devil's own day, haven't we?" Sherman remarked. "Yes," replied Grant with a drag on his cigar. "Lick 'em tomorrow though."[49] The statement expressed Grant's intestinal fortitude, which communicated itself to his officers. He had already told Sherman that when both sides seem defeated in battle, the first to assume the offensive would surely win. He had already ridden to each division commander, ordering a 4 a.m. attack. "It is always a great advantage to be the attacking party," he said. "We must fire the first gun tomorrow morning."[50] Perhaps no other Union general at this stage of the war would have dared such a counteroffensive. Grant's decision came from more than visceral optimism and an unquenchable fighting spirit: he had made a sound calculation of his strength on the morrow. He would be replenished by Lew Wallace's wayward division and the arrival of Don Carlos Buell's Army of the Ohio, which was ferried across the river that night. This would give him 25,000 fresh troops, reinforcing his 15,000 available survivors and dwarfing the 25,000 able-bodied troops fielded by Beauregard.

The next morning, Grant, who had to be lifted into his saddle, began to redeem his errors of the preceding day. By sunrise, his soldiers were high-spirited from their new numerical advantage and began a concerted offensive, accompanied by what Sherman called "the severest musketry-fire I ever heard."[51] An enormous battle droned on for hours as the tide shifted decidedly against the rebels. Grant didn't burden division commanders with detailed instructions, giving them freedom to be spontaneous. The clatter of arms grew earsplitting as rain thickened the dense smoke hanging over the battlefield. Union troops regained territory lost the day before, tripping over numberless cadavers and groaning men abandoned on the battlefield overnight. Once again, Grant, in the throes of fighting, rode just behind the front lines.

Taken by surprise, Confederate soldiers yielded ground all morning. Although they rallied around noon, they were exhausted, unable to make a sustained stand against fresh troops that bore down relentlessly upon them. Grant implemented a trademark technique: simultaneously applying pressure in as many places as possible. At one point in the afternoon, he gathered two regiments, lined them up for battle, then personally led them forward—a novelty for him. He carefully stopped within range of Confederate muskets. "The command, *Charge,* was given," he reported, "and was executed with loud cheers and with a run; when the last of the enemy broke."[52] By around 2:30 p.m., a desperate Beauregard feared his army would dissolve and signaled a withdrawal, taking his troops back to their base in Corinth. After two days of fighting, Grant's fatigued troops were in no condition to pursue them. Buell's Army of the Ohio was in better shape, but Grant couldn't order them to chase Beauregard. Only recently promoted above Buell, Grant didn't feel comfortable giving him orders. Heavy rains descended that evening, making roads too soft and marshy to sustain heavy artillery and precluding any follow-up.

Everyone was stunned by the scale of carnage at Shiloh, which posted a new benchmark for mass slaughter. Deeming it the war's bloodiest battle, Grant commented "that the Fort Donelson fight was, as compared to this, as the morning dew to a heavy rain."[53] Men who survived it could never scrub its harrowing imagery from their memories. Americans found it hard to comprehend the dimensions of the losses, which were beyond any historical precedent. Of more than one hundred thousand soldiers who pitched into the fray, twenty-four thousand had been killed or wounded. Shiloh's casualties eclipsed the total of the Revolutionary War, the War of 1812, and the Mexican War *combined.*[54] William Hillyer conveyed the spreading tableau of death that greeted him and Grant: "For miles and miles wherever we rode we found dead bodies scattered through the woods in all directions."[55] As Grant wrote memorably, "I saw an open field . . . so covered with dead that it would have been possible to walk across the clearing, in any direction, stepping on dead bodies, without a foot touching the ground."[56]

Shiloh peeled away any lingering aura of romance from the war, showing the sheer destructive power of modern combat. An array of technical advances, such as the conical minié ball that ripped through flesh and bone or rifled muskets and cannon that displayed greater accuracy and range, ensured bloodier battles than ever before. No less hardy a soul than Sherman remarked that the corpse-littered battlefield "would have cured anybody of war."[57] Combat had been pushed to extremes of cruelty that banished any remnant of civilized behavior. "Men lost their semblance of humanity," wrote a reporter, "and the spirit of the demon shone in [the soldiers'] faces. There was but one desire, and that was to destroy."[58]

Before Shiloh, Grant had nursed hopes for a titanic battle that would triumphantly crush the rebellion. Now, stunned by the combative spirit of his foes, he knew there would be many more bloodbaths in a long, grinding war of attrition. This began his conversion to a theory of total warfare in which all of southern society would have to be defeated. Technically speaking, neither side won the battle, for neither had gained new territory. For Grant, however, Shiloh was an unquestionable victory that had averted devastating consequences: "It would have set this war back six months to have failed and would have caused the necessity of raising . . . a new Army."[59] With the benefit of hindsight, he told Dr. Oliver Wendell Holmes: "If [Shiloh] had been lost the war would have dragged on for years longer. The North would have lost its *prestige*."[60] Grant had fended off attempts by the South to regain its defensive line in Tennessee and Kentucky, thus shielding the North from invasion. At the same time, General John Pope had taken a Confederate bulwark called Island Number Ten on the Mississippi River. The twin Union victories meant the Confederacy surrendered a huge section of the Mississippi Valley, foreshadowing steeper losses to come.

For Grant, Shiloh represented a personal victory. He had rescued his army from his own errors, showing a gumption and an audacity that altered the battle's course. He had shown coolness under fire and a willingness to take monumental gambles. The battle also instilled lasting confidence in the Army of the Tennessee, shattering anew the fighting mystique of rebel soldiers. The South, Grant noted, had demonstrated dash and pluck at the outset of battle, but his own men had exhibited the true staying power. Reflecting on this after the war, he said, "I used to find that the first day, or the first period of a battle, was most successful to the South; but if we held on to the second or third day, we were sure to beat them, and we always did."[61] Grant's endurance in the face of unexpected setbacks perhaps owed something to having survived the ups and downs of his own improbable life before the war.

EVEN AS THE NATION debated Shiloh's meaning, teams of doctors descended
on the remote Tennessee woods to treat thousands left wounded or disfigured by
the battle. Because of the warm weather, Grant attempted to bury the dead
without delay, and cadavers in blue and gray were lined up in neat rows or gathered in heaps. Many soldiers were buried in anonymous mass graves so shallow
that wagon wheels from burial details ran over skulls and toes protruding from
the earth. By contrast the remains of officers from well-to-do families were embalmed, placed in sealed coffins, and shipped back to their hometowns. All day
long Mississippi steamboats ferried Shiloh victims, displaying death on a new
industrial scale. One British journalist winced at a stack of coffins waiting on a
jetty "with the dead men's names inscribed upon them, left standing in front of
the railway offices."[62]

After Shiloh, Grant was vilified in the press with a fury that surprised him.
He was shocked that the northern press construed the battle as a Union loss.
Never before had he faced such national scrutiny or virulent attacks. As the war
of words grew fierce, Grant was traumatized. Union camps swarmed with correspondents who wrote for partisan papers and weren't overly scrupulous in their
methods. They trafficked in rumors that quickly found their way into print. In
the absence of any public relations machinery in the field, legends sprang up
overnight, filling entire newspaper columns. With few exceptions, Grant adopted a sensible policy on censorship, giving reporters the liberty to report on
past actions while preventing statements about future troop movements. In areas
conquered by the Union army, he shut down pro-Confederate papers hawking
treasonous views.

In the press Grant was faulted for being caught off guard by the Confederate
attack, arriving late at the battle, and failing to chase Beauregard back to
Corinth. He was made to seem inept and insensitive to the massive slaughter of
his men. The most savage denunciations issued from politicians in Ohio and
Iowa, home states to many victims. Grant and his staff suspected that these
stories originated with craven soldiers who had fled the front lines on the first
day at Shiloh, taking shelter beneath the bluff. Governor David Tod of Ohio was
especially irate at such insinuations, portraying these skulkers as victims of criminal negligence by the high command. To prove his point, he sent Lieutenant
Governor Benjamin Stanton to talk to Ohio soldiers near Shiloh and the latter

claimed in a diatribe that there was "a general feeling among the most intelligent men that Grant and Prentiss ought to be court-martialed or shot."[63] It was now open season on Grant, with a chorus of voices calling for his removal. Senator James Harlan of Iowa insisted that "those who continue General Grant in active command will in my opinion carry on their skirts the blood of thousands of their slaughtered countrymen."[64]

Grant received his most damaging coverage when twenty-four-year-old Whitelaw Reid weighed in under the pen name AGATE in the *Cincinnati Gazette*. An Ohio native, slender and urbane, Reid had studied at Miami University where he absorbed a love of literature and philosophy. His voluminous Shiloh account ran to 19,500 words, occupying thirteen newspaper columns; widely reprinted elsewhere, it became the most influential account of the battle. Brilliant as a piece of narrative prose, it left much to be desired as a first draft of history. Reid took at face value myths peddled by disaffected soldiers. He gave birth to the canard that Union soldiers, caught unawares by rebels swooping down on their camps the first morning of Shiloh, were trapped in their tents and bayoneted in bed. He also falsely pictured Grant as arriving late on the scene from luxurious quarters in Savannah. In fact, Grant had galloped tirelessly across the battlefield that day, exhorting his commanders from early morning. He blamed Grant for not summoning Lew Wallace earlier and loaded Buell with praise for the second-day turnaround. There was more than a germ of truth to what Reid wrote—Grant *had* been caught by surprise at Shiloh, he *had* failed to fortify his position—but the bogus, misleading details marred the genuine reporting.

In light of this calumny, it was predictable that Grant would be accused of drinking at Shiloh. So widespread were these allegations that he told Julia, "We are all well and me as sober as a deacon no matter what is said to the contrary."[65] One Grant supporter told Washburne he was asked "twenty times a day" whether Grant was intemperate. "The public seem disposed to give Grant full credit for ability and bravery but seem to think it 'a pity he drinks.'"[66] The documentary record makes clear that Grant was sober during the battle. Jacob Ammen, who was with Grant the day before the battle and on its first day, jotted in his diary: "Note—I am satisfied that General Grant was not under the influence of liquor, either of the times I saw him."[67] Colonel Joseph Webster wrote of Grant: "He was perfectly sober and self-possessed during the day and the entire battle."[68] William Rowley disabused Washburne of any notion of Grant drinking at Shiloh and added that "the man who fabricated the story is an infamous liar."[69]

John Rawlins was incensed by the uproar. "Though charged with intemperance, a more temperate man [than Grant] is not to be found in the service," he told a relative and polled those with Grant at Shiloh to substantiate his case.[70] By this point, Rawlins had developed a powerful vested interest in protecting Grant's reputation publicly, while sometimes chastising him internally. Convinced of Grant's supreme importance to the Union effort, he was forced into playing an unwanted double game about his drinking. Grant's sobriety at Shiloh apparently did not last. Five months later, when Lieutenant James H. Wilson reported to Grant's headquarters, Rawlins took him aside and showed him Grant's broken pledge not to drink. "Now I want you to know the kind of man we are serving under. He's a God damned drunkard, and he is surrounded by a set of God damned scalawags, who pander to his weakness . . . The sword of Damocles is hanging over his head right now, and I want you to help me save him, and ourselves too."[71]

Coincidentally, two of Grant's chums from his Ohio school days met him within days of Shiloh. Both left fascinating accounts of Grant's frankness about the drinking charges. When Benjamin Johnson called on Grant in his tent, the latter asked what people said about the battle. "I told him they said he was drunk. He fired up a little and asked me if I thought he was drunk now. I said I knew he was not. He replied, 'Well, I was just as drunk then as I am now, no more and no less.'"[72] Still more revealing was Grant's confidential two-hour chat with R. C. Rankin, son of John Rankin, who recalled: "He spoke bitterly of being charged with drunkenness and denied that he had been drinking, said he had not drunk any for several years. Grant told me he was ruined once with liquor and now he had quit it he would not allow it to get the upper hand of him again."[73] Seldom did Grant bare his innermost thoughts about alcohol in this patently confessional vein.

Amid a clamor for Grant's removal, Elihu Washburne withstood intense pressure as he took up the cudgels for him: "There is no more temperate man in the Army than General Grant," he declared on the House floor. "He never indulges in the use of intoxicating liquors at all."[74] Washburne maintained that at Shiloh Grant earned "one of the most brilliant victories."[75] He made clear that Grant's patriotic contributions far transcended Shiloh: "Though but 40 years old, he has been oftener under fire, and been in more battles, than any other man living on this continent excepting Scott."[76] At moments Washburne seemed a lonely voice in Grant's defense, producing everlasting gratitude in his protégé. A Grant staffer asked Washburne to send one thousand copies of his speech "for distribution among *our* friends."[77] Julia Grant, who felt "hard and revengeful" about the flood of newspaper accusations, thanked Washburne for his crusade to exonerate her husband "from the malicious and unfounded slanders of the press."[78]

With his faith in George McClellan increasingly shaken, Abraham Lincoln monitored the controversy swirling around Shiloh. Grant served as a standing rebuke to Little Mac, proof that you could send inexperienced troops into battle and emerge victorious without months of laborious training. Lincoln already pinned hopes on Grant, but he needed reassurance. Edwin Stanton wired Halleck that Lincoln wanted to know "whether any neglect or misconduct of General Grant or any other officer contributed to the sad casualties that befell our forces."[79] In noticeably tepid language, Halleck defended Grant from insinuations of misconduct at Shiloh, but Midwest politicos still harried Lincoln about Grant. "Why, after Shiloh," Lincoln recounted to an editor, "a republican senator from Iowa denounced him to me as bloodthirsty, reckless of human life, and utterly unfit to lead troops; and because I wouldn't sit down and dismiss him at once, went out in a rage, slamming the door after him."[80]

At this perilous moment for Grant's reputation, Lincoln kept the faith and saved him for future service. Long before setting eyes on him, Lincoln was steadfastly loyal and fair-minded to Grant, perceiving his sterling courage, competency, and unusual willingness to do battle. This was to prove an essential partnership needed to win the war. As Washburne informed Grant, "When the torrent of obloquy and detraction was rolling over you . . . after the battle of Shiloh, Mr. Lincoln stood like a wall of fire between you and it, [and was] uninfluenced by the threats of Congressmen and the demands of insolent cowardice."[81]

Perhaps the most remarkable anecdote about Lincoln's trust in Grant came from Colonel Alexander K. McClure, who told of a late-night chat at the White House. The anecdote's accuracy has been questioned, but it appears to reflect Lincoln's thinking at the time. McClure said he tried to impress upon Lincoln "with all the earnestness I could command the immediate removal of Grant as an imperious necessity to sustain himself . . . When I had said everything that could be said from my standpoint, we lapsed into silence. Lincoln remained silent for what seemed a very long time. He then gathered himself up in his chair and said in a tone of earnestness that I shall never forget: *"I can't spare this man, he fights."*[82]

Grant always interpreted Shiloh as a northern victory. The New York diarist

George Templeton Strong speculated it would "probably turn out an important national victory with heavy loss"—a verdict most historians endorse.[83] Grant bristled at the campaign of abuse against him, believing southern generals had the immense advantage of a favorable press while northern generals were hounded by poison-pen reporters. With the stoicism of a true soldier, however, he kept up an imperturbable facade. "Your paper is very unjust to me," he told one correspondent, "but time will make it all right. I want to be judged only by my acts."[84]

While feigning indifference to the journalistic onslaught, Grant was terribly agitated, nothing in his life having prepared him for such strident criticism or the harsh glare of publicity. Earnest by nature, a stickler for truth, he was unaccustomed to people playing fast and loose with facts. Even before Shiloh, he resented unjust charges that he was corrupt, telling Julia, "It annoys me very much when I see such barefaced falsehoods published and then it distresses you."[85] Writing frankly to Washburne, Grant said he was tormented by the pain inflicted on his family by press libels: "To say that I have not been distressed at these attacks upon me would be false, for I have a father, mother, wife & children who read them and are distressed by them and I necessarily share with them in it."[86] Julia's cousin William Wrenshall Smith noted of Grant and the drinking stories: "He never grew angry concerning such malicious lies about himself, but he felt it very deeply on account of his family."[87] In this bruised state, Grant fantasized about moving out West, where the eastern press could never touch him. "I am not going to lay off my shoulder-straps until the close of the war," he told a journalist, "but I should like to go to New Mexico, or some other remote place, and have a small command out of the reach of the newspapers."[88]

Although Grant did not dignify press attacks with responses, his father harbored no such misgivings. On April 21, Hillyer wrote to Jesse Grant and denied that Grant's army was taken by surprise at Shiloh, blaming thousands of soldiers who had "ignominiously" fallen back to Pittsburg Landing for spreading false reports.[89] It was almost certainly Jesse who had this letter published in the *Cincinnati Commercial* along with a letter Ulysses had written to him. Compounding this indiscretion, Jesse sent a tirade to Governor Tod of Ohio, blaming "five thousand cowards" who had thrown down their arms and fled to safety at Shiloh to explain why Ulysses received bad press.[90] Such actions by his father infuriated Grant. In one letter, he lectured him, "I do not expect nor want the support of the Cincinnati press on my side."[91] In still stronger language, he wrote: "I would write you many particulars but you are so imprudent that I dare not trust you with them; and while on this subject let me say a word. I have not an enemy in the world who has done me so much injury as you in your efforts in my defense. I require no defenders and for my sake let me alone."[92] It was a measure of Grant's new wartime strength that he could sternly lecture his father not to meddle in his life instead of just swallowing his anger.

On April 11, with Grant still languishing under a cloud, Henry Halleck arrived at Pittsburg Landing to take personal command of the army there. One officer recorded this impression of him: "He was carefully dressed in a new uniform, wearing his sword, and carrying himself erect, with a distant and somewhat austere manner . . . as he walked down the steamer's gangplank."[93] Clad in a spiffy uniform, Halleck stood out in a muddy atmosphere produced by days of rain and was shocked by the chaos he discovered in the aftermath of battle. When General John Pope arrived with his 30,000-strong Army of the Mississippi, Halleck merged it with the Army of the Ohio under Buell and the Army of the Tennessee to create a unified force of 110,000 soldiers. On April 30, he suddenly demoted Grant to second in command of the whole, a thankless job that dealt a serious blow to his pride, leaving him to twist in a cruel limbo without clear authority. Although Grant brooded, he did not complain openly at first about this painful humiliation. As in his prewar business dealings, Grant was again deceived about his true friends.

Grant was already in a subdued mood after the death of his former West Point commandant, General Charles Smith, who never recovered from his boat injury. "In his death," Grant told his widow, "the nation has lost one of its most gallant and most able defenders."[94] However deeply Grant mourned Smith, his death eliminated a talented commander and potential rival in the western theater of war, and Sherman later speculated that "had C.F. Smith lived, Grant would have disappeared to history after [Fort] Donelson."[95]

Grant's sudden elevation had proven a mixed blessing for Halleck. To the extent it boosted his prestige, he delighted in it, but he also feared the emergence of a competitor. Halleck pretended to be Grant's champion while subtly stabbing him in the back. For all his bookish knowledge, Halleck had not experienced the slashing realities of war, whereas the intuitive Grant was now steeped in combat experience. Sherman thought that Halleck, being distant from battle, was too tough on Grant, yet a deeper gulf separated the two men. Obsessed with bureaucratic forms, Halleck could not appreciate the fighting skill of the slovenly, disorganized Grant. "Brave & able in the field," Halleck wrote of Grant, "he has no idea of how to regulate & organize his forces before a battle."[96] In Halleck's topsy-turvy world, it was more important to look and act the part of a general than to win battles and crush the enemy. In professorial fashion, he gave Grant a stinging critique of his management style aboard his headquarters ship. One officer recalled Halleck, in a black civilian suit, pacing back and forth and "scolding [Grant] in a loud and haughty manner." All the while, Grant "sat there, demure, with red face, hat in lap, covered with the mud of the field, and undistinguishable from an orderly."[97] Halleck showed scant respect for Grant, freezing him out of high-level strategic planning and talking alone to other commanders.

Grant lacked the air of a major military man, which counted against him with Halleck and others. One correspondent wrote of Grant after Shiloh that he "has none of the soldier's bearing about him, but is a man whom one would take for a country merchant or a village lawyer. He has no distinctive feature; there are a thousand like him in personal appearance in the ranks . . . A plain, unpretending face, with a comely, brownish-red beard and square forehead, of short stature and thick-set."[98] The journalist Henry Villard observed of Grant that his "ordinary exterior . . . made it as difficult for me as in the case of Abraham Lincoln to persuade myself that he was destined to be one of the greatest arbiters of human fortunes."[99]

By late April, Halleck was ready to march his vast force, the largest assembled in the war, southwest toward the Confederate railroad hub at Corinth. He divided his army into three sections, under Generals George Thomas, Buell, and Pope. Conspicuously missing was Grant, who found his "advice neglected and sneered at by those in authority," Pope related.[100] Halleck's soldiers slogged ahead in muggy weather along rainy country roads, their woolen uniforms clinging to sweating bodies. So slow and laborious was this cumbersome army that it lumbered along at one mile per day. Albert Sidney Johnston had raced north along the twenty-mile route to Shiloh in two days, whereas Halleck took a month to accomplish this in reverse. Where Grant sometimes seemed heedless of danger, the fearful Halleck made his men dig defensive trenches every night. Unable to escape fears of another Shiloh, he roused his men before dawn and had them stand guard to avoid surprise attacks. Whatever the wisdom of this approach, it gave the rebel army plenty of time to brace for his arrival. As one reporter wrote,

Halleck's "grand army was like a huge serpent . . . Its majestic march was so slow that the Rebels had ample warning."[101] Moving south through a desolate landscape, Grant absorbed glimpses of the poverty inflicted on the southern populace. "I pity them and regret their folly which has brought about this unnatural war and their suffering," he told Julia.[102]

Downcast, embittered by his fallen status, Grant sulked that "I have had my full share of abuse" and decided he couldn't stand it any longer.[103] As he explained in his *Memoirs,* he felt demeaned to an "observer" of the unfolding campaign: "Orders were sent direct to the right wing or reserve, ignoring me, and advances were made from one line of entrenchments to another without notifying me."[104] On May 11, Grant wrote to Halleck to request that his command be restored or he wished to be relieved from further duty. He explicitly absolved Halleck of responsibility for his plight, blaming "studied persistent opposition to me by persons outside of the army."[105] Since Grant had meditated returning to the West Coast, his aides maneuvered futilely to obtain a command for him there, which would have removed him from serious action for the rest of the war. Grant informed Julia he would apply for a leave of absence unless he were reassigned to a new command. Grant was talked out of this wrongheaded decision by two persuasive people: Rawlins and Sherman. By now Rawlins had attained extraordinary power on Grant's staff. As Grant wrote admiringly, he had "become thoroughly acquainted with the routine of the office and takes off my hands the examination of most all papers. I think he is one of the best men I ever knew."[106] Besides protecting Grant from drink, Rawlins gave his staff some semblance of the management order Halleck found so woefully lacking.

But it was Sherman's intercession that conclusively dissuaded Grant from resigning. Once he learned from Halleck that Grant had gotten permission to leave the department the next morning, he spurred his horse to Grant's tent and saw his camp chests and papers all bound up for departure. The embattled Grant was "seated on a camp-stool, with papers on a rude camp-table; he seemed to be employed in assorting letters, and tying them up with red tape into convenient bundles."[107] Distressed by a sense of injustice, Grant disclosed that he was heading to St. Louis. "You know that I am in the way here. I have stood it as long as I can, and can endure it no longer."[108] He added morosely, "If I can't command a brigade or a division, I can carry a musket."[109] Sherman pointed out the danger of going and said Grant might miss a chance to regain favor in the same way he, Sherman, had redeemed himself after newspapers asserted he was crazy.

He pleaded with Grant to withhold his resignation for two weeks. When his appeal worked, Sherman rejoiced: "[Grant] certainly appreciated my friendly advice, and promised to wait awhile; at all events, not to go without seeing me again, or communicating with me."[110] Grant stayed in the army and within two weeks Sherman fell under his command, staying there throughout the war. Sherman said flatly that his advice to Grant had been "the turning point of the war."[111] Few things secured the fate of the Union as much as the bond of loyalty struck between these two generals who believed themselves wronged by the world's estimation of them.

By May 28, Halleck's huge army had pulled within a mile of Corinth's defenses. Halleck loved the archaic art of the siege and proceeded to institute one with textbook precision. When Grant suggested that, with a well-timed bluff on the left and center of their lines, the right wing of the army could easily overrun Corinth, "General Halleck received the suggestion coldly and treated it as being entirely impracticable," wrote Augustus Chetlain.[112] Grant's suspicion of Confederate weakness was vindicated on the night of May 29–30, 1862, when Beauregard's army, ravaged by disease and struggling with Shiloh amputees, evacuated Corinth before Halleck could attack. They stole away to Tupelo while duping Union troops with fake guns, dummy cannon, and scarecrows stuffed into rebel uniforms. When Halleck saw towering columns of smoke curling above the town, he imagined Beauregard was being reinforced, whereas Grant drew the correct inference that the Confederates were fleeing, destroying anything that might fall into Union hands.

Halleck hailed Corinth's fall as a brilliant victory that confirmed his military genius, writing proudly to his wife how the soldiers had dubbed him "Old Brains."[113] Lew Wallace rendered a harsher but more accurate verdict: "Corinth was not captured; it was abandoned to us."[114] The Union army entered a town of burning houses, shattered windows, and rotting food dumped into the streets, all valuable supplies having been taken away or incinerated. Grant commiserated with the townspeople. "Soldiers who fight battles do not experience half their horrors," he lamented to Julia. "All the hardships come upon the weak . . . women and children."[115] Grant believed Corinth could have been taken two days after Shiloh if Beauregard's army had been vigorously pursued. If Halleck had possessed the faintest idea of the weakness of the Confederate army holed up there, he thought, he could have marched against it sooner. For Grant, the bloodless fall of Corinth strengthened his belief that only the conquest of

Confederate armies, not taking towns, would end the war. It also confirmed his sense that it was better to strike in timely fashion with a smaller force than lose the advantage awaiting reinforcements. Grant was still in a funk, plagued by his old headaches. To treat these, his doctor foolishly gave him brandy, which affected his system powerfully. "He immediately ordered his horse and rode away along the lines," said William Wrenshall Smith. "I went with him and after a ride of ten or fifteen miles, he returned and was all right."[116]

During this anxious period, Grant's future was being thrashed out in the White House. According to Augustus Chetlain, Lincoln withstood insistent pressure to get rid of Grant. "I can't stand it any longer," he proclaimed to Washburne. "I am annoyed to death by demands for his removal." Washburne retorted that Grant had won more important battles than any soldier in the West. Relenting, Lincoln replied, "Well, Washburne, if you insist upon it, I will retain him, but it is particularly hard on me."[117] Another version of this story has Washburne deserting Grant and Lincoln saving him, winding his long arm around the congressman's shoulder and saying in soothing tones, "Elihu, it is a bad business, but we must try the man a little longer. He seems a pushing fellow, with all his faults."[118]

Grant's patience was rewarded after federal troops occupied Memphis on June 6. Having been shamed by the artful Confederate escape at Corinth, Halleck climbed down from his high horse and returned to St. Louis, restoring Grant to his old command. Grant asked to move his headquarters to Memphis, and when Halleck approved, he set out for the city on June 21. Halleck's mercurial reversal had lasting consequences for Grant's career. As Rawlins explained, Grant's "reason for selecting Memphis was, that General Halleck said he expected he would have to give him the job of taking Vicksburg."[119] Now that New Orleans, Baton Rouge, and Memphis had been overtaken by Union forces, Vicksburg arose as the major fortress on the Mississippi blocking Union domination of the waterway.

Through two days of blistering heat, Grant rode from Corinth to Memphis on horseback, escorted by two dozen men. En route, he stopped at the home of a man named De Loche who had remained loyal to the Union. Grant barely escaped capture by Confederate cavalry colonel William H. Jackson, then prowling in the vicinity. Jackson's horses were spent from heavy riding and he therefore thought it fruitless to race after Grant, whom he pictured cantering fast toward Memphis. "Had he gone three-quarters of a mile farther," Grant recalled, "he would have found me with my party quietly resting under the shade of trees and without even arms in our hands with which to defend ourselves."[120]

When a dusty, tired Grant trotted into Memphis on June 23, he entered a turbulent city under the potent sway of secessionists. From the time he was a young man, Grant had been admired for his patient, judicial temperament, which was now tested. "It took hours of my time every day to listen to complaints and requests," he recalled.[121] The city teemed with Confederate spies who wanted to torch the city and with families of rebel officers who shrilly opposed federal rule. Suddenly forced to administer the town, Grant faced fiendishly difficult issues and feared overstepping the bounds of military propriety. "As I am without instructions," he alerted Halleck, "I am a little in doubt as to my authority to license and limit trade, punish offenses committed by citizens, and in restricting civil authority."[122] He also had to contend with bloody depredations from Nathan Bedford Forrest, whose cavalry conducted daring raids in northern Alabama and middle Tennessee. Grant cracked down on guerrilla activity, holding local communities responsible for damage done by partisans and confiscating their property to pay for it.

On July 11, out of the blue, Grant received a mysterious summons from Halleck to confer with him in Corinth. When Grant asked whether he should bring his staff, Halleck replied cryptically, "This place will be your Head Quarters. You can judge for yourself."[123] A major change of military leadership had shaken Washington. After the failure of the Peninsula Campaign in Virginia, Lincoln had wearied of the dilatory tactics and imperious personality of George B. McClellan and made Halleck his military adviser and general in chief. McClellan first heard of Halleck's appointment in the newspapers and told his wife, with his usual contempt, that Lincoln had "acted so as to make the matter as offensive as possible—he has not shown the slightest gentlemanly or friendly feeling and I cannot regard him as in any respect my friend."[124] In private, McClellan spewed more venom, snarling that Stanton was "the most depraved hypocrite & villain" he had ever known and, as for Halleck, it would be "grating to have to serve under the orders of a man whom I know by experience to be my inferior."[125] As Lincoln soon learned to his regret, Halleck had a brilliant theoretical mind, but was a world-class procrastinator on a par with McClellan and no less likely to disparage threatening subordinates.

Advising Halleck to come to Washington posthaste, Lincoln urged him to place the western army under Grant and Buell. When Grant arrived in Corinth,

Halleck kept him in the dark, slowly twisting in the wind about his promotion. Then, right before he left on July 16, Halleck signed an order placing a huge plot of real estate under Grant's control. His District of West Tennessee would be bounded by the Mississippi River on the west, the Ohio to the north, and the Tennessee to the east. Now added to Grant's previous Army of the Tennessee was the sizable Army of the Mississippi that Pope had headed. Six days after Halleck left for Washington, Grant was still guessing what was afoot with Halleck and what position he might occupy. As shown in a letter to Washburne, Grant repaid Halleck's condescension and secret betrayals with awed respect: "I do not know the object of calling Gen. H. to Washington but if it is to make him Sec. of War, or Commander-in-Chief, Head Quarters at Washington, a better selection could not be made. He is a man of gigantic intellect and well studied in the profession of arms. He and I have had several little spats but I like and respect him nevertheless."[126]

In restoring Grant's command, Halleck broke up the enormous army he had led to Corinth. Deprived of troops and resources that might have made his new position more significant, Grant was thrown on the defensive amid a hostile population. Cavalry officer Philip H. Sheridan remembered how Grant "plainly showed that he was much hurt at the inconsiderate way in which his command was being depleted."[127] Nonetheless, as he set up headquarters in Corinth, in a gracious house decorated with fragrant foliage, Grant was at last free of somebody staring over his shoulder and meddling with his decisions. In the fullness of time, Halleck's departure gave Grant much more room to maneuver. Remote from Washington, he was less ensnared in backbiting politics and less endangered by any party faction. Unfortunately he still hovered on the periphery of the nation's attention, which was riveted on events in Virginia, and this bias in perception would always harm his historic reputation.

In late August, federal fortunes took a disastrous turn at the second battle of Manassas. It was there that the snickers about Robert E. Lee, once mocked as the risk-averse Granny Lee, gave way to admiration that deepened into southern veneration. Having united disparate commands into the Army of Northern Virginia, Lee distilled Confederate fighting power into one supremely effective weapon. At Second Manassas, aided by talented generals such as Stonewall Jackson and James Longstreet, he gave the demoralized federals a thorough thrashing.

Hoping to import western élan to the eastern seaboard and with Grant shadowed by charges of drinking and insubordination, Lincoln had placed John

Pope in charge of the new Army of Virginia. A West Pointer with a round, open face and long jutting beard, prone to bombastic self-assertion, the garrulous Pope had seemed an attractive alternative to the slow-moving McClellan. Then at Second Manassas, he stumbled straight into the grand trap cunningly laid by Lee. The resultant defeat dented Pope's massive ego, vanity, and bluster and he was completely deflated. With the northern public plunged into unfathomable gloom, Lincoln fell into a terrible depression. In view of Pope's disgrace, Lincoln executed a startling volte-face and restored Little Mac to command the combined armies in Virginia. Despite a host of misgivings, the president believed McClellan alone could revive army morale shattered by the recent disaster. For McClellan, of course, the move made perfect sense. As he told his wife with typical modesty: "Again I have been called upon to save the country."[128]

Among the military men who disappointed Lincoln was Halleck, whose career went downhill after Second Manassas. He had been recommended for his new job by Pope and their reputations plummeted together. Afflicted by insomnia and hemorrhoids during the late-summer crisis in Virginia—he ingested opium to dull the pain—he fell apart under pressure. Later on Lincoln confided that Halleck "broke down—nerve and pluck all gone—and has ever since evaded all possible responsibility—little more than a first-rate clerk."[129] Just how low Halleck sank in Lincoln's estimation was made apparent that autumn when Attorney General Edward Bates ventured at a cabinet meeting that Halleck should command the army in person. According to Secretary of the Navy Gideon Welles, Lincoln said "that H. would be an indifferent general in the field, that he shirked responsibility in his present position, that he, in short, is a moral coward, worth but little except as a critic and director of operations, though intelligent and educated."[130]

CHAPTER ELEVEN

/////////////////////////////

Exodus

As DROUGHT SETTLED over northern Mississippi that summer, parching streams that might nourish soldiers and horses on the march, Ulysses S. Grant, ensconced in Corinth, settled in for a period of defensive operations distinguished by small, hard-fought skirmishes. With guerrilla bands marauding through his district, he had to defend long railway lines, telegraph wires, and wide rivers located deep in enemy territory. Local inhabitants acted as spies, monitoring his every move. All the while, Halleck hollowed out his command, forcing him to divert several divisions to Don Carlos Buell to fight rebels in eastern Tennessee. Grant no longer engaged in wishful thinking about latent pro-Union sentiment simmering in the region. As he saw southerners flocking to partisan cavalry units and smuggling contraband, the Confederacy struck him as more monolithic and formidable than ever.

Such civilian support for the rebellion would lead to a broadening of the war's scope, an evolution previewed by Washburne telling Grant how the Lincoln administration would pursue "a vigorous prosecution of the war by all the means known to civilized warfare."[1] On August 2, Grant was instructed to "live upon the land," possibly spawning clashes with farmers. Endorsing a ruthless new phase of operations, Halleck urged Grant to blur distinctions between southern soldiers and citizens: "If necessary, take up all active sympathizers and either hold them as prisoners or put them beyond our lines. Handle that class without gloves and take their property for public use."[2] However tough his style of warfare, Grant never behaved vindictively toward the southern people. "I do not recollect having arrested and confined a citizen (not a soldier) during the entire rebellion," he maintained.[3]

Colonel Theodore Bowers, new to Grant's staff, told how Grant protected local residents from rough handling by his soldiers. One day Grant "came across a straggler who had stopped at a house and assaulted a woman. The general sprang from his horse, seized a musket from the hands of a soldier, and struck the culprit over the head with it, sending him sprawling to the ground." From the time he was a boy, Grant had defended the weak and felt especially protective toward defenseless women. "He always had a peculiar horror of such crimes," his future aide Horace Porter remarked. "They were very rare in our war, but when brought to his attention the general showed no mercy to the culprit."[4]

Reluctantly accepting the arduous nature of a protracted conflict and knowing he might not return home for the remainder of the war, Grant brought Julia and the children to Corinth. Condemned to a vagabond existence, they had boarded with Jesse and Hannah in Covington, but Julia was no more popular now with her in-laws than before, when she was rejected as a spoiled southern belle. "Julia says that she is satisfied that the best place for the children is in Covington," Grant reported to his sister Mary. "But there are so many of them that she sometimes feels as if they were not wanted."[5] Grant hoped Julia and William Hillyer's wife might share housekeeping duties in St. Louis, where Julia could see Colonel Dent. That May, Grant had instructed Julia that he did not want her to own slaves any longer "as it is not probable that we will ever live in a slave state again."[6]

As the Union army pushed deeper into the Mississippi Valley, fugitive slaves sought asylum in Grant's camps; every time he sent out an expedition, it came back trailed by a flock of hopeful runaways. Ohio chaplain John Eaton likened the influx to "the oncoming of cities" and said "a blind terror stung them and an equally blind hope allured them, and to us they came."[7] "Masters and Mistresses so thronged my tent as to absorb my whole time," Sherman groused.[8] Grant's thinking underwent a metamorphosis about what to do with them. In early June, he still blamed intransigent abolitionists for prolonging the war, but action in Washington recast the issue. Congress had already passed legislation preventing the return of runaway slaves, even if their masters were loyal. Then, in July, Congress passed the Militia Act, which enhanced the status of free blacks by enabling them to serve at reduced wages in northern militia as part of each state's federally assigned quota of recruits. Lawmakers also approved the Second Confiscation Act, which declared "forever free of their servitude" slaves who fled from disloyal masters to Union lines. The act, however amorphous and poorly worded, was a step in the right direction. The two laws shifted the tenor of the war as Union armies in the South became instruments of liberation, not just agents of punishment. That same month Lincoln decided to issue his Emancipation Proclamation to cover slaves in areas not yet occupied by Union forces.

Writing to Grant on July 25, Washburne coached him on how to advance in the military by adhering closely to Lincoln's new policy. "The negroes must now be made our auxiliaries in every possible way they can be, whether by working or fighting. That General who takes the most decided step in this respect will be held in the highest estimation by the loyal and true men in the country."[9] Having received these marching orders from his political patron, Grant heeded his advice and succeeded in the war for far more than just his military prowess. By subscribing to administration policy on slavery, he stood apart from renegade generals like George McClellan, a reactionary Democrat and an open racist who hated the thought of abolition, or generals like John Frémont and David Hunter, who brazenly issued freelance emancipation proclamations in their departments.

On August 11, Grant issued new orders to bring his practice into conformity with federal guidelines. He laid down strict instructions that no runaway slaves should be returned to masters, and they should be employed as teamsters, cooks, hospital attendants, and nurses. Most important, large numbers were set to work erecting fortifications. For all that, Grant carefully warned his men not to woo slaves from their masters, but only accept them if they showed up of their own volition. Since the slaves were often ragged, ill-clad, and frightened, Grant made sure they were issued shoes, pants, and tobacco, and he wrote tenderly about them in letters: "I don't know what is to become of these poor people in the end."[10] What he did know was that spiriting away slaves would destroy the southern economy in a steady progression toward total warfare.

Too thinly manned to hold so much acreage in northern Mississippi and western Tennessee—fifty thousand men was a pittance in this huge territory—Grant had to postpone major offensive operations. In September, he eyed warily the movements of two Confederate generals in the area. Leading fifteen thousand men, Sterling Price seized from a Union garrison the town of Iuka, a critical supply depot and railroad junction near Corinth in northeast Mississippi. Price hoped it would serve as a platform for invading Tennessee. A lawyer and politician born in Virginia, who fought gallantly in Mexico and then resided in Missouri, the silver-haired Price was a portly man with a rosy complexion and receding hairline. Earl Van Dorn had a shock of unruly hair, a truculent glare, and a bold handlebar mustache. Educated at West Point, he had experience in Mexico and fighting Indians. Grant's main fear was that Van Dorn would roar up from the south while Price swarmed in from the east, the two Confederate armies squeezing Corinth in a pincer movement. To head that off, he prepared to seize the initiative and assail Price at Iuka before Van Dorn strengthened him. Had Price and Van Dorn acted swiftly, they might have trapped him. Instead they gave him the necessary time to fortify his forces and assume the offensive.

The Confederate pause also allowed Grant to recuperate from another bout of ill health. For several weeks, he had lost his appetite, shed pounds, and awakened with cold night sweats. Fatigued, he told Julia in mid-September that he never got more than five hours' sleep and had skipped sleep altogether twice the previous week. With his devout belief in concentrating forces, he was trying desperately to marshal his scattered troops before taking on Price at Iuka. His plan envisioned a double-pronged strike that would have General William S. Rosecrans sneak up on Iuka from the south while General Edward O. C. Ord crept in from the northwest. With his irrepressible optimism, Grant hoped to surround the Confederates and bag Price's army or annihilate it. It was a simple plan, albeit one that required pinpoint accuracy. Once Price was taken care of, Grant planned to turn his attention to Van Dorn.

For the battle of Iuka, Grant took up position in Burnsville, which lay between Corinth and the enemy town. Before dawn on September 19, Ord began to advance on Iuka from the northwest, but was told by Grant to delay his final push until he heard gunfire from the south, signaling Rosecrans's arrival. Ord halted four miles short of town. With the poor country roads of northern Mississippi, Rosecrans's movements were hampered by thick woods and plentiful streams and he didn't reach Iuka till late afternoon. Unfortunately, the wind blew the wrong way, and owing to this "acoustic shadow," neither Ord nor Grant heard Rosecrans engaging the enemy and being driven back that evening. In frustration, a baffled Rosecrans sputtered, "Where in the name of God is Grant?"[11] Not until nightfall did Grant even know a battle had occurred.

In his usual bold style—momentum was everything for Grant—he ordered Ord and Rosecrans to renew their attack at dawn and Iuka fell in short order. Once again, the second day of battle had determined the outcome. Exploiting a critical road overlooked by Rosecrans, Price and his troops fled the town with ghostly ease. Around 9 a.m. Grant arrived in the empty town and took over the storehouse of Confederate supplies. If he had little to show for his conquest, he had blocked Price from entering Tennessee, which, he believed, would have amounted to "a catastrophe."[12] For the moment, he retained a high opinion of Rosecrans, although it was about to be tested.[13] A West Point graduate, Rosecrans was a cordial, outgoing man who enjoyed debating the fine points of Catholic theology and was well liked by his troops, who referred to him affectionately as "Old Rosy" in homage to his rubicund complexion and name. Grant thought him "a fine fellow" and a brave soldier, but with his usual exaggerated trust in people, he found it hard to believe Rosecrans secretly planted newspaper stories against him and promoted himself at his expense.

Right after taking Iuka, Grant went to St. Louis to improve his health and lobby Major General Samuel R. Curtis for additional troops. One correspondent observed that he appeared "remarkably well, although bearing some marks of the fatigues of his summer campaigns."[14] While in St. Louis, according to one well-placed onlooker, Grant indulged in a drinking binge. Franklin A. Dick, a St. Louis lawyer, bumped into Grant's old friend Henry T. Blow, Taylor's brother, who said Grant was "tight as a brick," as Dick tattled promptly to Attorney General Edward Bates. "Believing, as I do, that much of our ill success results from drunken officers, I intend to do my duty in reporting such crime upon their part."[15] Bates duly conveyed to Stanton the letter, which wound up on Halleck's desk. If the incident occurred as Dick alleged, it conformed to the pattern of Grant allowing himself a spree, not at moments of responsibility, but in the aftermath of a major battle when he briefly traveled to another city and could relax his vigilance. His men would then never see him drink and he was temporarily free of Rawlins's supervision. Grant usually had enough control over his drinking urges that he could confine his binges to such occasions.

In Sterling Price, Grant had met a strong-willed adversary. Not resigned to the loss of Corinth—Grant had returned there on September 30—Price teamed up with Van Dorn, assembled a force of twenty-two thousand soldiers, and headed for the town. The battle began on October 3 with high-pitched yells from hell-bent rebel soldiers and proved of short duration but unusual savagery. Showing uncommon fury, the Confederates pounded their foes with waves of attacks that herded them back to the town's inner defenses. This first day featured such a broiling sun that soldiers were forbidden to cook on open fires. Old Rosy was all over the battlefield, rallying his men. After one day his clothing was sprinkled with blood and pocked with bullet holes. When night came, water wagons rumbled through the Union camp, dispensing water to dehydrated soldiers. By noon the next day, Rosecrans counterattacked, putting the thirsty, exhausted rebels to flight and leaving a battlefield strewn with corpses. For such a short time span, the death toll was gigantic: 2,500 for the blue, 5,000 for the gray.

For all his horseback heroics at Corinth, Rosecrans committed a costly error by not pursuing the retreating Confederates, whose escape was slowed by the Hatchie River. Instead of dashing in hot pursuit, Rosecrans waited fifteen hours, took the wrong road, then got bogged down by an unwieldy wagon train, allowing the enemy to escape. This began Grant's progressive disillusionment with Old Rosy, who had twice allowed Confederate armies to get away. Rosecrans didn't take well to direction and always fancied himself in command. Fortunately for Grant, Halleck soon transferred Rosecrans to the Army of the Cumberland in eastern Tennessee, replacing Buell. Julia Grant remembered the day her husband came back "smilingly holding up a slip of paper" that announced the transfer.[16]

By trouncing the enemy in northern Mississippi, Grant had inflicted a smashing blow against the Confederacy. "I congratulate you and all concerned on your recent battles and victories," Lincoln telegraphed Grant in their first direct communication.[17] Grant had also walled off western Tennessee from further northward encroachment, shutting down offensive Confederate operations in the Mississippi Valley for the rest of the war. Momentarily reverting to wild optimism, he told his sister Mary, "It does look to me that we now have such an advantage over the rebels that there should be but little more hard fighting."[18] Even though insufficient troops forced him into temporary inaction, he had ensured the safety of the area under his jurisdiction and began to covet the bigger prize of Vicksburg. As the South comprehended how much had been sacrificed at Iuka and Corinth, rage fastened on Van Dorn. As one southern politician observed, "He is regarded as the source of all our woes . . . The atmosphere is dense with horrid narratives of his negligence, whoring, and drunkenness."[19] A court of inquiry exonerated him of charges of being drunk at Corinth.

Grant rose on an upward trajectory that carried him ever higher. On October 16, he was appointed to command the Department of the Tennessee, with headquarters in Jackson, Tennessee. This enormous district encompassed parts of western Kentucky and Tennessee, northern Mississippi, and southern Illinois. Now replenished with troops, Grant was firmly on the offensive, his natural element, as his thoughts turned toward the Confederate citadel at Vicksburg, Mississippi. He conceived a plan for a major offensive that would sweep south from

Grand Junction, just across the state line in Tennessee, moving down along the Mississippi Central Railroad. To his great dismay, some soldiers engaged in widespread looting that eroded military discipline. The march to Grand Junction, said an appalled journalist, "was marked nearly every mile of the way by burned buildings and fences, and was literally shown by clouds of smoke in daylight and pillars of fire by night. It had an immense concourse of camp followers who stole horses, mules and vehicles along the route for their own transportation, and robbed houses of everything they fancied."[20] An indignant Grant lambasted soldiers who violated civilian property: "Such acts are punishable with death by the Articles of War and existing orders. They are calculated to destroy the efficiency of an army and to make open enemies of those who before if not friends were at least noncombatants."[21]

Assisted by promised reinforcements, Grant set his army in motion with his usual pugnacious, hard-driving spirit. Returning to Mississippi, he pushed south down the railroad tracks. He knew this was a perilous operation, for the farther south he penetrated, the longer the supply lines left behind; conversely, the Confederates, when falling back, collected all the garrisons that had formerly safeguarded railway stops. He also had to parry nocturnal guerrilla raids that constantly menaced his march. "I told the inhabitants of Mississippi . . . that if they allowed their sons and brothers to remain within my lines and receive protection, and then during the night sneak out and burn my bridges and shoot officers, I would desolate their country for forty miles around every place where it occurred. This put an end to bridge-burning."[22] In the march toward Vicksburg, Grant made steady progress and after five weeks had gotten as far south as Grenada.

Meanwhile, Robert E. Lee, emboldened by Second Manassas, contemplated a daring raid against the North, taking the war to the enemy heartland. When crossing the Potomac into Maryland, his often-shoeless army had the appearance of an unwashed rabble. One Frederick resident watched in disgust as they marched by: "I have never seen such a mass of filthy strong-smelling men . . . They are the roughest looking set of creatures I ever saw, their features, hair and clothing matted with dirt and filth, and the scratching they kept up gave warrant of vermin in abundance."[23] They encountered Union troops, led by McClellan, in the town of Sharpsburg, as the two armies faced off across winding Antietam Creek. On September 17, 1862, they clashed in a battle of staggering ferocity that produced more than twenty thousand casualties, making it the single deadliest day in American history. If by most measures the battle was a draw, it foiled Lee's plans to invade the North and banished him from Maryland, giving Unionists cause to celebrate. Though he had shamefully let Lee's army slip away across the Potomac, Little Mac could not refrain from crowing: "Those in whose judgment I rely tell me that I fought the battle splendidly and that it is a masterpiece of art."[24] In truth, McClellan had missed a magnificent chance to destroy a badly outnumbered army and it soon ended his military career.

Antietam represented an important juncture in the war. On the eve of battle, the British and French had seriously entertained recognizing the Confederacy, and an indisputable triumph by Lee might have tilted the scales toward such a decision. Now Confederate diplomacy was frozen in its tracks. Still more momentous was that Lincoln seized on the quasi-victory as the occasion to issue his preliminary Emancipation Proclamation, with the Confederate states given until January 1 to renounce rebellion or see their slaves freed. At Secretary of State Seward's suggestion, Lincoln had awaited good news from the Union army to make this decision public, lest it appear a sign of desperation. Although slavery in the border states remained untouched by the proclamation, the war aims now expanded to include emancipation. The conflict had edged past the point of no return, making compromise impossible. To Grant, Halleck telegraphed the seismic shift: "We must conquer the rebels or be conquered by them . . . Every slave withdrawn from the enemy is the equivalent of a white man put *hors de combat.*"[25]

Every northern commander was sucked into the vortex of the fugitive slave issue, none more so than Grant in the heart of the cotton kingdom. As plantation owners fled his advancing army, thousands of slaves raced to freedom in Grant's camps. Temporary towns of makeshift dwellings, overcrowded with frightened black refugees, sprang up on the fringes of army posts. The slaves' lamentable condition demanded urgent attention. "There were men, women, and children in every stage of disease or decrepitude, often nearly naked, with flesh torn by the terrible experiences of their escapes," wrote John Eaton, who saw slaves dropping by the wayside. "Sometimes they were intelligent and eager to help themselves; often they were bewildered or stupid or possessed by the wildest notions of what liberty might mean . . . Some radical step needed to be taken."[26]

At first Grant was perplexed by these masses of dislocated people. "Citizens south of us are leaving their homes & Negroes coming in by wagon loads," he wired Halleck, adding plaintively, "What will I do with them?"[27] Many northerners feared an abrupt influx of blacks, making it essential to employ them in the

South. Nobody stood under any illusions about the extent of northern bigotry. On November 13, 1862, Grant took his first historic step in dealing with runaway slaves, naming Eaton as superintendent of contrabands for the Mississippi Valley—"contraband" of war being the term of art for runaway slaves coined by General Benjamin Butler in 1861 as a way to bypass the Fugitive Slave Act, then still in effect. A farmer's son, born in New Hampshire, Eaton had graduated from Dartmouth College and served as school superintendent in Toledo, Ohio. After attending Andover Theological Seminary, he was assigned as chaplain to the Twenty-Seventh Ohio Volunteer Infantry. A caring, passionate advocate for the former slaves, he faced the daunting need to shelter, employ, and prepare them for the demands of freedom. He set up large contraband camps where slaves could be educated, treated for medical problems, and set to work picking cotton as hired hands. Eaton felt awed by the godlike responsibility thrust upon him—"There was no plan in this exodus, no Moses to lead it"—and sensed it would be "an enterprise beyond the possibility of human achievement."[28]

When Eaton first met Grant at La Grange, Tennessee, he expected to find "an incompetent and disagreeable man" whose weather-beaten face would betray signs of dissipation.[29] Instead, he was pleasantly surprised to discover Grant's innate modesty, simplicity, and sobriety. Other than the shoulder straps that signified a major general, Grant was indistinguishable from his officers. Grant knew that the deeper his army penetrated into cotton country, the more he would have to grapple with the destiny of a slave population fast emancipating itself. Eaton was stunned that Grant's thinking already "far outstripped" the "meager instructions" he had received from Halleck.[30]

In fact, Grant's imagination had charted the entire arc of the freed slaves from wartime runaways to full voting citizenship. This man who had so recently balked at abolitionism now made a startling leap into America's future. To Eaton, Grant delineated a lengthy list of useful tasks that "contrabands" could perform, with the men building bridges, roads, and earthworks or chopping wood for Mississippi steamers, while women worked in kitchens and hospitals. But this merely served as prelude to something much bigger. "He then went on to say that when it had been made clear that the Negro, as an independent laborer . . . could do these things well, it would be very easy to put a musket in his hands and make a soldier of him, and if he fought well, eventually to put the ballot in his hand and make him a citizen. Obviously I was dealing with no incompetent, but a man capable of handling large issues. Never before in those early and bewildering days had I heard the problem of the future of the Negro attacked so vigorously and with such humanity combined with practical good sense."[31] This sudden enlargement of Grant's thinking and concern for the ex-slaves shows how the war had reshaped his views on fundamental issues.

Grant gave Eaton orders to establish the first contraband camp at Grand Junction, Tennessee, where thousands of former slaves had congregated. A central aim was to have newly liberated blacks work on abandoned plantations, picking cotton and corn that could be shipped north to assist the war effort. "We together fixed the prices to be paid for the negro labor," Grant recalled, "whether rendered to the government or to individuals."[32] It was a remarkable moment—the sudden advent of a labor market for former slaves, who would now be rewarded for picking cotton. Grant found himself overseeing a vast social experiment, inducting his black charges into the first stages of citizenship. Taking the proceeds from their labor, he created a fund that was "not only sufficient to feed and clothe all, old and young, male and female, but to build them comfortable cabins, hospitals for the sick, and to supply them with many comforts they had never known before."[33] This brand-new Grant never wavered in his commitment to freed people. It would be army commanders in the field, not Washington politicians, who worked out many of the critical details in caring for the recently enslaved. Frederick Douglass never forgot the service Grant rendered to his people, arguing that General Grant "was always up with, or in advance of authority furnished from Washington in regard to the treatment of those of our color then slaves," and he cited the food, work, medical care, and education Grant supplied in the months before the official Emancipation Proclamation.[34]

In the fall elections, Lincoln paid a fearful price for that impending proclamation. Berating Republicans as "Nigger Worshippers," Democrats conjured up fantastic "scenes of lust and rapine" in the South and "a swarthy inundation of negro laborers and paupers" in the North as the likely consequences of emancipation.[35] Although Republicans retained their hold over Congress, they surrendered twenty-eight House seats to Democrats and lost governorships in New York and New Jersey as well as statehouses in Indiana and Illinois.

Lincoln's woes as a liberator were compounded by the ongoing disaster of Union military performance in Virginia. With elections safely behind him, he acted swiftly to sack George McClellan, who had responded neither to gentle nudges nor outright pressure to become more aggressive. Without referring to

McClellan by name, Grant later made a comment that seems to allude to him: "The trouble with many of our generals in the beginning was that they did not believe in the war . . . They had views about slavery, protecting rebel property, State rights—political views that interfered with their judgments."[36] It was Grant's stalwart faith in Lincoln's war aims, coupled with his military acumen, that made him the ideal commander.

To head the Army of the Potomac McClellan was succeeded by Ambrose Burnside, a West Pointer from Rhode Island, a balding, congenial man with fluffy side-whiskers that jutted from his face and formed a mustache across his upper lip. A military lightweight, Burnside was in way over his head, betraying as much self-doubt as Little Mac had flaunted conceit. Grant had a certain fondness for Burnside, even though he saw him as unsuited to command an army. "No one knew this better than he did," Grant remarked.[37]

Lincoln continued to be cursed in his choice of generals. On a frigid day in Fredericksburg, Virginia, on December 13, 1862, Burnside sent wave after wave of Union soldiers to their death against the well-fortified positions of Robert E. Lee's army. If there was one Union loss during the war that looked like outright suicide, this was it. In the one-sided battle, nearly thirteen thousand Union soldiers were killed or wounded. A distraught Burnside had the decency to admit responsibility, while Lincoln, Halleck, and Stanton were all blamed by a northern public fed up with shocking losses. In the resulting demoralization, cabinet members began to plot against one another. "If there is a worse place than hell," Lincoln admitted to a visitor, "I am in it."[38] On January 25, 1863, Lincoln axed Burnside and replaced him with Joseph Hooker, dubbed "Fighting Joe," another general who would be undone by overweening self-confidence. A weary despair fell over Union ranks. "Mother, do not wonder that my loyalty is growing weak," a New York corporal wrote home. "I am sick and tired of disaster and the fools that bring disaster upon us."[39] Repeated Union failures in the East opened the way for a military hero to emerge in the West.

THROUGHOUT NOVEMBER 1862, Grant maintained his steady progress south along the Mississippi railroad, seizing Holly Springs and constructing a supply depot there before advancing as far south as Oxford, where he established his headquarters in early December. He now stood halfway to his overriding objective, Vicksburg, burrowing deeper into enemy territory. For his army to survive, he had to keep open a railroad 190 miles long, threatened by bitter, hostile residents. Oxford was an oasis, ringed by danger, "an island surrounded by a sea of fire, the enemy in front and rear, opposing progress," wrote Rawlins.[40] Always sensitive to the war's tragic nature, he described for his sister the Union army's impact on the cloistered university town: "This city, the seat of science for the South, toward which they pointed with pride and exaltation as the place rivaling 'Yale' for the education of their sons and daughters, is now one vast camp, and the University buildings of which they so justly boasted are the hospital for the sick, wounded soldier."[41]

With his army deep in the land of cotton, Grant had to deal with swarms of northern traders who maneuvered to cash in on the North's consuming need for this major export. Southern planters, stymied by the Union blockade, searched for ways to sell their product. Union armies required prodigious quantities of cotton for articles such as tents, and northern mills were starved for the raw material. There was even fear Great Britain might lean toward the Confederacy to keep its textile mills humming. "See that all possible facilities are afforded for getting out cotton," Halleck instructed Grant. "It is deemed important to get as much as we can into market."[42] Grant was outraged that gold paid for southern cotton might be utilized by rebels to buy arms against his men. After Washington overruled his order to prevent gold from being used in such transactions, he abided by a decision that required cotton traders to possess two permits: one from the Treasury Department, another from the local army.

It proved tough to enforce these rules. Cotton fetched such exorbitant prices in the North that huge fortunes were reaped overnight, and army officers were regularly bribed to wink at smuggling. Assistant Secretary of War Charles A. Dana was shocked by the wholesale corruption infecting the Union army: "Every colonel, captain, or quartermaster is in secret partnership with some operator in cotton; every soldier dreams of adding a bale of cotton to his monthly pay."[43]

Such practices infuriated Grant, who also fretted that traders might transmit military intelligence to the enemy—a special concern with the Vicksburg Campaign under way. Instead of allowing private traders to enrich themselves through price gouging, he wanted the government to purchase cotton at fixed prices. One journalist remembered that "Grant and Rawlins abominated cotton buyers as a class. In private conversations to the end of the war [Grant] always spoke of them as a gang of thieves."[44] Not surprisingly Grant felt a special antagonism against war profiteers, who not only extracted southern cotton but

often vended useful articles, such as medicine, flour, and salt, to southern buyers. At a time of rampant anti-Semitism, "Jews" ended up as a shorthand for
unscrupulous traders. As Sherman wrote from Memphis, "I found so many Jews
& Speculators here trading in cotton . . . that I have felt myself bound to stop it.
This Gold has but one use, the purchase of arms & ammunition."[45] Of course,
the great majority of those involved in the illicit trade were gentiles, but Jews
were much easier to scapegoat.

By early December 1862, Grant had zeroed in on Jewish traders as the source
of the trouble. During his southward advance, he issued orders that all traders
should stay in the rear of his army, but on December 5 he complained to Sherman that "in consequence of the total disregard and evasion of orders by the
Jews my policy is to exclude them so far as practicable from the Dept."[46] In a
mood of mounting anger, Grant was not content to chastise Jewish traders: he
wanted to banish *all* Jews. On December 17, he issued the most egregious decision of his career. "General Orders No. 11" stipulated that "the Jews, as a class,
violating every regulation of trade established by the Treasury Department, and
also Department orders, are hereby expelled from the Department. Within
twenty-four hours from the receipt of this order by Post Commanders, they
will see that all of this class of people are furnished with passes and required
to leave."[47] It was the most sweeping anti-Semitic action undertaken in American history.

On the same day Grant issued the order, he wrote a letter expressing a conspiratorial view of Jewish traders, endowing them with almost diabolical powers,
saying "they come in with their Carpet sacks in spite of all that can be done to
prevent it. The Jews seem to be a privileged class that can travel anywhere. They
will land at any wood yard or landing on the river and make their way through
the country. If not permitted to buy Cotton themselves they will act as Agents
for someone else who will be at a Military post, with a Treasury permit to receive
Cotton and pay for it in Treasury notes which the Jew will buy up at an agreed
rate, paying gold."[48]

There are compelling reasons to think Grant promulgated his infamous order in a fit of Oedipal rage against his father, who materialized in Mississippi
with three Jewish merchants from Cincinnati, the Mack brothers, who hoped to
inveigle cotton-trading permits. All year, in an evolving family psychodrama,
Grant's anger had risen against Jesse, who sought to exploit his son's position to
gain appointments for relatives. Ulysses had also been annoyed when his father

tried to borrow money from Julia and scolded Fred for supposed misbehavior. "I feel myself worse used by my own family than by strangers," Grant protested to Julia, "and although I do not think father . . . would do me injustice, yet I believe he is influenced, and always may be, to my prejudice."[49] With Julia and the children rootless and adrift, the tension between her and her in-laws complicated life for Grant, the enforced separation from his family replicating the harrowing situation of his early army years. Worsening matters was the way Grant's sisters mistreated his itinerant family, complaining about the money he paid them to care for his children. "Such unmitigated meanness as is shown by the girls makes me ashamed of them," Grant told Julia.[50]

On November 23, Grant sent his father a scalding letter about his treatment of Julia. He tore away his inhibitions, venting his fury: "I am only sorry your letter, and all that comes from you speaks so condescendingly of everything Julia says, writes or thinks. You . . . are so prejudiced against her that she could not please you. This is not pleasing to me."[51] It was while Grant was seething over this matter that his father and the Mack brothers appeared seeking cotton-trading permits. Because the brothers were large clothing contractors who provided uniforms to the Union army, they desperately needed cotton. They promised to give Jesse Grant a quarter of the profits if he prevailed upon his son to bestow a permit to buy cotton for shipment to New York.

According to one version of the story, Jesse first appeared in Oxford alone and spent a pleasant day or two with his son, who never suspected his true intentions. Ulysses entertained the Mack brothers cordially when they arrived until he spied their true purpose. At that point, said one journalist, "The general's anger was bitter and malignant toward these men . . . because of their having entrapped his old father into such an unworthy undertaking."[52] Of course, Jesse was a willing accomplice in the whole scheme. Once he saw the plot that was afoot, Grant had them all shipped north by the next train. Another version of the story says Grant was tipped off by aides to Jesse's imminent arrival with the Mack brothers and issued General Orders No. 11 as a preemptive strike against them before they arrived.[53]

Whatever the exact sequence of events, Grant must have felt wounded by the situation, for he had railed at traders only to discover his father in cahoots with them. Grant's infamous order was a self-inflicted wound, issued at a moment of pique and over the objections of Rawlins. Besides pointing to the order's offensive nature, Rawlins predicted it would be countermanded by Washington.

"Well, they can countermand this from Washington if they like," Grant re-joined, "but we will issue it anyhow."[54] When he refused a trading permit to the Mack brothers, they pulled out of the agreement with Jesse, who then sued them for breach of contract. In undertaking the lawsuit, Jesse guaranteed more bad publicity for his son. The judge overseeing the case declared that "the whole of the Trade disclosed in this proceeding was not only disgraceful, but tends only to disgrace the country. It is the price of blood."[55]

Lincoln perceived the political damage and injustice of General Orders No. 11 and rescinded it two weeks after its issuance. When outraged Jewish leaders descended on the White House, he reassured them that "to condemn a class is, to say the least, to wrong the good with the bad. I do not like to hear a class or nationality condemned on account of a few sinners."[56] Hesitant to rebuke Grant harshly lest it damage their relationship, Lincoln was firm in his decision, if rela-tively gentle in his reprimand. He did not ask Grant for an apology, letting others handle it. On January 21, Halleck transmitted to Grant Lincoln's reaction to his order: "The President has no objection to your expelling traders & Jew ped-lars, which I suppose was the object of your order, but as it in terms Proscribed an entire religious class, some of whom are fighting in our ranks, the President deemed it necessary to revoke it."[57]

While the Jewish press vehemently denounced Grant, the mainstream press also criticized him, *The New York Times* noting that the war had revealed in many gentiles "degrees of rascality . . . that might put the most accomplished Shylocks to the blush."[58] At first, Elihu Washburne sought to transform General Orders No. 11 into an enlightened action, "the wisest order yet made," as he told Lincoln. He professed amazement at all the fuss. "Your order touching the Jews has kicked up quite a dust among the Israelites," he told Grant. "They came here in crowds and gave an entirely false construction to the order."[59] Nonetheless, Washburne faced considerable opposition in the House, where a resolution was introduced to censure Grant. Extolling him as "one of our best generals," Wash-burne got it tabled by a narrow margin of 56 to 53. Although Senator Lazarus W. Powell of Kentucky castigated Grant's order as "illegal, tyrannical, cruel and unjust," Republicans still defeated the censure effort by a 30 to 7 vote.[60]

Luckily, during the brief time Grant's obnoxious directive was in effect, it was weakly enforced. The sole exception came in Paducah, Kentucky, where thirty Jewish families received notice to leave the city within twenty-four hours. These shell-shocked Jews hastily collected their belongings, shuttered their homes and shops, and boarded an Ohio River steamer. Several Jewish merchants in the group fired off a message to Lincoln protesting Grant's order, calling it unconstitutional and asserting it would "place us besides a large number of other Jewish families of this town as outlaws before the whole world."[61] American Jews were highly patriotic—in a population of 150,000, ten thousand served the North or South in the war—and were horrified at being stigmatized. So painful was the abuse incited by Grant's order that Philip Trounstine, a Jewish captain in the Fifth Ohio Cavalry, resigned from the army, explaining, "I can no longer bear the taunts and malice, of those to whom my religious opinions are known, brought on by the effect that, that order has instilled into their minds."[62]

Julia Grant, who seldom breathed a syllable of criticism of her husband, pulled no punches about General Orders No. 11, terming it an "obnoxious order" and saying Grant afterward agreed that criticism of him was deserved "as he had no right to make an order against any special sect."[63] In his *Memoirs,* Grant passed over the incident in embarrassed silence. When Fred flagged the omission, Grant explained, "That was a matter long past and best not referred to."[64] As we shall see, Grant as president atoned for his action in a multitude of meaningful ways. He was never a bigoted, hate-filled man and was haunted by his terrible action for the rest of his days. Even on his deathbed, according to a friend, "it was a source of great regret to him that he had been instrumental in inflicting a wrong upon [the Jews]."[65]

WHEN NEW ORLEANS fell to a Union fleet under David Farragut in April 1862, it left Vicksburg as the last forbidding Confederate fortress towering over the Mississippi River. As hub of a railroad network radiating outward to many parts of the Confederacy, the town was central to the Confederate psyche as well as its military strategy. If the Union could capture Vicksburg, it could slice the Confederacy in two, separating eastern soldiers from western supplies. With Vicksburg conquered, the Union would again enjoy untrammeled navigation of the Mississippi. Lincoln understood Vicksburg's centrality, but committed a critical error in selecting the general for the task. That fall, he asked Admiral David D. Porter to recommend the best general for taking Vicksburg in conjunction with a naval force. "General Grant, Sir," Porter replied crisply. "Vicksburg is within his department, but I presume he will send Sherman there, who is equal to the occasion." "Well! Well! Admiral," said the president, "I have in my mind a better general than either of them: that is McClernand, an old and intimate friend of mine."[66] According to Porter, Lincoln made the absurd statement that John A. McClernand, not Grant, had saved the day at Shiloh. It should be noted that Secretary of the Navy Gideon Welles claimed it was *Porter* who wanted McClernand, hoping to be relieved from dealing with West Point generals.

Whether McClernand bamboozled Lincoln, or simply convinced the president to appoint him on political grounds, is unclear. With his lean, bearded face and keenly flashing eyes, the Kentucky-born McClernand could be crotchety and hotheaded one moment, funny and quick-witted the next. Before the war, he had served as a lawyer, a newspaper editor, and a congressman from Illinois. He had dealt extensively with Lincoln, having served with him in the state legislature and argued courtroom cases with and against him. McClernand's military experience was sparse, confined to three months in the Black Hawk War of 1832, but that did not shrink his swollen ambitions or prevent him from becoming a brigadier general in 1861. As a leading War Democrat and a rousing orator with a gift for intrigue, he attracted many western recruits to the cause, and Lincoln, eager to shore up war support in southern Illinois, was loath to rebuff him. Fearful of treasonous home-front dissension, Lincoln grew alarmed by talk among antiwar, or Copperhead, Democrats of forging a "Northwest Confederacy" that would enter into a separate peace with the Confederacy. He needed McClernand to scotch any such effort. Although McClernand had been one of his commanders at Belmont, Fort Donelson, and Shiloh, Grant did not like the way he attempted to grab credit for victories and often overstated his contribution.

What Grant likely did not know was the extent to which McClernand exploited the drinking issue against him. "McClernand was very bitter against Grant from the start," recalled one officer. "He tried to destroy Grant. He had Grant drunk at Belmont, drunk at Donelson, drunk at Shiloh. He had spies in every regiment. He and [General Benjamin] Prentiss gave rise to a good many of the tales concerning Grant's use of liquor."[67] James H. Wilson confirmed McClernand's condescending view of Grant as a drunken mediocrity: "[McClernand] naturally looked down on Grant as a poor little captain kicked out of service for drunkenness, and it galled him like the devil to serve under such a man."[68] The historian Kenneth P. Williams has documented that it was McClernand who instigated Captain William J. Kountz to level drinking charges against Grant at Cairo early in the war.[69]

By the fall of 1862, Lincoln regarded reopening the Mississippi as a paramount objective and was receptive when McClernand, unknown to Grant, lobbied him in Washington about leading a mission to take Vicksburg. With his customary vanity, McClernand proclaimed he was "tired of furnishing brains" for Grant's forces and grumbled about West Point generals who mistook strategy for fighting.[70] Backed by endorsements from eight governors, McClernand requested an independent command in Grant's territory. His plan was to raise midwestern volunteers, assemble them in Memphis, then take them down the Mississippi to conquer Vicksburg. Lincoln had misgivings about McClernand, complaining that he was "brave and capable, but too desirous to be independent of everybody else."[71] Nevertheless, on October 7, he informed his cabinet that he would accede to McClernand's request for an independent command. To please all parties, in his confidential order of October 21, Stanton resorted to creative ambiguity, telling McClernand his expedition would "remain subject to the designation of the General-in-Chief." He also advised him to launch his campaign "when a sufficient force, not required by the operations of General Grant's command, shall be raised."[72] So McClernand didn't escape entirely from Halleck and Grant's oversight. Gideon Welles suggested that Stanton and Halleck endorsed the McClernand plan because "Grant was not a special favorite with either. He had like Hooker the reputation of indulging too freely with whiskey to be always safe and reliable."[73]

McClernand's top secret mission leaked to the press and on October 30 *The New York Times* issued a paean to him: "Gen. McClernand has inspired the whole West with enthusiastic faith in his courage, uniting energy with military skill."[74] Grant was sourly aware of the rumors. "Two commanders on the same field are always one too many," he believed, "and in this case I did not think the general selected had either the experience or the qualifications to fit him for so important a position."[75] At this point, Grant did something clever, asking Halleck to restate the exact scope of his authority. He really wanted to know whether he could deploy troops at Memphis intended for McClernand. A West Point cabal now swung into action, with Halleck retaliating against McClernand by wiring Grant: "You have command of all the troops sent to your Department, and have permission to fight the enemy when you please."[76] This was all the encouragement Grant needed to thrust McClernand aside and reassert control. Now engaged in a race to take Vicksburg, he wanted to beat McClernand at his own game. On November 14, in a daring, provocative move, he authorized Sherman to "leave Memphis with two full Divisions," including regiments McClernand had raised for his own use.[77]

On December 8, Grant conferred with Sherman at Oxford and sketched out plans for the expedition down the Mississippi River in which Sherman would cooperate with a gunboat fleet under David Porter. He was to assail Vicksburg from a spot north of the city known as Chickasaw Bayou. Showing his usual teamwork with Sherman, Grant was to execute a parallel movement south along the Mississippi Central Railroad, marching all the way down to Jackson, which lay due east of Vicksburg. In this way Confederates in Vicksburg would be required to fight on two fronts, land and water, to save the city. On December 19, as he rushed to depart before McClernand arrived, Sherman, in a mood of heady optimism, left Memphis with a large army and boasted to Rawlins, "You may calculate on our being at Vicksburg by Christmas."[78]

Such premature optimism didn't reckon on the damage Nathan Bedford Forrest and Earl Van Dorn would inflict on Grant's supply network. In mid-December, Forrest initiated a terrifying campaign against Union garrisons and cavalry in western Tennessee, ripping up railroad and telegraph lines and killing Union troops. A handsome man with blue eyes and steel-gray hair, a former slave dealer and planter with little formal schooling and no military training, Forrest was legendary for his ferocity in battle. In one newspaper advertisement for recruits, he exhorted them: "Come on, boys, if you want a heap of fun and to kill some Yankees."[79] Like Grant, Forrest was known for demanding "unconditional surrender" from opponents. His rapid-fire, zigzagging movements on horseback perplexed Union cavalry. Though never intimidated by Forrest, Grant respected, even dreaded, his prowess. He thought him peerless among Confederate cavalry officers because his methods were so unorthodox and unpredictable.

On the morning of December 20, Grant was chatting with John Eaton when a telegram alerted him to a dreadful development: Earl Van Dorn, with 3,500 men, had audaciously swooped down at dawn on the Union supply depot at Holly Springs, torching millions of rations, dozens of train cars, and hundreds of bales of cotton, while also capturing 1,500 Union troops. Van Dorn regained the reputation he had lost at Corinth in an action that threatened to undermine Grant's move on Vicksburg. As Grant read the telegram, Eaton recalled, "there was on his face no sign of disturbance that I could see, save a slight twitching of his mustache. He told me very quietly and dispassionately . . . that the night before he had telegraphed Colonel [Robert C.] Murphy warning him of Van Dorn's approach and directing him to be on guard at every point. He had since been informed that Murphy was engaged at the time in some form of conviviality and let the warning pass unheeded."[80] Grant characterized the Holly Springs surrender as "the most disgraceful affair" that had occurred in his department.[81] His soldiers had shown little stomach for a fight and capitulated with unseemly haste, while the young, inept Murphy had displayed "disloyalty" or "gross cowardice."[82] One southern journalist described wanton destruction at Holly Springs with "tents burning, torches flaming, Confederates shouting, guns popping, sabres clanking, abolitionists begging for mercy."[83] Loss of the supply depot temporarily derailed Grant's overland campaign to Vicksburg, forcing him to retreat northward. Van Dorn had little time to luxuriate in his triumph. On May 7, 1863, he would be shot to death at his desk by a husband incensed at the license he had taken with the man's wife.

Mississippi residents rejoiced at the Holly Springs raid until they realized Grant would now supply his army's needs by living off the land. Rich foods began showing up in Union camps as wagons returned from countryside forays loaded with ham, corn, peas, beans, potatoes, and poultry. Herds of cattle were rounded up for slaughter. As Grant improvised these opportunistic methods to supply his army, he drew the invaluable lesson that his men could subsist for days, even weeks, off the produce of local farms, an insight that opened up the possibility of operating deep in enemy territory for prolonged periods.

As Sherman steamed toward Vicksburg with a huge flotilla of thirty-two thousand men, crammed aboard seventy transports, Grant lost communication with him for more than a week since Forrest had torn the telegraph wires to shreds. This meant that when Sherman launched his morning attack on the north side of Vicksburg on December 29, he had no inkling of the disaster that had befallen the Union entrepôt at Holly Springs or that Grant had retired northward. He faced the full strength of the enemy alone and his attack proved hopeless from the outset. First his soldiers had to traverse the treacherous terrain of Chickasaw Bayou, a maze of swamps and streams. When they reached high, dry ground on an open plateau, they made easy targets for Confederate marksmen firing from the bluffs. One Union general described being "mowed down by a storm of shells, grape and canister, and minié-balls which swept our front like a hurricane of fire."[84] More a massacre than a battle, the operation was over by noon, the Union side having suffered nearly 1,800 casualties. Sherman shouldered the blame. "Our loss has been heavy," he wrote, "and we accomplished nothing."[85] So total was the communication blackout between Grant and Sherman that on January 5, Grant reassured Halleck of his firm "belief that news from the South that Vicksburg has fallen is correct."[86] It would be another four days before Grant received irrefutable confirmation of the horrific failure of Sherman's mission.

The short-tempered McClernand was incensed when he realized Grant and Sherman had outsmarted him, stolen his troops, and excluded him from the Vicksburg operation. Erupting in indignation, he howled to Lincoln, "I believe I am superseded. Please advise me."[87] To remind Grant who was boss, McClernand took thirty thousand soldiers, packed them on fifty transports, and led them on what Grant termed "a wild goose chase" to attack Fort Hindman on the Arkansas River.[88] Although McClernand captured thousands of prisoners and believed he deserved high praise for his initiative, Grant regarded the fort as devoid of strategic value and protested the wasted effort to Halleck. In reply, he got the exact message he longed to receive: "You are hereby authorised, to relieve Genl McClernand from command of the Expedition against Vicksburg, giving it to the next in rank, or taking it yourself."[89]

Henceforth, Grant spearheaded the expedition down the Mississippi himself. While he would have preferred to hand the role to Sherman, the latter was junior in rank to McClernand; McClernand could hardly protest if Grant personally took command. In handling McClernand, Grant had shown tact in a thorny matter of rank and protocol and proved surprisingly adept at bureaucratic infighting. McClernand continued to rant against Grant and Halleck. On January 22, exasperated by his pushiness, Lincoln wrote to McClernand and laid down the law, hectoring him to accept as a fait accompli his subordinate position under Grant: "I have too many *family* controversies (so to speak) already on my hands to voluntarily take up another . . . Allow me to beg, that for your sake, for my sake, & for the country's sake, you give your whole attention to the better work."[90] Periodically McClernand would pretend he retained a command independent of Grant, but Lincoln had spoken decisively and Grant had neatly consolidated his power.

CHAPTER TWELVE

Man of Iron

O N JANUARY 1, 1863, Abraham Lincoln signed the Emancipation
Proclamation. His hand had grown sore from greeting guests at the
annual New Year's Day reception at the White House, and he waited
a short while for it to heal so he could sign the document for posterity with a
firm hand. Couched as a military order, the proclamation applied only to slaves
in Confederate areas, not to Union border states or pockets of the South under
federal control, but it was no less radical for all that. No longer did Lincoln mention schemes to compensate masters for their slaves. The time for halfway measures was over.

By expanding war objectives to include abolition of slavery, the proclamation
upped the stakes and guaranteed an uncompromising, winner-take-all struggle.
"The Union party in the South is virtually destroyed," Halleck warned
Grant. "There can be no peace but that which is forced by the sword."[1] More
than ever the war became a clash between two incompatible ways of life, an effort to remake the nation as well as to save it. Through the proclamation, Lincoln hoped to subvert the southern economy, bridge a widening rift in his own
party, and capture the allegiance of mass opinion in Europe. This would now be
modern warfare at its most ferocious, exploiting every stratagem, straining every
nerve, and mobilizing every resource to defeat the enemy. Grant was the general
best suited to exploit the numerical superiority of northern manpower and manufacturing, while his army was best positioned to destroy enemy property.

Though Grant was not an abolitionist at the war's outset, his thinking had evolved in tandem with Lincoln's and he now opposed slavery on practical, military, and religious grounds, taking on the president's agenda as his own. As early as the summer of 1861, he had told an army chaplain "he believed slavery would die with this rebellion, and that it might become necessary for the government to suppress it as a stroke of military policy."[2] Grant's soon-to-be brother-in-law Michael John Cramer confirmed that "as the war progressed [Grant] became gradually convinced that 'slavery was doomed and must go.' He had always recognized its moral evil, as also its being the cause of the war . . . hence General Grant came to look upon the war as a divine punishment for the sin of slavery."[3]

In a letter to Elihu Washburne, composed eight months after the Emancipation Proclamation, Grant explained that since slavery was the root cause of the war, its eradication formed the only sound basis for any settlement with the South. It had become "patent to my mind early in the rebellion that the North & South could never live at peace with each other except as one nation, and that without Slavery. As anxious as I am to see peace reestablished I would not therefore be willing to see any settlement until this question is forever settled."[4] In later years, Grant explained that many Union soldiers thought it "a stain to the Union that men should be bought and sold like cattle" and that an early end to the war "would have saved slavery, perhaps, and slavery meant the germs of new rebellion. There had to be an end of slavery."[5]

The wartime fate of four slaves owned by Julia Dent Grant showed the sea change in Grant's outlook. As Julia recorded: "Eliza, Dan, Julia, and John belonged to me up to the time of President Lincoln's Emancipation Proclamation"—implying they were then freed.[6] That they were indeed emancipated is shown by the fact that a year later one of the former slaves refused to return with Julia to St. Louis "as I suppose she feared losing her freedom if she returned to Missouri," Julia wrote.[7] Jesse Root Grant said his son had been converted to abolition even earlier, having already told Julia's slaves "before any Proclamation of Emancipation was issued to go free and look out for themselves."[8]

While it has often been glibly stated that the Emancipation Proclamation did not free a single slave at the time—those affected resided in Confederate territory—it had immediate consequences in the field, accelerating the exodus of slaves, inspired by the promise of freedom, from plantations to Union camps. Union troops were now encouraged to entice slaves from their masters. No less consequential was that the proclamation authorized the recruitment of black soldiers, provoking outcries from Democrats and Unionists in border states.

Eventually, 179,000 black troops would fight for the North, many of them having been slaves, a development that not only helped to win the war but began the slow, deep, if halting transformation of the United States into a multiracial society.

On January 10, 1863, Grant temporarily moved his headquarters to Memphis, taking up offices in a local bank while he and Julia occupied rooms at the Gayoso House. While there, Grant was leveled by the debilitating migraine headaches that had pestered him throughout the war. John Eaton found him at the hotel "with his head and neck all swathed in hot poultices, which his wife was applying in order to relieve the violent sick headache from which he was suffering."[9] Julia, who fretted about his condition, was particularly upset when a doctor tried to ease his pain with liquor. "I cannot persuade him [i.e., Grant] to do so," she said; "he says he will not die, and he will not touch a drop upon any consideration."[10] With Julia, Grant always emphasized his abstinence from drinking, exhibiting his best behavior. "The bottle of Bourbon sent by Mrs. Davies I sent over to Gen. Sherman," he informed her from Oxford. "Myself nor no one connected with the Staff ever tasted it."[11]

In explaining away stories of her husband's drinking, Julia often griped that people misinterpreted his migraine headaches as instances of alcoholic abuse. Whether coincidentally or not, their brief stay in Memphis coincided with fresh allegations of drinking against Grant. On February 11, General Charles S. Hamilton scribbled a damning letter to Senator James R. Doolittle of Wisconsin:

> You have asked me to write you confidentially. I will now say what I have never breathed. *Grant is a drunkard.* His wife has been with him for months only to use her influence in keeping him sober. He tries to let liquor alone—but he cannot resist the temptation always. When he came to Memphis he left his wife at LaGrange, & for several days after getting here, was beastly drunk, utterly incapable of doing anything. [Brigadier General Isaac F.] Quinby and I, took him in charge, watching him day & night, & keeping liquor away from him, & we telegraphed to his wife & brought her on to take care of him.[12]

It must be noted that Hamilton, a disaffected general, hoped to supplant the popular James B. McPherson as one of Grant's corps commanders and that Grant resisted his efforts, supplying Hamilton with a timely motive for slander.

By late March, Grant removed the embittered Hamilton, alluding to his "natural jealous disposition," and recommended to Washington that his resignation be accepted.[13]

If Grant wrestled with migraines, it may have been from grappling with the war's biggest headache, Vicksburg, which he described as "very strongly garrisoned and the fortifications almost impregnable."[14] With seven miles of elaborate fortifications strung along the Mississippi's east bank, it posed an insuperable obstacle. It stood at a hairpin bend of the river, an unavoidable bottleneck that slowed ships, making them easy prey for bulging guns lodged high on the citadel's crest. There was no handy way to surround or even approach a fortress that was both natural (two-hundred-foot cliffs, cut by ravines) and man-made. The low-lying delta around it, a trackless wilderness of bayous and backwater, overhung by trees and infested by snakes, alligators, and bears, seemed unfit for man or beast. Such inhospitable swamps were all but impenetrable to armies dragging heavy artillery and equipment. The only high, dry ground around Vicksburg lay to the north and southeast, which Grant and Sherman had failed to take after the unforeseen debacle at Holly Springs.

Adding to Grant's nervous strain was that both sides identified Vicksburg as a vital strategic asset whose fate might determine the war's outcome. "Vicksburg is the key," argued Lincoln, who had twice journeyed down the Mississippi as a young man. "This war can never be brought to a close until that key is in our pocket."[15] Lincoln heeded the clamor of midwestern farmers who needed the river outlet for surplus crops and now sent much of their produce east by canal or rail at extortionate rates. Jefferson Davis knew Vicksburg was the grand trophy sought by Union forces in the West and that its surrender might sacrifice a huge section of the Confederacy, including Texas, West Louisiana, and Arkansas. To safeguard the stronghold, Davis appointed Lieutenant General John Pemberton, fortifying him with a thirty-thousand-man army and setting the stage for a prolonged battle for this linchpin of Confederate hopes.

Grant realized that, however much the North yearned for a major victory, it would take time to reach the high ground around Vicksburg, and the public would grow weary awaiting action. The Copperhead press took dead aim at Grant, with the *New York World* alleging that "the confidence of the army is greatly shaken in Gen. Grant, who hitherto undoubtedly depended more upon good fortune than upon military ability for success."[16] In late January, Grant steamed down from Memphis aboard his flagship, the *Magnolia,* mooring at

Young's Point, Louisiana, twenty miles upstream from Vicksburg. He strode nonchalantly down the gangplank, reading a newspaper, an unlit cigar in his mouth. "There's General Grant," one Illinois soldier remarked to another. "I guess not," the other corrected him. "That fellow doesn't look like he has the ability to command a regiment, much less an army."[17]

During this trying time, Grant had to cope with incessant rains that produced flooding of biblical proportions, postponing a direct assault on Vicksburg. The west shore of the Mississippi was so low that the river overflowed it, forcing Grant's men to camp on levees, often the only dry land poking above omnipresent water. Stuck in this quagmire, his army was threatened more by the elements than by Confederate weaponry. "The swollen state of the river, the dreary wastes of oozy swamp and fen," wrote a British correspondent, were more potent "than sword or bullet."[18]

In this unwholesome atmosphere, smallpox, typhoid, dysentery, measles, malaria, and pneumonia flourished, landing a third of the army on the sick list at one point. As soldiers died, they had to be buried on levees, producing a ghoulish situation in which soldiers slumbered on moist earth a mere foot above the buried corpses of their comrades. "Go any day down the levee," wrote an Ohio soldier, "and you could see a squad or two of soldiers burying a companion, until the levee was nearly full of graves and the hospitals full of sick."[19] Not infrequently, wagon wheels would churn up a coffin, heaving it open and exposing its cadaver to view. Grant came under heavy criticism for inadequate soldier care, but he pointed to hospital boats he brought in expressly designed for the situation. "I venture the assertion that no Army ever went into the field with better arranged preparations for receiving sick and wounded soldiers than this," he insisted.[20] Grant's belief was supported in March by Frederick Law Olmsted of the U.S. Sanitary Commission, who came to inspect the situation: "You cannot conceive how well and happy the men in general looked . . . If I were young and sound, I would like nothing so well as to be one of them."[21]

Early on Grant knew his best chance of taking Vicksburg was to venture south of the city, scurry past its guns, then approach it from dry land on the east bank. "I hope yet to fool the rebels and effect a landing where they do not expect me," he told an aide. "Once on the East bank of the river, on high ground reaching Vicksburg, there will be a big fight or a foot race."[22] Such a landing could not take place until late March at the earliest and until then he worried about the idle state and grinding misery of his men. He therefore approved a series of quixotic engineering projects meant to take Vicksburg by expanding the water-ways of nearby bayous, allowing boats to sneak closer to the city. He later claimed these were more makeshift projects than realistic hopes, but he pursued them in an amazingly stubborn and inventive manner, suggesting that he thought one might actually succeed. Employing steam shovels and dredges as well as hand tools, these efforts also showed the modernity of his mind and his openness to innovation.

The first such project envisioned digging a wide canal across the peninsula formed by the river's sharp bend opposite Vicksburg. The idea was to allow the Mississippi to enter the ditch and gouge out a deep channel, enabling gunboats to enter safely from the west side of the peninsula before emerging on the east side south of the city and beyond the reach of its batteries. The concept intui-tively made sense to Lincoln. "Direct your attention particularly to the canal proposed across the point," Halleck urged Grant. "The President attaches much importance to this."[23] Unfortunately, it was a herculean effort undone by the rising river. At Grant's command, four thousand black workers, armed with spades and picks, set to work. "Grant requested me to make a careful observa-tion of the conditions provided for the comfort of the Negroes engaged on the work," Eaton recalled. "I found them fairly well supplied with food and blan-kets, and so reported the matter to General Grant."[24] As laborers dredged up sediment, they threw it aside in huge mounds, but the resulting dam collapsed from a swollen river and rains in early March, terminating the project. The river had proven mightier than the men trying to redirect its course.

The second experimental plan proved more intricate. Four hundred river miles north of Vicksburg, a waterway called the Yazoo Pass had once allowed boats to enter from the Mississippi, then travel south by a series of winding, interconnected rivers, ending up at the Yazoo River north of the city. Before the war, the state had built a levee that blocked the entrance of this inlet from the Mississippi. By rupturing the levee, Grant hoped to carve out a backdoor ap-proach to northern Vicksburg for his transports near the high ground of Haynes' Bluff. For this demolition job, he selected twenty-five-year-old First Lieutenant James H. Wilson, a topographical engineer who had graduated from West Point in 1860. "A slight person of a light complexion and with rather a pinched face," he was a fountain of strong opinions and described by one journalist as "quick and nervous in temperament, plain and outspoken on all subjects."[25] In early Febru-ary, in a spectacular explosion, Wilson blew the levee to smithereens, then

watched the river water pour "through, like nothing else I ever saw, except Ni-
agara Falls," he wrote. "Logs, trees and great masses of earth were torn away with
the greatest ease."[26] Whatever his initial pessimism, Grant grew enamored of
the project, exulting that the "Yazoo Pass expedition is going to prove a perfect
success."[27]

The successful first phase obscured severe difficulties ahead. So overgrown
with vegetation were the inner recesses of the pass, with cottonwood, sycamore,
and cypress trees branching overhead, that Union gunboats could scarcely slide
through these narrow channels. Confederates sent teams of slaves to fell huge
trees, further slowing Union progress. It was a never-ending task for Wilson's
men to saw down obstructions and clear a path. Rebel soldiers threw up a further obstacle at the junction of two rivers, an earthwork island known as Fort
Pemberton, stymieing any advance by Union boats. Three times in March
Union gunboats worked to reduce the fort and failed. Grant's reaction to the
abortive project shows he banked more hope on these long shots than he later
cared to admit when he portrayed them as so many diversionary maneuvers for
inactive men. He told Sherman, "I had made so much calculation upon the expedition down the Yazoo Pass . . . that I have made really but little calculation
upon reaching Vicksburg by any other than Haynes' Bluff."[28]

At first, the project that captured Grant's fancy was cutting open another
levee that would provide access from the Mississippi to Lake Providence on the
Louisiana side of the river, fifty miles north of Vicksburg. Once entry was gained
to the landlocked lake, it would be theoretically possible for Union gunboats to
coast down several rivers and bayous to the Red River, where it emptied into the
Mississippi above Port Hudson. This detour, costing hundreds of miles, would
enable Union vessels to bypass Vicksburg's big guns and reach the eastern shore
of the Mississippi unmolested. Grant could then unite his forces with those of
General Nathaniel Banks for an onslaught against the Confederate bastion at
Port Hudson. Unfortunately, the proposed route south was choked with fallen
timber and many trees had to be sawed underwater to free a path for Union
boats. Along with dredging, this was such an arduous task that James B. McPherson, Grant's main engineer, elected to scuttle the effort.

Yet another project attempted to probe Vicksburg from the north via Steele's
Bayou, which led by a series of waterways to the Yazoo River. Once again dense
foliage tore apart wooden gunboats that brushed past the canopied branches.
"Birds, fish, snakes, turtles and alligators were the only living things we saw

while traversing its dark and gloomy labyrinths," one journalist wrote of his hell-ish passage through the bayou.[29] As boats drifted through tangled branches, rats, mice, raccoons, and snakes were shaken loose from tree limbs onto the decks, forcing crew members to sweep them off with brooms. River steamers with tall smokestacks got so entangled in this jungle growth that they could be hacked free only with difficulty. Submerged tree stumps also made it impossible for boats to move more than one mile per hour. All the while, stalled ships were subject to sporadic sniper fire from rebel sharpshooters. The Steele's Bayou proj-ect was terminated as yet another costly fiasco.

These multiple missteps around Vicksburg and widespread stories of ill sol-diers stoked fury in the North over the impasse. Echoing a crescendo of criticism, *The New York Times* scoffed that Grant was "stuck in the mud of northern Mis-sissippi, his army of no use to him or anyone else."[30] The excruciatingly slow pace of the engineering projects aroused mockery, the *Indianapolis Daily Journal* snickering that "Grant is getting along at Vicksburg with such rapidity that, in the course of fifteen or twenty years, he will be ready to send up a gunboat to find out whether the enemy hasn't died of old age."[31] For many, the Vicksburg deadlock symbolized the North's stalled war effort. "This winter is, indeed, the Valley Forge of the war," moaned an officer.[32]

It was a miserable time for Grant, who also had to cope with the loss of his false teeth. He had dipped them in a washbasin overnight only to find that his servant had tossed them out with the water the next morning. He also suffered cruelly from hemorrhoids. Although Grant insisted to Julia that his confidence remained unshaken, the Vicksburg stalemate prompted a wholesale reappraisal of his earlier successes, which many now chalked off to luck. Joseph Medill of the influential *Chicago Tribune* dismissed Grant's victories as overblown, telling Washburne, "We could have made him stink in the nostrils of the public like an old fish had we properly criticized his military blunders. Was there ever a more weak and imbecile campaign?"[33]

By early 1863 the chronic weakness of northern armies was blamed not on ordinary soldiers but on their hopeless commanders. In the newspapers, Grant was unfairly lumped together with feckless generals in Virginia who had repeat-edly disappointed Lincoln with their craven, weak-kneed leadership. The pres-sure on Grant grew daily. "All eyes are centered on your army and there is no mistaking the fact that the anxiety is intense," a military friend warned. "Many almost feeling that the fate of the Republic now rests on your success or failure."[34]

It was an amazing development: the lowly figure who had clerked in a Galena leather goods store now bore the weight of the republic on his shoulders. With voluntary enlistments dwindling and public discontent rising, the politically savvy Grant understood the urgent need for a smashing victory. "There was nothing left to be done but to *go forward to a decisive victory*," he later wrote. "This was in my mind from the moment I took command in person at Young's Point."[35]

As his foremost paladin, Congressman Washburne felt the heat as searing criticism against Grant intensified. His brother Cadwallader, a brigadier general under Grant, bombarded him with alarming predictions of upcoming calamity in Mississippi. "All Grant's schemes have failed. He is frittering away time and strength to no purpose. The truth must be told even if it hurts."[36] Without accusing Grant of drinking, he added: "He is surrounded by a drunken staff."[37] Meanwhile William Rowley slipped Washburne disturbing, confidential reports of new colonels on Grant's staff who regularly resorted to alcohol. "I doubt if either of them have gone to bed sober for a week," he wrote.[38] From all directions, Washburne's mail bulged with drinking charges against Grant.

In late January, Edwin Stanton appointed Captain William J. Kountz, who had tried to discredit Grant with drinking charges in Cairo, to supervise river transports for McClernand. Kountz lost little time renewing his vendetta against Grant and McClernand gladly helped him. On March 15, McClernand forwarded to Lincoln a letter from Kountz, whom he touted as honest and reliable. Kountz wrote: "On the 13th of March 1863 Genl. Grant I am informed was Gloriously drunk and in bed sick next day. If you are averse to drunken Genls I can furnish the Name of officers of high standing to substantiate the above."[39]

No indictment against Grant was more savage than one penned by Murat Halstead, editor of the *Cincinnati Commercial*, to Secretary of the Treasury Salmon P. Chase, who dutifully passed it along to Lincoln. The letter blasted Grant as "a jackass in the original package. He is a poor drunken imbecile. He is a poor stick sober, and he is most of the time more than half drunk, and much of the time idiotically drunk. About two weeks ago, he was so miserably drunk for twenty-four hours, that his staff kept him shut up in a state-room on the steamer where he makes his headquarters—because he was hopelessly foolish."[40] In conveying this letter to Lincoln, Chase noted that "reports concerning General Grant similar to the statements made by Mr. Halstead are too common to be safely or even prudently disregarded."[41] While such a letter, composed in Cincinnati about Grant's behavior in Mississippi, is suspect, one notes in these nasty letters a recurring consistency in their portrait of an intoxicated Grant. He was always described as being foolishly or idiotically drunk, childish and even jolly in behavior, never angry or abusive. This makes one suspect that the letters contained a germ of truth, since the various authors described the drinking episodes in remarkably similar terms, even though they could not have coordinated their messages with one another.

By nature and background, Abraham Lincoln was an eminently sober figure, having published as an adolescent his maiden newspaper article on the evils of alcohol. Whatever his worries about Grant's drinking, he could not afford to sacrifice this uniquely successful general. He showed wisdom and fortitude in facing down naysayers who brayed for Grant's dismissal, perhaps sensing their malice. "I think Grant has hardly a friend left, except myself," he said. Nevertheless, "what I want . . . is generals who will fight battles and win victories. Grant has done this, and I propose to stand by him."[42] The president, who felt as beleaguered as Grant, may thus have had an extra measure of sympathy for him. Before long Lincoln would feel vindicated by his fidelity to Grant: "If I had done as my Washington friends . . . demanded of me, Grant . . . would never have been heard from again."[43]

Because most Washington politicians had never set eyes on Grant, he was a largely mythical figure, a cipher on whom they could draw caricatures. The person best placed to correct these distorted images and provide a vivid, personalized picture of Grant was Charles A. Dana, the assistant secretary of war, who arrived in Grant's camp at Milliken's Bend, north of Vicksburg, on April 6. Dana found unforgettable his first glimpse of the Union camp laid out along the delta: "The Mississippi at Milliken's Bend was a mile wide, and the sight as we came down the river by boat was most imposing. Grant's big army was stretched up and down the river bank over the plantations, its white tents affording a new decoration to the natural magnificence of the broad plains."[44]

Before he left Washington, Edwin Stanton gave Dana his mission with Grant plus a plausible cover story: "The ostensible function I shall give you will be that of special commissioner of the War Department to investigate the pay service of the Western armies, but your real duty will be to report to me every day what you see."[45] Stanton wanted an honest assessment of Grant's drinking habits and daily reports on the Vicksburg Campaign. A handsome man with a full beard and dark, wavy hair, Dana was a figure of considerable stature and investigative skills. He had a colorful background, having lived at Brook Farm, the utopian socialist community, and served as managing editor of Horace Greeley's *New York Tribune*. It was an open secret that he was in Mississippi to spy on Grant and report back to Stanton, a situation that hardly endeared him to Grant's staff. "Dana was about as popular in camp as a case of measles," said Captain Samuel H. Beckwith. "We knew why he had come and the role he was playing, and the knowledge didn't engender any warm-hearted enthusiasm for him among us."[46]

It attested to Grant's excellent political judgment that, instead of snubbing Dana, he received him with such disarming civility that the two men formed a warm friendship. At their first interview, Grant even disclosed his new plan for taking Vicksburg. Before long, Dana admitted the true purpose of his presence, and Grant wasn't fazed. Dana soon vouched to Washington that Grant was "the most modest, the most disinterested, and the most honest man I ever knew, with a temper that nothing could disturb, and a judgment that was judicial in its comprehensiveness and wisdom."[47] He recorded a lovely vignette of Grant's conviviality: "A social, friendly man, too, fond of a pleasant joke and also ready with one; but liking above all a long chat of an evening, and ready to sit up with you all night, talking in the cool breeze in front of his tent."[48] As to whether Grant drank, Dana delivered a categorical rebuttal: "I have been able, from my own knowledge to give a decided negative."[49] Dana later had to modify this sweeping declaration, but for the moment, it helped to mollify Lincoln and Stanton and buttress support for Grant. So trusted did Dana become that he was soon invited to ride with Grant's army, becoming a reliable confidant. His dispatches made for prized reading in Washington and Stanton relayed them to the White House, where they were "looked for with deep interest," the war secretary said.[50]

Not surprisingly, Dana quickly perceived the special intimacy between Grant and Rawlins. Rawlins invited Dana to pitch his tent right next to Grant's, thinking it foolish to behave as if they had something to hide. So highly did Dana rate his friendship with Rawlins that he furnished Stanton with this thumbnail sketch: "He is a lawyer by profession, a townsman of Grant's, and has a great influence over him, especially because he watches him day and night, and whenever he commits the folly of tasting liquor hastens to remind him that at the beginning of the war he gave him (Rawlins) his word of honor not to touch a drop as long as it lasted."[51] But if Dana admired Rawlins's hardworking patriotism, he criticized his writing skill and thought Grant's staff was populated with mediocrities chosen less for competence than their loyalty to Grant. As he wrote bluntly to Stanton, "If Gen. Grant had about him a staff of thoroughly competent men, disciplinarians, & workers, the efficiency & fighting quality of his army would soon be very much increased."[52] The staff problems Dana identified would haunt Grant during his presidency, when he needed strong personalities with broad policy expertise. In wartime, however, Grant was at liberty to keep his own counsel and trust his judgment, which was more often than not correct.

EVEN AS HE PURSUED circuitous approaches to Vicksburg, Grant remained holed up for hours aboard the *Magnolia,* puffing intently on cigars and studying maps unfurled on a mahogany table before him. With its succession of natural barriers, Vicksburg was a riddle that he pondered with all-consuming concentration. "Heretofore I have had nothing to do but fight the enemy," he explained to Julia. "This time I have to overcome obstacles to reach him."[53] During a party aboard the flagship, the convivial James McPherson worried that Grant, oblivious to the crowd, was wearing himself down with hard work and attempted to lure him away from his desk. "General, this won't do; you are injuring yourself; join with us in a few toasts, and throw this burden off your mind."[54] Grant smiled up at McPherson. "Mac, you know your whisky won't help me to think; give me a dozen of the best cigars you can find, and, if the ladies will excuse me for smoking, I think by the time I have finished them I shall have this job pretty nearly planned."[55]

On April 1, Dana informed Stanton that Grant had ditched plans for indirect moves on Vicksburg. Lincoln had foreseen the failure of such tortuous approaches, telling a reporter he considered "all these side exhibitions through the country dangerous."[56] Pale, haggard, the president suffered anxious moments as he impatiently awaited news of a breakthrough from Mississippi. His prayers were soon answered. As the Mississippi waters receded, exposing more dry land, Grant opted for a more direct approach to Vicksburg. In a stupendous leap of military daring, he decided to run his gunboats past its batteries at night, establishing a beachhead for his troops south of the city. Just how tough this would be was strikingly demonstrated on March 25, when Grant ran two steam rams past its oversize guns. The *Switzerland,* though it absorbed a shot in its boiler room, floated past the fortress largely unharmed. The *Lancaster,* by contrast, was pulverized by Confederate fire. "The wreck floated down and lodged at our lower pickets, bottom up," Grant told Halleck. "She was very rotten and worthless."[57]

In addition to scooting gunboats and transports past miles of batteries, Grant would have to march his troops down the western Mississippi shore, then ferry them to dry land on the other bank. From there they would have to cut themselves off from their supply base and live off the land as they drove inland, taking the state capital at Jackson before turning on Vicksburg from the east. The strategy was fraught with danger, raising the prospect that Grant, operating in enemy territory, might be trapped between two Confederate armies—the Vicksburg garrison and any Confederate army that raced to its rescue from the east. It was also questionable whether such a large army could simply batten off the bounty of southern agriculture. Nevertheless, Grant was confident he could subjugate Vicksburg. As Cadwallader Washburn (sic) informed Elihu, "I hear that he says he has a plan of his own which is yet to be tried in which he has great confidence."[58]

The self-reliant Grant, despite resistance from several key commanders, chose a plan he hatched in solitude. Sherman thought Grant should return to Memphis and reprise his December tack of traveling south to Vicksburg along the Mississippi Central Railroad in a double-pronged assault. The stubborn Grant would not budge. "I confess I don't like this roundabout project," Sherman confided to a commander, "but we must support Grant in whatever he undertakes."[59] Believing the new plan headed for disaster, Sherman took the unusual step of writing to Rawlins, who shared his anxieties, about the extreme risk involved. As ever, Grant was exquisitely attuned to the political repercussions of military acts, telling Sherman he opposed retracing his December steps because such a "move backward would further discourage the loyal North and make it difficult to get men or supplies . . . what was wanted was a forward movement to a victory that would be decisive."[60] With such insights, Grant's mind moved increasingly in tandem with Lincoln's.

Acting rear admiral David D. Porter, commander of the Mississippi Squadron, shared Sherman's skepticism, telling Assistant Secretary of the Navy Gustavus Fox, "I am quite depressed with this adventure, which as you know never met with my approval."[61] Porter knew Grant was staking everything on one enormous roll of the dice. As he warned Grant, "You must recollect that when these gunboats once go below [Vicksburg] we give up all hopes of ever getting them up again."[62] Nevertheless, Porter soon gave the plan all the support Grant could wish. Grant's entire scheme rested on naval cooperation, but he lacked direct power over Porter, who had an ingrained bias against West Point generals.

With his long, full beard and heavy eyebrows, Porter had a stern, fiery air. Many people found him insufferably vain and egotistical, but Grant and Porter had struck up a fine working relationship. Porter liked Grant's "calm, imperturbable face" and his absence of pretension, while Grant deemed Porter "as great an admiral as Lord Nelson."[63] Their rapport established a model for army-navy teamwork in the Civil War.

Right before ten o'clock on the night of April 16, Julia and the children joined Ulysses on the upper deck of a steamer to witness a historic event. Twelve-year-old Fred bustled about while ten-year-old Buck sat in James Wilson's lap. Julia and Ulysses held hands, like a young couple courting. As they sat on deck chairs behind a white railing, seven ironclads, one wooden gunboat, and three transport ships set out single file to sail south past the Vicksburg batteries. Having remained hidden in the undergrowth of the Yazoo River jungle, the fleet now emerged onto the darkened Mississippi waters. It was a clear, starlit night and Charles A. Dana evoked the passing squadron in painterly terms:

> First a mass of black things detached itself from the shore, and we saw it float out toward the middle of the stream. There was nothing to be seen except this big black mass, which dropped slowly down the river. Soon another black mass detached itself, and another, then another. It was Admiral Porter's fleet of ironclad turtles, steamboats, and barges. They floated down the Mississippi darkly and silently, showing neither steam nor light . . . The vessels moved at intervals of about two hundred yards.[64]

Numerous precautions were taken to buffer the ships from the drubbing they would soon undergo. Boilers and decks were packed with hay, logs, cotton bales, sacks of grain, and sandbags that could safely absorb fire or at least muffle it. Ship lights were dimmed and pets banished to prevent telltale sounds that might notify rebel gunners of ships floating by. The boats towed coal barges to have fuel once they cleared the batteries.

Grant watched the proceedings silently, a cigar tucked in his mouth. When the flotilla came within range of Vicksburg's arsenal, Confederate cannon ignited in a thunderous pyrotechnic display—"Magnificent, but terrible," Grant called it—for an hour and a half.[65] Sulphurous smoke drifted everywhere. Little Buck began to bawl in Wilson's arms and was put to bed. To illuminate their targets, the rebels kindled bonfires on the Vicksburg shore and burned a wooden house on the Louisiana side, casting a lurid reddish glow over the ships speeding by. Instead of trying to widen their distance from the batteries, the flotilla hugged the eastern bank, leading shore batteries to overshoot their marks. Dana clocked 525 discharges of fire, of which only 68 hit the target. One heavily bombarded steamer, the *Henry Clay,* went down in flames. "The boat itself took fire and burned to the water's edge and floated downstream a burning mass," Grant reported to Halleck.[66] One other transport was slightly harmed. Miraculously, that was the total damage. While most, if not all, of the gunboats were repeatedly hit, they came through this perilous stretch unscathed, with only fourteen people wounded and none killed.

At once Grant galloped off excitedly to get a firsthand glimpse of the ships downstream.

The next morning he mingled with the armada at New Carthage where crew members were in high spirits. For Grant it had been a sensational triumph, his huge wager paying off brilliantly. Best of all, Pemberton did not seem to realize that the gunboat operation represented the first step of an unfolding sequence that would bring Grant's army en masse to his doorstep. Prematurely celebrating, the *Vicksburg Whig* editorialized that Grant's gunboats "are all more or less damaged, the men dissatisfied and demoralized."[67]

On the cloudy night of April 22, 1863, Grant dispatched six more steamers and twelve barges to brave the Vicksburg armaments and rendezvous with the fleet now stationed farther south. He had concluded that his army could not transport sufficient supplies by wagon down the single narrow road on the western shore. Hence, these transports were packed with critical supplies, each containing one hundred thousand rations and a forty-day supply of coal. Once again Grant was the foremost spectator of the encounter, one Illinois private remembering him "standing on the upper deck of his headquarters boat, a man of iron, his wife by his side. He seemed to me the most immovable figure I ever saw." As a cannonade rained down on his boats from the Vicksburg heights, Grant, counting five hundred shots, remained a study in composure. "No word escaped his lips," recalled the private, "no muscle of his earnest face moved."[68] Once more the operation proved an overwhelming success, with only one steamer destroyed, two damaged, and nobody killed. Grant rode off to meet Porter at Grand Gulf below Vicksburg, the point from which he hoped to launch his massive invasion of Mississippi's interior.

Once the gunboats cleared Vicksburg, Grant focused on the next stage of his master plan: to march his army down the west bank of the Mississippi, starting from Milliken's Bend, under extremely adverse conditions. "This whole country is under water," Grant told his father, "except strips of land behind the levees along the river and bayous and makes operations almost impossible."[69] He committed the entire machinery of his army, putting it irrevocably in motion. That his army managed to march down a watery shoreline in stormy weather was a wonder. Alligators slithered in nearby bayous. Soldiers and wagons sank in the soft, oozing mud, and it sometimes took eighteen horses to dislodge a single heavy gun from the muck. The soldiers lacked time to wash or change mud-smeared clothing. In the amused view of one Iowa soldier, "We are all as dirty as hogs . . . we are all lousy."[70] Nonetheless, the raw recruits plowed ahead with a lusty sense of purpose, throwing off knapsacks and grabbing axes to construct roads. They drained swamps and stripped wood from houses and barns, laying corduroy roads across boggy turf. Since the volunteer ranks included mechanics and other skilled craftsmen, they succeeded in building two floating bridges, each more than three hundred feet, across flooded plains.

Proud of his resourceful soldiers, Grant had no qualms about dismounting from his horse to lend a helping hand. More and more he had developed a mystique as the unglamorous man who got things done. "There was no Bonaparte, posturing for effect," observed an officer. "There was no nonsense, no sentiment; only a plain business man of the republic, there for the one single purpose of getting that command across the river in the shortest time possible."[71] After maddening months of doomed canal projects, Grant seemed liberated by the forward movement, his latent talent quickened into action. As Brigadier General John B. Sanborn remarked, "None who had known him the previous years could recognize him as being the same man . . . From this time all his genius and his energies seemed to burst forth with new life."[72] Instead of proceeding at a trot, Grant sped from place to place at top velocity. By April 27, McClernand's corps had reached its destination, a place of rude cabins named Hard Times, Louisiana, almost directly opposite Grand Gulf, soon followed by McPherson's corps. Two-thirds of Grant's army had now congregated below Vicksburg.

Having mulled over his plans at length, Grant executed a mature, sophisticated strategy with many interlocking parts. While concentrating his forces at Grand Gulf, he would simultaneously disperse enemy forces guarding Vicksburg, proving a master of deception. Early in the war, he had been frustrated by the prowess of Confederate cavalry and now intended to show the North could surpass it. (Late in life, he argued that Stonewall Jackson stood out only because he had fought inexperienced Union troops early in the war and would have been destroyed by Phil Sheridan later on.) Grant tapped Colonel Benjamin H. Grierson to spearhead a bold cavalry raid in eastern Mississippi. This former music teacher and Illinois bandmaster was an improbable choice. Ever since being kicked in the head as a child, he had heartily disliked horses. On April 17, he set out from La Grange, Tennessee, with seventeen hundred horse soldiers on a historic expedition that would cover six hundred miles in sixteen days. Pushing southward, he captured five hundred rebel soldiers and laid down a pell-mell path of destruction that uprooted fifty miles of railroad tracks. Most critical of all, he confused Pemberton about Grant's real intentions, damaged his vital rail links between Jackson and Meridian, made him divert cavalry, and distracted him from Grant's momentous operation at Grand Gulf. As Grant wrote, Grierson had "spread excitement throughout the State, destroyed railroads, trestle works, bridges, burning locomotives & rolling stock taking prisoners destroying stores of all kinds."[73] The stunning raid sent shock waves through the Confederacy as Grierson gave southern towns a taste of the terror that had been so liberally meted out by Nathan Bedford Forrest.

In this campaign of dazzling deceptions, Grant had another trick up his sleeve. He had Sherman take ten regiments and eight gunboats left behind by Porter and feign an attack north of Vicksburg, at Haynes' Bluff, not far from his failed assault at Chickasaw Bayou in December. For two days in late April, Union gunboats lobbed shells, Sherman's artillery chimed in with sporadic fire, and infantry lined up as if girding for a major attack. "The enemy are in front of me in force such as has never before been seen at Vicksburg," a Confederate commander implored Pemberton. "Send me reinforcements."[74] Exactly as Grant had hoped, Pemberton proved a sucker for the ruse and summoned back three thousand troops who had gone to do battle with him.

At 8 a.m. on April 29, as Grant, his son Fred, and Congressman Washburne stared agog from a tugboat, eight gunboats commanded by Admiral Porter began pounding the Confederate batteries at Grand Gulf, forty miles below Vicksburg. The plan called for the navy to soften up the bastion, providing cover for Grant as he whisked his men across the river. As Porter had warned Grant, the Confederate defenses were imposing, set on steep bluffs, and they now dealt a shellacking to Union gunboats. One Iowa soldier remembered "the batteries covering the face of the bluff, tier upon tier, belching forth streams of flame."[75] In the end, Porter did not knock out a single Confederate gun and his flagship absorbed a devastating hit. Grant arrived at the battered ship toward dusk. "The sight of the mangled and dying men which met my eye as I boarded the ship was sickening."[76]

After five hours of fruitless effort, it grew clear that heavily fortified Grand Gulf would not submit, confronting Grant with a tough predicament: he already had ten thousand men boarded on transports, floating in the middle of the river, ready to storm the shore. He proposed a risky, high-stakes gambit to Porter: they would have the gunboats and transports run the Grand Gulf batteries that night, much as at Vicksburg. With some transports now disabled, he wanted to enlist Porter's gunboats as ferries to take his troops across the river afterward. Grant awaited Porter's response with some anxiety. "If he had been a touchy admiral, jealous of his rank, in a severe state of discipline, he would have objected to his boats doing ferry duty," Grant reminisced. Fortunately, Porter "relieved my anxiety by saying that all his gun-boats were at my disposal to be used as transports and ferry-boats for getting the troops over the river."[77]

Grant's unorthodox strategy paid off handsomely. Porter's fleet sprinted past the blockade that night, while Grant had McClernand land his troops on the west side of the river. He had decided to effect a surprise landing at Bruinsburg, Mississippi, a spot of steep hills and thick forest sixty miles south of Vicksburg. The unexpected choice of Bruinsburg came after a local slave informed Grant that the shoreline was unguarded there, enabling his army to travel straight into the interior on dry, elevated land, past fertile plantations.[78] Riding with Grant that night, Dana recorded Grant's extraordinary equanimity and horsemanship at this tense moment: "The night was pitch dark, and, as we rode side by side, Grant's horse suddenly gave a nasty stumble. I expected to see the general go over the animal's head, and I watched intently, not to see if he was hurt, but if he would show any anger. I had been with Grant daily now for three weeks, and I had never seen him ruffled or heard him swear . . . instead of going over the animal's head, as I imagined he would, he kept his seat. Pulling up his horse, he rode on, and, to my utter amazement, without a word or sign of impatience."[79]

The nocturnal maneuver was a tour de force of audacity. McClernand's "troops marched across the point of land [top of a levee] under cover of night, unobserved," Grant recalled. "By the time it was light the enemy saw our whole fleet, iron-clads, gunboats, river steamers and barges, quietly moving down the river three miles below them, black, or rather blue, with National troops."[80] By the morning of April 30, one corps under McClernand and one division under McPherson had floated across the Mississippi, and Grant never forgot the blissful moment when they all debarked safely on the eastern shore: "When this was effected I felt a degree of relief scarcely ever equalled since . . . I was on dry ground on the same side of the river with the enemy."[81]

Once on the eastern Mississippi bank, Grant engaged in a race against time. Knowing the Confederates would hustle troops from Grand Gulf to stop him, he swiftly set his troops in motion toward the interior highland, even before his army finished disembarking. Such precise timing was Grant's specialty. Although transports brought rations galore, he sent out raiding parties to corral wagons from local farmers to carry food and ammunition, and before long his men had commandeered a motley array of vehicles from fancy carriages to rude commodity carts. Herds of cattle were gathered for slaughter. Lest his Washington superiors lodge objections, Grant kept them in the dark until the operation was too far along to be revoked. For the direction of his march, he made a breathtaking decision. Instead of driving straight north toward Vicksburg, sticking close to the river and his supply base, he would veer inland in a northeast direction toward the state capital of Jackson. His basic concept was to throw his army between Pemberton's main force in Vicksburg and a collateral force in Jackson and defeat the enemy piecemeal. The danger was that he might get crushed between two converging armies, whereas his intent was a one-two punch: to destroy the Jackson force first, then turn west and finish off Pemberton in Vicksburg.

Free from swampy terrain, Grant pursued his quarry with a sure step. The first town to fall on May 1 was Port Gibson, where he routed eleven thousand soldiers in daylong fighting and established a bridgehead. As Washburne observed, "The boys went in with such a shout as you never heard, and the enemy ran like the very devil and our boys after them, closing up the day with perfect success."[82] Legend has it that Grant thought the town "too beautiful to burn."[83] He boasted to Halleck afterward that "our victory has been most complete and the Enemy thoroughly demoralized."[84] The road to the Big Black River and Jackson now lay wide open. Grant implemented his plan to have troops feed off local plenty and patrols gathered abundant hams, chickens, mutton, bacon, and molasses, accompanied by sweet potatoes, corn, and strawberries. When a disgruntled farmer rode up on a mule to complain that his farm was stripped bare, a Union general taunted him: "Well, those men didn't belong to my division at all, because if they were my men they wouldn't even have left you that mule."[85] As a rule, Grant tried to blunt any punitive behavior. One terror-stricken woman who fled from Port Gibson wrote and asked if she could return safely with her children. Grant replied: "MADAM— You are at liberty to return to Port Gibson whenever you wish; women and children are non-combatants—we do not make war upon them. U.S. Grant."[86]

For days after crossing at Bruinsburg, Grant stayed on horseback, traveling like a humble private, his saddle devoid of fancy trappings. Temporarily deprived of personal belongings, he had only the clothes on his back and couldn't change his underwear. As Washburne wrote whimsically, "I am afraid Grant will have to be reproved for want of style. On this whole march for five days he has had neither a horse nor an orderly or servant, a blanket or overcoat or clean shirt, or even a sword . . . His entire baggage consists of a tooth-brush."[87] Dana was startled when Grant bedded down for the night on moist grass. "I have an overcoat here; let me put it under you," Dana offered. "I'm too sleepy; don't disturb me," replied Grant, drawing his knees to his chest and nodding off in seconds. The message of Grant's businesslike bravery filtered down to average soldiers. "He could stand any hardship they could stand and do their thinking beside," reflected one officer. "They went with him like men to a game; no despondency, all alert and eager, glad to know inaction had ended and vigorous work had begun."[88]

Twelve-year-old Fred Grant, a stout but fearless boy, crossed the river on a gunboat and made his way to the front, proudly carrying his father's sword and sash. Grant thought his son would stay aboard Porter's flagship and was taken aback to see him riding with Dana, "mounted on two enormous horses, grown white from age, each equipped with dilapidated saddles."[89] It seems odd that Ulysses and Julia Grant allowed Fred's presence in an active war zone, but Grant liked to toughen up his sons and insisted Fred's presence "caused no anxiety either to me or to his mother, who was at home."[90] After Port Gibson, Grant boasted with fatherly pride that young Fred had "heard balls whistle and is not moved in the slightest by it," making him sound like Grant himself as a boy.[91]

On May 3, Union forces reached Grand Gulf, which had been evacuated by Pemberton. Grant was reunited with Admiral Porter and his fleet and for the first time in days indulged in a bath and fresh change of clothes. At first he had entertained a cooperative movement with General Nathaniel Banks to take Port

Hudson to the south. Succeeding Benjamin Butler as commander of Union forces in southern Louisiana, Banks was a former Massachusetts governor and Speaker of the House of Representatives, a prime example of the political generals who bedeviled Grant. Grant imagined that once he helped Banks take Port Hudson, Banks would then turn north for a rendezvous with him, contributing additional men to the onslaught against Vicksburg. Now Grant received a belated letter from Banks, effectively bowing out of the Vicksburg Campaign and saying he would journey up the Red River instead. This was a defining moment for Grant, who opted to skip Port Hudson, forget about Banks, and wager everything on the impending thrust into Mississippi's heartland. "To wait for his [Banks's] cooperation would have detained me at least a month," wrote Grant. "I therefore determined to move independently of Banks, cut loose from my base, destroy the rebel force in rear of Vicksburg, and invest or capture the city."[92] Grant could not afford to squander time by awaiting permission from Halleck and courageously took full responsibility for shucking conventional strategy. As usual, he did not disclose to his corps commanders the overall plan of the campaign.

At first, Sherman feared that Grant planned to supply the army of forty-five thousand men by a long, single road soon glutted with wagons. But an emboldened Grant had no intention of clinging to this supply route and bet everything on his radical departure of feeding off the land, although he never lost touch entirely with his supply base. To his commanders, he laid out a formula for crippling civilian productive capacity in their path: "Impress upon the Cavalry the necessity of keeping out of people's houses, or taking what is of no use to them in a Military point of view. They must live as far as possible off the country through which they pass and destroy corn, wheat crops and everything that can be made use of by the enemy in prolonging the war . . . In other words cripple the rebellion in every way without insulting women and children or taking their clothing, jewelry &c."[93] Faced with these immense logistical challenges, Grant drew on his old quartermaster experience as never before.

When Sherman floated his corps across the Mississippi on May 7, Grant's army was complete and ready for battle. If Grant ever had a go-for-broke moment in the war, it was now as he commenced his high-speed march to Jackson. He wanted to maintain the tempo and badger the enemy with unrelenting pressure. He sent small forces north toward Vicksburg to precipitate minor flurries of fighting and trick Pemberton into thinking that was his intended route, while he rallied his army with ringing words: "Other battles are to be fought. Let us fight them bravely. A grateful country will rejoice at our success, and history will record it with immortal honor."[94] It was a thrilling but terrifying moment as he set out for the interior and left behind communications with Washington and the outside world. The short general with the forgettable appearance infused a winning spirit into his elated troops. "O, what a grand army this is," wrote a young soldier. "I shall never forget the scene today, while looking back upon a mile of solid columns, marching with their old tattered flags streaming in the summer breeze, and harkening to the firm tramp of their broad brogans keeping step to the pealing fife and drum, or the regimental bands discoursing 'Yankee Doodle' or 'The Girl I Left Behind Me.'"[95]

Limited rations endowed Grant's movements with extra urgency. On May 11, he ordered McPherson to seize the town of Raymond, about a dozen miles southwest of Jackson, the next day. "We must fight the enemy before our rations fail," he urged him, "and we are equally bound to make our rations last as long as possible."[96] After McPherson took the town in a bout of spirited fighting, Grant set his sights on the state capital. To isolate Vicksburg and starve it into submission, he needed to obliterate the vital railroad link connecting it to Jackson.

On May 9, the War Department in Richmond had placed Joseph Johnston, a general whom Grant greatly respected, in charge of defending Mississippi, and by nightfall on the thirteenth he arrived in Jackson after an extended train trip from Tennessee. Although enriched by fresh regiments from Georgia and South Carolina, Johnston had only six thousand troops to repulse an imminent Union attack. That same night, Grant's soldiers waded through foot-deep puddles in a rainy, headlong rush toward the state capital. He ordered Sherman and McPherson to hit Jackson hard at dawn. Seeing that it was foolhardy to hold the town against overwhelming odds, Johnston beat a hasty retreat north, and Jackson collapsed with stunning speed, becoming the third southern capital after Nashville and Baton Rouge to succumb to the Yankee interlopers. By three o'clock on the afternoon of May 14, Union forces chased away the last Confederates. Six months earlier, Jefferson Davis had assured his followers that Mississippi citizens would "meet and hurl back these worse than vandal hordes."[97] Instead Grant had registered a hugely lopsided victory.

Seated on high ground in a rural area, Jackson seemed a civilized oasis, with stately public buildings and houses wrapped with wide verandahs. Fred Grant always remembered the Stars and Stripes being run up over the statehouse. In the topsy-turvy fortunes of war, Grant took up residence at Jackson's finest brick hotel, the five-story Bowman House, sleeping in the room occupied by Joseph Johnston the night before. Union soldiers erupted in an orgy of celebration. "If there ever was a jubilant army," said one gunner, "Grant's army in Jackson was that night."[98] In a grim atmosphere of retribution, poor whites and blacks looted stores, and when convicts were released, they set ablaze the local prison, feeding flames that engulfed parts of the town. There were bitter charges that Grant's men had vengefully desecrated the town. "The Yankees were guilty of every kind of vandalism," wrote one British correspondent. "They sacked houses, stole clothing from the negroes, burst open their trunks, and took what little money they had."[99] Rich whites, fearing Grant might incinerate the town, supposedly fled to the countryside for safety.

Grant set forth a very different account: "Joe Johnston set fire to every store house in Jackson before I reached it. That was perfectly justifiable, as he could not take his provisions and did not want them to fall into my hands, but I had to issue two hundred thousand rations to prevent the people from starving."[100] When Grant and Sherman strolled into a cotton mill, they were astonished to discover it going at full throttle, manufacturing tent cloth and other essential goods for the Confederate army. "I guess we shall have to burn this," Grant remarked, and the building was promptly burned to the ground.[101] Most important, Sherman smashed facilities that had allowed Jackson to function as a transportation hub. Previewing things to come, his men also razed arsenals, machine shops, foundries, and factories as well as homes, performing their task with brutal efficiency.

The same day Jackson fell, Grant gained access to a message Johnston had dashed off to Pemberton: "I am anxious to see a force assembled that may be able to inflict a heavy blow upon the enemy."[102] Johnston wanted Pemberton to break out of Vicksburg with a large column of soldiers and unite their two forces to stop Grant. As soon as he divined Confederate intentions, Grant started barking out rapid-fire orders. He knew his own mind and needed no consultation. The all-important goal was to separate Pemberton and Johnston. Two of Grant's corps commanders, McClernand and McPherson, would hurry west and confront Pemberton, while Sherman stayed behind and pinned down Johnston at a safe distance. Grant galloped west to meet McPherson's men, having accomplished his paramount objective: he had flushed Pemberton and a portion of his army from their Vicksburg defenses, forcing them to fight in the open.

The armies of Grant and Pemberton clashed at Champion's Hill, where

Pemberton massed about twenty thousand men. Dug in for miles along a wooded ridge seventy feet high, the rebel position presented distinct challenges to their twenty-nine thousand blue-coated foes. Grant's men would have to traverse ground broken by gullies and ravines. As the battle got under way, Grant found McClernand too timid and dilatory in his forward movements even as McPherson punched away with sure-handed gusto. Both sides discharged fire in thunderous, nonstop volleys. "The rattle of musketry was incessant for hours," wrote a journalist. "Cannons thundered till the heavens seemed bursting."[103]

Grant ordered Brigadier General A. P. Hovey to throw his brigades against the Confederate left. An Indiana lawyer in civilian life, Hovey was "ambitious, active, nervous, irritable, energetic, clear-headed, quick-witted and prompt-handed," as Dana described Hovey to Stanton.[104] In a bloody charge up the ridge, Hovey's men drove the Confederates back before a counterattack forced them to retreat. The seesaw battle was one of unremitting savagery, "one of the most obstinate and murderous conflicts of the war," one of Hovey's men said.[105] At this point, Grant saw his right wing endangered. Drawing on his cigar, he studied the situation with his usual masklike inscrutability. "I was close enough to see his features," said one soldier. "Earnest they were, but signs of inward movement there were none."[106] True to form, Grant dwelled on enemy weakness, spying an opportunity to reverse the battle's course. "If the enemy has driven them he is not in good plight himself," Grant reasoned. "If we can go in again here and make a little showing, I think he will give way."[107] His optimism was justified. Once reinforced, Hovey's soldiers retook the high ground. By midafternoon Pemberton's forces were routed and Grant's units tailed them until after sundown.

More than two thousand of Pemberton's men had been killed or wounded and three thousand prisoners taken, but the Union toll soared to staggering levels as well. In a matter of hours, the gallant Hovey had sacrificed a full third of his division, rendering it a bittersweet victory. As he said, "I cannot think of this bloody hill without sadness and pride . . . It was, after the conflict, literally the hill of death."[108] Grant's joy was somewhat constrained by knowledge that if McClernand had enacted his assigned role, they might have rolled up Pemberton's army. Nonetheless, Vicksburg was now severed from the outside world and it seemed a foregone conclusion that it would fall.

That night Grant slept on the porch of a house that had been converted into a Confederate field hospital and was crammed with dead and mutilated bodies from Champion's Hill. As at Shiloh, the horror of battle only hit him in its aftermath. Once again, death in individualized form affected him more power-fully than mass death. He later offered this candid admission: "While a battle is raging one can see his enemy mowed down by the thousand, or the ten thou-sand, with great composure; but after the battle these scenes are distressing, and one is naturally disposed to do as much to alleviate the suffering of an enemy as a friend."[109]

By the morning of May 17, Grant's army lay within ten miles of Vicksburg. It now squared off against a rebel army that had assumed advantageous positions on the Big Black River, a bayou choked with detritus and fallen trees. Pember-ton's men improvised defenses by stacking cotton bales from a nearby plantation and tossing dirt over them. Tired, their spirits deflated, those men were no match for the élan of Grant's invigorated troops. The big Union breakthrough came from the impetuous action of Brigadier General Michael Lawler. A hearty, corpulent Illinois farmer—"a fine type of the generous, rollicking, fighting Irishman," said an admiring journalist—Lawler brandished his sword and or-dered his men to charge at the enemy across a cotton field.[110] Deflecting a deadly torrent of musket fire, they struggled across the bayou in mud up to their arm-pits. Grant would never have ordered this risky maneuver, but the exhausted Confederates, unnerved by Lawler's daring, immediately stuck cotton on their bayonets in a sign of surrender. On the spot, nearly two thousand prisoners fell to Union forces. Grant refused to quibble with success. As he observed, "When it comes to just plain hard fighting, I would rather trust old Mike Lawler than any of them."[111] One victim was Fred Grant, who was grazed in the right thigh by a bullet, again raising questions about Ulysses's paternal judgment in permit-ting him to loiter in the vicinity of battle.

It had been another one-sided triumph for Grant. The Confederate army suffered 1,751 killed or captured while Grant's lost only 276 killed or wounded. Retreating rebels burned the main bridge over the Big Black—some drowned as they splashed in terror to the other side—and Grant constructed three tempo-rary bridges in one day, slapped together with wood taken from dismantled houses and barns in the area. That night, Grant and Sherman sat together on a log by the river, illuminated by bonfires of pitch pine, and watched their col-umns snake across the Big Black, a sight so vivid Sherman said it made "a fine war picture."[112]

In less than three weeks, Grant had traversed 130 miles on foot and handily won five consecutive battles in a bravura campaign that would be enshrined in military textbooks. He had shown true virtuosity in spontaneously coordinating many moving parts and adapting to shifting enemy positions. With the Army of the Tennessee, he had created the mobile, lightning-quick army for which Lincoln yearned in contrast to the hidebound eastern forces. As Lincoln's secretary John Nicolay exclaimed, "The praise of our western soldiers is on every lip, Illinois valor particularly receiving as it properly should, large honor."[113] Contrary to his image of securing victories at heavy cost, Grant had sacrificed 4,300 men versus 7,200 for the Confederates, even though he had tackled a combined Confederate force at Vicksburg, Grand Gulf, and Jackson of more than 60,000 men, much larger than the 43,000 he transferred across the Mississippi. "Grant is now deservedly the hero," Sherman proclaimed. "He is now belabored with praise by those who a month ago accused him of all the sins in the calendar."[114] One journalist traveling with Grant's army summed up his new stature: "Nothing like this campaign has occurred during this war. It stamps Gen. Grant as a man of uncommon military ability—proves him the foremost one in the west; if not in the nation."[115] *The New York Times,* noting that Grant had captured fifty guns and six thousand prisoners, stressed that this whirlwind operation had been accomplished "in a foreign climate, under a tropical sun ablaze with the white heat of summer, with only such supplies as could be gleaned from the country."[116]

As Grant's columns strode confidently toward Vicksburg, scenes of ecstatic jubilation greeted them as they passed abandoned plantations and were applauded by former slaves. One ex-slave, seated on a lawn, rocking back and forth in joy, kept shouting, "Glory, hallelujah, glory, hallelujah . . . Bless God, bless God. I never spected to see dis day."[117] As his defeated men slunk away from the Big Black, John Pemberton peered into his blighted future. Back at Vicksburg, fearing the worst, he had his men herd cows, sheep, and hogs into the city in anticipation of a prolonged siege. Those Vicksburg residents who thought the "Gibraltar of the West" unassailable were shocked by the tattered, defeated soldiers shuffling back into town. "I shall never forget the woeful sight of a beaten, demoralized army—humanity in the last stage of endurance," said one observer. "Wan, hollow-eyed, ragged, foot-sore, bloody, the men limped along unarmed, followed by siege guns, ambulances, gun carriages and wagons in aimless confusion."[118]

CHAPTER THIRTEEN

Citadel

B
Y MAY 18, Grant and his fifty thousand soldiers began to encircle Vicksburg, with thirty-one thousand Confederate soldiers trapped inside. As they rode toward the town, Grant and Sherman were so eager to secure supplies for their men on the Yazoo River that they rode ahead with advance skirmishers, exposing themselves to danger. As Grant conceded, "The bullets of the enemy whistled by thick and fast for a short time."[1] On May 19, the two men inspected Haynes' Bluff on the high plain north of Vicksburg that Sherman had failed to take in December. As he shifted men east to stem Grant's onrushing army, Pemberton had yielded this critical high ground. The seizure of this recently contested turf elicited a strong response from Sherman, who had been dubious about Grant's strategy. "Until this moment I never thought your expedition would be a success," he admitted to Grant. "I never could see the end clearly; but . . . this is a success if we never take the town."[2] Joseph Johnston had warned Pemberton that if Union troops ever occupied these strategic bluffs, Vicksburg's days would be numbered. In such an eventuality, Johnston advised Pemberton, he should surrender Vicksburg and save his men, assaying an exodus toward the northeast. Pemberton did not heed this timely advice and paid a terrible price with his troops bottled up inside a death trap.

Sure that Pemberton and his men had been disheartened by recent defeats, Grant ordered an assault for the afternoon of May 19, expecting the rebels to capitulate quickly. As an extra measure, he had Admiral Porter project shells into the lower part of the city. At precisely 2 p.m., Grant unleashed three rounds of artillery fire, the signal for his entire line to storm the bulwark with its earth-works linked by rifle pits. Pemberton had built nine forts with walls twenty feet thick. Somehow the defending soldiers, drawing on new reserves of energy, dealt Grant a bloody setback, inflicting almost a thousand Union casualties while suffering fewer than two hundred of their own. Perhaps no less amazed than Grant himself, Pemberton informed Jefferson Davis, "Our men have consider-ably recovered their morale."[3]

Grant would not be easily discouraged and scheduled a follow-up attack for 10 a.m. on May 22. As always, he believed delay would allow the other side to boost its defenses and absorb reinforcements. Ever since crossing the Mississippi, Grant's men had been famished for decent victuals and basic comforts, and be-fore this new assault he made sure they were outfitted with plenty of food, tents, and cooking utensils. Nevertheless, he worried what would happen if his men began to wilt in the Mississippi heat: "There was no telling what the casualties might be among Northern troops working and living in trenches, drinking sur-face water filtered through rich vegetation, under a tropical sun."[4]

The night before the second assault, Porter's gunboats terrorized the town with a blistering barrage of projectiles. Then, at the appointed hour, after Grant's three chief commanders synchronized their watches (a novelty in wartime), all three corps raced forward with fixed bayonets, scaling ladders and ropes to sur-mount the sheer Vicksburg parapets. Although some troops neared the works and even planted their flags, they had to ward off Confederate fire and could not puncture the thick shell that shielded Vicksburg. The result was a second bloodbath—one Illinois colonel called it "the most murderous fire I ever saw"—with 3,200 Union soldiers killed, wounded, and missing.[5] Grant's losses ap-proached his total casualties from the time his army had crossed the river until it approached the citadel.

During the battle, Grant's plan was marred by a misleading report from John A. McClernand, who claimed he had captured two rebel forts and, if given more men, could stage a dramatic breakthrough. This turned out to be an exaggera-tion. But to avoid political problems, Grant diverted much of McPherson's corps to support McClernand, even though he couldn't see that either fort had been taken. The troops he dispatched to McClernand's aid accounted for a full half of the day's casualties. One journalist remembered the reaction of Grant and Rawlins to the self-serving deception. "[I] shall never forget the fearful burst of indignation from Rawlins, and the grim glowering look of disappointment and disgust which settled down on Grant's usually placid countenance, when he was convinced of McClernand's duplicity, and realized its cost in dead and wounded."[6]

Grant wasn't bashful about blaming McClernand. Two days later he sounded off to Halleck, noting that McClernand's dispatches "misled me as to the real state of facts and caused much of this loss. He is entirely unfit for the position of Corps Commander both on the march and on the battle field."[7] Grant had heeded McClernand's call for more troops against his better judgment, and he came to rank the May 22 assault as one of two wartime decisions he most regretted, the other being the later attack at Cold Harbor in Virginia.

After this second assault, with wounded soldiers writhing at the foot of the Mississippi ridge and dead bodies decomposing in fierce sunlight, Grant had to make an excruciating choice. Lest it signal weakness, he was reluctant to submit a request for a truce to inter the dead and care for wounded soldiers who lay helplessly exposed on the battlefield. It was Pemberton on May 25 who suggested a two-and-a-half-hour cease-fire—his soldiers had begun to gag on the stench of corpses—and Grant agreed, doubtless with relief.

Having despaired of taking the fortress by storm, Grant settled down to a classic siege that would choke off every conduit of food, men, and ammunition for those walled up inside. Taking up shovels and spades, his men gouged parallel lines of entrenchment, some just fifty yards from the enemy. Grant trained 220 land guns and 100 naval guns on the beleaguered city. Embedding heavy cannon in embrasures was perilous work as Confederate marksmen zeroed in on Union soldiers. To allay the fear gripping his men, Grant "deliberately clambered on top of the embankment in plain view of the sharpshooters, and directed the men in moving and placing the guns," observed one journalist. "The bullets zipped through the air by dozens, but strangely none of them touched his person or his clothing. He paid no attention to appeals or expostulations . . . and smoked quietly and serenely all the time, except when he removed his cigar to speak to the men at work. His example shamed the men into making a show of courage."[8]

The prospect of Johnston hastening in from the east to lift the siege and rescue Pemberton haunted Grant, who told Sherman that Johnston "was about the only general on that side whom he feared."[9] To counter this threat, Grant assigned Sherman, his most trusted commander, to fend it off. "I never had a moment's care while Sherman was there," Grant reminisced. "I don't think Sherman ever went to bed with his clothes off during that campaign, or allowed a night to pass without visiting his pickets in person."[10] As Grant besieged

Vicksburg, Confederate generals knew he was far different from the pushovers they had trounced in the eastern theater. Johnston wrote soberly to the Confederate war secretary James A. Seddon: "Grant's army is estimated at 60,000 or 80,000 men, and his troops are worth double the number of northeastern troops. We cannot relieve General Pemberton except by defeating Grant, who is believed to be fortifying."[11] Abraham Lincoln's faith in Grant was being rewarded. "Whether Gen. Grant shall or shall not consummate the capture of Vicksburg," he wrote on May 26, "his campaign from the beginning of this month up to the twenty second day of it, is one of the most brilliant in the world"—a judgment in which military historians would concur.[12]

Grant's competence stood in striking contrast to the bumbling ineptitude of Fighting Joe Hooker, whose nickname had proven a sad misnomer at Chancellorsville, Virginia, in early May. Despite outnumbering Robert E. Lee by two to one, Hooker had been as timidly erratic as McClellan. When he received the telegram about the Chancellorsville debacle, Lincoln paced the room in despair, hands clasped behind his back. This fresh disappointment with an eastern commander was more than his frazzled nerves could bear. "My God! My God!" he wailed. "What will the country say! What will the country say!"[13] Edwin Stanton identified this as "the darkest day of the war."[14] The only consolation anyone in Washington could extract from Chancellorsville was that Stonewall Jackson had been wounded by friendly fire and died in its aftermath. By late June, Lincoln cashiered Hooker, telling his cabinet he had exhibited "the same failings that were observed in McClellan after the battle of Antietam—a want of alacrity to obey, and a greedy call for more troops which could not . . . be taken from other points."[15] Major General George Gordon Meade took command of the Army of the Potomac. Amid such disillusionment, Lincoln valued more highly Grant's distant victories. If occasionally vexed by his secrecy, Lincoln enjoyed the novelty of a general who took the offensive without any official prodding and had battle in his bloodstream.

By late May, Grant was ready to relieve McClernand for his erroneous May 22 dispatch. Sherman had warned him that McClernand was intriguing against him, circulating false stories in the press. Stanton gave Grant full power "to remove any person who by ignorance in action or any cause interferes with or delays his operations."[16] Nevertheless, Grant knew McClernand had the president's ear and bided his time until Vicksburg was taken, which would enhance his own stature and make it easier to sack his faithless subordinate.

Then McClernand committed a blunder that played straight into Grant's hands, delivering a self-congratulatory speech to his men that found its way into the press. Not only did McClernand try to steal the glory of the Vicksburg Campaign, he reiterated his bogus claim that the failure to reinforce him on May 22 had stopped him from taking the city. This bombastic, egotistical statement violated War Department rules about publishing such boasts. McClernand hadn't cleared its publication with Grant, making him insubordinate. Grant now had all the ammunition he needed to banish him. He also fretted that, if he were disabled, his army command would settle on McClernand, who never got along with Sherman and McPherson. He now fired McClernand, with Rawlins heightening the effect by sending Colonel James H. Wilson to his tent at two o'clock in the morning to notify him of the decision. McClernand evidently knew what was coming. Wilson found him seated behind a table, two tapers burning, his sword laid out before him. Grant hadn't consulted anyone in Washington before handing out this summary justice. Subject to Lincoln's approval, he replaced McClernand with Major General Edward O. C. Ord. With McClernand exiled, Grant enjoyed undisputed control over the Vicksburg siege, having eliminated all rivals in the west.

The one nemesis Grant could not escape was a whispering campaign about his drinking. The protracted Vicksburg operation had imposed excruciating stress on Grant, who must have been sorely tempted to drink. A remarkable photograph taken of him that spring tells a haunting tale. There is an indescribable look of suffering in his sad, woebegone eyes, showing the terrible toll taken by the previous months. It is less the portrait of a conqueror than of a troubled survivor.

Historians have studied allegations that Grant got roaring drunk at a town called Satartia, northeast of Vicksburg, on an inspection trip up the Yazoo River on June 6, 1863, an episode that has become encrusted with legend. In early June, Grant suffered headaches or a spell of ill health that prompted Dr. Charles McMillan to prescribe wine as a sovereign remedy, not an uncommon practice at the time. This apparently led to more indulgence by Grant. Learning he had strayed from the strict path of sobriety, John Rawlins, his resident conscience, drafted an extraordinary rebuke to him in the wee hours of June 6 that seethed with moralistic outrage:

> The great solicitude I feel for the safety of this army leads me to
> mention what I had hoped never again to do—the subject of your
> drinking . . . I have heard that Dr. McMillan . . . induced you,

notwithstanding your pledge to me, to take a glass of wine, and today, when I found a box of wine in front of your tent and proposed to move it, which I did, I was told that you had forbid its being taken away, for you intended to keep it until you entered Vicksburg, that you might have it for your friends; and tonight, when you should, because of the condition of your health if nothing else, have been in bed, I find you where the wine bottle has just been emptied, in company with those who drink and urge you to do likewise, and the lack of your usual promptness of decision and clearness in expressing yourself in writing tended to confirm my suspicions. You have the *full* control of your appetite and can let drinking alone. Had you not pledged me the sincerity of your honor early last March that you would drink no more during the war, and kept that pledge during your recent campaign, you would not today have stood first in the world's history as a successful military leader.[17]

Some historians question whether Rawlins actually delivered this letter, but he himself wrote that he gave it to Grant: "Its admonitions were heeded, and all went well."[18] Years later Charles A. Dana said that he was with Grant when Rawlins rode up and handed "that admirable communication" to him.[19] Far from bristling at such chastisement, Grant continued to embrace Rawlins as his most valuable staff officer, singling him out in July for his "gallant and meritorious services."[20]

Although Rawlins claimed his admonition was heeded, it seems to have been followed by a far more significant lapse by Grant. As his hold on Vicksburg strengthened, Grant still worried that Johnston would roar in from the east and raise the siege, leading him to mass a Union force east of Satartia to forestall that possibility. His fears were further inflamed when Johnston sent a large, threatening force that took Yazoo City, north of Satartia, leading Grant to take a steamer up the Yazoo River, in Dana's company, to investigate the developing situation for himself.

A distinguished correspondent for the *Chicago Times* and the *New York Herald*, Sylvanus Cadwallader, a loquacious but prickly man, later conjured up a notorious tale of Grant's mad, drunken escapade on this trip. Virtually alone among journalists, he lived at camp with Grant, often messed and rode with him, became an ostensible staff member, and was the only reporter with privileged access to headquarters. Despite later writing about Grant's indiscretions, Cadwallader had inordinate admiration for him, hailing him as "the greatest military chieftain his generation produced."[21] So close did the journalist become with Rawlins that they lived together after the war, and Cadwallader even named his son Rawlins. Grant reserved his highest accolade for Cadwallader, telling him in September 1864, "For two years past I have seen more of you personally probably than of all other correspondents put together," and he commended his exemplary work in adhering to the legitimate journalistic duties assigned to him.[22]

Not wishing to violate confidentiality, Cadwallader delayed composing his memoirs until the late 1880s and early 1890s, when he was tending sheep in California. Fred Grant encouraged him to write, saying that "you certainly occupied a position with the Army that gave you great insight into affairs."[23] When the book was belatedly published in 1955, the historian Bruce Catton greeted it as "one of the great books of the Civil War."[24] Far from attempting to debunk Grant, Cadwallader intended to "emphasize his virtues" and show how the "splendor of his achievements will prove amply sufficient to cover all minor imperfections."[25] If Cadwallader had any ax to grind, it came from his belief that Grant in his *Memoirs* had slighted the wartime contribution of their mutual friend John A. Rawlins.

What we know for certain about the Satartia trip is that on June 6, at Haynes' Bluff, Grant and Dana boarded a small craft, USS *Diligence*, which carried them up the Yazoo River. Soon after their departure, Grant became ill—this may have been a euphemism for drunk—and fell asleep in a cabin. When the *Diligence* approached within two miles of Satartia, it met two Union gunboats heading downstream. Their officers came aboard the steamer and warned that because of Confederate activity in the area and a federal withdrawal, it was too dangerous to proceed any farther. Dana said the officers tried to converse "with General Grant who was not in a condition to conduct an intelligent conversation"—a clear indication Grant was drunk.[26] Under the circumstances, it was Dana, not Grant, who made the decision to have the boat turn back and return to Haynes' Bluff, escorted by gunboats. When Grant awoke the next morning, perfectly sober, he imagined they were at Satartia. Dana had to explain that they had turned around and were back at Haynes' Bluff, suggesting Grant had blacked out during the trip.[27] Later Dana insisted that on the "excursion up the Yazoo River" Grant had gotten "as stupidly drunk as the immortal nature of man would allow; but the next day he came out as fresh as a rose, without any trace or indication of the spree he had passed through."[28] Ironically, Dana, originally sent by Stanton to spy on Grant's drinking, became, like Rawlins, an unexpected accomplice in concealing the problem.

In narrating this tale, Sylvanus Cadwallader made a startling imaginative leap, placing himself aboard the boat to Satartia in lieu of Dana, even though contemporary records confirm that Cadwallader was absent and Dana present. Cadwallader described Grant's clownish behavior when tipsy: "He made several trips to the bar room of the boat in a short time, and became stupid in speech and staggering in gait."[29] According to Cadwallader, he prevailed upon the captain to bolt the barroom, denying Grant access to more liquor. Casting himself in a heroic light, Cadwallader said he locked himself into a cabin with Grant and began to chuck whiskey bottles from the window to protect him. When Grant protested angrily, the journalist supposedly got him to lie down and behave. "As it was a very hot day and the State-room almost suffocating, I insisted on his taking off his coat, vest and boots, and lying down in one of the berths. After much resistance I succeeded, and soon fanned him to sleep."[30]

The wildest part of Cadwallader's story involved Grant mounting a horse named Kangaroo after they returned to Haynes' Bluff and then careering through the woods. "The road was crooked and tortuous, following the firmest ground between sloughs and bayous, and was bridged over these in several places . . . He went at about full speed through camps and corrals, heading only for the bridges, and literally tore through and over everything in his way." Cadwallader allegedly charged after him on horseback and overtook him. "I secured his bridle rein to my own saddle and convinced him that I was master of the situation. His intoxication increased so in a few minutes that he became unsteady in the saddle." So subordinates would not see Grant intoxicated, Cadwallader "induced the General to lay down on the grass with the saddle for a pillow. He was soon asleep."[31] Cadwallader summoned an ambulance to fetch them back to camp. As they arrived at midnight, an alarmed Rawlins stood waiting. When Grant emerged from the ambulance, he "shrugged his shoulders, pulled down his vest, 'shook himself together,' as one just rising from a nap, and seeing Rawlins and [Colonel John] Riggin, bid them good-night in a natural tone and manner, and started to his tent as steadily as he ever walked in his life."[32]

What to make of this fantastic tale? Aside from the fact that Cadwallader wasn't on the trip to Satartia, many preposterous details strain credulity. If

Grant engaged in a drunken, high-speed chase across bridges and through Union camps, many people would have noticed and recorded the shocking sight. No one did. It is also the only account of Grant drinking where he gets drunk, sobers up, then immediately gets drunk again. Grant also never allowed his men to see him drunk. It is impossible to take the Cadwallader story at face value.

At the same time, it shows remarkable consistency with other drinking stories about Grant—the granite self-command breaking down under the influence; the slurred speech, wobbly gait, and sudden personality change; the strange reversion to a babbling, childlike state; the straightening up and getting sober and resuming his official personality in a twinkling. These factors make one suspect that the story, though hugely embellished, may contain a kernel of truth instead of being concocted whole cloth by Cadwallader's overwrought imagination. In all likelihood, Cadwallader heard the story of the Satartia trip from Dana or Rawlins and presented it as his own eyewitness account for dramatic effect or self-aggrandizement.

In his memoir, Cadwallader did provide a sound analysis of Grant's drinking habits: how he would resolve after a bender never to drink again; how that pledge would hold for several months; how many people close to him never saw him drunk; how he sat soberly at banquets with his glass turned upside down. "He was not an habitual drinker. He could not drink moderately. When at long intervals his appetite for strong drink caused him to accept the invitation of some old classmate, or army associate, to take 'just one glass before parting,' he invariably drank to excess unless some one was with him (whose control he would acknowledge) to lead him away from temptation."[33] Cadwallader also noted the merciless retribution Rawlins visited on anybody who led Grant down the primrose path: "Later on it was no secret that any staff officer who offered the General a glass of liquor, or drank with him . . . would be disgracefully dismissed and actually degraded in rank."[34]

Like Cadwallader, Dana left a knowing description of Grant's drinking, arguing that he always had a degree of control over it—somewhat unusual for an alcoholic. He noted that Grant never drank when it might imperil his army, but "always chose a time when the gratification of his appetite for drink would not interfere with any important movement that had to be directed or attended by him."[35] Of the Satartia trip, he said, "It was a dull period in the campaign. The siege of Vicksburg was proceeding with regularity."[36] Dana provided a convincing explanation of why some people close to Grant claimed, in all honesty, that they never saw these drinking episodes: "The times were chosen with perfect judgment, and when it was all over, no outsider would have suspected that such things had been."[37] He asserted that Grant drank only at three- or four-month intervals and that he knew of only "two or three other occasions" when he got seriously drunk.[38] In other words, Charles A. Dana had arrived at the same conclusion as John A. Rawlins: that Ulysses S. Grant was so essential to the Union cause that it was better to shield his sporadic binges than expose him to official censure. The story of the Yazoo River bender was an isolated case of Grant's drinking in a dangerous war zone where enemy forces were concentrated.

Perhaps alarmed by his binge, Grant on June 9 invited Julia and the children to join him at Vicksburg, where they could stay on a steamer during the siege. His son Fred—now "a thoughtful, serious boy and very sensible," said one relative—had stayed by his side during the campaign and adored his father for showing such faith in his maturity.[39] "I had the happiness as a child and as a man of being his constant companion in peace and war."[40] Grant obtained a Shetland pony for his youngest boy, Jesse, who joined him on inspection tours, "often perched behind him," wrote Jesse, "and clinging to his belt as we thundered along upon a big buckskin horse that had been presented to him, called, because of its viciousness, Mankiller."[41]

Unable to find a comfortable wartime niche with the Grant family and condemned to a vagabond life, Julia welcomed her periodic stays with her husband, when she was known to pore over military maps and was said to possess an excellent grasp of military strategy. As Grant's influence grew, so did hers, and she exercised it benevolently. "She had a kindly, gracious way that captured us," noted one general. "The officers who had annoyances and grievances that they could not take to the General, appealed to Mrs. Grant . . . and many an officer could thank her for solving his grievances."[42] And when Julia Grant was around, the stories about her husband's drinking had a way of disappearing instantly.

As he blasted Vicksburg into submission, Grant had no doubt the town would submit. He now had more than seventy thousand men camped in the vicinity and was surprised Pemberton made no attempt to slash his way out: "I didn't think the rebels would be such fools as to shut up thirty thousand troops there for me to capture."[43] It was a gargantuan feat to strangle Vicksburg, hemmed in by ravines and fallen trees. Grant established a Union line fifteen miles long to contain seven miles of enemy fortifications. He watched as federal trenches crept close enough to Vicksburg that his soldiers, crouching behind bulletproof sandbags, could toss hand grenades into the Confederate forts. Union infantry was protected by sharpshooters with such expert aim that rebel soldiers dared not poke their heads above the parapets. All the while, Grant shelled the city at regular intervals, sowing terror among the inhabitants, who slowly regressed to a primitive state.

Plagued by early summer heat and steady rain, Grant worked hard to strengthen his men's morale, even though one British doctor concluded that "no man alive could have counteracted the effects of that climate. Malaria, salt pork, no vegetables, a blazing sun, and almost poisonous water, are agencies against which medicine is helpless."[44] After two aborted assaults and many casualties, Union soldiers willingly endured a siege that spared them further bloodshed. Grant constantly fraternized with his men. One newspaperman noted how he sauntered about in worn clothes, his left hand thrust in his pocket, an unlit cigar in his mouth, his brow contracted thoughtfully. Grant, he discerned, inspired more respect than affection: "They do not salute him, they only watch him . . . with a certain sort of familiar reverence."[45] Grant never assumed military airs and talked casually with his men, as if he were a peer. "He sat on the ground and talked with the boys with less reserve than many a little puppy of a lieutenant," wrote an Illinois soldier.[46] Everyone noticed Grant's strangely nonchalant demeanor in a war zone. One day he strolled about in full view of Confederate marksmen as enemy bullets raised the dust around him. A newspaper reporter who did not recognize him shouted: "Stoop down, *down,* damn you, down!"[47] Grant didn't flinch.

Inside Vicksburg, General Pemberton banked all hope for deliverance on Joseph E. Johnston, a short, dapper, elegant-looking Virginian with a graying goatee, finely trimmed side-whiskers, and sharply chiseled features. With a certain romantic dash, Johnston liked to ride into battle sporting a black feather in his hat. Whenever his troops cheered him, a Tennessee soldier claimed, "Old Joe smiles as blandly as a modest maid, raises his hat in acknowledgment, makes a polite bow, and rides toward the firing."[48]

By mid-June, Pemberton flooded Johnston with desperate pleas for relief from the relentless salvos, but despite the large army at his disposal, Johnston offered no consolation. "I consider saving Vicksburg hopeless," he replied.[49] Horrified by this defeatist attitude, Confederate secretary of war Seddon lectured Johnston that "Vicksburg must not be lost without a desperate struggle. The interest and honor of the Confederacy forbid it." Johnston said Grant had done his work too thoroughly to be defeated. "Grant's position, naturally very strong, is intrenched and protected by powerful artillery, and the roads obstructed."[50] The confident Grant, while he respected Johnston beyond other Confederate generals, said he would be thrilled if he dared to barge his way into Vicksburg: "If Johnston tries to cut his way in we will let him do it . . . You say he has 30,000 men with him? That will give us 30,000 more prisoners than we now have."[51] By June 11, Grant blocked the last road between Pemberton and Johnston, hermetically sealing off Vicksburg. Later he said he regretted not having been able to confront Johnston's army, which would have permitted him to destroy two armies at once.

Grant rejected pleas for more men from General Banks, who had laid siege to Port Hudson, farther south on the Mississippi, just north of Baton Rouge. The original plan called for Banks to overrun Port Hudson, then steam up the river and cooperate with Grant's operation against Vicksburg, but the effort to subdue Port Hudson proved long and hazardous. Halleck was enraged at Banks for failing to unite his forces with Grant's, yet he seemed powerless to rein in the political general.[52]

In Washington, Lincoln studied telegrams from Vicksburg as he anxiously awaited the siege's outcome. An Associated Press reporter watched in the War Department telegraph office as the president absorbed an erroneous dispatch bringing dreadful news from Vicksburg. At once Lincoln looked "nervous," his whole frame "shook violently," and his face whitened with a "ghastly" pallor.[53] Lincoln never wavered in his belief that Vicksburg represented the centerpiece of Confederate defenses in the west. "We can take all the northern ports of the Confederacy," he insisted, "and they can defy us from Vicksburg."[54]

With deserters pouring from the town daily, Grant had a precise image of the brutal condition of soldiers and citizens cooped up inside. Hunger had yielded to starvation as dogs, cats, and even rats vanished from the city. Soldiers accustomed to beef and bacon settled for leathery mule meat, supplemented by small portions of rice, corn, and peas. Many contracted scurvy, and by late June half the garrison was laid low by illness.

Although bombarding civilian populations would be commonplace in future conflicts, it still arose as a dreadful novelty in the Civil War. Fleeing nonstop shelling, Vicksburg residents sought shelter in cellars or man-made caves carved out of hillsides. People spent so much time in these improvised bunkers that they furnished them with carpets, beds, and easy chairs until they resembled rude

apartments. "Caves were the fashion—the rage—over besieged Vicksburg," recorded a survivor.[55] Nighttime bombardments made these cave dwellers shrink
in terror as they listened to the shrieking whistle of diving shells. "Morning
found us more dead than alive, with blanched faces and trembling lips," wrote
one young woman.[56] To perk up the failing spirits of residents, local newspapers
kept alive the dreamlike prospect that Joseph Johnston would materialize to
deliver them from blue-coated evil. Confronted with a newsprint shortage, local
papers published their columns on the backs of rectangular sections of wallpaper
with bright floral prints.

As the siege wore on, Grant presided over a vast expansion in the care of
runaway slaves, who now streamed into his camp in enormous numbers. Several
hundred thousand slaves were liberated by Grant's army, and he enlisted them to
perform vital military duties. Black auxiliaries engaged in dangerous, arduous
tasks: digging trenches and rifle pits around Vicksburg, enhancing Union defenses at Haynes' Bluff and Grand Gulf, and tearing up railroad tracks east of
the city. They became so indispensable that one colonel wrote to McClernand
and pleaded for more: "I hardly know how I am to get along unless I can have
some more Contrabands."[57]

Grant embraced the new policy of arming Negroes promulgated by Halleck
on March 30, 1863: "It is the policy of the government to withdraw from the
enemy as much productive labor as possible . . . it is the opinion of many who
have examined the question without passion or prejudice, that [former slaves]
can also be used as a military force."[58] Three weeks later, Grant reported to Halleck that he had equipped black soldiers for the first time: "At least three of my
Army Corps Commanders take hold of the new policy of arming the negroes
and using them against the rebels with a will . . . You may rely on my carrying
out any policy ordered by proper authority to the best of my ability."[59]

In late March, Lincoln had dispatched Brigadier General Lorenzo Thomas,
adjutant general of the U.S. Army, to confer with Grant about the plight of liberated slaves—the so-called freed people—and aid the recruitment of black troops,
a policy that formed a natural sequel to the Emancipation Proclamation. The
ulterior purpose of Thomas's trip was to assess Grant's military performance
at Vicksburg. On April 11, when he arrived in camp, he was bowled over by
Grant and soon confessed himself "a Grant man all over."[60] In cobbling together
black regiments, Thomas displayed a crusading style, delivering rousing speeches
to counter deeply rooted racial prejudice endemic in the northern army. The

bigotry was so ingrained that one Ohio soldier warned northern soldiers "would lay down their arms and unbuckle their swords" if Washington persisted in arming blacks.[61] By year end, Thomas had plucked twenty thousand young black men from contraband camps in the Mississippi Valley and absorbed them into African American regiments. Grant placed the full weight of his prestige into coaxing his commanders to flesh out these new regiments.

All the while, Grant maintained his enthusiastic backing of Chaplain John Eaton, the general superintendent in the Mississippi Valley, who provided education, shelter, medical care, and employment to people in contraband camps, where disease and despair proliferated and mortality rates often ran high. When Eaton met Grant on June 11, the chaplain immediately saw in the seamed face and crow's-feet around Grant's eyes the stress of the rugged Vicksburg Campaign. "He was dressed . . . in an old brown linen duster surmounted by an old slouch hat; his trousers showed holes worn by the boot-straps, where they had rubbed against the saddle."[62]

Even amid the siege, Grant devoted time to Eaton, who read aloud to him a report he had written covering thirty-four pages of foolscap. Grant "showed not a sign of weariness to the end," reported Eaton, "and when I had finished he remarked: 'That is a very important report. I must send you with it to the President, with a personal letter.'"[63] Grant wrote promptly to Lincoln, saying the document would bring him up to date on the "negroes . . . coming into our lines in great numbers." He described Eaton's conscientious supervision of contraband camps. "Mr. Eaton's labors in his undertaking have been unremitting and skillful and I fear in many instances very trying. That he has been of very great service to the blacks in having them provided for when otherwise they would have been neglected . . . the accompanying report will show."[64] Frederick Douglass stated that Lincoln received the report from its emissary "with the greatest satisfaction, asking many questions about General Grant's views upon the whole subject of the treatment of the colored people . . . he repeated the expressions of his gratification that a General who was winning such military successes over the rebels was able, from a military standpoint, to give him so many practical illustrations of the benefits of the emancipation policy."[65] This reaction says much about Grant's rising star in the Lincoln firmament, for he was fast becoming the president's beau ideal of a general: one who regularly beat the enemy while endorsing the expanded war aims.

John Eaton grew so intimate with Grant that they even touched upon the delicate subject of Grant's prewar drinking travails. "It was plain that the army life in Washington Territory and Oregon had been full of temptations, and it is more than probable that he followed the example of the other officers while there," Eaton wrote. "To escape from the environment was certainly one motive for his leaving the army."[66] Eaton was impressed by Grant's candor and came to believe that the early stories of his drinking were true, the later ones baseless.

Just how much Grant would support the newly emancipated slaves became evident at a fertile spot called Davis Bend, located on a Mississippi River peninsula, about twenty-five miles below Vicksburg. Jefferson Davis and his rich brother Joseph had owned huge slave plantations there. When Joseph fled in 1862, his slaves invaded the mansion house and divided clothing and furniture among themselves. Even before Union troops came on the scene, the onetime slaves already operated the plantation. Grant spied a prime opportunity to create a model community for blacks that would showcase their industry and self-reliance. As Eaton recalled, "It was General Grant's desire that these plantations should be occupied by the freedmen, and, to quote his own words, 'become a Negro paradise.'"[67] Grant wasn't responding to a Washington directive but undertook this on his own initiative.

The experiment fully corroborated Grant's expansive vision. The land was leased to the freedmen, who paid the government for their rations, mules, and tools. While men worked the cotton fields, women tended vegetable gardens and peddled their wares to steamboat traffic on the Mississippi. Residents showed skill and enterprise at every turn, building a church, a schoolhouse, and an infirmary that housed orphaned children and elderly, ailing residents. By 1865 the Davis Bend community produced two thousand bales of cotton, earning a $16,000 profit and proving to skeptics that freed people could be fully productive, self-supporting members of society.

Grant's transformation into an imaginative abolitionist arose partly from his conception of himself as a professional soldier who believed in military subservience to civilian rule; he was following a changed policy that flowed down from the president. The evolution in his thinking was influenced by other factors, however, including the battlefield performance of blacks. Although the Emancipation Proclamation made them eligible for military service, many northern commanders wondered whether they were capable of courage and discipline, a prejudice that seeped down to the common soldiers. "The idea of arming and equipping Negro Regiments for the purpose of making them soldiers is, to my mind, worse than ridiculous nonsense," said an Iowa soldier at Vicksburg. "Blacks would only work *if you made them do so*."[68] If Grant reserved any private doubts on the matter, a historic battle at Milliken's Bend on the Mississippi on June 7, helped to retire them forever.

On that day, two thousand Texan troops under Major General John Walker invaded a Union supply depot, garrisoned by a thousand, mostly black, troops recently mustered into regiments in Grant's district. Jefferson Davis had already warned that rebellious slaves in northern uniforms would be sent back to their old masters or hanged as criminals. Southern soldiers often reacted viciously when they encountered former slaves in uniform. Arming blacks trespassed on sacred taboos for many of them, and they now flew black flags as a sign they would give no quarter. The Union victory at Milliken's Bend was notable for its hand-to-hand savagery. "After it was over," wrote Charles Dana, "many men were found dead with bayonet stabs, and others with their skulls broken open by butts of muskets."[69] Rebel soldiers reportedly butchered blacks whom they captured and even sold some of them as slaves. Far from succumbing to terror, the novice black troops, stuck with outdated muskets, fought off the larger rebel contingent and won honor for blacks everywhere with their bayonet charge. Dana believed the engagement had "completely revolutionized the sentiment of the army with regard to the employment of negro troops. I heard prominent officers who formerly in private had sneered at the idea of the negroes fighting express themselves after that as heartily in favor of it."[70] The defeat shocked southern sensibilities, and one stupefied Confederate lady wrote it was "hard to believe that Southern soldiers—and Texans at that—have been whipped by a mongrel crew of white and black Yankees. There must be some mistake."[71]

Grant was profoundly impressed by his black troops' performance at Milliken's Bend. "This was the first important engagement of the war in which colored troops were under fire," he wrote. "These men were very raw, having all been enlisted since the beginning of the siege, but they behaved well."[72] He assured Lorenzo Thomas the black soldiers had been "most gallant and I doubt not but with good officers they will make good troops."[73] The word soon made the rounds that Grant had gone from being a reluctant recruit to abolitionism to an ardent convert. In late July, Senator Henry Wilson of Massachusetts reported on a conversation with Dana about Grant: "He says that [Grant] is in favor of destroying the cause of this civil war—of overthrowing Slavery and that his army is deeply imbued with the same feeling."[74]

That Grant, whose army occupied the region with the most black refugees, was an enthusiastic proponent of black regiments ingratiated him with Lincoln. "The colored population is the great *available* and yet *unavailed* of, force for restoring the Union," the president told Governor Andrew Johnson of Tennessee. "The bare sight of fifty thousand armed, and drilled black soldiers on the banks of the Mississippi, would end the rebellion at once."[75] That May, Lincoln mused aloud to visiting church leaders that he "would gladly receive into the service not ten thousand but ten times ten thousand colored troops."[76] Grant was the general best positioned to translate this wish into reality. On August 23, he sent Lincoln a remarkable letter in which he made it clear that he endorsed the recruitment of black regiments both as an order he was bound to obey and as something he *personally approved:*

> Gen. [Lorenzo] Thomas is now with me and you may rely on it I will give him all the aid in my power. I would do this whether the arming of the negro seemed to me a wise policy or not, because it is an order that I am bound to obey and do not feel that in my position I have a right to question any policy of the Government. In this particular instance there is no objection however to my expressing an honest conviction. That is, by arming the negro we have added a powerful ally. They will make good soldiers and taking them from the enemy weaken him in the same proportion they strengthen us. I am therefore most decidedly in favor of pushing this policy to the enlistment of a force sufficient to hold all the South falling into our hands and to aid in capturing more.[77]

Here Grant stepped outside a narrowly defined military role to declare himself in personal harmony with Lincoln's overarching political objectives. His letter had the intended effect. On August 29, Secretary of the Treasury Chase recorded in his diary that Lincoln came into his office carrying Grant's message and one of similar tenor from Banks about arming negro troops. "Both Generals express confidence in the efficiency of these troops and clear opinions in favor of using them. These letters give much satisfaction to the president."[78]

Black soldiers still faced innumerable indignities. Until June 1864, they pocketed less pay than white counterparts, discrimination that stung deeply. But their sacrifice for the Union cause gave them pride, political standing, and leadership skills. Frederick Douglass recognized that once the black man had "a musket on his shoulder, and a bullet in his pocket," there was "no power on earth" that could "deny that he has earned the right of citizenship in the United States."[79]

As late June approached, Grant continued to pummel Vicksburg, preparing his opponents for capitulation. Morale eroded inside the beleaguered fortress as Pemberton's men stripped wood from houses to construct a crude fleet of boats by which they hoped to escape to the Louisiana shore of the Mississippi River. Grant notified Admiral Porter to be on the lookout for clandestine nocturnal efforts to cross the waterway. "Had the attempt been made," Grant wrote, "the garrison of Vicksburg would have been drowned, or made prisoners on the Louisiana side."[80] All the while, Sherman tightened the Union stranglehold on the city by obstructing roads with fallen timbers to forestall any outside attack by Johnston's forces. Grant gave him thirty-four thousand soldiers to form a firewall around the city, a move that Sherman brilliantly executed.

Always open to technological innovations in warfare, Grant approved the explosion of a Union mine intended to topple one of the enemy forts. Into a network of trenches and tunnels General McPherson managed to load twelve hundred pounds of explosives. They were detonated with such force that they threw up a huge cloud of white smoke, gouging out a crater thirty-five feet in diameter. Several Confederate soldiers were whirled up into the air and tossed down, still alive, on the Union side. Unfortunately, for all the fireworks, the explosion failed to break open the nearby fort and the effort came to naught.

By the end of June, as Joseph Johnston marched four divisions toward the Big Black River, Grant braced for a huge fight. Meanwhile, daily rations inside Vicksburg dwindled, leading to starvation. With his light fieldpieces aimed at the fortress, backed by big naval guns and mortar boats floating in the river, Grant exercised a commanding position over the battered city. He set off a second mine explosion on July 1, bringing his army right up to the parapets in three different places. He ensured easy access to these ramparts for his men by laying planks and bags packed tightly with cotton over swampy ditches, enabling them to rush uphill with sure, rapid steps.

It was a misfortune for the South that John C. Pemberton was a Yankee with two brothers fighting on the northern side. A decent administrator, he lacked verve as a fighting general. A brusque, crusty Pennsylvanian who attended West Point, he had fallen under the spell of the South, having wed a Virginia woman whose fervent embrace of secession bound him to the Confederacy. Grant laughingly tagged him as "a northern man who had got into bad company."[81] Even

had he not aroused southern suspicions by his northern birth, Pemberton's curmudgeonly personality would have earned him a large quota of enemies. As Lieutenant General Theophilus Holmes pointed out, Pemberton had "many ways of
making people hate him and none to inspire confidence."[82] Where another general might have heeded Johnston's warning about not getting bogged down in
Vicksburg, Pemberton dreaded charges that he had abandoned the city because
of his northern background and feared a treason prosecution. As he mulled over
surrender to Grant and pondered the "vanity of our foes," he somehow fancied
that Grant might confer lenient terms if allowed to take the town on Independence Day, July 4.[83] Grant was neither vain nor tender in this regard.

By July 1, Pemberton saw his last hopes vanish amid a desperate food shortage for his army. "Unless the siege of Vicksburg is raised, or supplies are thrown
in," he warned his commanders, "it will become necessary very shortly to evacuate the place."[84] With his garrison verging on mutiny, Pemberton reluctantly
concluded he could not withstand an assault rumored for July 4. Hence, at
10 a.m. on July 3, white flags sprouted along rebel parapets and gunfire ceased.
Then two high-ranking emissaries, Major General John Bowen and Colonel
Louis Montgomery, Pemberton's aide-de-camp, were seen advancing on horseback toward Union lines under a fluttering white flag. Pemberton had selected
his messengers with care. Bowen, who had befriended Grant during his dark
days of hardscrabble farming in St. Louis, was grievously ill and would soon die
of dysentery, but Pemberton wished to gain every possible advantage with Grant.

Much as Grant had steeled himself against any sentimentality in favor of Simon Bolivar Buckner at Fort Donelson, he refused to receive Bowen, although he
perused closely the letter he bore from Pemberton: "I have the honor to propose
to you an armistice . . . with a view to arranging terms for the capitulation of
Vicksburg—To this end if agreeable to you, I will appoint three commissioners,
to meet a like number to be named by yourself, at such place and hour today as
you may find convenient." Pemberton gave way to false bravado: "I make this
proposition to save the further effusion of blood which must otherwise be shed to
a frightful extent, feeling myself fully able to maintain my position for a yet indefinite period."[85] Grant, guessing that Pemberton preferred to surrender rather
than be captured in a July 4 assault, was relieved the Confederate general chose to
avoid further fighting, which he thought would be "little less than murder."[86]
After consenting orally to meet between the lines at three that afternoon, Grant
wrote Pemberton a tough, uncompromising response—by now his trademark.

Your note of this date is just received, proposing an armistice for several hours for the purpose of arranging terms of capitulation through commissioners to be appointed, &c.

The useless effusion of blood you propose stopping by this course can be ended at any time you may choose, by the unconditional surrender of the city and garrison. Men who have shown so much endurance and courage as those now in Vicksburg, will always challenge the respect of an adversary, and I can assure you will be treated with all the respect due to prisoners of war.

I do not favor the proposition of appointing commissioners to arrange terms of capitulation, because I have no terms other than those indicated above.[87]

For all his politeness, Grant knew he had the upper hand and played it to the hilt.

At 3 p.m., under a slightly overcast sky, Grant rode through the trenches toward a designated hillside spot beyond the city walls, accompanied by Generals Ord, McPherson, John Logan, and Andrew J. Smith. There he encountered Pemberton, who remembered him from their joint service in the Mexican War. While Grant attempted to be civil, greeting his Confederate counterpart "as an old acquaintance," the testy Pemberton spurned any pleasantries. He said he understood that Grant had "expressed a wish to have a personal interview with me" and Grant promptly denied any such thing.[88] When he asked Grant for the terms he would give if his army surrendered, Grant reiterated his uncompromising stand. Pemberton snorted in response, "The conference might as well end," and wheeled about as if to go. "I can assure you, sir," he threatened Grant, "you will bury many more of your men before you will enter Vicksburg."[89] Coolly puffing on a cigar, Grant was adept at a poker face, and not a muscle twitched as he stared at his foe. "Very well," said Grant, who did not care to tip his hand, especially when Pemberton was so full of bluster.[90] After Bowen suggested he should parley with a Union general, Grant agreed, and Bowen and Smith talked while Grant and Pemberton stepped aside under the shade of a stunted oak. Bowen put forth a proposal by which Confederate soldiers would march out of Vicksburg with full honors of war, bearing their small arms. As usual, Grant refused initially to yield an inch to his adversaries and said he would send final terms by ten o'clock that night.

That evening, as northern and southern soldiers socialized between the lines,

Grant gathered his officers for a war council, one in which he alone would wield ultimate power. The debate hinged on whether the Confederate garrison should be ferried north as prisoners or paroled, sending them home and effectively excluding them from the war. Despite Grant's reservations, his generals convinced him of the wisdom of the parole option; instead of tying up Union soldiers and monopolizing transports to steer more than thirty thousand rebels to northern prisons, Grant's army would immediately be freed up for fresh military adventures. As the years went by and his name became synonymous with reconciliation, Grant tended to forget that he had started out favoring harsher treatment for Pemberton's men. As he wrote in 1884, "The men had behaved so well that I did not want to humiliate them. I believed that consideration for their feelings would make them less dangerous foes during the continuance of hostilities, and better citizens after the war was over."[91]

Once the war council ended, Grant presented Pemberton with generous terms, which would enable Confederate soldiers to save face and surrender with traditional war honors: "As soon as rolls can be made out and paroles signed by officers and men you will be allowed to march out of our lines the officers taking with them their side arms and clothing, and the Field, Staff & Cavalry officers one horse each."[92] Turning up the pressure on Pemberton to accept these honorable terms, Grant slyly leaked the news to Confederate pickets. Once the rebel rank and file realized Grant was offering them a chance to head home, it would be difficult for Pemberton to reject his offer. He largely accepted the terms and said his men would march out the next morning with colors flying and stack their arms, but he tried to widen one loophole: "Officers to retain their side arms, and personal property, and the rights and property of citizens to be respected."[93] Grant knew slaves counted as personal property and had no intention of allowing them to be hauled back into bondage. Before dawn, Grant informed Pemberton he had vetoed this last request and gave him until 9 a.m. to abide by his terms or he would open a full-throttle attack on Vicksburg. Sometime around dawn Pemberton saw the light and the siege ended. At breakfast time, Grant sat in his tent, composing dispatches on a small table, when an orderly arrived with Pemberton's submission to his final terms. Wan, exhausted from the siege, Grant stood up and said with tangible relief to his son Fred, "W-e-e-e-ll, I'm glad Vicksburg will surrender."[94]

CHAPTER FOURTEEN

Deliverance

A S ALWAYS AFTER A GRANT VICTORY, Union soldiers engaged in no gloating as they watched their enemies being humbled. On the morning of July 4, a hot, steamy day, Union men stared in respectful silence as their Confederate counterparts, one regiment at a time, marched out of Vicksburg, deposited their arms in stacks, then retreated to their lines. The hush seemed palpable after weeks in which the navy had punished the town with more than twenty thousand rounds of shell and shot. Grant wrote that "not a cheer went up, not a remark was made that would give pain. Really, I believe there was a feeling of sadness just then in the breasts of most of the Union soldiers at seeing the dejection of their late antagonists."[1] The extreme heat made the prolonged ritual an ordeal for both sides. As Grant's telegraph operator, Samuel Beckwith, recalled: "The tramping of myriads of feet had stirred up a fine, yellow clay dust that coated our garments and filled our eyes and ears and nostrils until it was almost unbearable."[2]

Grant had not simply notched another major victory: he had bagged a gigantic army, and nothing pleased him more, said an aide, than "to reduce the enemy's strength by captures than by slaughter."[3] The speed, daring, and sophistication of the Vicksburg Campaign eclipsed anything Grant had accomplished before. More than thirty-one thousand southern soldiers fell under his control, joining six thousand captured during the siege and six thousand more in earlier battles after the river crossing. Adding to this bountiful harvest, Grant collected seventeen rebel cannon and sixty thousand muskets and rifles. By contrast, he had sacrificed fewer than ten thousand of his own men, prompting Bruce Catton to remark: "The legend of Grant as the heedless, conscienceless butcher finds nothing to feed on in the story of the Vicksburg campaign."[4]

Once the last Confederate surrendered, Grant ordered John Logan to lead his division into the fallen citadel and hoist the Stars and Stripes over Vicksburg's courthouse for the first time in two and a half years. The siege damage was manifest everywhere in toppled walls, shattered windows, and the emaciated faces of inhabitants. The town was "one vast cemetery," said one aide, with skulls and limbs of buried soldiers protruding from the earth.[5] Soldiers on both sides gazed at one another in wonder, the prosperous appearance of the Yankees no less surreal than the haggard faces of the famished Confederates. A Vicksburg woman, setting eyes on well-appointed Union men, wrote sadly, "What a contrast to the suffering creatures we had seen so long were these stalwart, well-fed men, so splendidly set up and accoutered. Sleek horses, polished arms, bright plumes—this was the pride and panoply of war."[6] Union soldiers were roused to pity by their "gaunt and hungry" foes, and one officer started handing out hardtack, sugar, and coffee to every rebel soldier he saw.[7] Grant was struck by how quickly the two sides began to mingle, retrieving their common nationality. Mortal hatred gave way to friendly banter. "I myself saw our men taking bread from their haversacks and giving it to the enemy they had so recently been engaged in starving out."[8] For the first time Grant toured the prehistoric apartments dug from the deep clay of the Vicksburg hills by residents driven underground by his incessant bombing.

Grant and his entourage repaired to a fine mansion whose front lawn had grown rank with weeds during the siege. As he mounted the wide front steps, Pemberton stepped onto the verandah and "stood for a single moment glaring upon his conqueror," Beckwith said.[9] The Confederate commander gruffly unbuckled his sword, belt, and revolver and "thrust more than offered" them in surrender to Grant, who reacted with punctilious restraint. "Retain your side arms, General," he told Pemberton, placing his hand softly upon the sword.[10] When Grant offered him a cigar, Pemberton took one with exaggerated reluctance. He refused to offer Grant a seat, and when Grant asked for a glass of water, a rebel officer told him he could get it himself. Behaving with his congenital aplomb, Grant did not stoop to anger, and the contrast between the two generals struck observers. According to Charles A. Dana, Grant "was received by Pemberton with more marked impertinence than at their former interview.

Grant bore it like a philosopher, and in reply treated Pemberton with even gentler courtesy and dignity than before."[11] Based on his prewar experience, Grant knew a thing or two about the tender ego of a defeated man.

As Pemberton foresaw, Vicksburg proved a full-blown catastrophe for his career and he was busted from lieutenant general to a lowly lieutenant colonel of artillery. In reporting on operations in Mississippi, Joseph Johnston loaded him with blame, noting that he had been told under no circumstances to allow himself to be besieged. The South needed a scapegoat, and the northern-born Pemberton presented the ideal target. Jefferson Davis did not allow Johnston to wriggle free, criticizing him for his failure to attack Grant. Such was the success of Grant's parole program that much of Pemberton's army withered away, many demoralized men swearing never to fight again. While some soldiers violated their paroles and returned to the war, most headed home, further depleting the limited stock of southern manpower.

With none of the conquistador in his nature, Grant impressed most folks in Vicksburg with his unassuming, egalitarian nature. When he went to a barbershop for a haircut, an aide tried to shove Lieutenant Frank Parker from a chair to make room for him, but Grant refused to brush aside a junior officer. "You are all right, my friend; go ahead," Grant said. "You feel just as much like getting cleaned up as any general, and you have got as much right to your turn as I have to mine." Parker was touched, since the hirsute Grant desperately needed a barber's attention. "He looked rough . . . his beard was long and his hair was ragged and his clothes were dusty and faded, but he never put on airs and never assumed to be a general."[12]

The short, plain man with the history of business failure now reigned as the leading northern general, although he still did not receive the adulation he might have garnered in the East. Armies in the western theater roamed a vast, sprawling territory with comparatively scant newspaper coverage. The fall of Vicksburg rendered indefensible Port Hudson on the lower Mississippi, and on July 9, its seven thousand defenders surrendered to Nathaniel Banks. Once again the Mississippi became an open thoroughfare for commerce from the northern states. As Lincoln phrased it more poetically, "The Father of Waters again goes unvexed to the sea."[13] Union control of the waterway sheared off Texas and Arkansas from the rest of the Confederacy, depriving it of western horses and cattle that had sustained its soldiers.

For many southerners, the loss of Vicksburg seemed to portend the demise of

the Confederacy itself, and a fatalistic tone crept into their commentary. Dazed
by this defeat, Jefferson Davis was more profoundly depressed by Vicksburg's
loss than by Lee's simultaneous defeat at Gettysburg, moaning, "We are now in
the darkest hour of our political existence."[14] Josiah Gorgas, head of Confederate
ordnance, saw the South skidding on a permanent downward spiral: "Yesterday
we rode on the pinnacle of success—today absolute ruin seems to be our portion.
The Confederacy totters to its destruction."[15] Grant could now force his way into
the vitals of the Confederacy instead of chipping away at its periphery.

The glad tidings brightened the mood of Lincoln, who had been so worried
about Vicksburg that his eyelids drooped and dark rings encircled his eyes. He
was studying a map of Mississippi when a beaming Gideon Welles pranced in
with a telegram from Admiral Porter fluttering in his hand. He executed a little
jig and threw his hat into the air: "I have the honor to inform you that Vicksburg
has surrendered to the U.S. forces on this 4th day of July."[16] With a double dose
of fantastic news from Vicksburg and Gettysburg, Lincoln, nearly euphoric, embraced Welles, proclaiming, "I cannot, in words, tell you my joy over this result.
It is great, Mr. Welles, it is great!"[17] Lincoln directed Halleck to inform General
Meade of what had happened, hoping it might inspire him to complete the demolition of Lee's army. The news produced such jubilation in official Washington that work ground to an abrupt halt. In government buildings, wrote the
journalist Noah Brooks, "the announcement of the news was received with cheer
upon cheer from the crowds of officers and clerks, and I do not believe that there
was much work done . . . during the rest of the day."[18] When a band serenaded
Lincoln at the White House that evening, he toyed with a theme he would later
rework into the Gettysburg Address: the idea of a war that would deliver on the
unfinished promise of the Declaration of Independence.

Until Vicksburg, the western theater had been something of a sideshow. Now
Ulysses S. Grant, an uncomplaining man of proven competence, found a new
place in Lincoln's affection. "He isn't shrieking for reinforcements all the time,"
Lincoln said. "He takes what troops we can safely give him . . . and does the best
he can with what he has got."[19] The lesson of self-reliance Grant had learned
before the war, when circumstances forced him to depend entirely on himself,
now came in handy. "Grant is my man," the president insisted, "and I am his the
rest of the war."[20]

Perhaps the highest honor bestowed on Grant was the privilege of direct correspondence with the president. Previously their communication was mediated

through Halleck and others. On July 13, thankful for Vicksburg, Lincoln composed a noble letter to Grant: "I do not remember that you and I ever met personally. I write this now as a grateful acknowledgment for the almost inestimable service you have done the country." Lincoln admitted magnanimously that he had faulted Grant's strategy, believing that, after crossing the Mississippi, he should have moved south and hooked up with Banks instead of shooting northeast toward Jackson. "I feared it was a mistake—I now wish to make the personal acknowledgment that you were right, and I was wrong. Yours very truly. Abraham Lincoln."[21] This lovely letter forged a bond between the two men that only grew stronger. With Grant, Lincoln no longer had to second-guess maneuvers or play the armchair general. Had he traveled west and gotten to know Grant personally, he might well have speeded up Grant's ascent to the top post and spared himself his frustrated dealings with several inept eastern generals.

Chaplain John Eaton met twice with Lincoln and reported back to Grant on the president's cordial feelings toward him, how he quoted from his dispatches and propped up a map of his operations on a tripod in his office. In a secondhand report from Dana, Lincoln had heard that Grant claimed he could not have taken Vicksburg without the Emancipation Proclamation, and the delighted president wished to have that verified. Once again Grant's sympathy with the broad political aims of the war formed no minor part of his attraction in Washington.

The magnitude of Grant's Vicksburg triumph helped to quiet temporarily the drinking issue. Admiral Porter told how Grant came aboard his ship at Vicksburg. "Wine was served but Grant took none, only a cigar, and let me say here that this was his habit during all the time he commanded before Vicksburg."[22] Lincoln dubbed Grant his "fighting general" and told Eaton of a congressional delegation that had lobbied for his ouster. "I asked why, and they said he sometimes drank too much and was unfit for such a position. I then began to ask them if they knew what he drank, what brand of whiskey he used, telling them most seriously that I wished they would find out . . . for if it made fighting generals like Grant, I should like to get some of it for distribution."[23] (Lincoln himself questioned the authenticity of this famous statement. "That would have been very good if I had said it," he told a cipher operator in the War Department, "but I reckon it was charged to me to give it currency."[24]) When Lincoln met General John Thayer, he quizzed him about Grant's drinking habit. "I have seen him often, sometimes daily," Thayer reassured him, "and I have never noticed the slightest indication of his using any kind of liquor . . . The charge is atrocious, wickedly false."[25] Lincoln felt supremely vindicated by his implicit faith in Grant: "No man will ever know how much trouble I have had to carry my point about him. The opposition from several of our best republicans has been so bitter that I could hardly resist it."[26]

The grand victory at Vicksburg also retired all residual doubts about Grant's skills as a general. Whether dealing with overall strategy or tactical minutiae, he had excelled. Vicksburg was a comeuppance for skeptics who had derided him. Halleck, having perversely turned against Grant after earlier victories, was swept along in the chorus of praise. "In boldness of plan, rapidity of execution, and brilliancy of results," he announced to Grant, the Vicksburg "operations will compare most favorably with those of Napoleon at Ulm."[27] (In the Bavarian town of Ulm, Napoleon had trapped the Austrian army, which surrendered without a fight.) Even so waspish a critic as Henry Adams lauded Vicksburg as "a military scheme such as Napoleon himself might have envied."[28] In retrospect, Grant asserted that he could have improved upon every one of his Civil War campaigns save one: Vicksburg. Many military historians rate it his masterpiece, the preeminent campaign waged by any general during the war.

On July 7, 1863, Ulysses S. Grant was named major general in the regular army, placing him firmly in control of his own military destiny. For a man drummed out of the regular army in disgrace a decade earlier, the move completed the spectacular transformation of his life. The promotion held deep psychological reverberations for the forty-one-year-old Grant as a West Pointer and career military man, who called it the "only promotion that I ever rejoiced in."[29] After a lifetime of chronic insecurity, the promotion conferred recognition, a comfortable salary, and a lifelong cushion of financial support. Grant had long entertained the notion of taking Julia and the children to California someday, and being made a major general emboldened him to think he might do so after the war. Wartime hardship had dispersed his family. In the autumn he thought of sending his two oldest sons to a boarding school in St. Louis, while Nellie stayed with Mrs. Boggs. "This breaking up of families is hard," he lamented after Vicksburg. "But such is War."[30]

That the Vicksburg conquest coincided with Lee's bloody defeat at Gettysburg leaned the war toward the Union side. No longer could Jefferson Davis seek legitimacy in European capitals. Vicksburg possessed deeper strategic meaning— Sherman called it the war's "most *decisive* event"—but Gettysburg received more extensive coverage in the eastern press, leaving a more durable imprint on northern opinion.[31] The mystique of Robert E. Lee was dealt a heavy blow at Gettysburg. Spoiled by success, succumbing to hubris after Chancellorsville, he had come to believe the myth of his own invincibility. Unlike his Virginia battles, his foray into Maryland and Pennsylvania had forced him to fight on enemy territory. For once it was the northern army that staked out an advantageous defensive position and Lee who had to improvise. It was hard to see how even a string of southern victories could defeat the North if Lee sustained such heavy losses. Confederate forces were being whittled down and could not be replaced by the South's smaller population. The sheer weight of northern numbers began to tell. Although Lee assumed full responsibility for his baffling failure at Gettysburg, his reputation definitely suffered. After Vicksburg and Gettysburg, northern soldiers were no longer quite so petrified of their southern foes.

Where Vicksburg had produced an acknowledged hero in Grant, Gettysburg produced a more dubious hero in George Gordon Meade, who had wanted to withdraw before Pickett's Charge but was overruled by his generals, then failed to follow up against the badly routed Confederates, allowing them to escape across the Potomac. Perhaps underestimating the difficulties involved, the president was furious at the missed opportunity. "If I had gone up there, I could have whipped them myself," he insisted. "Our army held the war in the hollow of their hand and they would not close it."[32] To make sure Meade got the message, Halleck wired him "that the escape of Lee's army without another battle has created great dissatisfaction in the mind of the President."[33] Curiously enough, Grant, who followed up victories aggressively, sympathized with Meade's sluggish response after Gettysburg and emphasized charitably that he had been placed in charge of the Army of the Potomac only days before the battle. "If [Meade] could have fought Lee six months later, when he had the army in his hand . . . I think Lee would have been destroyed . . . He was new to the chief command. He did not know how the army felt toward him, and, having rolled back the tide of invasion, he felt that any further movement would be a risk."[34]

Lincoln and Stanton thought of elevating Grant to the helm of the Army of the Potomac. But aside from his attachment to the western armies, Grant feared he would be ostracized as an interloper in the cliquish world of Virginia generals and, encouraged by Sherman, stoutly resisted the move. As Grant told Dana on August 5, "It would cause me more sadness than satisfaction to be ordered to the command of the Army of the Potomac. Here I know the officers and men and what each Gen. is capable of as a separate commander. There I would have all to learn. Here I know the geography of the country, and its resources. There it would be a new study."[35] Grant also feared leading an army that had ruined the career of a string of other generals. "I had seen so many generals fall, one after another, like bricks in a row, that I shrank from it," he commented in hindsight.[36]

From the time he emerged into the national spotlight, Grant disavowed political ambition as alien to his nature. "I am pulling no wires, as political Generals do, to advance myself," he attested. "I have no future ambition."[37] Yet Vicksburg conferred instant fame that could be parlayed into political success. According to some sources in the nation's capital, Congressman Washburne touted Grant for president with the same assiduity with which he had promoted his military career. General Benjamin Butler heard reports from Washington that Washburne was "making a business already of committing men to Grant for the Presidency . . . I hear good men say he will go into the nominating convention stronger than Lincoln went."[38] Washburne did nothing to dampen the boomlet, telling a friend that "after old Abe is through with his next four years, we will put him [i.e., Grant] in."[39] The impetus for this came entirely from Washburne, not Grant, who wanted none of it. Perhaps it was the fear of advancing Grant's presidential prospects that made Lincoln hesitate in bringing him east as chief general in a more timely fashion.

Grant worried that his firing of John McClernand still rankled Lincoln. A wily, persistent politician, McClernand stood ready to discredit Grant in government circles. To counter that, in late July, Grant dispatched his alter ego, John Rawlins, to deliver his Vicksburg report to the cabinet. Since Lincoln had never set eyes on Grant, Rawlins served as his proxy and during a two-hour presentation swayed the cabinet with his intelligence, sincerity, and self-evident passion. Incapable of guile, Rawlins disarmed skeptics. "His honest, unpretending and unassuming manners pleased me—the absence of pretension and I may say the unpolished and unrefined deportment of this earnest and sincere patriot and soldier interested me more than that of almost any officer whom I have met," Secretary of the Navy Welles told his diary.[40] Rawlins satisfied Lincoln that McClernand had obstructed operations at Vicksburg. Grant's timing here was superb: Lincoln could hardly indulge McClernand at the expense of the victor of Vicksburg. According to an officer who accompanied Rawlins, Lincoln paid an outstanding tribute to Grant: "That man Grant has been of more comfort to me than any other man in my army . . . [He] has few enemies and he is not a politician. It don't [*sic*] matter where he turns up, he is on the side of victory . . . Things move wherever he is."[41] Around this time, Grant sent in Rawlins's name for promotion to brigadier general of volunteers, claiming no officer had won "a more honorable reputation."[42] Rawlins duly received the appointment that August, testimony to his military skills and special protective relationship with Grant, and he also officially became his chief of staff.

After Vicksburg fell, Rawlins discovered love in an unlikely place. Grant had set up headquarters in the roomy home of merchant William Lum and his wife, Anna, who had taken in a governess from Danbury, Connecticut, Mary E. Hurlbut, always known as Emma. She had traveled south with friends before the war, entering the Lum household. Rawlins was a rather prudish man who had now been a widower with three children for two years. He became captivated by the "ringlets" and "laughing nature and rich good sense" of Miss Hurlbut, who blushed furiously and fluttered her eyelids around him.[43] She professed her loyalty to the Union, perfecting the romantic portrait for Rawlins, who married her in Danbury before Christmas. Unfortunately, the event that promised to restore happiness to Rawlins's life coincided with a continuing bout of bad health for him. By now he had developed a rasping cough and other bronchial symptoms, contracting pleuropneumonia during the Vicksburg siege. Whether from stoicism or escapism, Rawlins refused to acknowledge the illness and remained on active duty. For a long while, as the disease lengthened its tragic shadow over his life, Rawlins explained away his symptoms as something minor.

Even as Grant bemoaned the stifling heat, dust, and drought of Mississippi in July, he oversaw the final phases of the Vicksburg Campaign. To Sherman he had assigned the task of dismantling Joseph Johnston's army and eliminating any supplies and rolling stock it might possess. Grant's relations with Sherman had grown even more harmonious, and Sherman told visiting dignitaries how he had wrongly opposed Grant's Vicksburg Campaign. "Nothing could be more generous than his treatment of me," said Grant, who successfully recommended Sherman for brigadier general in the regular army.[44] Meanwhile, Sherman's foraging parties stripped the countryside of "Corn, Cattle, Hogs, Sheep, Poultry . . . and the new growing Corn." Driven by ideological zeal, previewing a muscular style for which he became notorious in the South, Sherman informed Grant, "The wholesale destruction, to which this country is now being subjected, is terrible to contemplate," but the moralistic Sherman blamed the South for not employing the "learned and pure Tribunals" established by America's forefathers to settle their grievances lawfully.[45] He wanted northern armies to impose military rule on the South, teaching it a lesson it would never forget.

On the night of July 16, after days of heavy shelling by Sherman, Johnston evacuated Jackson and fled east with his demoralized army, leaving Grant in undisputed control of the Mississippi heartland. "Jackson, once the pride and boast of Mississippi," Sherman observed, "is a ruined town."[46] Less truculent than Sherman, though widely in agreement with his goals, Grant took a more lenient view of how to treat the local populace: "Impress upon the men the importance of going through the State in an orderly manner, abstaining from taking anything not absolutely necessary for their subsistence while traveling. They should try to create as favorable an impression as possible upon the people."[47] To this end, Grant distributed food and medicine to needy residents.[48]

While both Grant and Sherman proved overly optimistic about the potential contrition of southern citizens, the North experienced a vicious backlash against emancipation during New York City draft riots in mid-July. In March, Congress had enacted legislation that allowed men to escape the draft by hiring substitutes or paying $300 bounties to the government. Those eligible for the draft in New York's poor Irish Democratic neighborhoods vented their class rage against Republicans rich enough to evade the war and racial prejudice against free blacks who threatened them with economic competition. The ugliest aspect of the riots, which took more than one hundred lives over four days, involved the outright murder of blacks on New York streets and the horrendous burning of the Colored Orphan Asylum. Lincoln refused to rescind the draft and brought troops fresh from victory at Gettysburg to restore order.

The New York riots magnified the glaring need to recruit more black soldiers, a policy Grant embraced with growing fervor. Once Vicksburg fell, he set about arming black soldiers with captured weapons and assigned them to reinforce the city's earthworks, collect and capture Confederate property, and police the city. Far from questioning their ability, Grant extolled them, telling Halleck that "negro troops are easier to preserve discipline among than our White troops and I doubt not will prove equally good for garrison duty. All that have been tried have fought bravely."[49] Grant had gotten religion on the issue. "I am anxious to get as many of these negro regiments as possible and to have them full and completely equipped," he told Lorenzo Thomas. "The large amount of arms and equipment captured here will enable me to equip these regiments as rapidly as they can be formed."[50] Grant's conversion to this cause reflected his common-sensical approach to things: he had tested and observed black troops and was honest enough to credit their high-caliber performance.

Also focusing Grant's mind on black recruitment were steady reminders from Washington. Now that he enjoyed direct correspondence with the president, Lincoln's priorities impressed themselves even more forcibly upon his mind. On August 9, Lincoln told Grant that black recruitment was "a resource which if vigorously applied now, will soon close the contest—It works doubly, weakening the enemy & strengthening us."[51] With the Mississippi open to commerce, Lincoln hoped one hundred thousand black soldiers could be assembled along its shores. In reply, Grant brought his views in exact conformity with national policy and presidential direction. "I have given the subject of arming the negro my hearty support," he assured the president. "This, with the emancipation of the negro, is the heaviest blow yet given the Confederacy."[52] Lincoln was so pleased with this statement that he quoted it in a letter read aloud at a mass rally in Illinois in September, deepening the political bond between the two men. Intent on furthering Lincoln's vision, Grant planned to send an expedition into Louisiana to gather black recruits. As the results of the draft showed more people than expected buying their way out of service or flunking physicals, the drive to arm and equip black soldiers acquired fresh urgency.

The most immediate issue demanding Grant's attention after Pemberton's surrender was what to do about slaves kept by rebel officers. A member of Pemberton's staff informed Grant that some slaves desired to return home to their masters and that forcing them to separate was "like severing families." Grant believed the decision should rest entirely with the blacks affected and "that no compulsory measures would be used to hold negroes. I want the negroes all to understand that they are free men."[53] If slaves decided to return to their masters, Grant thought, there might be collateral benefits as they told others how Yankees offered to set them free—something that might incite further rebellion in the South. Grant's policy was revoked when Confederate officers openly coerced their slaves into returning home, and it became clear that no free choice was involved. "Give instructions that no passes are to be given to negroes to accompany their masters on leaving the City," Grant ordered.[54]

For his services to the black community, Grant began to bask in some of the adulation lavished upon Lincoln. A few days after Vicksburg fell, a northern woman, Annie Wittenmyer, a sanitary agent from Iowa, invited Grant and

McPherson to dine in a house that had been damaged by Union shells. That morning, she recalled, the colored children "danced a jubilee" when they found out Grant was coming and began to throng around the house. "Black faces were peeping out from the near houses and the fences were black with colored people. It was perhaps the one chance of their lives to see their deliverer, the great captain who had opened the prison-house of Vicksburg, and given liberty to all the people."[55] By the time Grant and McPherson left the house, every black person in the neighborhood knew that the shorter man was their hero.

ULYSSES S. GRANT was a man of action par excellence for whom idleness remained an enemy. Not content merely to hold conquered territory or retreat into summer quarters, he meditated fresh schemes for further campaigns, including an attack on Mobile, but he had to bow to certain realities that stalled his progress. For one thing, his weary troops could not manage extended marches in midsummer heat. For another, Lincoln and Halleck retained separate priorities, including checking European pretensions in Mexico and foreign meddling in the war. This meant that, for the sake of foreign policy, Grant had to divert an entire division to Nathaniel Banks to beef up the Union presence in Texas. In consequence, the restless Grant had to "settle down and see myself put again on the defensive as I had been a year before in west Tennessee. It would have been an easy thing to capture Mobile at the time I proposed to go there."[56]

The temporary lull in fighting afforded him an opportunity to see the public adulation his success had generated. In late August, he went to Cairo to spend time with Julia before she placed their three eldest children in school in St. Louis. Grant seemed aglow with his new military renown, boasting to brother-in-law Fred Dent that "I feel younger than I did six years ago" when business troubles smothered his spirits.[57] Paying homage to Grant's talents, Memphis honored him with two dinners on consecutive nights. At the first, Grant responded with pitch-perfect brevity to a toast offered in his praise, having a staff officer reply crisply, "General Grant believes that he has no more than done his duty, for which no honor is due."[58]

For the rest of his life, banquets posed a challenge to Grant, who had to shield himself from alcoholic temptation. At the second Memphis dinner, John Eaton watched Grant handle this threat, especially when the mayor grew tipsy, spilled soup on Lorenzo Thomas, then splashed Grant while uncorking a champagne bottle. Amid the revelry, Grant made a point of abstaining from drink. "His wine glasses and those of General Rawlins, his chief of staff, remained inverted throughout the dinner," noted Eaton, "although there was even more than the usual freedom in the use of wines among the other guests."[59] Grant again showed himself a master of pithy expression, acknowledging a toast with just two lines: "I thank you, gentlemen, for your kindness. All that will add to your prosperity, that it is in my power to do, I will grant you."[60] At the same time Julia was being regaled as a newfound celebrity. Staying at a St. Louis hotel, she was entertained by serenaders and a huge crowd burst into uproarious cheers when she appeared on the balcony. The one family member who tried to exploit Grant's renown was, predictably, his father, who had been barred from doing deals in his son's district after the notorious meddling that provoked General Orders No. 11. Now, in a virtual replay of that egregious incident, Jesse had the gall to lobby General Nathaniel Banks to yield commercial rights to a Mr. L. Block, "one of a firm of five Brothers doing business in Cincinnati."[61] It seems unlikely Grant knew of this latest example of his father's unsavory business affairs.

The unholy trinity of circumstances that inevitably challenged Grant—inactivity, a side trip to a distant town, and relaxation after the unbearable pressures of a major campaign—occurred on September 2 when he journeyed to New Orleans to confer with Banks, stopping at the St. Charles Hotel. The visit's purpose was to review proposed operations west of the Mississippi. Grant's stay started with a magnificent reception for him at the Banks residence. "For hours streams of people poured through the spacious parlors," reported a local paper. "Grant received the 'storming party' with as much coolness and calmness as he conducted those which assaulted the stout walls of Vicksburg."[62] The next day, Grant hired a carriage with "two spanking bays" and drove Banks around the city at an exhilarating clip, leaving both horses drooping by the end.[63]

On September 4, Banks staged a grand review in Grant's honor in the nearby suburb of Carrollton. By all accounts, it was a poignant moment for Grant, who at first trotted so briskly by the assembled troops that other generals had difficulty keeping pace. Then he paused on horseback in the shade of an oak tree, wearing his black felt hat and drawing on a cigar. As he surveyed passing troops, regiments carried banners inscribed with the names of his famous victories and Grant tipped his hat to the veterans flashing by. Once the review was over, Grant and other participants repaired to "a handsome *déjeuner*—music, wine, choruses, etc.," and the wine mentioned may have been his undoing.[64]

Perhaps aware of Grant's reputation for taming frisky animals, Banks gave him a spirited but unbroken mount for the festivities, praising it as "the fleetest and best." Grant characterized the steed as "vicious and but little used.[65] One observer noted the ominous detail that when the horse was first presented to Grant, it "took two men to hold" it.[66] Afterward, Grant and other generals rode back to New Orleans on a road rutted by passing artillery, which had carved a gaping hole. Despite this, Grant's horse "grew quite unmanageable and flew like the wind," said an observer.[67] According to one version of what happened, Grant and the others engaged in a horse race with Grant sprinting ahead of the pack. Then came disaster. "General Grant's horse in jumping that hole in the road fell and threw the general clear over his head," said Lieutenant Frank Parker. "Grant fell on his head and shoulders and lay flat out on the ground. We thought he was dead."[68] In Grant's recollection, his horse reared at a shrill whistle issued by a locomotive. "This frightened the animal so that he plunged into a carriage that was coming from the opposite direction and was thrown to the ground with me under."[69] Ever the agile rider, Grant remained welded to his saddle as he fell, possibly aggravating the damage. His leg lay crushed and immobile, and his hip may have been dislocated. Yet another account asserted that a speeding horse came up behind Grant and trampled him severely. Whatever the case, he was knocked unconscious and carted on a litter to a nearby inn where he was confined to bed, unable to move his leg. "My leg was swollen from the knee to the thigh, and the swelling, almost to the point of bursting, extended along the body up to the arm-pit," he recalled. "The pain was almost beyond endurance."[70] Grant would rely on crutches for two months and tapped Sherman as his preferred deputy in an emergency.

Several—though hardly all—of the officers present attributed Grant's accident to drinking. "I am frightened when I think that he is a drunkard," Banks told his wife. "His accident was caused by this, which was too manifest to all who saw him."[71] No less damaging in historical annals was a letter General William B. Franklin, a former West Point classmate of Grant's, subsequently wrote to McClellan about Grant's visit. "He at once got into the most tremendous frolic, was drunk all over the city for forty-eight hours." After reviewing troops and eating lunch, Grant had "galloped over an exceedingly dusty road full split, tumbled head over heels & was badly hurt."[72] This report reverberated through the years and as late as 1885 Mark Twain reported that "Franklin *saw* Grant tumble from his horse drunk while reviewing troops in New Orleans."[73] In another letter, Franklin blamed Grant's lapse on Julia's absence. "When I saw Grant in Vicksburg about Aug. 1, he was perfectly straight & told me that he had drunk nothing during the war. I was as you can imagine somewhat surprised when I saw him in New Orleans. But Mrs. Gr[ant], a cross-eyed *very* ugly woman was at Vicksburg, and there was no such woman at New Orleans."[74] Sylvanus Cadwallader, the unreliable journalist who embellished Grant's drinking at Satartia, remembered gossip swirling around Grant's headquarters that he was "thrown from his horse on his return from a review of Gen. Banks's troops" and that it "was solely due to his drinking."[75]

As with many Grant drinking stories, the most lurid versions emanated from generals hostile to Grant. Franklin was a protégé of McClellan and had bungled two battles in the eastern theater before Lincoln banished him to Louisiana for scheming to get McClellan reinstated. Friendlier generals, such as Cadwallader Washburn (*sic*), made no allusion to drinking, even when writing to his brother Elihu about the fall. And if Grant was drunk, how did he have enough self-command to remain in the saddle? What lends most credence to the tale that Grant *had* been drunk was that John Rawlins heard it from people present and believed it. A couple of months later, suspecting a new drinking spree, he sent his fiancée an exasperated letter: "I had hoped but it appears vainly his New Orleans experience would prevent him ever again indulging with this his worst enemy."[76] The episode stands out because Grant usually had enough self-control to drink only in private, far from inquisitive eyes, whereas the New Orleans incident occurred in full view of high-ranking officers, some of them sworn rivals.

While the accident handicapped Grant for a couple of months, it did not interfere with any battles. Propped up by hotel pillows, Grant smoked, read a humorous book, and soldiered on with his usual equanimity, but mostly he lay flat on his back, unable to leave bed without assistance for several weeks. By September 16, taken back to Vicksburg, he settled in an upstairs bedroom of the beautiful Lum mansion, enjoying a fine view of the river. Here Julia and their youngest boy, Jesse, lent a hand, Julia taking up nursing duties beside his bed and fanning him in the oppressive heat. Not until the end of the month did Grant start to maneuver with crutches. During this period of enforced rest, an overriding concern was the formation of black regiments, and he urged Eaton to create a "colored military force" that would "resist attacks from the bands of guerillas that infested the country and threatened the plantations."[77] From these bedside discussions arose the Sixty-Third and Sixty-Fourth United States Colored Infantry Regiments, enhancing the status of black soldiers in the Union army.

While Grant recuperated, momentous events were reshaping the war in eastern Tennessee. On September 2, Ambrose Burnside captured Knoxville, and William Rosecrans took Chattanooga on September 9. These twin victories seemed to fulfill Lincoln's dream of prying loose eastern Tennessee from the enemy. Confederate leaders decided to contest this terrain vigorously, and Jefferson Davis expanded Braxton Bragg's army by transferring from Virginia two divisions under James Longstreet. On September 19, this strengthened force clashed with the Army of the Cumberland under Rosecrans at Chickamauga Creek, near Chattanooga, in northwestern Georgia. At first the battle seemed a furious, bloody struggle, devoid of strategic design, "a mad, irregular battle . . . in which one army was bushwhacking the other, and wherein all the science and the art of war went for nothing," said a Union general.[78] Then, on September 20, Union resistance crumbled as Confederates pierced a gap that opened in the enemy line. The dispatch that Charles Dana filed with Edwin Stanton evoked the enormity of the disaster that had befallen Union forces:

> My report today is of deplorable importance. Chickamauga is as fatal a name in our history as Bull Run . . . Never in any battle I have witnessed was there such a mass of cannon and musketry. [Confederate troops] came through with resistless impulse . . . Before them our soldiers turned and fled. It was wholesale panic. Vain were all attempts to rally them . . . the road is full of a disordered throng of fugitives . . . We have lost heavily in killed today. The total of our killed, wounded, and prisoners can hardly be less than 20,000 and may be much more.[79]

Besides the rebels' capture of more than eight thousand Union prisoners, a rich trove of weaponry tumbled into their hands. For the federal side, the sole redeeming feature came when the quietly determined General George H. Thomas and his men refused to buckle under Confederate assault. For his bravery Thomas chalked up legendary status as "the Rock of Chickamauga."

As Rosecrans's ragged, dispirited army retreated to the safety of Chattanooga, his reputation lay in ruins. Grant had shared the general affection for him, telling Halleck the previous year: "There are two men in this army whom I would just as soon serve under as to have them serve under me. One is Sherman, the other is 'Rosy.'"[80] Another time Grant spoke of Rosecrans tenderly as his "warm personal friend" and "one of the ablest & purest of men, both in motive and action."[81] For all that, Rosecrans was weak, vain, and irresolute, lacking Grant's superlative drive and focus, a terrible procrastinator who constantly clamored for more troops. At Chickamauga, he behaved with such shocking cowardice as he fled the battlefield that even Lincoln sneered he was "confused and stunned like a duck hit on the head."[82] One officer who saw Rosecrans said he would "not soon forget the terrible look of the brave man, stunned by sudden calamity."[83]

The situation of his army in Chattanooga, left with only a ten-day supply of rations, was fraught with peril. Enemy forces had seized the commanding heights of Missionary Ridge, on the city's eastern side, and Lookout Mountain to the southwest, leaving him dependent upon a single, often impassable road through the mountains to sustain his large army. The threat of starvation loomed with winter's approach. Chattanooga was also a critical railway hub and the Union could ill afford to lose it. Stanton rushed off a telegraph to the bedridden Grant to relieve Rosecrans with all available forces, and he promptly dispatched two divisions. Led by Sherman, one division set off by steamer from Vicksburg to Memphis only twelve hours after Grant got the order. Sherman never forgot this dreadful voyage. He had dragged along his family, including his oldest son, Willy, who became feverish and began to lose strength rapidly. A regimental doctor diagnosed him with typhus, and Willy expired not long after the boat docked at Memphis, leaving Sherman disconsolate. "This is the only death I have ever had in my own family, and falling as it has so suddenly & unexpectedly on the one I most prized on earth has affected me more than any other misfortune could," he confided to Grant. "I can hardly compose myself enough for work but must & will do so at once."[84] Sherman, though he persevered in his duties, was haunted by the specter of the dead boy. "Sleeping, waking, everywhere I see poor Willy," he told his wife.[85]

Stanton placed such a premium on rescuing Rosecrans that he undertook the war's most strenuous logistical feat to save him. At a late-night War Department meeting, he proposed sending twenty thousand troops from the Army of the Potomac to Tennessee—a proposal of such fiendish complexity that Lincoln laughingly said the army could not "get one corps [from northern Virginia] into

Washington in the time you fix for reaching Nashville."[86] In no mood for droll-ery, Stanton rejoined that "the danger was too imminent and the occasion [too] serious for jokes."[87] With his formidable energy, Stanton studied railway timeta-bles and proceeded to shift twenty thousand men and three thousand horses to Chattanooga in eleven days. The obstacles were daunting—the troops had to cover 1,233 miles, including crossing the Appalachian Mountains and twice ford-ing the Ohio River—making the successful move a tour de force of military organization.

On October 3, Halleck alerted Grant that Stanton wished him to travel at once to Nashville, via Cairo, and supervise the transfer of troops from the west. It took a week for the message to reach Grant. "I was still very lame," recalled Grant, who needed help getting on and off horses, "but started without delay."[88] Eaton accompanied him on the six-day steamboat ride from Vicksburg to Cairo and remembered how Rawlins hectored the skipper with manic urgency: "The old river boat was rushed along at a speed which seemed as if it might prove fatal at any moment, and the keel would scrape and grind the river bottom in the most disturbing fashion."[89]

As Grant journeyed east, the drumbeat of criticism of Rosecrans swelled in volume. Posted at Chattanooga, Charles Dana plied Stanton with critical com-ments about Rosecrans, stating that despite his well-known affability, he lacked "firmness and steadiness of will" and should be sacked.[90] Dana's dispatches grew more sardonic, then downright insulting. On October 12, he opined that "the practical incapacity of the general commanding is astonishing, and it often seems difficult to believe him of sound mind. His imbecility appears to be con-tagious."[91] All the while, Rawlins badgered Grant with reminders of Rosecrans's "general spirit of insubordination."[92] Lincoln grew convinced that Rosecrans had to be cashiered, but for political reasons wanted to wait a short while. The popular Rosecrans hailed from Ohio, and Lincoln preferred to temporize until after the Ohio gubernatorial election on October 13, which Republicans won.

When Grant reached Cairo on October 16, leaning on a crutch, he learned that an unnamed War Department official planned to meet him at the Galt House in Louisville. Setting off for Kentucky, he changed trains at Indianapolis and was about to leave the station when a messenger rushed up to notify him that Stanton and Governor John Brough of Ohio had arrived on an adjoining track. While Grant and Stanton had communicated via telegraph, they had never set eyes on each other. Short of breath, asthmatic, snuffling with a heavy cold, the short, stout

Stanton barged brusquely into Grant's car, eyed the officers present, then began to pump the hand of a bearded man with an army hat whom he assumed was Grant. "How do you do General Grant?" he cried. "I recognize you from your pictures."[93] Stanton was embarrassed to learn he was shaking hands with Grant's medical director, Dr. Edward Kittoe. If Grant was amused by the confusion, Stanton was badly flustered, and it darkened his mood for the rest of the journey to Louisville with Grant. Stanton later admitted that in guessing which officer was Grant, he had eliminated the real Grant because he looked much too ordinary and wasn't the prepossessing figure he had imagined.[94]

The war secretary presented a picturesque foil to the general. With thick spectacles that he wiped incessantly and a long gray-tinged black beard that almost seemed to rest on his chest, Edwin McMasters Stanton was easy to admire, hard to love. Heedless of political pressure, impatient with special pleading, he was a snappish, short-tempered man who enjoyed barking orders at terrified subordinates. He had been something of a surprise choice to replace Simon Cameron a year before. Back in 1855, Lincoln, a junior lawyer, was brought in to defend a client in a patent suit and had tangled with Stanton, a high-priced Pittsburgh practitioner who acted as one of the main defense attorneys. Stanton was contemptuous of Lincoln and made no attempt to conceal it. "Why did you bring that d—d long armed Ape here," Stanton allegedly asked his chief co-counsel; "he does not know anything and can do you no good."[95] Later on, he added "the original gorilla," "a low, cunning clown," and "that giraffe" to his litany of colorful epithets for Lincoln.[96] A Democrat who served briefly as attorney general under President Buchanan, Stanton seemed to have the wrong résumé for Lincoln's cabinet, but the War Department under Cameron was tarred with corruption allegations, and Stanton was exactly the scourge needed to clean it up.

To introduce bureaucratic transparency, Stanton stood behind a high desk in a public space in the War Department, delivering stern lectures to shady contractors or self-promoting officers. He came across as an unstoppable force with an overbearing sense of mission that brooked no dissent. If many people thought him an ogre, nobody ever questioned his incorruptible honesty or ruthless efficiency. His memory was prodigious, as was his capacity for work and scrupulous attention to detail. He was the managerial genius of a war that made stupendous logistical demands on the northern army, with its long supply lines, extensive rail and telegraphic networks, and distant factories. He developed a surprisingly good relationship with Lincoln because he got things done and was not especially concerned with legal niceties. He could be tyrannical in exercising power and heedless of civil liberties. "If I tap that little bell," he pointed out to one visitor, "I can send you to a place where you will never hear the dogs bark."[97] Stanton cared little for the feelings of others. Grant was fascinated by how Lincoln got his way through charm and sensitivity while Stanton prevailed through uncompromising truculence.

With his imperturbable calm, Grant was a little leery of Stanton's high-strung, domineering nature, yet the two men struck up an excellent working accord. "I don't think that Stanton was what I might call a cordial friend," Grant explained. "He was always courteous. Our friendship grew very slowly. I liked him very much better than he liked me, I think; but I must say, as Secretary of War he was extremely loyal and true."[98] Especially important to Grant was the ample leeway Stanton gave him: "He has never dictated a course of campaign to me," Grant testified, "and never inquired what I was going to do."[99] Grant stood in awe of Stanton's efficiency. "He was a man who never questioned his own authority, and who always did in war time what he wanted to do. He was an able constitutional lawyer and jurist; but the Constitution was not an impediment to him while the war lasted."[100] Until the end of his life and despite many strains that later marred their relationship, Grant deemed Stanton "one of the great men of the Republic" and a "martyr" to the Union cause.[101]

Throughout the train ride, Grant and Stanton remained locked in a deep, searching conversation. By the time they pulled into Louisville that night in "a cold, drizzling rain," Stanton had handed Grant two orders from Lincoln.[102] One created a brand-new Military Division of the Mississippi that consolidated the Armies of the Ohio, Cumberland, and Tennessee. Grant was placed atop this grand structure, giving him power over a huge western territory stretching from the Appalachian Mountains to the Mississippi River, with the exception of Banks's southwest command. With his headquarters in the field, there was no chance Grant could vegetate in an office. Sherman became head of the Army of the Tennessee and Burnside kept the Army of the Ohio. As for the Army of the Cumberland, Stanton gave Grant the option of replacing Rosecrans with George Thomas.

People flocked to the Galt House in Louisville to glimpse Grant, and some were taken aback that he seemed so much smaller in life. "I thought he was a large man," proclaimed a puzzled observer. "He would be considered a small chance of a fighter if he lived in Kentucky."[103] Grant, still lame, leaned on a crutch or cane, but was so comfortable in the saddle that one reporter believed "even in his feeble condition it would require a strong effort on the part of a horse to unseat him."[104] After a day of intense consultation with Stanton, Ulysses and Julia Grant took the evening off to attend the theater. Their short-lived leisure was interrupted by an emergency summons from Stanton, who had been frantically trying to locate Grant. When Grant arrived at the hotel at about eleven o'clock, he found Stanton, with a severe cold, "pacing the floor rapidly in his dressing-gown."[105] His agitation had been precipitated by a letter from Dana, saying Rosecrans planned to abandon Chattanooga unless stopped from doing so. Grant thought a retreat would be catastrophic, surrendering a strategic spot and threatening the loss of an entire army with irreplaceable artillery. At this critical juncture, he assumed official command of the Military Division of the Mississippi, replaced Rosecrans with Thomas, and told the stalwart Thomas to cling to Chattanooga at all hazards. Thomas sent back a message that throbbed with determination: "We will hold the town till we starve."[106]

After numerous mistakes in selecting generals, Lincoln and Stanton had weeded out the weak reeds and began to assemble the team that would win the war. Grant's ascent was simply stunning. As Rawlins told his fiancée, "This is now the most important command in the United States, involving immense labor, unceasing watchfulness and anxiety . . . I feel a confidence in General Grant's ability to master the whole and turn again as heretofore the tide of defeat and disaster."[107] The general public was amazed by Rosecrans's swift fall from grace. "Rosecrans is superseded by Grant!" the diarist George Templeton Strong exclaimed in New York. "The change astonishes everyone—its alleged reasons are still more startling. Opium-eating, fits of religious melancholy, and gross personal misconduct at Chickamauga are charged by newspaper correspondents."[108] Increasingly sure-footed in military strategy, Lincoln displayed growing toughness in hiring and firing generals. As the journalist Noah Brooks observed, "It is hard to give up a popular idol . . . no man in the nation was more pained at the necessity of the removal of General Rosecrans than was the President himself."[109] Whatever his earlier fondness for Rosecrans, Grant grew withering in his contempt for him, telling Halleck a year later that any general "will be better than Rosecrans" and advising Dana that Rosecrans should be shipped off to "the northern frontier with the duty of detecting & exposing rebel conspiracies in Canada."[110] Rosecrans turned into an impassioned foe of Grant, later penning a venomous article entitled "The Mistakes of Grant."

On October 20, Grant proceeded as expeditiously as possible to Chattanooga, making the first leg of his journey by train. Passing through Nashville, he saw that Grant mania had overtaken the army, with soldiers crowding the tracks and craning their necks to spot him. He disembarked from the train to meet a man who would figure significantly in his future: Andrew Johnson, the military governor of Tennessee. The laconic Grant had his first experience of Johnson's long-winded style. As they stood together before the St. Cloud Hotel, Johnson delivered a lengthy welcome speech while Grant, by his own admission, stood "in torture . . . fearing something would be expected from me in response. I was relieved, however, the people assembled having apparently heard enough."[111] Grant charmed the throng by admitting he had "never made a speech in his life, and was too old to learn now."[112]

Far from enjoying his glory, Grant sometimes exhibited a melancholy air, as if burdened by responsibility. After spending the night in Nashville, he boarded a train, and, as it slid through Tennessee, a soldier named Harvey Reid saw Grant sitting alone, wrapped in thought. "He had on an old blue overcoat, and wore a common white wool [hat] drawn down over his eyes, and looked so much like a private soldier, that but for the resemblance to the photographs that can be seen on every corner in this town, it would have been impossible to have recognized him . . . He was either tired with riding all night, or had something on his mind for he appeared almost sad as he looked vacantly without seeming to see anything that he was passing."[113]

By early evening, Grant reached Stevenson, just across the border from Tennessee in northern Alabama. With difficulty, he dismounted from the train and stood on the platform, resting on his crutches and awaiting a train that would bear the disgraced Rosecrans. One Union soldier noted the absence of any grand aura surrounding Grant: "An army slouch hat with bronze cord around it, quite a long military coat, unbuttoned no sword or belt, and there was nothing to indicate his rank . . . When the boys called for a speech, he bowed and said nothing."[114] While at the train station, Grant conferred with Rosecrans, who energetically disputed Dana's accusation that he planned to desert Chattanooga. Far from being despondent, Grant found Rosecrans "very cheerful . . . as though a great weight had been lifted off his mind."[115] Rosecrans outlined plans to supply his isolated army, and Grant found it a highly productive meeting with the demoted general laying out "some excellent suggestions as to what should be done. My only wonder was that he had not carried them out."[116]

At Stevenson, Grant also met General Oliver Otis Howard, who had lost an arm in Virginia the year before and was nicknamed the "Christian General" for his piety and aversion to alcohol. Howard was surprised by the slight, diminutive Grant, finding him "rather thin in flesh and very pale in complexion, and noticeably self-contained and retiring."[117] Grant spent the night sharing Howard's tent, which was pitched on a muddy flat. Howard remembered one comical, if slightly awkward, moment: "When [Grant] first came in there was hanging against the wall of my tent an empty liquor flask. His eyes twinkled and I saw a faint smile creep over his face. Before he could speak, I said, 'General, that flask is not mine. It was brought here by an officer from Chattanooga. I do not drink.' Grant answered quietly, 'Neither do I,' and surely at that period of his career he was not drinking, and I never knew him to take even a glass of wine during the Chattanooga campaign."[118] Howard came away enormously impressed with Grant. "He is modest, quiet, and thoughtful," he informed his wife. "He looks the picture of firmness."[119]

The last sixty miles to Chattanooga had to be made on horseback and constituted the most harrowing ride of Grant's life. Rawlins portrayed the trail as "the roughest and steepest . . . ever crossed by army wagons and pack mules."[120] This wretched mountain road, which constantly rose and fell, was the only supply route still open linking the besieged Union army in Chattanooga with the outside world. Grant had to be lifted onto his horse—Rawlins deposited him gently "as if he had been a child"—with his crutches strapped to the side.[121] Heavy rains stirred up the road into a froth of knee-deep mud, and in some places the path was washed away by mudslides. At the worst spots, Grant had to be taken off his horse and lifted over hurdles, an ordeal he endured with stoic fortitude. He also had to contend with the appalling sight of smashed wagons everywhere and the potent stench of thousands of dead mules and horses, which had been killed by rebel bayonets or starved to death. As the cavalcade approached Chattanooga, torrential rains left the beleaguered party "dark, wet and hungry," as Dr. Kittoe told Julia Grant.[122] Just as they made their way into Chattanooga, Grant's horse tipped over and fell flat on his side, but by a miraculous stroke of luck, he was spared further injury.[123]

//////////////////////////////////

CHAPTER FIFTEEN

Above the Clouds

W HEN GRANT REACHED the headquarters of General George
Thomas on the dark, rainy night of October 23, he was spent and
bedraggled from his arduous journey. To those who set eyes on the
sodden general, he seemed to be stoically grappling with pain. "As he arose and
walked across the floor," said a spectator, "his lameness was very perceptible."[1]
Grant's initial encounter with the Rock of Chickamauga was frosty. As the two
men sat wordlessly beside a fireplace, Grant smoked a cigar and hunched forward quietly, water trickling from his mud-spattered clothes, forming a puddle
beneath his chair. Thomas, who was loyal to Rosecrans and thought Grant had
treated him disgracefully, seemed unconcerned with his new commander's
wretched state. "Rawlins . . . was white with anger at the cool reception the general and staff had received," said James H. Wilson. "They had made a long and
tiresome ride and were soaking wet, but as yet nothing had been done to relieve
their discomfort." Wilson piped up. "General Thomas, General Grant has been
on the road two days . . . he is wet and suffering from a bruised leg; besides, he
is tired and hungry. Can't you get him some dry clothes from one of your staff
and order some supper to be provided for him?" Reminded of his duty, the
courtly Virginian replied, "Of course, I can," and he extended dry clothes and
an ample supper to Grant.[2]

Grant's rough-hewn style had an impact upon a man destined to be a key aide:
Captain Horace Porter, who had graduated third in his West Point class in 1860.
The images he had seen of Grant made him envision "a burly beef-contractor," not

the gentle, "slightly stooped" man, who stood five foot eight and weighed 135 pounds. Porter picked up many subtle traits: how Grant thoughtfully stroked his beard; the "perceptible twinkle in his eyes" when he was about to utter something amusing; the "square-shaped jaws" that expressed his willpower; the creased brow that disclosed a "serious and somewhat careworn" mood behind an otherwise cheerful facade; his surprisingly clear, melodious voice; his slow, rolling gait; and how he behaved civilly to everyone, never snubbing those of lesser rank.[3] But it was the mind, beautifully organized and well prepared, that most dazzled Porter as a torrent of ideas suddenly issued from this reputedly silent man. A keen listener and close observer, Grant "began to fire whole volleys of questions at the officers present. So intelligent were his inquires, so pertinent his suggestions, that he made a profound impression upon every one by the quickness of his perception and the knowledge which he had already acquired regarding important details of the army's condition."[4] Grant's instant grasp of complicated logistical issues astounded Porter.

With a reticence reminiscent of Grant, Thomas had a cool relationship with him. The commander of the forty-five-thousand-strong Army of the Cumberland had a broad, meaty face, bushy beard, tensely arched brows, set mouth, and stern gaze. With his dignified manner, commanding appearance, and superb judgment, "he had more the character of George Washington than any other man I ever knew," said Dana.[5] Unlike Robert E. Lee, the heavyset Virginian had decided that the treasonous nature of secession surpassed loyalty to his home state and stayed with the Union. As Grant recalled from West Point, Thomas had been tarred with the name "Old Slow-Trot"—he had a spinal injury that forced him to gallop slowly—which got to the heart of Grant's dilemma with him. Thorough in preparation for battle, dogged on defense, Thomas swung into action reluctantly. "He is possessed of excellent judgment, great coolness and honesty, but he is not good on a pursuit," concluded Grant, who often said, "Thomas is too slow to move, and too brave to run away."[6] Despite an absence of personal warmth between them, Grant carefully paid homage to his colleague in public, later calling him "one of the great names of our history, one of the greatest heroes in our war, a rare and noble character, in every way worthy of his fame."[7]

The morning after his arrival in Chattanooga, Grant mounted his horse and scouted the terrain with Thomas and his chief engineer, Brigadier General William Farrar "Baldy" Smith. (Surprisingly enough, riding in the coming days

completely healed Grant's leg and he soon dispensed with a cane.) Lincoln assigned high priority to retaining the town, viewing it as an entryway to the industrial heartland of the South, the booming arsenals and factories of Georgia
and Alabama. Things looked pretty ghastly as Grant took stock. Chattanooga
stood at the northern end of a valley bounded by Missionary Ridge, a steep slope
that rose as high as 400 feet, to the east, and Lookout Mountain to the southwest, which soared 1,400 feet above the valley floor. With both heights manned
by Confederates, Union troops were bottled up down below without ammunition for a single day's fighting. As Baldy Smith observed, the rebel army "believed
that they held the [Union] army at their mercy, and its destruction was only a
question of time."[8] Grant could see why: "It looked, indeed, as if but two courses
were open; one to starve, the other to surrender or be captured."[9]

Since nearly ten thousand horses and mules had perished from starvation,
not a single draft animal remained to haul artillery or transport the sick. Desperate soldiers, subsisting on half rations of leathery meat and hard bread,
prowled the ground searching for scraps of corn or oats. Many faced cold weather
without shoes and overcoats and had felled virtually every tree for fuel, even
grubbing up stumps in their desperation. Sick soldiers were stashed away in
makeshift hospitals. All the while, enemy pickets patrolled less than a hundred
yards away in some places.

The first order of business, Grant concluded, was to restore health and troop
morale by prying open a new water and land route to bring in food from the key
rail juncture at Bridgeport, Alabama. The Union army controlled the railroad all
the way from Nashville to that spot. The new route would be nicknamed the
"cracker line," a tribute to the hard biscuits munched by the men. Smith and others
had devised a plan to seize control of the serpentine Tennessee River at a point
north of Lookout Mountain. Supplies would be taken by a direct wagon road to a
spot known as Brown's Ferry, shifted across the Tennessee by pontoon bridge, then
moved across a spit of land known as Moccasin Bend. However tortuous this route
seemed, it promised a much shorter road to Bridgeport than the forbidding, rocky
mountain road now inadequately serving that purpose. Grant, Thomas, and Smith
inspected Brown's Ferry and confirmed that it stood well beyond the range of
powerful Confederate guns staring down from Lookout Mountain.

Grant gave Smith's ingenious plan his blessing and issued a host of orders to
implement it. As ever, his whole physiology sprang into action: his pulse quickened, his mind sharpened, and Porter remembered a dynamo of concentrated

energy that night. "He sat with his head bent low over the table, and when he had occasion to step to another table or desk to get a paper he wanted, he would glide rapidly across the room without straightening himself, and return to his seat with his body still bent over at about the same angle at which he had been sitting when he left his chair. Upon this occasion he tossed the sheets of paper across the table as he finished them, leaving them in the wildest disorder. When he had completed the despatch, he gathered up the scattered sheets, read them over rapidly, and arranged them in their proper order."[10]

On the spot Grant infused a fighting spirit into the army, and men received him with "a rousing cheer" as he made the rounds.[11] He tolerated no sloppiness. That first day he passed by soldiers packing cracker boxes into wagons in perfunctory fashion. "That won't do, men," he reprimanded them. "Those crackers are going to men who are starving. Every cracker is precious, and the more boxes you get into that wagon the more hungry men you will feed tonight."[12] He gestured with his crutch to indicate where more boxes could be stored. Such stories sparked new vitality in the hitherto sluggish, downcast army.

On the moonlit night of October 27, in predawn hours, Grant's men, loaded on barges, slipped past Confederate positions and stealthily landed at Brown's Ferry, overwhelming a meagerly defended Confederate post. Smith's men were ferried over and handily laid down a pontoon bridge across the Tennessee River. General Hooker arrived with another sixteen thousand men, consolidating Union control of the area. The upshot was that Union forces broke open the route from Bridgeport to near Chattanooga, ending the isolation suffered by semistarving federal troops, who whooped with joy. "The Cracker Line's open," they cried. "Full rations, boys!"[13] Food, clothing, and forage poured in, and suddenly Union men were better fed, better clothed, and more numerous than the rebels. This daring move threw into turmoil the Confederate camp, which shifted from confidence to alarm. "The question of supplies may now be regarded as settled," Grant telegraphed proudly to Halleck, saying he could switch his attention to offensive operations.[14] His old logistical skills, dating back to the Mexican War, had rejuvenated the army under his command, which felt a new guiding intelligence. "We began to see things move," explained Colonel L. B. Eaton, brother of the chaplain. "We felt that everything came from a plan . . . Everything was done like music, everything was in harmony."[15] Grant strengthened the entire supply chain. Drawing on the expertise of General Grenville M. Dodge, he rebuilt 182 interior bridges, many spanning chasms, and restored

102 miles of railroad tracks destroyed by rebel armies in northern Alabama and middle Tennessee—a stupendous engineering feat, often accomplished with elementary axes, picks, and spades.

At Chattanooga, Grant profited from knowledge of his Confederate counterpart, Braxton Bragg, a North Carolina native and West Point graduate, who had met Grant during the Mexican War and later worked as a Louisiana sugar planter. A cold martinet with a gaunt, narrow face and beetling brows, Bragg had flashing eyes that suggested his combustible temperament. However much Grant respected his professionalism, he knew "he was possessed of an irascible temper, and was naturally disputatious."[16] A stickler for rules, Bragg took sadistic delight in punishing people for violations, forcing fellow soldiers to witness executions of deserters. "He loved to crush the spirit of his men," said a soldier. "Not a single soldier in the whole army ever loved or respected him."[17] Whatever the dislike of his troops, Bragg had won significant victories at Perryville, Stones River, and Chickamauga and never shed the unqualified trust of his main supporter, Jefferson Davis.

Scarcely had Grant broken the semi-siege than reports drifted back that Bragg had made a critical error by dispatching twenty thousand men under James Longstreet to attack General Ambrose Burnside and his Army of the Ohio, holed up in Knoxville, in eastern Tennessee. Lincoln had lavished an almost paternal regard upon the loyal residents of eastern Tennessee, reflected in a flurry of telegrams from the capital to Grant, demanding urgent action to rescue Burnside. Although Grant shared their anxiety, he felt powerless to relieve Burnside directly. He still had to wrestle with a troublesome shortage of artillery horses, and, even had he posted soldiers to Burnside, there would have been no supplies or ammunition to equip them when they arrived. Stuck on the horns of this dilemma, Grant believed the most efficacious way to save Burnside was by thrashing Bragg in Chattanooga, possibly forcing him to summon Longstreet back to his side. On November 7, Grant was tempted to pummel a weakened Bragg at Missionary Ridge until Thomas convinced him the attempt was hazardously premature due to Confederate strength and a dearth of draft animals. He also didn't know if his men were ready. In the meantime, Grant exhorted Burnside to banish any thought of retreat and hold eastern Tennessee at all costs.

Working from a modest white frame house overlooking the Tennessee River, Grant believed the war hinged on saving Chattanooga—"the vital point of the rebellion"—as it had on Vicksburg before.[18] By mid-November, he enjoyed robust health, having recuperated from his accident, when William Tecumseh Sherman rode into town and made a beeline for headquarters. He and his seventeen thousand soldiers had tramped six hundred miles from Vicksburg. Grant's first action upon arriving in Chattanooga had been to telegraph Washington and request that Sherman be given command of the Army of the Tennessee, with his headquarters in the field. By now, an easy camaraderie joined the two men who immediately fell into good-natured repartee. Grant extended a cigar to Sherman, ushering him toward a rocking chair. "Take the chair of *honor,* Sherman." "Oh no—that belongs to you, General," Sherman retorted. "Never mind that," Grant replied slyly. "I always give precedence to age." "Well," said the slightly older Sherman, "if you put it on that ground I must accept," and he sat down and lit a cigar.[19] Grant held an animated discussion with Sherman and Thomas, lasting well into the night, about how best to bring Braxton Bragg to bay.

The next morning, escorted by Grant and Thomas, Sherman received his first sobering glimpse of military realities in Chattanooga when they strolled out to a promontory east of town that afforded "a magnificent view of the panorama," Sherman wrote. He saw rebel tents clearly stretched along Missionary Ridge and rebel flags aflutter atop Lookout Mountain, while rebel sentinels strode their posts "in plain view, not a thousand yards off." For the first time, Sherman comprehended the dire, claustrophobic plight of federal forces. "Why, General Grant," he remarked, "you are besieged." Grant confessed, "It is too true." Until that moment, Sherman said, "I had no idea that things were so bad."[20] Grant gave Sherman a complete rundown of the deficiencies he dealt with, including his fear that Thomas's army, whipped at Chickamauga, had shed their fighting élan and that Sherman's men would have to assume the offensive. Grant believed he had detected a weak link in Bragg's defenses—the northern portion of Missionary Ridge—and he and Sherman diligently reviewed the ground. The grand outline of Grant's strategy now emerged: Sherman and Hooker would attack the flanks of Bragg's position on Missionary Ridge—Sherman's attack on the northern end being the main thrust—while Thomas bulldozed the butternut center, then joined forces with Sherman.

By November 16, Longstreet laid siege to Burnside at Knoxville and Grant, concerned about this situation, stayed up past midnight to fire off dispatches. At the same time, he grew increasingly sanguine about his chances against Bragg. Projecting high spirits, he retailed old war stories as he rode about inspecting fortifications. "In general he is extremely reserved," the visiting William Wrenshall

Smith wrote in his diary, "but with one or two friends he is very entertaining and agreeable."[21] Charles Francis Adams Jr. found Grant's appearance uninspiring, saying he could easily pass for a "slouchy little subaltern." Yet he saw that the "cool and quiet" Grant radiated confidence and "in a crisis he is one against whom all around . . . would instinctively lean."[22] Grant's clear sense of purpose enabled him to enlist the energies of a giant army in a common task. "For good sense, strong judgment and nerve, he cannot be surpassed," Wilson wrote. "He is a tower of strength."[23]

The tower of strength struggled with one fateful flaw—his intermittent weakness for alcohol—and Rawlins did yeoman's duty policing Grant's staff to create a safe zone of sobriety around his boss. He grew irate when aide Colonel Clark B. Lagow—described by Dana as "a worthless, whisky-drinking, useless fellow"—held a raucous, late-night drinking party that Grant himself had to break up at 4 a.m.[24] Smith observed the rough justice meted out by Rawlins to Lagow: "He saw that General Rawlins wanted him off the staff, and after the unfortunate spree that the General himself broke up, he saw that he was treated coldly by him. He today heard his resignation had been approved and sent to Washington for acceptance."[25] Smith arrived in camp with a bottle of wine for Grant from his mother. When he turned it over to Rawlins, the latter snapped, "Who brought that?" Smith answered, "I did. The General's mother sent it." Rawlins spluttered, "The General's family are all damn fools."[26] That Hannah Grant sent wine to her son meant she was either unaware of his drinking history or refused to believe the prevalent stories.

Grant remained inordinately proud of Rawlins, having recently boasted to Elihu Washburne that he was "no ordinary man" and had matured amazingly as a military strategist. "As it is he is better and more favorably known than probably any other officer in the Army who has filled only staff appointments."[27] That November, Rawlins again sounded the alarm after two nights of apparent drinking by Grant, writing to him with his usual messianic fervor:

> I again appeal to you in the name of everything a friend, an honest
> man, and a lover of his country holds dear, to immediately desist
> from further tasting of liquors of any kind . . . This very moment
> every faculty of your mind should be clear and unclouded, the
> enemy threatens your lines with immediate attack, Burnside one
> of your Generals trembles where he stands, the authorities at

Washington fear he will yield, they look to you to save him. Since the hour Washington crossed the ice-filled Delaware with his bare-footed patriots to the attack of Trenton, so much of weighty responsibility, has not been imposed by your Government upon one man as it has now imposed upon you . . . Two more nights like the last will find you prostrated on a sick bed unfit for duty. This must not be, You only can prevent it, and for the sake of my bleeding country and your own honor I pray God you may.[28]

Upon reflection, Rawlins decided not to transmit this letter and talked to Grant instead, believing afterward it had the desired effect. If Grant imbibed at this interval, it deviated from his standard pattern of drinking on side trips; here his army was distinctly endangered. Rawlins began to feel oppressed by the eternal burden of being Grant's watchdog. "I am the only one here (his wife not being with him) who can stay [the drinking] . . . & prevent evil consequences resulting from it," Rawlins told his fiancée.[29] He was eager to visit Emma in Connecticut, but only if he could persuade "the General to send for Mrs. Grant. If she is with him all will be well and I can be spared."[30] In that same letter, Rawlins disclosed another reason for his extreme vigilance over Grant: his dread that he himself might turn into a drunkard. "I tell you, my dearest Emma, un-less the blighting shadow of intemperance once had hung like a pall over one's pathway all his life . . . and made him . . . fear to ask himself the question—'Am I to die a drunkard?'—he can poorly appreciate my feelings on this subject."[31] So Rawlins, under the guise of watching over Grant, seemed to be scrutinizing himself as well. That Rawlins's rebuke of Grant had a salutary effect can be seen from a comment made by Major General David Hunter, who stayed with Grant for three weeks, starting in Chattanooga. At the end of that period, Hunter reas-sured Stanton that Grant was "modest, quiet, never swears, and seldom drinks, as he only took two drinks during the three weeks I was with him."[32]

By November 18, Grant had eighty thousand men and stood ready to assault Missionary Ridge, notwithstanding that he still felt handicapped by a shortage of horses and supplies. As he told an aide, "I am tired of the proximity of the enemy and do not intend to stand it if it can be helped . . . And one more good whipping will virtually end the war. Unfortunately I am not in a condition to give them that."[33] The main attack was slated for November 21, with Sherman approaching the ridge at daylight from its extreme northern end. It would be a daring amphibious undertaking: Sherman and his men would cross the Tennessee River via a long pontoon bridge and aboard three large rafts.

Heavy rains on November 20 heaved roads around Brown's Ferry into muddy wastes, impeding Sherman's wagons, livestock, and artillery and making it impossible for him to get into position in time for an attack the next day. To Grant's extreme frustration, it was not even certain that Sherman, despite "almost superhuman efforts," would be ready by November 22.[34] Adding to Grant's worry was that hard fighting had broken out in Knoxville. He knew Lincoln and Stanton chafed in suspense over Burnside's fate and that he would be compelled to provide some relief. He also worried that Bragg might break loose from Chattanooga and rush to join the fray against Burnside. Longing to fight Bragg now, Grant found delay insupportable, telling Halleck that "I have never felt such restlessness before as I have at the fixed and immovable condition of the Army of the Cumberland"—a dig at George Thomas.[35] Meanwhile, scruffy Confederate soldiers languished in woeful misery that made the plight of Union forces look like paradise in comparison. "The soldiers were starved and almost naked, and covered all over with lice and camp itch and filth and dirt," wrote the Confederate soldier Sam Watkins. "The men looked sick, hollow-eyed, and heartbroken, living principally upon parched corn, which had been picked out of the mud and dirt under the feet of officers' horses."[36]

EARLY IN THE AFTERNOON of November 23, the Army of the Cumberland under George Thomas swept across the open plain in front of Missionary Ridge and overran a small cluster of hills, including an elevation called Orchard Knob that gave Grant the perfect command post for the coming battle. The next day all of the interlocking pieces of his strategy began to unfold, albeit with critical improvisations along the way.

On the cold, rainy morning of November 24, Sherman ordered his four divisions to cross a swollen Tennessee River with pontoons and occupy the undefended northern end of Missionary Ridge. It turned out to be sheer illusion that he had staked out a piece of the ridge called Tunnel Hill. Whether from defective maps or Sherman's having misread the geography, his men had conquered a freestanding hill, detached from the main ridge by a deep ravine. At a separate command post, he was initially unaware of what had happened and reported a successful move to Grant. Because of this error, Grant was fooled about the precise location of Sherman's army and sent an erroneous message of triumph to Thomas: "General Sherman carried Missionary Ridge as far as the tunnel with only slight skirmishing."[37]

The day's most scintillating action belonged to Joe Hooker. Tall, muscular, and ramrod straight, with blue eyes and tousled hair, he seemed perfectly cast as a general, with a self-confidence that many found appealing, but that also savored of self-promotion. A West Point general who fought in Mexico, he had failed in farming and engineering on the West Coast before the war plucked him from obscurity. Boastful, unable to muzzle opinions, he had waded into troubled waters with indiscretions. After he said the North needed a dictator, President Lincoln, who had appointed him commander of the Army of the Potomac, cautioned him, "Of course it was not for this, but in spite of it, that I have given you the command."[38] In many ways, the hard-drinking Hooker, whose louche headquarters were called "a combination of barroom and brothel," stood poles apart from the prudish Grant.[39] Right on the eve of the Chattanooga battle, Grant tried to get rid of Hooker and only held back because he had been sent by Lincoln. In his *Memoirs,* Grant admitted that he regarded the egomaniacal Hooker as "a dangerous man. He was not subordinate to his superiors. He was ambitious to the extent of caring nothing for the rights of others."[40]

On the morning of November 24, Hooker flung parts of three divisions against Confederate forces on Lookout Mountain. The scene couldn't have been more picturesque—or forbidding—for Union troops. The steep mountain was lined with chasms, rocks, and fallen trees and ringed with trenches and rifle pits. The battle was fought through sporadic haze, mist, and rain that at first veiled the upward movement of Hooker's men. "But the sound of his artillery and musketry was heard incessantly," wrote Grant, who watched from his command post at Orchard Knob.[41] Clad in black hat and coat, his trousers tucked into Wellington boots, Grant squatted and wrote dispatches while balancing his order book on one knee, sending messages to reinforce Hooker and cut off any enemy retreat. At other moments, he sat on a stool, behind a log barrier, calmly watching the action. One British journalist recorded his peerless tranquillity: "There he stood in his plain citizen's clothes looking through his double field-glasses apparently totally unmoved. I stood within a few feet of him and I could hardly believe that here was this famous commander, the model, it seemed to me, of a modest and homely but efficient Yankee general."[42] Grant always considered the pageantry of the Chattanooga fight beyond anything he had experienced, telling Washburne it was "the first battlefield I have ever seen where a plan could be followed and from one place the whole field be within one view."[43]

Once Hooker ascended the western face, he circled Lookout Mountain to take the northern slope, driving away Confederate soldiers. The peak was high enough that clouds congregated at lower levels, with Hooker's men intermittently visible above them; hence the colorful label attached to the conflict: the Battle Above the Clouds. Grant, who praised Hooker's handling of the maneuver, denied that fierce fighting ever took place. "The battle of Lookout Mountain is one of the romances of the war," he scoffed. "There was no such battle and no action even worthy to be called a battle on Lookout Mountain. It is all poetry."[44] When Hooker later heard such comments, he resented what he saw as an attempt to demean his achievement, saying he could "account for [it] in no other way than that [Grant] was in his cups."[45] Hooker had dexterously used feints and deceptions to coax rebel forces off the mountainside. As darkness descended, the sky was clear, a full moon shone—except for a lunar eclipse—and Union campfires dotted the slope in brilliant array. During the night, the last Confederate forces on Lookout Mountain melted away, rushing to the asylum of their comrades on Missionary Ridge. The next morning, Hooker's men planted the American flag atop the summit, drawing universal hurrahs from Union troops down below.

On November 25, a bright and glorious day, Sherman's army attacked the enemy, colliding with a small but proficient force under General Patrick Cleburne and absorbing numerous casualties. For many hours, the Army of the Tennessee made little headway, fighting fiercely at close range. Sherman was thus stymied in his quest for glory. "Go signal Grant," he instructed a staff officer at midafternoon. "The orders were that I should get as many as possible in front of me, and God knows there are enough. They've been reinforcing all day."[46] At the southern end of Missionary Ridge, Joseph Hooker was delayed when rebels retreating from Lookout Mountain burned a key bridge across Chattanooga Creek, costing Hooker four precious hours.

Originally, Grant hoped Sherman would reap the lion's share of glory at Chattanooga. But with Sherman and Hooker stalled at the far ends of Missionary Ridge, Grant turned his attention to George Thomas at the rebel center. He ordered Thomas, with his twenty-three thousand troops, to grab the base of Missionary Ridge and seize the first line of enemy rifle pits on the lower portion.

He held modest expectations since the ridge was steep, well fortified, and seemingly impregnable. Union soldiers would have to march across a perilously exposed plain, then overtake the lowest rifle pits at the foot of the ridge. One hour after Grant gave the order to march, the slow-moving Thomas still had not complied. When he saw Thomas conversing with Thomas Wood, a division commander, Grant gave way to an uncommon moment of pique. Summoning Wood, he said, "I ordered your attack an hour ago. Why has it not been made?" "I have been ready for more than an hour," Wood said defensively, "and can attack in five minutes after receiving the order." Grant shot back: "I order you to attack."[47]

Triggered by a signal—six consecutive cannon shots—nearly twenty-three thousand men sprang forward with lusty cheers. They moved with panache, urged on by rolling drums and bugle calls, their long, undulating columns and gleaming weapons providing a splendid spectacle in the afternoon sunshine. Fifty guns opened fire on them from the ridge. Far from being disheartened, as Grant had feared, Thomas's army was stimulated to superior performance. Relegated to an ancillary role, they had something to prove and made quick work of the first rung of rifle pits. "The troops moved under fire with all the precision of veterans on parade," an elated Grant informed Halleck.[48] Many Confederate defenders stood in poor condition, one observer describing them as "rough and ragged men with no vestige of a uniform."[49] Grant had good reason to crow about his men. "The assaulting column advanced to the very rifle pits of the enemy and held their position firmly without wavering."[50] All the while, Grant maintained his nonchalant, no-nonsense manner. "He seems perfectly cool," wrote William Wrenshall Smith, "and one could be with him for hours, and not know that any great movements were going on."[51]

Then, as Grant watched through field glasses, something unexpected— indeed miraculous—happened. Three blue-coated regiments found themselves on a spur of the ridge hidden from enemy soldiers peering down from the top. As Confederates at the lower level started a panicky retreat up the mountainside, Union men, by a common impulse, began to clamber up after them, their regimental colors streaming in the wind. Many federals fled higher to avoid enemy fire. Before long eighteen thousand blue-clad soldiers raced helter-skelter up the steep slopes. According to one version of the battle, it was the lowly soldiers who first heeded the impulse to scamper upward and their superiors who belatedly followed. Bravery was suddenly the path of least resistance. The northerners

taunted the fleeing rebels with derisory cries of "Chickamauga! Chickamauga!"—the humiliating defeat they sought to avenge.[52] All the while, surging
Union forces were saved from fire because Confederate marksmen feared they
might accidentally spray with bullets their retreating comrades down below. Before long sixty regimental Union flags streaked up the mountainside toward the
crest, chevrons of flying soldiers floating upward in an infectious outbreak of
mass courage. As they scrambled hastily for cover, Confederate soldiers left behind a trail of cannon, wagons, horses, and supplies. One Union commander
who reveled in the thrilling ascent was Phil Sheridan, who flapped his hat in the
air and brandished his sword. "Forward, boys, forward!" he admonished his
men. "We can go to the top . . . Come on, boys, give 'em hell!"[53] At the mountain
peak, it was young Arthur MacArthur Jr. of Wisconsin—father of World War II
general Douglas MacArthur—who drove in the first regimental flag.

Agog, Grant later admitted he had never seen anything like this extemporaneous rout of the enemy. Originally he had expected his men to pause at the first
trenches, regroup, then climb up the mountain in orderly stages, and he was
initially disconcerted by the spontaneous upward push. "Thomas, who ordered
those men up the ridge?" he demanded. "I don't know," said Thomas, his voice
level. "*I* did not."[54] Not about to argue with such success, Grant clamped down
hard on an unlit cigar and decided not to countermand the impulsive action.
"The boys feel pretty good," he observed. "Let them alone awhile."[55] He then
gave orders for the entire line to storm the ridge. Entranced by the amazing occurrence in progress, Grant hurried off a message to Sherman. "Thomas has
carried the hill and line in his immediate front. Now is your time to attack with
vigor. DO SO!"[56] By the end, ground observers saw one regimental color after
another unfurled on the summit. Grant was astonished at how few casualties his
men had endured. "I can account for this only on the theory that the enemy's
surprise at the audacity of such a charge, caused confusion and purposeless aiming of their pieces," he wrote.[57]

Once Grant saw the last Confederate defenses crumple, he spurred his horse
to the front. He always considered Shiloh and Missionary Ridge his two most
satisfying battles. As he rode along the ridgetop, he was cheered by jubilant
troops with "tumultuous shouts," said Dana, who described the storming of the
ridge as "one of the greatest miracles in military history."[58] Grant thought Bragg
might stand and fight, but he was already in headlong retreat, fleeing into nearby
Georgia. "An Army never was whipped so badly as Bragg was," exulted Grant,

who regretted not having captured the opposing army and thought he could have done so had he known the geography better.[59] Nonetheless, Grant had accomplished his foremost objective, pushing Bragg into Georgia and away from Burnside in Knoxville.

As befit a battle marked by theatrics, Bragg's escape sketched a memorable tableau. "Bragg is in full retreat, burning his depots and bridges," Dana told Stanton. "The Chickamauga Valley, for a distance of 10 miles, is full of the fires lighted in his flight."[60] One Union soldier recorded thousands of rebel soldiers fleeing in a disorderly rout down the rear slope of Missionary Ridge, jettisoning battle paraphernalia in their haste. "Gray clad men rushed wildly down the hill into the woods, tossing away knapsacks, muskets, and blankets as they ran."[61] For Braxton Bragg, the disgrace was total. "Bragg looked scared," one Confederate soldier remarked. "He had put spurs to his horse, and was running like a scared dog . . . Poor fellow, he looked so hacked and whipped and mortified and chagrined at defeat."[62] When Bragg forwarded his resignation to Richmond, the Confederate government hastened to accept it.

Endearing himself to Grant, Sheridan and his men pursued Bragg to his supply depot at Chickamauga Station, a quick-witted decision that yielded a windfall in prisoners and weaponry. Ecstatically joyful, Sheridan straddled one cannon, waved his hat, and emitted a loud cheer. Luckily for Bragg, nightfall made it difficult to overtake the defeated rebels. Grant chased Bragg as far as Ringgold, Georgia, twenty miles southeast of Chattanooga. Ely Parker, a newcomer to Grant's staff, was struck by the relentless way Grant rode, unfazed by bullets whistling around him. "When at Ringgold, we rode for half a mile in the face of the enemy, under an incessant fire of cannon and musketry . . . not once do I believe did it enter the general's mind that he was in danger . . . he requires no escort beyond his staff . . . Roads are almost useless to him, for he takes short cuts through field and woods, and will swim his horse through almost any stream that obstructs his way . . . he will ride from breakfast until one or two in the morning, and that too without eating."[63]

As was his wont, Grant proved generous in victory. When he and his officers trotted past a downtrodden contingent of enemy prisoners, he reacted with simple decency. "When General Grant reached the line of ragged, filthy, bloody, despairing prisoners . . . he lifted his hat and held it over his head until he passed the last man of that living funeral cortege," recalled a prisoner. "He was the only officer in that whole train who recognized us as being on the face of the earth."[64]

Once again the man badly stereotyped as a butcher showed more sensitivity toward his fallen adversaries than his colleagues.

Grant's reputation zoomed to new heights after Chattanooga. Within a month, he had done what seemed impossible: he had gone from being besieged by opponents to ejecting them, and his victory had pried open more rebel territory to Union penetration. Grant and his colleagues had cleaned out the enemy from most of Tennessee, laying the groundwork for a critical incursion into Georgia. "The Slave aristocracy broken down," trumpeted Quartermaster General Montgomery Meigs. "The grandest stroke yet struck for our country."[65] In New York, George Templeton Strong pronounced the Chattanooga Campaign "the heaviest blow the country has yet dealt at rebellion."[66] Grant thought his victory had driven "a big nail in the Coffin of rebellion."[67] Southerners recognized that if they couldn't hold Chattanooga, with its many natural advantages, they would have trouble resisting the Union juggernaut in future encounters.

For the first time Grant had taken elements of three Union armies—the Army of the Tennessee, the Army of the Cumberland, and the Army of the Potomac—and merged them into a cohesive fighting force despite rivalries that sometimes strained relations between western and eastern soldiers. "So far as I can understand the subject," wrote the historian John Lothrop Motley, "Ulysses Grant is *at least* equal to any general now living in any part of the world, and by far the first that our war has produced on either side."[68] As Grant reached a new apogee of fame, his praise was echoed in newspapers that had criticized the war effort, the *New York Herald* maintaining that "Gen. Grant is one of the great soldiers of the age . . . without an equal in the list of generals now alive."[69] The sweetest praise arrived in a letter from Washington: "I wish to tender you, and all under your command, my more than thanks—my profoundest gratitude—for the skill, courage, and perseverance, with which you and they, over so great difficulties, have effected that important object. God bless you all. A. Lincoln."[70]

All along Grant had worried about Ambrose Burnside in Knoxville, having vowed to send him speedy relief after disposing of Bragg. On November 23, Burnside sent Grant an alarming report that he had only ten or twelve days of supplies left, at the expiration of which he would need to surrender to Longstreet. "Do not be forced into a Surrender by Short rations," Grant beseeched him. "Take all the citizens have, to enable you to hold out yet a few days longer."[71] Grant decided to send twenty thousand soldiers to break the siege, one column consisting of Sherman and his men, who were exhausted from the tough assignment at Chattanooga. In a shrewd bit of psychological warfare, Grant outlined for Burnside the steps he had taken to raise the siege, deliberately allowing it to fall into Longstreet's hands. The ruse worked: the day after receiving the letter, Longstreet gave orders to lift the Knoxville siege and return to Virginia, realizing Lincoln's long-held dream of regaining control over eastern Tennessee with its strong pro-Unionist elements.

When Sherman arrived in Knoxville, he discovered that Grant had been badly bamboozled by Burnside, who had warned that his men faced starvation. Instead, Sherman found Burnside luxuriating amid plenty, with access to a fine herd of cattle. Burnside and his staff had taken up residence in a handsome mansion. Instead of finding bare cupboards, Sherman sat down to a generous dinner of roast turkey. When he told Burnside he expected to find him starving, the abashed Burnside confessed he had been able to obtain "a good supply of beef, bacon, and corn-meal" from the surrounding countryside.[72]

Hating to keep his army idle for extended periods, Grant immediately conceived new plans for taking Mobile. He wanted to steer his army down the Mississippi to New Orleans, then move east to Pascagoula in southeastern Mississippi and strike at Mobile and the Georgia and Alabama interiors. The idea was vintage Grant, moving beyond isolated battles to a boldly expansive blueprint for taking state after state and terminating hostilities. His great strength was that he thought in terms of sequence of battles. However meritorious, his plan was vetoed by Lincoln, Stanton, and Halleck, who feared it might leave eastern Tennessee vulnerable and reverse recent success there.

By this point, Lincoln stood firmly in Grant's corner, especially since his Tennessee victories had aided Republicans in carrying pivotal elections in Iowa and Ohio. "No man can feel more kindly and more grateful to you than the President," Washburne told Grant.[73] Once Lincoln received word that Chattanooga and Knoxville lay safely in Union hands, he advised the northern public to congregate in churches and praise the Lord "for this great advancement of the national cause."[74] After many hideous bloodbaths, Lincoln felt grateful that Knoxville was liberated without more slaughter. In Washington, politicians vied to decorate Grant, and both houses of Congress passed unanimous resolutions thanking him for the eastern Tennessee victories. On December 18, Lincoln asked Washburne to supervise the forging of a commemorative gold medal for Grant while the citizens of Jo Daviess County decided to give him a diamond-hilted sword, the names of his victories engraved on its gold scabbard. For all his hand-wringing over the flawed generals running the Army of the Potomac, Lincoln hesitated to bring Grant east, reluctant to dislodge him from the scene of so many stunning victories: "I do not think it would do to bring Grant away from the West."[75]

One reason Lincoln resisted any impulse to elevate Grant was the sudden chatter about Grant as a presidential candidate—perhaps inevitable for a conspicuously successful general. That November, Lincoln began to entertain more openly the idea of a second term, but his reelection, or even renomination, was no foregone conclusion. He had to reckon with the prospect that George McClellan might be the Democratic nominee, and he did not care to groom another possible military rival. The man banging the drum most loudly for Grant was James Gordon Bennett, the self-aggrandizing editor of the *New York Herald,* who editorialized that "the whole country looks up to [Grant] as the great genius who is to end this war, restore the Union and save us from the danger which the end of the war may bring upon us."[76]

The pro-Grant boom that germinated in December 1863 enjoyed no support from its supposed beneficiary, who was aghast at being thrust into the political spotlight. When approached by the chairman of Ohio's Democratic state central committee to be the presidential candidate of the War Democrats, Grant promptly squelched such scuttlebutt: "I do not know of anything I have ever done or said which would indicate that I could be a candidate for any office whatever within the gift of the people . . . Nothing likely to happen would pain me so much as to see my name used in connection with a political office."[77] Knowing it would find its way to the White House, Rawlins chimed in with a letter to Washburne that Grant was "unambitious for the honor" of the presidency.[78] On a train trip that winter, Grant explained to the wife of a Union officer why he preferred his generalship over the presidency. "That is for life and my family would be provided for"—no minor consideration for a man who had suffered such economic uncertainty.[79]

The person who eased Lincoln's late-night worries about Grant's electoral plans was J. Russell Jones, a U.S. marshal in Chicago and an intimate friend of Grant's who managed his investments. As speculation about a Grant candidacy gathered steam in January, Jones urged Grant to tamp down such talk. He thought that, with patience, Grant would be appointed lieutenant general, smoothing his way to the presidency four years later. In response, Grant spiked any discussion of his political leanings: "I am receiving a great deal of that kind of literature, but it soon finds its way into the waste basket. I already have a

pretty big job on my hands, and my only ambition is to see this rebellion suppressed. Nothing could induce me to think of being a presidential candidate,
particularly so long as there is a possibility of having Mr. Lincoln re-elected."[80]
By disavowing any political agenda and reaffirming his loyalty to Lincoln, Grant
showed his political astuteness. He already knew how to send clear but discreet
political messages. Jones received this missive just as he set out for Washington
to meet Lincoln, whom he found brooding about Grant's political intentions. As
they sat alone in the White House, Jones gave Grant's letter to the president,
who pored over it with infinite care, finishing with "a deep sigh of relief," according to Jones. "Then putting both hands on my shoulders, he said: 'My son, I can't
tell you how deeply gratified I am. You don't know how deep the Presidential
maggot can gnaw into a man's brain.'"[81] It made a remarkable statement about
Grant's meteoric ascent that Lincoln now warily appraised the former Galena
store clerk as a potential competitor.

One person who obsessed about Grant's rise to power was Sherman. Historians always laud their fraternal wartime bond, but where the affection was unalloyed on Grant's part, Sherman developed unspoken reservations about Grant.
When he returned home to Ohio that December, he saw Grant catapulted to a
new plateau of celebrity. "Our army is on all lips," he told Grant, "and were you
to come to Ohio, you would hardly be allowed to eat a meal, from the intense
curiosity to see you and hear you."[82] Sherman always made sarcastic comments
about politicians and feared Grant would be corrupted by power. "Your reputation as a general is now far above that of any man living," he reassured Grant,
"and partisans will maneuver for your influence; but if you can escape them, as
you have hitherto done, you will be more powerful for good than it is possible to
measure."[83] This letter marked the start of a slow-motion schism between the
two men, for Grant, unlike Sherman, *had* political ambitions and later allowed
himself to be swept into office. Sherman also harbored some secret doubts about
Grant as a general, not so much in individual battles but as a possible chieftain
of the overall war effort. "Grant has qualities Halleck doesn't," he told his
brother, Senator John Sherman, "but not such as would qualify him to command the whole army."[84]

Whatever Sherman's reservations, Elihu Washburne shared none of them
and lionized his protégé. So outsize were Grant's victories that many Washington admirers thought he merited a rank higher than a mere major general. On
December 14, Washburne presented a bill in the House to resurrect the grade of

lieutenant general, a rare honor conferred only on George Washington and by brevet on Winfield Scott. Grant was clearly intended as the recipient, which would jump him above Halleck to the pinnacle of military power. "I want [Grant] in a position where he can organize *final* victory and bring it to our armies and put an end to this rebellion," declared Senator James Doolittle of Wisconsin.[85] Grant, having done nothing to provoke this, played the bashful hero, disclaiming ambition and telling Washburne, "I have been highly honored already by the government and do not ask, or feel that I deserve, anything more in the shape of honors or promotion. A success over the enemy is what I crave above everything else."[86] Contrary to Grant's wishes, the lieutenant general bill spurred further speculation about him as a presidential candidate. Now persuaded that Grant didn't hanker after the presidency, Lincoln had no qualms about backing the lieutenant general bill.

On December 20, Grant relocated his headquarters to Nashville, a good spot for overseeing military operations in his jurisdiction that also enjoyed excellent telegraphic communication with Washington. During a winter respite in the fighting, Grant devoted his attention to mapping out future campaigns against Atlanta, Montgomery, and Mobile as his thoughts bent decidedly toward the eastern seaboard, the core of Confederate industrial strength. "Let us crush the head and heart of the rebellion," he told Halleck, "and the tail can be ground to dust or allowed to die . . . All possible results that can not be gained by moving west, will accrue necessarily when our objects are gained in the east."[87]

Grant's main organizational concern was to guarantee supplies for his armies for their spring campaigns. Just how capable he was is shown in the recollections of Colonel James Rusling of the quartermaster's department. He found Grant's appearance unprepossessing, with an "unbuttoned coat and a battered hat" reminiscent of "a country storekeeper or a western farmer." Then Rusling beheld Grant's extraordinary grasp of military detail, how "every night he knew precisely where the enemy was, and what he was doing, and what we were able to do and dare."[88] He also noticed how decisively Grant acted under pressure. When brought a request for a major expenditure, Grant approved it with startling speed. Rusling asked Grant if he was sure he was correct. "No, I am not," Grant shot back, "but in war anything is better than indecision. *We must decide.* If I am wrong we shall soon find it out, and can do the other thing. But *not to decide* wastes both time and money and may ruin everything."[89]

As part of his logistical emphasis that winter, Grant sought to ensure adequate supply routes for his armies. Never content to rely on secondhand information, he toured Chattanooga, Knoxville, and Lexington, by way of the Cumberland Gap, which entailed hard riding over desolate, badly pitted roads. In general, he enjoyed rugged exercise, but the unsightly remains of war rendered it a grisly experience. "The road over Cumberland Gap . . . was strewn with *debris* of broken wagons and dead animals, much as I had found it on my first trip to Chattanooga . . . The road had been cut up to as great a depth as clay could be by mules and wagons, and in that condition frozen . . . the road was a very cheerless one, and very disagreeable."[90] Grant was heartened to see loyal admirers lining the route and was amused by their mistaken reaction to his entourage. "The people naturally expected to see the commanding general the oldest person in the party. I was then forty-one years of age, while my medical director was gray-haired and probably twelve or more years my senior. The crowds would generally swarm around him, and thus give me an opportunity of quietly dismounting and getting into the house."[91] Despite Grant's self-effacing description, the ride illustrated what Sherman had recently said: Grant was now a national hero and viewed as a future president. As a colleague recalled, "*Hail to the Chief,* both words and air, greeted him at every stopping place."[92]

The winter provided a needed reprieve for Grant, allowing him to spend time in Nashville with Julia, who had been living in Louisville because "it was not particularly pleasant for me at Father Grant's house," as she expressed it.[93] During that frigid winter, Nashville provided few distractions from war. As Rawlins wrote, "If ever there was a city over which the shadow of gloom hung darkly, it is this. It is literally the City of Woe. Nineteen out of twenty of the inhabitants are in mourning for friends who have been killed in battle."[94] The kindhearted Julia, deeply moved by the plight of wounded and dying soldiers, thought of little else. "I went to visit the hospitals on several occasions and saw many sad sights," she said. "I returned each time laden with petitions for discharges." Then she discovered that her overworked husband, who needed a break from the unbearable grimness of war, chided her for bringing home distressing tales from sick wards: "I hear of these all day long and I sent for you to come that I might have a rest from all this sad part. I do not want you to know about these things. I want you to tell me of the children and yourself. I want and need a little rest and sunshine."[95] Sympathetic to her husband's deep-rooted sadness about the war, so visible in wartime pictures of him, Julia stopped visiting the hospitals, and they often attended a small Methodist church together.

In Nashville, Grant pursued the incorporation of black soldiers into his army. In his year-end address to Congress, Lincoln boasted that one hundred thousand former slaves now participated in military service, about half bearing arms, and he credited them with a goodly share of Union victories. Around the same time, when Grant recommended the appointment of Brigadier General Augustus L. Chetlain to command black troops, Lincoln seconded this choice. Chetlain's job was to recruit and organize "colored troops in Tennessee and West Kentucky."[96] In discussing the assignment with Grant, Chetlain found him a wholehearted convert to Lincoln's policy: "He then said that it was the policy of the government, which he fully endorsed, to place a large force of colored troops in the service at once; that the experiment of using colored men in the South in the army so far had proved satisfactory. After a pause, he added: 'I believe the colored man will make a good soldier.'"[97] That winter, Grant also expanded the use of black troops to guard plantations on the west side of the Mississippi River.

Grant had allowed his eldest son, Fred, to join him during the Vicksburg Campaign. During the siege, Fred had contracted typhoid fever that only worsened in subsequent months. In late January, Grant sped off to St. Louis, where Fred's condition had grown perilous. He was so pessimistic that he did not expect to find his son still alive. The military situation in eastern Tennessee unavoidably detained him—Longstreet had resumed menacing activities in that end of the state—but by the time Grant saw Fred, he was on the mend, if still looking skeletal. Once given proper medications, Fred recovered at such a rapid pace that he returned to Nashville with his parents.

While in St. Louis, Julia consulted Dr. Charles A. Pope to see if he could possibly correct her strabismus—a serious enough problem that it caused her physical distress and interfered with travel—but he said it was too late in life to perform this operation. When she mentioned the visit afterward to her husband, he was thunderstruck as to what had made her entertain such an idea. "Why, you are getting to be such a great man and I am such a plain little wife," Julia replied, "I thought if my eyes were as others are I might not be so very, very plain, Ulys; who knows?" Grant's response was piercingly tender. "Did I not see you and fall in love with you with these same eyes? I like them just as they are, and now, remember, you are not to interfere with them. They are mine, and let me tell you, Mrs. Grant, you had better not make any experiments, as I might not like you half so well with any other eyes."[98] The anecdote, as well as many others, attests to the depth of Grant's unconditional love for his wife, and vice versa.

Ulysses and Julia Grant received proof in St. Louis that they had been transformed into significant public figures. One night they attended the theater to see a drama called *Richelieu* and sat far enough back in their box that the audience didn't realize until intermission that Grant was there. At that point they took up a chant, "Grant! Grant! Get up!" He finally got up and made an awkward bow, but the crowd wouldn't stop cheering until he brought his seat to the front edge of the box, making him visible to the entire house.

Two nights later, Grant was feted at the new Lindell Hotel, where Colonel Dent joined the admiring throng. The colonel, now a white-haired old man, listened as nine major and brigadier generals and numerous orators extolled his son-in-law's victories. Grant warmly greeted old friends and responded modestly to their sustained applause, a typically inscrutable expression on his face. Incapable of making a speech when a toast was given—"Gentlemen," he replied, "it will be impossible for me to do more than thank you"—he stood and lit a cigar to the crowd's delight.[99] Waiters kept placing wineglasses at Grant's side from which he would not partake. "I dare not touch it," he told General John M. Schofield. "Sometimes I can drink freely without any unpleasant effect; at others I could not take even a single glass of wine." Schofield, impressed, thought, "A strong man indeed, who could thus know and govern his own weakness!"[100] Afterward, a huge crowd gathered outside Grant's hotel as celebratory bonfires burned and rockets streaked skyward. Grant appeared on the balcony to acknowledge the great fuss made over him. It must have been hard for his St. Louis friends to believe that this man, who had left town destitute a few years earlier, now rode such a wave of national adulation.

One person who followed Grant's growing fame with apprehension was John Rawlins, who behaved like a nervous mother fretting over a potentially wayward son. When traveling on a train with Grant in Kentucky, two St. Louis society ladies tried to push a bottle of wine on Grant, which he refused. Grant's physician, Dr. Kittoe, described Rawlins's outraged reaction: "Rawlins watched his chief with fear and trembling lest he should yield to the temptation, and gave vent to his indignation at the course pursued by the St. Louis females in terms more profanely forcible than elegant and in so loud a tone that the two objects of his wrath plainly heard what he said and bore evidence of their mortification by their looks."[101] The ever-watchful Rawlins feared Grant had given way to drink at the festive St. Louis dinner and was relieved when he returned unharmed to Nashville. "I feared everything was not as it should be with him, but his appearance has agreeably disappointed me, and for once I have done him injustice in my thoughts," he wrote.[102]

One reason Rawlins thought so despondently about Grant may have been his depressed view of his own medical condition. He was beginning to suspect that his long-standing cough might mean that, like his first wife before him, he was infected with tuberculosis. He would shortly leave on an extended western trip to try to recapture his health. In the meantime, he consumed opiates to deal with the pain, complaining to his new wife that "the quantity of opium has affected my whole system inasmuch as to produce a sensation of numbness and drowsiness."[103] When shown a photo of himself, he was taken aback to see himself looking "sad and death-like," yet he admitted to Emma that the image was accurate and that in every photo there was "that same sad and sorrowful expression."[104]

CHAPTER SIXTEEN

Idol of the Hour

A S HIS FATE WAS debated in Washington that February, Grant continued to direct his department's operations from Nashville, where he lodged comfortably with a family that "consists only of an elderly gentleman & his wife, son-in-law and his wife besides a young school Miss," Grant told Julia. "I usually take a ride for an hour in the evening on horseback or in the buggy. This you know always keeps me feeling well."[1] He would not enjoy this tranquil interval for long.

Grant felt ambivalent toward the congressional bill that would elevate him to lieutenant general and likely install him as chief of the northern war effort. Conflicted about his own ambition, he nonetheless had a way of making himself available for promotion. Although he did nothing to advance the bill in Congress, neither did he do anything to stop it. He feared that becoming lieutenant general would snatch him from the battlefield and chain him to a desk, weakening his contribution to the war effort. He made clear that he would accept no post that tethered him to Washington or prevented him from leading armies in combat. Finding political machinations distasteful, Grant dreaded becoming a bureaucratic captive, mixed up in legislative intrigue. He also worried that as lieutenant general, he would suddenly outrank and supersede Halleck. Even though Halleck had been two-faced toward him, Grant still treated him with great respect and balked at leapfrogging over him in the military hierarchy. The one feature Grant wholeheartedly embraced was that promotion would boost his salary to $8,640 per year. On some level, he still feared a reversion to financial failure after the war.

It came as no surprise that Grant's main cheerleader on the House floor was Elihu Washburne, who informed colleagues that Grant had "captured more prisoners and taken more guns than any general in modern times."[2] He cited Grant's modesty, lack of pretension, and devotion to the Union. There was some grumbling in Washington about Washburne's patent self-interest in promoting a man with whom he was so closely identified. Even his brother Cadwallader warned him he could be a bore and monomaniac on the subject of Grant: "Touching Ulysses S. Grant I think you have crowded him about as hard as he will bear and anything more looks fulsome. He's a good man, and we all know it, and we don't want to be told many times what we know already."[3] In the Senate, James Doolittle led the charge for Grant, enumerating how he had won seventeen battles and taken one hundred thousand prisoners and five hundred artillery pieces. Another persuasive argument for tapping Grant as lieutenant general was that it would topple Halleck, who was loathed by the more radical Republicans in Congress.

Some legislators didn't want a specific name attached to the lieutenant general bill, fearing it would encroach on presidential prerogatives, setting a harmful precedent. While the version that passed the House contained Grant's name, the Senate excised it. Opposition to the bill centered on the idea that such a lofty rank should be conferred only *after* the Union won the war. As Congressman Thaddeus Stevens colorfully put it, "Saints are not canonized until after death."[4] Everyone knew the sacred nature of the lieutenant general title, indelibly associated with George Washington. Congressman James Garfield worried that if the new lieutenant general failed in his assignment, he might have to be deposed a few months later and noted that Lincoln already had full authority to name a new general in chief. Washburne pressed the argument that Grant, with a free hand, could wind up the war more quickly. "I want this now," the congressman insisted. "Grant must fight out this war, and he will never leave the field!"[5]

To some extent, the drinking charges against Grant that passed through congressional corridors counted against him. Being an unknown entity to most legislators made him susceptible to damaging rumors about his prewar history. As the commissary chief Michael R. Morgan explained, "The reason for Grant's resignation in 1854 . . . was known. Grant's case was unusual at the time and was discussed by the Army . . . The prominent officers in the Eastern armies were mostly of the Old Army."[6] Rawlins believed his vigilance in saving Grant from drink was an open secret in Washington and those who knew it included "several gentlemen of great influence . . . who are to be found both in Congress and in the War Department and belonging to both political parties."[7]

On February 26, both houses of Congress agreed to a bill that followed the Senate's lead in expunging Grant's name. After Lincoln signed it three days later, he promptly named Grant to the position, perhaps believing promotion would neutralize a presidential rival. Events moved apace, the Senate confirming the appointment so swiftly that on March 3 Grant received a telegram, summoning him to Washington to receive his new commission from the president's own hands. He had mastered the art of not grasping for power, but letting it come to him unbidden. Beyond satisfying his aversion to lobbying, this approach allayed the ingrained American fear of the Man on Horseback, who might exploit his military laurels and turn tyrant after the war. As lieutenant general, Grant knew, his life would whirl into an altogether different orbit. "Nothing ever fell over me like a wet blanket so much as my promotion to the Lt. Generalcy," he later confessed.[8]

The two men who knew Grant best, Rawlins and Sherman, dreaded his fate in Washington. They sensed that this guileless man could get sidetracked in the crooked paths of power. They had good reason to agonize over him: Grant's fame had been sudden, massive—a torrential rain after years of drought. It says much about Grant's character that, at this moment of supreme triumph, instead of advertising his own virtues, he paid unstinting tribute to his colleagues, telling Sherman, "Whilst I have been eminently successful in this war . . . what I want is to express my thanks to you and McPherson as *the men* to whom, above all others, I feel indebted for whatever I have had of success."[9] In a gracious reply, Sherman paid tribute to Grant:

> You are now Washington's legitimate successor and occupy a position of almost dangerous elevation, but if you can continue as heretofore to be yourself, simple, honest, and unpretending, you will enjoy through life the respect and love of friends, and the homage of millions of human beings that will award to you a large share in securing to them and their descendants a Government of Law and Stability . . . I believe you are as brave, patriotic, and just, as the great . . . Washington—as unselfish, kindhearted and honest, as a

man should be, but the chief characteristic in your nature is the simple faith in success you have always manifested, which I can liken to nothing else than the faith a Christian has in a Savior. This faith gave you victory at Shiloh and Vicksburg.[10]

Sherman ended this warmhearted letter with a stark warning that Grant should beware the perils of Washington—a plea from one western man to another to avoid the insidious snares of the East. "Don't stay in Washington. Halleck is better qualified than you are to stand the buffets of Intrigue and Policy. Come out West, take to yourself the whole Mississippi Valley . . . Here lies the seat of the coming Empire, and from the West when our task is done, we will make short work of Charleston, and Richmond, and the impoverished coast of the Atlantic."[11]

Rawlins wondered what would happen to his beloved boss in the rarefied atmosphere to which he now ascended, telling his wife, "I grow dizzy in looking from the eminence he has attained and tremble at the great responsibility about to devolve upon him."[12] He also mused darkly about his own medical future, confessing to Grant that he feared his health "would require me to leave the service, that I should get no better when warm weather comes."[13] Rawlins's military career had soared along with Grant's, and for the first time he worried they might have to part company. When he was named brigadier general in the regular army on March 3, occupying the new post of chief of staff to the commanding general, some senators groused about his lack of credentials. Rawlins thought the ruckus boiled down to a charge that "my military education is not such as to fit me for his chief of staff" and that the brigadier rank should be reserved for field officers, not staff. Other senators thought it superfluous to have Rawlins as chief of staff in the field since Halleck would enact this role in the capital.[14]

Refusing to discard him, Grant made a persuasive case for Rawlins's confirmation as brigadier general. "General Rawlins has served with me from the beginning of the rebellion," he explained to Senator Henry Wilson. "He comes the nearest being indispensable to me of any officer in the service. But if his confirmation is dependent on his commanding troops, he shall command troops at once."[15] Having saved Grant from the bottle, Rawlins expected to be accorded special status in Washington. Testimonials to him invariably contained the code word "indispensable." As Captain Ely Parker wrote to Washburne of Rawlins: "His unwavering fidelity, judicious counsel, untiring energy and inflexible integrity, have no doubt contributed largely to the uninterrupted success of Gen. Grant's armies . . . It is my opinion that he is absolutely indispensable to Gen. Grant."[16] Lieutenant Colonel William R. Rowley chimed in to Washburne: "You know of how much importance I have always considered it to be to keep Rawlins with the General . . . It is unnecessary for me to particularize as I have talked with you on the subject."[17] Whether due to his guardian angel role or outstanding military judgment, Rawlins was confirmed as brigadier general by the Senate on April 14.

On the morning of March 4, 1864, Grant left Nashville for the nation's capital, accompanied by Rawlins and Cyrus Comstock, a West Point graduate who had become a trusted staff officer. It was a journey to a brand-new existence for Grant, who could tell from crowds blossoming at train stations along the way that his life had changed in an almost inconceivable fashion. "The General received a good deal of attention on the route, crowds waiting to see him at the depots," Comstock jotted in his diary.[18] Grant did not yet fathom that his center of operations would switch irrevocably to the eastern seaboard. Within two weeks, he imagined he would be back commanding western armies. What he knew for certain was that he would remain a fighting general in the field. As he promised Sherman, "I shall say very distinctly on my arrival" in Washington "that I accept no appointment which will require me to make that city my Head Quarters."[19]

En route, Rawlins maintained a proprietary scrutiny of his boss. One side of him was cheered by the "hearty and enthusiastic manner" in which varied people greeted Grant.[20] But his deeply puritan side descried a canker of corruption taking root in his pure-hearted boss. For all of Grant's humility, Rawlins perceived, some tincture of vanity in him adored the adulation, however flustered he outwardly appeared. Grant never declined invitations to honor him and glowed before worshipful crowds. When they stopped in Louisville, Rawlins attended the theater with Grant and sat beside him in a private box. Back in his hotel room, he wrote a letter to his wife laced with mounting exasperation. During the performance, he said, "I was supremely disgusted . . . with the eagerness or willingness rather, of him we love to say is so modest and unassuming to acknowledge the notice people are taking of him. In one who had less reputation for modesty it would be pardonable."[21]

When Grant arrived in Washington in the late afternoon on March 8, no official delegation greeted him at the train depot. Over his uniform he wore a well-worn linen duster, soiled with western dirt. Besides Rawlins and Comstock, he was escorted by thirteen-year-old Fred. Hewing to military protocol, Grant called on Halleck in his office, discovered he was gone, then called at his Georgetown home, where he was also out. Having done his duty, Grant headed straight to the Willard Hotel. The last time Grant was in the capital, he was on the humble mission of trying to convince the War Department that he hadn't stolen the missing thousand dollars as a quartermaster in the Mexican War. Now he confronted a sadder, busier Washington, reshaped by wartime exigencies. Churches and stables were enlisted as hospitals, while soldiers pitched their tents everywhere, even on the White House lawn. The city's sanitary conditions were atrocious with the Potomac River degraded into a receptacle for sewage, spreading filth and disease whenever it overflowed. Soldiers trudged down muddy streets, past the newly completed Capitol dome and the unfinished Washington Monument—apt symbols of both the finished and remaining business of the war.

Political life in Washington flowed through the thronged corridors of the Willard Hotel, down the block from the White House. Lincoln's secretary John Hay criticized the place as "miraculous in meanness; contemptible in cuisine," but that was beside the point.[22] Political deals were sealed in this watering hole, office seekers and war contractors buttonholed legislators, and senators socialized over free-flowing whiskey. "Everybody may be seen there," Nathaniel Hawthorne observed. "You exchange nods with governors of sovereign states; you elbow illustrious men, and tread on the toes of generals; you hear statesmen and orators speaking in their familiar tones."[23]

When Grant, short and shabby, entered the lobby of this haven for the city's power brokers, he brought into its elegant precincts the rough garb of the western theater of war. He was known only by his rank and reputation, and few capital denizens had ever seen him in the flesh. Hence he and Fred created no stir as they slipped unnoticed into the hotel. Grant was an easy man for easterners to patronize, and the desk clerk treated him with casual contempt, telling him a small top-floor room might be available. Unfazed, Grant said that would do and signed the hotel register "U. S. Grant and son, Galena, Ill."[24] When the clerk spun around the register and saw Grant's name, he changed on the spot from haughty to fawning, giving him Parlor 6, the most luxurious suite, where Lincoln had stayed prior to his inauguration.

Once Grant and his son had stowed away their bags, they descended to the dining room, Grant clutching Fred's hand. For a few minutes, nobody recognized him, and then pandemonium erupted. "Ladies and Gentlemen: The hero of Donelson, of Vicksburg, and of Chattanooga is among us," a congressman announced. "I propose the health of Lieutenant-General Grant."[25] Hundreds of diners cheered, stomped, twirled handkerchiefs, and banged knives on tables. Grant, who had never created a sensation like this, rose "looking very much astonished and perhaps annoyed . . . awkwardly rubbed his mustache with his napkin, bowed, and resumed his seat."[26] So many people came over to grab Grant's hand and say hello that he scarcely had time to eat and finally gave up the attempt. As people gawked and gossiped, he must have realized he had shed his privacy forever. He and Fred fled the unwanted attention of the dining room.

Many in the crowd commented on the celebrated newcomer. Richard Henry Dana Jr., a well-known writer, attorney, and politician from Massachusetts, reacted snobbishly to Grant, as educated easterners often did. He was disgusted by Grant's seedy appearance. Grant "had no gait, *no station,* no manner," Dana huffed. "He gets over the ground queerly. He does not march, nor quite walk, but pitches along as if the next step would bring him on his nose." He noted snidely that Grant had "rather the look of a man who did, or once did, take a little too much to drink."[27] Other spectators gave Grant a more searching look, spying hidden strength beneath the lackluster exterior. The renowned Shakespearean actor Edwin Booth grew enamored of the new lieutenant general: "Grant looks like the man he is—solid, true and honest."[28] Theodore Lyman, a young officer on General Meade's staff, described his appearance: "He is rather under middle height, of a spare, strong build; light-brown hair; and short, light brown beard; his eyes are of a clear blue; forehead high; nose aquiline; jaw squarely set, but not sensual."[29]

The hubbub at the Willard Hotel paled beside the glittering soiree that awaited Grant at the president's weekly reception at the White House. Having misplaced the key to his trunk, Grant wore the same grubby outfit in which he had traveled that day. Because one newspaper had announced he would attend the reception, the White House was packed with spectators eager to snatch their first glimpse of Grant, who arrived around 9:30 p.m. He slowly worked his way toward the lanky president, looming distantly in the Blue Room. Lincoln had prepared for the meeting by studying a Grant portrait by John Antrobus that hung in the Capitol, showing him on Missionary Ridge in Chattanooga. It had been commissioned by Grant's friend J. Russell Jones, who sent Antrobus there to sketch Grant in person.

Horace Porter recorded the historic encounter between Lincoln and Grant: "Lincoln recognized the general at once from the pictures he had seen of him. With a face radiant with delight, he advanced rapidly two or three steps toward his distinguished visitor, and cried out: 'Why, here is General Grant! Well, this is a great pleasure, I assure you,' at the same time seizing him by the hand, and shaking it for several minutes with a vigor which showed the extreme cordiality of the welcome."[30] The two formed a strange pair: Lincoln tall and rangy, loquacious with countrified good humor, whereas Grant was small and self-contained, as taciturn as Lincoln was talkative. Porter noted the comical discrepancy in height: "Grant's right hand grasped the lapel of his coat; his head was bent slightly forward, and his eyes upturned toward Lincoln's face. The President . . . eight inches taller, looked down with beaming countenance upon his guest."[31]

Lincoln chatted alone with Grant for a while, then had Secretary of State William Seward shepherd him into the East Room, which broke into brisk applause and wave after wave of cheers. So boisterous did the gathering grow that Noah Brooks labeled it "the only real mob I ever saw in the White House."[32] The room shook in the throes of Grant mania. Because the crowd swallowed up the diminutive Grant, people twisted their necks to spot the bashful hero, chanting "Grant! Grant! Grant!"[33] Finally at Seward's behest, Grant stood on a couch, enabling everybody to ogle the hero. "For once at least," Brooks noted, the president "was not the chief figure in the picture. The little, scared-looking man who stood on a crimson-covered sofa was the idol of the hour."[34] The moment capped Grant's improbable progression since Fort Sumter.

Never cut out for such social duties, a prisoner of this pandemonium, an embarrassed Grant admitted that the time he stood on the couch was the hottest campaign he ever fought. To Julia, he confessed, "I heartily wish myself back in camp."[35] One reporter captured vividly the flustered Grant standing amid the hubbub: "He blushed like a girl. The handshaking brought streams of perspiration down his forehead and over his face."[36] The war years hadn't improved Grant's social graces, but his gaucheness only heightened his appeal. "It indicated an absence of conceit, a lack of pretense," said an aide, "and a modesty almost unexampled in a man of his achievements."[37] For an hour, Grant remained a captive of the adoring crowd before extricating himself to confer with Lincoln and Seward in a small dining room.

Lincoln explained to Grant that, at a brief ceremony the next day, he would formally bestow the lieutenant general commission upon him. "The Secretary of

War and yourself may arrange the time to suit your convenience," Lincoln said. "I am all ready, whenever you shall have prepared your reply." Lincoln must have been startled when Grant retorted, "I can be ready in thirty minutes."[38] They agreed upon 1 p.m. the next day. As a courtesy to Grant, Lincoln furnished him with a four-sentence statement that he would read aloud to him the next day, enabling Grant to prepare his reply. Lincoln made two suggestions about Grant's response, both pertaining to the morale of soldiers and officers. Back at Willard's, Grant promptly scribbled his statement in pencil on a sheet of paper. Determined to establish his independence, he pointedly ignored Lincoln's two suggestions. Wary of pressure from Washington, he was bent upon resisting it from the outset.

At the cabinet meeting the next day, the guests included John Nicolay, Halleck, Rawlins, Comstock, and Fred Grant. With deep feeling, Lincoln expressed what the lieutenant generalship signified. Reading aloud from a paper, he proclaimed, "With this high honor devolves upon you also, a corresponding responsibility. As the country herein trusts you, so, under God, it will sustain you. I scarcely need to add that with what I here speak for the nation goes my own hearty personal concurrence."[39] In response, Grant seemed visibly nervous. Fishing his speech from his pocket, he seemed to decipher his own handwriting with some difficulty. Then he straightened his spine, settled his nerves, and recited his statement with clarity. He was brief and self-effacing: "With the aid of the noble armies that have fought on so many fields for our common country, it will be my earnest endeavor not to disappoint your expectations. I feel the full weight of the responsibilities now devolving on me and know that if they are met it will be due to those armies, and above all to the favor of that Providence which leads both Nations and men."[40] Although Nicolay was disturbed that Grant hadn't heeded Lincoln's two suggestions, the president himself voiced no complaint, and when he introduced Grant to his cabinet, they almost all applauded.

Afterward, Lincoln sat down with Grant for a strategy session, stating exactly what Grant wished to hear: "he had never professed to be a military man," had no desire to meddle further in military strategy, and had done so reluctantly in the past.[41] As Grant recounted, Lincoln said that "he did not care to know what I was to do, only to know what I wanted; that I should have all I required. He wished me to beat Lee, how I did it was my own duty. He said he did not wish to know my plans or to exercise any scrutiny over my plans; so long as I beat the rebel army he was satisfied."[42] Lincoln greatly overstated the degree of his future detachment. Almost immediately, he unrolled a map of Virginia and pointed out, in "his curious, high, piping voice," a path of attack lying between two streams that emptied into the Potomac.[43] Grant responded candidly that, if his army followed that direction, it would wind up in the mud or woods. "The route was an impossible route, and was never mentioned again by Mr. Lincoln," said Grant, who stressed that Lincoln and Stanton "did everything in the world to assure my success."[44] (In his *Memoirs,* Grant said he listened tactfully, but refrained from noting Lincoln's amateurish error.)[45] In short order, Grant had established his independence and taken full responsibility for the war's course. At the same time, he established a warm, cordial relationship with Lincoln, whose "affable and gracious manners" and humorous powers of mimicry pleased him.[46]

If Grant was in a hurry, Lincoln was equally impatient for results. He talked of his frustration with the whining, procrastinating generals who had tested his patience for years. Where Grant had hoped to make his headquarters out west, Lincoln emphasized the need for him to move east and rescue the sagging fortunes of the Army of the Potomac. He also stressed the urgent need for action. As Grant later quoted Lincoln, "The government was spending millions of dollars every day; that there was a limit to the sinews of war, and a time might be reached when the spirits and resources of the people would become exhausted."[47] Grant's swift, relentless military style would conform exactly to the president's desires. That night Grant was invited to dine with Secretary Seward. Rawlins, zealous as ever, trailed him doggedly, seeing temptations for his boss lurking everywhere. "I shall accompany [Grant] though it is not my pleasure to do so," he told his wife with a slight trace of martyrdom. "You know where I am wine is not drunk by those with whom I have any influence."[48]

THE SOUTH UNDERSTOOD the portentous meaning of Grant's promotion to lieutenant general: the North would have a fearless, aggressive commander who would ferociously exploit the North's full resources in manpower and matériel. "They say at last they have scared up a man who succeeds, and they expect him to remedy all that is gone," wrote the South Carolina diarist Mary Chesnut.[49] Meanwhile the North imposed correspondingly lofty expectations on Grant. Below a headline that blared, "We Have Found Our Hero," the *New York Herald* said Grant's advent "materially strengthens our hopes that the great campaign about to open will substantially put an end to the rebellion."[50]

For Grant, the first order of business on March 10 was to visit the troubled

Army of the Potomac, headquartered at Brandy Station, southwest of Washington, near the town of Culpeper, Virginia. That army's commander, George Gordon Meade, was temporarily grounded with a cold, so when Grant arrived in a driving rain, he was met at the train station by Meade's chief of staff, Andrew Humphreys. As Grant knew, the Army of the Potomac brimmed with suspicion of him as a newcomer, a westerner, and an outsider, and Humphreys expected to take an instant dislike to him. Instead Grant won him over handily, Humphreys informing his wife that Grant was "good looking, with an intellectual face and head which at the same time expresses a good deal of determination."[51] Meade showed respect for Grant by having a Zouave regiment, with red fezzes and exotic flowing trousers, salute him as a band struck up martial airs. The tall, slim Meade strode from his tent, eyed Grant beneath a slouched felt hat, and gave him a friendly handshake even before Grant dismounted. The two men had last met during the Mexican War, when they were both young lieutenants.

In many ways, George Gordon Meade was the antithesis of Grant. A patrician figure from Philadelphia, fluent in French, he had graduated from West Point and was well versed in military literature. With a gaunt, sallow face, bald pate, and graying beard, he had bags drooping below eyes that bulged behind oversize spectacles. Meade was forever jealous of his reputation. Thin-skinned and cantankerous, he seldom enjoyed calm moments and grew easily upset, spluttering with ungovernable rage whenever his pride was injured. This led to his nickname, the Old Goggle-Eyed Snapping Turtle, and it wasn't meant affectionately. His battlefield style was frenetic: he would explode with colossal energy, curse a blue streak, then pace with fury behind the lines. "No man, no matter what his business or his service, approached him without being insulted in one way or another," Charles Dana wrote, "and his own staff officers did not dare to speak to him unless first spoken to, for fear of either sneers or curses."[52] Meade later became notorious among the press corps when he seized a reporter who had criticized him, hung a scurrilous sign around his neck that said "Libeler of the Press," placed him backward on a mule, and ran him out of camp.[53] For all his flaws, Meade was a competent commander and an experienced professional and was recognized as such by his peers. When apprised the year before that Meade had taken command of the Army of the Potomac, Robert E. Lee reacted respectfully, saying Meade "would commit no blunders on my front, and if I make one he will make haste to take advantage of it."[54] Still, his failure to pursue Lee after Gettysburg revealed that Meade was not a bold, enterprising leader in the mold of either Grant or Lee.

Once Grant and Meade were seated in the latter's tent, they lit cigars and got down to business. Grant sized up Meade well, acknowledging his bravery and loyalty while noting his temperamental outbursts. "No one saw this fault more plainly than he himself," Grant wrote, "and no one regretted it more. This made it unpleasant at times, even in battle, for those around him to approach him even with information."[55] While Grant imagined at first that he would oust Meade, he needed to win over the goodwill of the skeptical Army of the Potomac and didn't want to appear high-handed. Many people had warned Grant he would be surrounded by backbiting jealousy in the East. "I have just come from the West," Grant noted, "and if I removed a deserving Eastern man from the position of army commander, my motives might be misunderstood, and the effect be bad upon the spirits of the troops."[56] Meade knew Grant might replace him with his own man, especially since Grant was "indoctrinated with the notion of the superiority of the western armies and that the failure of the Army of the Potomac to accomplish anything is due to their commanders."[57]

Nonetheless, Grant showed an open mind. As the two men chatted, Grant was hugely impressed with Meade's self-effacing manner. Saying he understood if Grant wished to replace him with a western officer close to him, Meade offered his resignation, arguing that the cause should take precedence over personal feelings. Grant was struck by his exemplary character. "He spoke so patriotically and unselfishly that even if I had had any intention of relieving him, I should have been inclined to change my mind after the manly attitude he assumed in this frank interview."[58] On the spot, Grant asked Meade to retain command of the Army of the Potomac and said he would appoint Phil Sheridan to take over the cavalry, with Sherman leading the western armies. Grant chose an unorthodox arrangement with Meade. He would make his headquarters in the field and travel with the Army of the Potomac, while Meade would remain, at least nominally, in command of the Virginia force. Grant would issue broad orders, leaving detailed execution to Meade. It was an awkward situation, with Meade operating in Grant's shadow, but it obtained for Grant the dawning respect of the Army of the Potomac. Grant always felt vindicated in his decision to retain Meade: "Meade was certainly among the heroes of the war, and his name deserves all honor . . . Under this harsh exterior Meade had a gentle, chivalrous heart, and was an accomplished soldier and gentleman."[59] The two men would have an excellent, though not flawless, working relationship.

Grant disarmed people's expectations with his interpersonal skills. If he did not overflow with charm, neither did he ruffle people's feathers or threaten them with rivalry. If needed, he could handle people as delicately as he did his horses, and this formed a major part of his military success as he assembled the team of people required to end the war. Meade had gone into the meeting somewhat dubious about Grant. During the Mexican War, he had found Grant "a clever young officer, but nothing extraordinary" and not particularly well educated. He was acquainted with the dark side of Grant's history, recalling how Grant had been "compelled to resign some years before the present war, owing to his irregular habits." He condescendingly attributed Grant's success to "indomitable energy and great tenacity of purpose," not subtlety of mind.[60] Now, Meade discovered new virtues in this somewhat clumsy, reticent man. "I was much pleased with Grant," he told his wife. "You may rest assured he is not an ordinary man."[61] He did detect one critical, lifelong failing in Grant: "a simple and guileless" nature that placed him "under the influence of those who should not influence him and desire to do so only for their own purpose."[62]

After this flying visit to Brandy Station, Grant returned to Washington, where he spurned an invitation from the president to attend a fancy dinner in his honor, followed by a performance of Edwin Booth in *Richard III*. Grant explained that he was anxious to set off for the West and put his military plans in motion. "We can't excuse you," Lincoln insisted. "Mrs. Lincoln's dinner without you would be *Hamlet* with Hamlet left out." Tactful but firm, Grant reminded Lincoln that time was important and that the dinner would mean a million dollars lost to the country. "And really, Mr. Lincoln, I have had enough of this show business."[63] Lincoln cordially bowed to his decision, perhaps secretly delighted by a general in chief so eager to finish the war.

By the time he left for Nashville the next day, Grant had started to reconfigure the upper echelons of the war effort, crafting a modern command structure. Halleck was demoted to army chief of staff, while Sherman would head the Military Division of the Mississippi and McPherson the Department and Army of the Tennessee. Lincoln did not regret seeing Halleck taken down a peg. He wasn't the enterprising commander he had expected, but had "shrunk from responsibility whenever it was possible," Lincoln complained.[64] Probably relieved by the change, Halleck now found his ideal position, bound to his desk and thrust into an advisory role, where he could shield Grant from Washington intrigue, free him from tedious paperwork, and provide a crucial liaison with Lincoln. He would also relay Grant's orders to eighteen departmental commanders.

Instead of bypassing Halleck, Grant made him the conduit for communications with Stanton and the administration. After a sometimes bumpy past, Grant and Halleck now developed a superb partnership. Halleck had excellent analytic powers and gave Grant invaluable intelligence about the political calculations of Lincoln and Stanton. He was deferential to Grant while reserving the right to register dissent. In Grant's later view, Halleck "was loyal and industrious, sincerely anxious for the success of the country, and without any feeling of soreness at being superseded."[65] The new structure was so well ordered by Grant that Lincoln could finally step back a bit from military matters.

When Grant arrived in Nashville on March 14, Sherman greeted him soberly. "I cannot congratulate you on your promotion; the responsibility is too great."[66] While there, Grant received the War Department order that officially made him commander of the Armies of the United States, his headquarters in the field. His decision to make Sherman chief of the entire western army was a daring one. Sherman had not yet attained his later celebrity (or notoriety), and his selection wasn't an obvious choice. Grant's new aide, Adam Badeau, recalled Sherman as "tall, angular, and spare . . . sandy-haired, sharp-featured; his nose prominent, his lips thin, his grey eyes flashing fire as fast as lightning on a summer's night; his whole face mobile as an actor's . . . No one could be with him half an hour and doubt his greatness, or fail to recognize the traits that have made him world-renowned."[67]

In Nashville, Grant met with the talented commanders who would be instrumental in winning the war: Sherman, McPherson, Sheridan, Rawlins, Dodge, and Logan. Over the next couple of days, Grant laid out the broad strokes of his general strategy, which called for applying maximum pressure simultaneously to Robert E. Lee and Joseph Johnston so they could not rush aid to each other. The western commanders were hungry for scuttlebutt about the Army of the Potomac, and Grant assured them it was "the finest army he had ever seen, far superior to any of ours in equipment, supplies, and transportation."[68] But he also told them of an army cowed by the overblown specter of Robert E. Lee. "He said . . . that the officers told him, 'You have not faced Bobby Lee yet,' and as he said it," Grenville Dodge noted, "I could see that twinkle in Grant's eye that we often saw there when he meant mischief."[69]

Grant's Nashville stay allowed time for a statehouse meeting with Governor Andrew Johnson and a theater trip to see *Hamlet*. The audience was noisy and Sherman, an avid theatergoer, complained how the actors were butchering the text. In the graveyard scene, when Hamlet performed his soliloquy over Yorick's skull, one soldier hollered, "Say, pard, what is it—Yank, or Reb?"[70] This led to such tumult that Grant and his associates left the theater to dine on oysters in a local restaurant. Another comic scene ensued when Galena's mayor arrived to present the ceremonial sword to Grant from the citizens of Jo Daviess County. The folks of northern Illinois were eager to claim him, notwithstanding his brief one-year residence in Galena. Grant stood ill at ease during the presentation. At its close, the mayor handed him a parchment covered with resolutions in his honor, passed by the Galena City Council. Grant, who had written out his reply, could not locate it, no matter how hard he searched. An amused Sherman said Grant "began to fumble in his pockets, first his breast-coat pocket, then his pants, vest, etc., and after considerable delay he pulled out a crumpled piece of common yellow cartridge-paper, which he handed to the mayor." The speech was, in Sherman's view, "excellent, short, concise, and, if it had been delivered by word of mouth, would have been all that the occasion required."[71] The moment illustrated that, if the naive Grant lacked polish, he already had finely tuned political instincts, the product of native intelligence.

When Grant departed for Washington, Sherman accompanied him, but they had to shout at each other to be heard above the train's din. As a result, when they reached Cincinnati, they took a room at the Burnet House, posted a guard at the door, unfurled maps, and formulated military policy. The strategy Grant laid out envisioned assaults on enemy armies, not cities or territories. "He was to go for Lee and I was to go for Joe Johnston," Sherman wrote. "That was his plan."[72] They also discussed the operation that would win Sherman lasting fame, his march on Atlanta. Then Sherman retraced his steps westward to Nashville and Grant continued eastward. Years later, standing outside the hotel, Sherman waved his hand toward it and declared, "Yonder began the campaign."[73]

Before leaving Cincinnati, Grant took time to visit his parents in Covington, Kentucky. His father sent a carriage to the train station, but the driver, expecting someone magnificent, did not spot Grant. As a result, Jesse was startled to see his son, alone, padding up the path to the house, toting his carpetbag, attired in a plain army coat. Hannah Grant had reacted to the Civil War with religious fervor, convinced the Lord had chosen her son for a purpose. She had only one concern: how would her son fare against the toughest southern general? Was he afraid to attack Lee? "Not at all," Grant assured her. "I know Lee as well as he knows himself. I know all his strong points, and all his weak ones. I intend to attack his weak points, and flank his strong ones."[74] During Grant's stay, a highly unlikely story made the rounds that he was drunk and Jesse insisted to a reporter that his son "had not drank [sic] a drop of liquor in ten years, except a very small quantity on one occasion, by order of a physician."[75]

On March 22, Grant spent the day in Philadelphia and dropped by the Continental Hotel, where he met General Delos B. Sackett, who was about to travel west as an army inspector. His friend E. D. Keyes, seated at the table, recorded a telling comment by Grant: "We conversed pleasantly on various subjects, and when I offered to fill a glass with champagne for him, the general placed his hand over his glass saying, 'If I begin to drink, I must keep on drinking.'"[76] The same day this conversation occurred, Isaac N. Morris, a former congressman from Illinois, published an unsigned biography of Grant in the *National Intelligencer*, boosting him as a presidential prospect. Two months earlier, Grant had written to Morris and explicitly disavowed presidential ambitions, but Morris refused to heed his word and proudly sent copies of the newspaper to Grant, his parents, and his friends in Ohio and Missouri.

The next day, Grant reached Washington in the company of Julia, who suffered from an eye infection, and six-year-old Jesse; the other children still boarded with Harry and Louisa Boggs in St. Louis. Grant received the treatment befitting a newly coined celebrity when he and Stanton visited the photographic studio of Mathew Brady. With his curly hair and wire-rimmed spectacles, Brady had pioneered in battlefield photography. After seating Grant directly beneath a skylight, he ordered his assistant to climb up and remove a covering that blocked the fading sunlight of late afternoon. When this colleague slipped, his feet crashed through two-inch-thick glass panes, sending a drizzle of sharp fragments around Grant, who, according to Brady, gazed up slowly with "a barely perceptible quiver of the nostril." His coolness struck the photographer as "the most remarkable display of nerve I ever witnessed." Turning white, Stanton trembled to think what might have occurred had Grant perished. "Not a word about this, Brady, not a word!" he exclaimed. "You must never breathe a word of what happened here today . . . It would be impossible to convince the people that this was not an attempt at assassination!"[77]

Brady snapped a perceptive photograph of Grant, leaving the upper third of the canvas bare and placing his subject slightly below the picture's center, accentuating his short stature. There was no strutting, no bombast, no false bravado. Grant sat with one arm resting on a table, his hand dangling in the air, while the other hand curled loosely into a fist. His hair was swept back carefully, his beard relatively well trimmed. He had been posed with a somewhat stiff, upright carriage, but his pale, sad eyes seem to brood over years of military casualties.

As Grant moved about Washington, he was mobbed by crowds elated to catch a glimpse of him. He knew his promotion would tie him to Washington for a long time, scuttling plans to move to the Pacific Coast someday. "General Grant is all the rage," Senator Sherman reported to his brother William. "He is subjected to the disgusting but dangerous process of being lionized. He is followed by crowds, and is cheered everywhere." The senator feared the purehearted Grant would be spoiled by fulsome flattery. William defended Grant from such insinuations, even though he experienced similar fears. "Grant is as good a leader as we can find," he wrote back. "He has honesty, simplicity of character, singleness of purpose, and no hope or claim to usurp civil power . . . Don't disgust him by flattery or importunity. Let him alone."[78]

Shortly after returning to Washington, Grant established his headquarters in the field at Culpeper Court House and quickly prepared for the upcoming campaign against Lee. One of his first orders was to commission a map from Halleck showing with red lines the front occupied by Union forces at the start of the war and at present, while an ambitious blue line marked the territory he planned to occupy. As he labored, he was invited to attend a White House reception with Julia, but too engrossed to go, he dispatched Julia and Admiral Farragut instead.

In many ways, Julia Grant was more worldly and socially adept than her husband and could tutor him in the elevated circles in which he now traveled. She knew the intense scrutiny he would undergo and worked hard on his appearance. As Badeau wrote, "With a feminine insight she comprehended both the petty craft and the important ambitions that underlie so many of the ceremonies of official life at Washington as well as in aristocratic capitals."[79] Badeau escorted her to the White House and recounted how on the receiving line Lincoln overlooked her name until Badeau repeated more loudly, "Mrs. General Grant, Mr. President." At that point, "the tall, ungainly man looked down upon his visitor with infinite kindness beaming from his ugly, historic face; then placed both his hands on Mrs. Grant's and welcomed her more than warmly."[80] When Lincoln asked where her husband was, Julia answered with studied diplomacy: "I begged the General to remain and accompany me, but he said he must go to the front and he was sure the President and Mrs. Lincoln would excuse him."[81] Julia championed her husband unapologetically. When a group of ladies asked whether he would take Richmond, Julia replied, "Yes, before he gets through. *Mr. Grant always was a very obstinate man.*"[82]

Every week Grant traveled to Washington and sat down with Lincoln and Stanton for lengthy talks. Almost immediately, he developed a harmonious working relationship with the president. That Lincoln felt perfectly compatible with Grant politically was demonstrated one evening when an Illinois visitor alluded to party operatives pushing Grant for president. Lincoln replied, "He is fully committed to the policy of emancipation and employing negro soldiers; and with this policy faithfully carried out, it will not make much difference who is President."[83] Grant was profoundly influenced by Lincoln, who buttressed his idealism and his view that slavery was fundamental to the Union fight. "There had to be an end of slavery," Grant later explained. "Then we were fighting an enemy with whom we could not make a peace. We had to destroy him."[84]

By this point in the war, Lincoln looked haggard and woebegone. His high forehead, dark hair, high cheekbones, and long chin made his appearance as unforgettable as Grant's was nondescript. With his ever-flowing fund of yarns, Lincoln might have seemed unlike Grant, but Grant, too, could be a wry, charming storyteller. Lincoln was more openly driven than the sometimes indolent Grant, displaying an irrepressible ambition and lifelong thirst for learning as he strove to feed his eager mind.[85]

Lincoln and Grant shared much common ground. They were both westerners, awkward in their movements, rough and uncouth in manners. Both had domineering fathers and ambitious wives. Both had married into slaveholding families that evinced insufferable conceit about their standing in the world. Both were fastidious and had grown up refusing to hunt or swear; Lincoln also eschewed tobacco, alcohol, and gambling. These two prairie figures also suffered the condescension of toplofty easterners. Criticism of Lincoln took a peculiarly harsh tone, editorial writers ridiculing him as a coarse country fellow. He had grown up in deeper poverty than Grant but had attained more security. Nevertheless, before succeeding as an attorney and a politician, he had bounced from job to job, serving as a riverboat man, store clerk, and blacksmith, a checkered past that made him loyal to people who had faltered in life. Even in the 1850s, Lincoln sometimes arrived in his law office wrapped in impenetrable gloom. Afflicted by nightmares, seized by periodic depression, he had an innate melancholy that contrasted sharply with his moods of uproarious mirth.

While Lincoln seemed more extroverted than Grant, appearances could deceive. At heart, he was enough of a loner that his friend David Davis called him "the most reticent, secretive man I ever saw or expect to see."[86]

Lincoln was fascinated, if somewhat bemused, by Grant, whose unpretentious style he appreciated. He'd had his fill of egomaniacal generals, professional braggarts, and blowhards, such as McClellan and Hooker. One day, Lincoln's secretary, William O. Stoddard, found his boss stretched out on a sofa and asked for his impressions of Grant.

> Well, Stoddard, I hardly know what to think of him altogether. I never saw him myself until he came here to take command. He's the quietest little fellow you ever saw . . . makes the least fuss of any man you ever knew. I believe, two or three times, he has been in this room a minute or so before I knew he was here . . . The only evidence you have that he's in any place is that he makes things git! Wherever he is, things move![87]

Lincoln's one early brush with military service came briefly as a militia captain during the Black Hawk War of 1832, when, he admitted, he fended off more mosquitoes than bullets. After the firing on Fort Sumter, Lincoln had undertaken a crash course in the art of warfare, borrowing military manuals from the Library of Congress and staying up late to devour them. He also studied reports from the field and quizzed every general and admiral he could find. The miracle was that Lincoln ended up a fine military strategist who was, in many ways, superior to the chief generals who preceded Grant. Not only was he free from West Point dogma but he wasn't beholden to generals from the old regular army. His military sagacity was a triumph of native intelligence and supreme willpower. Lincoln had developed operating theories that dovetailed perfectly with Grant's views: that the Union army should destroy Confederate armies, not take cities or territory; that it should exploit its massive resources by simultaneous attacks against the enemy across many fronts; that military decisions were inseparable from political goals; and that only one final, savage, protracted burst of fighting could end the conflict. The Lincoln whom Grant met in March 1864 was a more mature military thinker than the callow, fumbling president of April 1861 and fully prepared for the remorseless warfare patented by Grant, Sherman, and Sheridan.

Lincoln was smart enough to see that he and Stanton had been forced to act as armchair generals, second-guessing military leaders in the field, whereas now was the time to recede. "You and I, Mr. Stanton, have been trying to boss this job, and we have not succeeded very well with it," Lincoln said. "We have sent across the mountains for Mr. Grant, as Mrs. Grant calls him, to relieve us, and I think we had better leave him alone to do as he pleases."[88] Grant was the antithesis of everything Lincoln had deplored in his predecessors—as eager to fight as they were reluctant; as self-reliant as they were dependent; as uncomplaining as they were petulant. Grant did not badger or connive for more troops or scapegoat others. There would be no more grumbling from Lincoln about dilatory generals as Grant converted the Union army into a scene of ceaseless activity. With his zest for combat, Grant was itching for a fight.

Lincoln felt a huge weight lifted from his shoulders. When William O. Stoddard asked whether Grant was the man to embolden the Army of the Potomac, Lincoln pointed his long forefinger at him and exclaimed, "Stoddard, Grant is the first general I've had! He's a general! . . . You know how it has been with all the rest. As soon as I put a man in command of the army, he'd come to me with a plan of campaign and about as much as say, 'Now I don't believe I can do it, but if you say so, I'll try it on,' and so put the responsibility of the success or failure on me. They all wanted me to be the general. It isn't so with Grant. He hasn't told me what his plans are. I don't know, and I don't want to know. I'm glad to find a man who can go ahead without me."[89]

By now Grant had piled up so many victories that any lingering prewar insecurity had vanished, and he wasn't fazed by the vast power delegated to him. He and Lincoln developed a deep mutual trust that transcended petty egotism or rivalry. Grant was not only the most competent of Lincoln's generals but the most trustworthy, following no covert agenda. "I was never interfered with," Grant reminisced. "I had the fullest support of the President and Secretary of War. No general could want better backing, for the President was a man of great wisdom and moderation, the Secretary a man of enormous character and will."[90] The pieces were now in place for a gigantic turn in the direction of the stalemated eastern war.

CHAPTER SEVENTEEN

Ulysses the Silent

B Y THE TIME Grant became the top general, the larger population of the North versus the South counted heavily in the war, making it a battle of attrition for northern commanders. Grant's new command was colossal: he presided over twenty-one army corps, spread over eighteen military departments, with a total of 533,000 battle-ready troops. "Over this force," wrote Badeau, "Grant was as absolutely supreme, as free to dictate its every movement, as any general . . . who ever took the field."[1] The North had the luxury of having more than twice as many men under age thirty as the Confederacy. Hence, Grant's strategy depended on simple but gruesome math: the South could not replace fallen soldiers while the North could. A month before Grant came east, Lincoln had ordered an additional 500,000 men drafted for three-year service, assuming the war lasted that long. The week after his arrival, Lincoln summoned another 200,000 draftees. That February, in a sure sign of southern desperation, the Confederacy extended conscription to all white males between seventeen and fifty as the critical shortage of men extended to the officers' corps. At the war's outset, the Confederacy had been richly endowed with gifted generals, but here, too, the ranks were being rapidly thinned by the death of such irreplaceable commanders as Stonewall Jackson.

Before Grant became chief general, the Union's military effort had been fragmented and disjointed, deprived of a single supervisory mind to govern the whole enterprise. "Eastern and Western Armies were fighting independent battles, working together like a balky team where no two ever pull together," Grant recalled.[2] Now he mapped out an overarching design that encompassed *all* Union armies, marshaling their resources to capture Lee's army in Virginia and Johnston's in Georgia. This comprehensive approach, imparting a new sophistication to American warfare, was roundly applauded by Sherman. "That we are now all to act in a Common plan, Converging on a Common Center looks like Enlightened War," he wired Grant.[3] Such centralized decision making was facilitated by modern technology, notably the telegraph, which gave Grant instantaneous power to command multitudes, expanding his reach across the country.

Unlike McClellan, Grant would pursue a policy of "desperate and continuous hard fighting," inflicting massive casualties and applying unrelenting pressure.[4] "I look upon the conquering of the organized armies of the enemy as being of vastly more importance than the mere acquisition of their territory," he instructed his generals.[5] Gone was the gentility of his predecessors. Adopting a modern style of combat, Grant would speed up the war's tempo, following up on victories and creating a sense of unending activity. By concentrating his forces, he would create two or three large armies so that his soldiers would never be, in Rawlins's words, "whipped in detail."[6] Most important, Grant would use his scattered forces simultaneously so the enemy could not shift troops to one threatened point without jeopardizing another. Union forces would pin down Confederate units that might otherwise have succored their colleagues. "Oh, yes! I see that," Lincoln responded gleefully to this strategy. "As we say out West, if a man can't skin he must hold a leg while somebody else does."[7] By spring 1864, the Confederacy had shrunk to a more compact area, allowing a greater concentration of Union forces on southern soil.

For three years, the Army of the Potomac had fought the same army in the same places along the same Virginia rivers. Grant devised an ingenious plan to reorient its mission. He would take a large section of it, perhaps as many as sixty thousand men, march it down to North Carolina, and menace railroad links that sustained Lee's army in Virginia. This would pull Lee's men down into North Carolina, leaving Richmond exposed to a Union takeover. Halleck, better attuned to Lincoln's and Stanton's thinking, argued strenuously against this plan. He noted that Lee, instead of rising to the bait, might march instead on Washington, where there were only eighteen thousand troops, or lunge at Baltimore, Harrisburg, and Philadelphia. Union forces in North Carolina might then have to hurry north to defend a helpless federal capital.

In the end, Grant scrapped the plan as overly hazardous. He later speculated that it could have shortened the war by a year, but it would have entailed excessive risk, and he did not yet know firsthand the capacity of the Army of the Potomac. Instead he adopted a plan for advancing simultaneously on five fronts. He and Meade would make a direct frontal assault on Lee, attempting to drive him back toward Richmond, while Major General Benjamin Butler, stationed on the James River, southeast of Richmond, would advance on Lee from that direction, trapping him in a pincer movement. All the while General Franz Sigel would plow through the Shenandoah Valley, destroying granaries and rail lines that nourished the Confederate army. Meanwhile, Sherman would whirl through Georgia, taking Atlanta, slicing vital railway links to Lee, and draining the South's interior of precious resources. Lincoln was thrilled by the new plan. "This concerted movement," he told John Hay, was exactly what he had envisaged "so as to bring into action to our advantage our great superiority in numbers."[8]

For his fifth front, Grant hoped Nathaniel Banks would take aim at Mobile. As a matter of foreign policy relating to Mexico and France, however, Banks was directed that winter to occupy a portion of Texas. In April, he conducted a campaign up the Red River in Louisiana that was, in Sherman's blunt appraisal, "one damn blunder from beginning to end."[9] By the time he suffered a catastrophic defeat in Mansfield, Louisiana, on April 8, Banks had delayed too long to hazard the move on Mobile Bay that Grant coveted. While Grant wanted to have Banks relieved, he was well connected, a personal friend of the president's, and something of a political untouchable. Therefore, instead of dismissing him outright, Grant deftly asked Lincoln to move Major General Edward R. S. Canby into a field command, leaving Banks in administrative control of the Department of the Gulf, thus limiting any damage he might commit.

Grant had a pronounced preference for professional soldiers, and political generals, such as Banks and Butler, were the bane of his life, a special curse on the Union cause. He was furious when they tried to circumvent him by lobbying Congress for more troops, rather than the War Department. "What interfered with our officers more than anything else was allowing themselves a political bias," Grant was to comment. "This is fatal to a soldier. War and politics are so different."[10] Although he wouldn't have stated it quite so baldly, he would likely have agreed with Halleck's statement that April: "It seems but little better than murder to give important commands to such men as Banks, Butler, McClernand, Sigel, and Lew Wallace."[11] Convinced that many generals (not just political ones) were inept, Grant recommended to Lincoln that he fire more than a hundred notorious offenders, and he was willing to take the heat for this move. Lincoln, on the other hand, had to ensure political support for the war, not to mention his reelection, and couldn't afford to create so many enemies at once. In the end, he fired only a few of the people Grant singled out for punishment.

In a mark of his magnanimity and professionalism, Grant tried to restore to commands high-ranking generals consigned to inactive roles, including George McClellan, Ambrose Burnside, John Frémont, and Don Carlos Buell. His motivation went beyond a shortage of capable generals and included a desire to unify the North behind the war: "The country belonged as well to the Democrats as to us, and I did not believe in a Republican war."[12] In the last analysis, resistance came from the disgraced, embittered generals themselves, who "were not in a humor to be conciliated," Grant wrote. "I soon saw my plan was not feasible, and gave it up."[13]

One of Grant's major innovations was to maximize the number of people on active duty in the field rather than having them man garrisons or protect supply lines. There would be no more shirkers or laggards; everyone would mobilize for war. In a controversial reform, Grant stripped troops from Washington and uprooted startled desk officers. "In all the northern states are many troops, kept mainly that some of our Major Generals might have commands in Peace Departments commensurate with their rank," Rawlins explained. "These are all being gathered up and brought to the front."[14] Grant was especially eager to transfer black soldiers from the western theater of war and deepen their involvement in the Virginia fighting.

Although Grant took the train weekly to Washington, he was shadowed by assassination threats, especially since the legendary Confederate raider John Singleton Mosby, a former Virginia lawyer, preyed on Union detachments in the area. So thoroughly did Mosby terrorize northern Virginia that it was branded Mosby's Confederacy. In mid-April, Grant narrowly escaped capture by Mosby's irregulars, who attacked railroad guards at one station minutes before Grant was scheduled to arrive. Mosby's partisans were such a menace that Grant decided that autumn to treat them without mercy. "When any of Mosby's men are caught, hang them without trial," he ordered. One who obeyed was George Armstrong Custer, who executed six of them.[15] The threat of Mosby's raiders reached the point that by April 17, Grant advised Julia of his reluctance to travel to Washington, saying, "It is not altogether safe. I cannot move without it being known all over the country, and to the enemy who are hovering within a few miles of the railroad all the time."[16]

Before initiating his spring campaign, Grant waited for the Virginia roads to dry out and become manageable. By staying with the Army of the Potomac, he guaranteed that Virginia would be the fulcrum of the war effort, and he directed his forces elsewhere with the ultimate aim of encircling Lee. Settling into field headquarters in a modest brick house at Culpeper Court House, Grant sounded upbeat, telling Julia he lived "plain and well, surrounded with mud."[17] Two years earlier, when Walt Whitman visited Culpeper, he found it "one of the pleasantest towns in Virginia," fondly noting the "thin blue smoke rising from camp fires," the Blue Ridge Mountains shimmering in the background.[18] Now white tents sheltering fifty thousand troops cropped up everywhere. Because Virginia had been a cockpit of war, the surrounding area had lost any picturesque charm, leaving many houses vacant and forlorn. Fighting had created an alien world, beaten down by tramping boots and the bare feet of marching men, while shot and shell denuded the landscape. "Outside the town," wrote Badeau, "not a house nor a fence, not a tree was to be seen for miles, where once all had been cultivated farm-land, or richly wooded country."[19]

Grant's headquarters stood no more than ten miles from Meade's. Inescapably Grant hovered over him, making it difficult for him to delegate authority. Signaling that he was no McClellan, Grant dispensed with grand reviews and had troops simply line up before their campgrounds. By late April, however, as grass appeared, he permitted General Winfield Scott Hancock to oversee a full-dress review of the Second Corps. As Rawlins watched men march with a "proud and elastic step," he was roused to patriotic fervor. "It was the finest display of troops I ever witnessed at one review, twenty-two thousand men in all, in one clear, open field, with their glittering arms, their banners . . . and bands of music, all conspired to fill one with emotions of pride that he, too, was an American soldier fighting for the perpetuation of the principles of civil and religious liberty for our Republican form of Government." These spirited men, Rawlins asserted, incontestably believed "they can whip Lee."[20]

With the Army of the Potomac, Grant did not inspire the adulation or hero worship that Little Mac had so easily called forth. Soldiers pasted no endearing nicknames on him. He moved among them, not as a superior being, shoulders thrown back, head held high, but merely as first among equals. Quiet, understated, Grant walked with the characteristic stoop that pitched him forward, a cigar clenched between his teeth. His visits to his men were businesslike, and they reacted with respect, not rapturous cheers. In response, he would simply tip his hat and bow.

Those soldiers seeking high-flown Napoleonic grandeur or a dash of foppery came away disappointed. The artillery officer Charles Wainwright protested how Grant "rode along the line in a slouchy unobservant way, with his coat unbuttoned and setting anything but an example of military bearing to the troops."[21] As always, stories about Grant's early army career surfaced. "It is hard for those who knew him when formerly in the army to believe he is a great man; then he was only distinguished for the mediocrity of his mind, his great good nature and his insatiable love of whiskey," Wainwright wrote.[22] For Charles Francis Adams Jr., who formed part of Meade's cavalry escort, Grant seemed an untested entity: "The feeling about Grant is peculiar; a little jealousy, a little dislike, a little envy, a little want of confidence."[23] This want of confidence, he thought, would only be eliminated by a string of battlefield victories. Provost Marshal General Marsena R. Patrick dismissed Grant as someone who smoked, whittled, and "let Genl. Rawlins talk Big."[24]

Nevertheless, Grant had his fair share of defenders. Theodore Lyman studied him closely: "He habitually wears an expression as if he had determined to drive his head through a brick wall, and was about to do it."[25] Or: "He is a man of a natural, severe simplicity, in all things—the very way he wears his high-crowned felt hat shows this: he neither puts it on behind his ears, nor draws it over his eyes; much less does he cock it on one side, but sets it straight and very hard on his head." Then came Grant on horseback: "He sits firmly in the saddle and looks straight ahead, as if only intent on getting to some particular point. General Meade says he is a very amiable man, though his eye is stern and almost fierce-looking."[26] One recent West Point graduate was immediately taken with the unruffled Grant, finding him the center of "a pervasive quiet which seemed to be conveyed to everyone around him."[27] Another officer wrote home how General John Sedgwick "was very favorably impressed with Grant, for when he last saw him . . . he was drunken & dirty to the last extreme."[28]

In dealing with the Army of the Potomac, Grant believed its fighting spirit had been drilled out of it and that it had "never been thoroughly fought," giving way to inbred caution.[29] However demoralized the army was, it still clung to its pride, and Grant injected new dynamism into it. As his influence spread, a psychological change took hold. The men no longer saw themselves as virgin troops, outclassed by southern opponents, but as seasoned veterans who would wring victory from battle. Grant had the inestimable advantage of not being associated with the history of dismal defeats in Virginia and could offer a fresh start. If he never quite succeeded in turning the Army of the Potomac into a fighting force with the esprit de corps of his Army of the Tennessee, the improvement was still tangible. Lieutenant Charles Wellington Reed of Massachusetts was convinced that putting "Grant in command is the grandest coup yet" and that he had "inspired all with that confidence that insures success."[30] Grant's new army was well equipped and well fed, and he attributed much of this to his old West Point pal, General Rufus Ingalls, who directed supplies and "could move and feed a hundred thousand men without ruffling his temper."[31]

To keep up morale, Grant did his best to retain existing commanders of the Army of the Potomac. The one thing he couldn't abide was the dejected state of that army's cavalry. It had long bothered Grant that southern cavalry was thought superior to northern. One day, chatting before the White House with Lincoln and Halleck, Grant stated his need for a new cavalry commander, adding that he wanted the best man he could find. "Then why not take Phil Sheridan?" Halleck asked. "Well," Grant replied, "I was just going to say Phil Sheridan."[32] Promptly summoned from the west, Sheridan at first resented the transfer, believing himself on the verge of promotion to corps commander. Like Grant, Sheridan struck people as too slight to be a fearsome warrior and was therefore underestimated. A man after Grant's own heart, he wanted to rescue the cavalry from guard and picket duty, deploying it instead as a prime fighting force. When he reported to the Army of the Potomac, a Grant aide recalled, he was "worn down almost to a shadow by hard work and exposure in the field; he weighed only a hundred and fifteen pounds, and as his height was but five feet six inches, he looked anything but formidable as a candidate for a cavalry leader."[33] Sheridan laughed in later years that he was then "thin almost to emaciation."[34] The next time Grant stopped by the War Department, someone teased him about Sheridan's size: "The officer you brought on from the West is rather a little fellow to handle your cavalry." Grant responded prophetically: "You will find him big enough for the purpose before we get through with him."[35]

Grant was adamant about keeping Rawlins as chief of staff. Whether he was fit to discharge this important duty was another matter. Besides lacking appropriate credentials, Rawlins had to deal with a cough that had become hacking and frequent over the winter. The day Grant first met Lincoln, Rawlins told him to organize his new staff without him, fearing his health "would require me to leave the service."[36] Grant refused to let Rawlins go and promised if he didn't recover by the time warm weather came, he could take an extended leave. Rawlins was deeply touched. "No man in the country is so great a friend to me," he told his wife, "and to feel that I have this friendship, is to me, a great satisfaction."[37] So solicitous was Grant of Rawlins's health that when they arrived at Culpeper Court House, Grant insisted he occupy the other bedroom in his brick house, which had a soft, comfortable feather bed. Afraid his health might be harmed by living in a tent, Rawlins was again awash in gratitude to Grant.

Rawlins yearned to participate in the coming campaign and the conquest of Richmond, but there was no mistaking that things had worsened for him. Forced to nap every afternoon, he was so sleepy after dinner he could scarcely stay awake. At first he pretended to be mystified by this, then could no longer disguise the reason. "I have not been well today, owing to the large doses of medicine I have taken for my cough," he confessed to his wife on April 12. "The quantity of opium has effected [sic] my whole system insomuch as to produce a sensation of numbness and drowsiness, and given me a bad headache. I have slept the whole day."[38] Doctors said he had chronic bronchitis, though he must have suspected worse. Only two weeks before the campaign began, he insisted to his wife that his cough was improving. "Unless I do get better I cannot think of trying to remain here, for I had better quit the Service than to permanently injure my health. Permanent injury of my lungs would of course be certain death; this however I do not seriously apprehend."[39] On April 28, he went riding without an overcoat and contracted a severe cold, leading him to contemplate a long leave of absence. Whether from Rawlins's medical condition or because he disliked insidious gossip in Congress that he needed Rawlins to stay sober, Grant began to pull away from his chief of staff. It was not overt, nor something perceived by most people, but it was keenly felt by Rawlins. According to his friend James H. Wilson, Rawlins believed "Grant was drawing away from him. Grant remained friendly to him, but there was a coldness between them. He didn't know everything that Grant was doing as in the old days."[40]

By this point, Grant had put together the staff of twelve people who would sustain him through the war, and many would trail him to the White House. Some of his choices were cronies, but others were highly competent staffers. In the fall, Ely Parker, the full-blooded Seneca Iroquois whom Grant had befriended in Galena, had joined the staff as a military secretary. He had fallen victim to anti-Indian prejudice when he tried to get an army commission.

Approaching Secretary of State Seward, he had received a rude lecture that the war was "an affair between white men" and hence none of his business. "Go home, cultivate your farm. We will settle our own troubles among ourselves without any Indian aid."[41] Then, in May 1863, Brigadier General John E. Smith, formerly a Galena jeweler, recommended Parker as an assistant adjutant general, with a captain's rank, and Grant enthusiastically endorsed his selection, writing, "I am personally acquainted with Mr. Parker and I think [he is] eminently qualified for the position."[42] Impressed by Parker's performance at Vicksburg, Grant brought him on board as his military secretary.

Like many others, Parker praised Grant's storytelling power, humor, and special gifts as a listener. "General Grant had a wonderful power of drawing information from others in conversation without their being aware that they were imparting it."[43] He found Grant's absorbent memory astounding. "His memory for facts was good, and for faces remarkable. He recognized people after a period of twenty years and recalled their names immediately."[44] Most of all he was taken with Grant's kindness and fairness. "He always sought to speak of the good in men rather than the evil, and if he had to speak of the bad qualities in a man he would close his remarks with the mention of his good points, or excuses why he did not have them."[45] It was this lovely quality, inherited directly from Hannah, that would make Grant the victim of unscrupulous men.

Of his four new aides, Grant especially warmed to Horace Porter. A handsome young man with a handlebar mustache and pointed beard, he had shown bravery at Chickamauga and Chattanooga. His rollicking jokes and stories helped to relieve wartime tension, making him valuable when Grant turned despondent. Early on, Porter discovered that Grant—anointed the "American Sphinx," "Ulysses the Silent," and the "Great Unspeakable"—was very circumspect about personal matters. "When questioned beyond the bounds of propriety, his lips closed like a vise, and the obtruding party was left to supply all the subsequent conversation."[46] Yet when it came to war stories, Grant captivated his listeners with his excellent stock of knowledge. Porter noted that Grant had refined manners, however bespattered he was with mud and dust. "He was always particularly civil to ladies, and he rose to his feet at once, took off his hat, and made a courteous bow."[47]

Grant struck Porter as the most reflective of generals, devoted to pure contemplation of battle plans: "He would sit for hours in front of his tent, or just inside of it looking out, smoking a cigar very slowly, seldom with a paper or a map in his hands, and looking like the laziest man in camp. But at such periods his mind was working more actively than that of any one in the army. He talked less and thought more than any one in the service."[48] Porter limned a comic portrait of Grant's disorganized nature. Heaps of paper piled up higgledy-piggledy on his desk and letters overflowed his stuffed pockets. Nonetheless, Grant kept track of the chaos and "even in the dark" could "lay his hand upon almost any paper he wanted."[49] Grant never raised his voice, lost his temper, or scolded people and did not abuse his power by indulging in moody behavior. Grant explained to Porter his aversion to profanities, saying "swearing helps to rouse a man's anger; and when a man flies into a passion his adversary who keeps cool always gets the better of him."[50] A by-product of Grant's equanimity was his enviable ability to fall asleep anywhere. Even on the eve of a major battle, Porter noted, Grant could "drop down in the mud and rain and be sound asleep in two minutes."[51]

Grant's self-confidence, his willingness to act on his own judgments and take responsibility, spread courage through the ranks. He was a superb communicator, making sure officers in one place knew what was happening elsewhere. Porter thought Grant's capacity to visualize the entire battlefield unmatched. "After looking critically at a map of a locality, it seemed to become photographed indelibly upon his brain, and he could follow its features without referring to it again."[52] Porter also noticed Grant's old superstition about never turning back, noting "he would try all sorts of cross-cuts, ford streams, and jump any number of fences to reach another road rather than go back and take a fresh start."[53]

Another holdover from Grant's early days was his extreme queasiness about food. "I never could eat anything that goes on two legs" was a habitual Grant refrain.[54] As had been the case since boyhood, Grant would only touch meat burned to a dry crisp: "If blood appeared in any meat which came on the table, the sight of it seemed entirely to destroy his appetite."[55] His eccentric tastes favored oysters and cucumbers, along with corn, pork and beans, and buckwheat cakes. "In fact," concluded Porter, "he seemed to be particularly fond of only the most indigestible dishes."[56] Given his high level of activity during campaigns, one might have expected Grant to enjoy a hearty appetite. Instead he ate sparingly. Porter observed that "he ate less than any man in the army; sometimes the amount of food taken did not seem enough to keep a bird alive."[57]

Another aide new to Grant showed a literary flair comparable to Porter's. Adam Badeau joined the team of military scribes whom Grant termed his "men with quills behind their ears."[58] A short, stout young man, with glasses and a ruddy complexion, Badeau was emotional, high-strung, and voluble, with a weakness for alcohol that later marred his career. Born into a wealthy family, he lost his parents at an early age, but inherited enough money to attend tony boarding schools. In New York in the late 1850s, he earned a reputation as a witty commentator on culture, fashion, theater, and society for the *Sunday Times*. He was also a social climber and sycophant who latched on to celebrities. After seeing him in *Richard III,* he became smitten with Edwin Booth's exceptional talent, which far outpaced that of his brother, John Wilkes.

Badeau became Booth's journalistic champion, literary tutor, and patron in New York society. There was something vain and pretentious about Badeau, who was prone to hero worship intermixed with underlying envy and resentment. He would attach himself to gifted, powerful men, only to turn against them. He presented himself as the trusted counselor who would groom Edwin Booth for higher levels of artistry, yet when Booth married in July 1860, Badeau felt displaced from his affection. When spurned, Badeau could turn vicious, and this, too, set a pattern later repeated with Grant. In June 1863, Badeau suffered a foot wound at Port Hudson and recuperated in New York City under the care of Edwin and John Wilkes Booth. He was still hobbling on crutches when he came to Grant and started a lasting relationship as his secretary.

In time, Badeau emerged as the authorized historian of Grant's military campaigns and was mesmerized by the huge riddle of Grant's personality. He detected a subtle tension between the inner and outer man, a "suppressed intensity," while "the whole man was a marvel of simplicity, a powerful nature veiled in the plainest possible exterior."[59] Long before Grant penned his *Memoirs,* Badeau noted his concise style of expression: "In utterance he was slow and sometimes embarrassed, but the words were well-chosen, never leaving the remotest doubt of what he intended to convey."[60] Grant's thoughts could seem closed and impenetrable until battle came and his entire mind sprang into action. Then his "utterance was prompt, the ideas were rapid, the judgment was decisive . . . the whole man became intense as it were with a white heat."[61]

ONCE NAMED LIEUTENANT GENERAL, Grant knew his foremost objective was to vanquish Robert E. Lee and his Army of Northern Virginia, which he deemed "the strongest, best appointed and most confident Army in the South."[62] The confrontation would be squeezed into the well-worn, hundred-mile strip between Washington and Richmond that had witnessed impassioned fighting for three years. On April 9, Grant focused Meade's thinking with a crystal-clear directive: "Lee's Army will be your objective point. Wherever Lee goes there you will go also."[63] Grant's only doubt was whether to cross the Rapidan River above or below Lee's camp. His final decision represented a political no less than a military strategy: he would cross the Rapidan above Lee, cutting him "off from all chance of ignoring Richmond and going North on a raid."[64] Grant knew Lincoln and Stanton would be relieved that the Army of the Potomac, while proceeding south, would block any escape route by which Lee could strike at Washington.

The war's climactic phase came down to a fateful showdown between Grant and Lee. For the jinxed Army of the Potomac, Lee was more than a brilliant Confederate general: he was a man endowed with almost supernatural powers, having decisively licked Pope at the second battle of Bull Run, Burnside at Fredericksburg, and Hooker at Chancellorsville. To anyone who cared to listen, Rawlins blustered that Meade had already defeated Lee at Gettysburg. *The New York Times* interjected a timely reminder that "if it be true that Grant has never fought Lee, it is equally true that Lee has never met Grant."[65] Still, the fearsome aura of Lee haunted the Army of the Potomac. In New York, George Templeton Strong noted that Grant's path was "whitened by the bones of popular reputations that perished because their defunct owners did not know how to march through Virginia to Richmond."[66]

Southern soldiers consoled themselves that Grant's six predecessors had foundered against Lee and fooled themselves into imagining that the western theater of war, where Grant had flourished, was a less severe testing ground. Confederate general Evander M. Law said the "universal verdict" among rebel soldiers asserted that Grant "was no strategist and that he relied almost entirely upon the brute force of numbers for success."[67] Awaiting the spring campaign, one of Lee's officers smugly assured his family that Grant would "shortly come to grief if he attempts to repeat the tactics in Virginia which proved so successful in Mississippi."[68]

The lone Confederate officer warning against dangerous complacency was Grant's old friend James Longstreet. When one of Lee's officers said Grant could be easily defeated, Longstreet countered any such premature gloating. "I was in the corps of cadets with [Grant] at West Point for three years," he objected. "I was present at his wedding, I served in the same army with him in Mexico, I have observed his methods of warfare in the West, and I believe I know him through and through; and I tell you that we cannot afford to underrate him . . . that man will fight us every day and every hour till the end of this war."[69]

Facing such self-confident foes, Grant's main task was partly psychological: to shatter the Lee mystique, bury the bad memories of Union defeats in Virginia, and stop his own men from magnifying Lee's powers in their minds. While Grant respected Lee, he was never intimidated by him and rated Joseph Johnston the superior general. In his *Memoirs,* Grant referred to Lee as "the acknowledged ablest general in the Confederate army."[70] In private, though, his criticisms of Lee grew more waspish as the postwar notion took hold that Lee had fought with elegant finesse while he, a brutal plodder, fell back on sheer numbers. "Lee was a good man, a fair commander, who had everything in his favor," Grant recollected in 1879 with a touch of wounded vanity. "He was a man who needed sunshine. He was supported by the unanimous voice of the South . . . Everything he did was right. He was treated like a demi-god. Our generals had a hostile press, lukewarm friends, and a public opinion outside."[71] If Grant sounded grudging, Lee reciprocated the sentiment. When queried after the war about the best Union general, Lee gave his highest accolade to a man thoroughly derided by historians: "McClellan, by all odds."[72] In a wartime letter to one son, Lee subscribed to the stereotypical southern view of Grant: "His talent and strategy consists in accumulating overwhelming numbers."[73]

Born in Stratford Hall, Virginia, Lee had a blue-blooded pedigree. His father, Henry "Light-Horse Harry" Lee, had distinguished himself as a cavalry officer under George Washington before becoming a Virginia governor and congressman. Reckless, improvident, Henry Lee was addicted to speculation and ended up imprisoned for debt. This scandalous history left his son with a stern sense of rectitude and a burning desire to rehabilitate the family name. At West Point, he received not a single demerit and graduated second in his class, enabling him to enter the prestigious Army Corps of Engineers. Both in the Mexican War and in engineering projects on the Mississippi River, he compiled an outstanding record. Adding to his social prominence was his marriage to Mary Custis, great-granddaughter of Martha Washington. From Mary's father, the couple inherited a stately Arlington mansion, stuffed with George Washington memorabilia and worked by nearly two hundred Custis slaves. For three years, Robert served as West Point's superintendent, affording him a chance to study closely Napoleon's campaigns.

A handsome man with a gray beard, the fifty-seven-year-old Lee was proudly patrician with impeccable dignity and unshakable poise. He belonged to that breed of generals whose command over soldiers emanates from their firm command over themselves. An abstemious man who seldom drank, he was not likely to sympathize with Grant's history with alcohol. Unlike Grant, he had a dignity that discouraged familiarity and could seem aloof. For all that, he shared many traits with Grant. Though more formal, Lee also wore simple uniforms and didn't flaunt his rank; was motivated by an unyielding sense of duty; showed a minute attention to detail; radiated confidence even in the darkest moments; had tremendous tenacity in battle; and was essentially reserved. In desperate situations, both Lee and Grant showed daring and imagination and never wanted to retreat. Both were reluctant warriors who seemed happiest with their families.

It is often said that Lee defected to the Confederate cause not from ideological support for slavery or secession but from duty to his native Virginia. He acknowledged that slavery was "a moral and political evil," but he also exhibited a paternalistic form of racism that condoned it. Slavery, he claimed, was "a greater evil to the white man than to the black race . . . blacks are immeasurably better off here than in Africa, morally, socially & physically. The painful discipline they are undergoing, is necessary for their instruction as a race, & I hope will prepare and lead them to better things."[74] He hoped slavery would wither away thanks to Christian charity and contested those who sought to abolish it through political action.

So highly regarded was Lee at the war's onset that he was offered command of the U.S. Army with the rank of major general, but couldn't bring himself to accept it. "I could take no part in an invasion of the Southern States," he stated before resigning from the federal army to return to Virginia.[75] He was distraught over the Union's dismemberment. Throwing in his lot with the South, he would later be placed in command of all armed forces in Virginia. His maiden military efforts in western Virginia faltered, and he was thought such a rule-book commander that one southern politician groused that Lee was "too much of a red-tapist to be an effective commander in the field."[76] Not yet burnished with victories, he was skewered in the southern press with a spate of nicknames— "Granny Lee," "King of Spades," the "Great Entrencher"—that mocked his cautious nature. Before long, Lee became military adviser to Jefferson Davis and didn't return to the battlefield until June 1862 when he took charge of the Army of Northern Virginia. While that army had lingering doubts about their new leader's appetite for risk, one officer vouched for Lee's courage: "His name might be

Audacity. He will take more desperate chances, and take them quicker, than any other general in this country, North or South."[77] At Fredericksburg, Second Manassas, and Chancellorsville, Lee amply vindicated that faith.

In the contest between Grant and Lee, Grant had the edge in manpower and resources, but Lee boasted many other advantages. He fought mostly on home turf in Virginia, enjoying intimate knowledge of the geography, not to mention a spy network of local residents. In the upcoming campaign, he would fight on the defensive, throwing up fortifications at a time of major advances in such warfare, and Grant would be repeatedly stymied by them. The replacement of smoothbore weapons by more accurate rifles favored soldiers hunkered down behind barriers. "We had the advantage in the Virginia campaign of being on the inside and knowing [the] ground," said James Longstreet. "We could concentrate double the troops in half the time that Grant required."[78] Military theory taught that offensive forces had to be up to three times larger than dug-in defensive ones, meaning that Grant's numerical advantage can easily be overstated. "The army operating against the South . . . had to protect its lines of communication with the North, from which all supplies had to come to the front," Grant observed. "Every foot of road had to be guarded by troops stationed at convenient distances apart."[79] In the two notable instances where Lee fought offensive operations on unfamiliar soil—Antietam and Gettysburg—he suffered crushing setbacks. By the time he encountered Grant, he had renounced broad offensive strikes.

There is no question that Robert E. Lee was a masterly tactician in individual battles, showing a keen relish for war. "It is well that war is so terrible," he famously commented at Fredericksburg. "We should grow too fond of it."[80] Accustomed to winning gigantic gambles, he displayed an uncanny ability to intuit the responses of opposing generals, projecting himself into their inmost thoughts and figuring out what they would hazard next. Like Grant, he had lightning-fast reflexes and could improvise in the heat of combat, jumping on enemy mistakes. He also had terrific rapport with even lowly soldiers, merging them into a single fighting unit that moved with speed and agility. Sometimes, as at Gettysburg, Lee became too wedded to a battle plan and was deaf to warning voices. Sometimes he trusted too much to subordinates, presiding over them with a light touch and giving vague instructions, but such flaws were inseparable from his deep soldierly bond with his officers.

If Lee was master of the individual battle, it was Grant who excelled in grand strategy. For all his brilliance as a general, Lee's vision was narrowly focused on his beloved Virginia. In one tearful outburst at an 1862 Confederate cabinet meeting, he blurted out, "Richmond must not be given up; it shall not be given up!"[81] His attachment to this real estate was perhaps more personal than strategic. Lee had no real plan to end the war other than to prolong it and make the cost bloody enough that the North would weary of the effort. Grant, by contrast, had a comprehensive strategy for how to capture and defeat the southern army, putting a conclusive end to the contest. The caricature of Lee as elegant and faultless whereas Grant was a clumsy butcher misses the point that Grant had much the harder task: he had to whittle down the Confederate army and smash it irrevocably, whereas Lee needed only to inflict massive pain on the northern army and stay alive to fight another day.

Grant was the strategic genius produced by the Civil War. He set clear goals, communicated them forcefully, and instilled them in his men. While Lee stuck to Virginia, Grant grasped the war in its totality, masterminding the movements of all Union armies. It was Grant who best apprehended the strategic interactions of the eastern and western theaters. The major victories of Sherman, Sheridan, and Thomas in 1864–65 would occur under Grant's direct supervision, yet he is frequently denied credit for his overall guidance of the Union war effort. His epic confrontation with Lee in 1864–65 was just one facet of his farsighted leadership. "Grant's strategy embraced a continent; Lee's a small State," wrote Sherman. "Grant's 'logistics' were to supply and transport armies thousands of miles, where Lee was limited to hundreds."[82]

By April 1864, Lee had been worn down by protracted warfare, suffering lumbago attacks the previous winter and probably experiencing the early stages of heart disease. He hoped upcoming battles against the Army of the Potomac would be therapeutic, stating in early April that "we have got to whip them, we must whip them, and it has already made me better to think of it."[83] Lee's army was beset by extreme shortages of meat, bread, clothing, shoes, and blankets, forcing him to operate in a circumscribed sphere. His most pressing need was for manpower, requiring the expansion of conscription to almost all able-bodied southern males. As John Jones, a War Department clerk in Richmond, wrote, "Old men, disabled soldiers, and ladies are to be relied on for clerical duty, nearly all others to take the field."[84] In his diary, Jones described the sight of conscripts in chains being carted off to fight for Lee and the bleak atmosphere that reigned in a Confederate capital forced to ration everything: "The FAMINE is still advancing, and his gaunt proportions loom up daily, as he approaches with gigantic strides . . . Every day we have accounts of robberies, the preceding night, of cows, pigs, bacon, flour."[85] Lee tried to set an austere example, allowing meat to be served only twice weekly to his staff. "His ordinary dinner consists of a head of cabbage, boiled in salt water, and a pone of corn bread," Jones wrote.[86]

On March 31, Grant left Washington aboard a steamer and journeyed to Old Point Comfort, Virginia, to confer with Major General Benjamin F. Butler at Fort Monroe. Grant brought an entourage that included Julia, Rawlins, Comstock, and Congressman Washburne. Placed at the mouth of the James River, the stone citadel seemed an ideal place for Grant to discuss with Butler the part his Army of the James would enact in the forthcoming drama. Whether Butler would be his ally or nemesis was to preoccupy Grant in the coming months.

Butler had legions of both admirers and enemies. Shrewd and scheming, he was half reformer, half demagogue. Born in New Hampshire, he lost his father early and spent his adolescence in Lowell, Massachusetts, where his widowed mother ran a boardinghouse. After being rejected for West Point, Butler graduated from Waterville College, earned rich fees as a Boston lawyer, and championed progressive reforms, including a shorter week for blue-collar workers. While a Democrat in the Massachusetts legislature, he sank money into a lucrative woolen mill in Lowell. After Fort Sumter, as Lincoln wooed "political generals" from the Democratic side, he named Butler a major general of volunteers, even though he had actively championed Jefferson Davis for the Democratic nomination in 1860 and voted for John C. Breckinridge. Before the war, Butler had little time for abolitionists, cheering the Dred Scott decision. Although he lost the Massachusetts gubernatorial race in 1860, it established him as a political force. Lincoln executed a delicate balancing act with Butler, keeping him happy while trying to deny him control of a major Union army. He was the sort of wily politician whom people learned to handle gingerly.

The short and pudgy Butler had a notably ugly face that usually wore an imperious scowl. He had a broad, bald pate, with lank hairs falling to the side, a walrus mustache, and a strange, cross-eyed stare that boded ill for anyone who defied him. His lids drooped heavily, as did bags below his eyes, so his eyeballs seemed to recede into thick nests of flesh. Mark Twain once said Butler was so "drearily homely" that when he smiled, it was "like the breaking up of a hard winter."[87] One soldier, revolted by Butler's unsightly form, wrote of him: "Call before your mental vision a sack full of muck . . . and then imagine four enormous German sausages fixed to the extremities of the sack in lieu of arms and legs."[88]

In 1862, when he acted as military governor of New Orleans, Butler's rule was so draconian that residents maligned him as "Beast Butler." He gained lasting infamy when he issued an order that local females, who were emptying chamber pots on passing Union soldiers, should be treated as "women of the town plying their avocations."[89] Whether true or not, an aura of corruption pervaded his New Orleans tenure. Incensed at his alleged misdeeds, Jefferson Davis issued a proclamation that any Confederate officer who collared Butler would be entitled to hang him posthaste. Despite southern abuse, many northern observers hailed Butler for efficient, even honest, management of the town, in addition to organizing black regiments. Northern liberals also applauded early in the war when Butler coined the term "contraband" to cover slaves who defected to Union lines, providing a legal rationale for protecting them when the Fugitive Slave Act was still in force.

As general in chief, Grant hoped to oust Butler until Lincoln and Stanton made clear that they could not alienate so powerful and vindictive a politician. Perhaps left unspoken was that Butler harbored presidential ambitions and might assay a run against Lincoln in the fall. Grant had grudging respect for Butler as an enterprising general of "courage, honor and sincere convictions" but was painfully aware that he lacked a "military education."[90]

In the fall of 1863, Lincoln elevated Butler to command what became the Army of the James. Grant now gave him instructions for this army as he sought to harmonize all military actions in Virginia. While Grant and the Army of the Potomac would drive from northern Virginia toward Richmond, he wanted Butler and his thirty-thousand-man force to travel up the James River, establish a base at City Point, then strike at Richmond's soft underbelly from the southeast. Grant was realistic enough to know he could not vanquish Lee's army all at once. Rather he would pound away at it, eroding its strength, and finally bottle it up inside Richmond, which he would then encircle. Eventually he sought to unite his army and Butler's on the James River. Grant wanted Butler to take Petersburg, due south of Richmond, and slash away at its railway links that connected Richmond to Petersburg and points south and west. Once cut off from these sources of supply, Lee and the Confederate government could not survive.

Grant's initial impression of Butler was favorable, and their visions of the upcoming campaign converged. Striding to a map, Butler outlined the movement of his army that Grant had already planned. Grant believed Butler's subordinate generals would compensate for his deficiencies. Writing to his wife,

Rawlins had good words for Grant's three new commanding generals: Sherman, Meade, and Butler. "They are all three loyal to their country, friends of the General, and consequently with no ambitions to be gratified that look not to the success of our arms in obedience to and in accordance with his orders and plans."[91] In his diary, Cyrus Comstock sized up Butler more coldly, calling him "sharp, shrewd, able, without conscience or modesty—overbearing. A bad man to have against you."[92]

While Grant and Butler conferred, they took time out to review a black brigade camped nearby. The subject of black soldiers still occupied Grant's mind. On April 15, he learned of a horrifying cavalry raid conducted by Nathan Bedford Forrest against Fort Pillow on the Mississippi River in Tennessee. Forrest had slaughtered dozens of black soldiers after they surrendered, slashing and bludgeoning the wounded till they succumbed. "The Fort Pillow Massacre is one of the most brutal and horrible acts of fiendishness on record," Rawlins reported to his wife.[93] Grant reacted with outrage. "If men have been murdered after capture," he warned Sherman, "retaliation must be resorted to promptly."[94] As proof of his foe's inhumanity, Grant liked to quote the boastful dispatch Forrest filed after the episode: "The river was dyed with the blood of the slaughtered for two hundred yards . . . It is hoped that these facts will demonstrate to the Northern people that negro soldiers cannot cope with Southerners."[95]

Further proof of Grant's continuing concern for black soldiers was his uncompromising stand on prisoner exchanges. The previous year, Jefferson Davis had announced his intention of either executing captured black soldiers or returning them to slavery. This double standard for black and white Union soldiers was intolerable to Grant. In negotiating prisoner exchanges, he told Butler no distinction should be made between "white and colored prisoners; the only question being, were they, at the time of their capture, in the military service of the United States."[96] To back up his point, Grant suspended prisoner exchanges with the Confederacy until black and white equality was established. Even though he didn't believe they had attained the same proficiency as the most experienced white troops, Grant continued to insist that black soldiers should be employed as widely as possible. In laying out instructions for Banks's expedition up the Red River, he had expressed hope that "a large number of [black] recruits of this class" would be used.[97] Having conferred with Butler, Grant was ready, at last, to take on Lee.

CHAPTER EIGHTEEN

Raging Storm

B Y LATE APRIL, with the northern Virginia roads drying out and permitting unimpeded movement, Grant celebrated his forty-second birthday and scheduled a date for the launch of his campaign. His vast army would cross the Rapidan River on May 4, and that same night Benjamin Butler and his Army of the James would push up that river as far as possible, gunning for Richmond. Meanwhile Sherman would lunge against Joseph Johnston in Georgia, destroying the southern infrastructure that supported Lee's army, while Franz Sigel invaded the Shenandoah Valley. Provided with good intelligence about Grant's intentions, Lee braced for his opponent's first move and grew fidgety waiting to see where he would strike first. For his part, Grant longed for a fight. "I am growing impatient to be off," he told Julia, "but must wait completion of preparations."[1] He had enough composure to ask how Buck and Nellie were progressing with their lessons and requested that the children send him weekly letters.

Awaiting the din of battle, Abraham Lincoln was glad to set down, at least a bit, the heavy mantle of military leadership that his earlier mediocre generals had forced him to shoulder. On April 30, he sent Grant a letter that exuded confidence in him and granted him total freedom. That confidence arose in part because he and Grant agreed on so many military matters.

> Not expecting to see you again before the Spring campaign opens, I
> wish to express, in this way, my entire satisfaction with what you

have done up to this time, so far as I understand it. The particulars of your plans I neither know, or seek to know. You are vigilant and self-reliant; and, pleased with this, I wish not to obtrude any constraints or restraints upon you. While I am very anxious that any great disaster, or the capture of our men in great numbers, shall be avoided, I know these points are less likely to escape your attention than they would be mine—If there is anything wanting which is within my power to give, do not fail to let me know it. And now with a brave Army, and a just cause, may God sustain you.[2]

Grant graciously replied that Lincoln and Stanton had responded to all his wishes and he had been "astonished at the readiness with which everything asked for has been yielded without even an explanation being asked. Should my success be less than I desire . . . the least I can say is, the fault is not with you."[3] Psychologically, this last sentence was a masterstroke, reaffirming that Grant, unlike his predecessors, wouldn't scapegoat Lincoln or Stanton for any failures.

On May 2, Grant mounted his powerful bay horse Cincinnati and rode around the war-flattened countryside and Union encampments with his friend Daniel Ammen. He discussed the enormous logistical challenge posed by moving 115,000 men with wagons, supplies, and weapons. To accentuate his point, he noted that if the soldiers and their supply trains were strung out single file along the road, they would stretch the entire route from the Rapidan River to Richmond. Grant planned to have his army carry enough supplies for two weeks: one million rations plus two hundred thousand forage rations for the animals. He knew he must snap the potent spell Lee had cast over the Army of the Potomac, telling Ammen that Lee "possessed the entire confidence, respect, and indeed affection of every one under his command, and such a man could not be an indifferent commander to meet."[4]

That same day, showing a superb fingertip feel for his adversary, Lee stood atop a nearby mountain with his infantry chiefs and identified, with oracular authority, two of the fords where Grant would cross the Rapidan. The next day, he suspected an imminent engagement when reports filtered back to him of billowing dust clouds on the Union side, the kind kicked up by marching soldiers, plus billowing smoke, the kind that rose from newly abandoned army camps. That night, Union columns were seen passing in silhouette in front of campfires, making it all but certain that Grant's crossing of the Rapidan neared.

On the other side of the river that night, Grant sat in his tent, composing a letter to Julia. Knowing the nation's eyes were riveted upon him, he sounded self-possessed and extremely confident: "I know the greatest anxiety is now felt in the North for the success of this move, and that the anxiety will increase when it is once known that the Army is in motion."[5] That Grant felt sanguine about his prospects was revealed by an unexpected flash of wit. "I believe it has never been my misfortune to be placed where I lost my presence of mind, unless indeed it has been when thrown in strange company, particularly of ladies. Under such circumstances I know I must appear like a fool."[6]

The following night, in his Culpeper headquarters, Grant reviewed with Washburne, Rawlins, and senior staff members the scope of the upcoming campaign. Folding his legs, kindling a fresh cigar, he reviewed the strategy for hurling simultaneous strikes against the enemy in multiple locations. That night his army would begin its historic march into hostile territory. Once safely across the Rapidan, he would have a critical decision to make: whether to move right or left. Always preferring interwoven movements, Grant opted for the leftward movement, which would enable him to cooperate better with Butler's army below Richmond and provide safeguards for Washington. If he got lucky, he might even sever Lee's link with Richmond. A world of tactical difficulties lay ahead, but the broad strategic arc of his campaign stood clearly engraved in Grant's mind. At one point, he strolled over to a wall map and traced with his forefinger a curve that connected Richmond and Petersburg. "When my troops are there," he said, "Richmond is mine. Lee must retreat or surrender."[7] To ensure maximum secrecy, Grant waited until dark to issue orders that set the colossal machinery in motion. When he went to bed at 11 p.m., Washburne "said that Napoleon often indulged in only four hours of sleep, and still preserved all the vigor of his mental faculties." Grant, who needed seven hours, sounded dubious. "Well, I, for one, never believed those stories. If the truth were known, I have no doubt it would be found that he made up for his short sleep at night by taking naps during the day."[8]

On May 4, the day his army was to cross the Rapidan, Grant rose to the historic occasion and sported for once fancy military duds: a uniform frock coat over a blue vest, three-star shoulder straps, yellow thread gloves, a black felt hat adorned with a gold braid, a midriff sash, and a sword clanking at his side.[9] Before dawn, Sheridan's cavalry crossed at one ford and other units sprang into motion after sunrise. It was an impressive spectacle as infantrymen lifted their weapons and waded across waist-high water while cannon and supply wagons rolled across four pontoon bridges, two crafted from cloth, two from wood. On this improbably beautiful day, clear and glistening, the sun's rays struck brightly off bayonets, drums rolled, trumpets blared, and regimental banners rippled in the breeze. "Never since its organization had the Army of the Potomac been in better spirits, or more eager to meet the enemy," a journalist wrote.[10] As the day warmed, the sprightly soldiers, anticipating summer weather, deposited excess clothing and baggage by the wayside—"an improvidence I had never witnessed before," Grant said, forgetting what had happened at Fort Donelson.[11]

In the early morning light Grant lingered at Culpeper, waiting until all his troops were on the road. Then, astride Cincinnati, he galloped off to the Rapidan with Washburne at his side, the congressman dressed in such funereal black that wags said Grant had enlisted his own mortician. Around noon, when he crossed the river at Germanna Ford, Grant was delighted by what he saw. Horace Porter described how fast-stepping soldiers with "lusty shouts . . . greeted their new commander as he passed . . . But as General Grant was neither demonstrative nor communicative, he gave no expression whatever to his feelings."[12] He set up headquarters at a vacant hilltop farm on the Rapidan's south bank, where he profited from splendid views to track the unceasing movements of his army. Although he manifested neither pride nor pleasure, he inwardly exulted that his army traveled twelve miles that day and that four thousand wagons would lumber across the river by the following evening. "This I regarded as a great feat and it removed from my mind the most serious apprehension I had entertained: how was so large a train to be carried through a hostile country and protected?" Grant told Stanton.[13] He would also need to track down forage for thirty thousand horses and twenty-three thousand mules as the army journeyed south.

After lunch, Grant enjoyed a cigar with his staff, sufficiently pleased with his progress that he allowed himself momentary banter. When a reporter inquired how long it would take to reach Richmond, Grant gave a mischievous reply: "I will agree to be there in about four days." After an astonished silence, Grant went on, "That is, if General Lee becomes a party to the agreement. But if he objects, the trip will undoubtedly be prolonged."[14] The joke drew hearty laughter. By this time Grant had probably learned from intercepted enemy signals that Lee knew the Army of the Potomac had poured across the Rapidan River, prompting Grant to send a message to Burnside to move his corps posthaste to

Germanna Ford. "Make forced march until you reach this place . . . require them [his troops] to make a night march."[15]

The triumphant mood soon faded. The Rapidan crossing inaugurated the Overland Campaign, seven weeks of brutal, remorseless fighting so steeped in gore that one Union officer would term it "a raging storm of lead and iron."[16] Immediately south of the Rapidan lay a bleak, uninhabited region of dense vegetation known as the Wilderness, closely packed with stunted trees, tangled shrubs, scrub oak, and pine trees. Loggers had once chopped down a mature forest to make charcoal for nearby iron smelters, leaving behind a forbidding realm of second-growth trees. At the battle of Chancellorsville a year earlier, Lee had trounced Hooker in this perilous region, mastering its mystifying terrain. As far as Lee was concerned, Grant was set to wander into the same trap as Hooker. Lee had only 64,000 men versus Grant's 115,000—a difference that could be fatal to Lee in an open field confrontation. In the trackless maze of the Wilderness, however, that advantage would vanish. The tricky topography would also neutralize Grant's superior artillery, its fire obstructed by trees. For that reason, Lee made no effort to thwart Grant's crossing of the Rapidan and was eager to encourage it. Hoping to avoid a collision with Lee in the Wilderness, Grant intended to march his men through it rapidly, then meet Lee in more open country.

That night, Grant and Meade smoked before a blazing fire and hatched plans for the morrow. Satisfied with the day's activity, Grant wired Halleck: "The crossing of Rapidan effected. Forty Eight hours now will demonstrate whether the enemy intends giving battle this side of Richmond."[17] The conversation of Grant and Meade was interrupted periodically by messages confirming that Sherman, Butler, and George Crook had advanced their armies as planned. True to his word, Grant viewed the war effort through a wide-angled lens that spanned the fighting in its entirety. Adam Badeau, who admired Grant's unflappable nature, applauded this: "It had never happened before in the history of war that one man directed so completely four distinct armies, separated by thousands of miles, and numbering more than a quarter of a million soldiers; ordering the operations of each for the same day, and receiving at night reports from each that his orders had been obeyed."[18] The man who wielded this unprecedented power was a model of simplicity. He slept that night in a tent furnished plainly with "a portable cot made of a coarse canvas stretcher over a light wooden frame, a tin wash-basin which stood on an iron tripod, two folding camp-chairs, and a plain pine table," Porter remembered. "The general's baggage was limited to one small camp trunk, which contained his underclothing, toilet articles, a suit of clothes, and an extra pair of boots."[19]

Also camped in a tent that night, Lee decided that the following day he would provoke an encounter before Grant could concentrate his enormous forces. Though he wanted to avoid a Wilderness clash, Grant was scarcely less eager to fight. He had three corps under Winfield Scott Hancock, Gouverneur Warren, and John Sedgwick at his disposal, while a fourth corps under Burnside endured a grueling all-night march to join the fray. As he tensely awaited Burnside, Grant made a revealing comment to Porter: "The only time I ever feel impatient is when I give an order for an important movement of troops in the presence of the enemy, and am waiting for them to reach their destination. Then the minutes seem like hours."[20]

The few roadways in the Wilderness were rough and narrow, obstructing troop movements. Lee started one corps eastward under Richard S. Ewell down the Orange Turnpike and another under A. P. Hill down the Orange Plank Road, hoping a third corps led by Longstreet would appear in time to assist them. Early in the morning, Grant received word from Meade that Confederate forces had been spotted on the Orange Turnpike. When Meade ordered Warren to pounce on them immediately, Grant endorsed this aggressive attitude: "If any opportunity presents itself for pitching into a part of Lee's army, do so without giving time for disposition."[21]

For once Lee proved a reluctant warrior, preferring to defer any general engagement until the next day, when Longstreet would strengthen him with approximately fourteen thousand men. Nonetheless, he wasn't one to duck a battle, especially after Union general Charles Griffin pounded hard into one of Ewell's advance brigades. Griffin's triumph was fleeting, stymied by a factor that would govern two days of Wilderness fighting: as dry leaves and branches caught fire from exploding shells, they produced a thick curtain of smoke that trapped and blinded Griffin's men, making them vulnerable to Ewell's counterattack. Union soldiers ended up fleeing the scene. Griffin, incensed, showed up on a hill where Grant sat smoking with Meade. In blistering tones, he let his superiors know his disgust at not being supported. Shocked that someone would berate his beloved general, Rawlins gave way to anger, but Grant reacted more matter-of-factly. "Who is this General Gregg?" he asked Meade. "You ought to arrest him." "His name's Griffin, not Gregg," Meade replied, "and that's only his way of talking."[22] Meade then leaned forward and buttoned up Grant's coat for him.

In midafternoon came another bout of furious fighting. Grant and Meade sent a division commanded by General George W. Getty and a corps under General Hancock to deal with an advance by A. P. Hill on the Orange Plank Road. This produced a searing firefight marked by such deafening musket clatter that one federal soldier remarked, "The steady firing rolled and crackled from end to end of the contending lines as if it would never cease."[23] Despite acrid smoke drooping over the battlefield, the federal troops acquitted themselves ably, and Hill's forces staggered backward under the fierce onslaught amid heavy casualties on both sides.

The May 5 fighting, however feverish, was inconclusive. The next morning dawned bright but hazy, veiled by hanging smoke. Showing his inborn fighting spirit, Grant sent orders through Meade to pummel Lee's army as early as possible, much as he had done the second day of Shiloh. "It was my plan then, as it was on all other occasions, to take the initiative whenever the enemy could be drawn from his intrenchments," Grant wrote.[24] Eager to fight, he planned to attack Lee at 4:30 a.m. until Meade pleaded that the men were exhausted and argued for 6 a.m. Grant grudgingly allowed an extra half hour of sleep and set the time at 5 a.m. Throughout the Overland Campaign, he would force Lee *to react to him*. Striking first, setting the pace, shaping the contours of battle—these were priorities dear to Grant's heart. He also knew that Longstreet and his fourteen thousand men were furiously converging on the Wilderness and hoped to inflict maximum damage before their advent.

At 4 a.m., Grant rose and breakfasted on a cucumber soaked in vinegar, washed down with black coffee. Then he stuffed his pockets with cigars and retreated to a little knoll to superintend the battle. He paced as he awaited the opening guns. At 5 a.m., right on schedule, Hancock led two divisions up the Orange Plank Road and smashed the enemy so hard the Confederate line reeled backward. Chased for a mile into the woods, it dispersed in confusion.[25] It seemed as if total victory lay within Hancock's grasp. "We are driving them, sir!" Hancock exclaimed to Theodore Lyman. "Tell General Meade we are driving them most beautifully."[26]

His gloating was premature. Finding himself in an exposed forward position, Lee saw hundreds of soldiers from A. P. Hill's corps streaming back toward him, and he endeavored on horseback to arrest their flight. He would have failed had it not been for the timely arrival of Longstreet's troops, who surged forward, quick time, in a double column. Overcome with emotion, Lee asked which brigade this was. "The Texas brigade, sir," someone responded. "Hurrah for Texas,"

Lee called, waving his hat with delirious joy.[27] Still gripped by powerful emotion, he scurried to spearhead the Texas brigade, leading the counterattack himself. The soldiers, observing this brave folly, rushed to curb it. "Lee to the rear! Lee to the rear!" they hollered and finally prevailed upon him to hang back, one soldier actually taking his bridle and escorting him rearward.[28] The extraordinary moment disclosed Lee's battlefield zest and mystic bond with his men.

Backed by Longstreet, Lee cobbled together a revived force. Favored with intimate knowledge of the terrain, one Confederate general identified an old roadbed built for a disused railroad. Longstreet's men crept furtively along it then exploded from the closed woods in a stinging assault against Grant's men. In two hours, they wiped out earlier Union gains. The Confederate advance halted when Longstreet was struck by friendly fire in the neck and shoulder, an injury that would paralyze his right arm and sideline him for five months. Bleeding profusely, he was borne in a stretcher to a waiting ambulance as soldiers wept openly. When he heard them bemoaning his death, Longstreet lifted his hat with his good arm to reassure them he was still alive. Lee seemed stunned. "I shall not soon forget the sadness in his face," wrote a Confederate captain, "and the almost despairing movement of his hands, when he was told that Longstreet had fallen."[29] Grant knew Longstreet's worth to Lee, reflecting that it "compensated in a great measure for the mishap, or misapprehensions, which had fallen to our lot during the day."[30] Losing his best deputy forced Lee to assume his command and gave the Union side critical time to retreat, regroup, and blunt the Confederate countermeasure.

In the convoluted web of the Wilderness, Grant had to form a picture of the battle in his mind, for there was no hilltop ledge from which to survey his men. Only two or three times in two days of combat did Grant ride out on Cincinnati and witness fighting firsthand. Seated on a tree stump, in a hilly clearing, he puffed through twenty cigars, smoked a briarwood pipe, wrote orders, examined maps, and chatted with Meade. He idly whittled so many branches with a penknife that he wore holes in his thread gloves. While some observers claimed his hands trembled, most were struck by his unnatural calm. He seemed undisturbed when enemy shells burst nearby, refusing to relocate to a safer place, saying, "It would be better to order up some artillery and defend the present location."[31] If Grant had to make an instant decision, Badeau wrote, "it was made and uttered instantly, and unflinchingly, though it involved the fate of a corps. At these supreme moments, the dullest perceived his intensity, the most unwilling admitted his power."[32]

On the thickly wooded knoll, Grant had to be guided by sound more than sight, combined with dispatches rushed into his hands by breathless couriers. Like Lee, he could adapt swiftly to a shifting array of battlefield forces. The dense foliage, which made artillery useless, led to hand-to-hand combat of an appalling character. This frenzied fighting was like a deadly game of blindman's buff, with both armies flailing wildly at each other, their visions blinkered by floating smoke.

After an early afternoon lull, the fighting resumed at 4:15 p.m. as Lee mounted a furious attack against Hancock. Within an hour Hancock had repulsed the movement, but not before a terrifying event intervened: the woods started burning again. Exploding shells ignited dry brush and pine needles, heating the forest into a raging inferno. Adding to the conflagration were wooden Union breastworks, which blazed up with stunning speed. Wounded men were roasted alive on the forest floor, their agonized cries audible everywhere; many committed suicide rather than burn to death. Swirling smoke asphyxiated soldiers on both sides and Porter remembered how "the wind howled through the tree-tops, mingling its moans with the groans of the dying, and heavy branches were cut off by the fire of the artillery, and fell crashing upon the heads of the men, adding a new terror to battle."[33] Blood-smeared, hideous garments clung to bushes, and many survivors said the scene approached as near to scenes of hell as they could ever picture. Stanton would christen the Wilderness "the bloodiest swath ever made on this globe."[34]

One thing Grant hoped to accomplish was to stamp out the legend of Lee's invincibility. Toward evening he learned the myth was still alive. The Confederate general John B. Gordon had discovered that Grant's right flank was vulnerable and got Lee's permission to attack it. Gordon's unexpected drive shoved back Union soldiers for a mile and bagged two northern generals. An agitated Union general burst into Grant's presence, babbling about Lee's prowess: "I know Lee's methods well by past experience; he will throw his whole army between us and the Rapidan, and cut us off completely from our communications." Grant sprang to his feet, snatched his cigar from his mouth, and chastised the panic-stricken officer. "Oh, I am heartily tired of hearing about what Lee is going to do," he said with uncommon vehemence. "Some of you always seem to think he is suddenly going to turn a double somersault, and land in our rear and on both of our flanks at the same time. Go back to your command, and try to think what we are going to do ourselves, instead of what Lee is going to do."[35] This tirade from the taciturn Grant was clearly something he had meditated for some time, and the moment must have felt liberating. He wanted to banish the defeatist mentality from the Army of the Potomac and get its officers thinking confidently instead of shrinking into a defensive posture.

By the time darkness descended, the Union line had re-formed on the right and Gordon and his men retreated to their entrenchments, ending the Wilderness battle after two days of hectic fighting and unspeakable carnage. Even having experienced Shiloh, Grant still wrote that "more desperate fighting has not been witnessed on this continent."[36] Characteristically the tightly buttoned Grant allowed himself release only once the crisis passed. He carried the full weight of the Union cause on his shoulders, an impossible burden for any man. So, perhaps not surprisingly, he submitted to an overflow of feeling. "When all proper measures had been taken," Rawlins related, "Grant went into his tent, threw himself face downward on his cot, and gave way to the greatest emotion." The man of extreme self-control surrendered to his feelings. Rawlins asserted he had "never before seen him so deeply moved" and that "nothing could be more certain than that he was stirred to the very depths of his soul." Charles F. Adams Jr. confirmed that he "never saw a man so agitated in my life."[37]

After Grant experienced this tremendous catharsis, he snapped back to his usual self, showing his recuperative powers. Others who saw him that night were no less struck by the calm that settled over him. Ten minutes later, Porter wrote, "I looked in his tent, and found him sleeping as soundly and as peacefully as an infant."[38] "Several times during the night I visited his tent to receive or deliver messages, and found him apparently unmoved by the direful rumors," said cipher operator Samuel Beckwith. "Even with some of these disquieting tales unrefuted, he retired to his cot to snatch a much needed rest, the least ruffled of the group about headquarters."[39]

For two years, the journalist Sylvanus Cadwallader had covered Grant admiringly, but the horror of the Wilderness momentarily weakened his faith. Wrestling with his pessimism, he chatted with Grant by a dying campfire. "His hat was drawn down over his face," wrote Cadwallader, "the high collar of an old blue army overcoat turned up above his ears, one leg crossed over the other knee, eyes on the ashes in front." Grant noted that Lee could choose his own ground, but he was ready to contest him wherever he found him. Slowly it dawned on the skeptical journalist that Grant wasn't deterred by the recent slaughter. Quite the contrary, his resolve had been hardened. In his memoirs, Cadwallader recounted that it was "the grandest mental sunburst of my life. I had suddenly emerged from the slough of despond, to the solid bedrock of unwavering faith."[40] Indeed, though shaken to the core, some deep-seated determination took hold of the doughty Grant. When a journalist asked if he had anything to say to higher-ups back in Washington, Grant came back with a succinct response that carried the force of a credo: "If you see the President, tell him, from me, that, whatever happens, there will be no turning back."[41] When Henry Wing of the *New York Tribune* relayed Grant's words to the president, Lincoln was so transported with joy that he wrapped his "great strong arms" around the journalist, kissing him on the brow.[42]

In the immediate aftermath of the Wilderness, Grant speculated that Confederate forces had suffered more casualties than his own, but the reality was the reverse: the 17,500 Union casualties exceeded 11,000 on the other side. Nevertheless, Rawlins deemed the Wilderness a clear-cut Union victory since Grant's men, by the end, found themselves "masters of the field, the enemy having withdrawn."[43] That Grant refused to concede victory to Lee may seem self-serving, but he had sound reasons. "Our victory consisted in having successfully crossed a formidable stream, almost in the face of an enemy, and in getting the army together as a unit," he maintained.[44] He saw the Wilderness as the opening act in a long drama. He thought in terms of the overall war, not individual battles, and he had succeeded in taking the necessary first step to push Lee toward Richmond, paring down his army in the process. He would now initiate a new style of warfare, an uninterrupted stream of battles such as the war had never seen.

Grant's response to the battle was no less important than his behavior during it. Neither disheartened nor dismayed, he didn't lick his wounds or go skulking back to Washington with excuses. The Wilderness only toughened his resolve. Lee had failed to tame or cow Grant, who didn't shrink from the seas of blood through which his men would have to wade. Nobody appreciated his resolute qualities more than Lincoln, who, during the Wilderness battle, summed up Grant's style: "The great thing about Grant is his perfect coolness and persistency of purpose . . . he is not easily excited . . . and he has the *grit* of a bull-dog! Once let him get his 'teeth' *in,* and nothing can shake him off."[45]

One other person who understood that Grant was quite unlike his predecessors was his chief antagonist: Robert E. Lee. As both sides buried their dead, General Gordon boasted that there was "no doubt but that Grant is retreating." "You are mistaken," Lee corrected him, "quite mistaken. Grant is not retreating; *he is not a retreating man.*"[46] The thought was expressed more poetically by Walt

Whitman, who ardently followed the Overland Campaign: "When did [Grant] ever turn back? He was not that sort; he could no more turn back than time! . . . Grant was one of the inevitables; he always arrived; he was invincible as a law: he never bragged—often seemed about to be defeated when he was in fact on the eve of a tremendous victory."[47]

BASED ON PAST EXPERIENCE, the Army of the Potomac, after the grisly death toll of the previous two days, expected to turn north and slink back in disgrace across the Rapidan. Under previous commanders, they had been forced into demoralizing retreats, victimized by a defeatist attitude. But Grant refused to "give [Lee] time to repair damages."[48] As always, he thought of what he would do to Lee, not vice versa. "If [Lee] falls back and intrenches," Grant informed his staff, "my notion is to move promptly toward the left. This will, in all probability, compel him to try and throw himself between us and Richmond, and in such a movement I hope to be able to attack him in a more open country, and outside of his breastworks."[49] Lee would be thrust permanently on the defensive by Grant, who would set the agenda for coming battles, defining the war's geography and scope. By shifting to the left in a bold flank movement, he hoped to shield Washington from raids and effect an early junction with Butler and his Army of the James, which had landed safely at City Point on the James River. One of Grant's overriding fears was that Lee might beat him to Richmond and annihilate Butler before he arrived.

Under cover of darkness, Grant planned the stealthy overnight evacuation of his entire army to Spotsylvania Court House, a dozen miles southeast. If successful, his army would get there first and be closer to Richmond than Lee. As was his habit, Grant confined his secret plans to a small circle of officers. After sundown, his army began to pack up their gear and prepare to march north. Then, around 8 p.m., Grant and Meade, obscure, shadowy figures in the dark, came barreling down a narrow road on horseback at a rapid clip. The big movement was under way. Sections of forest still burned, throwing a lurid glow into the sky, and the stench of charred human flesh permeated the air.

As long columns of Union soldiers began to stir that night, they found themselves suddenly wheeling around, not to the north but to the south, and realized with a flush of exhilaration that Grant was going on the offensive, leading them back into battle against Lee! The cry that went up, "Grant is moving to

Richmond," was echoed up and down the line.[50] In spontaneous joy, soldiers expressed their fond opinion of Grant with cheers so loud they resounded through the woods, leading Confederates to fear an attack. "Men swung their hats, tossed up their arms, and pressed forward to within touch of their chief, clapping their hands, and speaking to him with the familiarity of comrades," wrote Porter.[51] Grant hushed them. "This is most unfortunate," he warned. "The sound will reach the ears of the enemy, and I fear it may reveal our movement."[52] Nonetheless, the men were thrilled that they had such a redoubtable commander, had not been defeated, and were plunging toward the Confederate capital. "Our spirits rose," said a veteran. "We marched free. The men began to sing . . . That night we were happy."[53] Some even kindled leaves that flickered in the dark, turning the army march into a festive parade.[54]

Everyone sensed a turning point in the war. "Spirits of men and officers are of the highest pitch of animation," Dana reassured Stanton.[55] When Sherman learned of the movement, he labeled it "the grandest act of [Grant's] life; now I feel that the rebellion will be crushed." He saluted Grant for his courageous order, telling him "if Wellington could have heard it he would have jumped out of his boots."[56] Grant hadn't yet slain Lee, but he had done something as important—he had slain his specter. James Wilson recalled how Grant's summons to turn south toward Richmond "lifted a great weight from my mind. We who had known him best felt that the crisis was safely passed, and that we were now on the sure road to ultimate victory."[57]

The contagious high spirits even infected Washington, where, according to Noah Brooks, "the entire city was ablaze with joy upon learning that Grant had pressed the rebels past their old battle ground of the Wilderness, and was driving them before him toward Richmond."[58] A procession of citizens, brimming with excitement, accompanied a band to the White House, where they serenaded the president. When Lincoln appeared, looking sleepless with black circles under his eyes, he comprehended the significance of Grant's movements. "I think, without knowing the particulars of the plans of General Grant, that what has been accomplished is of more importance than at first appears. I believe I know—and am especially grateful to know—that General Grant has not been jostled in his purposes . . . and today he is on his line as he purposed before he moved his armies."[59] Privately Lincoln expressed abiding faith in Grant. "I believe if any other General had been at the Head of that army it would now have been on this side of the Rapidan."[60]

After hours of hard riding, Grant reached Todd's Tavern, northwest of Spotsylvania, where he bedded down for several hours on blankets spread on the
barroom floor. Endowed with eerie intuition, Lee had accurately forecast Grant's
next move to his generals: "Grant is not going to retreat. He will move his army
to Spotsylvania."[61] This hunch wasn't based on direct evidence so much as a
sense that the hamlet represented the strongest strategic point. Once Lee ascertained that Grant's army was in motion—dust clouds hurled aloft by tramping
feet disclosed this—he rushed his army south and beat the sometimes cumbersome Union army to Spotsylvania Court House. Grant knew Lee would stand
and fight at this advantageous spot, which lay athwart his path to Richmond.
Dismayed though not despondent, Grant was "in capital spirits and seems to
have no doubt of success," Washburne wrote to his wife.[62]

The heat was brutal, the troops were exhausted, and a pall of dust and smoke
hung everywhere. The landscape at Spotsylvania Court House presented complex challenges to Grant. It had pockets of forests thick with dwarf pine and
scrub oak, punctuated by clearings, swamps, and gently rolling hills that benefited an army on the defensive. Lee ordered his men to build elaborate fortifications unprecedented in their breadth and sophistication. Once mocked as "King
of Spades" for his predilection for digging trenches, Lee had now refined the art
of defensive warfare, which had progressed more quickly than offensive methods. Intricately hewn from earth, rails, and logs, thrown up with dazzling speed,
Confederate defenses at Spotsylvania featured loopholes that allowed marksmen
to fire safely at Grant's troops. In the opinion of one Union officer, Lee's line was
constructed "in a manner unknown to European warfare, and, indeed, in a
manner new to warfare in this country."[63] (These deep entrenchments anticipated the western front in World War I.) It would be the bane of Grant's campaign against Lee that he usually had to attack him in fortified positions,
whereas Lee could shift troops nimbly employing short, interior lines.

That Lee beat Grant to Spotsylvania partly stemmed from botched communications between Meade and Sheridan, two men with especially hot tempers.
Meade complained that Sheridan and his cavalry had interfered with his infantry advance, ignoring orders to get out of the way. The splenetic Sheridan
shot back that he never received Meade's message and expressed outrage that
Meade bossed around his cavalry. As Porter related, "Sheridan declared with
great warmth that . . . if he could have matters his own way he would . . . move
out in force against [J. E. B.] Stuart's command, and whip it."[64] In a huff,

Meade marched off to Grant and repeated his conversation with Sheridan, including the latter's boastful comment about whipping Stuart. Meade was taken aback by Grant's response. "Did Sheridan say that?" he asked, struck by Sheridan's gumption. "Well, he generally knows what he is talking about. Let him start right out and do it."[65]

Meade wrote orders for Sheridan and his ten thousand horsemen to ride past the rear of Lee's army, drive toward Richmond, and harass the enemy. Union cavalry had never attempted anything so ambitious. As Sheridan wrote, before this "the boldest mounted expeditions had been confined to a hurried ride through the enemy's country, without purpose of fighting more than enough to escape in case of molestation."[66] Now Sheridan issued a full-scale challenge to Stuart's cavalry. For the next sixteen days, detached from the Army of the Potomac, Sheridan, with matchless gusto, played havoc with Lee's army, even penetrating Richmond's outer defenses. Grant summed up Sheridan's storied achievements: he had "encountered [Lee's] cavalry in four engagements, and defeated them in all; recaptured four hundred Union prisoners and killed and captured many of the enemy; destroyed and used many supplies and munitions of war; destroyed miles of railroad and telegraph, and freed us from annoyance by the cavalry of the enemy for more than two weeks."[67] On May 11, at Yellow Tavern near Richmond, Sheridan's men routed Confederate cavalry under Stuart, who was mortally wounded, robbing Lee of a premier lieutenant. A flamboyant figure partial to ostrich-plumed hats and scarlet-lined capes in battle, James E. B. Stuart was an inspired warrior whom the South couldn't afford to lose. Upon hearing of his death, Lee fought off tears. "I can scarcely think of him without weeping," he said and took refuge in his tent.[68] Earlier in the war, the Confederate cavalry had been preeminent but now, thanks to Sheridan's slash-and-burn style, the Union cavalry matched and overtook it.

All day on May 8, Lee had fended off Grant's attacks and felt sufficiently confident to wire encouragement to Jefferson Davis in the early hours of the night. "With the blessing of God, I trust we shall be able to prevent General Grant from reaching Richmond."[69] The next day, Grant could only guess at Lee's next move and lamented to Halleck that his own movements were encumbered "by our immense wagon trains."[70] That morning he mounted a black pony named Jeff Davis that had been captured on a Mississippi plantation owned by the Confederate president's brother. He went to scan Lee's fortifications, came upon General John Sedgwick, and conferred briefly with him. According to

Ulysses S. Grant looking restless but unbowed after his devastating defeat at Cold Harbor.

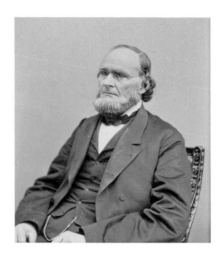

Jesse Root Grant, the overbearing and meddlesome father who constantly tried Grant's patience.

Grant's prim mother, Hannah Simpson Grant, in her later years, when she seldom saw her son.

Julia Grant with her adored father, Colonel Frederick Dent; her daughter Nellie; and her youngest son, Jesse. Grant found it difficult to share the adoration for his father-in-law.

Grant borrowed more of his strategy from Scott and more of his style from Taylor.

Old Fuss and Feathers,
General Winfield Scott

Old Rough and Ready,
General Zachary Taylor

John Rawlins, *left;* Grant, *center;* and Theodore Bowers. Rawlins functioned as Grant's chief of staff, adviser, and conscience throughout the Civil War, and the indispensable watchdog of his drinking problem.

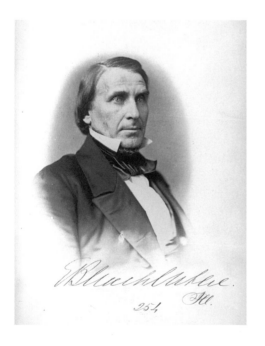

Congressman Elihu B. Washburne of Galena, Illinois, was the tireless sponsor of Grant's military career from the outset of the Civil War until the very end.

A full-blooded Seneca, Ely S. Parker, *below,* was one of Grant's military secretaries during the war and commissioner for Indian affairs during his presidency, the first time a Native American had been elevated to such a lofty government post.

A military secretary for Grant during the war and a diplomat during his presidency, Adam Badeau, *above,* was outwardly fawning and obsequious toward Grant, while secretly envious and resentful.

Grant with Orville E. Babcock, *right,* and Adam Badeau, *left.* After serving as wartime aide-de-camp to Grant, Babcock became his most confidential secretary in the White House but betrayed him with his duplicitous behavior during the Whiskey Ring investigation.

William Tecumseh Sherman in his later years. He revered Grant as a soldier but grew increasingly critical of his Reconstruction policies as president.

Philip H. Sheridan, *standing at left,* with his officers, including George Armstrong Custer, *seated at far right.* The high-spirited Sheridan overcame the early superiority that the Confederacy enjoyed in cavalry warfare.

For Grant, Benjamin F. Butler epitomized
the inept political generals who made
his life miserable during the war.

General John A. McClernand tried to trade on his
friendship with Abraham Lincoln to supplant Grant
in the military campaign against Vicksburg.

A brilliant armchair theorist, Henry W. Halleck
lacked Grant's visceral sense of battle and was often
two-faced in his treatment of his star general.

Robert E. Lee, *seated*, with eldest son Custis, *left*, and aide Walter Taylor, *right*. Lee's titanic struggle against Grant in Virginia formed the climax of the war.

Grant's old friend James Longstreet was Robert E. Lee's most dependable commander and showed genuine courage after the war in supporting Reconstruction.

Traditionally called "the last photograph of Abraham Lincoln from life," this picture was taken on February 5, 1865, two days after the president met with the three Confederate peace commissioners aboard the *River Queen,* anchored off Hampton Roads. The image shows a crack in the original negative.

Mary Lincoln's high-handed treatment of Julia Grant led the Grants to rebuff an invitation from the president to attend Ford's Theatre the night Abraham Lincoln was assassinated.

Abraham Lincoln and his son Tad glancing at a photo album on February 9, 1864, one month before Grant met the president at the White House. Lincoln brought Tad along when he visited Grant at City Point, Virginia.

Grant clashed with rough, brawling President Andrew Johnson, *above,*
over his dismissal of Secretary of War Edwin M. Stanton, *below,* a
controversial action that contributed to Johnson's impeachment.

President Grant, Julia, and their youngest son, Jesse, relaxing in 1872 at their cottage by the sea at Long Branch, New Jersey, often dubbed "the first summer White House."

The photograph of Julia Grant shows the remarkable force of her personality during the years of her husband's presidency, when she threw lavish dinners at the White House. Because she was cross-eyed, she always preferred to pose in profile.

Grant was a doting father to his four children. *Clockwise from top left:* Frederick Dent Grant, Ellen "Nellie" Grant, Jesse Root Grant Jr., and Ulysses S. "Buck" Grant Jr.

As secretary of state for eight years, Hamilton Fish compiled an outstanding record, including settlement of the *Alabama* claims, giving the administration much-needed stability.

As attorney general, the crusading Amos T. Akerman supervised the foremost accomplishment of Grant's administration, crushing the Ku Klux Klan by bringing indictments against thousands of members.

In his reelection campaign, Grant had no more ardent supporter than Frederick Douglass, who insisted that "to Grant more than any other man the Negro owes his enfranchisement."

The presidential standard-bearer of the Liberal Republicans and the Democrats, the eccentric Horace Greeley, *right,* urged a more conciliatory attitude toward the white South. Grant mocked the New York newspaper editor as "a genius without common sense."

In the 1872 presidential race, Susan B. Anthony cast an illegal vote for Grant—the only time she ever voted for a president—as a way to protest the absence of female suffrage.

As the imperious chairman of the Senate Foreign
Relations Committee, Charles Sumner defied
Grant's proposal to annex Santo Domingo.
Grant protested that Sumner "has abused
me in a way I have never suffered
from any other man living!"

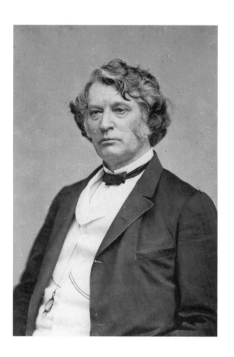

The flamboyant, dandyish Roscoe
Conkling, senator from New York,
was one of Grant's most faithful
champions in the Senate. The
president richly rewarded him with
patronage jobs in his state.

During his round-the-world tour, Grant met with Li Hung-chang, China's northern viceroy, in 1879 and pioneered a new role for ex-presidents by helping to mediate China's dispute with Japan over the Loo Choo (Ryukyu) Islands.

When Grant returned from his global tour, he sought an unprecedented third term as president. The cartoonist portrays a drunken Grant trying to stagger from a lamppost marked "2nd term" to one marked "3rd term." A policeman standing in the doorway wonders cynically, "Will he make it?"

FERDINAND WARD.—Photographed by F. E. Pearsall.

This engraving shows Ferdinand Ward in the early 1880s, at the time he swindled Grant and left him destitute.

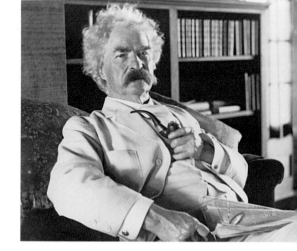

Operating as a publisher, Mark Twain helped to rescue Grant from poverty by boosting the royalty offered for his *Personal Memoirs* by an earlier editor. Twain called Grant "the most lovable great child in the world."

Less than a month from his death, a stoic Grant pens his *Personal Memoirs* on the porch at Mount McGregor, the fatal tumor on his neck shrouded by a scarf.

Porter, Sedgwick "seemed particularly cheerful and hopeful that morning, and looked the picture of buoyant life and vigorous health."[71] Shortly after Grant rode off, Sedgwick, a smart, good-natured, and much beloved bachelor, affectionately nicknamed "Uncle John," mocked his men for being afraid of Confederate snipers taking potshots at them. They didn't have to worry, he insisted, because the rebels "couldn't hit an elephant at this distance."[72] These were his last words as he toppled over dead, struck by a marksman's bullet to the head. At first, Grant could hardly take in the horrendous news. "Is he really dead?" he asked twice. Although he named the popular Horatio Wright to lead the Sixth Corps, he considered Sedgwick's loss irreparable. "His loss to this army is greater than the loss of a whole division of troops," he believed.[73]

At 9:30 a.m. on May 10, Grant prepared for a furious onslaught. He dashed off a telegram to Halleck with a vintage statement: "I shall take no backward step." He ordered another fifty rounds of ammunition for each of his one hundred thousand men. Still, he sounded less cocky than before and certainly more modest about thrashing Lee: "We can maintain ourselves at least and in the end beat Lee's Army I believe."[74] Grant probed for a chink in Lee's extended line and assailed his center, only to be thrown back with heavy losses. During this long day of bloody mayhem, he moved his headquarters tent to the margin of a wood. One adjutant remembered standing twenty feet from Grant when a shell "passed 3 inches from his ear." Without missing a beat, Grant told his new aide, Captain Peter Hudson, "Hudson, get that shell. Let's see what kind of ammunition they are using."[75] With his odd composure, Grant smoked and wrote dispatches, seemingly unaware of having barely escaped death. One wounded Wisconsin soldier, borne on a stretcher past Grant, observed approvingly, "Ulysses don't scare worth a damn."[76]

It was Grant's eternal assumption that when his adversary strengthened one part of his line, he weakened another. So upon learning that Lee had buttressed his left, Grant ordered an afternoon attack at the enemy's center under Hancock's direction. The fighting focused on an elevated spot called the Mule Shoe, named after its shape and the way it projected forward from Confederate breastworks. It was well guarded by artillery. Grant had long been frustrated by standard tactical manuals, translated from the French and poorly suited to wooded terrain. Now Colonel Emory Upton of New York, a West Point graduate and iconoclastic student of military lore, devised an ingenious solution. He took twelve regiments, arranged them into four lines, and had them race across open ground toward the Mule Shoe, howling like men possessed. The novelty of his method was this: when the first line reached the Confederate defenses, it split left and right, opening a path for the second line to rush in and take up the assault; this line, in turn, splayed left and right, creating an opening for the third and fourth in succession. To speed up the charge, soldiers were told to withhold fire until they reached the Confederate defenders. Badeau recalled this tour de force of tactical innovation: "Allowing nothing to stop them, creeping on hands and knees over all obstacles, even under fire, they climbed the hill and completely broke the lines in their front, capturing an entire brigade of infantry and a battery of artillery."[77] A thousand startled rebel prisoners fell into Union hands.

This major success was squandered when Upton didn't receive timely aid, the division assigned to support him having faced heavy artillery fire. Reluctant to subdue their fighting spirit, Grant was heartbroken to order a retreat by Upton's regiments, which had sacrificed a quarter of their men, with Upton himself severely wounded. As in the Wilderness, the forest burst into flames, frying to death many soldiers disabled on the battlefield. Before leaving Washington, Grant had been authorized to promote officers in the field for special acts of gallantry. On the spot, he made Upton a brevet brigadier general and in later years paid tribute to his sterling achievement at Spotsylvania. "He gave us the first really American system of tactics, a want our Army had long felt . . . his system of tactics adopted by the War Department made intelligent operations possible on any kind of ground."[78]

Of the late-afternoon attack against the Confederate line, Congressman Washburne wrote in his diary: "Genls. Grant and Meade . . . rode on to a ridge in front of the timber where the battle was raging. It was at its height just as the sun was going down. The roar of musketry and cannon and the cheers of our men as they rushed to the charge made an impression never to be effaced. It has been a day of continuous fighting and our losses have been heavy, but we have gained decided advantages."[79] In the waning daylight, other forays against Confederate positions miscarried. Despite the bright spot of Upton's tactics, it had been a rough day for Grant, marred by faulty coordination among commanders. He had insisted that Meade would lead the Army of the Potomac, but it was hard for him not to interfere and the awkward arrangement impaired operations. Nevertheless, Grant asserted that Meade had met his "most sanguine expectations" and a few days later recommended his promotion to major general in the regular army, even though it turned out no vacancies currently existed.[80]

That night, briefing a reporter on the day's action, Grant struck a rueful tone. "We have had hard fighting to-day, and I am sorry to say we have not accomplished much. We have lost a good many men, and I suppose that I shall be blamed for it." He struggled to augment public confidence without raising unrealistic expectations. "I do not know any way to put down this rebellion and restore the authority of the Government except by fighting, and fighting means that men must be killed. If the people of this country expect that the war can be conducted to a successful issue in any other way than fighting, they must get somebody other than myself to command the army."[81] Once again Grant showed well-tuned political instincts and found the right voice, honest and forthright, for addressing the northern public. By now, Rawlins had become a second Grant who internalized his tenacity and relentless sense of forward motion. "Our progress towards Richmond is slow," he wrote to his wife, "but we are on the way, and do not propose, unless some disaster overtakes us, ever taking a step backwards."[82]

The next morning, May 11, cold and rainy after two weeks of broiling weather, Grant enjoyed a spartan breakfast: a tiny piece of beef, cooked well enough to drain any juice from it, and black coffee. Around 8:30 a.m. he stood before his tent, smoking a cigar, and bid farewell to Washburne, who was returning to Washington. Washburne requested a message to take back to the capital— something to allay the anxiety of Lincoln and Stanton. Afraid of stirring false hopes, Grant hesitated. Then he disappeared into his tent and penned a letter to Halleck. Ely Parker said Grant wrote it on a tree stump, his head wreathed in cigar smoke that he swatted away with his hand. After Washburne left, Grant's staff examined a copy of the letter and found nothing exceptional. Grant referred to eleven generals and twenty thousand soldiers killed, wounded, or missing since crossing the Rapidan, while he had taken more than four thousand prisoners. Then came an immortal line that would be emblazoned in the press and trail him forever: "[I] propose to fight it out on this line if it takes me all summer."[83] In an artful piece of editing, Grant struck out the word "me," which might have sounded vain; that deletion turned him into an impersonal force of nature. Grant didn't realize the force of his line until it shouted from newspaper headlines several days later. Nothing since the "unconditional surrender" line at Fort Donelson had gripped the public imagination quite so powerfully.

Grant's words created a sensation in Washington. As Noah Brooks wrote, "Washington had broken loose with a tremendous demonstration of joy . . . There was something like delirium in the air. Everybody seemed to think that the war was coming to an end right away."[84] When crowds gathered at the White House, Lincoln uttered the famous line that had now become a watchword, a battle cry. A month later at a Philadelphia fair, he dilated upon Grant's theme: "Speaking of the present campaign, General Grant is reported to have said, 'I am going through on this line if it takes all summer.' I say we are going through on this line if it takes three years more."[85] Still, if the words delivered a needed fillip to northern spirits, they also risked fostering euphoric expectations. "The people are too sanguine," Lincoln lamented to a reporter. "They expect too much at once."[86]

Amid steady rain on May 11, Grant meditated his next step against Lee. The timing and place of his subsequent assault may have been dictated by a lapse in the seeming clairvoyance of Lee, who received intelligence that made him suspect Grant would suddenly pull out and march toward Richmond. To prepare for such a move, he withdrew twenty-two cannon from the Mule Shoe. When a rebel deserter alerted Grant to this news, he decided to attack the spot around daylight the next morning.

To lead the massive onslaught he selected Winfield Scott Hancock, the very image of a romantic, dashing officer, so high-spirited in battle that the press, taking a hint from McClellan, anointed him "Hancock the Superb."[87] In the view of one California soldier, Hancock was "the *beau ideal* of a soldier, blue-eyed, fair-haired Saxon, strong, well-proportioned and manly, broad-chested, full and compact."[88] Sheridan praised "his quick apprehension, his physical courage," and "soldierly personality."[89] Grant and Hancock had attended West Point together and served as Mexican War comrades. Grant admired the noble, aggressive way he dove into the thick of fighting, rallying his men by personal example. Hancock's renown had been enhanced by beating back Pickett's Charge from behind Cemetery Ridge at Gettysburg. By the end of the year, Grant would come to believe that Hancock, a Democrat, had been corrupted by political ambitions. "I have known [Hancock] for forty years," he said late in life. "He is a weak, vain man. He is the most selfish man I know. He could never endure to have anyone else receive any credit."[90]

Such cynicism was still far in the future on the foggy dawn of May 12 when Grant ordered Hancock and Burnside at 4 a.m. to lead "a prompt and vigorous attack."[91] Sitting around a campfire in a dell, pelted by sheets of rain and wrapped in an overcoat, Grant awaited the telltale musketry rattle that heralded the start of offensive operations. Porter portrayed Grant as "in excellent spirits" and even "jocose" that morning.[92] The charge came around 4:30 a.m., an uphill climb for Hancock and his men, who had to negotiate a marsh and wend their way through thickly wooded territory. They pressed toward the bulging Mule Shoe in constant rain, in early gray light, as morning mist helped to screen their movements. When they emerged into a clearing before the breastworks, fifteen thousand strong, they let loose a tremendous cheer and surged forward without firing a shot. One Union soldier recalled how "the great mass of men, with a rush like a cyclone, sprang upon the entrenchments and swarmed over."[93] Here, in a scene of wild turmoil, the two armies collided at such close quarters that they bashed each other to death with rifle butts and bayonets. In an hour of frenetic fighting, Hancock captured four thousand prisoners plus thirty cannon. Back in the dell, enthusiastic riders galloped up with news, eliciting cheers from Grant's staff, while Grant "sat unmoved upon his camp-chair, giving his constant thoughts to devising methods for making the victory complete."[94]

The captured division belonged to Major General Edward Johnson, soon hauled into Grant's presence as a prisoner. Tarnished with mud, prongs of hair jutting from a torn felt hat, Johnson must have been startled by the cordial greeting from Grant, who remembered him from the Mexican War. "How do you do?" said Grant, shaking his hand. "It is a long time since we last met." Continuing in this courteous manner, Grant offered Johnson a cigar and placed a camp chair for him by the fire. "Be seated, and we will do all in our power to make you as comfortable as possible."[95] The two men chatted, made no mention of the overwhelming conflict in progress, and confined their talk to reminiscences.

After Hancock's men plowed through the first line of Confederate entrenchments, they chased their opponents down woodland paths to a second. Over early morning breakfast, Lee heard the ominous clatter of guns from the Mule Shoe, realized he had misread Grant's intentions, and rode Traveller hastily toward the fighting. He encountered terrified soldiers, streaking back in chaotic flight. "Hold on!" Lee shouted, seeking to stem the rout. "Your comrades need your services." The terrified men refused to heed his admonition. "Shame on you men; shame on you!" he cried in desperation.[96] Lee was every bit as stubborn as Grant. Repeating his Wilderness performance, he hurried to organize a counterattack that would expose him to danger until his men shouted, "General Lee to the rear!" and he grudgingly obeyed.[97] The large force he assembled drove Union troops back to the front line they'd breached. Here Hancock, having seized Confederate defenses, turned them around to stop advancing rebel forces. The fight degenerated into a vicious stalemate that persisted for at least eighteen hours. With extraordinary zeal, Lee made five attempts to regain the front line he had lost and each time was flung back by Hancock's gallant determination.

Periodically Grant mounted little Jeff Davis and rode to observation posts to survey the bloodbath at the Mule Shoe. Nearby was a secluded clearing where zigzagging trenches formed a sharp angle known in historical annals as the Bloody Angle. As an emblem of the sheer hell of war, few places surpass this claustrophobic spot, its ground strangely corrugated by earthworks. Trenches filled with a soupy mixture of rain, mud, and blood, leading some wounded men to drown. Troops fought hand-to-hand atop the parapets in such squalid disorder that they often stood on dead men as they battled. One Massachusetts soldier remembered dead and wounded rebels "piled up in heaps three or four deep."[98] Each new wave of oncoming men trampled comrades fallen before them until the ground grew slippery with spilled blood. Frantic soldiers thrust swords and bayonets through gaps in the log parapets, killing foes only partly visible until a welter of mangled limbs accumulated. The incessant musket fire shredded trees and shrubs into twigs, leading Porter to comment memorably, "We had not only shot down an army, but also a forest." For Porter, the savagery "was probably the most desperate engagement in the history of modern warfare."[99] Union forces had managed to capture three thousand prisoners.

For those unlucky enough to fight there, the day furnished ghoulish vignettes they would never forget. As Charles Dana stared into a trench, "the leg of a man was lifted up from the pool and the mud dripped off his boot. It was so unexpected, so horrible, that for a moment we were stunned."[100] The jumble of dead bodies made it hard to extract the wounded, who lay gasping just below them. As Oliver Wendell Holmes Jr. wrote, the "wounded [were] often writhing under superincumbent dead."[101] It was long after dark when Confederate soldiers withdrew, leaving many dead to be buried in trenches where they had perished.

Grant interpreted the day's fighting as a victory and nominated Hancock for brigadier general in the regular army. In a telegram to Halleck, he noted that the Union army had captured an entire division, brigade, and regiment while keeping its own units intact. To Julia he boasted that the "enemy were really whipped yesterday."[102] Be that as it may, Grant had incurred heavy casualties since crossing the Rapidan: thirty-two thousand men killed, wounded, or missing, surpassing the total for all Union armies combined in any previous week of the war; the corresponding Confederate toll came to eighteen thousand. At the same time he had severely depleted the officer corps of Lee's army, taking, killing, or wounding twenty of the fifty-seven corps, division, and brigade commanders—irremediable losses for Lee. If Grant's main objective was to grind down the Army of Northern Virginia, he had made an effective if costly beginning. One Louisiana soldier voiced a dispiriting thought that began to sink in across the South: "We have met a man this time who either does not know when he is whipped, or who cares not if he loses his whole Army, so that he may accomplish an end."[103] Lee was sobered by his encounter with Grant. When he heard officers castigating Grant for "butchering" his men, Lee didn't let the comment pass unnoticed. According to General Henry Heth, he replied, "Gentleman, I think Gen. Grant has managed his affairs remarkably well up to the present time." As Heth noted, Grant "was wearing us out and starving us out. He hammered at us continually. He knew we couldn't replace our men and that he could."[104]

The heavy rain caused a two-day gap in the fighting, which Grant devoted to the sad duty of interring the dead and carting off the wounded to temporary field hospitals. Roads were churned into a muddy lather by the downpour, and by the night of May 14, Porter wrote, Grant was "a mass of mud from head to foot, his uniform being scarcely recognizable." At the same time, Porter noted that Grant was "scrupulously careful . . . about the cleanliness of his linen and his person," washed his own clothes, and sat down in a sawed-off barrel to bathe.[105] The pause in fighting gave Grant time to reflect and he seemed chastened by the barbaric intensity of the fighting. Pouring out his thoughts to Julia, he paid tribute to the indomitable grit of Confederate troops, which had clearly astounded him. The enemy, he reported, "are fighting with great desperation entrenching themselves in every position they take up . . . The world has never seen so bloody or so protracted a battle as the one being fought and I hope never will again . . . As bad as it is they have fought for [their cause] with a gallantry worthy of a better."[106]

CHAPTER NINETEEN

Heavens Hung in Black

ROM THE TIME Grant's men filed across the Rapidan, he assumed Ben Butler and his Army of the James would synchronize their actions with him, pushing up the James River, seizing territory south of Richmond, and wrecking critical railroads. Butler fielded a force of thirty thousand men, supplemented by five ironclads and seventeen gunboats. Unfortunately, he moved slowly, exhibited undue caution, and flubbed his chance for a lightning strike, permitting his opponent to rush reinforcements up from the Carolinas. Confederates had seeded the James River with hundreds of torpedoes, making progress treacherous. Both Richmond and Petersburg were insufficiently manned by troops and, had Butler acted with dispatch, he might have snared the Confederate capital while Lee was distracted farther north. Some historians believe Butler's failure to capitalize on this unmatched opportunity may have prolonged the war by nearly a year.

By mid-May, Grant's grand strategy, featuring simultaneous movements of his far-flung armies, appeared poised to reap huge rewards. His forward motion against Lee was temporarily arrested by endless rain, making Virginia's roads impassable. But en route to Atlanta, Sherman ousted Johnston from Dalton, Georgia; Sheridan smashed up major railroads serving Richmond; and Butler captured the outer defenses of Fort Darling, below Richmond. Then General Beauregard, exploiting Butler's laxity, defeated him decisively at Drewry's Bluff, driving him back down the river to a thin neck of land formed by the confluence of the James and Appomattox Rivers. In a bold stroke, Beauregard laid trenches across the land strip until Butler's army at Bermuda Hundred was, in Grant's acerbic image, "as completely shut off from further operations directly against Richmond as if it had been in a bottle strongly corked."[1] Later on, Grant regretted such harsh language against Butler, but his plan to trap Lee between his army and Butler's or starve his supply lines had been rudely upended. So neatly had Beauregard neutralized Butler that he could release several thousand soldiers to beef up Lee's army. Grant wearily told Halleck that Butler's army had failed to ruin the railroad running south of Richmond: "Under these circumstances I think it advisable to have all of it here except enough to keep a foothold at City Point."[2] A British soldier fighting with the Army of the James delivered this blunt assessment of Beast Butler: "There is no confidence felt in the *beast* at all."[3]

Around this time, another keystone of Grant's overarching design seemed to crumble. To curry favor with German Americans, Lincoln had appointed Franz Sigel as a brigadier general early in the war. Born in Germany, trained as a military officer, the versatile Sigel had worked as a journalist, teacher, and politician. A striking-looking man with high cheekbones and a fierce gaze, he was dedicated to the Union cause but destitute of military talent. Grant had dispatched him to the Shenandoah Valley with 6,500 men to harry Lee's supply base at Staunton. Instead, on May 15 at the battle of New Market, a smaller Confederate force under John C. Breckinridge trounced Sigel, aided by 250 cadets from the nearby Virginia Military Institute, sounding the death knell for Sigel's military career. "If you expect anything from him you will be mistaken," Halleck told Grant. "He will do nothing but run. He never did anything else. The Secty of War proposes to put Genl [David] Hunter in his place."[4] Grant heartily endorsed the move, which soon occurred.

The northern mood began to sour again and Noah Brooks speculated that the populace, "like a spoiled child," craved instant success, not a maddening deadlock.[5] If inspired by Grant's pluck, citizens were dismayed by the interminable casualty rolls. As Oliver Wendell Holmes Jr. wrote on May 16, "These nearly two weeks have contained all of fatigue & horror that war can furnish."[6] Grant knew he didn't enjoy the option of inaction. By the night of the sixteenth, with roads rapidly drying, he gave the signal for another round of dawn fighting at Spotsylvania. While he and Lee had absorbed reinforcements, Lee was strengthened by combat veterans while Grant had to deal with raw troops. If he was still beguiled by the notion of luring Lee to fight in the open, on the morning of May 18 Lee did not oblige, staying put behind his defenses as Grant attacked. The advancing Union infantry was raked by such blistering musket and artillery fire that by midmorning Grant called off the attack. All his maneuvering had come to naught, and he decided to abandon Spotsylvania.

The failure to ram through the Confederate line with frontal assaults inspired second-guessing and soul-searching on Grant's staff. Cyrus Comstock had been the supreme advocate of a fighting style he called "Smash 'em up! Smash 'em up!" Rawlins was so disgusted by this blunt approach, said James H. Wilson, that he "grew pale, and his form became almost convulsed with anger," as he inveighed against a strategy that was "the murderous policy of military incompetents."[7] Despite unstinting faith in Grant, Lincoln was agitated by the lengthy lists of dead soldiers. House Speaker Schuyler Colfax discovered him pacing his office, "his long arms behind his back, his dark features contracted still more with gloom." The distraught president let loose a terrible cri de coeur: "Why do we suffer reverses after reverses! Could we have avoided this terrible, bloody war! . . . Is it ever to end!"[8]

On May 19, in a rare offensive thrust against Grant, Lee unloaded a surprise attack in the late afternoon, which turned bloody for both sides. As usual, Grant perceived opportunity where others saw blind terror, instructing Porter to "ride to the point of attack . . . and urge upon the commanders . . . not only to check the advance of the enemy, but to take the offensive and destroy them if possible."[9] By nightfall, Confederate troops were driven back in what proved Lee's last offensive attack; henceforth he would exploit the advantages of fixed defensive positions. One feature of that sanguinary day has received insufficient attention: the bravery of black soldiers under Brigadier General Edward Ferrero. "It was the first time at the East when colored troops had been engaged in any important battle," wrote Badeau, "and the display of soldierly qualities obtained a frank acknowledgment from both troops and commanders, not all of whom had before been willing to look upon negroes as comrades."[10]

Unbowed, Grant decreed a secret midnight march south by his left flank, ordering Hancock "to get as far towards Richmond on the line of the Fredericksburg railroad, as he can make, fighting the enemy in whatever force he may find him."[11] For Grant, the important thing was the constant, inexorable push southward. Finding his progress delayed by slow-moving artillery, he shipped back one hundred pieces to Washington. He played a cat-and-mouse game with Lee, even pretending to commit an error that might tempt his rival to pounce. He deliberately kept Hancock's corps apart from the rest, dangling it as isolated bait that Lee might want to come out and snatch, but the stratagem didn't work.

For the next few days, energized by sunny weather, Grant and his army headed toward the railroad junction at Hanovertown, marching through prosperous, open countryside with elegant houses flanked by abundant fields of grain and tobacco. The prosperous air was misleading, for the region had been drained of life, abandoned by able-bodied men and left to the care of women, the old, and the infirm. As happened after the Wilderness fighting, Grant's dearest hope was to cover twenty-five miles fast enough to overtake Lee and insert his army between the Army of Northern Virginia and Richmond. Again aided by interior lines, the agile, alert Lee beat Grant to the North Anna River on May 22, digging in on its south bank. Never short of confidence vis-à-vis Grant, he predicted to his staff surgeon, "If I can get one more pull at him, I will defeat him."[12] Clearly Grant faced a far more self-assured rival than he had ever confronted before and one who seldom made mistakes.

During his race south, Grant lingered at Guiney's Station, throwing up tents on the ground of a country estate. When he paid his respects to the lady of the house, she told him that, by an extraordinary coincidence, Stonewall Jackson had died there two years earlier. Striking the conciliatory note he would sound at Appomattox, Grant complimented Jackson as a man and soldier. "I can understand fully the admiration your people have for him."[13] The woman sobbed in describing Jackson's last hour and Grant posted sentries around the house to shield it from harm. As courtly as any southern gentleman, he didn't force his way into the house but sat outside on the verandah.

Grant was no less courteous to his men. One Massachusetts regiment was marching down a railroad line when they spotted Grant sitting on a flatcar, devouring a ham bone. They let loose a cheer that he only acknowledged with a friendly wave of the bone before gnawing it again. As ever, Grant refused to parade his superior rank, and his skillful handling of people, no less than his military acumen, accounted for much of his success. As Charles Francis Adams Jr. wrote, "Grant had this army as firmly in hand as ever he had that of the Southwest. He has effected this simply by the exercise of tact and good taste."[14]

Having crossed the North Anna River first, Lee had established a strong position with troops who had recently opposed Butler and Sigel but were no longer needed against them. As Grant's men began to ford the river on May 23, they were "violently attacked," he informed Halleck, "but handsomely repulsed the assault without much loss to us."[15] The North Anna was a wide river with high bluffs and shallow enough that soldiers walked across in waist-high water. Grant's engineers also threw down pontoons and seized a wooden bridge with such electrifying speed that retreating Confederates jumped into the water, many drowning. That night, Lee's army dug fresh trenches and hardened their positions, and these fortifications again functioned as the great equalizer against superior numbers.

On May 24, Grant found his forces arrayed in a perilous configuration. The left and right wings of his army had crossed the North Anna, but with Burnside, in the center, having failed to do so, he feared Lee might pick off one wing of his divided army at will. In beautiful, summery weather, Grant's men spent the day finding new places to traverse the river. At this critical juncture, Lee was stretched out on a cot, laid low by intestinal problems as he meditated a knockout blow against Grant. His subordinates failed to capitalize on the opportunity presented by Grant's fragmented army. Lee grasped the danger of allowing Grant to press him back against the gates of Richmond. "We must strike them a blow," he told his commanders in frustration. "We must never let them pass us again."[16] Temporarily Lee retired Traveller and moved by ambulance for several days.

Spent from punishing night marches, battle smoke, sleep deprivation, and never-ending skirmishes, Grant's soldiers were dazed by the strain of the Overland Campaign. The cumulative pressures overwhelmed many, and Captain Oliver Wendell Holmes Jr. said that "many a man has gone crazy since this campaign began from the terrible pressure on mind & body."[17] "The men in the ranks did not look as they did when they entered the Wilderness," another soldier recalled. "Their uniforms were now torn, ragged, and stained with mud; the men had grown thin and haggard. The experience of those twenty days seemed to have added twenty years to their age."[18] Despite this outward change, Grant had wrought a profound alteration in the soldiers' psyche, making them believe in themselves. "This army has learned to believe that it is sure of victory," Dana told Stanton. "Even our officers have ceased to regard Lee as an invincible military genius."[19] The soldiers knew their movements weren't haphazard but integral parts of a well-thought-out plan. If anything, Grant seemed dangerously overconfident, telling Halleck, "Lee's Army is really whipped . . . I feel that our success over Lee's Army is already insured."[20]

Leavening the somber mood for Grant was the welcome return of a tanned, healthy-looking Sheridan after his memorable cavalry raid. With the exuberant, vivid gestures of a stage actor, he described for Grant the many clashes he had experienced. Darkly dramatic one moment, he burst into gales of laughter the next. The popular Sheridan had drawn off so many Confederate cavalry to cope with his raiders that the four thousand wagons of Grant's supply train had passed virtually unscathed.

The next day, Grant's men probed Lee's lines, finding them well defended and bristling with sharpened timbers. Grant despaired of breaching this barricade and again moved his army south, scuttling to the left, a move that kept his supply lines open by water. Lee knew his inability to inflict heavy damage on Grant's army meant a steady creep southward of the two armies toward Richmond, a move ultimately cataclysmic to the Confederacy. Grant's men tore up railroad tracks that supported Lee's army, heating and twisting crossties into crazy shapes to render them useless. Grant was greeted warmly by his soldiers, who were relieved he hadn't launched them in a suicidal rush against Lee's defenses on the North Anna. Grant's force was boosted by forty thousand reinforcements, replenishing men he lost, while the ten thousand Lee received didn't compensate for his losses.

Striding along in fine, clear weather, the Army of the Potomac tramped across streams and swamps as it penetrated to Hanovertown, seventeen miles from the Confederate capital. Richmond's citizens felt cornered as they eyed Grant's approaching movement and listened for artillery fire that might portend Armageddon for their city. Once again Lee was girding to meet Grant as a heated cavalry clash engaged the two armies. By the night of May 29, Grant's army had inched forward to Totopotomoy Creek, nine miles northeast of Richmond, where the Army of Northern Virginia stood aligned for battle.

At this point, Lee experienced something akin to panic. "We must destroy this army of Grant's before he gets to James River," he confided to a commander. "If he gets there it will become a siege, and then it will be a mere question of time."[21] Gradually Lee's army drifted south toward a place called Cold Harbor, where he hoped to intercept Grant if he made a sudden run for the James River. The name was derived from English roadside inns that advertised overnight stays without hot meals. True to this tradition, a tavern occupied the village crossroads. It was clear that this strategic spot, the nexus of five converging roads, would become a flashpoint in any looming fight.

On May 31, in a desperate cavalry conflict, Sheridan defeated the rebels near

Cold Harbor and Grant advised him to hold the place at all hazards. Lee's army had taken up positions north of the Chickahominy River. Grant wanted to herd his foes south of the river, while ravaging Richmond's northern railroad links and preventing Lee from sending men to curb Hunter's raids in the Shenandoah Valley. Riding beside Rawlins to Cold Harbor, Grant suffered one of his few recorded losses of temper when he spied a teamster flogging his horses. With his exquisite sensitivity for animals, Grant spurred his bay horse Egypt toward the perpetrator, shaking a clenched fist at him. "What does this conduct mean, you scoundrel?" Grant yelled. "Take this man in charge, and have him tied up to a tree for six hours as a punishment for his brutality."[22]

There was now an expectant sense that here, eight miles northeast of Richmond, a climactic battle was about to unfold and Grant's army might bulldoze its way through Lee's line and thunder straight into the outskirts of town. "A few days will solve the question of Richmond," Rawlins prophesied, "and whether a long siege, or a sharp decisive battle is to terminate it."[23] Soon after dawn on June 1, Lee's army administered a four-hour drubbing to Sheridan, who held out until Horatio Wright's corps arrived around 9 a.m. Late in the afternoon, Grant made successful forays against the rebels, who tried multiple times that night to recapture lost ground. Although the fighting had been savage that day, with the Union killed and wounded numbering two thousand, some tactical gains had been achieved. As Badeau observed, "The ground won, on the 1st of June, was of the highest consequence to the national army; it cost two thousand men in killed and wounded, but it secured the roads to the James, and almost outflanked Lee."[24]

As his army dealt with pitiless heat and choking dust—Oliver Wendell Holmes Jr. said he was "nearly dropping from my saddle with fatigue"—Grant revolved battle plans in his mind.[25] Charles Francis Adams Jr. described him "thinking very hard and looking abstracted, pulling his beard, whittling and smoking."[26] Lee fought on home turf, having bested McClellan on the peninsula two years earlier, while for Grant the swampy terrain of ravines and thickets was terra incognita. When Grant's brother Orvil arrived in camp, he brought along a friend, F. M. Pixley, who offered a portrait of Grant's smoldering intensity.

> At the evening mess table I met Gen. Grant, and after a very hasty
> meal, I watched him for an hour as he sat by the camp fire. He is a
> small man, with a square resolute thinking face. He sat silent among

the gentlemen of his staff, and my first impression was that he was moody, dull and unsocial. I afterwards found him pleasant, genial and agreeable. He keeps his own counsel, padlocks his mouth, while his countenance in battle or repose . . . indicates nothing—that is gives no expression of his feelings and no evidence of his intentions. He smokes almost constantly, and . . . has a habit of whittling with a small knife. He cuts a small stick into small chips, making nothing . . . There is no glitter or parade about him. To me he seems but an earnest business man.[27]

On the night of June 1, Grant pondered his next move. The northern public wanted bold action, not excuses. Keen to steal a jump on the enemy, Grant had two corps at Cold Harbor and a third expected at daybreak on the morrow. Lee had not had time to prepare elaborate defenses. Quick, decisive action, Grant thought, might produce a dramatic breakthrough to Richmond, routing the Confederate government. The alternative was to shuffle farther south, below the James River, in the neighborhood of Petersburg, and link up with Butler's army. Grant feared, however, that the northern public might quarrel with any delay as reminiscent of George McClellan's failed strategy. Writing to Julia at 9 p.m., Grant sounded shaken and uncertain, not like himself. He informed her the rebels were "making a desperate fight" and that he wouldn't see her and the children until the campaign had ended. He concluded on an atypically bleak note: "With the night booming of Artillery and musketry I do not feel much like writing you so you must excuse a short letter this time."[28]

On June 2, the weather was sweltering. Grant and his staff were quartered near Bethesda Church, and its pews were taken outside to provide seating for them before torrential rains drove them indoors. The idyllic scene gave scant warning of the disaster ahead. Grant had hoped for a dawn attack against Lee, but then put it off twice because of delayed troop movements, wrangling commanders, and hungry men exhausted from nocturnal marches. Grant wanted to make one last effort to flush Lee from behind miles of trenches and log parapets, forcing him into the open. In retrospect, it would seem a fool's errand. At Cold Harbor, Lee inhabited swampy terrain that played to his strong suit, his men crouching behind gullies and thickets that interposed natural barriers. The enforced delay in Grant's offensive enabled Lee's men to perfect a labyrinth of trenches that would defy any forward movement by the Army of the Potomac.

These defensive advantages more than offset the federal edge of 109,000 men versus 59,000 Confederates. To maximize his chances, Lee even stripped men from field hospitals.

Nobody underestimated the perils awaiting the Union army the next morning. As in many Civil War battles, fatalistic soldiers penned their names and addresses on snippets of paper, fastened to the backs of their coats, in case their corpses had to be identified. Grant believed that bloody warfare since the Wilderness had debilitated Confederate morale, making him willing to risk a colossal gamble, a frontal assault that would pierce a hole in Lee's line. He would throw three corps under Hancock, Wright, and William F. "Baldy" Smith against Lee's right, hoping to destroy that portion of the enemy army and blast an opening to Richmond. He bet big on a climactic battle that would obliterate Lee's army and end the war. He may also have hoped a resounding victory would secure the coming election for Lincoln. Finally, he may have feared that if fighting lasted into summer, hot weather and disease would decimate his army.

At 4:30 on the misty morning of June 3, sixty thousand Union soldiers dashed toward the center and right of the long Confederate line, braving a hail of musket fire and artillery that rained thickly down upon them. Some federal units had transient success, taking the first line of rifle pits and prisoners, but these bright spots were soon dwarfed by calamitous losses. Thwarted by marshy land, brush, and woods, the ill-fated charge ran straight into a many-layered defense system that was impenetrable. One journalist evoked the "intricate, zigzagged lines within lines, lines protecting flanks of lines, lines built to enfilade opposite lines . . . works within works and works without works."[29] Not a single Confederate soldier needed to venture outside these well-protected shelters. Meanwhile, Union soldiers, crashing through smoke and flame, proved easy prey for Confederate marksmen who mowed them down in dreadful numbers, turning the battlefield into a charnel house. The air grew dark with rifle bullets, shells, solid shot, and rolling smoke. "It seemed more like a volcanic blast than a battle," one soldier said, "and was just about as destructive."[30] So murderous was the Cold Harbor gunfire that Union soldiers dropped to the ground, using dead bodies of fallen comrades as defensive sandbags. The bulk of the fighting had ended by 7:30 a.m. At eleven that morning, Grant rode out from his rear position to confer directly with his commanders. After listening to their gloomy reports, he suspended further operations a little after noon. His army had paid a fearful price for the misguided assault, losing 7,000 men, mostly in the first

hour, against 1,500 casualties for Lee. In the lacerating verdict of the Confederate general Evander Law, Cold Harbor was "not war but murder."[31] One of Lee's
staff officers sneered at Grant's costly error, calling Cold Harbor "perhaps the
easiest victory ever granted to Confederate arms by the folly of Federal
commanders."[32]

There was plenty of blame to go around Union headquarters. Lee had been
more meticulous in preparation and thorough in reconnaissance than Grant,
who had issued vague orders to Meade. Grant and Meade had neglected to scrutinize the territory with sufficient care and badly coordinated the movements of
squabbling corps commanders. Grant had left the execution to Meade, leading
the latter to criticize him tartly for "honoring the field with his presence only
about one hour in the middle of the day," he grumbled to his wife.[33] Meade
sounded a still more cynical note about Grant: "I think Grant has had his eyes
opened and is willing to admit now that Virginia and Lee's army is not Tennessee and Bragg's army."[34]

It took time for Grant to fathom the full scale of the disaster. When he wired
Halleck at 2 p.m., from a place he called "Coal Harbor," he gave no hint of the
calamity. "Our loss was not severe nor do I suppose the Enemy to have lost heavily."[35] On the same day, writing to Stanton, Dana conveyed no sense of an infamous defeat with atrocious casualties, estimating the Union dead and wounded
at only three thousand.[36] That day Rawlins insisted to his wife that Cold Harbor
had been an "indecisive" battle with equal losses on both sides.[37] Still, by day's
end, many Union commanders grasped that they had lost four or five bluecoats
to every gray uniform. As Grant eventually admitted, with extreme understate-
ment, it was the one attack during the Overland Campaign that "did not inflict
upon the enemy losses to compensate for our own loss."[38]

In time, Cold Harbor became a byword for senseless slaughter, a club with
which Grant was beaten by opponents. It became the theme of every tirade contending that he was a filthy butcher. Lee, who refused to crow about his victory,
was genuinely perplexed as to what had provoked Grant into this supreme blunder. "I do not know what General Grant meant by his attack this morning," he
told a staff officer. "It was too heavy for a feint, yet I hardly think he expected to
break through here."[39]

In his *Memoirs,* Grant expressed special remorse for what had happened: "I
have always regretted that the last assault at Cold Harbor was ever made."[40] But
he didn't describe the scene in any detail. In his antiseptic description of

columns sent into battle, the casual reader derives no sense of the harrowing fighting. The manuscript of his *Memoirs* shows that Grant inserted the famous passage on Cold Harbor as an afterthought. It is written on paper of a darker color with a note Grant appended to his secretary: "Put this in after Cold Harbor. About the time the Army reached the James River probably would be best."[41] The belated incorporation suggests it took courage for Grant to include this blunt indictment of himself. In later years, he admitted that Cold Harbor was the one battle "that I would not fight over again under the circumstances."[42] If Grant's confidence made him an inspirational leader, it could also expose him to catastrophic mistakes engendered by overconfidence.

Some who saw Grant after Cold Harbor sensed a deep sadness. William Wrenshall Smith encountered him returning from the battle and depicted him as "much depressed. He dismounted and took a seat on the stone. What is the situation, I asked? Bad—very bad, he replied."[43] Samuel Beckwith noticed that after Cold Harbor Grant's face developed "a careworn expression that indicated sleepless nights and wearisome days." When he delivered a message to the general's tent, he found him sunk in thought. After absorbing the telegram, Grant sighed. "Beckwith," he said, "the hardest part of this General business is the responsibility for the loss of one's men. I can see no other way out of it, however; we've got to keep at them. But it is hard, very hard, to see all these brave fellows killed and wounded. It means aching hearts back home."[44]

As the nation meditated the death toll at Cold Harbor, the wounded lay squirming in misery on the battlefield next to the bloated, decomposing corpses of deceased comrades. In some places, according to Horace Porter, the ground was carpeted with fallen soldiers wedged so tightly together over thirty- or forty-yard areas that the revolting stench of mortality hung heavy in the blazing heat.[45] Since the slain and injured lay within easy range of snipers on either side, they couldn't be removed until a truce was declared, but this was held up by an unfortunate tussle over military protocol.

Most men stranded in the open were Union soldiers. Hence, on June 5, Grant suggested to Lee that "unarmed men bearing litters" be allowed to gather the dead and wounded during a cease-fire, and he declared his readiness to abide by any method suggested by Lee.[46] The next day, Lee quibbled over technicalities, suggesting these casualties should only be removed under a flag of truce— by which Grant would have to admit tacitly defeat at Cold Harbor. He seemed intent on teaching a lesson to Grant, who promised his stretcher bearers would carry "a white flag and not to attempt to go beyond where we have dead or wounded."[47] Sticking to military etiquette, Lee insisted upon a flag of truce instead of men waving white flags. Finally, at 7 p.m. on June 6, Lee agreed that Grant could send out orderlies to collect soldiers between 8 and 10 p.m. This message didn't reach Grant's headquarters until the allotted time had expired, leaving dead men rotting on the blood-soaked soil. The next morning, Grant regretted to Lee "that all my efforts for alleviating the sufferings of wounded men, left upon the Battle-field have been rendered nugatory."[48] By the time relief crews scoured the field on the night of June 7, all but two wounded soldiers had died as the generals bickered; another 432 men brought into Union lines were already dead. Historians sympathetic to Lee blame Grant in this affair, arguing that his ruffled pride could not accept the flag of truce proffered by Lee. Grant, for his part, blamed Lee's rigidity for the needless loss of life.

Cold Harbor culminated a four-week campaign distinguished by a savagery unseen in the war. Since May 4, the furious crescendo of fighting had produced appalling casualties: sixty-five thousand for the Union side versus thirty-five thousand for Confederates. Though his losses approached the size of Lee's entire army, Grant had inflicted comparable losses on Lee, equivalent to 40 percent of the Army of Northern Virginia. J. F. C. Fuller, the British military historian, and Bruce Catton have pointed out that Cold Harbor did a disservice to Grant's reputation since his armies tended to lose a smaller percentage of their men in battle than those commanded by Lee and most other Civil War generals. No statistical evidence buttresses the charge that Grant was needlessly careless with lives. For all the hand-wringing over Cold Harbor, it was no more disastrous an assault than that conducted by George Pickett under Lee's auspices at Gettysburg, although the death toll was then somewhat lower.[49]

Grant never apologized for the carnage, nor did he find his failure particularly surprising. He had to force Lee into the open, while the latter hid behind breastworks and rifle trenches. Lee "had the advantage of being on the defensive . . . and I had to attack and attack, but every blow I struck weakened him, and when at last he was forced into Richmond it was a far different army from that which menaced Washington and invaded Maryland and Pennsylvania. It was no longer an invading army."[50] Grant was resigned that this method would exact a huge tally in lost lives. "Fighting, hard knocks, only could accomplish the work."[51]

All the bloodshed made it easy to miss the significance of Grant's accomplishment. By steadily pushing Lee eighty miles south, he had robbed him of mobility and prevented him from assuming the offensive. Grant now controlled the direction of the contest, and, if he lost individual battles, he was winning the war. After Cold Harbor, his fighting spirit remained unquenchable and he insisted that "success was only a question of time."[52] He was rankled by charges that, during the Peninsula Campaign of 1862, McClellan took the same army by boat from northern Virginia down to Chesapeake Bay without incurring the grievous losses of the Overland Campaign. His rebuttal was terse: "I captured Lee's army; McClellan didn't."[53] By moving overland, Grant had shielded Washington from harm; had he gone by water, he would have been forced to leave behind ample forces to protect the capital. He cited the irreplaceable losses Lee suffered and the slow, inexorable grinding down of his army. He also took pride in the campaign as a logistical feat in which he moved a train of four thousand wagons "over narrow roads and through a densely wooded country."[54]

It was harrowing to see so many soldiers maimed, disfigured, and killed, and Gouverneur Warren undoubtedly spoke for many when he exclaimed, "For thirty days it has been one funeral procession past me, and it has been too much!"[55] Emory Upton recoiled in horror at Cold Harbor. "I am disgusted with the generalship displayed," he told his sister. "Our men have, in many cases, been foolishly and wantonly slaughtered."[56] The palpable dismay reached right into Lincoln's cabinet. Secretary of the Navy Welles shuddered that Grant had paved the road from Washington to Richmond "with the skulls of Union soldiers."[57] Even northern politicians advocating a more muscular military style blanched at Cold Harbor. "For god's sake try and arrange [peace] with the South," former congressman Martin Conway warned Lincoln, "on any basis short of their resumption of federal power on the cornerstone of slavery."[58] The opposition press feasted on Cold Harbor's casualties. "What is the difference between a *butcher* and a *general*?" a Copperhead editorial inquired. "A Butcher kills animals for food. A general kills men to gratify the ambition or malice of politicians and scoundrels."[59] After Cold Harbor, Grant could never cast off the butcher epithet, a mortifying burden for this plain, decent man. "They call me a butcher," he mused after the war, "but do you know I sometimes could hardly bring myself to give an order of battle? When I contemplated the death and misery that were sure to follow, I stood appalled."[60]

In the aftermath of the campaign, Lincoln faced almost unendurable pressure to stanch the bloodshed. He watched in despair as sick and wounded soldiers from Cold Harbor turned Washington into a vast infirmary, overrun with amputees and embalming establishments. Death was omnipresent in the capital. Mourning "our bleeding, bankrupt, almost dying country," Horace Greeley told Lincoln he feared "the prospect of fresh conscriptions, of further wholesale devastations, and of new rivers of human blood."[61] One particularly vitriolic critic of Grant resided in the White House. "He is a butcher," Mary Lincoln said of Grant, "and is not fit to be at the head of an army."[62] One evening, as he viewed ambulances transporting wounded soldiers, the president observed sadly, "Look yonder at those poor fellows. I cannot bear it. This suffering, this loss of life is dreadful."[63] To deal with the legions of dead, Quartermaster General Montgomery Meigs proposed the creation of a national military cemetery, surrounding the former Lee mansion at Arlington, and Stanton approved the measure the same day.

Despite the carnage, Lincoln never wavered in support of Grant or doubted his strategy. Two weeks after Cold Harbor, at a Philadelphia banquet, a gaunt, hollow-cheeked Lincoln quoted Shakespeare, telling listeners it could fairly be said "the heavens are hung in black."[64] Nevertheless, he refused to withdraw his belief in Grant. "I have never been in the habit of making predictions in regard to the war, but I am almost tempted to make one . . . If I were to hazard it, it is this: That Grant is this evening . . . in a position from whence he will never be dislodged until Richmond is taken."[65]

Enough people shared Lincoln's high regard for Grant that when Republicans—now called the National Union Party to garner more political support—convened their convention in Baltimore on June 7–8, Missouri's delegation cast its twenty-two votes for Grant. Before the final vote was announced, delegates switched their votes to Lincoln to make his nomination unanimous. Grant discouraged such political jockeying and tried to dispel the idea that he yearned for office. "I am not a candidate for any office," he quipped, "but I would like to be mayor of Galena long enough to fix the sidewalks, especially the one reaching my house."[66] Grant's apolitical stance surely endeared him to Lincoln. When entertained by a brass band after his renomination, the president gave him an unqualified endorsement: "What we want, still more than Baltimore conventions or presidential elections, is success under General Grant."[67] To strengthen Union sentiment in the border states and among War Democrats, the convention picked Andrew Johnson, the Democratic military governor of Tennessee, as its vice presidential nominee, a choice fertile with consequences for Grant's political future.

Everyone knew the presidential race would pivot on battlefield events. Grant,

Sherman, and their fellow Union generals had to convince skeptical voters that Lincoln should be reelected and that the current military strategy would succeed. The Democrats, slated to gather in August, planned to nominate someone on a platform of a negotiated peace acceptable to the South. Scattered voices feared Grant would be that Democratic nominee and cater to the Copperhead vote. Grant had no such plans. The *Chicago Tribune* editor Joseph Medill made a prediction to Elihu Washburne that proved startlingly accurate, saying if Grant remained lieutenant general and did not run, he would retain Republican Party loyalty "and four years hence will be their candidate and President for *eight years*. Nothing more certain."[68]

Before Grant left Cold Harbor, Mathew Brady, or someone in his studio, took a classic photo of the lieutenant general at his headquarters. Wearing rumpled, baggy pants and an unbuttoned coat, he stands with one arm resting against a pine tree, the other fist poised akimbo at his waist. His hat is pushed back slightly on his head while one foot is thrust forward. The contracted brow reflects the grim intensity of the Overland Campaign. It is an unusually candid shot of Grant, who seems a touch restless and unsettled, while still presenting the tough Grant the world knew: flinty and undeterred by setbacks. Although the photo was taken a little more than a week after Cold Harbor, he hardly looks defeated.

At this juncture, Grant executed a stunning volte-face in strategy. As shown by his prewar business speculations, he loved to gamble. He knew Lee would never emerge from his fortifications and that further frontal assaults would generate a suicidal rate of casualties, leaving him no choice but to adopt the slower course of a siege. It would be less romantic work, for which he was temperamentally unsuited, but it struck no less terror into Lee, who knew he couldn't survive a siege indefinitely. Grant had driven Lee into a box from which he could not escape easily as he defended Richmond and Petersburg.

Grant worried Lee might swoop down on Butler and the Army of the James before he could rescue them. For that reason, he elected to make a swift, secret movement to his left, taking his 115,000 men to a point south of the James River. There he would hook up with Butler's forces and be supplied by water. Grant had envisioned this from the beginning. If he could seize the vital railroad junction of Petersburg, twenty miles below Richmond, he could sever southern railroads that sustained Lee's army. With the surrounding countryside stripped bare of supplies, Lee depended heavily on produce sent by rail. As the hub for five railroads, Petersburg was the crucial portal for Richmond. If Petersburg fell,

Richmond and Lee's army fell, and the war would hasten to a speedy conclusion. For that reason, before moving his army south, Grant sent cavalry west under Sheridan to wreck the Virginia Central Railroad, eliminating that supply source for Lee. To complete his isolation, Grant ordered David Hunter's force in the Shenandoah Valley to disable the James River Canal, another wellspring nourishing the Confederate army.

By June 12, the weather had turned cool and windy. That night, after dark, Grant began to march his army toward the James. Staff officers noticed the tense way Grant relit cigars constantly and reacted with monosyllables. "Yes, yes," or "Go on—go on."[69] On this splendid night full of moonlight, the tramp of feet lifted swirling dust that soon obscured the stars. By the next morning, in a logistical masterpiece, the Army of the Potomac had vacated the Cold Harbor trenches. Lee was completely fooled by the exodus and thunderstruck to discover that Grant's entire army of 115,000 men had vanished in the night. While he had a hunch that Grant would swerve toward the James River, he could not be certain. To confound Lee further, Grant ordered some units to conduct diversionary feints toward Richmond.

Meanwhile, Grant's main army crossed the Chickahominy River and reached the formidable James River barrier. Grant needed to take his massive army across a waterway two thousand feet wide and eighty-four feet deep. To Julia, he described the operation as "one of the most perilous movements ever executed by a large army" since it involved "crossing two rivers over which the enemy has bridges and railroads whilst we have bridges to improvise." Ever the optimist, he shook off the settled gloom of Cold Harbor. "I am in excellent health and feel no doubt about holding the enemy in much greater alarm than I ever felt in my life."[70]

On the morning of June 14, Grant's engineers began to span the majestic James with a pontoon bridge measuring 2,100 feet in length and 13 feet in width, making it the longest such bridge in military annals. It was anybody's guess whether such a lengthy bridge, buoyed by 101 floats, could withstand tidal currents or gusts sweeping inland from Chesapeake Bay. Miraculously, the entire bridge was completed shortly after midnight. The next day, his hands joined behind his back, Grant gazed silently from a bluff on the river's north side as cavalry and artillery trains moved rapidly across the river. "He wore no sword or other outward trapping except his buttons and plain shoulder straps," one soldier had observed a day earlier. "His pants were tucked inside of a pair of long dusty boots and his whole attire looked dirty & travel stained."[71]

Grant officiated at one of the war's most stirring spectacles. On this cloudless day, brilliant sunshine sparkled off the water, gun barrels, and cannon trundling across the bridge. To the crisp beat of marching bands, troops stepped briskly onto ferry boats that plied the river at a dizzying pace. Nearby gunboats kept a watchful eye on any threatening enemy movements. Before the operation was over, an enormous herd of cattle swam across the river. From the capital, Lincoln applauded Grant, telegraphing at 7 a.m. on June 15: "I begin to see it. You will succeed—God bless you all!"[72] By around midnight the next day, the last remnants of Grant's army had crossed the river. Incredibly, Lee still had no idea Grant's army had slipped across the James in an operation so stupendous even one Confederate general dubbed it "the most brilliant stroke in all the campaigns of the war."[73]

On the day the pontoon bridge was laid down, Grant and Rawlins traveled by steamer up the James to Bermuda Hundred to consult with Ben Butler. As a general, Butler hadn't covered himself with glory, but as a noted Democratic politician, he was too useful for Lincoln to scrap. Grant found Butler covering the Appomattox River with another amphibious bridge to carry his men on a raid into Petersburg, only six miles away. Grant hoped to take Petersburg before Lee was alerted to his whereabouts.

On the evening of June 15, Baldy Smith and Winfield Scott Hancock achieved startling success when they overran the outer defensive rim of northeast Petersburg, seizing rifle pits, artillery, and several hundred prisoners. General Beauregard fielded a meager force to defend the town. Had Smith marched straight into the defenseless city, he might have scored a radical breakthrough and altered the war's course. Grant always believed that with such a move, "Lee would have at once been obliged to abandon Richmond."[74] Instead Smith tarried, spent the night in the same spot, then allowed his men a leisurely breakfast the next morning. He felt poorly, while Hancock was still ailing from an old Gettysburg wound. As Beauregard later reflected, "Petersburg at that hour was clearly at the mercy of the Federal commander, who had all but captured it."[75] The instant Lee learned of the attack by telegraph, he began loading troops onto railroad cars and sped them to the imperiled city. By June 16, rebel reinforcements filtered into Petersburg and soon reclaimed trenches taken by federal forces.

That day, Grant toured captured areas and was impressed by the strength of the Petersburg citadel, with its thick earthworks, deep moats, sharpened tree branches, and tangled telegraph wires. That night Union forces resumed their attacks, fighting in moonglow, but the main opportunity had already been squandered and only sporadic gains were recorded. Perhaps distracted by the James River crossing, Grant was not as deeply engaged at Petersburg as he should have been. True to his hardheaded style, he launched recurring attacks against the enemy, but lost more than twelve thousand men in four days without prying open Confederate defenses.

At noon on June 18, Meade ventured a last attempt to marshal his men against Petersburg's earthworks, but it miscarried. The haggard men had tired of blunt operations against the enemy and balked at more punishment. As the artillerist Charles Wainwright complained, "The attack this afternoon was a fiasco of the worst kind. I trust it will be the last attempt at this most absurd way of attacking entrenchments by a general advance in line . . . even the stupidest private now knows that it cannot succeed."[76] As the day progressed, Lee and his army appeared in full force, rendering further Union efforts futile.

Coming on the heels of Cold Harbor, the dismal failure at Petersburg disheartened Grant's soldiers. "Why have these lives been sacrificed?" Charles Francis Adams Jr. wondered. "Grant has pushed his Army to the extreme limit of human endurance."[77] Recognizing his men's exhaustion, Grant bowed to their human limitations: "We will rest the men and use the spade for their protection until a new vein has been struck."[78] The Army of the Potomac had sacrificed sixty-five thousand men killed, wounded, or missing since crossing the Rapidan on May 4, far exceeding anything experienced in the past. Averse to more frontal assaults, Grant now changed the war's character in Virginia, setting his men to work with pick and ax to construct defenses as expansive as those that guarded Petersburg. Whenever Grant extended his lines, Lee would have to match him and vice versa. The two would be locked into a partial siege of the city, a deadly stalemate that would test the nerves of both commanders. Grant would try to deny Lee's army freedom to strike and maneuver, guaranteeing bloody warfare at close range.

Grant established his headquarters on a high bluff over the James at the boat landing known as City Point, which soon evolved into the nucleus of the war effort. He selected the spot because it marked the crossroads of the James and Appomattox Rivers; provided easy water routes to Washington; sat at the eastern terminus of an important railway line; and stood ten miles northeast of Petersburg and twenty miles southeast of Richmond, enabling him to strike either city. Everybody commented on the spot's scenic beauty and the panoramic vista of river traffic. Within a year, the sleepy village would be transformed into one of the world's busiest ports. Grant attributed much of the logistical wizardry to Rufus Ingalls: "Through his supervision the Army of the Potomac has been supplied in a manner no army in the world has ever been supplied before."[79] Not only did City Point wharves teem with ships, but it had barracks, a hospital, railroad yards, fields of tents, bakeries, and a post office. Grant erected a signal tower 175 feet high, and Fred remembered mounting it with his father "to look upon the spires of Petersburg and Richmond."[80]

Initially Grant worked from a hospital tent atop the bluff, shaded by old trees, before moving to the middle of a humble row of log cabins. Stationed outside his door to ward off assassins was Ely Parker, a revolver at his side. Security was compromised by a plague of sightseers who descended as Grant became a local tourist attraction. Visitors reached him by mounting a long wooden staircase rising from the steamboat landing. This more fixed abode would allow Julia to spend a goodly portion of the summer with Grant, restoring a modicum of normality to their lives. On two occasions she went off to Burlington, New Jersey, to arrange schooling for their children, but she was otherwise able to provide emotional sustenance for her husband. That spring she had stayed with Colonel Dent in St. Louis as she grew accustomed to life without slaves. "Our colored people had all left," she recalled, "but their places were readily filled by German and French men and women, who were most excellent substitutes . . . We had a great deal of company, and then it was we missed the old family servants."[81] However brief the time allotted to family matters, Grant followed his children's affairs closely. The day after Cold Harbor, he wrote to eight-year-old Nellie, encouraging her study of German and hoping Fred would learn French to ease his way into West Point.

The northern public, having withstood multiple disappointments, was skittish about what was to come. Hoping to assess the state of Grant's army, Abraham Lincoln, clad in black, arrived with his son Tad at City Point on June 21. He had seldom strayed far from the White House during the war. With its sorrowful gaze, Lincoln's face registered inner emotion and was the opposite of Grant's poker face. Nevertheless, the two men enjoyed a fine rapport and Lincoln was warmly deferential toward Grant. When they met at the wharf, Porter remembered, "the President came down from the upper deck . . . and reaching out his long, angular arm, he wrung General Grant's hand vigorously, and held it in his for some time, while he uttered in rapid words his congratulations" for what Grant had done since their last meeting.[82] With a light touch, Lincoln conveyed that he came to learn, not to lecture. "I don't expect I can do any good, and in fact I'm afraid I may do harm, but I'll just put myself under your orders and if you find me doing anything wrong just send me right away."[83] Grant cheerfully agreed.

When they sat down for lunch, Lincoln told of the rough journey aboard his steamer, confessed to having been seasick, and complained of an upset stomach. "Try a glass of champagne, Mr. President," an officer said. "That is always a certain cure for seasickness." Lincoln's face crinkled with humor. "No, my friend," he replied. "I have seen too many fellows seasick ashore from drinking that very stuff."[84] Lincoln's witty retort provoked laughter. Aware of Grant's reputation for drinking, he had gracefully sidestepped the issue. After lunch, when Grant suggested the president might want to ride out to see Union troops at Petersburg, Lincoln cottoned to the idea. "Why, yes; I had fully intended to go out and take a look at the brave fellows who have fought their way down to Petersburg in this wonderful campaign, and I am ready to start at any time."[85]

Grant asked Lincoln to borrow his large bay horse Cincinnati, while he rode the small black pony Jeff Davis. Still attired in black, Lincoln wore his trademark headgear, a tall silk hat, which was promptly knocked off by a tree branch as they galloped along. The weather was so dry the president was coated with dust when they reached the Union line. "As he had no straps," wrote Porter, the president's "trousers gradually worked up above his ankles, and gave him the appearance of a country farmer riding into town wearing his Sunday clothes."[86] Lincoln's unexpected presence created a sensation among the soldiers, who cheered him lustily as he arrived to lilting band music. He had now drawn near enough to Petersburg to see church steeples in the distance. No mean politician himself, Grant suggested that Lincoln might want to see the black troops who had behaved gallantly during Baldy Smith's recent raid on Petersburg. "Oh, yes," Lincoln replied. "I want to take a look at those boys . . . I was opposed on nearly every side when I first favored the raising of colored regiments; but they have proved their efficiency, and I am glad they have kept pace with the white troops in the recent assaults."[87]

When Lincoln reached the camp of black soldiers, he witnessed a scene of overpowering emotion. The men who lined up two deep on each side of the road laughed, cried, and cheered, sending up hosannas for their beloved liberator. "They crowded about him and fondled his horse; some of them kissed his hands," wrote Porter, "while others ran off crying in triumph to their comrades that they had touched his clothes."[88] Badeau told Edwin Booth that the black troops "had never seemed so to realize the reality of their freedom as when they saw this incarnation or representative of it."[89] Lincoln peeled off layers of emotional reserve. Tears stood in his eyes as he bowed to the black soldiers, and his voice broke as he thanked them for their rapturous reception.[90]

That evening, Lincoln sat outside Grant's tent and unwound from the tensions of war, regaling Grant and his staff with humorous anecdotes, employing laughter to relieve the gloom that so often enveloped him. According to Porter, he "sat on a low camp-chair, and wound his legs around each other as if in an effort to get them out of the way, and with his long arms he accompanied what he said with all sorts of odd gestures."[91] Lincoln ate at a common table with the officers and fraternized informally with them in the same egalitarian spirit as Grant. After his frustrated dealings with a parade of intractable generals, Lincoln relaxed in Grant's amiable company and capable hands.

The next morning, Lincoln steamed up the James River for a meeting with General Butler and Admiral Samuel Phillips Lee and was shown places the Union army had seized. "When Grant once gets possession of a place," Lincoln commented approvingly, "he holds on to it as if he had inherited it."[92] The tour abounded in dreadful sights. "The weather was hot and the roads dusty beyond anything you can imagine," Badeau wrote; "dead horses filled the air with their stench, crowds of wagons and mules choked the way, and I was glad enough when the trip was over, for all the horror!!"[93] By the time Lincoln returned to Washington the next day, he and Grant "both felt that their acquaintance had already ripened into a genuine friendship," said Porter.[94] The sunburned Lincoln had benefited from the change of scenery, and when he got back to Washington, Secretary of the Navy Gideon Welles declared the trip had "done him good, physically, and strengthened him mentally."[95] Grant had lifted his morale and Lincoln enjoyed repeating his parting words: "You will never hear of me farther from Richmond than [I am] now, till I have taken it . . . It may take a long summer day, but I will go in."[96]

CHAPTER TWENTY

Caldron of Hell

B Y LATE JUNE, Grant wanted Union forces to stake everything on destroying the two principal Confederate armies under Lee in Virginia and Johnston in Georgia. He was resigned to the stalemate of a long siege in Virginia. For the moment, his army was stifled by oppressive heat, the mercury reaching 108 degrees as a plague of flies descended on his soldiers. A ubiquitous, drought-induced dust reached almost biblical proportions. Visiting City Point, George Templeton Strong gagged at the arid landscape: "Drought and travel have done their work on this region and pulverized the soil . . . beyond what I had dreamed possible. Miles and miles of what were meadow and cornfield are now seas of impalpable dust of unknown depth, and heated to a temperature beyond what the hand can bear."[1] The devastated terrain around Petersburg was a scene of deserted houses and flattened fences, with many soldiers buried in shallow graves that gave off a sickening odor. The war had reduced much of Virginia to a sterile wasteland, while drought choked off the harvest. "Indeed it would be difficult to form an idea of a territory more trampled and blasted by the hoof of war than the greater part of Virginia," Charles A. Dana reported from City Point.[2]

Awaiting the arrival of siege guns, Grant extended his line west and south of Petersburg, forcing Lee to imitate him, mile for mile, and throw up earthworks at every turn. Grant wanted to make Lee stretch his thinly staffed lines to the bursting point. Lee worried more about the steady provision of supplies for his men than an attack by Grant's army. Grant's overriding objective was to strike at the five railroads that crisscrossed Petersburg and fed Richmond. Starting on June 22, he threw cavalry units against the South Side and Danville Railroads, damaging vast stretches of the tracks but incurring heavy losses.

Grant hoped to choke Richmond through a slow, stealthy process of strangulation. "Every road leading from Richmond is now destroyed," he reported to Halleck, "and the Danville road so badly I hope, as to take a long time for its repair."[3] Grant erred in his optimism, for the rebel army had grown proficient at repairing tracks quickly. He drew encouragement from the fact that Lee's army was starting to include the very young and old, an unmistakable sign of desperation. As he told his father, his opponents had robbed "the grave and the cradle. Old men like yourself, and little boys like my Fred are now fighting; the Grandfather and Grandson side by side."[4] No less fervently Grant wrote, "The last man in the Confederacy is now in the Army. They are becoming discouraged, their men deserting, dying and being killed and captured every day."[5] With the South unable to replace lost men, Grant thought it only a matter of time before the Confederacy yielded.

To replenish the Army of the Potomac, he had appropriated a large number of soldiers previously manning Washington's defenses. In an emergency, he thought he could transfer an entire corps northward from Virginia in two days. Halleck feared that when Grant moved south of the James River, Lee would be tempted to dispatch a raiding party against the capital. Indeed, Lee imagined such a strategy would force Grant to divert a significant fraction of his army to defend the capital, contracting his presence outside Petersburg. In a fortuitous development for Lee, General David Hunter withdrew from the Shenandoah Valley into West Virginia, opening the way for a Confederate force to tear into Baltimore or Washington, defended only by militia, invalided soldiers, and convalescents. On June 12, Lee sent Jubal Early, with a considerable corps, to storm through the valley and deal a stinging blow to the federal capital. After defeating Hunter at Lynchburg, Early advanced steadily north, reaching Harpers Ferry by July 3.

A balding, full-bearded West Point graduate, riddled with arthritis, Early had functioned as a lawyer and politician in his native Virginia. Fiercely moralistic and notoriously ill-tempered, he didn't suffer fools gladly. Lee referred to him as "my bad old man."[6] Urged on by a crusading fervor, Early now led his fifteen thousand men toward Washington, their numbers magnified in the minds of panicky northerners. By July 4, Grant was informed by a deserter of the threat

posed by Early and warned Halleck the Confederate general would try to punish
Washington. He ordered cavalry and an infantry division to hasten to the capital's defense. "We want now to crush out & destroy any force the enemy dares
send north," Grant told Halleck in a midnight telegram on July 5.[7] As always,
the two-faced Halleck was quick to distance himself from Grant if things went
wrong and equally quick to grab credit if things prospered. He now reproached
Grant behind his back. "I predicted this to Genl Grant before he crossed the
James River," he told a friend, "and that Lee would play the same game of
shuttle-cock between him & Washington that he did with McClellan."[8]

On July 8, alarm mounted in the capital as Early's raiders penetrated western
Maryland, spreading terror as they ripped up railroad tracks, torched mills and
workshops, and sent local residents fleeing toward Washington and Baltimore.
The hysteria intensified the next day as Union soldiers retreated toward Washington after Early administered a beating to a Union force under General Lew Wallace at the Monocacy River, outside of Frederick. With a far smaller contingent,
Wallace slowed Early's march by a day, giving Grant precious time to transfer
more troops to Washington. "If Early had been but one day earlier," Grant wrote,
"he might have entered the capital before the arrival of the reinforcements I had
sent."[9] Train traffic was halted in and out of the city, government clerks packed
weapons at work, and Lincoln had a boat ready to spirit him away if Confederates
ransacked the city. The situation was grave enough that an unusually nervous
Grant volunteered to go to Washington, if Lincoln thought it advisable.

Lincoln felt queasy enough to suggest that Grant leave sufficient men to
guard his position at Petersburg and bring the rest to the capital. He saw an opportunity to protect Washington and destroy an invading army at once. Having
worked hard not to interfere with Grant, Lincoln made a point of treading gingerly. "This is what I think, upon your suggestion, and is not an order," he told
Grant.[10] This was the closest Lincoln ever came to handing Grant orders. Upon
reflection, Grant decided that traveling to Washington was "probably just what
Lee wants me to do," and refused to allow Lee to divert him from his plans.[11]
Rawlins was insistent that Grant's "appearance in Washington would be heralded all over the country as an abandonment of his campaign, a faltering at
least in his purpose," and Grant was swayed by his typically assertive viewpoint.[12] It spoke to the personal strength that Grant developed during the war
that he didn't agree with the president merely to placate him and that Lincoln
abided by his decision.

On July 11, Lincoln appeared at Fort Stevens, north of Washington, which was under fire from Early's men. To soothe an alarmed populace, Lincoln and Stanton rode there in an open carriage. The tall, angular president, peeping over the fort's parapet, made a prime target for Confederate marksmen, and one Union soldier (possibly Captain Oliver Wendell Holmes Jr.), unaware it was Lincoln, shouted, "Get down, you fool."[13] It was the only time in American history a sitting president came under fire in combat. Luckily for the Union side, the corps sent by Grant under Horatio Wright arrived at Fort Stevens that afternoon and the national capital was spared. Early made no further inroads, fading back into Virginia. "Well Major," he told an aide, "we haven't taken Washington, but we scared Abe Lincoln like hell."[14] Lincoln expressed annoyance that Wright didn't pursue the retreating rebels, saying sardonically the general feared "he might come across the rebels and catch some of them."[15] Grant sent troops to harass Early and leave a trail of devastation in their wake or, in his indelibly ghoulish words, "to eat out Virginia clear and clean as far as they go, so that Crows flying over it for the balance of this season will have to carry their provender with them."[16] At the War Department, Halleck faced serious internal criticism for not better coordinating Washington's defenses.

Although Early never entered Baltimore or Washington, he delivered a psychological jolt not soon forgotten. Grumbling against Grant broadened into a critique of his whole campaign. On July 15, unnerved by Early's raid, Dana let loose a blast about him to Rawlins. Without quite endorsing them, he set down critical shafts that could be directed at Grant—how he had stripped Washington of troops, rendering it vulnerable; how he had allowed Early to advance up the Shenandoah; how he had dallied in sending troops to Washington until it was too late to do anything other than chase the enemy back across the Potomac. He even disparaged the Wilderness Campaign as a costly fiasco with nothing to show but mass casualties. Dana warned that Grant's troubles might lead to Lincoln's defeat in the upcoming election, installing McClellan in the White House. "The black & revolting dishonor of this siege of Washington with all its circumstances of poltroonery & stupidity," Dana concluded, "is yet too fresh & its brand is too stinging for one to have a cool judgment regarding its probable consequences."[17]

Realizing that he needed to shore up Washington's defenses without compromising his plans against Richmond, Grant proposed that newly recruited troops be trained there to solidify its protection. He also proposed consolidating several departments under a lone commander who could single-handedly deal with threats to Maryland or Pennsylvania, suggesting General William B. Franklin. Most important, and contrary to customary practice, Grant sent a cipher telegram to Lincoln calling for another three hundred thousand men in the field. Noting widespread Confederate desertions, he predicted: "With the prospect of large additions to our force these desertions would increase. The greater number of men we have the shorter and less sanguinary will be the war."[18] Lincoln anticipated this plea, calling for *five hundred thousand* more men, "which I suppose covers the case," Lincoln told Grant. "Always glad to have your suggestions."[19]

Ever since Chattanooga, Grant had esteemed Brigadier General William F. "Baldy" Smith, a Vermont native who attended West Point with him. Short and stout, with a Vandyke beard, Smith had a sharp analytic mind that he applied to opening the "cracker line" that fed ravenous Union troops in Chattanooga. Grateful for this breakthrough, Grant endorsed his elevation to major general. "[Smith] is possessed of one of the clearest Military heads in the Army, is very practical, and industrious," he told Stanton. "No man in the service is better qualified than he for our largest command."[20] But Smith frequently made enemies, sniped privately at other generals, and fumed whenever Grant ignored his advice. His subordination to Ben Butler so grated on him that he swore to his wife that "I cannot live under this man much longer."[21] Smith was no less antagonistic toward Meade, complaining to Grant that he was "as helpless as a child on the field of battle and as visionary as an opium eater in council," and he challenged Grant to explain why he tolerated such barefaced ineptitude.[22]

Gradually Grant's enthusiasm for Smith cooled since he didn't care for grumblers and Smith was a professional malcontent. That May, Grant had written that Smith was "obstinate, and is likely to condemn whatever is not suggested by himself."[23] In mid-June, Smith sat down with Grant and delivered a harsh critique of the Overland Campaign, pouring blame on Meade: "I tried to show [Grant] the blunders of the late campaign of the Army of the Potomac, and the terrible waste of life that had resulted from what I had considered a want of generalship in its present commander. Among other instances, I referred to the fearful slaughter at Cold Harbor on the 3d of June." According to Smith, Grant conceded there had been "butchery" at Cold Harbor, but thought it pointless to criticize Meade.[24] Smith believed his rank entitled him to such candor, though it must have strengthened Grant's view of him as notoriously quarrelsome and vindictive. The touchy relationship between the two men formed the backdrop to a controversy that now unfolded.

With Grant's drinking history, it would have been surprising had he not re-
lapsed in the aftermath of Cold Harbor. At the end of June, he visited the headquarters of Ambrose Burnside and, allegedly egged on by Ben Butler, asked for
a drink to relieve a migraine headache. When Grant subsequently visited Baldy
Smith's headquarters, he told him the earlier drink had helped and asked for
another. As Smith recounted the incident:

> My servant opened a bottle for him, and he drank of it . . . I was
> aware at this time that General Grant had within six months pledged
> himself to drink nothing intoxicating . . . After the lapse of an hour
> or less, the general asked for another drink, which he took. Shortly
> after, his voice showed plainly that the liquor had affected him, and
> after a little time he left . . . as soon as I returned to my tent I said to
> a staff officer of mine who had witnessed his departure, "General
> Grant has gone away drunk. Gen. Butler has seen it, and will never
> fail to use the weapon which has been put into his hands."[25]

Smith claimed Grant mounted his horse with some difficulty and rode off "in a
most disgusting state after having vomited all over his horse's neck & shoulders."[26] This detail is highly suspect since it would have been the talk of the army
and nobody else recorded the incident. Grant's departure from abstinence that
day is echoed in a lament from the ever-vigilant Rawlins to his wife: "The General
was at the front today, and I learn from one of his staff he deviated from the only
path he should ever travel by taking a glass of liquor." Pained that he hadn't accompanied Grant to the front, Rawlins vowed, "I shall hereafter, under no circumstances, fail to accompany him."[27] Butler denied having seen Grant touch a drop
of hard liquor and contested the allegation that he had cajoled him into drinking.
Had he done so, Butler wrote, "I should have expected Grant to dismiss me from
the service at once, as he ought to have done, and as I would have done to him
under the same circumstances."[28]

In early July, when Smith asked for a leave of absence, Grant disclosed he had
lost faith in Butler, was trying to get rid of him, and wanted to replace him with
Smith. Indeed, on July 1, Grant wrote a damning letter to Halleck, citing Butler's lack of military knowledge and inability to execute orders. Instead of sacking Butler outright, Grant wanted to allow him to save face by transferring him
to another theater of war, perhaps Kentucky. In a neat piece of sarcasm, Halleck

replied, "To send him to Kentucky would probably cause an insurrection in that state."[29] Halleck suggested that Grant keep Butler in place but neutralize his battlefield influence.

When Halleck suggested that Baldy Smith replace Butler on the battlefield, Grant liked the idea and Lincoln endorsed it on July 7. This would exile Butler to administrative purgatory at Fort Monroe, giving Smith a free hand with field troops. But on July 9, before the order was published, Butler met with Grant at City Point to discuss the decision, which he thought a plot cooked up by Halleck and Smith. Whatever Butler said at the meeting, the offending order was rescinded the next day. When Smith returned from his furlough, he learned, to his everlasting suspicion, that Grant had overturned his decision, reinstated Butler to his former command, and dispatched him, Smith, to New York. In meeting with Smith on July 19, Grant referred to Smith's habit of slandering colleagues and creating mischief as the primary reason behind the reversal. It may have been that Lincoln decided he could not afford to alienate the politically powerful Butler and intervened to save him. At the end of the interview, Grant rebuked Smith flatly: "You talk too much!"[30]

The only way Smith could explain Grant's change of heart was that Butler had blackmailed Grant about the drinking episode: "I was convinced that General Butler had used his knowledge of the fact that General Grant . . . had temporarily become the victim of a habit which had at one time disqualified him for command, to force him to act against his judgment and inclination."[31] Eleven days after being relieved, an irate Smith wrote to Senator Solomon Foot of Vermont—the letter's authenticity has been questioned—laying out his case for what had happened. After the colossal deaths of the Overland Campaign, Smith speculated, Grant felt vulnerable to dismissal: "At that gloomy time, the blackest in the history of the war, when General Grant's movements in the East had been attended with awful sacrifices of life and with little substantial success, an indictment against him, based upon these failures and a recurrence of his old habit [i.e., drinking], supported by General Butler, might have swept him from power."[32]

What Smith didn't acknowledge were the many factors that might have compelled Grant to yield to Butler. It was widely thought that McClellan would emerge as the Democratic nominee for president at the August convention in Chicago. Grant might have feared political repercussions if he crossed swords with Butler at such a delicate moment, harming Lincoln's reelection chances. According to Adam Badeau, from the time Grant became general in chief he

wanted to get rid of Butler, but at a meeting with Lincoln and Stanton "was informed that political considerations of the highest character made it undesirable
to displace Butler."[33] In a newspaper interview in 1887, Smith admitted that
"General B[utler] had threatened to make public something that would prevent
the President's reelection. General Grant told me that he had heard that Gen. B.
had made some threat with reference to the Chicago convention which he said
he 'had in his breeches pocket.'"[34]

For Grant, morale and teamwork were always vitally important, and the venomous Smith had violated that code of soldierly conduct. It was his berating of
Meade that Grant mentioned in relieving Smith from command. Smith had
declared he could not serve with Butler, and when it was decided to retain Butler, his days were numbered. With his backbiting tendencies, Smith had simply
overplayed his hand. As Rawlins wrote, Grant dismissed Smith "because of his
spirit of criticism of all military movements and men . . . and his disposition to
scatter the seeds of discontent throughout the army."[35] Rawlins, never shy about
Grant's drinking, made no mention of liquor entering into the decision. Whatever his reasons for keeping Butler, the need for it surely rankled Grant. As Dana
told Rawlins: "I see that the General has backed down on Butler but I hope that
he will fix it so that that military lawyer will not be able to ruin the end of the
campaign as he has ruined and foiled the beginning."[36]

By the summer of 1864, northern victory seemed tantalizingly close, if only
Richmond or Atlanta were taken. Given the outsize casualties under Grant,
Republicans needed a major southern city to fall before the election to demonstrate genuine progress. By now Sherman preached a doctrine of total warfare
that grew ever more militant. By late 1863, his letters to Grant throbbed with a
burning sense of vengeance as he planned to widen the war to engulf civilian
society, obliterating the South's productive capacity. When Grant gave Sherman
his marching orders in April 1864, he provided him with extraordinary autonomy in his impending campaign against Joseph Johnston's army and Atlanta.
The brief orders allowed Sherman to fill in the blanks as he attacked Johnston
in the mountainous terrain of northwest Georgia. From afar Grant followed
Sherman with admiration, later contending that his campaign toward Atlanta
had been "managed with the most consummate skill, the enemy being flanked
out of one position after another all the way there."[37]

As his men trooped south, Sherman took note of enemy resilience. "No
amount of poverty or adversity seems to shake their faith; niggers gone, wealth

and luxury gone, money worthless . . . yet I see no sign of let up."[38] Only violence on a massive scale, he believed, could subdue such a hardy and refractory breed. "I begin to regard the death and mangling of a couple of thousand men as a small affair, a kind of morning dash," he wrote. "The worst of the war is not yet begun."[39] Sherman wanted to implant in his men a fighting spirit that would alter the whole balance of the war. He also wished to inflict psychological damage on the southern people because the North was "not only fighting hostile armies but a hostile people, and must make old and young, rich and poor, feel the hard hand of war, as well as the organized armies."[40] Better to bring the war to a speedy conclusion by hard fighting, he thought, than prolong the suffering of the conflict.

Atlanta beckoned as the peerless prize, home to arsenals and foundries, munition plants and machine shops, a place so crammed with manufacturing facilities that Sherman prophesied "its capture would be the death-knell of the Southern Confederacy."[41] Its extensive railway network sped food to Lee's faraway army. As Sherman's army moved forward it was a force of nature, an unstoppable juggernaut, pushing Johnston's army closer to Atlanta, and Jefferson Davis monitored its progress with "intense anxiety."[42] Many running battles Sherman fought with Johnston were inconclusive, but they had a common denominator: they brought him inexorably closer to Atlanta's outskirts. He wanted to circle the city, cut off its rail links, isolate it, and starve it out.

On July 20, Sherman notified Grant that Johnston had been replaced by John Bell Hood. While Grant respected Hood as "a gallant brave fellow," he greeted the news with quiet jubilation and smiled knowingly.[43] Much like Lee, Johnston had fought cautiously, sticking to defense and buying time for the Confederacy, while Grant thought Hood "would dash out and fight every time you raised a flag before him, and that was just what we wanted."[44] In Grant's view, Hood was prone to "rash and ill-advised attacks," and he was certain Sherman would outgeneral him.[45] Grant and Sherman hoped Hood would stand and fight in Atlanta rather than recede into the hinterland, a move that would yield the city but not the gray-coated army. Sherman's arrival on the city fringes provoked an exodus of fear-stricken residents. He believed it crucial that Grant keep Lee pinned down, unable to assist the rebel army in Atlanta—exactly the sort of integrated strategic thinking Grant had favored.

Whatever high spirits Grant experienced at Hood's advent were shortly dashed by a shocking development as the Atlanta contest got under way: the

death of thirty-five-year-old General James B. McPherson, who commanded the
Army of the Tennessee. On July 22, he was felled by a bullet while out surveying
Confederate defenses. Riding straight into a band of rebel skirmishers, he waved
his hat at them as he rode away and they shot him in the back; evidently he died
within an hour, his bloodied horse limping back riderless into camp. A tall, genial young man, McPherson had graduated first in his class at West Point. At his
death, he was engaged to a young woman in Baltimore. A courteous Methodist
who never cursed, he had endeared himself to Ulysses and Julia Grant. Sherman
had imagined that if anything ever happened to him and Grant, McPherson
would be summoned to direct the Union war effort, and Grant eulogized him as
one of the "ablest, purest and best generals" he had.[46]

It fell to Captain Samuel Beckwith, the chief cipher operator, to deliver the
heartbreaking news to Grant in his tent. He handed the dispatch to Grant, who
"read it silently. He was hard hit, I could readily see that. His mouth twitched
and his eyes closed as if he were shutting out the baleful words. Then the tears
came and one followed the other down his bronzed cheeks as he sat there without
a word of comment."[47] Shaken to his core, Grant wrote a rare condolence letter
to McPherson's grandmother that belied Grant's image as stolid and unemo-
tional. With simple eloquence, he expressed "personal love for the departed. He
formed for some time one of my military family. I knew him well. To know him
was but to love him . . . Your bereavement is great, but cannot exceed mine."[48]

By July 1864, with spirits slumping in the North and Lincoln's election prospects dampened by the abysmal rate of casualties in Virginia, Grant dreamed of
the bold breakthrough that would replenish the Union cause. After frenetic
spring fighting, the pace had slackened and Grant took advantage of this hiatus
to improve his entrenchments. The long Petersburg siege led to slow-motion tor-
ment for soldiers in the dank, filthy trenches, who had to duck to avoid bullets.
As Grant wondered how to end this stalemate—his aggressive temperament
chafed at the tedium of a siege—he was extremely open to any unconventional
ideas that appeared.

During the Vicksburg siege, he had experimented with digging a mine under
enemy defenses and blowing them up. The aborted explosion had left only a gaping crater. Nonetheless, in late June 1864, Grant endorsed a similar plan from
Ambrose Burnside. The impetus came from Colonel Henry Pleasants, whose

Pennsylvania volunteers included miners skilled at excavating tunnels, one of whom boasted, "We could blow that damn fort [at Petersburg] out of existence if we could run a mine shaft under it."⁴⁹ On June 25, these erstwhile miners began gouging out a tunnel that would secretly span the hundred yards separating Union and Confederate lines. Repeating the reason he had invoked for the quixotic schemes at Vicksburg, Grant wrote in his *Memoirs* that he approved the plan "as a means of keeping the men occupied."⁵⁰ It exercised a special fascination for Burnside, who wished to exorcize the stigma of his ruinous performance at Frederickburg. The mining scheme promised to punch a hole in Petersburg's defenses and possibly deliver the entire city to Union forces.

At first Meade thought Burnside would complete his mine in a little more than a week, but the work proved laborious, hampered by underground springs and quicksand. The miners, wielding primitive tools, had to figure out how to ventilate galleries with fresh air. Burnside planned to have the main tunnel branch off into chambers, with gunpowder stored in each. While some officers had misgivings about the project, Grant understood his men's restlessness in the baking heat and allowed it to proceed.⁵¹ Many of Grant's soldiers were unaware of the surreptitious plan, but by July 17, Grant heard reports that the other side had learned of it and launched a similar project in reverse. As the date of the mine detonation neared, Confederate soldiers sank shafts to plumb where the Union galleries stood.

On July 23, the excavation ended its initial phase. The main gallery ran 511 feet long, terminating 23 feet below the Confederate parapet. All that remained was to pack the tunnel with eight thousand pounds of explosives and blow the rebels to kingdom come. To set the stage for this, Grant concocted a characteristic ruse: he sent out a corps under Hancock with Sheridan's cavalry to wreck the Virginia Central Railroad, drawing a large portion of Lee's troops to the north side of the James. Sheridan proved adept at deception: under cover of night, he sneaked his men back across the James, carpeting a pontoon bridge with moss and earth to muffle the tramp of soldiers. Then by day he sent them across the James again to create the illusion that most of Grant's army was being evacuated. Steamboat captains blew shrill whistles, adding to the charade of a sudden retreat. The main aim of this subterfuge was to weaken Petersburg's defenses, making them vulnerable to the hole Grant hoped to blow through them. When this maneuver was completed, he was ready to ignite the mine and pour fifteen thousand troops into the fray.

Aside from the drubbing Lee gave him at Fredericksburg, Ambrose Burnside is best known to history for his flourishing side-whiskers, called "sideburns" in homage to him, and the massive bald dome of his head. Elegant, gracious in his manners, he was, like Rosecrans, popular and respected, but, in Grant's estimation, scarcely "fitted to command an army. No one knew this better than himself. He always admitted his blunders, and extenuated those of officers under him beyond what they were entitled to."[52] With the mine set to explode on July 30, Burnside planned to employ a division of highly motivated black troops, who wanted "to show the white troops what the colored division could do," said an officer.[53] They had distinguished themselves guarding Grant's huge wagon train, but stood somewhat apart from the rest of the Army of the Potomac. Black soldiers still had to contend with the ingrained prejudice that they couldn't perform complex maneuvers. At the last minute, Meade objected "that if we put the colored troops in front . . . and it should prove a failure, it would then be said, and very properly, that we were shoving those people ahead to get killed because we did not care anything about them."[54] Agreeing with Meade, Grant decided to use Burnside's three divisions of white soldiers at the mine blast. It was an ill-fated change, for the black division had received special training while the whites hadn't. Their three commanders drew slips to see who would lead the charge and the choice fell on General James H. Ledlie. In the estimation of one officer, "Ledlie was a drunkard and an arrant coward . . . It was wicked to risk the lives of men in such a man's hands."[55]

On July 28, in yet another tactical deception, Grant ordered a cessation of artillery fire against Petersburg as an eerie silence fell over the front line. He wanted to dupe the enemy into thinking he was furtively slinking away. At the same time, Rawlins, just back from Washington, was irked to learn that Grant had taken advantage of his absence to indulge in alcohol. "I find the General in my absence digressed from his true path," the long-suffering Rawlins told his wife. "The God of Heaven only knows how long I am to serve my country as the guardian of the habits of him whom it has honored. It shall not be always thus."[56] The time had long since passed when he had vowed to quit his staff if Grant touched a drop of forbidden liquor.

Grant and his staff eagerly awaited the mine explosion, hoping for a spectacular turn in the fighting. After a false start, the mine was triggered a little before 5 a.m. on July 30. With a fearsome roar, the earth was torn asunder, spewing a colossal cloud of dirt, dust, and smoke as broken muskets whirled into the sky, killing a rebel regiment and demolishing an artillery battery. Body parts lay scattered everywhere. One observer compared the lethal cloud to "an immense mushroom whose stem seemed to be of fire and its head of smoke."[57] The blast carved a crater 30 feet in depth, 60 feet in width, and 170 feet in length. One Confederate gunner remembered the dust column "hurtling downward with a roaring sound, showers of stones, broken timbers and blackened human limbs . . . the gloomy pall of darkening smoke flushing in an angry crimson" before the rising sun.[58] Then came the thunderous boom of 110 Union cannon and 50 mortars swinging into cooperative action.

Initially staggered by the blow, the Confederates fled in disarray instead of mounting a response. All seemed to proceed according to plan until Ledlie's division rushed into the breach and lost its way. Ledlie was nowhere to be found as his men milled around amid the smoking debris. Although Cemetery Hill commanded a direct route into Petersburg and was a mere three hundred or four hundred yards away, it wasn't taken. As Grant explained, he hadn't wanted Burnside's corps "to stop in the crater at all but push on to the top of the hill."[59] Burnside ignored these instructions while Ledlie was holed up in a bombproof trench, taking refuge in a bottle of rum. Instead of circumventing the breach, the troops had tried to rush through it and were trapped by the Crater's steep sides. They stood there adrift, defenseless, exposed to Confederate fire. "The shouting, screaming, and cheering," wrote Horace Porter, "mingled with the roar of the artillery and the explosion of shells, created a perfect pandemonium . . . the crater had become a caldron of hell."[60]

Simply dressed in a blue blouse and trousers in the blazing heat, Grant rode down to the front after the detonation, negotiating the final portion on foot, his face pasted with dust and sweat. Distracted soldiers brushed past him, not knowing it was Grant. He jumped over the parapet, exposing himself to enemy fire, and saw that the chance to advance had been fumbled. "These troops must be immediately withdrawn," he ordered. "It is slaughter to leave them here."[61] Even though the Confederates had been caught off guard, giving Burnside's men plenty of time to rush forward and capture Petersburg, the opportunity had been squandered. It was not so much the conception of the plan as its execution that had proven gravely defective.

Belatedly Burnside threw his black division, commanded by Brigadier General Edward Ferrero, into the maelstrom. By this time Union soldiers stood entrapped in a deep hole, easy targets for Confederate grenades. The black troops, who behaved gallantly, simply swelled the churning mass of soldiers meandering around. By now, the rebels, yelling racial epithets, had counterattacked and hurled grenades down at the black troops, who had no place to hide. In a burst of sadistic behavior, rebel soldiers responded with "a bayonet thrust" to cries for water from injured black soldiers.[62] Those who attempted to surrender were killed. Union forces suffered nearly four thousand dead, wounded, or missing—more than twice the number of their opponents—five hundred of them black.

Horace Porter recalled a sepulchral silence as Grant rode away from the scene of the disaster. He knew he had frittered away a chance to level a crippling blow at the Confederacy. When he finally broke the stillness, he remarked, "Such an opportunity for carrying a fortified line I have never seen, and never expect to see again."[63] In his *Memoirs,* he blamed Burnside and Ledlie without detailing the hideous carnage. In later years, he also claimed Gouverneur Warren had fatally hesitated to exploit the advantage opened by the Crater: "If Warren had obeyed orders we would have broken Lee's army in two and taken Petersburg."[64] Grant was not blameless, having given these incompetent officers too much latitude, then compounded his error by remaining curiously detached from the operation in its early stages. In time he confessed that he was culpable in allowing Ledlie—the worst division commander in Burnside's corps—to spearhead the fatal charge. "I knew that fact before the mine was exploded, but did nothing in regard to it. That is the only thing I blame myself for."[65]

Theodore Bowers, an aide, watched the toll taken on Grant, writing that "as the evidences of the disgraceful conduct of all concerned develop and thicken, Grant grows sicker at heart."[66] With his army enveloped by "gloom and despondency," Grant lay helpless with grief, confined to bed, his hopes deflated.[67] He came to consider the Crater disaster "the saddest affair I have witnessed in this war."[68] Meade and Burnside immediately descended into a round of mutual recriminations. Meade favored a court-martial for Burnside, whereas Grant just wanted him to exit quietly while a court of inquiry parceled out blame. In the end, Burnside was discreetly eased out of service.

After Cold Harbor and earlier fruitless attempts to take Petersburg, Grant knew the northern public would interpret the horrifying episode in an unforgiving mood. Many journalists wrote him off as no better than his predecessors. "Who shall revive the withered hopes that bloomed at the opening of Grant's campaign?" the *New York World* asked tartly.[69] Inside Lincoln's cabinet, Gideon Welles confessed to "an awakening apprehension that Grant is not equal to the position assigned him. God grant that I may be mistaken, for the slaughtered thousands of my countrymen who have poured out their rich blood for three months on the soil of Virginia from the Wilderness to Petersburg under his generalship can never be atoned in this world or the next" should he "prove a failure."[70]

On July 31, with wounded men still lying in the bloody chasm, Grant and Rawlins conferred for five hours with Lincoln and Assistant Secretary of the Navy Gustavus Fox at Fort Monroe. Grant asked to tour Norfolk, which he had never seen, before the party boarded a steamer. "The visit was very short for the heat was terrible," Fox explained, "so we pushed off towards the open ocean to get a sniff of the ocean air." Lincoln may have needed a chance to express his grave apprehensions to Grant in private. Nevertheless, he kept up his implicit trust in his ability to win the war, Fox noted, because Grant frankly owned up to the obstacles. "Neither Grant or the Pres[iden]t seemed cut down by the Petersburg affair . . . Genl Grant in our former visit told the Pres[iden]t that he should meet with several rebuffs but that he would finally get the place."[71]

The Crater wasn't the only atrocity exciting public comment. A day earlier, Jubal Early had torched Chambersburg, Pennsylvania, leaving three thousand residents homeless. For Lincoln and Grant, it was the last straw. Philip H. Sheridan, Grant's bantam cavalry commander, recalled that his assignment was to confront Early and "put an end to incursions north of the Potomac," which had hitherto turned Grant's army from its main purpose of destroying Lee and capturing Richmond.[72] The next day, Grant wired Halleck: "I want Sheridan put in command of all the troops in the field with instructions to put himself south of the enemy and follow him to the death."[73] On August 3, Lincoln, alarmed that Washington might be needlessly exposed, dissented sharply, telling Grant to "please look over the despatches you may have received from here . . . and discover if you can, that there is any idea in the head of any one here, of 'putting our army *South* of the enemy' or of following him to the *death* in any direction."[74] Nevertheless, Lincoln confirmed Sheridan's appointment. Grant was determined to stop Jubal Early and lay waste to the Shenandoah Valley, which had furnished its agricultural bounty to Lee's army for too long.

With Grant, Sherman, and Sheridan in place, the North now possessed an unbeatable team that surpassed Robert E. Lee and Joseph Johnston in its eagerness for combat and winning ways. The whole dismal parade of career hacks and self-promoting political generals on the Union side had been weeded out, giving way to a new fighting breed. Phil Sheridan, a pint-size man of cocky ferocity, was especially spoiling for a fight, convinced his cavalry could ride roughshod over anybody. Sheridan would command thirty thousand men in the Shenandoah Valley, eight thousand of them cavalry.

Born to poor Irish parents and reared in Somerset, Ohio, Sheridan, thirty-three, had fiery eyes, high cheekbones, and a handlebar mustache. He had been a middling student at West Point, his stay troubled by disciplinary problems. Already betraying a turbulent nature, he was suspended for a year after menacing a Virginia student with a bayonet. People tended to find "Little Phil," bow-legged and five feet five inches tall, risible in appearance, and Lincoln famously mocked him as "a brown, chunky little chap, with a long body, short legs, not enough neck to hang him, and such long arms that if his ankles itch he can scratch them without stooping."[75] George Templeton Strong wisecracked that Sheridan had "hair so short that it looks like a coat of black paint."[76]

Sheridan moved with a vigorous stride. An inspirational force in battle, mounted on his black horse Rienzi, he seemed to be everywhere at once, a whirl-wind of martial ardor. It was a matter of pride with him to fight in the front ranks, to which his men responded with adoration. "With the first smell of powder," said a journalist, "he became a blazing meteor, a pillar of fire to guide his own hosts."[77] Hotheaded, profane, excessively sure of himself, he never backed down or ran from trouble and was known for his salty comments. Like Grant, Sheridan had a pugnacity that refused to quit, and Sherman described him as "a persevering terrier dog, honest, modest, plucky and smart enough."[78] Quite unlike Grant, Sheridan was blunt and hard-drinking and almost foamed at the mouth when angry.

A superb judge of military talent, Grant made few errors in the generals he selected or cashiered. When he first met Sheridan at a railway station early in the war, Grant found him "brusque and rough," but he came to glory in his high spirits.[79] Most of all, he prized Sheridan's thorough preparations for battle and magnetic presence, sometimes rating him higher than Sherman. "He belongs to the very first rank of soldiers, not only of our country but of the world," Grant later commented. "I rank Sheridan with Napoleon and Frederick and the great commanders in history."[80] If there was an element of fraternal rivalry in Grant's relationship with Sherman, he displayed a purely paternal regard for Sheridan and was "as proud as a mother of a handsome son," said Augustus Chetlain.[81] Sheridan reciprocated this high regard, saying Grant "inspired me with confidence; he was so self-contained, and made you feel that there was a heap more in him than you had found out."[82]

Lincoln's telegram sent Grant rushing north for consultations to straighten out the command structure in the Shenandoah Valley. At Monocacy Junction in Maryland, Grant accepted the resignation of David Hunter, giving Sheridan undisputed control of troops in the Shenandoah Valley and Maryland. Grant gave him license for total warfare in the valley—a view congenial to Sheridan. "As war is a punishment," the latter believed, "if we can, by reducing its advocates to poverty, end it quicker, we are on the side of humanity."[83] Now Grant ordered Sheridan and his Army of the Shenandoah to ransack the valley so "that nothing should be left to invite the enemy to return . . . Such as cannot be consumed destroy."[84] Sheridan had few qualms about incinerating farms, destroying crops, and propagating terror. By August 8, a British soldier fighting with Confederate forces reported "columns of smoke . . . rising in every direction from burning houses and burning barns."[85]

Grant didn't endorse promiscuous destruction. Previously he had issued orders to Hunter stating that "indiscriminate marauding" should be avoided, that only supplies absolutely necessary for troops should be taken, and that receipts should be issued so loyal people could be reimbursed.[86] The order was perhaps more honored in the breach than the observance, as when Hunter's men looted and burned Lexington, Virginia, that June. Now in early August, Grant wrote: "It is not desirable that the buildings should be destroyed, they should rather be protected, but the people should be informed that so long as an Army can subsist among them, recurrences of these raids must be expected."[87]

Grant felt vindicated during his brief trip north, having redirected troops in Maryland to northern Virginia. He was also heartened by Admiral David Farragut's victory at Mobile Bay on August 5, achieving a long-sought objective. Grant knew, as he told Sherman, that Sheridan would "push the enemy to the very death."[88] Sherman wired back his pleasure that Sheridan would "worry Early to death. Let us give these southern fellows all the fighting they want and when they are tired we can tell them we are just warming to the work."[89] Whatever the gloom hanging over the North, Grant, Sherman, and Sheridan exhibited a combative spirit that would ultimately lead to victory. Grant had also won a major bureaucratic showdown, neutralizing Halleck's power. As Bowers told Rawlins, "He has settled Halleck down to a mere staff officer for Stanton. Halleck has no control over troops except as Grant delegates it. He can give no orders and exercises no discretion. Grant now runs the whole machine independently of the Washington directory."[90] Simplifying the command structure and concentrating power in Grant's hands would work to speed up Union victory.

By late August, Lee felt the pain of the terrifying tourniquet Grant was applying to his army, telling Jefferson Davis, "I think it is [the enemy's] purpose to endeavor to compel the evacuation of our present position by cutting off our supplies . . . It behooves us to do everything in our power to thwart his new plan of reducing us by starvation."[91] In early September, Lee confirmed that Grant was forcing him to fly blind in his own territory and react to Union initiatives. It was clear that Grant was in charge, setting the tempo and agenda and cramping Lee's style. "The enemy's position enables him to move his troops to right or left without our knowledge," Lee said, "until he has reached the point at which he aims, and we are then compelled to hurry our men to meet him, incurring the risk of being too late to check his progress."[92]

On the morning of August 9, Grant had just returned to City Point when the war came unexpectedly to his headquarters on the James River. A Confederate agent, John Maxwell, slipped through Union lines, clambered aboard a barge loaded with shells and ammunition, and planted gunpowder and a timing mechanism. As he hurried from the scene, a huge explosion threw up a towering shower of shells, bullets, splinters, iron bars, and human limbs, flinging them so high and far that fragments littered the ground a quarter mile away. By coincidence, Grant was then sitting in front of his tent, chatting with General George Sharpe, who had fretted about possible plots being hatched by nearby Confederate spies. Grant lived up to his image by exhibiting perfect sangfroid amid the mayhem. As the commissary chief Michael R. Morgan recalled, "I saw General Grant at his usual gait, walking up from his tent toward the adjutant-general's tent, taking things coolly, and seemingly not thinking anything out of the ordinary was taking place."[93] Grant took no precautions aside from ducking behind a large tree. Theodore Lyman remembered things differently. "The only man who, at the first shock, ran *towards* the scene of terror was Lieutenant-General Grant."[94]

Five minutes later, with his yard full of splinters and shell fragments, Grant filed a report with Halleck, claiming the death toll had reached fifty-three men, including thirty-eight black laborers. At first it was thought human error had triggered the mishap; seven years later, when Grant was president, a Virginian admitted the sabotage to Porter. The episode alerted Grant's staff to shortcomings in headquarters security and how readily a rebel assassin could snuff out Grant's life. Since Grant was congenitally heedless of danger and resisted extra security, his staff secretly organized a night watch to protect him. Grant never learned about this special layer of security until his second term as president.[95]

Despite the debilitating heat of a Virginia summer—"marching troops is nearly death," Grant observed—the headquarters staff tried to make life as tolerable as possible.[96] One commander attempted to divert Grant with a band that played patriotic and sentimental songs each evening, then discovered the lieutenant general was completely tone-deaf. "I've noticed that that band always begins its *noise* just about the time I am sitting down to dinner and want to talk," Grant protested.[97] The food at headquarters, though not lavish, was far superior to the grub of ordinary soldiers. "We live very well," Ely Parker reported. "Ice cream and all sorts of nice cakes cover our table at every meal."[98]

The one jarring note was the health of Rawlins, whose cough steadily worsened, exacerbated by dust from the constant procession of supply wagons. Grant expressed "no little anxiety about his illness," said Porter.[99] Rawlins's condition became so incapacitating that he took a three-month leave to recuperate with his family in Connecticut. Some observers feared he had consumption from which he would never recover and wondered darkly what that would mean for the man who had ridden herd on Grant's drinking problem for three years. "I fear [Rawlins] is permanently disabled, though I still hope he may recover," James H. Wilson told Badeau. "His loss would be irreparable, particularly when the surroundings of the General are considered. Heaven help us when some of the influences I know to be at work shall attain the ascendancy."[100]

Someone else might have resigned, but beyond unwavering loyalty to Grant and solicitude for his sobriety, Rawlins had an undying love of country. "Its greatness and glory is the one idea of my heart," he told his wife, "after my love and duty to you and our little ones."[101] While on leave, Rawlins consulted a New York medical specialist who reassured him that his cough was merely chronic bronchitis. Others were far more skeptical, including Charles Dana, who met Rawlins in Washington and detected "signs of increasing disease." Writing to Wilson, he did not mince words: "I fear there is no escape for him."[102]

Grant was no stranger to psychosomatic symptoms, and his bitter disappointment at the Crater was mirrored in lassitude and jangled nerves, as his body expressed what his mind could not admit. "Grant is not at all well," Provost Marshal Marsena R. Patrick wrote on August 18, "and there are fears that he is breaking down."[103] Bowers saw Grant's military frustration mirrored in poor health over a ten-day period: "He feels languid and feeble and is hardly able to keep about, yet he tends to business promptly and his daily walk and conduct are unexceptional."[104] For Bowers, Grant's low spirits bespoke his predicament as a man of action paralyzed by the lethargic tempo of the extended Petersburg siege. "I never before saw Grant so intensely anxious to do something," he informed Rawlins. "He appears determined to try every possible expedient . . . The failure to take advantage of opportunities pains and chafes him beyond anything I have ever before known him to manifest."[105]

Without Rawlins, Grant desperately needed Julia and the children, who visited City Point in August, staying for a day aboard a steamer. Grant still couldn't entirely shake depression when apart from his family. Now briefly buoyed by their company, he was emotionally carefree in a way he seldom managed alone. Porter left a charming vignette of him roughhousing with his boys: "The morning after their arrival, when I stepped into the general's tent, I found him in his shirt-sleeves engaged in a rough-and-tumble wrestling-match with the two older boys. He had become red in the face, and seemed nearly out of breath from the exertion. The lads had just tripped him up, and he was on his knees on the floor grappling with the youngsters, and joining in their merry laughter, as if he were a boy again himself."[106] Whenever she came to camp, Julia, a sprightly presence, enjoyed taking meals with the officers' mess and was widely appreciated for her geniality. In the evening, when she and Ulysses sat alone in the corner, they appeared to Porter "as bashful as two young lovers spied upon in the scenes of their courtship."[107] In company, Julia called him "Mr. Grant" and "Ulyss" to his face and sometimes added a private name she had coined for him after Vicksburg's fall—"Victor."

Grant's losses from Cold Harbor to the Crater left him leery of launching a major attack against Lee, and his men were equally gun-shy of direct assaults. The alternative was to draw the Confederates from their substantial entrenchments, which was no easy matter. Failing that, Grant could only tighten the pressure on Lee by cutting railroads linking Petersburg and Richmond and points south, sacking the Shenandoah Valley. He believed he had made it impossible for Lee to send troops to Atlanta and forced him to reinforce Petersburg by recalling men from the Shenandoah Valley as Confederate recruits ran short. "Unless some measure can be devised to replace our losses," Lee alerted the Confederate war secretary James Seddon, "the consequences may be disastrous."[108]

"The rich men and slave owners are but too successful in getting out, and in keeping out of the services," lamented the rebel war clerk John Jones in Richmond.[109] Southerners knew that, unlike Lee, Grant could replenish his army. Whatever his frustrations, his tenacious choke hold on Lee's army preyed on the minds of the southern populace, who knew Grant would never relent. In South Carolina, Mary Chesnut wrote resignedly that August, "Grant's dogged stay about Richmond is very disgusting and depressing to the spirits."[110]

Chew & Choke

A S AUGUST PROGRESSED, searing heat gave way to cooler weather and continual rain. Impatient to make headway, Grant pounded away at the rebels besieged in Petersburg, testing every chink in their armor. "Grant is striking out boldly in every possible direction . . . like a mad dog in a meat house," said one soldier.[1] Always fond of "demonstrations," Grant feigned fresh troop movements on the James River to goad Lee into recalling troops sent to aid Jubal Early.

Abraham Lincoln delighted in Grant's uncommon tenacity. In mid-August, fearful that a new draft would stoke more unrest in northern cities, Halleck urged Grant to send troops to deal with this eventuality. Grant balked from reluctance to relax his tight hold on Petersburg or give Lee a chance to send men to Georgia against Sherman. When Lincoln saw this response, he rejoiced in Grant's grit and wired him: "I have seen your despatch expressing your unwillingness to break your hold where you are. Neither am I willing. Hold on with a bull-dog gripe, and chew & choke, as much as possible."[2] Grant was seated in front of his tent, conversing with staff officers, when he read this dispatch. Horace Porter recorded his gratified reaction: "He opened it, and as he proceeded with the reading his face became suffused with smiles. After he had finished it he broke into a hearty laugh . . . 'The President,'" Grant announced, "'has more nerve than any of his advisers.'"[3] Despite the Crater disaster, Grant felt sufficiently secure in his position that he suggested to Stanton that Halleck be transferred to Oregon and Washington, which would have effectively removed him from the war.

The summer of 1864 represented the nadir of northern hopes as spreading disillusionment with the war threatened Lincoln's reelection. The appalling Virginia carnage had soured the public mood for further bloodshed. George Templeton Strong expressed the subdued mentality: "People seem discouraged, weary, and faint-hearted. They ask plaintively, 'Why don't Grant and Sherman do something?' . . . Such is the talk of not only Copperhead malignants, but of truly loyal men with weak backbones."[4] No incumbent since Andrew Jackson had won a second term and it looked as if Lincoln might have to settle for one. New York power broker Thurlow Weed assured William Seward that Lincoln would lose in November. "Nobody here doubts it; nor do I see anybody from other states who authorizes the slightest hope of success . . . The people are wild for peace."[5] Horace Greeley was categorical: "Mr. Lincoln is already beaten. He cannot be elected."[6]

There was constant speculation that Lincoln might have to withdraw his nomination in favor of Salmon Chase, Benjamin Butler, or even Grant, whose name figured in many such theories. In late May, disgruntled anti-Lincoln Republicans had met in Cleveland, formed a new party under the banner of Radical Democracy, and nominated John C. Frémont for president. When Democrats postponed their convention until late August, Noah Brooks thought this suggested the party might nominate "Grant or some other man whose availability will be made apparent by the campaign now in progress."[7] Of course, nobody knew Grant's exact political affiliations, multiplying the number of election theories. Grant himself rebuffed all efforts to groom him as a prospective candidate. When asked to furnish material for a biography, he scoffed, "I could not think of such a thing. It would be egotistical and I hope egotism is not to be numbered among my faults."[8] James Wilson told Badeau that Grant "would rather see Sherman President than any man in the country, if Mr. Lincoln cannot be reelected."[9]

On August 12, Lincoln summoned Colonel John Eaton to the White House and, after desultory conversation, unburdened his mind. "Do you know," Lincoln inquired, "what General Grant thinks of the effort now making to nominate him for the presidency? Has he spoken of it to you?"[10] No longer in close contact with him, Eaton agreed to go to City Point and sound out Grant. When he arrived, the two men talked past midnight, Grant pouring out his sorrows about the Crater episode and the botched chance to take Petersburg in June. They then discussed rumors that Stanton might be replaced, and while Grant hoped Stanton would be retained, he favored Rawlins as his successor. Finally,

Eaton gently nudged the conversation to whether Grant might be tempted to run for president. Eaton was startled by his unwonted vehemence. "We had been talking very quietly, but Grant's reply came in an instant and with a violence for which I was not prepared. He brought his clenched fists down hard on the strap arms of his camp-chair. 'They can't do it! They can't compel me to do it!'"[11] Once again, Grant understood the war's intertwined military and political dimensions. "I consider it as important for the cause that [Lincoln] should be elected as that the army should be successful in the field," he insisted.[12] When Eaton saw Lincoln again, the president pumped him for Grant's answer and he told how forcefully Grant had disavowed all political ambition. "The President fairly glowed with satisfaction," Eaton wrote. "'I told you,' said he, 'they could not get him to run until he had closed out the rebellion.'"[13]

What Grant did next attests to new political maturity, or perhaps new calculation: he began to write shrewdly crafted letters showing his complete agreement with the Lincoln administration. Previously he had shied away from such pronouncements. Now he thundered forth about southern perfidy and his unwillingness to compromise with slaveholders. All the while, he reaffirmed his distance from politics while, paradoxically, signaling sympathy with Lincoln. On August 16, he issued a plea for northern unity to Elihu Washburne, denouncing those who would divide the North and warning explicitly against any political settlement that preserved slavery:

> Our peace friends, if they expect peace from separation, are much mistaken. It would be but the beginning of war with thousands of Northern men joining the South because of our disgrace allowing separation. To have peace "on any terms" the South would demand the restoration of their slaves already freed. They would demand indemnity for losses sustained, and they would demand a treaty which would make the North slave hunters for the South. They would demand pay or the restoration of every slave escaping to the North.[14]

When Lincoln saw this statement, he promptly sent Washburne to secure Grant's permission to release it. Two days later, Grant expressed similar sentiments in a missive to Daniel Ammen, stating emphatically that "it would be better to be dead than to submit longer" to terms dictated by the South.[15]

The moment marked a watershed in Grant's life as he developed an avowed ideological commitment to the war as profound as his military contribution. Widening his outlook, he transcended the ethic of a mere soldier and, under Lincoln's tutelage, showed a touch of statesmanship. His new militance on abolition, coupled with his encouragement of black recruitment and devotion to "contraband" welfare, established a political outlook that would govern the rest of his career, setting an agenda from which he never deviated.

On August 18, twenty-five Radical Republicans met in New York City at the home of former mayor George Opdyke and agreed to call for a new Republican convention, with many pinning their hopes on Grant. Less than a week later, the Republican National Committee, also meeting in New York, decided that Lincoln's reelection prospects were nil. As their emissary, the journalist Henry J. Raymond, told Lincoln bluntly, "The tide is setting against us," and he advised the president to dispatch a peace commissioner to Richmond to negotiate an agreement that wouldn't obligate the South to renounce slavery.[16] To his eternal credit, Lincoln refused to trim his views on emancipation or contemplate a craven settlement. Against this backdrop, he asked his cabinet in late August to sign a document they were not allowed to read. Its opening sentence stated: "This morning, as for some days past, it seems exceedingly probable that this Administration will not be re-elected."[17] In the event he became a lame-duck president, Lincoln said, he wished to have a free hand to cooperate with the incoming administration to save the Union.

When the Democratic National Convention met in Chicago in late August, it brushed aside the militant views of War Democrats. Instead a determined peace faction pushed through a platform that renounced the war as an outright failure, demanded a "cessation of hostilities," called for a convention to restore peace, and reaffirmed states' rights. Many in this group believed abolition posed an insuperable obstacle to peace. On August 31, the convention nominated for president George B. McClellan, who was perfectly willing to trade emancipation for peace. Twenty years later, when composing his *Memoirs,* Grant still seethed over those distant events in Chicago, not deigning to mention McClellan by name: "The convention which had met and made its nomination of the Democratic candidate for the presidency had declared the war a failure. Treason was talked as boldly in Chicago at that convention as ever it had been in Charleston."[18] Grant was no less shocked by the vanity of General Winfield Scott Hancock, who garnered a single vote in Chicago. "He was so delighted that he smiled all over," Grant reminisced. "You could not even sit behind him without seeing him smile. He smiled all over. It crazed him. Before that we got on well. After that he would hardly speak to me."[19]

All predictions about the presidential race became obsolete on September 2 when Sherman marched into Atlanta. Fanatically determined to take the town, Sherman had promised he would leave Atlanta "a used up" community when he got through with it.[20] The next day, Sherman greeted Lincoln with the news that would help reelect him: "Atlanta is ours and fairly won."[21] Following a rough summer, Lincoln's prayers were answered, his despair abruptly converted into joy. After turning Atlanta into a military garrison, Sherman did not want to have to feed its citizens or assign extra troops to guard a sullen, restive population and ordered the evacuation of all residents. When the mayor pleaded that such an exodus would result in "appalling and heart-rending suffering," Sherman replied in lapidary prose: "War is cruelty, and you cannot refine it . . . You might as well appeal against the thunder storm as against these terrible hardships of war."[22]

Jefferson Davis knew that Atlanta, as a critical railway hub, had acted as linch-pin of the southern war economy and that its loss would "close up those rich granaries from which Lee's armies are supplied. It would give [the Union] control of our network of railways and thus paralyze our efforts."[23] The psychological effect was incalculable: Lincoln would be swept into office amid surging confidence while the South experienced a corresponding sense of doom. "I have never seen such a sudden lighting up of the public mind as since the late victory at Atlanta," wrote Theodore Tilton, the northern editor of the *Independent*. "This great event, following the Chicago platform—the most villainous political manifesto known to American history!—has secured a sudden unanimity for Mr. Lincoln."[24] Toppled by this tonic to northern spirits, John C. Frémont abandoned his insurgent candidacy, Republicans fell into line behind Lincoln, and McClellan disavowed the "peace plank" in the Democratic platform in short order.

On the evening of September 4, when he transmitted the official news of Sherman's victory, Samuel Beckwith found Grant smoking quietly before his tent with Rawlins. Grant already had an inkling of what had happened in Atlanta since rebels in Petersburg shouted the news to Union pickets. Now he perused the telegram "silently at first, and then, in a loud voice and with much satisfaction, he informed his companions of the contents. They greeted the announcement with a cheer. Of course the news spread like wildfire and the rejoicing soon became general."[25] Grant sent a congratulatory dispatch to Sherman and then, in an act of psychological warfare, fired a salute that evening from every battery near rebel lines.

Atlanta's conquest cemented the bond uniting Grant and Sherman, who spoke generously of each other. Grant told Sherman, "You have accomplished the most gigantic undertaking given to any General in this War and with a skill and ability that will be acknowledged in history as unsurpassed if not unequalled. It gives me as much pleasure to record this in your favor as it would in favor of any living man myself included."[26] In a reciprocal spirit, Sherman assured Grant that "I have always felt that you personally take more pleasure in my success than in your own and I appreciate the feeling to its fullest extent."[27]

Grant often doesn't receive the credit that properly belongs to him for Atlanta's fall. He was Sherman's boss and authored the interconnected strategy that guided Sherman's campaign. With Grant's advent as general in chief, the Union theaters of war no longer functioned as separate realms. Most important, Grant had kept up his harassment of Lee to prevent him from reinforcing Hood in Atlanta. Aside from Grant's strategic acumen, Sherman credited the telegraph network with "the perfect concert of action between the armies in Virginia and Georgia during 1864. Hardly a day intervened when General Grant did not know the exact state of facts with me, more than fifteen hundred miles away as the wires ran."[28] Grant's strategic achievements were inseparable from the advanced telegraphy of the Union side, which strung 15,389 miles of wire during the war, operated by an army of 1,500 linemen and operators.[29]

Since the essence of Grant's style of warfare was to exert unceasing pressure on his opponents, he didn't allow Sherman to rest on his laurels. "So soon as your men are sufficiently rested, and preparations can be made," Grant instructed him on September 10, "it is desirable that another campaign should be commenced. We want to keep the enemy constantly pressed to the end of the war."[30] Two days later, with discussions of a march to the sea in the air, Grant dispatched Porter to Atlanta to confer with Sherman. "I do not want to hamper him any more in the future than in the past with detailed instructions," Grant said. "I want him to carry out his ideas freely in the coming movement, and to have all the credit of its success."[31]

Aside from Sherman, the other potent weapon in Grant's arsenal was Sheridan, and on September 15 he left to confer with him in Charles Town, West Virginia, near Harpers Ferry. Sheridan had conducted a wild spree of devastation, burning wheat and hay and rounding up sheep, cattle, and horses. Grant's visit was propelled by a message from Lincoln, who expressed dismay that Early still controlled the Shenandoah Valley and wanted Grant to beef up Sheridan's forces to attack him. Grant set out with such a plan and also intended to prod Sheridan into disrupting two railroads and a canal that nourished Lee's army. As Grant chatted with Sheridan, a sergeant loitering outside growled about Grant: "I hate to see that old cuss around. When that old cuss is around there's sure to be a big fight on hand."[32] Before Grant could produce his battle plan, Sheridan unpacked a parcel of maps and, while the two men paced, spoke confidently about his ability to confront Early's army at Winchester, in north-west Virginia. Impressed by his confidence, Grant didn't even bother to take his own plan out of his pocket. "Could you be ready to move by next Tuesday?" he asked. "Oh, yes," Sheridan reassured him. "I can be off before daylight on Mon-day."[33] This was an assertive commander after Grant's own heart, and he decided not to linger in West Virginia "for fear it might be thought that I was trying to share in a success which I wished to belong solely to him."[34] Perhaps Grant re-membered Halleck trying to steal credit from him and shrank from committing the same error. He again showed he knew how best to motivate commanders by delegating authority to them—a trust that worked well with the talented, but could backfire with incompetents.

Grant went next to Burlington, New Jersey, to make provision for sending his children to school there. All summer long, he had thought of settling his family in Princeton because of its proximity to Philadelphia and Washington. In his elevated status, he set aside his old daydream of living on the West Coast and now thought exclusively in terms of residing in the corridor of politics and busi-ness along the eastern seaboard. When he and Julia were unable to find a suit-able house in Princeton or Philadelphia, her brother Fred had found them a "nice cottage pleasantly situated" in Burlington, a two-story house with a wide verandah and ivy creeping up the sides.[35] The boys would go to a military school while Nellie attended Miss Kingdon's School. During his day in Burlington, Grant was mobbed by the townsfolk. As he strolled toward the train station, a young woman said, "General, you have already done so much for us, that we expect a great deal more." When Grant replied, "I expect from Gen. Sherman more than from any other man in the country," the remark popped up in the *New York Tribune*.[36] Having lost his privacy, Grant confessed a touch ruefully to Julia: "It is but little pleasure now for me to travel."[37]

Upon returning to City Point, Grant told his officers how he had instructed Sheridan to "whip" Jubal Early. The verb "whip" struck one officer as unorthodox. "I presume the actual form of the order was to move out and attack him," he said. "No, I mean just what I say," retorted Grant. "I gave the order to whip him."[38] And that is exactly what thirty-three-year-old Sheridan did. On September 19, in an all-day battle, he clashed with Early's army at Winchester, and this bloody, seesaw contest climaxed with a classic infantry charge that sent Confederate soldiers "whirling through Winchester,"[39] wrote Sheridan's chief of staff, in a phrase soon parroted by the northern press. While both sides suffered 4,500 casualties, Sheridan's victory was unmistakable. Grant recommended his promotion to brigadier general in the regular army and he ascended to this new rank with lightning speed. As usual, Grant wanted his victorious commander to capitalize on victory, urging him to "push your success and make all you can of it."[40]

On September 22, Sheridan scored another triumph against Early at Fisher's Hill. He battered the rebel army with a shattering blow in the late-afternoon light, only darkness saving it from total destruction. Grant knew these Union triumphs in the Shenandoah Valley would have extensive ramifications for Lee's army. "Keep on," Grant exhorted Sheridan, "and your work will cause the fall of Richmond."[41] In a sign of Grant's expanding power in Washington, Stanton kept Julia closely apprised of events. "Sheridan fought another great battle yesterday," he wired her on September 23, "and won a splendid victory."[42] Thanks to Sheridan, Grant knew the rebel army wouldn't endanger Washington any time soon. On October 7, Sheridan boasted to Grant of having burned more than two thousand barns and seventy mills and rounded up three thousand sheep, a scorched-earth policy that prompted a massive flight of residents from the Shenandoah Valley and effectively depopulated it. Even the most hardened skeptics in Grant's army began to feel sanguine, even ebullient, about Union chances in the war.

On October 19, Sheridan capped his stellar campaign in the Shenandoah Valley with the battle of Cedar Creek. At dawn Confederate forces struck hard at Sheridan's men in a surprise attack, driving them back four miles and capturing twenty pieces of artillery. Sheridan had been in Washington, but when he returned to the fray that afternoon, he rallied his panic-stricken men on horseback in masterly fashion. Spying one division on rising ground, "I rode to the crest of the elevation, and there taking off my hat, the men rose up from behind their barricade with cheers of recognition," Sheridan recalled.[43] Riding along the line of battle, he led a counterattack that nearly caused Early's army to evaporate under pressure. Confederate soldiers flung away their weapons as they fled, bringing down the curtain on the war's last major battle in the valley. "Affairs at [the] time looked badly," Sheridan wired Grant, "but by the gallantry of our brave officers and men disaster has been converted into a splendid victory."[44] Sheridan's famous ride would be enshrined in art and poetry, converting him into a national hero.

Grant had loaded enormous responsibility upon Little Phil's shoulders, a trust amply repaid. When he received a dispatch about the Cedar Creek victory, he decided to have some fun with his staff, telling them first the sad news of how Sheridan's forces that morning had been "driven in confusion" from the battlefield. "That's pretty bad, isn't it?" he asked his staff, who echoed, "It's too bad, too bad!" "Now just wait till I read you the rest of it," he said, a mischievous gleam in his eye, then related the afternoon victory. As Porter said, "The general seemed to enjoy the bombshell he had thrown among the staff almost as much as the news of Sheridan's signal victory."[45] In homage to Sheridan, Grant ordered another hundred-gun salute. With the Shenandoah Valley in ruins, Grant no longer had to agonize over offensive threats from that direction and could concentrate his troops around Petersburg.

With Sherman and Sheridan on the move, Grant didn't remain idle. On September 29, in a surprise raid, the Army of the James under Ben Butler had captured Fort Harrison, which formed part of Richmond's outer defenses and was studded with big guns. Typically for Grant, he had an ulterior strategic motive: to force Lee to strengthen Richmond and thereby weaken Petersburg. When Grant rushed over to the captured fort, he found himself stepping gingerly over dead bodies strewn across the ground. "He turned his looks upward to avoid as much as possible the ghastly sight," wrote Porter, "and the expression of profound grief impressed upon his features told, as usual, of the effect produced upon him by the sad spectacle."[46] Despite Confederate bombardment, Grant clambered to the fort's parapet and was vouchsafed a closeup glimpse of church spires rising in central Richmond. Then, with his legs folded under him and projectiles bursting around him, the placid Grant sat down on the grass and penned orders for further attacks. According to Badeau, "A dead man lay at his feet whose head had been taken off; the blood and masses of hair from the scalp of wounded Rebels were scattered around; while Grant wrote, shells flew over the fort by the score . . . two burst immediately over his head, but he never looked up, tho' men and officers . . . ran for cover from the fragments."[47]

  The upshot of the victory was that Grant threw up a new line of entrenchments, forcing Lee, exhausted and suffering from sciatica, to broaden his defensive line despite waning manpower. Grant's strategy was working better than he
knew. Lee's lines were stretched so taut that on November 2 he warned Jefferson
Davis that without a fresh infusion of troops, "I fear a great calamity will befall
us."[48] Adam Badeau marveled at how coolly Grant directed all the moving pieces
of the war machinery from City Point. "While here, Grant goes out to the very
front, is under fire for hours together, and at the same time he receives despatches
from Sherman a thousand miles away, and directs the movements of his army at
Atlanta, of another in Louisiana, of the forces at Mobile; and smokes his cigar in
calm and quiet all the while," he informed Edwin Booth.[49]

  By the time Porter visited Atlanta in late September, Sherman had already
broached to Grant the idea of crossing Georgia with sixty thousand men, breaking loose from his supply lines and battening off rich farmland so that "Grant
will have to learn of my whereabouts . . . by means of scouts . . . and possibly
depend largely upon the news obtained from rebel newspapers," Sherman said
presciently.[50] Not quite sure what Sherman would do next, Grant fortified his
army with new recruits. Meanwhile Jefferson Davis blustered that he would
maul Sherman's supply lines and force him into an ignominious retreat, reminiscent of Napoleon from Moscow, which Grant found amusing. "Davis has not
made it quite plain who is to furnish the snow for this Moscow retreat through
Georgia and Tennessee," he joked.[51] Grant's major reservation about a march to
the sea, shared by Lincoln, was that John Bell Hood's army might lurch northward and jeopardize Tennessee unopposed. Unfazed, Sherman promised he
would dispatch George Thomas to the state with sixty thousand men to safeguard its security. In his flamboyant style, Sherman assured Grant he would
accomplish the "utter destruction" of Georgia's roads, houses and people. "I can
make the march and make Georgia howl."[52]

  On October 11, when it looked as if Hood would veer into middle Tennessee,
Grant gave Sherman the option of pursuing Hood—the choice he favored—or
setting out across Georgia for Savannah. Sherman preferred Georgia and "smashing things to the sea."[53] He aimed to shift the whole calculus of the war, lunging
across a broad swath of southern territory, not to hunt down an army but to demolish the civilian foundations of the war. His fiery procession would make a
major statement about unmatched northern might versus southern weakness.
This wasn't a European war, with two mercenary armies fighting each other,

Sherman contended, but a civil war where the pride of the southern populace had to be humbled. "If we can march a well appointed Army right through [Jefferson Davis's] territory, it is a demonstration to the World, foreign and domestic, that we have a power which Davis cannot resist," he told Grant.[54]

Recognizing Sherman's zeal, Grant let him pursue his favored course. "Sherman is a man with so many resources," Grant later said, "and a mind so fertile, that once an idea takes root it grows rapidly."[55] He gave Sherman credit for the idea of the march to the sea and its superb execution. He showed guts and daring by allowing Sherman to patent this new style of warfare despite stubborn opposition from Halleck and, more surprisingly, from Rawlins. Grant later declared he would only have trusted Sherman and Sheridan to accomplish such a hazardous undertaking. Lincoln registered grave misgivings. "The President feels much solicitude in respect to Sherman's proposed movement and hopes that it will be maturely considered," Stanton notified Grant.[56] Despite this, Grant sided with Sherman's audacity. "On mature reflection," he telegraphed Stanton, "I believe Sherman's proposition is the best that can be adopted . . . Such an Army as Sherman has, (and with such a commander) is hard to corner or capture."[57]

Grant loaded rations and ammunition aboard vessels that would steam down the eastern seaboard and rendezvous with Sherman at Savannah or another coastal spot. He approved Sherman's campaign of robust destruction, but within specified limits. When Sherman inquired if Grant was "willing that I should destroy Atlanta and the railroad," Grant advised, "Destroy in such case all of *military* value in Atlanta" (italics added).[58] Braced to lay down a ribbon of destruction, Sherman exhibited a bravado that contrasted sharply with Grant's solemnity. As he telegraphed on October 19, "I propose to abandon Atlanta, and . . . sally forth to ruin Georgia and bring up on the sea-shore."[59]

By November 1, with Hood's army marching north, Grant reversed position and told Sherman his first order of business should be to destroy that army. An anguished Sherman replied that Thomas could check any adverse moves by Hood: "If I turn back the whole effect of my campaign will be lost."[60] Always hesitant to second-guess field commanders, Grant wired him to proceed with his plan to traverse Georgia. By November 15, having destroyed everything of military value in Atlanta, Sherman inaugurated his three-hundred-mile march to the sea. He left a town "smouldering and in ruins," he wrote, "the black smoke rising high in air, and hanging like a pall over the ruined city."[61] The departing rebels also contributed to the destruction of the city. Sherman's army largely followed the railroad, plucking up rails as they went, heating them in bonfires, then twisting them around nearby trees or telegraph poles. He also had "bummers" fan out across the countryside to collect every morsel of food they could find. As he had warned Grant, Sherman and his army vanished into a black hole, severing telegraphic communication with City Point and Washington and cutting loose from any supply base. Grant scanned Richmond papers for any snippets of news about the march. Unnerved by the news blackout, Lincoln turned to Grant for reassurance, then told listeners, "Grant says they are safe with such a general [as Sherman], and that if they cannot get out where they want to, they can crawl back by the hole they went in at."[62] A confident Grant expected Sherman to crack the South wide open. "The Confederacy is a mere shell," he told a reporter. "I know it. I am sure of it. It is a hollow shell, and Sherman will prove it to you."[63] The more he later learned about the unity and esprit de corps of Sherman's army, the more enamored Grant grew of the sixty thousand men who were "as good soldiers as ever trod the earth; better than any European soldiers, because they not only worked like a machine but the machine thought."[64]

ASIDE FROM RANDOM FIGHTS and skirmishes between pickets, the Virginia war wound down to the low-level intensity of a siege in autumn 1864. By late October, colder weather and impassable roads hindered major troop movements. Mired in this stalemate, Grant lobbied for more troops and entertained visiting dignitaries at City Point. Stories of his drinking still circulated, Gideon Welles writing in December that "[Assistant Secretary of the Navy Gustavus] Fox says Grant occasionally gets drunk . . . There were such rumors of him when in the West."[65] With Rawlins's return, such rumors mostly subsided. When Grant sat for a portrait by the Norwegian painter and Union officer Ole Peter Hansen Balling, he asked Grant why he served only water to visitors. "How could I permit a drop of liquor or wine in my camp," Grant replied, "with all the newspaper slander I receive?"[66]

In September and October, Grant derived patent excitement from sitting around the campfire in the evening and reading aloud to fellow officers the spirited dispatches from Sheridan in the Shenandoah Valley. He was especially heartened by the reappearance of Rawlins, whose health had marginally improved during his furlough, but who was immediately bothered by the damp weather. "The day he arrived General Grant saw that he was still far from well, and said with much distress, when Rawlins was out of earshot, 'I do not like that cough,'" wrote Porter.[67]

All year long, Grant had remained foursquare behind black recruitment and aiding runaway slaves. "Every negro that comes in is taken into the service now, the best specimens physically being enlisted in companies already organized and the others are employed as laborers in some of the Departments or sent North," Grant informed Halleck that summer. "I will add also that every expedition going out brings back all the negroes they can find."[68] He supported recruiting the maximum number of black soldiers, telling Sherman to arm as many as possible on his swing through Georgia: "As far as arms can be supplied either from surplus on hand or by capture I would put them in the hands of negro men."[69] By late September, even Robert E. Lee had to entertain the idea of enlisting free blacks and slaves as teamsters and laborers.

That summer, Grant made a difficult decision to suspend prisoner exchanges. Prison camps on both sides teemed with a hundred thousand prisoners, many confined under deplorable conditions. With the rebellion running short of able-bodied men, such exchanges, Grant thought, could only benefit the Confederacy. "Every man released, on parole or otherwise, becomes an active soldier against us," he argued. "If we commence a system of exchanges which liberates all prisoners taken we will have to fight on until the whole South is exterminated."[70] A policy that could seem heartless to northern soldiers languishing in southern prisons, Grant reasoned, was only fair to northern soldiers in the field. He also believed devoutly that he held Lee's best soldiers in captivity and he did not care to release them.

On October 1, Lee proposed a prisoner exchange of soldiers captured outside Richmond. To his credit, Grant confronted Lee about whether he planned to exchange black troops on the same basis as whites. Lee responded that he had no intention of handing over fugitive slaves turned Union soldiers and said those "belonging to our Citizens are not Considered Subjects of exchange."[71] Grant rebuffed these obnoxious conditions, notifying Lee that "the Government is bound to secure to all persons received into her Armies the rights due to soldiers."[72] As the correspondence wore on, Lee treated Grant to a frosty lecture on the right of southern slave owners to reclaim black soldiers who had been their slaves, and his stilted language revealed something about his bad faith in defending this abhorrent practice: "The constitutional relations and obligations of the Confederate government to the owners of this species of property, are the same as those so frequently and so long recognized as appertaining to the government of the United States, with reference to the same class of persons, by virtue of its organic law."[73] The insistence on retaining black prisoners remained official Confederate policy until June 1865.

In a mark of Grant's confidence in the war's successful finale, he foresaw that, before too long, he would be able to switch his headquarters to Washington and spend the bulk of his time with his family in Burlington. "How anxious I am that this time should come," he told Julia, allowing his mind to wander to more pleasant times. "There has not been one hour since this war commenced that I have been relieved from anxiety."[74] For the foreseeable future, he knew his duties would restrict him to the eastern seaboard. As he pondered domestic matters for the first time in years, he urged Julia to bring to Burlington the able young woman who had cooked for them in Galena. "I want of all things good cooking when I get back home. It makes the greatest difference in my feeling well."[75] His thoughts strayed to his investments in railroad and copper stocks and his wish to have an annual income of $6,000 at the war's close. In a startling act of generosity, he informed Julia that he had written to Colonel Dent, who was ailing, and invited him to live with them. Aside from his love for Julia, this invitation perhaps reflected the newfound confidence and exalted stature Grant had attained during the war, making him less vulnerable to any bullying from his hypercritical father-in-law.

Grant had been offended that Julia's brother John defected to the Confederacy to manage a Mississippi plantation. When he was captured near Vicksburg by Union soldiers, Grant thought his imprisonment a salutary lesson and made little effort to free him. By August 1864, when it looked as if Dent would be sent north in a prisoner exchange, Grant remained caustic, telling his brother-in-law Fred, "I hope John has been thoroughly cured of his *secesh* sympathies by the long sojourn he has been forced to submit to with the people he defends."[76] In the end, Grant relented and negotiated John Dent's release in early March 1865.

In Grant's letters to Julia, there appeared a noticeable increase in his advice about their children, as if he were now overly compensating for lost time. He lectured his sons on spelling, urging them to write letters with a dictionary by their side, an ironic emphasis in light of Grant's own erratic orthography. The most mischievous child was still young Jesse, who had contracted a sudden allergy to school. "As to Jess refusing to go to school I think you will have to show him that you are *boss*," Grant advised Julia. "How does he expect ever to write letters to his Pa, or get to be Aide de Camp if he does not go to school and learn to write."[77]

With a presidential election in the offing, Grant was drawn into a contro-versy over whether soldiers in the field should be allowed to cast ballots. Writing to Stanton on September 27, he displayed growing political maturity and made an eloquent argument for permitting this. Conceding that in the past this prac-tice was faulted as "dangerous to constitutional liberty and subversive of Mili-tary discipline," he noted the novel circumstance of having a large portion of the electorate under arms. "In performing this sacred duty, [soldiers] should not be deprived of a most precious privilege. They have as much right to demand that their votes shall be counted, in the choice of their rulers, as those citizens, who remain at home; Nay more, for they have sacrificed more for their country."[78] However much he wished to see Lincoln reelected, Grant remained studiously nonpartisan. Even though newspapers and campaign literature flowed freely in Union camps, he barred political meetings or attempts to harangue soldiers for particular candidates. In the end, many states permitted absentee ballots, although Grant, a Galena resident, couldn't vote because Illinois didn't allow that. At Stanton's behest, Grant allowed Delaware soldiers to return home on furlough to vote in a state that denied voting rights in the field.

The election posed a major test of whether American democracy could per-sist under stringent wartime conditions, and everybody acknowledged the over-riding importance of the outcome. "Seldom in history was so much staked on a popular vote," Ralph Waldo Emerson said, articulating a familiar sentiment. "I suppose never in history."[79] Grant might consider a Union victory a foregone conclusion, but skeptics wondered how the North, with twenty million citizens, had been held at bay for two and a half years by five million recalcitrant white southerners. With so much at stake, the election dove straight down into gutter politics, with Democrats accusing "Black Republicans" of promoting "miscegenation"—a loaded word they introduced into the political lexicon dur-ing the campaign.

In the end, Lincoln received a resounding vindication, winning by a land-slide 212 electoral votes versus 21 for McClellan, while the popular vote told a much less encouraging tale. Lincoln surpassed McClellan by fewer than half a million of four million votes, drawing only 55 percent of the popular tally. A later analysis of absentee ballots in twelve states showed soldiers helped to tip the scales toward Lincoln, favoring him with 78 percent of their votes versus 53 percent among civilian voters.[80] Clearly soldiers wished to endow their service with transcendent meaning that would be negated by a Democratic victory and a negotiated settlement. Lincoln celebrated his win with a paean to American democracy, stating that the election "demonstrated that a people's government can sustain a national election, in the midst of a great civil war. Until now it has not been known to the world that this was a possibility."[81]

Grant and his staff displayed considerable anxiety as they awaited election returns on November 8. That night, they gathered around a campfire and listened as Grant read aloud a succession of telegrams updating the results. With his puckish humor, Grant again played the prankster and kept telling officers that each new dispatch showed McClellan in the lead. Only after midnight—by which time many dejected officers had drifted off to bed—did he admit delightedly that it had all been a hoax and Lincoln had been ahead the whole time. The results endorsed Grant's leadership no less than Lincoln's. Through Stanton, Grant conveyed his congratulations to the president. "The election having passed off quietly," he wrote, "no bloodshed or riot throughout the land, is a victory worth more to the country than a battle won. Rebeldom and Europe will so construe it."[82]

As Lincoln and Grant hoped, the Confederacy gazed with dismay at the election results since its whole strategy had been predicated on fomenting northern fears and defeating Lincoln at the polls. The southern shortage of manpower grew urgent. Every time another soldier in gray died, deserted, or was wounded, it meant a permanent shrinkage in rebel ranks. On November 7, in a shocking ideological reversal, Jefferson Davis endorsed a plan to buy forty thousand slaves who would take up arms for the South and receive freedom at the end of the war—that is, if the South won. The only alternative to this radical concession was total defeat, Davis concluded, but the response of constituents was overwhelmingly hostile. In the words of Howell Cobb of Georgia, who helped to create the Confederacy, "The day you make soldiers of [slaves] is the beginning of the end of the revolution. If slaves will make good soldiers, our whole theory of slavery is wrong—but they won't make good soldiers."[83] The plan to arm slaves was the reductio ad absurdum of the entire war. In his bones Grant knew the Confederacy's days were numbered, insisting in November that the rebels couldn't "recover from the blow he hopes to give them this winter."[84]

With the election safely behind him, Grant permitted himself a flying visit to Burlington, bringing in tow Samuel Beckwith to guarantee uninterrupted telegraphic contact with his army. His train pulled into the Burlington station after dark, and he was flustered and embarrassed that he had no idea where to go. "They say I live here," he confessed to two men on the platform, "but I don't know where."

When the local police chief caught a glimpse of him under a lantern, he exclaimed, "Thunder, it's General Grant," and escorted him to his house on Wood Street. Because Grant had no key, he rapped at the door like a stranger, even though it was past midnight. From an upstairs porch, Julia called down: "Is that you, Ulyss?" When he replied, "Yes," she came down and admitted him to his new home.[85]

After a brief stay, Grant collected Julia, the children, and Badeau and stopped at the Astor House in Manhattan. For reasons of modesty and possibly security, Grant issued no formal announcement of his arrival—Badeau asked the local press to ignore him—yet the moment he showed up, he caused a sensation. Hundreds of admirers encircled his hotel, staring up at his windows, trying to spot him. When he entered the hotel dining room, arm in arm with the New York governor-elect Reuben Fenton, he received a foretaste of the pandemonium that would greet his postwar appearances. People leapt on chairs and tables, roaring, cheering. Garbed in his threadbare blue army overcoat, Grant toured the city streets for the first time in two decades until crowds recognized him, making strolling impossible. He also rode a streetcar, hanging on a strap and unable to sit down because no passenger believed his escorts that this really was General Grant. As prominent figures trooped to his hotel, Badeau had fresh cause to extol Grant's unassuming demeanor. "He is a more unselfish man than [George] Washington, and is free from vanity," he wrote. "I have never seen anyone comparable to him in public life . . . Hundreds of years hence, some actor will be studying his character and 'making up' for him instead of Hamlet."[86] For the more cynical Rawlins, Grant seemed to engage in a gaudy show of fake modesty, stage-managed by the limelight-craving Badeau, and he grumbled that Grant should never have permitted Badeau to "ostentatiously announce his desire that his presence should not be noticed."[87]

On his way back to City Point, Grant stayed at the Willard Hotel to confer with Lincoln. Stanton felt poorly from overwork and, in the election's aftermath, some enemies schemed to oust him. Lincoln promised Grant that, if any change occurred, he would be consulted about his successor. Gruff though Stanton was, Grant transcended petty politics and judged the war secretary on his true merits. "I doubt very much whether you could select as efficient a Secretary of War as the present incumbent," Grant assured Lincoln. "He is not only a man of untiring energy and devotion to duty, but even his worst enemies never for a moment doubt his personal integrity and the purity of his motives."[88] With election-year politics over, Grant submitted a list of eight major generals and thirty-three brigadiers whom he wanted drummed out of the service. Some were political generals, including Franz Sigel, John McClernand, and Carl Schurz, whose military ability Grant had long questioned, and he would pay dearly after the war for their enmity. Some names on the list frankly surprised Lincoln. "Why, I find that lots of the officers on this list are very close friends of yours; do you want them all dropped?" Grant's response was patriotic: "That's very true, Mr. President; but my personal friends are not always good generals."[89]

When Grant bestowed his seal of approval on Sherman's march to the sea, it was premised on the idea that George Thomas would handle the army of John Bell Hood that Sherman had left behind. However disabled Hood was—he had an injured arm and an amputated leg and stumped about on crutches strapped to his saddle—Grant still deemed him a formidable threat. On November 30, at the battle of Franklin, south of Nashville, a portion of Thomas's army savaged Hood, producing seven thousand Confederate casualties, triple the number of federal victims. Despite the severe damage, Hood was undeterred, and by December 2 he confronted Thomas and the Union defenses at Nashville. A resolute commander with a faulty strategic sense, Hood hoped to defeat Thomas, take Kentucky and Tennessee, then possibly link up with Lee's army or turn north to the Ohio River. Implausible though this scenario might be, Grant began to pester Thomas to show no mercy to Hood's army, the Lincoln administration being hugely alarmed by its progress. To his extreme frustration, Thomas said he needed to await the arrival of more cavalry before taking on Hood, and he planned in the interim to hunker down in a defensive posture.

Grant had long criticized Thomas for dilatory behavior and Nashville only strengthened his case. As always, Grant thought it wrong to await reinforcements when the enemy might perfect his defenses in the interim. "Time strengthens [Hood] in all probability as much as it does you," he warned Thomas.[90] He burned with the conviction that Thomas already had enough men to "annihilate [Hood] in the open field."[91] In Grant's opinion, the hapless Hood had committed an egregious blunder in trying to take Nashville, and he wished to capitalize on it. Later on, Grant contended that, had he been Hood, "I would have gone to Louisville, and on north until I came to Chicago. What was the use of his knocking his head against the stone walls of Nashville? If he had gone north, Thomas never would have caught him."[92]

Until December 6, despite persistent coaxing of Thomas, Grant only *suggested* that he attack Hood posthaste. Now, in an uncharacteristic fit of pique and fearful Hood would make a dash for the Ohio River and the North, Grant gave direct orders to attack at once. When Thomas did not comply the next day, Grant, his ire mounting, told Halleck to get ready to supplant him with General John M. Schofield. "There is no better man to repel an attack than Thomas," Grant wired Halleck, "but I fear he is too cautious to ever take the initiative."[93]

On December 8, Grant ratcheted up the pressure on Thomas with an impassioned telegram. By this point he fairly breathed fire: "Now is one of the fairest opportunities ever presented of destroying one of the three Armies of the enemy. If destroyed he can never replace it."[94] The next day, Thomas swore he was set to attack when "a terrible storm of freezing rain" immobilized him. From Halleck, Thomas knew of Grant's wrath, telling the latter stoically, "I can only say I have done all in my power to prepare, and if you should deem it necessary to relieve me I shall submit without a murmur."[95] Regarding Thomas as a man of rock-solid rectitude and ability, Grant wrestled with a quandary. He was eager to salvage the pride of this valiant warrior but he also didn't wish to let slip a major chance to destroy a southern army. The Petersburg siege could only have heightened his yearning for a dramatic victory. "I was never so anxious during the war as at that time," Grant wrote, and Porter confirmed the "mental torture" Grant endured.[96] In these trying days, he seemed short-tempered, but even as his emotions simmered at a slow boil, he decided to give Thomas one last chance.

On December 13, caving in to anxiety, Grant ordered Major General John A. Logan to proceed to Nashville with instructions to relieve Thomas *unless* he had already attacked Hood, in which case the order was nullified. Stretched on a rack of worry, Grant couldn't relax, which was unusual for him with his outwardly even temper. "His uneasiness of mind was revealed in his drawn features," recalled Beckwith.[97] Finally, on December 14, Grant made a snap decision to relieve Thomas in person in Nashville. "Beckwith," he ordered, "you've got just fifteen minutes to pack your knapsack and get on that boat. Hustle."[98] Filling his pockets with cigars, Grant left City Point by a special dispatch boat, intending to talk with Lincoln and then grab a train to Nashville. Though reluctant to second-guess Thomas, Lincoln didn't stand in Grant's way.

As Grant tarried in Washington, the War Department received a late-night telegram that Thomas had initiated the long-delayed attack, slammed into the enemy force, and thoroughly routed it. "It was along toward midnight when [Grant] returned to the [Willard] hotel, and I noticed that his face wore a smile of satisfaction that betokened good tidings," said Beckwith. "He came to me directly and there was a note of cordiality in his voice that had been missing for many a day as he said: 'Beckwith, I guess that we won't go to Nashville after all. Thomas has licked Hood.'"[99] An overjoyed Stanton bustled off to the White House where a "highly delighted" Lincoln pored over the victory news by candlelight, standing in his nightshirt.[100] A potential threat had been averted and irreparable harm inflicted on a major rebel force.

Grant entreated Thomas to follow up on victory and punish his foe further. "Push the enemy now and give him no rest until he is entirely destroyed."[101] Astride his horse, in the rear of the action, a chastened Hood reflected that "I behold for the first and only time a Confederate army abandon the field in confusion."[102] Just as Grant hoped, Hood's Army of Tennessee was whittled down from forty thousand to fewer than twenty thousand men and was pummeled into such panicky disarray that it effectively ceased to exist as a single army. To celebrate Thomas's achievement, Grant ordered a two-hundred-gun salute, topping the one-hundred-gun standard of earlier victories.

At the time Sherman left Atlanta, Grant predicted Hood would refuse to follow him and turn north into Tennessee and that Thomas would then vanquish him. The sequence of events made Grant again look startlingly prophetic, and the demise of Hood's army left the battered Confederacy with only one truly powerful army in the field—Lee's Army of Northern Virginia. In congratulating Thomas, Grant revealed the motive behind his urgency to defeat Hood. He had long operated on the theory that the southern army could only shrink in size, but now Davis and Lee had floated the idea of arming slaves. "Let us push and do all we can before the enemy can derive benefit either from the raising of Negro troops or the concentration of white troops now in the field," Grant implored Thomas, who came away from the December events with bruised feelings that never entirely healed.[103]

Though they had temporarily lost telegraphic contact, Grant never forgot that Sherman and his men were charging toward the seacoast, and he made a point of keeping Lee trapped in Petersburg and Richmond, unable to detach troops to prevent it. "My own opinion," Grant wrote, pinpointing his foe's strategic flaw, "is that Lee is averse to going out of Va. and if the cause of the South is lost he wants Richmond to be the last place surrendered."[104] But if Lee moved south to block Sherman, Grant was prepared to trail his army down to Georgia. Whenever Lincoln expressed jitters about Sherman, Grant assuaged his fears, saying, "There was no danger but [Sherman] would *strike* bottom on Salt Water some place. That I would not feel the same security, in fact would not have entrusted the expedition to any other living commander."[105]

From the rebel press, Grant gleaned shards of information about Sherman's whereabouts and in late November read a proclamation by General Beauregard in a Savannah newspaper, summoning Georgia residents to block his progress: "Arise for the defense of your native soil. Rally around your patriotic government and gallant soldiers, obstruct and destroy all roads in Sherman's front, flank and rear and his Army will soon starve in your midst."[106] Even as Sherman was demonized in the South, the black community welcomed him as their liberator. White folks might stare with stony contempt at the endless columns of northern troops striding through their towns, but their slaves, wrote Sherman, "were simply frantic with joy. Whenever they heard my name, they clustered about my horse, shouted and prayed in their peculiar style, which had a natural eloquence that would have moved a stone. I have witnessed hundreds, if not thousands, of such scenes."[107] Many rapturous blacks saw Sherman's army as an instrument of the Lord, come to deliver them from bondage. "Us looked for the Yankees," one said, likening them to "de host of angels at de second comin'."[108] Sherman feared that if too many former slaves joined his march, they would encumber it, and he noted apprehensively that "fifty negroes and footsore soldiers" seemed to follow every regiment.[109] In all, an estimated twenty thousand slaves deserted their plantations to travel on the edges of Sherman's army.[110]

By mid-December, Grant deduced from southern newspapers and a dispatch from Sherman's army that reached Washington that his colleague was closing in on Savannah. He pondered what Sherman should do when the town fell. At first he wanted him to establish a coastal base, then embark by sea with a large portion of his troops, traveling north to join him on the James River. Then, on December 16, with Savannah under siege, Sherman wrote to Grant and described the spectacular success of his novel strategy of living off the land. He depicted his ruddy troops gorging on sweet potatoes and cornmeal, as well as turkeys, chickens, sheep, hogs, and beef. Having started out with five thousand head of cattle, his army, as if by some miracle, arrived outside Savannah with ten thousand, having seized many along the route. "Our whole Army is in fine condition as to health, and the weather is splendid."[111]

Sherman was reluctant to move his army by water to the James River. When he learned that Grant had so few ships to ferry his soldiers northward that the operation would take two months, he touted his plan to march up through the

Carolinas and Grant concurred. Aware of being the South's bête noire, Sherman hoped to take advantage of this terrifying image and foresaw the psychological effect a march would have in demoralizing the enemy. He wanted southerners to "feel the hard hand of war" and realize that, contrary to southern propaganda, the North was winning. To Grant, Sherman talked of visiting havoc on the Carolinas, boasting, "I can go on and smash South Carolina all to pieces."[112] With his former love of southern culture, Sherman both feared and favored a policy of revenge. "The truth is, [my] whole army is burning with an insatiable desire to wreak vengeance upon South Carolina," he informed Halleck. "I almost tremble at her fate, but feel that she deserves all that seems in store for her."[113]

By December 20, 1864, the Confederate garrison evacuated Savannah, leaving behind a large trove of invaluable supplies in their haste to leave. Sherman's entrance into the city released an outpouring of joy among liberated blacks. "Shout the glad tidings o'er Egypt's dark sea," cried an elderly man. "Jehovah has triumphed, his people are free."[114] Sherman's letter notifying Lincoln of what happened became an instant classic: "I beg to present you as a Christmas-gift the city of Savannah, with one hundred and fifty heavy guns and plenty of ammunition, also about twenty-five thousand bales of cotton. W. T. Sherman, *Major-General*."[115] Lincoln cherished this holiday gift, remarking that the combined triumphs of Thomas and Sherman "brings those who sat in darkness, to see a great light."[116] Grant transmitted copies of Sherman's victory telegram to his corps commanders. Henceforth Sherman, once stigmatized as incurably insane in the northern press, would be lionized as "Tecumseh the Great." Amid all the hoopla and talk of elevating him to a new rank, Sherman admonished his brother, "I will accept no commission that would tend to create a rivalry with Grant."[117]

Grant remained the presiding genius of the war effort. Sheridan's successful rampage through the Shenandoah Valley, Thomas's demolition of Hood's army at Nashville, Sherman's conquest of Atlanta and Savannah—all formed part of the scheme he had envisaged when he became general in chief. He had accomplished exactly what he had set out to do, interweaving his far-flung armies so they cooperated in a single strategy and moved with a common purpose, the result being that the Confederacy was sliced into ever smaller pieces. The only stalled part of his scheme was Virginia, but that effort had bottled up Lee and stopped his army from aiding embattled rebel forces in Tennessee and Georgia. Now Grant set his sights on finishing off the most fearsome Confederate army.

Her Satanic Majesty

EVEN AS HE masterminded the land campaigns, Grant investigated ways to shut down the few remaining southern ports that defied the Union blockade. A major objective was to capture the port of Wilmington, North Carolina, a move Gideon Welles thought might damage the Confederacy almost as much as losing Richmond. The last major harbor east of the Mississippi River still available to blockade runners, it provided ammunition and other essential imports that went straight to bolster Lee's army. Grant cited a compelling diplomatic need to seize Wilmington "because foreign governments, particularly the British Government, were constantly threatening that unless ours could maintain the blockade of that coast they should cease to recognize any blockade."[1] The key obstacle to any operation against Wilmington was Fort Fisher, a mammoth earthwork redoubt guarding the mouth of the Cape Fear River, just below the port. When Grant discovered that Confederate soldiers in North Carolina were being shunted off to fight Sherman in Georgia, he spotted a chance to deprive the Confederacy of its last Atlantic outpost.[2]

By early December, Ben Butler had concocted a far-fetched scheme for taking Fort Fisher by loading an old vessel with 215 tons of gunpowder, towing it near the fort, then igniting it. Grant was dubious: "Whether the report will be sufficient even to wake up the garrison in the fort, if they happen to be asleep at the time of the explosion, I do not know. It is at least foolish to think that the effect of the explosion could be transmitted to such a distance with enough force to weaken the fort."[3] Lincoln acquiesced to the plan without placing much credence in it, saying mockingly, "We might as well explode the notion with powder as with anything else."[4] Grant couldn't banish Butler from the expedition, which would occur under the aegis of his Department of Virginia and North Carolina. Rear Admiral David D. Porter gathered an enormous fleet of sixty ships while Butler readied 6,500 men to sail to Fort Fisher under General Godfrey Weitzel. Grant's confidence in Butler was minimal, and he hoped the twenty-nine-year-old Weitzel would perform the actual fighting, but the headstrong Butler insisted on going along and taking personal control, which boded ill for the venture. Meanwhile, weather-related delays enabled the rebel garrison to replenish its numbers.

The day before Christmas, the USS *Louisiana*, bulging with gunpowder, drifted close to Fort Fisher, but true to Grant's prediction, the explosion inflicted little harm, leading to much merriment at Butler's expense. Most of the blast's explosive shock dissipated in the air. When Porter unleashed a furious cannonade at the fort, many shells landed with a harmless thud in surrounding soil. On Christmas morning, he sprayed the fort with ten thousand rounds of shot and shell, which was supposed to be followed by a spirited infantry assault from the fort's land side. Unfortunately, Butler, observing Confederate artillery on the parapet, got cold feet and called off the mission. An irate Porter blasted Butler for "not attempting to take possession of the forts, which were so blown up, burst up, and torn up that the people inside had no intention of fighting any more . . . It could have been taken on Christmas with 500 men, without losing a soldier."[5] Porter may have overstated his case: while he had ravaged the fort's water side, many heavy guns on the land side had survived his onslaught.

Joining Porter in blaming Butler, Grant now had sufficient cause to fire him and demanded his removal as "an unsafe commander for a large Army."[6] Having won reelection, Lincoln no longer feared political reprisals from Butler and approved. Butler was replaced at the helm of the Army of the James by a West Point graduate, General Edward O. C. Ord.

Butler was not one to leave quietly. As his parting shot, he explained to his soldiers what he discerned as the true reason for his dismissal: "I have refused to order the sacrifice of . . . soldiers and am relieved from your command—The wasted blood of my men does not stain my garments."[7] Ord asked Grant whether he should suppress this inflammatory statement. Perhaps thinking this vengeful farewell would hurt Butler more than help, Grant allowed its release. Butler rushed off to protest to a congressional committee that he had wisely called off the Fort

Fisher attack and been victimized for his courage. Well into his postwar career, Butler spewed venom at Grant, telling one friend before Grant became president that he had been "the most unpopular soldier in the whole Army" and was "the weakest feeblest creature . . . that ever was thought of for any public office."[8]

Prodded by Lincoln, Grant prepared for a second action against Fort Fisher, where he would enjoy "the largest naval force ever assembled," said Welles.[9] Having demonstrated the power of land and sea operations throughout the war, Grant advised General Alfred Terry, a classically educated lawyer, of the paramount need for "unity of action" with Admiral Porter.[10] On January 6, 1865, the new expedition set sail for Fort Fisher, only this time the seamen and marines hit the ground running; following a heavy navy bombardment, they grabbed the fort and took more than two thousand prisoners. This dramatic turning point in the war ended the heyday of blockade runners and left Galveston the sole port open to the shrinking Confederacy. Reeling from the Fort Fisher debacle, the Confederate vice president, Alexander Stephens, mourned it as "one of the greatest disasters that had befallen our Cause from the beginning of the war," and Confederate desertions in North Carolina leapt dramatically.[11] Once again Grant hovered as the tutelary spirit behind a major victory. "Grant stands very much higher for the Fort Fisher affair; it showed the stupid world what it had forgotten that he really controls the armies of the U.S.," Badeau told James Wilson. "They are just beginning to realize that all these stupendous combinations which have resulted so splendidly are the fruit of one master mind."[12]

Despite the fort's capture, Admiral Porter chose to criticize Grant mercilessly in a letter to Gideon Welles that castigated Grant for allowing Butler to accompany the first expedition. He portrayed Grant as ungrateful for the signal role played by the navy at Fort Fisher, reviling him as a shallow opportunist "always willing to take the credit when anything is done, and equally ready to lay the blame of the failure on the navy, when a failure takes place." Porter also claimed Grant had always stolen credit from him and that without his help, Grant "never would have been Lieutenant-General."[13] When Grant, as president, nominated Porter to be a full admiral, this blistering letter was published, and Julia Grant claimed it hit her unprepared husband hard. "General Grant felt dreadfully hurt, as he really thought a great deal of Porter," who "vowed he never wrote the letter, but there it was in his own handwriting."[14] Implausibly Porter pretended to have no recollection of writing the letter, telling Grant he regretted "exceedingly the loss of your friendship."[15]

By December 1864, Grant had tightened the noose around Richmond, severing its southern rail links and isolating the town. Sheridan was able to transfer
his entire corps from the Shenandoah Valley to Petersburg. As it grew clear that
final victory glimmered in the distance and as snow fell thickly and temperatures dipped below zero, summer tents at City Point headquarters gave way to
durable log huts. Grant's wooden quarters consisted of an office in the front
portion, a private area in the rear. Horace Porter described the atmosphere as
neat and spartan: "An iron camp-bed, an iron wash-stand, a couple of pine tables, and a few common wooden chairs constituted the furniture. The floor was
entirely bare."[16] In the dank, gloomy days before Christmas, Grant was laid up
with a stomach disorder and hemorrhoids, his condition troubling enough that
he made the ultimate sacrifice: he briefly renounced cigars. He shouldered so
much responsibility that he was upset at being confined to bed and confessed to
Julia how much he relied on sheer willpower: "I know how much there is dependent on me and will prove myself equal to the task. I believe determination can
do a great deal to sustain one and I have that quality certainly to its fullest
extent."[17]

On Christmas Day, Fred appeared and immediately saddled up for a ride
with his father. Julia lingered in Burlington with the other children until January, when she joined her husband at City Point. The Grants were now a celebrated couple with many worldly temptations dangled before them. They were
delighted by the gift of a fully equipped house in Philadelphia, given to them by
several dozen grateful citizens. Neither then nor later was Grant nagged by the
possible impropriety of such gifts, regarding them as a reward commonly bestowed upon victorious generals. Indeed, such gifts were then seen not as nefarious but as generous gestures to patriotic heroes for the sacrifices they had made.
Still, such gifts would accumulate in the future and raise uncomfortable questions about Grant's judgment in accepting them. For the most part, Grant had a
well-developed ethical sense, as evidenced by his response when offered a free
stake in shady oil properties. "I have a perfect abhorrence of having any interest
in anything which might prove speculative at the expense of a confiding public,"
he wrote back.[18]

When Julia joined him in January, she domesticated the rough-hewn cabin
where her husband lived and worked, much as she had at Hardscrabble, and took
her meals on equal terms with his officers. She brightened up the table by draping
a makeshift cloth over it and had a way of cheering the men with her vivacity and

attending to anyone who was ailing. Having spent much of the war apart from Ulysses, she didn't mind the austere military milieu. "I am snugly nestled away in my husband's log cabin," she confided to a friend and told of long nocturnal chats with him. "Am I not a happy woman?"[19]

It was also clear that she stood guard over her husband's drinking. Right before she arrived at City Point, Henry W. Bellows of the U.S. Sanitary Commission visited Grant and speculated privately that he might have taken "just a little too much soup"—a wording that suggests he was tipsy.[20] Gideon Welles, that inveterate chronicler of invidious gossip, recorded in his diary on December 29 that Grant had recently sailed back to Virginia from Washington, accompanied by Senator Zachariah Chandler, and the boat's skipper, a Captain Mitchell, had related that "both Grant and Chandler were very drunk. Grant got into Mitchell's berth and slept off the fumes. Chandler was continuously and all the time drunk."[21] As always when Julia was around, rumors of Grant's drinking vanished on the spot.

On New Year's Day 1865, Grant issued orders to observe a day of peace with nearby rebel soldiers and refrain from firing upon them unless fired upon first. For Thanksgiving, donors in New York had shipped eighty thousand pounds of turkey for distribution among Union troops and Lee had allowed them to enjoy it in peace; now Grant repaid the courtly gesture. "We are never to be outdone," Rawlins wrote proudly, "either in fighting or magnanimity."[22]

With 124,000 well-fed soldiers at his disposal, Grant felt hopeful about his prospects against Lee's dwindling force of 57,000 men. Normally not inclined to boast, Grant wrote on January 2, "We now have an Army of Soldiers such as the world never saw before."[23] The high rate of Confederate desertions—entire squads now melted away—strengthened his confidence. Lee's officers would have begged to differ, one affirming that Lee had "60,000 of the best soldiers in the world and they have unbounded confidence in him . . . we will storm Grant in his breastworks if they were twice as strong."[24] But this was so much whistling in the dark and some Confederate officers began to voice hitherto taboo feelings. "The wolf is at the door here," said a staff officer in Richmond. "We dread starvation far more than we do Grant or Sherman. Famine—that is the word now."[25] The manifold attacks by Grant against railroads, canals, and ports had impoverished the Confederate supply chain. Lee, fearing his army would fall apart from hunger, railed at the dangerous complacency of southern politicians. After returning from a visit to Richmond, he strode his room in agitation and vented his spleen to his son. "I have been up to see the Congress and they do not seem able to do anything except eat peanuts and chew tobacco, while my army is starving. I told them the condition my men were in, and that something must be done at once, but I can't get them to do anything."[26]

In early January, Grant was made privy to a plan, sanctioned by the president, to have Francis P. Blair Sr., an old Jacksonian Democrat, pass through City Point en route to secret talks with Jefferson Davis. In all likelihood, Grant heard from Blair what was afoot, Blair having come up with a chimerical scheme to reunite North and South by having them engage in a joint operation to eject the French from Mexico. If Lincoln scoffed at the idea, he was curious to see what it might yield. Jefferson Davis, a proud and testy man, assumed Lincoln would stick by his old demand for "unconditional surrender." Still, he thought the southern populace might be reinvigorated by Lincoln's intransigence and peace proponents discredited, and so he authorized Blair to inform Lincoln of his willingness to "enter into conference with a view to secure peace to the two countries." Lincoln communicated his readiness to enter into informal talks "with the view of securing peace to the people of our one common country."[27] For his negotiating team, Davis chose three prominent figures to proceed to Washington: Vice President Alexander H. Stephens, president pro tem of the Senate Robert M. T. Hunter, and Assistant Secretary of War John A. Campbell. All had occupied high positions in the old federal government. All three had also expressed dissatisfaction with Confederate conduct of the war and couldn't be dismissed as mere flunkies or pliant tools of Jefferson Davis.

On Sunday, January 29, the three emissaries crossed the outer perimeter of Petersburg's defenses under a flag of truce. After years of grueling warfare they were hailed as messengers of peace, and a surprisingly festive mood reigned as their carriage rolled from Confederate to federal lines, both sides greeting the ambassadors with "prolonged and enthusiastic applause" and ecstatic cries of "Peace! Peace!"[28] To cheers from their respective armies, the southern band played "Dixie" and the northern band "Yankee Doodle," before young men on both sides responded with mutual appreciation to "Home, Sweet Home." Because Grant was at Fort Fisher, the three emissaries indicated to a Lieutenant Colonel Hatch that Grant had been forewarned of their journey to Washington as peace commissioners. Hatch contacted Ord, who contacted Stanton, who said to await Lincoln's instructions. In a quandary over what to do, Hatch returned to the three commissioners and blurted out, in what may have been a delaying tactic, "that Grant was on a big drunk and it might be some time before there was any reply."[29] The next morning, the three men directed a letter to Grant himself.

Back at City Point on January 31, Grant sent Lincoln a copy of the letter, which expressed the commissioners' wish to confer with him in Washington. Shortly afterward Grant got a telegram from Stanton alerting him that Major Thomas T. Eckert was on his way to Virginia, bearing presidential instructions. That night Grant had Colonel Orville Babcock escort the three commissioners to his log cabin, where they found him scribbling at a small table in the glow of a kerosene lamp. When Babcock tapped at the door, Grant called out "Come in" in a cordial voice that Alexander Stephens said he would never forget.[30]

Chatting with the three men, Grant conspicuously avoided any political talk. He treated them in a courteous manner that concealed his deep indignation at what the South had wrought. "For my own part I never had admitted, and never was ready to admit, that they were representatives of a *government*," he wrote in his *Memoirs*. "There had been too great a waste of blood and treasure to concede anything of the kind."[31] Nevertheless, Grant hospitably installed the three men in well-appointed staterooms on the steamer *Mary Martin*, where they remained for several days. Grant assigned no guards to watch over them, invited them to dine with his officers, and allowed them to saunter about freely, fostering tremendous goodwill. He bore little resemblance to the fearsome ogre conjured up by the southern press.

Though he established rapport with all three men, Alexander Stephens, a pale, wizened little man with a keen mind and boyish face, was especially enchanted by Grant. "I was instantly struck with the great simplicity and perfect naturalness of his manners, and the entire absence of everything like affectation, show, or even the usual military air . . . of men in his position."[32] The observant Stephens noted Grant's economical speech and the exceptional intelligence that lay behind his taciturn style: "I saw before being with him long, that he was exceedingly quick in perception, and direct in purpose, with a vast deal more of brains than tongue, as ready as that was at his command."[33] Despite Grant's circumspection, Stephens discerned that he wished peace talks to occur and was "exceedingly anxious for a termination of our war."[34] Stephens decided that Grant was "one of the most remarkable men" he had ever met and would someday "exert a controlling influence in shaping the destinies of this country."[35]

The next afternoon, Major Eckert arrived and Secretary of State Seward made his way separately to Fort Monroe. Eckert was instructed to send the three peace commissioners to meet Seward only if they agreed they had come "with the view of securing peace to the people of our one common country."[36] Not surprisingly, the three men winced at this explosive formulation, which violated the "two countries" position dictated by Jefferson Davis. That night, Eckert wired Lincoln that the three commissioners refused to comply with his terms. When he met Seward the next morning, he informed him the commissioners wouldn't be able to come.

Just as it looked as if the peace talks had struck an insurmountable obstacle, Grant did something entirely out of character that bespoke his increased trust and intimacy with the president. He wired Stanton that his talks with Stephens and Hunter persuaded him that "their intentions are good and their desire sincere to restore peace and Union . . . I fear now their going back without any expression from any one in authority will have a bad influence."[37] Clearly Grant trespassed into the forbidden sphere of public policy, even subtly reproaching Lincoln and Stanton for their intransigence. The supposedly bloodthirsty man of war craved peace. The telegram hit the bull's-eye, confirming Grant's sound political instincts and new intimacy with Lincoln. About to recall Eckert and Seward, Lincoln not only scratched that notion but decided, on the strength of Grant's message, to travel to Fort Monroe to meet with the commissioners even though he doubted anything productive would ensue. Grant promised Lincoln not to relax military pressure as the talks progressed.

By the time Lincoln and Seward met the commissioners on February 3 aboard the steamer *River Queen,* anchored at Hampton Roads, the war's calculus had been altered by congressional passage of the Thirteenth Amendment outlawing slavery. On January 31, the final vote in the House of Representatives was received with tumultuous cheers and applause. Hats were hurled in the air, ladies in the galleries flapped handkerchiefs. At the White House, Lincoln lauded the amendment as "a king's cure-all for all evils."[38] To try to kill the vote, amendment opponents had pointed to rumored peace talks, but Lincoln saved the day by stating ambiguously that there were no peace commissioners "in the city [Washington] or likely to be in it"—true as far as it went.[39] The stirring Republican victory strengthened the northern commitment to blotting out slavery and made any backsliding on the issue unthinkable. Lincoln also hoped the vote would alert southerners that their struggle to save slavery was now doomed.

For several hours Lincoln and Seward parlayed with the commissioners in the *River Queen*'s saloon. As a member of the military, Grant was expressly excluded.

"There was a determination on the part of Mr. Lincoln and Mr. Stanton to ex-clude the military authorities altogether from the final settlement, after submis-sion should be secured," wrote Badeau.[40] No notes were taken, no secretaries allowed. Lincoln respected the head of the delegation, Alexander Stephens, hav-ing once praised a speech he made against the Mexican War as "the very best speech of an hour's length I ever heard."[41] But Lincoln, no pushover, immedi-ately made clear he had three nonnegotiable conditions: permanent restoration of the Union; an end to slavery; and no cessation of hostilities until all rebel forces were disbanded. The peace commissioners had expected concessions and were taken aback by these unbending terms. The North was winning the war and Lincoln knew he played a strong hand. Hunter interjected: "Mr. President, if we understand you correctly, you think that we of the Confederacy have com-mitted treason; that we are traitors to your government; that we have forfeited our rights, and are proper subjects for the hangman. Is that not about what your words imply?" Lincoln didn't sugarcoat the truth. "Yes. You have stated the proposition better than I did. That is about the size of it."[42] Nonetheless, at mo-ments Lincoln sounded more conciliatory, expressing a willingness to compen-sate southerners for forfeited slaves. While Seward objected to this, Lincoln persisted: "If it was wrong in the South to hold slaves, it was wrong in the North to carry on the slave trade and sell them to the South."[43] Despite such state-ments, it grew clear that an unbridgeable gulf now yawned between Lincoln and the commissioners and that the talks had encountered a dead end.

When Lincoln gave him a postmortem on the meeting, Grant was struck by the president's "generous and kindly spirit toward the Southern people" and the absence of "a revengeful disposition"—attitudes to be reflected in Grant's own charitable behavior toward the South.[44] Lincoln delighted Grant with his de-scription of how the shriveled Stephens was bundled up in a gray woolen over-coat several sizes too large. As Lincoln recalled, "The cabin soon began to get pretty warm and after a while [Stephens] stood up and pulled off his big coat. He slipped it off just about as you would husk an ear of corn. I couldn't help thinking as I looked first at the overcoat and then at the man, 'Well, that's the biggest shuck and the smallest nubbin I ever laid eyes on.'"[45]

Grant's bond with Lincoln deepened when he helped to resolve a family di-lemma concerning twenty-one-year-old Robert Lincoln, the president's eldest son, who had graduated from Harvard College. Good-looking and genial, Robert had been criticized for evading war service—criticism all the more mortifying since he was eager to serve. Mary Lincoln, having already lost two children, didn't care to risk a third and grew wildly emotional on the subject. Lincoln hesitated to cross her as her mental instability grew more evident. Although he tried to steer Robert to Harvard Law School, the ploy didn't succeed. With relations already awkward and distant with his eldest son, Lincoln hit on an ingenious way to appease both Mary and Robert. On January 19, he sent Grant a tactful letter that began with a beautiful, if slightly unrealistic, line: "Please read and answer this letter as though I was not President, but only a friend." He then stated his son's wish "to see something of the war before it ends" and asked if Robert could join Grant's military family.[46] Lincoln even extended an unusual offer to pay his army expenses. From Annapolis, Grant hastily replied on the blank bottom half of Lincoln's letter, offering Robert an adjutant's job on his staff with the rank of captain. On February 21, Robert Lincoln reported for duty at Grant's headquarters. Sympathetic to the president's predicament, Grant guarded Robert from perilous situations and often relegated him to meeting visiting dignitaries. With his bright, amiable manner, Robert Lincoln became a popular figure at headquarters whose presence only made the president more eager to visit City Point, as perhaps Grant had hoped.[47] It is unlikely that Mary Lincoln was ever reconciled to her son's presence in the war, even at such a relatively safe spot.

EARLY 1865 WITNESSED the slow-motion unraveling of the Army of Northern Virginia, which was gradually thinned out by massive desertions amounting to about a regiment per day. Tattered men in large groups appeared in Grant's camps, surrendering their weapons. "Hundreds of men are deserting nightly," Lee confessed to Jefferson Davis as such departures shaved off 8 percent of his army in January, followed by a further 8 percent in February.[48] Driven by poor food, withheld pay, and rapidly depreciating Confederate currency, rebel soldiers were rendering their own bleak verdict on the war's future course. In early February, Grant obtained a poster showing Lee reduced to begging from local farmers, pleading with them "to sell or loan as much Corn Meal & Molasses as they Can spare."[49] Southern conscription covered boys as young as fourteen and men as old as sixty.[50]

Grant believed the southern people, once ardent to fight, had shed their taste for bloodshed. "Everything looks to me to be very favorable for a speedy termination of the war," he predicted in mid-February, wondering whether rebel leaders would flee or be ousted by their citizens.[51] Inside the Confederate cabinet,

Secretary of State Judah Benjamin argued strenuously that blacks must be recruited or Lee would have to abandon Richmond.[52] The Confederate legislature
approved a bill to enlist slaves in the army, sidestepping the explosive question of
whether to emancipate them. Its most eloquent proponent was Lee, who urgently
needed fresh troops. "I think those who are employed [as soldiers] should be
freed," he argued. "It would be neither just nor wise, in my opinion, to require
them to serve as slaves."[53] The *Charleston Mercury* noted the absurdity of the
whole enterprise: "Assert the right in the Confederate Government to emancipate slaves, and it is stone dead."[54] After the Virginia legislature endorsed the bill
for recruiting black soldiers, one or two black companies were assembled and
briefly paraded in the Richmond streets, but they came too late to prop up the
beleaguered cause. Grant tracked with consuming interest this controversy in
Richmond newspapers. Slavery was slowly crumbling, as evidenced by a precipitous drop in the market price for slaves. As the Richmond war clerk John Jones
indicated in his diary, "Here the price of slaves, men, is about $5000 Confederate
State notes, or $100 in specie. A great depreciation. Before the war they com-
manded ten times that price."[55]

All the while, plowing remorselessly through the Deep South, Sherman erad-
icated supply bases and transportation networks that kept Lee's army alive. By
early January, with Savannah secure, Sherman was ready to "sally forth again,"
telling Grant of his plans to carve a path of destruction through Columbia and
Camden, South Carolina, followed by Wilmington and Raleigh in North Carolina. "The game is then up with Lee," Sherman stated, "unless he comes out of
Richmond, avoids you, and fights me: in which event, I should reckon on your
being on his heels."[56] His options vanishing, Lee would soon face an unpalatable
choice: either stay in Richmond and sacrifice the rest of the South, or head
southward, fight in the open, and be squeezed between Sherman's and Grant's
converging armies. Lincoln allegedly gave humorous expression to this by saying,
"Grant has the bear by the hind leg while Sherman takes off the hide."[57]

Rolling through Georgia, Sherman's army had collected fugitive slaves at
every turn. When the question arose of shipping them to City Point, Halleck
interceded to stem any such movement: "Our experience is that negroes brought
north during the cold weather from a warm climate are almost useless; moreover, they suffer very much from cold."[58] Sherman still complained that jubilant
blacks flocking to his army hampered its progress. To deal with this surplus
population, he devised one of the war's most innovative measures. The federal

government had confiscated four hundred thousand acres of land. In mid-January, Sherman issued Special Field Order No. 15, which set aside the Sea Islands and a large strip of territory along the Georgia, South Carolina, and Florida coasts for settlement by landless black families. They would be offered forty-acre plots in self-governing communities. By June, this remarkable experiment in reconstruction offered new life to forty thousand former slaves, although the land titles given out had not yet acquired lasting legal power. Sherman was an improbable author for this most progressive order and later explained that he had done it as a temporary wartime measure at the behest of Stanton.

On February 1, Sherman began his march through the Carolinas, candidly trumpeting his intention to make the inhabitants "fear and dread us."[59] True to his words, his campaign would be indelibly engraved in southern memory, feeding a deep-seated hatred of Yankees. As a precaution, Grant shipped supplies to predetermined spots along the coast in case Sherman needed them and he promised to reinforce him, if necessary, with thirty thousand men. Exactly as Grant had hoped, Lee diverted troops to halt Sherman's progress, critically undermining his defense of Richmond. Like Grant, Sherman thought that Lee, however fine a tactician, was a poor strategist who would play straight into their hands. "If Lee is a soldier of genius," Sherman lectured, "he will seek to transfer his army from Richmond to Raleigh or Columbia. If he is a man simply of detail, he will remain where he is and his speedy defeat is sure. But I have little fear that he will be able to move; Grant holds him in a vise."[60] Lee's circumscribed vision became a matter of even greater moment when he was elevated to command all Confederate armies in early February 1865.

Like Sherman, Grant recognized the psychological value of a Union army streaking through southern towns hitherto spared a firsthand glimpse of war. Southern newspapers, Grant noted, proclaimed that Sherman's army "was nothing better than a mob of men who were frightened out of their wits." As the hard-charging army then passed their way, showing an invincible spirit, "the people became disabused and they saw the true state of affairs."[61] Sherman mapped a route through South Carolina, cradle of the rebellion, that would take him to the state capital at Columbia, which he endowed with special strategic worth. "I expect [Jefferson] Davis will move Heaven & Earth to catch me," Sherman told Grant. "Richmond is not more vital to his cause than Columbia and the heart of South Carolina."[62] Sherman's sixty thousand battle-tested veterans, now tough, wiry, and resilient, had to ford numberless swamps and rivers in all sorts of weather. They stormed ahead with crusading fervor, burning everything of strategic value in their path. Although their rapacity in Georgia can be exaggerated, they directed a special animus against South Carolina for having started the war.

Sherman's march formed only one element of Grant's multifaceted plan to end the conflict. The latter announced a new Department of North Carolina, with John Schofield in command, its mission to take Wilmington and Goldsboro and create new supply sources for Sherman. Grant secretly dispatched twenty-eight thousand troops to New Bern and the Cape Fear River on the Atlantic coast with orders to get a railroad there in working shape to speed the movement of Union troops. This would enable Schofield's army to team up with Sherman in case Lee abandoned Richmond and brought the war farther south. On the surface, Grant seemed idle in Virginia when, in reality, he was spinning intricate webs to catch Lee. "I shall necessarily have to take the odium of apparent inactivity, but if it results, as I expect it will, in the discomfiture of Lee's Army, I shall be satisfied," Grant notified Stanton.[63] To counter his initiatives, the Confederate government on February 22 appointed Joseph Johnston to oversee all Confederate forces in the Carolinas.

Sherman's push through South Carolina reached a new phase of heightened intensity on February 17 when his army entered Columbia, the small but charming state capital. Many residents of Charleston and Augusta had mistakenly repaired there as a sanctuary from Sherman's wrath. For vengeful Union troops, the South Carolina capital was a fit place to punish the hotbed of sedition. Grant and Sherman always insisted that the fire that engulfed large sections of Columbia was set by retreating Confederates, describing this as standard practice when southern armies surrendered towns. Sherman and his staff pitched in to quell the sudden conflagration, but charges also arose that Sherman's soldiers, giving way to a rowdy spirit, spread the flames with cotton dipped in turpentine. By the time Sherman and his entourage left the town on February 23, much of it lay in smoking ruins.

While Grant defended Sherman's behavior, neither man seemed unduly disturbed by what had happened. In his *Memoirs,* Grant commented drily that Union troops had helped to save Columbia, but that "the example set by the Confederates in burning the village of Chambersburg, Pa., a town which was not garrisoned, would seem to make a defense of the act of firing the seat of government of the State most responsible for the conflict then raging, not imperative."[64] Sounding more like an avenging angel, Sherman insisted that he hadn't ordered the destruction of Columbia, but "I have never shed any tears over it, because I believe that it hastened what we all fought for—the end of the war."[65] With Columbia gone, Charleston soon succumbed, and the two losses spread fear and lamentation through the South. The scenes that now unfolded heralded not simply impending Confederate defeat, but a brave new biracial world. In a sight scarcely credible to southern eyes, the black Fifty-Fourth Massachusetts Infantry arrived in Charleston, lustily singing "John Brown's Body." The headline in *The Liberator*, William Lloyd Garrison's abolitionist paper, captured the extraordinary symbolism: "Babylon Is Fallen!"[66] Grant felt the war careering toward its climactic scene: "Everything looks like dissolution in the South. A few days more of success with Sherman will put us where we can crow loud."[67]

A swelling cascade of Union victories ensued, with Wilmington falling to Schofield on February 22, shutting down the last major southern port. A restless Grant never quite knew Sherman's location, but assumed he was hurtling toward Goldsboro and would soon join forces with Schofield. Belatedly Richmond newspapers awoke to the realization that Grant traced Sherman's mysterious movements through their own columns. "The papers are requested to say nothing relative to military operations in South and North Carolina," wrote the rebel war clerk John Jones on February 25, "for they are read by Gen. Grant every morning of their publication."[68]

A winter of freezing Virginia temperatures meant that Grant's campaign against Lee was paralyzed by snow and record cold. Heavy rains washed out roads, forcing Grant to wait until they dried. By late February, Grant assigned Sheridan to lead an expedition to wreck the railroads and the James River Canal that supported Lee's army. In sending Sheridan toward Lynchburg, he contemplated that his cavalry would clear the Shenandoah Valley of Confederates, then link up with Sherman as the latter advanced north, "eating out the vitals of South Carolina," as Grant phrased it.[69] Sheridan's horsemen rode through a heavy downpour that plastered their uniforms with mud. Sheridan balked at the idea of teaming up with Sherman to defeat Lee, thinking it essential that eastern soldiers from the Army of the Potomac should share in Lee's defeat.

One day Grant spread out a map for Julia to show her the deployment of his armies and display his grand design. "You observe it is a perfect cordon from sea to sea again," he told her. When she asked what came next, he replied, "Well, I am going to tighten that cordon until the rebellion is crushed or strangled."[70] Grant had reached his peak powers as a strategist, and Horace Porter noted that his operations now "covered a theater of war greater than that of any campaigns in modern history, and . . . required a grasp and comprehension which have rarely been possessed even by the greatest commanders. [Grant] was at this period indefatigable in his labors, and he once wrote in a single day forty-two important despatches with his own hand."[71]

In late February, General Ord met with General Longstreet about prisoner exchanges and the problem posed by barter of newspapers, tobacco, and other items between pickets on opposing sides. Before long their talks touched on the possibility of their commanding generals hashing out a peace settlement. Ord argued that since northern politicians balked at such talks, only generals could make it happen. The honest Longstreet called it "a great crime against the Southern people and Army for the chief Generals to continue to lead their men to hopeless and unnecessary butchery."[72]

The two men discussed a rather fanciful plan in which Longstreet's wife would pass through Union lines with Confederate officers to meet with her cousin and old girlhood friend Julia Grant, who would reciprocate with a return visit to Richmond with Union officers. Julia, at City Point, seemed wildly excited by this diplomatic gambit. "Oh! How enchanting, how thrilling!" she told her husband. "Oh, Ulys, I may go, may I not?" Grant reined in her enthusiasm. "No, you must not . . . The men have fought this war and the men will finish it."[73] Initially Grant blessed the talks, and on March 2, Lee wrote to propose a meeting dealing with "the subjects of controversy between the belligerents."[74] Aware he was treading on tenuous ground, Grant submitted the matter to Stanton, who sharply disapproved and informed him that Lincoln "wishes you to have no conference with Gen Lee unless it be for the capitulation of Lee's army . . . He instructs me to say that you are not to decide, discuss, or confer upon any political question."[75] In response, Grant reassured Stanton he wouldn't venture into politics and would continue to prosecute the war "to the utmost of my ability."[76]

The secessionist cause lay dying everywhere in the South. All through February, as the social life drained out of Richmond, those who could afford it fled in massive numbers toward outlying areas or safe havens in North Carolina. The Confederate government braced for the capital's surrender, collecting tobacco that could be set ablaze at the entrance of Union troops. With something close to panic, government officials and their families prepared for an evacuation. At the War Office, clerks stockpiled boxes and got ready to pack up the archives and move them away from prying northern eyes.

Grant's main fear wasn't that Lee would stand and fight. Rather he worried that Lee's mobile army would suddenly take flight and dart south to North Carolina or drive west toward Lynchburg and eastern Tennessee, prolonging the war for a year. However passive he might appear, Grant knew his main job was to keep Lee's army cooped up in Richmond and Petersburg until Sherman and Schofield merged their forces in North Carolina. If he applied too much pressure prematurely, the move could backfire, prompting Lee to scuttle south from Richmond and break up the crucial rendezvous of Union forces farther south.

Back in Washington, Lincoln signed a flurry of last-minute bills passed by the outgoing Congress, including one to create a Freedmen's Bureau meant to last one year and help provision freed slaves with food, clothing, housing, and fuel. To avoid any appearance of favoritism, it was also supposed to assist white refugees in the South. Significantly, it was authorized to extend the sort of program that Sherman had launched along the southern coast to assign forty-acre plots to landless ex-slaves.

On March 4, 1865, a wretched, rainy day in the capital, Abraham Lincoln was sworn in as president for his second term. Despite cold gusts that buffeted the Capitol's east portico, thirty thousand onlookers showed up and the London *Times* estimated that at least "half the multitude were colored people."[77] A company of black soldiers—a first for an inauguration—marched in the parade. Standing beneath the Capitol dome, looking especially thin and gaunt, Lincoln delivered an inaugural address that talked of retribution against the South but also tried to set a forgiving tone for the peace Grant would soon bring about: "With malice toward none; with charity for all; with firmness in the right, as God gives us to see the right, let us strive on to finish the work we are in; to bind up the nation's wounds; . . . to do all which may achieve and cherish a just, and a lasting peace, among ourselves, and with all nations."[78]

Perhaps no less consequential for Grant's political future than Lincoln's speech was the boorish behavior of the new vice president, Andrew Johnson of Tennessee. When he took the oath of office in the Senate chamber, he gave a rambling, twenty-minute speech, shot through with populist overtones, that left more than one bemused spectator thinking him "in a state of manifest intoxication."[79] Allegedly to soothe his nerves because of a recent illness, Johnson had imbibed a few glasses of whiskey before the ceremony, and this showed all too plainly. When Johnson was done, Lincoln whispered to the parade marshal, "Do not let Johnson speak outside."[80] Joining the inaugural festivities was Frederick

Douglass, and, when Lincoln pointed him out to Johnson, Douglass saw only
"bitter contempt and aversion" for him etched in the vice president's face.[81]

The day after the inauguration, Grant received welcome news that Phil Sheridan had not simply defeated Jubal Early near Charlottesville but had captured
his officers, stores, and wagons. The Shenandoah Valley was now stripped bare
of Confederate troops and produce for Lee's army. Provided with a clear field to
move east toward Richmond, Sheridan's cavalry unleashed a rampage of destruction against the infrastructure supporting Lee, crippling the Virginia
Central Railroad and locks, dams, and boats on the James River Canal. "Negroes had joined [Sheridan's] column to the number of two thousand or more,"
recalled Grant, "and they assisted considerably in the work of destroying the
railroads and the canal."[82] Grant received news of Sheridan's conquest in an
unorthodox manner. During dinner in the officers' mess, a teenage scout was
hustled into his presence. "He had on a pair of soldier's trousers three or four
inches too short, and a blouse three sizes too large," recalled Porter. The intelligence he brought was "written on tissue-paper and inclosed in a ball of tin-foil,
which the scout had carried in his mouth."[83] Grant unwrapped the three-page
message and read aloud Sheridan's exuberant description of the dismantling of
enemy assets. The catalogue of destruction—including canal locks, aqueducts,
railroad bridges, warehouses, and factories—was simply staggering. Only two
railroads were left to service Lee at Richmond, and Grant now ordered Sheridan
to finish up the job. As he felt his army being slowly encircled and squeezed to
death, Lee knew he would have to give up Richmond and Petersburg or risk losing his entire army.

By mid-March, Grant knew the South's war machine was winding down, its
people weary and disillusioned. At some point, Grant assumed, the isolated
Lee would fall back to Lynchburg or execute a frantic effort to hook up with
Johnston's army in North Carolina. To deal with this contingency, he put his
commanders on high alert, ready to move out troops on short notice.

In this mood of coolheaded optimism, convinced the rebel army would collapse in a matter of weeks, Grant learned of the death of his oldest sister, Clara
Rachel, who had died on March 6 and was the second sibling to pass away during the war. "Although I had known for some time that she was in a decline yet
I was not expecting to hear of her death at this time.—I have had no heart to
write earlier," Grant told his father.[84] With the war fast approaching its denoue-
ment, Grant could spare no time for rites of mourning.

Union armies scented victory in the air. On March 11, Sherman took Fayetteville, North Carolina, invading its bountiful arsenal, and his men grew
ruddy with conquest. "The Army is in Splendid health, condition and Spirit," he
wrote to Grant, with characteristic brio, "although we have had foul weather and
roads that would have stopped travel to almost any other body of men I ever read
of."[85] Huge crowds of ex-slaves gravitated joyously to his banner, while Sherman,
who still had a war to fight, continued to regard them as an encumbrance. Grant
told Sherman he would consider his army "entirely safe" once he learned it had
joined forces with Schofield's.[86] Speeding across North Carolina at a northeastern diagonal, Sherman's army reached Goldsboro and the long-awaited union
with Schofield's on March 23. With justice, he hailed his march as "one of the
longest and most important marches ever made by an organized army in a civilized country."[87] The combined armies of Sherman and Schofield numbered
nearly 90,000 men, eclipsing fewer than 20,000 fielded by Joe Johnston. And
when those 90,000 men were added to Union forces positioned outside Petersburg and Richmond, Grant oversaw a colossal force of 217,000 well-fed, well-
armed soldiers ready to crush Lee and stamp out the rebellion for good.

With his second inauguration behind him, Abraham Lincoln underwent a
spell of illness and exhaustion, doubtless from the cumulative fatigue of four
harrowing years of war. "I'm a tired man," he admitted to one visitor. "Sometimes I think I'm the tiredest man on earth."[88] By mid-March, unable to rise
from bed, he convened a cabinet meeting in his bedroom where he lay braced by
pillows. His deeply scored face reflected the hardships he had endured. "It
looked care-ploughed, tempest-tossed and weather-beaten," Horace Greeley remarked.[89] Julia Grant, noticing frequent newspaper references to Lincoln's rundown appearance, suggested her husband invite him for a visit. By this point,
Grant was keenly sensitive to the president's moods and agreed that a vacation
from Washington would refresh his sagging spirits. From Robert Lincoln he also
knew that the president didn't care to intrude on his chief general and would require a gentle nudge. "Can you not visit City Point for a day or two?" Grant wired
Lincoln on March 20. "I would like very much to see you, and I think the rest
would do you good."[90]

Eager to escape the capital and see his son, Lincoln readily accepted. "He was
really most anxious to see the army," Grant explained, "and be with it in its final
struggle."[91] Aboard the side-wheel steamboat *River Queen,* Lincoln traveled to
Virginia with Mary and their youngest son, Tad. As the war approached its end,

he reverted to a cheerfulness unseen for many years. During this poignant interlude, Mary Lincoln said the president "was almost boyish, in his mirth & reminded me, of his original nature, what I had always remembered of him, in our
own home—free from care surrounded by those he loved so well."[92]

On the night of March 24, the *River Queen* docked at City Point, and Lincoln's bodyguard William Crook remembered the splendid scenery with "the
many-colored lights of the boats in the harbor and the lights of the town straggling up the high bluffs of the shore, crowned by the lights from Grant's headquarters at the top."[93] Accompanied by Julia and Robert Lincoln, Grant ambled
down to the gangplank and welcomed the president, who clasped his hand
cordially. The socializing didn't last long since the Lincolns, spent from their
journey, wished to retire to bed.

At dawn the next morning, a sad-eyed Robert E. Lee assayed his last offensive battle, sending a large force east of Petersburg to seize a bulwark known as
Fort Stedman. More than a last-ditch effort to shatter the siege, it represented
the first step in a strategy to blast out an escape route to reinforce Joseph Johnston in North Carolina. Even though his men overran Fort Stedman, they
couldn't retain it and fell back before a heavy Union onslaught, losing nearly five
thousand men, with two thousand taken prisoner. Lee's desperate gamble, Grant
knew, meant the war had entered its endgame. Between rebel soldiers slaughtered and captured, Lee had sacrificed a significant fraction of his army when he
could ill afford additional losses.

Lincoln was scheduled to review troops that morning, and it said much about
Grant's confidence in the military situation that he didn't cancel the outing but
merely rescheduled it for the afternoon, not far distant from where the fighting
had unfolded. After breakfast, Robert Lincoln briefed his father on Fort Stedman
and the president telegraphed the news to Stanton in oddly jocular tones: "Robert
just now tells me there was a little rumpus up the line this morning, ending about
where it began."[94] Apparently Lincoln did not fathom the severity of the fighting
until he surveyed the bloodstained field where it unfolded. "The ground immediately about us was still strewn with dead and wounded men," a member of the
entourage recalled.[95] When a knot of Confederate prisoners marched by, "Lincoln remarked upon their sad and unhappy condition . . . his whole face showing
sympathetic feeling for the suffering about him."[96] By the time Lincoln reviewed
the troops, said a Confederate captive, he had regained his composure, was
buoyed by the appreciative soldiers, and appeared "seemingly not in the least

concerned and as if nothing had happened."[97] Lincoln toted a map that he consulted frequently, showing his exact knowledge of the positions assumed by Union forces.

Always sensitive toward Grant, Lincoln made a point of not pestering him for predictions about the war's conclusion, for which Grant was grateful: "I never would have risked my reputation with Mr. Lincoln by any such prophecies."[98] As they spent considerable time together, Grant came to respect Lincoln as "a fine horseman" and allowed him to use his horse Cincinnati, an excellent trotter, riding with him on swampy roads to far-flung camps.[99] Lincoln's presence lifted the spirit of Union troops, who warmly received him, and he reciprocated with kindly words and gracious salutes. When he met soldiers chopping wood for a cabin, the old rail-splitter, wielding an ax, sliced open a hefty piece of timber to enthusiastic cheers from the men. One day, Lincoln devoted five hours to patients at an army field hospital and, in a tender spirit of reconciliation, shook hands with wounded Confederates. Even the most patronizing officers fell under his spell. Colonel Theodore Lyman described Lincoln as "the ugliest man I ever put my eyes on," with an "expression of plebeian vulgarity in his face."[100] Nonetheless, his brief conversation with Lincoln satisfied him that he was "a very honest and kindly man" who resembled "a highly intellectual and benevolent Satyr."[101]

At night, Lincoln reveled in the camaraderie of the campfire and luxuriated in this respite from the pressures of the executive mansion. There were no office seekers to pursue him, no legislators to lobby him, no reporters to hound him. Despite his proximity to battlefield perils, he was surprisingly relaxed, and Porter observed that as Lincoln "sat in a camp-chair with his long legs doubled up in grotesque attitudes, and the smoke of the fire curling around him, he looked the picture of comfort and good-nature."[102] With inexhaustible good humor, he traded quips and stories and reminisced about the war. When someone asked if he had ever doubted the North's final victory, he shot back, "Never for a moment." He quoted Seward, saying "that there was always just enough virtue in this republic to save it; sometimes none to spare, but still enough to meet the emergency, and he agreed with Mr. Seward in this view."[103]

Grant derived special pleasure from Lincoln's expansive fireside mood. As he later said, the president "talked, and talked, and talked, and the old man seemed to enjoy it and said: 'How grateful I feel to be with the boys and see what is being done at Richmond' . . . He would sit for hours tilted back in his chair, with his hand shading his eyes, watching the movements of the men with the greatest interest."[104] By this point, the Lincoln-Grant relationship had ripened into genuine friendship. Both men had been caricatured as simpletons from the western prairies and greeted with contemptuous sneers by detractors. A certain self-deprecating modesty deceived people into underrating both of them, causing them to miss an underlying shrewdness.

Grant always treated Lincoln with tremendous love and reverence. Unlike some earlier generals, Grant had been completely honorable in his dealings with him, never bad-mouthing him behind his back. "He was a great man, a very great man," was his final verdict. "The more I saw of him, the more this impressed me. He was incontestably the greatest man I ever knew." He rejected the idea that Seward or Chase or Stanton governed Lincoln's decisions. "It was that gentle firmness in carrying out his own will, without apparent force or friction, that formed the basis of his character."[105] He was especially taken with Lincoln's quick, intuitive mind. "Long before the statement of a complicated question is finished his mind will grasp the main points, and he will seem to comprehend the whole subject better than the person who is stating it."[106]

Relations between the Grants and the volatile Mary Lincoln were unfortunately strained. With her round, open face, Mary was as short and plump as her husband was tall and thin. When his train whistle-stopped to Washington for his first inauguration, Lincoln would materialize on the platform, the compact Mary at his side, and joke to the crowd "that now they could see 'the long and short of it!'"[107] The daughter of a Lexington, Kentucky, banker, Mary had grown up in surroundings not dissimilar from Julia Grant's comfortable St. Louis home. She had slaves at her beck and call and was well educated at fine private schools where she learned French. This sociable woman aspired to mingle in tonier society than her husband, who put on no airs and had the common touch. Even in the early days with Lincoln, an imperious streak marred Mary's witty, vivacious manner. "This woman was to me a terror," said Lincoln's law partner, William Herndon, who perhaps unfairly labeled her "imperious, proud, aristocratic, insolent witty and bitter."[108] The spendthrift Mary struggled with the frugality imposed by Lincoln's comparatively lean years as a lawyer. From their earliest days of marriage, she exhibited a sharp tongue and fiery temper that made household help and even her husband wary of her stormier moods. Yet despite flashes of acrimony and troubling undercurrents, the marriage was marked by deep mutual devotion and loyalty, and Mary Lincoln greatly assisted her husband's rise in the world.

The role of president's wife suited her ambitions and she proved a convivial hostess at gatherings. Still, she managed to alienate some people with her pretensions as she lavishly refurbished the executive mansion. One newspaper editor mocked her as "the laughing stock of the town, her vulgarity only the more conspicuous in consequence of her fine carriage and horses and servants in livery and fine dresses, and her damnable airs."[109] Lincoln's secretary John Nicolay dreaded her unruly temper, christening her "her Satanic Majesty."[110] Mary Lincoln grew deeply envious of Kate Chase, the beautiful young daughter of the treasury secretary, and insisted on striking her name, along with those of her husband and father, from the list of a cabinet dinner in January 1864. When Lincoln vetoed this action, Nicolay said, "there soon arose such a rampage as the House hasn't seen for a year."[111]

Four of Mary's five Kentucky brothers fought with the Confederates, which did not endear her to the northern public, feeding scurrilous commentary about "treason in the White House."[112] That one brother died at Shiloh and the other at Vicksburg may have unconsciously contributed to her pronounced dislike of Grant. Elizabeth Keckley, the black seamstress who worked for Mary, recorded her invective against him: "'He is a butcher' she would often say, 'and is not fit to be at the head of an army.'" When Lincoln rebutted her, citing Grant's victories, Mary insisted that "he loses two men to the enemy's one. He has no management, no regard for life." Lincoln, who disliked confrontation, sought to mollify her with a mixture of mild humor and forgiving tolerance. "Well, Mother, supposing that we give you command of the army. No doubt you would do much better than any general that has been tried."[113] In 1864 Adam Badeau was amazed to learn from Mrs. Stanton that she had stopped seeing Mary Lincoln altogether. That was not possible, Badeau responded. "I do not go to the White House," she repeated. "I do not visit Mrs. Lincoln."[114]

Mary's fragile mental health was damaged in 1850 when her three-year-old son Eddie died. Even though she had two more boys, Willie and Tad, in addition to Robert, she never quite recuperated from the loss. Her behavior grew more erratic in February 1862, when Willie, age eleven, died from typhoid fever, contracted by drinking polluted water from White House faucets. For three weeks Mary languished in bed and was unable to attend the funeral. So potent was her grief that she never again set foot in the bedroom where Willie died or in the Green Room where his corpse lay embalmed. Seeking comfort from spiritualists, who conducted up to eight séances in the White House, Mary came to believe she could commune with her two dead sons and drifted into a dream world of fantasied reunions. "Willie lives," she told a relative. "He comes to me every night and stands at the foot of the bed with the same sweet adorable smile he always has had . . . Little Eddie is sometimes with him."[115] For almost a year, subdued by mourning, the Lincolns mostly stopped entertaining while Mary distracted herself shopping for clothing and jewelry in New York and Philadelphia, running up unpaid bills.

During the City Point stay in late March 1865, Mary Lincoln's behavior seemed to regress from the bizarre to the almost pathological. When Julia paid a courtesy call on her, she was coldly received. As she sat down on the sofa next to Mary, the latter shot her a look of protest, as if she were guilty of lèse-majesté. Julia sprang to her feet. "I crowd you, I fear," she said quickly. "Not at all," Mary replied, encouraging Julia to sit down. Julia took a chair instead, not daring to risk Mary's wrath again.[116] The Dent family grapevine kept the story alive. "Emma Dent Casey [Julia's sister] often told the story that Julia was outraged because Mrs. Lincoln had expected her to back out of the room and to treat her like royalty," wrote an early biographer of Julia Grant. "In any event there were cool relations between the two women from the start."[117]

Grant invited the Lincolns to travel to the north side of the James River and review the Army of the James under General Ord. The latter was one of Grant's favorites, a twice-wounded West Point veteran whom he appreciated as "skillful in the management of troops . . . brave and prompt."[118] To reach the parade ground at Malvern Hill, Grant rode on horseback with a high-spirited Lincoln, General Ord, and the general's pretty young wife, Mary. Mary Lincoln and Julia Grant lagged behind in an ambulance, accompanied on this bumpy ride by Badeau and Horace Porter. At one point on the uneven road, the half-open carriage struck a deep rut that threw the ladies violently against the top, smashing their heads and bonnets. The incident rattled the high-strung Mary, who had suffered a serious carriage accident in 1863, and it may have triggered a migraine headache as well.

During the ride, Mary discovered that Mrs. Ord had ridden ahead with her husband and flew into a jealous rage. "What does the woman mean by riding by the side of the President? And ahead of me? Does she suppose that *he* wants *her* by the side of *him*?" When Julia Grant tried to settle her down, Mary turned her wrath on Julia. "I suppose you think you'll get to the White House yourself, don't you?" Mary Lincoln was watchful, even paranoid, about potential rivals to her husband and had resented newspaper references to Grant as a possible presidential nominee the year before. Maintaining her dignity, Julia replied that she was quite satisfied with her present position, but Mary refused to relent. "Oh! You had better take it if you can get it. 'Tis very nice,'" she said and went back to maligning Mrs. Ord.[119]

At Malvern Hill, Mary was enraged that the review had started in her absence—the troops had awaited Lincoln's arrival for hours—with her husband trotting down the line beside the fetching Mrs. Ord, who wore a plumed hat. As the band played, Grant's horse pranced and reared its head while Lincoln, in top hat and black frock coat, rode his mount with stately calm. When Mrs. Ord, at Julia's behest, galloped over to greet Mary, the First Lady lashed out at her in a vituperative outburst. "Mrs. Lincoln positively insulted her, called her vile names in the presence of a crowd of officers, and asked what she meant by following up the President," wrote Badeau. "The poor woman burst into tears and inquired what she had done, but Mrs. Lincoln refused to be appeased, and stormed till she was tired." To no avail, Julia gallantly tried to defend Mrs. Ord.[120]

That night, the Lincolns entertained the Grants aboard the *River Queen* when Mary again erupted in a tantrum and "berated General Ord to the President, and urged that he should be removed," Badeau continued. "He was unfit for his place, she said, to say nothing of his wife. General Grant sat next and defended his officer bravely."[121] Mary accused her husband of flirting brazenly with Mrs. Ord. Though Lincoln tried to deflect these attacks, Mary would not desist. Throughout the City Point visit, Badeau claimed, Mary Lincoln kept attacking her husband in front of other officers: "He bore it as Christ might have done; with an expression of pain and sadness that cut one to the heart, but with supreme calmness and dignity."[122] The embarrassed president would hang his head, call his wife "Mother," attempt to soothe her, then stroll away when all else failed. For the remainder of her visit, Mary Lincoln mostly stayed incommunicado in her cabin before returning to Washington on April 1, leaving her husband and Tad behind. In her memoirs, it should be noted, Julia Grant criticized Adam Badeau for having embellished the story of her contretemps with Mary Lincoln.

On March 27, William Tecumseh Sherman, who hadn't set eyes on Grant for a year, arrived at City Point for an overnight visit devoted to strategy sessions with Grant, Admiral Porter, and Lincoln. Sherman, having consummated his long-sought juncture with General Schofield at Goldsboro, was ready to launch the next stage of war. In fine fettle, he jested that he wanted to see Grant and "stir him up" out of fear that the long Petersburg stalemate had "fossilized him." With typical zest, he said, "I'm going up to see Grant for five minutes and have it all chalked out for me, and then come back and pitch in."[123] When Sherman arrived aboard the steamer *Russia,* Grant hurried to the wharf to embrace his foremost colleague. According to Horace Porter, the hyperactive Sherman didn't simply step ashore but "jumped ashore and was hurrying forward with long strides to meet his chief." Such was the bonhomie of Grant and Sherman as they shook hands that they reminded Porter of two schoolboys fondly reunited after summer vacation.[124] For an hour, as Grant enjoyed a cigar by the campfire, Sherman entertained his staff with tales of his march to the sea and through the Carolinas before Grant decided it was time to pay court to the president. "I know he will be anxious to see you," Grant assured him. "Suppose we go and pay him a visit before supper?"[125]

Based on an encounter earlier in the war, the headstrong Sherman wasn't prepared to like Lincoln, but he was now utterly beguiled as they chatted aboard the *River Queen.* The president wasn't the simple rube he had imagined so much as a man of feeling, wisdom, and sincerity. Sherman noted how the careworn Lincoln came alive when he spoke, his face growing animated, his long, slack arms flying into motion. "Of all the men I ever met," he concluded, Lincoln "seemed to possess more of the elements of greatness, combined with goodness, than any other."[126] Insatiably curious about the historic march, Lincoln listened raptly to Sherman's sparkling rendition. According to Sherman, the president "seemed to enjoy very much the more ludicrous parts—about the 'bummers,' and their devices to collect food and forage when the outside world supposed us to be starving."[127] Overshadowed by the talkative Sherman, Grant was content to sit back and say relatively little during two meetings with Lincoln.

The first meeting lasted an hour. When Grant and Sherman returned to Julia Grant, who had readied tea for them, she asked if they had seen *Mrs.* Lincoln. Grant confessed they had not asked for her. "Well, you are a pretty pair!" she chided them. "I do not see how you could have been so neglectful."[128] The two men, conceding their faux pas, pledged to ask after her the next day. It speaks well of Julia Grant that, despite her treatment by Mary Lincoln, she still observed the social amenities and remained concerned about her mental state. When Grant duly inquired after Mrs. Lincoln the next day, the president bore the message to her stateroom and returned to say she was indisposed and begged the gentlemen to excuse her.

At the second session, the military men got down to business with Lincoln. Grant described how Sheridan was crossing the James River by a pontoon bridge with plans to shatter the South Side and Danville Railroads that propped up Lee's army. If Lee responded by striking out for North Carolina, Lincoln feared he might escape by southern railroads. Sherman insisted his men had destroyed their tracks beyond redemption. "What is to prevent their laying the rails again?" Grant probed. "Why, my 'bummers' don't do things by halves," Sherman explained. "Every rail, after having been placed over a hot fire, has been twisted as crooked as a ram's-horn, and they never can be used again."[129] Sherman insisted he could defeat the joint forces of Lee and Johnston if Grant came up behind them in a day or so. On the other hand, if Lee mistakenly clung to his Richmond defenses, Sherman would roar up from North Carolina and he and Grant would starve out Lee or drub him in open combat. Whatever happened, Grant and Sherman saw an inescapably bloody battle ahead, and Lincoln reacted with anguish. "Must more blood be shed?" he cried. "Cannot this last bloody battle be avoided?"[130] On this the generals could promise nothing.

As they pondered postwar reconciliation, Lincoln preached leniency toward the South, saying he didn't want reprisals. Facetiously he added that he didn't want to *hang* Confederates so much as hang *on* to them. Though he couldn't say so publicly, he hinted he would be happy if Jefferson Davis fled the country, avoiding a treason trial that might inflame sectional tensions. "I want no one punished; treat them liberally all round," Lincoln advised. "We want those people to return to their allegiance to the Union and submit to the laws."[131] While the pacific spirit of his postwar policy seemed clear, the specifics were maddeningly vague, as befit a president still bent on winning the war. Grant came away believing that in dealing with Lee's army, he should be magnanimous in his terms of surrender. "Let them have their horses to plow with, and, if you like, their guns to shoot crows with," Lincoln stated.[132] Sherman came away with a sense of a broad mandate that extended to more political matters, remembering Lincoln's belief that "to avoid anarchy the State governments then in existence, with their civil functionaries, would be recognized by him as the government *de facto* till Congress could provide others."[133] Sherman soon had reason to cling to this recollection.

The afternoon session lasted three hours, at the end of which Lincoln, Sherman, and Grant, having been cooped up all afternoon, rambled by the riverside. A reporter captured the vivid contrasts presented by the three men: "Lincoln, tall, round-shouldered, loose-jointed, large-featured, deep-eyed, with a smile upon his face, is dressed in black and wears a fashionable silk hat. Grant is at Lincoln's right, shorter, stouter, more compact; wears a military hat with a stiff, broad brim, has his hands in his pantaloon pockets, and is puffing away at a cigar. Sherman, tall, with a high, commanding forehead, is almost as loosely built as Lincoln; has sandy whiskers, closely cropped, and sharp, twinkling eyes, long arms and legs, shabby coat, slouched hat, his pantaloons tucked into his boots."[134] As they strolled, Lincoln suddenly presented an odd question. "Sherman, do you know why I took a shine to Grant and you?" Abashed, Sherman replied, "I don't know, Mr. Lincoln. You have been extremely kind to me, far more than my deserts." "Well, you never found fault with me."[135] Lincoln had been betrayed by so many generals, he was endlessly grateful for the loyalty of Grant and Sherman. It was the last time William Tecumseh Sherman ever set eyes on Lincoln.

On the morning of March 29, in a farewell imbued with poignant emotion, Lincoln returned to Washington. For Julia Grant, it amounted to a double farewell since her husband was switching headquarters to Gravelly Run for the opening of the Appomattox Campaign, which he would personally direct. Horace Porter recounted how Grant "bade an affectionate good-by to Mrs. Grant, kissing her repeatedly as she stood at the front door of his quarters. She bore the parting bravely, although her pale face and sorrowful look told of the sadness that was in her heart."[136]

When Grant and his staff escorted Lincoln to the train station, the president's mood turned grave. Porter thought the lines were more deeply incised in his face, the rings darker beneath his eyes. Lincoln gave each officer an affectionate handshake. As his train began to move, Grant and his officers lifted their hats in unison in a gesture of profound respect, and Lincoln repaid them with a salute. "Good-by, gentlemen," he said, his voice cracking with emotion. "God bless you all! Remember, your success is my success."[137]

Dirty Boots

D URING LINCOLN'S STAY AT CITY POINT, Phil Sheridan and his
hard-charging cavalry rode in with many jaded, even shoeless, horses,
exhausted from operations on muddy plains in ceaseless rain. Grant
knew it would take several days before the animals were freshly shod and replenished. The rangy Lincoln had been agog at the exploits of the doughty little
Sheridan. As they shared a boat ride on the James River, the president had stared
down at the diminutive general. "General Sheridan, when this peculiar war began I thought a cavalryman should be at least six feet four inches high, but I have
changed my mind. Five feet four will do in a pinch."[1]

Grant issued written instructions for Sheridan to move his cavalry against
Lee's right flank and, if this misfired, to break off, proceed to North Carolina,
and assist Sherman to destroy Johnston before circling back to help take Richmond and Petersburg. After absorbing these instructions, a disgruntled Sheridan, who didn't relish a long trek into North Carolina, slunk off in a terrible
funk. Sensing his displeasure, Grant drew him aside and confided thoughts he
dared not commit to paper. The northern public had grown so eager to end the
war, Grant explained, that unless the current Virginia campaign proved an unqualified success, "it would be interpreted as a disastrous defeat."[2] For that reason, he had stated, *for the record only,* that Sheridan might move south. Now
Grant elaborated privately, saying he "intended to close the war right here, with
this movement, and that he should go no farther." Sheridan's "face at once
brightened up, and slapping his hand on his leg he said: 'I'm glad to hear it, and

we can do it.'"[3] Convinced the war neared its close, Sheridan wanted his cavalry "to be in at the death."[4]

Several political realities colored Grant's thinking in these waning days of battle. He had already informed Lincoln of his plan to attack Lee's extreme right flank, blocking Lee's ability to aid Johnston, when the roads dried up. Some skeptics wondered why he didn't wait until Sherman finished off Johnston and could then fortify him against Lee. The true motivation was political. For much of the war, western armies had won the lion's share of acclaim, and Grant, like Sheridan, thought it imperative that the Army of the Potomac claim the main credit for the demise of Lee's army. In that way, each section of the nation would share the final victory laurels, helping to restore postwar unity. The fear of Sherman dashing north and stealing their glory pervaded the Army of the Potomac. (Some also suspected Grant didn't want Sherman to upstage him.) Not only did Grant show political instincts that matched his military reflexes, but he demonstrated how seriously he meditated the shape of postwar politics. He also knew the war cost a stupendous $4 million a day and, if it persisted, could easily bankrupt the federal government.

With fifty thousand men lined up behind a creek called Hatcher's Run, Grant prepared for his final campaign, a major offensive southwest of Petersburg. On March 28, Lee knew something big was afoot. "Genl Grant is evidently preparing for something," he told his daughter, "& is marshalling & preparing his troops for some movement, which is not yet disclosed."[5] The next day, before dawn, riding on boggy roads, Sheridan shifted west around Lee's right with nearly ten thousand cavalry, hoping to knock out two railroads that formed Lee's lifelines. Lee swung his troop strength to the south to confront this massive threat, dispatching George Pickett with eleven thousand soldiers to guard a crucial crossroads at Five Forks. "Hold Five Forks at all hazards," Lee instructed him.[6] Bowing to Grant's overwhelming strength, Lee decided to commit everything to a desperate gamble and abandon Petersburg. Reflecting his dire predicament, he admitted to Jefferson Davis that Grant's move "seriously threatens our position, and diminishes our ability to maintain our present line."[7] No reasonable alternative existed except to discard the Confederate stronghold on the Appomattox River. With Richmond menaced, Jefferson Davis's wife and children fled, feeding rumors that the capital might be transferred to Georgia.

With so much riding on the outcome, Grant paced in a "profoundly anxious" state, keeping Lincoln minutely informed by telegraph.[8] Never before had he enjoyed such daily, almost hourly, access to the president, signaling that the climactic battle lay just ahead. Grant was haunted by the prospect that Lee and his men might flee to the mountains and fight on in scattered, irregular units, a guerrilla force difficult to run aground. "The General feels like making a heavy push for everything we have hoped for so long, and I am not slow in seconding all such feelings," Rawlins wrote.[9] With everything set for a major advance the next morning, Grant blustered to Sheridan that "I now feel like ending the matter."[10] Then the skies opened and heavy rains drenched roads already flooded with standing pools. So many horses and mules were swallowed by quicksand and had to be yanked from thick muck that the army laid down corduroy roads to advance artillery and wagon trains. Writing to Julia amid a heavy downpour on March 30, Grant allowed himself a witticism, saying it was "consoling to know that it rains on the enemy as well."[11]

Plunging through sheets of rain, Sheridan galloped to Grant's headquarters, hoping to steel Grant's wavering resolve and lobby for the final thrust against Lee. When he arrived, a pall had settled over the officers in Grant's tent. Supported by Rawlins, Sheridan sought to embolden them. According to Horace Porter, he stalked up and down "like a hound in the lash," asserting that, if strengthened by infantry, he could crush Lee's right wing or "break through and march into Petersburg." He summed up his stance with a dash of bravado: "I tell you, I'm ready to strike out tomorrow and go to smashing things."[12] Badeau related that Sheridan "talked so cheerily, so confidently, so intelligently of what he could do, that his mood was contagious" and Grant's low spirits evaporated.[13] "We will go on," he informed Sheridan, ordering him to seize Five Forks.

The next day, Grant sent Lincoln a running commentary on the fierce fighting, based on dispatches Sheridan transmitted from a spot near Dinwiddie Court House. Plagued by "heavy rains and horrid roads," Union forces had retreated before two infantry divisions commanded by George Pickett, but Grant was sure Sheridan would retrieve lost ground.[14] He was ecstatic at having coaxed Lee from his fortifications, giving him a fair chance to end the war. He trusted only one general to complete the job: Phil Sheridan, who, with his bottomless courage, seemed heedless of death. "I have never in my life taken a command into battle," Sheridan maintained, "and had [not] the slightest desire to come out alive unless I won."[15] This encapsulated why Grant reposed such supreme confidence in him.

At 10:45 that night, he directed Sheridan: "You will assume command of the whole force sent to operate with you, and use it to the best of your ability to destroy the force which your command has fought so gallantly today."[16]

On April 1, 1865, at Five Forks came the swift blow from which Robert E. Lee never recovered, the encounter one southern officer eulogized as the Confederacy's Waterloo. Late in the afternoon, an impatient Sheridan sent his dismounted cavalry crashing into Confederate lines, aided by Gouverneur Warren's corps on his flank. Sheridan was as energetic as a storybook soldier, riding Rienzi up and down the line, shaking his fist at the enemy and inspiring his men with pungent oaths. "The cowardly scoundrels can't fight such brave men as mine," he roared, or "Kill that infernal skulker."[17] Porter recorded a horrifying moment when a Union soldier was struck by a bullet in his neck, which spouted blood. "I'm killed!" the man exclaimed, slumping to the ground. "You're not hurt a bit!" Sheridan expostulated. "Pick up your gun, man, and move right on to the front." So commanding were Sheridan's words that the stricken man hoisted his musket and stumbled forward a dozen paces before keeling over and dropping dead.[18] In another extraordinary moment, Sheridan vaulted on horseback over a Confederate barrier only to drop down in the middle of astounded enemy soldiers.[19]

Pickett's army didn't simply reel under the bluecoats' onslaught but disintegrated, allowing Sheridan to capture thousands of prisoners, almost half the rebel soldiers, while the other half fled in fright. When Porter rode into Grant's camp with the glad tidings, he found the officers grouped around "a blazing campfire," with Grant "wrapped in a long blue overcoat and smoking his usual cigar."[20] Not waiting to dismount, Porter shouted the news from horseback to electrifying effect: all the officers except Grant leapt to their feet, shook hands, spun their hats in the air, and engaged in backslapping. Typically, Grant reacted in businesslike fashion. Eager to exploit enemy weakness and knowing Lee would now have to abandon Petersburg and Richmond, he disappeared into his tent and scratched out orders to batter the entire Petersburg front at 4:45 the next morning. As ever, he reasoned that because Lee had shored up forces on his left, he must have weakened his center. It represented a huge military gamble, but Grant was eager to move in for the kill.

Despite the moment's high drama, he slumbered peacefully on his camp bed that night. As dawn broke and hundreds of Union guns boomed simultaneously, the attack was launched while Grant waited at headquarters. A vast flying wedge of soldiers descended on all points of the Confederate lines. After the grinding

misery of a four-year war, the tempo speeded up in an almost unimaginable manner. Union troops under Generals Ord, Andrew Humphreys, and Horatio Wright
stormed Petersburg, slashing openings and taking the outer ring of defenses.

As soon as Grant heard of this triumph, he mounted his horse "to join the
troops who were inside the works. When I arrived there I rode my horse over the
parapet just as Wright's three thousand prisoners were coming out."[21] When
Grant encountered Wright's men, they burst into cheers unlike anything he had
ever heard. Once inside Petersburg's fortifications, he dismounted and gazed at
the sophisticated ramparts with something akin to awe. "They are exceedingly
strong," he told Julia, "and I wonder at the success of our troops carrying them
by storm."[22] By his own estimate, he had captured twelve thousand prisoners
and fifty pieces of artillery from a southern army once deemed unbeatable. The
scene unfolding on the rebel side was a mirror image of such elation. Submitting
to the inevitable, Lee ordered his crippled, depleted army to retreat from Petersburg; to save the remnant of this force, he needed to evacuate Richmond as well.
As he informed Secretary of War Breckinridge: "I see no prospect of doing more
than holding our position here till night. I am not certain that I can do that; if
I can I shall withdraw tonight north of the Appomattox."[23]

Late that afternoon, Grant transmitted to Lincoln news of his victory, inviting him to tour the captured Petersburg works the next day. Julia was at City
Point with Lincoln when he received the message and noted his "radiant" expression.[24] "Allow me to tender to you and all with you the nation's grateful thanks
for this additional & magnificent success," Lincoln replied to Grant. "At your
Kind suggestion I think I will meet you tomorrow."[25] Some officers urged Grant
to pierce Petersburg's inner lines that afternoon, but Grant argued that Lee
would evacuate the city that night, sparing them any need for further bloodshed. Sheridan had choked off the last railroad into Petersburg, making Confederate survival there impossible. True to Grant's prediction, the Confederate
army stole westward at nightfall and Grant issued orders to overrun the town at
dawn the next day.

Once Lee decided to retreat from Petersburg, he wired Jefferson Davis and
advised him to leave Richmond at once. The messenger who bore this telegram
crept down the aisle of St. Paul's Episcopal Church in Richmond and handed it
to Davis, who turned deathly pale, bolted from his pew, and left. As alarmed
whispers spread through the church, government officials fled and soon the
whole congregation poured into the street, where pandemonium broke loose.

People scurried about frantically, desperate to desert the town. At the train station, officials scrambled to load treasury gold and government archives onto
trains bound for Danville. The cabinet rode off by two in the afternoon. People
clambered onto roofs of overloaded trains or clung feverishly to their sides. Determined to deny the Yankees anything of value, residents set ablaze cotton and
tobacco, and flames enfolded the town by nightfall.[26] In the early morning of
April 3, retreating Confederate troops exploded ordnance depots, causing thousands of shells to burst until "a vast column of dense black smoke shot into the
air . . . several bright jets of flame . . . augured the breaking forth of that terrible
conflagration which subsequently swept across the heart of the city," wrote a
British correspondent.[27] Shattered glass spilled across sidewalks. By the time
Yankee troops under Godfrey Weitzel arrived at 8:15 the next morning, their
first order of business was to douse towering sheets of flame that had burned
hundreds of buildings in what came to be known as the Burnt District. In South
Carolina, Mary Chesnut penned an epitaph for the Confederacy: "Everything is
lost in Richmond, even our archives. Blue-black is our horizon."[28]

As word of the Petersburg and Richmond surrenders spread to northern cities, the joy was as profound as the pent-up misery of the war had been deep. In
Washington crowds filled the streets with raucous people laughing and bellow-
ing hurrahs. Philadelphia residents broke out flags and flapped them deliriously.
Even in the sober precincts of Wall Street, George Templeton Strong found a
euphoria that transformed pure strangers into instant comrades: "I walked about
on the outskirts of the crowd, shaking hands with everybody, congratulating
and being congratulated by scores of men I hardly know even by sight."[30]

On the morning of April 3, Grant entered Petersburg and, with bullets still ric-
ocheting off walls, took shelter with Meade in a deserted brick house at 21 Market
Street that offered cover from enemy fire. Members of the town council—"old
men, in homespun, butternut clothing . . . bearing an improvised flag of truce that
looked suspiciously like a dirty linen table cloth," said one journalist—surrendered

Grant was hardly surprised that Lee had abandoned Richmond; his only
surprise was that he had held it for so long at such dear cost. In later years, he
expounded on Lee's error in holding on to Richmond: "After I crossed the James,
the holding of Richmond was a mistake . . . Lee sacrificed his judgment as a
soldier to his duty as a citizen and the leader of the South. I think Lee deserves
honor for that, for if he had left Richmond when Sherman invaded Georgia, it
would have given us another year of war."[29]

to the new authorities.[31] In the distance, Grant discerned the Confederate army escaping across a bridge over the Appomattox River. He deliberately refrained from bringing up artillery to mow it down. "At all events I had not the heart to turn the artillery upon such a mass of defeated and fleeing men," he explained, "and I hoped to capture them soon."[32] Instead of trailing Lee's army, Grant preferred to let them withdraw and then race ahead of them, obstructing their access to remaining food supplies in western Virginia and blocking their access to Johnston in North Carolina. Few white residents poked their heads out of doors, while small knots of blacks rejoiced at their Union liberators. As Grant sat on the porch of the house, curious white pedestrians studied the man who had been their constant nemesis and now suddenly turned up in their midst.

Taking up Grant's offer, Lincoln, with Tad in tow, slowly made his way on horseback to Petersburg, garbed in a black suit, a silk hat, and trousers that inched up his legs as he rode. Despite anguished concerns about his personal safety, he reassured Stanton, "I will take care of myself."[33] He traversed battlefields covered with mutilated, bloated bodies, and William Crook noted that the president looked upon "one man with a bullet-hole through his forehead, and another with both arms shot away." As Lincoln mused on these dreadful visions, his "face settled into its old lines of sadness."[34]

On the fringes of Petersburg, Robert Lincoln met his father with horses and a cavalry escort, and the retinue proceeded through eerily deserted streets, passing dozens of skeletal houses with gaping holes blown through their walls. When they reached the brick house where Grant awaited them, the general in chief descended the stairs to greet the president. A beaming Lincoln bounded forward, grasping Grant's hand robustly, his joy gushing to the surface. With a droll smile he declared, "Do you know, General, I have had a sort of sneaking idea for some days that you intended to do something like this."[35] As they conversed on the porch, neither Lincoln nor Grant knew of Richmond's downfall. In an expansive frame of mind, Lincoln expatiated on his ideas for southern Reconstruction. Grant felt he could be open with Lincoln about upcoming battle plans. He expressed pleasure that the eastern army was defeating Lee. Otherwise western congressmen might have lorded it over their eastern counterparts after the war. Lincoln confessed he had never given the matter much thought "because his anxiety was so great that he did not care where the aid came from, so the work was done."[36] It is interesting to note that the astute Lincoln never weighed this question while the supposedly apolitical Grant volunteered this insight. As the

two men chatted, the little yard before them filled with former slaves emancipated by the triumphant troops in blue. Lincoln and these freed people stared at
one another in silent wonder. It would have been hard to say which was more
surprising: the sudden freedom of the slaves or the fact that the president who
brought forth the Emancipation Proclamation was there to greet them personally in their first hours of freedom.

Lincoln and Grant talked for ninety minutes, hoping to hear the momentous
news of Richmond's fall, which didn't arrive. When the two parted, Lincoln
pumped Grant's hand, wishing him "God-speed and every success."[37] Grant rode
off to join Sheridan, Ord, and Meade in hot pursuit of Lee. The last great chase
of the Civil War was on. As Grant sped west, he surveyed the wreckage deposited
by Lee's fleeing army: discarded artillery, ammunition, clothing, burned wagons,
and ambulances. Union forces had taken twelve thousand Confederate prisoners,
with large numbers of stragglers rounded up everywhere. Grant spent the night at
Sutherland Station, where he received word that Richmond had fallen into Weitzel's hands. The surrounding generals reacted with jubilation, one soldier emit-
ting a cry of joy: "Stack your muskets and go home."[38] True to his nature, Grant
showed no emotion, merely saying: "I am sorry I did not get this information
before we left the President. However, I suppose he has heard it by this time."[39]

The riven portions of Lee's army, pared down to thirty-five thousand men
and separated on opposite sides of the Appomattox River were set to converge at
Amelia Court House, thirty-five miles west of Petersburg. The fond hope of
these famished men was to find stores of rations awaiting them there; instead,
due to a bureaucratic snafu in Richmond, they came upon ammunition of little
value without rested horses to carry it. The day Lee sacrificed in waiting for supplies proved costly. He had planned to move along the railroad tracks toward
Danville and merge with the northward-moving army of Joseph Johnston, defeating Sherman before Grant intervened. Once Grant got wind of this, he ordered Sheridan to move west on the railroad with all possible speed, and Meade
traced the same route the next morning.

By the time Lincoln returned to City Point, he had learned of Richmond's
capture, erasing four years of inexpressible heartache. "Thank God I have lived
to see this," he told Admiral Porter. "It seems to me that I have been dreaming a
horrid dream for four years, and now the nightmare is gone. I want to see Richmond."[40] Grant had prevailed upon Lincoln to extend his City Point stay, promising that he would soon be able to tour the liberated Confederate capital.

Intent upon capturing Lee's army, Grant was never tempted to enter Richmond and play the swaggering conquistador, a piece of symbolism as profound as his upcoming mercy at Appomattox. The historian John Lothrop Motley praised this exemplary restraint: "There is something very sublime to my imagination in the fact that Grant *has never yet set his foot in Richmond,* and perhaps never will."[41] With poetic justice, black soldiers joined the entrance of Union troops into the ravaged capital on April 3. The message wasn't lost on the townspeople. "The white citizens felt annoyed that the city should be held mostly by negro troops," wrote the rebel war clerk John Jones.[42]

The next day, escorted by Admiral Porter and a mere ten sailors equipped with carbines, Abraham Lincoln bravely strode Richmond's streets, past hundreds of charred, blasted buildings, his steps shadowed by black people who shouted with rapture, as if suddenly beholding the Messiah. One elderly black man exclaimed, "Glory, hallelujah!" and knelt reverently at his feet. Lincoln stood chagrined. "Don't kneel to me," he admonished the man tenderly. "That is not right. You must kneel to God only, and thank Him for the liberty you will hereinafter enjoy. I am but God's humble instrument."[43] Lincoln traveled to the Confederate White House—his face "pale and haggard," said one observer, with "a serious, dreamy expression" said another—and occupied the chair so recently warmed by Jefferson Davis.[44]

During these stirring days, one disaffected spectator was Julia Grant, who felt snubbed by Mary Lincoln and frozen out of her social circle once Ulysses departed. The Lincolns still stayed aboard the *River Queen,* anchored in the James River, but Julia enjoyed virtually no contact with them, even though she occupied a boat only a hundred yards away. "I saw very little of the presidential party now, as Mrs. Lincoln had a good deal of company and seemed to have forgotten us. I felt this deeply and could not understand it, as my regard for the family was not only that of respect but affection." Her bitter sense of exclusion sharpened after Petersburg and Richmond fell: "All of these places were visited by the President and party, and I, not a hundred yards from them, was not invited to join them."[45] Accompanied by other ladies, Julia rolled in a carriage through Richmond's empty streets. Back in her stateroom, she lamented the terrible devastation wrought by the war. "How many homes made desolate! How many hearts broken! How much youth sacrificed!" Suddenly she gave vent to tears and realized that she also mourned the vanished way of life that had bred her in Missouri. "Could it be that my visit reminded me of my dear old home in Missouri?"[46]

With the war's end in sight, questions emerged as to whether the Confederate leaders should be treated leniently or harshly. While Lincoln seemed inclined
toward leniency, Vice President Andrew Johnson, in a speech celebrating Richmond's fall, previewed a more vindictive spirit. When his allusion to Jefferson
Davis elicited shouts of "Hang him! Hang him!" Johnson appeased the bloodthirsty crowd. "Yes, I say hang him twenty times." He then extended his retribu-
tive wrath to include other ringleaders of the rebellion. "When you ask me what
I would do, my reply is—I would arrest them, I would try them, I would convict
them, and I would hang them . . . Treason must be made odious."[47]

By April 4, 1865, Grant had decided to give Lee no respite until he knocked
out his army and terminated the war. Nothing mattered any longer except track-
ing down the enemy army and destroying it. Rawlins applauded his boss's fighting spirit, his determination to end the protracted struggle. "I had feared he
might not so decide," he told his wife, "but all is well now and promising early
brightness of the national sky."[48] With Sheridan and his cavalry thundering
ahead, straining to overtake the enemy, Grant sorted through intelligence reports to figure out the exact route Lee would take from Amelia Court House.
Grant rode through a disorderly landscape swarming with rebel deserters—
dazed, exhausted men, often sprawled by the roadside next to wounded brethren. "Houses through the country are nearly all used as hospitals for wounded
men," he informed Stanton.[49] At noon, Sheridan reported that Lee's army, crossing to the north side of the Appomattox River, seemed to be retreating toward
Lynchburg in western Virginia.

With the finely honed instinct of a hunter seeking wounded prey, Sheridan
wrote to Grant from Jetersville on April 5, saying Lee was at nearby Amelia
Court House, had nearly exhausted his rations, and the time had come to
trounce the enemy. Lee had ordered rations to be brought up from Danville to
the railway junction at Farmville, which now beckoned as his last hope for salva- ·
tion. He had been reduced to headlong flight to secure food and avert outright
starvation. By moving aggressively, Sheridan thought he could foil any move Lee
made to Farmville.

That evening, after a wearisome day in the saddle, Grant received a letter
from Sheridan that had profound repercussions. It arrived in an unconventional
form: a Union scout, tricked out in Confederate garb to dupe the enemy, held a

tinfoil pellet in his mouth with a message wrapped inside. Sheridan entreated Grant: "I wish you were here yourself—I feel confident of capturing the Army of Northern Va. if we exert ourselves—I see no escape for Lee."[50] As the great drama hastened to its climax, Grant decided to make his headquarters with his advance troops and, without pausing for supper, set off with Rawlins and a dozen orderlies to join Sheridan.

Even though Sheridan's camp lay ten miles off, Grant had to traverse hazardous countryside and skirt rebel lines, logging more than thirty miles on horseback: "I remember being challenged by pickets, and sometimes I had great difficulty in getting through the lines. I remember picking my way through the sleeping soldiers, bivouacked in the open field."[51] Around 10 p.m., Grant reached Sheridan's small frame headquarters in Jetersville where he found aides toiling by candlelight while Sheridan dozed in an elevated loft. When Grant entered, Sheridan climbed down a ladder "with no clothing but a shirt, pants, and boots," said an observer.[52] After supplying his weary guests with beef, chicken, and coffee, Sheridan again implored Grant to make the supreme push for victory. An intense debate had divided Sheridan and Meade, with Meade wanting to guard Richmond to the east, while Sheridan feared this would facilitate Lee's escape to the west. Sheridan wished to clobber Lee's army *now*. With his inimitable gusto, he pored over maps and sketched diagrams, showing the positions of Lee's columns and how he could capture his entire army. "Lee *is* in a bad fix," confessed Grant, who tried to tamp down expectations, resisting premature euphoria. "It will be difficult for him to get away." "Damn him," Sheridan spluttered, "he *can't* get away," then he let fly a volley of profanities.[53] These words rattled around in Grant's mind. He knew Sheridan would stalk Lee with his usual febrile intensity. "My judgment coincided with Sheridan's," Grant recalled. "I felt we ought to find Lee, wherever he was, and strike him. The question was not the occupation of Richmond, but the destruction of the army."[54]

Accompanied by Sheridan, Grant consulted with an ailing, dyspeptic Meade, arguing the time had come to scrap prudence and stake everything on victory. Reiterating his wartime credo, Grant insisted he did not want to take Richmond, which was "only a collection of houses," but grab Robert E. Lee's army, "an active force injuring the country."[55] Among other things, Grant hoped to throw his army between Lee and Johnston's army in the Carolinas, isolating both and ruling out any cooperation. "I explained to Meade that we did not want to follow the enemy; we wanted to get ahead of him, and that his orders would allow the enemy to escape."[56] It was now too late for Grant to pretend that Meade made the major decisions for the Army of the Potomac. On the spot, he took out a pencil and handed Meade orders for his entire infantry to move on Amelia Court House early the next morning.[57]

That night, Lee abandoned his position there and raced to stay ahead of the Union army, his abject soldiers reduced to pleading for food from spectators lining the route. At the battle of Sayler's Creek (sometimes spelled Sailor's Creek) the next day, Sheridan isolated a corps of Confederate infantry under General Richard S. Ewell, shattering a solid quarter of Lee's army. "The enemy, seeing little chance of escape, fought like a tiger at bay," Sheridan wrote.[58] After furious fighting, Sheridan collared six rebel generals and six thousand prisoners. George Armstrong Custer helped to capture and burn hundreds of Confederate wagons. Like disoriented sleepwalkers, Lee's gallant but now spent soldiers could scarcely function any longer, one correspondent telling how "hundreds of men dropped from exhaustion, and thousands let fall their muskets from inability to carry them any further."[59] These dazed retreating figures had the extra handicap of having to stop and turn to fire, making them ready targets for Union marksmen. With his army eroded, Lee understood the terrible meaning of the defeat, destined to be the last major engagement between the Army of the Potomac and the Army of Northern Virginia. As he sat astride Traveller, watching in horror as his noble band of soldiers broke down into a chaotic rabble, he let forth a poignant lament: "My God! Has the army been dissolved?"[60]

Even before receiving news from Sayler's Creek, Lincoln had narrowly monitored developments. At noon on April 6, he summoned Mary and others into a drawing room of the *River Queen* to regale them with the flow of uplifting bulletins from Grant. Once again Lincoln seemed to possess limitless energy, shucking off the war's oppressive weight. "His whole appearance, pose, and bearing had marvelously changed," noted Senator James Harlan. "That indescribable sadness . . . had suddenly changed for an equally indescribable expression of serene joy, as if conscious that the great purpose of his life had been attained."[61] When Sheridan rushed off a message to Grant—"If the thing is pressed I think that Lee will surrender"—Lincoln endorsed this audacious declaration: "Let the *thing* be pressed. A. Lincoln."[62]

The latest victory effected a critical transformation in Grant's outlook. Quite unlike Sheridan, he hadn't expected to capture Lee's army in its entirety. Now he had to revise his thinking. Upon reaching Sayler's Creek, he observed prisoners "coming in by shoals, I saw there was no more fighting left in that army."[63] He reflected on a conversation he had with a Virginia doctor named Smith, who relayed a startling pronouncement made by Richard Ewell, now in captivity. Ewell regarded the Confederate cause as so helpless that he thought "that for every man that was killed after this in the war somebody is responsible, and it would be but very little better than murder."[64] Spending the night at Burkeville, Grant decided the time had come to propose to Lee the surrender of his army.

By the afternoon of April 7, riding in light rain, applauded by soldiers as he passed—he lifted his hat and nodded in response—Grant arrived at Farmville and heard the clock ticking down toward the end of the war. "Every moment now is important to us," he warned Meade.[65] Galvanized by the fast-moving situation, Grant traveled without baggage, his clothes soiled from squalid roads. Separated from his headquarters wagons, he didn't even transport a dress sword, making it pure happenstance that he was not grandly appareled for his rendez-vous with Lee two days later. In the town hotel, an ample brick building with a wide porch, he set up temporary headquarters. However fine in better days, the dowdy hostelry now appeared "almost destitute of furniture," Grant wrote.[66] That morning, Lee had passed through Farmville, where he tried to resuscitate his faltering army with waiting rations. Having abandoned plans to escape south toward Danville and the North Carolina border, he planned to drive west to Appomattox Station, where the next batch of supplies, he prayed, would await him in railway cars. If all went according to plan, he would reach Lynchburg and still more abundant supplies and maybe vanish into the vast hinterland of the Blue Ridge Mountains. Sheridan intended to make sure Lee never reached Appomattox Station and wrote Grant with that pledge.

At five in the afternoon, Grant conferred on the hotel verandah with Generals Ord and John Gibbon. Before they hurried off to assist Sheridan, Grant said in a disarmingly soft-spoken voice, "I have a great mind to summon Lee, to surrender."[67] Taking up his dispatch book, he wrote on its thin yellow pages, interleaved with carbon sheets. In his usual concise style, he began his letter to Lee: "GENERAL, The result of the last week must convince you of the hopelessness of further resistance on the part of the Army of Northern Va. in this struggle. I feel that it is so and regard it as my duty to shift from myself, the responsibility of any further effusion of blood by asking of you the surrender of that portion of the C. S. [Confederate States] Army known as the Army of Northern Va. Very respectfully your obt. svt U. S. Grant Lt. Gn."[68] Riding under a flag of truce,

Brigadier General Seth Williams and an orderly disappeared down darkening country lanes to deliver this momentous message to Lee.

Awaiting the reply, Grant eased into a chair on the verandah, which afforded him a front-row seat as emboldened soldiers from Wright's Sixth Corps moved by with a crisp, elastic step. It developed into one of the war's more theatrical scenes. The soldiers, who had learned to love Grant, spotted him on the porch and saluted him with exultant cheers as they swung by, crooning "John Brown's Body." When Grant rose and stood by the banister, puffing his cigar, the ovation swelled in volume. As night fell, a starry sky stood revealed, washed clean by the day's rainfall. The soldiers tramped by in bright moonshine, their movements thrown into silhouette by the powerful glow of bonfires bordering the route. They grabbed sticks, thrust them into the blaze, then strode on with flaming torches, as if participating in a candlelight election parade. "The night march had become a grand review," noted Horace Porter, "with Grant as the reviewing officer."[69]

Grant's message reached Lee around 10 p.m. at a little cottage where he was bedding down for the night. He perused it with a blank face that would have done credit to Grant at his most inscrutable, then handed the sheet to his most reliable deputy, James Longstreet, who instantly vetoed surrender with the admonition, "Not yet."[70] Now a study in contradiction, Lee was convinced the war was hopeless, yet was reluctant to fall on his sword. "I have never believed we could, against the gigantic combination for our subjugation, make good in the long run our independence unless foreign powers should, directly or indirectly assist us," he mused aloud to General William Pendleton. A devout believer in the Confederate cause, Lee had braced himself to fight until the last moment: "We had, I was satisfied, sacred principles to maintain and rights to defend, for which we were in duty bound to do our best, even if we perished in the endeavor."[71] The comment belies the notion that Lee fought simply from loyalty to his home state of Virginia and betokens a more militant attachment to Confederate ideology.

Lee sat down and formulated his thoughts to Grant: "GENERAL:—I have received your note of this date. Though not entertaining the opinion you express of the hopelessness of further resistance on the part of the Army of N. Va. I reciprocate your desire to avoid useless effusion of blood & therefore before Considering your proposition ask the terms you will offer on condition of its surrender."[72] A courier galloped off into the night. Grant was resting in his room, well after midnight, when he was given Lee's response. He wisely chose to sleep on his response. The next morning, he sent Lee a delicately worded note that dropped the defiant tone that had earned him the nickname "Unconditional Surrender Grant":

> GENERAL, Your note of last evening, in reply to mine of same date, asking the conditions on which I will accept the surrender of the Army of N. Va. is just received. In reply I would say that *peace* being my great desire there is but one condition I insist upon, namely: that the men and officers surrendered shall be disqualified for taking up arms again, against the Government of the United States, until properly exchanged.
>
> I will meet you or will designate Officers to meet any officers you may name for the same purpose, at any point agreeable to you, for the purpose of arranging definitely the terms upon which the surrender of the Army of N. Va. will be received.
>
> Very respectfully your obt. svt. U. S. GRANT Lt. Gn[73]

By April 8, Grant felt confident enough about the outcome that he assured Stanton he expected to compel Lee's surrender the next day. Far from being exhausted, Sheridan's men operated on the spare reserves of energy armies muster in the last spurts of winning wars. Many of Lee's soldiers, by contrast, who came from the surrounding region, began to dissolve back into the countryside from whence they came. As northern politicians tingled with expectation, future president Rutherford B. Hayes noted that "the glorious news is coming so fast that I hardly know how to think and feel about it. It is so just that Grant, who is by all odds our man of greatest merit, should get this victory."[74] Still, Grant grappled with tremendous anxiety at this pivotal juncture. Lee was approaching supplies sent by railroad at Appomattox Station while his own supply base receded uncomfortably in the rear. He figured that he had, at most, a day to close the contest before he would need to retreat and feed his own army. Lee, in turn, knew that if his army could survive another day, he might penetrate farther west to Lynchburg and find a haven in the Virginia and Tennessee mountains.

Grant's morning letter reached Lee after dark when he read it in a roadway by the uncertain glare of a candle held aloft by an aide. He pondered the message with an impassive face before passing it to the aide. "How would you answer that?" he inquired. The young man, with southern pride, responded, "I would answer no such letter." Lee knew such intransigence would no longer suffice.[75] Under the surface, he had been gripped by turbulent feelings all day, striding about in a black mood. Always in tight control of his emotions, Lee sat down by the road and composed his reply to Grant as he clung to his last shred of dignity.

> I received at a late hour your note of today—In mine of yesterday I did not intend to propose the Surrender of the Army of N. Va—but to ask the terms of your proposition. To be frank, I do not think the emergency has arisen to call for the Surrender of this Army, but as the restoration of peace should be the Sole object of all, I desired to know whether your proposals would lead to that end. I cannot therefore meet you with a view to Surrender the Army of N–Va—but as far as your proposal may affect the C. S. [Confederate States] forces under my Command & tend to the restoration of peace, I should be pleased to meet you at 10 A m [sic] tomorrow on the old stage road to Richmond between the picket lines of the two armies—[76]

As Grant awaited the reply, the bottled-up tension inside him had triggered a pounding migraine headache. Settled in a farmhouse for the night, he turned to his usual sovereign remedies, soaking his feet in hot water mixed with mustard and slapping mustard plasters on his wrists and neck. The tormenting headache would not pass. That staff officers banged out tunes on a parlor piano surely aggravated the misery for the tone-deaf Grant.[77]

Around midnight, Rawlins brought in Lee's letter, which Grant read aloud. "It looks as if Lee still means to fight," he commented, regretting his foe's obstinacy. "I will reply in the morning."[78] A heated exchange ensued with Rawlins, who, uncompromising as ever, blamed Lee for shifting the negotiating ground from outright surrender to peace talks. "No, sir. No, sir," he declared hotly. "Why, it is a positive insult—an attempt, in an underhanded way, to change the whole terms of the correspondence." Grant interpreted Lee's statement more charitably, not simply from the standpoint of military advantage but from human sympathy for what his chastened opponent must be feeling. "It amounts to the same thing, Rawlins," Grant explained. "He is only trying to be let down easy." He had no doubt of prevailing in his upcoming encounter with Lee. "If I meet Lee he will surrender before I leave."[79] Rawlins reminded Grant that Lincoln and

Stanton had delegated no power to him to arrange terms of peace. "Your business is to capture or destroy Lee's army."[80]

Perhaps disturbed by this or else tormented by his headache, Grant, usually an excellent sleeper, managed only a few fitful hours of rest. When Horace Porter checked on him at 4 a.m., he discovered an empty room, finding Grant instead "pacing up and down in the yard, holding both hands to his head. Upon inquiring how he felt, he replied that he had had very little sleep, and was still suffering the most excruciating pain."[81] Once again an agonizing headache manifested the extraordinary stress under which Grant labored.

The next morning, Palm Sunday, was unseasonably cold and damp. After downing coffee at Meade's headquarters, Grant sent Lee a note that spurned his proposed meeting and yielded no concessions. It did, however, exhibit a softer, more personal side.

> GENERAL, Your note of yesterday is received. As I have no authority to treat on the subject of peace the meeting proposed for 10 a.m. to-day could lead to no good. I will state however General that I am equally anxious for peace with yourself and the whole North entertains the same feeling. The terms upon which peace can be had are well understood. By the South laying down their Arms they will hasten that most desirable event, save thousands of lives and hundreds of Millions of property not yet destroyed.
>
> Sincerely hoping that all our difficulties may be settled without the loss of another life I subscribe myself very respectfully your obt. svt. U. S. GRANT Lt. Gn[82]

When this letter reached Lee, he was in the proper frame of mind to receive it. Sheridan's cavalry had outraced him to the Appomattox depot, capturing four railroad cars, Lee's last hope for subsistence, while the Union army stood astride the westward route by which he planned to escape. Rebel soldiers were stuck fast in a thicket of Union bayonets. Although they tried one last time to escape the deadly trap, they were badly outnumbered and saw resistance as futile. When one officer suggested to Lee that his army should disband and soldier on as guerrillas, he spiked such dangerous thinking, noting that guerrillas "would become mere bands of marauders, and the enemy's cavalry would pursue them and overrun many sections they may never [otherwise] have occasion to visit. We would bring on a state of affairs it would take the country years to recover from."[83]

With his letter sent, Grant mounted Cincinnati and trotted west to Sheridan, who had captured Appomattox Station. Bypassing Lee's army, Grant took a long, roundabout route along boggy lanes that spattered his already grimy garments. Toward noon, his progress was halted when a high-spirited officer from Meade's staff galloped toward him, flapping his hat wildly and brandishing a sealed letter, one of the most consequential in American history. Grant broke it open and mutely weighed its meaning. "There was no more expression in Grant's countenance than in a last year's bird nest," observed a journalist. "It was that of a Sphinx."[84] Allowing himself the barest trace of a smile, Grant requested that Rawlins read it aloud. As he complied, his eyes flashed and his voice resonated with solemn emotion:

> I sent a communication to you today from the picket line whither I
> had gone in hopes of meeting you in pursuance of the request con-
> tained in my letter of yesterday. Maj Gen Meade informs me that it
> would probably expedite matters to send a duplicate through some
> other part of your lines. I therefore request an interview at such time
> and place as you may designate, to discuss the terms of the surrender
> of this army in accordance with your offer to have such an interview
> contained in your letter of yesterday[.][85]

Now admitting that surrender was the crux of the matter, Lee had capitulated. Grant's headache vanished the instant he set eyes on these words and he couldn't resist gently ribbing Rawlins. "Well, how do you think that will do?" he inquired of his petulant friend. "I think *that* will do," Rawlins allowed happily.[86] Only one staff officer openly rejoiced at the extraordinary news; celebration seemed cheap and tasteless after so many years of epic bloodshed. Sitting down on a grassy slope by the roadside, Grant composed a letter to Lee that struck a conciliatory note, agreeing to meet him at any place he proposed. Orville Babcock delivered it under a flag of truce and found Lee leaning against an apple tree, his feet in the road, chatting with Longstreet beyond Appomattox Court House. Based on his long-standing relationship with Grant, Longstreet persuaded a skeptical Lee that his old friend would behave honorably at any parley and not inflict humiliating conditions.

After replying to Lee, Grant hurried to meet Sheridan, who was eager to thrash the Confederate army into final submission. The impetuous Sheridan had been disappointed when a messenger, white flag in tow, announced Lee's surrender. "Damn them," Sheridan blurted out. "I wish they had held out an hour longer and I would have whipped hell out of them." Grabbing his gloved hand, he swore, "I've got 'em like that."[87] Grant never made such boasts, nor did he revel in a blood-thirsty desire for vengeance. In chatting with Grant, Sheridan dismissed Lee's talk of surrender as a patent ruse. He was, Grant recalled, "anxious and suspicious about the whole business, feared there might be a plan to escape, that he had Lee at his feet, and wanted to end the business by going in and forcing an absolute sur-render by capture. In fact, he had his troops ready for such an assault when Lee's white flag came within his lines."[88] To his credit, Grant conquered any feelings of revenge and, knowing that Lee's overture was genuine, acted on that assumption.

With the Confederate army bivouacked in a nearby valley, Sheridan directed Grant to a brick house on the outskirts of Appomattox Court House where Lee awaited him. It was owned by Wilmer McLean, who had owned a house at Bull Run damaged during the first battle there; he had fled to the sleepy hamlet of Appomattox Court House, hoping to escape further hostilities, and would now claim the odd distinction of witnessing the beginning of the Civil War in his backyard and its ending in his parlor. Approaching the historic rendezvous, Grant was painfully aware of how poorly costumed he was to enact this lofty scene; his slovenly appearance had come about merely from being detached from his head-quarters wagon. He had no inkling that later historians might be charmed by his outfit or assume that his mud-caked clothes made a political statement. Quite simply, Grant hadn't expected to meet Lee this soon: "I had an old suit on, with-out my sword, and without any distinguishing mark of rank, except the shoulder straps of a Lieutenant General on a woollen blouse . . . I was afraid Lee might think I meant to show him studied discourtesy by so coming—at least I thought so."[89] Later asked what was uppermost in his mind at this sublime moment, a sheepish Grant said prosaically: "My dirty boots and wearing no sword."[90]

Grant, now forty-two, had no trace of gray in his dark brown hair. Neverthe-less, his beard was fuller than at the start of the war, his face broader, and the bags heavier beneath his eyes, their somber expression bordering on depression. So earthy was his appearance that one officer said with a laugh that he "looked like a fly on a shoulder of beef."[91] However self-conscious Grant may have been about his appearance, he projected authority as he approached the McLean house. Joshua Lawrence Chamberlain, a hero of Gettysburg, was awestruck as Grant trotted by:

Slouched hat without cord; common soldier's blouse, unbuttoned,
on which, however, the four stars; high boots, mud-splashed to the
top; trousers tucked inside; no sword, but the sword-hand deep in
the pocket; sitting his saddle with the ease of a born master, taking
no notice of anything, all his faculties gathered into intense thought
and mighty calm. He seemed greater than I had ever seen him,—a
look as of another world about him. No wonder I forgot altogether
to salute him. Anything like that would have been too little. He rode
on to meet Lee at the Court House.[92]

Lee dreaded the encounter and only submitted when informed that Sheridan
had checkmated his army. "Then there is nothing left me to do but go and see
General Grant," he concluded wearily, "and I would rather die a thousand
deaths."[93] As befit a man about to step onto the brightly lit stage of history, Lee
startled his officers by appearing in a spotless gray uniform, buttoned tightly to
the throat. At fifty-eight, he still cut a tall, erect, and imposing figure. Every
garment he wore had been chosen with extreme care: the intricately wrought
dress sword with the gilded hilt; long, embroidered buckskin gauntlets; silk sash
fitted around his waist; and high boots with an ornamental design of red silk, set
off by prominent spurs. When his officers questioned him about this magnificent display, Lee confided, "I have probably to be General Grant's prisoner, and
thought I must make my best appearance."[94] Longstreet saw Lee's ceremonial
glitter as so much emotional armor. "At first approach his compact figure appeared as a man in the flush vigor of forty summers, but as I drew near, the
handsome apparel and brave bearing failed to conceal his profound depression."[95] Another spectator noted how Lee's hair and beard had grown "as white
and as fair as a woman's."[96] There was a Roman severity, a patrician air of rectitude, about Robert E. Lee, and at Appomattox Court House he was determined
to look the victor, even if he could not be one.

Appomattox Court House consisted of a single street or two of straggling
houses. When Grant arrived at the brick McLean house around 1:30 p.m., the
blue and gray armies faced off uneasily outside of town, set to resume hostilities
the second talks failed. Nothing outwardly marked the house as the venue for
talks except that Traveller and another horse munched grass in the front yard.
Having dismounted, Grant marched up the wooden steps, crossed the verandah,
then entered the front hallway alone. Lee, who was waiting, sat in a small front

room with a single aide, Lieutenant Colonel Charles Marshall. Mildly irritated by the delay, Lee rose to greet Grant, shook hands civilly, and ushered him into the room. A stiff, unbending dignity about the unsmiling Lee threw into relief Grant's down-to-earth nature. Pulling off his tattered, dark yellow gloves and noting Lee's spruce appearance, Grant apologized for his "rough garb."[97] As he appraised the Union general, Marshall thought "he looked as though he had had a pretty hard time."[98] Perhaps with mild embarrassment, Lee explained that his new uniform had been sent by some Baltimore admirers and was the only one he had available for the occasion.

Because Grant had left his entourage outside, Orville Babcock went out and invited Ord, Sheridan, Rawlins, and other generals into the parlor. They shuffled discreetly into the room, "very much as people enter a sick chamber where they expect to find the patient dangerously ill," one noted.[99] The officers then withdrew as they awaited an agreement. With a large fireplace, two small tables, a wicker armchair, and a leather swivel chair, the McLean parlor was cramped but adequate for negotiations. Characteristically, Grant tried to exchange pleasantries with Lee, who sat there with Olympian gravity. In a slightly fumbling manner, Grant said deferentially, "I met you once before, General Lee, while we were serving in Mexico, when you came over from General Scott's headquarters to visit Garland's brigade, to which I then belonged. I have always remembered your appearance, and I think I should have recognized you anywhere." Fifteen years his senior, Lee didn't bother to pretend that he recalled Grant. "Yes, I know I met you on that occasion, and I have often thought of it, and tried to recollect how you looked, but I have never been able to recall a single feature."[100] The comment surely reminded both men of their highly unequal ranks in Mexico, a difference in status equalized by subsequent events.

On the surface, their conversation seemed amiable, but Grant was perceptive enough to discern that Lee struggled with strong feelings behind a mask of cordiality. As he observed in an eloquent passage of his *Memoirs* notable for its empathy:

> What General Lee's feelings were I do not know. As he was a man of much dignity, with an impassible face, it was impossible to say whether he felt inwardly glad that the end had finally come, or felt sad over the result, and was too manly to show it. Whatever his feelings, they were entirely concealed from my observation; but my own

feelings, which had been quite jubilant on the receipt of his letter, were sad and depressed. I felt like anything rather than rejoicing at the downfall of a foe who had fought so long and valiantly, and had suffered so much for a cause, though that cause was, I believe, one of the worst for which a people ever fought, and one for which there was the least excuse.[101]

The tone of Grant's reminiscence confirmed the Duke of Wellington's adage that "next to a battle lost, there is no spectacle more melancholy than a battle won."[102]

Doubtless with some exaggeration, Grant claimed, "Our conversation grew so pleasant that I almost forgot the object of our meeting."[103] While Grant tried gamely to converse about friends and old times, Lee seemed to find socializing unendurable under the circumstances and resolutely resisted any show of surface camaraderie. What preyed on his mind were the exact terms of surrender. He cut short small talk in a slightly brusque manner. "I suppose, General Grant," he interrupted, "that the object of our present meeting is fully understood. I asked to see you to ascertain upon what terms you would receive the surrender of my army." Fully prepared, Grant said both officers and men would be "paroled and disqualified from taking up arms again until properly exchanged, and all arms, ammunition, and supplies [were] to be delivered up as captured property." Lee nodded in agreement. "Those are about the conditions which I expected would be proposed." Grant added his fond hope that such terms would "lead to a general suspension of hostilities, and be the means of preventing any further loss of life."[104] Lee bowed his head in approval. When Grant sought to digress, dwelling on the prospect of peace, Lee firmly steered him back to business. Clearly he didn't care to prolong this torture. "I presume, General Grant, we have both carefully considered the proper steps to be taken, and I would suggest that you commit to writing the terms you have proposed, so that they may be formally acted upon." "Very well," Grant responded. "I will write them out."[105]

Chewing a cigar, writing fluently, Grant drafted the surrender terms on a small, oval wooden table, while Lee sat at a squarish, marble-topped table. With no premeditated formula, Grant trusted to the moment's inspiration. Wreathed in cigar smoke, he scribbled the terms rapidly in a "manifold order book" that enabled him to make three copies. Using magnanimous language, he began his transformation from scourge of the South to its unlikely champion: "The Arms,

Artillery and public property to be parked and stacked and turned over to the officer appointed by me to receive them . . . This done each officer and man will be allowed to return to their homes not to be disturbed by United States Authority so long as they observe their parole and the laws in force where they may reside."[106] This last sentence was significant, making southern soldiers immune from treason prosecutions and setting the stage for postwar reconciliation—or so it was hoped. Afraid Lee would become a martyr and his sword a holy relic, Grant made a point of *not* asking Lee to surrender his sword; he also didn't care to humiliate him. Finally, Grant omitted the noxious words "unconditional surrender," lest they grate on Lee's proud sensibility. With no tinge of malice, Grant's words breathed a spirit of charity reminiscent of Lincoln's second inaugural address.

When he finished writing, Lee cleared the small table before him, wiped his steel spectacles, crossed his legs, and reviewed the language with close scrutiny, asking for only minor revisions. With special delight he saw that officers would be allowed to save face by retaining their sidearms and horses and could return home to resume their lives unmolested. With quiet fervor, he said this "would have a most happy effect, and accepted the terms," Grant recalled. "I handed over my penciled memorandum to an aide to put into ink, and we resumed our conversation about old times and friends in the armies."[107] Lee seemed hugely relieved. When Grant asked if the terms were satisfactory, he answered, "Yes, I am bound to be satisfied with anything you offer. It is more than I expected."[108]

The business concluded, Grant brought in his staff officers, but Lee only deigned to engage in conversation with General Seth Williams, his former adjutant when he was West Point superintendent. Apart from this exchange, Horace Porter wrote, "Lee was in no mood for pleasantries, and he did not unbend, or even relax the fixed sternness of his features."[109] At first Grant assigned Theodore Bowers to prepare a fair copy of the surrender agreement, while Marshall drew up an acceptance letter for Lee to sign. Because Bowers's hand quivered nervously and he botched three or four sheets, Grant reassigned the task to his Senecan aide, Ely Parker. When introduced to the swarthy Parker, Lee blushed deeply, eyeing tensely his complexion. "What was passing in his mind no one knew," Porter said, "but the natural surmise was that he at first mistook Parker for a negro, and was struck with astonishment to find that the commander of the Union armies had one of that race on his personal staff."[110] Another onlooker thought Lee momentarily offended since he believed "a mulatto had been called on to do the writing as a gratuitous affront."[111] Evidently Lee relaxed when he realized Parker was a Native American. "I am glad to see one real American here," he ventured, shaking his hand. To which Parker retorted memorably: "We are all Americans."[112]

The terms of surrender settled, Lee alluded to his hungry army, which had subsisted for days on parched corn, and asked for food and forage for it. Unhesitatingly Grant consented to provide rations and wondered how many were needed, to which Lee replied, "About twenty-five thousand."[113] Grant directed Lee to send his commissary and quartermaster to Appomattox Station, where they could gather plentiful stocks of beef, salt, hardtack, coffee, and sugar. "I think it will be ample," said Lee, touched by Grant's generosity, "and it will be a great relief, I assure you."[114] M. R. Morgan, Grant's commissary chief, later commented, "Were such terms ever before given by a conqueror to a defeated foe?"[115] Grant showed genuine compassion for the Confederate soldiers, saying he assumed most were farmers and wanted to plant crops to tide them over during the winter. To this end, he issued a directive that rebel soldiers who owned their horses or mules should be allowed to take them home. "This will have the best possible effect upon the men," Lee said. "It will be very gratifying, and will do much toward conciliating our people."[116]

The afternoon fast approached four o'clock when the final documents were signed and Lee and Marshall strode onto the porch. The bright lamp of the Confederacy was now nearly extinguished. For all intents and purposes, the war had ended, although Johnston's army in North Carolina, Richard Taylor's in Alabama, and Edmund Kirby Smith's in Texas remained at large. During the encounter, Lee had maintained his marble composure, but as he waited for Traveller to be bridled, he gazed wistfully toward his army and gave way to emotion. Horace Porter registered the lone gesture that disclosed his unspoken despair: "He thrice smote the palm of his left hand slowly with his right fist in an absent sort of way, seemed not to see the group of Union officers in the yard, who rose respectfully at his approach, and appeared unaware of everything about him."[117] Only Traveller's approach snapped him from this trance. When Lee sat up straight in the saddle, Grant descended the front steps and lifted his hat in homage to his vanquished foe, as did other Union officers. In response Lee tipped his hat and rode off slowly toward his army while a Pennsylvania regimental band across the way played "Auld Lang Syne." The scene was no less solemn when he reached his soldiers, who crowded the wayside, doffing their hats in respect. Lee stared fixedly ahead as he passed and many men called good-bye or stroked affectionately Traveller's flanks.

When he at last spoke up, Lee simply said, "Men, we have fought through the war together. I have done the best that I could for you."[118] At this, he and his soldiers wept openly. The moment underscored the loving bond Lee had forged with his men. Many of them had assumed Grant would mete out punitive conditions and were pleasantly surprised. As one said, "The favorable and entirely unexpected terms of surrender wonderfully restored our souls."[119]

Grant's handling of his own soldiers was equally sensitive. Once Lee was out of earshot, the Union army surrendered to jubilation. In marked contrast to Grant, George Meade went wild with exultation, galloping hatless through his camp, shouting madly, "It's all over, boys! Lee's surrendered! It's all over."[120] Everything not nailed down was twirled in the air. Such a celebration was anathema to Grant, who stopped his artillery from firing a hundred-gun salute. After the war, afraid that the North would seem to be bragging about the South's downfall, he even objected to a painting being placed in the Capitol that depicted Lee's surrender. He now reminded his army that the rebels had been restored as their countrymen. Thanks to this, the unseemly rejoicing was stopped, replaced by stunned silence. To prevent scuffles that might upset a conciliatory mood, Grant heeded Lee's request that the two armies be kept apart.

Some fraternizing ensued between officers and old feelings of camaraderie suddenly welled up. The most memorable came when the tall, hirsute James Longstreet shuffled into the McLean household.[121] As soon as Grant saw his old pal, he sprang to his feet, shook his hand, offered him a cigar, and invited him to play brag, the card game they had enjoyed before the war. As Longstreet told a reporter, he was bowled over by Grant's generous spirit: "Great God, thought I to myself, how my heart swells out to such a magnanimous touch of humanity! Why do men fight who were born to be brothers? . . . His whole greeting and conduct toward us was as though nothing had ever happened to mar our pleasant relations."[122]

Grant's courtesy at Appomattox became engraved in national memory, offering hope after years of unspeakable bloodshed that peace, civility, and fraternal relations would be restored. It was a fleeting, if in many ways doomed, hope, which may be why it has had such staying power in the American imagination. Although Grant would do everything in his power to make it happen, the promised era of postwar forgiveness and tranquillity never truly came to fruition. For the South surrendering was one thing, but acceptance of postwar African American citizenship and voting rights would be quite another.

Whatever his reservations about Lee as a general, Grant applauded his "manly course and bearing" at Appomattox. Had Lee resisted surrender and encouraged his army to wage guerrilla warfare, it would have spawned infinite trouble, Grant believed.[123] Such was Lee's unrivaled stature that his acceptance of defeat reconciled many diehard rebels to follow his example. At the same time, it was Grant who set the stage for Lee's high-minded behavior by treating him tactfully, refusing to humiliate him, and granting him generous terms that allowed him to save face in defeat.

Once Lee had disappeared, Grant's officers stooped to a rapacious frenzy as they snapped up every conceivable memento of the meeting. Wilmer McLean pocketed $20 from Sheridan for the table on which Grant composed the surrender agreement; the next day, Sheridan gave it as a gift to Libbie Custer, wife of George Armstrong Custer, who, legend says, flew off with the prize on horseback. General Ord paid $40 for Lee's table and later tried to give it as a gift to Julia Grant, who diplomatically redirected it to Mrs. Ord. In retrospect, Wilmer McLean forfeited his treasures at bargain prices, and his family claimed that Union officers ransacked the house for souvenirs without paying compensation. One journalist left a vignette of this crazed hunt for sacred relics: "Cane bottomed chairs were ruthlessly cut to pieces . . . Haircloth upholstery was cut from chairs, and sofas was [sic] also cut into strips and patches and carried away."[124] The episode presaged a postwar rapacity that would supersede the noble sentiments enunciated at Appomattox.

Curiously absentminded, Grant forgot to notify Washington of Lee's surrender and had to be prodded by his staff. At 4:30 p.m., he stopped by the roadside, sat down on a boulder, and wrote a message to Stanton that was singularly devoid of self-congratulation: "Gen. Lee surrendered the Army of Northern Va this afternoon on terms proposed by myself. The accompanying additional correspondence will show the conditions fully."[125] Stanton replied with fervor: "Thanks be to Almighty God for the great victory with which he has this day crowned you and the gallant army under your command."[126]

The previous day, Abraham Lincoln had left City Point for Washington. Prior to departing, he had unexpectedly requested the military band aboard the *River Queen* to play "Dixie." "That tune is now Federal property," he declared, adding it was "good to show the rebels that, with us in power, they will be free to hear it again."[127] Back in the capital, Lincoln spent the night of April 9 commiserating with William Seward, who had been badly mauled in a carriage accident. Lincoln lay beside him on the bed, delighting him with tales of Grant's victories. "I think we are near the end at last," he concluded.[128] Later at the White House, as the president prepared for bed, Stanton materialized, waving Grant's telegram, and Lincoln embraced him with undisguised joy. Elated by the generous Appomattox agreement, Lincoln kept saying "Good!," "All right!," and "Exactly the thing!" in happy appreciation.[129] As Lincoln went to inform Mary, Stanton rushed to Seward's house with the electrifying news. "Don't try to speak," Stanton told him. "You have made me cry for the first time in my life," came Seward's heartfelt response.[130]

Then, on the misty evening of April 11, with buildings brightly lit throughout the capital, Washingtonians took to the streets to celebrate. On the north portico of the White House, Lincoln appeared at his favorite window and "men fairly yelled with delight," reported Noah Brooks, and "tossed up their hats and screamed like mad." Hundreds of enthusiastic citizens gathered to sing to Lincoln and applaud Lee's surrender. Lincoln again requested "Dixie" and proposed "three cheers for General Grant and the officers and men under him."[131] Standing in a candlelit glow, Lincoln, in his last public speech, touched on the fraught issue of "reconstruction" in the seceded states—a word that connoted sweeping changes ahead for the southern social order. The Union army, he noted, would likely linger in the South for an extended period to deal with "disorganized and discordant elements," a prospect that would define Grant's career for many years.[132] At a time when only six northern states granted blacks the right to vote, Lincoln expressed partial support for black suffrage: "I would myself prefer that [the vote] were now conferred on the very intelligent, and on those who serve our cause as soldiers."[133] These words buzzed angrily in the brain of one spectator, John Wilkes Booth, who supposedly snarled: "That means nigger citizenship. Now, by God, I'll put him through. That is the last speech he will ever make."[134]

Julia Grant long remembered the moment at City Point when a breathless telegraph operator handed her news of Lee's surrender. The James River was packed with passenger boats, and the atmosphere grew festive as the information reached them. These boats drew alongside Julia's steamer, and people "came aboard to congratulate me and to tell me that General Grant would certainly be the next President." Later on, Julia stoutly supported her husband's presidential ambitions, but at this moment she derived no joy from the possibility, preferring to savor his new renown as chief "of this great and victorious army."[135]

Around the campfire on April 9, Grant expressed cautious optimism that the remaining Confederate commanders would soon lay down their arms. While his staff officers thought he might want to see the army he had defeated, he refused to lord it over them and planned to head to Washington. It was a measure of his humility that, instead of seeking to exploit his army's strength, he wished to demobilize it and end weapons purchases as soon as possible. Having defeated the Army of Northern Virginia, he felt a solicitude for its well-being, and years later admitted to a young Virginian that Lee's army came to hold a place in his heart second only to the paternal care he harbored for his own men. "Curious sort of feeling, isn't it?" he remarked with wonderment.[136]

On the rainy morning of April 10, Grant rode out to meet Lee a second time, bringing a bugler and staff officer waving a white flag. On a small hillside beside the road, he and Lee held a parley alone on horseback while their staff officers, in "a most beautiful semi-circle," said Parker, kept a respectful distance.[137] The two men behaved with impeccable courtesy, each lifting his hat to the other. They spoke frankly. Lee claimed the war had reduced him to poverty. Grant's main concern was that Lee should exert his moral authority to bring the war to a speedy conclusion, inducing other commanders to relinquish their weapons. Lee endorsed the need to pacify the country and bring the South back into the Union fold. At heart, he asserted, he had always been a Union man and blamed extremist politicians for bringing on the war. He contended that southerners stood resigned to the end of slavery.

Despite these encouraging generalities, Lee balked at specifics. As Grant recollected: "General Lee said that his campaign in Virginia was the last organized resistance which the South was capable of making—that I might have to march a good deal and encounter isolated commands here and there; but there was no longer an army which could make a stand. I told Lee that this fact only made his responsibility greater, and any further war would be a crime."[138] While conceding that the war had ended, Lee insisted he couldn't undertake helpful measures without consulting Jefferson Davis, now a fugitive from justice. Grant regretted Lee's inability to break free from his benighted leader: "I saw that the Confederacy had gone beyond the reach of President Davis, and that there was nothing that could be done except what Lee could do to benefit the Southern people."[139] When Grant urged Lee to go and speak directly with President Lincoln, Lee again invoked the need to confer with Davis, missing a historic opportunity.

After thirty minutes of discussion, Grant and Lee reenacted the courtly ceremony of lifting their hats to each other and Lee rode off to bid farewell to his army. A couple of days later, after surrendering their arms and folding their colors, the Army of Northern Virginia dispersed in a peaceful manner that demonstrated the wisdom of Grant's clemency. Led by Joshua Lawrence Chamberlain, the soldiers in blue lifted rifles to their shoulders in a respectful gesture that touched southern hearts. Grant allowed the defeated men to ride home free of charge on government transportation and military railroads.

After parting with Lee, Grant relaxed on the McLean porch before proceeding to City Point, the first stop on his journey to Washington. He traveled slowly east on a special train that was repeatedly detained by derailed cars and other somber vestiges of war. He didn't reach City Point until the next morning, when he sprinted up to Julia's stateroom and breakfasted with her aboard the steamer. Someone inquired whether Grant planned to visit Richmond and Julia urged him to do so, but he showed, as always, exquisite sensitivity to the psychology of a defeated people. "Hush, Julia," he responded. "Do not say another word on this subject. I would not distress these people. They are feeling their defeat bitterly, and you would not add to it by witnessing their despair, would you?"[140] It was the observation of a man who had known terrible shame in his own life and understood the extreme need for self-respect at moments of failure.

Grant had grown immeasurably during the war and now possessed a broader understanding of people and politics than his earlier provincial life had ever allowed. One adjutant disagreed: "All through the war I never noticed him change at all, except to become a little sadder . . . He felt a terrible responsibility and he expressed it in his face, in every feature."[141] It was remarkable that Grant had borne so much responsibility for four years despite his alcohol problem and amid unbearable stress. The credit must go first to Grant, who managed to keep his demons at bay enough to win the war, but also to Rawlins. Grant's Galena physician, Dr. Edward D. Kittoe, noted that Grant had been surrounded by constant temptation and praised his "repeated efforts to overcome the desire for strong drink while he was in the army, and . . . his final victory through his own persistency and the encouragement and advice so freely given him by Rawlins."[142] In the war's final days, the country acknowledged an immense debt to Rawlins by making him a brigadier general in the regular army, then a major general by brevet, honors recommended by Grant, who called him "an officer who has won more deserved reputation in this war than any other who has acted throughout purely as a Staff Officer."[143]

A certified failure in civilian life, Grant had entered the war with everything to gain and nothing to lose. The erstwhile leather goods clerk from Galena now had more than one million men under his command. A new American military power had come into being that could compete with almost any European army. Grant had been the mainspring of the Union effort, imposing order and giving cohesion to far-flung armies. In summarizing his salient qualities, *The New York Times* foresaw that in future generations "if a great soldier is indomitable in purpose and exhaustless in courage, endurance, and equanimity; if he is free from vanity and pettiness, if he is unpretentious, truthful, frank, constant, generous to friends, magnanimous to foes, and patriotic to the core, of him it will be said, 'He is like Grant.'"[144]

The Civil War had been a contest of incomparable ferocity, dwarfing anything in American history. It claimed 750,000 lives, more than the combined total losses in all other wars between the Revolutionary War and the Vietnam War.[145] The historian James M. McPherson has calculated that, as a portion of the total population, the Civil War killed seven times as many American soldiers as World War II.[146] While the North lost more men in absolute terms, death took a far graver toll in the South, where the population was smaller, with young and old alike indiscriminately conscripted; by the end, more than one-fifth of the southern white male population had perished. Grant was sobered by the horrifying roster of casualties, saying future generations would look back at the Civil War "with almost incredulity that such events could have occurred in a Christian country and in a civilized age."[147]

For the rest of his life, Grant had to deal with the charge that he had merely been the lucky beneficiary of superiority in men and resources. He grew touchy on the subject because it addressed the larger question of whether he had crudely consigned young men to their death, winning by overwhelming force. The plain fact was that six Union commanders before him had failed, with the same men and matériel, whereas Grant had succeeded. It vexed him that the North denigrated its generals, while southern generals were idealized. As he remarked bitterly, "The Southern generals were [seen as] models of chivalry and valor—our generals were venal, incompetent, coarse . . . Everything that our opponents did was perfect. Lee was a demigod, Jackson was a demigod, while our generals were brutal butchers."[148]

Over the years, Grant adduced many reasons why the South had the advantage in the war, starting with its political unity versus constant northern divisions. "We had to send troops to suppress riots in New York; we had enemies in our midst. In every Northern State there was a strong party against the war; always rejoicing over disaster, always voting to paralyze our forces; ready for any concession or surrender."[149] The South, by contrast, could mobilize fully, recruiting all able-bodied men. Four million slaves had worked the farms, supported the economy, and freed the white population for military service—at least before they flocked in large numbers to Union lines. And the Confederacy almost always fought on home turf, with all the obvious advantages that entailed for Lee.

What Lee thought of Grant as a general is somewhat contradictory. As already mentioned, he later said George McClellan was the foremost Union general. But the Reverend George W. Pepper, a chaplain in Sherman's army, said Lee named Grant as the premier Union general: "Both as a gentleman and as an organizer of victorious war, General Grant has excelled all your most noted soldiers."[150] Another story, printed years later, said Lee was distressed when somebody argued that Grant had merely profited from fortunate circumstances. "Sir," Lee upbraided him, "your opinion is a very poor compliment to me. We all thought Richmond, protected as it was by our splendid fortifications and defended by our army of veterans, could not be taken. Yet Grant turned his face to our capital, and never turned it away until we had surrendered. Now, I have carefully searched the military records of both ancient and modern history, and have never found Grant's superior as a general."[151] The authenticity of this quote has been questioned.[152] What has never been doubted is Lee's gratitude to Grant for his behavior at Appomattox, which he commended as "without a parallel in the history of the civilized world."[153]

Grant betrayed only qualified admiration for Lee: "Lee was of a slow, conservative nature, without imagination or humor, always the same, with grave dignity. I never could see in his achievements what justifies his reputation. The illusion that nothing but heavy odds beat him will not stand the ultimate light of history."[154] Strangely enough, Grant derided Lee as a desk-bound general even though Lee was almost invariably engaged in the field. It seemed to bother Grant that Lee was reserved and aloof while he himself had "always kept open house at head-quarters, so far as the army was concerned."[155] Perhaps the person who best explained Grant's strategic superiority was Sherman, who stated that while Lee attacked the front porch, Grant would attack the kitchen and bedroom. In his earthy way, Sherman expressed the view that Grant engaged in total warfare that eroded enemy supply lines and infrastructure, while Lee remained tightly focused on the battle at hand, without a long-term strategy for winning the war.

For all the endless horrors of that war, Grant believed the country was stronger for having endured it: "We are better off now than we would have been without it and have made more rapid progress than we otherwise should have made."[156] The country had become more cosmopolitan, its citizens more worldly, its economy more productive, its military more potent. Most important, Union forces had struck a major blow for freedom and equality. Like Lincoln, Grant deemed the war "a punishment for national sins that had to come sooner or later in some shape, and probably in blood."[157] Four million slaves had been emancipated and would shortly receive the right to vote, send their children to public schools, and enjoy the benefits of citizenship—progress that would be savagely resisted. For Grant, the war had validated the basic soundness of American institutions. Before, he noted, "monarchical Europe generally believed that our republic was a rope of sand that would part the moment the slightest strain was brought upon it. Now it has shown itself capable of dealing with one of the greatest wars that was ever made, and our people have proven themselves to be the most formidable in war of any nationality." He added the important caveat that the war had been "a fearful lesson, and should teach us the necessity of avoiding wars in the future."[158]

A Singular, Indescribable Vessel

W HEN ULYSSES AND JULIA GRANT docked in Washington on the sunny morning of April 13, 1865, they found a capital bedecked with patriotic imagery. Julia remembered how "all the bells rang out merry greetings, and the city was literally swathed in flags and bunting."[1] The pair went straight to the Willard Hotel, where Grant had been snubbed by a patronizing desk clerk a year earlier. As word leaked out that the Grants were guests, huge crowds milled in the surrounding streets, avid to snatch a glimpse of their war hero. Grant hadn't come to town to glory in adulation, but to dismantle the army and reduce national expenses. The police had to clear a path for Grant to visit the War Department, where he advised Stanton to cease recruiting activities and the purchase of new weaponry. Such was the spellbinding power of Appomattox that even the dour Stanton no longer appeared quite so grumpy. "Mr. Stanton was in his happiest mood," Julia wrote, "showing me many stands of arms, flags, and, among other things, a stump of a large tree perforated on all sides by bullets, taken from the field of Shiloh."[2]

In honor of Lee's surrender and the city of Mobile's fall the previous day, the capital was to be grandly lit that evening, and the Lincolns wanted Grant to accompany Mary Lincoln in a coach to view the sights. Julia was pointedly excluded, but after the dreadful parade ground incident with Mrs. Ord, she was relieved to be spared the First Lady's trying company. Grant and Mary Lincoln rolled through a capital bathed in the brilliant glow of lights, while rockets and fireworks augmented the effect, streaking skyward over the Potomac. On the ride, Grant received ovations everywhere. "The people were wild with enthusiasm," wrote Horace Porter, "and wherever the General appeared he was greeted with cheers, the clapping of hands, waving of handkerchiefs, and every possible demonstration of delight."[3] Mary Lincoln, suspecting a possible rival to her husband in Grant, disliked the idolatry lavished on him. When crowds chanted "Grant," she asked the driver to let her get out; only when they cheered the president did she allow the journey to resume. Grant found the experience so unsettling, he later confided, that it entered into his decision to spurn the president's offer to escort him to Ford's Theatre the next evening.

That night, the Grants attended a party at the Stanton household with military bands performing outside. Before they arrived, Sergeant John Hatter, standing guard on the doorstep, was accosted by a mysterious man in a dark suit who inquired whether General Grant was inside. In a portrayal perhaps colored by later events, the stranger was described as a "small, delicate-looking man with pleasing features, uneasy black eyes, bushy black hair, and an imperial, anxious expression shaded by a sad, remorseful look."[4] Hatter pegged him as a curiosity seeker out to glimpse Grant. "If you wish to see him," Hatter said, "step out on the pavement, or on the stone where the carriage stops, and you can see him."[5] The man reacted oddly, stopping to muse a moment before he disappeared. Later on he returned as the Stantons and Grants filed onto the front steps to witness fireworks. Approaching Major Kilburn Knox, who was stationed in front of the two prominent couples, he inquired, "Is Stanton in?" "I suppose you mean the Secretary?" replied Knox. "Yes. I am a lawyer in town. I know him very well."[6] Although Knox warned him not to bother Stanton, the stranger spotted Stanton and stood behind him for a time. Finally he entered the house and was asked to leave, especially since he seemed to be intoxicated. He turned out to be Michael O'Laughlen, a former Confederate soldier and boyhood friend of John Wilkes Booth who had plotted with him to kidnap Lincoln. Later fingered by Hatter and Knox, he was charged with stalking Stanton and Grant, with intent to kill, and was sentenced to life in prison. It's quite possible that O'Laughlen was guilty as charged, but his lawyers argued that he had "walked away" from the Booth conspiracy and gone unarmed to the Stanton household.[7] One historian has even claimed it was "far more likely that he stopped at Stanton's house to warn him of Booth's plot, but lost his nerve."[8]

On the morning of Good Friday, April 14, Lincoln shared a breakfast with his son Robert, who provided him with firsthand details of Lee's surrender at Appomattox. It seemed as if the day would be noteworthy in American history as the fourth anniversary of the evacuation of Fort Sumter. Northern dignitaries and abolitionists congregated in Charleston to watch General Robert Anderson hoist above the harbor ruins the same American flag hauled down in shame on April 14, 1861. On that same day four years later in Virginia, Major General John Gibbon wired Grant that Lee's army had yielded its artillery, small arms, and flags, with somewhere between twenty-five thousand and thirty thousand men paroled. In a hopeful vein, he wrote, "I have Conversed with many of the surrendered officers & [am] satisfied that by announcing at once terms [of] a liberal merciful policy on the part of the Govt we can once more have a happy united Country."[9] It seemed as if the war was ending and might give way to amity on both sides.

Invited to the weekly cabinet meeting at 11 a.m., Grant was treated as an honored guest and cabinet secretaries applauded his entrance. Uplifted by recent events, Lincoln was in a cheerful, extroverted mood. However eager he was to absorb ex-Confederate states back into the Union by December and restore normal trade relations with them, he had decided not to recognize existing rebel governments. On the other hand, he admitted, "We can't undertake to run State governments in all these Southern States. Their people must do that,—though I reckon that at first some of them may do it badly." Stanton proposed a plan that envisioned an interim period in which military rule would prevail, with Virginia and North Carolina merged into a single military district. When Gideon Welles squawked at annulling state boundaries, Lincoln asked Stanton to redraw his plan before the next meeting and implored his cabinet to ponder the knotty topic of Reconstruction for "no greater or more important one could come before us, or any future Cabinet."[10]

The discussion turned to Appomattox and Grant's pledge to Lee that defeated soldiers would not be prosecuted for treason so long as they abided by their paroles. Someone inquired about the terms extended to ordinary soldiers, and Lincoln smiled broadly as Grant explained, "I told them to go back to their homes and families, and they would not be molested, if they did nothing more."[11] Lincoln made it abundantly clear that Grant had operated within the spirit of his wishes and that he "hoped there would be no persecution, no bloody work, after the war was over. None need expect he would take any part in hanging or killing those men, even the worst of them."[12]

A fine raconteur, Grant narrated for the cabinet his hot pursuit of Lee and described the dramatic finish at Appomattox. He confessed he hadn't heard from Sherman in North Carolina and couldn't verify the fate of Joe Johnston's army. He was certain news from Sherman would shortly arrive. In his diary Welles recorded Lincoln's startling response:

> The President remarked [that the news from Sherman] would, he had no doubt, come soon, and come favorable, for he had last night the usual dream which he had preceding nearly every great and important event of the War. Generally the news had been favorable which succeeded this dream, and the dream itself was always the same . . . he seemed to be in some singular, indescribable vessel, and . . . was moving with great rapidity towards an indefinite shore; that he had this dream preceding Sumter, Bull Run, Antietam, Gettysburg, Stone[s] River, Vicksburg, Wilmington, etc. General Grant said Stone[s] River was certainly no victory, and he knew of no great results which followed from it. The President said however that might be, his dream preceded that fight. "I had," the President remarked, "this strange dream again last night, and we shall, judging from the past, have great news very soon. I think it must be from Sherman."[13]

Contrary to Grant's sarcastic gibe that Stones River "was certainly no victory, and he knew of no great results which followed from it," the battle (known as Murfreesboro in the South) had been a Union victory, if a terribly bloody one.[14] The victor had been Grant's old nemesis, General William S. Rosecrans, and Welles thought Grant's carping betrayed his "jealous nature."[15] Certainly Grant's willingness to quibble with the president at a cabinet meeting showed anew the confidence he had attained during the war and Lincoln's respect for his opinion.

The session droned on until 2 p.m., and Grant lingered afterward to chat with the president, who invited him and his wife to see Laura Keene in *Our American Cousin* at Ford's Theatre that evening, with Mary Lincoln forming part of the group. The newspapers had already announced that Grant would accompany the president and the theater had distributed handbills to that effect; the house would be liberally draped with flags and bunting. For security reasons, Stanton protested heatedly that such a public event would endanger both Lincoln and Grant. As Samuel Beckwith recalled, Stanton issued a vociferous warning: "He had for some months been aware that threats of assassination were being made by certain evil minded persons against the leaders of the Federal government and army . . . The presence of the President of the nation and the Lieutenant-General of the armies at any public function at such a critical hour was simply courting disaster." Lincoln reacted flippantly, chaffing Stanton "for his lack of faith in human nature."[16] The president of a democracy, he averred, had to show himself to the people, and some danger was an inescapable hazard of office. "To be absolutely safe," he told John Nicolay resignedly, "I should lock myself up in a box."[17] Lincoln knew dangers always lurked in the shadows—his office desk had a pigeonhole stuffed with more than eighty threatening letters— but not until November 1864 were four plainclothes policemen assigned to the White House.

Lincoln urged Grant to accompany him to the theater, hinting that the nation expected to see the victorious president and general united at such a moment. Having just been in the public spotlight, Grant wished to escape town. At this awkward moment, a message from Julia arrived, listing her reasons for wanting to set out for Burlington in the late afternoon. Fortified with these excuses, Grant politely declined to attend Ford's Theatre, joking that he now had a command from Mrs. Grant. As he subsequently said, "I was glad to have the note, as I did not want to go to the theater."[18] Lincoln, who was disappointed, understood. "Of course, General, you have been long from home, fighting in the field, and Mrs. Grant's instincts should be considered before my request. I am very sorry, however, for the people would only be too glad to see you."[19] As Porter later commented, "It was probably this declination which saved the general from assassination, as it was learned afterward that he had been marked for a victim."[20]

Shortly afterward, Lincoln drove out with Mary in an open carriage ride, pouring forth bittersweet reflections as they recaptured a particle of their prewar happiness. To Mary, the president seemed lighter, carefree, more like his younger self. "Dear Husband," she announced, "you almost startle me by your great cheerfulness." "And well I may feel so, Mary," he answered. "I consider *this day,* the war, has come to a close." He tried to turn the page on the dark chapter of the past four years. "We must *both,* be more cheerful in the future—between the war and the loss of our darling Willie—we have both, been very miserable."[21] Having been spurned by the Grants, the Lincolns invited a young couple to the theater: Clara Harris, the daughter of a New York senator, and her fiancé and stepbrother Major Henry R. Rathbone. The Lincolns had an early dinner at the White House and Noah Brooks recalled that, as they left for Ford's Theatre, the president's last thought turned to Grant: "Grant thinks that we can reduce the cost of the army establishment at least a half million a day, which, with the reduction of the expenditures of the Navy, will soon bring down our national debt to something like decent proportions."[22]

For Julia Grant, this eventful day was shot through with baleful omens. To close friends, she would candidly confess that she had refrained from going to Ford's Theatre that night because "she objected strenuously to accompanying Mrs. Lincoln."[23] Her memories of Mary Lincoln's diatribes against Mrs. Ord and high-handed treatment of her at City Point still grated, and Julia elected not to subject herself to her sharp temper again. Julia wasn't the only one who had felt the lash of Mary Lincoln's tongue. According to Adam Badeau, Lincoln had also invited Stanton and his wife to the theater that night. Mrs. Stanton suddenly called on Julia and told her that "unless you accept the invitation, I shall refuse. I will not sit without you in the box with Mrs. Lincoln."[24] The two women decided jointly to boycott the theater outing.

Around midday, a messenger tapped at Julia's door at the Willard Hotel, purporting to bear tidings from Mary Lincoln. "Mrs. Lincoln sends me, Madam, with her compliments, to say she will call for you at exactly eight o'clock to go to the theater." Somewhat flustered by the message, Julia replied, "You may return with my compliments to Mrs. Lincoln and say I regret that as General Grant and I intend leaving the city this afternoon, we will not, therefore, be here to accompany the President and Mrs. Lincoln to the theater." Julia found something disquieting about the man, who was "dressed in [a] light-colored corduroy coat and trousers and with rather a shabby hat of the same color," but she couldn't specify what seemed so disturbingly amiss.[25] Only later did she suspect the man hadn't been dispatched by Mary Lincoln at all.

After packing her bags for Burlington, Julia and son Jesse lunched with Mary E. Rawlins and her little girl. Across the dining room Julia saw four shifty-looking characters and thought one was the queer messenger who had rapped on her door. As she studied this motley quartet, her gaze was arrested by one of them, "a dark, pale man," who "played with his soup spoon, sometimes filling it and holding it half-lifted to his mouth, but never tasting it." Because he seemed to eavesdrop on their conversation, Julia thought he must be mad. "Be careful," Julia whispered to Mrs. Rawlins, "but observe the men opposite to us and tell me what you think." Mrs. Rawlins glanced at them and also found them peculiar. "I believe they are a part of [John Singleton] Mosby's guerrillas," Julia speculated, "and they have been listening to every word we have said. Do you know, I believe there will be an outbreak tonight or soon. I just feel it, and am glad I am going away tonight."[26] As it turned out, Julia's intuitions served her exceedingly well.

By the time the Grants took a carriage to the station to catch a 6 p.m. train, the weather had turned cool and gusty. Julia sat in the backseat beside the wife of General Daniel Rucker while her husband democratically shared the front with the driver. The journey was forever imprinted on the memory of young Jesse Grant: "I remember clearly the drive down Pennsylvania Avenue to the depot, the iron-tired wheels of our carriage rattling and bumping over the cobblestones. It was in the early evening, but the Avenue was deserted and quiet as midnight. We were nearing the railway station when a man on horseback overtook us, drew alongside, and, leaning down, peered into our carriage. Then he wheeled his horse and rode furiously away."[27] Julia Grant also had lasting memories of the horseman who flashed by twice "at a sweeping gallop on a dark horse," then circled around and dashed back toward them, thrusting his face at Grant and glaring at him both times.[28] Julia recognized the rider as the same dark, pale man who had menacingly toyed with his spoon at lunch and told her husband so. Grant was likewise disturbed by this stranger flitting by and eyeing them. "I do not care for such glances," he remarked. "These are not friendly at least."[29] Grant later learned the glowering horseman was John Wilkes Booth, who had been conferring on the sidewalk with his actor friend John Mathews when the Grant carriage sped by and he set off in pursuit of it. From the heaped-up baggage, he must have confirmed that the Grants were leaving town and would not be at Ford's Theatre. "It seems I was to have been attacked," Grant stated, "and Mrs. Grant's sudden resolve to leave deranged the plan."[30]

At the train station, the Grants boarded a private railroad car, furnished by the president of the Baltimore & Ohio Railroad. They were accompanied by Samuel Beckwith, the telegraph operator who functioned as Grant's shadow. In a fortuitous move to ensure Grant privacy, the train conductor locked the doors of his compartment. Somewhere in northeast Maryland, a man attempted without success to barge into the car. A few days later, Grant said, "I received an anonymous letter from a man, saying he had been detailed to kill me, that he rode on my train as far as Havre de Grace, and as my car was locked he could not get in. He thanked God he had failed."[31] That Grant was slated to be killed cannot be dismissed since he was cited as a potential target at the subsequent trial of the Booth conspirators. Whether the nameless author was genuine or a crank cannot be determined since his identity was never ascertained. Subsequently, a witness testified that he knew someone who heard conspirator George A. Atze-rodt say emphatically over dinner, "If the fellow that had promised to follow Grant had done his duty, we would have got General Grant, too."[32]

At about 10:13 p.m., John Wilkes Booth entered Lincoln's box at Ford's The-atre and executed the gentle president with brutal efficiency. The lone Washing-ton police officer assigned to guard the presidential box had left his post, leaving only a White House footman. "I struck boldly" was Booth's cheap boast in his diary.[33] At that moment, the Grants were sliding through the night, oblivious that the tide of history had just shifted its course. While changing trains in Philadelphia, they stopped at Bloodgood's Hotel for a late supper shortly after midnight. They noticed that the hotel lobby was packed with people who seemed suspiciously silent. A hotel employee thrust a telegram into Grant's hand. "We walked into the parlor and the three of us, General and Mrs. Grant and I, sat down upon a sofa in one corner of the room," Beckwith recalled. "He read the despatch and without comment passed it to his wife, who in turn read it and with an exclamation of painful surprise handed it to me. I shall never forget the dumb horror of that moment. My heart seemed to leap into my throat. None of us spoke a word. We simply sat there and wondered. Lincoln was shot."[34]

A slightly different account emerged from Charles Bolles, then a messenger boy at the American Telegraph Company, assigned to carry urgent messages. Julia, he said, had already seated herself on a couch and taken off her bonnet as her husband "remained standing and reached out his hand for the message. As he read the words which bore such sorrow to the nation that night not a muscle of his face quivered or a line gave an indication of what he must have felt at that great crisis. Turning to Mrs. Grant, seated behind him, he handed her the mes-sage without a word. She could not have read more than a line or two before her feelings overcame her, and burying her face in her hands, she burst into tears."[35]

Horace Porter provided yet a third version of this watershed moment. Grant stood still, not speaking as he absorbed a series of telegrams. As ever at moments of extreme stress, some stoic composure hardened his features. Finally Julia could tolerate the suspense no longer. "Ulyss, what do the telegrams say? Do they bring any bad news?" "I will read them to you," he said, with unwonted emotion, "but first prepare yourself for the most painful and startling news that could be received, and control your feelings so as not to betray the nature of the despatches to the servants."[36] The most important telegram came from Major Thomas T. Eckert in Washington, who disclosed that Lincoln had been wounded with a pistol shot to the head and would not survive. He noted a simultaneous attack against Secretary of State Seward, who lingered in critical condition. "The Secretary of War desires that you return to Washington immediately."[37]

This saddest day of his life would be etched in black in Grant's memory. Aside from losing the greatest leader he had ever known, he had lost a dear friend of the past thirteen months: "To know [Lincoln] personally was to love and respect him for his great qualities of heart and head, and for his patience and patriotism."[38] Because the South sorely needed Lincoln's broad understanding, his death was "the greatest possible calamity to the country, and especially to the people of the South."[39] He feared for the peace process consecrated at Appomattox: "I did not know what it meant. Here was the rebellion put down in the field, and starting up in the gutters; we had fought it as war, now we had to fight it as assassination."[40] Another cause for concern arose when Julia asked whether Andrew Johnson would ascend to the presidency. "Yes," Grant replied, "and for some reason I dread the change."[41] Before long Grant would criticize Johnson for his excessively cozy relationship with white southerners. At this point, however, he worried that his hostility toward former rebels "would be such as to repel, and make them unwilling citizens . . . I felt that reconstruction had been set back, no telling how far."[42] Soon after, it was learned that George A. Atzerodt, who had been assigned to kill Johnson, had roamed around the capital and gotten drunk instead.

Just when Grant imagined he could breathe easier, with the crisis atmosphere of wartime subsiding, the pressure of events now returned with a swift, terrible rush. The Lincoln assassination ushered in an anxious, fragile peace, fraught with fresh dangers, perhaps unimaginable new forms of violence. After Grant took the train north to Burlington, safely depositing Julia and Jesse there, the tracks were cleared so a train could transport him back to Washington, with pickets and patrols guarding the route. At the behest of Assistant War Secretary Charles A. Dana, a special engine preceded the train to detect any explosives embedded along the way. Grant traveled to the capital with Julia's brother Fred. In Philadelphia, Beckwith said, Dent purchased a pint of champagne that he shared with Grant on the journey. It was a shockingly inappropriate time for Grant to imbibe, with his services so urgently required in Washington, but perhaps he needed to calm his shaken nerves after the shock of Lincoln's death. Beckwith's story gains credibility because he typically defended Grant from all drinking allegations and called this the sole time he ever witnessed his "indulgence in liquor of any kind."[43]

Grant would long wonder if his presence at Ford's Theatre might have altered things and whether Julia's dislike of Mary Lincoln had inadvertently modified the direction of American history. Would Grant, with his acute battlefield instincts, have sensed the assassin's tread? Would he have been more attentive to security concerns and brought his own security guard? Would the omnipresent Beckwith have sat outside the box, buffering his boss from harm? Such questions surely rattled around endlessly in Grant's uneasy mind on that long train ride.

The president had been carried to a small boardinghouse across Tenth Street, his long frame laid out in a cramped back room on the ground floor. Cabinet members came to pay their respects while crowds outside awaited word of the president's condition. Their vigil ended when Lincoln died at 7:22 a.m. and Andrew Johnson was sworn in as president within hours. The battle-toughened Stanton lost no time supervising a comprehensive response to the crisis, briefly acting as de facto president. By the time Grant learned of the assassination, the hyperefficient war secretary had already notified nearby forts to seal off the capital and shut down bridges, posted roadblocks, and halted Potomac River traffic. He threw his department's resources into investigating the conspiracy, interrogating witnesses and casting a huge dragnet across the city that netted Atzerodt and Lewis Powell, who had ferociously slashed Seward. Both men were in custody by the time Grant reached Washington. Despite a sizable reward for his apprehension, Booth escaped and remained at large for another eleven days.

Grant entered a bleak, rainy capital already clothed in mourning, with church bells chiming dolefully, flags drooping at half-mast, and hundreds of former slaves gathered before the White House "weeping and wailing their loss," wrote Gideon Welles.[44] The lieutenant general was hurried into the presence of the new president. While Grant knew the original plot had contemplated killing more than Lincoln and Seward, he didn't expect fresh episodes of violence to unfold, reassuring Julia that the plot had "expended itself and there is but little to fear."[45] For all that, Grant adopted unusual precautions, returning to the Willard Hotel twice daily for meals and staying indoors at night. When he set eyes on images of John Wilkes Booth, he immediately recognized the sinister horseman who had shadowed his path to the train station and knew that he himself had stood on the death list of intended victims. By mid-May, the Grants had moved into the vacated Georgetown residence of General Halleck, where three officers and fifteen privates functioned as constant sentinels around the house.

Events conspired to pile huge new burdens on Grant's shoulders. He had to oversee the formal rituals of grief, with every post draped in mourning for thirty days. Many field commanders refused to believe the calamitous reports of Lincoln's murder and Grant had to verify the awful news for them. With possible military threats still hanging in the air, he reviewed the preparedness of nearby forts, Stanton instructing him that "I feel it my duty to ask you to consider yourself specially charged with all matters pertaining to the security and defense of this National Capital."[46] As he toiled to secure Washington, Grant couldn't shake off the deep grief that had seized him. A man named Charles H. Jones was unwinding balls of crepe at the War Department, when he entered a third-floor office where the lights were dimmed and the occupant sat at his desk with his head slumped forward. "Pardon me," Jones said. When the man lifted his eyes, Jones realized with astonishment that it was Grant in a state verging on exhaustion. "Don't mind me," Grant told him. "Carry out your orders."[47]

Just a week earlier, Grant had behaved with exceptional generosity toward Lee and his men. Now, as apocalyptic fears convulsed Washington, worries arose that the disbanding rebel army might be teeming with secret conspirators and assassins. Executing a temporary volte-face, Grant was especially preoccupied with Virginia. John T. Ford, manager of the theater where Lincoln was slain, was in Richmond. Grant had Ord arrest him and send him under guard to Washington. In a striking retreat from his recent forgiving mood, Grant submitted to atypical rage, rashly asking Ord to arrest the mayor and members of the old Richmond city council as well as paroled officers who had not taken oaths of allegiance. "Extreme rigor will have to be observed whilst assassination remains the order of the day with the rebels."[48] Ord sent back an admirably coolheaded reply, noting that if he arrested Lee and members of his staff in Richmond, the Civil War might resume. Upon reflection, Grant tempered his hasty response, telling Ord that arresting the Richmond politicians was merely a suggestion, not an order.

The post-assassination hysteria attained such a fever pitch that Grant feared Joseph Johnston might be tempted to resume the fight. Not taking any chances, he dispatched Sheridan to move promptly with six to eight thousand cavalry men to join Sherman and stymie any chance for Johnston's army to escape. Nonetheless, he continued to believe that a just policy toward Confederate soldiers was far more likely to reconcile them to Union victory than a punitive one. When a group of Mosby's partisans asked to surrender and be paroled, Grant leapt at the chance, telling Stanton, "It will be better to have Mosby's . . . men . . . as paroled prisoners of War than at large as Guerrillas."[49]

In the days after Lincoln's death, Julia Grant behaved with all due decorum and "went many times to call on dear heart-broken Mrs. Lincoln, but she could not see me."[50] Mary Lincoln hadn't relented in her feelings toward Julia and perhaps nursed a grudge that the Grants had snubbed the Ford's Theatre invitation; in any event, she chose to be alone with her grief. Among the many tasks heaped on Grant was organizing the obsequies to Lincoln when his casket lay in state in the White House. With Lincoln dead, a new responsibility had settled upon Grant, who became the foremost symbol of the Union and the political agenda ratified by the war, most notably justice for the freed slaves. Already carrying on the Lincoln legacy, which would shape his worldview in future years, he came up with an ideal gesture to honor the dead president, commanding Ord to send up one of the best black regiments from Virginia for the funeral ceremony. At ten o'clock on the morning of April 19, a solitary Grant took up his position by Lincoln's catafalque in the East Room of the White House and with the ramrod-straight posture of a soldier stood guard as tears coursed freely down his cheeks, a highly unusual show of emotion for him. Sheltered by an open black canopy that afforded views from all four sides, the walnut coffin rested on a raised platform. Mary Lincoln was too grief-stricken to attend, and Captain Robert Lincoln ranked as the sole family member present. Many years later, attending the dedication of a Lincoln museum, Grant summed up the importance of the dead president, the first in American history to be assassinated: "His fame will grow brighter as time passes and his great work is better understood."[51]

At 2 p.m., the presidential entourage, Grant included, accompanied the coffin to the Capitol, where it remained on view for several days in the rotunda. Then the presidential remains began a lengthy, roundabout journey to Springfield, Illinois, for the burial. Pausing in many cities, it covered seventeen hundred miles, an estimated seven million people converging on the railroad tracks to pray and weep and tip their caps in homage as the train rode by. The nation had never witnessed such a mass outpouring of emotion, not even for George Washington, who had died from natural causes at a more advanced age. As the train wound toward Illinois, a New York cavalry detachment cornered John Wilkes Booth in a tobacco shed in Port Royal, Virginia. After the wooden structure was set ablaze, Booth was shot and dragged to the porch of a nearby farmhouse, where he died, but not before he attempted to lay claim to Confederate martyrdom. At the end, he supposedly said, "Tell my mother I die for my country."[52]

ABRAHAM LINCOLN WAS RUDELY SNATCHED away just as many Americans had learned to appreciate his benevolence and farsighted wartime leadership. Nobody could have served as a fit successor to Lincoln, but the rise of Andrew Johnson to the presidency was an especially cruel stroke for the nation. About five feet ten inches tall and solidly built, Johnson was a humorless, pugnacious man, thin-skinned and vindictive, with a fiercely turbulent expression and close-set, beady black eyes. He was placed on the ticket with Lincoln in 1864, not for outstanding talent or intelligence, but because Republicans hoped to broadcast their status as a full-fledged Union party by drafting a border state Democrat from Tennessee. As the only senator from a secession state to retain his seat in the U.S. Congress—a courageous stand that endeared him to Republicans—a heroic aura had burnished Andrew Johnson for a time.

His accidental presidency started promisingly enough when he announced plans to retain members of Lincoln's cabinet. Widely accused of being drunk at Lincoln's second inaugural, he worked to project a more presidential demeanor. When George Templeton Strong visited his temporary office at the Treasury Department, where Johnson had hung two flags—the one draped over Lincoln's box at Ford's Theatre, the other showing the long gash where Booth's spur had slashed the fabric as he leapt to the stage—he was pleasantly surprised by Johnson's sedate behavior, finding him "dignified, urbane, and self-possessed."[53]

The early life of this rough-hewn president contained remarkable features. Born in a log cabin, reared by poor, illiterate parents in North Carolina, he was apprenticed to a tailor and ran away as an adolescent to Tennessee, where he opened a tailor shop. In future years, he would always be faultlessly dressed, at least looking the part of a model politician. At age eighteen, he began to leave behind the trappings of frontier life when he married sixteen-year-old Eliza McCardle, a shoemaker's daughter, who taught him to read and write. Like Lincoln, Johnson became a fanatic for self-improvement, avoiding theater, gambling, and horse races and admitting he "never had much time for frivolity."[54] As he prospered, he came to own five slaves, whom he freed in late 1863. Living among large landowners who condescended to him, he always felt like an outsider. Their patronizing attitude deposited a bitter residue in his nature, a seething resentment and profound ambivalence toward the planter class, whom he longed to ape and punish at once.

A gifted debater, Johnson rose fast through the political ranks in Tennessee, starting as mayor of Greeneville before going to the state legislature and shifting from Whig to Democrat. He was determined to soar in politics, and a friend depicted his tumultuous career as "one intense, unceasing, desperate upward struggle."[55] Before the Civil War, he progressed from congressman to two-term Tennessee governor to U.S. senator. The obstinate Johnson barged ahead with sharp elbows, and President James K. Polk, who came from his state, perceived him as "vindictive and perverse in his temper and conduct."[56] An abrasive quality to Johnson's ambition tended to offend people and later left him isolated in the White House, where he trusted few people and dispensed with confidants. Although Johnson portrayed himself as a tribune of the common people, his selective populism encompassed poor whites but excluded blacks. After John Brown's raid on Harpers Ferry, he made a speech that held up slavery as beneficial. His talk was larded with tributes to "honest yeomen," mingled with tirades against the "pampered, bloated, corrupted aristocracy" that owned slaves.[57] Somehow his sympathy never extended to the slaves themselves.

When it came to preserving the Union during the war, Andrew Johnson was a brave, stalwart supporter. A rabble-rousing orator, he didn't mince words when South Carolina seceded, calling it "levying war against the United States" and accusing southern rebels of "treason."[58] It took immense courage for him to maintain this view, and he confronted threats and was burned in effigy for his outspoken stand. When the state capital of Nashville fell to the Union, Lincoln named Johnson military governor of the state, hoping he would mobilize support for the federal cause.[59] He enforced Unionism in a bullheaded manner that antagonized people. As the journalist Henry Villard wrote, "He was doubtless a man of unusual natural parts, [but] had too violent a temper and was too much addicted to the common Southern habit of free indulgence in strong drink."[60] By late 1863, Johnson had converted to abolitionism as part of his vendetta against the slavocracy, but not from any real regard for those in bondage. "Damn the Negroes," he insisted, "I am fighting those traitorous aristocrats, their masters."[61] Influenced by the Emancipation Proclamation, he told a delegation of free blacks in Nashville he would stand as their Moses, leading them "through the Red Sea of war and bondage to a fairer future of liberty and peace."[62] For Republicans, Johnson's nomination was perilous because he was a racist at heart and a robust Democrat—two flaws that could no longer be papered over once he became president.

In his initial comments about Johnson, Grant sounded mildly optimistic. "I have every reason to hope that in our new President we will find a man disposed and capable of conducting the government in its old channel."[63] In moments of crisis, he thought, people should rally around the president, affording him the benefit of the doubt. On April 21, he offered this generous assessment of Johnson:

> It is impossible that an ordinary man should have risen to the position which Pres. Johnson has and have sustained himself throughout. His start was in the South where he had an aristocracy to contend against without one advantage except native ability to sustain him. I am satisfied the country has nothing to fear from his administration. It is unpatriotic at this time for professed lovers of their country to express doubts of the capacity and integrity of our Chief Magistrate.[64]

Before long, Grant's stouthearted faith would be severely tested as the new president went from being too harsh toward Confederate leaders to being too obliging. During his first week as president, Johnson issued a statement that "instigators of this monstrous rebellion" would pay the full price for their actions, seemingly the antithesis of Grant's large-hearted spirit at Appomattox.[65]

Once sworn in, Johnson had to cope with the last remnants of war. The news of Lee's surrender had not penetrated many corners of the rural South, and Sherman still had to negotiate the surrender of Joseph Johnston's army in North Carolina. While Sherman knew he could overpower his opponent, he feared the defeated army might splinter into marauding guerrilla bands. "There is great danger that the confederate armies will dissolve and fill the whole land with robbers and assassins," he told Grant.[66] Jefferson Davis, still blinded by zeal, wanted to prosecute a now hopeless war, telling Johnston and Beauregard, "I think we can whip the enemy yet, if our people will turn out." With soldiers deserting in droves, Joseph Johnston brushed aside this attitude as purely delusional. "My views are, sir, that our people are tired of the war, feel themselves whipped, and will not fight."[67] Convinced Johnston would surrender when he learned Lee had done so, Grant authorized Sherman to offer him the identical terms, which Sherman commended as "magnanimous and liberal." He promised Grant: "Should Johnston follow Lee's Example, I shall of course grant the Same."[68] Had Sherman stuck to this promise, he would have spared himself a world of trouble.

On April 17, Sherman met with Johnston northwest of Raleigh. Far from confining himself to the narrow military terms hammered out at Appomattox, Sherman extended to Johnston a sweeping political settlement. However demonized as a scourge of the South, Sherman furnished terms of shocking leniency. Overplaying his hand, he agreed that southern soldiers should stack their arms in state capitals; existing state governments would be recognized and carry on as before; and the Constitution would protect the "rights of person and property" of citizens in the former Confederacy, even though that might seem to condone slavery.[69] In framing this agreement, Sherman claimed to rely on memories of his meeting with Lincoln at City Point, arrogating to himself civilian powers that rightly belonged to the president and Congress in fixing the postwar status of seceded states.

On April 18, Sherman sent the agreement to Grant and Stanton for presidential approval, appending a breezy note that promised peace and gave no forewarning of the storm about to break. Sherman believed he had wisely bolstered existing state governments in the South, preventing an upsurge of guerrilla violence. When he dispatched Major Henry Hitchcock to Washington with the agreement, Grant, instead of going to Burlington for a brief rest, stayed behind in Washington to await his arrival. "It looks as if I was never to have any rest," he grumbled to Julia.[70] On the afternoon of April 21, as soon as Grant set eyes on Sherman's dispatch, he knew instantly that Sherman had vastly exceeded his authority and committed a colossal blunder by negotiating a full-blown peace treaty. Grant had known where to draw the line between military and civilian matters, whereas Sherman had blurred the two worlds.

Grant promptly contacted Stanton and suggested that Johnson summon an emergency cabinet session to discuss the new agreement. That evening, Grant stood before a tense cabinet and read aloud Sherman's message, which was roundly condemned. Only days after Lincoln's funeral, members still sulked in a hawkish, unforgiving mood. Johnson called Sherman an outright traitor and Stanton was especially vocal, ticking off on his fingers his many objections to Sherman's decision. Gideon Welles noted that while Grant was "decidedly opposed" to Sherman's agreement, he carefully retained personal loyalty to "his brother officer and abstained from censure."[71] Still fuming, Stanton instructed Grant to have Sherman resume hostilities immediately. In his *Memoirs,* Grant argued that Sherman thought he had followed the Appomattox agreement and the wishes of the slain president, who had authorized the convening of the Confederate Virginia legislature.[72] That order had been revoked, but Sherman didn't know it. Wasting no time, Grant secretly departed for Raleigh at midnight to confer with Sherman, imagining a personal visit would draw the sting from Stanton's reprimand. Wild rumors flew through the capital. "Sherman's conduct is that of a madman," wrote Senator Charles Sumner. "Stanton was disposed to recall him & send him before a court-martial; but Grant was full of tenderness for his lieutenant & undertook at once to go down & relieve him, thus breaking his fall."[73]

Stanton seized on Sherman's surrender agreement to pursue a vendetta against him. Despite Sherman's extraordinary record, Stanton attempted to turn him into a public pariah, leaking the story to the press. Aside from their clashing personalities, Stanton may have regarded Sherman as a political threat, accusing him of angling for the "Copperhead nomination for President."[74] Two days after the cabinet meeting, newspapers printed Sherman's dispatches along with Stanton's slanted version of events. The war secretary was not content to lambast Sherman's agreement with Johnston, but insinuated that Sherman had fallen under malevolent Confederate influences and might even help to aid Jefferson Davis's escape. Grant was appalled that Stanton had turned so savagely on Sherman, telling Badeau it was "infamous" that four years of meritorious service should be thus rewarded.[75] He came to characterize Stanton's scurrilous campaign as "that inexplicable and cruel storm of defamation."[76]

Stopping at Fort Monroe en route to Sherman, Grant reverted to battlefield mode, giving orders that Sheridan and his cavalry should move to Greensboro, North Carolina, with all possible haste. Perhaps not wishing to alarm him, Grant did not telegraph to Sherman that he was coming. He had a difficult boat journey to New Bern, North Carolina, where he disembarked having been "dreadfully seasick and he looked sad and careworn," noted a spectator.[77] Grant showed tact by going only as far as Raleigh, instead of continuing a bit farther to Sherman's headquarters, because he still hoped his friend would receive full credit for Johnston's surrender and did not mean to upstage him. On April 24, when Major Hitchcock appeared back at Sherman's headquarters, an officer quizzed him as to whether "you bring peace or war?" "I brought back General Grant," he disclosed.[78]

By the time Sherman met Grant, he already anticipated stiff opposition to his agreement but for the wrong reason. Unaware of the ruckus raised by Stanton, he had received a batch of northern newspapers reflecting northern wrath over Lincoln's assassination. Passing them along to Johnston, he noted ruefully that

"I fear much the assassination of the President will give such a bias to the popular mind, which . . . may thwart our purpose of recognizing 'existing local governments.'"[79] Sherman, professing pleasure at Grant's arrival, must have been
startled all the same. Grant explained that the original deal with Johnston had
been scuttled in Washington, pointed to the furor over Lincoln's death, and said
Sherman should offer Johnston the identical terms extended to Lee at Appomattox. Johnston was duly notified that the truce was terminated. Even while rein-
ing in Sherman, Grant handled the situation with consummate finesse, allowing
Sherman to save face by negotiating the surrender, while he stayed discreetly in
the background. On April 26, Sherman extracted from Johnston the same agreement Lee had signed and an undoubtedly relieved Grant scrawled across the
bottom, "Approved: U.S. Grant."[80]

Grant's brief southern sojourn opened his eyes to widespread misery in the
region. As he awaited the results of Sherman's dealings with Johnston, he sent
Julia a letter notable for its tenderness, mercy, and forgiveness toward his former foes:

> Raleigh is a very beautiful place. The grounds are large and filled
> with the most beautiful spreading oaks I ever saw. Nothing has been
> destroyed and the people are anxious to see peace restored so that
> further devastation need not take place in the country. The suffering
> that must exist in the South the next year, even with the war ending
> now, will be beyond conception. People who talk now of further
> retaliation and punishment, except of the political leaders, either do
> not conceive of the suffering endured already or they are heartless
> and unfeeling and wish to stay at home, out of danger, whilst the
> punishment is being inflicted.[81]

His mission complete, Grant returned to Washington and may have survived
an assassination plot as he headed northward. With a small entourage of officers,
he traveled on a train consisting of a single car that was thrown from the track.
Adam Badeau, for one, thought the derailment "left little doubt of the design"
behind the accident.[82] The episode received little attention, likely because nothing was ever proven. Stopping at Goldsboro, Grant saw scathing newspaper reports about Sherman planted by Stanton and was outraged. As he pored over
Stanton's comments, Badeau wrote, "his face flamed with indignation, his fist

was clenched, and he exclaimed: 'It is infamous—infamous! . . . After four years of such service as Sherman has done—that he should be used like this!'"[83] As Grant foresaw, Sherman was shocked when he saw the press clippings and learned Halleck was telling Union troops not to obey him. He criticized Stanton vehemently for failing to advise him to "limit our negotiations to purely military matters."[84] In his view, Stanton had deliberately humiliated him by informing the press of the cabinet's flat rejection of his peace deal. With deep anguish Sherman wrote to Grant that his officers would now "learn with pain and amazement that I am deemed insubordinate & wanting in common sense" and that someone who brought "an army of seventy thousand men in magnificent condition across a country deemed impassable, and placed it just where it was wanted almost on the day appointed have brought discredit to our Governm[en]t."[85]

Trapped in the Sherman-Stanton cross fire, Grant did not answer this letter or send his friend any message after leaving Raleigh. The silence gnawed at Sherman, and on May 10 he sent Grant a scalding telegram, spilling out his rage with Stanton, Halleck, and, implicitly, Grant himself. He had waited to receive guidance from Grant, he said, but had received none. By now Sherman had brought his army up to Manchester, Virginia, near Richmond. Citing the "great outrage" perpetrated against him, he forbade Halleck, now posted to Richmond, from reviewing his army. He went further and warned Halleck that he would march through Richmond and "asked him to Keep out of sight lest he should be insulted."[86] He also warned that he would ignore his orders unless issued in the president's name. "I deny his right to Command an Army," he told Grant. "No amount of retraction or pusillanimous excusing will do. Mr. Stanton must publicly confess himself a Common libeller."[87] If Grant didn't vindicate him from Stanton's insults, Sherman warned, he would have to do the job himself. "No man shall insult me with impunity, even if I am an officer of the Army."[88]

With Grant being discussed as a future presidential candidate, Sherman concluded his message by warning him, in almost Shakespearean language, against the wiles of the intriguing Stanton: "He seeks your life and reputation as well as mine. Beware, but you are Cool and have been most skillful in managing such People, and I have faith you will penetrate his designs . . . The lust for Power in political Minds is the strongest passion of Life, and impels Ambitious Men (Richard III) to deeds of Infamy."[89] Aside from ventilating his anger, Sherman clearly believed Grant was entering an alien world where he might be led astray by the dangerous allure of power.

The feud between Sherman and Stanton exposed a deep fissure that would shortly divide the country over Reconstruction. With the war ending, Sherman's old fondness for the South became more apparent. His views on slavery had remained strictly reactionary. When teaching in Louisiana before the war, he had written, "I would not if I could abolish or modify slavery . . . Negroes in the great numbers that exist here must of necessity be slaves." He also wrote: "Niggers won't work unless they are owned, and white servants are not to be found in this parish."[90] Now he was flabbergasted that Stanton gave serious consideration to granting blacks the right to vote. In many ways, Sherman wanted to re-create the status quo ante in southern states, minus slavery. "The South is broken and ruined and appeals to our pity," he told Rawlins. "To ride the people down with persecutions and military exactions would be like slashing away at the crew of a sinking ship."[91]

When Sherman appeared in Washington for the Grand Review of the Union armies, he met with President Johnson, who claimed he had not known in advance about the bulletins published by Stanton attacking Sherman. Almost everyone in the cabinet reprised the same sentiment. Stanton never offered any apology or explanation. To his credit, Grant tried to mediate a truce between the two men, telling Sherman, "I want to talk to you upon matters about which you feel sore. I think justly so, but which bear some explanation in behalf of those who you feel have inflicted the injury."[92] Sherman nursed his wounds and vowed "to resent what I considered an insult, as publicly as it was made."[93]

With Johnston's surrender, the Civil War effectively ended, but isolated pockets of resistance remained in Tennessee, Alabama, Texas, and Arkansas. Grant tracked the movements of Jefferson Davis as he fled south incognito. On May 10, he was captured in a pine forest in Irwinville, Georgia. For the next two years, he languished in Fort Monroe, sometimes shackled, becoming a southern martyr. Lincoln's prediction that it would be best if Davis quietly left the country was posthumously vindicated. Grant believed an overriding strategic necessity governed Davis's capture: "I feared that if not captured, he might get into the trans-Mississippi region and there set up a more contracted confederacy. The young men now out of homes and out of employment might have rallied under his standard and protracted the war yet another year."[94]

The capture of Jefferson Davis didn't cause quite the sensation expected because it competed with another drama riveting the nation's attention that day. Just as he was taken into custody, eight defendants charged with the attempted murder of Lincoln, Johnson, Seward, and Grant went on trial in Washington in the grim precincts of the Old Arsenal Penitentiary, a place of barred windows and thick walls. Johnson made a controversial decision to try the defendants before a military court, which decided to conduct the trial in secret and brief one reporter at the close of each day. Alarmed by this precedent of a secret trial, Grant, after testifying on May 12, went to the White House to protest these opaque proceedings. Although Johnson was noncommittal, Grant's intervention seems to have had the desired effect, for the court soon opened proceedings to visitors for the first time.

The trial wasn't the finest hour of American justice as the treatment of the prisoners seemed medieval in its barbarism. Almost all of the male prisoners were dragged into the courtroom with linen masks shielding their faces and chains and heavy iron balls strapped to their ankles. With clanking irons, they shuffled in and, once seated, their hoods were removed. The military commission took testimony for seven weeks and ultimately found all eight defendants guilty, with four of them (Mary Surratt, Lewis Powell, David Herold, and George Atzerodt) sentenced to hang while three others (including Michael O'Laughlen) were given life imprisonment and one a six-year term. Mary Surratt, who ran a boardinghouse where Booth colluded with other conspirators, went down in historical annals as the first woman ever executed by the federal government.

On May 18, orders were issued for a festive march of the victorious Union armies, which would last two days and feature on the first day, May 23, George Gordon Meade and the Army of the Potomac, followed by William Tecumseh Sherman and his Army of the Tennessee and Army of Georgia on the second. Because of the widely discussed brouhaha between Stanton, identified with the eastern army, and Sherman, identified with the western army, Grant made sure their camps were cleanly separated by the Potomac River.

The Grand Review would commence at the Capitol and proceed down Pennsylvania Avenue past a grandstand erected before the White House, where Johnson, Grant, Stanton, and other cabinet members would survey the troops. For the first time since Lincoln's death, the emblems of mourning that had decorated the capital—flags flying half-mast, masses of funereal crepe—were withdrawn, superseded by a spirit of jubilation.

In all, two hundred thousand soldiers were slated to participate. On the first morning, with becoming modesty, Grant sauntered over to the temporary bleacher from army headquarters at Seventeenth and F Streets; he didn't wish to arrive by horse or coach or attract any fuss. The entire city seemed adorned with flags and bunting, and every window and doorway was jammed with expectant spectators. Poor whites and blacks alike jostled on the sidewalks. At 9 a.m., on a morning of spectacular sunshine, a signal gun announced the parade's start and martial bands began to thump and blare. With flowery garlands wreathing his horse, Meade set off at the head of the Army of the Potomac. His army had been chosen to lead the extravaganza because of its seniority and because it had been charged with defending the capital. Upon reaching the White House, Meade on horseback delivered to Johnson and Grant a brisk salute, then joined them to watch his army march past. By common consent, Andrew Johnson was at his presidential best: as each regiment passed and presented their colors, he acknowledged them with salutes and handshakes and formally tipped his hat.

Ulysses S. Grant held an honored spot in the day's festivities. As soldiers passed him, they lustily chanted, "Grant! Grant! Goodbye Old Man!"[95] To those who searched his face for special emotion, there shone only serene dignity and quiet joy, consistent with his modest demeanor at Appomattox. As one Ohio lawyer remembered, "There was no vindictiveness in his face; the fires that lighted up his eyes were not those of grim satisfaction at being the conqueror, but rather those of a man who was pleased to know that the country was once more united and that the war, with all its horrors, had ceased."[96] Julia Grant savored the tributes tendered to her beloved husband, who had emerged from deep obscurity to lead a million-man army. "How magnificent the marching!" she wrote. "What shouts rent the air!"[97]

For more than six hours, close ranks of cavalry (twelve abreast) and infantry (twenty-five abreast) flowed down the broad avenue with all the pride and élan of their hard-earned victory, parading on a thick carpet of flower petals strewn in their paths by spectators. It was a brilliant pageantry of war, stripped of its bloodshed, horror, and disease. The sights that stirred onlookers most were battle flags, many shredded by bullets, that had fluttered through the smoke of war. Some people in the crowd, overcome with emotion, rushed forward to kiss and embrace the banners. For soldiers in the surging mass moving down the boulevard, the experience was enthralling. As Joshua Lawrence Chamberlain wrote: "At the rise of ground near the Treasury a backward glance takes in the mighty spectacle: the broad Avenue for more than a mile solid full, and more, from wall to wall, from door to roof, with straining forms and outwelling hearts."[98] Among many colorful figures prancing down the avenue on horseback, perhaps none was more captivating than George Armstrong Custer, whose horse suddenly bolted forward, tearing the hat from his head. "His long golden locks floating in the wind," wrote Horace Porter, "his low-cut collar, his crimson necktie, and his buckskin breeches, presented a combination which made him look half general and half scout, and gave him a daredevil appearance which singled him out for general remark and applause."[99]

The next day's parade was devoted to Sherman's western army. Everyone knew the trouble brewing between him and Stanton and wondered whether a blowup was at hand. Once again at 9 a.m., in ideal weather, the troops began to march in dense columns from the Capitol, Sherman proudly riding at their head. Especially prominent were black pioneers, toting picks, axes, and spades, stepping lively to the music. For easterners Sherman was more legend than reality and they were thrilled that he resembled the leathery warrior they had imagined. The crowds cheered him, showering flowers on him. "When I reached the Treasury-building, and looked back, the sight was simply magnificent," Sherman wrote. "The column was compact, and the glittering muskets looked like a solid mass of steel, moving with the regularity of a pendulum."[100] As he reached a corner brick house on Lafayette Square, his gaze rose to an upper window, where Secretary of State Seward sat swathed in bandages from his recent attack. With a flourish, Sherman waved his hat and Seward saluted in return. As Sherman and his men rode past the presidential grandstand, they saluted the assembled dignitaries with their swords.

When Sherman approached the reviewing stand, the band broke into "Marching Through Georgia" with special oomph. It was then that the long-anticipated showdown took place. After Sherman dismounted, he bounded up the steps and exchanged handshakes with Johnson and Grant and chatted courteously with cabinet members. Then he drew near his foe. Stanton extended his hand and Sherman, with an infallible flair for the dramatic, refused to grasp it. (Charles Dana claimed Stanton didn't offer his hand but merely inclined his head.) Sherman's snub went even further. "What a defiant and angry glance he shot at Stanton," Julia remembered.[101] Another observer claimed "Sherman's face was scarlet and his red hair seemed to stand on end."[102] The whole contretemps lasted a few seconds before Sherman brushed past Stanton brusquely and shook the hands of other cabinet secretaries.

For Grant, this second day of marching was the more emotional, for his roots lay in the western army, which had first carried him to military glory. In comparison, the eastern army had been an adopted one. The western men, who looked more ragged and weather-beaten than the easterners, had once been dismissed as an ill-bred rabble, but they displayed an unmistakable swagger and panache that only years of victory could produce. For Grant, "their marching could not be excelled; they gave the appearance of men who had been thoroughly drilled to endure hardships . . . without the ordinary shelter of a camp."[103] Sherman likewise swelled with pride as he watched his "well organized, well commanded and disciplined" army and thought "there was no wonder that it had swept through the South like a tornado."[104]

The two-day affair represented the high-water mark of Grant's career to that point. "He was unquestionably the most aggressive fighter in the entire list of the world's famous soldiers," observed Porter.[105] Perhaps to prolong the celebratory mood, Grant and Orville Babcock took a sunset ride on horseback down Pennsylvania Avenue. Crowds still mingled on the sidewalks and recognized and applauded Grant, who simply nodded and lifted his hat. One of those who set eyes on him was Walt Whitman, who told his mother about seeing Grant. "He is the noblest Roman of them all—none of the pictures do justice to him— about sundown I saw him again riding on a large fine horse, with his hat off in answer to the hurrahs—he rode by where I stood, & I saw him well, as he rode by on a slow canter, with nothing but a single orderly after him—He looks like a good man—(& I believe there is much in looks)."[106]

PART THREE

A Life of Peace

CHAPTER TWENTY-FIVE

Soldierly Good Faith

U NDER GRANT'S AEGIS the federal government had mustered a fearsome army, a million strong, that may well have been, as he claimed,
the best trained and equipped in the world. Yet his first task as general
in chief in the postwar era was to contract that army dramatically, and within
six months its numbers had dwindled to 210,000 men. The brick building at
Seventeenth and F Streets, from which Grant ran the army and received an unending parade of visitors, was small and unprepossessing and scarcely seemed an
imposing seat of power. With its yard and tree in front, Grant's son Jesse thought
it exuded a sedate residential air: "Washington side streets were not paved in
those days, and army teams were often stalled, hub-deep in the mud, before
headquarters."[1] Showing the loyalty to his staff that was both his blessing and
his curse, Grant kept on John Rawlins as chief of staff; Cyrus Comstock, Orville
Babcock, Horace Porter, and Fred Dent as aides-de-camp; Adam Badeau and
Ely Parker as military secretaries; and Theodore Bowers and Robert Lincoln as
assistant adjutant generals.

Only gradually did Grant adapt to the murky ways of Washington—"I have
a horror of living in Washington," he warned Julia, "and never intend to do
it"—but residence there proved inseparable from high command.[2] He fantasized
about living in Philadelphia and commuting to the capital weekly, a dream
nearly realized in January 1865 when a group of Philadelphia dignitaries gave
him, gratis, a fully furnished house on Chestnut Street "in gratitude for eminent

services."³ These rich citizens spared no expense, outfitting the opulent quarters with an excellent piano, velvet carpets, and lace curtains. However hard it might be to picture the hard-bitten Grant stomping about in this prissy place, he envisioned it as his new home. To her horror, Julia discovered that the new abode came with a complete wine cellar, well stocked with costly wines, brandies, and whiskies, and she quietly consulted Rawlins about how to get rid of such temptation. "Send for some responsible broker . . . have him dispose of the entire stock at once; and put the money in your pocket," Rawlins advised her, and Julia acted swiftly before her husband was waylaid into fresh temptation.⁴

Upon occupying the house in May, Grant discovered he had woefully underestimated the time he had to spend in Washington. Predictably he became a prisoner of his heavy workload and Julia, after four years apart from her husband, hated being stranded in another city. In Washington Grant stayed at the Willard Hotel, where he was so hounded by job supplicants that Julia perceived he needed "a home where these petitioners could not penetrate."⁵ Also, the upkeep of the tony Philadelphia home was so expensive Grant feared he would be saddled with debt for a decade. Consequently, the Grants rented out the Philadelphia house in November and relocated to Washington, decorating their new home with furniture from Philadelphia. The residence at 205 I Street NW was an ample, four-story place with two acres and a fine Potomac view. Hung with banners, swords, bugles, and other wartime trophies, the house contained engravings of Washington, Sherman, and Sheridan, along with a bust of Lincoln.

If the Philadelphia house posed a financial burden for Grant, it never presented an ethical one. Showered with gifts by adoring businessmen, he didn't question such generosity, accepting it as standard recompense for war heroes. Julia reacted to these gifts as so much manna dropped by a bountiful heaven: "a home, a lovely home, given to my dear, brave husband by a number of strange gentlemen of Philadelphia!"⁶ In fairness to Grant, one should note that the Duke of Wellington had received a dukedom and a vast fortune from a devoted nation, while Sherman pocketed money and a St. Louis home. But presents from private donors could easily shade over into subtle sources of corruption, especially since Grant's name was now being bandied about as a future president.

The Georgetown home came from a coterie of well-heeled New York admirers, led by Major General Daniel Butterfield, who transferred $105,000 to Grant in February 1866. Since the money far exceeded the $34,000 mortgage, these rich gentlemen furnished Grant with $55,000 in government bonds and the remainder in cash. No judicial rules yet governed such gifts. One donor was Abel Rathbone Corbin, the former editor of a Missouri newspaper, who later married Grant's sister Jennie. As we shall see, Corbin wasn't bashful about trading on his connection with Grant. Grant took this largesse without any apparent misgivings. Once again, what looked like patriotic munificence from one standpoint might look like buying future influence from another.

In Washington, people were struck by how lightly Grant wore his postwar fame. When John Eaton brought two British clergymen to meet him, they expected a profusion of ribbons and medals, but found him dressed instead in a "plain business suit" with a battered old army hat "lying on the table before him."[7] Showing a democratic style, Grant grabbed a streetcar to work each morning and in fair weather pounded the pavement at a rapid clip, smoking and tipping his hat to pedestrians as he whizzed by. The cigar still served as his trademark, though he scaled back consumption from twenty per day during the war to ten, feeling virtuous in his self-restraint. An active, curious pedestrian, he was often caught window-shopping by an amused Sherman. "Hello, Grant," Sherman would interrupt him, "what are you doing?" Grant would give an embarrassed little laugh. "Taking a little exercise, as usual, and looking around," he declared.[8] The one thing about Washington that seemed to cramp Grant's style was the absence of long straightaways for racing fast horses.

Julia Grant came alive in the heady atmosphere of Washington politics and was fondly received by the new First Lady, the sickly and reclusive Eliza McCardle Johnson. "Mrs. Johnson was a retiring, kind, gentle old lady," Julia wrote, "too much of an invalid to do the honors of the house . . . but she always came into the drawing room after the long state dinners to take coffee and receive the greetings of her husband's guests."[9] After the Grants bought the I Street house, Julia emerged as an ambitious social hostess, with a clear case of Potomac fever. Her receptions were packed with powerful visitors, leading Cyrus Comstock to growl at one gathering about "a horrid jam in which it took about an hour to get from stairway to parlor."[10] At loose ends as a host, Grant seemed misplaced in these fancy gatherings. He "was a quiet, undemonstrative man," noted a visitor, "whose immobile face rarely relaxed into a smile, and who displayed slight interest in social affairs."[11] If a trifle unsophisticated, Julia was well-meaning and eager to please. "Mrs. Grant is an unpretending, affectionate, motherly person who makes a good impression on everybody," wrote Rutherford B. Hayes. "Her *naivete* is genuine and very funny at times."[12]

Grant's postwar fame didn't spare him the bane of his father-in-law's glaring presence. After he and Julia settled into their Georgetown home, Colonel Dent had no qualms about moving in with them, forcing the victorious Union general to tolerate under his roof a cranky, unrepentant rebel who pontificated about the North violating southern rights. "Occasionally I get into a discussion against my will with Mr. Dent," wrote Comstock, who resided with the Grants. "He was a rebel sympathizer during the war & now is always abusing the Yankees & crying 'unconstitutional.' It makes me furious once in a while."[13]

Many Colonel Dents remained scattered throughout the South, unreconciled to the war's outcome. As the charitable victor at Appomattox, Grant stood as the foremost symbol of a merciful attitude toward the defeated states. At the same time, as the leading Union general, fully committed to the war's agenda of preserving the Union and ending slavery, Grant was no less associated with protecting the four million freed people. How to reconcile these two often incompatible impulses as they clashed in postwar America would define the rest of Grant's life and would prove, in many ways, as baffling a problem as winning the war. Nearly two weeks after Appomattox, Grant had written to Julia, "I find my duties, anxieties, and the necessity for having all my wits about me, increasing instead of diminishing. I have a Herculean task to perform."[14]

Lincoln had left behind only vague hints about how to pursue Reconstruction. He had bequeathed no immutable master plan, leading to educated guesswork about what he might have done. "Grant only knew the general magnanimity of the President's views and his disposition toward clemency," wrote Badeau.[15] In Andrew Johnson, Grant had to deal with a new president who would swing from excessive hostility toward the South to excessive leniency, alienating him at both ends of the spectrum.

Grant's relationship with Johnson started out amicably despite their differing styles. Grant was circumspect and reserved whereas Johnson blurted out oaths and tirades, heedless of the consequences. Grant disclaimed interest in politics or the presidency. "If I supposed that President Johnson believed that I desired to be President, I would be so ashamed that I could not look him in the face," he confided.[16] With Grant a bona fide war hero, Johnson cultivated the relationship, naming Jesse Root Grant postmaster of Covington, Kentucky. In the view of one lawmaker, Johnson "seemed not exactly to stand in awe of [Grant] but anxious to conciliate rather than resolved to command."[17] From the outset, Grant held decidedly ambivalent feelings toward the hotheaded Johnson, finding him "revengeful, passionate, and opinionated."[18]

Complicating their relationship was head-scratching about whether Grant was a Democrat or a Republican. Many Democrats sensed an allied spirit and possible presidential nominee for their party. Later, when their relations soured, Johnson insisted that Grant had started out a stalwart supporter of his policies who was then seduced by Radical Republicans catering to his dawning presidential ambition. "He meant well for the first two years, and much that I did that was denounced was through his advice," said Johnson. "He was the strongest man of all in the support of my policy for a long while."[19] Johnson overstated his case, conveniently forgetting many points of disagreement. Grant saw himself as a soldier, not a politician, narrowly defining his duties as general in chief. He was allowed to attend cabinet meetings about Reconstruction but piped up only when addressed about specific military issues. Still suffused with the Appomattox spirit, he lobbied Stanton to release Confederate prisoners and argued that former rebel soldiers who qualified as loyal citizens should be eligible for the regular army.

With Congress out of session until December, Andrew Johnson spurned calls for a special session to deal with Reconstruction. Grant thought it a profound error to make such momentous decisions by presidential fiat. At first Johnson appeared tailor-made to appeal to poor southern whites and juggle the conflicting interests of North and South. In Grant's view, he was "one of the ablest of the poor white class" and started out his presidency as if he "wished to revenge himself upon Southern men of better social standing than himself."[20] With a broad streak of class rage, Johnson seemed to breathe fire against patrician southern planters. Radical Republicans in Congress even thought the president a kindred soul who might support black equality and suffrage. "It was supposed," Sherman recalled, "that President Johnson would err, if at all, in imposing too harsh terms upon these [southern] states."[21]

Fresh from Appomattox, Grant was initially dismayed by the way Johnson lashed out at ex-rebels. "They surely would not make good citizens," he later wrote, "if they felt that they had a yoke around their necks."[22] Before long, however, he grasped the hidden psyche of Andrew Johnson and saw lurking behind his grievances against southern planters a burning wish to emulate them. Instead of punishing his social betters, he would pose as their champion to win them over. As Grant put it, "As soon as the slave-holders put their thumb upon him . . . he became their slave."[23] A Democrat with a devout faith in limited government and states' rights, Johnson wasn't ready to extend federal power to protect blacks. Before long, Grant wrote, Johnson came "to regard the South not only as an oppressed people, but as the people best entitled to consideration of any of our citizens."[24] The new president planned to win a second term through an alliance of southern white Democrats and moderate northern Republicans.

What pretty much guaranteed that Johnson would side with white supremacists was his benighted view of black people. No American president has ever held such openly racist views. "This is a country for white men," he declared unashamedly, "and by God, as long as I am President, it shall be a government for white men."[25] In one message to Congress, he contended that "negroes have shown less capacity for government than any other race of people."[26] He privately referred to blacks as "niggers" and betrayed a morbid fascination with miscegenation. In his inverted worldview, he wanted to ensure that the "poor, quiet, unoffending, harmless" whites of the South weren't "trodden under foot to protect niggers."[27] Not only did he think whites genetically superior to blacks but he refused to show the least respect to their most brilliant spokesmen. When Frederick Douglass came to the White House with a black delegation, Johnson turned to his secretary afterward and sneered: "He's just like any nigger, & would sooner cut a white man's throat than not."[28] Such a president could only picture southern blacks picking cotton for low wages on their former plantations.

In May, Johnson unveiled his Reconstruction program with a pair of proclamations. One promised to restore full citizenship to most southerners who agreed to take an oath of allegiance. The second outlined steps by which rebel states would be readmitted to the Union. The president would name provisional governors who would call elections to assemble conventions that would bring forth new state constitutions. These elections, of course, would be limited to white male voters. Whatever hopes Radical Republicans cherished about Johnson were rudely thwarted as he began granting wholesale pardons to white southerners. The conservative men he chose as southern governors showed he didn't intend to "reconstruct" the South at all or upset its traditional power structure. With presidential acquiescence, the old slave owners would reclaim their firm hold on power.

Grant and Johnson clashed sharply over a possible treason prosecution for Robert E. Lee. Johnson's amnesty proclamation excluded Confederate military leaders, who were required to apply directly to the president for pardons. Grant knew he would never have extracted the Appomattox agreement if it hadn't exempted Confederate officers from future punishment, but many northerners still bristled at coddling Lee. As Ralph Waldo Emerson protested, "General Grant's terms certainly look a little too easy, as foreclosing any action hereafter to convict Lee of treason."[29] A vociferous campaign in the northern press advocated trying Lee on treason charges, with Ben Butler assuring the president that Grant "had no authority to grant amnesty" at Appomattox.[30] The issue was a highly charged one. Memories of the war were fresh, the wounds were still raw, and many dead bodies lay unburied around Appomattox Court House and Sayler's Creek. Johnson insisted that as commander in chief he could override anything done by Grant at Appomattox. Grant objected that the rebels had surrendered on these terms, Lincoln had honored them, and there would have been "endless guerrilla warfare" without this leniency.[31]

Everybody knew that the treatment of Lee, with his tremendous moral authority, would sway southern opinion during the postwar era. In early May, Halleck informed Grant that many of Lee's officers had lined up to take amnesty oaths and that Lee himself contemplated petitioning Johnson for a pardon. "Should he do this, the whole population with few exceptions will follow his example," Halleck insisted.[32] Willing to take heat on the issue, Grant showed courage and fairness in endorsing merciful treatment for Lee. "Although it would meet with opposition in the North to allow Lee the benefit of Amnesty," Grant told Halleck, "I think it would have the best possible effect towards restoring good feeling and peace in the South to have him come in."[33]

Any chance for such a harmonious outcome was shattered in late May when federal judge John C. Underwood, a northern abolitionist, convened a grand jury in Norfolk, Virginia, for the express purpose of indicting Lee and other Confederate leaders for treason. Underwood belittled the Appomattox agreement as "a mere military arrangement" that "can have no influence upon civil rights or the status of the persons interested."[34] Following the judge's lead, the grand jury returned indictments against Lee, Joseph Johnston, James Longstreet, and other high-ranking Confederate generals.

Lee was stunned. Having pledged his sacred honor at Appomattox, Grant was no less flabbergasted that his agreement was being retroactively nullified. Lee sent out feelers to determine whether Grant would support his clemency request and word filtered back that Grant would stand by his solemn pledge at

Appomattox. On June 13, Lee wrote to Grant and asked for confirmation that officers and men of the Army of Northern Virginia had surrendered under terms protecting them "from molestation, so long as they Conformed to its conditions."[35] He enclosed a pardon application "with the earnest recommendation that, this application of Gen. R. E. Lee for amnesty and pardon may be granted him."[36] Grant saw a battle royal ahead with Johnson as to whether he had exceeded his authority at Appomattox. He jogged Stanton's memory that "the terms granted by me met with the hearty approval of the President at the time, and of the country generally. The action of Judge Underwood in Norfolk has already had an injurious effect, and I would ask that he be ordered to quash all indictments found against paroled prisoners of war, and to desist from further prosecution of them."[37]

On June 16, Grant met with Andrew Johnson at the White House and the two men engaged in a testy exchange about the fate of Lee and other Confederate generals. Johnson reiterated his vow to make "treason odious" and demanded, "When can these men be tried?" "Never," answered Grant, "unless they violate their paroles."[38] Grant summarized the dispute:

> Mr. Johnson spoke of Lee, and wanted to know why any military commander had a right to protect an arch-traitor from the laws. I was angry at this, and I spoke earnestly and plainly to the President. I said, that as General, it was none of my business what he or Congress did with General Lee or his other commanders . . . That did not come in my province. But a general commanding troops has certain responsibilities and duties and power, which are supreme. He must deal with the enemy in front of him so as to destroy him . . . His engagements are sacred so far as they lead to the destruction of the foe. I had made certain terms with Lee . . . If I had told him and his army that their liberty would be invaded, that they would be open to arrest, trial, and execution for treason, Lee would never have surrendered, and we should have lost many lives in destroying him. Now my terms of surrender were according to military law, and so long as Lee was observing his parole I would never consent to his arrest . . . I should have resigned the command of the army rather than have carried out any order directing me to arrest Lee or any of his commanders who obeyed the laws.[39]

Grant didn't lightly throw down a gauntlet in this way. When he returned to the War Department, he notified his staff, "I will not stay in the army if they break the pledges that I made."[40] Johnson must have known the damage Grant's resignation would do to his administration and Grant won the confrontation hands down. On June 20, at Johnson's behest, Attorney General James Speed ordered the U.S. attorney in Norfolk to abandon Lee's prosecution. On the same day, Grant informed Lee that no further actions would be taken to place him behind bars. Lee predicted that the government would procrastinate in granting his pardon, though he couldn't have predicted that his civil liberties and right to vote would not be restored until Johnson's broad amnesty in December 1868. His citizenship wasn't fully restored in his lifetime and more than a hundred years passed before it was posthumously accomplished through a joint congressional resolution in 1975.

As news spread that Grant had saved Lee, it confirmed his special status as a forgiving, merciful northern general. As one southern editorial writer said, "Though a past uncompromising enemy of that successful Captain, we now take a special pleasure in recording this our testimony to his soldierly good faith." The paper quoted a ringing paean from the Alabama politician Clement Clay: "Gen. GRANT is not disposed to oppress the South; on the contrary he is striving to lighten her burden."[41]

With the treason indictment behind him, Lee accepted the presidency of Washington College in Lexington, Virginia, a quiet town in the shadow of the Blue Ridge Mountains, where he hoped to dodge the spotlight. But the war's passions hadn't subsided. William Lloyd Garrison wondered how "the vanquished leader of the rebel armies" could inculcate in his students loyalty to the Union "which he so lately attempted to destroy!"[42] Lee ducked attempts to draft him into politics, calling it "extremely unpleasant" that his "name should be unnecessarily brought before the public."[43] Although he preached acceptance of the war's verdict, he remained an unreconstructed southerner. Where he had once emphasized his original opposition to secession, he now stressed states' rights and constitutional principles to justify the South's action, clinging to a prejudiced view of blacks. As he told a cousin, "I have always observed that wherever you find the Negro, everything is going down around him, and wherever you find the white man, you see everything around him improving."[44] In February 1866, he testified before Congress to oppose suffrage for former slaves: "My own opinion is that, at this time, they cannot vote intelligently, and that giving them

the right of suffrage would open the door to a great deal of demagoguism, and
lead to embarrassments in various ways."[45]

Most consequential for Grant's historic reputation was the way southerners of
the Lost Cause school would begin to idealize Lee, portraying him as a gallant,
noble general who had far outshone Grant and lost the war only because his opponent was backed by limitless manpower and industrial machinery. Even in the
North, praise for Lee grew so effusive that Frederick Douglass would complain in
the 1870s, "We can scarcely take up a newspaper that is not filled with *nauseating*
flatteries of the late Robert E. Lee."[46] However statesmanlike he outwardly appeared, Lee remained a southern partisan, privately lamenting "the vindictiveness
and malignity of the Yankees, of which he had no conception before the war."[47] He
never retreated from his retrograde views on slavery, signing a manifesto during
the 1868 presidential campaign that proclaimed: "The idea that Southern people
are hostile to the negroes and would oppress them . . . is entirely unfounded . . .
They have grown up in our midst, and we have been accustomed from childhood
to look upon them with kindness."[48] The signers proposed a restoration of the
"'kindness and humanity' of their former social system."[49] Grant came to believe
that Lee, far from accepting the war's outcome gracefully, was secretly hostile to it
and abetted southern fantasies that their defeated cause would rise anew.

While Lee's case was the most celebrated, Grant furnished legal protection to
scores of southern generals who turned to him for pardons. One by one the top
brass of the Confederate army besieged him with doleful letters. Grant's most improbable intervention came on behalf of John Singleton Mosby, the notorious
"Gray Ghost," whose raiders had bedeviled his army in northern Virginia. Mosby's
wife went to President Johnson in distress and pleaded that her husband couldn't
earn a living as a lawyer because his freedom of movement was restricted. Grant
issued a safe conduct that allowed Mosby to move about, rescuing him financially.
Mosby repaid the surprising kindness by becoming a steadfast friend and ally of
Grant, who later described him as "an honest, brave, conscientious man."[50]

For Grant, there remained an unfinished piece of business from the Civil
War: Mexico. In 1862, Napoleon III began to send an army of occupation to
Mexico, under the pretext of collecting overdue debts, to topple the legitimate
government of Benito Juárez and install a puppet regime under Ferdinand Maximilian, an Austrian archduke. Lincoln had grown alarmed for multiple reasons:

the invasion had flouted the Monroe Doctrine, provided potential asylum for Confederate soldiers, and might lead France to side with the Confederacy. Refusing to recognize this forcibly imposed government, Lincoln rushed to shore up Union forces in Texas to stem any possible French incursion from Mexico.

Ever since Grant had fought there as a young soldier, Mexico had exerted a powerful romantic charm over his imagination. A confirmed republican, he feared the French action was "a foothold for establishing a European monarchy upon our continent . . . I, myself, regarded this as a direct act of war against the United States."[51] There was so much cross-border skulduggery between France and the rebels during the Civil War—the Confederacy regularly smuggled supplies across the Rio Grande while its soldiers used Mexico for sanctuary—that Grant classified Napoleon III as "an active part of the rebellion."[52] Convinced his position reflected the sentiments of many Union soldiers, he lobbied President Johnson and Secretary of State Seward for postwar action against Mexico. Right after Appomattox, a young staff officer recalled, Grant returned to his office one day and announced, "Now for Mexico."[53] According to Matías Romero, a Mexican minister allied with Benito Juárez who plotted with Grant to liberate his country, the lieutenant general told him that "60,000 veterans from the United States would march into Mexico as soon as they were mustered out, and this government would not oppose that action."[54]

With such decided views on Mexico, Grant allowed his political judgment, which could be faulty, to supersede his military caution. During the war, he had been exemplary in bowing to civilian leadership, whereas he now tried to circumvent the secretary of state. On May 17, 1865, he dispatched Phil Sheridan with fifty thousand men to pacify Texas and parts of Louisiana still controlled by the Confederate general Edmund Kirby Smith, offering him the same surrender terms granted to Lee and Johnston. Such actions fell well within Grant's jurisdiction as general in chief, but he had an ulterior motive in advising Sheridan to line up a strong force along the Rio Grande. He pictured Sheridan fording the Rio Grande, joining up with Juárez, and proceeding to overthrow Maximilian. Better a small war now, Grant reckoned, than a larger one later on. Like Grant, Sheridan regarded Maximilian's downfall as the war's final phase and subscribed wholeheartedly to the plan. It was atypical of Grant to defy the avowed wishes of the secretary of state. "With regard to this matter," Sheridan recalled, Grant had said it would be necessary "to act with great circumspection, since the Secretary of State, Mr. Seward, was much opposed to the use of our troops along the border in any active way that would be likely to involve us in a war with European powers."[55]

During the war, Grant had grown acquainted with Seward when he visited the City Point headquarters. Henry Adams thought the secretary possessed "a head like a wise macaw," with its gray hair and thickly tufted eyebrows.[56] Disfigured by a knife attack the day Lincoln was shot, Seward still bore an enormous scar on his right cheek. A short, affable man, he liked to smoke, drink, and hold court in a rasping voice, issuing oracular statements. Perhaps it was inevitable that Grant and Seward would clash: Grant was blunt and straightforward in style, while Seward prided himself on being a master of diplomatic wiles. In time, Grant came to think that Seward had sacrificed his principles to retain his influence under President Johnson.

With Mexico Grant played a dangerous game, hoping to reunite North and South under the banner of a popular foreign war. Under Sheridan's invigorating leadership, he thought such a war would be "short, quick, decisive, and assuredly triumphant," smashing Napoleon's Mexican empire with one blow.[57] Seward imagined he could accomplish the same goals bloodlessly through patient diplomacy. On June 30, Grant received a message from Sheridan that vindicated his most vivid fears: defeated Confederates were sacking federal arsenals and hauling artillery across the border into Mexico. "Everything on wheels artillery horses mules . . . have been run over into Mexico. Large and small bands of rebel soldiers and some citizens amounting to about two thousand have crossed the Rio Grande into Mexico."[58] This evoked the specter that renegade rebels might perpetuate the war in exile, producing the very guerrilla chaos Grant had worked so hard to avoid. A rump group of rebel soldiers formed a colony west of Vera Cruz called Carlota, which soon burgeoned into a community of five thousand people. Among southern generals flocking to sanctuary in Mexico were Jubal Early, Edmund Kirby Smith, Sterling Price, J. B. Magruder, and Joseph Shelby as well as governors of three southern states and members of the Confederate cabinet. With Maximilian's connivance, these refugees began to advertise in southern newspapers that cheap land and labor were plentiful in Mexico.

At a June 16 cabinet meeting, Grant made a vigorous case for a confrontational approach with Maximilian, arguing that Confederate refugees would join the latter's imperial army and precipitate hostilities with the U.S. government. He predicted a long, bloody war, fueled by thousands of former Confederate soldiers, and proposed that the federal government issue a solemn protest against the Mexican monarchy. Seward, in an eloquent rebuttal, said this tough approach would "wound French pride and produce a war with France." In his estimation, Maximilian's reign "was rapidly perishing, and, if let alone, Maximilian would leave in less than six months, perhaps in sixty days, whereas, if we interfered, it would prolong his stay and the Empire also."[59] After this debate, Gideon Welles issued his private verdict that "Seward acts from intelligence, Grant from impulse."[60] Cynical and curmudgeonly, Welles spied in Grant's concern for Mexico a concealed taste for power, writing that he "naturally perhaps, desires to retain a large military force in service."[61] The war had certainly made Grant far more accustomed to exercising power, but he had been active in disbanding troops ever since Appomattox.

The Mexican question roiled Johnson's cabinet and grew only more heated when the president read aloud on July 14 a truculent letter from Sheridan that was endorsed by Grant. Sheridan bragged that his army was in "magnificent trim" and hoped shortly to "have the pleasure of crossing the Rio Grande with them with our faces turned towards the city of Mexico."[62] Secretary of the Treasury Hugh McCulloch warned that a Mexican war might bankrupt the U.S. government. For his part, Seward was astounded by Sheridan's bellicose message. "Said if we got in war and drove out the French, we could not get out ourselves," Welles recorded.[63] Meanwhile, Grant advocated deeper involvement in Mexico by sending a general there to act as a liaison with liberal forces and sell them arms from federal surplus stock. When General John Schofield was chosen as the intermediary, Seward adroitly steered him to Paris instead, telling him "to get your legs under Napoleon's mahogany and tell him to get out of Mexico."[64] Grant's hawkish stand on Mexico helped Seward's dovish diplomatic efforts since the latter could present himself to the French as a peaceful alternative to Grant's belligerence.

Even though Seward made clear that the United States would rely on diplomacy to settle differences with Mexico, Grant clung to a more muscular policy. On August 10, *The New York Times* carried an interview in which Grant warned that "the French would have to leave Mexico peaceably, if they chose, but forcibly if they refused."[65] Grant denied making any such explicit threat, but he was clearly applying pressure on the administration instead of passively serving as its chief soldier. In early September, he renewed his obsessive campaign against Mexico, telling Johnson that the United States should serve notice on the French to withdraw their troops. Sheridan found it difficult to restrain his men from crossing the Rio Grande. All the while, imperial French troops continued to extend their control over Mexico.

OUTSIDE OF WASHINGTON, Grant remained a celebrity, smothered with adulation everywhere. It was impossible to restrain admirers who surged around him at every turn. On June 8, he attended commencement exercises at West Point and was embraced by Winfield Scott, gray eminence of the army, who lived in a hotel on the academy grounds. "Thank God you have passed through so much peril unharmed," Scott exclaimed upon seeing Grant. "Welcome to my bachelor home!"[66] Such camaraderie must have seemed dreamlike to Grant, who had first glimpsed the majestic Scott as a West Point plebe. Now the two men strolled arm in arm, as comfortable as well-worn pals. Still tremendously tall, Scott was white-haired, corpulent, and wrinkled and sat with Julia on a verandah while Grant surveyed marching cadets. Having recently published his memoirs, he gave Grant a copy with a warm inscription that must have bowled him over: "From the oldest to the greatest General of the Army of the United States."[67] Before long, Fred Grant would enter the academy and Grant noted proudly he was "full three inches taller than I was when I entered West Point and better prepared."[68]

From July 24 through October 6, Grant embarked on a tour of the East and Midwest with Julia, the four children, and an entourage that included Babcock, Badeau, Parker, and Porter. The trip brought home how much the modest Grant had become a helpless casualty of his own fame. William Wrenshall Smith left this impression of a beleaguered Grant on the road:

> He was so famous and so celebrated that everyone wanted to stare at him and shake him to death . . . crowds gathered by the 50,000 to look at him. He seemed to shrink away from them, to be pained by the attentions paid to him, but the people loved him better for it. When the crowds would gather thick and fast, he sometimes clenched his hands together, as if pained by it all. He also liked to have his young son Jesse stand in front of him because Jesse was a little show off and seemed to deflect the people. Grant stood with his hands on his small son's shoulders, never seeing anything, just mechanically shaking and looking on absently. It was a terrible drain on him.[69]

Admitting to a poor memory for speeches, though not for faces, Grant declared that public speaking was "a terrible trial for me."[70] He considered the political custom of shaking hands "a great nuisance" that should be abolished and complained that the 1865 trip left his right arm sore.[71] At a Chicago fair, Grant announced that his hands were so swollen he would shake no more hands. A woman protested loudly that it didn't matter, since the women wanted to kiss him. "Well," Grant joked, "none of them have offered to do it yet."[72] The women called his bluff by rushing forward in considerable numbers to give him a buss. Being the object of such female adoration was a completely novel experience for Grant.

The most rapturous reception came in Galena, where he arrived aboard a private car provided by the railway company. When a fellow passenger noted the contrast between this luxurious conveyance and the Wilderness, Grant retorted, "Yes, it is very fine; and but for the suffering of the men I greatly prefer the wilderness."[73] Five years before Grant had arrived in Galena in a state of shame and misery. Now ten thousand people greeted him, backed by brass bands, thunderous cannon, and blizzards of bunting. A political agenda informed the town's decision to honor Grant. Elihu Washburne and local officials had grown worried when he accepted the Philadelphia house and declared he would reside there. In Galena this was regarded as a serious breach of faith, even though Grant had resided there only one year before the war. In May, Washburne reminded Grant that he first "commanded an Illinois regiment" and "was appointed a brigadier general, a major general and a lieutenant general, all from Illinois, and I may say all, through Illinois influences."[74] This was a not-so-subtle reference to Washburne's steadfast sponsorship. In reply, Grant promised Washburne he would vote in Galena at the next election and officially proclaim it as home.[75] But Grant, having scaled national heights, wasn't eager to crawl back into the prosaic life of a small town in western Illinois.

Grant strode through Galena's streets beneath flowery arches, one emblazoned with the names of his famous victories. He had once quipped that he wanted to be town mayor so he could put in a new sidewalk from his house to the station, and one arch announced in floral lettering: "General, *the sidewalk is built*."[76] Near the old leather goods store where he had labored, Grant was pelted with bouquets by thirty-six girls, representing the states of the Union. After Washburne delivered a speech, the Grants were ushered to a fully furnished house, a gift of local businessmen costing $16,000 and designed to tether them to the town. Beautifully situated on a prime hilltop location, it had lawns sloping away to afford fine vistas. Grant was moved by the transformation four years had wrought and one neighbor spotted "tears trickling down his cheeks" as he left the house.[77] Grant told Rawlins he found the Galena reception "flattering though somewhat embarrassing" and wished the generosity had been lavished on him when he most needed it.[78] Another time, upon receiving a costly overcoat, he commented, "There have been times in my life when the gift of an overcoat would have been an act of charity. No one gave it to me when I needed it. Now when I am able to pay for all I need, such gifts are continually thrust upon me."[79] The Galena house remained something of a showpiece for Grant, grand and a trifle stuffy, and it never showed the true imprint of his residence.

Whenever he visited Galena, Grant shied away from the leather goods store, which didn't stop Jesse Root Grant from cashing in on his son's presence in the most mercenary fashion. He wrote this advertising jingle for the *Galena Gazette:* "Since Grant has whipped the Rebel Lee / And opened trade from sea to sea / Our goods in price must soon advance / Then don't neglect the present chance / To Call on GRANT and PERKINS. J.R.G."[80] Old family jealousies still festered and Orvil's wife, Mary, reacted to Grant's visit with her old tart-tongued perspective about her brother-in-law. "He was the same, maybe a little more self impressed, but Julia was much worse," she said. "She still ran after him, bragged on him, told me, 'Isn't he ever more handsome with his three-star boards?' and like nonsense. She togged herself in expensive clothes, but he still was dressed like he rolled out of bed, though Julia always said he was the handsomest soldier, always fussing and hovering over him, which he lapped up like a boy in a confectionery."[81]

Later in the trip, returning to another scene of dismal failure, Grant visited St. Louis and was feted by ten thousand people in Lafayette Park, culminating in a congratulatory speech by Missouri's lieutenant governor. On the way back to Washington, he made a side trip to Covington to visit his parents. Hannah Grant was as hesitant to bask in her son's fame as Jesse was eager. She had been horrified on July Fourth when she was coaxed onto a political platform outside Cincinnati amid earsplitting applause. Now she wanted to make sure her son wasn't spoiled by idolatry. "Well, Ulysses," she said in her no-nonsense style, standing in her apron, "you've become a great man, haven't you?"[82] Then she proceeded with her usual round of chores, avoiding any show of maternal warmth.

BACK IN WASHINGTON in early October, Grant compiled a report that charted the army's reorganization from a war footing to peacetime conditions. He proudly informed Stanton that the Armies of the Potomac and the Tennessee had been disbanded in July without major disruptions. Grant already had a premonition that the army would occupy a central role in Reconstruction and suggested an eighty-thousand-man peacetime force to deal with "unsettled questions between the white and black races at the south."[83] He wanted the president to have authority to raise an additional twenty thousand black troops if necessary. "Colored troops can garrison the sea coast entirely," he told General George Thomas, "and the number of interior posts may be reduced as low as you deem expedient."[84] In the end, prodded by Stanton, Grant reduced the projected army to fifty-three thousand soldiers.

As Grant toiled under heavy burdens, Rawlins felt duty-bound to assist him. He assembled much of the material for the army report, which Grant wrote in his home library. With the war over, Rawlins had hoped to devote time to recovering his health, but Grant's crammed schedule made that difficult. Grant remained solicitous of Rawlins's health, urging him to spend several months recuperating at his new Galena home. "The house presented to me by the kindness of the Citizens is entirely at your service if you choose to do so," he told Rawlins. "You will find it very comfortable and containing everything necessary for housekeeping."[85] But Rawlins found it difficult to tear himself away from Washington as the debate over the military and Reconstruction grew ever more acrimonious.

With the army report off his desk, Grant allowed himself another interval of hoopla and hero worship in New York, arriving there by private railway car and staying for ten days. On November 20, flanked by General Joseph Hooker and magnate William B. Astor, he attended a reception in his honor at the posh Fifth Avenue Hotel that seemed to contain every luminary in the city. Suddenly Grant was the darling of the city's plutocrats. Generals galore were there, including Winfield Scott, John C. Frémont, George Gordon Meade, Ambrose Burnside, and Lew Wallace, as well as poets, journalists, and five senators. Three thousand people supped on oysters and champagne before watching a fireworks display outside. The Grants also hobnobbed with high society, attending a dinner party thrown by George Templeton Strong. "Mrs. Grant is the plainest of country women," Strong wrote, "but a lady, inasmuch as she shows no trace of affectation or assumption, and frankly admits herself wholly ignorant of the social usages of New York."[86] While Grant's aides tired of this social whirl, Grant soaked up the attention, perhaps showing the first signs of political ambition. His intimates feared this might look like grandstanding or even a blatant attempt to upstage President Johnson. "If everybody knew him as you and I do, it would be different," wrote Washburne to Badeau, "but as they do not, they attribute to him motives that we know never entered his head." Happy that Grant and Johnson seemed in "perfect accord," Washburne hoped Grant would succeed him as president in the 1868 race.[87]

As the year progressed, Grant was drawn ever more deeply into the debate on Reconstruction. In early March 1865, the federal government had assumed responsibility for aiding freed slaves through the creation of the Freedmen's Bureau. Since it was set up as a War Department agency, drawing funds and staff from it, Grant was directly involved in its operations. The bureau's mandate was to feed, clothe, and educate former slaves, providing them with medical supplies and legal protection and relocating them on more than 850,000 acres of land the federal government came to control during the war. It was overseen by General Oliver O. Howard, whom Grant had met outside Chattanooga and who later helped to found Howard University.

Because southern slaves had inhabited a rural culture, the pivotal issue for their future was whether they could receive land from the federal government. With a plot of land, they had a chance for an independent life; if condemned to remain landless, they would be thrown back into servitude to the same plantation barons who had owned them. On August 16, Johnson issued an order that allowed southern whites to recapture land confiscated from them during the war—a move that made him heroic to whites while dealing a crushing blow to black hopes. It forced freedmen to abandon the forty-acre plots they had started to work, turning the men into powerless sharecroppers, bound to land owned by whites. Within weeks, a white delegation from the former Confederacy rushed to the White House to express "sincere respect" for Johnson's desire "to sustain Southern rights in the Union."[88]

By the end of 1865, so-called Black Codes began to forge a new caste system in the South, a segregated world where freed slaves worked as indentured servants, subject to arrest if they left jobs before their annual contracts expired. It was a cruel new form of bondage, establishing the foundations of the Jim Crow system that later ruled southern race relations. In South Carolina, blacks were confined by law to their plantations, forced to work from sunup to sundown. In Florida, blacks who showed "disrespect" to their bosses or rode in public conveyances reserved for whites could be whipped and pilloried. In Mississippi, it became a criminal offense for blacks to hunt or fish, heightening their dependence upon white employers. Thus, within six months of the end of the Civil War, there arose a broadly based retreat from many of the ideals that had motivated the northern war effort, reestablishing the status quo ante and white supremacy in the old Confederacy.

During the summer of 1865, President Johnson sent Carl Schurz, the Prussian-born journalist and Union general, to the South to report on the progress of Reconstruction. His forty-six-page report didn't present the rosy view of a reconciled South that Johnson preferred. Instead he painted the white South as angry and defiant, still insisting that secession had been legitimate. His portrayal of freed blacks described them as languishing in wretched conditions of poverty, reinforced by Black Codes that trapped them in a new subservience. For Radical Republicans, the Schurz report crystallized their discontent with Johnson's approach to Reconstruction, which seemed to favor whites instead of blacks. Even though Johnson blocked the document, excerpts appeared in the *Boston Daily Advertiser.* So strongly did the president deplore the report that he said his sole error thus far as president had been to dispatch Schurz to the South.

To undo the damage, Johnson decided in late November to exploit Grant's prestige and send him south on a fact-finding tour. Grant was already fielding reports from southern commanders that suggested a resurgence of violence in the region, with many white atrocities against blacks. George Meade warned that withdrawing federal troops "would very likely be followed by a war of races," while General Peter J. Osterhaus said white militias, with telltale names such as the Jeff Davis Guards, were springing up across Mississippi.[89] At first, Grant wavered as to whether he should undertake such a risky assignment and was perhaps swayed by Cyrus Comstock's advice that "he had better go so that he might be able to speak decidedly on questions of reconstruction."[90]

As he pondered the region's future, Grant was mildly sanguine that with slavery's demise, a widespread social transformation would overtake the region. Had the Confederacy won the war, he thought, it would have become a pariah state in the world economy, doomed to stagnation. Slavery, he later wrote, had been a barbaric system that "degraded labor, kept it in ignorance, and enervated the governing class."[91] He hoped that poor downtrodden whites who had never owned slaves would now make common cause with northern liberals rather than the large planters who had conspired to keep them in an impoverished, dependent state.

On November 27, Grant headed south along with Comstock, Babcock, and Badeau. The two-week trip was terribly brief and superficial, taking them through Virginia, the Carolinas, Georgia, and Tennessee, before returning to Washington on December 11. The ruinous state of southern railroads made the journey slow and oppressive. Eager to rush back to Washington for the opening of Congress, Grant felt himself a prisoner to an overly tight schedule. In many towns his time was consumed by ceremonial visits from mayors, aldermen, and merchants as well as ex-rebel governors and former Confederate cabinet members. While he reviewed a black regiment on the Sea Islands of Georgia, he spent most of his fleeting trip huddled with white leaders. In Raleigh, North Carolina, he met with committees from both houses of the legislature and sent this bland synopsis to Julia: "There seems to be the best of feeling existing . . . by both original Secessionists and Unionists, to act in such a way as to secure admittance back and to please the general Government."[92] Everywhere Grant was lavishly complimented by white southerners who honored his charity at Appomattox. Badeau summed up the fawning treatment: "The man who had done most to subdue the South was universally recognized as its protector and savior from further suffering."[93] Unfortunately, such reverence made it impossible for Grant to deliver the astringent, cold-eyed critique the situation required.

Cyrus Comstock kept a diary of the trip that provides glimpses of the South that tally with Carl Schurz's assessment, not Grant's. In Charleston, he spoke to Oliver O. Howard's brother, who told him that "the feeling between whites & negroes is bad, the negroes having no trust in the whites & the latter fearing a rising."[94] He noted that many southern ladies made angry faces at Yankee officers. En route to Augusta, when they were all squeezed into an ambulance car, they passed a former rebel soldier who called out, "Well if there ain't a whole coach full of full blooded Yankees."[95] At the close of the trip, Comstock came up with a blunt assessment: "There is much bitter feeling still at the south . . . the government will have to exercise some control over the south for a year to come to secure the best treatment of the negro."[96]

On December 18, the Thirteenth Amendment, which banned slavery, went into effect. Until then slavery had remained legal in most southern states, making the amendment more than merely symbolic. It presented a pivotal moment in attitudes toward Reconstruction. William Lloyd Garrison closed up shop at *The Liberator,* believing the work of emancipation done. With the amendment and the creation of state governments in the South, Seward imagined Reconstruction would soon be completed. For Radical Republicans, however, the hard work had only just begun. "Liberty has been won," contended Senator Charles Sumner. "The battle for Equality is still pending." Unless freed blacks received the vote, warned Frederick Douglass, "we should have slavery back again, in spirit if not in form."[97]

On the same day the amendment was ratified, Grant filed his report on his southern trip with Andrew Johnson, presenting his findings in unconvincingly Panglossian terms. "I am satisfied that the mass of thinking men of the South accept the present situation of affairs in good faith. The questions which have heretofore divided the sentiment of the people of the two sections, Slavery and States Rights . . . they regard as having been settled forever."[98] To assure the safety of blacks and whites, Grant suggested the maintenance of small garrisons in the South. In a controversial passage, he recommended that only white troops should be stationed in the southern interior, appeasing white fears that black soldiers might "instigate" their southern brethren: "The presence of Black troops, lately slaves, demoralizes labor both by their advice and furnishing in their camps a resort for the Freedmen for long distances around. White troops generally excited no opposition."[99] Grant opposed land redistribution, which had excited so much hope among freedmen, saying "the late slave seems to be imbued with the idea that the property of his late master should by right belong to him."[100] Such thinking could incite dangerous collisions, he was persuaded, and he blamed agents of the Freedmen's Bureau for fomenting such incendiary ideas. On the other hand, he urged the bureau's continuance to safeguard black rights.

In his laudable desire to restore goodwill between North and South and remain the grand conciliatory figure of Appomattox, Grant had submitted a remarkably naive, anodyne report. While presuming to know the thoughts of freed people, he hadn't spent much time with them. He showed a desire to protect black civil liberties, but recapitulated the party line fed to him by white planters when he wrote that unrealistic fantasies about receiving land from their former plantations discouraged blacks from signing labor contracts. Pleased that Grant had submitted a report endorsing his conservative policies, Johnson sent

it to the Senate along with the antithetical one by Carl Schurz. White southerners were predictably pleased by Grant's report, while Radical Republicans in
Congress, who had their own plans for Reconstruction, denounced it as a white-
wash of presidential policies. Close readers of the report noted that Grant hadn't
relinquished his desire to protect freed slaves, and the radical *Boston Daily Advertiser* emphasized his statement that the federal government "shall stand as the
guardian of those whom it has freed, until it sees them firmly established in the
rights of citizenship."[101]

Historians have been quick to pounce on the blind spots in Grant's report.
Less noticed is that he almost immediately recanted what he wrote. As early as
January 12, 1866, Carl Schurz informed his wife that "Grant feels very bad
about his thoughtless move and has openly expressed regret for what he has
done."[102] When Schurz encountered Grant at a soldiers' reunion in December
1868, Grant was still more regretful, admitting that on his southern tour "I traveled as the general-in-chief and people who came to see me tried to appear to the
best advantage. But I have since come to the conclusion that you were right and
I was wrong."[103] Here Grant echoed a famous line Abraham Lincoln had written
to him, showing he was a big enough man to confess frankly to past error. In the
future, he wouldn't pull his punches about black-white relations in the South or
the need for decisive military action to safeguard freed people.

Swing Around the Circle

W HEN THE NEW CONGRESS met in December 1865, it grew crystal-clear to Radical Republicans that Andrew Johnson's Reconstruction policies were slanted toward the entrenched white South. Southern states sent white representatives to Washington who reflected the old Confederacy, not a newly reconstituted region, leading Radicals to take matters into their own hands. Congress set up a Joint Committee on Reconstruction, cochaired by a moderate Republican senator, William Pitt Fessenden of Maine, and Representative Thaddeus Stevens of Pennsylvania, an ardent abolitionist. Johnson saw this as an attempt by the legislative branch to wrest away prerogatives that properly belonged to the executive. Radicals advanced the argument that Confederate states, by seceding, had relinquished their former rights as sovereign states and should be treated like territories, their terms of readmission defined by Congress. Guided by this perspective, they refused to seat new southern congressmen or admit their states back into the Union. For all their excessive zeal, these militant Republicans would produce some of the most powerful legislation in American history to accord equal rights to African Americans.

Instead of the bromides Grant had doled out about southern harmony, the Joint Committee delved into violence inflicted on two particular groups. One was the so-called carpetbaggers, tens of thousands of young northerners who flocked southward to earn money and aid freed people. They built schools and churches, bought plantations, and often risked their lives to assist blacks. In southern mythology, they would be demonized as corrupt parasites, but many were motivated by idealism and paid a steep price for their courage. Southern whites who supported Reconstruction, called "scalawags," faced similar antipathy.

Carpetbagger harassment was tame compared with the outright terror inflicted on blacks. One former Louisiana slave testified that whites flogged blacks as if they were still enslaved and that more than two thousand had been killed around Shreveport in 1865 alone. Blacks enjoyed little recourse to local sheriffs, who were often Confederate veterans and seldom acted against whites charged with crimes against blacks. It grew patently obvious that southern blacks could count on protection only from federal troops. As one Mississippi observer pleaded: "Take away garrisons from this Southern Country, and the negroes will be subjected to every outrage."[1] From Georgia came warnings of a new breed of nocturnal terror unleashed against blacks. General Rufus Saxton reported a black man killed "by a band of disguised men at midnight"—a grisly scene reenacted many times in coming years.[2] As southern blacks came to rely on the U.S. military for protection, Grant was thrust smack into the middle of the controversy. A man of fixed purpose, he never faltered in his deep concern for the fair treatment of freed people. On January 12, 1866, he took aim at anti-black discrimination when he issued General Orders No. 3, which protected "colored persons from prosecutions" in any southern state "charged with offenses for which white persons are not prosecuted or punished in the same manner and degree."[3]

Supplied with copious and quite graphic reports by southern commanders, Grant soon realized that the hopeful tenor of his December report had been a pipe dream. After dispatching Cyrus Comstock to New Orleans to confer with Generals Edward Canby and Phil Sheridan, he received a sobering report in late January: "Saw Gen. Canby who says feeling is worse now than at close of war. He & Sheridan both say northern men could not stay south if martial law were revoked or troops withdrawn, as they could get no justice from courts . . . Canby says if troops were withdrawn, the negroes would be far worse off than before the war, being no longer property to be cared for."[4]

On February 7, President Johnson met at the White House with five black leaders, including Frederick Douglass, who came to lobby for a civil rights bill. The black leaders were treated in a tasteless, abusive manner. After they shook hands with the president, their spokesman, George T. Downing, said they hoped he would support voting rights for blacks, which elicited a bizarre, rambling monologue from Johnson. He admitted to having owned slaves, but boasted of never having sold one, as if that would somehow ingratiate him with his visitors. He presented himself as a kindly master who had been "their slave instead of their being mine." To promote civil rights, Johnson went on, would "result in the extermination of one [race] or the other." If given the vote, "the colored man and his master, combined," would conspire to keep poor whites "in slavery," denying them a portion "of the rich land of the country."[5] After the bewildered delegation filed out, Johnson boasted to his secretary, "Those damned sons of bitches thought they had me in a trap."[6]

Around this time, cracks appeared in the facade of unity between Grant and Johnson. In mid-February, Grant shut down the *Richmond Examiner* for stridently disloyal editorials, lifting the order only when the president protested. Nonetheless, Grant instructed southern commanders that the "persistent publication of articles calculated to keep up a hostility of feeling between the people of different sections of the country cannot be tolerated."[7] He disputed a resolution of the Mississippi legislature demanding that federal troops be withdrawn, saying local authorities refused to execute the law and maintain order for blacks. He also plied the president with statistics showing that whites committed far more crimes against blacks than the reverse—44 more murders and 78 more assaults.[8]

That February, Johnson's relations with congressional Republicans soured further when Johnson vetoed a bill to extend the Freedmen's Bureau. In his veto message, he cast scorn on the bureau as an "immense patronage" scheme that only cosseted indolent blacks.[9] In fact, the bureau was poorly financed and chronically understaffed, never fielding more than nine hundred agents in the South. Under slavery, more than 90 percent of the adult black population had been illiterate, and the bureau had performed superlative work in helping young evangelicals and northern aid societies to teach them to read. The former slaves reacted with an unquenchable thirst for education. By early 1866, a bureau official calculated "that half a million of these poor people are now studying the spelling-book, or advanced readers."[10] Outraged by the veto, Radicals retaliated with a joint resolution stating that no senator or representative from former Confederate states should be readmitted until Congress decided they were entitled to representation, thus sharpening the battle lines with Johnson.

On the night of February 22, Washington's birthday, a large throng of Johnson's supporters streamed to the White House to congratulate him on his veto message. The president exploited the occasion to rant against his foes in a wild-eyed, intemperate, egotistical manner, inveighing against Radical Republicans and the Joint Committee on Reconstruction. George Templeton Strong thought the president was intoxicated with "Old Bourbon" on the occasion: "He avowed himself at war with radicalism, and denounced Sumner in the Senate and Stevens of the House and [abolitionist] Wendell Phillips . . . as disunionists and traitors. He talked of Senators going about 'with assassination in their hearts' . . . This may result in an impeachment of the President within thirty days!"[11] It would take much longer to accomplish that goal, but the rabidly partisan speech polarized the capital in a way that foreshadowed that harrowing outcome.

In early March, Grant applied to Johnson to have his fifteen-year-old son Fred admitted to West Point and he was promptly accepted. Grant and longtime aide Theodore Bowers shepherded Fred to the academy for his entrance exams a few days later. Bowers was a thirty-three-year-old bachelor and former newspaperman from Illinois, a handsome, bearded young man with dark, wavy hair and expressive eyes. The Grant family had delighted in his self-deprecating humor. On the way home, Grant boarded the train at Garrison Station, across the Hudson River from the academy, but Bowers, running late, tried to leap onto the train as it left the station. Unable to find a solid footing, he got trapped between the train and the platform and was dragged along, then fell to the tracks and was run over by one wheel, which mangled his face, severed his arms, and killed him on the spot. When Grant got off the train to see what had happened, the rails were streaked with blood, his friend's body twisted beyond recognition. Those with Grant admired his stoic calm as he drafted orders to dispose of the body. Crushed by the calamity, he told Sherman, "The loss of poor Bowers is one that I feel more keenly than it is usually possible for anyone to feel for another not an immediate member of their own family."[12] It was typical of Grant to respond profoundly to death with inner grief but no outward show of emotion.

After attending Bowers's funeral at West Point, Grant returned to a capital preoccupied with the civil rights bill introduced by Radical Republicans to nullify Black Codes in the South that prevented freedmen from owning property, making contracts, and filing lawsuits. Though silent on voting rights, the bill sought to bring the full blessings of citizenship to anyone born in the United States, including blacks, protecting them by the "full and equal benefit of all laws."[13] (Native Americans were excluded.) This landmark legislation defined citizenship rights in a new manner that made the federal government, not the states, the guarantor of basic liberties.

On March 27, Andrew Johnson vetoed the bill, denouncing it for trespassing on states' rights. Instead of viewing it as a brave attempt to remedy historic injustice, he denigrated it for surpassing anything the federal government "has ever provided for the white race." Perversely, he interpreted it as a case of reverse discrimination "made to operate in favor of the colored and against the white race."[14] He heaped further insults on the black community by stating that immigrants had superior claims to American citizenship because they better understood "the nature and character of our institutions."[15] The veto was a reckless move by Johnson, the original bill having passed both houses by overwhelming margins. In a stunning rebuke, Congress dealt a resounding defeat to Johnson by overriding his veto. Johnson had damaged his standing, leading even moderate Republicans to distance themselves from him. "The feud between Johnson and the 'Radicals' grows more and more deadly every day," observed George Templeton Strong, "and threatens grave public mischief."[16]

Grant was caught in the dispute as both sides worked hard to lay claim to his incomparable prestige. Thinking it improper for army officers to take public stands on legislation, Grant had kept a punctilious silence on the civil rights bill, but Johnson was bent on enlisting his support whether he liked it or not. When Grant threw a glittering soiree at 205 I Street, President Johnson ventured outside the White House to stand between Ulysses and Julia Grant on the receiving line, and Radical Republicans were taken aback by his presence.

Grant's team of commanders in the South enforced the new Civil Rights Act. General Daniel Sickles abolished South Carolina's Black Code, stating that "all laws shall be applicable alike to all inhabitants," while General Alfred Terry barred Virginia's vagrancy law as an effort to restore "slavery in all but its name."[17] A backlash arose among white southerners, producing stepped-up vigilante activity as robed, hooded figures beat and murdered blacks. White northern teachers working with the Freedmen's Bureau faced death threats and black schools and churches were burned with impunity in North Carolina, Mississippi, and Alabama. Grant continued to present Johnson with statistics documenting racially motivated violence against blacks and added two new categories of coercion: driving off blacks "without compensation for labor" and "retaining freedmen without compensation."[18]

In early May, a vicious race riot in Memphis resulted in forty-eight blacks killed, seventy injured, and five black women raped in three days. On May 12, Major General George Stoneman reported to Grant from Memphis that the unrest was touched off when white policemen arrested two "boisterous" black men and hauled them to the station house, whereupon black bystanders wounded a police officer with a pistol shot. In retaliation, police gathered a mob of white citizens, some outfitted in Confederate uniforms, and "proceeded to shoot, beat, and threaten every negro met with in that portion of the city."[19] The next day, these white vigilantes set ablaze black schools, churches, and homes, one black witness alleging that white arsonists chanted calls for a "white man's government" as they spread mayhem.[20] "Thank heaven the white race are once more rulers of Memphis," the *Memphis Avalanche* editorialized with satisfaction.[21]

Grant empaneled a body to probe the Memphis riots. In reporting to Stanton, he showed that local authorities had tolerated a bloody vendetta by policemen and firemen against black citizens. What resulted "was a scene of murder, arson, rape & robbery in which the victims were all helpless and unresisting negroes, stamping lasting disgrace upon the civil authorities that permitted them."[22] Grant noted that the only protection afforded black citizens came from a small body of federal troops. He recommended that the riot instigators be held by the military until civil authorities in Memphis proved willing to prosecute them. Dispatching several cavalry companies, he gave them these pointed instructions: "If the Civil Authorities fail to make arrests for past violence let the troops make them and hold the parties in confinement until they, the Civil Authorities, give satisfactory evidence that justice will be done."[23] In General Orders No. 44, he generalized this policy to all southern states: "A strict and prompt enforcement of this order is required. By command of Lieutenant General Grant."[24] In the face of a recalcitrant president, Grant was rapidly emerging as the foremost protector of persecuted southern blacks.

He exhibited increasing militance in his view that only federal troops could provide safety for former slaves. On May 31, the *Missouri Democrat* ran an interview with Grant that he thought was off the record. His voice differed markedly from the soothing tone of his December report and was the more striking because of it. "Troops must be kept at all the principal points in the South for some time to come," he said. "This will be necessary to repress the turbulence of a class of the South very dangerous to well-disposed persons, and also to protect the rights of the freedmen, who are looked upon with deep hatred by a large proportion of the people."[25] He was incensed at the sudden defiance of southerners he had thought chastened. "A year ago they were willing to do anything; now they regard themselves as masters of the situation."[26] Then, most shockingly,

Grant pitched into Robert E. Lee: "Lee is behaving badly. He is conducting himself very differently from what I had reason, from what he said at the time of the surrender, to suppose he would. No man at the South is capable of exercising a tenth part of the influence for good that he is, but instead of using it, he is setting an example of forced acquiescence so grudging and pernicious in its effect as to be hardly realized."[27] Though he regretted his remarks were published, Grant never disavowed their authenticity.

Grant's belief that only federal troops could give southern blacks "a feeling of security" ran afoul of the conservative consensus hardening inside Johnson's cabinet.[28] On July 13, Attorney General Speed admitted to the president that the "most disgusting scenes of murder, arson, rape and robbery" had been practiced in Memphis against "helpless and unresisting colored citizens." But he forswore federal responsibility, wrapping himself in the righteous rhetoric of states' rights. He conceded that Grant's soldiers had done a creditable job in suppressing mob violence. "Having done that," Speed added, "they have . . . nothing to do with the redress of private grievances, or prosecutions for public wrongs."[29] This hands-off attitude was completely antithetical to the assertive use of federal power so strenuously expounded by Grant.

In June, Radical Republicans enacted the centerpiece of their legislative efforts to defend freed blacks, passing the Fourteenth Amendment, which engraved in the Constitution the principle of equal citizenship before the law regardless of race. It declared that all persons born or naturalized in the United States enjoyed both federal and state citizenship and prevented states from denying freedoms mandated by the Bill of Rights. Seeking to scotch the Black Codes, it denied states the right to deprive "any person of life, liberty, or property, without due process of law" and guaranteed all citizens "equal protection of the laws."[30] Andrew Johnson, who now gloried in taunting Congress, not only opposed the amendment but urged southern states to reject it, which they did. Nevertheless, the Fourteenth Amendment was ratified on July 9, 1868.

During the growing tug-of-war between Congress and Johnson to curry favor with Grant, Johnson recommended and Congress passed on July 25 an act to create especially for Grant the new grade of "General of the Army of the United States," with an annual salary of $20,000. As Mark Twain said, it gave Grant "that supreme and stately and simple one-word title, 'General,'" placing an unprecedented four stars on his shoulder straps and making him the first person since George Washington to hold the full general title.[31] In the reshuffling of military ranks that followed, Sherman became lieutenant general while Rawlins retained his chief of staff post.

Grant's elevation and the George Washington analogy inevitably spurred discussion about his possible ascent to the presidency. During the House debate, Thaddeus Stevens drew laughter when he volunteered his willingness to lift "this Marlborough, this Wellington" to "a higher office whenever the happy moment shall arrive."[32] When Sherman told Grant that spreading disillusionment with politicians was leading to a popular groundswell for him as president—a move Sherman thought would harm his pure-hearted friend—Grant did his best to reassure him: "All that I can say to discourage the idea of my ever being a candidate for an office I do say."[33] As a Democratic-leaning president and a Republican-dominated Congress vied for his favor, Grant tried to tiptoe modestly along the political tightrope suspended between them.

Of course, the one person who claimed to read Grant's mind with telepathic clarity was his father. In a published letter, Jesse ruled out a near-term presidential run by his son: "You know ULYSSES is not and never was an aspirant for any personal favor or promotion . . . to accept the Presidency would be to him a sacrifice of feeling and personal interest." At the same time, Jesse brashly opened the door for a future presidential race for his son, asserting that "if there should seem to be the same necessity for it two years hence, as now, I expect he will yield."[34] This letter appeared in *The New York Times* on September 24, 1866, as Grant labored to spike such speculation. As he had long since learned, it was impossible to curb these eruptions from his self-important, busybody father.

Political tensions flared on July 30 when racial violence broke out at a mostly black convention at the Mechanics' Institute in New Orleans, convened to remodel the state constitution and secure black voting rights. Goaded by Mayor John Monroe, a Confederate pardoned by Johnson, the local press had published inflammatory stories about the gathering. Around 1 p.m., a procession of black delegates marched to the institute, brandishing an American flag, when it clashed with a white mob, backed by police, many of them Confederate veterans. The whites stomped, kicked, and clubbed the black marchers mercilessly. Policemen smashed the institute's windows and fired into it indiscriminately until the floor grew slick with blood. When blacks inside shook a white flag from a window, the white policemen ignored it and invaded the building. They emptied their revolvers on the convention delegates, who desperately sought to escape. Some leapt from windows and were shot dead when they landed. Those lying wounded on the ground were stabbed repeatedly, their skulls bashed in with brickbats. The sadism was so wanton that men who kneeled and prayed for mercy were killed instantly, while dead bodies were stabbed and mutilated. Dr. Anthony Dostie, a well-known white Republican, was shot five times and slashed with a sword for good measure. "Let Dostie's skin be forthwith stripped and sold to [P. T.] Barnum," the *Mobile Tribune* taunted, "the proceeds to go to the Freedmen's Bureau and negro newspapers."[35]

In the end, the riot left 34 blacks and 3 white Republicans dead, with 160 wounded, in a chilling display of racial hatred. The son of Hannibal Hamlin, Lincoln's first vice president, commented on the sickening butchery: "I have seen death on the battlefield but time will erase the effects of that; the wholesale slaughter and the little regard paid to human life I witnessed here on the 30th of July I shall never forget."[36] This violence seemed a grotesque continuation of the Civil War by other means, and one member of the white rabble went so far as to brag, "We have fought for four years these god-damned Yankees and sons of bitches in the field, and now we will fight them in the city."[37]

The melee had occurred in the military bailiwick of Phil Sheridan, who was in Texas at the time. At first Sheridan branded the black delegates "political agitators & revolutionary men," vowing to arrest them.[38] Yet when he hurried back to New Orleans to investigate, he was revolted by the white mob's behavior, telling Grant how two hundred blacks were attacked with "fire-arms, clubs & knives in a manner so unnecessary & atrocious as to compel me to say it was murder."[39] The next day, Sheridan delivered a sterner indictment. "It was no riot, it was an absolute massacre by the police which was not excelled in murderous cruelty by that of Fort Pillow."[40] This was provocative language, Fort Pillow having witnessed the most notorious slaughter of black soldiers during the war. On August 13, after further probing, Sheridan wrote that "I believe that at least nine tenths of the casualties were perpetrated by the police & citizens stabbing and smashing in the heads of many who had been already wounded or killed by policemen."[41] Only the presence of federal troops restored order to the turbulent city.

To Stanton, Grant recommended that New Orleans "be kept under martial law until the causes of the riot are ascertained and the guilty parties brought to punishment"—an action Stanton readily endorsed.[42] After conferring with Johnson, Stanton informed Sheridan that he had "full authority for the maintenance of the public peace and safety."[43] It is important to note that such military rule by the North was not imposed lightly or capriciously but in direct response to a total collapse of southern justice in its treatment of defenseless blacks. As chief general at a time when the South gradually fell under military rule, Grant could not escape a central role, try though he might to be neutral. As attention focused on which side he would choose, one worried Louisiana Republican lectured, "Gen. Grant must be told not to listen to the cowardly dog Andrew Johnson."[44] It was already apparent that Grant's sympathies lay with the threatened black community and the need for a forceful military presence in the South.

On August 6, Sheridan sent the president a detailed account of the veritable orgy of sadism unleashed against blacks at the New Orleans convention, which he saw as a turning point in the question of whether the South would respect the rule of law. "No steps have as yet been taken by the Civil Authorities to arrest Citizens who were engaged in this Massacre, or policemen who perpetrated such cruelties," he reported a week after the violence.[45] It was bootless to appeal to Andrew Johnson on this issue; even before the riot, he had notified Louisiana's lieutenant governor that the black convention could be disrupted. Instead of blaming police for atrocities, he assailed "the radical Congress" and its misguided desire to enfranchise the "colored population."[46] In response, Radical Republicans began to wonder darkly whether they would need to impeach the president. Reflecting their extreme apprehension, Thomas Nast published a scathing cartoon in which a grinning President Johnson stood in a doorway, watching as white men hacked to death a host of helpless black figures.

In the wake of the New Orleans riot, Grant found President Johnson and his policies increasingly intolerable. On August 18, 1866, Johnson entertained at the White House a delegation from the National Union Convention in Philadelphia, his chosen vehicle for packing Congress with conservative supporters, and invited Grant. Although Abraham Lincoln ran under the National Union banner in 1864, its Republican membership had dwindled and it had settled solidly into the Democratic camp. The gathering had acquired such a "coppery" hue, said one journalist, that Confederate general Nathan Bedford Forrest, the perpetrator of the Fort Pillow massacre, was named a vice president. Profoundly unsettled by this summons to a baldly political event, Grant felt duty-bound to honor Johnson's request. Outwardly it would appear—as Johnson clearly intended—that Grant was lending the event his prestige. Greeted by applause at his entrance, Grant strode up to Johnson and shook hands amid a round of cheers. To one reporter, Grant's behavior seemed to imply, "I am with you gentlemen. I endorse your proceedings."[47]

Appearances could be grossly deceiving: an outraged Grant was persuaded that the president had selfishly manipulated him. As Badeau explained, Grant went "to the White House with the intention of excusing himself, but the President had already taken his place in the East Room, and sent for the General-in-Chief to join him there. Again Grant thought that without positive rudeness he could not refuse. So he stood by Johnson's side during the entire demonstration, greatly to his own disgust and chagrin, and returned to his headquarters afterwards full of indignation . . . and beginning to detest the policy of the President."[48]

Grant's relationship with Johnson soon worsened. Against the warnings of his advisers, the president planned a speaking tour of northern states, popularly dubbed a "swing around the circle," to publicize his pro-southern policies, berate congressional Republicans, and woo Democrats in the fall elections. The pretext for this three-week, two-thousand-mile extravaganza was to dedicate a monument to the late Stephen A. Douglas in Chicago, but the whole thing soon smacked of crude political theater. Johnson dragooned Grant into joining the cavalcade so it would seem as if Grant subscribed to his views. Repeatedly Grant rebuffed Johnson's offer until the president grew so insistent that Grant felt "it would be indecorous any longer to object," wrote Badeau.[49] Many Americans believed Grant adhered to the president's policies, when he actually detested Johnson's chicanery and "was in reality doing more than all the country besides to thwart Johnson's designs."[50] In addition to Grant, Admiral David Farragut, William Seward, Gideon Welles, and George Gordon Meade made up the retinue.

On August 29, the presidential caravan reached New York City, where large, boisterous crowds turned out. Preceded by his distinguished entourage, Johnson stood in an open carriage, bowing and playing melodramatically to the masses. When the group went for a drive in Central Park, Grant took the reins of his carriage and challenged another driver to a race, winning easily. Rawlins, who accompanied the tour, hoped it would "fix [Grant] in the confidence of Mr. Johnson, enabling him to fix up the Army as it should be."[51] It soon grew apparent, however, that Grant and Farragut, not the president, received the bulk of applause, and newspapers gleefully recounted how Johnson writhed with envious embarrassment. "He Becomes Incensed at the Repeated Cheers for Grant," read one headline. "The People Cry Aloud for Grant, and do not want to hear A.J.," said another.[52]

By August 31, a disenchanted Grant wrote to Julia from Auburn, New York, hometown of William Seward: "I am getting very tired of this expedition and of hearing political speeches. I must go through however."[53] The visit was marred by a freakish incident: a young boy named Clarence Richardson was so eager to rush up and meet Grant that he slipped under a carriage, crushing his leg. Once Grant learned of this, he went to console the boy. Later on he was devastated when he heard his leg had been amputated and promptly wrote to him: "How sad now to hear that you have suffered amputation! and then too that I should have been innocently the cause of this mishap!"[54] Grant kept in touch with Clarence, swapping photographs with him.

As the tour wound through midwestern cities, it degenerated into a public relations nightmare for the president, showcasing the coarse, vulgar side of his nature. Some observers thought he was frequently drunk, and Senator John Sherman snickered that the trip had "sunk the Presidential Office to the level of a Grog House."[55] When angry crowds heckled him, the boorish Johnson lashed out in return. As Johnson aired his disgust with Radical Republicans and expressed disdain for blacks, Grant, feeling mortified and exploited, attempted to shrink into the background. Running into his old friend Daniel Ammen, he openly declared his disgust with the tour. "Perhaps on no other occasion [save this one] have I seen General Grant discomposed," Ammen commented.[56] To a reporter Grant complained that he didn't "consider the Army a place for a politician."[57] To another he grumbled that "I am disgusted at hearing a man make speeches on the way to his own funeral."[58]

Since the war Grant had steered clear of the bottle, but the trip so unnerved him that en route from Buffalo to Cleveland, he began to indulge with Surgeon General Joseph Barnes, who had attended to Abraham Lincoln on his deathbed. His omnipresent watchdog, Julia, was absent, but even Rawlins, part of the retinue, could not stave off the binge, underscoring Grant's extreme distress. According to Sylvanus Cadwallader, "The Cleveland Reception Committee on the train had a refreshment car loaded with eatables and potables, and waiters passed constantly through the cars, plying everybody to eat and drink. Gen. Grant had to be taken into a baggage car; compelled to lie down on a pile of empty sacks and rubbish; and remain there . . . till we reached Cleveland. Gen. Rawlins and myself stood guard over him, alternately, every mile of the way; locked out all callers for him; and protected him from observation as far as possible."[59] This sounds exaggerated—Cadwallader had embellished the Satartia story—until we note that Postmaster General Alexander Randall claimed to see Surgeon General Barnes "go up to Grant to feel his pulse" only to find Barnes "so drunk that he tumbled down on him."[60] Gideon Welles confirmed that Grant had grown "garrulous and, stupidly communicative" on the way to Cleveland.[61] The episode fits Grant's pattern of drinking on visits to distant cities, far from the critical eyes of his staff and wife, and it was one of the last times it happened.

On September 3, an especially hostile audience baited Johnson in Cleveland, where his behavior flirted with new lows. When a heckler yelled that Johnson should "hang Jeff Davis," the president rejoined, "Why not hang Thad Stevens and Wendell Phillips?"[62] When someone in the crowd hollered, "Is this dignified?" Johnson shot back: "I care not for dignity."[63] Welles said Grant was "somewhat inebriated" in Cleveland and Johnson explained that he was "extremely ill."[64] To hide their drunken binge, Grant and Barnes were smuggled aboard a steamer bound for Detroit—"both of them intoxicated," noted Welles—in the hope that the bracing Lake Erie air might sober them up.[65] Writing to Julia from Detroit, Grant admitted that, for an unspecified reason, he had broken away from the tour. "Gen. Rawlins, Dr. Barnes and myself switched off from the party at Cleveland last night and came here by boat. The balance of the party stayed overnight there and will reach here this evening."[66]

On September 9 the tour touched its nadir in St. Louis when Johnson, in another intemperate outburst, had the gall to blame Congress for the New Orleans riot: "Every drop of blood that was shed is upon their skirts, and they are responsible for it."[67] Turning himself into a martyr, he proclaimed, "I have been traduced. I have been slandered. I have been maligned. I have been called Judas Iscariot."[68] To Julia, Grant transmitted his horrified reaction: "I never have been so tired of anything before as I have been with the political stump speeches of Mr. Johnson . . . I look upon them as a National disgrace."[69] Even many northern papers that had supported his presidency turned against him, believing he had demeaned the office with these scurrilous screeds.

Contrary to Johnson's plan to promote himself, the tour provoked a spontaneous boom for a Grant presidency. In Newark, Ohio, spectators interrupted Johnson's speech with calls for Grant. "You cannot insult the President through General Grant," George Armstrong Custer chastised them.[70] However much Grant abhorred Johnson's behavior, he refused to countenance actions that presented him as a presidential hopeful and asserted he would never allow the American military to "be made a party machine."[71] When a Chicago crowd gathered outside his train to further his candidacy, Grant refused to encourage the demonstration or even leave his car.

In Cincinnati, Grant arrived earlier than Johnson and was enjoying a theater outing when a military company showed up, wanting to support him and dump Johnson. Taciturn on the tour, Grant abruptly found his tongue, lecturing the group's leader: "SIR: I am no politician. The President of the United States is my Commander-in-Chief. I consider this demonstration in opposition to the President of the United States, ANDREW JOHNSON. If you have any regard for me you will take your men away."[72] The next day, Grant may have regretted such misplaced loyalty when the president had a well-known St. Louis Copperhead, Congressman John Hogan, introduce him to various crowds—a gaffe the victor of Appomattox simply couldn't abide. Grant told Welles he had no desire to associate with the man: "A Rebel he could forgive, but not a Copperhead."[73]

Pleading ill health, Grant departed from the tour and returned early to Washington. Compared with Johnson, he seemed the soul of sanity and thus benefited politically from the trip, even if he had not sought that outcome. As Badeau reported, "People have talked to us of Grant being made Dictator; and at any rate makes it more certain . . . that nobody else can be next President; which for him is not a consummation devoutly to be wished for."[74] Johnson confided to Secretary of the Interior Orville Browning that Grant connived for the presidency and that "there was a conspiracy on foot among the radicals to incite . . . another rebellion, and especially to arm and exasperate the negroes in the South."[75] Some Washington observers floated scenarios of a constitutional showdown in which Johnson would deploy Grant and the military to silence Congress. Suddenly Grant's political tendencies became of more than theoretical interest. Ben Butler, now a Radical Republican, wondered privately whether "Grant can be trusted to disobey positive orders of his chief? When the hour of peril comes, shall we not be leaning on a broken reed?"[76] Grant knew of this high-stakes guessing game. "No matter how close I keep my tongue," he informed Sherman, both parties "try to interpret from the little let drop that I am with them."[77] He was so dismayed that he wanted to yield his command and travel abroad but felt obligated to stay home at such a perilous moment for the nation.

On September 22, Grant performed an act that spoke volumes about his secret sympathies: he quietly ordered the chief of ordnance, General Alexander Dyer, to empty surplus weapons from five southern arsenals and send most of their small arms to New York Harbor. He also spurned a request from Virginia to furnish ten thousand weapons for white militias to confront a supposedly better armed black population. In addition, he opposed rearming former Confederate states.[78] Writing confidentially to Sheridan, Grant warned that few people who fought for the North exerted any influence over the pro-southern president. Johnson, he feared, would declare Congress as a body "illegal, unconstitutional and revolutionary. Commanders in Southern states will have to take great care to see, if a crisis does come, that no armed headway can be made against the *Union*."[79] The outside world may have wondered about Grant's sympathies, but his private statements leave no room for conjecture about his inexorable drift toward Radical Republicanism. Welles later speculated that by fall 1866, Grant "was secretly acting in concert with the Radicals to deceive and beguile the President."[80] Grant didn't regard it as deception so much as adhering to bedrock principles, telling Badeau he had "never felt so anxious about the country."[81]

As it happened, Grant swam in a strong political tide. Johnson's "swing around the circle" was such an indescribable fiasco that Republicans registered stunning gains in the fall elections, winning substantial majorities in both houses of Congress. The election also resoundingly endorsed the Fourteenth Amendment. These electoral gains prompted speculation about whether Johnson would seek by force to block the new Congress from meeting. Taking advantage of their election mandate, Radical Republicans planned to initiate a period of Congressional Reconstruction, helping blacks and white Republicans in the South and supplanting Presidential Reconstruction, with its heavy bias toward southern white Democrats.

Rawlins was upset by talk that Grant might be seduced by Radical Republicans and not only because he was more conservative than his boss. Like Sherman, he believed Grant was "not a politician or statesman," but only a man who knew how to fight well. For Rawlins, Grant "was not a man of ability outside of the profession of arms, and was a man of strong passions and intense prejudices . . . [Rawlins] thought Sherman a great man—a statesman as well as a soldier— Grant was the soldier only."[82] The fraternal protectiveness Rawlins had shown toward Grant's drinking now extended to what he deemed the equally corrupting influence of politics.

By February 1866, Napoleon III announced plans to withdraw troops from Mexico—an apparent victory for the diplomatic approach advocated by Seward versus Grant's more robust desire to go to war. On the other hand, Grant's decision to send a military force to the Rio Grande had helped the liberal opposition there to survive. Grant's worries about Mexico as a haven for renegade rebels hadn't abated, especially after Sheridan warned in February that "if the scheme is not broken up, every act of our Government which is distasteful to these people, will cause a fresh exodus to Mexico."[83] For Grant, Mexico was a hotly emotional topic. Unpersuaded that Napoleon III would budge, Grant badgered President Johnson to supply arms to liberal forces in Mexico to rid the country of the French-imposed emperor, assuring a reporter that Sheridan, with two thousand American troops, would "clean Maximilian out of Mexico in six months."[84]

On October 18, at the president's behest, Grant sent a cryptic letter to Sherman in St. Louis, asking him to come to Washington and intimating he might be named acting secretary of war. Like Rawlins, Sherman saw Washington as a cockpit of intrigue and preferred to steer clear of it. Grant couldn't say so in a letter, but he had experienced growing friction with Johnson, who feared that in a constitutional confrontation with Congress, Grant would lean toward the legislature. Hence, Johnson wanted to ease Grant out of town, sending him on a diplomatic mission to Mexico. Grant was supposed to escort the new American minister to Mexico, Lewis D. Campbell of Ohio, and meet with Benito Juárez. Campbell had a well-known fondness for drink and some thought Johnson wished to expose Grant to temptation and tarnish his reputation. Of this unwanted assignment, Grant told the president flatly, "It is a diplomatic service for which I am not fitted either by education or taste."[85] Grant believed he would be damaged by a failed Mexican mission, while Seward would take credit for a successful one. He also believed Johnson had no right to send a military man on a patently political trip. When Sherman reached Washington, Grant told him that "he had thought the matter over, would disobey the order, and stand the consequences." In emotional tones, he characterized the order as "a plot to get rid of him."[86]

Backing Grant fully, Sherman marched off to see the president, who received him cordially and said he wished him to command the army in Grant's absence in Mexico. "I then informed him that General Grant *would not go*," Sherman recalled, "and he seemed amazed."[87] Sherman pointed out that Hancock in New Mexico or Sheridan in Texas could easily handle the job and, if neither was satisfactory, he would gladly go himself. "Certainly," said the president, "if you will go, that will answer perfectly."[88] Sherman saw Johnson manipulating Grant as a mere pawn in a power play. "I have no doubt there is some plan to get Grant out of the way, & to get me here, but I will be a party to no such move," Sherman informed his wife.[89] He suspected the president harassed Grant "because he was looming up as a candidate for President."[90] Badeau also thought Johnson meditated replacing Grant with the more conservative Sherman, who would be more "supple" in supporting his Reconstruction policies.[91]

Even though the importunate Johnson hectored Grant to take the job, he remained unyielding. He then invited Grant to a cabinet meeting at which he exploded with rage when Grant declined the Mexican mission. According to Julia, the president raised his voice and struck "the table with his clenched hand with considerable force."[92] Johnson asked the attorney general whether any reason existed "why General Grant should not obey my orders? Is he in any way ineligible to this position?" Grant sprang to his feet in protest. "I am an officer of the army, and bound to obey your military orders. But this is a civil office, a purely diplomatic duty that you offer me, and I cannot be compelled to undertake it."[93] Amid shocked silence, Grant stormed from the room. Realizing that he was unmovable, Johnson reluctantly let Sherman go to Mexico instead. The president could no longer doubt Grant's opposition. "[Grant] was as anxious to frustrate Johnson's maneuvers as he had ever been to thwart those of Lee," wrote Badeau.[94] In the end, William Seward was correct that Maximilian's empire rested on shaky turf and that patient diplomacy in Mexico worked better than force. In June 1867, liberal forces loyal to Benito Juárez executed Maximilian by a firing squad in a move applauded by Grant.

JOHNSON DID EVERYTHING in his power to dissuade southern states from accepting the Fourteenth Amendment. Unlike the president, Grant believed they should adopt it before readmission to the Union and grew progressively more alarmed that black and white Republicans were being murdered with abandon in southern states. On January 18, 1867, he wrote a confidential letter to Oliver O. Howard that showed what a flaming militant he had become in protecting freedmen and how closely he now identified with Radical Republicans. Grant asked Howard to compile a list of "authenticated cases of Murder" committed against freed people and white Republicans in the South during the previous six months. "My object in this is to make a report showing that the Courts in the states excluded from Congress afford no security to life or property . . . and to recommend that Martial Law be declared over such districts as do not afford the proper protection."[95] On February 8, Grant handed Howard's findings to Stanton. In a cabinet discussion a week later, Howard's evidence was gruffly dismissed by Welles as mere "rumors of negro murders," unworthy of serious consideration.[96] This would become a standard Democratic defense in future years. Johnson and Welles worked to bury the explosive document. If it went to Congress, Welles feared, certain "mischievous persons" would say that "here was information of which Grant complained, but of which the President took no notice."[97]

All the while a movement to impeach the president gathered strength in Republican circles. Since people imagined Johnson might be suspended from his official duties before being convicted, the conflict portended a crisis of the first magnitude. By now Johnson had surrendered any lingering solicitude for poor southern whites in favor of the old slaveholding elite, making the former slaves the villains of his administration. When the journalist Charles Nordhoff met him at the White House, he described the president as sure that "the people of the South . . . were to be trodden under foot to 'protect niggers.'"[98] Grant believed that Johnson strove to form a coalition of northern Peace Democrats and former Confederates to nullify the war's outcome. So plausible did it seem that the conflict between Johnson and Congress would end in violence that Congressman John Logan of Illinois wrote discreetly to Colonel N. P. Chipman in the War Department, warning him to "quietly and secretly organize all our boys that can assemble at a given signal . . . ready to protect the Congress of the U.S."[99] For many in Washington, the great mystery was how Grant would act in such a crisis. President Johnson didn't know the answer, wrote Gideon Welles, and "I doubt if Grant himself knows. The Radicals, who distrust him, are nevertheless courting him assiduously."[100]

The Radicals succeeded in attracting him to their camp, for only they could offer continuity with the deeply held values that had informed his wartime service. Alarmed by the punishment being inflicted on former slaves and Union men in the South, Grant recommended to Stanton on January 29, 1867, that Texas be placed under martial law. Such a measure, he thought, would be a warning to other southern states "and if necessary could be extended to others."[101] A few weeks later, *The New York Times* printed a candid interview in which Grant chided southern states for their recalcitrance. If they "had accepted the [Fourteenth] Amendment instead of rejecting it so hastily, they would have been admitted by Congress in December, but now I think they will have to take the Amendment, and manhood suffrage besides."[102] In many parts of Texas, Grant asserted, a Union man wasn't safe outside the umbrella of federal military protection. When asked whether a Union man could travel safely in the South, he replied frankly that if he got into "angry political discussions, there would be danger in some places no doubt. In that case shooting would probably be passed off as justifiable homicide, if the murderer was arrested at all."[103]

On March 2, 1867, the Radical Republicans, having scored stunning gains in the fall elections, engineered a backlash against Andrew Johnson that crystallized with passage of what became known as the First Reconstruction Act. In shaping the bill, Congress consulted closely with Grant. The legislation carved up ten Confederate states (Tennessee, having ratified the Fourteenth Amendment, was exempt) into five military districts. Appointed by the president, the general commanding each district would exercise enormous power, overseeing conventions to draft new constitutions before their states were readmitted to the Union. States were required to ratify the Fourteenth Amendment and grant voting rights to black men. Betraying his ingrained racial prejudice, Johnson vetoed the act. "The negroes have not asked for the privilege of voting," he stated, and "the vast majority of them have no idea what it means."[104] Grant scorned this message as "ridiculous" and large House and Senate majorities quickly overrode the veto.[105] Johnson deferred to Grant's wishes in picking the first five military district commanders—John Schofield, Dan Sickles, George Thomas, Edward Ord, and Phil Sheridan—although Gideon Welles griped that in choosing these men Grant had been "swayed by Radical influence."[106]

The First Reconstruction Act represented an extraordinary effort to invest former slaves with full citizenship rights, delivering a stark rebuke to southern whites who wanted to hurl them back into a new form of bondage. "What a bitter dose for their arrogant aristocracy of only seven years ago!" George Templeton Strong gloated. "Was there ever a more tremendous and searching social revolution?"[107] For many southern whites it seemed that, having endured wartime defeat, they now had to submit to a second military humiliation. Summarizing this view decades later, H. L. Mencken claimed the South was subjected "to the supervision and veto of the rest of the country—and . . . enjoyed scarcely more liberty, in the political sense, than so many convicts in the penitentiary."[108] Yet for southern blacks and white Republicans the First Reconstruction Act promised sorely needed protection against the indiscriminate white terror directed at them with alarming frequency.

Privately Grant endorsed the legislation as "a fitting end to all our controversy."[109] Southern intolerance, as revealed by the Memphis and New Orleans race riots, had led him to revise his lenient attitude at Appomattox in favor of more drastic measures to protect freed people. "General [Grant] getting more & more radical," Comstock noted in his diary.[110] With military oversight of the South and district commanders reporting directly to him, Grant now wielded unprecedented power over the region—probably more domestic power than any other general in chief in American history. In enforcing the new legislation, he increasingly took his cues from Congress and bypassed an intransigent president. Still a relative novice in Washington politics, Grant managed at first to maintain decent relations with both Johnson and Congress, Welles speculating that he would "not be surprised if Grant, in whom [Johnson] still has [great] confidence, and possibly Stanton, are the only persons whom he consults."[111] Grant performed a nimble balancing act that would be tested as strains between the president and Congress grew unmanageable.

On the day the Reconstruction bill passed, Congress also enacted the Tenure of Office Act, a future flashpoint in its relations with the president. From the earliest days of the Republic, presidents had been obligated to seek the advice and consent of the Senate in appointing cabinet members, while retaining full power to remove them. Radical Republicans feared Johnson would seek to eviscerate Reconstruction by ousting Stanton, and the new bill, specifically designed to protect him, required Senate approval before firing cabinet members. With some justice, Johnson saw the law as impinging squarely on his constitutional prerogatives. After objections from congressional moderates, the bill was modified to apply only to cabinet members appointed by sitting presidents, exempting those appointed by previous presidents. Since Stanton had been named by Lincoln, the tantalizing question hung fire: Was he covered by the act? As president, Grant would acknowledge the law's absurdity and work to repeal it. When it became the law of the land in 1867, however, he felt legally bound to obey it.

Congress imposed other punitive restraints on the president. A rider to a military appropriation bill prevented him from issuing orders directly to the army, lest he tamper with Radical Reconstruction and pressure southern commanders. All such orders had to be routed through Grant, lodging extra power in his hands. The rider further stipulated that Grant could be cashiered only with Senate consent. Taken together, these rules chipped away at Johnson's power and converted Grant and Stanton into protected wards of Congress, presaging a constitutional showdown between Johnson and Radical Republicans that would hinge on the political sympathies of the two men.

Of the five military commanders in the South, none supported Congressional Reconstruction more militantly than Sheridan, who was in charge of Louisiana and Texas and especially bewailed conditions in Louisiana: "Government is denounced; the Freedmen are shot and Union men are persecuted if they have the temerity to express their opinion."[112] Within a week of his appointment, Sheridan showed how briskly he would enforce the First Reconstruction Act by removing from office the Louisiana attorney general, the New Orleans mayor, and a federal district judge in the city—all of whom had condoned recent racial violence. He believed they had egged on the rioters, then prosecuted victims instead of perpetrators. Two days later, Grant applauded Sheridan's action: "I have just seen your order . . . It is just the thing, and meets the universal approbation of the loyal people at least."[113] When Sheridan contemplated removing the Texas and Louisiana governors, Grant cautioned him against doing so, saying its constitutionality was questionable.

Never cavalier about constitutional issues, Grant believed the First Reconstruction Act provided military governments "for the rebel states until they were fully restored in all their relations to the general government."[114] Until then, military commanders should regard "present state governments as provisional," tolerating them "just so far as they could be used in carrying out the will of Congress."[115] On March 23, the Second Reconstruction Act expanded the powers of district commanders over southern election procedures and allowed them to register voters, a move that enraged Andrew Johnson, who blocked further removal of southern officials by the military in early April. Although Grant sent this order to Sheridan, he secretly dissented from it, informing Sheridan "there is a decided hostility to the whole Congressional plan for reconstruction, at the 'White House,' and a disposition to remove you from the command you now have. Both the Secretary of War and myself will oppose any such move, as will the mass of the people."[116] Far from seeing himself as high-handed or dictatorial, Grant pictured himself as a soldier loyally carrying out congressional directives.

By virtue of his position, Grant received panoramic accounts of conditions in the South that portrayed a region seething with white hatred and sometimes black as well. In mid-April, he dispatched Orville Babcock and Horace Porter to report on southern Reconstruction. The two men gave an optimistic verdict on the progress of blacks, who had embraced citizenship with an enthusiasm that heartened northern abolitionists and terrified white supremacists. As Babcock wrote from New Orleans, "The negro is learning very fast. they will soon be the best educated *class* in the South, if they continue at their present rate of progress."[117] The Freedmen's Bureau had helped to sign up 130,735 students in classes, but teachers, white and black, continued to be murdered and burned out of schools and homes. Babcock and Porter witnessed an ominous upsurge of Confederate sentiment, with Confederate symbols employed to intimidate blacks. In Georgia, wrote Babcock, "the police in most of the cities are in a grey uniform, the real *confederate* uniform."[118] Certain states resisted Reconstruction more passionately than others. After visiting three Texas cities, Porter wrote, "This is, by far, the worst State in the Union, and it is only by the adoption of strict and decided measures that it is kept from giving a great deal of trouble."[119]

Antiblack animus in the South now assumed more sinister forms. In mid-1866, Confederate veterans in Pulaski, Tennessee, founded a club called the Ku Klux Klan, its arcane name derived from the Greek word *kuklos,* for band or circle. By the time of the First Reconstruction Act, what had started out as a social club began to shade into a quasi-military organization, recruiting Nathan Bedford Forrest as a leader. It was less a tightly structured organization than a free-floating network of thuggish white groups adopting similar methods and rituals to terrorize blacks. Members vowed to support "a white man's government" and carry weapons at all times.[120] Before long, former privates in the Confederate army were taking orders from their old officers in the Klan. To hide their identities, Klansmen donned outlandish hoods to terrorize their former slaves into believing they represented the ghosts of dead Confederate soldiers. They carried out murders and mutilations in a grotesque spirit of sadistic mockery. Despite these disguises, the freedmen often knew and feared the identities of their tormentors. By no coincidence, the Klan would spread rapidly across the South during the 1868 elections, targeting as it did black voters.

The actions taken by Sheridan were detested by the Klan. He ordered mayors in Louisiana and Texas to draw at least half their police officers from former

Union soldiers, meaning black veterans would be hired. He also presided over a budding civil rights revolution, starting with the desegregation of New Orleans streetcars. Previously blacks had been forced to ride on separate streetcars with stars stamped on their sides. When they crowded onto white streetcars in protest, transport companies appealed to Sheridan to banish these black passengers. Instead Sheridan warned that if companies permitted discrimination, he would bar them from the streets. Sheridan informed Grant that once the original hubbub over desegregated streetcars subsided, the locals had "cheerfully adopted" the new system and "the excitement died out at once."[121] This startling early revolution in civil rights would be all but forgotten by later generations of Americans.

Never a man for halfway measures, Sheridan in early June removed Governor James M. Wells of Louisiana, who had brazenly defied Reconstruction. In typically hot-blooded language, Sheridan blasted Wells as "a political trickster and a dishonest man," whose "conduct has been as sinuous as the mark left in the dust by the movement of a snake."[122] Many people concurred—the *New Orleans Times* quipped that "All's well that ends Wells"—but the action remained highly controversial.[123] Sheridan believed that if civil officers could flout military commanders with impunity, Reconstruction was bound to fail. Writing to him in confidence, Grant emphasized that Stanton supported the Wells removal, while he himself rendered a more qualified judgment. "I have no doubt myself but that the removal of Governor Wells will do great good in your command if you are sustained, but great harm if you are not sustained."[124]

Already irate with Sheridan, Johnson reprimanded him and told him to defer his action. Bent upon foiling the Congressional Reconstruction pushed by Radical Republicans, he elicited from Attorney General Henry Stanbery an opinion that flagrantly challenged the policy, alleging that military commanders should refrain from suspending political officials. This provoked a bruising cabinet battle with Stanton hotly denouncing this crabbed interpretation of the law. When Johnson ordered Grant to circulate Stanbery's opinion to district commanders, Grant betrayed his true sympathies by letting them know they could freely interpret it as they chose. Although Grant was usually dutiful in following civilian policy, he believed Johnson had subverted the will of Congress in a way that bordered on treason. It grated on Johnson that Grant, a mere subordinate, had been endowed with such godlike powers over Reconstruction.

By this point, there was no magical way to balance ambitious Reconstruction policies mandated by Congress with the obstructive arts of a hostile president. On June 27, Welles reported a "nervous and apprehensive" Johnson living "in constant dread of impeachment."[125] However much he disagreed with the president, Grant prayed this extreme remedy would be averted "unless something occurs hereafter to fully justify it."[126] While Radical Republicans were ready to banish the hated president, party moderates remained skittish about forcing him from office. On July 18, Grant testified before the House Judiciary Committee, which had begun to consider possible impeachment, and he contrasted his humane treatment of Lee and other paroled officers with the harsh action favored by Johnson, who thought "they should be tried and punished" and treason "made odious."[127] He reiterated his long-standing contention that Lee wouldn't have surrendered had he believed "he was going to be tried for treason and hanged."[128] Grant was honest without being vindictive toward Johnson and won plaudits from the press. "The responsibility, the fidelity, the sagacity of Gen. Grant constitute the only guarantee . . . for the adequate enforcement of the conditions dictated by Congress in the spirit in which they were conceived," wrote *The New York Times*.[129]

The day after Grant testified, Congress approved the Third Reconstruction Act, which confirmed the power of district commanders to fire civilian officials and expanded their supreme power over voting rights. When Johnson vetoed the bill, Congress promptly overrode it. Though the legislature adjourned the next day, a committee lingered in the capital to take testimony that might yield grounds for impeachment. Instead of focusing on Reconstruction—the true issue—they chose a more roundabout method, hoping to find Johnson guilty of improper conduct. Specifically, they hoped to prove he had corresponded with Confederate politicians, misappropriated federal funds, and chosen unqualified figures to govern southern states.

Stymied in his bid to hobble Congressional Reconstruction, Andrew Johnson was especially enraged by his belief that Edwin Stanton had authored the new Reconstruction bill. Armed with the new powers, Grant took strong measures to deal with looming racial strife in Memphis. Nothing alarmed the white South more than black power at the polls, which was why most terror was directed there. Stanton had received warnings of "a formidable and bloody riot" in Memphis, scheduled for its August 1 election, "to prevent negroes voting."[130] Grant didn't care to "wait until people are killed and the mob beyond control" and sent troops in advance of the election.[131]

After his testimony, Grant felt badly in need of a breather from the poisonous atmosphere of Washington. For the first time, he and Julia took a seaside cottage in Long Branch, New Jersey, a hideaway where Grant could revert to a life that suited him more. The town had recently become a fashionable watering hole for millionaires. The waterfront house on Ocean Avenue was three stories high with a shingled roof and two glassed-in observatories. Twice a day Grant rode in a carriage to breathe in tangy salt air before returning to the house and poring over mail and newspapers on the verandah. Staying in Long Branch struck him as a guilty pleasure. "Every day that I am absent from Washington," he informed Stanton, "I see something in the papers or hear something, that makes me feel that I should be there." At the same time, he admitted wistfully that "I have got so tired of being tied down that I am nearly ready to desert."[132]

Grant had many things to ponder about his future since second-guessing his presidential aspirations had become a popular parlor game. With the benefit of hindsight, Andrew Johnson said Grant had supported him for two years then saw the "Radical handwriting on the wall, and heeded it . . . Grant did the proper thing to save Grant, but it pretty nearly ruined me."[133] Grant was outwardly a sphinx upon whom people could project their preferred ideology, and Radical Republicans searched for assurances that Grant stood on their side. With a select group of people he was frank about his views, but never in public. People knew he had cast his lone vote for president for James Buchanan and still wondered whether he was a Republican or a Democrat. But for Grant, the Democrats had nothing to offer him, only a repudiation of the war and all its sacred goals.

To unravel the mystery of his political affiliation, Radical Republicans dispatched Senator Benjamin Wade to Covington to quiz Jesse Root Grant about his son's politics. Jesse and Hannah were out of town and Michael John Cramer, Grant's brother-in-law, received the senator instead. Once seated in the parlor, Wade pressed Cramer for Grant's views on Reconstruction, saying he wished to know whether Grant was "a good Republican; for we desire to bring him forward as our candidate for the presidency; yet we do not exactly know where he stands on these questions." When Cramer replied that Grant was "a thorough Republican" who could be fully trusted, Wade twirled his hat into the air and accidentally smashed a chandelier, then proclaimed, "That settles the matter; we shall propose Grant as the candidate for the Republican Party for the presidency. I am greatly relieved . . . With him we are sure to win."[134]

For those seeking clues to Grant's political opinions there was no surer source
than a speech on Reconstruction delivered in Galena that June by John Rawlins.
Knowing people saw Rawlins as his surrogate, Grant reviewed the speech carefully and gave it his private imprimatur. The speech was so detailed and corresponded so perfectly with the Radical Republican agenda that it was widely
reprinted. Rawlins said it made no sense to emancipate slaves if they weren't
entitled to the law's full protection. Because southern governments failed to
adapt their constitutions to new political realities, Congress had a duty "to sweep
from existence any and all governments in any States that were anti-Republican."
He applauded Congress for barring former Confederate states that hadn't guaranteed suffrage to all "without distinction of race or color." Only through voting
could freed people protect their liberties. In a rousing peroration, Rawlins described Radical Reconstruction as "the result of a wise exercise of the unquestionable power of the law-making branch of the Government . . . the South must
accept the situation fully and unreservedly."[135] That Grant allowed Rawlins to
make this fervent speech removed any residual doubt as to where he stood on the
cardinal issue of the day.

Volcanic Passion

RELATIONS BETWEEN GRANT and Edwin Stanton had never been noticeably warm. Partly the problem stemmed from Stanton's dyspeptic personality and brusque treatment of Grant and partly it reflected turf disputes. After Appomattox, Grant wished to retain his supreme wartime powers and have army orders funneled through him, leaving Stanton to handle military matters requiring presidential approval. Stanton wanted the War Department to reclaim its traditional prewar powers, thus weakening Grant. At one point, Grant threatened to resign if Stanton continued to usurp what he deemed his rightful authority. Despite such conflicts, Grant retained unalloyed respect for Stanton's wartime accomplishments, deeming him an irreproachable patriot with a fiercely "volcanic" passion for the Union.[1] He sided with Stanton on Reconstruction and shared his dismay over Johnson. As he noted, Stanton "believed that Johnson was Jefferson Davis in another form, and he used his position in the Cabinet like a picket holding his position on the line."[2]

Because of Stanton's cordial relationship with congressional Republicans, his dealings with the president deteriorated during the summer of 1867. On August 1, Johnson summoned Grant for a lengthy talk—he fancied Grant had "just come off a debauch"—and expressed his intention to fire Stanton.[3] Grant hesitated as he mulled over his response. Later that day, he sent the president a tough, candid letter, laying out legal and political arguments against Stanton's ouster. Such a move, he asserted, would violate the Tenure of Office Act, expressly designed to protect the war secretary. He wondered why Johnson had not requested Stanton's removal while the Senate was in session. Grant concluded his blunt missive with a blazing declaration: "I know I am right in this matter."[4] For Grant, there was now no turning back. He had declared his true allegiance, leaning toward the Radical Republican fraternity, and could no longer pretend he was intimately allied with administration policy.

Such was Grant's popularity that Johnson could not dismiss Stanton without Grant's support. Grant was still adored in the North for his wartime leadership, in the South for his clemency. Johnson searched for a legal means to fire Stanton without running afoul of the Tenure of Office Act. On August 5, he sent Stanton a one-sentence letter: "Public considerations of a high character constrain me to say, that your resignation as Secretary of War will be accepted."[5] Johnson knew that if Stanton resigned, instead of being sacked, the troublesome legislation would be a dead issue. That same day, in a tart response, Stanton lectured Johnson that "public considerations of a high character . . . constrain me not to resign the office of Secretary of War before the next meeting of Congress."[6] Radical Republicans trooped to the War Department, stiffening Stanton's spine as he took issue with the president. They knew that he was a primary shield for their Reconstruction policies. The stage was set for a constitutional impasse between Congress and Johnson, with Grant likely caught in the middle.

On Sunday morning, August 11, Johnson told Grant unequivocally that Stanton would be *suspended,* not fired, to bypass the Tenure of Office Act, and he asked Grant to become the temporary secretary of war. Grant didn't spurn the appointment, but stipulated, according to Badeau, that "on no account could he consent to hold the office after the Senate should act" on Stanton's suspension.[7] In other words, he saw himself as merely a temporary placeholder, awaiting a Senate ruling on Stanton when it reconvened. Johnson took away a quite different impression: that if the Senate overturned Stanton's dismissal, Grant would hand the job back to *him,* not Stanton. Johnson assumed Stanton wouldn't dare to override someone of Grant's stature.

Why did Grant take a job so fraught with peril? As a soldier, he felt the need to submit to civilian direction. He also feared that if he turned down the job, Johnson might offer it to someone who shared his conservative agenda on southern policy. As Grant told Julia, "I think it most important that someone should be there who cannot be used."[8] By holding the office, he reasoned, he could protect the army from political meddling in executing Reconstruction. Even some Grant intimates questioned his wisdom in taking a post that enmeshed him in a dense web of partisan politics. "Had I been there," Rawlins told his wife, "I might have prevailed upon the General not to accept the position."[9] He feared Johnson would manipulate Grant in his ongoing tussle with Congress. Badeau thought Johnson wanted to destroy Grant as a presidential candidate by binding him to his administration, undercutting him while pretending to advance him.

That same day, Grant drove to see Stanton and informed him of the president's decision. Though a crushing blow for Stanton, it was not unexpected. When Grant received official notice of his appointment the next day, he sent Stanton a conciliatory message designed to draw the sting from the moment. "I cannot let the opportunity pass without expressing to you my appreciation of the zeal, patriotism, firmness and ability" with which Stanton had served as war secretary.[10] In reply, Stanton admitted he had "no alternative but to submit, under protest, to the superior force of the President."[11] Branding the president's action illegal, he was convinced Congress would restore his position when it reconvened in late November.

Occupying two positions simultaneously, Grant now spent mornings at the War Department, then strolled across the street and passed afternoons at his old army headquarters, where he was still chief general. Formal in the morning, he became more casual and unconstrained among his staff officers in the afternoon. On August 13, Grant attended his first cabinet meeting as war secretary ad interim, thrusting him squarely into the political arena. He lost no time establishing that he was a confirmed supporter of Congressional Reconstruction and would stand by his military commanders in the South. When Gideon Welles challenged him and asked if the latest Reconstruction law wasn't "*palpably* unconstitutional and destructive of the government and of the Constitution itself . . . ?" Grant countered: "Who is to decide whether the law is unconstitutional?"[12]

The exchange went to the heart of the dispute that led to Johnson's impeachment. However unwise the Tenure of Office Act, were not government officers obligated to heed it until the courts overturned it as unconstitutional? Grant thought so. In cabinet meetings, he showed a self-assurance that antagonized some secretaries. "This is the second meeting of the cabinet Grant has attended," wrote Secretary of the Interior Browning, "and both have been marked by a rather ridiculous arrogance. He has been swift to deliver his crude opinions upon all subjects, and especially upon legal questions, as if they were oracles and not to be controverted."[13] Grant was no longer the bumbling clerk from Galena. Wartime experience had acquainted him with a wide array of issues and he could be quite forceful in expressing his opinions.

In dealing with Johnson, Grant perceived himself as embodying the Union cause and preserving Lincoln's legacy. Less than a week after Grant became acting war secretary, Johnson decided to replace Sheridan in New Orleans with General George Thomas, who was suffering from a liver ailment. In the end, Winfield Scott Hancock replaced Thomas. For Grant, Sheridan's removal was a barefaced attempt to eviscerate Congressional Reconstruction. Usually unflappable, he sent the president a letter glowing with passion: "I . . . urge, earnestly urge, urge in the name of a patriotic people who have sacrificed Hundreds of thousands of loyal lives, and Thousands of Millions of treasure to preserve the integrity and union of this Country that this order be not insisted on . . . [Sheridan's] removal will only be regarded as an effort to defeat the laws of Congress. It will be interpreted by the unreconstructed element in the South, those who did all they could to break up this government by arms . . . as a triumph."[14]

Clearly, in Grant's eyes, the country was slouching toward a crisis that required him to ride to the rescue. He regarded Reconstruction as the Civil War's final phase and believed Johnson had cast his lot with the disloyal South. Nonetheless, Johnson not only transferred Sheridan to Missouri but sent Grant an explanatory letter that insulted Sheridan, stating he had "rendered himself exceedingly obnoxious" and that his "rule has . . . been one of absolute tyranny, without reference to the principles of our government or the nature of our free institutions."[15] The letter left Grant both blue and badly disillusioned with politics. "All the romance of feeling that men in high places are above personal considerations and act only from motives of pure patriotism . . . has been destroyed," he told Sherman.[16] To mitigate the president's order, he told his commanders *not* to reinstate southern politicians ousted by Sheridan and he publicized his letter to Johnson disputing Sheridan's removal. Grant's standing promptly soared in military circles, the *Army and Navy Journal* celebrating a letter whose "every word is golden."[17]

With tensions running at a high pitch between the president and Congress, leading administration figures again fretted that Johnson would be arrested even before his conviction in an impeachment trial, with Benjamin Wade or another Radical Republican installed in his stead. Along with conservative cabinet members, Johnson toyed with replacing Grant with Sherman, who was more perturbed by the Radical tumult in Congress. On October 8, Secretary of the Interior Browning sounded out Sherman as to whether Grant would cooperate with a Radical congressional coup d'état against the president. Sherman reassured him that Grant "might be relied upon to prevent violence. He would not allow a mob of the 'grand army of the Republic' to execute the revolutionary measures of Congress."[18] Again showing solidarity with Grant, Sherman refused to entertain any appointment placing him in a superior position.

To plumb Grant's views more deeply, Johnson took an unaccustomed step on October 12: he visited Grant at the War Department for a frank discussion. The president cut straight to the crux of the matter: What would Grant do if Congress tried to depose or arrest him before an impeachment conviction? Grant said "he should expect to obey orders," Welles reported, "that should he (Grant) change his mind he would advise the President in season, that he might have time to make arrangements."[19] Although Johnson came away from the discussion heartened, Grant had subtly inserted political distance between himself and the president. Welles believed Grant lobbied key Radical Republicans to tamp down any talk of arresting Johnson.

In early October, Democrats won decisive victories in Pennsylvania and Ohio, throwing fear into the Republican Party, which paid a steep penalty with voters for promoting black suffrage. This enhanced Grant's appeal as a versatile presidential candidate who might attract moderate Democratic voters while keeping die-hard Republicans in line. Blessed with this bipartisan veneer, he became the supreme prize in American politics, sought by all parties. Carl Schurz even thought his "nomination for the presidency appears to have been rendered practically certain by the October elections."[20] The *New York Times* editor Henry J. Raymond courted Grant with equally emphatic predictions: "Nothing in the world can prevent your nomination by the Republican party, as things are now. They dare not and cannot nominate anybody else . . . All you have to do is to *stand still*. Say nothing, write nothing & do nothing which shall enable any faction of any party to claim you."[21] This suited Grant, who had a clever way of placing himself in the pathway to success, then calling it fate. True to Raymond's advice, *Harper's Weekly* ran a cartoon that depicted Grant as a sphinx with a cigar clenched firmly in his mouth.

To an obsessive extent, the political world speculated about the political complexion of Grant's mind. Prodded by Senator John Thayer of Nebraska, John Forney, the editor of the *Washington Daily Chronicle,* printed a lengthy article on November 7 that examined Grant's political utterances since leaving Galena, removing any doubts about his Republican leanings. The two men took an advance copy to Rawlins, who marched into Grant's office with it. Grant sat closeted with the piece for some time before Rawlins emerged to say that "General Grant is quite pleased with your statement of his political record, and surprised that he proves to be so good a Republican."[22] If this encouraged the visitors, Rawlins also relayed the sobering message that Grant didn't care to be president, for he worried about the monetary consequences. "He is receiving from seventeen to twenty thousand dollars a year as General . . . a life salary. To go into the Presidency at twenty-five thousand dollars a year is, perhaps, to gain more fame; but what is to become of him at the end of his Presidency? . . . Eight years from the 4th of March, 1869, he will be about fifty-six years old."[23] It was revealing that Grant, still haunted by his prewar fear of poverty, analyzed the presidency through the lens of financial security.

When the new Congress assembled in late November, the House Judiciary Committee, by a 5 to 4 vote, called for Johnson's impeachment. Some allegations against him were relatively trivial, revolving around vetoed bills or signed pardons. More consequential was the charge of disobeying the Tenure of Office Act, but the crucial underlying issue remained Congressional Reconstruction. Representative John Churchill of New York, who cast the committee's decisive vote, explained that he had voted against Johnson because the president intended to "prevent the reorganization of the southern states upon the plan of Congress."[24]

On November 30, President Johnson read aloud to his cabinet his shrill defense against any attempted impeachment or arrest: "You no doubt are aware that certain evil disposed persons have formed a conspiracy to depose the President of the United States, and to supply his place by an individual of their own selection." After issuing articles of impeachment, he warned, these conspirators might move to arrest him or remove him from office, and he accused them of plotting "a revolution changing the whole organic system of our Government."[25] An unrepentant Johnson served notice he would fight any impeachment effort. "I cannot deliver the great charter of a Nation's Liberty to men who, by the very act of usurping it, would show their determination to disregard and trample it under foot."[26]

When he sent a defiant annual message to Congress in early December, it polarized the situation even further. He accused Congress of burdening southern states with black voting rights even though blacks had demonstrated little capacity for government and "wherever they have been left to their own devices they have shown a constant tendency to relapse into barbarism."[27] This message claimed the dubious distinction of being the most racist such message ever penned by an American president. But the central issue was whether Johnson had committed a serious crime that met the lofty constitutional standard of "high crimes and misdemeanors" or was simply being hounded for irreconcilable political differences with Congress.

Against this impeachment backdrop, there emerged a crescendo of voices clamoring for Grant to run for president, presenting him as the nation's potential savior. On December 5, a huge rally at the Cooper Institute in New York, attended by business moguls Alexander T. Stewart and William B. Astor, endorsed Grant's nomination for the high office. As his name was bandied about for president, powerful figures schemed to stop him. Rumors had raced about that Ben Butler, having never forgiven Grant for his wartime dismissal, had stooges spying on him to scrounge up a host of past indiscretions. "Butler has had detectives following the Genl. and the story is that they will at the proper time prove 'Grant is a drunkard after fast horses women and whores,'" Orville Babcock tipped off Elihu Washburne.[28]

Johnson played a cunning game with Grant, praising his performance publicly to bind him to the administration, while surreptitiously driving a wedge between him and Stanton. When on December 12 he asked the Senate to approve Stanton's suspension, he seized the opportunity to puff up Grant's stature: "Salutary reforms have been introduced by the Secretary *ad interim,* & great reductions of expenses have been effected under his administration of the War Department, & the saving of millions to the Treasury."[29] Gideon Welles urged the president to go further and declare his confidence in Grant so he would be permanently "hitched" to the administration. "It would have made an issue between him and the Stanton Radicals," he wrote in his diary.[30]

In many ways, Welles was typical of the conservative cabinet members who vilified Grant. A prolific diarist, he issued scathing denunciations of Grant that have long been trotted out by historians. A Connecticut lawyer, journalist, and politician, he had a white beard of biblical breadth, wore a queer wig parted down the middle, and voiced a curmudgeonly outlook. During the war Lincoln had dubbed him "Old Father Neptune." In his diary, he offered so many diatribes against Grant that they come to sound almost pathological. He denounced Grant as "a political ignoramus," ignorant of the workings of government, and "severely afflicted with the Presidential disease" that warped his judgment.[31] He reviled him as someone of "sly cunning, if but little knowledge," a passive, credulous tool

in the hands of Radical Republicans, too stupid to exercise independent judgment.[32] "The race-course has more attractions for [Grant] than the Senate or the
council room," the quotable Welles wrote. "He loves money, admires wealth, is
fond of power and ready to use it remorselessly."[33] As Lincoln's navy secretary,
Welles had performed ably in blockading southern ports and building up the
navy, but Grant thought him an opportunist who had defected to the Democrats to please Andrew Johnson.

Welles's clash with Grant was at bottom a political one. He adored the president and his family. "No better persons have occupied the Executive Mansion,"
he later wrote.[34] Like Johnson, he identified with the southern white elite and
lacked sympathy for the emancipated slaves. When the subject of food relief for
hungry freed people emerged in the cabinet, Welles groused that "feeding the
lazy and destitute negroes for a few weeks was an absurdity."[35] After discussing
Reconstruction with Grant, he declared: "The Radical policy is to proscribe the
intelligent, the wealthy, the moral portion of the South, and to place over them
the ignorant and degraded and vicious."[36]

Grant considered Reconstruction a noble experiment while Welles and other
cabinet members condemned it as a misguided disaster that would put shiftless
blacks in power. Conventions now began to meet in southern states to draw up
new constitutions, which would allow them to be readmitted to the Union. At
the Louisiana and South Carolina conventions, blacks made up a majority of
delegates. Never before in American history had there been such racially integrated governmental meetings, and they pioneered in establishing public schools
and contesting discrimination. In Alabama, a racially mixed convention guaranteed voting rights to "all colored male persons of the age of 21 years."[37] The
Louisiana convention enacted a provision calling for equal access to public
transportation "without distinction of race or color or previous condition."[38] In
Charleston, seventy-six black delegates made up a majority of the state convention, many of them former slaves. Such a spectacle was anathema to many terrified whites, prompting the *Charleston Mercury* to jeer at this assembly as the
"Congo Convention."[39] More than 80 percent of black delegates were literate,
but the handful of illiterates provided endless fodder for vicious satire in the
white press, creating an enduring caricature of Reconstruction as a period of
misrule by inept black politicians.

Nothing alarmed white southerners more than the specter of blacks casting
votes. The united power of blacks, carpetbaggers, and scalawags produced a

stunning string of Republican election victories in fall 1867 across a region long solidly Democratic. Blacks embraced voting rights and registered amazingly high participation rates: a 70 percent turnout in Georgia and almost 90 percent in Virginia, casting virtually unanimous Republican votes. In Alabama, there were 89,000 black voters versus 74,000 whites, while 95,000 black voters in Georgia nearly equaled the 100,000 white voters. In a startling reversal for an area once dominated by slavery, the elections spawned black sheriffs, school board members, state legislators, and congressmen. That yesterday's slave laborer was today's state legislator horrified many white southerners who refused to accept this extraordinary inversion of their bygone world.

Several of Grant's district commanders expressed deep admiration for how freed people adapted to their new status. One was General John Pope, an unabashed Republican, whose military district encompassed Georgia, Alabama, and Florida. The South might complain of "bayonet rule," but Pope was spurred by idealism and an unflagging desire to protect black welfare. As he told Grant, "It may safely be said that the marvelous progress made in education and knowledge by these people, aided by the noble charitable contributions of Northern Societies and individuals, finds no parallel in the history of mankind . . . It becomes us therefore to guard jealously against any reaction which may and will check this most desirable progress of the colored race."[40]

Pope was too sympathetic to Congressional Reconstruction for the conservative taste of Andrew Johnson. After Pope insisted that blacks be allowed to serve on juries, Johnson fired him, overriding fierce objections from Grant and sparking fresh calls for his impeachment. In a valedictory letter to Grant, Pope argued that in his district the Confederate spirit of rebellion was still abroad and "nearly as powerful as during the War . . . You can scarcely form an idea of the spirit of malice & hatred in this people—It is a misnomer to call this question in the South a political question—It is *War* pure & simple . . . The question is not whether Georgia & Alabama will accept or reject reconstruction—It is, shall the Union men & Freedmen, be the slaves of the old negro rebel aristocracy or not?"[41]

Never cavalier about military rule in the South, Grant wanted to terminate it as soon as possible, but without sacrificing black welfare. As he told one district commander, "The best way, I think, to secure a speedy termination of Military rule is to execute all the laws of Congress in the spirit in which they were conceived, firmly but without passion."[42] Grant had to deal with hysterical denunciations of Reconstruction policy from white southerners, including Colonel

Dent, who predicted "all sorts of disasters to the Country," he told Sherman. Far from viewing carpetbaggers as greedy, predatory figures, Grant pictured them going with "brain in their heads, money in their pockets, strength and energy in their limbs" to "make the South bloom like the rose."[43]

Just how pessimistic Grant was about the southern mood was revealed by an unpublicized episode. Adam Badeau received a letter from his friend Edwin Booth, the illustrious Shakespearean actor and older brother of John Wilkes Booth. Unlike his brother, Edwin had been a faithful Union man and came to Badeau with a humble request from his elderly mother, who wished to have the remains of John Wilkes, now buried under the Old Arsenal Penitentiary, transferred to a family plot. To Grant, Badeau made an eloquent case to honor the family's wishes. "But he was immutable," wrote Badeau. "He said the time had not yet come."[44] Grant's response shows his reaction to the frightening upsurge in Confederate sentiment prevalent in the region under his personal military supervision.

THE DRAMA OVER Stanton's dismissal spiraled toward its fateful climax when the Senate Committee on Military Affairs issued a report on January 10, 1868, calling for his immediate reinstatement. Soon the entire Senate launched into a blistering debate. For Radical Republicans, nothing less than the future of the Republic lay at stake. Only Stanton's presence at the War Department "will prevent the employment . . . of this office on the side of the Rebellion," wrote Charles Sumner, adding that Andrew Johnson was "now a full-blown rebel, except that he does not risk his neck by overt acts; but in spirit he is as bad as J.D. [Jefferson Davis]."[45]

The committee's action sent Grant scurrying to study the Tenure of Office Act. He was shocked to discover that if the Senate sustained the decision to restore Stanton and Grant then refused to hand the office back to him, he faced a $10,000 fine and a five-year prison term—risks he didn't care to run. At Sherman's prompting, Grant made his way to the White House on Saturday, January 11, to alert Johnson to his concerns. Exactly what happened at that meeting would divide Grant and Johnson—and future historians—forever after.

Grant explained to Johnson that if the Senate stood by Stanton, Grant would have to vacate his office, citing the possible fine and prison term. He and Johnson quarreled bitterly over the meaning of the Tenure of Office Act. Grant believed bad laws trumped presidential directives and must be obeyed until judges rescinded them. "I stated that the law was binding on me, constitutional or not, until set aside by the proper tribunal," Grant wrote.[46] Dismissing the act as unconstitutional, Johnson refused to be bound by it and grew agitated over Grant's unbending position. With a melodramatic flourish, he promised that if Grant clung to his office when Stanton tried to retake it, he would pay the fine himself and serve the jail term. When Grant demurred at this outrageous idea, Johnson pleaded with him to resign and return the office to him before Stanton regained it. Grant came away with the clear impression that he had promised to give the office back to Stanton, while Johnson came away with an equally clear impression that Grant would hold on to it until the courts ruled otherwise. Grant said he would call on Johnson on Monday with a final decision. That meeting never took place—Congress would act in the interim—and his failure to appear formed part of Johnson's savage indictment against Grant.

Johnson thought of naming a new war secretary who stood a fair chance of Senate confirmation. Sherman suggested Governor Jacob D. Cox of Ohio, whose term would shortly expire. As a former Union general with a commendable war record, he would find favor with Grant and Republicans, while as an opponent of universal black suffrage, he might also entice moderates. According to Sherman's recollections, Grant "urged me to push the matter all I could, saying that Governor Cox was perfectly acceptable to [him], and to the Army generally."[47] Johnson evinced scant enthusiasm for the idea.

On January 13, the full Senate ratified the judgment of the Military Affairs Committee and overwhelmingly voted for Stanton's restoration as secretary of war. That evening, to the astonishment of official Washington, Grant attended a reception at the executive mansion. Julia had female friends staying with them who were eager to go, but when she asked her husband to escort them, he balked. "I would like to gratify you, but, really, under the circumstances, I do not think I ought to go."[48] Nevertheless, he yielded gallantly to the ladies. As they were leaving, a messenger arrived with news of the Senate vote, which Grant perused by the flickering glow of gaslight. He found himself in the excruciating bind he had feared, trapped between Stanton and Johnson. When he reached the White House, Johnson shook his hand genially and the two men chatted for several minutes; Grant later admitted his embarrassment at the show of presidential cordiality. At another dreadful Washington soiree that evening, Sherman chatted with Secretary of the Interior Browning, who wrote afterward that Sherman "spoke bitterly of Stanton's restoration and seemed to think the President blame-able, as he might, he said, have prevented it by nominating some moderate Re-publican for Secy of War who would have been confirmed by the Senate, and the whole subject disposed of in that way."[49]

In Grant's view, his tenure as temporary war secretary ended when he read the Senate announcement by gaslight. Early the next morning, he showed up at his War Department office, locked the door from the outside, then transferred the keys to the adjutant general. "I am to be found at my office at army headquarters," he announced.[50] Never a man to tarry, Stanton was back at work in an hour, con-verting his old office into a gloomy fortress, buttressed by guards. Though Grant had saved him, the graceless Stanton immediately started bossing him around. Grant resented his "discourteous mode" and the uncomfortable situation Stanton had created by his obstinacy.[51] Even young Jesse Grant recollected Stanton's boor-ish behavior. "Small boy that I was, I remember the rudeness of his manner."[52] Grant notified the president that he had vacated the office and no longer func-tioned as war secretary. Faced with this fait accompli, Johnson was furious, believ-ing Grant should have resigned his post and allowed him to name a successor.

Bent on showing that Grant was still war secretary, Johnson demanded his presence at a cabinet meeting, one of the most rancorous in American history. After everyone was seated, Johnson canvassed the room, asking each secretary to name a subject for discussion. When he came to Grant, the latter reminded him that he was no longer a cabinet member and attended only at his request. An enraged Johnson began to grill Grant like a prosecutor, castigating him for abandoning his office, then asked point-blank: "Why did you give up the keys to Mr. Stanton and leave the Department?"[53] According to Johnson loyalists, he reminded Grant of their understanding "that if you did not hold on to the office yourself, you would place it in my hands that I might select another?" "That," said Grant, "was my intention. I thought some satisfactory arrangement would be made to dispose of the subject." Browning quoted Grant as confessing he had agreed to hold the office until courts ruled on the Tenure of Office Act.[54]

Grant left a strikingly different version. As diplomatically as possible, he told the president he "might have understood me in the way he said, namely that I had promised to resign if I did not resist the reinstatement. I made no such promise."[55] He wondered aloud why Johnson had passed over the opportunity to appoint Governor Cox, which would have created a convenient exit from the impasse. He also explained that after his original talk with Johnson on the subject, he had read the Tenure of Office Act and learned of the severe penalties for violating it. Once again Johnson volunteered to pay the fine or serve the prison stretch. Feeling his integrity questioned, Grant abruptly asked to be excused from the meeting. According to Welles, he left in an "almost abject" state after enduring the president's "cold and surprised disdain."[56] When he was gone, Johnson inveighed against his "secret intrigue in this business" and blasted him for having acted "under the direction of the chief conspirators."[57]

During these critical days, Grant knew he was going to be damned by either the Radical Republicans or the president. Through studied ambiguity, he had tried to keep his options open until the last moment. In the end, he couldn't please both sides and wound up antagonizing the president. By this point, both his political future and fundamental principles led him to line up with Radical Republicans against Johnson, who had so patently sabotaged the work of his southern commanders. Grant wasn't being opportunistic, only true to his principles.

No longer needing to appease Grant, Johnson broadcast his anger against him to the press. The next day, an editorial in the *National Intelligencer* recounted the cabinet meeting and damned Grant for supposed duplicity. Upset by the leak, Grant and Sherman went to the White House to protest. Johnson claimed he hadn't read the article and insisted that Grant had betrayed him. In Johnson's recollection, Grant had said he would make an effort to prevail upon Stanton to resign; Grant insisted he had only said he thought Stanton *would* resign.

Two days later, Johnson had the *Intelligencer* piece read aloud to his cabinet and asked them to comment on its authenticity. While they all agreed on its accuracy, one wonders how anyone could have dissented knowing Johnson's desired response. All four cabinet supporters of Johnson's version of the truth were his rabid partisans. Only William Seward disputed the consensus, maintaining that Grant's statements had been ambiguous and his admissions "rather indirect and circumstantial."[58] Grant had not lied but he may well have equivocated, which to Johnson amounted to the same thing. The president demanded that Grant obey no orders from Stanton unless issued by presidential direction, a move that Grant would rebuff. When Grant went to Stanton and discussed his possible resignation, he realized such advice was useless with the headstrong Stanton. Welles maintained that Stanton assumed "an imperious and angry look" toward Grant and spoke "loud and violently," leaving Grant not "daring to make known the object of his mission."[59]

In the firestorm of charges and countercharges, the press divided along predictably partisan lines. Pro-Johnson papers dredged up old drinking charges against Grant, asserting he was inebriated during the Stanton imbroglio. The Republican press refused to accept that Grant, a stickler for the truth, would ever stoop to dishonesty. "In a question of veracity between U.S. Grant and Andrew Johnson, between a soldier whose honor is as untarnished as the sun, and a President who has betrayed every friend, and broken every promise, the country will not hesitate," wrote the *New York Tribune*.[60]

On January 28, Grant sent Johnson a letter on Stanton's suspension and attempted to show he had consistently denied he would defy a Senate ruling in the matter. He reiterated that his views had changed after studying the Tenure of Office Act. Far from tugging his forelock, Grant adopted a waspish tone that accelerated the break between the two men. He "in no wise admitted the correctness" of Johnson's recollection of events and denied he had ever made a promise to resign as war secretary.[61] When the letter surfaced around town, Radical Republicans seemed jubilant as any appearance of amity between Johnson and Grant vanished. "He is a bolder man than I thought him," Thaddeus Stevens said of Grant. "Now we will let him into the church."[62] At a stroke, Grant had virtually guaranteed he would be the Republican nominee for president.

Rawlins had returned from Galena to support Grant in the controversy. On February 3, dropping any pretense of impartiality, Grant sent Johnson an impassioned letter that essentially called him a liar, a coward, and a lawbreaker. To have resisted Stanton's reinstatement, Grant alleged, would have meant breaking the law. "And now, Mr. President, where my honor as a soldier and integrity as a man have been so violently assailed, pardon me for saying that I can but regard this whole matter, from the beginning to the end, as an attempt to involve me in the resistance of law . . . and thus to destroy my character before the country."[63] These were shockingly bold words from Grant, who accused the president of smearing his reputation and attempting to bully him into committing a crime. According to Badeau, Rawlins told Grant that neutrality with Johnson was impossible and that the time had come for an open breach. To that end, Rawlins redrafted Grant's February 3 letter, making its language even more scorching. Rawlins had always exercised an outsize influence on Grant, but this intervention seemed extraordinary. "I never in my intercourse with Grant saw another instance where another exercised so direct and palpable and important an influence with him," wrote Badeau. "It made [Grant] a Republican. Rawlins knew this."[64] Rawlins again functioned as Grant's alter ego, his conscience, his better self.

A week later, the president sent Grant a reply that matched his blunt vehemence: "First of all, you here admit that from the very beginning of what you term 'the whole history' of your connection with Mr. Stanton's suspension, you intended to circumvent the President. It was to carry out that intent that you accepted the appointment."[65] Even by the lowly standards of Washington blood sport, this was bare-knuckled politics. All the while, said Senator George Williams, Grant had remained "cool and undisturbed, though his honor was at stake, and undismayed by the formidable array of power and influence against him."[66]

Increasingly desperate, Johnson turned to Sherman, hoping to enlist the army on his side in a showdown with Congress. On February 12, he ordered Grant to create a new military division that would encompass Washington, with Sherman as its commander and its headquarters located in the capital. By this transparent subterfuge, Johnson hoped to neuter Grant and control the army through Sherman. Having tried to divide Grant and Stanton, he now attempted to do the same with Sherman, who again feared the arrangement would jeopardize his long-standing relationship with Grant. In distress, he told Grant that "I never felt so troubled in my life" and objected to "the false position I would occupy as between you and the President."[67] Sherman composed a deeply felt letter to Johnson, expressing discomfort at being placed in a rivalrous position with his old friend. If difficulties arose between them, he would have "no alternative but resignation."[68] In an earlier letter to the president, Sherman had noted the unfortunate changes wrought in the trusting Grant by Washington's corrosive atmosphere. He had been with Grant through "death and slaughter . . . and yet I never saw him more troubled than since he has been in Washington, and been compelled to read himself a 'sneak and deceiver,' based on reports of four of the Cabinet, and apparently with your knowledge."[69] In the end, Johnson decided that he couldn't afford to alienate the two leading war heroes and withdrew his controversial order.

THE WORSE THINGS LOOKED FOR Andrew Johnson, the brighter was the political future for Grant. In early February, when the New York Republican Convention endorsed him for president, it gave a tremendous fillip to his potential candidacy. His actions during this pivotal time have been interpreted in two ways: that he either kept his head down and didn't dabble in politics or, under the cloak of serving Congress, cannily angled for Radical Republican support

for president. The two interpretations perhaps reflect his own ambivalence. After the war he had attained an exalted stature in North and South that transcended party labels and a political career could threaten that appeal. Still a
relative newcomer to politics, he recoiled from the dishonest wrangling in Washington. "Indeed, the spectacle of Johnson dishonored, impeached, almost deposed, was not calculated to make one who stood so near at all eager to become
his successor," wrote Badeau.[70] When people inquired about his presidential aspirations, Grant met them with perfect silence and a blank, stony face that mystified even the most penetrating observers.

Badeau thought the Democratic sympathies of the Dents may have held
Grant back, but this seems highly unlikely since Julia, who had been brought up
to daydream of a higher destiny, was always ambitious for her husband. Ideology
was less important to her than power, whose trappings she now craved. When he
considered a presidential run, Grant told Julia he didn't relish being president
but considered himself well situated to effect a rapprochement between North
and South. "The South will accept my decision on any matters affecting its interests more amiably than that of any other man. They know I would be just and
would administer the law without prejudice."[71] Julia didn't prod him to run—
she bristled at the idea she was a pushy wife—but once he made the decision, she
followed him most devoutly. "I became an enthusiastic politician," she would
recall. "No delegation was too large, no serenade too long."[72]

It goes without saying that Jesse Root Grant promoted his famous son with
unashamedly bumptious pride. When the *New York Ledger* assigned a reporter
to collect stories about Ulysses's boyhood, Jesse furnished a bumper crop of three
letters recounting favorite anecdotes. They soon appeared in weekly newspaper
installments under the rubric "The Early Life of Gen. Grant." Once Grant
found out about his father's latest escapade, he was predictably outraged and
interceded to block publication of further letters. The newspaper's editor assured
Jesse that his letters contained no political allusions to his son and couldn't be
misconstrued as "writing him up as a Presidential candidate," but they indeed
looked like a blatant campaign ploy.[73]

The prospect of a Grant candidacy led to microscopic scrutiny of his personal behavior, producing fresh drinking allegations. After New York Republicans endorsed him, the *New York World* branded him "a commonplace man. He
has no military talent . . . is hated by the army. He is generally drunk."[74] It's hard
to know whether these rumor mills simply rehashed wartime chatter. That

January, a woman named Helen Griffing, who resided in Washington, told the New York editor Theodore Tilton that she had walked down F Street on a recent evening and "passed two gentlemen, one of them very intoxicated, leaning on the arm of the other. The one who was intoxicated I believe to be Gen. Grant."[75] In March, Elihu Washburne, long a clearinghouse for Grant drinking stories, heard from his friend Rufus P. Stebbins that Grant had reportedly been "seen reeling on the street." After stating with alarm that "twenty millions of the best men women and children would weep at the bare *possibility* of this being true," Stebbins suggested that Grant agree to a total abstinence pledge.[76]

After President Johnson despaired of luring Sherman to Washington, he moved swiftly to banish Stanton. On February 21, without consulting the Senate, he fired him and replaced him as secretary of war ad interim with General Lorenzo Thomas, the army adjutant general. Grant saw Stanton soon afterward and told him to hold his ground as secretary. As word spread to the Capitol, Charles Sumner fired off a telegram to Stanton with a single imperative syllable: "Stick."[77] Stanton turned his office into a veritable locked bunker, pocketing the key. Thomas notified Grant that he would operate from his H Street residence, while Stanton remained "camped in the war office," as one editor phrased it.[78]

Johnson had unleashed the political equivalent of an act of war against Congress. Retaliating against the president's violation of the Tenure of Office Act, the House introduced a resolution to impeach Andrew Johnson for high crimes and misdemeanors. Three days later, the resolution passed by an overwhelming 126 to 47 vote, with every Republican aligned against the president. Until recently, Grant had frowned upon impeachment as an extreme remedy, but Johnson's press vendetta against him and their wounding exchange of letters had changed his mind. Badeau observed that "when the motion for impeachment was finally passed he heartily approved it."[79] Grant now harbored deep antagonism toward Johnson that burst out when he rode a streetcar with Senator John Henderson of Missouri. "I would impeach [Johnson] . . . because he is such an infernal liar," Grant exclaimed.[80] Rawlins was openly indignant against the president, while Grant, no less enraged, was more circumspect in style.

Eleven impeachment articles were filed against Johnson, all but two revolving around Stanton's firing. Those two struck closer to the source of congressional discontent, accusing the president of refusal to implement Reconstruction laws and employing "intemperate, inflammatory and scandalous harangues" against legislators.[81] As Congressman William Kelley of Pennsylvania proclaimed: "The unsheeted ghosts of the two thousand murdered negroes in Texas, cry . . . for the punishment of Andrew Johnson."[82] Radicals took a broad view of impeachment, hoping Johnson would stand trial for combating Reconstruction, sparing them the need to document violation of a particular law. Moderates championed the narrower view that a president could only be removed for committing a specific crime; hence their emphasis on the Tenure of Office Act.

For pro-impeachment forces one complicating factor was that Johnson had no vice president, so that if he were removed, the office would fall to the president pro tempore of the Senate, Benjamin Wade of Ohio, whose Radical Republican views offended moderate Republicans and Democrats alike, one chiding him for being "the first to secure the nigger suffrage enactment."[83] As the impeachment trial approached, an apocalyptic mood seized the country, arousing fears of a violent confrontation. For weeks, Gideon Welles had warned Johnson that Congress meditated a military coup, employing Grant as its cat's-paw. After Johnson was impeached, General Ord told Grant that someone had asked him "what I thought would be the course of Army officers if the President should . . . call on them to support him as against the Congress—and I told him that nine tenths or perhaps more of the officers would Certainly support Congress."[84]

When the Senate impeachment trial began on March 5, Chief Justice Salmon P. Chase officiated in his judicial robes, while Grant's bête noire, Benjamin F. Butler, acted as a snarling chief prosecutor. Everybody recognized the historic nature of the occasion: this was the first time the House had impeached and the Senate tried a sitting president. Instead of testifying in person, Johnson followed events by a telegraph wire hooked up between the Capitol and the Willard Hotel, leaving his defense to William Evarts, who complained, "The managers conduct the trial as if it was that of a horse thief."[85]

The Senate chamber grew tense as congressmen and cabinet members crowded in behind senators while packed galleries erupted in prolonged waves of partisan applause. Grant had hoped to escape to Missouri, but felt nervous leaving the capital in such an uproar and minutely monitored proceedings from his office. Although consulted regularly by party leaders, he thought it inappropriate to appear at the trial. As odds-on favorite to be the Republican presidential nominee, his presence would appear unseemly. During the war he had learned that it was better to let power seek him rather than to pursue it; a good general waited to be summoned by his superiors. Nevertheless, he remained far from inactive during the trial. "He not only conversed with those whose action he thought he could affect, arguing in favor of the conviction of Johnson and demonstrating his guilt," wrote Badeau, "but he visited at least one Senator at his house with this purpose."[86] Despite his reticence in public, Grant's position was widely bruited on Capitol Hill, Charles Sumner citing Grant as "earnest for the condemnation of the [president]."[87]

Despite legitimate grievances against the president, the impeachment case ultimately rested on a slender base. Evarts pointed out that the Tenure of Office Act violated the Constitution. Even if constitutional, he argued, it did not apply to Stanton, who had originally been appointed by Lincoln. He presented Andrew Johnson as a statesmanlike figure who had challenged the act in a judicious manner, dismissing Stanton and waiting for the courts to decide. The legal arguments were dwarfed by the larger political context since many voters viewed the impeachment trial as a referendum on the war and Reconstruction, abolition and civil rights. As the attorney Edwards Pierrepont wrote to Grant from New York City: "Let no man be deceived—This is the trial of an issue which determines whether true men or rebels shall rule."[88] Several weeks into the trial, Grant thought the Senate would convict Johnson, terminating his career and casting him into outer darkness. "Impeachment seems to grow in popularity," he wrote, "and indications are that the trial will not be protracted."[89]

By May 15, Grant concluded that "impeachment is likely to fail."[90] The next day, amid extraordinary drama, the first vote was taken on whether to convict President Johnson on the eleventh impeachment article. One representative recalled legislators looking "pale and sick" from the intolerable suspense, while a senator remembered how his colleagues "leaned over their desks, many with hand to ear."[91] A conviction required a two-thirds vote of the Senate. Johnson was acquitted by a single vote when Edmund G. Ross, a junior senator from Kansas, cast the vote that rescued him. Seven Republicans voted to acquit, effectively ending the crisis. Subsequent votes merely reproduced these results. Many senators had feared a conviction would lead to legislative tyranny and presidential impotence in the future. Some thought Johnson's misdeeds didn't rise to the level of high crimes or misdemeanors. Others worried that Ben Wade, as president pro tempore of the Senate, would ascend to the presidency and capture the Republican nomination instead of Grant. With Johnson acquitted, everyone knew, Grant would get the party nod. Significantly, the seven Republicans who voted for acquittal all campaigned for Grant after he secured the nomination. They also extracted a critical pledge from Johnson that he would cease interfering with congressional action on Reconstruction.

Initially Grant regretted the acquittal, but he conceded with hindsight that a conviction would have done lasting harm. With the power of the Radicals eroded by the decision, Grant became a shoo-in for the Republican nomination. Julia Grant, too, came to applaud the decision. "I could not free myself from the thought that the trial savored of persecution and that it was a dangerous precedent," she later wrote.[92] Acknowledging his bitter defeat, a discredited Stanton resigned and John Schofield, with Grant's ready endorsement, was easily confirmed in his stead. Andrew Johnson never forgave Grant for backing his tormentors, accusing him of "standing behind the seven managers of impeachment, with Butler in the lead, urging them on to impeachment and declaring conviction and deposition indispensable to save the country . . . In this encounter he was again repulsed and driven back in . . . disgrace."[93] The next stage of Grant's career would signify anything but disgrace.

Trading Places

THOUGH TRANQUILLITY DESCENDED BRIEFLY on Washington after Andrew Johnson's acquittal, he disappointed Republicans who imagined he would prove more pliant on Reconstruction. Whether issuing amnesty proclamations or appointing conservative southern commanders, he showed that he wouldn't water down his views during his nine months left in office. Most upsetting to Grant was that Johnson turned a deaf ear to anguished pleas from blacks and white Republicans that armed terror from the Ku Klux Klan had proliferated and met no resistance from white lawmen. He transmitted to the president a letter from a Tennessee representative who described gangs of mounted men "scouring the country by night—causing dismay & terror to all—Our civil authorities are powerless."[1] In response, Johnson hid behind the shield of states' rights and declared that, having received no direct aid requests from the Tennessee legislature, the federal government lacked all jurisdiction in the matter.

Grant did what he could to counter this brazen show of presidential indifference. He was especially concerned about terror in New Orleans. "Loyal men are being murdered in many parishes . . . revenge and murders are rampant in our state," an informant wrote. "Can nothing be done to protect our loyal people from assassination?"[2] The commander there was Grant's old West Coast bogeyman, Robert C. Buchanan, who had refused to stanch the bleeding. "If Civil government fails to protect the Citizen," Grant reprimanded him, "Military government should supply its place."[3] Once again, Grant did not see himself as disobeying Johnson so much as heeding the dictates of Congress, which had laid down the laws on military occupation.

Throughout the South, conventions had spawned new constitutions to protect freed people's rights, qualifying their states for readmission to the Union. In late June, six states were folded back into the Union, resuming congressional representation. On July 9, 1868, the Fourteenth Amendment was ratified, bestowing citizenship rights upon blacks as well as women and children born in the United States of immigrants, guaranteeing them due process and equal protection of the law and prohibiting state infringement on those rights. The amendment specified that federal or state officials who had sworn to uphold the Constitution and then joined the rebellion could only be eligible for government jobs through a two-thirds vote in Congress.

Grant's boldness in upholding Radical Reconstruction surely arose from the knowledge that he would soon be the Republican nominee for president, even though he never openly declared his candidacy. In his political life, there had always been an illusion of passivity, the sense of a massive wave lifting him to the next plateau without corresponding effort on his part, while all the time he had quietly positioned himself to ride its crest. He did not exactly want the presidential job, but neither did he exactly *not* want it. "I wasn't sorry to be a candidate," he later said, "but I was very sorry to leave the command of the army."[4] Still viewing events through the dark prism of the war, he equated the Republican Party with the Union cause and believed only he could unify it, even as he identified the Democratic Party with the white supremacist South: "I believed that if a democratic president was elected there would be little chance for those who fought for the Union."[5] If Republican leaders wondered about Grant's true convictions—and his private actions as chief general had long confirmed his Republican credentials—the rank and file adored him, and it was hard to argue with such popularity as an aura of inevitability began to surround his candidacy.

As Republican delegates set off for their Chicago convention—it met days after Johnson's acquittal—the prospective nominee and his wife debated their future in private. When Julia asked if he wished to be president, Grant exhibited less than gushing enthusiasm. "No," he replied, "but I do not see that I have anything to say about it. The convention is about to assemble and, from all I hear, they will nominate me; and I suppose if I am nominated, I will be elected."[6] In part Grant's response can be attributed to native modesty and a strict

Methodist upbringing, but it also marked a transitional moment in a life hitherto devoted to military protocol and following orders. Henceforth he would need to learn the wily and aggressive arts of a politician instead of simply retreating behind the pose of a self-effacing soldier.

Right before the convention, a "Soldiers and Sailors" gathering met in Chicago and symbolically nominated Grant for president. Doubtless fulfilling a long-suppressed fantasy, Jesse Root Grant rose to address the crowd in support of his son. It astonished him, he confessed, that he "who had done nothing in particular in the great war for the country, should be called upon by the braves of the nation to speak." "You had a boy," shouted an audience member. "That is enough."[7] Alarmed by Jesse's forwardness, Elihu Washburne and his circle had conspired to intercept him before he traveled to Chicago, even enlisting his son Orvil in the effort, but only brute force could have prevented the loquacious Jesse from droning on before a large, enthusiastic assembly.

The next day, with Jesse proudly in attendance, eight thousand Republicans crammed into Crosby's Opera House for a veritable coronation of Ulysses S. Grant. To play on wartime memories, General John "Black Jack" Logan was designated to place his name in nomination. His speech was followed by a well-staged extravaganza: hats and handkerchiefs fluttered, rounds of applause rippled across the house, and a pigeon, dyed red, white, and blue, flapped through the cavernous space. As a huge ovation for his son gathered strength, Jesse Grant stood before the speaker's platform in "mute astonishment," said a reporter.[8] Then a curtain rose to reveal huge images drawn by Thomas Nast of the Goddess of Liberty, juxtaposed with Grant. To no one's surprise, Grant won by acclamation on the first ballot. Nobody else was even nominated. Abiding by the custom of nominees staying away from conventions, Grant remained in Washington, hard at work and seemingly in harness at army headquarters.

The suspense in Chicago centered upon the choice of a vice presidential candidate. At the time, presidential nominees had no real say in selecting running mates. After several ballots, the convention settled upon House Speaker Schuyler Colfax of Indiana, a man so amiable he was known as "Smiler" Colfax. One delegate described him as a "good-tempered, chirping . . . real canary bird."[9] According to Gideon Welles, Lincoln had scorned Colfax as "a little intriguer—plausible," but "not trustworthy."[10] Although Colfax had supported Edward Bates for the Republican nomination in 1860, he had then become an ardent Lincoln adherent. "Colfax is a young man, is already in position, is running a brilliant career and is sure of a bright future in any event," wrote Lincoln, who considered naming him to his cabinet.[11] After the war, Colfax became a fervent booster for Reconstruction and black voting rights.

Grant learned of his nomination when Edwin Stanton came panting up the stairs and burst into his office. "General! I have come to tell you that you have been nominated by the Republican party for President of the United States."[12] Grant was probably less astonished by the news than by Stanton's unwonted ebullience. He reacted with his usual poker face, repressing a smile. "I did not want the Presidency, and have never quite forgiven myself for resigning the command of the army to accept it; but it could not be helped," he reminisced. "I owed my honors and opportunities to the Republican party, and if my name could aid it I was bound to accept."[13] He feared the Democratic Party had become a haven for rebel sympathizers who refused to accept the basic tenets of Unionism, and he saw it as his duty to stand as the Republican nominee. Taking a bitter swipe at Johnson, Phil Sheridan had promised him that "the period is not distant when loyalty to the government will not be considered a crime at the White House."[14]

Grant was elected on a platform very congenial to him. The Republican Party had drifted to the right on economic issues, while maintaining an unalterable commitment to black equality before the law and the right of freed people to participate in southern politics. The platform forged an amalgam of old and new, harking back to the party's founding abolitionist principles and ahead to the conservative economics of its future. The pragmatic Grant could embody this new synthesis without fear of contradiction.

Conforming to tradition, the convention sent a delegation to Grant with official notice of his nomination. In return, he scratched out a statement that mostly dealt in standard rhetoric, concluding with four words that formed the slogan of his campaign and remained irreversibly associated with him: "Let us have peace."[15] These words, an inspired piece of phrasemaking, were gobbled up by the public and showed Grant's sound political instincts. Translating this motto into practice, however, would prove far more daunting for it spoke to two competing themes: the need for reconciliation between North and South and the need to consolidate the war objectives. For some, the credo sounded blandly vacuous and Henry Adams wisecracked that "Let Us Have Peace" meant only "Leave Me Alone."[16]

Backed by southern supporters, Andrew Johnson vainly hoped that the Democrats would nominate him at their July convention in New York. He managed to place second on the first two ballots before his candidacy faded altogether. On the twenty-second ballot, the delegates chose the colorless Horatio Seymour, a protégé of Martin Van Buren, who had been close to Boss Tweed and Tammany Hall and a notorious Copperhead as wartime governor of New York. His résumé confirmed Grant's stereotype of the Democrats as the party of reaction. Seymour had denounced the Emancipation Proclamation as "a proposal for the butchery of women and children, for scenes . . . of arson and murder."[17] During the 1863 draft riots in New York, Seymour had praised the responsible hooligans as "my friends" in what some deemed treasonous behavior.[18] His record threw into bold relief Grant's heroic stature and ability to capitalize on Unionist sentiment.

For vice president, the Democrats picked the irascible Francis Preston Blair Jr. of Missouri, who had fought gallantly as a Union general before emerging as a biting critic of Reconstruction. Right before the convention, Blair published a letter that contested black suffrage in the South, proposing a plan to raze the entire scaffolding of Reconstruction. He wanted the new president to "declare the reconstruction acts null and void; compel the army to undo its usurpations at the South; [and] allow the white people to reorganize their own governments."[19] Once nominated, Blair freely bashed Grant, accusing him of wanting to uphold military "usurpations over the eight millions of white people at the South, fixed to the earth with his bayonets."[20] Though his brother Montgomery had represented Dred Scott before the Supreme Court, Frank Blair was an unabashed racist who vowed that as vice president he would "prevent the people of our race . . . from being driven out of the country or trodden under foot by an inferior and semi-barbarous race."[21] Walt Whitman summed up the Democratic ticket by calling it "a regular old Copperhead Democratic ticket, of the rankest kind—probably pleases the old democratic bummers around New York and Brooklyn—but everywhere else they take it like a bad dose of medicine."[22]

As befit the political custom of the time, Grant did not actively campaign or make formal speeches. Lacking the big, overflowing personality or oratorical skills of a lifelong politician, he was lucky to have that custom in effect. Dating back to the early days of the Civil War, he had maintained a firm belief that one's worth should be recognized instead of being crassly promoted, and he refused to allow party leaders to hatch any deals to secure his election. Back in Washington, Rawlins and other party stalwarts drafted letters and gave speeches as his surrogates, while James H. Wilson and Charles A. Dana pumped out laudatory campaign biographies.

In early June, Grant traveled to St. Louis, where he had gained possession of White Haven and an additional 280 acres from the Dent family. It was another strange, dreamlike transformation of his life from his dreary years there in the 1850s. Now he was master of the plantation he had first visited fresh out of West Point, and Colonel Dent, having suffered a crippling stroke, depended upon him and Julia. Grant planned to spend several weeks there yearly, planting strawberries and other fruits and breeding blooded horses. To banish any lingering remnants of slavery, he had his steward, William Elrod, demolish a dozen slave cabins. As president, he would closely manage the farm through Elrod.

After St. Louis, Grant moved on to Fort Leavenworth, Kansas, where he joined Sherman and Sheridan for a two-week western tour. Although they inspected forts, they participated in a new type of military campaign, this one to garner votes, with a crew of reporters tagging along to chronicle the journey. Grant, having never set eyes on the Great Plains, wanted his son Buck to see them "whilst still occupied by the Buffalo and the Indian, both rapidly disappearing now."[23] Like many travelers of the day, the party carried carbines to shoot buffalo, helping to hasten their demise. When they journeyed by stagecoach to Denver, they took frequent potshots through the windows at herds of antelope, killing two of them. Grant rhapsodized about the beauty of the American West, only regretting the "three epidemics" that had plagued it: the pistol, the bowie knife, and whiskey.[24]

Circling back to the Midwest, he gave a brief speech to well-wishers in St. Louis before arriving at his Galena house on August 7. "After an absence of three years from your midst," he told a gathering, "it affords me great pleasure to return here again to see you all, and, as I hope, spend an agreeable and quiet fortnight with you."[25] Wherever he went, Grant encountered swarms of people who longed to see him. Whether from genuine or fake modesty, he professed to be startled by these swelling, enthusiastic crowds. Visiting a friend in Quincy, Illinois, he was amazed by the throngs who engulfed his every step. "What was my surprise to find what seems to be not only the whole city, but the county of Adams, turned out to welcome me to your midst," Grant told the appreciative townspeople.[26]

By August 18, Grant had settled into Galena for a prolonged stay, assisted by Adam Badeau and Cyrus Comstock. Galena gave Grant a convenient residence in the American heartland, where he could lie low and shun publicity. He read newspapers attentively each morning, then drove and visited old friends in the afternoon or stopped by the DeSoto House Hotel. Friends and party managers wanted him to stay in the East so he could easily be consulted. Grant isolated himself, however, leaving instructions that official business should be referred to Rawlins, who forwarded only urgent letters to him. It was the first troubling sign that Grant, in his new political incarnation, might ignore professional advice and prove unwilling to modify his traditional style to accommodate new political realities. Grant would hail the summer of 1868 as his most balmy and restful since the war began.

Despite his seeming indolence, his campaign flourished and by midsummer Senator Charles Sumner wrote, "Everything is auspicious politically. Grant will surely be elected."[27] For an increasingly fragmented Republican Party that wanted to remember the war and rally around a common hero, Grant possessed an irresistible appeal. Something of a political cipher, he enabled moderates to imagine he might weaken the Radicals, while Radicals believed he would perpetuate Reconstruction. Grant's minions busily cultivated the top plutocrats of the day, and northern business leaders piled into the campaign, with the financier Jay Cooke and others disgorging large donations into party coffers, while Democrats aimed to exploit a populist backlash against the big-business coloring of their opponents.

Toward the end of the campaign, when Horatio Seymour delivered a handful of campaign speeches, a joke made the rounds that "Grant takes his cigar—Seymour takes the stump."[28] Democrats conducted a defamatory campaign, portraying Grant as a drunken dolt. Seymour supporters invented new lyrics to a ditty called "Captain Jinks of the Horse Marines," with words that went: "I am Captain Grant of the Black Marines, / The stupidest man that ever was seen." The song also featured this nasty couplet: "I smoke my weed and drink my gin, / Paying with the people's tin."[29] Nobody was more disgusted by the drinking tales than Julia Grant. One morning in Galena, she read a newspaper story that her husband was "in a state of frenzy and is tearing up his mattress, swearing it is made of snakes." Then she gazed up from her paper and scrutinized her sober husband "dressed in his white linen suit, calmly smoking and reading his paper and smiling at my wrathful indignation, saying, 'I do not mind that, Mrs. Grant. If it were true, I would feel very badly, perhaps as badly as you do.'"[30]

Ideologically, Democrats identified Grant as a tool of Radical Republicans and their Reconstruction program. "This is a white man's country," ran the party's motto, "let white men rule." Frank Blair spewed forth incurably racist remarks, claiming Republicans in the South had promoted "a semi-barbarous race of blacks" who yearned to "subject the white women to their unbridled lust."[31] Thanks to Blair's vile rhetoric, Democrats ran what the historian David W. Blight has branded "one of the most explicitly racist presidential campaigns in American history."[32] Grant railed at the "desperate and unscrupulous" tactics of Democrats, but Republicans didn't shy away from invective either, spreading rumors that Horatio Seymour was insane.[33]

Everybody knew the Jewish issue would surface because of Grant's notorious General Orders No. 11 during the war, when he had temporarily banned Jews as a class from his military department. A year earlier, Schuyler Colfax had argued against Grant's nomination because of "the danger of losing at one blow the whole Jew vote, by his having banished the whole of them publicly from his lines at Paducah" during the war.[34] The party feared that large concentrations of Jewish Republicans in Cincinnati, St. Louis, and Chicago might defect to the Democrats, dragging entire states down with them. During the campaign, Grant received hundreds of letters from Jewish voters, seeking reassuring explanations for his wartime order.

The publisher Joseph Medill was so upset by a possible Jewish crossover vote to the Democrats that he suggested to Elihu Washburne that Grant submit an expiatory letter to "leading and influential" Jewish leaders as a way of "smoothing the matter over."[35] Grant took personal responsibility, disavowing his wartime order as a thoughtless, misguided action that a moment's reflection might have blocked. To Isaac Morris, who was Jewish, he insisted in September, "I have no prejudice against sect or race but want each individual to be judged by his own merit." He admitted that General Orders No. 11 "does not sustain this statement . . . but then I do not sustain that order. It never would have been issued if it had not been telegraphed the moment penned, without one moment's reflection."[36] This letter traveled widely in the Jewish community. Grant also sat down with David Eckstein, a Jewish leader from Cincinnati, and convinced him that he regretted his wartime action and was free of any anti-Semitic taint. He told the lawyer Simon Wolf that his wartime order was "directed simply against evil designing persons, whose religion was in no way material to the issue."[37] In the end, Jewish voters across the country forgave and endorsed Grant, who began a systematic effort to atone for his atrocious decision.

The black population loaded enormous expectations on Grant, one hopeful black editor predicting that when "Grant becomes President, a great many wrongs would be made right."[38] Blacks still couldn't vote in many northern states, whereas they could vote in most formerly Confederate states. Blacks associated the Democratic Party with the slaveholding South, making them natural Republican adherents. "Does anybody want a revised and corrected edition of Andrew Johnson in the presidential chair for the next four years?" Frederick Douglass asked rhetorically.[39] In an influential essay, he reminded readers that for decades the Democratic Party had existed "to serve the great privileged class at the South." The marching orders for the black electorate were now clear: usher in Grant "by a vote so pronounced and overwhelming as to extinguish every ray of hope to the rebel cause."[40] One black woman in California so zealously supported Grant that she deferred all clothing purchases for several months, telling a reporter that if "Grant was not elected, she would never want anything more to wear, for she would die."[41]

The campaign's most chilling feature was the huge wave of murder and arson orchestrated by the Ku Klux Klan against black and white Republicans in the South. As state conventions drafted new constitutions that endowed blacks with the franchise, the white South acted to stamp out that voting power through brute force. Nathan Bedford Forrest boasted that the Klan had recruited forty thousand men in Tennessee alone, half a million across the South. This bloodthirsty backlash grew out of simple arithmetic: in South Carolina and Mississippi, blacks made up a majority of the electorate, while in other southern states, the substantial black populace, joined with white Republicans, appeared set to prevail during Reconstruction.

In some southern states, white employers threatened blacks with job losses if they voted Republican, and elsewhere whites resorted to naked violence to dampen Republican electoral prospects. In Opelousas, Louisiana, armed mobs of Democrats wrecked a Republican newspaper office, expelled its editor, and shot as many as two hundred blacks. So egregious was the ubiquitous terror in the state that Grant estimated that between fraud and violence, the Republican vote had been whittled down to a few thousand.[42] In Camilla, Georgia, hundreds of armed whites shot indiscriminately into a black election parade, murdering or wounding many marchers. Throughout the South, black organizers were gunned down with impunity and President Johnson, having purged Grant's best regional commanders, did nothing to halt the mayhem.

Until Election Day, Grant remained secluded in Galena, preferring to be a distant spectator of the campaign and telling Washburne that someone living in

Galena would have no idea of a presidential race "if it were not for the accounts we read in the papers of great gatherings all over the country."[43] Grant withdrew into a shell from which he seldom emerged, deferring the "evil day" of returning to Washington until after the election.[44] He still urged his Washington staff to withhold letters he received, knowing the majority would come from people badgering him for jobs. One noteworthy reason Grant provided for his Galena isolation was his fear that he might be assassinated before the election.[45] Once elected, he thought the incentive to kill him would decline. In typical Grant fashion, he mentioned this to a friend in a matter-of-fact way without elaboration, but Badeau later revealed that Grant received several letters bearing death threats.[46]

Such fears aside, the one thing that marred Grant's relative calm was press speculation about his strained relations with Sherman. For Sherman, politics had always been anathema, but he understood that Grant might think otherwise and believed that as president he would give the country "eight years of calm, quiet, firm administration."[47] A purist in his loathing for politics, Sherman refused to provide Grant with a public endorsement that might have swayed some veterans. To subdue talk of a rift in their friendship, Grant went to stay with Sherman at his farm outside St. Louis and professed to understand his reluctance to issue a statement of support. Still he was disappointed Sherman never openly aided his campaign. The problem was less personal than a clash of radically divergent worldviews—Sherman opposed Reconstruction and military occupation of the South—and the gap would only yawn wider in coming years.

The drift of the election was dramatically disclosed in mid-October when Republicans scored victories in Pennsylvania, Ohio, and Indiana, virtually ensuring Grant the presidency. For Orville Browning, Johnson's conservative interior secretary, such a prospect guaranteed that Reconstruction, which he hated, would be preserved: "Grant will be the next President, and the Country is yet to have darker days, and heavier afflictions than have been endured in the past. The troubles in the Southern States will be aggravated and armies must be kept there to maintain the despotisms of Reconstruction."[48]

On November 3, Grant marched off to the polls and voted a straight Republican ticket, omitting only the vote for president. That evening he wandered over to the home of Elihu Washburne, where a telegraph was installed near the front window to speed election results to Galena. Aside from Washburne and a couple of Republican correspondents, it was mostly townspeople who mingled excitedly in the house, Grant being the most imperturbable. "I often saw him show more interest over a game at cards than on that night when the Presidency was played for," Badeau commented.[49] Well after midnight, when Grant learned he had been elected president, he appeared on Washburne's doorstep to address dozens of citizens who had gathered to celebrate. His speech was curt, as usual. "The responsibilities of the position I feel, but accept them without fear, if I can have the same support which has been given to me thus far." With a placid demeanor, he promised to make an "annual pilgrimage" back to Galena, which was always afraid of losing him.[50]

Grant had captured the popular vote by a comfortable but not overwhelming margin, collecting 3,013,000 votes versus 2,709,000 for Seymour. Nonetheless, he won all but eight states and trounced Seymour in an electoral landslide of 214 to 80. Bolstered by black and white carpetbagger votes, all southern states, with the notable exception of Georgia and Louisiana, where Klan violence was rife, tumbled into the Republican column. White violence had also diminished Republican turnout in Tennessee, Alabama, and South Carolina. Grant probably lost the majority of white votes, but hundreds of thousands of black votes made up the difference, an outcome that would add self-interest to idealism as he and other Republicans mobilized to grant black citizens the ballot.

Wending his way back to Washington, Grant remained heedless of death threats, even though his route was widely reported. His less sanguine aides packed guns without telling him. Since Grant had not campaigned, the future course of his administration was unclear. Would he be the Grant of Appomattox or the Grant of Reconstruction? "Already the bitterness and animosity, always engendered by a Presidential campaign, are subsiding," he wrote a week after the election, sounding like the candidate who had intoned the soothing slogan "Let us have peace." "I hope now for national quiet and more looking after material interests."[51] But the electorate had divided along sectional and racial lines with no compromise in sight, portending a period of profound turbulence ahead. The South, so often the wartime battleground, had now become a different kind of killing field. Thomas Nast published an election cartoon entitled "Victory!" that showed Grant mounted on a white horse, waving a flag bedecked with the words "Union" and "Equal Rights," as he thrust his sword into the throat of Horatio Seymour, who sat astride a black horse with the initials "K.K.K." branded ominously on its flank.[52]

When President-elect Grant returned to Washington on November 7, he slipped so unobtrusively into the capital, taking a public coach from the train station to his house, that reporters didn't know he had returned until they saw him ambling near army headquarters the next day. The first thing awaiting his attention was a stack of more than six hundred letters soliciting jobs. With his old distaste for self-promotion, Grant suspected people who promoted themselves and refused to sift through this tall backlog of letters. Nor did he warm to people who tried to worm their way into his administration. When his brother-in-law Abel Corbin drafted an inaugural address for him, Grant told Badeau to lock it up unread until after his March 4 swearing-in.

Grant preserved an inscrutable silence about his cabinet appointees, declining invitations to dine with people, lest they corner him for information. In one of the more curious interregnums in American history, the tight-lipped president-elect kept the country in suspense as he mulled over his choices. At a time when the spoils system dominated American politics, Grant favored silence to ward off pressure from party bosses, hoping to make selections based purely on merit. With his pronounced streak of autonomy, he regarded any attempt to influence his cabinet choices as unwarranted meddling. "If announced in advance, efforts would be made to change my determination," he explained, "and, therefore, I have come to the conclusion not to announce whom I am going to invite to seats in the Cabinet until I send in their names to the Senate for confirmation."[53] To guarantee secrecy, he didn't even deign to discuss appointments with Julia. Henry Adams, debuting in his role as an acerbic gadfly of Grant's administration, wrote that politicians were "furious at not being consulted."[54] Dubbing the president-elect "Ulysses the Silent," George Templeton Strong observed that "Odysseus knows how to keep his own counsel, and shuts up, close as an oyster."[55]

Grant wasn't entirely a political neophyte. He had survived four years as general in chief in a superheated political atmosphere and had made many wartime decisions with distinctly political overtones. Yet he brought to the job no deep knowledge of statecraft and had a special need for experienced advisers. Instead he adopted the secretive, intuitive decision-making style of a general who feared his war plans might leak out. As a West Point graduate, Grant had enjoyed an insider's knowledge of military personnel during the war, but as a Washington outsider, he needed the valuable advice of seasoned professionals about appointments. So far had the pendulum swung in Grant's life that the insecure man of the pre–Civil War era now radiated a confidence that could verge on complacency. He wrongly assumed that the skills that had made him successful in one sphere of life would translate intact into another. He entered into no consultative process, engaged in no methodical vetting of people, and sent up no trial balloons to test candidates, making his decisions maddeningly opaque. Only in hindsight did Grant fathom his own limitations upon taking office. "I entered the White House as President without any previous experience either in civil or political life," he admitted. "I thought I could run the government of the United States, as I did the staff of my army. It was my mistake, and it led me into other mistakes."[56]

Outwardly Grant remained his modest, unassuming self. After chatting with him in December, Rutherford B. Hayes wrote that Grant was "cheerful, chatty, and good-natured, and so sensible, clear-headed, and well-informed . . . he remains unspoiled by his elevation."[57] While he refrained from public statements, his private pronouncements exuded optimism. James McCosh, president of Princeton College (then called the College of New Jersey), said after a conversation with Grant that he "spoke freely, and he expressed his determination to pay the national debt, to reduce the national expenditure, to do what was possible for the Indians, and above all was determined to have peace."[58] Such blithe generalities gave few direct hints of the likely path of his administration.

At a Chicago army reunion in December, James H. Wilson was charmed at how natural Grant remained, unspoiled by his new eminence. "He was as good and plain, and frank, as he always was," Wilson told a friend. "I never saw so modest or so unselfish a man—and I am sure he will make one of the best presidents we have ever had."[59] Yet Grant struggled with more inward pressure than he admitted and achieved his unexampled calm at a steep psychological price. When he got up to thank his old army comrades, he confessed, "I am now suffering from one of those neuralgic headaches with which I am periodically afflicted, and which prevents me, even were I so inclined, from saying anything farther on this occasion."[60] To Julia, he was more forthcoming about his anxiety. "I have been shaken to pieces . . . and will be glad to get started home."[61] Back in Washington, a perceptive reporter detected an "expression of sadness" in Grant, who seemed "borne down with cares" as he strode about in an ordinary black suit."[62] Doubtless adding to his discomfort was an awkward distance from the lame-duck president with whom he never met. To forestall any unpleasant encounter with Johnson, Grant spent New Year's Day 1869 in Philadelphia, avoiding the customary call at the executive mansion, and he refused to allow his children to attend a special children's party there.

About his cabinet decisions Grant kept even Rawlins and Washburne at bay until near the inauguration. The most suspense hung over Rawlins's fate. "All seem to take it for granted that the General is going to do something very handsome," Rawlins told his wife, "more than he has ever done for me."[63] When Grant procrastinated in making a decision, Rawlins fell prey to nagging doubts. His medical condition had worsened and he looked haggard and sickly, debilitated by lung congestion coupled with a hacking cough. To alleviate these symptoms, he soaked in salt water and took daily horseback rides on Grant's black pony Jeff Davis, which did little to retard the course of his tuberculosis. By October 1868, as Rawlins fell apart under the strain of work, Grant wondered whether he could cope with the exacting demands of a cabinet job. His gratitude to Rawlins was boundless, but he didn't want to burden a gravely ill man with intolerable responsibility.[64]

Grant decided to assign Rawlins to the military command of the Department of Arizona, where the hot, dry climate might relieve his suffering. When Rawlins learned of this, he grew indignant and said he deserved to be secretary of war. Wilson communicated his displeasure to Grant, who replied at once, "You can tell Rawlins he shall be Secretary of War."[65] Rawlins's appointment was extremely important, for Grant required a deputy who would protect his reputation and serve as a fearless truth-teller, saving him from personal blunders and protecting his innocent nature from designing politicians.

Grant's elevation to the presidency opened a vacancy for general of the army with Sherman the clear front-runner. He had monitored Grant's rise with decidedly mixed emotions, believing that "if forced to choose between the penitentiary and the White House for four years, I would say the penitentiary, thank you."[66] At the Chicago army reunion, Grant, refusing to be coy, pretty much offered him the top army job. Then, in early January, Grant informed Sherman of a startling proposition: a group of New York City businessmen, led by the retail mogul Alexander T. Stewart, had offered to buy his I Street residence for $65,000—"which I insisted was more than the property was worth," Grant admitted—and then donate it to Sherman.[67] Even though he admitted the price was excessive, Grant expressed no scruples about the windfall, which almost doubled the price he had paid. On the day of his inauguration, Grant would nominate

Sherman as general of the army and Philip H. Sheridan as lieutenant general, jumping them over George Gordon Meade and a deeply offended Henry W. Halleck.

Intense speculation swirled around what would happen to Grant's chief patron, Elihu Washburne, who had suffered medical problems and to whom Grant incontestably owed more than anyone else in Washington. In Washburne's present medical state, Grant doubted that he could handle a taxing job and happily acceded to his desire to become minister to France. At the same time, coveting the prestige of a temporary cabinet position, Washburne advanced a bizarre proposal: he wanted to serve briefly as a cabinet secretary so he could forever claim the title. When he suggested treasury secretary, Grant proposed instead a fleeting stint as secretary of state and Washburne agreed. Even though this arrangement devalued the position of secretary of state, Grant didn't believe he could reject Washburne's wishful thinking out of hand. It was a well-meant, but politically maladroit, decision. Washburne would hold the post for only five days, leading one senator to wisecrack, "Who ever heard before of a man nominated [as] Secretary of State merely as a compliment?"[68] This odd temporary appointment added to a general impression of Grant as a rank amateur.

Perhaps because business success had eluded Grant, he held wealthy folks in high esteem and selected Alexander T. Stewart for treasury secretary. The Irish-born department store merchant had amassed a colossal fortune in the luxury trade, had faithfully supported Grant, and had spearheaded the money collected for his Washington house. Far from seeing a political payoff involved, Grant saw only a talented businessman willing to sacrifice his economic interests for the sake of public service.

Grant's fealty to Reconstruction appeared in his choice of an attorney general, whose portfolio would be central to protecting black rights in the South. He turned to Ebenezer Rockwood Hoar, a bespectacled Republican with a grizzled beard, who was born in Concord, Massachusetts, and attended Harvard College and Law School. A former member of the Free-Soil Party, an upright gentleman of starchy integrity, he had served on the Massachusetts Supreme Judicial Court where he used sarcasm to savage lesser mortals. "When on the bench," wrote an observer, "he was said to be unhappy because he could not decide against both litigants."[69] In Boston, he belonged to the so-called Saturday Club with Ralph Waldo Emerson, Henry Wadsworth Longfellow, and Oliver Wendell Holmes. One group luminary, James Russell Lowell, was enamored of

Hoar's intellect: "The extraordinary quickness and acuteness, the *flash* of his mind (which I never saw matched but in Dr. Holmes) have dazzled and bewildered some people so that they were blind to his solid qualities."[70] Even so hearty a Grant hater as Henry Adams allowed that "in the Attorney-General's office, Judge Hoar seemed to fill every possible ideal, both personal and political."[71] Hoar loathed the spoils system and Grant would back him in appointing high-caliber judges. Because many of Andrew Johnson's judicial appointees had shown little concern for black citizens, Congress had introduced nine new circuit judgeships and Grant would name some distinguished progressives to occupy them, including Hugh Lennox Bond, a Republican judge and abolitionist from Baltimore, who championed black education after the war.

For navy secretary, Grant tapped a genial, well-to-do Philadelphia businessman named Adolph E. Borie, a card-playing companion who lacked credentials for the job, injecting a touch of cronyism into the administration. He had contributed to the Philadelphia house given to Grant after the war. Grant portrayed Borie as "a merchant who had amassed a large fortune" and was "perfectly fitted for any place"—another example of Grant preferring to view rich businessmen through rose-colored glasses.[72] A modest man, Borie tried to decline the office: "I told [Grant] that I did not consider that I knew enough about the navy and naval affairs . . . He said that was all nonsense; that I knew about ships and one thing and another."[73] Borie was in poor health, but Grant intimated he would serve as a figurehead while David Dixon Porter ably ran the department and so he consented to take the job. Borie "is now a mere clerk to Vice-Admiral Porter, not the Secretary of the Navy," Gideon Welles jeered.[74] Borie would last just four months, replaced by the attorney general of New Jersey, George M. Robeson, a roly-poly Princeton graduate with muttonchop whiskers and a sociable bent, who had been a brigadier general in the war. He would prove a capable if often slipshod administrator, shadowed by suspicions of corruption.

For interior secretary, Grant recruited Jacob Dolson Cox, a Union major general and highly literate Oberlin graduate who had rendered distinguished service at Antietam and whom Grant and Sherman had wanted to succeed Stanton as war secretary. As Ohio governor, Cox preached against black suffrage and for racial segregation, making him a conservative member of Grant's administration. On the other hand, he enjoyed a reputation as an efficient administrator and energetic ally of civil service reform, favoring a merit system for the Department of the Interior, a notorious mare's nest of corruption. It is important to note that corruption was rife in many departments *before* Grant took office. In January 1869, the journalist John Russell Young told Washburne that somebody was needed in the Interior Department "who will take the many-headed serpent of robbery and strangle it in its various shapes—Indian Rings, Patent Rings, Stationery Rings and Railroad Rings. This work will, of course, make a tremendous howl among Congress-people."[75]

For postmaster general, Grant made a superb choice, selecting John A. J. Creswell of Maryland. A Dickinson College graduate, he had practiced law in Maryland and served as a representative and U.S. senator from the state. Having started out a Democrat, he joined the Radical Republican ranks and became a protégé of Henry Winter Davis, a militant on Reconstruction. There was no job richer in patronage positions than the postmaster general's—he would employ a veritable army of sixty thousand employees—and Creswell appointed a record number of African American postal workers.[76] He introduced new efficiencies into mail delivery by rail and steamship, innovated with a penny postal card, and expanded mail routes.

The frosty relations that had marked Grant's dealings with Andrew Johnson ever since the feud over Stanton had never thawed. Hence the change of administrations represented one of the more acrimonious power transfers in American history, and the two men traded petty snubs. For two months before the inauguration, the outgoing president dithered over whether to attend. In January, he grumbled that Grant was "a dissembler, a deliberate deceiver" and swore he would not "debase" himself by going to the ceremony.[77] Grant failed to extend friendly overtures and refused to share a carriage with Johnson at the inaugural parade. Johnson passed on the chance to ride in a separate carriage. Gideon Welles reminded Johnson that President-elect Andrew Jackson had never called upon John Quincy Adams, who retaliated by boycotting Jackson's swearing-in. "The President said he was not aware of that fact," Welles wrote. "It was a precedent for us which he was glad to learn."[78] The upshot was that Johnson stayed doggedly put in the White House until noon on March 4, distracting himself with signing bills and tying up loose ends. A few minutes after noon, he escorted his cabinet to the main entrance portico, where carriages awaited them. "I fancy I can already smell the fresh mountain air of Tennessee," Johnson said as he departed from the White House forever.[79] It was a fitting end to a sad, sometimes shabby, presidency. In future years, bent on a comeback, Johnson was defeated in contests for the U.S. Senate and House of Representatives, although the Tennessee legislature made him a U.S. senator in 1875. "Thank God for the vindication," Johnson remarked, then died five months after being sworn in.[80]

In the inaugural parade, Grant and Rawlins, with the Fifth Cavalry as their escort, rode together in an open carriage despite cold, rainy weather, presenting a portrait of the unique partnership that had won the war. At the last moment, Grant relented and stopped his carriage at the White House, inviting Johnson to come along, but the lame-duck president sent back word that he was too busy to comply. The cavalcade then proceeded to Capitol Hill, passing hordes of spectators who had poured into the capital for days. Since Grant was a military hero, the parade possessed a suitably martial air, with eight divisions of marching soldiers, including several black companies. Once at the Capitol, Grant strode into the Senate chamber, where he saw Schuyler Colfax sworn in as vice president, then emerged onto the building's eastern facade before a vast multitude of perhaps fifty thousand people gathered under gray, gusty skies. He stood calmly during a twenty-two-gun salute in his honor. At forty-six, Grant was still trim and fit, the youngest man elected president until then. Having weathered the crucible of war, he was a more worldly figure than in earlier years, his face showing curiosity, intelligence, and skepticism. Lacking the tall, upright carriage or silver mane of a prototypical politician, Grant, in black suit and yellow kid gloves, looked more like a man on a minor business errand than a statesman embarking on high office. To those who knew him well, he seemed a bit tense, perhaps awed by his removal to a wholly new realm. "That day," wrote Badeau, "there was no geniality, no familiar jest, hardly a smile."[81]

Shortly after noon, just as Andrew Johnson vacated the White House, Grant was sworn in as eighteenth president by Chief Justice Salmon Chase. For Grant, it had been an improbable journey to this moment, with many setbacks intermixed with vaulting triumphs. Jesse Root Grant sat prominently among dignitaries on the eastern portico. He had grown quite deaf and learned to compensate with a booming voice. In the course of the day, he suffered a severe fall, tumbling down a flight of stairs. "It is not probable that his injury will shorten his life," Grant told his sister Mary, "but will probably make him lame for life."[82] Despite the leg injury, Jesse was hounded by office seekers who saw him as their most convenient conduit for reaching his son.

Despite Jesse's wealth, he and Hannah still lived in a plain two-story brick house on an unfashionable block in Covington. Hannah didn't accompany her tightfisted husband to the inauguration, occasioning much press speculation, especially since she never visited Washington during her son's two terms in office. With her silver hair and kind, maternal face, she remained reticent, shy, and self-contained. "In her old age," said a journalist, "she had calm winning manners, and a face still sweet and still young."[83] Her absence from Washington may have sent a political message since she came from a family of Jacksonian Democrats. More likely it had to do with the eternal Dent-Grant psychodrama: Hannah detested the Dent clan and didn't care to meet them in Washington. Jesse tried to coax her into going, but she decided firmly against it when informed she would have to sit among dignitaries. "Do you think I want to set [sic] up there for 50,000 people to gaze & point at?" she told her husband. "I would rather go when there are no strangers there."[84] This attitude says much about Hannah Grant's plainspoken, homespun ways. Rumors later ran around Covington that at the hour when her son took the oath of office, Hannah was spotted "on the rear porch of her residence, with broom in hand sweeping down the cobwebs."[85]

Once the swearing-in ended, Grant fished from his coat pocket the inaugural address that he had kept a secret, releasing no advance copies. In composing it, Grant again displayed the extreme self-reliance that had marked his career. Three weeks earlier, he had given Badeau a handwritten copy, told him to stash it in a drawer, and even hid it from a frustrated Julia. Now he delivered that speech almost verbatim. Once again the secretive Grant had forgone the insights of old political hands who might have made some constructive suggestions. As he began his speech, the huge throng pressed forward to hear his soft, almost inaudible, voice. Most of the speech, a mere twelve hundred words, was businesslike and uninspired. Grant declared himself an independent, not a professional politician: "The office has come to me unsought, I commence its duties untrammeled."[86] Striking the conciliatory Appomattox note, he drew a discreet veil over the violence tearing apart the South and promised to approach remaining war issues "calmly, without prejudice, hate or sectional pride."[87] No one knew better than Grant the war's cost and he left no doubt that, as a hard-money man, he wished to bolster American credit and pare down debt. "To protect the national honor every dollar of Government indebtedness should be paid in gold unless otherwise expressly stipulated in the contract."[88]

The speech lacked soaring cadences or memorable lines, yet it touched on two explosive issues at the finale. He advised Native Americans that their days as a hunting, gathering people were numbered and that he favored "civilization,

christianization and ultimate citizenship" for them.[89] Then, in sharp contrast to
his predecessor, Grant championed black suffrage. "It seems to me very desirable
that the question should be settled now, and I entertain the hope . . . that it may
be by the ratification of the fifteenth article of amendment to the Constitution."[90] All winter long, he had stood foursquare behind the amendment, telling
delegates from the first national black political convention in Washington that
as president he would ensure that "the colored people of the Nation may receive
every protection which the law gives them."[91] By late February, the amendment,
having won the needed two-thirds vote in Congress, went to the states for ratification. It suffered from decided limitations—it disappointed feminists, who
hoped it would encompass women, and didn't bar discriminatory tests to keep
blacks from voting—but it qualified as a stunning triumph nonetheless. "Nothing in all history," William Lloyd Garrison wrote, equaled "this wonderful,
quiet, sudden transformation of four millions of human beings from . . . the
auction-block to the ballot box."[92] Grant termed it "the most important event
that has occurred, since the nation came into life."[93] George Boutwell, who had
introduced the proposed amendment in the House, said Grant had thrown his
immense prestige behind it and that "its ratification was due, probably, to his
advice . . . Had he advised its rejection, or had he been indifferent to its fate, the
amendment would have failed."[94]

When Grant finished his speech, a wild cheer went up from the crowd and he
bowed gratefully. He then bent over, planted a kiss on Julia's cheek, and handed
her the address. "And now, my dear," he said facetiously, "I hope you're satisfied."[95] Thirteen-year-old Nellie bounded over in a bright blue dress, golden
tresses tumbling down her shoulders, to kiss her father. In a charming gesture, the
new president left the platform holding her by one hand and Schuyler Colfax by
the other. Grant's speech was derided as flat and platitudinous. It didn't announce
a transformative presidency, nor did it articulate a sweeping vision or enlist followers in a grand social movement. Still Republicans thought it true and honest,
a reflection of Grant's pragmatic authenticity. "I think it the most remarkable
document ever issued under such circumstances," said James Wilson. "The
beauty of it is, that every word of the address is Grant's."[96] Grant would prove a
far more assertive president than his modest inaugural address had suggested.

With the ceremony over, Grant climbed back into his carriage and headed to
the White House. He was accompanied by a military escort and joyous black citizens, who celebrated his endorsement of the Fifteenth Amendment, trailing in

his wake. By the time he reached the now-empty executive mansion, he was greeted by General John Schofield, his temporary holdover as secretary of war. A small group followed the new president to his office where they partook of drinks and cigars.

When the committee formed to arrange the inaugural ball had convened in January, the bashful Grant had startled them by saying it might be best to skip the affair altogether. Far from heeding his advice, the committee brought forth a ball of unusual opulence, held in an unfinished new wing of the Treasury Department and conducted with something less than military precision. By the time the Grants arrived at 10:30 p.m., with Julia decked out in a white satin dress, it was clear the function had degenerated into an expensive fiasco. More than a thousand guests crowded into an airless space, thick with marble construction dust, and several ladies celebrated the incoming administration by fainting on the spot. Although a blizzard hit the city, nobody had worked out a system to check coats or hats or arrange carriages for departing guests. Some people ended up spending the night in frantic searches for missing wraps, while others slogged home through the snowy mess without their overcoats. Some surely wondered whether these slipshod arrangements presaged trouble ahead for the Grant administration.

Spoils of War

O N HIS FIRST FULL DAY IN OFFICE, March 5, Grant, with brisk, military efficiency, produced his first list of cabinet appointees—Washburne, Stewart, Borie, Creswell, Hoar, and Cox—and John Rawlins materialized on the Senate floor to present it. Grant, it turned out, had overlooked an antiquated statute, introduced by Alexander Hamilton in forging the Treasury Department in 1789, that no treasury secretary could be directly or indirectly involved in trade or commerce. A flustered Grant discovered this provision only after Alexander T. Stewart was unanimously confirmed by the Senate. Stewart offered to place his profits in a trust while in office, with the proceeds donated to charity, but that didn't solve the predicament. Grant pursued a failed effort to have Congress pass a resolution exempting Stewart from the law. In the end, he withdrew the nomination, the whole debacle reflecting his inexperience and refusal to seek counsel before selecting cabinet secretaries.

Instead of Stewart, Grant proposed Congressman George Boutwell of Massachusetts, the first commissioner of Internal Revenue during the war. Heavily touted by Radicals, the former Massachusetts governor had been an early backer of the Republican Party and a stout supporter of Reconstruction. A fire-breathing house manager in the Andrew Johnson impeachment, he had excoriated the president as an "apostate and a traitor."[1] As a confirmed abolitionist, he had been instrumental in passing both the Fourteenth and Fifteenth Amendments. Boutwell was not an endearing personality—one colleague found him "cold, calculating, and without confidences"—but he reflected Grant's emphasis on

defending the rights of newly freed blacks.[2] Within days Grant sent to Capitol
Hill the names of a second batch of appointees, including Boutwell and Rawlins, and they were duly rubber-stamped. Elihu Washburne, having served as
secretary of state for all of five days, was now confirmed as minister to France,
with Hamilton Fish chosen to run the State Department on a permanent basis.
With his long face, wide mouth, wavy hair, and scraggly side-whiskers, Fish was
Grant's most inspired choice. The squire of a Hudson River estate where Grant
had stayed, the sixty-year-old Fish was a former New York governor and senator,
a cultivated patrician fluent in four languages. With his Whig background, impeccable judgment, and long experience, he described himself as an old fogey
with traditional notions of honesty. In a cabinet plagued by high turnover, he
would labor for eight years, lending gravity to American foreign policy and riding out many controversies. He functioned on such confidential terms with
Grant that he almost ranked as his prime minister. Steeped in statecraft, he
would master reams of information, keep a voluminous diary, and tutor Grant
in the mysterious ways of diplomacy. For Grant, Fish was a godsend, compensating for his own glaring inexperience in foreign affairs. Grant later boasted, with
some justice, that Hamilton Fish was the best secretary of state in fifty years.

While historians have tended to mock Grant's cabinet as a bunch of
mediocrities—and Borie certainly qualified as such—it was actually weighted
with former congressmen, senators, governors, and judges. It had figures of real
distinction (Fish), Radical Republicans (Boutwell, Creswell), men of exceptional
intellect (Hoar), and advocates of civil service reform (Cox). Rutherford B. Hayes
was enraptured by Grant's freedom from party hacks: "His Cabinet looks like a
revolution . . . It is an attempt to put fitness and qualification before what is
called 'claims' and 'political services.' If anybody could overthrow the spoils doctrine and practice, Grant is the man."[3] The trouble lay less with the caliber of
choices than an absence of any ideological cohesion. Grant didn't want his cabinet ruled by a monolithic party line, which was praiseworthy, but this sometimes
resulted in a fragmentation of views that would bedevil his administration.

In this heyday of the spoils system, Grant had thrown down a gauntlet to
party leaders. In response, they patronized him as a dunderhead and lashed out
at his choices. Senator John Sherman said Grant's "attempt to form a cabinet
without consultation with anyone, and with very little knowledge, except social
intercourse with the persons appointed" cast doubt on his presidency.[4] After seeing Grant, Ben Butler growled that "he is stupidly dull and ignorant and no

more comprehends his duty or his power under the Constitution than that dog," indicating a small dog nearby.[5] Charles Sumner, the all-powerful chairman of the Senate Committee on Foreign Relations, took special umbrage at not being consulted about the secretary of state, perhaps because he coveted the plum assignment himself. Unfortunately, Grant's reforming spirit backfired, since he had to make amends to spurned politicians on Capitol Hill and only ended up more beholden to them.

Grant exhibited another serious defect in managing appointments. In the fast-moving world of warfare, it was a virtue to act decisively and make snap judgments based on intuition. In the White House, by contrast, he was too quick to hire people, then too quick to fire them. If this style served Grant well in the fog of war, where improvisation was vital, it led to some rough clashes and bruised feelings in the political sphere. Instead of seeming simple and direct, he could come across as brusque and even insensitive. Where he should have deliberated and calculated, he sometimes rushed into headlong action, as if storming an enemy fort.

Critics have faulted Grant for applying a rigid military model to his cabinet secretaries, treating them as so many staff officers. Ebenezer Hoar later complained that Grant had "the most crude and imperfect notions" of the proper relationship with his cabinet, leading to his interfering "with the duties which the law imposes upon a Cabinet officer."[6] But this was far from a universal impression among his cabinet. Boutwell believed that Grant gave him ample leeway, as he had given his wartime commanders. Fish disputed that Grant was a naive, bumbling president, saying he was "the most scrupulously truthful man he had ever known" and had earnestly educated himself in every great question laid before him.[7]

For his White House entourage, Grant imported pretty much the same coterie of staff officers who had served him during the war and its aftermath. As with his cabinet, he favored personal secretaries with whom he felt comfortable, including Frederick Dent, Adam Badeau, Orville Babcock, Cyrus Comstock, and Horace Porter, as well as Robert Douglas, son of the late senator Stephen Douglas. In these appointments Grant demonstrated commendable loyalty for past services. As Ely Parker phrased it, "After the war was over, Grant showed his love for his military family by doing kindness[es] for them whenever he could. When he became President he sought them out, and without solicitation on their part, provided for many of them."[8]

Yet it was sometimes difficult to distinguish personal loyalty from cronyism.

Many observers were disturbed by all the uniformed men striding the White House corridors. In a broad-brush indictment, Charles Sumner disapproved of the way the White House "assumed the character of military head-quarters. To the dishonor of the civil service and in total disregard of precedent, the President surrounded himself with officers of the army, and substituted military forms for those of civil life."[9] Among the administration's clandestine critics was William T. Sherman, who saw an unprepared Grant gravitating into a political sphere where he operated as a dangerous amateur.

During the war, Grant had been a superb talent scout, winnowing out unqualified officers and advancing enterprising ones. Nevertheless, he had proven credulous with some personalities who didn't deserve his trust, and as president he again showed little inkling of the opportunism that could afflict his staff as they faced the lure of peacetime riches and power. One such opportunist—although it took Grant many years to see it—was Adam Badeau. The onetime theater critic had an agile pen and was given his own White House room to compose an elaborate, three-volume *Military History of Ulysses S. Grant,* meant to enshrine his boss in the history books and contest Lost Cause southern analysts who glorified Lee at his expense. In time, Grant elevated Badeau to several diplomatic posts abroad, even as an underlying resentment festered inside the younger man. As early as March 1869, one White House staffer noted that Badeau had "violently" offended Grant "by his pushing and presumption"—the start of a rift that would silently widen in future years.[10]

In the end, the most troubling aide was Orville E. Babcock, who enjoyed the most intimate access to Grant. A popular, congenial thirty-three-year-old with a Vandyke beard, he was born in Vermont, graduated from West Point, and was a skilled engineer. For Grant, he had been a genuine war hero, fighting with gallantry at the Wilderness and Petersburg. Much like a chief of staff, Babcock occupied a second-floor White House office that enjoyed direct admittance to Grant's private study, so that, in General Sherman's words, he became "a kind of intermediator between the people and the President."[11] Grant trusted him so much that Babcock opened mail addressed to him and often sent replies himself. Babcock's influence rivaled that of cabinet secretaries and only Rawlins enjoyed more confidential relations with the president. Unfortunately, where Rawlins qualified as a man of fiery principles, Babcock came to personify the looser morals of the Gilded Age.

Though sometimes hoodwinked by close acquaintances, on other occasions

Grant managed to combine personal favors with first-rate appointments. He made an excellent choice by tapping his old pal and ex–Confederate general James Longstreet as surveyor of customs for New Orleans. The rich patronage position seemed well merited, for Longstreet was that rare southern general who had preached cooperation with Reconstruction and been traduced as a scalawag for his outspoken courage. "Our new president has done many acts for which his country will hold him in grateful remembrance," wrote Horace Greeley, "but he never did a wiser or nobler act than his nomination yesterday of General James Longstreet."[12] Grant personally shepherded the nomination through the Senate. "The Senators have as many favors to ask of me as I have of them," he told Longstreet, "and I will see that you are confirmed."[13]

The Grants and Dents showed no scruples about badgering Grant for jobs and he found it hard to avoid the perils of nepotism. Such favoritism was commonplace in the freewheeling atmosphere of nineteenth-century America. During the Civil War, the New York World had rapped Lincoln on the knuckles for having "appointed his whole family to government posts."[14] With an eye on the main chance, Jesse Root Grant had his son renew his appointment as postmaster of Covington. The pushy Jesse also lobbied for patronage jobs for friends, sought a fancy new post office in Covington, and bragged about his Washington connections. Not content to control Covington, he set himself up as a power broker in Ravenna, Ohio, where he favored for postmaster Eliza F. Evans, a soldier's widow and the daughter of an old friend, over an aspirant preferred by Congressman James A. Garfield. When Grant backed Mrs. Evans, Garfield didn't challenge him, but he disliked a meddling interloper such as Jesse Grant. In sketching this brawl, the New York World said archly that in future civil service exams, the Grant administration should list just two questions: "Were you a contributor to either of Grant's three houses, in Philadelphia, Washington, or Galena?" and "Are you a member of the Dent family or otherwise connected by blood or marriage with General Grant?"[15]

Grant was kept busy supplying jobs for Michael John Cramer, the Swiss-born Methodist clergyman who married his youngest sister, Mary. During the war, Grant had wangled him a job as a hospital chaplain, followed by another at an army barracks in Covington after the war. As if such generosity were not enough, Grant conferred upon his brother-in-law the honor of being resident minister and chargé d'affaires in Denmark, where he would reside for eleven years.

In many ways, the most lavish beneficiary of such largesse was the man least entitled to it, Colonel Dent, who had been invited by Grant to live in the White House. "The General was always so, so lovely to my dear father, and papa was so proud of him," Julia wrote in her sometimes unreal, flowery style.[16] Now in his early eighties, the Colonel had never modified his Confederate views and remained a rabid Democrat. Before becoming president, Grant had paid off such sizable debts accumulated by his father-in-law that it mired him in financial obligations. For visitors to the executive mansion in the Grant years, Colonel Dent was ubiquitous, whether sunning himself on the porch or occupying his favorite spot near Grant's office and lecturing waiting politicians. At Blue Room receptions, he sprawled in an easy chair behind the president and First Lady, as if he were the grand old man of the administration. Despite a surface charm, the Colonel was still dogmatic about politics and said his son-in-law was "really a stanch Democrat; but he doesn't know it."[17]

As in past years, the self-absorbed Jesse Root Grant and equally self-absorbed Colonel Dent continued to find each other insufferable and Grant took refuge in his old strategy of passive detachment. With Colonel Dent monopolizing the White House, Jesse stayed at an inexpensive hotel when he visited Washington. The two men took turns insulting each other, pretending the other was a doddering old fool. "You should take better care of that old gentleman, Julia," Dent would say of Jesse Grant. "He is feeble and deaf as a post, and yet you permit him to wander all over Washington alone. It is not safe; he should never be allowed out without an attendant."[18] To insult Jesse, Colonel Dent would pop out of his armchair whenever Jesse entered the room. "Accept my chair, Mr. Grant," he would say with elaborate courtesy, as if humoring a senile old man. Stiffly indignant, Jesse would reply in a stage whisper to a grandson, "I hope I shall not live to become as old and infirm as your Grandfather Dent."[19]

Relations between the Dents and Grants, at a low ebb for twenty-five years, regressed even further. Cyrus Comstock reported that Julia was "aggrieved by that old good for nothing J R Grant, abusing her firmly to some correspondent."[20] Grant's childhood friend Eliza Shaw reflected the rancor of the Grant family when she observed that "Old Man Dent was a man without tact or respect for anybody. He was a fat old man, drank a good deal." She confirmed that Hannah Grant thought the Dents had captured the White House and boycotted Washington to avoid meeting them. "Julia Grant was not on good terms with the General's mother. The General's mother was never in Washington because of this. She never came to see her son at the capital."[21]

As the Dent family guzzled freely at the patronage trough, the president more or less willingly catered to their thirst. One of Julia's brothers-in-law was made a bank examiner in Missouri, another a District of Columbia marshal, a third the collector of the Port of New Orleans. Her brothers also lined up for posts, with one made a customs appraiser in San Francisco, a second an Indian trader in New Mexico, and brother Fred one of Grant's secretaries. "A dozen members of the family billeted upon the country!" Senator Sumner snorted in disgust.[22]

The subject of Grant and nepotism remains a puzzle. The practice hurt his standing and detracted from his better cabinet appointments. As Carl Schurz protested, Grant showed "a disposition to give offices to all his relatives and to a great number of old personal friends; and in these instances to consult the members of Congress very little. That makes bad blood here and there."[23] As Grant had shown during the war, he was personally incorruptible and never desired promotions that stemmed from wire-pulling. To keep the selection process pure, he had even refrained from consulting politicians about his cabinet choices. Yet he also had an unremitting sense of fidelity to family, even when they scarcely deserved it, and seemed unable to perceive how unfair such partiality might appear to most Americans. Having been battered by the world in his earlier years, he had come to rely on family and friends and never forgot that lesson. When he offered an appointment to a former St. Louis friend, the man felt obliged to point out that he was a Democrat. Grant waved away this concern. "Just before the Civil War," he said, "when I was standing on a street corner in St. Louis by a wagon loaded with wood, you approached and said: 'Captain, haven't you been able to sell your wood?' I answered: 'No.' Then you said: 'I'll buy it; and whenever you haul a load of wood to the city and can't sell it, just take it around to my residence . . . and I'll pay you for it.' I haven't forgotten it."[24]

Many of Grant's appointment problems also resulted from the absence of a true civil service as patronage lubricated the system. In the motto enunciated by New York senator William L. Marcy, "To the victor belongs the spoils."[25] As *Harper's Weekly* noted on the eve of Grant's election, "The chief business of the executive had become the distribution of patronage."[26] In an era when strangers could walk straight into the White House, Abraham Lincoln had been besieged by job seekers who cluttered the stairs and corridors day and night. One day a friend asked Lincoln whether he was depressed because the Union army had suffered a military setback. He smiled wanly and said, "No, it isn't the army. It is the post office in Brownsville, Missouri."[27] When an officer accompanied Lincoln to the opera and noticed how tired he looked, he asked the president whether he was enjoying the opera. "Oh, no, Colonel; I have not come for the play, but for the rest. I am being hounded to death by office-seekers, who pursue me early and late, and it is simply to get two or three hours' relief that I am here."[28] Corruption was so endemic under Andrew Johnson that the 1868 Republican platform claimed he had "perverted the public patronage into an engine of wholesale corruption."[29]

Grant quickly saw he would spend disproportionate time in fights over revenue collectors, Indian agents, postmasters, marshals, and customs collectors. Within weeks of becoming president, a harried Grant was already worn down by throngs of job claimants, who stalked him everywhere. "I scarcely get one moment alone," he told his sister Mary. "Office-seeking in this country . . . is getting to be one of the industries of the age. It gives me no peace."[30] Grant knew that, for every friend he won through an appointment, he earned a hundred enemies in rejected suitors. Under the spoils system, the president had to appease congressmen who dispensed patronage in their districts and grew powerful perpetuating this unsavory system. Gideon Welles observed that "corruption is not confined to one party. It is the disgrace and wickedness of the times."[31]

Despite such pressures, Grant made extraordinary strides in naming blacks, Jews, and Native Americans to federal positions—a forgotten chapter of American history. The minor story of nepotism has overshadowed this far more important narrative. Forty years before Theodore Roosevelt incurred southern wrath by inviting Booker T. Washington to dine at the White House, Grant welcomed blacks there. On April 2, he met with the first black public official ever to visit the White House, Lieutenant Governor Oscar J. Dunn of Louisiana. On New Year's Day, citizens always lined up to pay their respects to the president. Before crowds started to arrive on January 1, 1870, the police asked Grant whether they should honor the custom of having blacks and whites enter separately and he said yes. When informed, however, that "a number of colored people" wished to come in with whites on an equal basis, Grant "at once gave direction to admit all who wished to come," Babcock recalled.[32]

George T. Downing of the National Convention of the Colored Men of America told Grant that his followers placed special emphasis on black appointments, for they "would give a death blow to objections against our holding such positions in the South, by convincing the South that it is not true that the North wishes to force a policy upon them which it is not willing to accept itself."[33] In response, Grant appointed Ebenezer D. Bassett as minister to Haiti, making him the first African American diplomat in American history. The grandson of a slave, the Yale-educated Bassett had been principal of the Philadelphia Colored High School, where he joined with Frederick Douglass in enlisting thirteen black regiments during the war. In soliciting Grant for the job, Bassett wrote that his appointment "as a *representative colored man* . . . would be hailed . . . by recently enfranchised colored citizens, as a marked recognition of *our* new condition in the Republic and an auspicious token of our great future."[34] Frederick Douglass, who had entertained hopes for the Haitian post, graciously conceded defeat. "Your appointment," he told Bassett, "is a grand achievement for yourself and for our whole people."[35] Two years later, Grant expanded this precedent by naming James Milton Turner as minister to Liberia. Downing extolled Grant for surpassing Lincoln in naming "numbers of our race to important positions" and giving "a rebuke to vulgar prejudices against a class. In this you have gone far beyond our late lamented President."[36] .

Grant's efforts transcended high-profile appointments as he named a record number of ordinary blacks to positions during his first term in office.[37] During the 1872 presidential campaign, Frederick Douglass toted up black employees sprinkled throughout the federal bureaucracy, citing customs collectors, internal revenue assessors, postmasters, clerks, and messengers, and was simply staggered by their numbers: "In one Department at Washington I found 249, and many more holding important positions in its service in different parts of the country."[38] Grant integrated the executive mansion, appointing Albert Hawkins as his stable chief and coachman; he also cared for a Grant menagerie that included dogs, gamecocks, and a raucous parrot. For his personal servants, Grant picked George W. "Bill" Barnes and John Henry Whitlow. The able Barnes had been a runaway slave who showed up when Grant was in Cairo in 1861 and had turned himself into an indispensable valet.

Mortified at memories of General Orders No. 11, Grant compiled an outstanding record of incorporating Jews into his administration, one that far outstripped his predecessors'. The lawyer Simon Wolf estimated that Grant appointed more than fifty Jewish citizens at his request alone, including consuls, district attorneys, and deputy postmasters, with Wolf himself becoming recorder of deeds for the District of Columbia. When Grant made Edward S. Salomon governor of the Washington Territory, it was the first time an American

Jew had occupied a gubernatorial post. (When Salomon proved corrupt, Grant handled his case leniently, letting him resign.) Elated at this appointment, Rabbi Isaac Mayer Wise said it showed "that *President* Grant has revoked *General* Grant's notorious order No. 11."[39]

Grant also introduced a crusading spirit in protecting Jewish rights abroad, even if it clashed with other foreign policy interests. In the past, such concerns had been criticized as interfering with the internal affairs of other nations. Now Grant set a new benchmark for fostering human rights abroad, growing out of his concern for persecuted Jews. In November 1869, reports surfaced that Russia had brutally relocated two thousand Jewish families to the interior on smuggling charges—an episode faintly reminiscent of Grant's own wartime order. After conferring with American Jewish leaders, Grant responded in exemplary fashion. "It is too late, in this age of enlightenment," he told them, "to persecute any one on account of race, color or religion."[40] He protested to the czar while the American ambassador in Russia formulated a state paper documenting coercion against Russian Jews. The *New York World* professed satisfaction at how superior this Grant was to "that General Grant who issued . . . an order suddenly exiling all the Jews from their homes within the territory occupied by his armies."[41]

A still more menacing episode of anti-Semitism emerged in June 1870 with reports of "fearful massacres" against Romanian Jews, at least a thousand of whom were said to have been murdered in a pogrom. (The reports proved exaggerated.) Walking over to the State Department, Grant ordered Fish "to obtain full and reliable information in relation to this alleged massacre, and in the meantime to do all in his power to have the [neighboring] Turkish government stop such persecution."[42] In discussing this Romanian bloodletting with Simon Wolf, Grant declared that "respect for human rights" was the "first duty" of any head of state and that blacks and Jews should be elevated to a rank of "equality with the most enlightened." Grant showed surprising passion on the subject, saying "the story of the sufferings of the Hebrews of Roumania profoundly touches every sensibility of our nature."[43]

In December, Grant appointed Benjamin Franklin Peixotto, a Sephardic Jewish lawyer and journalist from San Francisco, as U.S. consul general to Romania. Grant spelled out Peixotto's mission in a groundbreaking statement that stands as a landmark in American diplomatic annals: "Mr Peixotto has undertaken the duties of his present office more as a missionary work for the benefit of the people who are laboring under severe oppression than for any benefits to accrue to himself . . . The United States knowing no distinction of her own citizens on account of religion or nativity naturally believe in a civilization the world over which will secure the same universal liberal views."[44] For the next five years, without an official salary, Peixotto performed major work investigating conditions in Romania and the Balkans, opposing anti-Semitism, and even providing sanctuary in his own home for Jews menaced by oppression.

The unceasing pressure for federal jobs that confronted Grant at every step mirrored a far larger phenomenon: the vast transformation of American government wrought by the war. Federal power had expanded immeasurably, testing the president's ability to manage the change. The National Bank Acts, the Homestead Act, the Morrill Act setting up land-grant universities—such wartime measures dramatically broadened Washington's authority. Boasting fifty-three thousand employees, the federal government ranked as the nation's foremost employer. Before the war, it had touched citizens' lives mostly through the postal system. Now it taxed citizens directly, conscripted them into the army, oversaw a national currency, and managed a giant national debt. As James M. McPherson has pointed out, eleven of the first twelve amendments to the Constitution constrained governmental power; starting with the Thirteenth Amendment, six of the next seven enlarged it.[45] The war also centralized power, welding states closer together and forging a new sense of nationhood. As Grant told a relative, "Since the late civil war the feeling of nationality had become stronger than it had ever been before."[46] When the first transcontinental railroad, aided by land grants and government bonds, was completed two months after Grant took office, it heralded a new geographic unity in American life.

Fueled by war contracts, the northern economy had burgeoned into a mighty, productive engine that exploded with entrepreneurial energy, eclipsing the small-scale, largely agricultural antebellum economy and catapulting the country into the front ranks of world powers. As the flush of wartime idealism faded, the Grant presidency ushered in the Gilded Age, marked by a mad scramble for money and producing colossal new fortunes. During the postwar boom, industrial trusts began to dominate one industry after another, creating growing inequalities of wealth and spawning a corresponding backlash from labor unions and the general public. New technologies, especially the railroad and telegraph, made the economy continental in scope, bringing forth modern industries and flooding the country with a cornucopia of consumer goods.

The rise of big business required government assistance, providing fresh opportunities for graft to abound. With the federal government bound up in new moneymaking activities, there arose a gigantic grab for filthy lucre that affected statehouses as well and saturated the political system with corruption. Businesses bargained for tax breaks, government contracts, land grants, and other favors, undermining democratic institutions that found it hard to withstand this assault. The mounting wealth also meant the dominant Republican Party was torn between its idealistic, abolitionist past and its business-oriented future.

In dealing with these changes, Grant inevitably bore a sizable load on his shoulders. He knew the postwar economic boom was uneven, the South having surrendered half its wealth, while four million freed slaves struggled to find their niche in American society. He had to deal with the paradox that while demands upon the presidency had grown exponentially, the Congress-dominated system of the Johnson years had drastically weakened the executive branch. In the nineteenth century, Congress was infinitely more powerful than in the twentieth and senators ruled as headstrong barons whose power often rivaled that of presidents. Grant had a special political conundrum to figure out. The Radical Republicans who formed his power base were the very people who had asserted congressional power during Andrew Johnson's impeachment. The deep-seated habit of promoting congressional prerogatives against the president would be fiendishly difficult to subdue, many senators having grown accustomed to exercising unchecked power.

ALTHOUGH ITS POPULATION WAS SWELLING, much of the Washington over which Grant presided languished as undeveloped wasteland. "It is out at the elbows, shabby at the toes, generally dingy and neglected," griped a lady visitor. "There are vast, dreary, uninhabited tracts, destitute of verdure and roamed over by herds of horse cars and hacks."[47] The soldiers who camped there during the war had leveled grass and bushes, leaving barren patches instead of parkland. Grant remembered the capital that year as "a most unsightly place . . . disagreeable to pass through in Summer in consequence of the dust arising from unpaved streets, and almost impassable in the winter from the Mud."[48]

Perhaps more than any other president, Grant oversaw the evolution of Washington from a straggling village into a modern city with well-paved sidewalks, sewers, and water and gas mains, enabling him to claim that it became "one of the most sightly cities in the country, and can boast of being the best paved."[49] Working with the vice chairman of the board of public works, Alexander R. Shepherd, Grant adorned public parks with trees and shrubbery, straightened a third of the city's roads, laid sidewalks where none had existed, introduced many streetlights, and signed legislation to finish the Washington Monument. With Orville Babcock heading the office charged with public buildings and grounds, Grant showed a surprisingly keen eye for government architecture and became so identified with a heavy, ornate design—the best example being the State, War, and Navy Building, now the Eisenhower Executive Office Building, adjacent to the White House—that it would be dubbed the "General Grant style" as it was replicated at post offices and courthouses across America.

The White House—then styled the executive mansion—required such thorough renovation that Julia Grant decided they should wait two weeks to move in while new wallpaper and carpets were installed. Because no West Wing or Oval Office yet existed, Grant held his cabinet meetings and kept his office on the second floor. His most noticeable additions to the mansion were a wood-paneled billiard room, rather solemnly decorated with stained glass windows and illuminated by gaslight chandeliers, and a pool set up on the south lawn that erupted with decorative water spray. Reflecting Republican hegemony, Grant removed the Thomas Jefferson statue from the north lawn, relegating it to Statuary Hall in the Capitol.

Julia Grant expressed shock at her predecessors' housekeeping and son Jesse recoiled at "the dingy, shabby carpets and furniture in this new home."[50] Since Grant was devoid of interest in interior decorating, Julia refurbished the White House, sprucing it up at considerable expense. She lavishly redecorated the East Room, swathing it in blue satin curtains and upholstery. Instead of Gilbert Stuart's portrait of George Washington in the Red Room, she hung a Grant family portrait that showed her grandly surrounded by her children, her uxorious husband standing stiffly to one side, a bit upstaged. Grant managed to get an equestrian portrait of himself hung in the Green Room. Finding the ushers and messengers unkempt in appearance, Julia decided to turn them out "in dress suits and white gloves."[51] She also cleared the south lawn, which had been a haunt for public loungers, slammed shut the iron gates, and created a "beautiful lawn" for her and the children, often overseen by the president as he smoked cigars on a porch rocking chair.[52] Few First Ladies—and the name wasn't yet commonly used—have so reveled in the White House or developed such a proprietary

feeling about it. "Eight happy years I spent there—so happy!" Julia would remi-
nisce. "It still seems as much like home to me as the old farm in Missouri, White
Haven."[53]

By January 1, 1870, with the remodeling complete, Julia began to play hostess
with a vengeance. The first and most brilliant early dinner came on January 26
when the Grants entertained Prince Arthur, third son of Queen Victoria. Both
British and American flags hung in the State Dining Room as guests munched
their way through a dinner of Gilded Age luxuriance, twenty-nine courses in all.
Grant had imported an army chef whose idea of fine cuisine consisted of heavy
slabs of roast beef and cheese piled high atop apple pie. Julia fired him and hired
an Italian steward named Valentino Melah, who still plied groaning guests with
up to thirty-five dishes in an evening, with a new wine introduced at every third
course; he replaced roast beef with partridge and lighter delicacies. At the center
of the State Dining Room stood a horseshoe-shaped table with a large flower-
draped mirror that when angled allowed Grant to screen himself from guests he
especially wished to dodge.

Because of the Civil War, the White House had acquired a lugubrious atmosphere under Lincoln while the Johnson impeachment trial had further eroded
social festivities in the capital. Now, with Julia's exuberant hospitality, the
mansion emerged as the center of a splendid social scene. Each Tuesday afternoon she received visitors while her husband held evening receptions every other
week. Julia developed the winning idea of inviting wives of cabinet secretaries,
senators, and friends to assist her in greeting visitors on the receiving line and,
reversing long-standing tradition, she made sure they were incorporated into
state dinners. Although faulted for extravagance, she never felt the least twinge
of guilt on the subject: "I have visited many courts and, I am proud to say, I saw
none that excelled in brilliancy the receptions of President Grant."[54]

Julia also helped to democratize the White House. With her sociability off-
setting her husband's shyness, she drew praise for her cordiality and openness to
all guests. "Of all the public receptions at the capital . . . Mrs. Grant's weekly
audiences are perhaps the most enjoyable, and certainly the most peculiarly republican gatherings," wrote one journalist, noting "the poorest working woman"
was invited to join them. The conversation was lively and often unexpectedly
provocative. "Woman suffrage was the burning question of the hour; and in this
Mrs. Grant showed great interest."[55] One army officer believed Julia's strabismus
handicapped her as a hostess: "Her somewhat impaired vision, with perhaps

inability to recall the crowded past promptly, interfered in later years with her recognition of persons in power."[56] Still self-conscious about being cross-eyed, Julia tended to pose for photographs in profile. To deal with her correspondence, she required a private secretary to assist her. Despite this drawback, she became a popular First Lady who impressed the vast majority of visitors. As one cabinet member wrote after dining next to her, "She is intelligent, lady-like, and particularly pleased me by speaking of her husband as 'Mr. Grant.'"[57]

A touch of restlessness still characterized Mr. Grant, who rebelled against the hidebound etiquette that forced presidents to socialize only on their home turf. Scrapping this custom, he dined out regularly at the homes of cabinet members and old army comrades. Large numbers of friends were happy to reciprocate, stopping by the White House in the evening. After dinner Grant loved to wander across Lafayette Square and drop by Hamilton Fish's house for casual conversation. "Few men had more powers of conversation and of narration than he when in the company of intimate friends," Fish remarked.[58]

As a result of interminable dinners, the once-slender Grant developed a sleek, portly look and his beard grew flecked with gray. Though conversational with close friends, he didn't look especially comfortable at White House social functions, trussed up in black evening coat and white tie, a onetime warrior ambushed by a sudden outbreak of peace. Shedding his levity, he nonetheless wore a downcast expression. "I observed a greater dignity of feeling," wrote Badeau, "a conscious and intentional gravity, an absence of that familiar, almost jocular mood which once had been so frequent."[59] Grant lacked the useful glibness of many presidents and could sometimes seem like a grudging prisoner of duty. He didn't impose himself upon people or thrust himself into conversations or demand to be the center of attention. As Badeau put it, Grant "had little small talk, and could not make conversation without a theme; but he observed closely under his mask of silence, and I always relished his criticisms of people and manners."[60]

Grant has labored under the charge of being an errand boy for plutocrats, turning his back on his roots in small-town America. Without question he enjoyed fraternizing with prosperous businessmen, but he was also extraordinarily charitable toward the indigent, even though he never advertised his generosity. "He gave to all who asked him, being often unnecessarily and unwisely profuse in his donations," said Fish. "I have not infrequently known him to give sums from five to ten times the amount of what the applicant could have reasonably or probably expected."[61] His papers show a steady solicitude for the poor, the money routed anonymously through the Metropolitan Methodist Episcopal Church in Washington, where he worshipped regularly. "Please give $10 to the blind man and $10 to the soldier's widow," went one note in 1869.[62] In another he wrote to the Reverend John P. Newman, "Please find enclosed my check for $100, for distribution among the poor."[63]

While wine flowed freely at state dinners, Grant didn't partake and no alcohol was served when he dined in private. For New Year's Day receptions, he ordered that coffee instead of liquor be distributed. His political enemies still delighted in branding him a drunkard, the label now being the stock-in-trade of Grant critics. Ben Butler mocked Andrew Johnson as the "drunken tailor" and Grant as the "drunken tanner."[64] When Orville Browning called on Grant one day, he found him "very much bloated, eyes red and watering, and looking very much as if he were drunk, and I think he must have been pretty full."[65] But such random accusations were now more conspicuous by their absence and occurred with nowhere near the frequency of wartime drinking charges. The precise circumstances required for Grant's drinking binges—visits to distant cities, the absence of his wife—seldom applied during his presidency when he was constantly surrounded by people, especially Julia. Admiral Daniel Ammen summed up Grant's presidency thus: "During all of these years I never saw General Grant in a condition that would give rise even to a suspicion that he had indulged too freely in liquor, and only on one occasion have I ever had a glass of liquor in the White House."[66] It was an extraordinary achievement that Grant, despite the almost unbearable tensions of his presidency and undoubted temptations to drink, largely conquered an alcohol problem that had beset him through much of his adult life.

An active man, Grant often felt cooped up in the White House where he worked from 10 a.m. to 3 p.m. before escaping for a carriage drive. He showed his usual fondness for speedy trotters, sometimes driving so fast the timid Julia begged him to return her to the safety of the executive mansion. As Grant careened down roadways, pedestrians occasionally imagined he steered a runaway carriage. One day, riding down Pennsylvania Avenue with Sherman, Grant inquired, "Sherman, what special hobby do you intend to adopt?"[67] Sherman was perplexed until Grant explained that newspapers liked to pin pet interests on people and he had chosen horses as his hobby. That way, if a reporter pressed him for information he didn't wish to share, he could deflect the conversation to horsemanship. The anecdote suggests Grant was more artful and sophisticated in dealing with reporters than is commonly supposed.

Perhaps his most remarkable extracurricular activities were his solitary walks around Washington, sometimes covering five or six miles. Grant disbanded his personal guard and sauntered around town alone, hands clasped behind his back, smoking a cigar. On these rambles, he often passed Walt Whitman, then working in Washington. The poet told his mother, "I saw Grant to-day on the avenue walking by himself—(I always salute him, & he does the same to me.)"[68] He often spotted Grant frequenting "a little cottage on the outskirts" of town, where he had struck up a friendship with an elderly couple. "I would see him leaning on their window sills outside: all would be talking together: they seeming to treat him without deference for place—with dignity, courtesy, appreciation."[69] Far from seeing Grant as an elitist president or toady of the rich, Whitman thought he embodied a common, democratic spirit. "Grant was the typical Western man—the plainest, the most efficient . . . the least imposed upon by appearances."[70]

For Grant, the walks pierced the bubble inevitably isolating a president. On his constitutional one day, he noticed a commotion among a knot of government construction workers. When he asked what was the matter, he was told they were being forced to work ten-hour days even though Congress had recently passed legislation introducing an eight-hour day for laborers employed by the federal government. Grant summoned the responsible figure, a Mr. Benjamin, for a dressing-down and notified him "he should never again exact above eight hours labor a day from his men."[71] However frugal with government funds, Grant didn't allow it to interfere with his sense of justice for these workmen. On May 19, 1869, he issued a proclamation endorsing an eight-hour day for government laborers without any diminution of pay.[72] It was yet another example that belies the charge that Grant had turned his back on ordinary working people.

In his early days in Detroit, Grant had befriended Colonel James E. Pitman, who told the following tale of Grant on one of his walks:

> He used to meet a lady every morning as she was coming out of the Treasury building. He bowed to her and she bowed to him, but never spoke. One day, he stepped before her. "See here, why don't you stop and speak to me?" "But General," she answered, "I supposed you

wanted to be alone, and I didn't want to intrude." Grant smiled and said, "Don't you suppose I would rather have people stop and talk with me than let me walk alone?" There is a hint here of Grant's admiration for a pretty woman and also a hint of his essential loneliness. This trait he had even as a young officer in Detroit.[73]

As part of his health regimen, Grant escaped from the sweltering Washington summers by withdrawing to Long Branch. A miasmic breeze, he believed, blew from flats south of the White House, communicating disease to its occupants. His friend George W. Childs, the editor of the *Philadelphia Public Ledger,* had joined with George Pullman and other well-off friends to purchase the shingled, three-story cottage on Ocean Avenue, perched on a bluff, which effectively became the first summer White House. Grant was allowed to use the house free of charge for life and bought it in his name.[74] Described by one reporter as a "mixture of English villa and Swiss chalet," it was encircled by verandahs and dormer windows that provided fine ocean vistas.[75] Not nearly as fancy as Newport, Long Branch exuded an informal charm and gaiety, despite its heavy contingent of bankers and industrialists. Brass bands thumped out tunes on the local hotel lawn, while scores of red, white, and blue flags rippled in the salt air. Grant responded to "the genial sea breeze, fine roads and beautiful surrounding villages, and pleasant and hospitable neighbors."[76] At Long Branch he felt blithe as a schoolboy and loved to flaunt feats of strength. There was a chin-up bar at the ferry house where he startled his family by performing twenty-five or thirty repetitions. Clad in a linen duster, he drove fast buggies on the beach or scooted off to neighboring towns, often logging in twenty miles before breakfast. Other times he drifted down to the ocean alone and stared pensively at the sea, smoking his cigar. Grant ran into criticism for spending too much time at his Long Branch hideaway, but he kept up an ample work schedule there and was often visited by cabinet secretaries. The beach house became for him an irreplaceable sanctuary from the pressures of office.

Ever since the war, the Grant family had suffered from a vagabond existence. With the two eldest boys away at school, Long Branch provided a cherished haven where the Grants functioned as a true clan, bathing in the surf, enjoying clambakes, and entertaining visitors. Since Grant was a young president, the press delighted in the rambunctious antics of his teenage children, ranging from

eighteen-year-old Fred to eleven-year-old Jesse. "I have never seen a more devoted family or a happier one," observed the White House usher William Crook.
"There never seemed to be the slightest jar."[77] As in Galena days, Grant would
playfully knead his bread into little balls at meals and fire them at Nellie and
Jesse, who resided in the White House. "When the missile hit, he went over and
kissed the victim on the cheek," said Crook. "He was a most loving father."[78]
Grant's oldest son, Fred, who was at West Point, showed strikingly similar interests to his father's. He excelled at math, adored horses, and loved parade ground
drills; besides the physical resemblance, he had his father's laconic style and bullheaded drive. The second son, Buck, displayed his father's strength and simple,
straightforward manner. Nellie was pretty and sweet and pampered by her doting father. At one point, to instill more discipline in her, the Grants sent her to
Miss Porter's School in Farmington, Connecticut, where she revolted at her unwanted exile and soon returned to the mad flurry of Washington parties.

The child providing reporters with the most captivating copy was Jesse,
whom his father called "a saucy little rascal" and who didn't go to school until
age nine, having had private tutors instead.[79] Inheriting his father's taste for fast
horses, Jesse drove a pair of Shetland ponies in a little buggy crafted by his father. He was constantly at Grant's side during his White House rounds: "Father
was with me on walks, talks, star gazing, stamp collecting, raising pets, playing
ball and other pastimes."[80] The "star gazing" referred to a telescope Jesse had
mounted on the White House roof where he and his father studied the universe.
Stamp collecting was another of the boy's hobbies, and he was outraged when he
sent $5 to a Boston company for foreign stamps that never arrived. Grant pre-
vailed upon a local police officer named Kelly, assigned to the executive mansion, to see justice done. "I am a Capitol Policeman. I can arrest anybody,
anywhere, at anytime for anything," Kelly wrote on White House stationery
with mock menace to the company. "I want you to send those stamps to Jesse
Grant right at once."[81] Jesse shortly got a bumper crops of stamps.

It wasn't yet the custom for First Ladies to champion causes, but Julia Grant
exerted quiet influence behind the scenes. She didn't try to butt in on policy
decisions, where her knowledge was limited, but she readily detected false or
treacherous figures and strove to protect her husband from the pervasive intrigue around a president. "She soothed him when cares oppressed him," wrote
Badeau, "she supported him when even he was downcast."[82] Whenever she
thought he needed advice or support, she would scribble a little note and slip it

into an envelope marked on top, "The President, immediate."[83] Whereas Grant accepted his presidential tenure with a certain ambivalence, the stout, buxom Julia thrived during her White House stay, referring to it as "a bright and beautiful dream" that she hoped might last forever.[84]

Julia made varied impressions on people. Before she became First Lady, one journalist commended her as a "sunny, sweet woman; too unassuming to be a mark for criticism," while many others complimented her tact, warmth, and hospitality.[85] Another vein of commentary chided her, however, for being bossy and autocratic, too impressed with her own prerogatives. Some remembered her berating servants; Eliza Shaw recalled her "scolding her coachman because the carriage was muddy."[86] The author Olive Logan was blunt about her shortcomings: "She was not well liked . . . she applied herself at once to finding out her privileges, and was not slow in asserting them."[87]

Since he adored his wife, Grant was largely blind to these flaws, treating her like a young bride. He escorted her, arm in arm, to breakfast each morning and reenacted the same ceremony for the evening meal. Julia conjured up images of domestic bliss, leaving this vignette of the family's quiet time together before dinner: "I was generally lying on the bed resting among my pillows before making my toilet. The General usually sat near the head of the bed, smoking his favorite cigar. Fred, feeling sure of his welcome, stretched himself across the foot. Ulysses [Buck] sat on a lounge at the foot of the bed, while Nellie and Ida [later Fred's wife] took their comfort in great cushioned chairs."[88]

CHAPTER THIRTY

//////////////////////////////

We Are All Americans

I F THERE WERE MANY small things Grant didn't know about the presidency, he knew one big thing: his main mission was to settle unfinished business from the war by preserving the Union and safeguarding the freed slaves. As Walt Whitman noted, Grant had signed on for "a task of peace, more difficult than the war itself."[1] The first issue involved money. During the conflict, the federal government had issued reams of bonds and paper currency styled "greenbacks," running up enormous debt. Grant and Secretary of the Treasury Boutwell were united in wanting to retire that debt. For northern veterans, redeeming the debt counted as a sacred matter, rewarding those who had invested in the war effort. The wartime Congress had promised to pay interest in gold, but a postwar movement took hold to repay money in greenbacks instead. "Every greenback," Senator Sumner protested, "is red with the blood of fellow-citizens."[2] So it came as no surprise that the first major piece of legislation signed by Grant on March 18, 1869, committed the government to paying off bondholders in "gold or its equivalent" and redeeming paper money "at the earliest practicable period."[3] Persuaded that the restoration of American credit should be his first priority, Grant established his bona fides as a conservative, hard-money man and upheld the honor of the Union cause.

No less committed to the Radical side of the Republican agenda, he signed a bill on March 19 conferring equal rights on blacks in Washington, D.C. The fate of blacks and white Republicans in the South was a far more vexed matter that would dominate Grant's tenure in office. Everybody agreed that readmitting former Confederate states to the Union was long overdue. Three states—Virginia, Mississippi, and Texas—had yet to resume their rightful place, and Grant saw their harmonious return as an overriding objective. As ever, he had to tread a fine line between retribution and reconciliation. On April 7, he asked Congress to authorize elections in Virginia and Mississippi to ratify new state constitutions, while insisting that those constitutions should "secure the civil and political rights of all persons within their borders," black and white alike.[4] Between January and March 1870, Virginia, Mississippi, and Texas returned to the Union as they pledged to protect black rights.

Virginia seemed the easy success story, electing a northern-born Republican governor, Gilbert C. Walker, allied with Democrats and moderate Republicans. Mississippi, by contrast, with its black majority, would turn into an overheated furnace of violently competing interests. Hope for Reconstruction rested on its provisional Maine-born governor, Adelbert A. Ames, whom Grant also named commander of the Fourth Military District, which encompassed Arkansas as well. With his thick handlebar mustache, long goatee, and high forehead, the thirty-three-year-old Ames had graduated high in his West Point class and won the Medal of Honor for his valor at the first battle of Bull Run. By war's end he had attained the rank of brevet major general. Soon he would be married to Ben Butler's daughter. Fired by a crusading spirit, Ames saw carpetbaggers as apostles of "northern liberty" who had "a hold on the hearts of the colored people that nothing can destroy."[5] He oversaw elections for a new Mississippi constitution that made the state eligible for readmission to the Union. "When I took command of this military district," he recalled, "I found that the negroes who had been declared free by the United States were not free, in fact that they were living under a code that made them worse than slaves; and I found that it was necessary, as commanding officer, to protect them, and I did."[6] Delivering on his promise, Ames appointed the first black officeholders in Mississippi history. Upon entering the U.S. Senate in February 1870, he combated segregation in the U.S. Army and stood in the forefront of the campaign waged against the Ku Klux Klan. For his efforts on behalf of downtrodden blacks, Ames was to brave years of unremitting violence from the white power structure in the state.

One of Grant's most vocal Mississippi critics was his brother-in-law Judge Lewis Dent. Conservative Republicans had nominated Dent for governor against the more liberal James Alcorn, a prominent planter, hoping Dent's association with Grant might mislead credulous blacks into supporting him. In fact, far from being sympathetic to black suffrage, Dent believed southern whites possessed a God-given right to rule and that black voting would "inevitably lead to a black-man's party and eventually to a war of races," he told Grant. The upshot would be "to alienate from the planters, the ancient confidence and affection of this race."[7] Refusing to bow to nepotism this time, Grant issued a stern warning to Dent that he would resist him. "Personally, I wish you well, and would do all in my power proper to be done to secure your success; but in public matters, personal feelings will not influence me."[8] Dent lost the election.

Grant also began to commit critical federal resources to ensuring black welfare. In 1867 the Bureau of Education had been created to educate freed people, but Congress had consistently slashed its budget, threatening to shut it down. Grant intervened to save it. "With millions of ex-slaves upon our hands to be educated," he stated, "this is not the time to suppress an office for facilitating education. The Bureau shall have another trial."[9] To guarantee its success, Grant drafted John Eaton, the chaplain who had done superlative work resettling freed slaves during the war and who again enjoyed Grant's unconditional support. Without Grant, Eaton declared, "the Bureau could hardly have become—what it has been said to be—the most influential office of education in the world."[10]

On a personal level, Grant extended an olive branch to Confederate generals. In May 1869, Robert E. Lee came to the White House to discuss a railroad venture. As at Appomattox, Grant attempted to smooth over an awkward situation with a little levity and small talk. "You and I, General," said Grant, "have had more to do with destroying railroads than building them."[11] Lee would not be drawn into this sort of pleasantry. According to Badeau, he "refused to smile, or to recognize the raillery. He went on gravely with the conversation, and no other reference was made to the past."[12] The diplomat John Lothrop Motley, who was there, detected "a shade of constraint" in Lee's manner.[13] On political matters, Lee worked hard to sound reasonable, expressed approval of the Fifteenth Amendment, and professed to see no "prodigious harm" in permitting blacks to vote. "All the Southern States should be in harmony with the National Government," he declared.[14] But before too long, Lee rose to his feet, bid Grant a frosty farewell, and departed. The two wartime titans were destined never to meet again. Lee died on October 12, 1870.

In another stunning reversal wrought by the war, General Ely Parker, the full-blooded Seneca sachem, emerged as a leading personality in the new administration. On April 13, Grant elevated him to commissioner of Indian affairs, the first Native American to hold the job and the first nonwhite person to ascend to such a lofty government post. With nearly three hundred thousand Indians in the United States and its territories, Parker's job promised to be one of unfathomable complexity. Indian communities reeled under remorseless threats as railroad, stagecoach, and telegraph lines pushed steadily westward, crisscrossing Indian territory. As settlers traversed Indian hunting grounds, they set off deadly clashes. Gradually Indian tribes were shoved off the Great Plains, where they had hunted buffalo, and herded into drastic new patterns of resettlement.

Aided by Parker, Grant embarked on a Peace Policy with the Indians that was full of high-minded intentions. Outraged by injustices perpetrated against Native Americans, he aimed to clean up a corrupt system of licensed government traders who cheated Indians on their supplies of food, clothing, and shelter and grew indecently wealthy through a veritable sinkhole of graft called the Indian Ring. These lucrative jobs were prime sources of congressional patronage. Grant believed the best way to root out such scoundrels was to remove the whole network of shady agents from the political sphere, relocating the Bureau of Indian Affairs into the War Department. Right before his inauguration, he received a Quaker delegation and asked them to nominate Indian agents from their members. "If you can make Quakers out of the Indians, it will take the fight out of them," Grant told them. "Let us have peace."[15] Aside from his respect for Quaker pacifism and integrity, Grant knew the society had coexisted peacefully with Indians in Pennsylvania. By the end of his first year in office, Grant had ferreted out many crooked Indian agents, replacing them with Quakers and honest army officers, eliciting howls from congressmen who had once controlled those jobs. At Grant's behest, Congress also formed a ten-man Board of Indian Commissioners, a civilian watchdog agency staffed by dedicated, nonsalaried figures, to police wrongdoing in the Indian Bureau and reform its procedures.

Many of the same generals who had defeated the Confederacy were now assigned to pacify Native Americans and often betrayed a punitive, bloody attitude, exemplified by Phil Sheridan's infamous remark "The only good Indians I know are dead."[16] Convinced Native Americans must succumb to a stronger race of white men, Sheridan reviled them as "the enemies of our race and of our civilization," who had to be confined on reservations or killed.[17] During one Indian war in 1867, Sherman advised Sheridan, "The more [Indians] we kill this year, the less we would have to kill next year."[18] Many in Congress had few qualms about pursuing a policy of outright genocide, with one Nevada congressman calling for "extinction. And I say that with a full sense of the meaning conveyed by that word." A Texas legislator warned that "he who resists gets crushed. That is the history of the wild Indian."[19]

Cut from a different cloth, Grant had always shown sympathy for the underdog. Ever since his exposure to West Coast Indians in the 1850s, he had exhibited a touching compassion for their plight, perhaps more than any previous president. "I have lived with the Indians and I know them thoroughly," he said. "They can be civilized and made friends of the republic."[20] He blamed white settlers for many problems wrongly attributed to Native Americans. Right after Appomattox, he remarked that "the Indians require as much protection from the whites as the white does from the Indians. My own experience has been that little trouble would have ever been had from them but for the encroachments & influence of bad whites."[21] He thought peace with the Indians could be achieved if only the latter renounced their "roving life" and agreed to "fixed places of abode" on reservations.[22] Parker espoused an end to the treaty system, contending that treaties could only be made between two sovereign states, whereas Indian tribes were "wards" of the American government.[23]

Even as he enunciated his Peace Policy, Grant knew frightened settlers demanded tough federal protection and they constituted his ultimate political constituents. Over time, his genuine concern for Indian justice had to reckon with an incessant clamor from railroads, ranchers, and miners for more troops and frontier forts. Spurred by the 1862 Homestead Act and the transcontinental railroad, the country had made a tremendous investment in westward expansion, providing land for white settlers and masses of immigrants. Indians and federal soldiers would trade blows and engage in atrocities across a wide swath of territory. While preaching how it was "much better to support a Peace commission than a campaign against Indians," Grant would be summoned repeatedly to send arms to western states to defend them against Indian raids.[24]

In the long run, Grant and Parker planned to extend citizenship to Indians through a gradual, paternalistic process of "humanization, civilization, and Christianization," as Parker expressed it.[25] "A system which looks to the extinction of a race is too abhorrent for a Nation to indulge in," Grant told Congress in his first annual message in December 1869. As with all his presidential addresses, he composed it himself. "I see no remedy for this except in placing all the Indians on large reservations, as rapidly as it can be done, and giving them absolute protection there."[26] This hopeful, idealistic path, paved with good intentions, had been touted by well-meaning presidents from George Washington to Abraham Lincoln. Grant saw absorption and assimilation as a benign, peaceful process, not one robbing Indians of their rightful culture. Whatever its shortcomings, Grant's approach seemed to signal a remarkable advance over the ruthless methods adopted by some earlier administrations.

Urging Native Americans to resettle on reservations and take up an agricultural economy was an ultimately quixotic idea that never gained much traction among the tribes. Most Native Americans didn't care to be "civilized" on Grant's terms. For them, any renunciation of their hunting traditions meant an unrelenting annihilation of their ancient culture. At the same time, the butchery of vast buffalo herds on the Great Plains by white men, many killed for commercial leather or pure sport, spelled doom for the Indian way of life. Grant favored mercy toward Indians who abided by his solution, but ended up having to deal severely with those who roamed beyond their reservations and clashed with westward settlement by whites.

Government relations with Indians soured in January 1870 after the U.S. cavalry under Major Eugene M. Baker massacred 173 Piegan Blackfeet in the Montana Territory, the vast majority of them women, children, and the elderly. Many were roasted alive when their tepees were set ablaze or hacked apart with axes. Sheridan had likely contributed to the ferocity by hectoring Baker to "strike them hard!" and he blithely characterized the massacre as "well-merited punishment."[27] The episode mocked Grant's Peace Policy and prompted a congressional backlash against the army's handling of Indian relations. This led to banning military officers as Indian agents, a move that was partly Congress's way of reclaiming the lucrative patronage powers lost to it.

Grant refused to regress to the seamy ways of the past. Building on his successful experience of employing Quaker agents, he expanded the idea to encompass other Protestant denominations and Roman Catholics. Religious groups would nominate people and the interior secretary selected them. When Grant's go-between with the Jewish community, Simon Wolf, protested the exclusion of Jews, Grant said he would be glad to recognize the "Israelites," naming Dr. Herman Bendell as superintendent of Indian affairs for the Arizona Territory.[28] He was later celebrated as the first Jewish settler to plant stakes in Phoenix, Arizona. The presence of Jewish agents fit incongruously with the Christianizing mission proclaimed by Grant. Within a few years, Grant hoped his policy would "bring all the Indians on to reservations, where they will live in houses, have schoolhouses and churches, and will be pursuing peaceful and self sustaining avocations."[29] Again Grant seemed well-meaning but naive in thinking nomadic Indians would repudiate their past and suddenly mimic the ways of the white men who had forcibly dispossessed them of their tribal lands.

ULYSSES S. GRANT had an obsessive side to his nature—a *quietly* obsessive side, but no less tenacious for all that. This pit-bull vigor had served him well in the military, making him the scourge of the Confederacy. Yet in politics, where a certain lightness of touch and flexibility were essential, such obstinacy could easily backfire. During his presidency, Grant came to dwell obsessively on annexing Santo Domingo—the Spanish-speaking half of the island of Hispaniola, today's Dominican Republic—and found it hard to let the controversial issue drop.

As with many large mistakes, it stemmed from deceptively small beginnings. Early in the new administration, Colonel Joseph W. Fabens, a New England expatriate and speculator, filed a glowing report with Secretary of State Fish that idealized the rich mineral, agricultural, and timber resources of Santo Domingo. Serving as an emissary from President Buenaventura Báez, he peddled the Caribbean country to the United States as if it were a high-priced real estate parcel: "The annexation of this country to the United States should be an acquisition of great value."[30] The proposal envisaged nothing less than the final conversion of Santo Domingo into a full-fledged American state, or series of states. Fabens and his ally General William L. Cazneau were, in fact, shady operators who had booked considerable land holdings on the island and stood to pocket large profits if the United States absorbed the small country.

Fish was annoyed by Fabens's persistence. Still, as a dutiful secretary of state, he conveyed the proposal to the cabinet in early April while withholding even tepid support. Grant showed no special partiality for the idea and seemed "a listener rather than a participant in the debate," recalled Secretary of the Interior Cox.[31] But Grant *was* intrigued by the magnificent harbor at Samaná Bay, which had the makings of a coaling station for naval ships. During the war, the Lincoln administration had recognized the strategic advantages of a Caribbean naval base in guarding sea lanes for boats bound for the isthmus of Panama, protecting East Coast trade with the Pacific.

No sudden whim of Grant's, American involvement with Santo Domingo stretched back into earlier presidencies. In 1846 President Polk had dispatched

David Porter to scrutinize Samaná Bay as a possible American naval depot. In 1854 President Pierce named Cazneau a special commissioner to Santo Domingo. Taking up residence there, he inveigled lucrative concessions for himself from the local government while urging the Dominican government to lease the bay to the United States.

For an assortment of reasons good and bad, the Caribbean had long been scouted as a haven for freed American slaves. While some racists simply wanted to export as many blacks as possible, many abolitionists had approved "colonization" plans as long as they were voluntary and fully protected blacks. In 1858 Abraham Lincoln joined the board of managers of the Illinois Colonization Society and three years later lobbied Congress to allocate funds for territory outside the United States to relocate freed slaves. In 1862 the United States established diplomatic relations with Haiti and Liberia with an eye to their being future destinations for emancipated slaves. By the time Lincoln promulgated the Emancipation Proclamation, he foresaw a biracial America and had cooled forever on such colonization schemes.

After Spain withdrew from Santo Domingo in 1865, it became one of the few West Indian islands free of European control. With a tiny population of 150,000, it had an educated elite of Spanish ancestry along with mulattoes and Indians, many of whom welcomed an American protectorate. In 1866 Secretary of State Seward sent his son Frederick and Admiral Porter, fortified by a boatload of gold, to negotiate the purchase or extended lease of Samaná Bay. They were entertained by that man for all seasons, William L. Cazneau. The negotiations failed because of a recent revolutionary struggle. It is important to note that after the Civil War, territorial expansion and imperialism were very much in the air, William Seward having bought Alaska for $7.2 million and begun maneuvers to acquire Hawaii.

By October 1868, the Báez government arrived at a favorable view of American annexation. Fervent support sprang from Congressman Ben Butler, who had been liberally bribed by Joseph Fabens with land on Samaná Bay. In January 1869, Butler promised Fabens he would see President-elect Grant to "secure his friendly cooperation."[32] Meanwhile, President Johnson told Congress he favored annexing all of Hispaniola—Haiti and Santo Domingo combined. In the administration's waning days, Seward worked tirelessly for annexation, so that the Santo Domingo scheme was in some respects a holdover from previous administrations.

Grant portrayed himself as a passive spectator of the scheme's evolution. In his first year as president, he explained, "the proposition came up for the admission of Santo Domingo as a territory of the Union. It was not a question of my seeking but was a proposition from the people of Santo Domingo . . . which I entertained."[33] The project began to cast a peculiar spell over his tenacious imagination. In a handwritten memorandum entitled "Reasons why San Domingo should be annexed to the United States," he showed just how fully he had pondered the issue.[34] Noting the country's land area of twenty thousand square miles, he praised its mineral wealth, stores of timber, tobacco, tropical fruits, and dyes and cited plentiful sugar and coffee supplies that could slash prices for American consumers. With considerable prescience, he foresaw that the "Isthmus of Darien" would someday have a canal drawing a substantial share of world commerce and a naval base at Samaná would command its gateway. Annexing Santo Domingo could also break British domination of the Caribbean, which forced American vessels "to pass through foreign waters."[35]

But for Grant the most potent argument related to the aftermath of American slavery. Santo Domingo, he asserted, was "capable of supporting the entire colored population of the United States, should it choose to emigrate."[36] He emphasized that this was not a colonization or deportation scheme. He was by no means urging African Americans to emigrate to the Caribbean island, but simply acknowledging that it could function as a critical safety valve if white Americans refused to honor their rights: "The present difficulty in bringing all parts of the United States to a happy unity and love of country grows out of the prejudice to color. The prejudice is a senseless one, but it exists."[37] If a black person could resort to a Caribbean sanctuary, Grant reasoned, "his worth here would soon be discovered, and he would soon receive such recognition as to induce him to stay."[38] Or, as he subsequently wrote: "If two or three hundred thousand blacks were to emigrate to St. Domingo . . . the Southern people would learn the crime of Ku Kluxism, because they would see how necessary the black man is to their own prosperity."[39] The memorandum shows Grant in a visionary frame of mind, grappling with large issues of racial justice. Blacks would enjoy the option of resettling outside the continental United States, yet remain citizens under the full jurisdiction of the federal government: "I took it that the colored people would go there in numbers, so as to have independent states governed by their own race. They would still be States of the Union, and under the protection of the General Government; but the citizens would be almost wholly colored."[40]

Although one thousand blacks had emigrated to Liberia in 1866 and 1867 under the aegis of the American Colonization Society, the idea of such emigration lost support among many blacks during Reconstruction as they gained full rights to citizenship. This progress limited, but by no means eliminated, black support for annexing Santo Domingo. Still, Grant's policy contained a substantial element of wishful thinking. A black asylum in the Caribbean could create an incentive for whites to expel blacks from the continental United States, while Caribbean states with all-black constituencies might not fare very well in the domestic political arena.

As Santo Domingo emerged as a potent political issue, its supporters issued a stream of articles presenting it as a tropical paradise—"the garden of the Antilles" and the "finest part of the whole West Indies."[41] A steady drumbeat of criticism arose from those who spied a huge boondoggle being foisted on the country by unscrupulous speculators. "The signs are," warned the *New York World*, "that there is a powerful combination in this country to annex the [West Indian] islands by some hook or crook, not from any considerations of public advantage, but merely as a large speculation in real estate and colonial debts."[42] There also emerged sotto voce grumbling against a Caribbean country where Spanish was spoken, many people were of mixed race, Roman Catholicism was practiced, and there was no history of American-style democracy.

In July 1869, Grant took a decisive step that moved Santo Domingo from theoretical question to practical reality. Meeting his cabinet, he "casually remarked that the navy people seemed so anxious to have the bay of Samana as a coaling station that he thought he would send Colonel [Orville] Babcock down to examine it and report upon it as an engineer," wrote Secretary of the Interior Cox.[43] Babcock, with his background as a military engineer, seemed a logical choice for the assignment. Even those opposed to the trip didn't object vociferously and Babcock slipped away without publicity. On July 13, Grant wrote to President Báez apropos of Babcock: "I have entire confidence in his integrity and intelligence, and I commend him to your excellency accordingly."[44]

Before Babcock sailed, Grant startled his cabinet by announcing that a group of New York merchants who traded with Santo Domingo had offered him free passage on one of their ships. When Fish objected to such a flagrant conflict of interest, Grant backed down and agreed that a naval vessel should carry him to the Caribbean instead. With that conversation, the cabinet began to suspect that unseen business forces were operating upon Grant and that he had established a

series of back channels to Santo Domingo. Traveling there without special diplomatic authority from Fish, Babcock was only authorized to gather information, but Grant gave him orders to sound out Báez on annexation and Babcock
happily complied.

When Babcock arrived in Santo Domingo in late July, his hand strengthened
by an escort of American warships, he found local denizens "ignorant but not
indolent."[45] When he posed the question of annexation, not everyone greeted
the idea, but he thought they would reverse course once the first steps were
undertaken. Babcock ended up grossly exceeding his authority, negotiating a
full-dress agreement instead of merely gathering facts. On September 4, President Báez signed a treaty by which the United States would annex Santo Domingo and assume its public debt of $1.5 million or else purchase Samaná Bay
outright for $2 million. It included an understanding that Grant would apply all
his power to lobby the treaty in Congress in a secretive atmosphere. Santo Domingo would be admitted as a U.S. territory, then eventually as a state.

When Babcock returned to Washington, bearing this unexpected document, the news elicited a shocked reaction from Grant's cabinet and Fish was
horrified that Babcock had exceeded his directions. "What do you think!" he
exclaimed to Cox privately. "Babcock is back, and has actually brought a treaty
for the cession of San Domingo; yet I pledge you my word he had no more
diplomatic authority than any other casual visitor to the island!"[46] According to
Cox, an exasperated Fish wished to bury the whole matter in "oblivion as a state
secret."[47]

When secretaries arrived at the next cabinet meeting, they discovered that
Babcock had laid out mineral samples from the island, openly advertising its
wares. Fish and Cox had expected Grant to repudiate the treaty, but he endorsed
it instead. "I suppose it is not formal," he confessed, Babcock having "had no
diplomatic powers; but we can easily cure that. We can send back the treaty, and
have Perry, the consular agent, sign it; and as he is an officer of the State Department it would make it all right."[48] Cabinet members sat there in thunderstruck
silence. "But Mr. President," Cox inquired, "has it been settled, then, that we
want to annex San Domingo?" Cox said that Grant blushed, "smoked hard at his
cigar," and finally ended a painful pause by changing the subject. Henceforth,
Grant took diplomatic matters into his own hands. He instructed Fish to draw
up two treaties: one for annexation, another for taking over Samaná Bay. Fish
had a racial aversion to absorbing the Dominican Republic and was, at best, a

lukewarm supporter who humored Grant to gain a freer hand on other matters. By December, Grant had in hand the two treaties negotiated by Babcock.

The president didn't anticipate what a hard sell Santo Domingo annexation would be, involving a tropical, Spanish-speaking, Roman Catholic nation inhabited by dark-skinned people. He committed fatal errors by pursuing this momentous policy in a closed-door, top-down style that made sense in wartime, but not in politics. He didn't prepare the American electorate or mobilize public opinion or rally voters to his side. Grant hadn't yet learned the art of appealing to the public over the heads of Washington legislators, presenting himself as steward of a broader public interest. The absence of a systematic marshaling of public opinion hurt Grant in jousting with senators who had to approve the treaty, especially Charles Sumner, august chairman of the Committee on Foreign Relations. Fearing that Haitian independence would be compromised by Dominican annexation next door, he emphatically opposed U.S. expansion there. Sumner's pronouncements were decrees that other political figures defied at their peril. Headstrong and imperious, he resented any treaty hatched without his personal blessing, and Grant would experience the full force of his towering fury before the Santo Domingo imbroglio was finally laid to rest.

Cuba was the other locus of controversy in the Caribbean. As with American attitudes toward Santo Domingo, it was sometimes hard to differentiate between humanitarian concerns and imperialist swagger. Right before Grant became president, Cuban insurgents launched a campaign to oust their Spanish colonial overlords, provoking brutal reprisals. In Grant's cabinet, a stentorian voice for aiding the rebels and recognizing their provisional government was the emaciated John Rawlins. As always, he approached the issue with evangelical conviction, arguing for the expulsion of all European authority from the Western Hemisphere. As Grant's right-hand man, he commanded special respect in the cabinet and remained as outspoken as during the war. Although severely depleted by the tuberculosis that had harried him for years, Rawlins rallied during his first months as war secretary, perhaps stimulated by his new powers, and promoted his ideas in his usual animated style.

Never one to traffic in halfway measures, Rawlins wanted to champion Cuban rebels as the first step in a policy that foresaw annexation of the island. The prospect of war with Spain didn't seem to frighten him. Before the Civil War, the impetus for Cuban annexation had come from the South, which saw a new outpost for slavery. After the war, many northerners, including prominent blacks, favored ending Spanish domination of Cuba to rid the island of slavery, casting Cuban rebels in a heroic light. Believing the rebels would prevail, Grant leaned toward Rawlins's views and considered recognizing the insurgents as a belligerent power. They had to contend, however, with the ever-cautious Fish, who thought it foolhardy to risk war with Spain right after the Civil War. With the United States preparing for major negotiations with Great Britain on wartime claims, Fish was in no mood to engage in side battles in the Caribbean. Having already given anemic support to Grant's Santo Domingo venture, he chose to go no further in the region. He was disturbed that filibustering expeditions against Cuba set sail from American ports with Union and Confederate veterans signed up by the Cuban revolutionary junta in New York.

However much he was exasperated by John Rawlins, who kept poaching on his territory, Fish recognized that the ailing war secretary was a good-hearted soul, motivated by pure feelings. "He is a generous, high-spirited, and right-minded (impulsive) man," Fish wrote, "instinctively right in the direction of his impulses, even if occasionally extravagant."[49] At the same time, Fish realized that Rawlins's bombastic rhetoric and impetuous nature could lead to reckless moves in the Caribbean that undermined his own work at State.

Despite sympathy for the Cuban rebels, Grant tread a fine line between neutrality and intervention. He was outraged in June when Spanish authorities executed two Americans in eastern Cuba, inflaming American public opinion. Still, Grant acted swiftly to end anti-Cuban raids originating on American soil, and, prodded by Fish, threatened to use military force to halt them. Grant was always willing to listen to contrary opinions. A year later, profoundly grateful to Fish, he thanked him for his restraint on Cuban intervention, saying, "You led me against my judgment at the time . . . and I now see how right it was—and I desire most sincerely to thank you."[50] It was owing to Fish's professionalism that Grant refrained from recognizing Cuban belligerency, which might have resulted in war with Spain.

In late August 1869, when Spain perpetrated fresh atrocities in Cuba, the American press seethed with denunciations. In the *New York Sun,* Charles Dana declared that America was now duty-bound "to interfere in Cuba" and terminate the heinous bloodshed wrought by Spain.[51] Internecine battles over Cuba in Grant's cabinet came to a head on August 31, when Rawlins and Fish arrived for a showdown. Rawlins appeared with a deathly pallor, his eyes starting in their deep-set sockets. After visiting his pregnant wife in Connecticut, he had suffered a hemorrhage en route to Washington, then another after he arrived. Cabinet members were stunned by his cadaverous visage. Seated next to Grant, looking ravaged, he mustered enough energy for one final diatribe on behalf of Cuban insurgents. More overwrought than usual, he turned to Grant and asked forgiveness for his sustained outburst. "I have been your adjutant," he apologized, "and I think you will excuse me for being earnest." "Certainly," Grant said tenderly, "and you are still my adjutant."[52]

While the discussion percolated at a low boil, Grant scribbled on a sheet of paper, setting down conditions under which the United States could mediate peace between Spain and Cuba and buy Cuba in the process. As at Appomattox, Grant drafted a letter-perfect document in an attempt to bring a complex situation, fraught with danger, to a peaceful termination. When finished, he shoved the paper across the table to Fish, saying, "There is my decision."[53] The peace process would start with an immediate armistice, Cuba would compensate Spain for public property, and Spaniards on the liberated island would be free to remain or leave. Once slavery was abolished, the United States would purchase Cuba. When these terms leaked to the press in Madrid, the Spanish public reacted with explosive outrage, appalled at having to bicker with the United States over Cuba. The ferocious reaction snuffed out any hopes of a negotiated end to the conflict.

In his year-end speech in December 1869, Grant reviewed the star-crossed Cuban initiative, explaining that he had not recognized the insurgents as a belligerent power because they lacked ports, courts, or a permanent seat of government. He lamented that Spain had spurned his deal and stressed that he wasn't swapping American for European colonialism, invoking self-determination as his guiding principle: "These [Caribbean] dependencies are no longer regarded as subject to transfer from one European power to another. When the present relation of Colonies ceases they are to become independent powers, exercising the right of choice, and of self-control in the determination of their future condition."[54]

John Rawlins put on a brave front as he struggled with his terrible cough and alarming medical troubles. "My health is much improved this summer," he told a friend on August 19, whistling in the dark, "though for two weeks past I have been a little under the weather."[55] He had already soldiered on far longer than friends had thought possible. In making his militant case for Cuba, Rawlins believed "he had over-exerted himself . . . for from that excitement his disease redoubled its violence, and his frame, already exhausted, was too weak to resist," wrote Ely Parker.[56] Rawlins remained the earnest figure he had always been, motivated by deep patriotism and personal fidelity to Grant, but the strain now proved overwhelming. Right after the Cuban cabinet debate, his health collapsed altogether and death seemed imminent. "Poor Rawlins at this moment is very ill," wrote Fish. "I fear that his disease (consumption) has the *entire* mastery of him, and that he has not long to labor."[57] Unable to visit the War Department, he had aides transfer urgent papers to his residence. As he lay dying, a flock of generals—Ely Parker, William T. Sherman, Oliver O. Howard, and Montgomery Meigs, among them—stood vigil by his bedside, visibly distraught. "If the love of my friends could do it," Rawlins remarked sadly, "I would soon be a healthy man."[58]

With time running out, Rawlins, thirty-eight, brooded about his young family's future. His wife had just given birth to a stillborn baby, news carefully withheld from him. He began to dictate a will to Parker, appointing "my friend Genl Ulysses S. Grant" as guardian of his three children and his wife. It was a poignant tribute to the man who had transformed his life and by whom he had stood so ably. As he lay dying, Rawlins yearned to see Grant one more time and seemed pained by his absence. "Hasn't the old man come yet?" he asked plaintively.[59] Rawlins was so palpably upset by his absence that when he inquired, "When will he get here?" Sherman had to console him with a lie: "In about ten minutes."[60] Sherman secretly dashed off a telegram to Grant, now in Saratoga, describing Rawlins's anxiety to see him one last time. When Grant got the telegram, the last train for the day had already left, forcing him to postpone his departure. "The most recent dispatches scarcely leave a hope that I may see [Rawlins] alive," he told a colleague.[61]

Those present at Rawlins's bedside kept promising the dying man he would see Grant one last time. Thwarted by logistical mishaps, Grant's train didn't arrive in Washington until 5:20 p.m. on September 6. Rawlins had expired an hour earlier, with an attendant physician intoning, "The soul of Grant's Cabinet is gone."[62] When Grant arrived at the deathbed, he stared mournfully at his friend's ashen face and declared he had hoped to be there earlier. The doctor mentioned that Rawlins had frequently spoken his name. Overcome with emotion, Grant could only refer to the train delays that had stalled him. His failure to be at the bedside when Rawlins died led to wounding charges of neglect. "I knew personally of [Grant's] constant and devoted attentions to his friend," said

John Eaton, "but many people chose to believe the sensational and libellous reports."[63] Likely feeling guilty, Grant wished to maintain a vigil by the corpse during the night, but Sherman, knowing he was exhausted by the journey and shaken by the death, convinced him to go to the White House, where he wrote to Emma Rawlins of her husband's demise: "Your beloved husband expired at twelve minutes after four o'clock this afternoon, to be mourned by a family and friends who loved him for his personal worth and services to his country, and a nation which acknowledges its debt of gratitude to him."[64]

The death provoked a vast outpouring of grief, and Senator George Spencer of Alabama said, "I have never known a man more universally mourned."[65] "Poor Rawlins has gone to a happier office!" sighed Adolph Borie. "A noble fellow, truly, he was so pure zealous and earnest."[66] On the day of the funeral, the route from the War Department to the Congressional Cemetery was crowded with mourners tipping their hats or bowing in homage as the cortege rolled by. It was a remarkable tribute to a man never elected to office who had thrived in Grant's shadow. No organization chart could evoke the influence he had wielded as Grant's trusted counselor. A month later, James Wilson sent an appreciation of him to Orville Babcock:

> The death of Rawlins is more deeply regretted by the thinking and knowing men of the country than it otherwise would have been, on account of the fact that it had come to be recognized by them, that he was the President's best friend & most useful counsellor when engaged in renouncing rascality, which the President's unsuspicious nature has not dreamed of being near. You and I know how necessary, the bold, uncompromising, & honest character of our dead friend, was to our living one—and how impossible it is for any stranger to exercise as good an influence over him, as one who has known him from the time of his obscurity till the day he became the foremost man of the nation. The long and short of it is that Rawlins, was his Mentor—or if I may say it, his conscience keeper.[67]

After Rawlins died, Sherman served briefly as acting secretary of war, encouraging Grant to name William W. Belknap, a tall, burly Iowan with curly hair and a long, square-shaped beard and a background in law and politics, as permanent secretary. Born in Newburgh, New York, and educated at Princeton and Georgetown, Belknap had fought with distinction at Shiloh and Vicksburg and joined Sherman on the march to the sea, ending the war as a brevet major general. Sherman had bristled at how Rawlins had lodged power in the War Department, reducing his own influence as chief general. He was shocked that when he complained to Grant, the latter sided with Rawlins, and their friendship never quite recovered from the difference of opinions. Even though Sherman had recommended Belknap as war secretary, he shuddered at how Belknap also circumvented him on military matters. Grant promised to arbitrate, but never did, further deepening Sherman's disenchantment with his old comrade.

With his unrivaled candor, Rawlins had occupied a special niche in Grant's life that nobody could re-create. Selflessly protective of Grant's reputation, Rawlins would have warned the president against predatory, designing figures who encircled him in Washington. He would have detected wrongdoers and been a stalwart voice against corruption, elevating the ethical tone at the executive mansion. With Rawlins gone, Grant lacked that one trusted adviser upon whose judgment he could implicitly rely. Stung by criticism, Grant would retreat into silence and lick his wounds. Rawlins might have penetrated that reserve. Into the vacuum left by Rawlins moved crafty, cynical politicians for whom the credulous Grant was often no match.

In future years, Grant discharged many offices of friendship to his fallen comrade. He successfully prodded Congress to appropriate money for a bronze equestrian statue of Rawlins in the capital. He also served as guardian of the three young Rawlins children, contributed liberally to their support, paid for their boarding schools in Connecticut, and helped them obtain jobs.

John Rawlins inspired intense affection among friends, a feeling heightened by his premature death. A small cult sprang up dedicated to the proposition that Rawlins had been the unacknowledged genius of the Civil War—that it was Rawlins's military insights that had been decisive and that Grant cheated Rawlins of his just deserts. The main acolytes for this view were James H. Wilson, the journalist Sylvanus Cadwallader, and General William S. Hillyer, who had served on Grant's wartime staff.

Those who tended the sacred flame of Rawlins believed Grant came to resent his dependency on him, especially when people gave Rawlins credit for his own success. General John E. Smith contended that certain people "did succeed in alienating Grant from Rawlins. He, Rawlins, felt it keenly and often complained of it."[68] Wilson was "sure that Rawlins's domination over Grant was so pronounced that when Rawlins died Grant felt relieved."[69] The Rawlins acolytes believed Grant had destroyed incriminating letters that might have cast Rawlins in a better, and Grant in a lesser, wartime light, although this allegation has never been proven.

This belief in Rawlins as the war's neglected genius flamed into a full-blown crusade when Grant later published his *Memoirs* and only made brief, fleeting references to his dead comrade. Sherman thought the omission deliberate, but not for the reasons advanced by Rawlins's admirers: "Some of Rawlins' flatterers gave out the impression that he, Rawlins, had made Grant, and had written most of his orders and dispatches at Donelson, Shiloh and Vicksburg—Grant disliked to be patronized—and although he always was most grateful for all friendly service he hated to be considered an 'accident.'"[70]

It does no disservice to the estimable John A. Rawlins to state that his importance lay in his auxiliary services to Grant. Through four years of fighting, Rawlins kept Grant's drinking problem within manageable bounds. He was an inspired choice as chief of staff and extremely valuable as a vocal devil's advocate, sometimes questioning Grant's tactical moves where others feared to tread. He was also an indispensable intermediary to a man who could be taciturn and inhibited. Nevertheless, in the last analysis, Rawlins could never have substituted his judgment for Grant's superior military acumen.

CHAPTER THIRTY-ONE

Sin Against Humanity

ULYSSES S. GRANT, who had often shown signs of a speculative bent, could never quite resist the allure of buccaneering tycoons of the Gilded Age. This most trusting of men was perhaps destined to draw the wiles of two of Wall Street's most conniving moguls, Jay Gould and James Fisk Jr. In spring 1869, Gould concocted a plan to corner the market in gold, driving up its price. As it duly rose, Secretary of the Treasury Boutwell spoiled the scheme by selling additional gold from government coffers. He had embarked on weekly gold sales in exchange for greenbacks, using the proceeds to shrink the large federal debt. This overhang of government gold always threatened to undo any advance in gold prices. Faced with this impediment, Gould and Fisk undertook a campaign of seduction aimed at persuading Grant to restrict gold sales by the Treasury Department.

Both directors of the Erie Railroad, Gould and Fisk, made up an unlikely duo. A short, neat man with a full beard and piercing eyes, Gould had grown up as a poor farmer's son in upstate New York. As a young man, he had devised a better mousetrap, foreshadowing the damage he would later do to Wall Street rivals. Coldly exacting, shunning the limelight, he had amassed a colossal fortune through a railroad network spanning the nation and came to personify the predatory instincts of contemporary tycoons. "The people had *desired* money" before Gould, Mark Twain observed, "but *he* taught them to fall down and worship it."[1] Indeed, Gould's audacious moves riveted and appalled the nation in equal measure.

With his handsome blond mustache, bloated frame, and diamond rings, the flashy Jim Fisk was the antithesis of the saturnine Gould. The son of a Vermont peddler, he collected prostitutes and chorus girls no less promiscuously than he bought railroads and steamships and exulted in the attention his flamboyance aroused. Such was his roguish charm that people were captivated even as they were horrified by his total lack of scruples. As George Templeton Strong sketched him: "Illiterate, vulgar, unprincipled, profligate, always making himself conspicuously ridiculous by some piece of flagrant ostentation, he was, nevertheless, freehanded with his stolen money, and possessed, moreover, a certain magnetism of geniality that attracted to him people who were not particular about the decency of their associates."[2]

Every decent conspiracy demands a saintly cover story, and Gould had cleverly devised one that identified his personal avarice with the national interest. He argued that higher gold prices would produce a corresponding decline in the value of greenbacks and thus artificially cheapen exports, allowing American farmers to reap bountiful sales abroad. Inasmuch as Gould also functioned as a major proprietor of east-west railroads, he stood to make a double killing, profiting from levitating gold prices and rising freight loads to eastern ports.

To peddle this self-serving economic theory, Gould needed a conduit to Grant and found a willing one in Abel Rathbone Corbin, a slippery man who had dabbled in law, journalism, and politics, even investing money for Julia Grant in New York real estate. Gould saw him as "a very shrewd old gentleman," while a less charitable journalist sneered at him as the "most consummate old hypocrite I ever saw."[3] Most important, he had recently married Grant's sister Virginia, known as Jennie. In her late thirties, Jennie was suffering the fate of an old maid and living with her parents in Covington when the sixty-one-year-old Corbin wooed her. Grant, who was fond of his sister, had known Corbin since his St. Louis days in the 1850s and gave away the bride at the wedding. "You will be surprised when I tell you I have just finished a letter of congratulation to Miss Jennie Grant," Julia informed a friend in late April. Thrilled by the match, she noted that Corbin was "an old friend of ours & we are all well pleased."[4] Julia would shortly have reason to eat these words.

Gould had indoctrinated Corbin with his pet theory about the benefits of higher gold prices and Corbin, acting his part to perfection, began to flog it to Grant. The cynical Fisk saw Corbin as the cat's-paw of the whole conspiracy. "Why damn it! Old Corbin married into Grant's family for the purpose of working the thing in that direction. That's all he married for this last time."[5] Whatever the scheme's genesis, Gould traded brazenly on his supposed intimacy with Corbin, who traded on his supposed intimacy with Grant, even as Grant seemed oblivious to the web of intrigue being sedulously spun around him. When the post of assistant treasurer in New York fell vacant, Corbin and Gould lobbied successfully for the appointment of Major General Daniel Butterfield, who lacked any background in finance. He had been chief of staff for Joseph Hooker during the war and was credited with creating the bugle call "Taps." The assistant treasurer post was critical to the machinery of Gould's plot because the all-important gold sales were conducted through his Wall Street office. When Butterfield started work on July 1, Gould offered him a $10,000 bribe, binding him to the conspiracy. Butterfield preferred to characterize the money as an unsecured real estate loan.

The plot tempo quickened in mid-June 1869 when Grant, after visiting Fred at West Point, stopped by the Corbins' West Twenty-Seventh Street town house. While he was there, Jay Gould dropped by to say hello and extended an offer to the president to cruise to Massachusetts the following evening aboard Fisk's steamboat *Providence,* an offer that Grant, headed for Boston, naively accepted. Grant could sound cynical about the self-made men of his time, saying they "worship money rather than country," but he found it hard to fend off their unctuous overtures.[6]

Once afloat, Gould and Fisk sprang their trap on Grant, steering the conversation to crop exports and Boutwell's weekly gold sales. They wanted to convince Grant that Boutwell should halt such sales and galvanize the economy. For a long time, Grant listened silently, then hazarded the opinion that the current prosperity had a fictitious air and the speculative bubble might as well be pricked one way or another. His attitude—that the economy was excessively inflated and needed no stimulus—stopped the conspirators dead in their tracks. "We supposed from that conversation that the President was a contractionist," said Gould. "His remark struck across us like a wet blanket."[7] Disheartened, Gould let his gold purchases lapse for a while until a more auspicious opportunity arose.

Gould went on plying Grant with favors and Grant, heedless of appearances, accepted them. In mid-August, the Grants and the Corbins left New York aboard a private railroad car, furnished by the Erie Railroad, to travel to Kane, a scenic spot in western Pennsylvania, where the president went trout fishing. Gould and Fisk boarded the luxurious car to make sure the accommodations suited the president. In the town of Susquehanna, Gould and Fisk gave Grant a private tour of their locomotive works and repair shops. Around this time, the two speculators resumed their gold purchases. After touring Pennsylvania, Grant headed for Newport, Rhode Island, and was lobbied en route by Jim Fisk, who told him that unless the Treasury Department withheld gold, the Republican Party would be blamed for heavy losses sustained by farmers and railroad workers across America. Grant responded in an exemplary manner, saying it would not be fair to tell any private citizen what the Treasury Department planned to do.

In early September, Gould heated up the plot, purchasing $1.5 million in gold for the Corbins and a like sum for General Butterfield. When Gould again met him at the Corbin home, Grant said reports of an abundant harvest had persuaded him gold prices should be kept high to aid crop exports. Gould was delighted: Grant had finally jumped at the bait. Grant wrote to Boutwell and argued the need to keep gold high to accelerate crop sales abroad. With good reason, Gould imagined he had recruited Grant to his scheme. To mask his trading moves, he executed gold purchases through a byzantine network of brokers.

During the second week of September, Grant returned to the Corbins' town house and Jay Gould called anew. Grant at last sensed something terribly amiss and told their servant never to admit Gould again. "Gould was always trying to get something" out of him, Grant complained.[8] On September 12, he dashed off a letter to Boutwell about "the bulls and bears of Wall Street" that showed his awareness that people on both sides of the gold trade were trying to manipulate him. "The fact is, a desperate struggle is now taking place, and each party wants the government to help them out. I write this letter to advise you of what I think you may expect, to put you on your guard."[9] Whatever his earlier naïveté, Grant now grasped the designs upon him, and Boutwell adhered to his liberal policy of selling gold. Meanwhile rumors of financial skulduggery floated freely in New York, Horace Greeley warning that "certain financiers" were colluding to push gold up to "an exorbitant rate."[10]

On September 13, the Grants left New York to spend several days in southwest Pennsylvania. Three days later, Gould made a bald-faced effort to bribe Horace Porter: "We have purchased half a million gold on your account." Porter responded impeccably: "I have not authorized any purchase of gold, and request that none be made on my account."[11] On September 17, Abel Corbin wrote Grant a letter urging a curb on government gold sales, and warning of calamitous consequences without it. This letter was whisked off to the president by William Chapin, an Erie Railroad employee in the pay of Jim Fisk. That Grant had banned further visits from Gould should have alerted Corbin that the scales had belatedly fallen from his eyes and that such a letter would be seen as one entreaty too many.

When Chapin reached southwest Pennsylvania a day later, he spied Grant playing croquet on the lawn with Porter. He waited in the house, then hand-delivered the letter to Grant, who absorbed its contents silently before disappearing for a while. When he returned, Chapin asked for his response to the message. "Is it all right?" he asked. "All right," Grant echoed, indicating he would have no response.[12] It was a studiously neutral reply, but Chapin sent Fisk an ambiguously worded telegram that stated "Delivered. All Right," which implied, to Gould's cold raptor eyes, that Grant had heeded Corbin's admonition to check gold sales, turning him into an unwitting accomplice of the conspiracy.[13]

The stratagem boomeranged on Gould and Corbin since Grant found it highly suspicious that they had dispatched a messenger to western Pennsylvania to deliver a simple letter. At once, Grant asked Julia to send a message to his sister Jennie, warning about the gold purchases. As Julia remembered its gist: "The General says, if you have any influence with your husband, tell him to have nothing whatever to do with [Gould]. If he does, he will be ruined, for come what may, he (your brother) will do his duty to the country."[14]

Grant blamed himself for not having stopped Corbin sooner in his mad spree of unwanted advice about boosting gold and saving the country. "I always felt great respect for Corbin," he told Julia, "and thought he took much pleasure in the supposition that he was rendering great assistance to the administration by his valuable advice. I blame myself now for not checking this (as I thought) innocent vanity. It is very sad. I fear he may be ruined—and my poor sister!"[15] Grant never broke off relations with Corbin and would prove surprisingly forgiving toward him, exchanging pleasant letters with him before too long.

Julia's letter had the intended impact on Jennie Corbin, who pleaded with her husband to desist from further gold speculations. When Gould visited the Corbin house, Corbin tried to unload his gold position. "Ulysses thinks it wrong," he explained, "and that it ought to end." Gould quickly fathomed the significance of Grant's letter to the Corbins. "Mr. Corbin," he announced, "I am undone if that letter gets out."[16] He decided to liquidate his position before Boutwell made his next gold sale, which would shatter the conspiracy. Gould still made small gold purchases, but only to gull traders as he dumped gold. Meanwhile, gold prices consistently rose, thanks to steady buying and voluble encouragement from Jim Fisk, who knew nothing of Gould's planned sales. On September 22, Fisk appeared in the Gold Room—a specialized commodity market next to the stock exchange—and loudly brayed buy orders to rally gold bulls, claiming Grant was solidly on their side. Large throngs milled outside, eager to witness the climax of the Gold Corner.

After markets closed on September 23, Boutwell came to Grant, who had just returned from Pennsylvania, to discuss the gyrating gold prices unsettling Wall Street. That day, Fisk and his allies had driven gold prices sky-high, damaging many bears and inciting frenzied trading in the Gold Room. A hundred short sellers covered their losses by bidding gold to unimaginable heights. It was expected to soar even more the next day. As Boutwell recalled, "I then said that a sale of gold should be made for the purpose of breaking the market and ending the excitement." Grant "asked me what sum I proposed to sell. I said: 'Three million dollars will be sufficient to break the combination.'" Whether wishing to punish Gould and Fisk or simply alarmed by the turbulent trading, Grant replied: "I think you had better make it $5,000,000."[17] In the end, Boutwell placed an order with General Butterfield in New York to sell $4 million worth of gold. According to one version of the story, Butterfield tipped off Gould before traders learned the news. Another claims Gould and his cronies tapped telegraph wires that carried news of the Treasury's action and exploited a brief twenty-five-minute window to jettison more than $60 million in gold before prices crashed.

In the interval before the news hit, the price of gold zoomed sharply higher. Many in the Gold Room didn't simply suspect that the Grant administration had turned a blind eye to the price manipulation, but that it had cooperated with its perpetrators. "Friends of the Administration openly stated that the President or yourself must have given these men to feel you would not interfere with them or they would never dare to rush gold up so rapidly," a Wall Street operative told Boutwell. "In truth, many parties of real responsibility and friends of the Government openly declared that somebody in Washington must be in this combination."[18] Grant and Boutwell were set to refute, with a dramatic flourish, these malicious rumors noised abroad by Fisk and his myrmidons.

Shortly after Boutwell's telegram was received on Friday morning, September 24, the surging gold market collapsed, the price plummeting from $160 to

$133, plunging the trading world into chaos. Gould emerged unscathed from a debacle that wiped out many Wall Street dealers and went down in history as Black Friday. Fisk described the chaos in the Gold Room as "the wildest confusion and the most unearthly screaming of men."[19] By day's end, it was "each man drag out his own corpse."[20] Gould and Fisk fled for their personal safety. The Gold Room was shut down for a week to restore order and deal with the wreckage. The economic repercussions were extensive. The Gold Room mayhem shaved 20 percent from stock market prices and cut trading volume in half for months, while fourteen stock exchange firms failed.

Grant's dealings with Gould, Fisk, and Corbin show that even as president, he was still the same trusting rube who had been hoodwinked by business sharpers before the war. His sin was one of naïveté, not malice or lack of scruples, his sole concern being the welfare of the country. "This is only one of a thousand instances in which the President has been duped," James H. Wilson wrote, regretting Rawlins's sudden absence.[21] The Gold Corner set the pattern for future Grant scandals. The personal integrity of the president was never questioned, only his judgment in consorting with unsavory characters, oblivious to the impression it might create. He was a soft touch for schemers and this began to tarnish his public image. Robert Bonner, the editor of the *New York Ledger,* pleaded with Grant to make a public statement disclaiming "all foreknowledge of that combination, in order to relieve yourself entirely from all responsibility for the acts of others."[22] Lincoln had been a master at sending letters to newspaper editors that gave important glimpses into his thinking. Now Grant penned a letter to Bonner that said, "I had no more to do with the late gold excitement in New York City than yourself, or any other innocent party, except that I ordered the sale of gold to break the ring engaged, as I thought, in a most disreputable transaction."[23] Bonner wired back that his statement had struck the bull's-eye. "Your letter has already done a vast deal of good."[24]

Butterfield was never charged with a crime and always maintained his innocence, but his reputation had been sullied and Grant asked for his resignation. The House Committee on Banking and Currency launched an investigation, with some members hoping to tar Grant himself, but the worst charge they could level was his lack of judgment in accepting the hospitality of Gould and Fisk. Though innocent himself, Grant had allowed himself to be carried briefly in the talons of two of Wall Street's most rapacious financiers. "With the conventional air of assumed confidence," wrote Henry Adams, "everyone in public assured every one else that the President himself was the savior of the situation, and in private assured each other that if the President had not been caught this time, he was sure to be trapped the next, for the ways of Wall Street were dark and double."[25]

By this point Adams had emerged as the most waspish critic of the Grant administration. He rated Grant "the greatest general the world had seen since Napoleon," but his political behavior was another matter.[26] It wasn't surprising that a fastidious Boston Brahmin such as Adams would find Grant uncouth and boorish, a common reaction among the eastern intelligentsia. The grandson of John Quincy Adams and the son of former U.S. minister in London Charles Francis Adams Sr., Henry Adams counted William Dean Howells, Henry James, and John Hay among his glittering galaxy of friends. A thoroughgoing snob and Washington resident, he found the capital a social backwater and groaned that no "literary or scientific man, no artist, no gentleman . . . had ever lived there."[27] Adams must have sensed that Grant loathed his entire clan. In one letter, Grant wrote that "I confess to a repugnance to the appointment of an Adams," and in another he protested that the family did "not possess one noble trait of character that I ever heard of, from old John Adams down to the last of all of them, H. B."[28]

Henry Adams's failure to secure a niche in the Grant administration dealt a blow to his family vanity and amour propre. The chief of the spurned literati, he became a scathing critic of the spoils system under Grant and savaged his appointees with a pen dipped in vitriol. He damned Grant's cabinet as mediocrities, especially Boutwell, although he saved kind words for Secretary of the Interior Cox and Attorney General Hoar. "My family is buried politically beyond recovery for years," he complained. "I am becoming more and more isolated as far as allies go."[29] Adams didn't receive from Grant the social deference to which he felt entitled and recorded this mordant impression of a White House reception in December 1869: "At last Mrs. Grant strolled in. She squints like an isosceles triangle, but is not more vulgar than some Duchesses. Her sense of dignity did not allow her to talk to me, but occasionally she condescended to throw me a constrained remark."[30]

Adams got his revenge with a series of withering aperçus about Grant that have clung like barnacles to his historical reputation. He said the initials "U. S." stood for "uniquely stupid."[31] His most barbed comment was that Grant had single-handedly refuted Darwinian evolution: "The progress of evolution from

President Washington to President Grant, was alone evidence enough to upset Darwin."[32] The comments, both hilarious and totally unfair, have been irresistible fodder for historians. Adams saw Grant as lacking a guiding sense of purpose as he piloted the ship of state, reducing governance to discrete issues devoid of an overarching design.

By an extraordinary coincidence, Adams occupied the same G Street boardinghouse as Adam Badeau, whom he recalled as a stout, red-faced, bespectacled little man. They shared a common fascination with the Grant enigma. Badeau boasted that only he and John Rawlins had truly understood the general. Adams and Badeau agreed that Grant came alive amid wartime danger, then lapsed back into inertia when the threat subsided. As Adams expressed it: "When in action he was superb and safe to follow; only when torpid he was dangerous."[33] He summarized Badeau's similar view: "To him, Grant appeared as an intermittent energy, immensely powerful when awake, but passive and plastic in repose."[34]

For all his hero worship of Grant, Badeau harbored secret reservations that he voiced to Henry Adams, who summarized them thus:

> [Badeau] said that neither he nor the rest of the staff knew why Grant succeeded; they believed in him because of his success. For stretches of time, his mind seemed torpid. Rawlins and the others would systematically talk their ideas into it, for weeks, not directly but by discussion among themselves, in his presence. In the end, he would announce the idea as his own, without seeming conscious of the discussion; and would give the orders to carry it out with all the energy that belonged to his nature. They could never measure his character or be sure when he would act. They could never follow a mental process in his thought. They were not sure that he did think.[35]

Though the portrait was overdrawn—Grant clearly thought a great deal about many matters—he did pick up ideas by a strange process of osmosis and made them fully his own. Many people said they could not follow the steps of his mental development because they were often secretive, interior, and hidden from view, the result of a powerfully intuitive process. Grant didn't have a systematic mind, nor did he arrange his ideas inside a larger theoretical scaffolding, and he was therefore a mystery to himself and others. When Henry Adams probed people about Grant's extraordinary success, they all seemed dumb-

founded: "'We do not know why the President is successful; we only know that
he succeeds.'"[36]

WHILE HE PROVED a constant irritant to Grant, Adams was merely a gadfly
who posed no enduring threat beyond his wickedly funny pen. Far more fraught
was the relationship with another prickly Bostonian, Senator Charles Sumner,
whose differences with Grant would fester and assume the dimensions of a pathological feud that bloodied both participants. As shown in his zeal for Andrew
Johnson's impeachment, the redoubtable Sumner could be motivated by idealism and implacable hatred at once. He was, in many ways, a kindred spirit to the
curmudgeonly Adams. "The boy Henry worshipped him," Adams wrote, "and
if he ever regarded any older man as a personal friend, it was Mr. Sumner."[37]

Handsome, Harvard-educated, a cosmopolitan traveler, Sumner had long
been adored by abolitionists. Right before the Civil War, his antislavery crusade
led the South Carolina representative Preston Brooks to thrash him severely
with a cane on the Senate floor, transforming him into a secular saint. As he
droned on in endless, windy speeches, the sanctimonious Sumner was easier to
admire than to love. A cold, humorless bachelor, he sashayed around Washington with his walking stick, glorying in his self-importance. As Grant's son Jesse
recalled, he "was a tall man of commanding appearance, rendered doubly conspicuous by the garments he wore . . . He always wore the most glaring clothes I
have ever seen on a civilized man: heavy plaids in vividly contrasting colors,
looming above a foundation of white spats."[38] Sumner's mandarin hauteur stood
opposed to Grant's modesty and his baroque language was a world apart from
Grant's spare eloquence.

Grant had admired Sumner's statesmanship and ardent abolitionism. Sumner, for his part, had high praise for Grant as a soldier, but reluctantly endorsed
him for president and only belatedly threw his weight behind him during the
1868 race. Dismissing Grant as an intellectual lightweight, he fancied he would
function as Grant's tutor on foreign policy and expected to be named secretary
of state as a reward for his support. His hopes were dashed when his friend
Fish beat him out for the post, and he bristled further as Grant toed an independent line in foreign policy. With a sense of senatorial privilege, Sumner
expected to dominate American foreign policy and suggested appointments.
"Mr. Sumner . . . who is the idol of the reformers, was among the first senators

to ask offices for his friends," Grant noted. "He expected offices as a right."[39] Chairing the Foreign Relations Committee, he also expected his views to prevail. Sumner typified a Senate that had grown arrogant and imperious, demanding patronage as the price of its cooperation with the president. The press and reformers expected Grant to tame the headstrong Senate, a clash that would come to a head in his conflict with Sumner.

Although Sumner failed to become secretary of state, he scored a major victory in April 1869 when Grant named, at his recommendation, the historian John Lothrop Motley as minister to England. A graduate of Harvard, Motley had studied in Germany, served in the diplomatic corps in St. Petersburg, and written a magisterial history of the Dutch republic. Learned but irascible, a habitué of aristocratic drawing rooms, he had acted as American minister to the Austrian Empire until he started to find fault with Johnson administration policy and surrendered his post.

When Motley returned to the United States, he delivered stirring campaign speeches for Grant, whom he had idolized during the war. Before the inauguration, he cultivated Grant's company, even reading manuscript chapters of Badeau's military history of Grant's wartime service. He impressed Grant as "a gentleman, a scholar and a man of ability, fully capable of representing his government in any capacity."[40] Still, Grant had private reservations, complaining that Motley "parts his hair in the middle and carries a single eye glass."[41] "In truth," wrote Henry Adams, "Grant disliked Motley at sight, because they had nothing in common."[42] Although he chafed at Sumner's pressure, Grant succumbed to his lobbying and appointed Motley, making Adam Badeau his assistant secretary of legation in London. Sumner prided himself on Motley's appointment, but it was to embroil Grant in protracted controversy with the self-aggrandizing senator.

The flashpoint in their fractured relationship revolved around the CSS *Alabama* claims, which dated from the war. This incendiary issue dredged up potent emotions. Constructed in a British shipyard, the *Alabama* had been the most lethal Confederate blockade runner preying on Union ships, seizing or demolishing dozens before being destroyed by the USS *Kearsarge* off Cherbourg in June 1864. As Grant reminded people, the depredations of the *Alabama* and other Confederate raiders outfitted in England had wreaked havoc with Union shipping, driven up insurance costs, prolonged the war, and forced desperate American exporters to resort to foreign ships. In these ways, the *indirect* costs of the *Alabama* raids added up to stupendous sums, dealing a blow to America's merchant marine and forcing it to cede shipping supremacy to Great Britain. British dependence upon southern cotton for its textile mills had engendered a pro-southern bias in certain circles, and the *Alabama*'s activities seemed to belie British claims to wartime neutrality. Grant had been incensed by this betrayal, complaining that the British government had supplied torpedoes, fuses, and guns to the Confederacy, all crafted in its arsenals.

In the waning days of the Johnson administration, William Seward had pursued an indemnity from England, asking for all of Canada as recompense for crippled Union shipping. In the end, he settled for much less compensation incorporated into the Johnson-Clarendon Convention, which he submitted to the Senate as Grant was about to assume power. The agreement outraged the American electorate, which found it too timid in its demands upon the British. Grant believed that Seward had usurped his prerogatives as an incoming president by trying to arbitrate the *Alabama* claims at the close of the Johnson regime.

The Johnson-Clarendon Convention still lay before the Senate when Grant became president and Sumner delivered its coup de grâce. On the Senate floor, he issued a flaming denunciation of the treaty, contending the Civil War had been "doubled in duration" by Britain's treacherous support for the Confederacy.[43] Not simply wanting compensation for destroyed American vessels, he added a still more explosive demand: that Britain pay a staggering $2 billion in indirect damages for extending the war and undermining America's merchant marine. He wanted Canada thrown in as a lagniappe and inflamed the situation further by calling for a British admission of guilt and an apology; Grant and Fish would have settled for an expression of regret. Sumner's words stirred up fellow senators, arousing such bellicose passions that the Senate defeated the Johnson-Clarendon Convention by a huge margin. With his speech, Sumner staked his claim to leadership in foreign policy under Grant.

The British were shocked by Sumner's intemperate language. Lord Clarendon, Britain's foreign secretary, denounced him for the "most extravagant hostility to England," while *The Times* of London called him a demagogue.[44] The Grant administration was taken unawares by Sumner's screed. While sharing his indignation and seeking substantial reparations, Grant and Fish saw a chance for a negotiated solution with William Gladstone's new liberal government and a rapprochement with England. Should this *not* occur, they feared war with England and an erosion in credit extended by British banks to American industry. Fish also hoped to push for Canadian independence, expecting the United States then to annex the country peacefully. Grant, although bitter over England's wartime duplicity, was a true-blue anglophile at heart. "England and the United States are natural allies, and should be the best of friends," he declared in his *Memoirs*. "They speak one language, and are related by blood and other ties. We together . . . are better qualified than any other people to establish commerce between all the nationalities of the world."[45]

That Sumner intended to oversee *Alabama* negotiations was underscored when Motley, before sailing to England, drew up a fifteen-thousand-word memorandum that would govern his diplomacy on the issue. It exuded the same venom as Sumner's speech, decrying British policy as "a sin against humanity, a disgrace to civilization."[46] It was undoubtedly influenced, if not partly drafted, by the senator himself. Fish found the document belligerent, suppressed it, and drew up more circumspect instructions. Sumner then confronted Fish and tried to induce him to accept the paper. Fish could be tough in a low-key way and refused to submit to Sumner's bullying. When Sumner threatened that he would urge Motley to resign, Fish refused to be blackmailed. For Grant it came as a harsh initiation into the trouble an insolent senator could cause. By early June, the London *Times* reported that a "social breach" had opened between Grant and Sumner.[47]

Grant placed a high priority on something that should have pleased Sumner, the welfare of black citizens, to whom he offered unprecedented White House access. On December 11, 1869, he received a delegation from the mostly black National Labor Convention. While he couldn't gratify all their wishes, especially their desire to redistribute land to black laborers in the South, he left no doubt of his extreme solicitude for their concerns. "I have done all I could to advance the best interests of the citizens of our country, without regard to color," he told them, "and I shall endeavor to do in the future what I have done in the past."[48]

Grant designated November 30 as the date for Mississippi and Texas to vote on new state constitutions that would guarantee black rights and readmit them to the Union. When Mississippi's new, heavily Republican, legislature gathered in January, it signaled a radical shift in southern politics in its selection of two new senators. One was Adelbert Ames and the other Hiram Revels, a minister who became the first black person to serve in the U.S. Senate. In a powerful piece of symbolism, Revels occupied the Senate seat once held by Jefferson Davis. Former slaves looked on with wonder as they gained a new place in state legislatures and in Washington. For many southern whites, however, the idea that their erstwhile slaves could now hold office and even gain the upper hand in their political lives was intolerable. It reinforced their growing conviction that secession had been, as *The Nation* phrased it, "not wicked, but holy and glorious."[49]

Each step in black emancipation had led ineluctably to the next, and the controversial next goal was granting black males the right to vote. After the Thirteenth Amendment abolished slavery and the Fourteenth conferred citizenship rights upon blacks, the Fifteenth prevented states from denying voting rights based on race, color, or earlier condition of servitude. For Grant this last amendment embodied the logical culmination of everything he had fought for during the war. In Badeau's words, he thought that "in order to secure the Union which he desired and which the Northern people had fought for, a voting population at the South friendly to the Union was indispensable."[50] He watched ratification of the Fifteenth Amendment with the keenest sympathy. "You will see by the papers that the ratification of the Fifteenth Amendment is assured!" he exulted to Elihu Washburne in late January 1870. "With this question out of politics, and reconstruction completed, I hope to see such good feeling in Congress as to secure rapid legislation and an early adjournment."[51]

On February 3, the Fifteenth Amendment was ratified and its acceptance required for every southern state readmitted to the Union. On March 30, as one hundred guns boomed in the capital in celebration, Grant composed an unusual message to Congress celebrating that the amendment had become part of the Constitution that day, and his words fervently embraced black suffrage: "A measure which makes at once Four Millions of people heretofore declared by the highest tribunal in the land, not citizens of the United States, nor eligible to become so, voters in every part of the land, the right not to be abridged by any state, is indeed a measure of grander importance than any other one act of the kind from the foundation of our free government to the present day . . . The adoption of the 15th Amendment . . . constitutes the most important event that has occurred, since the nation came into life." It was a stunning statement of Grant's faith in the new black electorate. He further urged Congress to promote popular education so that "all who possess and exercise political rights, shall have the opportunity to acquire the knowledge which will make their share in the government a blessing."[52]

That evening, to commemorate the landmark amendment, thousands marched down Pennsylvania Avenue in a torchlight procession. When they gathered outside the White House, Grant came out to address them and stressed the extraordinary importance he attached to the amendment, lauding it as a seminal act and saying there had been "no event since the close of the war in which I have felt so deep an interest . . . It looked to me as the realization of the Declaration of Independence."[53] Grant's brother-in-law Michael John Cramer later explained that Grant had initially worried about bestowing voting rights upon black citizens, some of them still illiterate. Ku Klux Klan terror wiped away that hesitation, for as the Klan "endeavored to suppress the political rights of the freedmen of the South by the use of unscrupulous means, etc., he, the head of the army, became convinced . . . that the ballot was the only real means the freedmen had for defending their lives, property, and rights."[54]

This fateful moment presented Grant with a domestic challenge as daunting as that faced by any American president, for it inspired hope among blacks and smoldering resentment among many whites. Before long, southern blacks held office as lieutenant governors, militia officers, state legislators, and secretaries of state, not to mention coroners, constables, judges, and county magistrates; six hundred served as southern legislators during Reconstruction. Black gains can be overstated and certainly were by an alarmed white community: fewer than 20 percent of state political offices in the South were held by blacks at the height of Reconstruction. Still, these represented spectacular gains for people so recently chained in bondage.

The dread of black suffrage drove many former secessionists to new heights of indignation. Although blacks made up 13 percent of the total U.S. population, they constituted 36 percent of the South, with outright majorities in Mississippi and South Carolina. The Fifteenth Amendment meant that blacks, armed with the vote, could exercise real power and invert, in an astonishingly short period, the power structure that had long suppressed them. Many southern whites found this insupportable and argued that hapless, newly enfranchised blacks were being manipulated by scheming northern Republicans. Woodrow Wilson would express this stereotypical view: "Unscrupulous adventurers appeared, to act as the leaders of the inexperienced blacks in taking possession, first of the conventions, and afterwards of the state governments . . . [Negroes] submitted to the unrestrained authority of small and masterful groups of white men whom the instincts of plunder had drawn from the North."[55] Not surprisingly, the Fifteenth Amendment incited a violent backlash among whites whose nerves were already frayed by having lost the war and their valuable holdings of human property.

Hardly had the ink dried on the new amendment than southern demagogues began to pander to the anxieties it aroused. In West Virginia, an overwhelmingly white state, Democratic politicians sounded the battle cry of electing a "white man's government" to gain control of the governorship and state legislature. "The spirit of the late rebellion is in the ascendant," one Republican politician admitted. "Hostility to negro suffrage was the prime element of our defeat."[56] To circumvent the Fifteenth Amendment, white politicians in Georgia devised new methods of stripping blacks of voting rights, including poll taxes, onerous registration requirements, and similar restrictions copied in other states. With a violent backlash well under way, the party of Lincoln began to pay a price for being the vocal paladin of African Americans. As Senator Henry Wilson observed in 1869, there was not "a square mile of the United States" where Republican advocacy of black rights hadn't resulted in the loss of white votes.[57]

Behind the Fifteenth Amendment's idealism lay the stark reality that a "solid South" of white voters would vote en masse for the Democratic Party, forcing the Republicans to create a countervailing political force. Under Article I, Section 2, of the Constitution, slaveholding states had been entitled to count three of every five slaves as part of their electorate in computing their share of congressional delegates. Now former slaves would count as full citizens, swelling the electoral tally for southern states. This was fine as long as freed people exercised their full voting rights. Instead, over time, the white South would receive extra delegates in Congress and electoral votes in presidential races while stifling black voting power. "It was unjust to the North," Grant subsequently lamented. "In giving the South negro suffrage, we have given the old slave-holders forty votes in the electoral college. They keep those votes, but disfranchise the negroes. That is one of the gravest mistakes in the policy of reconstruction."[58]

Just as the Fifteenth Amendment was enacted, Grant was given an unusual opportunity to reshape the Supreme Court. Shortly after taking office, he had signed a bill expanding the current team of justices from eight to nine, effective December 1869. To fill the new vacancy, on December 14 he nominated his attorney general, Ebenezer Hoar. Uneasy with two Massachusetts men, Hoar and Boutwell, in his cabinet, Grant imagined a court appointment for Hoar offered an elegant solution to the problem. An estimable jurist, with extensive experience on the Massachusetts high court, Hoar seemed an unexceptionable choice, but a week later, the Senate tabled his nomination. Senators were irked by Hoar's stiff opposition to the spoils system and his sparring with Radical Republicans over Reconstruction. Instead of withdrawing the nomination, the stubborn Grant dug in his heels and became combative as he took on entrenched senators. In his diary, Hamilton Fish noted that Grant had decided to "withhold political patronage" from senators opposed to "the policy or attitude of the Administration."[59] Nevertheless, Hoar was voted down decisively. The episode perpetuated the tension between the president and the Senate that had flared up so unforgettably under Andrew Johnson.

Meanwhile, an elderly associate justice, seventy-five-year-old Robert C. Grier, who was elevated to the court by President Polk in 1846, notified Grant that he was resigning for medical reasons, opening a second vacancy. At this point, Grant turned to a well-known aspirant for the court, Edwin Stanton, who had enjoyed a prosperous prewar legal career, arguing cases before the high court. His wish to join the court was fiercely held, dating back to Lincoln's cabinet, and he now hungered for the honor, aided by his congressional admirers. Stanton was still weak from his wartime labors and had recently suffered from poor health. When he made a courtesy call at the White House soon after Grant became president, Julia was shocked that he "looked pale and feeble."[60] Because of his shaky medical condition, she claimed, her husband was eager to give Stanton his last shot at the court.

Never slow in self-assertion, Stanton boasted to a friend in October 1869: "There is a vacancy on the Supreme Bench for which I have adequate physical power, & so far as I can judge of my intellect, its powers are as acute & vigorous as at any period of my life—and perhaps more so."[61] Some in the press wondered whether the cantankerous Stanton possessed an even judicial temperament. Nonetheless, he enlisted enthusiastic supporters on Capitol Hill, including Vice President Colfax and House Speaker James G. Blaine, who bombarded Grant with lists of legislators clamoring for his appointment. On December 20, bowing to pressure, Grant nominated Stanton to replace Grier. Thanking Grant, Stanton reflected that a Supreme Court seat was "the only public office I ever desired, and I accept it with great pleasure."[62]

Stanton's name flew through the Senate confirmation process, winning approval by a 46 to 11 vote; then he died of heart failure days later, at age fifty-five. Whatever his reservations about Stanton's abrasive personality, Grant eulogized him as one of America's "most distinguished citizens and faithful public servants" and ordered the White House draped in mourning and government offices shut for the funeral.[63] Stanton's death gave the country a chance to pay tribute to one of the gigantic figures generated by the war. It also left Grant in a forgiving mood, and he attempted to advance the fortunes of Stanton's son, making him his personal attorney. "If I were asked to name the greatest men of the Republic," Grant later opined, "I certainly should include Stanton among them."[64] Although Stanton never served a day on the high court, Grant sent his widow, Ellen, as a keepsake, his lapsed commission as a Supreme Court justice.

In the end, Grant named two new members to the Supreme Court: Joseph P. Bradley and William Strong. Strong was a proficient attorney from Philadelphia, a product of Yale College and Law School. Because he was a solid Unionist and a Republican Party member since the late 1850s, Lincoln had contemplated appointing him chief justice after Roger B. Taney died in 1864. Never a judicial statesman, he was nonetheless widely respected for legal competence, and Justice Grier commended him as "an accomplished and sound lawyer."[65] He also had the right political credentials, one newspaper praising him for being "sufficiently Radical for even the most Radical Senators."[66] The other new justice, Joseph P. Bradley, son of a farmer from upstate New York, had worked as a lawyer in Newark, New Jersey, representing railroads and insurance companies. Like Strong, he had been an ardent Unionist, having written that "secession has always been treason."[67] With a court composed solely of justices from north of the Mason-Dixon Line, Grant came under pressure to add a southerner, completing the reentry of the former Confederate states, but he was deterred by skeptics. "If you yield to the clamor to nominate a southern man," Elihu Washburne warned, "ten to one you will be sold out in the end. See how Lincoln came out in his appointments of Supreme Judges."[68] Grant appears to have heeded the advice.

/////////////////////////////////

The Darkest Blot

I N HIS YEAR-END MESSAGE to Congress in December 1869—Congress-man George F. Hoar said Grant wrote it "without pause or correction, and as rapidly as his pen could fly over the paper"—the president evoked a thriving nation of nearly forty million people that, spurred on by the war, an industrial boom, and westward expansion, had blossomed into a global power, strong in manufacturing and stretching across the continent.[1] To bind the eastern and western seaboards more tightly, he proposed a survey of the Isthmus of Darien as a possible site for a canal connecting the Atlantic and the Pacific—a visionary project that possessed his imagination for the rest of his life. The need for inter-nal unity was paramount for Grant. He chided Georgia, which had ratified a new constitution, for having "unseated the colored members of the legislature." Striking a very different tone from Andrew Johnson, he paid tribute to the im-pressive strides registered by former slaves: "The freedmen . . . are making rapid progress in learning, and no complaints are heard of lack of industry on their part where they receive fair remuneration for their labor."[2] With the Republican Party now straddling former abolitionists and conservative businessmen, Grant gave voice to both impulses. A hard-money man, he favored a gradual return to a dollar redeemable in gold, a moderate tariff to raise government revenue and protect business, and a modest income tax. He professed pleasure that the federal budget enjoyed a robust surplus.

Grant's message showed marks of inexperience. Inordinately long, it delved into too many policy details and quoted verbatim from internal reports. It papered over blunders he had committed during his first year in office. Still he seemed to learn from his errors and sounded sanguine about the country's mood. "Everything seems to be progressing well in the United States," he informed Elihu Washburne. "Our currency is increasing in value . . . and on the whole I think a very healthy political feeling is springing up."[3]

Grant was about to grapple with a grave challenge from Charles Sumner on Santo Domingo. He now had in hand the two-part treaty, negotiated by Orville Babcock, for a fifty-year lease of Samaná Bay and a gradual absorption, after a national referendum, of the Dominican republic into the United States. Grant's cabinet was allowed to speak openly about the Samaná Bay deal, but was sworn to secrecy about Dominican annexation until the New Year. When President Báez worried about his future, Grant dispatched seven American warships to Dominican waters to assuage his concerns. In late February, Báez conducted the promised plebiscite on the American treaty and resorted to strong-arm tactics. The one-sided tally of 15,169 for annexation and only 11 against highlighted the vote's coercive nature. It was a foolish act of bullying by Báez, since many observers agreed that the Dominican people genuinely favored an American union and would have delivered a safe majority through honest methods.

On Sunday evening January 2, 1870, Grant swallowed his presidential pride, suppressed his distrust of Sumner, and strolled across Lafayette Square to pay an impromptu call at the senator's house. It was an extraordinary move by a president on behalf of a treaty. Grant insisted he did not go to persuade Sumner to support the treaty but only to explain why it was conducted in secrecy: he feared that if word leaked out, harmful speculation in Dominican debt might ensue. He also wanted to outline for Sumner the island's ample resources and convey the Dominican people's desire for American annexation. Then dining with John W. Forney, a newspaper publisher and recent secretary of the Senate, and the journalist Ben Perley Poore, Sumner was startled by Grant's sudden appearance. When proffered a glass of sherry, Grant declined while assuring the two guests they could stay during his chat with Sumner.

After some talk about the treaty, Sumner broached a seemingly unrelated topic. He had received a letter from his friend James M. Ashley, who was being ousted by Grant as governor of the Montana Territory. He issued a plea to retain him or name him to a new position. Grant, visibly annoyed, couldn't understand why on earth he should appoint a man he had just fired. Sumner read aloud two pages from Ashley's letter, later admitting he had been crass, "taking too great a liberty with [Grant] in my own house, but I was irresistibly impelled by loyalty to an absent friend."[4] Slow to fathom Sumner's ploy, Grant never dreamed of any quid pro quo between keeping Ashley and senatorial assent to the treaty. "It never occurred to me that [Sumner] tried to purchase a commission for Ashley by giving his support to the San Domingo treaty," Grant told Hamilton Fish. "But in the light of his subsequent conduct, and the readiness of his friends to impute improper motives to you and I, it is a much fairer inference to impute such motives to him."[5] Wisconsin senator Timothy Howe corroborated Grant's suspicion: "I have never doubted that Mr. Sumner . . . resolved to make his support of the treaty conditional upon Ashley's restoration." When Grant replaced Ashley with Ohio politician Benjamin F. Potts, Howe witnessed Sumner's incandescent display of wrath: "I never saw him so excited as when Potts was confirmed in place of Ashley."[6]

Grant left the talk with the decided impression that Sumner was "pleased" with the proposed treaty, having expressed a desire to see a draft.[7] John Forney walked away with a similar impression that Sumner admitted he "would cheerfully support the treaty." The intransigent Sumner would hotly contest this. He insisted the language was "fixed absolutely in my memory: 'Mr. President,' I said, 'I am an Administration man, and whatever you do will always find in me the most careful and candid consideration.'"[8] Secretary of the Treasury Boutwell, who dropped by Sumner's house while Grant was there, corroborated his boss's memory. When Sumner ended his defense of Ashley, Boutwell said, "the President rose, moved toward the door and repeated his remark that he would send the papers in the morning by Gen. Babcock. Mr. Sumner then said, after thanking the President, 'I expect Mr. President to support the measures of your administration.'"[9] When Babcock laid the treaty before Sumner a day or two later, the senator again—in Grant's recollection—expressed unequivocal approval of it.

The misunderstanding between Grant and Sumner was to be, in the words of a Sumner biographer, "the turning point in Grant's administration and in Sumner's career as well."[10] By now, the Santo Domingo treaty had become Grant's pet policy, his private obsession, and Sumner's betrayal would rankle for years. He had also been offended by Sumner's condescending manner. Perhaps recollecting that night, Grant made this telling remark: "Sumner is the only man I was ever anything but my real self to; the only man I ever tried to conciliate by artificial means."[11]

On January 10, Grant conveyed two documents to the Senate—one to lease
Samaná Bay, the other to annex the Dominican republic. For Grant, annexation
was a patently good thing and he was mystified why it didn't generate more
popular enthusiasm. However wrongheaded, the treaty was an ambitious undertaking upon which Grant staked his prestige, and any resistance to it aroused his
fighting instincts. "When he was once engaged in battle," Badeau noted, "he
was always anxious to win."[12] But it was much harder to win a legislative than a
military battle and the Senate was in no mood to compromise. Grant chafed at
legislative obstacles thrown into his path. When James Russell Lowell studied
his face at dinner that February, he detected "a puzzled pathos, as of a man with
a problem before him of which he does not understand the terms."[13]

The first sign of trouble on Capitol Hill came when Sumner procrastinated
in considering the treaty. He contended that a large majority of his committee
already opposed Dominican annexation and he ranted at the autocratic President Báez: "I know his history intimately. He is a usurper, whose hands have
been red with innocent blood."[14] If the treaty wasn't approved by March 29, it
would expire, and on March 14 a worried Grant requested prompt action from
Sumner. The next day, the Foreign Relations Committee handed him a severe
blow when it voted down the Dominican treaty by a 5 to 2 margin. As the matter shifted to the full Senate, Grant doggedly took charge of the lobbying campaign. Two days later, he marched up to the Capitol—"somewhat in the style of
Oliver Cromwell," the *New York World* archly noted—and summoned fifteen
senators who might sympathize with the treaty.[15] Such presidential leadership
was highly unusual at the time, leading to accusations of executive interference
with the legislative branch, and Sumner grunted that his visit was "as unconstitutional in character as that warlike intervention on the island."[16]

Grant had given Báez his personal pledge that he would apply his influence
to carry the treaty. With military thoroughness, he drew up a list of senators
opposed to or undecided about the treaty, inviting them to the White House.
His lobbying skills weren't finely honed and his laconic personality was poorly
suited to such moral suasion. Senator Carl Schurz, a new member of the Foreign
Relations Committee, described Grant's gauche effort to win him over: "At first
the President listened to me with evident interest, looking at me as if the objections to the treaty which I expressed were quite new to him, and made an impression on his mind. But after a while I noticed that his eyes wandered about
the room, and I became doubtful whether he listened to me at all."[17]

Grant's soldierly instincts made him persevere in a lost cause instead of trimming his losses. In politics a fight-to-the-finish mentality could be unsound strategy. Grant was trapped in a controversy whose dynamics he didn't understand, and all his frustrations as a novice president crystallized around this one issue. So fierce was his commitment to the flawed treaty that the British ambassador thought it "strange that he should be so tenacious with regard to its acceptance."[18] Instead of opposing the treaty openly, Sumner deftly moved to strangle it through dilatory tactics. He wanted his vanity stroked, but Grant, pure in his sense of rectitude, refused to appease him with patronage or cool him off with an appointment for Ashley.

On March 24, when the Senate began secret deliberations on the treaty, Sumner let loose a four-hour tirade against it. Senate opposition to annexation blended idealism with the basest form of racism. When Carl Schurz rose to eviscerate the treaty, he presented a demeaning view of Dominicans as lazy, shiftless tropical people, a theme picked up by General Joseph R. Hawley of the *Hartford Courant,* who complained to Sumner: "We *don't want any* of those islands just yet, with their mongrel cutthroat races and foreign language and religion."[19] To annex Caribbean territory beyond the continental United States was hard for many Americans to countenance, and opponents exploited the xenophobic reaction. Before the debate ended, John Logan denounced the Dominicans as a "naked and half-savage people."[20] Opponents also lambasted the fraudulent plebiscite and venal agents promoting the scheme.

By May 14, Hamilton Fish had extracted from Dominican representatives an extension of the treaty's expiration date. Grant received timely warnings of the rocky road ahead. In early April, Senator Lot Morrill of Maine had advised Hamilton Fish "that the President should not press the treaty—says it has no 'earnest' friends in the Senate—that the weight of Argument & fact is against it."[21] Although Fish passed along this advice, Grant had personalized the issue and would not budge. By mid-May, as the treaty floundered in the Senate, Fish suggested amendments to make it more palatable by presenting statehood as only one possibility. An alternative would be something like commonwealth status, a protectorate enjoying a looser affiliation with the United States than a state. Although Grant toyed briefly with this idea, his pride was wounded and his dander up and he doubled down on his bet.

On May 31, the frustrated president sent a message to the Senate asking to extend the time for its consideration. His support for annexation now flew into the realm of fantasy. On the one hand, he admitted the Dominican republic was a weak nation, with fewer than 120,000 inhabitants; on the other, he prophesied that it was "capable of supporting a population of 10,000,000 of people in luxury." Even though he had never visited the place, Grant advertised it as paradise on earth: "It possesses the richest soil, best and most capacious harbors, most salubrious climate and the greatest abundance of [most valuable] products of the forest, mine and soil, of any of the [West India] islands."[22] The free labor market in Santo Domingo, he claimed, would sound the death knell for slavery in Puerto Rico and Cuba as escaped bondmen sought sanctuary there.

The extra Senate time spent on the treaty in June hardly added to its luster. Early in the month, Fish privately transmitted to Grant allegations from Major Raymond Perry, who spied double-dealing in Babcock's promotion of Dominican annexation. Perry dubbed Babcock a "damned rascal" who had connived with Joseph Fabens and William Cazneau and stood to profit royally if the treaty went through.[23] Grant served warning upon Babcock "that if anything dishonorable or dishonest was proved" against him, "he should answer it with his Commission."[24] Despite repeated warnings, Grant never overcame a blind spot toward Babcock, missing a shady side to his character. Babcock's papers confirm that he was hip-deep in machinations with Fabens as they conspired to send money and arms to President Báez.[25]

In June, a further blot stained the treaty when Senator Orris Ferry of Connecticut condemned the treatment of Davis Hatch, a Connecticut businessman residing in Santo Domingo who had been imprisoned by President Báez. Hatch had protested to Washington that Báez was a scoundrel. A trial in Santo Domingo City ended in a death sentence for Hatch, commuted to banishment by Báez. Despite this verdict, he suffered in jail for six months. When Babcock visited the island, he did nothing to spring Hatch from jail, apparently fearing that when released, he might poison American public opinion against Báez. When Senator Ferry leveled charges against Babcock, Charles Sumner roared that the general should have his name "struck from the army, and struck from the roll of honorable men."[26] Sumner began telling fellow senators that when Grant had stopped by his house in early January, he had been under the influence of alcohol—of which there was no evidence.

The Hatch fiasco prompted a Senate investigation. The majority report cleared Babcock, but a minority report said he had turned a blind eye to Hatch's mistreatment. Under intense questioning by Carl Schurz, it emerged that both

Babcock and Grant's old pal Rufus Ingalls had received land on Samaná Bay that would appreciate prodigiously if the treaty passed. The whole enterprise had ensnared its supporters in the machinations of an island permeated with corruption. By now in a surly, defensive mood, Grant did nothing to discipline Babcock, but cast him as the innocent victim of a witch hunt. "I never saw father so grimly angry," son Jesse later commented.[27]

In frustration, Grant lashed out at cabinet members for failing to sustain him on the treaty. On June 13, when Fish saw him on unrelated business, Grant went on a rampage against his supposedly disloyal cabinet. Fish replied that only the treasury secretary opposed the treaty, but Grant was adamant that "the Secretary of the Interior is opposed to it; the Attorney-General says nothing in its favor, but sneers at it; and the Secretary of the Treasury does not open his mouth."[28] Never before had Grant demanded unswerving loyalty in the White House. And just as he spied a host of hidden enemies in his midst, he failed to see the one truly betraying him. As Fish wrote in his diary, Grant referred "warmly and affectionately to Babcock, whose innocence of the charges against him he firmly believes."[29]

When Ohio governor Rutherford B. Hayes visited the White House on the sweltering evening of June 27, the two men sat out on the south portico with its fine view of an unfinished Washington Monument. Grant brooded at what he perceived as the rank injustice of the Senate Foreign Relations Committee. Hayes recorded Grant's reflections: "*Sumner* as chairman, a man of very little practical sense, puffed-up, and unsound. *Carl Schurz,* an infidel and atheist; had been a rebel in his own country—as much a rebel against his government as Jeff Davis." What riled Grant most deeply were the savage attacks on Babcock, and "he felt 'much embittered' against Sumner" for his unjust remarks about him. He gave Babcock a "fine character," complaining that he was given no opportunity to defend himself against Sumner.[30] Having felt unfairly accused before the war, when he was hounded from the army, Grant instinctively sided with the victims of character assassination, even when that sympathy was sorely misplaced.

Grant's laborious efforts to enact the treaty came to naught. On June 30, the Senate split evenly on a 28 to 28 vote—a far cry from the two-thirds necessary for passage. Nineteen Republicans and nine Democrats teamed up to kill the measure in a resounding setback for Grant. Having been a successful general made it hard for him to reconcile himself to such crushing defeats. When his son Jesse asked why Santo Domingo was so important, an injured Grant replied: "Because it should belong to us. There is not one sound argument against annexation, and one day we shall need it badly."[31] He had expended too much of his political capital on the battle and badly miscalculated the strength of hostile forces arrayed against him.

In impotent rage, Grant turned against the man he had appointed at Sumner's behest: John Lothrop Motley in London. For some time, Grant and Fish had been displeased with Motley, who had espoused Sumner's hard line against England in the *Alabama* claims rather than their own more conciliatory posture. In fall 1869, Adam Badeau had resigned his post as secretary in London and returned to White House duties. To replace him, Grant planned to send Nicholas Fish, the secretary's son, but Motley fiercely resisted the appointment. As Badeau recalled, Grant "was extremely angry; he looked upon the refusal as another piece of insubordination, a proof that Motley was determined to do as he pleased, and not as the President desired."[32] Once again a president accustomed to the automatic obedience of huge armies had to brook the vagaries of petty politics and wayward personalities.

With ambitious plans in the works for settling the *Alabama* claims, Grant needed a cooperative representative in London. He aimed at nothing less than annexing Canada, a much less risible prospect than taking over Santo Domingo. Clearly the expansion-minded Grant envisioned some glorious addition to the country on the scale of the Louisiana Purchase. Standing in the way was Motley and his truculent language with the British. Exceeding his instructions from Grant and Fish, Motley told Lord Clarendon that Britain's neutrality proclamation early in the Civil War had been "the fountainhead of the disasters which had been caused to the American people . . . by the hands of Englishmen."[33]

In mid-May 1870, Grant sent Badeau back to London for another tour of duty, this time as consul general. As Grant saw him off at the White House door, the talk turned to Motley. "He was persuaded that the Minister was un-American in spirit," recalled Badeau, "and not a fitting representative of democracy."[34] Grant believed he had gotten precious little thanks from Sumner for appointing his protégé. On the eve of the Senate vote on Santo Domingo, Grant told Fish that Motley "represented Mr. Sumner more than he did the Administration, & spoke with much warmth of feeling, about Sumner."[35] Fearing repercussions from Sumner, Fish urged Grant not to fire Motley summarily. By the next day, Sumner had gotten wind of Grant's intention to cashier Motley and was incensed.

On July 1, the day after his Santo Domingo treaty went down to humiliating defeat, Grant acted on his vengeful feelings and fired Motley. The move had been contemplated by Grant for a while, but the timing made him look extremely vindictive. Fish was afraid the public would attribute the move to pure spite, but Grant didn't seemed fazed. When Fish pleaded with him to retain Motley for a spell, Grant replied vehemently, "That, I will not do—I will not allow Mr. Sumner to ride over me." When Fish pointed out that Grant was lashing out at Motley, not Sumner, Grant brusquely retorted, "It is the same thing."[36] In general, Grant wasn't one given to grudges and festering wounds, but Sumner had pushed him into a dark frame of mind, and he still had the thin skin of a novice president. He also considered Motley a faithless, rogue diplomat.

When Fish informed Motley of his dismissal, he offered him "the opportunity of resigning, in case you feel inclined to do so."[37] In reply, Motley obstinately declined to resign. He pointed out that he had been unanimously approved by the Senate and had faithfully served the president for fifteen months. "I fail to perceive why I should offer my resignation."[38] On July 15, Grant sent to the Senate the name of former senator Frederick T. Frelinghuysen of New Jersey to replace Motley and he was confirmed. Motley first learned of this from the London newspapers and was shocked. He admitted he had erred in departing from administration instructions, "but he held that his offense had been condoned," Badeau wrote. "But Grant did not often condone. The crisis finally came."[39] Frelinghuysen rejected the appointment, as did several other people, and in the end Grant turned to General Robert C. Schenck, a former Ohio congressman and minister to Brazil, who accepted the post and put Grant out of his misery. All the while, Motley refused to quit his station, becoming a pariah in London, a minister without portfolio, banished from polite society. In December, bowing to the inevitable, he finally stepped down.

Needless to say, Senator Sumner was apoplectic over Motley's recall. "My allegation is that the removal of Mr. Motley was an act of sheer brutality & utterly indefensible," he contended.[40] He called Motley's firing "the most atrocious crime in diplomatic history."[41] In September, Sumner protested to Fish that sacking the illustrious Motley was "the most grievous personal wrong ever done in the Depart. of State, & from the character of the victim not to be forgotten."[42] He professed shock that nobody in Grant's cabinet had shown the decency to resign in protest. Even people who thought Grant was entitled to cashier Motley faulted how he had handled it. The *New York Times* editor John Bigelow, who believed Motley had been dealt with "very shabbily," noted that it was customary to give "even a footman 30 days notice."[43]

When it came to his uncompromising feud with Sumner, Grant lived up to his nickname "Unconditional Surrender" Grant. Usually reticent about criticizing people, he unleashed a volley of invective against Sumner, branding him "dogmatic, opinionated, infallible in his own estimation . . . he believed his own illusion without regard to the facts. It really amounted to a mental delusion."[44] Mocking Sumner's vanity, he said: "Mr. Sumner could never have been bribed but in one way. That would be by flattery."[45] Once asked if he had heard Sumner converse, he replied, "No, but I have heard him lecture."[46] Told that Sumner didn't believe in the Bible, Grant retorted, "Well, he didn't write it."[47] Although the handwriting on the wall proclaimed in glaring letters the demise of the Santo Domingo treaty, Grant refused to concede defeat and contemplated further measures to keep it alive. He still had something to prove to Sumner, to the Senate, and to himself.

ONE OF THE FIRST CASUALTIES of Grant's colossal feud with Sumner was Attorney General Ebenezer Hoar, who had been rejected for the Supreme Court. Although the president found him smart, charming, and able, he was uncomfortably close to Sumner and withheld support on Santo Domingo. Grant remained on the warpath against disloyal cabinet members. As he told Hamilton Fish, "I have said to Senators & others that I mean to recognize my friends—& those who sustain my policy."[48] In promoting the treaty, Grant had come under intense pressure from white Republican leaders in the South whose black constituents revered Sumner and who had paid a price for defying him. In exchange, they demanded a southerner in the cabinet and touted the attorney general post as the best place to start.

On June 15, 1870, out of the blue, Grant scratched out a frosty note to Hoar, asking for his resignation, a letter that shook him like a thunderclap. "I sat for a while wondering what it could mean," he wrote, "why there had been no warning, no reference to the subject."[49] He imagined someone had unjustly maligned him and was tempted to protest. Instead he sent Grant a short, diplomatic letter of resignation. That afternoon, when he saw Grant at the White House, he was mollified by his warm words and explanation for what had happened. For Hoar's partisans, his dismissal was shocking. Secretary of the Interior Cox believed Grant decided "to sell his best friends . . . for support in the San Domingo or any other scheme in which he might set his heart." He later questioned Grant's "good purposes" and glimpsed "a low & unscrupulous cunning" as the "ruling motive of his public life."[50] Whatever Hoar's injury, he departed in gentlemanly fashion, sending Grant a gracious farewell note. In private, however, he broadcast his anger and "wished the government might be destroyed."[51]

On June 16, Grant tapped Amos T. Akerman of Georgia to replace him and he was approved by the Senate a week later. Although a somewhat obscure figure on the national scene, he was a brilliant choice, the first cabinet selection from the Confederate states. Honest and incorruptible, Akerman was a tall, slim man with a balding pate, eyebrows that jutted over deep-set eyes, and a pencil-thin mustache. The penetrating intensity of his gaze led one reporter to discern a "face of learning and disposition to deep meditation."[52] A native of New Hampshire and a Dartmouth graduate, Akerman had taught at a boys' academy in North Carolina and practiced law in antebellum Georgia before serving in the Confederate quartermaster corps. After Appomattox, he switched to the Republican Party, endorsed black voting rights, and maintained that the South should renounce slavery and its extreme interpretation of states' rights. Solidly progressive, devoted to the rule of law, he took part in Georgia's constitutional convention of 1867–68, which overturned the old white supremacist constitution. Horrified by white vigilantism, Akerman, as federal district attorney for Georgia, showed a zealous dedication to black rights by prosecuting violators of the Civil Rights Act of 1866, costing him the support of many white southerners.

The same week that Grant appointed Akerman, Congress created the Department of Justice. Before then, the attorney general had functioned as the president's legal adviser, operating from the Treasury building without the dignity of a separate department. Now he would head an active department with a substantial array of new powers. In part its creation was a practical measure to consolidate government lawyers and litigation in one department, sparing cabinet members the expense of hiring outside attorneys and thus reducing conflicts of interest. Civil service reformers also spotted a chance to streamline the government's legal capacity and enhance efficiency. The new department immediately faced a pressing task to ensure compliance with the Thirteenth, Fourteenth, and Fifteenth Amendments, which had sparked an explosion in litigation. That racial justice stood very high among Akerman's priorities was underscored when he set up Justice Department headquarters in the new Freedman's Savings Bank building.

In shaping the department, Congress provided for a solicitor general who would act as the government's main attorney, arguing cases before the Supreme Court and offering counsel to U.S. attorneys and marshals. The first occupant was another outstanding choice—the bearded Benjamin Helm Bristow, a crusading U.S. attorney from Kentucky. Educated at Jefferson College in Pennsylvania, Bristow had been a "Kentucky bluejay" who bucked local sympathy for the Confederacy, helped to assemble two federal regiments in Kentucky, and fought with Grant at Fort Donelson and Shiloh before joining the state senate. He had "a bluff, frank" personality, said one reporter, who thought he conveyed "a very marked impression of personal strength."[53] After the war, he worked to assemble a moderate Republican Party in Kentucky and won plaudits as a U.S. attorney of high integrity and legal excellence, committed to black civil rights. Just before Akerman's appointment, Bristow wrote from Kentucky to Attorney General Hoar: "It is a matter of first importance to the 225,000 Colored people of this state that the so-called 'Civil Rights' law of Congress should be maintained and enforced."[54]

The new Justice Department would forge its identity in the battle to slay the Ku Klux Klan and such offshoots as the Knights of the White Camellia. Having disbanded Confederate armies, the North had not stopped the emergence of quasi-military organizations throughout the South. In describing the Klan's tight grip over the region, Grant summoned his most emphatic language, saying its purpose was "by force and terror . . . to deprive colored citizens of the right to bear arms and of the right to a free ballot, to suppress schools in which colored children were taught, and to reduce the colored people to a condition closely akin to that of slavery."[55]

Grant constantly received desperate pleas from southern governors for help with the Klan. In March 1870, Governor William W. Holden of North Carolina warned of a rising tide of Klan terror in his state: "Bands of these armed men ride at night through various neighborhoods, whipping and maltreating peaceable citizens, hanging some, burning churches and breaking up schools which have been established for the colored people."[56] By July, Holden feared his paltry force of six hundred soldiers would be overwhelmed by Klan marauders. Grant acted vigorously to stem the North Carolina violence, promising Holden "to send more troops to the State without delay."[57] Holden pinpointed the essence of the problem: witnesses were too terrified to testify against Klan members, and juries to convict them, enabling the secret society to flout local courts with impunity. Those who cooperated in Klan prosecutions were almost guaranteed to suffer vicious reprisals. One district attorney in Mississippi despaired when five of his main witnesses were murdered. "I cannot get witnesses as all feel it is sure death to testify before the Grand Jury," he wrote.[58]

At election time, the Klan acted to intimidate black voters and elect white Democrats. It tried to undo Reconstruction and re-create the status quo ante of a submissive black workforce, lorded over by white masters. In October 1870, Governor Robert K. Scott of South Carolina told Grant his state had endured an election campaign that "for rancor and virulence . . . has never been excelled in any civilized community . . . Colored men and women have been dragged from their homes at the dead hour of night and most cruelly and brutally scourged for the sole reason that they dared to exercise their own opinions upon political subjects."[59] A shaken Scott added: "I have within a few moments witnessed in my own office a spectacle that has chilled my blood with horror." Four citizens were "at the dead hour of night dragged from their homes and lashed on their bare backs until the flayed flesh hung dripping in shreds, and seams were gaping in their mangled bodies large enough to lay my finger in."[60]

Organized in thousands of scattered groups and billing itself as the Invisible Empire, the Klan launched a new civil war by clandestine means. The menace had spread to every southern county. As Governor William H. Smith of Alabama informed Grant, "Things look here very much as they did in 1860 . . . If Alabama can be carried by intimidation & fraud so can every other state South, & the whole south will be lost to the Republican party."[61] One southern Unionist described things unequivocally: "The Ku Klux business is the worst thing that ever afflicted the South."[62] It became hard to see how the Republican Party could survive in the South without the shield of federal protection. Former abolitionists latched on to the new cause of combating the KKK. If the Civil War had to be fought over again, they favored Grant back in the starring role. "There [is] still a state of war with the South," declared Wendell Phillips. "Let General Grant lay his hand on the leaders in the South, and you will never hear of the Ku-Klux again."[63]

Grant was swamped with letters from southern blacks and white Republicans who graphically described the nightmare descending on their towns. Typical was a letter from a Mrs. S. E. Lane in South Carolina, who said she and her husband were "true & hearty Republicans . . . but Sir, we are in terror from Ku-Klux threats & outrages . . . our nearest neighbor—a prominent Republican now lies dead—murdered, by a disguised Ruffian Band, which attacked his

House at midnight a few nights since—his wife also was murdered . . . & a daughter is lying dangerously ill from a shot-wound—my Husband's life is threatened . . . we are in constant fear & terror—our nights are sleepless, we are filled with anxiety & dismay."[64] From senior politicians down to lowly share-croppers, people sent Grant hair-raising descriptions of night riders that gave him a comprehensive grasp of the terror. However clumsy his handling of Dominican annexation, he was sure-footed when it came to protecting freed people and handling other matters arising from the war. In pursuing the Klan, he showed to advantage his persistence, simplicity, and innate stubbornness. Through the Justice Department, the federal government would emerge as the undisputed champion of civil liberties in the southern states, carving out a new role.

Battle lines hardened in the 1870 election, which represented a worrisome setback for the Grant administration. Democrats coasted to victory in New York, Indiana, Missouri, West Virginia, and Tennessee, while the Republican majority in Congress shrank drastically. The election was noteworthy for having six black candidates elected to Congress from the Deep South, including three from South Carolina, cradle of the Confederacy. Of the six black congressmen, four were born into slavery. The election of black Republicans fed a continuing white backlash, one New York newspaper noting snidely that Congress "will soon have its full proportion of darkey members."[65] In the South, violence directed against Republicans allowed the Democrats to reclaim—or as they preferred to call it *redeem*—power lost in Georgia, Alabama, and Florida. "It seems that we are drifting . . . back under the leadership of the slave holders," a black Republican moaned.[66] The southern states had now been readmitted to the Union with full congressional representation, but far from adumbrating a new era of harmony, it signaled the start of a deepening era of polarization.

In Mississippi, the troubled situation was thrown into bold relief as scores of black churches and schools were burned without prosecutions. In March 1871, three blacks in the small town of Meridian were brought up on charges of delivering "incendiary" speeches. At the court hearing, the Republican judge and two black defendants were killed. The violence spilled over into gruesome riots in which thirty blacks were gunned down, including "all the leading colored men of the town with one or two exceptions."[67] During the first three months of that sanguinary year, sixty-three blacks were murdered in Mississippi and nobody served a day for these crimes.

In May 1870, Congress had passed the first Enforcement Act to protect the

voting rights granted by the Fifteenth Amendment by banning the use of force
or intimidation to abridge the right to vote because of race. Widespread voting
irregularities in the South led Grant on February 28, 1871, to sign yet another
Enforcement Act, which strengthened federal oversight of the voting process,
especially in large cities. Henceforth, federal judges could appoint election officials to supervise registration and voting methods and certify the accuracy of
returns, insisting upon the use of written ballots.

But all such reforms would die aborning if the root problem was not eradi-
cated: the Ku Klux Klan. Increasingly Grant was flooded with appeals from
Republican southern governors to slay the epidemic of Klan violence in their
states. "This organized conspiracy is in existence in every County of the State,"
Governor Holden of North Carolina warned. "It is believed that its leaders now
direct the movements of the present Legislature."[68] Governor Scott of South
Carolina notified Grant that two counties, Spartanburg and Union, had experienced such a "reign of terror" by Klansmen that "but few Republicans dare sleep
in their houses at night."[69] Every night thousands of blacks fled into the woods
for asylum. From two Carolina congressmen, Grant heard how members of a
black militia had been arrested for allegedly killing a white man. The Klan invaded the jail and murdered the black captain and five of his men. Upon learning that the remaining eight black militiamen were to be transferred to another
county, five hundred masked Klansmen raided the jail, overpowered the jailer,
and lynched the defendants. The congressmen concluded that South Carolina's
government was "powerless to preserve law and order . . . the constituted authorities invoke the strong arm of the United States to do so."[70]

In late February, Grant read aloud to his cabinet a horrifying report about
the murders, whippings, and violence overtaking South Carolina. He sent troops
to the state to halt the spreading disorder and swore that federal cavalry would
remain even if they had to stay "during the remainder of his administration."[71]
Soon Major Lewis Merrill, a man with "the head, face, and spectacles of a German professor and the frame of an athlete," was sent to South Carolina to protect the black community as part of Attorney General Akerman's grand strategy
for demolishing the Klan.[72] In a controversial move, Merrill had army officers
arrest Klan members while he enlisted U.S. attorneys to try their cases and lined
up federal judges to oversee their trials. These were groundbreaking decisions
that for the first time enabled the federal government instead of state and local
governments to punish "private criminal acts."[73]

Klan violence was unquestionably the worst outbreak of domestic terrorism in American history and Grant dealt with it aggressively, using all the instruments at his disposal. To strengthen the federal arsenal, he urged Congress to widen his executive powers and insisted the new Forty-Second Congress meet on March 4, 1871, instead of waiting until that December, to do so. So strongly did Grant feel about Klan atrocities that he beseeched House Speaker James G. Blaine to focus exclusively on legislation to uproot these domestic terrorists: "If the attention of Congress can be confined to the single subject of providing means for the protection of life and property . . . I feel that we should have such legislation."[74] While conservative Republicans and Democrats squawked that Grant trespassed on states' rights—a sacred cause in the South—he employed every weapon in his repertoire to suppress Klan violence. To accentuate just how deeply he felt, he marched up to Capitol Hill, accompanied by virtually every member of his cabinet, and lobbied for an explicitly anti-Klan bill, leaving the particulars up to legislators. He was so fixated on the Klan that Representative James A. Garfield of Ohio complained privately that Grant was "very anxious that Congress shall do nothing else, but legislate, concerning the Ku Klux."[75] The purpose of the proposed legislation was to force state compliance with the new constitutional amendment. "It seems to me, that this will virtually empower the President to abolish the State Governments," Garfield protested. "I am in great trouble about the whole matter."[76]

Refusing to backtrack, Grant plunged ahead. When Congress formed a select committee to consider Klan legislation, it encountered extraordinary resistance. Democrats construed the Ku Klux bill not as an effort to save southern blacks from wanton terror, but as a political swindle to extend Republican rule in the South. As Congressman James B. Beck of Kentucky said, "Many of you would rather see the President dictator to-day than to see the Democratic party come into power and expose the outrageous acts your party has committed."[77] Grant was dubbed "Kaiser Grant" and derided as a power-hungry, lazy, and negligent president, who wielded patronage to advance his fortunes. Senator Garrett Davis of Kentucky ridiculed him as incompetent and unfit for office while Representative John B. Hawley of Illinois labeled him "a despot; a dictator," who would "override the liberties of this great people."[78] The press debate was no less heated, and the *Chicago Times* blasted Grant as "the chief of a Ku Klux Klan more powerful than that of the South."[79] One of his most scathing critics was none other than William Tecumseh Sherman. "If Ku-klux bills were kept out of Congress, and the army kept at their legitimate duties," he told a New Orleans audience, "there are enough good and true men in all Southern States to put down all Ku-klux or other bands of marauders."[80] Many Democrats claimed that Klan atrocities were so many fairy tales dreamed up by Republicans for political expediency and denounced the Klan legislation as unconstitutional.

Fortunately for Grant, the fervor on his side was equally passionate. Frederick Douglass wisely saw that the random corruption cases that tarnished the administration's reputation were far less consequential than the president's unqualified support for southern blacks. Reconstruction was the essential sequel to the Civil War, completing its mission. "If we stand by President Grant and his administration," he wrote, "it is from no spirit of hero worship or blind attachment to mere party, but because in this hour there is no middle ground. [Grant] is for stamping out this murderous *ku-klux* as he stamped out the rebellion."[81]

On April 20, 1871, Grant returned victorious to Capitol Hill to sign the third Enforcement Act, commonly known as the Ku Klux Klan Act. He had planned a California trip that spring, but canceled it in the belief that he couldn't sidestep this historic moment. The strong new measure laid down criminal penalties for depriving citizens of their rights under the Fourteenth Amendment, including holding office, sitting on a jury, or casting a vote. The federal government could prosecute such cases when state governments refused to act. The law also endowed Grant with extraordinary powers to suspend habeas corpus, declare martial law, and send in troops. To halt night riders, the act made it illegal "to conspire together, or go in disguise upon the public highway . . . for the purpose . . . of depriving any person . . . of equal protection of the law."[82] However loathed in the South, the law stood as a magnificent achievement for Grant, who had initiated and rallied support for it, never wavering. To further strengthen it, he issued General Orders No. 48, allowing federal troops to arrest violators of the Ku Klux Klan Act and break up and disperse "bands of disguised marauders."[83]

The man who implemented this bold agenda was Akerman, who thought Reconstruction best served the long-term interests of the enlightened South, properly understood. To those who protested its severity, he responded that nothing was "more idle than to attempt to conciliate by kindness that portion of the Southern people who are still malcontent. They take all kindness on the part of the Government as evidence of timidity."[84] For Akerman, the Klan's actions "amount to war, and cannot be effectually crushed on any theory."[85] The metaphor didn't seem excessive, for the Klan resisted by force any effort to restrain it, reflected in Nathan Bedford Forrest's bloodthirsty injunction to his followers: "If they send the black men to hunt those confederate soldiers whom they call kuklux, then I say to you, 'Go out and shoot the radicals.'"[86]

On May 3, Grant issued a proclamation containing a ringing defense of the Ku Klux Klan Act, calling it a "law of extraordinary public importance."[87] Never mentioning the Klan by name, he alluded to "combinations of lawless and disaffected persons." To those who bridled at the enhanced use of federal power, denounced "bayonet rule," and brandished the states' rights banner, he implored them to use local laws to suppress the Klan and obviate the need for federal troops. If that didn't happen, the inaction of local communities "imposes upon the National Government the duty of putting forth all its energies for the protection of its citizens of every race and color."[88] If states abdicated responsibility, Grant was prepared to use the full panoply of federal power in response. At the same time, he issued orders to federal troops in South Carolina and Mississippi "to arrest disguised night marauders and break up their bands."[89] In countering the Klan, Grant found himself back in familiar territory, operating as general in chief. Whenever he returned to war-related issues, Grant showed a sure grasp of both his values and methods. He knew that the Klan threatened to unravel everything he and Lincoln and Union soldiers had accomplished at great cost in blood and treasure.

When a joint congressional committee traveled to South Carolina to gather testimony on the Klan rebellion, many of the witnesses were threatened. They made it abundantly clear that the Klan's word was law in many counties. As one witness from Union County testified, "The county was in effect under Ku-Klux rule; that no order issued by the Klan would be disregarded."[90] Grant received the same message from petrified citizens, such as Javan Bryant of Spartanburg County, who assured Grant that "it is a common thing for men to say in the country that they will kill anybody who reports them as Ku Klux."[91]

To aid the anti-Klan effort, Akerman fielded a vast array of resources, including federal marshals and attorneys of the brand-new Justice Department. Members of the nascent Secret Service pitched in with undercover detective work. On September 12, Akerman left for South Carolina to take personal supervision of the campaign, Grant placing federal troops at his disposal. The following month, Akerman sent him a sobering report on Klan activity in South Carolina that portrayed the Klan not as bands of isolated, wild-eyed ruffians but as a comprehensive movement that spanned the entire white community. It embraced "at least two thirds of the active white men of those counties, and have the sympathy and countenance of a majority of the other third. They are connected with similar combinations in other counties and States, and no doubt are part of a grand system of criminal associations pervading most of the Southern States."[92] Bound by secret oaths, Klansmen perjured themselves to escape prosecution and terrorized witnesses and juries. Akerman estimated that the Klan had committed thousands of criminal acts during the previous year.

On October 12, the anti-Klan assault entered a new phase when Grant, at Akerman's bidding, issued a proclamation calling upon "combinations and conspiracies" in nine South Carolina counties to disperse and retire peacefully to their homes within five days.[93] Five days later, when the groups did not disarm, Grant suspended habeas corpus there. Akerman explained to Grant the legal rationale for doing so: it was impossible to prosecute Klan members if witnesses dreaded reprisals. With habeas corpus suspended, those threatening reprisals could be held in custody long enough to protect witnesses and obtain convictions. Akerman greeted Grant's move, saying blacks can "sleep at home now."[94] By late November, he informed the cabinet that he had taken two thousand prisoners in South Carolina for violating the Ku Klux Klan Act.

Under Akerman's inspired leadership, federal grand juries, many interracial, brought 3,384 indictments against the KKK, resulting in 1,143 convictions.[95] The conviction rate was even better than it sounded. The federal court system was burdened with cases and many federal judges, appointed before Grant, didn't sympathize with the anti-Klan crusade. Furthermore, the act that created the Department of Justice had reduced the federal legal staff by a third and curbed its ability to hire outside lawyers as needed. With witnesses offered protection, Klansmen began to name other Klansmen, stripping off the secret veil that cloaked their activities. Many Klansmen, facing arrest, fled their states. Several hundred pleaded guilty in exchange for suspended or lenient sentences. Sixty-five Klansmen wound up in the federal penitentiary in Albany, New York. The goal was not mass incarceration but restoring law and order. To his district attorneys, Akerman made plain that more than convictions were at stake: "If you cannot convict, you, at least, can expose, and ultimately such exposures will make the community ashamed of shielding the crime."[96]

A southerner by choice, Akerman found it sobering to verify the depth of Klan penetration in the region, which "revealed a perversion of moral sentiment among the Southern whites which bodes ill to that part of the country for this generation."[97] On a single day in November, 250 people in one South Carolina county confessed affiliation with the group. As Akerman expressed the matter with deep feeling: "I doubt whether from the beginning of the world until now, a community, nominally civilized, has been so fully under the domination of systematic and organized depravity."[98] To another correspondent, he denounced the Klan as "the most atrocious organization that the civilized part of the world has ever known."[99]

Grant pushed the anti-Klan crusade despite sturdy resistance within his own administration. At cabinet meetings, he repeatedly allowed Akerman to expatiate on Klan horrors even though some members could not have cared less. After one session, Hamilton Fish complained wearily in his diary: "Akerman introduces Ku Klux—he has it 'on the brain'—he tells a number of stories—one of a fellow being castrated—with terribly minute & tedious details of each case—It has got to be a bore, to listen twice a week to this same thing."[100] Akerman's speeches were hardly a bore to Grant or the terrified people victimized by Klan thuggery in the South.

By 1872, under Grant's leadership, the Ku Klux Klan had been smashed in the South. (Its later twentieth-century incarnation had no connection to the earlier group other than a common style and ideology.) He had employed forceful, no-holds-barred actions to loosen the Klan's grip. As southern violence subsided, southern Republicans regained confidence and cast votes with an assurance of their safety, and for southern blacks the changed mood was palpable. "Peace has come to many places as never before," wrote Frederick Douglass. "The scourging and slaughter of our people have so far ceased."[101] It was a startling triumph for Grant, who had dared to flout what southern states considered their sacred rights to enforce the law within their borders.

Just how profoundly the atmosphere changed was revealed by a letter written by Senator Adelbert Ames, the Mississippi Republican, six months after Grant signed the Ku Klux Klan Act:

> Had it not been for the Ku Klux law . . . we would not have had any showing at this election. At one time, just previous to the passage of that law, the K.K. organizations were being perfected in every county in the state. It is believed by our friends that had the law not been passed, not one of them would have been safe outside of a few of the larger cities. As it is, the K.K.'s, cowards as they are, have for

a time at least suspended their operations in all but the eastern parts
of the state. Recent convictions in North Carolina and the President's
action in putting a part of South Carolina under martial law has had
a very subduing effect all over the South. It is perceptible here.[102]

For Grant's admirers, the routing of the Klan eclipsed the lesser failures of his
first term as president. "I do not know where to look for a worthier or more
popular candidate than President Grant," Akerman wrote. "The objections to
his administration . . . are of the most frivolous sort. They do not go to essen-
tials."[103] For the implacable Charles Sumner, however, Grant could do nothing
right, and he scoffed "that the much-criticized Ku Klux legislation . . . would
have been *entirely unnecessary,* if this Republican President had shown a decent
energy in enforcing existing law."[104] One wonders whether Sumner thought
Grant had done too little or feared that the president had upstaged him as the
foremost protector of African American rights.

Despite Grant's stunning success, a certain moral fatigue began to afflict the
North, where racism remained widespread. Segments of the Republican Party
pulled away from the idealism of earlier days, and nobody sensed this seismic
shift more acutely than Amos Akerman. "The real difficulty is that very many
of the Northern Republicans shrink from any further special legislation in regard to the South," he wrote in December. "Even such atrocities as KuKluxery
do not hold their attention as long as we should expect."[105] Democrats, meanwhile, slammed Grant's actions as dictatorial, and one South Carolina newspaper portrayed the men arresting Klan members as "Grant's 'night riders.'"[106]

Even as he rendered superlative service in squashing the Klan, Akerman
clashed with the railroads, the country's most powerful industry. In June, he had
turned down an application by the Union Pacific for a huge land subsidy and incurred the enmity of railroad barons such as Jay Gould and Collis P. Huntington. He rebuffed an attempt by one railroad company to bribe him and wouldn't
back down in his regulatory decisions. Grant came under enormous pressure to
replace him and on December 12, he requested Akerman's resignation. He hinted
at nameless forces behind the request and expressed his "approbation of the zeal,
integrity and industry" Akerman had shown in performing his duties.[107] For
many months, Akerman had known special interests were gunning for him and
even considered resigning to spare Grant this pressure. Now he fell on his sword,
thanking Grant for the kindness he had shown and conveying his "ardent wishes

for the continued success of your administration."[108] Their exchanged letters
show affection and mutual respect. Akerman declined Grant's offer of a judge-
ship and returned to private life in Cartersville, Georgia. He remained loyal to
Grant and insisted that his administration had been the best since the days of
John Quincy Adams.

To replace him, Grant named George H. Williams, a judge and former U.S.
senator from Oregon, who was speedily confirmed. Williams was well qualified
to be attorney general, having served as a district judge and chief justice in Oregon before establishing a lucrative law practice in Portland. Always sensitive to
regional demands for representation, Grant was glad to have someone from the
Pacific Coast in his cabinet and for a long time enjoyed a fine rapport with Williams, who valued the president as a "serene, self-reliant, conscientious man and
officer."[109] Although Solicitor General Bristow resigned in November 1872—he
felt bruised when Grant elevated Williams instead of him to replace Akerman—
the war against the Klan never ground to a halt. Thanks to zealous work by U.S.
attorneys in the South, Williams brought three times as many cases and chalked
up four times as many convictions against Klansmen in 1872 as Akerman had
attained in 1871 and did even better in 1873.[110] The retreat from Klan prosecutions came later. Grant deserves immense praise for hiring Akerman, the greatest ornament of his cabinet and one of the outstanding attorneys general in
American history, but he also deserves blame for letting him go much too soon.
Nevertheless, the campaign against the Klan was now in full swing, had generated enormous momentum, and would only expand during the next two years.

CHAPTER THIRTY-THREE

//////////////////////////////

A Dance of Blood

T HE SAME FLINTY DETERMINATION that informed Grant's spectacular campaign against the Klan harmed him when dealing with the
Santo Domingo treaty, an obsession he could not discard. In October
1870, he reassured President Báez that he would pursue the issue when Congress
reconvened. Hamilton Fish was eager to wriggle free from the whole sordid
mess, but he found it difficult to do so without offending Grant. Meanwhile,
Charles Sumner still stewed over Motley's recall and threatened to foil Grant at
every turn.

In early December, when Grant sent his annual message up to Capitol Hill, it
contained many fresh, forward-looking features. He wanted to rejuvenate America's merchant marine through shipbuilding subsidies and proposed two new
bureaus in the Interior Department, one for education, the other for agriculture.
What was downright stale was his renewed plea to annex the Dominican nation.
Far from backing down, he upped the stakes. "So convinced am I of the advantages to flow from the acquisition of San Domingo, and of the great disadvan-
tages, I might almost say calamity, to flow from non acquisition," he wrote in his
draft message, "that I believe the subject has only to be investigated to be approved."[1] The more Grant pushed the issue, the more critics pushed back. "The
President's message is good," observed Rutherford B. Hayes. "With the exception
of San Domingo, it is approved by all fair-minded Republicans."[2]

Grant requested a joint resolution of Congress that would empower him to
appoint a three-man commission to investigate annexation of the island nation.

Such a resolution required a simple majority vote, not the higher two-thirds bar to pass a treaty. Not surprisingly, Sumner refused to introduce such a resolution. Instead Grant turned to another member of the Foreign Affairs Committee, Senator Oliver P. Morton of Indiana, who presented the resolution on December 12. Sumner reacted with ferocity and for two weeks assailed Grant in closed-door sessions of the committee. On December 20, *The New York Times* reported that several senators had failed to effect a truce between Grant and Sumner: "Mr. Sumner remains as bitter as ever, and the President maintains a firm attitude, inconsistent with anything like an approach toward conciliation."[3] Far from calming down, Sumner worked himself up to his most grandiloquent indictment yet. On December 21, with an early winter storm swirling about the Capitol, he delivered a salvo against the treaty that had become a casus belli for him with Grant. It was known as the *Naboth's Vineyard* speech, for he referred to Ahab, the Israeli king whose wife, Jezebel, had Naboth stoned to death to procure his vineyard. For sheer histrionics and gratuitous insults, it was one of the most vitriolic speeches in Senate annals.

"The resolution before the Senate commits Congress to a dance of blood," Sumner thundered. "It is a new step in a measure of violence."[4] He noted that Grant didn't need congressional authorization to send agents to foreign countries but had done so "to commit Congress to the policy of annexation."[5] He took deadly aim at Báez, saying American warships in Dominican waters sustained his government: "You call him 'president,' they call him there 'dictator.'"[6] At this point, Senator Morton objected that Sumner had raised a frivolous point, since all groups in Santo Domingo favored annexation, not just the president. In response, Sumner unleashed his full cannonade of rhetoric: "Frivolous! Is it frivolous when I see the flag of my country prostituted to an act of wrong? Is it frivolous when I see the mighty power of this Republic degraded to an act of oppression?"[7] Sumner went on melodramatically about America bullying Haiti, claiming Grant wanted to annex the entire island, not merely the Dominican side. Stooping to a new low, he identified Grant with three former presidents who had appeased the South—Pierce, Buchanan, and Johnson—and sought "the oppression of a weak and humble people." In closing, Sumner made a bizarre racial argument that the island of Hispaniola had been consecrated "to the colored race. It is theirs by right of possession; by their sweat and blood mingling with the soil; by tropical position; by its burning sun, and by unalterable laws of climate."[8]

Many senators were appalled by Sumner's ugly attack, which Zachariah

Chandler of Michigan termed a "brutal assault."[9] To rebut his charges, Senator Roscoe Conkling of New York rose to defend Grant and pointed out that the three-man commission was merely one of inquiry to confirm or deny the charges directed against annexation. He countered Sumner's indignation with his own. "Why, sir," he protested, "if the charges made by the Senator today against the President be true, it would be necessary to convict him of being a fool in order to acquit him of being a knave." At first Conkling seemed to mock the notion that Grant wanted to eject Sumner from the Foreign Relations Committee, then he endorsed it by saying it should no longer be chaired "by a Senator who has launched against the Administration an assault more bitter than has proceeded from any Democratic member of this body."[10] Morton backed up Conkling, protesting that Grant had been treated with "a bitterness of persecution and a torrent of calumny" not seen "since the days of Thomas Jefferson."[11]

In a rowdy debate, opposing senators roared through the night and it was around dawn when they wearily approved Morton's resolution for an inquiry commission. Vice President Colfax went to the White House to congratulate Grant, who received a parade of jubilant lawmakers. In the following days, Sumner told Fish and Boutwell that he had always been courteous to Grant. Afterward, at the White House, the two men analyzed Sumner's manic behavior. Though an old friend of his, Fish said the Massachusetts senator was "crazy" and "a monomaniac upon all matters relating to his own importance and his relations toward the president." For Boutwell, Sumner had fired charges against Grant "so outrageous and violent" that he dared not repeat them.[12] He recalled Sumner's charge that Grant was drunk when he stopped by his house for the famous dinner chat. As proof, Sumner had cited the fact that Grant addressed him as chairman of the *Judiciary* Committee. "He was no more drunk, or excited," recalled Boutwell, "than he was when we left him upstairs five minutes since—no more than Sumner himself."[13] Sumner now took to calling Grant "a colossus of ignorance" and defamed Fish as "a gentleman in aspect with the heart of a lackey."[14] He said he would have no further dealings with the secretary of state, a rupture that threatened the very workings of government.

Among those who believed Sumner trafficked in unfair invective was Frederick Douglass, who wrote to the senator and berated him for lumping Grant's name "with the infamous names of Pierce, Buchanan and Johnson. These names in the minds of all loyal and liberty loving men stand under the heaviest reproach—and I candidly think you did wrong to place Grant in that infamous category even by implication."[15] Only a group of neutral commissioners, Douglass argued, could engage in dispassionate analysis of the Santo Domingo question and report honestly to the American people.

In defending Grant, Fish insisted that the president had maintained cordial relations with senators who opposed the Santo Domingo treaty. He paid a remarkable tribute to Grant, stating that "no man living is more tolerant of honest and manly differences of opinion, is more single or sincere in his desire for the public welfare, is more disinterested or regardless of what concerns himself, is more frank and confiding in his own dealings, is more sensitive to a betrayal of confidence, or would look with more scorn and contempt upon one who uses the words and the assurances of friendship to cover a secret and determined purpose of hostility."[16] In short, Fish thought Sumner had gone way beyond legitimate disagreement and behaved in a false, duplicitous manner.

On January 9, the resolution for an inquiry commission passed the House and was approved by the Senate three days later. For all of Sumner's bombastic invocation of black rights, opposition to the Dominican annexation had taken on a racist tinge. Carl Schurz regretted that annexation would soon bring the absorption of Cuba, Puerto Rico, and other Caribbean islands in its wake. He described these islands as populated mainly by indolent black people and issued this challenge to treaty proponents: "Show me a single instance in any tropical country where labor when it was left free did not exhibit a strong tendency to run into shiftlessness, and where practical attempts to organize labor did not run in the direction of slavery."[17]

Once the joint resolution cleared Congress, Grant tapped three figures of unimpeachable integrity for the commission: Andrew White, the president of Cornell University; Dr. Samuel Gridley Howe, who had done excellent work for the blind; and Benjamin F. Wade, the former Ohio senator and Radical Republican. Grant had chosen impartial men of high character and didn't stack the deck in favor of annexation; White and Howe actually opposed it. Grant also chose Howe because he was a longtime abolitionist, married to the poet Julia Ward Howe, and a Bostonian friend of Sumner, who would be outflanked if Howe opted for annexation. Emotions didn't cool down between Grant and Sumner. When intermediaries proposed that the abolitionist Gerrit Smith act as peacemaker between them, Grant replied, according to Sumner, that if he weren't president he "should demand personal satisfaction of Mr. Sumner"—in other words, a duel. Sumner, playing the innocent, professed complete ignorance as to why Grant was so upset with him: "I have done nothing but my duty;—nor have I ever made any personal impeachment of him."[18]

Stealing the moral high ground, Grant summoned to the White House Frederick Douglass, who agreed to become secretary to the commission. When it sailed to the Caribbean on January 18, the group also included a State Department geologist, a government botanist, and a *New York Times* photographer. On the eve of Douglas's departure, a friend described him as "enchanted at the prospect of visiting a tropical island."[19] At Grant's behest, he enjoyed every courtesy extended to the three commissioners, joining them for meals in the admiral's cabin. At a time when this was hardly taken for granted, Douglass marveled at his equal treatment, commenting that "while all the fools are not dead yet, the American people are rapidly outgrowing their slavery-engendered prejudices, and will one day wonder how they could have so long lived under its degrading spell."[20] Douglass's assignment was yet another example of Grant's appointing African Americans in far greater numbers than any previous president.

Grant hoped that if the commission filed an unfavorable report on Santo Domingo, it would put the entire matter to rest. Some observers saw the commission as a charade, a face-saving way for Grant to disengage from a failed initiative. "The commission was intended merely to let the administration down 'easy,'" wrote former attorney general Hoar. "It cannot report in season to do anything in this Congress—and the next will be strong against it."[21] On the other hand, Grant hoped that if the commissioners arrived at a favorable conclusion, annexation might ensue. In fact, the commissioners reacted ecstatically to the island nation. "There is no more fruitful Country on Earth," Benjamin Wade wrote, "and they are so far all without exception crazy to be annexed—All that Grant said about it is true—all that Sumner said is false."[22]

With the commissioners away, the marathon feud between Grant and Sumner redoubled in fury. Relations had also deteriorated between Sumner and Hamilton Fish, whom Sumner anointed "Mephistopheles."[23] Fish not only thought Sumner "bitterly vindictive and hostile," but believed he suffered from "mental derangement," succumbing to wild, paranoid delusions that Grant and Orville Babcock had threatened to assault him.[24] Boutwell thought Sumner's days as chairman of the Foreign Relations Committee were numbered "when he declined to have any intercourse with the Secretary of State outside of official business."[25] The State Department kept sending minor treaties to Sumner, who then sat on them for months, and watched as the senator pompously issued instructions to foreign diplomats in Washington.

In February, after Sumner strove to thwart confirmation of Grant's brother-in-law Michael John Cramer as minister to Denmark, the president despaired of any improvement in the situation and threw his considerable weight behind efforts, spearheaded by Senators Morton, Conkling, and Chandler, to oust Sumner as chairman of the Foreign Relations Committee when Congress convened in early March. In a momentous shift, Grant made common cause with party bosses, who increasingly formed the backbone of his support on Capitol Hill.

When Congress came back into session, in a rare spectacle of a mighty senator being humbled by his peers, the Republican caucus voted to depose Sumner as head of the Foreign Relations Committee. The full Senate approved by a 33 to 9 vote, with twenty-five senators abstaining. Even though Schurz defended Sumner and John Logan objected to intrusive executive power, the will of the body had turned unmistakably against Sumner, who was replaced by Senator Simon Cameron of Pennsylvania, a Grant supporter. By now well schooled in Washington intrigue, the president had shown he would not be pushed around by an arrogant senator. He insisted he had nothing to do with Sumner's dismissal, but admitted he "was glad when I heard that he was put off, because he stood in the way of even routine business, like ordinary treaties with small countries . . . It was a sad sight to find a Senate with the large majority of its members in sympathy with the administration, and with its chairman of the Foreign Committee in direct opposition to the foreign policy of the administration."[26] Like many shy, reserved men, Grant was slow to take offense, but once provoked he could be implacable in his bitterness. Walking past Sumner's house with Grant after the senator's removal, George Hoar was flabbergasted to see the president shake a fist at his window and manifest his anger. "The man who lives up there has abused me in a way I have never suffered from any other man living!"[27] Most of the time, Grant was a tactful, forgiving man, but there were limits to his patience.

The self-righteous Sumner absolved himself of all responsibility for what had happened. "The Pres[iden]t has such relations with me as he chooses," he explained smugly. "I have never declined to see him or confer with him. If there is a quarrel it is all on his side."[28] On March 27, Sumner spewed forth another three-hour speech against Grant, accusing him of trampling senatorial rights and even likening him to a Klan wizard, saying it was "difficult to see how we can condemn . . . our own domestic Ku Klux with its fearful outrages while the President puts himself at the head of a powerful and costly Ku Klux operating abroad."[29] Even those who sympathized with Grant worried about the impact Sumner's expulsion would have on Republican unity, an early sign of the schism that would split the party in the 1872 election.

By the time the commissioners returned from Santo Domingo in late March, they were convinced the Dominican people wanted annexation and were surprised to concur with Grant about the wisdom of that policy. The final leg of their journey aboard a Potomac mail packet was marred by a racial incident when the captain refused to admit Douglass into the dining room with the three commissioners. Andrew White was irate that "a man who had dined with the foremost statesmen and scholars of our Northern States and of Europe" was banished from the table. In protest he refused to touch his food and stormed from the dining room with Samuel Gridley Howe. Later on, Sumner tried to smear Grant with the incident, saying that "almost within sight of the Executive Mansion," Douglass had been rejected from the white man's table. Thus "was the African race insulted, and their equal rights denied but the President . . . neither did nor said anything to right this wrong."[30] The insult was compounded, according to Grant's critics, when the president invited the three commissioners to dine at the White House on March 30 and excluded Douglass.

There's only one problem with the story of the supposed presidential snub: the man who most conspicuously defended Grant's behavior was the man allegedly victimized. "There is something so ridiculous about this dinner affair," Douglass told a friend, noting that Grant was well within his rights not to invite him.[31] Douglass made many good points to disarm critics. He pointed out that Grant had "never withheld any social courtesy" from the Haitian ambassador, "a man of my own complexion." Every day for ten weeks, Douglass had dined with the commissioners "and this doubtless by the President's special direction." Finally, he thought the public misunderstood the circumstances of the dinner. Messrs. White, Howe, and Wade had called on the president, who invited them on the spot to dine with him. "Had I been in company with the Commissioners," Douglass wrote, "I have no question but that an invitation would have been extended to me as freely as to any of the gentlemen of the Commission."[32] Not only had Grant been uniformly cordial to him, but "after Lincoln and Sumner no man in his intercourse with me gave evidence of more freedom from vulgar prejudice."[33] Douglass *did* believe, however, that Grant had thrown away a splendid opportunity to rebuke the ship captain who had snubbed him by welcoming him to a White House dinner.

The president invited Douglass to the executive mansion to deliver his personal views on the mission. Sumner had reproached annexation on the ground that despotic Dominicans threatened black Haitian republicans. Douglass stood this argument on its head, stating that "the Dominicans are a far superior people to the Haitians; that there is no republicanism whatever in Haiti, and that the Government there is an absolute despotism of the most oppressive character," a reporter jotted down. Douglass thought Santo Domingo annexation would "strike a blow" at tropical slavery and raise the "world's opinion of the mental and moral possibilities of the colored race."[34] Douglass hoped Sumner would soften his opposition, fearing it would tear apart the Republican Party. If Sumner persisted, Douglass regretted, "I shall . . . regard him as the worst foe the colored race has on this continent."[35]

On April 5, Grant submitted the commissioners' report to the Senate and happily observed that the findings sustained his views on annexation. No less important, it refuted corruption charges and "fully vindicates the purity of the motives and action of those who represented the United States in the negotiation."[36] Grant had privately bemoaned the "insinuations of fraud, corruption, crime" attributed to those negotiating the treaty and he yearned for this vindication.[37] For Grant the controversy had become a matter of honor as well as duty, a means to reestablish his personal reputation for incorruptibility. He didn't ask for congressional action on the report and merely requested that it be printed and disseminated, which would end "all personal solicitude upon the subject."[38] Thumbing his nose at Sumner, Grant ended by saying that a faithful public servant, when sustained by his own conscience, "can bear with patience the censure of disappointed men."[39]

If Grant thought the report might salvage the treaty, he was sorely mistaken. A public consensus had already coalesced against annexation. "The Pres. . . . is as *stubborn as ever,* and seems determined to risk his all upon that one card," Schurz observed. "He seems to have a genius for suicide."[40] Many annexation foes still exploited racist and xenophobic fears and Sumner fulminated against the treaty at every opportunity. "Nothing has aroused me more since the Fug[itive] Sl[ave] Bill & the outrages in Kansas," he swore.[41]

Usually circumspect in comments about people, Grant found it hard to be politic about Sumner, whose betrayal brought strong, censored feelings bubbling to the surface. Eight months after Sumner was toppled as Foreign Relations chairman, Grant refused to heal the breach, telling Senator Henry Wilson:

> Mr. Sumner has been unreasonable, cowardly, slanderous, unblushing false. I should require of him an acknowledgment to this effect, from his seat in the Senate, before I would consent to meet him socially. He has not the manliness ever to admit an error. I feel a greater contempt for him than for any other man in the Senate. Schurz is an ungrateful man . . . and one who can render much greater service to the party he does not belong to than the one he pretends to have attachment for.[42]

Nor was Sumner in a forgiving mood. To embarrass Grant, he introduced a Senate resolution calling for a constitutional amendment to limit presidents to a single term. Although it didn't apply to the current occupant, it was clearly meant as a slap at Grant. On the Senate floor, to rousing cheers, Roscoe Conkling said that despite attacks from "presses and demagogues," Grant remained "secure, as no predecessor for forty years has been secure, against detraction and defeat."[43] The proposed amendment faded away, along with Grant's treaty for annexing Santo Domingo.

The treaty debate had been a bruising lesson in Washington power politics for Grant. He had been subjected to unconscionable attacks by Sumner, but had also made the mistake of personalizing the issue and matching the senator's animus. As Julia Grant once said of her husband, he had "lots of friends and no enemies until political ones came on."[44] This was not quite true, for he had enemies during the war who tried to injure him. But the politicians now plotting his downfall were craftier and more ruthless and had played the game far longer than he had. Grant lacked the normal human quota of cynicism and had paid for it. Some people thought he had mishandled his relationship with the vain Sumner. The senator himself complained that Grant "may have sought my vote, which I did not promise; but he never sought 'advice & counsel.'"[45] Sumner had demanded a show of deference, a bend of the knee, which Grant refused to give. The president, of course, could point to his unprecedented stroll over to Sumner's house to talk about the treaty, a novel show of deference that had clearly backfired.

THE DEMOTION OF CHARLES SUMNER and the dismissal of John Lothrop Motley greatly simplified Grant's task in negotiating an end to the controversial *Alabama* claims. Their settlement took a dramatic leap forward in autumn 1870 when Sir Edward Thornton, Britain's ambassador, went to Fish's house for a friendly chat. Thornton surmised that Grant was eager to reach a settlement to advance his reelection prospects and that Fish, too, craved a touch of diplomatic glory. Over cigars in his study, Fish made two statements that transformed the discussion. First, he said Washington would drop its insistence upon Canadian independence if Great Britain made satisfactory concessions on other issues. Second, instead of a timid, piecemeal approach, he proposed a far grander solution with all outstanding disputes between the United States and Great Britain, including fisheries, boundaries, and tariffs, negotiated at once.

One evening in early November, Grant dropped by Fish's house and the two conversed for a couple of hours. Fish persuaded Grant that it was futile to pursue Canadian annexation. Many Britons ascribed to Grant a deep-seated hostility toward them, and he indeed later wrote that the British ruling class had "shown an indecent haste in their recognition of a southern confederacy."[46] Still, he retained a fondness for Anglo-Saxon culture, telling a friend, "It has always been my desire to cultivate the best of feeling between the two English speaking Nations . . . the most enterprising as well as freest Nations of the world."[47] By late December, he had given Fish his blessing to hammer out an *Alabama* settlement with the British.

Fish had already received notice from Sir John Rose, a Canadian diplomat, that the other side was ready to bargain. In late January, the cabinet endorsed negotiations with the caveat that Great Britain "admit her liability for the losses sustained by the acts of the *Alabama*," Fish noted.[48] In his annual message in December, Grant expressed his "firm and unalterable" conviction that the British should admit their guilt.[49] Fish knew they would consent to no such confession and that insistence on this would only wreck the discussions. Toward the end of January, Grant and Fish responded warmly to a proposal from Sir Edward Thornton for a joint commission that would arbitrate the differences between the two nations, heralding a peaceful new way of solving international disputes.

At the time, Charles Sumner still chaired the Senate Foreign Relations Committee and made preposterous demands upon the English. Not only did he want all of Canada but a total British withdrawal from the Western Hemisphere, including its Caribbean islands and the Falkland Islands off the Argentine coast. Circumventing Sumner, Fish lobbied other committee members and secured their support for a joint commission. On February 9, Grant announced its creation to iron out differences with England.

By the end of the month, the British-American Joint High Commission held its first meeting on the State Department premises, with five representatives from each side. Grant and Fish had scored a major breakthrough in bringing the British to the table: their participation tacitly admitted guilt that they could not publicly avow. It also meant the administration had prevailed over Sumner, Ben Butler, and other Republicans hankering for a collision with Great Britain. Acting on Fish's suggestion that his commission appointments show a bipartisan spirit, Grant included Samuel Nelson, an associate justice of the Supreme Court and a Democrat. For the next nine weeks, Grant and Fish, who served as an American commissioner, crisscrossed Lafayette Square innumerable times to consult each other. The commission sessions proceeded amicably, and the British were pleasantly surprised to find the Americans "a very gentlemanly good set of fellows socially" and Fish "quite English in manner and appearance."[50] One British commissioner thought Grant's reelection "the mainspring of the whole machine of the Commission."[51] While the diplomats deliberated, Sumner was ousted as chairman of the Foreign Relations Committee, markedly improving the prospects for treaty ratification.

While not admitting guilt over the *Alabama,* the British commissioners conceded that, as a neutral government, they should have used "due diligence" to ensure that British-built vessels weren't armed for combat against another nation. When they confessed to negligence and regret, Grant and Fish were satisfied. The British also agreed to submit damages claimed by the United States to binding arbitration. The Joint High Commission recommended the creation of a five-man arbitration tribunal, based in Geneva, with members chosen by a cluster of world dignitaries: President Grant, Queen Victoria, the king of Italy, the president of the Swiss Confederation, and the emperor of Brazil. On May 8, the British and American commissioners gathered in a flower-bedecked room at the State Department and affixed their signatures to the Treaty of Washington. One British commissioner dropped scalding sealing wax on the fingers of a harried clerk preparing the final treaty document, leading the latter to burst into tears. With this mishap safely resolved, the commissioners celebrated their achievement over plates of strawberries and ice cream.[52]

Presented to a special Senate session in early May, the treaty was so imaginatively fair-minded that even Sumner, that eternal skeptic, couldn't fault it. The American press registered enthusiastic support and on May 24, it won Senate approval by a lopsided margin. Its ratification ushered in a new era of closer relations between the United States and Great Britain while offering a precedent for settling disputes peacefully among leading nations. Enshrined as a milestone in diplomatic annals, it established Hamilton Fish as one of the most innovative secretaries of state in American history and Grant as a major mediator and consensus builder. Grant felt liberated from the curse of Charles Sumner, who had choked off treaties and other pressing diplomatic measures. After the agreement passed, Fish wrote to Simon Cameron, "Since you took charge in the Senate of the business from this Department, I have felt that important measures . . . were no longer to be smothered, & pigeonholed in the Committee Room."[53]

For much of Grant's first term, Fish had been restless, periodically threatening to quit. Grant could be abrupt and impulsive, and Fish, with his smooth professionalism and thorough preparation, had saved him from many errors. From the outset, Fish had expected to serve only a brief period and knew the *Alabama* settlement would qualify as the high-water mark of his tenure. Once the Senate approved it, he told Grant he would like to depart on August 1. Grant, who knew Fish's worth, was taken aback and pleaded with him to reconsider, saying he would rather forfeit any other cabinet member. "I urge reasons for my resigning," Fish recounted in his diary, "& he meets them, by admitting that it involves great sacrifice, to me, to remain, but he could not replace me to his own satisfaction."[54] Grant admitted to Vice President Colfax that he kept Fish in his cabinet through sheer persistence, but "seeing as I do that he is suffering in health, I have not the heart to urge him stronger than has already been done to remain longer than he has consented to."[55] Though a newcomer to politics, Grant had learned the lesson of heeding professional counsel.

Already meditating a second term, Grant prevailed upon Fish to stay past the November elections. Congressional Republicans also applied pressure, fearing he would be succeeded by Senator Oliver P. Morton of Indiana. "If Morton succeeds you or otherwise goes into the Cabinet," Senator Chandler warned Fish, "it will be impossible for the Republican Party to carry the next Presidential election, for nobody has any confidence in him."[56] In July, Fish complained about the "severe & confining duties of my office" and tendered his resignation anew, only to have Grant rebuff it again.[57]

With such a capable secretary of state, Grant made sure the American public knew how deeply he himself had been involved in shaping the Treaty of Washington. As he told a reporter, "The facts are that every article of the treaty was submitted to me after it was adopted by the Commission and approved by me; and that each article was in the same way submitted to the British Cabinet and approved by the Ministers of the Crown at once." The treaty, he boasted, had done nothing less than stave off war with Great Britain. "Settlement or war were the alternatives," he told one reporter flatly, punctuating his conclusion by brusquely tossing aside his cigar.[58]

Because only one American would be appointed to the Geneva tribunal, the selection was consequential. At first Grant resisted naming Charles Francis Adams Sr., betraying his old grudge against the Adams clan. "I confess to a repugnance to the appointment of an Adams," Grant advised Fish, "which I would not feel to the ap[pointmen]t of an out-and-out democrat."[59] In the end, Fish convinced him nobody was better acquainted than Adams with the history of rebel cruisers built in England and Grant bowed to his advice. He balked, however, at appointing William Evarts as counsel to the Geneva tribunal. A suave, masterful lawyer who had served as Andrew Johnson's private counsel during the impeachment trial, Evarts was too associated with Johnson to be acceptable in Grant's mind. Yet when Fish cited the imperative need for a distinguished counsel, Grant "yielded all personal feeling, and cordially agreed to his appointment," said Fish. "As a general rule, he asserted his own views tenaciously and firmly."[60]

On December 5, Fish, having drafted instructions for the tribunal counsel, handed Grant his resignation after a cabinet meeting and Grant grew flustered. In his diary, Fish said Grant "was very sorry &c did not know what he should do—referred to the good feeling existing through the Country, & the confidence of the public & of the Republican Senators, & Congressmen in me."[61] Grant didn't want to force Fish to stay unwillingly, but dreaded his departure. As rumors surfaced that he might resign, Senators Conkling, Cameron, and Frelinghuysen issued strenuous pleas for him to stay. Such was the lofty esteem in which Fish was held that Vice President Colfax, along with forty-four senators, signed a letter begging him to stay in office.

By December 20, Fish informed Grant he wouldn't retire as secretary of state and the president's relief was immediately visible, as Fish informed his diary: "He replies with great warmth thanking me, & says 'I cannot express to you what a great gratification it affords me. I could not fill your place—& the Country has as I have the greatest confidence in your Administration of the Foreign Policy of the Govt.'"[62] Grant's reaction was understandable. Fish had provided expert judgment, reflecting more credit upon Grant than perhaps any other cabinet member. He stood as a one-man rebuke to charges of mediocrity leveled at the administration. On Reconstruction issues, Grant operated from deep knowledge and long experience, but when it came to the niceties of diplomacy, he was an amateur at sea, sorely needing a veteran hand. For Grant, Fish was the ideal cabinet member because he never hesitated to disagree or warn of dangers inherent in a given course of action. At the same time, once Grant made up his mind he was unshakable, and Fish loyally carried out his directives, whether he supported them or not.

No sooner did the arbitration tribunal hold its inaugural session in mid-December at the Hôtel de Ville in Geneva—an American, a Briton, a Swiss, a Brazilian, and an Italian composed the polyglot crew—than it foundered on the explosive issue of indirect damages. American representatives pointed out that the treaty had stipulated that *all* issues could be presented for arbitration. Aside from seeking payment for vessels directly damaged by the *Alabama* and other raiders, the United States wanted Great Britain to foot the bill for the *entire* war cost after Gettysburg, some $2 billion, the logic being that after Gettysburg, the Confederacy had abandoned offensive operations, except at sea. If the British hadn't provided naval aid, the South couldn't have prolonged the war and Great Britain was therefore liable for the extra astronomical expenses incurred. The ghost of Charles Sumner, who ranted that Great Britain had extended the war by two years, reared its ugly head in Geneva. Despite private reservations on the issue, Grant knew his reelection chances would be imperiled if he retreated entirely on indirect damages. As for Fish, he knew the Senate would recoil at any agreement that ignored it.

As American demands cropped up in the London press, they met with a shrill outcry from the Tory opposition, fostering an almost warlike mood. Prime Minister Gladstone gave his opinion to Queen Victoria "that the conduct of the American Government in this affair is the most disreputable he has ever known in his recollection of diplomacy."[63] His cabinet sent a stinging protest to Washington while Gladstone reassured the British public that it would be "insane to accede to demands which no nation with a spark of honour or spirit left could submit to even at the point of death."[64] Benjamin Moran, secretary of the American legation in London, was stunned by the decline of American support even among Britons who had fervently embraced the Union cause: "They look upon this claim for consequential damages as dishonest and as confirming the popular English opinion . . . that we are a tricky people."[65]

On February 6, 1872, with stock markets gyrating wildly, Grant's cabinet met to ponder the British protest and refused to yield on indirect claims. "We must go on," Grant intoned, prompting unanimous nods from his department heads. "I want you, Mr. Fish," he added, "to instruct Mr. Adams to remain and sign the award *alone* if all the others withdraw!"[66] Ever truthful, Fish reminded Grant that the treaty required approval of the majority of the tribunal. Writing to Badeau, Orville Babcock explained that the presidential campaign had strengthened Grant's hard line on indirect claims: "If England backs out all our people will stand by the President. If she stands by the treaty, all will say 'it is because Grant stood firm.'"[67]

In the end, Grant instructed Charles Francis Adams to travel to London and offer quiet guarantees to the British that the United States wouldn't insist on gigantic payments for indirect damages, but would settle for a tribunal statement that it possessed the right to pass judgment on the question. As the Geneva agreement came to a vote in May 1872, Grant showed a growing mastery of the legislative process, inviting members of the Senate and House Foreign Relations Committees to meet him at the State Department, where they pored over diplomatic correspondence from Switzerland. Eager to show that he sought advice and consent from the Senate, he accepted an invitation from the Senate Foreign Relations Committee to consult with them. On May 18, Grant climbed into his carriage and was about to depart for the Capitol when Fish intercepted him and advised "that as a mere matter of Etiquette & courtesy the Comm[ittee] should call upon him, not he on them." At the time, presidents weren't supposed to dabble in legislation in this way and Fish worried that treaty opponents would charge Grant with exerting "undue influence" over its passage.[68] After considering, Grant dismounted from the carriage.

In taking a tough stance on the *Alabama* claims, Grant played a winning hand with the American public. Thomas Nast published a cartoon in which Grant and Fish stood beneath a sign warning: "No More Concessions. U.S. Grant—Let Us Have Peaceful Arbitration." At their foot crouched a big, whimpering British lion and the caption: "Our President Puts His Foot Down, and the British Lion Will Have to Wriggle Out."[69] Grant achieved a historic diplomatic triumph. In September, the Geneva tribunal handed down a judgment that Great Britain was culpable in allowing the *Alabama* and other raiders to be built in British shipyards and owed the United States $15.5 million. The indemnity helped Grant redeem outstanding public debt left from the war and he basked in the immense success of the outcome. "We are quite content with the Geneva Award," Fish informed Elihu Washburne. "It decides that Great Britain was culpable."[70]

Settling the *Alabama* claims is an obscure episode that has receded in history and sounds a trifle dated and musty, of interest only to professional historians. Yet its dramatic importance cannot be overstated, for it showed the value of international arbitration, banished lingering ill will between the United States and Great Britain, and launched a new fraternal relationship of major consequence. As the United States emerged as the world's foremost industrial power, Great Britain served as the premier banker to American railways and factories, powering the country's economic growth at a time when American finance could not have managed the feat alone. Adam Badeau noted that while much credit for the *Alabama* settlement belonged to Fish, Adams, Evarts, and other American diplomats, "Grant was the head; it was for him always to decide. If he had been backward or uncertain, if he had failed in judgment or nerve or sagacity or decision—the achievement would have been impossible. If there were no other measure of his Administration worthy of praise, this one makes it well for America that Grant was President."[71]

///////////////////////

Vindication

I T IS SADLY IRONIC that Grant's presidency became synonymous with corruption, since he himself was impeccably honest. Some found Grant truthful to a fault. "In the White House one day he was busy and a stranger called," a visitor remembered. "The man on duty, knowing that Grant was busy, said to the servant at the door, 'Tell the gentleman that the President is out.'" Grant, overhearing this, said, 'No, don't tell him that. Tell him I am engaged and must be excused. I never lie for myself and do not want anybody to lie for me.'"[1]

The mystery of Grant's presidency is how this upright man tolerated some of the arrant rascals collected around him. Again and again he was stunned by scandals because he could not imagine subordinates guilty of such sleazy behavior. "He thought every man as sincere as himself," said childhood friend Eliza Shaw.[2] This reputation for credulity had clung to him through the rigors of war. "The soul of honor himself," said James Longstreet, "he never suspected others either then or years afterward."[3] Grant was a strange amalgam of wisdom and naïveté about human nature. As he admitted, "I could never bear to think illy of anyone whom I had selected for responsible positions, unless proven guilty."[4]

Grant's record in selecting colleagues was uneven, mixing brilliant and disastrous choices. "He sometimes seemed to know men marvelously well . . . but at other times he was absolutely blind to arts and traits . . . apparent to many lookers on," Badeau observed.[5] Occasionally susceptible to flattery, Grant didn't guard himself with a shell of protective cynicism against venal people. If slow to make friends, once he admitted them into his inner circle, they could perform no wrong in his eyes.

Some of this trust came from a soldierly loyalty to his comrades. "It was a principle with [Grant] never to abandon a comrade 'under fire,'" said West Point classmate James B. Fry, "and a friend in disgrace, as well as a friend in trouble, could depend upon him until Grant himself found him guilty."[6] He stood by people whom he thought unjustly slandered, giving them the benefit of the doubt. "I have made it the rule of my life," he said, "to trust a man long after other people gave him up."[7] This noble trait was bound to be abused by unscrupulous types. "In political life the more bitterly his friends were attacked the more stoutly he clung to them," said his son Fred. "This was at times most unfortunate."[8] Grant reacted defensively when friends were attacked, often retreating into hurt silence, and he never learned to develop a thick rind in the face of such criticism. When he realized he had been duped by valued associates, he was invariably crestfallen. "He was sincere and devoted in his friendships," said Boutwell, "but when he discovered that his confidence had been misplaced, a reconciliation became impossible."[9]

Grant had the misfortune of presiding over America in the corrupt Gilded Age. Syndicates known as "rings" reigned in many areas of society, and newspapers covered their larcenous escapades with relish. The corruption arose from numerous sources: the enormous wartime expansion of government; the unbridled growth of heavy industry; the buccaneering tactics of big business; the rise of ruthless political machines; the protracted rule of the Republican Party; helter-skelter settlement of the West. The railroads represented a festering source of corruption, issuing free passes to Grant and other public figures, who accepted such largesse as legitimate perks of their jobs. With the postwar boom and a universal thirst for riches came a complete breakdown of public and private morality. Grant couldn't inoculate his administration against this epidemic, which infected both parties and every state legislature.

In many ways, Grant should have been a natural convert to civil service reform. From the time he was a boy, he had exhibited a meritocratic streak as he reacted against his father's chronic wire-pulling; as president-elect, he had distanced himself from congressional pressure in assembling his first cabinet. Once sworn in, he was deluged with patronage requests, which consumed the bulk of his correspondence. Such was the daily crush of office seekers that he said he scarcely had time "to read the current news of the day."[10] The wholesale hunt for government jobs submerged him in the minutiae of local politics, forcing him to arbitrate among warring factions. He had to deal with job seekers and their congressional patrons, whose support he needed for legislation. "The real vice of the present system is the patronage of members of Congress," wrote Amos Akerman. "Many of them think that their business here is not to make laws but to make appointments."[11]

With so many appointments based on connections, civil service reform was a contentious issue. One of its foremost proponents was Secretary of the Interior Jacob D. Cox, who favored competitive exams for selected positions. The interior secretary saw Grant as the victim of artful politicians who cajoled him with their "skillful advocacy and impassioned manner."[12] Cox ran afoul of party bosses when he implemented a merit system at Interior; rebuffed demands that political appointees make mandatory party contributions; and resisted lawmakers wishing to meddle with Indian agent appointments. His days were numbered when he disobeyed Grant's orders about a patent dispute on mineral lands that Grant thought involved frauds on both sides. Defending his action, Cox told Grant that as he "only fought fraud with such vigor as I could, I can make no compromise, & if I fail to secure to the fullest extent your approval of my course, I must beg you to relieve me at once."[13] Proud of his integrity, Grant said Cox's blatant insinuation that he was corrupt "cut him severely."[14]

In October 1870, he accepted Cox's resignation. "My views of the necessity of reform in the civil service have brought me more or less into collision with the plans of some of our active political managers," Cox wrote to him, "and my sense of duty has obliged me to oppose some of their methods of action through the Department."[15] In reply, Grant paid tribute to "the zeal and ability" shown by Cox in discharging his duties.[16] Under the surface, he thought Cox the victim of a swollen ego: "The trouble was that General Cox thought the Interior Department was the whole government, and that Cox was the Interior Department."[17] Cox was replaced by Columbus Delano, an Ohio politician who would presumably be more submissive. Subsequently Cox took every opportunity to malign Grant, telling Sumner he had "no confidence in any real purpose of Civil Service Reform on the part of President Grant."[18]

With Cox's resignation and the loss of Ebenezer Hoar, Grant had sacrificed members of the high-minded liberal reform wing of the Republican Party who opposed party bosses, thereby exposing profound new fault lines in the party. It was a watershed moment for Grant, who had to deal with a widening split

common to parties long in power. Writing privately to Cox about his resignation, Congressman James Garfield didn't mince words: "It is a clear case of surrender on the part of the President to the political vermin which infest the
government and keep it in a state of perpetual lousiness."[19]

To contain the damage of Cox's departure, Grant made a concerted push for
civil service reform in his second annual message to Congress in December
1870: "There is no duty which so much embarrasses [the] Executive, and heads
of departments, as that of appointments; nor is there [any such] arduous and
thankless labor imposed on Senators and representatives as that of finding places
for constituents."[20] Heeding his plea, Congress gave him power to impanel the
nation's first Civil Service Commission, headed by George William Curtis, a
New York reformer who had lectured widely on the subject. Born in Rhode Island, Curtis had resided at the utopian community of Brook Farm before becoming a newspaper and magazine editor. Having objected to the departure of
Hoar and Cox, he was a daring choice for Grant. Curtis's board would recommend drastic measures to clean up the civil service, ranging from competitive
exams to an end of forced political payments by civil servants. It was still a novel
idea to hire civil servants based on pure merit in lieu of party affiliation.

Addressing Congress in December 1871, Grant portrayed himself as an advocate of civil service reform, his naysayers notwithstanding. In transmitting a
fifty-page report from Curtis's advisory group, he adopted many rules it recommended. He asked for an extension of the Civil Service Commission, making it
a permanent body that would oversee new civil service exams. Perhaps with an
eye on the upcoming race for president, he sounded like a full-fledged convert to
reform and even elicited praise from Sumner, but Congress refused to back him
up. As *The New York Times* noted, civil service reform had failed "due to a lack
of support from Congress, strong pressure from politicians, and the absence of a
sufficiently mature and vigorous public sentiment on the subject."[21] In the end,
new guidelines implemented by Grant were more honored in the breach than
the observance. Congressmen simply balked at surrendering their most potent
source of power—patronage. As Garfield said, party bosses backing Grant were
"furious against the Civil Service Report, and the indications are that Grant
must back down or offend his defenders."[22]

Grant talked a good game on civil service reform despite a multitude of private reservations. When Joseph Medill of the *Chicago Tribune* attempted to resign from the advisory board, Grant refused to heed his request: "It is my

intention that Civil Service reform shall have a fair trial. The great defect in the past custom is that Executive patronage had come to be regarded as the property of individuals of the party in power."[23] On April 11, 1872, Curtis submitted a second report to Grant, stressing that political activity shouldn't factor into hiring government workers. Within a week, Grant promulgated an executive order adopting civil service regulations that reflected Curtis's views. No longer would government workers be required to fork over payments to political parties to retain their jobs. "Political assessments . . . have been forbidden within the various Departments . . . honesty and efficiency, not political activity, will determine the tenure of office," wrote Grant, echoing language long cherished by Curtis.[24] Later in the year, when awarding an honorary doctorate to Grant, Harvard president Charles W. Eliot singled out "reforming the civil service" as one reason behind the honor.[25] Grant differed from most proponents of civil service reform in believing that competitive exams should be administered *after* hiring, not before, as a better way to test the fitness of workers for their jobs.

Grant's reforms never worked out as planned, and he blamed the fact that they were neither binding nor respected by Congress. In future years, he bared his true feelings about civil service reforms, even debunking them as "humbug."[26] Patronage might be the bane of a president's life, but he came to think of it as a necessary evil in a democratic system: "You cannot call it corruption—it is a condition of our representative form of government—and yet if you read the newspapers, and hear the stories of the reformers, you will be told that any asking for place is corruption."[27] Presidents who wanted government to proceed smoothly, he believed, had to be able to win over congressmen and did so by complying with their patronage demands.

Thus, while Grant paid lip service to reform and became the first president to urge creation of a professional civil service, he ended up willy-nilly a captive of the spoils system. His detractors sensed that his heart wasn't really in reform and that he privately questioned their methods. For reformers, Grant came to embody the system they despised. Whatever his inward dismay at the patronage mess, he learned to manipulate the levers at his disposal to get things accomplished on Capitol Hill. After personal betrayals suffered over the Santo Domingo treaty, he decided to reward loyalty above ideology and came to view reformers as two-faced troublemakers while party bosses, however corrupt, at least stuck to their word. By March 1873, as appointments were made that violated the spirit of new civil service regulations, George William Curtis handed in his resignation and Grant accepted it. Grant had made a genuine effort at civil service reform and deserves credit as the first president to do so, but he hadn't produced lasting change. Only with the 1883 Pendleton Act would competitive exams be required to fill a portion of federal jobs.

The ideals behind Grant's presidency were often enlightened, even if the backroom tactics sometimes seemed ignoble. He had to thrust himself into the middle of byzantine political maneuvering, becoming the true son of his father and accepting the spoils system for the sake of party unity. Grant has suffered from a double standard in the eyes of historians. When Lincoln employed patronage for political ends, which he did extensively, they have praised him as a master politician; when Grant catered to the same spoilsmen, they have denigrated him as a corrupt opportunist.

Part of Grant's need to placate party bosses was that he presided over government in the heyday of senatorial power. Senators were still elected by state legislatures controlled by party machines and business interests. The new political machines, many concentrated in northern cities, made politics a lucrative business for their acolytes. Meanwhile, safely entrenched in their posts, senators ruled Washington like feudal barons, jealously guarding their turf from presidential interference. Not having to face voters for reelection, they stood as formidable barriers to any progressive legislation.

During Grant's presidency, the Radical Republicans who dominated the Senate under Lincoln and Johnson gave way to Stalwart Republicans, men of a different stripe. Such power brokers as Roscoe Conkling of New York, Oliver Morton of Indiana, Zachariah Chandler of Michigan, and Simon Cameron of Pennsylvania were motivated less by ideology than amassing power. "I fear that such advisors as Chandler, Cameron and Conkling are too influential with Grant," Rutherford B. Hayes complained in May 1871. "They are not safe counselors."[28] Their ascent reflected the Republican Party's gradual metamorphosis from the party of abolition to a more business-oriented one. Once the maverick party of outsiders, the Republicans had evolved into the comfortable political establishment, with all the corruption that goes with the territory. Grant cooperated with the Stalwart Republicans not only because they supported him but because they shared his fundamental view of the Democratic Party as battling against southern Republicans and trying to reverse the outcome of the war, fostering the need for a solidly Republican North. Many of the party bosses boasted fine records on Reconstruction.

Of all the Stalwarts with whom Grant forged an alliance, perhaps the most improbable was Roscoe Conkling, a foe of civil service reform. Born in Albany, Conkling had trained as a lawyer and served as mayor of Utica before being elected to the House in 1858 and the Senate in 1867. Grant made peace with Conkling at a time when New York's large block of electoral votes was critical to winning national elections. Tall and handsome with a theatrical air, Conkling was a strutting peacock with foppish curls. He wore white flannel trousers and yellow vests and strolled about with his nose in the air, betraying a dandified sense of his own grandeur. An early fitness buff, he liked to ride and box and slug a punching bag drooping from his office ceiling. His female conquests were so numerous that John Hay derided him as "a patriot of the flesh-pots."[29] Conkling was an eloquent orator who could be charming with friends, but he was a relentless enemy when crossed. Master of numerous patronage jobs, he laughed at morality as something that bound lesser mortals.

Despite his superior manner, Conkling's political acumen made him a useful mentor for Grant, who detected virtues in Conkling that escaped others, regarding him "as the greatest mind . . . that has been in public life since the beginning of the government."[30] Hamilton Fish understood the attraction, saying Conkling's advice to Grant was always smart, if distinctly partisan.[31] The journalist John Russell Young noted how Conkling and Grant grew strangely enamored of each other: "For Conkling Grant has a romantic affection, and this was returned by Conkling in a manner almost womanly, which was curious considering his imperious, high-toned, impetuous, yet noble character."[32] Grant's son Jesse echoed this assessment: "Conkling and my father loved each other. They were devoted; and Conkling's devotion was quite unselfish."[33] Even Julia Grant shared her husband's fawning admiration for Conkling, once urging his selection as chief justice because she thought his fair curls would look stunning when set off against black judicial robes.[34]

Conkling typified Stalwart Republican contradictions in the 1870s. Though a quintessential party boss, he had been a vocal abolitionist, a supporter of civil rights, and a draftsman of the Fourteenth Amendment who saw eye-to-eye with Grant on Reconstruction. By no accident Frederick Douglass alluded to Conkling as a great senator and would eulogize him at a memorial service after his death. Conkling fully reciprocated Grant's admiration for him, telling a friend in August 1871: "He has made a better President than you and I, when we voted for him, had any right to expect . . . He has given the country the best practical administration, in many respects, [that] we have had for a quarter of a century and people know it."[35]

The biggest favor Grant bestowed upon Conkling was control of the New York Custom House, which generated a huge chunk of customs revenues, its fifteen hundred jobs making it the richest fountain of patronage in the federal system. The immense sums that flowed through its corridors could be siphoned off by crooked officials. Power over the custom house made any politician kingpin of New York's machine politics and Conkling was determined to seize that power.

On July 1, 1870, Grant nominated Thomas Murphy as New York customs collector. He was a genial Irishman and lover of horse flesh whom Grant had befriended in Long Branch, but he had a reputation as a shady wartime contractor. When New York senator Reuben Fenton contested the nomination, Conkling spotted an opportunity to ingratiate himself with Grant by throwing his support to Murphy. A massive power struggle ensued. *The New York Times* described Murphy's nomination as "the sensation of the Capitol" and reported that "Senator Fenton and his friends seem to accept it as a direct blow at them."[36] Cynical about this intramural battle of spoilsmen, the paper concluded: "On both sides the contest at Washington has been conducted with[out] the slightest possible reference to the wishes and welfare of this City, or even the welfare of the Republican party. The whole affair has narrowed down to a struggle for . . . advantage between the two New York Senators."[37]

Politics was played as an unforgiving blood sport in the Gilded Age and Conkling resorted to character assassination. When the Senate went into executive session to ponder Murphy's nomination, Fenton dug up newspaper clippings that chronicled his sordid business adventures. Not to be outdone, Conkling secretly unearthed a startling discovery: Fenton, as a youth, had stolen $12,000 that he was supposed to carry from New York to Albany. He had pretended to be robbed and stashed the money in his bedclothes. In rising to defend Murphy, Conkling said, "It is true that Thomas Murphy is a mechanic, a hatter by trade; that he worked at his trade in Albany supporting an aged father and mother and a crippled brother. And while he was thus engaged there was another who visited Albany and played a very different role."[38] At this point, Conkling withdrew with a flourish the incriminating court documents from his pocket and Fenton, understanding their meaning, slumped over at his desk in defeat.

With that gesture, the Murphy nomination won handily. In reviewing the imbroglio, *The Nation* credited the "skill and ferocity" with which Conkling had joined the fray but condemned Tom Murphy as "a hack politician, unfit for any trust."[39]

With Murphy's appointment, Grant dealt a crushing blow to the Fenton forces and installed Roscoe Conkling as the supreme power in New York. The subsequent messages Murphy received from the White House telegraphed mixed signals. Babcock advised Murphy that he had a batch of letters asking for administration support to obtain jobs in the New York Custom House: "I do not wish to embarrass you . . . and I have therefore given [you] no such letters, nor shall I do so."[40] This sounded scrupulously honest. But Horace Porter sent a far more ambiguous message, stating that "my only desire is to see you distribute the patronage of your office as to render the most efficient service to the country and the cause of the Administration"—which sounded unashamedly political.[41] In November, Grant met with Murphy and applauded "his efforts to secure the success of the Republican ticket in the late campaign in New York," reported the *New York Tribune.*[42]

Shadowed by corruption charges, Murphy staffed the New York Custom House with Republican operatives beholden to Conkling. After the November 1871 elections, he left office against a backdrop of scandal. Showing a pattern he later repeated, Grant defended Murphy until the critical chorus became insupportable. In accepting his resignation, Grant praised the "efficiency, honesty and zeal" with which he had fulfilled his duties.[43] Seeking a replacement, Grant turned to another henchman of Conkling's, Chester Arthur, who was more efficient than Murphy and a capable lawyer, launching the career of a future president. Seated on his new patronage throne, Arthur would make $50,000 a year, a salary equal to the president's. Increasingly disgruntled with Grant, Horace Greeley snorted that the new collector of customs was "Tom Murphy under another name."[44]

Appointing Arthur didn't silence the hubbub over the New York Custom House, and Garfield denounced Stalwarts supporting Grant as "superserviceable lackeys that sneeze whenever their master takes snuff."[45] Amid a growing furor, congressional investigators launched a probe of New York's port, which Republicans suspected was politically motivated to sway the 1872 elections. One villain investigated was George K. Leet, formerly on Grant's wartime staff, whose firm enjoyed the custom house monopoly on warehousing imported goods. Shocked by committee disclosures, Grant ordered his treasury secretary and attorney general to prosecute "all persons in New York, who have testified that they gave bribes to Govt Officials," Fish noted in his diary.[46] Despite this, the hearings damaged Grant as Greeley testified that approximately a hundred Fenton men were cashiered to make room for Conkling minions. The patronage war seemed to mock Grant's modest pretensions to being a civil service reformer and the press gleefully ballyhooed his troubles. "The New York *World* and the New York *Tribune* have entered into a partnership for the throwing of dirt at Grant," George Templeton Strong noted. "They merely disgust and alienate the public."[47]

In the lengthy roll of corruption cases, perhaps the most distressing for Grant centered on Ely Parker, whom he had appointed as commissioner of Indian affairs to extirpate corruption among Indian agents. Instead, Parker ended up being trailed by accusations of fraud. Grant's Indian advisory board, headed by reformer William Welsh, accused him of failing to open Indian contracts to competitive bidding; in response, Parker cited emergency conditions that warranted this approach. Welsh's charges seem to have been part of a racially inspired vendetta. As a beef contractor recalled, Welsh spoke of Parker as "the representative of a race only one generation from barbarism, and he did not think that he should be expected to be able to withstand the inducements of parties who were his superiors in matters of business."[48] In February 1871, a House investigating committee uncovered "irregularities, neglect, and incompetency . . . in the Indian Department," but exonerated Parker of wrongdoing.[49] Nevertheless, hurt by the unfair charges, Parker submitted his resignation and on July 13, 1871, Grant accepted it with regret: "Accepting it severs official relations which have existed between us for eight consecutive years, without cause of complaint as to your entire fitness for either of the important places which you have had during that time."[50]

While Parker may have exhibited bad judgment, his behavior had been far from egregious and he had admitted to gaffes from inexperience. Welsh believed Grant allowed personal fondness and abiding loyalty to cloud his judgment. "Parker was . . . an infatuation heightened by a sentiment in favor of an Indian civilizing his brethren," he told Cox.[51] A few years later, Welsh published an open letter to Grant that portrayed him as irredeemably blinded by his love for friends: "Every suggestion I ever made to you was promptly responded to, save only the investigation of frauds allowed by your appointees. Even this lamentable trait I believe springs from a distorted virtue. Your protection of General Parker . . . seems wholly unaccountable, except on the hypothesis that love in you is blind."[52]

Despite Grant's wish to bring probity to Indian affairs, the Indian Ring, with its legion of swindling agents, went on fleecing its clients, and Grant continued to express uncommon sympathy for the victims' plight. "I don't like riding over and shooting these poor savages; I want to conciliate them and make them peaceful citizens," he told a reporter.[53] When one reformer asked if he planned to modify his Indian policy, Grant replied, "I do not believe our Creator ever placed different races of men on this earth with the view of having the stronger exert all his energies in exterminating the weaker."[54]

From the start, Parker had endorsed Grant's policy of dealing with Indian tribes humanely, guiding the Indian Bureau "with a view to the maintenance of peace, and the avoidance of expensive and horrible Indian wars."[55] He believed the days of unlimited Indian freedom were over and that roving bands of Plains Indians must be sequestered on reservations. Lobbied by railroads, Congress revoked the treaty system that regarded these areas as independent states, with no more treaties signed after 1871. Along with Grant, Parker had worked to incorporate Indian tribes into the United States as partially self-governing territories, but many tribes resisted the imposition of any outside form of government.

In pursuing peace with Native Americans, Grant was trying to square the circle. It was hard to be just to the Indians and protect railroads and white settlers at the same time. As a military man, he didn't wish to constrain the style of his commanders, but some of them dealt with Indian incursions in a bloodthirsty manner. In the end, Grant had to show the velvet glove and iron fist at once. Issuing instructions to General Schofield in 1872, for instance, Grant warned that "Indian hostilities should be avoided in the future," giving way to "a policy to civilize and elevate" the Indians. On the other hand, "Indians who will not put themselves under the restraints required will have to be forced, even to the extent of making war upon them, to submit to measures that will insure security to the white settlers of the Territories."[56]

In the last analysis, land speculators and railroad companies, in cahoots with their congressional allies, almost guaranteed that punitive policies would supersede Grant's humane intentions. As Indian commissioner Samuel Tappan told Grant, these powerful forces "rush blindly and madly on, evidently intent upon robbing the Indian of every inch of his land, and forcing the last of his race into the grave by the cowardly and bloody hand of betrayal and massacre."[57] In meeting with Red Cloud, Red Dog, and other Oglala Sioux chieftains in Washington in May 1872, Grant evoked the burgeoning American population, the westward tidal flow of immigrants, and the demise of Indian hunting culture as unstoppable forces: "The time must come when, with the great growth of population here, the game will be gone, and your people will then have to resort to other means of support; and while there is time we would like to teach you new modes of living that will secure you in the future and be a safe means of livelihood."[58] Grant promised to send the Oglala Sioux large herds of sheep and cattle for raising stock and to build schools that would teach them English. For the Indians, however, this didn't mean salvation so much as the wanton destruction of their traditional culture.

Grant had a complicated relationship with the American West, one that foreshadowed the competing impulses of future federal land management. He handed over millions of acres to settlers and miners and promoted the growth of railroads. At the same time, sensitive to scenic beauty, he established Yellowstone as the first national park on March 1, 1872. President Lincoln had signed a bill in 1864 that permitted California to preserve the Yosemite Valley and the giant sequoias of the Mariposa Grove, but it was Grant who initiated the modern national park system.

AFTER A TUMULTUOUS first term in office, Grant occasionally dreamed of returning to his farm in St. Louis. "I was not anxious to be President a second term," he confided to a reporter, "but I consented to receive the nomination simply because I thought that was the best way of discovering whether my countrymen . . . really believed all that was alleged against my administration and against myself personally."[59] While Grant said memorably that he "probably had the least desire for [the office] of anyone who ever held it," the habit of power, perhaps imperceptibly, had acquired an inescapable hold over him.[60] As Adam Badeau observed drily, "After he had been long in power he was not insensible to the sweets of possession, and was decidedly averse to relinquishing what he had enjoyed."[61] Like most presidents, he yearned for affirmation and a general vote of confidence from the electorate.

Such was Grant's personal popularity—his wartime prestige stood quite apart from his administration's record—that his renomination by Republicans was a foregone conclusion. Yet a growing number of disaffected party members questioned whether he could be reelected. In March 1871, the nucleus of a breakaway party met in Cincinnati, led by Jacob Cox, Grant's disgruntled former interior secretary, and one hundred Republicans signed its declaration of principles. One ringleader was Senator Carl Schurz of Missouri, who predicted that "the superstition that Grant is *the* necessary man is rapidly giving way."[62] By September, Schurz clamored openly for a new Liberal Republican Party and espoused a general amnesty for former Confederates. He inveighed against "Negro supremacy" and referred to Reconstruction as "the horror, the nightmare, of the Southern people."[63]

The new movement represented a curious blend of progressive and reactionary impulses, all trotted out under the rubric of reform. These dissenting Republicans recoiled at the scandals that tarnished Grant's first term—what newspapers had now christened "Grantism"—and the advent of political bosses. They favored civil service reform, sound money, low tariffs, and states' rights. Led by Brahmins, who felt threatened by urban machines and party bosses who cooperated with immigrants and laborers, the movement had a decidedly elitist tinge. Associating Reconstruction with political corruption and shabby government, these "reformers" espoused the withdrawal of federal troops from the South and railed against "bayonet rule." Many identified with the white southern elite. To understand Grant's position it is worth stressing that it was Liberal Republicans— self-righteous, good-government folks—not conservative businessmen and Stalwart Party bosses who decided that black citizens were suddenly expendable.

The new party included such presidential hopefuls as Charles Francis Adams Sr. of Massachusetts and Senator Lyman Trumbull of Illinois, who caustically observed of Grant, "The people are tired of a man who has not an idea above a horse or a cigar."[64] It boasted a smattering of abolitionists, including Theodore Tilton and Salmon P. Chase. There was also a healthy representation of those who nursed personal grievances against Grant, including Sumner, Motley, and Fenton. Then came old journalistic nemeses such as Whitelaw Reid, who penned the damning description of Shiloh, and Murat Halstead, who blasted Grant for wartime drinking. Many blue bloods still patronized Grant as a commoner with western roots who lacked their cosmopolitan touch.

On May 1, 1872, the Liberal Republican convention met in Cincinnati. In his keynote speech, Schurz asserted they would no longer "permit themselves to be driven like a flock of sheep."[65] The unruly gathering went through six ballots before choosing *New York Tribune* editor Horace Greeley as their presidential candidate and Missouri governor B. Gratz Brown as his running mate. Greeley's selection was greeted with jeers and laughter. Despite the abolitionist credentials of many delegates, the convention endorsed "home rule" in the South under the old white elite, and faulted the Ku Klux Klan Act as an unwarranted federal intrusion upon state liberties. Greeley intended to make Grant's Reconstruction policy the centerpiece of his campaign "in the confident trust that the masses of our countrymen, North and South, are eager to clasp hands across the bloody chasm which has too long divided them."[66]

Grant was incensed at the apostasy of old friends. In the Cincinnati convention, he discerned mischief perpetrated by Democrats wishing to divide Republicans. When the time came, he thought the Democratic convention would refuse to adopt Greeley as their candidate as well, forcing him out of the race. Many onlookers thought Greeley would march the new party straight off a cliff. "I don't know whether you are aware what a conceited, ignorant, half-cracked, obstinate old creature he is," E. L. Godkin of *The Nation* told Schurz. Schurz needed no reminding. He was astounded by the turn to Greeley, who opposed free trade and hard money and was lukewarm toward civil service reform. Schurz fruitlessly prodded Greeley to withdraw, saying his nomination was simply "a successful piece of political hucksterism."[67] Some people bolted the new party and returned to Grant. "That Grant is an Ass," remarked an Ohio Liberal, "no man can deny, but better an Ass than a mischievous Idiot."[68]

A couple of years earlier, Grant had judged Greeley an "honest, firm, untiring supporter of the republican party."[69] By 1872 he had settled into private contempt for him, believing he had tried to foist disreputable appointments upon him. He even thought Greeley suffered from a "mental disease" that led him to propose unsuitable characters for office.[70] "Mr. Greeley is simply a disappointed man at not being estimated by others at the same value he places upon himself," Grant wrote to Henry Wilson. "He is a genius without common sense. He attaches to himself, and reposes confidence only, in the fawning, deceitful and dishonest men of the party."[71] Grant wasn't alone in detecting something faintly ludicrous about the new nominee. Thomas Nast made a cottage industry out of caricaturing the mercurial editor, while one newspaper taunted him as a "ridiculous political mouse."[72]

Originally from New Hampshire, Greeley had been a printer's apprentice in

Vermont before moving to New York and commencing his journalistic career. Even before Thomas Nast set pen to paper, Greeley resembled a cartoon with his round face, wire-rimmed spectacles, ghostly pallor, and faint wisps of white hair straggling across a bald pate. With a shambling walk, he was slovenly in dress and partial to white dusters. A prophet of lost causes, he had identified himself with pet theories ranging from profit sharing to vegetarianism, temperance to utopian socialism. Even ardent admirers could find Greeley's quixotic crusades infuriating. One of the original celebrity editors in American journalism, he showed a genius for self-promotion, as when he wrote, "Go West, young man." Though based in New York, his newspaper boasted the largest circulation in the nation, making Greeley a force to be reckoned. "Meek as he looks," commented Harriet Beecher Stowe, "no man living is readier with a strong sharp answer."[73]

Greeley had been admirably consistent in fighting slavery. But during the war he had been a volatile figure, now for war, now for peace, driving Lincoln to distraction. "He is the most vacillating man in the country, or was during the war," said Andrew Johnson.[74] Greeley now executed a startling reversal away from African Americans. From being a wholehearted abolitionist, he became an exponent of southern amnesty who opposed the Ku Klux Klan law. "Not as much violence occurs in Texas as in New York City," he assured an Arkansas paper in 1871. "There are more desperadoes in that city than in Texas, and it is harder work to manage them."[75] He typified northern Republicans who experienced moral fatigue on race issues and expressed newfound sympathy with southern whites, assailing black legislators in South Carolina as a "mass of ignorance and barbarism."[76] He resorted to racial stereotypes about freed people, reproving them as "an easy, worthless race" who took "no thought for the morrow."[77] For this reason abolitionist Wendell Phillips declared in disgust, "Liberal Republicanism is nothing but Ku-Klux-Klanism disguised," and William Lloyd Garrison hotly disavowed the movement.[78]

After Greeley was chosen as the Liberal Republican standard-bearer, Charles Sumner renewed his campaign against Grant. On May 31, 1872, he delivered a lengthy Senate speech entitled *Republicanism vs. Grantism*, in which Grant was puffed up into a modern Caesar. In overheated language, he called Grant's promotion of the Santo Domingo treaty "more unconstitutional and more illegal than anything alleged against Andrew Johnson on his impeachment."[79] He said the "august trust" of the presidency had been demeaned by nepotism, "fast horses, and sea-side loiterings," and patronage to reward friends. He stirred up old charges that Grant had accepted houses and other gifts from people who wound up in his cabinet. In conclusion, Sumner said mockingly that Grant was "first in war," but also "first in nepotism, first in gift-taking repaid by official patronage, first in presidential pretensions, and first in quarrel with his countrymen."[80] Sumner lived another two years, but his desertion of the Republican Party and endorsement of Greeley exiled him to the political wilderness.

In the weeks before the Republican convention in Philadelphia in early June, Grant remained passive, doing nothing to further his nomination, but he didn't need to fret about the outcome, which would amount to an elaborate coronation. Although Liberal Republicans had fled, the Philadelphia convention showed Grant with a firm grip on those remaining. Former congressman Shelby M. Cullom of Illinois placed Grant's name in nomination. The moment he uttered it, a huge, appreciative roar reverberated through the hall. From a hidden ceiling nook descended a giant portrait of Grant, transfixing the thousands assembled and kindling a wild tumult of enthusiasm. "The recent vindictive attacks on General Grant have created a strong reaction in his favor," wrote Rutherford B. Hayes, "which accounts for the unexpected feeling in his behalf, I mean the unlooked-for enthusiasm."[81] Unanimously nominated, Grant received the votes of every state and territory, while the party platform made no apologies for his presidency. "This glorious record of the past is the party's best pledge for the future," it proclaimed.[82]

The only suspense in Philadelphia concerned the vice presidential nominee. Schuyler Colfax had been tainted by accepting stock in the Crédit Mobilier scandal, which had tarred many politicians, and he declined reelection. Since delegates worried about the impact of Sumner's scathing words on Massachusetts voters, they opted for Senator Henry Wilson of Massachusetts, a Radical Republican and supporter of Reconstruction. An orphan trained as a shoemaker, he ended up operating a shoe factory, acquiring the nickname of the "Natick Cobbler." To reporters Grant sounded diplomatic about the merits of both men: "Personally I have a great affection for both Wilson and Colfax. Mr. Colfax . . . has been a firm friend, and we have always entertained the most affectionate relations toward one another."[83] Since Colfax came from Indiana, Grant thought a ticket with Wilson would provide more geographic balance.

In early July, Democrats gathered in Baltimore knowing they had to join forces with Liberal Republicans to beat Grant. With their visceral dislike of the president, they followed the lead of Liberal Republicans, adopting their platform verbatim and nominating Greeley for president and Brown for vice president. Greeley was famous for his withering slurs against Democrats, having once said that while not all Democrats were horse thieves, all horse thieves were Democrats. He had denounced them as "traitors, slave-whippers, drunkards and lecherous beasts."[84] So in nominating Greeley, the convention had to take refuge in an awkward gallows humor. "If the Baltimore convention puts Greeley in our hymn book," said one delegate, "we will sing him through if it kills us."[85] Even Democratic National Chairman August Belmont declared Greeley's selection "one of those stupendous mistakes which it is difficult even to comprehend," although he urged the party faithful to rally around him.[86] Ex-senator James R. Doolittle of Wisconsin, who chaired the convention, gave the game away when he said the true aim of the novel fusion ticket was the "overthrow of Negro supremacy"—the anti-Reconstruction agenda, however thinly masked by reform rhetoric.[87] Most Republicans stood aghast at the unsavory bargain struck in Baltimore. "It does not seem possible that such an unholy and corrupt alliance could possibly succeed," remarked Elihu Washburne.[88] Still, the electoral math showed that if Greeley could siphon off a significant fraction of Republican votes, added to unanimous Democratic support, he might indeed prevail.

For Grant, the election was about more than personal vindication. He had long warned that a Democratic victory in 1872 would overturn the result of the Civil War, degrading the Thirteenth, Fourteenth, and Fifteenth Amendments into "dead letters."[89] So deeply did he believe this that he stated "it would have been better never to have made a sacrifice of blood and treasure to save the Union than to have the democratic party come in power now and sacrifice by the ballot what the bayonet seemed to have accomplished."[90] Grant had striven to protect the black community, met regularly with black leaders, and given them unprecedented White House access, making global abolitionism an explicit aim of American foreign policy. In his annual message of December 1871, he applauded emancipation efforts in Brazil, deplored ongoing bondage in Cuba and Puerto Rico, and asked Congress for legislation to forbid Americans from "holding, owning, or dealing in slaves, or being interested in slave property in foreign lands"—a practice that hadn't ceased with emancipation at home.[91]

Black leaders echoed Grant's view that the merger of Liberal Republicans and Democrats threatened their welfare. Their views were vitally important because some southern states possessed enormous black populations that, coupled with Republican votes in the North, could easily determine the electoral outcome. Philip A. Bell told the black readership of his San Francisco newspaper, the *Elevator,* that Liberal Republicans were "the same men, who ten years ago, flung the lash at the slave markets of the South, they are the men who refused sitting in a street car, alongside with a colored man, and who now, when aware of your growing political importance, pretend to be your friends and claim your votes."[92] For the black community, Grant's unstinting allegiance to the Fifteenth Amendment made him the hands-down favorite. *"Grant secured to us the privilege* of exercising that franchise," a black Mississippian told Senator Adelbert Ames.[93] In April, a black convention in New Orleans voted two-to-one to support Grant. That same month, while entertaining a delegation of black church leaders, Grant told them "that no one except themselves could be more gratified than he was that four millions of persons who had been held in bondage and disposed of as chattels were now free to think for themselves and worship God as they thought proper, and that civil rights for all were fast becoming recognized throughout the land."[94] Small wonder that civil rights leader George T. Downing reaffirmed that when it came to respecting black rights, "we have not had Grant's equal in the Presidential chair."[95]

Perhaps the most remarkable tribute to Grant came in a letter that September from leaders of the Convention of Colored Citizens of New England. It began: "Allow us to offer you a tribute of grateful hearts." It praised his wartime service for helping to free "four millions of our race"; for making the Emancipation Proclamation a reality; for suppressing "the midnight murderous bands" who had perpetrated atrocities against southern blacks; and "for appointing men of our color Ministers Plenipotentiary, thus establishing the fact of your practical recognition of the equality of all men before the law."[96]

The 1872 presidential race provoked deep cleavages among abolitionists. When Sumner published an open letter to black voters, summoning them to abandon Grant, many erstwhile allies were speechless. "If the Devil himself were at the helm of the ship of state," the abolitionist and women's rights activist Lydia Maria Child responded, "my conscience would not allow me to aid in removing him to make room for the Democratic party."[97] She believed that when Liberal Republicans endorsed "state sovereignty," it meant "when the Ku Klux renew their plans to exterminate Republicans, white and black, they shall be dealt with by Southern civil authorities—that is, by judges and jurors who are themselves members of the Ku Klux associations."[98] William Lloyd Garrison agreed that "home rule" meant "a blow aimed at the exercise of power entrusted to the President by Congress for the . . . protection of the Southern freedmen and loyalists against robbery, assassinations, and lynch-law barbarities."[99] Wendell Phillips exhorted black voters in the South: "Vote, every one of you, for Grant . . . If Greeley is elected, arm, concentrate, conceal your property, but organize for defense. You will need it soon."[100] Gerrit Smith invoked Grant's thousands of anti-Klan indictments and warned that "the spirit of Kukluxism will not die out so long as the Democratic Party exists to sympathize with that spirit."[101] In the end, more than three-quarters of abolitionists closed ranks behind Grant.[102]

By far the most important black endorsement came from Frederick Douglass, who actively campaigned for the president. He was dismayed by the betrayal of his hero, Charles Sumner, in supporting Greeley and asked him not to "give up the almost dumb millions to whom you have been mind and voice during a quarter of a century."[103] For Douglass, the black alliance with the Republican Party remained an inviolable trust. "If as a class we are slighted by the Republican party," he noted, "we are as a class murdered by the Democratic party."[104] He swore he would rather blow his brains out than destroy the Republican Party.

For Douglass, Grant was the general who had effected with the sword Lincoln's emancipation policy, then extended those gains by backing the Fifteenth Amendment. "To Grant more than any other man the Negro owes his enfranchisement," Douglass stated.[105] Grant enjoyed a special niche in his pantheon, the assorted blemishes in his administration paling before his anti-Klan crusade in which "thousands have openly acknowledged the crimes charged . . . and peace had come to many places as never before. The scourging and slaughter of our people have so far ceased."[106] For readers, Douglass rattled off the unprecedented number of blacks Grant had appointed as ambassadors, customs collectors, internal revenue agents, postmasters, and clerks. Grant had also consistently welcomed him at the White House. "I have called upon him often . . . and have always found him to be easily accessible, gentlemanly, and cordial."[107]

Despite his unflagging advocacy for black rights, Grant never forgot the spirit of Appomattox and his desire for harmony between North and South. In May 1872, he signed legislation that extended amnesty and a restoration of rights to all former Confederates, except for a few hundred ex–rebel officers. He was willing to forgive any political offense as long as people were left free "to vote, speak & act" despite their "views, color or nativity."[108] He continued his relationship with the onetime Confederate partisan John Singleton Mosby, the

"Gray Ghost" who had mercilessly harassed his troops in northern Virginia. After Appomattox, Grant insisted upon extending the same generous surrender terms to Mosby as to Lee. Mosby returned the favor by outlining a southern strategy for Grant that would help him carry Virginia in 1872, and the two became fast friends during Grant's second term when Mosby turned into a frequent dinner guest at the White House.

In the nineteenth century, it was still thought unseemly for a presidential candidate to campaign, and Grant gladly stayed on the sidelines. In justifying his decision to Roscoe Conkling, Grant noted that, in recent memory, only Stephen A. Douglas and Horatio Seymour had violated this custom and "both of them were public speakers, and both were beaten. I am no speaker and don't want to be beaten."[109] Second terms had become a rarity, nobody having managed two full terms since Andrew Jackson. As Grant sat out the campaign, he repaired to Long Branch and journeyed periodically to Washington for cabinet meetings, often making the trip in a regular passenger train, where he smoked cigars and conversed with ordinary people.

Despite his seeming detachment from the race, Grant possessed a finely honed political sense and an excellent grasp of state-by-state politics. When Henry Wilson told Grant's friend George Childs that his ticket with Grant would likely be defeated, Childs conveyed this forecast to Grant. "The general said nothing, but sent for a map of the United States," recalled Childs. "He laid the map on the table, went over it with a pencil, and said, 'We will carry this State, that State, and that State' . . . When the election came, the result was that Grant carried every State that he said he would."[110] Hamilton Fish confirmed his uncanny predictive powers: "I never met anyone who formed, in advance, better estimates of elections that were about to take place than General Grant."[111] Buoyed by this confidence, Grant was relaxed, even a bit cocky, as the campaign progressed. "There has been no time from the Baltimore Convention to this when I have felt the least anxiety," Grant insisted in September.[112] When one politician visited him in early October, he found Grant "just as easy as tho' he were driving horses on a smooth road with a good cigar in his mouth."[113]

Grant was a formidable incumbent if only because his foe was so lackluster. Greeley campaigned from the back of a train, delivering scores of speeches and previewing the whistle-stop style that later marked presidential campaigns. His campaign stumbled from the start and never found a secure footing. He was kept busy explaining his history of derogatory statements about Democrats. "I never said all Democrats were saloon keepers," he protested. "What I said was that all saloon keepers were Democrats."[114] The more Greeley talked, the lower he sagged in public esteem. "Greeley's foolish speeches must surely weaken him," wrote Rutherford B. Hayes, "and destroy what chances he had."[115] Greeley was a ready target for ridicule. Declaring open season on his candidacy, Thomas Nast drew Greeley scaling an enormous monument, "The Whited Sepulchre," with the slogan "This is a white man's government" scrawled across it.[116] The hapless Greeley was subjected to such a personal pounding that he afterward sighed, "I hardly knew whether I was running for President or the Penitentiary."[117]

Grant projected a different image from the sturdy, independent Grant who had captured national attention in 1868. With less of a halo around his head, he was now a power broker chummy with influential barons, ankle-deep in patronage and deal making. As political machines lined up behind him, his sophisticated campaign included a "correspondent's association" that supplied newspapers across the country with favorable editorials. Telegrams endorsing Grant were cranked out by Capitol Hill Republicans to constituents back home. Business interests applauded Grant's stewardship of the country, his preference for low debt, high tariffs, and sound money. The Wall Street financier Henry Clews explained why he banged the drum for Grant: "Because I believed the sacredness of contracts, the stability of wealth, the success of business enterprise, and the prosperity of the whole country depended on the election of Grant for President."[118] Reflecting Grant's appeal to business leaders, Jay Cooke funneled more money into Grant's campaign coffers than anybody else. With these new magnates so influential, the Republican Party was now a house divided, and Wendell Phillips complained that oligarchs and monopolists meant the party made "the rich richer, and the poor poorer, and turns a republic into an aristocracy of capital."[119]

However beholden to business interests, Grant knew the touchstone issue for the party remained Reconstruction. Even if wrapped in gauzy reform rhetoric, Greeley's speeches dwelled on the damage Grant had done in the South and the need to restore "home rule" in the former Confederacy. For this reason, Grant predicted, "I do not think [Greeley] will carry a single Northern State," although he thought his opponent might pick up southern and border states.[120] When it came to Reconstruction, Grant was not the tool of moguls, but the champion of oppressed blacks, leading Henry Ward Beecher to proclaim there "had never been a President more sensitive to the wants of the people."[121] Despite conspicuous blunders in his first term, notably cronyism and the misbegotten Santo Domingo treaty, Grant had chalked up significant triumphs in suppressing the Klan, reducing debt, trying to clean up Indian trading posts, experimenting with civil service reform, and settling the *Alabama* claims peacefully. He had appointed a prodigious number of blacks, Jews, Native Americans, and women and delivered on his promise to give the country peace and prosperity.

Like many adversaries in Grant's past, Greeley supporters resuscitated old drinking rumors, which haunted the president even after the reality had largely vanished. The abolitionist Anna Dickinson claimed Grant had a "greater fondness for the smoke of a cigar and the aroma of a wine glass" than for running the country.[122] So many New York newspapers harped on Grant's putative drinking that George Templeton Strong erupted in indignation: "If it be true that a beastly drunkard, without a sense of decency, can successfully conduct great campaigns, can win great battles, and can raise himself from insignificance to be a lieutenant-general and President, what is the use of all this fuss about sobriety?"[123] That Grant had largely been sober for four years testifies to his remarkable willpower and his wife's vigilance and constant presence. When a southern correspondent asked Fish about Grant's drinking, he replied that he had been with Grant at all hours but had never seen him influenced by liquor; any insinuations to the contrary were "utterly and wantonly false."[124]

Grant was the first president to confront the feminist movement as a viable political force. The same fervor for equality that generated abolitionism had spurred on feminists, who created the National Woman Suffrage Association in 1869. While Grant showed sympathy for women's rights, he didn't cover himself with glory on the issue. Susan B. Anthony, Elizabeth Cady Stanton, and other feminist leaders had opposed the Fifteenth Amendment unless the sequel was a Sixteenth granting women the right to vote. They wanted black and women's suffrage to advance hand in hand. In spring 1872, a New York conference composed predominantly of women, under the banner of the Equal Rights Party, nominated thirty-four-year-old Victoria Woodhull as its first female candidate for president—she was legally too young to be president—on a platform dedicated to female voting rights. Two years earlier, Woodhull, a prophetess of free love, and her sister Tennessee Claflin had opened the first female brokerage house on Wall Street, secretly aided, it was said, by Cornelius Vanderbilt. On

Election Day 1872, Woodhull wound up in jail, imprisoned for sending obscene materials through the mail, her paper having broadcast salacious details of Henry Ward Beecher's alleged philandering.

When the Republican Party met in Philadelphia that June, Susan B. Anthony implored the platform committee to take a stand for women's suffrage. She got a rhetorical nod in that direction, what she termed a "splinter" in the platform, urging "respectful consideration to the rights of women."[125] Anthony, a temperance advocate, associated Grant with drink. When a reporter asked if he was her favorite candidate, she replied, "So far, yes. Personally, I do not admire Grant, and do not care to see a 'fast man' at the head of the nation; but . . . principles to me are more than individual character." When the reporter asked whether Grant was friendly to the women's movement, she answered, "Yes, and his wife, who is said to influence him greatly, is with us heart and soul. Grant's letter of acceptance pleases me, inasmuch as the last paragraph recommends 'equal rights to all citizens,' which is evidently a sop thrown to us women."[126] When Democrats met in Baltimore to nominate Greeley, an opponent of female suffrage, Anthony came out foursquare for Grant: "The mountain has brought forth its mole, and we are left to comfort ourselves with the Philadelphia splinter as best we may."[127]

Making good on her pledge, Anthony, Stanton, and other feminists held a women's rally for Grant at the Cooper Institute in New York in early October. The newspaper coverage was typically condescending, but transmitted some sense of the excited gathering: "The hall was packed to suffocation. The lady speakers were ranged in a row, all dressed to kill . . . They have fine, large, intellectual heads and small bodies, and they seemed more fitted to be speakers on the rostrum than to fulfill the domestic duties of wives and mothers."[128]

That November, Anthony registered to vote in Rochester, New York, planning to cast her ballot for Grant for president. Women around the country were starting to issue such challenges to laws barring them. When registrars allowed Anthony to sign in, even though illegal voting was a crime, she went for Grant—the only time she ever cast a vote for president. She was arrested, tried, and found guilty. She pilloried the trial as the "greatest outrage History ever witnessed" and balked at paying the prescribed fine.[129] Although she was never imprisoned, the election registrars spent five days in jail. When Anthony appealed to Grant, he pardoned the men. On the eve of his second inaugural, Julia Ward Howe, Louisa May Alcott, and other feminists petitioned Grant to embed women's suffrage in his inaugural address. In reply, Grant stated equivocally that "he had completed his inaugural, but he looked with favor and approval on all efforts for the enlargement of woman's sphere of work and influence."[130]

Susan B. Anthony never ceased trying to lure Grant to the feminist cause. One day she buttonholed him while he was out strolling in the capital. Grant greeted her politely and asked what he could do. "I have only one wish, Mr. President, and that is to see women vote." "Ah, I can't do quite as much as that for you," Grant confessed, laughing. "I can't put votes into the hands of you women, but it may comfort you to know that I have just appointed more than five thousand postmistresses."[131]

Grant retained an imperturbable confidence about the voting outcome right up until Election Day. The only suspense concerned whether violence might mar the results, and Solicitor General Bristow alerted southern officials to be vigilant about intimidation at the polls. Federal scrutiny paid off: blacks voted Republican in overwhelming numbers in the fairest presidential election in southern states until 1968. Nonetheless, there were unfortunate exceptions, especially in Louisiana, where local Republicans claimed that more than two thousand supporters were "killed, wounded, or otherwise injured" in the weeks leading up to the election.[132] Republican ballots plummeted to half the level of previous elections. The contested race left the state with two governors and two legislatures. More than a little suspiciously, Grant didn't register a single vote in three Georgia counties with a solid majority of black voters.

For all the vitriol expressed in the race, Grant ended up breezing to a resounding victory. "There were no arrangements at the White House for receiving the election returns, no waiting reporters, no scurrying aides," said his son Jesse. "Father was apparently unconcerned, and we retired at the usual hour, content to read of the result in the morning papers."[133] The morning papers yielded astounding news: Grant had overwhelmingly won the electoral vote, and had garnered the largest popular majority of the century, nearly 56 percent of the vote, the biggest percentage between Andrew Jackson and Theodore Roosevelt. It constituted an unequivocal endorsement of Grant, who had drawn six hundred thousand more votes than four years earlier. Buttressed by southern blacks, he carried every state in the region except Georgia and Texas, although he lost the border states of Kentucky, Maryland, Missouri, and Tennessee. Every northern state was folded into his winning column. Republicans would now control the Senate and House with commanding majorities. "I was the worst beaten man that ever ran for that high office," Greeley glumly conceded.[134]

After all the hubbub, Grant was understandably gratified by the election results and felt vindicated in the course he had pursued as president. "The second nomination was almost due to me . . . because of the bitterness of political and personal opponents," he said.[135] But his first term in office hadn't been flawless and opponents braced for worse ahead. A *New York Sun* headline jeered: "Greeley Defeated: Four More Years of Fraud and Corruption."[136] Second terms were notoriously difficult to negotiate and even steady Grant supporters foresaw serious pitfalls.

Grant would have to contend with waning faith in Reconstruction among Republicans, combined with a mounting white backlash in the South. Thanks to peaceful elections, black and white Republicans had won a majority of seats in the South Carolina legislature, while the governor was a white Republican and former brigadier general from Ohio, Robert K. Scott. The spectacle of black legislators seemed intolerable to many southern white voters, who skewered the state as "a new Liberia," while Louisa McCord, a prolific essayist, satirized the new legislature as the "crow-congress" and the "monkey show."[137] This was perhaps less surprising than growing northern agreement that many Reconstruction governments were mercenary and incompetent, an attitude that reflected an ebbing tide of Republican idealism. The bitter passions of Reconstruction had broken the bonds of affection, polarizing the nation.

For Greeley, the election's aftermath was calamitous. His wife had died right before the vote, he faced loss of control of his newspaper, and the shattering defeat to Grant perfected his downfall. "My house is desolate, my future dark, my heart a stone," he wailed.[138] Doleful and exhausted, Greeley died three weeks after the election on November 29, 1872, before the Electoral College had even cast its votes. In a magnanimous gesture, Grant led funeral mourners down Fifth Avenue in New York and skipped a reception for Elihu Washburne in town the same day. "I came here really to attend Mr. Greeley's funeral," he explained. "If I stayed here to Mr. Washburne's reception, it might be misinterpreted."[139]

That the stain of corruption in Washington spread beyond Grant's cabinet was confirmed right before the election when the *New York Sun,* exposing "The Kings of Frauds," uncovered the electrifying Crédit Mobilier scandal, which involved the building of the transcontinental railroad. During the Johnson administration, the Union Pacific Railroad had set up a dummy construction company, Crédit Mobilier, with the same executives as the parent railroad. The directors of Crédit Mobilier awarded themselves lavish salaries, all covered by government payments that far exceeded the actual cost of constructing the railroad. As Charles Francis Adams Jr. explained: "They receive money into one hand as a corporation, and pay it out into the other as a contractor."[140] Attaching fellow legislators to the swindle, Massachusetts congressman Oakes Ames had distributed Crédit Mobilier stock to them at knockdown prices. After the story broke, Congress instituted an investigation in December 1872 that tainted House Speaker James G. Blaine, Congressman James Garfield, and Grant's current and future vice presidents, Schuyler Colfax and Henry Wilson. President-elect Grant rose above the scandal, which predated his administration. But the involvement of Colfax and Wilson and the fact that the investigation unfolded on his watch have unfairly linked Grant's name in the history books with a scandal in which he lacked any association.

Schuyler Colfax extricated himself from the charges until it was shown he had deposited $1,200 in his bank at the same time Ames recorded on his books a payment for that amount. Colfax lied about the transaction, which some thought more incriminating than the transaction itself. Because they were warm personal friends and perhaps feeling guilty that Colfax had been dropped from his ticket, Grant sent him a supportive letter, showing the same misplaced confidence in wrongdoers that had marred his first term: "Allow me to say that I sympathize with you in the recent Congressional investigations; that I have watched them closely, and that I am as satisfied now as I have ever been, of your integrity, patriotism and freedom from the charges imputed as if I knew of my own knowledge [of] your innocence."[141] Grant sent this on the day of his second inauguration, authorizing Colfax to publish it. When Grant's letter became known, Benjamin Bristow shook his head over the unfortunate impression it created: "It occurred to me that if [Grant] could have been deprived temporarily of the power to wield his pen the time he wrote the Colfax letter, it would have been better for his reputation."[142]

Another congressional scandal shadowed Grant's reelection: a 50 percent raise from $5,000 to $7,500 per annum that the Forty-Second Congress gave itself at its last session in March 1873. Congress also awarded Grant a sizable jump in salary from $25,000 to $50,000. Congress hadn't received an increase in a generation, so that provoked no special outrage. What raised hackles was that it declared the increase retroactive to the start of the Forty-Second Congress two years earlier, producing a $5,000 windfall in back pay to every member. "Let Republicans and Democrats alike own the facts with shame," *The New York Times*

reprimanded legislators.[143] The bonus so enraged the country that Congress rescinded the raise, although Grant's salary hike remained in effect, the president's
salary having remained unchanged since George Washington's time. (Grant, who
was $25,000 in debt, badly needed the money.) The "salary grab" wasn't Grant's
handiwork, but as with Crédit Mobilier, it became identified with his tenure.
Because it formed part of a general appropriations bill, Grant had been unable to
veto it without shutting down the government. After signing it, he properly asked
for a line-item veto that might have enabled him to strike out the salary grab—
making him the first president in American history to request one.[144]

On the night of March 3, the eve of his second inauguration, Grant toiled
until midnight, signing a last pile of bills from the outgoing Congress. The next
day the capital was gripped by frigid temperatures as low as four degrees, making it the coldest inauguration day in history, worsened by biting winds that
gusted up to twenty-eight miles per hour. The Grant who emerged from the
White House at 10 a.m. looked grave and heavy-set compared with the wartime
general, his chest more massive, his paunch thicker, his body pear-shaped, suggesting a sedentary, overfed executive. In formal wear, he always looked as if he
had been imprisoned under extreme duress.

A custom-made black carriage with three senators pulled up to the driveway
and Grant clambered into the rear seat. The open carriage, exposed to fierce
winds, had unusually high springs and towered over the others in the procession.
Julia followed in a carriage with Vice President–elect Henry Wilson. The parade
route to the Capitol featured a heavy military presence, including West Point
cadets and Annapolis midshipmen who shivered without overcoats, and the cold
made it impossible for marching musicians to play in tune. When Grant arrived
at the Capitol's east portico, its pillars hung with icicles, the plaza below was
"black with a solid mass of people," wrote a reporter, estimating the throng as
"larger than any assemblage ever before gathered in Washington."[145] When
Grant appeared on the platform, doffing his hat, a huge cheer burst from the
audience as he was seated in a chair used by George Washington for his first
inauguration in New York City.

At 12:30 p.m., Salmon P. Chase, the bearded chief justice, haggard from a
stroke and two months from death, delivered the oath of office to Grant. After
a twenty-one-gun salute, Grant delivered his second inaugural address, braving
winds so brisk that the vast majority of the audience saw the speech in panto-
mime. Characteristically, Grant wrote it without consulting anyone. He started

with a paean to the peace and prosperity he had created along with lower taxes. Then he reaffirmed his commitment to the four million former slaves who had been made citizens. Still, the freed people were "not possessed of the civil rights which citizenship should carry with it. This is wrong and should be corrected."[146] He also praised the readmission of former Confederate states and tacitly signaled that there might be fewer federal interventions in the South in his second term.[147] He sounded charitable toward Native Americans, advocating "education and civilization" in place of war: "Wars of extermination . . . are demoralizing and wicked. Our superiority of strength, and advances of civilization, should make us lenient towards the Indian."[148]

Grant previewed other second-term themes, including civil service reform and a restoration of the dollar to a fixed value in gold. He seemed to apologize for mishandling the Santo Domingo treaty, saying future acquisitions of territory should enjoy the prior support of the American public. Then, in a stupendous leap, he expressed a belief "that our Great Maker is preparing the world, in his own good time, to become one nation, speaking one language, and when armies and Navies will be no longer required."[149] He ended on a peculiarly aggrieved note, stating that even though his life had been dedicated to public service since Fort Sumter, he had been "the subject of abuse and slander scarcely ever equaled in political history, which today I feel that I can afford to disregard in view of your verdict which I gratefully accept as my vindication."[150] It was a sour, churlish note, yet a very candid and human one. At the close, Grant climbed back into his carriage, returned to the White House, and, bundled up from the cold, watched the parade from a viewing stand.

Following a grand fireworks display, the elaborate inaugural ball that evening was a dismal affair that did not bode well for Grant's second term. A cavernous wooden building, lit with gas chandeliers, had been especially constructed for the occasion, with an enormous eagle, streaming the national colors from its claws, suspended from the ceiling. To camouflage the rough wood structure, the walls were draped with so much white muslin it was nicknamed "the Muslin Palace." Hundreds of canaries were imported to warble their greetings to three thousand guests. In a courageous move, Grant invited black guests, leading some members of the Washington beau monde to boycott the event in protest at this racial mixing.[151]

The whole ostentatious affair was undone by a simple design flaw: the big barnlike room lacked heat. As guests arrived, they were shocked by the frosty temperature and attempted to dance in their fur wraps, hats, and overcoats to keep warm. Champagne, food, and ice cream froze in the arctic air. By the time Ulysses, Julia, and Nellie Grant arrived at 11:30 p.m., canaries had started to keel over and die in droves on their perches, the first martyrs to Grant's second term. The presidential family decided not to tarry long and the dwindling crowd, seeing their chance to escape the deep freeze, had piled out of the hall by the stroke of midnight.

CHAPTER THIRTY-FIVE

A Butchery of Citizens

N O SOUTHERN STATE presented more insurmountable problems to Grant than Louisiana, which had become a hotbed of hatred and corruption. Henry Clay Warmoth served as the Republican carpetbag governor of the state during Grant's first term as president. "I don't pretend to be honest," he said. "I only pretend to be as honest as anybody in politics." For those who didn't grasp the point, Warmoth added, "Why, damn it, everybody is demoralized down here. Corruption is the fashion."[1] He ended up being impeached. Exasperated by Louisiana's political squalor, Grant confessed that "if he knew capable, honest men in Louisiana, who would accept office, he would appoint them, whether Republicans or Democrats."[2]

In November 1872, there arose a slashing race for governor between Senator William Pitt Kellogg, the Republican candidate backed by Grant, and Democrat John McEnery. Kellogg was allied with Grant's brother-in-law James F. Casey, collector of customs in New Orleans. Although Kellogg emerged victorious, his foes refused to concede the election, which had been marked by illegalities on both sides. For months, both Kellogg and McEnery claimed to be governor, holding competing inaugural celebrations and assuming similar trappings of office. For Grant, who had hoped to intercede less in southern states during his second term, the standoff presented a baffling dilemma. He decided that General William H. Emory, his New Orleans commander, should refrain from taking sides and only act "to maintain order should there be a disturbance."[3] At the same time, he thought the McEnery government should desist

from enacting legislation until the courts had decided which governor was legitimate. Despite election "frauds and forgeries," Grant professed he was "extremely
anxious to avoid any appearance of undue interference in State affairs."[4] His
statement is noteworthy for, despite southern charges of "bayonet rule," Grant
never lightly or capriciously intervened in the South, doing so only when he
discovered a sound constitutional basis for action. As an adroit politician, he was
very aware of the growing northern reluctance to get embroiled in these chronic
southern disputes.

A couple of days later, he informed his cabinet that in late March or early
April he planned to tour the southern states, culminating in unruly New Orleans. This signified a new stage in his presidency. He had been in the South as
a general on military business, but never as president; it spoke volumes that he
dared not set foot in the South for fear of violence against him or perhaps because he had been deterred by the legal complications of states being restored to
the Union. In late February, Grant canceled the proposed trip when a Nashville
friend advised him "there are evil disposed persons who may be inclined to do
harm to him & to his party," noted Fish, who said Grant received other alarming letters.[5] Julia Grant was resolutely against her husband hazarding the trip
and Grant soon told people, not quite truthfully, that "urgent public business"
necessitated that he postpone it indefinitely.[6]

The Louisiana situation deteriorated with resurgent Klan activity. On January 21, Joseph T. Hatch, a businessman, informed Grant that he was being
persecuted for having voted for Grant, Kellogg, and the Republican ticket. One
night up to twenty men in disguise had ringed his warehouse, emptied more than
one hundred shots into it, then threatened that unless his business "was moved,
that in a Short time they would apply the Torch."[7] In spite of Grant's reluctance
to meddle in Louisiana, the wholesale breakdown of law and order made it imperative. In early March, Governor Kellogg described how McEnery supporters
had seized a police station and said he would need to send in state militia under
General James Longstreet to recapture it. Grant reacted swiftly: "Instruct Military to prevent any violent interference with the state Government of La."[8]

After a federal judge ruled in favor of the Kellogg slate, the powder keg of
Louisiana politics exploded in April 1873. William Ward, a black Republican,
and Christopher Columbus Nash, a white Democrat, vied for control of Grant
Parish in the center of the state. Ward summoned his black supporters and warned
them that Democrats would try to seize by force the county seat of Colfax, a lush

place of swamps and bayous and a black Republican stronghold. To avert this, they threw up earthworks around the courthouse, guarding it for several weeks. This display of black power was anathema to the white community. On Easter Sunday, Nash led a mob of several hundred whites, armed with rifles and a small cannon, who opened fire on the courthouse, setting it ablaze. Even though its black defenders ran up a white flag of surrender, begging for mercy, the mob butchered dozens of them. Black families were afraid to claim the many corpses that thickly littered the ground. When Longstreet sent Colonel T. W. DeKlyne to Colfax, the latter found heaps of dead black bodies being scavenged by dogs and buzzards. "We were unable to find the body of a single white man," he reported. Many blacks "were shot in the back at the head and neck . . . almost all had from three to a dozen wounds. Many of them had their brains literally blown out."[9] It was the worst slaughter perpetrated against blacks during Reconstruction.

Staggered by this cold-blooded massacre, Grant told the Senate "a butchery of citizens was committed at Colfax, which in bloodthirstiness and barbarity is hardly surpassed by any acts of savage warfare."[10] A week later, Captain Jacob H. Smith of the U.S. Army arrived in Colfax with a hundred soldiers, arrested eight white perpetrators of the carnage, and counted seventy-three black victims; other estimates ran as high as three hundred. There was no possibility the culprits would be prosecuted under local laws. Invoking the Enforcement Act of 1870, a federal grand jury handed down seventy-two indictments, but only three men were convicted. In 1876, in *United States v. Cruikshank,* the Supreme Court determined that the perpetrators could not be prosecuted under the Fourteenth Amendment because it governed only state actions, not individual ones. The Colfax murderers thus walked off scot-free, sending a powerful message to white supremacists that they could slay blacks without any penalty.

In commenting on the Colfax brutality, Grant was enraged that the same southern Democrats who accused him of unwarranted federal intrusion did nothing to repudiate such unalloyed sadism. Only federal power, he believed, could protect freed people from abuses brazenly ignored by states. As he told the Senate, "insuperable obstructions were thrown in the way of punishing these murderers, and the so-called conservative papers of the State not only justified the massacre, but denounced as federal tyranny and despotism the attempt of the United States officers to bring them to justice. Fierce denunciations ring through the country about office-holding and election matters in Louisiana, while every one of the Colfax miscreants goes unwhipped of justice, and no way can be found in this boasted land of civilization and Christianity to punish the perpetrators of this bloody and monstrous crime."[11] Grant seldom spoke with such full-throated passion.

In early May, Grant received a dispatch from Kellogg that two or three Louisiana parishes were "in a state of insurrection against the state authorities."[12] Grant answered this appeal for troops with the carefully worded formula he invoked to justify southern intervention: "Now therefore, I, Ulysses S. Grant, President of the United States, do hereby make proclamation, and command said turbulent and disorderly persons to disperse and retire peaceably to their respective abodes within twenty days from this date."[13] Should they refuse to do so, Grant would send in federal troops. Perhaps as a reminder of who had won the war, he published a proclamation on May 21, shutting government offices for the day so that employees could honor Union graves on Decoration Day.

As Grant attempted to normalize federal relations with former Confederate states, he struggled with newly emergent white supremacist groups, hydra-headed offshoots of the Klan with names such as the White League, "rifle clubs," Red Shirts, and Knights of the White Camellia. They tiptoed around prosecution by claiming to be county militia. Unlike the Klan, which was a secret paramilitary group, the White League that formed in Opelousas, Louisiana, in 1874 operated with overtly political aims that included evicting the Republican Party from power. The league didn't refrain from undisguised violence—one historian described it as "the military arm of the Democratic Party"—and preached imminent race war, but it also engaged in economic pressure and terrorism against blacks who dared to vote.[14] Its credo could be seen in the preamble of the state Democratic platform, which began, "We the white people of Louisiana . . ."[15] Harper's Weekly wasn't far from the mark when it termed the White League "an unmasked Ku Klux."[16]

In August 1874, Governor Kellogg wrote to Grant about terror inflicted upon Republican voters in Louisiana and said he anticipated more before the next election. He noted that Grant had held back from intervening in Arkansas and Texas with his new policy "to let the South alone," but he predicted that federal troops would be necessary in his state so "that every republican voter should know that he will be protected if violently interfered with in the exercise of the rights conferred upon him by Congress and the Constitution."[17] Kellogg didn't overstate the threat: that same month, White Leaguers dragged six Republican officials from their homes in Coushatta and murdered them. Grant grew livid.

"No one has been punished," he told the Senate, "and the conservative press of the State [denounced] all efforts to that end, and boldly justified the crime."[18] These bloodcurdling events convinced Grant that despite northern fatigue and hypocritical indifference, he lacked the luxury of pulling federal troops from the South. Told they were "unnecessary and irritating to the people," he had withdrawn most of them from Louisiana, but he now revised his opinion.[19] In early September, he notified Secretary of War Belknap to have troops at the ready: "The recent atrocities in the South, particularly in Louisiana, Alabama and South Carolina, show a disregard for law, civil rights and personal protection that ought not to be tolerated in any civilized government."[20] Attorney General Williams advised U.S. attorneys and marshals in six southern states of Grant's fierce determination to stem violence against black and white Republicans.

This was the prelude to a state of anarchy that engulfed New Orleans on September 14. D. B. Penn, the Democratic lieutenant governor under McEnery, issued a provocative call for his militia to drive from power the "usurpers," as he billed Republican officeholders. In a veritable coup d'état, thousands of whites, many of them former Confederate soldiers instigated by the White League, barricaded the streets, overpowered black militia and the racially integrated Metropolitan Police Force led by Longstreet, and took over City Hall and the statehouse, killing more than twenty people. Afterward, they announced that Governor Kellogg had been overthrown. General Emory informed Grant that the rebellion had "embraced nearly every white man in the community."[21] The battle had witnessed an extraordinary event: James Longstreet now fired on men he had commanded during the war, his small army having killed twenty-one White Leaguers. "The streets of the city were stained with blood," wrote Grant, who released a proclamation that said "turbulent and disorderly persons" had conspired to overthrow Louisiana's government and he ordered them to disperse within five days.[22] To back up his words, he dispatched five thousand troops and three gunboats to reinstate Governor Kellogg. Almost overnight, the federal garrison in New Orleans swelled to America's largest. Grant's decisive actions pacified a dangerously unstable situation: the insurgents disbanded, the Penn forces surrendered state offices, and William P. Kellogg was restored as rightful governor.

While some northern newspapers roundly praised Grant's handling of the uprising, many Liberal Republicans had tired of the black community and its eternal discontents. Contrary to the evidence, E. L. Godkin of *The Nation* portrayed southern blacks as well protected by their white governments, while in states still controlled by black Republicans, "the blacks have themselves become, in the hands of white knaves, oppressors of the worst sort."[23] Many northerners were fed up with carpetbag governments in the South and wanted the federal government to disengage from the region, even if this meant transferring it to white supremacists bent on draconian Democratic rule. One American diplomat believed northern voters were impatient "with this worn out cry of 'Southern outrages'!!! Hard times & heavy taxes make them wish the 'nigger,' 'everlasting, nigger,' were in . . . Africa."[24] The ardent idealism that had informed the Civil War had been succeeded by a cynical, bitter revulsion.

To Grant, it looked as if the country might be lurching toward a second Civil War. He had felt so outraged by events in Louisiana that he hadn't bothered to consult his cabinet before issuing his proclamation. Fish and others grumbled about being excluded, but Grant's crisp, decisive actions stopped an insurrectionary movement in its tracks. He exhibited the same spirit of command as during the war, when he had rapidly dashed off orders to his officers under fire. At one point during the Louisiana crisis, Grant had his luggage at the White House door, ready for a trip to Long Branch, when cabinet members questioned the propriety of going at such a time. He realized he needed to remain and had his trunks brought back inside.

Grant remained in a quandary over the fate of the sometimes disreputable Kellogg. In an extraordinary cabinet session on September 16—maybe the most dramatic in Grant's presidency—he and his cabinet aired their grave doubts about the governor's honesty and competence. "Kellogg's weakness & imbecility were denounced" by Grant and others, Fish recorded, everyone agreeing that "great frauds" had been committed in the gubernatorial election on both sides.[25] At the same time, everyone believed the insurgent Democratic government shouldn't be recognized. As Marshall Jewell, the postmaster general, admitted, "Kellogg . . . is a first-class cuss, but there's no getting rid of him."[26]

Concerns about Kellogg's probity were dwarfed by the awareness that the Grant administration had to end the violent overthrow of a state government. "He is cool and collected," Jewell described Grant, "and thoroughly determined, and grows a little black in the face when talking about it."[27] Attorney General Williams glimpsed a vast, insidious conspiracy in the South, poised to retake governments by force. He warned that "large quantities of arms, & military equipments [*sic*] have been taken into La & other Southern States—that 'White leagues' & 'Rifle Companies' have been organized throughout the South, & are regularly drilled, meeting at night, & going through various Military evolutions, such as pitched fights, bayonet exercises &c."[28] Such fears were validated after the morning cabinet session when Judge James Lyons of Virginia informed Fish that "the entire white population of the South, would consider any force, to re-instate the Kellogg Govt as an act of War, which would be resisted."[29]

After federal troops were sent to Louisiana, Grant was besieged with death threats, often addressed to Julia as well. One New Orleans resident, signing himself "a Lover of Justice," let Julia know her husband would be "assassinated if he dont MAKE Kellogg resign . . . Men are now on their way to Washington to FULLY EXECUTE the DESIGN of putting U.S. Grant out of the way."[30] A Cincinnati correspondent told her, "If Grant *reinstates* Kellogg—he will suffer. Southerns, do no want to have Kellogg & niggers over them . . . Grant, may follow Kellog—if he does, he will be Shot at."[31] Grant received a raft of disturbing letters from Republicans as well. A petition signed "We the Colored people of New Orleans" claimed that the White League, in conjunction with the Democratic Party, had amassed a stockpile of up to thirty thousand guns and sworn to take control of the state "if they must kill every negro that is in the State they declares that Just as Soon as you Shall With drew the Troops from Louisanana there Will not be One republican to be found in the State."[32]

The elections that November were policed by federal troops and McEnery and the Democrats gained control of the state senate, while Kellogg retained the governorship. Once again both sides swapped vicious charges of election manipulation. It was alleged that Kellogg had blatantly reduced the number of Democratic legislators, while the black community said they had been threatened with physical harm and loss of jobs if they didn't exactly follow the Democratic line. Merchants refused to extend credit to planters who allowed their workers to vote Republican.

Resisting cabinet pressure to tread gingerly, Grant sent Phil Sheridan to assume command in Louisiana in early January. It wasn't a conciliatory choice, nor was it meant to be. So commonplace had black murders become in Louisiana that when Sheridan conducted an investigation, he came up with a gruesome tally of 2,141 blacks killed by whites since the war, with another 2,115 wounded—almost all crimes that had gone unpunished.

RIGHT AFTER GRANT'S REELECTION, Supreme Court Justice Samuel Nelson decided to retire and a delegation of jurists trooped to the White House to discuss his successor. They made this courtesy call with a clear favorite in mind, Benjamin Bristow, who said they "gathered around me and expressed their individual desires that I should be appointed Judge Nelson's successor."[33] Grant invited Bristow to dine later that day, raising expectations of his elevation to the top bench. Always bedeviled by appointments, Grant hated to be lobbied and preferred to meditate on his choices privately. "President is anxious to have the nomination made before the pressure upon him is made by the friends of the various Candidates," Fish wrote.[34] Grant had no consultative process in place with his staff or anything resembling modern-day vetting of court nominees. He came up with a surprise choice, Ward Hunt, a former Utica, New York, mayor who had served on the New York Court of Appeals and was associated with Roscoe Conkling. The Senate confirmed him without incident. The selection didn't please feminist groups: riding the circuit in New York, Hunt had overseen the conviction of Susan B. Anthony for illegally voting for Grant in Rochester.

Grant's next Supreme Court pick proved infinitely more complex. On May 7, 1873, Chief Justice Salmon P. Chase died after nine years of distinguished service. Five days later, Ulysses and Julia Grant rode in the funeral procession with Roscoe Conkling. Grant resolved to let the matter of a successor dangle until Congress reconvened in December, hoping to make the right choice and spare any nominee "the mortification of a rejection."[35] This seemed to represent a step forward for Grant: instead of making inscrutable snap judgments, he would throw open the process to a collaborative approach. As the time approached, the rumor mill kept churning out the name of Roscoe Conkling. It was then routine for presidents to nominate political figures instead of eminent jurists, but Liberal Republicans derided Conkling as a poor specimen of a politician. "To politics, in any good sense of the word, Mr. Conkling has not contributed a single useful or fruitful idea," sneered Godkin in *The Nation,* adding that "his political claims to the chief place on the bench of the greatest tribunal in the world are as paltry as his professional ones."[36]

Despite the expected criticism, Grant was swayed by personal loyalty and offered Conkling the job on November 8, 1873. The New York senator was too wedded to Washington intrigue to retreat to the contemplative solitude of the court. Incredibly, he saw the job of chief justice as contracting his considerable power and cramping his freewheeling style. "I could not take the place," he explained, "for I would be forever gnawing my chains."[37] On November 20, he sent Grant a short, cryptic letter, declining the offer without volunteering a reason; Conkling may have worried that with Democrats in control of New York's legislature, his Senate seat would fall into enemy hands. Grant then offered the job to Hamilton Fish, who turned it down in a more thoughtful manner: "I insisted that I could not accept it—that it was upwards of twenty years since I had had any connection with the bar or practice . . . I felt that it would be important to put a younger man in the place."[38]

Grant next turned to Caleb Cushing, a seventy-three-year-old Massachusetts lawyer and former attorney general under President Franklin Pierce, who was heavily touted by Congressman Benjamin Butler. After years of feuding, Grant and Butler had reached a rapprochement as evidenced by Butler's fealty to administration policy. Because Cushing's age posed an impediment, Butler proposed that Grant appoint him as a stopgap chief justice who would resign before Grant's term expired, thus entitling him to name a replacement. Grant canvassed his cabinet on the choice of Cushing and almost everyone balked. "I expressed a very high estimate of Cushing's ability and fitness . . . but felt the force of the objection to Cushing's age, and the question of the propriety of dispensing an office of that character on a conditional tenure," Fish wrote.[39]

By elimination Grant turned next to Attorney General George Williams, who bore no exalted status as a jurist and would be replaced by Benjamin Bristow. He sent their names to Capitol Hill along with his annual message. Behind the scenes, Horace Porter and Orville Babcock had schemed to secure Williams's nomination. To many observers, Williams had done fine work against the Klan, but he lacked the superior legal mind required for the court and was overshadowed by ethical questions about his personal finances, having gotten into a bad habit of paying personal checks with government money. The reaction to him was uniformly hostile and many senators couldn't understand why they had not been chosen instead. Editorial writers raked Williams over very hot coals. "The country should be ashamed and disgraced by the nomination of such a man," said the *Cincinnati Commercial,* while Louisville's *Courier-Journal* branded him "the worst appointment yet."[40]

Nevertheless, Grant, who often became obstinate when attacked, applied intense pressure on the Senate, making the Williams nomination a litmus test of party loyalty. Some Grant advisers told him that if he plunged ahead, victory would be assured. "The Judiciary Committee is sitting listening to every idle story, every lie told by political opponents, who arrive every day to feed the fight," wrote Porter. "It is simply a Slanderous rough-and-tumble political fight."[41] At the same time, in the Senate Judiciary Committee, where a solid phalanx of opposition awaited Williams, members urged the president to yank the name. Grant, an immovable object, refused to countenance the idea, and his storied persistence once again boomeranged. "The Gen[era]l has done nothing heretofore that has hurt him so much," Associate Justice Noah Swayne told Bristow. "Everyone *now* says that the *third term* is wholly out of the question if there Ever was a possibility of such a thing."[42] The next day, Bristow told Grant he was turning down the attorney general appointment.

In late December, Fish found Grant alone in the cabinet room in a highly agitated state. He had belatedly grown disenchanted with Williams, telling Fish he didn't think Williams "had done anything corrupt or illegal but that there had been indiscreet things done. That Mrs. Williams had given orders for the purchase of an expensive carriage and liveries for two servants and that the expenses for these had been paid out of the Contingent fund of the Department of Justice; as were also the wages of the two men who were employed as private servants. He manifested much regret at having learned this."[43] For Grant, this was a now-familiar tale of his trusting, innocent nature betrayed.

With the Senate prepared to reject Williams, Grant reluctantly withdrew his name. In another instance of errant judgment, he allowed Williams to retain his attorney general post, despite the damaging information that had come to light. In such embarrassing situations, Grant could be hurt and angry and submit to an impulsive side of his nature. Without consulting anyone, he reverted to his earlier pick and sent Caleb Cushing's name to the Senate. However charming and erudite he was, Cushing met instant opposition. One senator unearthed a friendly, if innocuous, letter he had written to Jefferson Davis three weeks before Fort Sumter, recommending a friend as a Confederate clerk, and this lessened his chances for confirmation. Feeling bruised, Grant withdrew Cushing's name as well.

Unable to afford another gaffe, Grant consulted the Senate leadership and came up with the name of Morrison R. Waite of Toledo, Ohio, who was, if not a brilliant lawyer, at least a proficient one, having recently chaired the Ohio constitutional convention. Assistant Attorney General C. H. Hill lauded him as "a prompt, energetic business man."[44] Appeased senators approved Waite's name within forty-eight hours, bringing general relief throughout the country. The Nation spoke for many when it wrote that Grant had "with remarkable skill, avoided choosing any first rate man . . . But considering what he might have done, we ought to be thankful."[45] The New York Tribune damned Waite with faint praise, describing him as "an honest man and a fair lawyer, and that is as much as can reasonably be expected from Grant."[46] Harper's Weekly penned a fitting epitaph for Grant's conspicuous mishandling of the chief justiceship: "In both the cases of Mr. Williams and Mr. Cushing the nomination was made not only without consultation, but without proper knowledge or inquiry, and it is evident therefore, without a due sense of the great character and importance of the office."[47]

THROUGHOUT HIS PRESIDENCY, Grant remained a doting father, husband, and son. As his health worsened in late 1872, Jesse Root Grant voiced an urgent wish to see his famous son. "My father is very old and infirm," Grant told a friend, "and has conceived the idea that unless he sees me this Winter he will never see me again."[48] Julia wasn't overjoyed about the trip. "I think it will be rather a doleful visit," she confided to a correspondent. "But still he has to go I suppose."[49] However frayed their relationship, Jesse Root Grant still loomed large in his son's mind. In late May, he went into a terminal decline and died on June 29, 1873, just as Ulysses was en route to Covington.

After the funeral, Grant consoled himself with the thought that his father had been resigned to his death, having "reached a ripe old age without pain or sickness," he wrote. "He had been so long gradually failing that my mother and sister . . . had discounted his death in advance."[50] Perhaps because of complex, unresolved feelings toward his father, Grant took his death very hard. "I went up . . . to see him and tell him I had been with his father," said Eliza Shaw. "The General could not speak a word he was so affected."[51] Grant's grief was understandable since Jesse, for all his many flaws, had never surrendered implicit belief in his son. "When his faculties waned," a family friend assured Grant, "his joy in your fame and his almost childish faith in you, were the unguarded gate through which interested persons imposed upon him. I am glad he never had

occasion to think you had failed him."[52] After Jesse's death, Hannah Grant decided to live in New York with her daughter Virginia and son-in-law Abel
Corbin. Grant's mother still hadn't visited the White House and seemed distant
from her son, perhaps feeling slighted by him or still uncomfortable with Julia
and the unreconstructed Dents. In 1880, she informed a relative that "U.S.
Grant," as she coolly referred to him, had paid her a short visit, then she added
tartly that "he Seldom Writes to any of us."[53]

Grant had long been caught between two willful, overbearing men—his father and his father-in-law. By a curious symmetry, Colonel Dent's health faltered
a month after Jesse Root Grant died. Long a White House fixture, granted an
honored, if undeserved, place at the head of the table in the private dining room,
he had made no effort to muffle his views and always spouted the Democratic
Party line. For five months, he hung on in a debilitated state. On the evening of
December 15, 1873, Grant, Julia, and their son Fred dined out and returned
near midnight to find the Colonel resting "in a quiet slumber." A few minutes
later, he expired "without a struggle or movement of a limb or muscle," Grant
wrote.[54] A funeral service was held in the Blue Room of the White House before
the Colonel's body was shipped back to St. Louis for burial. Julia, still enamored
of her father, was inconsolable and unable to make the trip, so Grant and Fred
accompanied the remains to St. Louis. Grant had been relieved of the heavy
burden of two impossibly difficult men, but Julia never fully recovered from the
blow of her father's loss.

Grant kept close tabs on his four children during his presidency. Fred had
developed into a handsome, muscular young man, with a mustache and his father's broad, open face. Grant never goaded him to join the military, but he believed that if his son chose an army career, he should enter West Point. Fred
fared poorly at the academy, studying, like his father, under the well-known
military theorist Dennis Hart Mahan, while piling up loads of demerits. Some
people thought he put on airs, trading on his father's name. The Hartford phi-
lanthropist David Clark claimed that Fred had "made himself obnoxious to the
professors by advising them of what 'his father' desired or did not desire."[55]
When Fred graduated in June 1871, he ranked thirty-seventh in a class of forty-
one and stood forty-first in discipline.

While at West Point, Fred was implicated in an ugly racial incident involving
a cadet named James W. Smith, the first black cadet accepted there. A graduate
of South Carolina's Freedmen's Bureau school, Smith had been sponsored and

educated by David Clark. From the time he entered West Point in May 1870, Smith contended that he was verbally abused by white cadets and called "nothing but a damned nigger."[56] On June 30, a sadly discouraged Smith told Clark that "I have borne insult upon insult, till I am completely worn out."[57]

Smith was ready to drop out in July when Grant met with Clark in Hartford and heard about the black cadet's daily persecution. Knowing Grant would be in town, Clark had published a letter in the local paper laying out the problem. "Such treatment of this noble Boy," Clark wrote, "is disgraceful to the country."[58] A distraught Clark told the president that Smith might resign from West Point. Showing sympathy, Grant insisted Smith should stay and that "the battle might just as well be fought now as at any other time."[59] Grant intimated he would shield the cadet from further abuse. But Fred Grant held decidedly more retrograde views, Clark recalled, telling his father "the time had not come to send colored boys to West Point."[60] Clark countered that if it was time for black senators, it was certainly time for black cadets at West Point. Fred sulkily retorted, "Well, no damned nigger will ever graduate from West Point."[61] Despite Grant's encouragement, Smith continued to endure blows and insults and got no satisfaction when he complained to the academy.

In September 1870, Cadet Smith was court-martialed for attacking a cadet named Wilson—he had hit him with a coconut dipper after being mocked as a monkey—and both young men were found guilty. Smith received a light sentence, but his misery had not ended. While he was marching, a cadet named Anderson kept stepping on his toes until Smith protested, "I wish you would not tread on my toes." To which Anderson rejoined: "Keep your damned toes out of the way."[62] According to Smith, Fred Grant was one of the white cadets who invaded the rooms of three black cadets on the night of January 3, 1871, driving them into the cold. For Smith this was "a most outrageous example of Lynch law," but he couldn't get the academy to punish the offenders and believed the inaction stemmed from the involvement of the president's son.[63]

According to Clark, when Smith was again charged that month with refusing to hold his head up while marching, Secretary of War Belknap consulted Grant about the composition of the court that would pass sentence. "I have received two or three letters from my son Fred," Grant supposedly said, "who informs me that the cadet is very objectionable there . . . Now, as this trial is to come off, Mr. Secretary, I trust that you will so make up the court as to cause his removal."[64] Smith was found guilty and ordered dismissed. Belknap forwarded the proceedings to Grant, who commuted the sentence to a one-year suspension, with Smith set back one year, forcing him to start over as a plebe. Despite this clemency, David Clark stuck to a conspiratorial view of events, writing on June 21, 1871, that "I feel that Cadet Smith has been outraged by the Secy of War and the President. Fred Grant a low miserable scamp has been the cause of much of his trouble."[65] Smith and Clark charged that Grant had condoned harsh treatment against Smith to protect his son. Smith never graduated from West Point. After suffering so much ostracism, he flunked a test given by a biased philosophy professor and was drummed out of the academy, dying two years later of tuberculosis.

As Fred ended an unhappy tenure at West Point, Grant soured on a military future for him. "I do not want Fred to stay in the Army longer than to report for duty and serve a week or two," he said, citing his many demerits.[66] Instead of assignment to a regiment after graduation, Fred surveyed the Rocky Mountains as an assistant civil engineer, receiving a leave of absence as an army officer. Prodded by Julia, Grant, at his most henpecked, arranged for Fred to join Sherman on a European tour and he wound up attached to his staff. Grant always showed an uncritical love of his children, a yearning that went back to his lonely days on distant western outposts. Sherman felt put upon by Grant, grumbling that being forced to hire Fred was "a positive violation of law . . . Fred Grant had . . . no claim to military distinction other than being his father's Son."[67] He remained unimpressed with Fred's talents. "He is a good natured fellow, but cares for little."[68] Ever the loving father, Grant appraised his eldest son most charitably. "Fred is a splendid fellow," he wrote, "and I think not the least spoiled yet."[69] Sherman described Grant's adoration for his children as an "amiable weakness, not only pardonable, but attracting the love of all who did not suffer the consequences."[70]

Starting in May 1873, Fred joined the Chicago staff of Lieutenant General Phil Sheridan, with the rank of lieutenant colonel. The next year, he accompanied George Armstrong Custer's expedition to the Black Hills. Custer, a martinet, had Fred arrested for drunkenness, and later on he committed himself to total abstinence. While in Chicago he met a pretty young woman named Ida Marie Honoré, daughter of a wealthy local plutocrat, and fell in love with her. She was an attractive, worldly young woman of French extraction with dark hair piled high on her head and a savvy, knowing look. The Grants were all enamored of her. "Fred's wife is beautiful and is spoken of . . . as being quite as charming for her manners, amiability, good sense & education as she is for her beauty," Grant reported.[71] The Grants attended their society wedding at an Honoré country residence before the young couple began their matrimonial life in the White House.

Grant expressed pride when his second son, Buck, entered Harvard, where he was a student of Henry Adams and got the lowest grade in his history class. Instead of having to upbraid Buck about bad behavior, Grant could dispense more grown-up advice. In a revealing letter, he told his son "to have the respect of all with whom you come in contact . . . To gain this never deceive nor act an artificial part. Be simply yourself . . . never resort to any means to make believe you know more than you really do."[72] It was as close to a statement of his philosophy as Grant ever came up with for his children. Buck was perhaps the most likable son, one family member finding him "a pleasing young man, a little nervous, but rather winning and gentle."[73] He excelled in German and French, spending his junior year in a small German village before returning to Harvard. When he left college, he apprenticed at a law office in New York while studying simultaneously at Columbia Law School. "Buck, who is a spare looking young man, weighs 160 lbs. twenty pounds more than I weighed at forty years of age," Grant told Badeau in 1874. "As my children are all leaving me it is gratifying to know that, so far, they give good promise. They are all of good habits and are very popular with their acquaintances."[74]

The youngest son, Jesse, the veteran mischief maker, was never as accomplished as his older brothers. Cursed with delicate health, he suffered from headaches and nosebleeds. Spoiled and overprotected, he received surprisingly little formal schooling, but in autumn 1873, the Grants packed him off to Cheltenham Academy near Philadelphia. When he lapsed into homesickness and complained of headaches, Grant allowed him to come home. Despite his limited education, Jesse was accepted at Cornell "without a condition," Grant wrote, "although he has never attended school but three years, then in an infant class."[75] Julia was delighted that Jesse had gained acceptance to such a respectable university. "Do you not think that is doing pretty well?" she asked a friend. "Having been tied to my apron string all his life? (As his papa says.)"[76] That Jesse was a president's son and might have something of an undue advantage didn't appear to cross Julia's mind.

When Grant was elected, his daughter, Nellie, was just thirteen, and a pretty young girl in the White House was bound to captivate the press. *Woodhull &*

Claflin's Weekly went so far as to publish her poetry. Short in stature, with dark eyes, a round nose, and a sweet expression, Nellie bore a striking resemblance to her father. Grant prized her as "my little sunshine" and everyone knew she ranked as his favorite. "My sister Nellie was his only daughter," Fred wrote, "and she was much petted and loved by him."[77] One journalist saw that Nellie's "girlish prattle was far more attractive to [Grant] than the compliments of Congressmen or the praises of politicians."[78] Charming, smart, and agreeable, a good dancer, Nellie was popular around the White House. In fall 1870, she was sent off to Miss Porter's School in Farmington, Connecticut, but, like Jesse, she fell homesick and came home quickly.

In 1872 the Grants suggested that Nellie accompany their Philadelphia friend Adolph Borie and his wife on a European holiday, little suspecting how the trip would profoundly alter her life. Emerging from her parents' protective cocoon, she blossomed into a young woman as Queen Victoria received her at Buckingham Palace and she toured Paris and other capitals. "She has been all her life so much of a companion of her mother that I feared she would want to return by the first steamer leaving Liverpool after her arrival," Grant noted with wonder. "But she writes quite the reverse of being homesick."[79] In sending Nellie abroad, her parents hoped to guard her from any amorous engagement, a strategy that had ironic consequences. On the voyage home, when the Bories fell sick and were confined to their stateroom, Nellie roamed the ship in search of adventure and found it with an Eton-educated young Englishman named Algernon Sartoris (pronounced Sar-tress). She fell in love with the handsome young man who parted his hair down the middle. He came from a family of minor gentry who owned a magnificent estate in Southampton and was wrapped in a romantic haze for Nellie. Algernon's father was a member of Parliament and had served as British minister at a European court. His mother, a former opera singer, was a sister of the renowned actress Fanny Kemble and had counted Charles Dickens and Henry James among the fashionable guests congregating at her London salon.

Grant was chagrined to discover that his pet of a daughter had escaped his paternal control and embarked on a shipboard romance. When Algernon Sartoris came to dine at the White House, Grant ushered him into the billiard room for a confidential chat over cigars. "I waited and hoped the President would help me, but not a word did he say," the young man recalled. "He sat silent, looking at me. I hesitated, and fidgeted, and coughed, and thought I would sink through the floor. Finally, I exclaimed in desperation—'Mr. President, I want to marry your daughter.'"[80] Both Grants had a queasy premonition of something wrong with the dashing, bearded young Englishman. Grant griped "that he would prefer Nellie to be an old maid, but if she must marry, he thought she should choose an American husband."[81] Julia sighed every time Algernon's name was mentioned and at last confronted her daughter: "Nellie, is it possible you are willing to leave your father and me, who have loved and cherished you all of your life, and go with this stranger for *always*?" Nellie replied sweetly: "Why, yes, mamma. I am sure that is just what you did when you married papa and left grandpa."[82]

On July 7, 1873, the president sat down at Long Branch and composed a heartfelt letter to Algernon's father that bespoke deep love of his daughter and country: "Much to my astonishment an attachment seems to have sprung up between the two young people; to my astonishment because I had only looked upon my daughter as a child, with a good home which I did not think of her wishing to quit for years yet."[83] His letter sounded a defiantly patriotic note. "It would be with the greatest regret that I would see Nellie quit the United States as a permanent home. It is a country of great extent of territory, of fertility, and of great future promise . . . May I ask you therefore in all candor . . . to state to me whether your son expects to become a citizen of the United States? And what has been his habits? And what are his business qualifications."[84] Grant confessed that he had to live off his presidential salary and could not provide for his daughter financially. Unable to deny her ardent wishes, he reluctantly consented to the match. The one condition was that Algernon and Nellie should wait a year before announcing their engagement, but that didn't seem to arrest the romance.

On May 21, 1874, 250 guests shuffled into the East Room of the White House for a wedding minutely chronicled by reporters voracious for details. A multitude of spectators circled the White House while across the street Treasury Department clerks pressed their faces to the windows to catch glimpses of arriving celebrities, including Grant's cabinet, Supreme Court justices, and a column of generals and senators. Even Walt Whitman was susceptible to the frenzy, penning a poem that concluded: "O sweet Missouri rose! O bonny bride! Yield thy red cheeks, thy lips, today, Unto a Nation's loving kiss."[85]

While renovating the White House, Julia had converted the East Room into a sumptuous ballroom that was now garlanded with flowers, evergreens, and potted palms. Fred Grant, immaculate in military dress, served as groomsman and entered with Algernon Sartoris. When Nellie swept in on her father's arm, he was, wrote Jesse, "silent, tense, with tears upon his cheeks that he made no movement to brush away."[86] Grant had approved the marriage, but lacked the guile to mask his true misgivings. Julia seemed disconsolate as she trailed along with Jesse and Buck on her arms. Officiating at the wedding was the Reverend O. H. Tiffany of the Methodist church. Beneath a canopy of white blossoms shaped like a bell, Nellie, eighteen, and Algernon, twenty-two, took their vows while Grant stared moodily at the floor. Once the ceremony ended, the guests adjourned to an elaborate wedding breakfast in the State Dining Room. The young couple were showered with costly gifts, estimated to cost $60,000, that accumulated in the library, including an eighty-four-piece silver service from George W. Childs and a silver dinner service from the financier Anthony J. Drexel.

The Gilded Age ostentation barely concealed the president's dismay, which broke through his usually stolid exterior. Buck left a telling remembrance: "The saddest I ever saw my father was when my sister Nellie was married. It was a lavish White House ceremony and she married a foreigner. He was very downcast for a long time about it. That evening I found him sitting with mother upstairs in my mother's dressing room and he was sobbing like a boy. I was so in awe of my father I couldn't think of what to say, so I withdrew, deeply shaken."[87] Others claimed Grant disappeared after the wedding guests left and was discovered crying alone in Nellie's vacant bedroom.

Grant thought he had extracted a pledge from Algernon to become an American citizen and reside in the United States. Then Algernon's elder brother died and he became heir to the Sartoris estate. In a cruel twist for Grant, Nellie moved to England with her new husband. The marriage soon began to unravel thanks to Algernon's drinking and womanizing, and one wonders whether Grant had intuited all along his son-in-law's alcohol problem. Although the Grants tried bravely for years to pretend that Nellie was happily married as she bore a succession of children, they admitted their extreme regret that they had lost her to England.

After meeting her, Henry James evoked a forlorn Nellie, stranded among strangers, unable to keep pace with the sophisticated repartee of her mother-in-law. After one meeting, James lamented the "poor little Nelly Grant" and her "three very handsome but rather common youngsters. She is illiterate, lovely, painted, pathetic and separated from a drunken idiot of a husband. The Sartorises don't like her very much, but they like her more, I suppose, than they do their disreputable 'Algie.' Whenever I see her there is something rather touching and tragic to me in this eminently chubby vision of the daughter of a man" who was president "in a strange land, quite without friends, ignorant, helpless, vulgar, untidy, unhappy, perfectly harmless and smeared over with fifteen colours."[88]

The American press wallowed in salacious gossip about Nellie's marriage, much of it unfortunately true. Articles said that Algernon gallivanted around England, leaving Nellie for months at a time; that he had a farm in Green Bay, Wisconsin, and brought his mistress to Milwaukee; that Nellie's father-in-law settled property on her children on condition that they be educated in England; and that Grant had to send remittances to provide for Nellie and the children. Finding it too painful a subject, the president never talked publicly about the catastrophic failure of his daughter's marriage. For so protective and loving a parent, it must have been unmitigated torture to watch her being abused by a young scoundrel, especially since Grant had sensed something amiss with the young man. To make his beloved daughter happy, he had overcome his doubts about the marriage only to see Algernon Sartoris turn into a cad far worse than anything his innocent imagination could ever have conceived.

꧁꧂

The Bravest Battle

I N AUGUST 1873, Grant's new treasury secretary, William A. Richardson—a Harvard-educated lawyer from Lowell, Massachusetts, who had replaced Boutwell—contemplated the American economy with unruffled satisfaction: "I have devoted considerable time this summer to the investigation of the condition of the commerce of the country . . . and am very much pleased at the favorable exhibit."[1] To buttress his rosy appraisal, he cited mounting exports in cotton, bread, iron, steel, leather, and shoes. The government boasted a small surplus and had refinanced outstanding debt at reduced interest rates. In short, the boom that had powered the postwar economy appeared intact. Modern mass industries, such as steel and petroleum, and ever-expanding railroads had introduced new vigor but also instability into the economy. Only in retrospect would it be clear that the boom had been built on a flimsy scaffolding of speculation and that excessively generous credit had overextended the nation's railways.

On September 8, Wall Street banks started to fold in a cascading series of closures that sparked chaos in the financial district. Gold prices dove, stocks collapsed, and a general panic seized the city. Coincidentally, Grant found himself with a front-row seat for the foremost bankruptcy. He had gone to place Jesse in Cheltenham Academy outside Philadelphia and stayed at Ogontz, the estate of Jay Cooke, whose firm had marketed Union bonds during the war and bankrolled the Northern Pacific Railway. Grant and Elihu Washburne had even made stock investments through him. Ogontz was a gloomy five-story pile, smothered in heavy, Victorian furniture, but Cooke, with his long, patriarchal beard, proved a warm and charming host. On the morning of September 18, as Grant got ready to leave for Washington, Cooke pocketed several ominous telegrams, giving Grant no hint of their contents.

It turned out that Jay Cooke & Company, unable to sell Northern Pacific bonds, had gone bust. Such was the firm's incomparable prestige that its failure fanned a jittery situation into a full-blown panic, toppling one Wall Street house after another. On September 20, the New York Stock Exchange halted trading for ten days. Grant received emergency pleas for purchases of Treasury bonds to add liquidity to national banks, while Thomas Murphy, the former New York customs collector, wired: "Relief must come immediately or hundreds if not thousands of our best men will be ruined."[2] Not since 1837 had such a spasm of fear flashed through Wall Street.

In this heyday of laissez-faire economics, citizens didn't automatically expect the president to manage the economy or cushion downturns. Economic fluctuations were regarded almost like vagaries of weather. Nevertheless, on September 20, Grant and Richardson journeyed to New York, staying at the Fifth Avenue Hotel, where desperate businessmen besieged them. As *Harper's Weekly* described the scene, "The corridors swarmed with a multitude of frenzied people, who supposed that incalculable disaster impended, and that the President had the power of staying it by a word."[3] Any credit breakdown, Grant knew, would threaten produce shipped to the eastern seaboard for export, and he feared the crisis would soon migrate from Wall Street to Main Street. At the behest of New York bankers, he agreed to purchase Treasury bonds, but in the absence of a central bank, the government couldn't function as a lender of last resort, and he balked at more stimulative measures. As he put it, the government would "take all legal measures at its command; but it is evident that no Government efforts will avail without the active co-operation of the banks and moneyed corporations."[4] Boldly deviating from precedent, Grant allowed Richardson to reissue $26 million worth of greenbacks to satisfy those who thought some measure of inflation might revive the economy. In an interview, Grant sought to soothe the nation, describing the panic as a "passing event."[5] Writing privately to the banker Anthony J. Drexel, he sounded equally sanguine: "I hope the worst of the panic is over, and that general good may flow from it."[6]

Far from being transitory, the crisis was deep and intractable and persisted for more than five brutal years. It would be termed "the Great Depression" until eclipsed by the 1930s downturn. Much of the industrial landscape lay in ruins: half the nation's railroads went into receivership and half its iron furnaces shut down. In farming areas, crop and land prices plunged. In New York City alone, a quarter of all workers were tossed from their jobs. Before the depression ran its course, deflation had dragged down wholesale prices by 30 percent. Industrial leaders banded together to cut production and stabilize prices, leading to monopolistic practices in many industries and spawning a corresponding concentration in labor. Many workers joined unions that engaged in railway, textile, and coal strikes and flirted with radical movements. For the first time, America began to resemble the stratified, class-ridden societies of Europe. As unions demanded public works projects and easy money, Grant had to deal with a constellation of political forces unknown to earlier presidents in a simpler, agrarian America.

No clear theory dictated how government should steer the economy through such a profound downturn. "I look on the coming session [of Congress] as the most troublesome and uncertain of any that I [have] ever seen at this distance from it," Garfield wrote that November. "The great financial panic which has swept and is still sweeping over the country will be the most difficult element to handle."[7] The business community favored a cleansing of speculative excess by clinging to a tight money policy, forcing prices and wages to drop. Within Grant's cabinet, Hamilton Fish argued forcefully for austerity: "Any expansion would only bolster up some now tottering concerns, and would encourage new speculations."[8] Garfield and Richardson talked Grant out of an ambitious and farsighted plan to combat unemployment through a large-scale public works project, which would have anticipated Franklin Roosevelt's New Deal.[9]

As president, Grant had taken pride in being a scrupulous custodian of the nation's finances, cutting taxes, reducing expenditures, saving money on interest payments, and working toward restoring gold as the currency basis. The Panic of 1873 gave fresh urgency to the question of what to do about the circulation of greenbacks, which had helped the North to finance the Civil War and taken the country off the gold standard. Traditionally Americans had harbored deep suspicion of paper money, which wasn't backed by gold reserves. Yet greenbacks were championed by western farmers and railroads, who had borrowed heavily and therefore favored expansionary monetary policy. In contrast, bankers and other eastern creditors wanted Grant to resume the gold standard, giving money an imperishable value, a course backed by Lincoln, who had called for "a return to specie payments . . . at the earliest period compatible with due regard to all interests concerned."[10]

In general, Grant deemed it "one of the highest duties, of government, [to] secure to the citizen a medium of exchange of fixed, unvarying value."[11] At the same time, he feared a tight money supply might impose a straitjacket on the economy. He held surprisingly modern views on the need for an elastic currency that would expand and contract with seasonal trade. On the other hand, when surplus funds existed, he didn't want excess money to flow into speculative Wall Street loans and stock market gambling.

The seemingly esoteric topic of greenbacks became one of the most fraught issues of Grant's second term. By early 1874, the unemployed surged into the streets in mass protests, and they wanted more money in circulation to prime the economic pump. When Grant took office there were $356 million in greenbacks in circulation, with Boutwell and Richardson adding small amounts to that sum. Any further moves in that direction raised the specter of inflation, eliciting strident protests from hard-money men. "Now that no war threatens us, and no overmastering necessity is to be pleaded," proclaimed Roscoe Conkling, "guilty and mad will be the hour when Congress can find no better way to conduct the finances of the nation than to print an unlimited issue of irredeemable promises to pay."[12] Nevertheless, the House and Senate rushed through legislation to boost the greenback currency to $400 million and the national bank note circulation to $400 million—a sharp increase in the nation's money supply.

By April 14, this legislation, known as the Ferry bill, after its sponsor, Senator Thomas W. Ferry, but commonly dubbed "the inflation bill," sat on Grant's desk with every expectation of his endorsement. As he considered the bill, he was being vilified for corruption and cozy ties to congressional bosses. "Discontent is everywhere," Vice President Wilson warned him. "We are passing through a Storm of criticism and denunciation. You can carry us through the Wilderness as you once did."[13] Factory workers, farmers, and westerners clamored for the inflation bill, but *The Nation* deplored Senate complicity in the legislation, regretting how "that body is given over completely to inflation in its maddest form."[14]

Reviewing the bill with painstaking care, Grant found himself in a terrible quandary. He knew more greenbacks would make it difficult to resume specie payments—that is, allow Americans to redeem paper currency for gold or silver. At the same time, the bill enjoyed widespread approval from his Stalwart cronies in Congress, especially John Logan, Oliver Morton, and Ben Butler, plus members of his own cabinet. When it assembled on April 17, all but two of his secretaries wanted him to put his signature to the bill. Grant sat, listened, and said nothing, a poker player refusing to tip his hand. That day, the telegraph entrepreneur Cyrus Field bombarded him with a petition signed by 2,500 leading businessmen, pleading for a veto of the bill. Grant replied that "he had watched the progress of this bill through Congress with more interest than he had any other measure before that body since he had been President," but he still refused to commit himself.[15] Albert Redstone, president of the National Labor Council, squeezed Grant from the other side, anxiously urging him to approve the inflation bill and telling a reporter that Grant "will show that the people did not make him President to prevent their will and prevent their prosperity."[16] Some Republican leaders conjured up visions of wholesale western defections from the party because of a veto—a compelling argument for Grant and a frightening one. As he wrestled with the monetary riddle, he experienced such turmoil that he suffered bouts of insomnia. Even on blood-soaked battlefields he had slept more soundly.

On April 21, Grant summoned his cabinet and made a startling confession. The night before, he had resolved to sign the inflation bill and sat up late drafting an accompanying message, listing his most cogent arguments. But the more he wrote, he said, the more specious his own arguments sounded. "The only time I ever deliberately resolved to do an expedient thing for party reasons, against my own judgment, was on the occasion of the . . . inflation bill," Grant confessed years later. "I never was so pressed in my life to do anything as to sign that bill, never."[17] The more he wrote that night, the less he was persuaded by his own reasoning. Finally, he thought, "What is the good of all this? You do not believe it. You know it is not true."[18] So he tore up his message, tossed it into the wastebasket, and decided to veto the bill. It was an impressive display of Grant's intellectual honesty, candor, and exemplary courage. He had examined the bill dispassionately from many angles and found it wanting.

Grant refrained from asking for advice from his cabinet. Fish and Postmaster General Creswell applauded him—Fish said Grant had given America nothing less than "the foundation of a restored credit, & a sounder Currency"—but other cabinet secretaries fired back with a battery of protests.[19] Secretary of the Interior Delano reminded Grant that vetoes were usually reserved for declaring acts unconstitutional. Secretary of the Navy Robeson predicted a detrimental outcome in upcoming congressional elections. Attorney General Williams and Secretary of War Belknap foresaw untold damage to the fortunes of the Republican Party. Yet Unconditional Surrender Grant proved adamant. "I dare say the first result will be a storm of denunciation," he admitted. "But I am confident that the final judgment of the country will approve my veto."[20]

Though Grant always viewed the inflation bill veto as a proud accomplishment, ushering in a new age of sound money, he braced for fierce attacks. Surprisingly enough, his veto was sufficiently popular, even in parts of the West, that opponents fell short of the votes needed to override it. Not surprisingly, bankers and businessmen flooded the White House with congratulatory telegrams. The attorney Edwards Pierrepont wired from New York: "God almighty bless you. The bravest battle and the greatest victory of your life."[21] Garfield hurried to the White House to offer up a whiff of incense. "For twenty years no President has had an opportunity to do the country so much service by a veto message as Grant has," he wrote, "and he has met the issue manfully."[22] Grant had made a timely statement about his integrity, and the malaise that infected the administration seemed to vanish overnight. "We shall be able to stick to Grant to the end," rejoiced Rutherford B. Hayes.[23] The veto restored Grant's image as a simple, decent, straightforward president, every inch his own man. "He has a wonderful amount of good sense," Fish commented, "and when left alone is very apt to follow it."[24]

If the veto solidified the Republican Party's growing reputation as a bastion of sound money, free markets, and economic conservatism, it did not sit well in all quarters. A meeting of Indianapolis merchants took Grant to task for having sold himself to those "whose god is the dollar" and said it was "utterly shameful" that he should "do their bidding."[25] By the light of modern economic theory, it is hard to justify a veto that tightened money amid a severe economic contraction and likely worsened it. It also stoked populist movements, especially among eastern immigrants and western farmers, providing a major new opening for the Democrats in this era of Republican hegemony. But the veto did offer beneficial effects. It reassured European investors, who financed railroads and heavy industry, that they could plow funds into American business and be repaid in sound money. In this way Grant's decision, which likely had severely deleterious effects on deflation in the short run, set the stage for America's emergence as the world's supreme industrial power.

Not long after Grant's veto, Secretary of the Treasury Richardson left the cabinet, trailed by scandal. A Massachusetts politician, John D. Sanborn, had been hired by the Treasury Department to track down tax evaders and was allowed to retain half the back taxes collected. He extorted money from companies by falsely accusing them of tax evasion. Richardson had signed the contract with Sanborn and came in for sharp criticism. "Since I have been in Washington the past few days," Vice President Wilson notified Grant, "I have heard the strongest condemnation of [Richardson's] unfitness."[26] In early June 1874, Grant banished Richardson by exiling him to the U.S. Court of Claims—a peculiar penalty for official misconduct, probably explained by the fact that Richardson hadn't profited from the transactions in question.

Benjamin Bristow, the first solicitor general and a spirited booster of Grant's inflation bill veto, was tapped as the new treasury secretary. With his upright reputation, Bristow seemed a superb choice. "Grant can do more unexpected things in the same length of time than any man I know," observed the diplomat Marshall Jewell.[27] If Bristow claimed little financial expertise, he was honest and competent, hailed from a key border state, and had excelled in the Klan prosecutions. A tall, heavyset man, he had an elegant appearance and a "firm sweep of the jaw" that, one reporter predicted, promised an "aggressive performance" at Treasury.[28] Hamilton Fish came away pleased by their first cabinet meeting, lauding Bristow as "masterful, energetic, and ambitious."[29] A zealous advocate of civil service reform, Bristow soon expelled hundreds of political appointees from his department.

As Grant reshuffled his cabinet, he replaced Postmaster General Creswell, who had done an excellent job, lobbying for a postal telegraph while incurring the wrath of the Western Union monopoly. He was succeeded by Marshall Jewell, a former Connecticut governor and minister to Russia. Like Bristow, Jewell had crusaded for civil service reform and immediately started cleaning up his department with Grant's blessing. The appointments of Bristow and Jewell were seen as triumphs of good government, and the Union League of America congratulated them for "inaugurating a new and healthier order of things in their Departments," ridding them "of corrupt and inefficient Officers."[30] Their appointments formed part of Grant's rebuttal of Liberal Republican critics who saw him as much too lax on scandal.

Having killed the inflation bill, Grant completed his monetary program with a return to the gold standard, which would enable any citizen who walked into a Treasury office to exchange greenbacks for gold coins. The policy remained explosive amid a depression that many populists blamed on scarce money. After Grant outlined his views in a memorandum, House Speaker James G. Blaine cautioned Fish that "if carried out it would be ruinous to the Republican party and the country."[31] Even hard-money men worried about moving too quickly, arousing popular ire. Despite this, Bristow urged Congress to pass legislation to return the currency to a specie basis. Because many Republican leaders feared the political impact of an overly hasty return to gold, the Specie Payment Resumption Act of 1875 postponed resumption to January 1, 1879, slowly scaling back greenbacks in circulation. In signing the bill, Grant reiterated his belief that with a currency of "fixed, known, value," business would revive and "the beginning of prosperity, on a firm basis, would be reached."[32] The act flew through Congress, encountering scant opposition. Republicans might disagree on Reconstruction, but they heartily concurred on preserving the perpetual strength of the Almighty Dollar.

THE MIDTERM ELECTION RESULTS in autumn 1874 proved nothing short of calamitous for the Republican Party, a stunning repudiation of Grant and his inflation bill veto. Republicans relinquished their sizable majority in the House of Representatives—the first time they had surrendered control since the war—and Democrats took charge by a huge margin. This scarcely seemed the same Democratic Party trounced so handily by Grant two years earlier. It was small consolation to the Republicans that they retained a majority of Senate seats. The Democrats chalked up major triumphs in New York, New Jersey, Massachusetts, Pennsylvania, Ohio, Missouri, and Illinois. The main reason for the electoral landslide was the economic slump, which left voters in a surly mood, and Grant's refusal to countenance a dose of inflation to conquer it. The aura of corruption around the White House had also contributed to a sense of an administration adrift. Some observers believed that speculation about a possible third term for Grant—something he dismissed "in ridicule and contempt"—made him seem selfish, encouraging disgruntled voters to turn against him.[33] The first act of the new House would be to pass a resolution that exhorted Grant to refrain from seeking a third term, which would be "unwise, unpatriotic, and fraught with peril to our free institutions."[34]

Another disaffected spectator was William T. Sherman, who was far less intimate with Grant than in the palmy days of their wartime comradeship. Sherman was irate when Grant allowed Secretary Belknap to interfere with his chain of command and he moved his headquarters to St. Louis in protest. "My faith in [Grant's] friendship is shaken," Sherman told an editor, "and when again he wants it, it may be less than he supposes."[35] Privately Sherman was scathing about his old friend, pinning the electoral defeat on Grant: "Genl Grant and his immediate surroundings have been selfish and mean, and have alienated the Country and many of his Old Friends are not only alienated but deeply angry." He mentioned his many sacrifices for Grant. "You have seen how he has returned it. I am not sorry that he has caught the inevitable consequence."[36] Sherman never understood that Grant had graduated from the narrow, provincial outlook of a military commander to embrace a broader leadership role. Despite Sherman's bitterness, Ulysses and Julia Grant were the soul of hospitality when he lunched with them at the White House in November.

In the congressional elections, northern voters had sent a clarion message of retreat from black civil rights, protesting Grant's decision to send troops into Louisiana. Racism was omnipresent in the North as well as the South. "There is a deep and a growing restlessness and jealousy of Military influence, & ascendancy," Fish noted, "and this jealousy is being fostered . . . by the Democratic press."[37] As the northern public, beset by economic troubles, soured on Reconstruction, they latched onto a book, *The Prostrate State: South Carolina Under Negro Government,* which portrayed southern Reconstruction governments as populated by corrupt carpetbaggers and illiterate black legislators. The author, James Shepherd Pike, had worked for Greeley at the *New York Tribune* and become disillusioned with Grant. After Greeley died, his successor, Whitelaw Reid, sent Pike on a southern tour, which produced this racist diatribe. "Sambo takes naturally to stealing," Pike told readers. "Seven years ago these men were raising corn and cotton under the whip of the overseer. Today they are raising points of order and questions of privilege."[38]

In this new dispensation, Grant was increasingly fair game. Democratic control of the House had far-reaching consequences for him. Armed with investigative powers, committees turned a glaring searchlight on executive departments to ferret out corruption, a tactic used to discredit the administration on Reconstruction. Half the House committee chairmanships were handed over to southerners, who attempted to block further racial progress by Grant. In the South,

Democrats regained control of Alabama as the old white elite restored their antebellum primacy. White and black Republicans in the region reacted with shocked dismay. "What sorry times have befallen us!" wrote Adelbert Ames, now Mississippi's governor. "The old rebel spirit will not only revive, but it will make itself felt. It will roam over the land, thirsty for revenge . . . the war is not yet over."[39]

Through it all, Grant remained imperturbable. He had won battles precisely because he never succumbed to panic, but his congenital calm now made him seem out of touch to some colleagues. When Postmaster General Jewell dined at the White House, he didn't find the president as gloomy as he had expected, telling Fish that Grant had "no appreciation of the results of the late election, which have been overwhelmingly adverse to the Republican party."[40] Other Republican leaders were equally alarmed, Vice President Wilson calling Grant "the millstone around the neck of our party that would sink it."[41] So despairing was Garfield that he felt "all the Gods had conspired to destroy the Republican Party," while Bristow interpreted the elections as "a perfect Waterloo to Republicans."[42]

By late November, Grant labored several hours a day over his annual message to Congress, writing it, as usual, by himself. That August, when he attended a Methodist camp meeting at Martha's Vineyard, the mogul Russell Sage had invited him aboard an iron steamship built by his company. This encouraged Grant to revive a proposal he had floated a year earlier to connect American canals and rivers into a national network, lowering transport costs and stoking business. He also wanted to revive American shipbuilding, which had been badly damaged during the war, by paying "ample compensation" to American ships that carried mail domestically and abroad.[43] Grant expanded this vision by again endorsing a canal to connect the Atlantic and Pacific Oceans and he had surveys conducted to locate the most feasible site. Quite visionary about this pathway, Grant maintained that "it would add largely to the wealth of the Pacific coast, and, perhaps, change the whole current of the trade of the world."[44]

As he struggled with his annual message, all issues paled beside the baffling subject of race relations. In a bluntly eloquent appeal, he reproached white southerners for condoning vigilante violence against black citizens. He acknowledged that they fancied themselves law-abiding citizens. "But do they do right in ignoring the existence of violence and bloodshed in resistance to constituted authority?" He railed against those who denied federal responsibility to halt abuses on the state level: "The theory is even raised that there is to be no further

interference on the part of the general government to protect citizens within a
state where the state authorities fail to give protection. This is a great mistake.
While I remain Executive all the laws of Congress, and the provisions of the
Constitution . . . will be enforced with rigor."[45] In short, Grant pleaded with
white southerners to do justice to blacks or he would have no choice but to send
in unwanted federal troops. He issued a prophetic warning of the perils facing
America's two parties:

> Under existing conditions the Negro votes the republican ticket be-
> cause he knows his friends are of that party. Many a good citizen
> votes the opposite not because [he] agrees with the great principles of
> state which separate party, but because, generally, he is opposed to
> Negro rule. This is a most delusive cry. Treat the Negro as a citizen
> and a voter—as he is, and must remain—and soon parties will be
> divided, *not on the color line,* but on principle.[46]

From southern Republicans, Grant heard heartrending pleas for help, a sorrowful chorus of concern. From a black minister in Tennessee, he learned of
blacks flocking to his town because so many had been murdered by night riders
elsewhere. He promised Grant that "these Colored peopel will all die for you to
day. they have a great love for you. So we want you to do all [you] Can for us."[47]
A Houston resident complained of Democrats riding roughshod over Texas Republicans. "Send your Bayonets to Texas—and break up the assemblage of
Maniacs—Ruffians—and Thieves At Austin." The writer asserted that Democrats wouldn't hesitate to make a constitution that placed "the colored man in a
peonage worse than Slavery—But they fear the mighty Ulysses might Break up
there Government."[48]

Unfortunately, Grant was progressively hamstrung in coping with this sudden rash of crises. The newly resurrected Democrats launched a congressional
investigation into Justice Department spending that imposed steep cuts in enforcing Reconstruction. The three Enforcement Acts that had given muscle to
the anti-Klan battle clashed with growing southern resistance, bolstered by
northern neglect. Attorney General Williams, who had continued the crusading
militance of Amos Akerman against the Klan, faced growing hostility and the
press disparaged him as "Grant's Secretary of State for Southern Affairs."[49] He

began to plead for more caution in southern prosecutions, insisting the Klan had already been smashed. With major cases about Reconstruction's constitutionality pending before the Supreme Court, Williams instructed district attorneys that "criminal prosecution under these acts ought to be suspended until it is known whether the Supreme Court will hold them constitutional or otherwise."[50] When issued in spring 1876, those court decisions would slam the door shut on Reconstruction.

The situation grew more perilous in March 1875 when Postmaster General Jewell asked Grant if he could speak to him plainly about a troubling matter. "I always wish the Cabinet to feel entirely free to make confidential communications to me," Grant replied.[51] Jewell then told of whispers that the Judiciary Committee, probing the Justice Department, had generated facts about Attorney General Williams that could tarnish the administration. Williams's Supreme Court nomination had foundered in part because of his wife Kate's extravagant spending. Now it was alleged that after the Justice Department brought suit for evasion of customs duties against the New York merchant house of Pratt & Boyd, a "certain lady" had extorted $30,000 from them in exchange for a promise to drop the suit. When Grant conferred with Fish on April 12, he preferred to view Williams as an innocent dupe, showing the sympathy for human frailty that was his tragic undoing. As Fish wrote, Grant "had a high respect for Williams but feared that he had been entrapped, or that transactions had passed through his hands without his notice, for which he could not fail to be held officially responsible, of a very disreputable nature."[52] Nonetheless, frightened by a potential probe into the attorney general's office, Grant suggested that Williams depart at once. In accepting his resignation, Grant gave no hint of the scandalous backdrop: "My sincere friendship accompanies you in the new field of life you have chosen and best wishes for your success. Very respectfully yours U. S. GRANT."[53]

In choosing a successor, Grant searched for someone of unimpeachable honesty to forestall further snooping by House Democrats. He picked Edwards Pierrepont, a popular New York lawyer, who had gained reformist credentials combating corruption in Tammany Hall. To avoid unpleasant surprises, Grant made sure to canvass his cabinet, all of whom warmly approved the choice. In adding Pierrepont, Bristow, and Jewell to his cabinet, Grant temporarily silenced detractors who had portrayed his administration as riddled with corruption. *Harper's Weekly* said that by recruiting these three men of "the highest character," Grant had shown his commitment to "good government and honest administration."[54]

PERHAPS NO STATE EXPOSED more graphically the irremediable clash between the old South and Republican rule than Mississippi. The state legislature's composition was shockingly alien to many Mississippi whites—55 of 115 state representatives were black, as were 9 of 37 senators. In the summer of 1874, Grant received a steady flow of warnings that white agitators, operating under the People's Party or White Man's Party banner, would attempt to purge the legislature by intimidating black voters and officeholders. Especially alarming was violence predicted in Vicksburg, where armed whites prowled the streets before municipal elections on August 4. On July 4, the anniversary of Grant's Vicksburg victory, white thugs pounced on a patriotic celebration held by black Republicans and opened murderous fire on the crowd, with several killed in the subsequent melee. Peter Crosby, the first black county sheriff in Vicksburg, appealed to Lieutenant Governor Alexander K. Davis, who then pleaded with Grant to send two companies of U.S. soldiers. "Armed bodies of men are parading the streets both night and day," he informed Grant.[55]

Governor Ames grew desperately worried. Knowing only federal troops could safeguard black voters, he described for Grant the openly military character of the white Democrat threat, organized into infantry, cavalry, and artillery units. Departing from the assertive actions of his first term, Grant hesitated and refused to send in federal soldiers. "I have tried to get troops, but the President refuses," Ames told his wife. "It is thought he wants the support of the Southern Democrats for a third term. Most true it is that they are generally for him in this state. And they in Vicksburg who are rioting, who are ready for murder and frauds, laud him to the skies."[56]

The August election passed without violence. "The election just closed was the most peaceable and orderly ever held here" came the reassuring message to Grant from a Mississippi senator.[57] But the eerie quiet merely proved that white intimidation had succeeded, with blacks terrorized into staying home; white supremacists expelled Republicans from local offices without firing a shot. "Had there been a doubt as to the issue," Ames concluded, "a bloody riot would have resulted."[58] It was a turning point in Reconstruction, much as Vicksburg's fall had been during the war. White Democrats had demonstrated that without the protection of federal troops, they could resurrect the prewar power structure. The Vicksburg vote showed the fundamental weakness of a political revolution that had relied heavily on force applied by outsiders in Washington—something that couldn't be maintained indefinitely. The lesson was well learned by armed White League and White Line militia in Mississippi, Louisiana, Arkansas, Alabama, and South Carolina, who mobilized to retake control of their states.

Grant was peppered with conflicting reports from white Democrats and black Republicans in Mississippi, who seemed to reside on different planets. One white complained to Grant about "ignorant brutal" black voters; griped that "the scum of the North" had "flooded this country in pursuit of offices & plunder"; and, referring to Grant himself, observed, "We have a Dictator who claims to be President under the constitution."[59] Yet black citizens told Grant they felt utterly powerless. A black sergeant who had fought with Grant at Vicksburg said of the black community in Mississippi: "We are all most Povity stricken to death . . . We are dependin on you for help." The Democrats, he said, wanted "to starve the dam negros out that vote the Radical ticket."[60]

On December 5, a bloodless coup occurred in Vicksburg when armed members of the Taxpayers' League (the White League in some accounts) seized the Warren County courthouse, forced the black sheriff, Peter Crosby, to flee, then chased out the board of supervisors. As a column of black militia approached Vicksburg, the mayor declared martial law and appointed a former Confederate officer, Colonel Horace Miller, to enforce it. Black and white militia confronted each other at a bridge south of town; as blacks began to retreat, armed whites fired and killed several blacks. Whites then went on a homicidal spree, pulling blacks from their homes and killing them. Some violence occurred on the very spot where Pemberton had surrendered to Grant. "They were shot down like dogs," wrote Blanche Ames, the governor's wife, "and those that fell wounded were murdered."[61] A congressional investigatory committee concurred: "It was no battle; it was a simple massacre."[62] The death toll approached that of a small battle: at least twenty-one blacks dead and two wounded. As one observer recalled, "Others were killed and eaten by buzzards . . . The birds had got all the meat off their bodies, and the only way you could recognize them was by their clothes."[63] In the days ahead, armed white men initiated a campaign of killing in the nearby countryside that took up to three hundred black lives.

On December 17, Governor Ames summoned the state legislature to an emotional special session. He now faced an armed uprising that he described as an "insurrection in the fullest sense."[64] Without the military means to curb this "reign of terror," he feared the insurgents would impose a new order "founded entirely upon the degradation and serfdom of a class."[65] Both houses of the legislature endorsed a resolution calling upon Grant to hasten federal troops to Vicksburg. There was no way Grant could back down before a military putsch on American soil, and he now showed flashes of his gritty old panache. First he acted to protect the Mississippi legislature, telling the federal commander in Jackson that if "threatened with violence from unauthorized persons they must be protected in the proper discharge of their duties."[66] On December 21, he issued a proclamation that repeated charges made by Ames and Mississippi legislators and ordered the "disorderly and turbulent persons to disperse and retire peaceably within five days."[67] Grant now followed the well-polished script of his first term.

When Ames requested federal troops on January 4, Grant promptly ordered his commanders to "comply with the request of Govr Ames as far as practicable."[68] His decisive response contrasted starkly with congressional wavering. "I fear that Congress will not give the President power to put down the White Leaguers of the South," Jesse Ames told his son Adelbert. "If not, there can be nothing but a reign of terror in the South until the nation is involved in a Civil War from one end of the land to the other of which the last war is a mere trifle compared to it."[69] When a congressional committee reported in February on the Mississippi bloodshed, it concluded that the nation had arrived at a crossroads and "must either restrain by force these violent demonstrations by the bold, fierce spirits of the whites" or tell newly enfranchised black citizens, "we have made you men and citizens . . . now work out your own salvation as others have done."[70] It had become flagrantly obvious that no common ground existed between the white and black communities in the South, no middle position that allowed for compromise. Any federal action would either inflame the white community or victimize the black. There was simply no neat solution as a violent gulf yawned open between Democrats and Republicans.

The other southern warfare that winter was in Louisiana, where blacks were terrified by marauding White Leaguers. An attempt to integrate New Orleans schools resulted in a wave of violence as squadrons of white men and boys severely beat black students, hauling them forcibly from integrated schools and marching them off to black schools. "The city superintendent was attacked by a posse of half grown boys and insulted, beaten and even threatened with hanging," Grant heard from a student.[71] Dismayed by the simultaneous violence in Louisiana and Mississippi, Grant sent Phil Sheridan to Vicksburg, Jackson, and New Orleans to collect information and report back on his findings.

Sheridan's advent coincided with one of the stormiest moments in New Orleans annals. The 1874 election had created a stalemate in the Louisiana legislature. The Conservatives—a fusion of Democrats and Liberal Republicans—had ostensibly won the legislature, but the returning board, which certified elections, tried to forge a Republican majority by vacating several seats won by Conservatives. The upshot was that when the lower house of the state legislature gathered in early January, both sides claimed to rule by a two-seat majority. Anticipating violence, eighteen hundred federal troops ringed the statehouse. At noon, with great turmoil in the chamber, the house convened, elected a Conservative as the temporary speaker, and prepared to fill five undecided seats with Conservatives. This prompted Republicans to march out in protest.

What happened next shocked the nation. Governor William Pitt Kellogg requested that General Philippe R. de Trobriand remove "all persons not returned as legal members of the house of representatives by the returning-board of the State."[72] Accompanied by twenty bayonet-wielding soldiers, Trobriand burst into the chamber, brandishing papers from Governor Kellogg. One declared the house an illegal body while another gave him authority to eject the five new members not confirmed by the returning board. The five Conservatives were escorted from the chamber amid a show of bayonets and Republican cheers. By the time the general left, Kellogg Republicans controlled the disputed house and Conservatives had withdrawn, refusing to take dictation from federal soldiers.

Sheridan was ready to hand out rough justice to white vigilantes. "I think that the terrorization now existing in Louisiana, Mississippi, and Arkansas could be entirely removed . . . by the arrest and trial of the ringleaders of the armed White League," he informed Belknap. "It is possible that if the President would issue a proclamation declaring them banditti, no further action need be taken except that which would devolve upon me."[73] Sheridan's remarks became public, touching off a national furor. Without consulting Grant's cabinet, Belknap sent back a supportive telegram: "The President and all of us have full confidence and thoroughly approve your course."[74] Sheridan's remarks and Belknap's response would haunt the administration. Not given to legal niceties, Sheridan told a visiting Massachusetts congressman that the best way to vanquish the

White League was to "suspend the what-do-you-call-it"—otherwise known as the writ of habeas corpus.[75]

In tampering with a legislature, the rambunctious Sheridan had crossed a line, hitherto invisible, that was now clearly marked out for irate citizens. His high-handed behavior was a publicity bonanza for southern Democrats. The spectacle of soldiers entering a statehouse left northern opinion aghast, leading to vociferous demands for Sheridan's ouster. Major Republican newspapers in the North denounced Grant. William Cullen Bryant thought it high time for Sheridan to "tear off his epaulets and break his sword and fling the fragments into the Potomac."[76] The strident headline in the *New York World* distilled northern hysteria: "Tyranny! A Sovereign State Murdered!"[77] *The Nation* joined the apoplectic chorus, damning the New Orleans action as "the most outrageous subversion of parliamentary government by military force yet attempted in this country."[78] Before long, death threats against Grant, most emanating from the South, swamped the White House.

The New Orleans events presented Grant with an issue as tough and intractable as any he had faced as president. He felt outraged at the injustices white Democrats perpetrated in Louisiana and Mississippi. Yet even sympathetic northerners cringed at the image of federal soldiers barging into a state legislature and ousting elected officials. George Templeton Strong spoke for many when he wrote, "I have stood up for Grant through evil report and good report for ten years," but he would not condone the Louisiana blunder.[79] A couple of days later, Strong ran into General John Dix, who remarked, "It's only the other day that they murdered a score or two of niggers at Vicksburg. Why didn't these gentlemen get up an indignation meeting about *that*?"[80] Other isolated voices in the North roundly applauded the hard line in Louisiana, especially Wendell Phillips, who commended Grant's "decision & sagacity in dealing with the White League. One firm decisive hour will scatter the whole conspiracy."[81]

Sensitive to public opinion, Grant worried about alienating supporters on whom he had relied to reform southern society. On January 9, he assembled his cabinet for a highly contentious debate on Louisiana. One of Grant's saving graces was his ability to listen, and he did just that. Attorney General Williams likened the federal troops in New Orleans to a *posse comitatus* summoned to maintain peace under the U.S. Constitution—an interpretation Grant applauded. Fish protested that whether Democrats had committed fraud or not, Governor Kellogg had no right to interfere with the legislature. When he suggested that Grant repudiate Trobriand's action, Grant snapped he would "'certainly not denounce' it nor would he censure Sheridan."[82] But Fish thought Grant's support of Sheridan waned as the discussion progressed, and "he seemed to be somewhat impressed with doubt as to the entire correctness of what had been done."[83]

The Louisiana hubbub did not subside. Two days later the Pennsylvania legislature passed a resolution condemning "so heinous an abuse of the power committed to the President."[84] At first Grant refused to bend. Events in the South struck bedrock principles that he would not compromise. As he contemplated a message to the Senate, he told Fish "he was determined under no circumstances to apologize for anything that had been done."[85] Fish pleaded that a fundamental constitutional principle was at stake that the president had to defend. Grant replied that his message would "recapitulate the events which he thought would show the necessity of what had occurred."[86]

In his speech sent to the Senate on January 13, 1875, Grant spoke straight from the heart. He summoned his innermost feelings from the war and frustration over the bloody punishment inflicted on southern black and white Republicans and his message rose to unusual heights of eloquence. Instead of restricting himself to recent Louisiana history, he reconstructed earlier outrages perpetrated in the state. He recounted the six Republicans murdered in cold blood in Coushatta in August 1874—a crime that had gone unpunished. He recalled how D. B. Penn, who claimed election as lieutenant governor in 1872, issued an "inflammatory proclamation" calling upon state militia to "drive from power the usurpers," as he termed Republican officeholders. "The White Leagues, armed and ready for the conflict, promptly responded."[87] Governor Kellogg had requested troops and Grant had issued a proclamation to restore order. By then, insurgents "had taken forcible possession of the State House, and temporarily subverted the government. Twenty or more people were killed, including a number of the police of the city."[88] Grant implied that people had forgotten the bloody prelude to the violence inspired by Democrats, which had produced the legislative standoff.

Turning to recent events in New Orleans, Grant pointed out that he hadn't known beforehand of Trobriand's action, but he described a military coup hatched by Conservatives, who had employed fraud and violence to engineer a majority in Louisiana's lower house. "I am credibly informed that these violent proceedings were part of a premeditated plan to have the house organized in this way, recognize what has been called the McEnery senate, then to depose Governor Kellogg, and so revolutionize the State government."[89]

In conclusion, Grant expressed his extreme distaste at having to interfere in the domestic affairs of Louisiana: "I have deplored the necessity which seemed to make it my duty under the Constitution and laws to direct such interference." Nothing, he added, would afford him greater satisfaction than to sweep federal troops from the South. But he stated, in tough, unsparing, language, that "to the extent that Congress has conferred power upon me to prevent it, neither Ku-Klux-Klans, White Leagues, nor any other association using arms and violence to execute their unlawful purposes, can be permitted in that way to govern any part of this country."[90]

Grant had refused to mince words about Democratic injustices in Louisiana. As Fred Grant told Sheridan, the Grant family had stood up for him "and mother carries her endorsement almost to an absurdity. Father is very strong in his feelings but more quiet."[91] That Julia Grant, erstwhile southern belle, felt so outraged by Democratic misbehavior in Louisiana says something about the militant mood in the Grant household. From official Washington, Grant received welcome encomia on his address. "You have never been more forcible or felicitous in the presentation of a great public question!" House Speaker Blaine assured him.[92] John Singleton Mosby told Grant his message was "a triumphant vindication of your conduct."[93] At Faneuil Hall in Boston, a large protest meeting, addressed by Wendell Phillips, applauded Grant and Sheridan, but the national mood was swinging rapidly in the other direction. The president was running out of room to maneuver as the country backed away from further federal interference in the South. The outcry over Louisiana began to ring down the final curtain on Reconstruction. Southern whites increasingly substituted the word "Redemption"—a restoration of white rule—for the hated term "Reconstruction."

In New Orleans, the atmosphere remained so combustible that newspapers openly advocated Sheridan's murder and he was heckled when he appeared in his hotel dining room. "Some of the Banditti made idle threats last night that they would assassinate me because I dared to tell the truth," he informed Belknap. "I am not afraid and will not be stopped . . . the very air has been impregnated with assassinations for some years."[94] Grant refused to hurl Sheridan to the wolves and reiterated to two congressmen his high esteem for the diminutive general: "I believe General Sheridan has no superior as a general, either living or dead, and perhaps not an equal."[95] When a congressional delegation went to Louisiana to collect evidence, Sheridan noted that more than two thousand political murders had been committed in Louisiana since 1866. The congressmen brokered a compromise whereby control of the lower house was returned to Democrats, who promised not to impeach or overthrow the Republican governor Kellogg.

Many saw the Louisiana violence as the opening shot of a second Civil War and a revitalized Confederacy, albeit clothed in a new form. Discussing the mood in New Orleans, Sheridan told Orville Babcock, "I have so often heard expressions that the new rebellion was to be fought under the stars & stripes and in the north as well as the South—that the mistake made in 1861 was to have had their own flag."[96] So darkly violent was the outlook that a former Georgia governor advised Babcock: "*Confidential* . . . the time has arrived when the President is in danger of assassination, and extraordinary caution should be exercised."[97] As the whole edifice of Reconstruction cracked apart, fueled by a northern backlash, those most fearful were the freed people of the South. Reflecting their anxiety, more than two hundred Louisiana blacks petitioned Grant about their wish to emigrate to a foreign nation: "We cannot get upon a mans Stemboat and make a round trip but what Some of us are whipped or Beat or Killed or Driven ashore. if we Stand up as men for the protection of our Wives and our Daughters . . . these white men . . . Says that we must die."[98]

One of the last hurrahs of Reconstruction was passage of the Civil Rights Act of 1875, enacted by lame-duck Republicans. For several years, such a bill had been a will-o'-the-wisp for Charles Sumner, who hoped it would be "the capstone of my work."[99] As he lay dying in early 1874, he clasped the hands of visitors to his bedside and croaked passionately, "You must take care of the civil-rights bill . . . don't let it fail."[100] Despite its association with Sumner, Grant endorsed the measure and signed it into law on March 1, 1875. It outlawed racial segregation in public accommodations, schools, transportation, and juries. The law had many flaws in its enforcement provisions, but was revolutionary in its principles of equal treatment for all. "This bill is a simple declaration of the equality of the citizens of the United States," declared *Harper's Weekly*.[101] Democratic governors never bothered to enforce it. Nonetheless, however toothless, it struck fear into those opposed to interracial justice, as evidenced by a new wave of death threats that Grant promptly received from the Klan.[102] The Civil Rights Act of 1875 was struck down as unconstitutional by the Supreme Court in 1883. Not until 1957 would Congress dare to pass another civil rights bill, and it was only with the long-overdue Civil Rights Act of 1964 that many of the 1875 legislation's protections for blacks became the enduring law of the land.

Let No Guilty Man Escape

HARDLY HAD THE Louisiana furor died down than Grant found his administration descending into a scandal that would eclipse all previous scandals, which had soiled individual cabinet members but had not touched the president himself. This new one would widen, surround Grant, and threaten him directly.

To finance the war, the Lincoln administration had levied steep taxes on whiskey and evading those taxes had become a national pastime. Whiskey barons had emerged as major forces in American politics, channeling vast amounts of money to the Democratic Party under Andrew Johnson. "The revenues of the Country are in the hands of the enemy," Grant was told during the 1868 campaign, "and the whiskey ring alone can raise from now until the close of the canvas a million a day should they need so much for political purposes."[1] In 1868 Congress created internal revenue supervisors to clean up fraud arising from the whiskey tax. Nevertheless, the Treasury Department remained an asylum for corrupt agents, who siphoned off money from distillers eager to avoid taxes. The methods of the Whiskey Ring were fairly straightforward. Distillers would falsify figures of the amount of liquor brewed and treasury agents would then certify those bogus returns. The upshot was that in major brewing centers taxpayers were cheated of millions of dollars in government revenues.

The system was perfected in St. Louis, where Grant maintained the White Haven farm and where he and Julia thought they might retire. As he explained, he kept close watch on his irregular farm income because it was "largely what I must depend on for a support when retired from public duties."[2] In October 1874, Grant attended a St. Louis agricultural fair, and his sentimental homecoming again underscored the indescribable changes in his life since 1860, when he had left the town impoverished. Horace Porter rode over to Hardscrabble with Grant and recorded this fascinating vignette:

> When visiting St. Louis with him . . . he made a characteristic remark showing how little his thoughts dwelt upon those events of his life which made such a deep impression upon others. Upon his arrival a horse and buggy were ordered, and a drive taken to his farm, about eight miles distant. He stopped on the high ground overlooking the city, and stood for a time by the side of the little log house which he had built partly with his own hands in the days of his poverty and early struggles. Upon being asked whether the events of the past fifteen years of his life did not seem to him like a tale of the *Arabian Nights,* especially in coming from the White House to visit the little farm-house of early days, he replied, "Well I never thought about it in that light."[3]

Grant's host in St. Louis was his old friend General John McDonald, a former steamboat operator slated to play a notorious part in the upcoming whiskey scandal. Grant had appointed him supervisor for internal revenue for Arkansas and Missouri, with headquarters in St. Louis, but instead of rooting out crooks, McDonald became the kingpin of the local whiskey cabal. For every seventy-cent tax dodged on a gallon of whiskey, thirty-five cents went to the distiller and an equal amount to the ring. These colossal sums propped up Republican politicians in Missouri, shady activity unknown to Grant.

Never known for subtlety, McDonald entertained Grant lavishly during his stay, allowing him to use for free an entire floor at a local hotel. While there, Grant entered two of his horses in a competition at the local fair. Shaded by a pagoda in the center of the arena, Grant smoked his cigar and studied the horses. As a connoisseur, he knew the Kentucky Thoroughbreds on display far outshone his own horses and he was resigned to losing. He didn't reckon on McDonald's role as judge; the latter approached Grant's colt and gaudily draped a blue ribbon around its neck. Far from being pleased, Grant was disgusted at the unfairness, a friend recalling that Grant "flushed, took his cigar out of his mouth, threw it on the ground and said in a low voice: 'That is an outrage.' He turned and walked away."[4] McDonald also strove to ingratiate himself with Grant by giving him a pair of fast horses, equipped with wagon, harness, and gold breastplates engraved with his name. The Whiskey Ring made sure Grant's aide Orville Babcock enjoyed an unforgettable interlude with the blonde Louise Hawkins, nicknamed "Sylph." Waxing poetic about her beauty, Babcock said, "She was, indeed, a sylph and siren, whose presence was like the flavor of the poppy mingled with the perfumes of Araby."[5]

Grant told McDonald that he worried about Republicans losing Missouri, and McDonald, to remedy that, doled out whiskey funds and patronage jobs to favored politicians. So much whiskey money flowed through his operation that he directed funds to candidates in other states. The ring spread its bribes liberally among Washington insiders, who warned distillers whenever anyone from the capital came snooping. Because of Grant's friendship with McDonald, it was commonly asserted in the St. Louis cabal that "the old man knows"—meaning Grant. McDonald fostered this misconception, giving his conspirators an illusory sense of safety, but he alone alleged that Grant knew of these machinations.[6]

In June 1874, when Benjamin Bristow became treasury secretary, he brought his prosecutorial zeal to bear against the ring. In his robust style, he embarked on a mission "to purge the [Republican] party of all the rogues that have fastened themselves upon us and to satisfy the people that we mean to have honest government."[7] That October, when he sent revenue inspectors to St. Louis, somebody in Washington tipped off the ring with an oblique telegram: "Put your house in order. Your friends will visit you."[8] Thus forewarned, the conspirators averted detection. The oracle in the capital spoke again to the conspirators on February 3: "We have official information that the enemy weakens. Push things. Sylph."[9] It wasn't yet apparent to investigators that the Whiskey Ring had a confederate ensconced in a high place and that his name was Orville Babcock. Grant grew wary of Bristow's crusade, having been warned by Ben Butler that the treasury secretary was a self-seeking man who sought publicity to further his own presidential ambitions.

By December 1874, Bristow believed Babcock and Secretary of the Interior Delano plotted to oust him. "I am struggling along in the Treasury Department as best I can," he told a friend, "and assure you I find it a very hard place to fill."[10] He was aided by Solicitor of the Treasury Bluford Wilson, brother of General James H. Wilson. Bristow secured a major breakthrough in February, when

George W. Fishback, publisher of *The St. Louis Globe-Democrat,* alerted him to a monstrous system of fraud in St. Louis distilleries and promised to supply a well-placed source. Bristow hired a secret agent, Myron Colony, to delve into nefarious doings in St. Louis, while James J. Brooks, assistant chief of the Secret Service, did the same in Chicago and Milwaukee. Before long, Bristow possessed evidence that St. Louis distilleries ran clandestinely at night, paying taxes on only a third of the whiskey they shipped, and similarly incriminating findings cropped up in Chicago, Milwaukee, Louisville, and other brewing centers where millions of gallons of whiskey escaped taxation. The scope of the scandal broadened just as Grant had labored to improve the ethical tone of his administration.

On May 7, Bristow and Wilson sketched for Grant a massive pattern of collusion between distillers and revenue agents, pinpointing McDonald's central involvement. Suitably appalled, Grant demanded that suspect agents be dismissed and pledged his "hearty cooperation."[11] Bristow and Wilson were very heartened. Grant "stated that McDonald had been a friend of his, and had grievously betrayed, not only that friendship, but the public," Wilson later testified. "As to the others . . . he said they were either knaves or fools, and in either case should go out."[12] When Bristow apprised Grant of imminent plans to seize distilleries in St. Louis, Chicago, and Milwaukee, Grant approved. Although the plan was hatched in strictest confidence, Babcock, writing as Sylph, alerted distillers. "Lightning will strike on Monday," he informed St. Louis. "Be prepared for it."[13] When the intercepted telegram was returned to Washington, Bristow knew the ring had a confederate lodged in the upper echelons of the administration, although he didn't yet know the culprit was Babcock.

On May 10, Bristow struck hard at the ring, raiding distilleries and tax offices in St. Louis, Chicago, and Milwaukee. Reams of paper fell into his hands that documented systematic tax evasion and yielded dozens of arrests. Confiscated ledgers confirmed John McDonald as a mastermind of the scheme. He turned up in Washington to try to contain the damage, but when Bristow showed him irrefutable evidence against him, McDonald broke down and admitted to swindling in his district. McDonald resigned his St. Louis post along with John A. Joyce, the local revenue agent. They would be sentenced to three and three and a half years in prison, respectively.

The growing scandal mesmerized the reading public. Investigators started out by interrogating foot soldiers of the conspiracy—distillers, gaugers, and storekeepers—then worked their way up the ladder to internal revenue agents. Bristow confided to a friend that "I am in a fight up to my eyes with tremendous combinations of money and unscrupulous thieves."[14] At first, Grant was angry at McDonald until Babcock persuaded him of his innocence. In late May, Grant told Bristow that "there was one honest man [McDonald] upon whom they could rely, as he was an intimate acquaintance and confidential friend of Babcock's." Horrified, Bristow pointed out that McDonald was at the "center of the frauds; that he was at this time in New York with $160,000 of money fraudulently obtained, ready to take a steamer on the first indication of any effort to arrest him."[15] By now Bristow had concluded that Babcock was a thorough scoundrel. "Bristow tells me that Babcock is as deep as any in the Whiskey ring," Fish wrote, "that he has most positive evidence he will not say of actual fraud but of intimate relations and confidential correspondence with the very worst of them."[16] An honest man in a corrupt age, Grant could not conceive of such dishonesty by his most confidential aide.

When the president withdrew to Long Branch that summer, Orville Babcock was at his side. With his black goatee, handlebar mustache, and suave, insinuating manner, the Vermont-born Babcock was a capable man, having graduated high in his class at West Point, but he was a dangerously devious one. When a newspaper reporter wrote a damning piece about McDonald and Joyce, Babcock reassured McDonald that "I do not believe in joining in abuse of you and Joyce (Who have always been kind to me) now that you are in trouble."[17] Babcock's papers at the Newberry Library in Chicago show just how slyly duplicitous he was. Writing two years later to his lawyer, Thomas C. Fletcher, Babcock claimed that he thought the legal pursuit of McDonald and Joyce "a piece of persecution" and that he had "tried to help them all I could and wrote them a few letters and notes, in pencil, I think." He insisted that his letters contained nothing "that any honorable mind could misconstrue, but you know how hellish the press is." At the same time he disclosed that McDonald had a letter from him that might be used to threaten him. Convinced McDonald would part with these letters "for a consideration"—that is, a bribe—he instructed Fletcher to have McDonald "Destroy *them* in your *presence*" or "Place them in your possession so that as attorney no person can ask them from you."[18] It was a shocking letter: Babcock was advising his lawyer to buy and destroy evidence while pretending to be an innocent soul whose words might be unfairly misconstrued by vindictive reporters.

How had such a rascal insinuated himself into Grant's good graces? Even

fifty years later, Grant's son Jesse still paid homage to the saintly altruism of
Orville Babcock, whom he thought incapable of guile:

> Never for a moment did father question Colonel Babcock's honesty.
> We all knew and loved him. He fought under father, he was a mem-
> ber of the family on I Street. Not only would it have been impossible
> for Colonel Babcock to have been guilty as charged, but father ap-
> preciated just what had happened. Colonel Babcock was the most
> disinterestedly friendly person I have ever known. His was almost a
> passion for helpfulness. The slightest acquaintance was sufficient
> motive for Babcock to respond ardently to any request within his
> power to grant. He was never so happy as when exerting himself in
> behalf of his friends, and to Colonel Babcock every acquaintance
> was a friend.[19]

By late July, as a grand jury handed down indictments, Bristow established
that the Sylph messages were in the handwriting of Babcock, who had notified
McDonald of upcoming investigations in St. Louis. In one letter, Babcock had
told McDonald that he had intervened to block the probe. "I have succeeded," he
wrote. "They will not go. I will write you. Sylph."[20] Around this time, Grant received a letter from a St. Louis friend, William D. W. Barnard, that contained
alarming news. The attorney for McDonald and Joyce had asked him how far he
thought prosecutions would proceed and Barnard, a devout believer in Grant's
honesty, replied indignantly "until the last man made restitution to his utmost
ability to pay and were punished to the extent of the law." The attorney shot
back that McDonald and Joyce had assured him Grant would "not give them
up, or Babcock was lost."[21] When Grant read this, he was outraged at the shocking suggestion that he had subverted justice. He handed the letter to Bristow
with a passionate admonition scrawled across it: "Let no guilty man escape if it
can be avoided—Be specially vigilant—or instruct those engaged in the prosecutions of fraud to be—against all who insinuate that they have high influence . . .
to protect them."[22] Grant couldn't have supplied Bristow with a more invigorating statement. Bristow asked if Grant's statement could be published to silence
doubting critics and, when he agreed, it appeared in the *Washington Chronicle*
on August 10. Bristow warned Grant that efforts were being made to show a
"want of harmony" between them in the Whiskey Ring prosecutions. "Of course

I know how utterly false all such statements are . . . but it cannot be denied that the frequent repetition of them by parties who *profess* to have your confidence has done some mischief."[23]

Relations between Grant and Bristow worsened after the treasury secretary confronted Babcock with a Sylph telegram. A smooth liar, Babcock confessed to having written it, but alleged it was unrelated to the Whiskey Ring. Bristow told Babcock he would probably be indicted and felt duty-bound to show the president the telegram. When Bristow did so, it was clear Grant had already been bamboozled by Babcock. "It doesn't refer to the whiskey business," Grant said flatly. "It refers to an order for the transfer of a supervisor." "Unfortunately, Mr. President," Bristow noted, "that transfer order was not issued until February, 1875, whereas this telegram was sent in December, 1874!"[24] Even though Bristow predicted that Babcock would be indicted when the grand jury met in St. Louis, Grant refused to force his resignation. Afterward, Bristow bemoaned that Grant was "being misled by men who profess friendship for him, but who are acting treacherously."[25] As in the past, Grant identified with the embattled man, worrying more about wrongly accusing an innocent person than pardoning a perfidious one.

In September, escorted by Babcock, Grant spent four days in St. Louis and was furious to discover that Bluford Wilson had forewarned John B. Henderson, the special counsel there, to keep a close eye on Babcock. The shameless Babcock had no scruples about meeting with John McDonald. Even Grant met with him, despite the unfortunate impression this might create.[26] Grant received fresh warnings about Babcock's treachery when William L. Burt, the Boston postmaster, told him of a report from Marshall Jewell that Babcock was aiding Whiskey Ring villains and "was a friend of bad men and protected them." He named two prominent men in Washington who, he said, "were corrupt and Babcock was shielding them."[27]

Things looked ghastly for the Grant administration in early November when a St. Louis grand jury pored over names closely associated with the president: his brother Orvil, his brother-in-law Fred Dent, as well as Babcock, prompting Republican talk of a "rebel grand jury" out to embarrass and discredit the president.[28] On November 29, U.S. Attorney David P. Dyer notified Attorney General Pierrepont that he was preparing to indict Babcock, adding, "It is painful to me . . . that the President of the United States should be betrayed by those so close to him as Gen. Babcock. I know that there is no one more anxious than the President himself to see the plunderers of the public Treasury punished."[29] Grant stood squarely behind the prosecutions, even as they crept closer to his own office. At the same time, he knew the popular Bristow eyed the Republican presidential nomination and feared he was exploiting the Whiskey Ring investigation as a national platform for doing so.

On December 3, Henderson obtained a conviction of William O. Avery, chief clerk of the Treasury Department. He introduced damaging evidence against Babcock and dragged Grant's name into the fray. "It is very far from the opinion of myself or any of my associates that the President of the United States knew anything about the Ring," he said in the courtroom, but he thought that Grant had "been grossly deceived and imposed upon by men who professed to be his friends, here and in Washington."[30] In an indiscreet closing statement, Henderson came perilously close to accusing Grant of complicity in attempting to halt the Whiskey Ring investigation: "What right has the President to interfere with the honest discharge of the duties of a Secretary of the Treasury? None whatever."[31]

When this speech reached Washington, Grant's cabinet reacted with shock, pronouncing it "an indecency and an outrage upon professional propriety."[32] For Grant it represented proof that "Henderson was a personal enemy of his and was disposed to abuse him when opportunity offered." According to Fish, the cabinet concurred: "The indecency of a Counsel specially designated by the President abusing him was severely denounced by all."[33] With Grant's approval, Pierrepont sternly reprimanded Dyer, noting that Grant was not on trial and had imposed no impediments to speedy punishment of the whiskey villains. He instructed him to dismiss the offending Henderson, who was replaced by an able lawyer, James O. Broadhead.

With an indictment now looming, Babcock tried to head off trouble by requesting that a military court of inquiry consider his case and Grant agreed. Everybody knew the consequences if Grant was perceived as tampering with criminal proceedings in St. Louis. Pierrepont gave his opinion that a military inquiry wouldn't "interfere with the pending criminal proceedings at St. Louis," which would have been "ruinous to Babcock, the President and the Administration."[34] Grant performed an immense favor for Babcock by naming three sympathetic generals—Phil Sheridan, Winfield S. Hancock, and Alfred Terry—to oversee the military inquiry in Chicago, but it was disbanded when St. Louis prosecutors refused to share their evidence against Babcock.

On December 9, Dyer secured a fraud and conspiracy indictment against Babcock. When Babcock insisted that he would be exonerated, Grant clung with a childlike devotion to complete faith in his innocence. On December 17, he sat down to allay the fears of Babcock's wife, Annie:

> My Dear Mrs. Babcock, I know how much you must be distressed at the publications of the day reflecting upon the integrity of your husband, and write therefore to ask you to be of good cheer and wait for his full vindication. I have the fullest confidence in his integrity, and of his innocence of the charges now made against him. After the intimate and confidential relations that have existed between him and myself for near fourteen years—during the whole of which time he has been one of my most confidential Aides & private Sec.—I do not believe it possible that I can be deceived. It is scarcely possible that he could, if so disposed, be guilty of the crime now charged against him without at least having created a suspicion in my mind . . . My confidence in Gen. Babcock is the same now [as] it was when we were together in the field contending against the known enemies of the government.[35]

On Christmas Day, Grant summoned Bluford Wilson, accused him of attempting to have his brother Orvil and son Fred indicted for whiskey frauds, and expressed "his earnest belief in Babcock's innocence and his sense of the great outrage perpetrated on him," Wilson said.[36] A week later, Chicago and New York newspapers fingered Orvil and Fred Grant as involved in the Whiskey Ring. Indignant at the feeding frenzy in the press and protective toward his family, Grant exploded in fury, saying he had "heard enough through talk like this from Treasury officials, and wanted it either stopped or proven true."[37] At a cabinet session he ordered Pierrepont to haul reporters before grand juries and force them to substantiate their charges. He said he was prepared to let his brother and son be prosecuted, if the rumors proved true, but he strongly questioned their veracity. Treasury officials then confirmed that Orvil and Fred Grant bore no connection to the Whiskey Ring.

At this point, Grant took active steps to guard Babcock. In late January, he had the attorney general issue a circular letter to U.S. attorneys in St. Louis, Chicago, and Milwaukee, advising them not to allow witnesses to turn state's evidence. Granting immunity had formed an essential part of the prosecutions, which would be crippled without them. Grant reiterated his position in a petulant exchange with Bluford Wilson, lecturing him that "when I said let no guilty man escape, I meant it, and not that nine men should escape, and one be convicted." Wilson countered: "Pardon me, Mr. President, we are not in this battle counting heads."[38]

As Liberal Republicans talked up Bristow for president, Grant regretted that the secretary's "zealous young friends" promoted his nomination.[39] Bristow now felt a peculiar chill in the air around Grant. Bothered by this, he stopped by Hamilton Fish's home on February 6 for a confidential talk. He recounted how he had gone to Long Branch the previous September to present Grant with his resignation and Grant had assured him that "he was more likely than any one person to be named as his successor, and that there was no one whom he would prefer, and he begged him to take back his resignation, which he did."[40] Since that time, relations with Grant had soured and the president was now "*cold, distrustful and at times offensive, and severe in his insinuations and his remarks.*"[41] Fish urged Bristow not to resign, pointing out that Grant sincerely believed in Babcock's innocence and was persuaded "the prosecution of persons who were appointees of his reflected upon the Administration."[42]

By February 5, 1876, Babcock had checked into a St. Louis hotel along with former attorney general Williams, who served as his defense counsel. Three days later, opening arguments began in his trial. Horace Porter tried to convince Grant that his testimony alone could save Babcock from the "scoundrels" bent on persecuting him.[43] As the trial progressed, Grant's worries about Babcock only deepened when prosecutors introduced evidence showing his secret communications with McDonald, one ring conspirator even claiming that John Joyce stuffed $500 into an envelope for Babcock and brazenly mailed it to him in the White House.

In a cabinet session of extraordinary drama, a distraught Grant said betrayal by Babcock was inconceivable to him. The wounded president submitted to outright paranoia. As recorded by Fish, Grant said that "the prosecution was aimed at himself, & that they were putting him on trial; that he was as confident as he lived of Babcock's innocence."[44] If Babcock were guilty, he insisted, it would be the basest ingratitude and trickery ever known. Grant not only said he was ready to give a deposition in the case but stunned the meeting by claiming he wished to travel to St. Louis to testify at once, dragging at least two cabinet

members with him. Fish protested that this would place him in the embarrassing predicament of testifying against a case prosecuted by his own administration. "The Cabinet were unanimous in the opinion that the President ought not
to leave Washington during the session of Congress to be made a witness," wrote
Fish, and "ought not under any circumstances to consent to appear in Court as
a witness."[45] A flustered Grant then admitted he had already promised Babcock's lawyers he would testify. The cabinet decided he should give a deposition
instead, which he did on February 12 before Chief Justice Morrison Waite—an
unprecedented step for a president in a criminal proceeding.

During the five-hour deposition, Grant described how he knew Babcock
"intimately" and regarded him "as a most efficient and most faithful officer."[46]
He denied Babcock had tried to obstruct the Whiskey Ring investigations and
would not relent one iota on his innocence. "I have always had great confidence
in his integrity . . . and as yet my confidence in him is unshaken."[47] When Grant
was read Babcock's suspicious messages to McDonald, he disclaimed any knowledge of them at the time and insisted Babcock had explained them to him to his
satisfaction. Grant didn't commit perjury, but he did show a willful refusal to
open himself up to the facts. At the same time, he repeatedly exhorted Pierrepont, "If Babcock is guilty, there is no man who wants him so much proven
guilty as I do, for it is the greatest piece of traitorism to me that a man could
possibly practice."[48] Despite his epic success in life, an atavistic side of Grant still
identified with battered, beaten-down, and besieged people, and Orville Babcock now fell into that category of folks worthy of his sympathy.

Two days later Grant unburdened himself to Hamilton Fish. He thought
St. Louis prosecutors were gunning for him and that Babcock was a convenient
decoy as they took dead aim at him. Bristow, he believed, "had become possessed with the idea of the complicity of the President, and was using his office
for the purpose of annoying him." Bristow's colleagues wanted to elevate him to
the presidency and he "was yielding to it and allowing himself to be made a
party to these proceedings."[49] So persuaded was Grant that personal attacks
against him emanated from Bristow's hostile circle that Badeau termed his mood
"one of the most intense" he had ever seen.[50] Persuaded that Grant would dismiss him after Babcock's trial, Bristow pondered his resignation. He had always
esteemed Grant "a good man, motivated by patriotic desire and unselfish devotion" to his country, but he believed he had fallen under the potent spell of bad

advisers.[51] Now the two men had arrived at an irrevocable break, one that threatened to split the Republican Party.

On February 24, Babcock's trial closed with an acquittal and many observers believed Grant's affidavit had helped to influence the outcome. The prosecution had suffered under the additional handicap that Babcock's cryptic letters to St. Louis suggested guilt but offered no foolproof evidence. Just when it seemed Grant might be vindicated in his rosy view of Babcock, the gods decided to disabuse him savagely. While Babcock was returning to Washington, Grant received evidence that in 1869 he had invested in gold speculations that ended disastrously with the market crash on Black Friday, losing $40,000 in the transactions. The disclosure that Babcock had connived in tandem with Jay Gould and Jim Fisk devastated Grant. As Bluford Wilson wrote, "The President then, for the first time, comprehended . . . that if [Babcock] had betrayed him in the Black Friday transactions, he was quite capable of betraying him in connection with the whisky frauds."[52] Grant had received a sudden and terrible education in misplaced loyalty. As Buck recalled, Grant thought Babcock "could not properly come back into his family."[53] Needing someone in whom he could repose a rock-solid trust, a shaken Grant drafted Buck as his secretary to replace Babcock. The scales had fallen much too late from the president's eyes.

For a couple of days, Babcock lingered at his White House desk. Horrified to see him there, Fish pleaded with Grant to send him away. On March 1, Grant finally got rid of him, although Babcock stayed on as superintendent of public buildings in Washington. Exactly a year later, Grant handed him a humiliating assignment, shunting him to the lowly job of inspector for the fifth lighthouse district, an extraordinary comedown for a man once seated at the throne of power. To sweeten the pill somewhat, Grant wrote to Babcock and assured him of his confidence in his "integrity and great efficiency."[54] In 1884 Babcock, age forty-eight, drowned while performing his duties at Mosquito Inlet in Florida.

Even though Grant had expelled the serpent from the garden, peace didn't return to the executive mansion. Bristow found the atmosphere "irksome and disagreeable," thought Grant remained under Whiskey Ring influence, and decided to resign.[55] According to one story, Bristow tendered Grant his letter of resignation as the president mounted his carriage for a drive; Grant pocketed the envelope in frosty silence and departed. Bristow's letter pulled no punches. It said corrupt people had convinced Grant the prosecutions were "really aimed at you and are prompted by a mixture of base & ambitious motives . . . Utterly false as I know such statements to be . . . it is painfully apparent that they are not so regarded by you." He faulted Grant for "withdrawal of your confidence & official support."[56] In a decidedly cool reply, Grant accepted Bristow's resignation and hoped he would "find that peace in private life denied to anyone occupying your present official position."[57]

After Bristow resigned, he was summoned by a congressional committee investigating the whiskey frauds. He declined to appear, citing executive privilege and the confidential nature of cabinet communications. Grant, showing exceptional confidence in his own integrity, urged Bristow to waive executive privilege and testify, declaring his desire "not only that you may answer all questions . . . but wish that all the members of my Cabinet . . . may also be called upon to testify in regard to the same matters."[58]

Grant refused to surrender his suspicion that Bristow's whiskey crusade was designed to position him as the Republican presidential candidate in 1876. From Fish's diary entries, one can see that Grant's famous composure was breaking down under pressure, and that he had become irritable, short-tempered, and impatient. On October 12, Fish recorded Grant's astonishing private appraisal of Bristow. Fuming, he described Bristow's nature as one of "intense selfishness and ambition and of extreme jealousy and suspicion and that from the time he entered the Cabinet he had set his eye on the Presidency with a distrust and hostility to himself (the President) and to every member of the Cabinet."[59] He later repented of this jaundiced, unfair view of Bristow.

Grant had succumbed to the curse of second-term presidents: spreading scandal. He himself was never tied to knowledge of the Whiskey Ring. In fact, his administration had brought more than 350 indictments against the whiskey culprits—an astounding feat for which Grant seldom gets credit.[60] His fault was again one of supervisory judgment rather than personal corruption. The world of politics was filled with duplicitous people and Grant was poorly equipped to spot them, remaining an easy victim for crooked men. "They studied Grant, some of them, as the shoemaker measures the foot of his customer," wrote George Hoar.[61] Many years later, David Dyer issued this verdict: "General Grant had no knowledge of the existence of the Whiskey Ring when the prosecutions began, and therefore was not in the remotest manner a party to or in any wise connected therewith. His great mistake was in trusting men who did know . . . and this after their connection with the ring was a matter of common information.

Grant was an honest man and implicitly trusted those he believed to be his friends . . . At no time during the prolonged inquiry . . . was anything discovered that reflected upon General Grant's integrity."[62] In later years, when an acquaintance inquired what had pained him most in the course of his eventful life, Grant responded readily, "To be deceived by a friend."[63]

DESPITE THE SCANDALS that had rocked his administration, Grant's wartime heroism clung to him like an honored, if somewhat faded, old cloak and the American public retained faith in his personal integrity. But he suffered ongoing criticism from Liberal Republicans who favored civil service reform, disliked Reconstruction, and were discomfited by his disgraced cabinet members. One unsparing critic remained his steadfast wartime comrade William T. Sherman. In July 1875, the former interior secretary Orville Hickman Browning recorded this indictment by Sherman against Grant:

> He thought Grant's administration a failure—said the President was very deficient in the qualities of a statesman—that he had no comprehension of the fundamental principles of civil governments, constitutions and laws—that he had been surrounded by a weak cabinet, and had failed to restore harmony and fraternity among the different sections of the Country—that a great mistake had been made in putting all the political power of the Souther[n] states in the hands of the ignorant, and substantially disfranchising the intelligent classes, and the South was in a worse condition to-day than at the close of the war.[64]

Sherman's views were colored by his close identification with the white southern establishment he had known and admired before the war.

Despite his detractors, Grant remained popular enough to provoke conjecture that he might hazard a run at a third term, defying the two-term custom that had ruled American politics since George Washington. Although Stalwart senators prodded him to run, a worn-out Grant demurred. Sixteen years of public service, he later confided, had exerted a "constant strain" upon him.[65] His silence on a third term perpetuated so much speculation that Jesse pressed him to issue a statement, opting out of another term. "Do you want me to decline something that has never been offered to me," Grant asked, smiling sadly. "If the effort is made, I shall refuse to permit my name to be brought before the next national convention. Until then it would be futile for me to speak."[66]

In early 1875 Grant reconsidered this silence amid chatter in Republican circles that a third term might injure the party. When a Republican convention in Pennsylvania approved a resolution opposing a third term, Grant knew he had to issue a categorical denial. To convention president Harry White, he admitted that the "fire of personal abuse, and slander" of his first term had made him seek vindication in the 1872 election. Now "I am not, nor have I been, a candidate for a renomination."[67] Grant's pledge made newspaper headlines across America. Writing to Edwin Cowles of the *Cleveland Leader,* Grant showed the same reluctance to seek power that he had manifested after Fort Sumter, when he thought it beneath his dignity to lobby for an army commission: "I left a life position of which I was very proud, to accept a first term, very much against my inclination. Twice I have been nominated to the office with great unanimity by Conventions convened to make the nomination." It wasn't in his nature "to struggle for position," he said, and he would never accept a nomination tendered grudgingly by his party.[68]

Grant summoned his cabinet informally to show them his letter to Harry White. When Julia Grant demanded to know the reason for this impromptu gathering, Grant stalled, lit a cigar for courage, then marched into her room, explaining he had just composed a letter squelching rumors he would seek a third term. His wife, he knew, was hell-bent on remaining in the White House and he was prepared for her wrath. "Bring it and read it to me now," she demanded. "No," he replied, "it is already posted; that is why I lingered in the hall to light my cigar, so the letter would be beyond recall."[69] Julia would gladly have stayed for one more term and had no qualms about scrapping George Washington's precedent. "Oh, Ulys! was that kind to me?" she protested. "Was it just to me?" "Well," he replied, "I do not want to be here another four years. I do not think I could stand it." Rather than feel sympathy for her husband's plight as a profoundly overburdened president, Julia chose to feel "deeply injured."[70] She had relished being First Lady as only someone could whose social ambitions had been cruelly mocked during their early years of marriage. In the White House, she had finally attained a grandeur that satisfied her White Haven upbringing and she had radiated pleasure in the spotlight. "She enjoyed her presidential life," observed a guest, "and good naturedly said so."[71] Julia surely wondered what life would offer without the salary and perquisites that came with the three eminent positions her husband had held since the war.

Grant remained an observant Methodist and was never reluctant to profess his faith. In August 1875, he assisted John Heyl Vincent, his former Galena pastor, at the Chautauqua movement of Christian summer camps, addressing a crowd of thirty thousand. He also attended a revival meeting officiated by Dwight Moody, a leading evangelist. During the 1876 centennial, when asked to supply a statement for Sunday school children, he wrote: "Hold fast to the Bible as the sheet-anchor of your liberties; write its precepts in your hearts, and PRACTISE THEM IN YOUR LIVES. To the influence of this book we are indebted for all the progress made in true civilization."[72] Yet Grant never exploited religion for partisan gain or pandered to the political agenda of any religious group. At a time when some Protestants wanted to Christianize the country and some Catholics lobbied for state funding for parochial schools, he produced a landmark statement reaffirming the separation of church and state.

The occasion was a trip in September 1875 to Des Moines, Iowa, where he held an afternoon meeting at Moore's Opera House, greeting 2,500 children who had been cautioned that the visiting president "was a man of deeds not words."[73] The taciturn Grant lived up to his billing, spoke briefly, and spent the rest of the afternoon touring the city with Judge C. C. Cole. As they viewed various schools, they discussed the tremendous strides the nation had made in free public education. The sight of the schoolchildren had stirred some latent impulse in Grant yearning for expression. That evening he was scheduled to address an Army of the Tennessee reunion and asked Cole if they might return to his house early so he could jot down some thoughts for his dinner speech. In only forty minutes, scribbling in pencil, Grant drafted a speech "on the backs of envelopes and the stray scraps of paper at hand in his room."[74] It was a historic plea for public education and the need to save the nation's classrooms from religious interference.

Grant started out by emphasizing the importance in a republic of a knowledgeable citizenry: "The free school is the promoter of that intelligence which is to preserve us as a free nation." With an unaccustomed rhetorical flourish, he affirmed that in the near future "the dividing line will not be Mason & Dixons but between patriotism, & intelligence on the one side & superstition, ambition

& ignorance on the other."[75] He wound up with an eloquent appeal for separating church and state: "Encourage free schools and resolve that not one dollar of money appropriated to their support no matter how raised, shall be appropriated to the support of any sectarian school . . . Leave the matter of religion to the family circle, the church & the private school support[ed] entirely by private contribution. Keep the church and state forever separate."[76]

Some observers construed the speech as a transparent attack on the Catholic Church and one Catholic periodical said Grant sought to "ostracize" Catholics "socially and disfranchise them politically."[77] Thomas Nast drew a cartoon that showed Grant smoking a cigar as he coolly stepped on the foot of a prelate crossing the church-state divide. Many Catholics supported the speech, however, which proved so popular in Iowa that it revived Republican Party fortunes there. Traveling elsewhere in Iowa, Grant proselytized for a wider agenda to promote public education. When asked about state support for higher education, he endorsed it as long as free, universal education was provided for younger children, elementary schools being the system's cornerstone. Doubtless with Reconstruction in mind, Grant advanced a broader vision of free education as the most effective means to assimilate immigrant masses and heal lingering wartime wounds. Students should be taught that "while loving the home State, they should love the country more. Hard sectional feelings should give way to brotherly love for the whole American family."[78]

In his annual message to Congress that December, Grant embroidered this theme of the need for mass public education to resist "tyranny and oppression . . . whether directed by the demagogue or by priestcraft."[79] Educating the citizenry, he asserted, was the optimal way to protect democratic institutions. Making a dramatic leap, he advocated a constitutional amendment that would require each state "to establish and forever maintain free public schools adequate to the education of all the children . . . irrespective of sex, color, birthplace, or religions; forbidding the teaching in said schools of religious, atheistic, or pagan tenets; and prohibiting the granting of any school-funds, or school-taxes . . . in aid . . . of any religious sect or denomination."[80] Grant worded his message to remove any suspicion that he spoke for a particular religious denomination. Also buried in his statement was a courageous, farsighted plea for free, universal education for black children. The laconic Grant's crusade for public education was a unique event in his presidency, the result of a riveting speech that had forced an issue on the national consciousness through powerful oratory.

EVEN AS GRANT'S ENTOURAGE rolled through western states, violence against Republicans flared up again in the Deep South. The target of terror continued to be black citizens who had the temerity to exercise their voting rights. On September 4, Mississippi Republicans threw an alfresco barbecue in Clinton, west of Jackson, scheduled to rally voters in upcoming elections. Intruders from a White Line rifle club showed up to harass them, murdered a black citizen, then opened fire on other blacks, who quickly grabbed pistols and returned fire. The gunfight left seven or eight blacks sprawled dead in the dust, with three white men killed in retaliation. William H. Harney, sheriff of Hinds County, reported to Governor Adelbert Ames that the incident stemmed from squads of white men bushwhacking through the countryside, "murdering and driving the colored people from their homes . . . The colored people are unarmed and defenseless . . . I appeal to your excellency . . . to stop this slaughter of an innocent and defenseless people."[81] Local law enforcement seemed powerless to curb the cresting wave of white violence.

On September 7, Ames pleaded with Grant for federal help, noting that illegal bands of armed white men were sowing terror in several counties and boldly defying sheriffs. Grant acted decisively to stanch the violence, telling his adjutant general, "You may instruct commanding officer of troops in Mississippi that he may assist the governor in maintaining order and preserving life in case of insurrection too formidable for him to suppress."[82] Then, on vacation in Long Branch, Grant began to dither in an uncharacteristic fashion. In the altered political climate, with northern support for Reconstruction waning, he agonized over the legality of intervention and sought the opinion of his conservative attorney general, Edwards Pierrepont, who urged inaction, unfurling the banner of states' rights. Meanwhile, Mississippi Democrats blandly assured Washington of the absence of any violence. "There are no disturbances in this State," the Democratic Executive Committee told Pierrepont, "and no obstructions to the execution of the laws."[83]

Pierrepont believed the federal government should act only if state forces failed to quell the bloodshed. On September 11, he sent Grant a soothing message that state authorities had "no difficulty in putting down the riot, and that the sending of Federal troops would do great mischief. I am satisfied that the war is over."[84] This was an extreme case of Panglossian thinking. When Pierrepont inquired of Ames if an uncontrollable insurrection existed, he confirmed that was the case. Ames knew a pivotal moment had arrived and that northern opinion had given up on protecting freed people. Sticking to his convictions, he made a forthright political stand: "I am aware of the reluctance of the people of the country to national interference in State affairs . . . Permit me to express the hope that the odium of such interference shall not attach to President Grant or the Republican Party . . . Let the odium, in all its magnitude, descend upon me. I cannot escape the conscious discharge of my duty toward a class of American citizens whose only offense consists in their color."[85]

On September 13, Grant composed a long, handwritten letter to his attorney general. He had to decide whether to issue a proclamation and send troops to Mississippi. He seemed poised on a knife edge, torn between popular revulsion against Reconstruction and his fervent wish to aid threatened blacks. He admitted to being "perplexed" as to the ideal course of action. "The whole public are tired out with these annual, autumnal outbreaks in the South, and . . . the great majority are ready now to condemn any interference on the part of the government."[86] But having noted that he didn't intercede lightly in southern affairs, he came down forthrightly for intervention. "I do not see how we are to evade the call of the governor, if made strictly within the Constitution."[87] Grant showed a painstaking concern for the constitutional propriety of such a move. At the same time, to mollify critics, he encouraged Ames to exhaust all state resources before receiving federal help. Whatever his misgivings, Grant wanted to rescue Ames and the black people of Mississippi even if it meant defying his attorney general. He was fully prepared to risk the political backlash against Reconstruction.

His letter written, Grant departed for a veterans' reunion in Utica, New York, leaving the matter to Pierrepont, who sent Ames a message that substituted his own conservative judgment for the president's, while pretending he and Grant acted in unison. He struck out a line saying that Grant had agreed to an intervention proclamation. Instead he chastised the Mississippi governor for not having proven the existence of an insurrection—the legal requirement for sending troops—or taken sufficient steps to stop the violence on his own, a rebuke that left Ames feeling "disgusted" and "quite exasperated."[88] The letter concluded that "if there *is such a resistance to your State authorities as you cannot, by all the means at your command, suppress,* the President will swiftly aid you in crushing these lawless traitors to human rights."[89] Two days later, Pierrepont advised Grant that the federal government should back off. "No proclamation needed," he counseled.[90] Grant approved the suggestion, which he would regret as the single greatest error he made during Reconstruction. He shortly departed on his western trip, leaving Pierrepont in charge. One wonders whether, had he stayed in Washington, the Mississippi crisis might have unfolded differently.

Although Ames decided to raise a volunteer company of black and white militia, White Liners decided to scare blacks from the polls and install a Democratic government through naked terror if necessary. The black community in Vicksburg conjured up their lawless methods in a letter to the governor: "They are going around the streets at night dressed in soldiers clothes and making colored people run for their lives. They are drilling every night with the wharf boat guns. They have got 2 or 3 thousand stand of arms here in this city. They say they will either carry this election by ballot or bullet."[91] Ames surmised that Democrats and their White Line allies would temporarily lay low to forestall any proclamation from the president. "It is believed that white-liners will delay violence till one or two days before election," he apprised Grant.[92]

The White Liners didn't bother with any such pretense of civility or restraint. On October 7, John Milton Brown, the sheriff of Coahoma County, reported a "perfect state of terror" had seized his jurisdiction. "I have been driven from my county by an armed force. I am utterly powerless to enforce law or to restore order."[93] Disheartened by Grant's refusal to rush troops to Mississippi, Ames sat brooding and besieged in the governor's mansion in Jackson. He concluded that Reconstruction was a dead letter, white supremacists in his state having engineered a coup d'état. "Yes, a *revolution* has taken place—by force of arms—and a race are disfranchised—they are to be returned to a condition of serfdom—an era of second slavery," he lamented to his wife.[94] Sarcastically referring to Grant's and Pierrepont's words, he wrote, "The political death of the Negro will forever release the nation . . . from such 'political outbreaks.' You may think I exaggerate. Time will show you how accurate my statements are."[95] To head off threatened impeachment, he decided to resign after the election. His darkly prophetic letter previewed the nearly century-long Jim Crow system that would cast blacks back into a state of involuntary servitude to southern whites.

Ames worked hard to effect a truce between white Democrats and white and black Republicans in his state and even offered to strip black militia of their weaponry if Democrats respected black voting rights in the November elections. Attorney General Pierrepont dispatched to Mississippi George K. Chase, who moved into the governor's mansion to arbitrate the bloody dispute. On October 16, Ames thanked Pierrepont for this timely assistance, saying that Chase "has succeeded in inspiring us all with confidence, and . . . by his wisdom and tact has saved the state from a catastrophe of blood"—news that drew relieved sighs from Grant and his cabinet.[96] But Chase was hornswoggled by southern Democrats—White Liners had cynically suspended violence during Ames's peace conference—and he was frank enough to admit it. On October 27, he alerted Pierrepont that it would be "impossible to have a fair election on November 2nd" without the aid of U.S. troops.[97]

Grant and Pierrepont, having fatally wavered, had failed to quash the campaign of intimidation that left black and white Republicans cowering across Mississippi. With Chase's blunt warning in hand, Grant and Pierrepont now belatedly sent troops to Mississippi to ensure fair elections, holding them ready for swift deployment in the event of Election Day disorder. Far from being uplifted by this news, Ames dismissed it as too little too late. "The election ceases to have any interest for us," he told his wife. "It is lost. Gone forever. The republican candidate for the presidency next year may want this state, but he as well might want the moon for a toy."[98] The violence on Election Day vindicated Ames's dire scenario. As he informed his wife: "The reports which come to me almost hourly are truly sickening. Violence, threats of murder, and consequent intimidation are co-extensive with the limits of the state. Republican leaders in many localities are hiding in the swamps or have sought refuge beyond the borders of their own counties. The government of the U.S. does not interfere, and will not, unless to prevent actual bloodshed."[99] Democrats emerged triumphant in the state, boasting that they had rooted out malfeasance and bad government. Even Hiram R. Revels, the first black U.S. senator from Mississippi, applauded the outcome as a victory over "corruption, theft, and embezzlement," and he wasn't the only black official who complained that Ames had surrounded himself with mercenary officials.[100]

Still, there was little doubt that the Democrats had won by crushing black turnout. In Yazoo County, only seven Republican votes were cast in a black population that exceeded twelve thousand. Ames saw the election as a referendum on race, pure and simple: "In one phrase—hostility to the negro as a citizen. The South cares for no other question. Everything gives way to it. They support or oppose men, advocate or denounce policies, flatter or murder, just as such action will help them as far as possible to recover their old power over the negro."[101] He scoffed at Grant's hollow promise to send troops as "a sham and the election a fraud."[102] The election had mocked the U.S. Constitution and guaranteed a prolonged night of terror for freed people. When a Senate committee investigated the election, it decided it had been won "by the Democrats by a preconceived plan of riots and assassinations," in the words of Senator George Boutwell.[103]

Why had Grant retreated so shamefully from Reconstruction in the final stages of his administration? Again and again, he had declared southern counties in a state of insurrection and sent federal troops to protect black citizens. His actions had been courageous, exemplary. The solution to this mystery came years later from John Roy Lynch, the sole black Mississippi congressman to survive the Democratic onslaught in the state. A rousing orator, the biracial Lynch was the son of a white plantation master and an enslaved woman. Almost forty years afterward, living in Chicago, he told of a talk at the White House in November 1875. When he asked Grant why he had refused action in Mississippi, he had replied that as soon as Ames's plea for succor came in early September, he had prepared to issue a proclamation for action in Mississippi—something confirmed by Grant's own papers. Before signing it, however, he conferred with Ohio Republicans who warned that if Grant intervened in Mississippi, Republicans would lose Ohio elections on October 13, the state having already lost faith in Reconstruction. Grant decided it was more important to retain Ohio than save Mississippi. Republicans won the Ohio elections, returning Rutherford B. Hayes to the governorship and setting the stage for the next president. "I should not have yielded," Grant told Lynch. "I believed at the time I was making a grave mistake. But as presented, it was duty on one side, and party obligation on the other. Between the two I hesitated, but finally yielded to what I believed was my party obligation. If a mistake was made, it was one of the head and not of the heart."[104]

Grant's personal tragedy was simultaneously an American tragedy. Tormented by his decision, steeped in a meditative mood, Grant reflected on the deep changes wrought in northern Republican circles. He predicted to John Roy Lynch that the northern retreat from Reconstruction would lead to Democrats recapturing power in the South as well as "future mischief of a very serious nature . . . It requires no prophet to foresee that the national government will soon be at a great disadvantage and that the results of the war of the rebellion will have been in a large measure lost . . . What you have just passed through in the state of Mississippi is only the beginning of what is sure to follow. I do not wish to create unnecessary alarm, nor to be looked upon as a prophet of evil, but it is impossible for me to close my eyes in the face of things that are as plain to me as the noonday sun."[105] This wasn't a minor statement: the victorious Union general of the Civil War was saying that terror tactics perpetrated by southern whites had nullified the outcome of the rebellion. All those hundreds of thousands dead, the millions maimed and wounded, the mourning of widows and orphans—all that suffering, all that tumult, on some level, had been for naught. Slavery had been abolished, but it had been replaced by a caste-ridden form of second-class citizenship for southern blacks, and that counted as a national shame.

Saddest of the Falls

THE LAST THING Grant needed after the Whiskey Ring scandal was more cabinet wrongdoing, but the bloodletting had not yet ceased. The tenure of Secretary of the Interior Columbus Delano had been shadowed by controversy. His department was rife with fraud, suffering from accusations of an "Indian Ring" of corrupt agents who exploited Native Americans. To worsen matters, his son was accused of blackmail and corruption in the Wyoming Territory. As charges against Delano mounted, Grant resisted pleas to sack him. "If Delano were now to resign," he told Fish, "it would be retreating under fire and be accepted as an admission of the charges."[1] Bristow was especially upset that Grant failed to clean house and force Delano's resignation.

Before long congressional scrutiny turned to Orvil Grant, who had received four profitable Indian trading posts at a time when such trading licenses were virtual presses to print money. *The New York Times* conjectured that for two years not "a single important tradership had been secured without the payment of large sums."[2] In July 1875, press speculation suggested that Delano was privy to misdeeds involving Orvil. One newspaper presumed to know that at a heated Long Branch session between Grant and Delano, the interior secretary had "made threats of exposure concerning privileges granted Orville [*sic*] Grant, a brother of the President, if his [own] resignation was enforced, but gave assurances that if not molested until after the Indian frauds investigation had been concluded, he would quietly step down and out."[3]

The scandal around Indian trading posts edged closer to Grant in February

1876 when the *New York Herald* charged Orvil with taking kickbacks from a sutler. "Let the President send for his own brother," the paper intoned, "and question him about the money that was made in the Sioux country by starving the squaws and children."[4] Summoned by a House committee delving into War Department expenditures, Orvil testified that he had told his brother of his desire to secure Indian trading posts in 1874 and had gotten one at Fort Peck and a second at Standing Rock: "I suppose I feel grateful to my brother, and indebted to him for getting that post at Standing Rock." The interrogator pressed him: "You consider, then, that you do have influence with the President to manage these matters to some extent?" "To some extent I have," replied Orvil breezily, "though I am sorry to say they are of very little profit to me."[5] In fact, Grant had told Orvil about four trading posts that would soon be vacated; Orvil had applied for and received all four, installing "partners" who shared half the proceeds with him without a shred of work on Orvil's part.

Orvil's testimony vastly embarrassed his brother, though he admitted that the president was ignorant that he had skimmed money from these transactions. A cheerfully amoral man, Orvil betrayed not one scintilla of remorse about his misdeeds. What nobody knew—except possibly his brother—was that Orvil was slipping into madness. Its main symptom would be a manic appetite for speculation that veered off into extravagant fantasies about cornering markets and gobbling up businesses. That Orvil was such an affable witness, seemingly unaware of the harm he caused his brother, suggests the madness had already taken root. The press had a field day with his rambling ruminations. *The Nation* commented that he "told his own story of his jobs as an Indian trader in a simple, artless way that would be diverting if it were not for the picture it presents of the views entertained by the Presidential family on 'the science of politics.'"[6] Nor was the president spared journalistic venom. "Under an honest and high-toned civil service," the *New York Tribune* lectured, "the President would consider it his first duty . . . to see that traders at Indian posts are responsible men, and that their trade is regulated for the best interests of the Indians."[7] In fact, starting with Ely Parker and the Quakers, Grant had worked long and hard to ban corruption on the reservations.

The last cabinet secretary enveloped by scandal was Secretary of War William W. Belknap, who had shown little sympathy for Reconstruction or Grant's Peace Policy toward the Indians. From his earliest days as war secretary, Belknap had entertained sumptuously at his Lafayette Square home with his second wife,

Carrie, a beautiful Kentucky belle, who captivated guests. When Mrs. Belknap exhibited a conspicuous taste for luxury, it seemed mysterious to Washington observers how she managed it. It turned out she had helped businessman Caleb P. Marsh to obtain a trading post at Fort Sill in Indian Territory that was currently held by a John S. Evans. To keep his lucrative position, Evans agreed to make quarterly payments to Marsh and Mrs. Belknap, who split a $12,000 annual kickback. When Carrie Belknap died of tuberculosis in December 1870, her husband went on pocketing the extorted money, feigning ignorance of its source. In December 1873, he married his sister-in-law Amanda, nicknamed "Puss" and famous for her gowns and costly jewels. The war secretary still banked the illegal payments made to the previous Mrs. Belknap, albeit now at a reduced rate. In time the new Mrs. Belknap became a recipient of this satisfying flow of largesse. In all, the Belknap household received $20,000 from Evans, the equivalent of two and a half years' salary for the war secretary, another example of Gilded Age gluttony in Washington.

In early March 1876, a House committee, headed by Hiester Clymer of Pennsylvania, pieced together evidence that Belknap had taken hefty payments for an Indian trading post and prepared to release a report recommending his impeachment. A Democrat and a confirmed racist—one of his campaign posters proclaimed "CLYMER'S platform is for the White Man"—he was eager to discredit Reconstruction and savaging the war secretary was a handy way to do so.[8] Not masking his hatred for Grant, Clymer declaimed against "the corruption, the extravagance, the misgovernment which has cursed this land for years past."[9] At 10 a.m. on March 2, Belknap, knowing the congressional committee would present its critical report that afternoon, rushed to the White House in an unholy panic to tender his resignation. Rumors even made the rounds on Capitol Hill that Belknap had shot himself.

At breakfast, Bristow had tipped off Grant that Congress had gathered incriminating evidence on Belknap, which came as a complete surprise to him. He was distracted by the Orville Babcock case and blindsided by the sudden appearance of this new scandal. According to Julia Grant, he was heading out to have his portrait painted when a White House steward informed him that Belknap and Secretary of the Interior Zachariah Chandler wished to see him in the Red Room. "I cannot now," Grant said, "but will when I return." "Oh, Mr. President, do see [Mr. Belknap] before you go," the steward urged. "He is in some trouble and looks very ill."[10] In the Red Room, a wildly discomposed

Belknap—Julia described him as hoarse and "deadly pale"—offered to resign. "Accept it at once," Belknap cried. "Do not hesitate, Mr. President. For God's sake, do not hesitate." "Certainly," Grant conceded, slightly mystified, "if you wish it."[11] Belknap fostered the impression that he was acting gallantly to save his wife, not his own scalp. Years later, Jesse Grant said his father suggested the resignation to Belknap and that the two of them always thought Belknap "an upright, chivalrous man, worthy of all respect."[12]

In a curt letter, Grant accepted Belknap's resignation: "Your tender of resignation as Secretary of War, with the request that it be accepted immediately, is received, and the same is hereby accepted with great regret."[13] "Thank you, you are always kind," said Belknap, beating a hasty retreat from the room.[14] His unseemly haste should have alerted Grant that something was grievously amiss. The president had acted impetuously, unaware of the full legal ramifications of his action. In typically unflappable style, Grant strode off to the studio of Prussian-born artist Henry Ulke, oblivious to the tremendous hubbub now shaking Capitol Hill. When impeachment articles against Belknap passed that afternoon, Grant's premature acceptance of his resignation threatened to sabotage the process, having made Belknap a private citizen at the time he was impeached. This fresh scandal renewed questions about Grant's judgment. As the Washington correspondent for the notoriously anti-administration *New York Herald* sketched events that day in Congress:

> When the letter of the President was read, stating that he had accepted the Secretary's resignation at half-past ten o'clock, there was a murmur of amazement at what looked to everybody then like an act deliberately intended to shield Mr. Belknap, but when the terms of the letter were read, in which the President tells Mr. Belknap that he accepts his resignation with great regret, people turned to each other with indignation at something which seemed to them an open defiance of decency and of public opinion . . . The discussion turned mainly on the question of the power of the House to impeach a person who had resigned office.[15]

The next day, in a confessional mode, Grant informed his cabinet that when Belknap first arrived, he hadn't fathomed the scandal's magnitude. Belknap had been so overcome with emotion, he said, that he could hardly spill out his words.

Only later in the day, when Grant learned that Belknap hoped to escape impeachment, did he recognize the gravity of what he had done. As so often with Grant, he saw the Belknap case in personal rather than political terms. "He spoke of his long continued acquaintance with Belknap in the Army," Fish wrote, "of his having known his father as one of the finest Officers of the Old Army, when he himself was a young lieutenant."[16] Profoundly shaken, Grant instructed Attorney General Pierrepont to pursue Belknap in criminal or civil court. John Eaton recalled that the episode "had a very disturbing effect upon the President. I remember his asking me in connection with it, if I had any knowledge or suspicion of corruption in any of the other Departments."[17] Although the cabinet recommended Rutherford B. Hayes as Belknap's successor, Grant turned instead to Senator Lot M. Morrill of Maine. In an ominous sign for the lame-duck president, Morrill refused, confiding to Fish that he was deterred by Orville Babcock and other unsavory White House characters.[18] Grant gave the job to Yale-educated Alphonso Taft of Cincinnati, an influential judge and father of William Howard, the future president.

Even in a capital inured to scandal, Belknap's downfall produced deep reverberations. "The corruptions of this administration seem to permeate every Department of the Government," wrote Orville Hickman Browning, a sturdy Grant hater, with grim satisfaction.[19] More sympathetically, Amos Akerman declared that he had thought Belknap "to be thoroughly upright. This is to me the saddest of the falls of our public men."[20] While William Tecumseh Sherman had long grumbled that Belknap bypassed him in military matters, he had never suspected malfeasance. "I feel sorry for Belknap—I don't think him naturally dishonest, but how could he live on $8000 a year in the style that you all beheld?" he wondered aloud to his brother.[21]

Amazingly, Grant soon reverted to his childlike belief in Belknap's innocence. By March 7, a U.S. attorney had issued the first subpoenas for witnesses to appear before a grand jury. When this subject arose at a cabinet meeting, Grant suddenly expressed his faith that Belknap was not guilty. The cabinet was so taken aback, wrote Fish, that "no response of assent was made by anyone present."[22] Julia Grant had exercised restraint as First Lady, saving political judgments for private talks with her husband. But her friend Amanda "Puss" Belknap had been ostracized since the scandal and Julia, like her husband, tended to side with the victim. On March 21, she personally summoned cabinet members to an extraordinary meeting, imploring them and their wives to visit poor Mrs. Belknap.

"She says that Mrs. Belknap was very much distressed and had expressed a wish to see her and that she would come so as not to be either seen or recognized," Fish recorded. "Mrs. Grant had refused to let her come in secret; but had seen her when she called on Sunday last during the day."[23] The soul of honesty, Fish told Julia he hadn't called on the Belknaps "because I thought it better for both the Belknaps and the Administration that I should not."[24] Secretary of the Navy Robeson hinted at political embarrassments and legal complications that might emerge from such contacts. Reluctantly Julia agreed to stop seeing Mrs. Belknap. Fish observed that "Mrs. Grant [was] overcome and in tears said she supposed this was right—but she felt so sorry for them."[25] From a human standpoint, it was a poignant display of empathy, but a shocking case of political naïveté. In their psychological makeup, both Ulysses and Julia Grant too readily identified with troubled souls, leaving them exposed to manipulation.

On March 31, Pierrepont broached to the cabinet the prospect of a criminal prosecution of Belknap. Not hedging his words, Fish said candidly "that the Administration owed it to itself and to the country to press the indictment."[26] Other cabinet secretaries concurred. Whatever his reservations, Grant gave Pierrepont full permission to proceed with a criminal indictment of Belknap. In the end, the evidence didn't justify criminal proceedings. By April, the Senate began to sit as an impeachment court under the tutelage of Chief Justice Waite and the case dragged on through July. In making his closing statement, Belknap's counsel, Jeremiah S. Black, drew a false analogy between Belknap's accepting gifts and Grant's accepting houses from admirers after the war. His speech showed how poorly Grant's loyalty to Belknap had been repaid:

> That the present Chief Magistrate has taken large gifts from his friends is a fact as well known as any other in the history of the country. He did it openly, without an attempt at concealment or denial. He not only received money and lands and houses and goods amounting in the aggregate to an enormous sum, but he conformed the policy of his administration to the interests and wishes of the donors. Nay, he did more than that; he appointed the men who brought him these gifts to the highest offices which he could bestow in return. Does anybody assert that General Grant was guilty of an impeachable crime in taking these presents even though the receipt of them was followed by official favors extended to the givers?[27]

Of course, Grant received gifts for wartime sacrifice whereas Belknap had taken money from men profiting from his protection. On August 1, he was acquitted on all five impeachment articles, but it was something less than a total vindication. Many senators believed him guilty and only refused to convict him because he had resigned hours before being impeached, returning him to the status of a private citizen. Grant's blunder in accepting his resignation had saved him.

A perfect torrent of scandal had swept over the administration and Grant seemed powerless to stem the rushing, foaming tide. In the face of such overwhelming facts, a few points are worth emphasizing. Grant had not been personally involved in any scandal. His failure had been one of poor selection of cabinet officers and how he handled their downfalls. He never stopped prosecutions of guilty parties and was often insistent about having them prosecuted. It is also important to emphasize that the manufactured outrage over the scandals came from legislators eager to discredit Reconstruction and the moral underpinnings of the administration. Finally, the Grant scandals, which have so clouded his historical reputation, were largely confined to the second half of his second term, obscuring his earlier signal successes as president. Still, endings have a disproportionate influence on any narrative and this holds true for presidencies as well. Grant's maladroit response to scandal reflected the lack of sophistication in a man who had been a stranger to politics before the war. He could recognize evil in his enemies, but not in those who posed as his friends. Many Americans understood this, and, through the many vicissitudes of his administration, retained respect and affection for Grant.

GRANT SHUFFLED HIS CABINET one last time in spring 1876. Attorney General Pierrepont was shipped off to London as minister to England, replaced by Alphonso Taft, who had served fleetingly as secretary of war. Replacing Taft at War was James D. Cameron of Pennsylvania, a Princeton graduate with a background in banking and railway businesses. A man of substantial wealth, Cameron, forty-three, was little known in political circles, except as the son of Senator Simon Cameron, the disgraced war secretary under Abraham Lincoln. Despite his earlier reluctance to replace Belknap, Senator Lot M. Morrill agreed to follow Benjamin Bristow at Treasury. He was an apt choice, having agreed with Grant on financial matters, such as opposing the inflation bill, and had also firmly supported Reconstruction.

The final cabinet shakeup came in July when Marshall Jewell was unexpect-edly asked to resign as postmaster general, an abrupt decision that prompted intense speculation about Grant's motives. "The true reason for the President's action is . . . that Gov. Jewell made too many apologies for the administration, and was not disposed to stand before all the world as a member of it," *The New York Times* conjectured.[28] Something about Jewell grated on Grant, who told Fish "he could stand his annoyance no longer."[29] In appointing his successor, Grant displayed the mischievous side of his nature. He called in James N. Tyner, second assistant postmaster general, and announced, "I have decided, Mr. Tyner, to ask for your resignation." Tyner blushed, his head drooping. "And to appoint you Postmaster-General," Grant added, to Tyner's sudden, brightening delight.[30] Thus ended the topsy-turvy history of Grant's many cabinet appointments.

Although Grant had rejected a third term and refrained from involvement in choosing a successor, he was hardly indifferent to the fate of a party he had pi-loted for nearly eight years. Hamilton Fish had been his most intimate confi-dant, showing cool, superlative judgment and forming the perfect counterweight to Grant's sometimes unaccountable moods. Grant deemed him the foremost statesman of the age and favored him as his successor. Without telling Fish, Grant secretly drafted a letter of support to be disclosed at the Republican con-vention if the favorite-son candidacies of James Blaine, Oliver Morton, and Ros-coe Conkling misfired. While Grant would have happily embraced any of these party regulars, he was still infatuated with Conkling, holding "his great charac-ter and genius in profound respect" and believing he had been fiercely loyal.[31] Conkling chafed at Grant's refusal to endorse him openly and maintain surface neutrality in the race.

The one man Grant didn't care to see nominated was Bristow, who had be-come a darling of Liberal Republicans. In the minds of reformers, Grant re-mained associated with party bosses who would get their just comeuppance with civil service reform. In mid-April, Carl Schurz rallied Republicans concerned by "widespread corruption in our public service" and they met in New York a month later.[32] These insurgents didn't endorse Bristow openly, but agreed to work qui-etly for him at the Republican convention. For Grant, Bristow was the treacher-ous cabinet secretary who had connived to discredit him, and he wasn't a man to forget such a supposed betrayal. As Louise Taft, wife of the new attorney general, confided to a friend: "The President's family naturally consider [Bristow] in league with his enemies, as Bristow's friends all abuse the Administration."[33]

Party Stalwarts agreed with the administration on Reconstruction and were prepared to turn the upcoming election into another contest of loyal Republicans versus disloyal Democrats. They would inveigh against the Klan and make emotional appeals that reminded voters of northern sacrifice and southern betrayal during the war. Yet a segment of the Republican Party establishment now wondered aloud whether troops should be withdrawn from the South, leading many blacks to yearn for a third Grant term. As Robert T. Kent of Atlanta wrote to him, "We the Colored Men and Women Boys & Girles yes Even the Litle Children Thank you dear Sir," and he ended with a plea for Grant to stand for reelection.[34]

When the Republican convention met in Cincinnati in June, it was feared Bristow's nomination would alienate Stalwarts, while Blaine, Morton, and Conkling would deter the party's Liberal reformers. The platform implicity criticized Grant, railing against "a corrupt centralism which, after inflicting upon ten states the rapacity of carpetbag tyranny, has honeycombed the offices of the federal government itself with incapacity, waste, and fraud."[35] The one man who seemed able to unify the party was Governor Rutherford B. Hayes of Ohio, who defeated Blaine for the nomination on the seventh ballot by a 384 to 351 vote; Congressman William A. Wheeler of New York joined him as the vice presidential candidate. Hayes had been wounded during the war and fought with sufficient gallantry to attain a rank of brevet major general. Grant, having known Hayes well as a congressman and admired him as "an honest, sincere man, and patriot," hurried off a telegram of hearty support.[36] "I congratulate you and feel the greatest assurance that you will occupy my present position from the Fourth of March next."[37] Serenaded by the Marine Band, Grant appeared on the White House balcony to address the party faithful crowded below: "I cannot withhold my approval of the excellent ticket given you by the National Republican Convention at Cincinnati—a ticket that should receive the cordial support of all races in all sections."[38] On July 4, he invited Hayes to stay at Long Branch and sample "the genial sea breeze, fine roads and beautiful surrounding villages, and pleasant and hospitable neighbors."[39] Perhaps distancing himself from the administration, Hayes studiously avoided such a visit.

Grant soon discovered Hayes wasn't the friendly, compromise candidate he had envisioned. As early as March 1875, Hayes had admitted privately he was "opposed to the course of Gen. Grant on the 3d term, the Civil Service, and the appointment of unfit men on partisan or personal grounds."[40] Now, in a letter accepting the nomination, Hayes embraced civil service reform, flayed the spoils system, and promised, in advance, to spurn a second term. Grant interpreted this last pledge as a backhanded swipe at him. Despite promises to protect southern blacks, Hayes resorted to code language to suggest a repeal of Reconstruction, telling southerners he would "cherish their truest interests" and assist them in obtaining the "blessings of honest and capable local government."[41] The *New York Tribune* reported that Grant thought Hayes's letter "in extremely bad taste" and that it "reflected upon the present Administration . . . The President's entire manner indicated complete dissatisfaction with the political situation, and much personal anger."[42] This coincided with reports portraying Grant as moody and temperamental in the twilight of his second term and hypersensitive to criticism. On July 14, Hayes wrote to Grant and denied that he had tried to insult him by renouncing a second term. Putting forth a lame argument, he said he had hoped to harmonize the Republican Party by reassuring younger presidential hopefuls that he wouldn't block their path.

When Democrats gathered in St. Louis in late June, they nominated for president Samuel J. Tilden, the New York governor and well-to-do lawyer, after two ballots. Having taken on Tammany Hall and the corrupt Tweed Ring, Tilden, like Hayes, laid claim to good-government credentials. Imitating Hayes, he also endorsed a one-term limit for presidents. Predictably for a Democratic candidate, he opposed Reconstruction and excoriated "the rapacity of carpetbag tyrannies."[43] With all but three southern states now back in the Democratic Party fold, it appeared that a political backlash of monumental proportions had taken hold against Reconstruction. Sensing an abandonment of Reconstruction, Frederick Douglass wondered what good abolition had been for the black man if "having been freed from the slaveholder's lash, he is to be subject to the slaveholder's shotgun?"[44]

Grant's last year in office was supposed to be a festive season for America, marking the nation's centennial. In 1873 he had announced that an international exhibit, the first such fair in American history, would open in Fairmount Park in Philadelphia in spring 1876. A convinced believer in American progress, Grant had caught the spirit of the age and wished to celebrate American economic gains and the advance of republican government across the globe. The exposition, he hoped, would showcase "our own and foreign skill and progress in manufactures, agriculture, art, science, and civilization."[45]

On May 10, 1876, with a crowd of 186,672 on hand, Grant opened the fair, flanked by the emperor and empress of Brazil. Following the "Centennial Inauguration March," composed by Richard Wagner, and a hymn by John Greenleaf Whittier, the president reviewed a century of development in which forests had been cleared and prairies subdued to make way for advancing settlement. He paid tribute to American industry and fine arts. Most important, he contended the United States now rivaled "older and more advanced nations in law, medicine and theology—in science, literature, philosophy, and the fine arts."[46] So softly did Grant mouth his speech that a frustrated reporter, stationed a mere twenty feet away, "could not catch a single word." Nevertheless, when Grant pronounced the exhibition open, his words set loose a burst of pandemonium: "A flag ran up the staff on the main building, the chimes began, the cannon boomed from George's Hill, and the orchestra and chorus pealed forth the majestic Hallelujah Chorus."[47]

Grant escorted his Brazilian visitors to Machinery Hall, where they set in motion the huge Corliss engine, the showpiece of the fair. Grant was annoyed that the emperor kept pausing to chat with mechanics, while Julia nursed her own grievances against the empress, who participated in starting up the engine. "I, too, was there on the platform with the President, the Emperor and Empress. I, the wife of the President of the United States—I, the wife of General Grant—was there and was not invited to assist at this little ceremony."[48] Julia Grant's pique and acute sense of entitlement show how accustomed she had grown to deference in the White House.

The exhibition advertised the technological prowess that had powered American progress and featured every mechanical marvel from Alexander Graham Bell's telephone to Remington's "Typographic Machine." George Washington's dentures and Ben Franklin's hand press were on display. Visitors could also inspect the right arm and torch of the Statue of Liberty before they were whisked off to New York Harbor for assembly into the completed monument. But tributes to America's startling ascent from frontier society to burgeoning industrial power had to contend with Indian troubles brewing on the western plains that belied this triumphant narrative.

THE PROBLEM CENTERED on the Black Hills in present-day South Dakota, where the Oglala Sioux and other tribal bands had been guaranteed a huge reservation under the 1868 Treaty of Fort Laramie. Serving as a site for many martial and religious rituals, the Black Hills occupied a special niche in the Sioux spiritual world. Despite Grant's pacific intentions, the leading enforcer of his Indian policy was Phil Sheridan, who considered Indian culture barbaric. Sherman's attitude was no less punitive. "Sooner or later these Sioux have to be wiped out," he observed, "or made to stay just where they are put."[49] In 1874, amid rumors of abundant gold seeded in the Black Hills, Sheridan sent George Armstrong Custer and his Seventh Cavalry to hunt out a site for a new fort. Custer led a column of a thousand men, armed with cannon and Gatling guns, which verified that gold existed. Predictions that the vein embedded there rivaled California's triggered a mad scramble of miners who wished to exploit it. Although Grant took steps to intercept the sudden onslaught of money-mad settlers, pleading with them to stay away, some commanders grew lackadaisical and allowed the prospectors to encroach on sacred Sioux turf. The magnetic tug of instant riches was irresistible in a country still mired in depression.

Even as this standoff simmered, Grant traveled to Indian Territory in October, becoming the first president to do so and praising efforts by four tribes to cultivate ranching and lead a more settled life. Though wanting to enforce the Treaty of Fort Laramie and safeguard the Sioux, he recognized that the army couldn't hold back rapacious miners. To resolve the impasse, he offered the Sioux $6 million if they ceded the Black Hills to the federal government. There lay some practical wisdom behind Grant's offer, but one can easily imagine the chiefs' horror at auctioning off their sacred lands.

In early 1875, Grant sent an expert geologist to the region to validate that it contained gold. If it were found in large quantities, Secretary of the Interior Delano informed Grant, his department would "protect the rights of the Indians as guaranteed to them by the treaty of 1868." But he also intended "to use every effort possible to extinguish the Indian title to the Black Hills country, and open the same to settlement and explorations for mineral wealth at the earliest day practicable."[50] Thus, the Grant administration pursued two contradictory missions: to protect Sioux treaty rights and to pave the way for the inexorable invasion of predatory miners. In case the Sioux didn't get the message, Sheridan prepared to establish a military post in the Black Hills, perched on the western edge of their reservation.

On May 26, 1875, Grant met Sioux leaders at the White House and entreated them to relocate farther south where, he claimed, the climate was better, the grass richer, the buffalo more abundant. He explained the extreme difficulty of interdicting white settlers, predicting the problem would only intensify and spur violent clashes. Under the Sioux treaty, the federal government had promised supplies, but, Grant warned, in the event of fighting, he would be forced to withhold them. "My interest is in seeing you protected," he continued, "while I have the power to make treaties with you which shall protect you." But the Sioux must "settle the question of the limits of your hunting grounds, and make preliminary arrangements to allow white persons to go into the Black Hills."[51] Federal payments for the Black Hills would take the form of government bonds, with semiannual interest applied to benefit the Sioux. Despite Grant's evident concern for their welfare, he was offering them a suicide pact for their culture, urging that he wanted to see their "children attending schools" and future generations "speaking English and preparing [themselves] for the life of white men."[52]

While Grant dealt with the nascent Sioux crisis, he received an explosive letter from Professor Othniel Marsh of Yale College, outlining pervasive corruption at the Red Cloud Agency that furnished Sioux supplies in northwest Nebraska, near the Black Hills. Marsh laid out a lurid tale of putrid pork, inferior flour, rotten tobacco, and other shoddy goods foisted upon the tribe. He stated categorically that the interior secretary and commissioner of Indian affairs worked not to correct fraud, but to suppress knowledge of it. Marsh directly challenged Grant: "You alone have the will and the power to destroy that combination of bad men, known as the Indian Ring, who are debasing this service, and thwarting the efforts of all who endeavor to bring to a full consummation your noble policy of peace."[53] Grant assured Marsh of his "earnest desire for an honest administration in every department of the Government, and willingness to ferret out and punish fraud wherever found."[54] That same day, he told Secretary of the Interior Delano that the agent at the Red Cloud Agency was "wholly incompetent" and "easily led without his knowledge to work the designs of bad and unscrupulous men."[55] Not standing on ceremony, Grant also directed Delano's attention to serious accusations against him.

Perhaps stung by criticism of the ethical shortcomings of his administration, Grant convened a commission to travel to Nebraska to study the Red Cloud Agency, one that included waspish critics of Delano. Clearly Grant meant business. Remarkably, he met with Marsh—a gadfly who had publicly chastised Indian policy—three times, giving him a warm reception in contrast to his frigid treatment at Interior. Grant accepted Delano's resignation, replacing him with the former Michigan senator Zachariah Chandler, a bluff, amiable man and a robust fund-raiser for the Republican Party. Since he had criticized civil service reform, his selection disappointed journalists seeking a purge of the scandal-ridden Interior Department.

When the commissioners arrived in Nebraska to confer with Sioux chiefs, their spokesman proceeded to tell them that Grant—"the Great Father in Washington"—had sent them to uncover wrongdoing: "If the agent or any of the contractors who have been employed by our Government to furnish you goods and supplies have cheated you, we want to find that out."[56] Red Cloud responded that he didn't want army officers acting as Indian agents. Then he turned to the momentous issue that overshadowed corruption. Facing the Black Hills, he said, "The people from the States who have gone to the Black Hills are stealing gold, digging it out and taking it away, and I don't see why the Great Father don't bring them back."[57]

In early November, a pastoral delegation met with Grant and expressed concern that he had renounced his Indian Peace Policy. Far from it, Grant insisted, he hoped "it would become so firmly established as to be the necessary policy of his successors."[58] After meeting with another critic, George H. Stuart, who had resigned from the Board of Indian Commissioners, Grant received a congratulatory letter from him, applauding how he had banished crooked Indian agents and installed "vastly superior" men who were "as faithful and honest as any class of men in the government Service."[59] Stuart foresaw a vindication of Grant's Indian policy: "The policy is doing what was never before really attempted,—it is teaching the Indians civilization and Christianity,—giving them books, schools, Homes and Churches, and the result . . . will be in a few years the settlement of the Indian question, and they will be as the colored people now largely are, able to take care of themselves."[60] Such euphoria would prove woefully shortsighted.

On November 3, 1875, Grant presided over a confidential White House meeting that soon left his Peace Policy in ruins. At a parley with Sheridan, Belknap, Chandler, and Brigadier General George Crook, Grant concluded they could no longer resist the wave of miners washing over the Black Hills. While he didn't rescind the order keeping them from the area, he indicated it should no longer be rigidly enforced since opposing the miners "only increased their desire and complicated the troubles."[61] Relaxing the order would open the floodgates of settlement and menace the Sioux. Still more threatening to them was the decision to force Sitting Bull—a brave warrior and holy man with an almost mystical following, who had opposed the sale of the Black Hills—and his band of

Sioux outside the reservation to relocate on agency land by the tight deadline of January 31, 1876. If they failed to do so, Grant would send a military force to ensure their compliance. When Sitting Bull flouted this unrealistic timetable, Chandler told Belknap that the Indians in question had been turned over to his War Department. After Belknap notified Sheridan to take action, Brigadier General Alfred H. Terry formed three columns to march against Sitting Bull and his quietly charismatic ally Crazy Horse.

Part of that force was to include George Armstrong Custer, a West Point graduate who had stood out during the Civil War as an intrepid cavalry officer. Feared by his men, Custer was also admired for his flair and flamboyant audacity. He struck colorful poses in combat, his fringed buckskin suits and blond hair flowing in the breeze as he led charges. His ferocity won Phil Sheridan's admiration, although Grant took a much more nuanced view, praising his "personal gallantry and valor" while condemning him as "not a very level-headed man."[62] Custer—vain, headstrong, narcissistic—was the very antithesis of Grant. A Democrat who had idolized George McClellan, he had often been insubordinate, intrigued against superiors, lobbied for his personal advancement, and gambled and womanized. He had also supported Andrew Johnson, opposed Grant for president, and worked against Reconstruction. So it came as no surprise that when Grant lauded Custer, he quoted Sheridan's opinion, not his own. As he wrote in 1866, there was no cavalry officer in whom Sheridan lodged greater confidence and no officer in whose "judgment I have greater faith than in Sheridan's."[63]

Not long after the war, Grant received reports of Custer's cruelty toward his men, one charging that Custer habitually inflicted "the most brutal & unusual punishments . . . for trifling offenses."[64] In 1867 Custer underwent a court-martial for ordering deserters to be shot and Grant seemed to consider him guilty.[65] The following year, Custer and his cavalry obliterated an Indian village on the Washita River, wantonly murdering more than a hundred Southern Cheyenne, including women and children. In late March 1876, Custer testified before Representative Hiester Clymer's committee on War Department expenditures and accused Belknap of corruption. Recklessly self-promoting, he insinuated that Grant had tampered with the Sioux reservation boundary to assist the corrupt practices of Belknap and Delano. Angered by these groundless accusations, Grant instructed Sherman and Sheridan that he didn't want Custer to supervise one of the columns in the impending campaign against Sitting Bull and Crazy Horse.

Eager to be part of the expedition, Custer worked to rally public opinion in his favor. Tamping down his pride, he went to the White House on May 1 to seek an interview with Grant and cooled his heels for five hours. According to one press account, Custer "sat in the waiting room unsent for until the President's calling hour was over, although he repeatedly sent in his card."[66] When Grant at last sent out a message that he couldn't see him, Custer stormed out in disgust. "Custer is trying to brow-beat the President," Belknap wrote. "He *may* succeed."[67] Press reports intimated that Sherman had pleaded with Grant that Custer was the best man to lead the Sioux campaign, but Grant replied that Custer had tried "to besmirch his administration, and he proposed to put a stop to it."[68]

Custer feared he would lose face with his regiment if he were sidelined during the Sioux campaign, and he begged Grant to spare him the "humiliation of seeing my regiment march to meet the enemy, and I not to share its dangers."[69] Phil Sheridan took his side. In the end, Grant wouldn't overrule Sheridan and on May 8 decided to allow Custer to join the expedition, leading his regiment in Brigadier General Alfred Terry's column. "Advise Custer to be prudent, not to take along any newspaper men who always work mischief, and to abstain from any personalities in the future," Sherman told Terry.[70]

The Sioux had acquired the reputation, Sherman said, of being "the most brave and warlike Savages of this Continent."[71] By late May, Phil Sheridan confessed that his two department commanders, Generals Crook and Terry, hadn't the foggiest idea where Sitting Bull and his Sioux warriors had fled. Sheridan took refuge in the illusion that a large body of hostile Indians couldn't remain cohesive for long and even imagined that the approach of three columns would herd them back onto the reservation. Shattering such naive expectations on June 17, Crazy Horse led a band of warriors against the thousand-man column under General Crook, dealing them a bloody setback and driving them rearward to their base camp. As Custer drifted westward toward his doom, he knew nothing of this stunning defeat.

As the nation got ready to solemnize its centennial on July 4, reports filtered back that Custer and 263 of his men in the Seventh Cavalry had been annihilated by Lakota Sioux and Northern Cheyenne warriors along the Little Bighorn River in southern Montana, their mutilated bodies strewn among the hills. Custer was found naked, a bullet hole in his head, a gash in his thigh, an arrow piercing his penis. Supposed to be marching toward a rendezvous with Generals Terry and John Gibbon, he had arrived too soon, failed to wait for other troops, and confronted alone an enormous Indian force favored with overpowering numbers. "I deeply deplore the loss of Custer and his men," Sheridan wrote. "I feel it was an unnecessary sacrifice, due to misapprehension and a superabundance of courage—the latter extraordinarily developed in Custer."[72]

People could scarcely fathom the shocking news and Custer soon acquired an aura of martyrdom. Some speculated that, unhinged by his feud with Grant, he had acted rashly to show his bravery. Grant refused to accept that. In a newspaper interview, he placed blame for the disaster squarely on Custer's shoulders:

> I regard Custer's massacre as a sacrifice of troops, brought on by Custer himself, that was wholly unnecessary . . . He was not to have made the attack before effecting the junction with Terry and Gibbon. He was notified to meet them on the 26th, but instead of marching slowly, as his orders required in order to effect the junction on the 26th, he enters upon a forced march of eighty-three miles in twenty-four hours, and thus has to meet the Indians alone on the 25th . . . General Crook is the best, wiliest Indian fighter in this country. He has had vast experience in Indian fighting . . . He is as wily as Sitting Bull in this respect, that when he finds himself outnumbered and taken at a disadvantage he prudently retreats. In Custer's case Sitting Bull had ten men to every one of Custer.[73]

Whoever was to blame for the Little Bighorn calamity, the national response was a ferocious outcry for Indian blood, bordering on the genocidal. E. L. Godkin of *The Nation,* who had embraced Grant's Peace Policy, reflected the altered sentiment: "Our philanthropy and our hostility tend to about the same end, and this is the destruction of the Indian race."[74]

By July 8, as he consulted at the White House with his military advisers, Grant rushed to shore up forces in the West while outraged Americans volunteered for service. "We must not have another massacre like Custer's and Congress is now in Session willing to give us all we want," Sherman advised Sheridan.[75] On August 11, Grant asked Congress to expand the cavalry by 2,500 men and requested authority to call up five more regiments to deal with the emergency created by the massacre. In the wake of the disaster, Grant was less reticent in talking about the gold found in the Black Hills. That August former governor Newton Edmunds of Dakota Territory brought gold samples to the

White House. "When the mines shall have been thoroughly explored," Grant predicted, "as much gold will be found there as in California."[76] Such remarks guaranteed a stampede of prospectors to the area. At the same time, Grant recommended that people "stay away until the present troubles are over and until we have extinguished the titles of the Indians to the lands which they sold by treaty."[77] That December, the federal government took legal possession of the Black Hills.

There was something profoundly contradictory about Grant's attitude toward the whole situation. In addressing Congress in December, he placed ultimate blame for what had happened to the Sioux on the white men: "Hostilities there have grown out of the avarice of the white man who has violated our treaty stipulation in his search for gold."[78] All along he had ardently desired to bring justice to Native Americans. This raised questions of why Grant had caved in to greedy miners. To answer this, he invoked force majeure, saying that "rumors of rich discoveries of gold" had drawn miners to the region and any effort to remove them would have led to desertion by the bulk of troops sent there.[79] In other words, U.S. troops would have refused to thwart the miners, even under direct orders from the president. Thus Ulysses S. Grant, an advocate of a Peace Policy toward the Indians, found himself, willy-nilly, on the side of those raping their lands and violating a sacred treaty commitment. In the last analysis, Grant had to favor the American electorate and sacrifice the Sioux. It was a terribly ironic coda to a policy premised upon humane treatment of Native Americans. The outcome was fine as far as Phil Sheridan was concerned. "This was the country of the buffalo and the hostile Sioux only last year," he wrote in 1877. "There are no signs of either now, but in their places we found prospectors, emigrants, and farmers."[80] Quite a different verdict was rendered by the U.S. Court of Claims in 1979. Reviewing the federal government's dealings with the Sioux, the court said of the Black Hills episode that "a more ripe and rank case of dishonorable dealing will never, in all probability, be found in our history."[81]

Lost amid recriminations over Little Bighorn was that on June 9 Grant had made amends to another oppressed group, attending the dedication of Adas Israel synagogue in Washington, home to an orthodox Jewish congregation. It was the first time an American president ever attended a synagogue consecration and yet another instance of Grant atoning for General Orders No. 11, his infamous wartime edict. A synagogue dedication was a small-time affair, yet Grant brought a distinguished retinue to the neat brick building, including his son

Buck, Senator Thomas Ferry of Michigan, the Methodist minister John P. New-man, and the lawyer Simon Wolf, all of whom were seated on sofas near the podium. (Because Vice President Henry Wilson had died on November 22, 1875, Ferry, who was president pro tempore of the Senate, would succeed Grant if he did not finish his term.) The American flag was draped on both sides of the Torah ark and the narrow, gaslit room was fragrant with bouquets.

Officiating was the Philadelphia rabbi George Jacobs, clad in black robe and cap. Since the prayers were in Hebrew, Grant sat through long portions chanted in a foreign tongue. With political tact, Jacobs offered a prayer to the president of the United States along with senators and representatives. He and the scroll bear-ers then circled seven times around the sanctuary as prescribed by ancient ritual. Jacobs delivered a sermon in English about the patriarch Jacob, who beheld in a dream a mystical ladder upon which angels went up and down. For three straight hours, Grant sat in the modest room, his hat on in homage to Jewish custom, as humble as a penitent in sackcloth. In a mark of respect, he never spoke. Congre-gation elders made clear that he need not feel obliged to sit through the entire ceremony, but he made a point of staying to the end. At the close, when he made a $10 donation, the congregation extended "heartfelt thanks" for his unusual presence and generous gift.[82] Grant's attendance at the dedication crowned the special solicitude he had shown for the Jewish community throughout his presi-dency. As Simon Wolf wrote during Woodrow Wilson's tenure, "President Grant did more on behalf of American citizens of Jewish faith at home and abroad than all the Presidents of the United States prior thereto or since."[83]

Redeemers

F OR THE MOST PART, Grant sat out the 1876 presidential contest, while his cabinet was far more actively engaged. Secretary of the Interior Chandler managed the campaign of Rutherford B. Hayes and chaired the Republican National Committee, while others pitched in with supporting speeches. With extreme trepidation Grant monitored a race that threatened to reverse gains made by the Republican Party and black voters across the South. In August, John Roy Lynch, the black Mississippi congressman, saw that the Democratic revival overtaking the South would make the electoral math very difficult for Hayes: "Every Southern state [the Democrats] propose to carry as they carried Mississippi last year . . . not by the power of the ballot, but by an organized system of terrorism and violence."[1]

However aloof he was from campaigning, Grant remained committed to the safety of black voters. While staying at the Pennsylvania home of William W. Smith in late September, members of a "colored men's marching club" came to serenade him.[2] Grant expressed pleasure that blacks had been so faithful to the Union and reiterated his belief that voting remained the cardinal right in a democracy. As reported in the *Pittsburgh Telegraph,* Grant said that "it was his purpose to see that every man of every race and condition should have the privilege of voting his sentiments without violation or intimidation. When this was secured we would then, and only then, deserve to be called a free *Republic.*"[3] Having long shied away from speeches, Grant, as a lame-duck president, seemed much more open and quicker to spout fundamental beliefs.

In the presidential race, Democrats feasted on the frequent scandals that had plagued Grant's second term and at times seemed to run against "Grantism" rather than Hayes. Republicans cast Democrats as thinly disguised slaveholders, one prominent Republican thundering: "Every man that loved slavery better than liberty was a Democrat . . . Every man that raised blood-hounds to pursue human beings was a Democrat."[4] Though more sympathetic to white southern concerns than Grant, Hayes nonetheless advised his campaign managers to exploit fears of "rebel rule and a solid South."[5]

As rebel banners were waved defiantly across the South, Grant worried that a rejuvenated Democratic Party would demand compensation for freed slaves. He especially dreaded a growing southern canard that the Civil War had been a war of northern aggression, with a moral equivalence drawn between the two sides. As he told a newspaper, he regretted Democratic claims that Confederate soldiers "fought honestly as American citizens for an honest purpose and in as good a spirit as the Northern soldiers who have been pensioned, and that they were provoked and driven into the War by the North."[6] This revisionist thesis was propagated by Lost Cause ideologues, who venerated Lee and depreciated Grant as a butcher who had only defeated his rebel counterpart by dint of superior manpower.

Grant knew that Reconstruction was imperiled and that the legal props were being kicked out from under it. In 1876 the Supreme Court handed down two rulings, *United States v. Cruikshank* and *United States v. Reese,* that gutted portions of the Enforcement Act of 1870 and narrowed the powers of the Fourteenth and Fifteenth Amendments. Grant did what he could to protect southern blacks and their threatened voting rights. When the House of Representatives passed a resolution to strengthen enforcement of the Fifteenth Amendment, he directed Sherman to hold forces ready "for protecting all citizens, without distinction of race, color, or political opinion, in the exercise of the right to vote as guaranteed by the Fifteenth Amendment."[7] But Reconstruction was clearly ebbing, the federal military presence in the South having waned to slightly more than three thousand officers and men.

The need for federal troops hadn't faded, as evidenced by havoc in Hamburg, South Carolina, on July 4, 1876, the date of America's centennial. South Carolina was one of three southern states remaining in the Republican column, Florida and Louisiana being the others, and it faced unrelenting pressure from whites to "redeem" their state for the Democrats. At Hamburg, a scuffle arose when two white farmers in a buggy protested that their path was barred by a parade of local black militia; before long, militia leaders were jailed for obstructing a public highway. White vengeance wasn't yet sated. In the coming days, armed whites from South Carolina and nearby Georgia, including members of rifle clubs and saber companies, gathered in Hamburg to demand that local black militia relinquish their weapons. The latter took refuge in a small brick building used as an armory and a drill room, but the swelling white mob blew out its windows with musket and cannon fire. Believing their assailants would soon blow up the building, blacks leapt from the windows or climbed down an escape ladder only to be gunned down in cold blood. Five men in a row were executed and three more wounded as they attempted to flee. James Cook, the black town marshal, was shot and his skull smashed in with muskets. The Republican governor, Daniel H. Chamberlain, was a lawyer from Massachusetts, a Yale graduate who had been an officer in a black Union regiment during the war. Writing to Secretary of War Cameron, he deplored the Hamburg massacre as a "butchery of unoffending and unarmed colored men by a brutal and bloodthirsty mob of white men."[8] He thought the episode more shocking than the massacre of Custer's men, who were at least "shot in open battle. The victims at Hamburg were murdered in cold blood after they had surrendered and were utterly defenseless."[9] The homes of nearly every black family in town were pillaged while mutilated bodies of the murdered men broiled in sunlight for days, their families too petrified to retrieve them.

On July 17, the U.S. marshal in Charleston appealed to Attorney General Taft to send federal troops to Hamburg. Without consulting the president, the conservative Taft dismissed the action as unconstitutional. On July 22, Governor Chamberlain wrote directly to Grant, portraying the Hamburg massacre as part of a systematic "campaign of violence and blood" to breed terror among black voters. The murders had bred "a feeling of triumph and political elation . . . in the minds of a considerable part of the white people and Democrats." The governor asked Grant to exercise federal power vigilantly in the state.[10] In an impassioned reply, Grant revealed the depth of his emotional commitment to black security:

> The scene at Hamburg, as cruel, bloodthirsty, wanton, unprovoked, and as uncalled for as it was, is only a repetition of the course that has been pursued in other Southern States within the last few

years—notably in Mississippi and Louisiana—Mississippi is governed
today by officials chosen through fraud and violence, such as would
scarcely be accredited to savages, much less to a civilized and christian
people—How long these things are to continue, or what is to be the
final remedy, the Great Ruler of the Universe only knows . . . There
has never been a desire on the part of the North to humiliate the
South—nothing is claimed for one State that is not freely accorded to
all the others, unless it may be the right to Kill negroes and republicans
without fear of punishment, and without loss of caste or reputation.[11]

Although Grant stopped short of dispatching federal troops, he promised, "I will
give every aid for which I can find law, or constitutional power."[12]

Historians have criticized Grant for not hastening troops to South Carolina,
but in the new, less forgiving political climate, he was obliged to demonstrate
that the state governor had done everything in his power to handle the problem
alone. That Grant was profoundly disturbed by the killings is unquestionable.
Transmitting to the Senate documents about the Hamburg "slaughter"—Grant's
term—he alluded to "murders & massacres" of innocent men in Louisiana as
well. "All are familiar with their horrible details, the [only] wonder being that so
many justify them or apologize [for] them."[13] Throttled by dwindling Republican support for Reconstruction, Grant compensated by expressing his frustration
in white-hot language.

That summer, white Democrats in South Carolina united around the
gubernatorial candidacy of Wade Hampton III, a former Confederate cavalry
officer, who was aided by paramilitary rifle clubs known as Red Shirts. L. Cass
Carpenter, an internal revenue collector in South Carolina, warned Grant in
August that Hampton and his followers were plotting to regain control of the
state government. When Carpenter attended Republican election meetings, he
shuddered at the spectacle of "hundreds of armed, mounted white men, members of rifle and saber clubs," who were there to "intimidate the speakers, and the
assemblage gathered to hear them."[14] David T. Corbin, U.S. attorney in Green-
ville, investigated the Hamburg butchery and told of insuperable obstacles to
prosecutions, blaming "the terror of the witnesses to testify, the constant fear of
assassination if they do." He concluded that "juries will not convict on any
proof, however good."[15]

The Hamburg carnage preceded far worse atrocities in October in Ellenton,

South Carolina. Two black burglars allegedly entered a white woman's home and struck her with a stick, prompting a murderous binge by hundreds of lethally armed whites from rifle clubs. They executed blacks ranging from a ninety-year-old man to a seventeen-year-old adolescent, who had his ear sliced off. Simon Coker, a black state legislator, was gunned down in an open field. At least seventeen blacks were slain within a week. So widespread was the savagery that the estimated death toll of black victims ran as high as 150. In its aftermath, black citizens of Aiken sent Grant a heartbreaking description of their plight: "We write to tell you that our people are being shot down like dogs, and no matter what democrats may say; unless you help us our folks will not dare go to the polls."[16]

On October 11, Governor Chamberlain employed the requisite language for tapping federal troops, notifying Grant that "insurrection and domestic violence" in three counties near the Georgia border exceeded the state's power to control it.[17] Six days later Grant ordered rifle clubs "who ride up and down by day and night in arms, murdering some peaceable citizens and intimidating others," to disperse and retire peaceably to their homes.[18] Secretary of War Cameron dispatched troops the same day. Now approaching the finale of his second term, Grant threw aside political caution and northern ambivalence to protect black and white Republicans in the South. It was a reminder to northern Republicans that, despite the scandals in his administration, Grant had almost always been most courageous where it counted: in protecting freed people. Many northern Republicans applauded his stand, although Democrats complained that he was favoring the Hayes slate. "Today I was again impressed with the belief that when his presidential term is ended, General Grant will regain his place as one of the foremost of Americans," James Garfield reflected.[19] About a thousand federal troops had shown up in South Carolina by Election Day, not sufficient to avert all violence, but enough to provide a modicum of safety to defenseless Republicans. As one grateful white Republican reassured Grant, without federal troops "any man *white* or colored who would have dared to cheer Hayes . . . would have had his head taken off."[20]

Mississippi remained a racial tinderbox. Blanche Ames, the outgoing governor's wife, pointed out that among the "principal men" in the state capital, "there is hardly one who has not, by counsel or action, taken some part in the Negro murders."[21] In September, the U.S. marshal in Oxford, James H. Pierce, informed Attorney General Taft that a "perfect reign of terror" existed in three Mississippi counties, making Republicans afraid to vote.[22] At least ten companies of federal troops, he estimated, would be required to suppress the mayhem. Hobbled by the hostile northern climate, the best Grant could do was to deploy three companies in the bloodstained counties. Aside from outright violence, White Liners terrified black voters by forcing them to reveal their employers before they voted, thus exposing them to economic reprisals. The terror tactics worked: on Election Day in November, only two Republicans dared to vote in all of Yazoo County, only one in Tallahatchie County.

In Louisiana, whites were set to purge the state and "redeem" it from Republican control. In September, Grant had received disturbing messages that electoral fraud would undermine presidential voting. The Republican senator Joseph Rodman West believed whites were reenacting the Civil War, organizing their local Democratic Party "with as much method and discipline as were the armies of the Confederacy."[23] As Louisiana Democrats took power by coercion, the resulting violence assumed horrific proportions. Rifle clubs and White Liners carried out a murderous vendetta against black Republicans on the Saturday before Election Day. As investigators later wrote:

> They visited the house of Abram Williams, an old colored republican, sixty years of age. He was taken from his house, stripped, and severely whipped. They visited the house of Willis Frazier, took him also from his bed and brutally whipped him. They visited the house of a son of Abram Williams. He had taken the precaution to spend the night in the cotton-field. Not finding him at home, they whipped his wife, and committed another outrage upon her person. Merrimon Rhodes, on that night, was killed. A few days later his body, disemboweled, was found in the bayou and was buried. They visited the house of Randall Driver. They took him from his bed and from his house and brutally whipped him. They visited the house of Henry Pinkston. He was taken from his bed, from his house, and shot to death. His infant child was killed. His wife was cut in different places; she was shot and nearly slain.[24]

On Election Day 1876, Western Union hooked up a telegraph to bring presidential results directly to the White House. Tilden decisively swept the popular vote with a quarter-million margin, but with 184 electoral votes, fell one short of the 185 required for victory. Nonetheless, as Grant gathered with Republican leaders, the prevailing sense was that Tilden had won and the White House mood darkened accordingly. "Sherman, with his usual impetuosity, was pacing the room," recalled John Eaton, "lamenting with some profanity the fate of the Nation—and especially of the army—should the Democrats . . . assume control, but Grant was perfectly calm and apparently serene."[25]

Slowly the extraordinary prospect dawned that Hayes, who could claim with certainty only 166 electoral votes, might pull off an upset victory. Disputed results in the three "unredeemed" southern states—Louisiana, Florida, and South Carolina—could, if all resolved in his favor, provide him with 19 votes, tipping him over the edge to a one-vote victory with 185 votes. The stage was now set for an electoral deadlock and an explosive constitutional crisis.

The day after the election, Grant traveled to Philadelphia for the closing ceremonies of the Centennial Exhibition. He stayed at the residence of George Childs, where Republican bigwigs pored over returns that documented the most closely contested presidential race in American history. They rejoiced when it appeared Hayes might win, but Grant sought to disarm their premature optimism. "Gentlemen," he pronounced, "it looks to me as if Mr. Tilden was elected."[26] Though scarcely pleased by an ostensible Democratic victory, Grant was fully prepared to bow to the electorate's wishes. "Everything depends now upon a fair count," he told the press.[27] While attending a closing banquet for the exhibition, Grant hurried from the hall when an emergency telegram arrived from Interior Secretary Chandler, who related a grisly saga of having dispatched a train southward to verify election returns only to have it "Kukluxed" and thrown from the track. "There is no doubt of our majority if we can secure an honest canvass," Chandler predicted, "but the indications are that violence is to be freely resorted *to, to* prevent any returns from remote points in the interior. We shall need an army to protect us."[28]

To deal with a spreading threat of disorder—Democrats began to rally to the cry of "Tilden or Blood!"—Grant mustered the stamina to weather one last crisis.[29] He rushed Colonel Thomas H. Ruger to Florida and backed him with troops to ensure a quiet, peaceful ballot count, while he ordered General Christopher C. Augur to do the same in Louisiana. Grant proved remarkably fairminded, declaring that "should there be any grounds of suspicion of fraudulent counting on either side it should be reported and denounced at once . . . Either party can afford to be disappointed in the result but the Country cannot afford to have the result tainted by the suspicion of illegal or false returns."[30] This remained his unswerving policy during the high-stakes drama now unfolding. The northern press cheered Grant's actions in sending troops to avert vote tampering in Louisiana, South Carolina, and Florida, but until final returns were certified in these states, it was impossible to name a new president and the political system wobbled in a dangerous limbo.

Though scrupulously evenhanded, Grant was demonized by southern Democrats and rumors proliferated that he would be killed. John Singleton Mosby advised him to heed this rash talk. "I met Mosby on my way to the President's," Hamilton Fish wrote, "and he told me that the language of the Democrats now was more desperate and more threatening and violent than that of the Southern men on the Election of Lincoln in 1860."[31] To illustrate the vengeful southern mood, Mosby told how he himself had been threatened with arrest "because he prevented a Democrat at the Poles from clubbing a colored voter and had insisted on the right of the negro to vote."[32] True to Mosby's prediction, Grant was peppered with death threats. One anonymous writer, signing himself "An Outlaw of the west," gave him three weeks to prepare for His Maker: "I am bound under oath to take your life."[33] Klan members sent a letter adorned with a skull and crossbones, warning, "You and your assistant thieves will soon be assassinated."[34] At the same time, rumors floated about that a secret Democratic army would stage a military raid on Washington and declare Tilden the winner. To guard against this menace, Grant and Sherman redeployed troops from the interior to Washington and secured the federal arsenal along with three critical bridges leading to the capital.

The crisis came to a head in South Carolina. After the election, Grant heard stories of rifle clubs ringing polling places, allowing only Democrats to vote.[35] Both the Republican governor Chamberlain and the Democratic contender Wade Hampton had claimed victory in the gubernatorial contest. On November 24, with the legislature slated to meet, Chamberlain told Grant that "armed and violent" Democrats would seek to block the session.[36] Two days later, Grant and several cabinet members pondered reports that up to eight thousand rifle company members in South Carolina might seize the state legislature. On the spot, Grant instructed Secretary of War Cameron that Chamberlain was still the legally constituted governor, facing "resistance too formidable to be overcome by the State authorities," and should have all necessary support against domestic violence.[37] A few days later, Democrats invaded the South Carolina legislature, installing their own speaker and clerk and leaving the state in turmoil. As one black railway porter told Grant, at every stop on the train white men sent up hosannas for Wade Hampton and "Damnation to Every Negro, Grant, chamberlain and Company—for God Sake, General . . . Help me, to Come out of this Country of assassins."[38] South Carolina now had two governors and two state legislatures, greatly complicating the electoral fight over the presidency.

Just when Grant thought he could disengage from turbulent racial politics and contemplate a tranquil, post-presidential life, he was thrust back into some of the thorniest dilemmas ever to confront an American chief executive. At a dramatic cabinet session, Cameron proposed that federal troops eject the Democratic speaker and clerk from the South Carolina legislature, reinstating their Republican counterparts. When he swore "this is war and Revolution," Grant retorted, "Decidedly no! no! It is no such thing."[39] Remembering the brouhaha over Sheridan's expelling legislators in New Orleans, Grant explained that the president should not tamper with state politics, but simply provide a safe, peaceful setting for states to resolve their own disputes. He relayed this advice to Colonel Ruger in South Carolina, imploring him to avoid "unlawful use of the Military" by "taking men claiming seats out of the legislative hall."[40]

On December 3, Grant received Tilden's campaign manager, Representative Abram S. Hewitt of New York, and made it clear he would accept Tilden as the next president if he were lawfully chosen. With unusual vehemence he defended his actions in South Carolina, where he thought Democrats had stolen the election from Hayes by scaring away black voters, and he cited the need for federal troops when white rifle clubs ruled the state. He also made it crystal clear that if an armed mob attacked Congress, he would defend it. So wound up was the taciturn Grant that he spoke for a straight hour, perhaps a record outburst for him. As The New York Times marveled, "The President himself told a Republican Congressman this morning that he made the longest speech he had ever made in his life."[41] Approaching the end of his presidency, Grant again seemed more vocal and expressive in his comments, providing glimpses into an emotional life ordinarily screened by his opaque personality.

The electoral crisis reached a new phase on December 6 when the Electoral College electors were scheduled to meet in their respective capitals and cast their votes for president. It quickly became apparent that a new president could not be named because three of the contested states with warring governments—South Carolina, Florida, and Louisiana—filed one set of election certificates for Hayes

and another for Tilden. Their returning boards, which verified the election returns, were in Republican hands, further tainting the results in Democratic
eyes. Faced with this agonizing dilemma, Congress in mid-December called for
a special bipartisan committee to settle the electoral crisis and favored the creation of "a tribunal whose authority none can question and whose decision all
will accept as final."[42]

Meanwhile, Grant had to deal with this dangerous stalemate. Repeatedly he
heard how Democratic ruffians, scraped off the Baltimore and New York streets,
would inflict mayhem on the capital, murdering the president and kidnapping
Hayes. When a patriotic delegation appeared at the White House, styling themselves the Stars & Stripes Association and offering to protect the capital, Grant
calmed them by saying there would be no disturbance. A cool hand at the helm,
he prevented a frightening situation from fraying into partisan violence. As always, Grant was at his most levelheaded in a crisis. With memories of the Civil
War still fresh, another bloody clash was far from unthinkable.

As in the past, Louisiana presented seemingly insurmountable problems. After the election, Grant heard of ballot boxes being destroyed there by Democrats
and sent Senator John Sherman, Congressman Garfield, and other prominent
observers to scrutinize the canvassers tallying the count. Sherman's report described a travesty of justice. So intimidated had black voters been by night riders
that overwhelmingly Republican parishes ended up in the Democratic column.
"Organized clubs of masked armed men, formed as recommended by the central
democratic committee, rode through the country at night, marking their course
by the whipping, shooting, wounding, maiming, mutilation, and murder of
women, children, and defenseless men."[43] A Senate investigating committee
later ascertained that in a single parish, more than sixty black Republicans had
been butchered before the election.

Louisiana Republicans and Democrats, in their eternal squabble, had formed
rival state legislatures. Grant promised to act in a nonpartisan fashion, but his
neutrality was tested when thousands of armed White League members laid
siege to the statehouse, trained their guns on the courthouse, and ejected the
sheriff. On January 11, Grant oversaw an acrimonious cabinet debate about
what to do. Solidly interventionist in the past, he momentarily allied himself
with conservatives. James D. Cameron and Zachariah Chandler grew exasperated that Grant wanted to wait until shots were fired before sending in federal
troops. Despite Grant's hesitation, he then came down hard on the side of the

new Republican governor, Stephen B. Packard, telling General Augur he would not tolerate a state government being taken over "by illegal means."[44]

Tired of the cutthroat politics in Washington, Grant labored under excruciating pressure as he confronted a choice of political poisons: either intervene in state politics and invite a northern outcry or stand back and allow thuggery to reign supreme in Louisiana. On January 17, Fish recorded an extraordinary conversation with a distraught Grant, who was so upset by Louisiana events that he couldn't sleep. He seemed to be edging toward a nervous collapse and even doubted for a moment the wisdom of his past policies. He railed against incompetent carpetbag governors in the South who "had no interests there, but had simply gone there to hold office and so soon as they should lose it, intended to come away." He also seemed to oppose the very black voting rights he had so courageously upheld: "He says he is opposed to the XV amendment and thinks it was a mistake; that it had done the negro no good, and had been a hindrance to the South, and by no means a political advantage to the North."[45] Two years later, in a discussion with the journalist John Russell Young, Grant clarified what he meant, saying that the Fourteenth Amendment had bolstered southern power by scrapping the rule that had once counted an African American as only three-fifths of a person for electoral purposes. Despite suppressing the vote of blacks, white southerners could now count them fully for election purposes, giving the "solid South" forty extra votes in the Electoral College and disproportionate influence in American politics. "They keep those votes, but disfranchise the negroes. That is one of the gravest mistakes in the policy of reconstruction."[46]

However eager Grant might be for a Hayes presidency, he knew he would be crippled if his election rested on the outcome in two or three questionable southern states.[47] In late January, Grant signed an act creating a bipartisan Electoral Commission, composed of five members of each house and five Supreme Court justices, to judge the validity of election returns from the contested states.[48] Grant saw this as a peaceful exit, "a wise and constitutional means of escape," from the political abyss into which the nation had sunk.[49] The final seat on the commission went to Joseph P. Bradley of New Jersey, the Republican Supreme Court justice chosen by Grant, and gave Republicans an eight-to-seven edge on the panel.

While the Electoral Commission deliberated in February, Grant longed to be free of the intolerable burdens of office. "But three weeks remain until I close my official career," he told Edwards Pierrepont. "Although so short a time, it appears to me interminable, my anxiety to be free from care is so great."[50] On February 9, Hayes won the Florida vote and on February 16 the Louisiana vote, stacking the odds heavily in his favor. "There is still some doubt, but apparently very little, of the result," a satisfied Hayes wrote in his diary. "I would like to get support from good men of the South, late Rebels. How to do it is the question."[51] Convinced Hayes would win, Grant sent him a cordial invitation to stay in the White House until the inauguration, but Hayes thought this unwise given the murky situation and he didn't arrive in Washington until March 2, right before the inauguration.

Consequential to the election outcome were the many private contacts in the capital between southern Democrats and Hayes's northern Republican supporters. At Wormley's Hotel on February 26, five Hayes people pledged that federal troops would be withdrawn from the South; new "redeemer" governments would be tolerated and "home rule" restored; the four southern Democrats promised, in return, fair treatment of the black community. The influence of the so-called Wormley Conference has been greatly overstated, for it merely culminated months of bargaining and confirmed what was already clear: that Hayes would bring an end to Reconstruction. It was a pyrrhic victory for Republicans, who sacrificed their idealism in exchange for perpetuating their rule. Shortly afterward, the special commission declared Hayes the winner in South Carolina, giving him a 185 to 184 victory in the Electoral College. Having ably presided over this troubled period, staying above the fray, Grant lauded the Electoral Commission as "a fine bit of self-government on the part of the people."[52]

The fifteen-member body had split eight to seven, leading one irate Democrat to object that "we have been cheated, shamefully cheated," while other Democrats bitterly emphasized Tilden's victory in the popular vote and satirized Hayes as "His Fraudulency" or "Rutherfraud B. Hayes."[53] Just as Grant got ready to leave office, the disputed election amplified Democratic animosity to a new level of verbal violence. Many thought the Electoral Commission had winked at cheating committed by Republicans in the South, but Democrats had clearly engaged in widespread voter intimidation and Grant later stated that "the real fraud has been perpetrated by those who are raising the cry of fraud."[54] Despite the rancor, the prospect of two warring presidencies had been averted and the inauguration of Hayes would proceed smoothly.

All in all, Grant's impartial handling of the election, in an extremely tense situation, had been one of his finest achievements. He had prevented bloodshed and ensured a peaceful transition of power. "If Tilden was declared elected I intended to hand him over the reins, and see him peacefully installed," Grant said afterward. "I should have treated him as cordially as I did Hayes, for the question of the Presidency was then neither personal nor political, but national . . . The day that brought about the result and enabled me to leave the White House as I did, I regard as one of the happiest in my life."[55] Grant's coolness in crisis and impeccable fairness reminded voters of why they had trusted him in the first place. "He comes up to the mark so grandly on great occasions," wrote Ebenezer Hoar, "that I wish he were more careful of appearances in smaller matters."[56] Resolution of the crisis brought immediate solace to a terribly overwrought, sleepless president. "The change was not so apparent to the world," wrote Jesse Grant, "but to the family it was more than evident. The brooding gloom that had enveloped him as a cloak was gone and with us, he was all animation."[57]

DURING HIS EIGHT YEARS IN OFFICE, Grant had been bedeviled not so much by his policies, where his record was often excellent, but by personalities, where his record left much to be desired. When the cartoonist Thomas Nast visited him in his last months as president, he found him in a chastened mood, scandalized by the misbehavior of his underlings: "The President was overwhelmed . . . wherever he turned some new dishonor lay concealed."[58] In his last annual message to Congress, he confessed with artless candor, "It was my fortune or misfortune, to be called to the office of Chief Executive without any previous political training . . . Under such circumstances it is but reasonable to suppose that errors of judgment must have occurred." His problems had stemmed from appointees, he said, many of them originally strangers. "It is impossible that where so many trusts are to be allotted that the right parties should be chosen in every instance."[59] Grant couldn't admit that some wayward appointees were old colleagues, notably Orville Babcock, whom he had known too well and stood by too long.

He rightly noted that, as a president coping with the daunting sequel to the Civil War, he had wrestled with herculean challenges: "Nearly one half [of] the states had revolted against the Govt. and of those remaining faithful to the Union a large percentage of the population sympathized with the rebellion and made an 'enemy in the rear' almost as dangerous as the honorable enemy in the front."[60] He had overseen the trajectory from slavery to full-fledged freedom for four million black citizens. As the first president to govern after the Fifteenth Amendment, he had guaranteed the exercise of brand-new black voting rights and opposed the spate of domestic terrorism it engendered. He had been a good steward of the nation's finances, having slashed taxes, trimmed debt, and watched the trade balance turn from deficit to surplus. He had shown that government could make good on its pledge to repay war debt and restore American credit. Unable to let go of Santo Domingo, he pleaded one last time that by its annexation "the emancipated race of the South would have found there a congenial home," where their civil rights might have stood unimpaired.[61]

At the end of the address, Grant acknowledged that his presidency would soon end, and he delivered a plaintive farewell to politics, a fickle world he had never fully mastered: "It is not probable that public affairs will ever again receive attention from me further than as a citizen of the republic, always taking a deep interest in the honor, integrity and prosperity of the whole land."[62] The address was an odd mixture of apologia and self-assertion, the *New York Tribune* describing it as the statement "of a man who is weary of public life and tired of political strife."[63] Grant was haunted by his diminished popularity and the loss of his heroic aura. To Congressman Abram S. Hewitt, he confided that for sixteen years he had borne the entire weight of the nation on his shoulders "without any interval of rest or any possibility of being free from great responsibility."[64] Now he was at last free to set down that awesome burden.

When Jesse Grant returned from Cornell University that Christmas, he found his father "wan and worn, and wrapped in a brooding silence that even the family could not dispel." "We're going, Jesse," his father said forlornly. "That's settled. We start as soon as possible after my successor is installed. We will take whatever money there is and we will go as far and stay as long as it lasts."[65] Only the thought of a round-the-world trip sustained his flagging mood. Whatever the cares of his presidency, Grant must have trembled at the specter of returning to private life, a world where he had stumbled so miserably.

While the presidency had contained its quota of nightmarish moments for Grant, it had been a fairy-tale existence for Julia, who now busied herself with stocking the larder and preparing the White House for the advent of the Hayes family. She was inwardly heartbroken and made no bones about the fact that she was wedded to their celebrity in the White House. One day her husband returned from Capitol Hill, exasperated by lawmakers, and exclaimed, "I wish this was over. I wish I had this Congress off my hands. I wish I was out of it altogether.

After I leave this place, I never want to see it again." Julia looked up, rather startled. "Why, Ulyss, how you talk! I never want to leave it."[66] For Julia, the White House sojourn had been not just a sacred public trust, but an enchanting social whirl. As she put it, "I wish it might have continued forever, except that it would have prevented others from enjoying the same privilege."[67]

A sense of tangible relief, coupled with a mood of wintry melancholy, took hold of Grant in his last days at the White House. Right before leaving office, he dined with General Augur, who was shaken by how downcast he was: "While smoking with the President after dinner, I spoke of his return to civil life, in which I said he would be free from the annoying burdens and vexatious attacks which were embittering his official career. To my dismay the President said, with deep feeling, that he welcomed the change, because his confidence was badly shaken. He added that it was the saddest hour of his life . . . because he had come to realize that he did not know where to go, outside of his family, to find a man to be his confidential secretary, in whom he could put entire trust."[68] The exchange shows how scarred Grant had been by the betrayal of Babcock and other faithless subordinates. A lifelong naïf, Grant had been seared by Washington's cynical politics, which left a bitter aftertaste.

On March 2, President-elect Hayes arrived at the White House, and, giving way to strong emotion, grasped Grant by both hands. Momentarily overcome, the president-elect stood there speechless. "Governor Hayes," Grant said, "I am glad to welcome you."[69] Under the law, the inauguration was supposed to take place on March 4, but that fell on a Sunday and Grant and Hayes balked at a Sabbath ceremony. Hence, on Saturday evening March 3, Hayes was privately sworn in by Chief Justice Morrison Waite before dinner in the Red Room of the White House, an action re-created for show on Monday before a multitude of thirty thousand citizens.

On March 5, Grant escorted Hayes to the Capitol for his public swearing-in. With a portly physique and silver-streaked hair, Grant had aged dramatically in the White House and looked more like the cartoon of a Gilded Age mogul than a battle-steeled general. After months of partisan turmoil, the inauguration proceeded without incident and Garfield wrote of "relief and joy that no accident had occurred on the route for there were apprehensions of assassination."[70] Perhaps motivated by a touch of pique, a teary-eyed Julia refused to escort her husband. "She did not accompany her husband to the Capitol to see another man installed in the place which he had held," wrote Adam Badeau, adding, "It may not be improper to say just here, that . . . Mrs. Grant was unwilling to have her husband retire; she had desired him to become a candidate for another term."[71] From later comments, we know the thoughts that buzzed through Grant's brain. As he told one newspaperman, "Personally I was weary of office. I never wanted to get out of a place as much as I did to get out of the Presidency."[72] He felt "like a boy getting out of school."[73] After the inaugural ceremony, he and Julia hosted a large luncheon for the new president and his wife as well as departing cabinet members. In taking leave of the new First Lady, Julia remarked, "Mrs. Hayes, I hope you will be as happy here as I have been for the last eight years."[74]

The luncheon over, the Hayeses ushered the Grants to the portico and bid them an emotional farewell as they stepped into a carriage that would take them to Hamilton Fish's home for a three-week stay. For all of Grant's avowed mistakes, Garfield was struck by what the nation owed him. "No American has carried greater fame out of the White House than this silent man who leaves it today," he told his diary.[75] As he left, Grant bore himself with a sturdy, soldierly composure, even though he stared into an indefinite future. Presidents didn't then qualify for pensions and Grant was uncertain where or how he would earn his livelihood after his projected global journey. "I have scarcely thought of where I will make my home on my return," he had told a friend. "I am free to go wherever it seems to be the most agreeable."[76] His itinerant army life had left him with no fixed abode, and, if he felt at home anywhere, it was in Washington. As for Galena, he had spent only a year there and almost all his old friends had died or moved. From a life excessively defined by duty, Grant was now free to abandon himself to wanderlust with all its attendant wonders and terrors.

Like many ex-presidents, Grant experienced shock when the new president didn't automatically defer to his opinions and appointed critics of Reconstruction. He was mortified when his old foe Carl Schurz became interior secretary, while William M. Evarts ascended to secretary of state. Much to Grant's chagrin, Hayes, an advocate of civil service reform, took issue with Roscoe Conkling and his New York patronage empire. Within a year, Hamilton Fish bemoaned to Grant that "poor Hayes, has . . . given himself up, 'body & breeches' to the control of the most embittered hostility, of the most disappointed of the 'Liberals' toward 'Grant' & 'Grantism'—he is amiable, I believe, but weak as dish water."[77] Hayes always denied there was any deal, but true to his informal understanding with the Democrats, he removed troops from the

South—or at least from the statehouses, returning them to their barracks— leaving blacks to the tender mercies of the vengeful white community. Reconstruction was now officially dead and the Democratic Party in charge across the South. "Half of what Grant gained at Appomattox," said Wendell Phillips, "Hayes surrendered for us on the 5th of March."[78] Yet many northerners cheered the change. "The negro will disappear from the field of national politics," *The Nation* pontificated with satisfaction. "Henceforth, the nation, as a nation, will have nothing more to do with him."[79] The so-called Liberal wing of the Republican Party had abandoned blacks while the Stalwart Grant had kept the faith.

Once he left office, some in the press rendered harsh judgments on his two terms. In an editorial brittle with patrician scorn, *The Nation* made quick work of him, calling him "coarse" and "blunt" and fond of "low company."[80] One of Grant's most lacerating, if covert, critics was Sherman. "When [Grant] leaves the White House I fear he will sink out of sight and maybe worse," he told a friend. "The transcendent fame he held at the close of the war, will be clouded by the acts of his Political Administration which History may stamp as corrupt and selfish."[81] Decades later, Woodrow Wilson, a southerner who detested Reconstruction, consigned President Grant to the dustbin of history: "The honest, simple-hearted soldier had not added prestige to the presidential office . . . He ought never to have been made President."[82]

At moments, Grant had indeed been his own worst enemy, crossing the line that separates tenacity from obstinacy. But a class-ridden condescension accounts for some of the negative verdicts on Grant's presidency. "It is easy to see why Grant is so often belittled," wrote David Herbert Donald, the eminent Lincoln biographer. "He was not well educated, was not articulate in arguments, was not flashy, and had no connection with the Eastern world of intellect and power. On the other hand, he was not merely a remarkable general but . . . a skillful and successful politician. After all, he was the only President between Abraham Lincoln and Woodrow Wilson [besides McKinley] to be elected to two consecutive terms of office."[83] Donald singled out Grant as the most underrated American president.

Grant has been vilified as an incompetent president for the scandals on his watch. Attacking him on that issue became a convenient tool for Reconstruction opponents who sensationalized his failings through congressional hearings and a strident press. But corruption had flourished in American politics since the heyday of Andrew Jackson. Partly Grant's problem arose from poorly chosen appointees, but the main cause of the corruption under his aegis was the postwar expansion of the federal government with its myriad opportunities for graft. Although Grant took the first halting steps toward civil service reform, he should have championed the movement more vigorously and freed himself from the onus of patronage. His administration's reputation for cronyism and nepotism has obscured his exemplary record in appointing many groups hitherto excluded from American government, including African Americans, Jews, and Native Americans. It also overlooks the many outstanding figures, including Hamilton Fish, Amos Akerman, Benjamin Bristow, and John Creswell, whom he appointed.

In his final annual address, Grant affirmed that his Indian policy had largely been a success, notwithstanding the massacre at Little Bighorn. He had made a good-faith effort to eradicate corruption on reservations by appointing agents chosen by religious groups. In sharp contrast to Sherman and Sheridan, who spoke of Native Americans with cold-blooded contempt, Grant spoke of them sympathetically and frequently blamed the rapacity of white settlers for Indian misdeeds. His Peace Policy of trying to "Christianize and civilize" Native Americans, however flawed, had been pursued with honesty and must be given high marks for good intentions. Before he left office, Grant received a delegation of Choctaws, Chickasaws, Cherokees, and Creeks, who said, "On the eve of your retirement from Office, we desire to express our appreciation of the course you have pursued towards our people while President of the United States—At all times just and humane you have not failed to manifest an earnest wish for their advancement in the arts and pursuits of civilized life, a conscientious regard for their rights and the full purpose to enforce in their behalf, the obligations of the United States."[84]

Unfortunately with Indian policy, as with southern policy, there was no safe middle ground for Grant to stake out. To save Native Americans, he offered them a chance to retreat to reservations and copy the folkways of the white man, abandoning their traditional hunting economy. For many Indian tribes, this was unacceptable. In the end, neither Grant nor any American president could have resisted the massive flow of westward expansion, the political power of settlers, the money lust of mining companies, and the inexorable spread of railroads. Grant probably offered the tribes the best possible deal, although it fell dreadfully short of what they deemed necessary to their survival as a people. There was a tragic gap between what President Grant could reasonably propose and what the Indians could reasonably accept.

Thanks to the diplomatic skills of Hamilton Fish, Grant had racked up a remarkably good record in foreign affairs. During his presidency, there was no war, no military swagger, no saber rattling, and he stayed true to his motto: Let us have peace. The Treaty of Washington settling the *Alabama* claims prevented war with England and opened the way for a close economic partnership, with British capital powering the rise of American industry. It also established a new benchmark for employing peaceful arbitration to settle international disputes instead of the traditional resort to warfare. It is no coincidence that Grant scored his foremost triumphs as president with two issues that grew out of the Civil War—settling the *Alabama* claims and fighting the Klan—for he had become the embodiment of that conflict and its mission to reunite the country and achieve justice for freed slaves.

Ultimately, the appraisal of Grant's presidency rests upon posterity's view of Reconstruction. Grant took office when much of the South still lay under military rule; by the time he left, every southern state had been absorbed back into the Union. For a long time after the Civil War, under the influence of southern historians, Reconstruction was viewed as a catastrophic error, a period of corrupt carpetbag politicians and illiterate black legislators, presided over by the draconian rule of U. S. Grant. For more recent historians, led by Eric Foner, it has been seen as a noble experiment in equal justice for black citizens in which they made remarkable strides in voting, holding office, owning land, creating small businesses and churches, and achieving literacy. About two thousand blacks served as state legislators, tax collectors, local officials, and U.S. marshals, while fourteen served in the House of Representatives and two in the Senate. The South witnessed a civil rights movement that briefly introduced desegregation and vouchsafed a vision of a functioning biracial democracy. Since Grant was president during this period, his standing was bound to rise with this revisionist view. Even as his party and cabinet became bitterly divided over Reconstruction, he showed a deep reservoir of courage in directing the fight against the Ku Klux Klan and crushing the largest wave of domestic terrorism in American history. It was Grant who helped to weave the Thirteenth, Fourteenth, and Fifteenth Amendments into the basic fabric of American life.

When Reconstruction was pilloried as a byword for political abuse, Grant was accused of going too far in advancing black civil rights and foisting "bayonet rule" on the South. Recent revisionist historians have sometimes swung to the other extreme, criticizing him for backtracking on Reconstruction during the last two years of his presidency, when he hesitated to send troops to police elections in Mississippi, South Carolina, and Louisiana. They condemn him for not undertaking extensive land reform in the South—a fine idea, but perhaps quixotic in a region dominated by the Klan and other terrorist groups. The true wonder is not that Grant finally retreated from robust federal intervention, but that he had the courage to persist for so long in his outspoken concern for black safety and civil rights as he faced a ferocious backlash from Democrats and even his own party. By the end of his second term, northern support for Reconstruction had largely disappeared. As the Indiana senator Oliver P. Morton recognized, if Reconstruction failed, it was not because of Grant, but because it had been "resisted by armed and murderous organizations, by terrorism and proscription the most wicked and cruel of the age."[85]

Americans today know little about the terrorism that engulfed the South during Grant's presidency. It has been suppressed by a strange national amnesia. The Klan's ruthless reign is a dark, buried chapter in American history. The Civil War is far better known than its brutal aftermath. Without knowing that history, it is easy to find fault with Grant's tough, courageous actions. For Grant, Reconstruction amounted to a tremendous missed opportunity: "There has never been a moment since Lee surrendered that I would not have gone more than halfway to meet the Southern people in a spirit of conciliation. But they have never responded to it."[86] To protect blacks, Grant had been forced to send in federal troops whose presence provoked a virulent reaction among southern whites who believed their home states had been invaded by hated Yankees a second time. Despite Grant's best efforts at Appomattox, the breach of the Civil War never healed but became deeply embedded in American political culture.

By the end of Grant's second term, white Democrats, through the "redeemer" movement, had reclaimed control of every southern state, winning in peacetime much of the power lost in combat. They promulgated a view of the Civil War as a righteous cause that had nothing to do with slavery but only states' rights—to which an incredulous James Longstreet once replied, "I never heard of any other cause of the quarrel than slavery."[87] In this view, Reconstruction imposed "an oppressive peace on honorable men who had laid down their arms."[88] But the South never laid down its arms. When it came to African Americans, southern Democrats managed to re-create the status quo ante, albeit minus slavery.

Reconstruction was a fine but ultimately doomed experiment in American life. The tragedy of this intractable issue was that there was finally no way for blacks to enjoy their rights without a prolonged military presence, and that became politically impossible. Could even Abraham Lincoln have appeased the white South while simultaneously protecting its black population? It seems unlikely. Grant saw a double standard at work: the country tolerated terror by whites, but not by blacks. As he wrote after leaving office: "If a negro insurrection should arise in South Carolina, Mississippi, or Louisiana, or if the negroes in either of these States . . . should intimidate the whites from going to the polls . . . there would be no division of sentiment as to the duty of the President. It does seem the rule should work both ways."[89]

Once Reconstruction collapsed, it left southern blacks for eighty years at the mercy of Jim Crow segregation, lynchings, poll taxes, literacy tests, and other tactics designed to segregate them from whites and deny them the vote. Black sharecroppers would be degraded to the level of debt-ridden serfs, bound to their former plantation owners. After 1877, the black community in the South steadily lost ground until a rigid apartheid separated the races completely, a terrible state of affairs that would not be fixed until the rise of the civil rights movement after World War II.

Grant deserves an honored place in American history, second only to Lincoln, for what he did for the freed slaves. He got the big issues right during his presidency, even if he bungled many of the small ones. The historian Richard N. Current, who also saw Grant as the most underrated American president, wrote: "By backing Radical Reconstruction as best he could, he made a greater effort to secure the constitutional rights of blacks than did any other President between Lincoln and Lyndon B. Johnson."[90] In the words of Frederick Douglass, "That sturdy old Roman, Benjamin Butler, made the negro a contraband, Abraham Lincoln made him a freeman, and Gen. Ulysses S. Grant made him a citizen."[91] Or in the simple prose of T. Jefferson Martin of Michigan, who wrote to Grant after he left office: "As a colored Man I feel in duty bound to return you my greatful and heart felt thanks, for your firm stedfast and successful administrations of our country, both as Millitary chieftain and civil Ruler of this nation . . . My Dear friend to humanity."[92]

PART FOUR

///

A Life of Reflection

CHAPTER FORTY

The Wanderer

U PON QUITTING THE FISH RESIDENCE in late March, Ulysses and Julia Grant conducted a sentimental tour of familiar haunts from early days, including Cincinnati, St. Louis, Chicago, and Galena. Huge crowds waylaid them everywhere. In Cincinnati, Grant was toasted as a figure second only to George Washington in American history. "I feel that I have considerable life, health and strength left," he told one gathering, "notwithstanding the past sixteen years of labor and toil I have undergone."[1] Afterward, he rode a pair of "fine trotters" into Brown County, Ohio, scene of his boyhood, a place he hadn't visited in decades.[2] A forward-looking man, never prone to introspection, Grant was left unnerved by his brush with aging friends. As he explained, "The changes that I saw in others is so great that I felt no desire to tarry long."[3]

During his presidential years, Grant had accumulated heavy expenses while entertaining guests, saved little, and was now beset by financial worry. His salvation came from the money admirers had given him after the war, a windfall he had luckily invested in a mining venture that yielded a tidy $25,000 profit. He planned to disburse this bonanza in foreign travel for two years, or until the money ran out. All the while, Buck would manage his investments through a pair of select banking houses, J. & W. Seligman and Drexel, Morgan.

Sixteen years earlier, Grant had been seized by a historical whirlwind that had carried him through the war and his presidency and now deposited him uneasily in the terra incognita of retirement. To fill the void that yawned open in his life, he decided to indulge a long-standing fantasy and visit Europe. A few years earlier, Jules Verne had published *Around the World in Eighty Days,* lending new glamour to extended foreign travel. Some historians have speculated that Grant undertook this globe-straddling tour for want of anything better to do, but Grant was a plucky traveler at heart—"the greatest traveler that ever lived," in Adam Badeau's view.[4] A newcomer to Europe and the Grand Tour, he overlooked the small matter of securing a passport and, at the last minute, Hamilton Fish had to appeal to Secretary of State Evarts to rush passports to J. S. Morgan & Co. in London. Although Grant planned to tour as a private citizen, he would travel on U.S. warships and could scarcely pass himself off as a lowly tourist. Before long the trip would assume the dimensions of a major diplomatic event, with Evarts instructing American consuls around the world to furnish Grant with all necessary assistance.

For a week before departing for Liverpool, Grant stayed at the Philadelphia home of George Childs. He had stopped off to see his mother in Elizabeth, New Jersey, and was outraged when his son Jesse failed to appear as well, showing disrespect for the elderly woman. "You young worthless," he scolded Jesse, with atypical anger, "I expected to see you at your grandma's . . . You know we sail on the 17th and if you should not be here you will be left without visible means of support."[5] In Philadelphia, Grant was feted at so many banquets that he must have been worn out from all the jubilation. At a reception at Independence Hall, 2,500 people per hour streamed past him, eager to snatch a glimpse.

On May 17, as he boarded a cutter that carried his party to the steamship *Indiana,* Grant got a resounding send-off from the city. Thousands of well-wishers piled onto the wharves while scores of ships, streaming with flags and bunting, blasted their horns. Many observers thought it the greatest ovation Philadelphia had ever extended. Now that Grant was out of office, the cloud that had lowered over him lifted, and the public was reminded of the inestimable service he had performed in winning the war and reuniting the country after Appomattox. Aboard the cutter, William T. Sherman, upset by Lost Cause theorists who canonized Robert E. Lee as a military genius, delivered a speech that placed Grant securely in the pantheon of American heroes, saying, "If the name of Washington is allied with the birth of our country, that of Grant is forever identified with its preservation."[6] Momentarily, Grant and Sherman recaptured their old wartime camaraderie and Grant credited his success to "the assistance of able lieutenants . . . I believe that my friend Sherman could have taken my place as a soldier . . . and the same will apply to Sheridan."[7]

One triumph not commemorated was Grant's remarkable victory over alcohol. "Even before his voyage around the world," wrote Admiral Daniel Ammen, "the ordinary use of liquors, or even of the lightest wines, had been laid aside."[8] Though Grant had conquered this problem through his exceptional determination and Julia's steadfast love, he was perturbed by the alcoholic relapses of his black manservant, Bill Barnes, who had served him since the war. Grant had fired him several times over the issue only to relent and rehire him. If his own history made him sympathetic to Barnes's drinking troubles, it may also have made him wary. Perhaps Grant feared a long sea voyage, followed by dinners in foreign capitals, trapped with an alcoholic who flouted his pledge of sobriety. When he boarded the *Indiana,* he was shocked to discover Bill Barnes in his stateroom, unpacking his luggage, and he swiftly sought out the captain. "There is a colored man down in my cabin, Captain. His name is Bill Barnes . . . either you arrange for the departure of Bill Barnes, or I go, but Mrs. Grant must not know until Bill is safely ashore."[9] Barnes was promptly removed from the boat. To compensate, Grant saw to it that he was awarded a lifetime pension.

For the trip, Grant jettisoned his official Washington retinue and brought along only Julia, the truant Jesse, an oversize maid, and a polyglot guide. That Grant still cared devoutly about public opinion was manifest in his decision to incorporate John Russell Young, a thirty-six-year-old journalist, into the small, informal party. Like many veteran politicians, Grant could no longer picture his life apart from its constant reflection in the national press. The prospect of returning to public life was never entirely distant from his mind and, perhaps far more than he cared to admit, he had come to crave the limelight. The coverage of his foreign escapades would burnish his credentials at home during his extended stay abroad.

A hearty Irishman with blue eyes, brown hair, and reddish side-whiskers, Young soon fell into a filial relationship with Grant. He had covered Bull Run for a Philadelphia paper and later become managing editor of Horace Greeley's *New York Tribune.* Such was his journalistic renown that Walt Whitman classed him among "the higher type of newspaper man."[10] In 1870 he had endeared himself to President Grant when he founded the *New York Standard* "to compete directly with *The Sun* by those friends of your administration who resented its brutality and cowardice towards yourself," he informed Grant.[11] The paper survived only two years before Young landed a high-profile job with James Gordon Bennett's *New York Herald.*

As the *Indiana* steamed into the Atlantic Ocean, Young entered into a close study of Grant, who sauntered about the deck in a cloth cap, puffing cigars. He observed how he sloughed off presidential cares and the hurly-burly of politics and, freshened by sea breezes, reverted to the genial private citizen of yore: "On the first morning at sea, General Grant said 'that he felt better than he had for sixteen years, from the fact that he had no letters to read, and no telegraphic dispatches to attend to.'"[12] Like many before him, Young learned that Grant's storied reticence was belied by a bottomless trove of anecdotes and that while his fame was "that of a silent man those who know him at all know that in reality we have few better talkers in America."[13] He found Grant an honorable man thirsting for peace: "You might have known him for a year and never learned that he had fought a battle in his life."[14] Far from being solitary, Grant seemed to be someone yearning for late-night intimacy. "He read much, smoked rather from restlessness than love of tobacco and disliked to go to bed. To be a midnight, or two o'clock in the morning companion was the shortest road to his esteem."[15]

The trip would flower into a royal procession continually lengthened until it spanned two years and four months. Grant's extraordinary reception by potentates, prime ministers, and moguls would testify to what a giant figure he had become in the world's imagination, exceeded only by Lincoln. The quintessence of the American spirit, he would walk through other lands in his matter-of-fact style, a plainspoken, democratic figure. His hosts would smother him with official protocol and fawning receptions—exactly the stifling stuff one might have expected him to evade—but he would handle himself with admirable tact. He also displayed inexhaustible curiosity about the daily habits of ordinary people, seeking out obscure nooks of cities where he could watch them incognito. Julia would seem more dazzled by the glamour and glitter, devoting a full third of her memoirs to the trip, describing each stop along the way with a smattering of superlative adjectives.

On May 28, after a crossing marked by "unusually stormy weather and rough seas," the Grants landed in Liverpool.[16] If Grant reserved any hopes that he could travel abroad as an anonymous tourist, they were instantly dispelled on the River Mersey, where people excitedly packed the docks on a sparkling day, American flags flapping from every ship. He was greeted by the mayor and Adam Badeau, now U.S. consul in London. "It had not occurred to father that anything like an official reception awaited him, save, perhaps, from our own representatives abroad," Jesse Grant recalled. "Now we found that, in effect, we were expected to be guests of the city of Liverpool."[17] During Grant's stay, the mayor bore him off to the Custom House, where he faced ten thousand expectant British citizens. With a start, Grant discovered he had to pioneer in freelance diplomacy and actually deliver some speeches.

A Pullman car at his disposal took him next to Manchester, where the Liverpool bedlam was reproduced. Grant began to polish his oratorical skills, showing a real knack for extemporaneous speaking, a change first apparent during his last year or two in office. Knowing the British working class had supported abolition and the North during the Civil War, he appealed to his audience with perfect pitch. He was now an accomplished politician. "I was very well aware during the war . . . of the sentiments of the great mass of the people of Manchester towards the country to which I have the honour to belong, and of your sentiments with regard to the struggle in which it fell to my lot to take a humble part."[18] At 339 words, Grant's speech rated as a veritable marathon for him, shattering his previous record.

From the outset the British were mostly charmed by Grant, who showed a becoming modesty. "I cannot help feeling that it is my country that is honored through me," he told one audience.[19] A British newspaper averred that with his firm, open face and "blunt, bluff and honest" manner, "everybody at once settled in his own mind that the General would do."[20] As his trip progressed, observers draped many symbolic meanings on it, seeing him as an emblem of free labor or abolition or American democracy or peace with the Indians, and his superb handling of the *Alabama* claims exalted him in British esteem. "Here he will find that his eminent services to the cause of international peace are not forgotten," *The Times* of London editorialized. "He will be welcomed, not only as an illustrious soldier, but as a statesman who has always been friendly to England."[21] Two weeks later, the paper affirmed that "after WASHINGTON, General GRANT is the President who will occupy the largest place in the history of the United States."[22]

When his entourage proceeded to London, Grant was cheered by street crowds. As befit the foremost living American, he was honored by the second Duke of Wellington with an Apsley House banquet. A wide-eyed Julia surveyed with some envy the vast residence, its magnificent halls bedecked with Napoleonic trophies. "This great house was presented to Wellington by the government for the single victory at Waterloo," Julia mused, "along with wealth and a noble title which will descend throughout his line. As I sat there, I thought, 'How would it have been if General Grant had been an Englishman?'"[23] Grant fared somewhat better than Julia among the many luminaries they met. After William Gladstone encountered Grant at a reception, he confided that Grant "fulfills his ideal as a taciturn, self-possessed, not discourteous, substantial kind of man. Mrs. Grant [was] kind but alas 'dowdy.'"[24] Grant, reciprocating the admiration, branded Gladstone "the greatest living Englishman" and professed he had become "greatly attached" to him.[25] As for Gladstone's supreme rival, Prime Minister Benjamin Disraeli, Grant found him uncommonly clever and well versed about foreign affairs. Disraeli threw a "colossal American dinner" to honor Grant, but found his guest sadly deficient and "more honorable than pleasant. I felt so overcome that I escaped as soon as possible."[26]

As he squired Grant around London, Badeau was struck by how the presidency had expanded Grant's intellectual range. He had always exhibited a surprising capacity for self-improvement. When the Lord Mayor of London gave him the Freedom of the City at a Guildhall dinner, Grant entranced a glittering audience. "I was brought up a soldier—not to talking," he explained. "I am not aware that I ever fought two battles on the same day in the same place, and that I should be called upon to make two speeches on the same day under the same roof is beyond my comprehension."[27] A galaxy of literary grandees, including Thomas Huxley, Matthew Arnold, Robert Browning, and Anthony Trollope, turned out to breakfast with him. Arnold frowned silently on Grant, scorning him as "ordinary-looking, dull and silent . . . A strong, resolute, business-like man, who by possession of unlimited resources in men and money . . . had been enabled to wear down and exhaust the strength of the South."[28] Arnold might have been surprised by how little Grant cared for war. When the Duke of Cambridge asked him to review troops at Aldershot, Grant replied "that the one thing I never wanted to see again was a military parade"—a recurrent theme of his trip.[29]

Queen Victoria received the Grants at Windsor Castle for a private supper and overnight stay on June 26 and had to swallow a stiffer dose of republican pride than she had anticipated. The visit got off to a rocky start when the Grants were informed that nineteen-year-old Jesse and Adam Badeau had to dine with the royal servants. Her Highness pleaded vertigo in dealing with large groups. Jesse, growing irate, said he would rather return to town than suffer this indignity. Ever the adoring father, Grant endorsed this position: "I think that is what

I would do, if I were in Jesse's place."[30] Finally the queen backed down, sending word that "she would be happy to have Mr. Jesse dine at her table."[31]

Like her youngest son, Julia administered stern lectures on republican virtue. Before supper, two noblewomen stopped by to school her in palace etiquette. "Mrs. Grant," one said, "I hope you will not feel fatigued. Our Queen always receives standing." Julia replied breezily, "Oh, I am sure I will not feel the fatigue. You must remember I *too* have received for the last eight years and always standing."[32] Julia was at pains to remind the two women that they were dealing with *American* royalty.

The cultural tension continued during the meal at the queen's private table, deemed a signal honor for visitors. As Grenadier Guards entertained them in the courtyard, the queen cast a critical eye on her uncouth American guests. She considered Julia "civil & complimentary in her funny American way," but griped that the upstart Jesse was "a very ill-mannered young Yankee."[33] Meanwhile, the Earl of Derby shuddered at the boorish general from America. "He is certainly the roughest specimen we have yet had from the west," he commented. "Anyone who had seen him today would have said that his manners & intelligence were about on a par with those of a bulldog."[34] The Grants must have sensed the snobbery, for Julia turned unusually feisty. When the queen referred to her myriad duties as monarch, Julia feigned sympathy. "Yes, I can imagine them: I too have been the wife of a great ruler."[35] Privately Grant criticized the queen's behavior for an unexpected reason. "He said her Majesty seemed too anxious to put him at his ease," wrote Badeau, "and he implied that the anxiety was unnecessary."[36]

Despite the small snubs, the trip to Windsor Castle strengthened the budding Anglo-Saxon alliance. Two days later, Grant expressed pleasure at "the good feeling and good sentiment which now exist between the two peoples who of all others should be good friends. We are of one kindred, of one blood, of one language, and of one civilization, though in some respects we believe that we, being younger, surpass the mother country."[37] The visit was minutely chronicled by the American press, and Union soldiers believed that tributes lavished upon Grant were paid in absentia to them as well. Perhaps because of his English ancestry, Grant maintained that his visit there was arguably the most enjoyable segment of his global tour. "Next to my own country, there is none I love so much as England."[38]

Grant's fondness may have been enhanced by his daughter's temporarily happy marriage to Algernon Sartoris. Three months earlier, Nellie had given birth to a son and the Grants visited her at the Sartoris estate in Southampton for several days, gadding about the countryside. The marriage as yet offered no signs of the coming disaster and the Grants felt relieved as they left their daughter. "Nellie appeared very happy in her beautiful country home," wrote Jesse, "and we returned to London greatly cheered by her content."[39]

In July, Grant crossed the English Channel, met King Leopold II in Belgium and Richard Wagner in Heidelberg (Julia remained fuzzy as to whether it was Wagner or Franz Liszt), and drank in the sublimity of the Swiss Alps. While ensconced at Lago Maggiore in northern Italy, Grant announced, "There is one Italian whose hand I wish especially to shake, and that man is General Garibaldi."[40] Everywhere Grant drew enormous crowds, but his elaborate tour rested on a tenuous financial base and he fretted continually about money. Writing to Buck from London in late August, he inquired about his shares in Consolidated Virginia Mining Company, a silver producer: "The length of my stay abroad will have to depend in some degree upon the length of time it continues to pay dividends, or the price at which my stock in it sells."[41] Grant's mind drifted to political events at home and he stoutly opposed the huge strike by Baltimore & Ohio Railroad workers who objected to pay cuts. As the stoppage migrated to other railroads, he told Abel Corbin, "My judgment is that it should have been put down with a strong hand and so summarily as to prevent a like occurrence for a generation."[42]

Grant's harsh stance stood in sharp contrast to the enraptured reception he received from British labor. Upon arriving in Newcastle in late September, he encountered crowds dwarfing anything he had ever seen. As the mayor greeted him at the train station, thousands of eager people milled about outside, avid to catch a look at him. As ceremonial guns fired salutes, foghorns blared, and church bells chimed, Grant boarded a steamer on the River Tyne and gaped in disbelief at the immense crowds lining the docks—a throng estimated at 150,000 people, mostly workmen who had poured from mines and factories to see him. Grant handled this unforeseen adulation with perfect aplomb, never losing his composure.

On September 22, as he mounted a platform on the town moor, the assembled laborers cheered so lustily that their roar could be heard a mile away. He delivered a speech that breathed a fine spirit of solidarity, confirming that Grant had never forgotten his simple midwestern roots: "We all know that but for labor we would have very little that is worth fighting for, and when wars do come, they fall upon the many, the producing class, who are the sufferers. They not only have to furnish the means largely, but they have, by their labor and industry, to produce the means for those who are engaged in destroying and not in producing."[43] The speech touched a profound chord and one reporter spotted a black man, his face awash with tears, "devouring Grant with a gaze of such fervid admiration and respect and gratitude that it flashes out the secret of the great liberator's popularity."[44] While Grant was celebrated as a victorious wartime general and the president who had peacefully settled the *Alabama* claims, most gratifying to him was being honored as the protector of freed people. A delegation of painters marched by, hoisting a picture that depicted the shackles of slavery being struck off beside the words "Welcome to the Liberator."[45]

ON OCTOBER 24, 1877, Ulysses S. Grant arrived in a rain-swept Paris and checked into the Hotel Bristol for five weeks. Elihu Washburne had briefed him on the frenzied politics of the Third Republic with its bitter strife between Republicans and monarchists: "No man not present can have an idea of the violence, the madness and the ruffianism of the opposition to the Republicans."[46] Recent elections had brought a republican victory but also fed rumors of a right-wing military coup. "Paris never looked more beautiful, more self-composed, but never was more anxious," said John Russell Young.[47] The situation reminded Grant of the irreconcilable split between American Unionists and secessionists. Upon arrival he paid a courtesy call at the Élysée Palace, meeting with President Patrice de MacMahon, a former field marshal in the French army, who told Grant his people preferred a monarchy. The two men developed a warm rapport, strolling arm in arm down the Champs-Élysées, but Grant believed the French were Republicans at heart and would never settle for a royal regime. Misreading his American visitor, MacMahon cordially invited Grant to review military facilities across the country and was taken aback that the famous warrior evinced no nostalgia for combat.

In contrast to his British Isles tour, Grant was received coldly by Victor Hugo and other militant Parisians who believed he had tilted toward Prussia during the Franco-Prussian War, a view strengthened by the heroic actions of Washburne who, as American minister, had rescued Germans stranded in Paris during the conflict. The French view had more than a grain of truth: Grant had detested Napoleon III and the entire Bonaparte family, affecting his view of the conflict. "The third Napoleon was worse than the first, the especial enemy of America and liberty," Grant later said. "Think of the misery he brought upon France by a war which . . . no one but a madman would have declared."[48] The man who most impressed him was the Republican leader Léon Gambetta, interior minister during the Franco-Prussian War, who had escaped from Paris by balloon. Grant saw Gambetta as a spotless patriot and one of the premier European statesmen, occupying the same rarefied realm as Gladstone.

Grant's aversion to Napoleon kept cropping up during his Parisian stay. Young tried to steer him to Les Invalides to see Napoleon's tomb and nearly succeeded before Grant swerved away and kept on walking. "I never admired the character of the first Napoleon; but I recognize his great genius," Grant wrote.[49] In part his revulsion arose from his hatred of any romanticizing of warfare. "I never saw a war picture that was pleasant," he remarked. "I tried to enjoy some of those in Versailles, but they were disgusting."[50] Grant's dislike of Napoleon didn't extend to Julia, who fell prey to unabashed hero worship at his tomb: "I never read of his gallant deeds but it thrilled my girl's heart." As she approached the tomb, she was seized with a "violent shivering" of pure awe. "There lay Napoleon, not twenty steps from me in that great black sarcophagus."[51]

The chilly political atmosphere encouraged Grant to sample the everyday delights of Paris and eavesdrop on ordinary people. When he visited Versailles, he deliberately took a third-class train to mingle with the working people. He loved to study idlers on the Champs-Élysées or watch a Punch-and-Judy show in the park. He stopped by the studio of Frédéric Bartholdi and watched him sculpt the Statue of Liberty. Sometimes he visited the local bureau of the *New York Herald* to scan the newspapers and didn't seem bothered by press attacks against him.

Julia Grant recorded one Parisian incident that offers a revealing perspective on Grant's famous habit of never turning back, instead always plunging ahead. She had grown enamored of a jeweled butterfly she spotted in the Tiffany store, but before she made up her mind to buy it, Grant glanced at his watch. "My time is up," he stated. "I have an engagement and must go now."[52] As they descended the stairs, Julia belatedly realized how cheap the broach was and decided to go back and buy it. "The General refused to turn back, said he was superstitious about turning back, and reminded me that I was about to make a purchase on Saturday, which he knew I was always superstitious about."[53] Although refusing to retrace his steps, Grant agreed to buy her the butterfly for Christmas. The

Grants' belief in dreams and superstition, so evident in their early letters, never entirely deserted them. However much Grant enjoyed his Parisian rambles and glimpses of quotidian life, he was mystified about the charms American expatriates found there. "I have walked over the city so thoroughly that the streets are quite familiar to me," he told Buck, his provincial roots showing. "The city is beautiful, but I do not see the inducements for so many Americans remaining here year after year who are not engaged in business. I certainly should prefer any of our large cities as a residence."[54]

In December, Grant's trip entered a new phase when the U.S. government allowed him to use the *Vandalia,* a man-of-war cruising in the Mediterranean, giving him his own private warship as he steamed to Italy, Egypt, and the Holy Land. That Grant traveled aboard a government vessel disclosed the growing political importance of his trip: he was traveling as the representative of his country, an emerging power in the world. As diplomatic expert Edwina Campbell has written of this novel venture, "Grant was his country's ambassador at large, the first practitioner of postpresidential diplomacy."[55] The accommodations were rougher than on a transatlantic liner, but Grant delighted in them, as if launched on a boyish lark. "The lines of worry were gone from his face," recalled Jesse, "and he looked younger than I could remember him. For the first time in his life he was free from worry and care."[56] Young noticed how the Mediterranean sun had bronzed Grant's face, erasing the "tired, weary, anxious look" of his second term as president.[57] Albert G. Caldwell, who commanded the *Vandalia,* detected Grant's split personality—the silent mask he donned for others, his conviviality among family and friends. He "looks grim & does not talk when strangers are about but is quite chatty with us on board . . . bright & witty when he wants to be but diffident as a young girl in company & silent as a post before the world."[58] Caldwell estimated that Julia and Grant *both* weighed about 180 pounds; that she was "very cross eyed: always kind & pleasant"; and that Grant and Jesse treated her with sweet solicitude.[59]

Grant had plenty of time to read, perusing *The Innocents Abroad* by Mark Twain and reading aloud excerpts from Homer's *Odyssey* to Julia. Pompeii's ruins charged his imagination, although he prudishly refused to tour the ancient brothel that had beguiled so many sightseers. Egypt's khedive, Ismail the Magnificent, gave Grant the run of a palace and a vessel to transport him up the Nile. Whether clad in Turkish fez or pith helmet wrapped in silk, Grant showed inexhaustible energy and curiosity as he toured ancient tombs and temples. He rode

on a camel, which he found tougher than weathering heavy seas. He was trans-
fixed by the Sphinx, whose silence surpassed his own. "It looks as if it has kept
on thinking through all eternity without talking too much," he noted with approval.[60] Grant bounded healthily from place to place, but the stout Julia proved
less nimble. As Grant informed Fred, "Your Ma balances on a donkey very well
when she has an Arab on each side to hold her, and one to lead the donkey."[61] Not
blind to the hardships of Egyptian life or the filthy condition of Alexandria's
poor, he still rhapsodized his weeks on the Nile "as among the happiest in my
life."[62]

In February 1878, Grant braved rain, wind, and snow to become the first
American president to visit Jerusalem. He met with a delegation of American
Jews who distributed relief to their suffering brethren in the Holy Land and he
promised to carry their message to Jewish leaders at home. As they entered religious sites, Julia was susceptible to powerful emotions, her active imagination a
perfect foil for her husband's skeptical, deadpan humor. After entering a beautiful chapel, Julia set eyes on an intriguing sign: "Anyone who will say a prayer for
the soul of Pope Pius IX will receive absolution." At once she fell to her knees
and heard her husband quip, "You see, Young, Mrs. Grant is taking all the
chances"—that is, taking no chances in the afterlife.[63]

By early March, the Grants reached Constantinople, went ashore, and viewed
the sultan's stable of pure-blooded Arabian stallions, magnificent creatures that
"pick up their feet like a cat & so quickly that one can scarcely follow their mo-
tions," said Caldwell.[64] Grant was instantly entranced by the animals, and, when
the sultan pressed him to take home a pair, he selected two dappled grays that
were shipped to New York. He was startled to discover how thoroughly Otto-
man officers had studied his military campaigns. When the *Vandalia* anchored
off Athens, the king of Greece came on board to while away an afternoon with
Grant and sought his advice on relations with Turkey—another sign that Grant
was far more than just a private citizen flitting about on vacation. In a special
tribute, the Greeks illuminated the Parthenon in his honor. After Greece, when
Grant left the *Vandalia,* Caldwell was saddened to see him go, saying he was
"chock full of information . . . Grant knows what it costs to make a yard of cotton south or in Providence—the bushels of grain exported for years—the fluctuations of exchange—the Army & Navy ration to an ounce & all such
information & he is *never* wrong about a figure or a date."[65]

Grant's eventful tour had many wonders in the offing. The morning he arrived in Rome, an emissary from Pope Leo XIII tracked him down and invited him to a private audience at 2 p.m. King Umberto I had sought the honor of greeting him first, so Grant agreed, with diplomatic finesse, that he and Jesse would stop by the palace en route to the Vatican and pay their respects to the monarch. Grant wasn't fazed that a king and a pope vied for his company. "We're simply tourists, Jesse," he said. "We'll have an early lunch and then we'll go."[66] With Jesse guiding them with a map, father and son set out for the palace only to barge in at the wrong gate. After they located the right courtyard, they chatted with the king and queen for nearly an hour. At the Vatican, they were joined by Julia, and Grant found Pope Leo XIII impressively robed in white. The new pontiff blessed Julia's little diamond cross and chatted with Ulysses in French as Jesse translated. Well-briefed on American affairs, the pope regretted that Grant's Des Moines speech on separating church and state had prevented Roman Catholic instruction in public schools, but he admired the impartial way Grant had applied his policy across all religious denominations.

Although Grant absorbed Rome's beauties, taking in the Colosseum and the Arches of Titus and Constantine, his taste in art was impoverished. In the Vatican, he whizzed past famous marble statuary, as if traversing barren territory on a rapid military march. Adam Badeau stood amused and appalled by Grant's indifference to artistic treasures: "He got tired of the Sistine Chapel, and poked fun at me when I wanted to look once more at the Last Judgment of Michael Angelo. He would not pretend. He was blind always to the beauties of art. I don't think he could ever tell a good picture from a bad one."[67] In Venice, Grant let slip a remark that would provide fodder for many satirists: he told a young woman what a fine city it would be if only the canals were drained. Henry Adams adduced this as damning evidence of Grant's philistine nature, but he may only have meant that the canals should be cleansed of sewage.

Returning to Paris in May in time to browse the Universal Exposition, Grant thought that it didn't measure up to the Centennial Exhibition he had presided over as president. When he and Julia stepped on a newfangled scale at the fair, he registered 165 pounds and she weighed 10 pounds more. The couple now swapped children on the trip, sending Jesse home to attend Columbia Law School, while welcoming Fred to the party. "I had enough of it," an exasperated Jesse confessed to reporters on the New York dock. "I got tired of those foreign countries."[68] For the first time in a year, Grant admitted to being homesick and Julia had wearied of this vagabond life. Still, the indefatigable Grant had a lengthy list of places he wanted to see. There was also the bizarre circumstance that he possessed no true American home, making him feel like a stateless, latter-day Flying Dutchman. He also knew that certain friends would shanghai him back into politics as soon as he returned home. For this reason, he decided to extend the trip until the following year. His silver mining dividends sustained the voyage, and he added two thousand shares of Yellow Jacket Silver Mining Company, whose terrain formed part of the Comstock Lode. With his future so uncertain, Grant pondered how he would support himself upon his return. In declining an offer in late May to become president of the Atlantic and Great Western Railroad, a firm associated with Jay Gould, he specified that, should the offer be renewed when he got home, he would certainly reconsider it.

Perhaps Grant's most stimulating European encounter came with Otto von Bismarck. Upon arriving in Berlin, Grant boarded an ordinary streetcar and rode around the town, enjoying unfettered views of the working population. Back in his hotel, he discovered that Prince Bismarck had sent his card over four times to arrange a meeting. "I do not want Bismarck running after me," Grant told Young; "he has a great deal of business to do, while I am simply a wanderer." He made himself available to Bismarck at any hour.[69] He ended up seeing him at four the next afternoon, showing up at his palace on foot—the liveried servants, aghast, had expected him to pull up in a stately coach—and after throwing away his cigar butt, he ascended a marble staircase.

With snow-white hair and a massive forehead, Bismarck, in military uniform, welcomed Grant with both hands extended. Turning on the charm, he expressed surprise that Grant was only seven years his junior. "That shows the value of a military life," he remarked, "for here you have the frame of a young man, while I feel like an old one."[70] Grant was entranced by the flow of wit that emanated from the worldly Bismarck with his imposing physique, beautiful manners, ready laugh, and penetrating insights. As they sat in his study, smoking cigars, with the window thrown open to a gorgeous park, the conversation turned to the varied exercises in nation building in which both men had so strenuously engaged.

Bismarck commiserated with Grant upon the countless fatalities of the Civil War. "But it had to be done," Grant replied. "Yes," said Bismarck, "you had to save the Union just as we had to save Germany." "Not only save the Union, but destroy slavery," Grant added. "I suppose, however, the Union was the real sentiment, the dominant sentiment," Bismarck inquired. "In the beginning, yes," agreed Grant, "but as soon as slavery fired upon the flag . . . we all felt, even those who did not object to slaves, that slavery must be destroyed. We felt that it was a stain to the Union that men should be bought and sold like cattle."[71] Grant's comments reflect the militance he had felt as president about protecting black civil rights. He now interpreted the four-year war as providential, since a shorter war might have ended up preserving slavery. They had been "fighting an enemy with whom we could not make a peace. We had to destroy him. No convention, no treaty was possible—only destruction."[72] This meeting led to several more between Grant and Bismarck, who enjoyed a surprising rapport. Bismarck assumed his place alongside Disraeli and Gambetta in Grant's personal gallery of the leading men of Europe.

Somewhat reluctantly Grant accepted an invitation from the crown prince to review troops outside of Berlin, but he was disturbed by the regimented militarism of Prussian society. Nagged by a bad cold on a dank, drizzly day, Grant watched as soldiers executed bayonet charges. A great modernizer in military science, he had always favored light, quick, efficient troops, unburdened by antiquated armor, and lectured his hosts to drop the bayonets: "The bayonet is heavy, and if it were removed, or if its weight in food or ammunition were added in its place, the army would be stronger. As for the bayonet as a weapon, if soldiers come near enough to use it they can do as much good with the club-end of their muskets."[73]

In July, Grant explored Denmark and Scandinavia, where he received universal cheers and admired the honest industry of the people. His brother-in-law Michael John Cramer, the U.S. chargé d'affaires in Copenhagen, was struck by how studiously Grant approached his travels, as befit a former head of state who had brushed up on each country through diplomatic reports. Grant exhibited a precise knowledge of Danish history and society and was especially taken with their public school system. When he was received by the king and queen, Cramer noted that Grant refrained from alcohol: "It was noticed that General Grant drank no wine, except a few drops of champagne when the king proposed his health." When the minister of foreign affairs proposed a banquet in his honor, Grant declined, saying they were "tired of being 'banqueted'" and "had come here to rest for a week."[74]

By late July, the Grants arrived in St. Petersburg, where an imperial carriage whisked them to a meeting with Czar Alexander II at his Summer Palace. The czar stood tall and erect in military uniform, but Grant detected a nervous energy about the man, who had been targeted by assassination attempts. (He would succumb to one in March 1881.) Oddly enough, the czar was mostly interested in warfare with American Indians and Grant tried to satisfy his curiosity. Meanwhile, the czarina gave Julia a tour of the Peterhof outside of St. Petersburg, laying special emphasis on the carriage and other objects employed by Peter the Great. "I could not help drawing a comparison between this great man and another great man I knew," wrote Julia, never bashful about exalting her husband.[75] When the U.S. minister, Edwin W. Stoughton, took the Grants to see the Russian man-of-war *Peter the Great,* it fired a seventeen-gun salute. "Madam," said Stoughton, "they are saluting your husband." "Oh, no, that salute is for you, Mr. Minister," Julia objected, as ever a bit touchy about matters of status. "General Grant's salute is twenty-one guns always."[76] With his democratic interests, Grant followed his customary practice of exploring St. Petersburg on foot, studying everyday life.

Grant finished the summer in Vienna, where he met with Emperor Franz Joseph I, and in Salzburg, where he met the German emperor Wilhelm I. After fifteen months abroad, Grant concluded that nobody had ever covered so many countries in that length of time. Writing from the Austrian Alps, he confessed that "I miss English speaking people. I find that I enjoy European travel just in proportion as I find Americans to associate with."[77] Many countries that Grant visited levied onerous taxes on their subjects to service massive debt and maintain standing armies, giving him a fresh appreciation of republican government in America. "The fact is we are the most progressive, freest and richest people on earth, but don't know it or appreciate it. Foreigners see this much plainer than we do."[78]

In Madrid, James Russell Lowell, the American minister there, left priceless vignettes of the Grants as rustic innocents. When Lowell took them to the opera, Grant could scarcely endure the high-pitched screeching. "Haven't we had enough of this?" he asked after five minutes.[79] Despite the royal attention bestowed on Grant, Lowell saw that his supreme pleasure was slipping off and exploring the streets incognito: "After being here two days I think he knew Madrid better than I did . . . He is perfectly natural, naively puzzled to find himself a personage, and going through the ceremonies to which he is condemned with a dogged imperturbability."[80] He also noticed how Julia, when stuck with dinner companions who spoke no English, simply chattered away in English, sure she would be understood. Her "confidence in the language of Shakespeare & Milton as something universally applicable . . . was sublime."[81]

Hanging over Grant's trip was the vexed question of whether he should chance a bid for a third term upon returning home. Those who favored such a course advised him to linger abroad, where his exploits were widely reported and he could dodge reporters' questions. "Most every letter I get from the states . . . ask me to remain absent," Grant told Badeau in March. "They have designs for me which I do not contemplate for myself."[82] The wandering Ulysses deflected questions about a third term, answering "that he knew what the Presidency was, and had had all he wanted."[83] Nonetheless, he was mightily disturbed by the mounting sway of southern Democrats in Congress and sarcastically warned that Unionists might soon need "one of Andy Johnson's pardons to relieve us from responsibility as murderers, robbers, and illegal and unjustifiable invaders of the sacred soil of the South."[84] Grant's concern for African Americans never faltered. That summer in Paris, he met with the black Republican senator Blanche K. Bruce of Mississippi, who informed *The New York Times* that if it came down to a matter of duty "I have no doubt [Grant] would accept the nomination . . . Gen. Grant would be the first choice for the Presidency of nine-tenths of the colored voters of the South."[85]

Just as Grant contemplated a return home that fall, he received an irresistible invitation from the Secretary of the Navy Richard W. Thompson to sail on the government steamer *Richmond* for India, China, and Japan via the Mediterranean and the Suez Canal. Thompson frankly admitted the political agenda lurking behind the offer, arguing that Grant's presence on board the man-of-war would "so arrest public attention as to bring prominently into view, not merely the character and extent of our commerce, but the nature and value of our institutions."[86] Grant, seizing this "splendid opportunity," prolonged his stay abroad to visit Asia.[87] He calculated accurately that extending his tour would land him back in the United States in autumn 1879, just as things heated up for the 1880 presidential race. When the *Richmond* was temporarily delayed, the Grants set out on a commercial steamer to Asia, deciding to catch up later with the government vessel, which he would use for the trip between China and Japan.

By February 13, the party had touched down in Bombay, where Grant soldiered on through official visits with his colonial British hosts and was struck by the absence of beggars. When traveling to Jabalpur, he hoisted himself on an elephant for a ride to a nearby marble quarry, finding himself "much pleased with the intelligence of these animals."[88] The Grants, with Fred and former navy secretary Adolph Borie in tow, visited the Taj Mahal by daylight and returned to gaze at it in moonlight. Julia, sounding like a provincial chauvinist from a Mark Twain satire, said of the Taj: "Everyone says it is the most beautiful building in the world, and I suppose it is. Only I think that everyone has not seen the Capitol at Washington!"[89] While not uncritical of British rule in India, Grant believed they had taken a "benighted and downtrodden" country and improved its railroads, schools, farms, and factories.[90] He gazed with sorrow on the workings of the caste system and the absence of female rights, reflecting his lifelong concern for the dignity of women.

One high-ranking Briton whom Grant met in India, Lord Lytton, the viceroy, left a damaging account of a drunken Grant making an utter fool of himself:

> On this occasion "our distinguished guest" the double Ex-President of the "Great Western Republic," who got as drunk as a fiddle, showed that he could also be as profligate as a lord. He fumbled Mrs. A., kissed the shrieking Miss B.—pinched the plump Mrs. C. black and blue—and ran at Miss D. with intent to ravish her. [At last Grant was] captured by main force and carried (quatre pattes dans l'air) by six sailors . . . which relieved India of his distinguished presence. The marine officers . . . report that, when deposited in the public saloon cabin, where Mrs. G was awaiting him . . . this remarkable man satiated there and then his baffled lust on the unresisting body of his legitimate spouse, and copiously vomited during the operation.[91]

Grant biographers have rightly found this story suspect. Grant had no history of groping women, much less his wife, and Lytton left Calcutta the day before the dinner in question.[92] Still, one wonders whether this patently embellished story, obviously based on hearsay, may have had a kernel of truth. The description of a tipsy Grant contains disquieting echoes of the anonymous wartime letters accusing him of drunken indiscretions. This was the sole allegation of Grant's getting drunk on his extended trip, despite numerous temptations.

From India the Grants penetrated east to Burma and Singapore. As their ship glided across the smooth waters of the Bay of Bengal, John Russell Young began an interview with Grant about the war and his presidency, pumping him for opinions and producing a voluminous and invaluable transcript. "There are few men more willing to converse on subjects on which he is acquainted than General Grant," Young wrote. "The charm of his talk is that it is never about anything that he does not know, and what he does know he knows well."[93]

In Thailand, the royal family feted the Grants and in Hong Kong, one hundred thousand people jammed the streets to catch sight of him. Nobody's presence pleased him more than that of John Singleton Mosby, the Gray Ghost, and now the American consul there. "This is really the most beautiful place I have yet seen in the East," Grant wrote. "The City is admirably built & the scenery is most picturesque."[94] To Grant's amazement the Asian crowds that turned out to see him eclipsed in size those in Europe and the United States, their numbers inconceivable to a Westerner. When Grant went to see the viceroy of Canton, two hundred thousand people lined the route in a tumultuous reception, with Grant carried aloft in a sedan chair, curtained with green blinds, that swayed and jangled on its bamboo poles. "I regard this Canton procession, as among the most extraordinary scenes in my life," John Russell Young wrote in his diary.[95]

In late May, Grant spent a week in Shanghai, attending a torchlight parade and a ball in his honor. Repelled by the filth, squalor, and overcrowding he found in China, he also admired the industry and enterprise of the people and shrewdly sized up their economic potential. "My impression is that the day is not very far distant when they will make the most rapid strides toward modern civilization, and become dangerous rivals to all powers interested in the trade of the East."[96] Arriving in Peking on June 3, he spent the last five hours of the journey riding in a sedan chair borne by eight men. The next morning, while ascending the Great Wall, he took a comically pragmatic view of the structure: "It is hard to see any practical use these walls can serve in the present age unless they should be converted into drives."[97]

This closing phase of Grant's journey proved important as he became the first ex-president to undertake personal diplomacy abroad. Meeting with Prince Kung, the Chinese regent and de facto head of state, he touted the benefit of railroads and warned against excessive reliance on foreign debt. Then the prince directed Grant's attention to the fate of the Loo Choo (Ryukyu) Islands over which Japan and China had sparred for control, a conflict that had brought them to the brink of war. The Japanese had deposed the local sovereign and occupied the islands and Prince Kung wanted Grant's aid in reversing this. At first Grant begged off as someone out of office. "But we all know how vast your influence must be," the prince urged, "not only upon your people at home, but upon all nations who know what you have done."[98] Acknowledging that war between China and Japan would be a grave misfortune, Grant volunteered to serve as mediator between the two nations during his stop in Japan, invoking the *Alabama* settlement as his model. "An arbitration between nations . . . satisfies the conscience of the world, and must commend itself more and more as a means of adjusting disputes," he declared.[99]

The Grants steamed toward Japan aboard the *Richmond* in mid-June and at their first port of call, Nagasaki, received a twenty-one-gun salute—Julia's gold standard—in the harbor. Emissaries of the emperor escorted them to a fifty-course meal at an ancient temple. The Grants were invited to plant banyan trees at a local park to honor their visit, and Grant minted a beautiful message that would be etched in stone nearby: "I hope that both trees may prosper, grow large, live long, and in their growth, prosperity and long life be emblematic of the future of Japan."[100] Of all the countries included on his worldwide caravan, none captivated Grant quite like Japan, which he found a model of beauty, balance, and cultivation. He loved the green hills, fertile valleys, and fine streams and found the people "the most kindly & the most cleanly in the world."[101] The Japanese, he believed, had perfected their school system, educating all classes, male and female, and producing "the superior people of the East."[102] So smitten was Grant that he wanted the United States to negotiate a commercial treaty with the country.

The Japanese reciprocated his affection. After his arrival in Tokyo on July 3, a high-level reception committee paid homage to Grant's accomplishments: "How you crushed a rebellion, and afterwards ruled a nation in peace and righteousness, is known over the whole world."[103] The emperor wanted to receive his illustrious visitor on the Fourth of July, and Grant's carriage, flanked by cavalry, had to penetrate an enormous crush of people and ride under floral arches before reaching the emperor's summer palace. The young, slim emperor then did something unprecedented: he strode up to Grant and shook his hand in profound respect, after which Ulysses and Julia Grant exchanged bows with assorted princes. The emperor later said nobody during his reign had impressed him more than "the unassuming bourgeois Civil War hero and president."[104]

At a subsequent meeting with the emperor, Grant decried colonial exploitation of Asian countries, making an exception for British rule in India. "But since I left India I have seen things that made my blood boil, in the way the European powers attempt to degrade the Asiatic nations."[105] Grant made good on his pledge to mediate the dispute over the Loo Choo Islands, showing a deft, diplomatic touch. He succeeded in getting negotiations started between the two sides, and the Chinese acceded to Japanese control of the islands. Grant became the first American president to accomplish such a solo feat, and the Chinese and Japanese were deeply grateful, even though talks later foundered. Grant contrasted his selfless diplomacy with the self-interested approach of European powers who "have no interests in Asia . . . that do not involve the humiliation and subjugation of the Asiatic people."[106] It formed a fitting finale to a trip in which Grant defined a new role for ex-presidents abroad, showing how they could use their prestige to settle intractable foreign conflicts and promote peaceful arbitration.

ON SEPTEMBER 3, 1879, Grant and his party departed from Japan aboard the *City of Tokio*, bound for San Francisco. After two years and four months roaming the seas like a modern Ulysses, Grant was outwardly the same unadorned man with the placid exterior, but inwardly much transformed. He had shed the last vestiges of his provincial boyhood and seemed a far more cosmopolitan figure, his head stocked with exotic stores of information. He had become an accomplished speaker and diplomat, able to throw off witticisms with an effortless touch and offer cogent commentary on many cultures. *The New York Times* speculated that the trip had endowed him with "greater power to discern the true character of men."[107] Yet despite his manifold triumphs, Grant turned homeward with some trepidation, even a creeping sense of dread, unsure how he would make a living or where he would live. "I have no home, but must establish one after I get back," he told Elihu Washburne. "I do not know where."[108]

When he grew bored with playing cards on the boat, Julia inquired if he had ever read Victor Hugo's *Les Misérables*. "No," he said. "I started to read it on the James River but was interrupted so frequently that I read only a few pages."[109] He began reading it so voraciously that he disappeared for days, only popping up for meals. "He read it very slowly," said Young, "almost like a man who is studying rather than reading."[110] Then at eleven o'clock one night, Young was pacing the deck when Grant appeared, fresh from reading, and he asked him about Hugo's presentation of the battle of Waterloo. "It is a very fine account," Grant answered.[111] Then he astounded Young with his fine-grained knowledge of the weapons, troops, and tactics employed by Napoleon and Wellington. Despite his contempt for Napoleon, Grant concluded that "it was the finest planned battle of Napoleon, the best conceived battle that I know of, and nothing but Providence being against him defeated him."[112] For those who thought Grant ignorant of military history, Young delivered a salutary corrective, describing how Grant spoke at length about the art of warfare. He wasn't simply an intuitive general but a self-aware modernizer:

> Grant went on to describe all of Napoleon's campaigns . . . speaking of each battle in the most minute manner—the number of men engaged on either side; even the range of their guns and the tactics of both sides; why victory came and why defeat came, as thoroughly learned as a problem in mathematics. Then back to the battles of Frederick the Great, Leuthen, the campaigns of the Thirty Years' War, back to the campaigns of Caesar, and always illustrating as he talked the progress and change in the art of war, and how machinery, projectiles, and improvements in arms had made what would be a great victory for Napoleon almost impossible now. It simply meant this: that Gen. Grant, with his marvelous memory, had not forgotten his West Point education. In addition to his great common sense he knew the lessons of war as completely as any General that ever lived.[113]

Had Napoleon been thoroughly unselfish, Grant suggested, he would have been the greatest man in history, such was his military genius. When a young woman on board asked Grant to name the two figures he detested most in history, he shot back, "Napoleon and Robespierre."[114]

From the time he disembarked in San Francisco, Grant would be barraged with questions about his presidential ambitions, Hayes having made good on his pledge to serve only one term. During Grant's exile, his image had waxed ever larger thanks to favorable press coverage, much of it from the pen of John Russell Young. His absence had softened memories of his presidency's scandals and heightened appreciations of his many accomplishments. The Stalwart wing of the Republican Party meditated schemes to advance him as their presidential candidate in 1880. Grant always insisted that he had no heart for a third term, but Young spun quite a different tale. While sailing the Red Sea, Young wrote to the cartoonist Thomas Nast, "The General, Mr. Borie, and I spend most of our time looking out on the waves, and *scheming for a third term*!!!! You never knew such a schemer as the Gen. He sits up for hours and hours, late and schemes."[115] Yet when Young was later asked by a reporter about Grant's political plans, he replied, "If he is nominated by an enthusiastic convention, then he will decide what is the best thing to be done. He never plans ahead. He is not a schemer."[116] It was another example of Grant's inability to admit the extent of his own ambition.

Those who shared the dream of a third term had thought that Grant should linger abroad and only return right before the 1880 convention. In May, Badeau had advised Sherman that once Grant landed "in America the attacks will begin. Why should he not escape them for another year?"[117] Badeau and others thought that Grant's September 1879 return to San Francisco was too soon, allowing the publicity boom that would follow his arrival to cool off by convention time. Badeau therefore believed Grant "had neither expectation nor ambition to return to power."[118] Jesse Grant thought his father lacked the fiery desire to return to the White House, but that his travels had led him to believe he could now conduct America's foreign relations better than anyone else.

As Grant's ship steamed into San Francisco before a golden sunset on September 20, he received a rapturous reception as foghorns bellowed and flag-bedecked yachts swarmed around him. Julia recalled how "we saw a procession of ships which approached in pairs, separated as they neared us, passed on either side of us, closed in again after they passed, and escorted us in through the Golden Gate to San Francisco."[119] Cannon roared from Angel Island, Black Point, and Alcatraz, while thousands waved from Telegraph Hill. When Grant spotted Alcatraz, he remembered seeing it twenty-five years earlier after his hellish passage through Panama. "A year and a half ago I was thoroughly homesick," the peripatetic Grant told reporters, "but the variation of scene and the kindness which I have met with have almost done away with that feeling."[120] To inevitable questions about his residual presidential ambitions, Grant said simply, "Well, I don't aspire . . . My time is all my own and there is nothing to hurry me."[121]

During his trip, American readers had received vicarious pleasure that one of their own had been treated with such respect around the world, conducting himself with becoming modesty. Among Grant's many astonishing triumphs was that he had survived an endless round of banquets and receptions without slipping back into drinking. "I was present when the old man returned from around the world," said his friend Amos Webster, "and he told us he hadn't tasted liquor but once during the entire trip. He had turned down his glass everywhere."[122] One wonders whether that lone lapse was the one recounted by Lord Lytton in India. Doubtless much of the credit for Grant's abstinence goes to Julia and her strict vigilance over his sobriety. Now that he had landed in America, there would be more heavy-drinking receptions, and a person involved in one of them remembered how "Mrs. Grant had requested us not to have wine at the banquet."[123]

Adam Badeau surmised correctly that the moment Grant returned, he would be thrown into the red-hot crucible of politics. *The Nation* tagged him as a puppet of the Stalwarts and thought it "difficult to find words of condemnation sufficiently strong . . . for using this simple soldier as the head of The Machine."[124] "Ulysses S. Grant is a man driven mad by ambition," the *New York Sun* blustered. "He now seeks to grab the government of the United States—a thing unprecedented—for a third term."[125] While in San Francisco, Grant held a midnight meeting with James M. Comly, a confidant of President Hayes's. Grant said frankly he would prefer to see somebody else nominated as the Republican candidate for president and expressed sorrow that Hayes had restricted himself to one term. But for Comly, the startling thing was that Grant did not rule out a run. "The conversation changed my opinion entirely as to Grant's candidacy—his willingness I mean," he told Hayes confidentially. "I am convinced that he will not decline a nomination, if tendered with full acquiescence of leading Republicans."[126]

Grant was elated by his ecstatic reception in San Francisco, which had grown enormously since his last visit. "I cannot venture in the streets except in a carriage for the mob of good-natured and enthusiastic friends, old and young."[127] Leaving there in early October, he took a stagecoach tour of Yosemite Valley and tramped through giant sequoia groves before returning to scenes of his early army life in Oregon. In Portland, Grant addressed a veterans reunion and returned to the field where he had once planted potatoes. In Sacramento, Julia Grant had a curious encounter with a black woman who approached her gingerly, holding out her hand. "Miss Julie, I do not believe you know me. I am Henrietta, or Henny, as you used to call me at home."[128] Julia took the woman's hands and recognized one of her father's former slaves. "I was very glad to see Henny and told her to come to my room the next day, but I never saw her afterwards," Julia wrote in her memoirs.[129] One notes Julia's emotional response to the unexpected reunion, but also that Henrietta failed to materialize the next day—perhaps a telling reaction from a former slave of Colonel Dent's.

Having survived the world tour on dividends from the Consolidated Virginia Mining Company in Nevada, the Grants spent three days in mining country there. A photo shows a gray-bearded, burly Grant in a porkpie hat and rough miner's coat, carrying a lamp and preparing to descend into the mine. He looked more like a grizzled, weather-beaten prospector than a former president. When he bet Julia that she wouldn't dare to descend into the mine, located seventeen hundred feet below, it roused her fighting spirit and she proved him wrong. Grant surfaced from the deep mine, red-faced and perspiring, and joked that it was a good place "to leave the newspapermen." "Would you not leave the politicians, too?" asked John H. Kinkead, the Nevada governor. "Yes," Grant said drily, "but there ain't room for all that ought to be put here."[130]

As Grant moved east to Utah Territory, he presented a different public persona than before his trip, more verbal and gregarious, and in Ogden he conceded he had grown accustomed to public speaking abroad. "I think I am improving, for my knees don't knock together like they did at first."[131] Stopping next in Nebraska, he seemed to be campaigning very hard for a man who disclaimed any interest in a third term. As he whistle-stopped across the state, he was flabbergasted by the rapid growth of the Great Plains and discovered a new America with railroads and settlements spread across the prairies. "I am very glad to see you, but your towns in Nebraska are too thick for me to talk at every place the train stops. They are springing up here so rapidly that I scarcely know the country in passing through, although I have been out here three times before."[132] Pausing in Galesburg, Illinois, he hazarded a joke about his freshly honed oratorical skills. "I have only been in Illinois one hour, and during that time I have already made two speeches, and feel talked out."[133]

Grant's next destination was Galena, where he and Julia occupied their furnished house for several weeks. In an interview, Grant made a surprisingly open confession when he said he could reside more cheaply in Galena than a large city. He explained that he still had two farms near St. Louis; thirty-one acres of money-losing land outside Chicago; stock in Adams Express Company, which had appreciated; and a $50,000 to $60,000 profit from Nevada mining stock, which had underwritten his travel abroad. "My income is not large enough for me to live as I would like," he confessed, "and I will have to find something to do after a while."[134] Despite a huge reception in Galena, with its buildings decked out in bunting, Grant couldn't see dawdling there and complained that Galena, once a prosperous town, had regressed to a sleepy little rural backwater bypassed by new railroads.

Everything that happened to Grant between San Francisco and Galena was a mere warm-up for the tremendous reception that awaited him in Chicago, where he was the centerpiece of a celebration lasting several days. As one broadside put it, the town belonged to the "Man of Destiny, our own General Grant."[135] The person drafted to preside over this tribute was Grant's old mentor, Elihu Washburne, who declined the honor, pleading a lecture he had to give in Indiana. Nobody in the political world was hoodwinked by this excuse, which was attributed to his own presidential ambitions in 1880. "He was ostensibly for Grant, but was really a candidate," said Grant friend J. Russell Jones. "This Grant could never forgive."[136]

The Chicago festivities opened with a gigantic parade, with Grant riding in a carriage at its head, trailed by three thousand soldiers and fifteen thousand civilians. That morning a heavy rain had soaked the city and the crowd, ranging from bootblacks to businessmen, was "compelled to wade through the thickest mud which had disgraced Chicago for many a day."[137] When the rain stopped, a rainbow appeared and Grant mounted a flag-draped reviewing stand outside the Palmer House already occupied by Governor Shelby Cullom, Mayor Carter Harrison, and Mark Twain.

An excited Twain had geared up for this encounter with Grant, telling William Dean Howells, "My sluggish soul needs a fierce upstirring."[138] During Grant's first term, Twain had escorted Senator William Stewart of Nevada to the White House, where they found the president hunched over papers, scribbling away. When he finally raised his eyes, a flustered Twain said, "I seem to be a little embarrassed. Are you?" As Twain recalled "the General was fearfully embarrassed himself."[139] Now Mayor Harrison introduced Twain anew to Grant, who fixed the author with a wry smirk and said, in an amazing display of memory, "Mr. Clemens, I am not embarrassed—are you?"[140] Some banter ensued as Twain told Grant he would withdraw to the rear of the platform. "I'll step back, General. I don't want to interrupt your speech." "But I'm not going to make any," Grant told him. "Stay where you are," Twain insisted, "I'll get you to make it for me."[141]

Grant's history always provided rich food for Twain's imagination. They were both from the Midwest, having risen from humble roots. Perhaps from some nagging guilt at having fought briefly on the Confederate side early in the war, almost crossing paths with Grant in Missouri, Twain remained obsessed with him. Playing the buffoon, he liked to present himself as the anti-Grant, the congenital coward, underscoring his fascination with the valiant Grant. In Chicago, Twain had an opportunity to see Grant in action when the latter addressed a large reunion of the Army of the Tennessee. When Grant entered, wrote Twain, "a deafening storm of welcome burst forth which continued during two or three minutes. There wasn't a soldier on that stage who wasn't visibly affected, except the man who was being welcomed, Grant. No change of expression crossed his face."[142]

In a paternal, almost Lincolnesque style, Grant called in two speeches for national unity and the need to avoid "all bitterness and ill-feeling, either on the part of sections or parties toward each other."[143] At the same time, he tacitly rebuked the South for its hostile treatment of carpetbaggers: "We claim for [former Confederates] the right to travel all over this broad land, to locate where they please, and the right to settle and become citizens and enjoy their political and religious convictions free from molestation or ostracism, either on account of this, or their connection with the past."[144] At one of the tributes to him, Grant sat impassively through battle hymns and panegyrics about his service to his country before a thousand men lustily belted out "Marching Through Georgia." All the while, Twain said, Grant "never moved a hand or foot, head, or anything . . . an achievement which I should not have believed, if I had not seen it with my own eyes."[145]

The capstone of the Grant celebration was a banquet for six hundred people at the Palmer House, a Lucullan feast of Gilded Age extravagance featuring beef and venison, wild turkey and duck, intermixed with six hours of speeches. The room was plastered with shields that had Grant's major battles inscribed in gilded letters. "I doubt if America has ever seen anything quite equal to it," Twain wrote. "I am well satisfied I shall not live to see its equal again."[146] At two in the morning, the author rose to offer the sixteenth and final toast. Determined to convulse the imperturbable Grant with laughter, he adopted a risky comedic strategy, proposing a toast to "The babies—as they comfort us in our sorrows, let us not forget them in our festivities."[147] Exactly how Twain would relate this to Grant was unclear. Then he contrasted the Grant who faced "the death storm at Donelson and Vicksburg" with Grant in the nursery, a powerless infant who "clawed your whiskers, and pulled your hair, and twisted your nose."[148] In a daring twist, he then imagined the fifty-seven-year-old Grant as an infant, whose main goal in the cradle was "to find some way of getting his big toe in his mouth." Then, after a long pause for dramatic silence, he uncorked his showstopper: "And if the child is but a prophecy of the man, there are mighty few who will doubt that he *succeeded*."[149] Grant fell apart with laughter. "I fetched him! I broke him up utterly!" Twain exulted to his wife. "The audience *saw* that for once in his life he had been knocked out of his iron serenity."[150] To William Dean Howells, he added, "I shook him up like dynamite & he sat there fifteen minutes & laughed and cried like the mortalest of mortals."[151]

By the end of his Chicago stay, Grant had endured enough adulation and more than enough alcoholic temptation. Before the Palmer House banquet, Frances Willard, the head of the Woman's Christian Temperance Union, appealed to the organizers to "dispense with all intoxicating liquors at the approaching feast."[152] The plea was rebuffed and the banquet hall swam with booze. But Grant pleased temperance advocates in Harrisburg in December when they saluted his refusal "to take any stimulant at the close of the procession" in his honor and praised "the dignified example he set at the ban[q]uet on Saturday evening when he inverted his wine glasses and refused, with a few other gentleme[n] to partake of any intoxicating beverage—they endorsing the request of the W.C.T.U. of Allegheny."[153] It showed Grant's success in dealing with his alcohol problem that he was now able to endorse temperance so publicly.

After Chicago, Grant resumed his grand procession across the country, traveling in a private railroad car custom-made for George Pullman himself. He created a sensation in Louisville, Kentucky, where huge crowds defied rain and mud to welcome him. "The windows were crowded with ladies & children waving their handkerchiefs," Grant wrote, "and the houses all decorated with stars & stripes."[154] He made time for a black delegation, expressing hope "that all the rights of citizenship may be enjoyed by them as it is guaranteed to them already by the law and constitutional amendments."[155] Pushing on, he met soldiers' orphans in Xenia, Ohio, and business leaders in Pittsburgh and spoke before the governor's mansion in Harrisburg.

The most stupendous gathering came in Philadelphia, where the mayor declared a holiday in Grant's honor. From a reviewing stand, Grant oversaw a parade that stretched for a mile with 350,000 pedestrians blanketing the sidewalks. Ten days later, returning to Philadelphia, he enjoyed time alone with President Hayes. "A most agreeable talk with General Grant for two hours alone," Hayes told his wife. "He looks well and is in excellent spirits."[156] The most daring aspect of Grant's stay was his address to a pacifist organization, the Universal Peace Union, founded by the aptly named Alfred H. Love. It seems remarkable that the group embraced a famous warrior, but Grant had already received its plaudits for his Peace Policy with the Indians and arbitration of the *Alabama* claims. In his speech, Grant peered into the future, evoking something akin to the League of Nations: "I look forward for a day when there will be a Court established, that shall be recognized by all nations, which will take into consideration all questions of difference between nations, and settle by arbitration or decision of such court, those questions, instead of keeping up large standing armies as in Europe."[157]

Grant had stopped off in New Jersey to spend Christmas Eve with his mother, then staying with his sister, Virginia Grant Corbin. A few days earlier, the strait-laced Hannah Grant, with her silvery hair, shucked her inhibitions and gave an interview to *The Philadelphia Press,* expressing considerable interest in her son's cross-country pageant. "I was just reading about General Grant's reception in Philadelphia," she said. "What a time they are making over him." She said she hadn't seen him since his return. "I wonder what his plans are . . . he promised to come here before his departure for the South. How does he look? He must be tired . . . The General was always a good traveler. He possessed that characteristic from his boyhood." When told that her son had refrained from discussing a third term, she professed no surprise. "The General is not in the habit of giving himself up to conjectures. When a question arises he decides it, and I do not think he has given any thought to the possibility of his being nominated again."[158]

Master Spirit

EVEN AS HE CIRCUMNAVIGATED the globe, Grant had worried about resurgent southern Democrats back home, ex-Confederates who had recaptured control of every state in the region and threatened to undo everything he had accomplished. "It looks to me that unless the North rallies by 1880 the Government will be in the hands of those who tried so hard fourteen—seventeen—years ago to destroy it," he wrote.[1] Grant regretted the rise of the solid South and deemed it his duty "to save the results of the war."[2] He also feared that unreasoning southern resistance to northern capital doomed the region to economic stagnation. Grant's travels also made him eager to introduce consular reforms, international arbitration, closer ties between China and Japan, new trade agreements, and a more international role for the United States. Finally, he was concerned about labor unrest and the rash of railroad strikes that had roiled the Hayes administration, nearly paralyzing the economy.

For these reasons, Grant felt a direct personal stake in the 1880 election. As he traveled, he was rejuvenated by his renewed popularity at home. He had never lost the ability to draw on lingering affection from Appomattox. As *The Times* of London explained, American voters were disillusioned with President Hayes for failing to deliver on civil service reform and realized that Grant, for all his errors, had hewed to "a firm and honourable policy." This reevaluation made Grant "the most popular American, and, if the Republican nominating convention for 1880 were now to meet, would give him the nomination.[3] Julia Grant perked up at the exuberant crowds who turned out for her husband—"They understand now and are sorry," she told her children—and longed to reign again as Washington's social doyenne.[4] When the British governor in Singapore had asked about her plans to return to the White House, she had made no secret of her ardent wish for a comeback, adding that if her husband heard her say so, "he would knock my head off."[5]

Two people who watched Grant's resurrection with enthusiasm were his old comrades Sheridan and Sherman. "He has grown wonderfully in public confidence as an able and strong man," Sheridan wrote as Grant sailed the seas, "and it would not surprise me a bit, if he was called upon to again go to the White House."[6] More surprising had been the rediscovery of Grant's merits by Sherman. "No man of Either Party, Seems to rise above Mediocrity, or to Command public Confidence," Sherman wrote in October 1878. "If this Continues two years More Grant may again be President, and . . . too vigorous to remain idle he cannot well refuse."[7]

Right before Grant returned to America, Sherman posted to him a long, thoughtful letter, describing how southern leaders threatened to reverse the progress of Reconstruction and "ignore the laws made in pursuance of the new amendments to the Constitution."[8] Such inflammatory rhetoric, Sherman argued, would have made Grant an inevitable Republican candidate for 1880. But that Democratic threat had now receded and with it the need for a third Grant term. The underlying point of the letter was to notify Grant that, if Sherman's brother John should be a candidate for president, "it would be unnatural for me to oppose or qualify his purpose."[9] When he received this letter in Tokyo, Grant was deeply moved by Sherman's sensitivity in explaining why he might be forced to support his brother. With tears in his eyes, he told Young, "'People may wonder . . . why I love Sherman. How could I help loving Sherman. And he has always been the same during the thirty five years I have known him. He was so at West Point.'"[10]

In 1879 a book by an anonymous author appeared with the provocative title *The Great American Empire; or, Gen. Ulysses S. Grant, Emperor of North America.* Whether or not Grant lusted for power—and he was careful to conceal any evidence of that—he could never admit it and preferred to be carried along in the political current by friends more openly interested in power. He had a way of standing back and letting things happen—a tacit form of approval. Inaction had become his preferred form of action. That Grant leaned toward a third term was evident from his unending appearances across the country and the fact that John

Russell Young rushed out his book about Grant's round-the-world tour in time for Christmas 1879. At the same time, Grant pleaded with Badeau to speed up publication of his military history of his wartime campaigns. "I think you can not get it out too soon after your return to America," he lectured him in late November. "It will be the most authentic book published on the war, and I think the most truthful history."[11]

Buck advanced a subtler view of his father's ambivalent mood about another presidential race: "While father was abroad, his political friends arranged that he should try again for the third term and had gone so far in their arrangements, that when he returned he felt in justice to them, that he ought to go on. The Presidency was not a thing to be sought for, neither was it a thing to be refused. He never sought position. But when it came to him, he felt it his duty to accept if he could fill the place. He was also incapable of supposing his friends to be selfish."[12]

On December 19, President Hayes conceded in his diary that Grant was the "general popular favorite" in the Republican Party, trailed by Senator James G. Blaine of Maine and Secretary of the Treasury John Sherman. Washburne concurred that the Republican vote for Grant "will be so overwhelming . . . that Blaine will get out of the road."[13] Blaine and Sherman were favored by reform-minded party members who opposed machine politics and were dubbed Half-Breeds. Grant detractors already poured scorn on the idea of a third term. E. L. Godkin of *The Nation* mocked Grant's supporters as those seeking "a permanent, or nearly permanent, President" and ridiculed the notion that foreign travel had produced a new, improved version of the scandal-ridden Grant.[14]

Still searching for a permanent abode, Grant spent the final days of 1879 at a friend's home in Washington. He hoped Buck would make a speculative killing for him in an Arizona mine, enabling him to buy a suitable residence in the capital. In late December, Grant undertook an invasion of the South, this time a purely peaceful one, visiting Columbia, South Carolina, and addressing a black militia in Beaufort. The trip barely camouflaged his political agenda: to demonstrate that he could break the Democratic grasp on the region and carry some southern states, a view buttressed by endorsements from a handful of southern newspapers.

Delighted by his friendly reception in the South, Grant and Julia boarded a steamer to St. Augustine, Florida. While in Florida, Grant associated openly with the temperance movement for the second time, meeting in Fernandina with a black lodge of the Independent Order of Good Templars. "General Grant," a lodge spokesman said, "the black men are not unmindful of the great good you rendered in the darkest days of the race's history, when there was but one real peril that threatened our nation's glory, slavery." In reply, Grant dwelled on a topic he had never dared broach so freely before: that "he thought intoxicating liquors the chief cause of poverty and crime."[15] Once again, Grant's courage in identifying with the temperance cause suggests a mastery over his drinking problem and hence a new willingness to acknowledge it. During his two-week Florida stay, he also gushed about the state's economic future. "This is becoming a great resort for invalids and people who wish to avoid the rigors of a Northern Winter," he told his daughter.[16]

Grant decided to spend a goodly portion of the winter in Cuba and Mexico, taking Fred and his wife, Ida; Phil Sheridan and his wife; and Katherine Felt, the daughter of Galena friends. With John Russell Young, Grant had learned the art of taking along a chronicler who might convert a private trip to public advantage, and he now chose Byron Andrews of the *Chicago Inter-Ocean* as his secretary. In an oppressively hot Havana, the Grant party was handsomely entertained at the governor's palace, then toured tobacco and sugar plantations. After arriving in Vera Cruz, Mexico, on February 18, Grant was welcomed by Matías Romero, the former treasury minister. Writing home, Grant made clear that his absence from America had a patently political objective: "We will be back in the United States about the 22d of March by which time public opinion will be sufficiently developed for me to determine my duty."[17] Those backers who argued that Grant had returned prematurely from his foreign travels now hoped his southern detour would enable them to rekindle a Grant boom when he returned in the spring.

From the moment he set foot in Mexico, Grant was transported by the beautiful scenery, perfect climate, and hospitable people—exactly as during the Mexican War. On February 23, he and Sheridan held a cordial meeting with President Porfirio Díaz in Mexico City and Grant again showed his talent for defining a brand-new diplomatic role for superannuated presidents. He could speak more frankly than when in office and addressed long-standing Mexican suspicions about the United States, telling Díaz frankly that "our country had dealt harshly with his in years past, and that, although I had been in the military service at the time, I had always felt that the war was unjust."[18] A true friend of Mexico, Grant foresaw the day when it would "become a rich country, a good neighbor, and the two Republics would profit by the contact."[19] Most of Mexico stood as virgin territory for railroad development and Grant agreed to aid the country in developing a rail network with American capital.

While in Mexico City, Grant relived a pair of battles now three decades in the past. Riding in mule-drawn carriages, he and his retinue drove nine miles south of Mexico City to where Grant had fought at Churubusco in 1847. "Right here among these haciendas," he announced, alighting from his carriage, "my command lay all day waiting for the battle of Contreras to be fought."[20] He also revisited Molino del Rey and beheld ancient walls still pockmarked with bullets and cannonballs from that conflict. The spot had never shed its youthful romance for Grant. As the intervening years fell away, he came alive in relating the story. "As [Grant] stood up in the carriage," wrote a reporter, he talked about the fight "and his face wore an expression of eager animation such as I have never observed through its mask of immobility before."[21]

During Grant's Mexican sojourn, Washburne reassured him he would win the nomination by acclamation at the Republican convention in Chicago, but he also sounded some alarming notes. People worried about overturning George Washington's precedent of restricting the president to two terms. "Of course the copperheads howl over it," Washburne wrote, "and now the opposition of our own party is howling still louder."[22] Grant was being portrayed in the press as a captive of party bosses who manipulated him for their own ends. "Many of those who desired Grant . . . do not want him as the candidate of the Camerons and Conklings, secured by manipulated caucuses and pledged delegations," *The New York Times* cautioned.[23] About the auspices under which he might secure the nomination, Grant showed scant concern, having long ago cast his lot with the Conklings and the Camerons, and it was too late to undo the damage.

To Washburne, Grant insisted it was "a matter of supreme indifference" whether he was nominated or not.[24] But crossing the border into Texas in late March he looked suspiciously like an energetic, barnstorming candidate, sometimes giving four or five speeches a day that plainly declared his intentions, and he exhibited an oratorical prowess that floored those who remembered the old nervous, tongue-tied Grant. At a Galveston banquet, Grant invoked his service in Texas during the Mexican War, singing the state's praises: "I am glad to come back now on this occasion to behold a territory which is an empire in itself, and larger than some of the empires of Europe."[25] Visiting a school for African Americans, Grant promoted education for blacks and the vital importance of an educated citizenry: "I am glad to see that the colored children of Galveston have the opportunity of becoming useful citizens, and hope that you will improve it by obtaining a common school education, and that the white children will do likewise."[26] In Houston, hundreds of blacks mobbed Grant at the local hotel while one stooped, white-haired black preacher "spread out his long bony hand and pronounced his blessing upon him," said a spectator.[27]

Throughout the South, the ubiquitous Grant stopped at African American schools and churches, engendering a fervent outpouring of support from black citizens whom he had assiduously courted over the years. When he spoke to the black congregation of a Methodist church in New Orleans, the large, eager crowd spilled into the surrounding streets. "The South has been the home of the colored man," Grant stated, "and I hope he will always be permitted to live peaceably in the South, freely."[28] Grant's concern for the black community melded altruism with self-interest, for black Republican votes could wrest several southern states from Democratic hands. As James Longstreet told a reporter with enthusiasm, "There are Southern States which one Republican and one alone can carry and that one is General Grant—North Carolina, Louisiana, Georgia . . . Yes, it is possible for Grant to carry Georgia. Why not? Almost half the population of the State are negroes, every man of them Republicans at heart."[29]

Among whites, Grant's southern tour inspired divergent reactions. In Mobile, former mayor Jones Withers, once a Confederate general, extolled the tour as "the grand crowning act" of an eventful life in which Grant had exhorted his countrymen to rise above "sectional animosity and party strife to his own high level of pure patriotism and true statesmanship."[30] Striking a similar note, the *Memphis Appeal* wrote: "We are, let us hope, upon the threshold of the new era when all trace of the bloody contest will be blotted out."[31] But many southern whites resented Grant's presence, had not forgotten his wartime ferocity, and blamed him for Reconstruction, placing him beyond forgiveness or redemption. "Unless our people have eaten of the insane root and lost their reason, Grantism can have no foothold at the South," the *Mobile Register* declared. "We have not yet become dogs to lick the hand that smites us."[32] Reprising the familiar charge of "bayonet rule," the Louisiana Senate voted down a resolution welcoming Grant to the state.

Grant knew the symbolic importance of a peaceful trip through a region in which he had waged bloody war and balanced appearances before black audiences with amicable speeches before white ones. At numberless banquets, he expatiated on national unity and paid tribute to southern generals, who stepped forward to thank him for his generosity at Appomattox. The reconciliation theme crested in Vicksburg, where Grant joked he was "glad to go to Vicksburg through the front door; once, you know, I was forced to come in through the back door."[33] Seventeen years after bombarding the starving city, Grant personified a spirit of renewal. "I know that nothing can again array the blue against the gray. This fact is proven by the citizens coming here to-day, white and colored together."[34] Another emotional high point came in Cairo, Illinois, where Grant recalled that when he last inhabited the town it had been "a camp of bristling bayonets."[35] He reminded listeners that on his southern swing, former Confederate officers had expressed satisfaction with the war's outcome "and [I] in no wise felt inclined to attempt to disturb them."[36] Grant's newfound southern popularity made it seem feasible that, as a presidential candidate, he might peel away several states from the Democratic grip. The black community nationwide lined up wholeheartedly behind his candidacy, one black journalist calling Grant "the only man who can silence the *Copperhead* element in the South."[37]

Starting in Cairo, Grant's itinerary through Illinois was largely orchestrated by Washburne, who wished to expose the undeclared candidate to as many towns as possible. Grant suffered from a lost tooth and Julia's eye problem bothered her again, but otherwise the trip went well. The Stalwarts made no secret that Grant was their pet, their creature, their best bet for a return to power. "General Grant is in the hands of his friends," John Logan bragged to a reporter, "and they will not withdraw him until he is beaten, no matter how many ballots are taken."[38] On April 27, when Grant celebrated his fifty-eighth birthday in Galena, townspeople trooped through his house, now a temporary oasis for a former president with no fixed address. Young claimed that he and Grant "knocked about the country together like a pair of boys on a holiday. I never saw him better or in better form."[39]

By April 1880, Adam Badeau thought opposition to Grant's nomination had hardened because of his premature return from his world tour. He also believed Grant's reticence about a third term and ingrained passivity damaged his chances at the forthcoming convention. According to Badeau, "Men like Conkling, Cameron, and Logan declared in intimate conferences that Grant had never said to either that he would be a candidate . . . He had done nothing whatever to promote his first nomination, and nothing directly for his second; and he determined now to follow the same course in regard to a third."[40]

Months spent on the road had strengthened Grant's determination to return to the White House, as if acting at being president made him *want* to be president again. Staying at Fred's house in Chicago in May, weeks before the convention, Grant executed an atypical volte-face: he threw off all pretense of neutrality and declared his wish to nab the nomination. Badeau was thunderstruck: "Grant manifested as much anxiety as I ever saw him display on his own account; he calculated the chances, he counted the delegates, considered how every movement would affect the result."[41] The foreign policy ideas about China, Japan, and Mexico that fermented in his brain gave him a valid reason to want to return to the presidency instead of falling back on pure egotistical desire, which had never satisfied his Methodist soul. Painfully aware of his mistakes as president, Grant fantasized about reentering the White House to correct those errors and redeem his reputation. Beyond his sudden daydreams of returning to power, Grant was goaded to run by Julia, and it was widely bruited in the press that "the General would rather offend forty million people than Madame."[42]

RIGHT BEFORE THE CHICAGO CONVENTION, a filthy man in ragged clothes walked the city streets, making a public spectacle of himself. "I am U.S. Grant's brother," the drunken derelict told startled pedestrians, "don't I look like him?"[43] The shabby vagrant was Orvil Grant, and he spoke the plain truth. With a wife and four children, Orvil was a genial man with a full beard, large forehead, and close-set blue eyes. Right before Grant became president, Orvil's vindictive wife had tried to borrow money from Julia and gotten a rough reprimand. As she recalled, Julia "became indignant, she had a hot temper mind you, and said that Orvil had gotten a great deal of money from father Grant, that Ulysses had gotten none because he had 'earned his way,' and if Orvil had squandered such riches, that was not her fault and she would not make up the difference."[44] In 1872, after Grant appointed James McLean, Orvil's partner in the Galena leather business, collector of the port of Chicago, he was stunned to discover that McLean had forked over kickbacks to Orvil to procure the job. "I did not dream that such obligation existed," Grant protested.[45] Despite bad blood, he had promised a year later to give his younger brother $5,000 or $10,000 when he entered a new business. Still, Orvil proved an embarrassment, cutting shady deals for Indian trading posts, and he also seemed to share his brother's problematic drinking history. He was firmly in the mold of Jesse Root Grant, working every angle to exploit his brother's celebrity.

Orvil's erratic behavior acquired new significance in September 1878 when the Grant family had him committed to the State Asylum for the Insane in Morristown, New Jersey. Two constables grabbed him at a train station, a reporter describing him as "a rather tall man, who wore a somewhat seedy black beaver hat, and whose clothes were untidy."[46] Accompanied by a family physician, Dr. Morton, the constables hustled off a dazed Orvil to the Elizabeth jail and then to the asylum, where he feverishly paced the floor, jabbering about speculative ventures. The press exploded with stories about hallucinations that had seized him, all revolving around crazy moneymaking schemes. The outcast brother had turned into a walking caricature of Jesse Root Grant at his most avaricious. He imagined he had bought enormous quantities of calf skin or pianos or sewing machines or wheat, cornering the market. Dr. Morton called the delusions "purely an intellectual aberration" and denied they were related to alcohol.[47]

To discuss Orvil's case, a *New York Times* reporter sought out Hannah Grant, then living with the Corbins in Elizabeth:

> She is a gentle-mannered old lady, with an abundance of silver-gray hair, and a face as kind and motherly as it is delicate and finely cut. Mrs. Grant said that her son Orville [sic] had been a trouble to the family for some time. If he could have been persuaded to remain quietly at home, no restraint would have been put upon his actions, for he was a kind husband and father, and there was no apprehension that his mania would take a violent turn. His insanity consisted in a monomania for immense transactions without any capital . . . he had spent or invested in unremunerative enterprises nearly or quite all the $50,000 he had formerly made in the timber business, and she did not think there would be anything left for the maintenance of the family.[48]

According to the article, Grant had taken Orvil's case to a "distinguished alienist" who concluded that "quiet surveillance" by friends would suffice instead of forcible restraint.[49] During his global trip, Grant monitored Orvil's behavior at the asylum, finding nothing to hearten him. "I am sorry to say that I do not get favorable news from Orvil," he told a relative in December 1878. "He does not seem to improve."[50]

For reasons that are murky, weeks after Grant wrote this letter, Orvil was released from the asylum and turned up on Philadelphia's streets, boasting of big business plans ahead in San Francisco. "Not only was he going to open a great restaurant," reported *The New York Times*, "but he had several hundred thousand dollars invested in a Pacific slope tannery, another immense sum in a brewery, and was in partnership with several parties in other concerns."[51] Although shut up in a dream world, Orvil was affable as he endeavored to strike business deals, but his clothes were shabby, his shoes begrimed with mud. By August, he had drifted to Chicago, where he showed up right before the Republican convention, presenting a public relations nightmare for his brother. As one Grant supporter wrote, "'Brother Orville' [*sic*] is here & you ought to see him. A perfect wreck from liquor, and in a ragged, drunken, collarless [state], almost without shoes, & his clothes in the most disgusting condition. He walks the street, and is observed of everybody. It is an outrage upon the American people that the General should permit this."[52] Grant didn't spurn his brother, and his willingness to tolerate his presence typified his reaction to his most trying family members: whatever they did, he stuck loyally by them, or at least did not disown them. But Grant showed no enduring affection for his brother, who had disappointed him so many times. When Orvil died in August 1881, at age forty-six, Ulysses did not attend the funeral.

IN THE PRELUDE to the Republican convention, scheduled to convene in Chicago on June 2, 1880, Ulysses S. Grant exuded a confident air, convinced voters would give him a fresh chance at the White House. "The General is now here feeling first rate," wrote Elihu Washburne from Galena in late April, "calm as a summer morning and feeling fully assured of success, the same as we all feel."[53] Grant refused to campaign, wanting the nomination to come to him without any unseemly show of desire on his part. The ladylike Julia, by contrast, favored a more bare-knuckled approach. So hopeful were the pro-Grant omens that on May 21 *The New York Times* termed his nomination "certain," citing an influential politician who contended he had locked up a commanding 380 convention votes.[54]

One naysayer was John Russell Young, who met with Grant in late May and tried to convince him he couldn't be reelected. In response, Grant drafted a letter for the four politicians who would supervise his nomination in Chicago—Conkling, Boutwell, Cameron, and Logan—and volunteered to withdraw if needed to stem any bitterness generated by his candidacy. His one condition was that he would bow out only if James Blaine did so as well. When Julia got wind of this letter, she was irate, telling Young, "If General Grant were not nominated, then let it be so, but he must not withdraw his name—no never."[55] The letter was delivered in a large envelope to Fred Grant, who claimed he passed it on to Conkling. George Boutwell says Grant had already given the four men complete discretion to handle his candidacy as they thought advisable. In the end, Grant never withdrew.

Quite amazing was the ardor with which Julia Grant prodded her husband to take off the kid gloves and fight hard for the nomination. When she urged him to go to Chicago and appear on the convention floor, he said he would rather cut off his right hand. "Do you not desire success?" she asked. "Well, yes, of course," he answered, "since my name is up, I would rather be nominated, but I will do nothing to further that end." Julia harrumphed at what she considered misguided chivalry. "For heaven's sake, go—and go tonight. I know they are already making their cabals against you. Go, go tonight, I beseech you." Grant grew exasperated. "Julia," he declared, "I am amazed at you," and he strolled off to chat with a visitor.[56]

On June 2, Senator James D. Cameron banged the gavel to open the Chicago convention. The first big floor fight erupted over a procedural point that could theoretically swing the nomination to Grant. With Conkling leading the charge, Grant forces lobbied for the unit rule, which would guarantee that three large states in the Stalwart camp—New York, Illinois, and Pennsylvania—cast all their votes for a single candidate. James A. Garfield predicted a "fierce fight" over this seemingly technical issue.[57] In a preview of things to come, the unit rule was defeated by a 449 to 306 vote, substantially lessening Grant's chances for victory and disclosing the first chinks in his electoral armor.

The most conspicuous delegate on the convention floor was his manager, Roscoe Conkling, a tall, arresting figure who dominated attention. Blaine called him the "master spirit" of Grant's followers, and, with head held high, he lived up to that designation.[58] When several delegates offered to back Conkling instead of Grant, he sharply upbraided them: "I am here as the agent of New York to support General Grant to the end. *Any man who would forsake him under such conditions does not deserve to be elected, and could not be elected.*"[59] Lord Roscoe did not disappoint those who expected a flurry of showmanship. When he rose to nominate Grant, he leapt onto a table reserved for journalists, folded his arms across his chest, then waited until a hush had fallen. He began by softening up

the crowd with some light verse: "When asked what state he hails from, / Our
sole reply shall be, / He comes from Appomattox, / and its famous apple-tree."[60]
This set off an uproarious ten-minute celebration for Grant. "Never defeated in
peace or in war," Conkling resumed, "his name is the most illustrious borne by
living man."[61] When he mocked Grant's opponents and was greeted by derisory
shouts, he blithely sucked on a lemon until the uproar had subsided.

With his round-the-world tour, Conkling said, Grant had added knowledge
and experience to profound common sense. He laughed at criticisms leveled at
Grant—"The shafts and the arrows have all been aimed at him, and they lie
broken and harmless at his feet"—then confronted head-on the view that no
president should be entitled to a third term. "Who dares . . . to put fetters on that
free choice and judgment which is the birthright of the American people?"[62]
Conkling transported the delirious crowd beyond Grant's checkered presidency
to the glory days of the Civil War, arousing them with military imagery. Such
was the hysterical enthusiasm, a reporter wrote, that "the friends of Grant threw
away the characteristics of age and became boys once more."[63] For all his glittering flashes of oratory, Conkling's presence played into the hands of those who
thought Grant the cat's-paw of party bosses. For them, the messenger trumped
the message. After Conkling spoke, Garfield delivered a fine speech for John
Sherman that somewhat cooled off Grant mania sweeping the hall.

In the past, Conkling had clashed with Blaine, the darling of the Half-
Breeds, taunting him for "his haughty disdain, his grandiloquent swell, his majestic, supereminent, overpowering, turkey-gobbler strut."[64] A politician to his
fingertips, with a sonorous voice and magnetic personality, Blaine was cordial
but calculating. Sometimes Grant viewed him charitably as "a very able man, I
think a perfectly honest man, fit for any place."[65] But at other times he called
Blaine "a very smart man, and when I say that I do not mean talented, but
smart."[66] Grant blamed Blaine for venomous attacks launched against him and
their friendship didn't survive the convention. Grant had never warmed to John
Sherman, who reciprocated the feeling, warning that Grant's nomination "would
be fatal to us in the election."[67] Moving silently in the background was Elihu
Washburne, who claimed to favor Grant's nomination. Then articles surfaced in
The St. Louis Globe-Democrat that the two-faced Washburne secretly promoted
his own candidacy, leaving Grant hurt and dumbfounded. "Mr. Washburne is
my friend," Grant told a reporter. "He has always been a very warm and sincere
friend to me, and was [at] such a time when his friendship was so valuable that,

no matter what happens, I can never forget it nor cease to remember it with gratitude."[68]

The winning candidate needed 379 votes. On the first ballot, Grant drew a narrow lead of 304 votes versus 284 for Blaine, 93 for Sherman, 34 for George F. Edmunds of Vermont and—confirming Grant's worst fears—30 for Washburne. These last votes, the unkindest cut for Grant, denied him an insuperable lead. The convention then wore on through many wearisome ballots, marked by trifling changes in the vote count. On the third ballot, two new names appeared with a single vote apiece: the Indiana politician Benjamin Harrison and Congressman James A. Garfield. Finally came the fateful thirty-sixth ballot, which produced a political earthquake. Perhaps feeling the tremors, Conkling admonished the Grant delegates: "Keep steady, boys, Grant is going to win on this ballot."[69] During the roll call, Maine deserted Blaine, its favorite son, and switched all its votes to Garfield, setting off a delegate stampede in his direction. Grant's votes remained firm as Blaine and Sherman supporters alike defected to Garfield. When the counting ended, Garfield had 399 votes, Grant 306, Blaine 42, Elihu Washburne 5, and John Sherman 3. It was a startling victory for Garfield, who had never declared his candidacy, had stood foursquare behind Sherman, and was the most reluctant of dark horse nominees.

Grant was in the office of William Rowley of his wartime staff when he learned his last presidential hopes were snuffed out. He stepped outside, puffed thoughtfully on a cigar, then told friends, "I can't say that I regret my own defeat. By it I shall escape four years of hard work and four years of abuse, and gentlemen, we can all support the candidate."[70] One side of Grant was likely relieved, Grant telling Conkling he had "grown weary of constant abuse," much of it emanating from "former professed friends."[71] Buck told how his father had reacted to Conkling's speech and the thunderous ovation it received. As they walked home afterward, an uneasy Grant turned and said a little sadly, "I am afraid I may be nominated."[72] Buck claimed his father lost the nomination because he refused to cut a side deal to retain John Sherman as treasury secretary. That Grant felt his defeat deeply grew clear when he failed to send a congratulatory message to Garfield. He felt duped by his backers, telling friends he would never have allowed his name to be used if he thought victory uncertain: "My friends were not just to me in saying that it was only a matter of form."[73] With this defeat behind him, Grant would endorse a constitutional amendment limiting the president to one seven-year term. Julia Grant felt bitterly the injustice of her husband's loss.

Having been received with grand ceremony by monarchs and prime ministers around the world, she could not contemplate comfortably the return to a mundane, civilian life. "I take it as a personal grievance," she said of Garfield's victory, "and I am down on Washburne & the whole 'Caboodle' of them."[74] She told one friend, "You know I'm a Democrat. What's more, I'm *Secesh,* particularly as the Republicans wouldn't nominate Ulysses for a third term."[75]

Grant's loss perhaps owed less to insufficient popularity than to heavy-handed methods wielded by his henchmen Conkling, Logan, and Cameron, who ended up splitting the Republican Party. As Hayes wrote, "The immediately valuable result is the condemnation of the machine as organized by Conkling and Cameron . . . I greatly regret that Grant, our first soldier and a man of many sterling qualities, should be so humiliated and degraded as he has been by his unprincipled supporters."[76] The Stalwarts could claim one victory in Chicago: the choice of Conkling's protégé Chester Arthur, the former collector for the port of New York, as the vice presidential nominee, a consolation prize to Conkling. Arthur, having stuck by Grant to the last minute, refused to rebuff the overture from the Garfield forces. When he informed Conkling about the job, the latter grew outraged that Arthur would even consider such a disloyal thing. "Well, sir," Conkling roared, "you should drop it as you would a red hot shoe from the forge." Arthur, pained, would not be browbeaten. "The office of the Vice President is a greater honor than I ever dreamed of attaining . . . In a calmer moment you will look at this differently." Conkling was not appeased. Declaring his independence, Arthur accepted the nomination and his decision would shortly transform a New York political hack into a president of the United States.

A BIG, ROBUST MAN with a long beard, James Abram Garfield was a remarkable autodidact, born in a log cabin in Ohio. An industrious student who worked at menial jobs to pay his way through school, he ended up a professor of ancient language, literature, and math and a college president at age twenty-six. After Fort Sumter, his ascent in the Union army was no less rapid as he fought at Shiloh and Chickamauga and served as chief of staff for General Rosecrans. In 1863, soon after becoming a major general of volunteers, he resigned to serve in Congress and wound up a champion of emancipation and civil rights for blacks.

Though Garfield had long been a faithful Republican, Grant had never especially warmed to him, but neither had he criticized him. "He is a good man,"

Grant commented after the convention in a less than rousing endorsement. "Garfield has always been right."[77] During his southern tour, Grant had come to believe he could dent Democratic dominance in the region whereas he saw no chance of Garfield making such inroads. When Democrats gathered in Cincinnati in late June and nominated Winfield Scott Hancock as their standard-bearer, Grant's attraction to Garfield intensified overnight. To a reporter, he sardonically recalled Hancock's vainglorious reaction to receiving a single vote at the 1864 Democratic convention, recalling how "from that time [Hancock] had had the Presidential bee in his bonnet."[78] Mocking Hancock as an inexperienced political lightweight, Republicans printed up a pamphlet entitled "Hancock's Political Achievements," a work that contained nothing but blank pages.[79]

When the Chicago convention ended, Grant resumed his nomadic life, hoping to end up in New York City—if he could afford it. To escape hot weather, he returned to the Rocky Mountains, where Jesse had struck it rich in Arizona and New Mexico mining ventures. The newly extroverted Grant was much in demand, his appetite for public ceremonies never sated. In Fort Leavenworth, Kansas, Grant was asked if he ever tired of these events. "Oh, no," he replied. "I rather enjoy them if I could only get sleep enough."[80] Wherever his train stopped on the Great Plains, huge assemblies of welcoming people gathered and Democrats no less than Republicans honored him at banquets and parades.

Grant was especially pleased to visit Colorado, which had recently become a state, thanks to his signature on a bill late in his presidency. Inspecting gold and silver discoveries, he ventured some political humor when told that a Colorado creek was called Son of a Bitch Creek and he suggested it be renamed Carl Schurz Creek. He provisionally accepted the presidency of the San Pedro Mining Company, a gold and copper producer, hoping its dividends would sustain him. "One thing is certain: I must do something to supplement my income or continue to live in Galena or on a farm," he confided to Badeau. "I have not got the means to live in a city."[81]

On June 22, Grant spurned a lucrative offer to become president of the new Panama Canal Company that was extended by Ferdinand de Lesseps, who had overseen creation of the Suez Canal. Though a spirited advocate of an interoceanic canal, Grant favored Nicaragua as the most practicable route from an engineering standpoint. Ever mindful of the Monroe Doctrine, he also wanted a canal created under American auspices. By December, Grant had emerged as a charter member of the new Maritime Canal Company of Nicaragua with the expectation that he would soon become its president.

Wherever he went, reporters eagerly solicited his views on the presidential race. In mid-July, he issued a thumping vote of confidence in Garfield: "There is no reason why any Republican should hesitate to define his position, or not vote for Garfield. I know him to be a man of talent, thoroughly accomplished, and an upright man."[82] Garfield was gleeful at the zest with which Grant had suddenly embraced him. "Certainly no American is so well able, by an experience wholly unequalled in our history as you, to aid in bringing our people into harmony and ensuring the success of our party," Garfield flattered Grant.[83] Grant sent back a robust letter of support, disclosing that he would return east around September 20 and suggesting that he and Garfield travel partway together. Grant was back in the game. On September 28, he campaigned with Conkling in Warren, Ohio, and dazzled the crowd with a seven-minute speech. Startled by his sudden loquacity in public, the press began talking up the notion of a new Grant. He stayed at Garfield's home in Mentor, near Lake Erie, while Julia, resenting Garfield's triumph and believing her husband cheated of his rightful place in the universe, refused to join him. "The General went," she wrote with proud defiance, "but I would not go."[84]

Grant volunteered to campaign for Garfield in northeastern states and again blazed a new path for ex-presidents. Having sat out his own presidential races, he had never campaigned before or made speeches on the hustings and threw himself into the task with self-evident gusto. "We must elect Garfield," he exhorted a Cincinnati audience. "He is a great man. He has but few intellectual peers in public life."[85] With his uncanny knack for self-reinvention, Grant turned into a master of the stump speech, condensing his thoughts into brief talks and prompting prolonged bursts of applause. As Mark Twain recalled, Grant "was received everywhere by prodigious multitudes of enthusiastic people and . . . one might almost tell what part of the country the General was in . . . by the red reflections on the sky caused by the torch processions and fireworks."[86]

On October 16, Mark Twain escorted the born-again, whistle-stopping Grant from Boston to Hartford, where he introduced him to a vast audience in Bushnell Park. On the train, Fred Grant revealed to Twain that his father, "far from being a rich man, as was commonly supposed, had not even enough income to enable him to live as respectably as a third-rate physician."[87] Twain thought this disgraceful, and, in introducing Grant, contrasted his financial plight with that of the pampered Duke of Wellington, so richly rewarded after Waterloo. England had "made him a duke, and gave him $4,000,000. If you had done and suffered for any country what you have done and suffered for your own, you would have been affronted in the same sordid way," Twain joked to Grant, then added, "Your country loves you, your country is proud of you, your country is grateful to you."[88]

Grant had deployed his gift for dry humor in private, but now delighted audiences with droll commentary. At the New York Stock Exchange, he entertained brokers with humorous observations of their frenzied trading routines: "The first time I came here I thought you were all fighting with one another, and if that were so it was no place for me to be, among fighting men . . . I am pleased to see you all and wish both bulls and bears success, and that you will all come out of this without a scratch."[89] On October 21, the man renowned for stoic silence squeezed three speeches into one hectic day. "I am hoarse to-day," he told a crowd in Stamford, Connecticut. "Frequent speeches make one hoarse, I believe."[90] He kept up a brisk pace, more typical of lightning military strikes than electioneering forays, explaining in Franklin, New Jersey, that he believed the fate of the republic was at stake—that all the blood and treasure spilled during the Civil War would be squandered by a Democratic victory. "The great importance of this occasion has induced me to attend political meetings as I have never done before in my life. I have felt . . . that I could not see the Government in the hands of those who labored to destroy it."[91]

During his concluding ten days of electioneering, Grant spoke with unwonted ebullience, dropping deep-seated inhibitions. Flashing his trademark silk hat and cigar, he was hoisted on the shoulders of delirious crowds. What became clear as he crossed upstate New York was that Grant wasn't just campaigning for a candidate but for a cause. He was outraged that "our fellow-citizens of African descent" in the South couldn't vote "without being burned out of their homes, and without being threatened or intimidated." He would not allow Democrats to "control elections by the use of a shot-gun and by intimidation and assassination."[92] In Auburn, Grant spoke at two giant wigwams that held up to ten thousand people apiece and blasted the southern doctrine of states' rights, charging that the Democratic Party upheld the principles of Robert E. Lee and Andrew Johnson and stood under the control of "Rebel Brigadiers."[93] In a final burst of energy, he returned to New York City right before the election and stood with Chester Arthur at a nocturnal parade that lasted from midnight until 4 a.m.

On Election Day, all of Grant's campaigning appeared to pay off. Garfield won by a wafer-thin margin in the popular vote column, but did better in the Electoral College, and Grant had good reason to believe he had made a signal contribution to Garfield's election. "The country, in my judgment has escaped a great calamity in the success of the republican party," Grant told his daughter. "A month ago the result attained was not expected."[94] In a postelection interview, he again showed his newly acquired candor: "If the South had once obtained a firm hold of the Government they would have ruined the country and nothing short of a revolution would have rescued it from their hands again."[95]

A Miserable Dirty Reptile

A FTER THE ELECTION Grant picked up hearsay that he might receive a cabinet post or foreign mission from Garfield and he eased the president-elect's mind on the subject: "I want no reward further than the approval of the patriotic people of the land."[1] In reply, Garfield expressed disappointment at Grant's reluctance to serve, saying he had hoped to profit from his knowledge of Mexico, Japan, and China and welcomed his advice on cabinet appointees. Taking Garfield at his word, Grant fruitlessly recommended John Jacob Astor III for treasury secretary. In his inaugural address, Garfield seemed to satisfy Grant's expectations, stressing voting rights and economic opportunity for black citizens and reviving some of the bygone spirit of Reconstruction.

Grant's short-lived honeymoon with Garfield ended when he appointed James Blaine as secretary of state, a man Grant regarded as his political foe. Already he had warned Garfield: "I do not like the man, have no confidence in his friendship nor in his reliability."[2] He thought of yanking support from Garfield, then reconsidered. When he and Julia breakfasted with the new president in Washington, Garfield solicited his advice on policy matters and appointments. Grant huddled with his troika of Conkling, Logan, and Cameron and kept a weather eye out for their interests. Then came a series of Garfield appointments that infuriated Grant, notably that of Judge William H. Robertson—the man Grant thought engineered his downfall at the Chicago convention—as collector of the port of New York. It was the biggest plum in the patronage pie and Grant took umbrage. Having campaigned for Garfield at a torrid pace and helped him carry New York, Grant felt double-crossed. He thought he had earned a special place in Garfield's affections and had been penalized instead. In a published letter, he took a shot across Garfield's bow, alluding to "a deep laid scheme by somebody to punish prominent leaders for being openly friendly to me. I cannot believe that Garfield is the author of this policy."[3] Grant had violated an unspoken rule that presidents not chastise their successors so publicly and he had done so with unseemly speed.

On April 24, Grant sent Garfield a stinging letter, protesting that he had made New York appointments without consulting the state's two senators. "To select the most obnoxious man, to them, in the state is more than a slight."[4] The surly tone Grant adopted suggested he craved a return to power and wasn't ready to withdraw into the political wilderness. He had grown accustomed to exercising power and deeply felt its loss. Once again he misjudged the revulsion against old-style party bosses. Both New York senators, Conkling and Thomas C. Platt, resigned to protest Garfield's action. By May, Grant described himself as "completely disgusted" with Garfield's deeds and allowed their feud to play out in the press.[5]

On May 15, Garfield sent a strongly worded letter to Grant, defending Robertson's appointment and saying "worthy and competent men should not be excluded from recognition because they opposed your nomination at Chicago."[6] He tempered the note with a friendly ending. "My dear General, I can never forget your great services during the late campaign."[7] Instead of reacting with respectful silence, Grant spewed forth more harsh opinions in public, telling one paper that "Garfield is a man without backbone; a man of fine ability, but lacking stamina."[8] He pushed things past the point of a rapprochement. Instead of relaxing in the afterglow of his round-the-world trip, Grant fell back into the peevish, crabbed mood of his embattled last days as president, berating Garfield at every turn. As the New York Evening Post observed, "The role of the 'silent man' became him much better."[9]

On July 2, Grant was staying at Fred's cabin in Long Branch, across from the hotel where Garfield's wife, Lucretia, stayed, when word arrived that Garfield had been shot in a Washington train station by Charles Guiteau, a mentally disturbed office seeker. Grant had kept an icy distance from Mrs. Garfield, merely tipping his hat when he passed her. "I do not think he can afford to show feeling in this way," Garfield had complained in his diary. "I am quite certain he injures himself more than he does me."[10] Suddenly Grant found himself in the uncomfortable position of having vilified a badly wounded president. Almost as soon as Lucretia Garfield learned of the shooting, Grant knocked at her door, entered quietly, and took her hand. According to one observer, Grant was "so overcome with emotion, he could scarcely speak."[11] Forgetting his spat with Garfield, Grant sought to comfort his wife with a telegram from Washington, asserting that the president would survive the shooting, and recounted how many soldiers in wartime recovered from comparable bullet wounds. Grateful for Grant's intervention, Lucretia Garfield later told Julia her husband had been among the first to express sorrow.[12] Grant also wired Secretary of War Robert T. Lincoln, "Express to the President My deep Sympathy & hope that he may speedily recover."[13] Lincoln replied that Garfield was "perfectly clear in mind and desires me to thank you for your telegram which I gave to him in sub-stance."[14] The next day Lincoln plied Grant with rosy telegrams, charting the president's cheerful temper and medical improvements.

It turned out that before he had stalked Garfield, Charles Guiteau had stalked Grant. The previous winter, when Grant stayed at the Fifth Avenue Ho-tel in Manhattan, Guiteau had sent up his card and attempted to visit his room. Fred Grant had warned his father that Guiteau was "a sort of lawyer and dead-beat in Chicago. Don't let him come up. If you do he will bore you to death."[15] Grant couldn't shake the entreaties of this uncouth stranger, who accosted him persistently in the street. Finally Guiteau trailed a waiter to his hotel room and knocked on his door. Thinking it a servant, Grant said, "Come in." He instantly recognized Guiteau, who "looked seedy and like a dead-beat," and reprimanded him. "I said I would not see you." "All I want is your name," Guiteau rejoined. "I don't want you to trouble to write anything at all." "But I don't know you," said Grant with annoyance, "and I won't give you my name for any purpose whatever."[16] A disappointed Guiteau slunk off, only to resurface as the presi-dent's assailant.

Three days after Garfield was shot, Grant gave a newspaper interview and commented on Garfield's condition with perhaps more truth than wisdom. At first he had been hopeful about the president's medical condition, then learned physicians couldn't locate the bullet. "I have known a great many cases of men shot very much in the same way where the ball was lodged where it could not be found," he said. "The men would rally after the shock and then suddenly change for the worse, contrary to the expectations of the patient and physicians and then die in a few hours." Realizing his words might depress the nation, not to mention Mrs. Garfield, Grant ended on a more upbeat note. "If the President should live two or three days longer with his strong constitution and absolutely correct habits, I should expect he would eventually recover."[17] He also said that, if he could see the bedridden president, he would gladly board the next train for Washington.

Profoundly dispirited by the shooting, Grant argued that it had "produced a shock upon the public mind but little less than that produced by the Assassination of Mr. Lincoln."[18] He noted that the Constitution made no provision for an incapacitated president and sensibly suggested that the cabinet should consider a report from physicians about Garfield's disability and, if necessary, deputize the vice president as temporary president. For much of July, as Garfield hung on, Grant felt more sanguine about his recovery, then revised his opinion toward the end of the month. "Now however I fear the chances are largely against" his recovery, he told Badeau.[19] He applauded a belated decision to evacuate Garfield from the White House in early September and bring him by train to Long Branch. "During the months of August and September the White House is one of the most unhealthy places in the world," Grant told the press. "He should have been taken from there long ago."[20]

Garfield's physician seriously mismanaged the treatment, repeatedly probing the wound without antiseptic conditions, and the president died on September 19. A shocked Grant received the news at his New York hotel. "You will please excuse me from a consideration of this sad news at this time," he told a reporter. "It comes with terrible force and is unexpected."[21] Withdrawing to a private office, Grant wept such bitter tears that Fred Grant said "he had never known him to be so terribly affected."[22] It must have tormented Grant that he would never have a chance to heal the breach with Garfield, and he was probably reminded of the many death threats he himself had received during his presidency.

Garfield's death lifted Chester Arthur—scorned as Conkling's puppet with muttonchop whiskers—into the presidency. The Half-Breed press poured out its loathing for Arthur, who had stayed incommunicado as the president lay dying. Grant was scandalized by the "shameful and villainous manner" in which Arthur was slandered as "a monster . . . I know him to be a man of common sense and clear-headed, with good associates—a man of integrity."[23] When Grant attended Garfield's funeral, he followed Chester Arthur in the procession.

With Arthur's rise to the presidency, Grant found his influence reinstated at

the White House and was instrumental in the appointment of Frederick T. Frelinghuysen as secretary of state. Arthur seemed receptive to Grant's suggestions
and honored him with a dinner in March 1882. That same month he nominated
John Russell Young as minister to China. Then, without warning, Arthur asserted his independence from Grant and Conkling, becoming a proponent of
civil service reform. When he named William E. Chandler as secretary of the
navy—a man who had staunchly opposed Grant's third term—Grant's relations
with Arthur began to unravel. Although Arthur named him to negotiate a commercial treaty with Mexico and Grant accepted, he inwardly seethed that Arthur sought to allay his anger in this way. As Badeau recalled, Grant found in
Chester Arthur "a bearing more imperious than he thought necessary or appropriate in the new President toward the old."[24] At bottom, Grant's problem with
Arthur, as with Garfield, was that he couldn't relinquish his old hold on Washington or accept his diminished authority. The man who had felt so powerless in
his early years had acquired a taste for power and refused to quit the high-stakes
game of politics.

The practical details of Grant's future lay shrouded in uncertainty. He felt
the potent lure of New York City and its manifold opportunities, but noted the
prohibitive cost of living in the metropolis. Financial worries also beset Julia,
who had indulged in a gargantuan shopping spree on the global tour. The Grants
had spent the previous winter at the Fifth Avenue Hotel, even though they could
scarcely afford this grand establishment. "With an income of less than six thousand dollars per annum," wrote Julia, "we found it difficult to meet even the very
liberal terms made for us by the proprietor of the Fifth Avenue."[25]

Luckily for Grant, wealthy financiers were outraged that their hero lacked
the necessary funds for a proper retirement. A group of Wall Street admirers
created for Grant a $250,000 Presidential Retiring Fund, which would not only
yield $15,000 in annual interest but reinforce his image as overly beholden to the
rich. To supplement his income, Grant returned to his scheme for a Mexican
railway system and sketched out his blueprint at a fancy dinner at Delmonico's
in lower Manhattan, organized by his friend Matías Romero, the Mexican minister, and attended by twenty railroad tycoons. For Grant, his vision of a railway
network in Mexico dovetailed with his wish to deepen U.S.-Mexican relations.
Within a month he chaired a committee on the subject that included Collis P.
Huntington, Grenville Dodge, and Jay Gould, representing leading railway interests. Through Grant's influence, William Waldorf Astor introduced a bill in

the New York legislature to incorporate the Mexican Southern Railroad, with Grant, Gould, Porfirio Díaz, and Romero among its charter subscribers. Railroads already under way would connect the United States with Mexico City and the new venture would run additional lines south from the Mexican capital, extending to Central and even South America, along with east-west lines to the Gulf of Mexico and the Pacific.

In late March 1881, Grant gathered Julia, Buck and his pretty new bride, Fannie Josephine Chaffee, and Matías Romero and set out for Mexico to hammer out a contract for the new railroad, whose president he had become. Stopping off in Galveston, Texas, he admitted to a reporter that Jay Gould was a stockholder in the new company whose roads would radiate northward and intersect with Gould's railway empire. It seems strange that Grant, having been bamboozled by Gould in the Gold Corner scheme of 1869, should have entered into a business venture with him. By year's end, Grant boasted, fifty thousand workers would labor on new Mexican railways. Speaking at a Mexico City banquet in late April, he emphasized that his railway proposals would cement relations between the United States and Mexico, which "should be the warmest of friends, and enjoy the closest commercial relations."[26] By May 11, he had extracted a concession from the government for the Mexican Southern Railroad and returned home a voluble booster of the project. "The road will be in all about 700 miles long," he told one newspaper, "running from the City of Mexico through Pueblo [*sic*] to the Pacific Coast, while another branch runs down to the gulf."[27] Unfortunately, the railroad fared poorly, encountering numerous delays and setbacks.

By the time Grant got home, he could no longer evade the pressing question of where he would settle after four years of an unsettled life. Spending the summer in Long Branch, he expanded and refurbished the house to accommodate his grandchildren, then moved to New York City in the fall, where he hoped to engage "in some occupation giving me a good income."[28] To have a Manhattan residence was a decision that exposed Grant to the temptations of the Gilded Age metropolis, an atmosphere in which he could easily lose his moral bearings. Even blessed with bountiful gifts from rich benefactors, Grant couldn't afford a New York home and George Childs spearheaded yet another syndicate of donors who gave Grant $100,000 for a residence. When Childs and Anthony Drexel appeared at the Fifth Avenue Hotel and presented the Grants with this handsome gift, Julia wasn't fazed by their largesse: "So I was to have a beautiful home,

all my own, and how happy I was all that summer looking for a house and selecting paper, furniture, etc."[29]

The Grants made payment on a spacious four-story brownstone at 3 East
Sixty-Sixth Street, only steps from Fifth Avenue, its bay windows jutting out to
afford a view of Central Park, with a $98,000 price tag. "It was a much larger
and a more expensive house than we had intended (or had the means) to buy, but
it was so new and sweet and large that this quite outweighed our more pruden-
tial scruples," Julia wrote.[30] On September 29, 1881, the Grants occupied the
sparsely furnished house—their possessions filtered in piecemeal in the coming
weeks—and Fred and Ida and their two children formed part of the household.
The new home would be richly furnished, stuffed with trophies collected abroad
and assorted items shipped from the Galena house—"handsome parlor books,
an old brass bell, wooden sword rack, large black lacquer box . . . two flower
vases of silver bronze and cut glass," as Grant itemized them.[31] He had landed in
a world where he was bound to feel poor but entitled to be rich. In her memoirs,
Julia rejoiced at their warm reception at "the palaces on Fifth Avenue" and commented upon "how regally New York entertains. In our journey around the
world I saw nothing that excelled them in magnificence of elegance."[32]

The recipient of two generous gifts, Grant still felt a financial pinch and a
trace of bitterness that the presidency had impoverished him—the reason he
never expressed remorse about accepting gifts from rich admirers. In his mind,
private munificence had compensated him for public sacrifice. In refusing to
help a young friend obtain a government post, he made the telling remark that
"the worst thing that can be done for a young man is to get him a Government
position. Such places only give a man a mere support while he holds it, and un-
fits him for the battle of life when he is discharged."[33] Unable to retire on a presidential pension and having sacrificed his military pension to enter politics, he
discreetly supported efforts to restore him to the retired army roster with the
rank and pay of general. This proved a surprisingly hard sell in Congress, especially when the hefty gifts to him were publicized. As the Missouri senator George
Vest remarked, Grant was "surrounded by wealthy connections, living luxuri-
ously in the city of New York, and possessed, besides other fortune, of the income from $250,000 donated to him by the public."[34]

Perhaps reacting to the monetary drawbacks of government service, Grant's
sons had gravitated to the private sector. In 1881 Fred resigned his army commission to become president of a Texas railroad. Jesse, who had married Elizabeth

Chapman, joined the produce business with Fred's brother-in-law Henry H. Honoré Jr. and soon prospered enough to become a member of the American Yacht Club. At least materially, the most successful offspring was Buck, who had graduated from Exeter, Harvard College, and Columbia Law School, acted as his father's White House secretary, then served as assistant U.S. attorney for the Southern District of New York. With his broad, handsome face and handlebar mustache, he bore a striking resemblance to his father. So winning was his nature that a White House reporter described him as "a modest, retiring lad, as sensitive and kindly as a girl . . . so sensitive that a cross word was more of a punishment to him than a severe chastisement would be to most boys."[35]

Starting with the Comstock Lode, Buck had dabbled in speculative mining ventures, especially after marrying the daughter of the former Colorado senator Jerome B. Chaffee, who had reaped a fortune in banking and mining stocks. Grant reposed such trust in Buck that he had given him power of attorney and allowed him to handle his investments during his absence abroad. Buck seemed to thrive in the business world. By October 1881, when he was only twenty-nine, he became squire of a two-hundred-acre farm in Westchester with a twenty-one-room house and nearly one hundred head of horses and cattle. Grant had such implicit faith in Buck's business sagacity that he boasted he was "a man of some means, gathered by his own exertions."[36] Grant evinced a trust in all his sons, but especially Buck, who, like his father, seemed incapable of guile.

Buck entered into a partnership with a young financier named Ferdinand Ward and the stout, balding James D. Fish, president of the Marine National Bank. So bold and electrifying were Ward's forays on Wall Street that Buck, who left all business dealings to Ward, imagined he had amassed a $400,000 stake under his tutelage. Ulysses S. Grant had always avoided ethical shortcuts and never lent his prestige to business ventures, denying several efforts to name him president of sundry mining operations. But swayed by his tender confidence in Buck, on November 1, 1880, he entered into a partnership with him and Fish and Ferdinand Ward. Buck added $100,000 to his earlier investment, while Grant and his son Jesse chipped in $50,000 apiece. Grant expected to live comfortably off its income for many years. Later it turned out that James Fish hadn't contributed a penny in cash to the firm and Ward had bought his share with worthless securities. In other words, the entire working capital for Grant & Ward came from the Grants, who seemed to have a congenital weakness for confidence men. Before Ward's larceny was over, Fred Grant would contribute

nearly $1.5 million of his own money. Amazingly Grant's many disappoint-
ments with business partners and treacherous White House appointees had not
sharpened his instinct for fraud. Once again he would prove an incurably naive
man, defeated by his own fundamental decency.

Though he allowed his name to be exploited by a business for the first time,
Grant engaged in shockingly little study of the operation. He didn't review
transactions, leaving that to the supposed wizardry of young Ward. Instead he
functioned as so much high-priced decoration to lure in the carriage trade. One
last time he was touched by a tragic blindness. He never had a lawyer scrutinize
the agreement, seemed hazy on its details, and thought he was a limited partner
rather than a general partner with full liability if anything went wrong. Grant's
Mexican railway venture was also housed at 2 Wall Street and the association
immeasurably enhanced Ferdinand Ward's stature in the financial district.

In trading securities and commodities at Grant & Ward, Ferdinand Ward
enjoyed unlimited power. Only he was allowed to sign checks, manage the
books, and run the firm, using Grant's name as window dressing. Just twenty-
nine, but already lionized as the Young Napoleon of Finance, Ward had fair
hair, blue eyes, rosy cheeks, and a charming manner. A pathological narcissist,
he had no concern for anyone but himself. Cool and unflappable, he had the
psychopath's ability to counterfeit sincerity and present the exact image other
people wanted to see. Such was the hypnotic spell he cast that Ohio senator Allen Thurman had labeled him America's "most successful financier" and predicted the next president "would make a stupendous blunder if he did not make
Ferdinand Ward Secretary of the Treasury."[37]

Like many greedy personalities, Ward grew up in a threadbare home, steeped
in piety, in upstate New York, his parents having served as missionaries in India.
His father, a strict Presbyterian minister, inveighed against alcohol, gambling,
and "Popery." His mother was a morbidly self-pitying woman who steeled her
children against worldly temptations. "Ferdie" felt stifled by his father's religious
dogmatism and the family austerity. After moving to New York City in 1873, he
clerked at the Produce Exchange and learned to trade commodity futures. He
married a rich young woman from Brooklyn Heights whose father was a director
of the Marine National Bank, catapulting him into the tony sphere to which he
aspired. When his father-in-law died, Ward became coexecutor of his estate and
began to bilk his widowed mother-in-law. He also purloined money from the
Sunday school of the Church of the Pilgrims, where he acted as treasurer.[38] With

four Irish maids, a French chef, and rich artwork displayed in his home, Ward projected an air of bourgeois respectability and the Grant connection gave him the ideal camouflage for his larceny.

When Grant arrived for his first day at Grant & Ward, he pulled up in a carriage, entered the building arm in arm with Buck, and was swallowed up by an enormous throng of well-wishers. He thrust out his hand to greet Ferdinand Ward. "No one can realize the feeling of pride with which I greeted him, not only as a friend but as a partner," Ward said.[39] The young flimflam man studied his famous victim with scientific care, noting that Grant went to church regularly, deplored off-color stories, and largely abstained from alcohol: "He very seldom touched any liquor except ale, and he drank that sparingly and at rare intervals."[40] Ward made sure to have twenty-five of Grant's favorite cigars ready whenever he stopped by the office. Twice a week, he traveled uptown to join Grant's poker games. "I have known [Grant] to go to bed with a heavy Havana in his mouth, put out the lights and continue smoking for a time in the dark," he recalled. "He would never finish this nightcap cigar, but when it was about half done he would put it somewhere, where it might be reached easily in the morning."[41]

Ward sized up Grant as a "child in business matters" who would never be able to uncover his deceptions.[42] The firm paid Grant $2,000 monthly for living expenses and Ward funneled extra money to him as needed. Grant associates who invested with Ward walked away with dazzling profits. One friend invested $50,000, disappeared for six months on a European vacation, then came home to a whopping $250,000 check. As others reaped 15 percent to 20 percent profits per *month,* a mania to invest with Grant & Ward overtook Wall Street. The stupendous returns dulled investor curiosity about how these exorbitant returns were earned and dozens of Union veterans poured in money on the strength of Grant's name alone.

Going for broke, Ward quizzed Grant about other family members who might like to invest. "He questioned me about the outlying kin, and wherever he found a member of it that had saved up something in a stocking he sent for it and got it," Grant later said. "In one case, a poor old female relative of mine had scrimped and saved until she had something like a thousand dollars laid up for the rainy day of old age. Ward took it without a pang."[43] Far from being suspicious, Grant showered gifts upon his marvelous young partner, filling his home with exotic mementos—leopard skins, Japanese swords, hand-painted bamboo screens—culled from his global tour. Ward loved to flash a pocketknife engraved with the letters "U.S. Grant," custom made for the ex-president in Sheffield, England. So intertwined were their lives that Grant even kept a pair of Thoroughbred horses in Ward's stables.

Grant sternly lectured Ward that if the firm ever engaged in government business, he would terminate the partnership: "I having been President of the United States was not willing that my name should be connected at all with any such transactions."[44] When Buck advised Ward to avoid government contracts, "he said my father's honor was as dear to him as it was to me."[45] Buck and Fred Grant knew about the supposed government contracts, although their father remained in a state of blissful innocence. Whenever investors quizzed Ward about his mysteriously astronomical profits, he intimated that he had large government contracts for wheat or hay and hinted at the secret influence of Grant or President Arthur.[46] In this way, Ward purveyed an image of Grant not as an upstanding former president but as a swindling politician with a hand in procuring government deals. In fact, no government contracts existed and Ward used these fictitious transactions to extract more loans to feed his bottomless greed.

Ferdinand Ward operated what would later be termed a Ponzi scheme, paying off old investors with money from new ones. Violating every principle of sound finance, he piled up staggering debt, using the same securities as collateral for multiple loans. All the while, Grant acted as his unwitting dupe. Ward alone had access to securities in the firm's vault. Every day, Grant arrived punctually at ten o'clock and enjoyed the firm's success without devoting any time to business details. Either Ward or the chief clerk slapped letters in front of him, which he often signed without bothering to read. He signed one letter implying he knew of speculation in government contracts and sanctioned the use of his name. When James Fish asked how the firm was doing, Grant raved about its success. "'I think we have made more money during the past year than any other house in Wall Street, perhaps in the city.' He said Ward was the ablest young businessman he ever saw." Fish then asked Grant "whether he had ever examined the books of the firm. He said no; he had only looked over the monthly statements, which were satisfactory to him."[47] Grant's complacency was shocking. He seemed to think it perfectly normal that gigantic sums of money should fall from the sky without any effort on his part, even though family and friends had invested their life savings with Grant & Ward on the basis of his involvement.

No less gullible was Buck, who had his law office at 2 Wall Street. Ward rebuffed any snooping by Buck into the firm's internal workings. "I was reduced to doing nothing," Buck confessed. "I was sort of a customer of the firm."[48] For those who watched skeptically, there was something disturbingly vague and unreal about Grant & Ward's success. Grant would boast about the extravagant returns, not the way in which they were made. He traveled in a world of Gilded Age financiers who routinely made fortunes in short order and felt himself a lucky newcomer to this privileged class. Although Julia had queasy feelings about Ward, her husband reflexively defended his young partner. "Mother," he advised her, "I'd give anything in this world if our boys were as smart as that young Ward."[49] He told Julia not to worry about setting aside money for their children's future. "Ward is making us all rich—them as well as ourselves."[50] The general who had impressed Abraham Lincoln and vanquished Robert E. Lee was powerless to defend himself before the infinite wiles of a shameless young trickster. As Mark Twain later remarked, "It was the unimpeachable credit and respectability of [Grant's] name that enabled [Fish and Ward] to swindle the public. They could not have done it on their own reputations."[51]

On May 11, 1883, Hannah Simpson Grant died in New Jersey. She went as quietly as she had lived, having maintained a mostly independent existence and refused to exploit her son's fame. She hadn't been estranged from Ulysses's life, but certainly detached. In advising the pastor at the funeral, Grant said he should "speak of her only as a pure-minded, simple-hearted, earnest, Methodist Christian; make no reference to me; she gained nothing by any position I have filled or honors that may have been paid me. I owe . . . all that I am to her earnest, modest and sincere piety."[52]

On August 30, the rotund Grant, who had bulked up to two hundred pounds, embarked on a three-week train excursion across the country to celebrate completion of the Northern Pacific Railway. Thirty years earlier, as a young officer, he had helped to outfit an expedition to survey the railway. Now he would hammer in the golden spike uniting two wings of the road and lay the cornerstone for the new capitol at Bismarck in Dakota Territory. With his continental perspective, Grant had toured virtually every state and territory; no other nineteenth-century president traveled so widely or glimpsed so much of the country. As his train sped west, he was astonished that every ten or fifteen miles, the spire of another church or schoolhouse pierced the sky. To Nellie he described the many cities with "horse cars, streets lit with gas, daily papers, and large hotels . . . making it possible to drive from one end of the [rail]road to the other . . . without camping out a single night."[53]

Never again did Grant undertake such an arduous journey. On Christmas Eve, he returned home after midnight from dinner with friends. After alighting from the cab, he turned to give his driver a Christmas tip and stumbled on the icy pavement. He may have fractured his left hip or torn a thigh muscle and he was confined to bed for several weeks. Days later pleurisy set in, headaches flared up, he was troubled by boils and bedsores, and he suffered insomnia. Through it all, he remained stoical and uncomplaining, even as visitors noticed a profound alteration in him. "He had grown very old-looking," recalled General George Stannard, "and his face looked as though some great sorrow had befallen him."[54] By February, he moved about the house on crutches, despite rheumatism in his legs, and felt well enough to grouse that he opposed Chester Arthur's renomination for president, preferring his old Stalwart comrade John Logan.

In March 1884, at the behest of doctors, Grant went with Julia to Old Point Comfort, Virginia, hoping warm weather and physical therapy would alleviate his condition. Later in the month, he traveled to Washington, held court at a local hotel, and received a parade of political visitors. When he ventured a surprise visit to the House of Representatives, a recess was called so that members could pump his hand. Still the symbol of North-South reconciliation, he entertained a delegation of black soldiers and sailors and lent his prestige to a new home for disabled Confederate veterans. Though still lame, Grant summoned up the strength to address veterans of the Grand Army of the Republic before heading back to New York City.

For all his medical troubles, Grant luxuriated in freedom from financial care. As Badeau recalled, "He told me that in December for the first time in his life he had a bank account from which he could draw as freely as he desired," and he liberally dispensed gifts to his children.[55] In this hopeful mood, Grant sketched out in an interview a rosy view of America's future, with the population booming to one hundred million and manufacturing surging in the South. He reserved fond words for his adopted city: "New York City will . . . retain her ascendancy over all other places in the country, and I expect the people living at the end of the present century will see New York the financial center of the world."[56] Much of this optimism arose from Grant's continuing delight with Ferdinand Ward, whose wife, Ella, gave birth in March 1884 to a boy named

Ferdinand Grant Ward. When a friend warned that Ward's profits were suspect, Grant didn't care to listen and pooh-poohed such pedestrian caution. "These are able and experienced businessmen who are engaged with Ward. They would not be likely to take part in any foolish scheme."[57]

On his journey through life, Grant had survived many toils and snares and been betrayed by false friends, but his innocent belief in people, inherited from Hannah, was now to suffer one final crushing blow. He would have benefitted from an atom of his father's cynicism. For three months, Ward had secretly raced about town, borrowing money from four big trust companies to stave off financial disaster. In this frenetic state, he grew pallid and thin. On Sunday afternoon May 4, he unexpectedly visited Grant at East Sixty-Sixth Street and disgorged a woeful tale of how the Marine National Bank had run into trouble and might fail, threatening the $660,000 Grant & Ward held there. To avert this and give the bank time to collect its loans, Ward appealed to Grant to raise $150,000 that would be repaid within twenty-four hours. "I know the General can borrow it if anyone can," Ward asserted.[58] In reality, Ward was rushing to rescue Grant & Ward itself, which owed $1.3 million to the Marine National Bank, premised on fictitious collateral. Of such knowledge, Grant was as innocent as a child.

Still hobbling on crutches, he agreed to see William H. Vanderbilt and plead with him for $150,000. The son of Commodore Vanderbilt, and heir to a vast railroad empire, William was a heavyset man with flaring sideburns. Unlike Grant, he paid dutiful attention to business. At first Grant balked at borrowing from Vanderbilt, afraid he wouldn't be repaid at once. But Ward insisted that Grant would simply be swapping guaranteed checks with Vanderbilt. Grabbing his crutches, Grant escorted Ward and Buck to Vanderbilt's palatial Fifth Avenue residence. Receiving the group in his ornate home, Vanderbilt was startled by their request. He had never done such a thing before, he said, but he revered Grant and handed him a check for $150,000. In exchange, Grant gave him a Grant & Ward check with the proviso that he not cash it for a day or two. With Vanderbilt's check in hand, Ward assured Grant everything was now fine. The former two-term president and hero of the Civil War had been reduced to an errand boy for a young charlatan. When a friend called on him that evening, Grant was in a cheerful mood and invited him to attend a poker game that Tuesday night. "Ward is certainly coming, and the party is made," he declared.[59]

The next day, a frantic Ward beseeched Buck to secure another $500,000 loan from William Vanderbilt: "I am very much afraid that the end has come and that, unless something is done to-night, everything will be over to-morrow . . . This is our last hope, Buck, so do all you can."[60] New York City had pulled $1 million from its Marine National account and the bank couldn't call in loans fast enough to cover the withdrawal. Ward had borrowed and written enormous checks on the bank, despite having nothing substantial on deposit there. The Marine National suffered a shortfall of nearly $1 million with the Clearing House. Armed with a satchel full of cash and securities, which he hoped to use as collateral for a large rescue loan, James D. Fish hastened to the bank association "acting like a man dazed with fright."[61] But his desperate move was insufficient to paper over the yawning deficit. On Tuesday, May 6, when the Marine National Bank closed, angry depositors swarmed outside its padlocked doors, desperate to retrieve their money. As a general partner of Grant & Ward, Fish next made his way to Brooklyn Heights, where Ella Ward told him Ferdie was too tired to see him. Fish brusquely shoved her aside and mounted the stairs only to discover that Ward had slipped out a basement door. Anticipating the collapse of his scheme, Ward had made over the deed of the house to his wife.

Around noon on May 6, Ulysses S. Grant arrived at 2 Wall Street with the serene confidence of a self-styled millionaire who thought he had reaped fabulous profits from his investment. He found a growing crowd mingling on the sidewalk in a strange hubbub of excitement. After entering, Grant moved steadily on his crutches toward Ward's office, an unlit cigar in his mouth. In a gesture that must have mystified him, people doffed their hats when they saw him. He was promptly intercepted by Buck, who blurted out, "Father, you had better go home. The bank has failed."[62] Grant was stunned, having had no forewarning of the disaster. When Badeau arrived, he found his dazed patron sitting alone. "We are all ruined here," Grant announced. "The bank has failed. Mr. Ward cannot be found. The securities are locked up in the safe, and he has the key. No one knows where he is."[63] A shattered Grant conferred with Roscoe Conkling, looking "weary and troubled," a reporter wrote.[64]

Grant expected Ward to materialize with a soothing explanation, but the young man had vanished and Grant took refuge in his upstairs office. He summoned the cashier George Spencer, who brought out ledgers that had recorded Grant & Ward's phantom profits. "Spencer," Grant asked, grasping his armchair, "how is it that man has deceived us all in this way?" The cashier could not elucidate for Grant the mystery of human nature. "I don't see how I can ever trust any human being again," Grant said, sinking his face in his hands.[65] The whole operation had been a monstrous hoax. As a Marine National director concluded, "The transactions of Grant & Ward constituted the most colossal swindle of the age."[66] Enlightenment came too late for Ulysses S. Grant, who left his Wall Street office for the last time at 2:15 p.m., offering no comment to waiting reporters. "I cannot deny or corroborate the reports current," Buck told them. "We are nearly $500,000 short. Our safes are locked and until we can find Mr. Ward I cannot say how we stand."[67] It was a damaging admission: Buck and his father lacked access to the firm's own safe, which they had assumed bulged with $1.3 million in blue-chip securities. As unsophisticated, in the last analysis, as his father, Buck kept reiterating to him that "Ferd would come out right yet; he had no doubt he would come out right."[68]

When Grant took a streetcar uptown, he ran into his old friend James B. Fry, whom he had invited to his poker party that evening. "We will not have the meeting I fixed for tonight," he informed Fry. "I have bad news." "Why, general," said Fry, "I hope it is nothing serious." "Yes," Grant said, "the Marine Bank has failed or is about to fail. It owes our firm a large amount, and I suppose we are ruined. When I went downtown this morning I thought I was worth a great deal of money, now I don't know that I have a dollar; and probably my sons, too, have lost everything."[69]

Grant was correct. He and his three sons had plowed their life savings into the criminal venture. Instead of being worth $1 million, Grant was suddenly worth $80 and Julia $130. The magical profits had evaporated overnight. In the coming days, as evidence of Ward's giant fraud emerged, Grant discovered that checks he had given to him for deposit in the Marine National Bank had been diverted into Ward's own bank account. Similarly, the rapacious Ward had taken money from Grant for railroad bonds that were never bought, even as Grant's bank books registered punctual dividend payments. The final reckoning revealed the wholesale looting of hapless clients: the firm owed investors $16,792,647 against a paltry $68,174.30 in assets.[70]

The day after it went bust, the Young Napoleon of Finance, in a paroxysm of weeping, hand-wringing hysterics, confessed his sins to Ulysses and Buck Grant. In later testimony, Buck said Ward broke down and admitted he had been "a wicked thief and a great rascal" who had cheated the Grant family from the outset. Grant then told Ward "that the least he could do would be to tell the truth in the matter. Ward promised to do so."[71] Just when he least expected it, the wheel of fortune had thrown Grant back into a forgotten world of hardship, reminiscent of prewar days. Dazed and stunned, he receded into a defeated solitude. When James Fish confronted Ward, he was far less patient than Grant. "I advised him to go and commit suicide," Fish said. "Drown himself, hang himself."[72] Fish unpacked a string of expletives, cursing Ward as "a miserable dirty reptile," then picked up a chair and threatened to smash it over his head. Ward "crouched down on the floor at my feet and held up his hands and whined like a puppy."[73]

The honorable Grant agonized over the $150,000 Grant & Ward had borrowed from William H. Vanderbilt. The day after the firm's failure, he went to Vanderbilt to convey to him title to his East Sixty-Sixth Street house. In a profound act of contrition, the ruined ex-president was ready to transfer his worldly possessions to one of America's richest men. Vanderbilt accepted Grant's East Sixty-Sixth Street residence on condition that the Grants stay there. He also decided that, after Grant died, he would take the swords, medals, trophies, and memorabilia Grant had gathered from the Civil War and his round-the-world trip and donate them to the federal government. Grant even deeded to Vanderbilt ownership of his St. Louis property. Meanwhile the push was renewed in Congress to place Grant on the retired army list with the rank and pay of general of the army.

For the moment, the Grants were flat broke, and, when they paid the domestic help, the checks bounced. By a grim irony, Grant couldn't collect anything from the $250,000 trust fund bestowed upon him by rich businessmen because the money had been invested by Ward in the bonds of a defaulted company. "We are all paupers now," Grant said bluntly as he and Julia awoke from their highfalutin dreamworld of riches.[74] "Imagine the shock to us," wrote Julia, "who thought we were independently wealthy."[75] The Grants returned to a state of misery they thought they had long ago escaped. Reeling from the shock, Grant succumbed to a murderous rage, recalled former senator Chaffee. "The General would suffer for hours in his large arm chair, clutching nervously with his hands at the arm-rests, driving his finger-nails into the hard wood . . . One day he said to me, 'Chaffee, I would kill Ward, as I would a snake. I believe I should do it, too, but I do not wish to be hanged for the killing of such a wretch.'"[76] Beyond financial hardship, Grant cringed with embarrassment at having been duped by Ward. He avoided society and stopped reading newspapers to spare himself the rage.

The business luminaries who had championed Grant now seemed to desert him and he had to scrounge for basic necessities. Had it not been for the kindness of a stranger and a foreigner he wouldn't have been able to pay household bills. His trusted Mexican friend Matías Romero came and offered a $1,000 loan that Grant rebuffed; in response, Romero simply walked out of the room, leaving the check on the table. Romero estimated that Grant had only $18 left. Out of the blue, a veteran named Charles Wood, manager of a brush factory in upstate New York, sent Grant a $500 check and offered him a $1,000 interest-free loan for a year, renewable if necessary. Grant accepted this charity with everlasting relief. In his note, Wood tipped his hat to Grant by saying the payment was "for services ending about April 1865."[77]

The ruin was general for the Grant family. Convinced he would be enriched quickly, Fred had borrowed heavily to invest with Ward and now stood $500,000 in debt. His daughter long remembered her father coming home pale and troubled and retiring to an upstairs bedroom with her mother. "Her cry of surprise and distress rang out, and then loud questions and quiet replies floated to the hall below, where we children sat, frightened."[78] Creditors foreclosed on their house, forcing them into cheaper lodgings in Morristown, New Jersey. Jesse had deposited all of his savings with Grant & Ward, some the day before the failure, and he too was wiped out. Across the Atlantic, Nellie suffered losses and not only because she had sacrificed her $12,000 investment with Ward. For two years, Grant had been sending her remittances for the children. "When the General became impoverished through the rascality of Ferdinand Ward," wrote one newspaper, he regretted "that his poverty would prevent him from assisting Nellie, who was practically supported by his bounty."[79] Even one of Grant's sisters and a nephew lost their investments in Grant & Ward.

Among Grant's children, Buck, who had imagined he was worth $1.7 million, was perhaps the most visible casualty. Hypnotized by Ward's legerdemain, he had invested income from his wife's fortune in the firm and borrowed money from his rich father-in-law that he could never repay. "So confident were we all that Grant & Ward were making piles of money that we invested everything we could get," he told a journalist.[80] After the failure, newspapers reported that Buck had fled to Canada to evade the law. When a reporter went to East Sixty-Sixth Street for confirmation, the stout Julia materialized in a black satin dress, her face flushed, her eyes bright with indignation. "Why should my son go to Canada?" she asked. "Why should he be afraid of being arrested? Why should anybody want to arrest him? Is my son a thief?" Tears stood in her eyes. "You have the thief under arrest," she said bitterly, "the man who has robbed and ruined us."[81]

As Grant shrank from the garish glare of unwanted publicity, the humiliation was excruciating. He had been employed as bait to attract victims to Ward's machinations, dealing a savage blow to his renown. "For the love of money," wrote the *New York Sun,* "the greatest military reputation of our time has been dimmed and degraded by its possessor."[82] Grant was exposed as the same hapless hayseed who had bungled business deals in his early years. One newspaper editorial noted that the imaginary government contracts obtained by Grant & Ward were instrumental in Ward's deceiving gullible investors: "The conclusion is inescapable that a large number of persons were drawn into the maelstrom by a belief that Gen. Grant's influence was used in some highly improper way, to the detriment of the government and the benefit of Grant & Ward."[83] Some in the Democratic press called for Grant's criminal prosecution and even some Republicans saw him as less a victim of fraud than an accomplice. An especially critical perspective issued privately from Sherman, who couldn't resist gloating over Grant's downfall, as if his friend's life were a morality play whose sorry ending he had long foreseen. "Look at *Grant* now," he wrote. "His experience in the White House poisoned his mind, and tempted his family to yearn for that Sort of honor."[84]

At the same time there emerged an immense outpouring of sympathy for Grant. He was still America's most famous man, the remarkable general who had won the war for Lincoln, protected the freed slaves, and kept America at peace during his presidency. *The Washington Post* expressed some of this compassion: "Compared with the distinguished services he has rendered, his faults are not to be considered. If he had possessed a broader but keener aptitude for business, he might never have been duped by a Wall Street adventurer; but the fact of his misfortunes in one direction can never eclipse the brilliancy of his successes in another."[85]

The demise of Grant & Ward had widespread repercussions. The stock market plunged, two banks shut down, and seven brokerage houses failed. On May 26, James Fish was arrested and, when released on bail, tried futilely to shift blame to his partners. Ferdinand Ward, arrested on May 21, described to a federal grand jury the inner operation of the scheme, telling how "he simply borrowed from Peter to pay Paul."[86] He fully exonerated Grant from complicity: "He knew nothing. He took my word. He had the same information the customers had—and he had the same happiness, while it lasted."[87] Ward was eager to blame his victims, who had lacked even minimal curiosity and never asked to see the government contracts he allegedly obtained. He was completely coldhearted about the ruin he had visited upon scores of people: "They were so pleased with the show of big profits that they were only too glad to have their apparent winnings pyramided."[88] Incapable of remorse, the delusional Ward maintained until his death that he had sought to protect Grant instead of ruining him. As late as 1910, he said, "I believe General Grant . . . knew that . . . I did not rob the firm, but rather that I did everything in my power to save it from downfall. He was a just man, and no matter how he might have suffered, I believe he was fair in his judgment of me and realized what a burden I had carried along for those years."[89]

//////////////////////////

Taps

G RANT HAD REFRAINED from following the example of other Civil War generals who published their memoirs with a haste he found preening and self-aggrandizing. He disliked talking about himself and professed that he lacked the literary ability and industry to hazard such a venture. "Oh, I'm not going to write any book," he told a reporter after leaving the White House. "There are books enough already."[1] The *Century Magazine,* which planned a series of articles entitled "Battles and Leaders of the Civil War," sought Grant's participation, but in January 1884 he vowed that "I have no idea of undertaking the task of writing any of the articles the Century requests."[2] With the collapse of Grant & Ward, the *Century* editors revived their offer to have him write on his battles, noting that the "country looks with so much re-gret and sympathy upon General Grant's misfortune."[3] Though touched by their concern for his plight, Grant resisted the invitation to oblige them.

With their finances in ruins, the Grants closed up the East Sixty-Sixth Street house and took up summer residence in Long Branch. The household staff had been dismissed and Julia, knocked from her high perch, was reduced to cooking in the twenty-eight-room cottage. On June 2, Grant swallowed a peach and suf-fered excruciating pain—the episode related at the start of this narrative. "He walked up and down the room and out to the piazza, and rinsed his throat again and again," Julia recalled.[4] Mystified, she thought an insect must have lodged in the peach. At first, Grant minimized a chronic sore throat that he had, but when the pain intensified in July, his next-door neighbor, George Childs, suggested he consult a Philadelphia doctor named Jacob Mendez Da Costa who was then visiting him. When he examined Grant, he discovered a growth on the roof of his mouth, prescribed pain medication, and advised Grant to consult his family physician, Dr. B. Fordyce Barker, as soon as possible. Barker was then on a European trip, which allowed Grant to stall for several months before seeing him. Was this another example of Grant's lifelong stoicism or a childlike escape from frightening news?

Weak and lame, still on crutches, Grant knew he needed to repair his finances and agreed to a visit from a *Century* editor. The magazine dispatched thirty-one-year-old Robert Underwood Johnson, who found Grant garbed in a curious outfit for a warm summer day. Because of his sore throat, he had wrapped a cape around his shoulders and a white silk scarf around his neck—details that would assume new significance in retrospect. Grant talked about his perilous financial state, venting anger at Ferdinand Ward. "In his direct and simple fashion," Johnson wrote, "he reviewed the *debacle* of his fortunes without restraint, showing deep feeling, even bitterness, as to his betrayal."[5] As Johnson listened and discovered Grant's sensitive nature, he mentally likened him to "a wounded lion."[6] Once he had cleansed himself of anger, Grant got down to business. "He told me, frankly and simply," wrote Johnson, "that he had arrived at Long Branch almost penniless."[7] In the end, Grant agreed to write four articles—on Shiloh, Vicksburg, the Wilderness, and Appomattox—for $500 apiece. Later on he decided to dispense with Lee's surrender in favor of the battle of Chattanooga.

Largely secluded in the house, Grant set up a white wooden table in a room facing the seaside porch and it soon became cluttered with maps, books, and military papers. By the end of June, Grant had completed his first article on Shiloh, but it sorely disappointed the *Century* editors. Written in Grant's pithy style, it was arid and compact and read like a bloodless report. Johnson hurried over to Long Branch for a pep talk with his new writer. A gifted editor, he drew Grant into personal reminiscences about Shiloh and made him see the difference between a dry recitation and one enlivened by personal impressions. This came as a revelation to Grant, who was an apt pupil and promised to start anew. As he did so, he felt a spurt of liberating energy. "Why, I am positively enjoying the work," he told Johnson. "I am keeping at it every night and day, and Sundays."[8] Under Johnson's tutelage, Grant discovered new dimensions to his writing, disclosing a huge literary gift that had lurked there all along.

Nothing if not dogged, Grant marched on to Vicksburg, averaging more than four hours of writing per day, one visitor recalling Grant's pen "racing over his pad."[9] Encouraged by Johnson to describe events more freely, he went from excessive concision to a more richly detailed style, completing a draft by the end of August. Grant's stunning burst of prose led the *Century* editors to contemplate something more ambitious: publishing a memoir by Grant. To reel in his catch, Roswell Smith, the company president, traveled to Long Branch and chatted with Grant as they sat on wicker chairs on the verandah. At first, Grant reacted coyly, wondering whether "anyone would be interested in a book by me." Smith replied, "General, do you not think the public would read with avidity Napoleon's personal account of his battles?"[10] He came away impressed by Grant's firm grasp of publishing: "I found him thoroughly intelligent in relation to the subscription book business, and very much disgusted with the way it is usually managed."[11] At this point, Grant made no contractual commitment, preferring to wait until he had made further headway with the articles, which would form the basis of the book. Spending the rest of the month writing, he experienced the pride of authorship, pleasure of craftsmanship, and delight of reliving past triumphs. Greatly preoccupied with money, Grant revised his will on September 2, bequeathing his entire estate to Julia, about whose financial future he worried incessantly.

By October, the Grants were back in New York, sharing their East Sixty-Sixth Street house with other refugees from the Grant & Ward debacle—Fred and Ida Grant and their children. Belatedly Grant consulted Dr. B. Fordyce Barker, who discovered a suspiciously swollen area on the back of his tongue and immediately referred him to Dr. John H. Douglas, a distinguished, white-bearded throat specialist, who had devised a wartime remedy for scurvy for Union soldiers. He examined Grant thoroughly, probing his mouth with his finger, and found a hard, swollen area at the base of the tongue. Using a mirror, he located three cancerous lesions on the roof of the mouth. At once, Grant suspected the worst. "Is it cancer?" he asked. Cancer was then routinely deemed a death sentence and the doctor shaded the brutal truth. "General, the disease is serious, epithelial in character, and sometimes capable of being cured."[12] Douglas was far more pessimistic than he let on. Using a cocaine and water mixture, he relieved some of the pain and swabbed out accumulated mucus and other debris, telling Grant to come back twice daily for treatment. Grant told neither Julia nor Fred what had happened, although he confided in Badeau. "When he returned he said the physician told him that his throat was affected by a complaint with a cancerous tendency. He seemed serious but not alarmed . . . Still there was disquietude and even alarm—the terrible word cancer was itself almost a knell."[13] When Grant confided in Julia, she fought the truth and refused to believe the ailment could be fatal.

Gradually Grant was ground down into a mass of pain. He had a severe attack of neuralgia and, to relieve it, his dentist extracted several teeth without anesthesia, only worsening his misery. Extracting the teeth also made it easier for Dr. Douglas to clean out his throat. Every day, Grant collected his crutches and took a horse-drawn streetcar to see the doctor, unable to afford private cabs any longer. Passengers must have been startled to find themselves sitting next to America's most renowned individual. Julia finally persuaded him to indulge in a carriage.

In early November, Douglas snipped a slice of tissue from Grant's throat and sent it to Dr. George Frederick Shrady, an eminent pathologist, who had treated President Garfield after the shooting. Douglas was careful not to identify the patient. When Shrady diagnosed the problem as cancer of the throat and tongue, Douglas asked if he was certain. "Perfectly sure," said Shrady crisply. "This patient has a lingual epithelioma—a cancer of the tongue." Douglas now disclosed that Grant was the patient. "Then General Grant is doomed," he replied.[14] He predicted that Grant would endure agonizing pain and be dead within a year.

When Dr. Shrady met with Grant, he suspected a connection between his compulsive smoking and his cancer and advised him to restrict himself to one cigar a day. Pretty soon Grant lost his taste for tobacco altogether and, after a lifetime of oral cravings, smoked his last cigar on November 20, 1884. A journalist named C. E. Meade, a nephew of George Gordon Meade, claimed Grant puffed on his last cigar while visiting a horse farm in Goshen, New York. "Gentlemen," Grant announced to his companions, "this is the last cigar I shall ever smoke. The doctors tell me that I will never live to finish the work on which my whole energy is centered these days . . . if I do not cease indulging in these fragrant weeds. It is hard to give up an old and cherished friend, that has been your comforter and solace through many weary nights and days. But my unfinished work must be completed, for the sake of those that are near and dear to me."[15]

Julia never seemed to draw the proper connection between her husband's smoking and his cancer. In her memoirs, she recounted a conversation with the emperor of Brazil at the 1876 Centennial Exhibition in Philadelphia. She had proudly pointed to bundles of American tobacco only to have the emperor object. "Humph, what is it good for?" Julia rushed to the defense of smoking in her high-spirited fashion. "Why, everything . . . It is a great pleasure to smoke. Smoking quiets the nerves. If one is wakeful it soothes one and promotes sleep. Smoking is a great assistant to digestion."[16] In other words, Julia still believed in the beneficial effects of tobacco long after her husband had likely died from it.

Even grimacing with pain, Grant tracked presidential politics intently. He rejoiced when Chester Arthur lost the Republican nomination to James G. Blaine, who he believed would trounce the Democratic candidate, Governor Grover Cleveland of New York, who had earned a reputation opposing political corruption. Grant had relented in his attitude toward Blaine: "To reject such a man in all the plenitude of his knowledge, ability and will for a man of Grover Cleveland's limited experience would be beneath the good sense of the American people."[17] The American people begged to differ and the rotund Cleveland became the first elected Democrat in the White House since the Civil War. A new national consensus took a more conciliatory view of secession and blasted Reconstruction as an outright failure, giving Grant an additional motivation to publish his memoir and counter this growing revisionist view.

The sudden intimation of his own mortality made Grant worry he would die and leave Julia impoverished. As a result, he told the delighted *Century* editors that he wished to publish his memoir with them. He recruited Fred as his researcher and editor and asked Adam Badeau to move into the house as his editor, promising to give him modest payments from the book royalties—the most Grant could afford in his straitened circumstances. He was so harassed by pecuniary worries that he gave up his pew in a Madison Avenue church, admitting sheepishly he did so "because of my inability to pay the rent."[18] Badeau had a host of unspoken reservations about assisting Grant. Having already published three volumes on Grant's wartime campaigns, he feared they would be overshadowed by Grant's work. He also disliked being sidetracked from a novel he was writing. A querulous man with an ever fragile ego, Badeau didn't voice his concerns, letting them fester beneath the surface. Grant was very clear that Badeau would provide research and that he himself would write. "I am going to do it myself," he told a visitor, flashing his old doughty independence. "If I do not do it myself it will not be mine."[19] Badeau agreed to Grant's terms and took a bedroom at the East Sixty-Sixth Street house.

By late November 1884, pain had become Grant's constant companion. Avoiding solid foods, he had his devoted black valet, Harrison Terrell, bring him milk on a tray twice daily. Even liquids were pure torture for him to swallow. As he told George Childs, "Nothing gives me so much pain as swallowing water," comparing it to drinking "molten lead."[20] His daily meals became harrowing ordeals and Adam Badeau left a graphic vignette of Grant's struggles at the dinner table:

> I shall always recall his figure as he sat at the head of the table, his head bowed over his plate, his mouth set grimly, his features clinched in the endeavor to conceal the expression of pain, especially from Mrs. Grant, who sat at the other end. He no longer carved or helped the family, and at last was often obliged to leave before the meal was over, pacing the hall or the adjoining library in his agony. At this time he said to me that he had no desire to live if he was not to recover. He preferred death at once to lingering, hopeless disease.[21]

Whenever Grant lay down, he suffered from a ghastly sensation of being strangled. He therefore preferred to sit in an armchair, his legs resting on a chair before him with a blanket thrown over them, a silk handkerchief wound around his neck, and a woolen cap on his head. Unable to lie down normally, he was tormented by insomnia. On one occasion, Dr. Shrady was summoned to calm and reassure him. "Pretend you are a boy again," he advised Grant. "Curl up your legs, lie over on your side and bend your neck while I tuck the covers around your shoulders." As a docile Grant obeyed, he said, "Now go to sleep like a good boy," and Grant soon fell fast asleep. But in his fitful sleep, he was often disturbed by nightmares. One night, as Fred stood listening, he heard his father bellow in his sleep, "The cannon did it."[22]

Always an active, enterprising man, Grant lapsed into unaccustomed apathy, sitting in his armchair, hands folded, staring blankly into space. "It was like a man gazing into his open grave," wrote Badeau.[23] That December, when Sherman visited, he found a disconsolate Julia, who worried that her husband had withdrawn "into a silent moody state looking the picture of woe."[24] Attempting to rally her, Sherman conjured up the distant war days when a taciturn Grant sat silently at headquarters as he himself paced, swore, and talked a blue streak. Sherman noticed that Grant warmed up in his presence and that of any other faithful comrade from yesteryear. Seeing his stricken friend transported Sherman back to their wartime camaraderie and the purer love he had once felt for Grant.

Grant's catatonic state didn't last. Soon he was devoting four or five hours daily to his memoirs, working in a second-floor room overlooking East Sixty-Sixth Street, surrounded by huge volumes that housed his military orders and maps. As he worked, Julia constantly replenished bouquets of fresh flowers. In the evening he sometimes read aloud to her from the manuscript. For a time, his pain eased, permitting more work as he wrote on loose sheets of lined paper in a clear, flowing hand. Lest she descend into depression, Julia struggled to keep her emotions in check and feigned a brisk, businesslike manner. "Her calmness and self-control almost seemed coldness," said Badeau, "only we knew that this was impossible."[25]

The *Century* editors offered Grant a standard 10 percent royalty for his memoir with projected sales of twenty-five thousand copies. That summer the *Century* editor Richard Watson Gilder told Robert Johnson that Grant "ought not to be permitted to get too high an idea of immediate sales and profits. We have never had such a card before as Grant . . . and we mustn't let that slip!"[26]

They didn't reckon on the intervention of another prospective publisher who was dropping by to see Grant. Grant had always been fascinated by Mark Twain, a frequent lunchtime guest at Grant & Ward. Three years earlier Twain had attempted to persuade him to compose his memoirs only to have Grant deprecate his own writing ability. In February 1884, Twain set up his nephew Charles Webster in a new publishing outfit known as Charles L. Webster and Company whose sole mission, at first, was to publish *Huckleberry Finn* and other Twain works. With this venture Twain was bogged down in debt from the outset. "I am like everybody else—everything tied up in properties that cannot be sold except at fearful loss," he told William Dean Howells that March. "It has been the roughest twelve-month I can remember for losses, ill luck, and botched business."[27] Twain had a money-crazed side to his nature in which he resembled many of the arrivistes he satirized, and he expected Grant's memoirs to be a bonanza that would salvage his endangered publishing firm.

In November 1884, after giving a speech, Twain enjoyed a late supper at the studio of Richard Watson Gilder, editor of the *Century Magazine,* and learned that Grant was preparing four articles for the magazine. Gilder boasted of having rescued Grant from poverty with a $500 check for his initial piece. Twain was aghast: he thought the amount scandalously small—the literary equivalent of buying "a dollar bill of a blind man and [paying] him ten cents for it."[28] When Gilder let slip the momentous news that Grant had agreed to write his memoirs, Twain, agog, made a silent resolution. "I wanted the General's book," he said, "and I wanted it very much."[29] He was instantly riveted by prospective riches from the project, although he didn't yet know that Grant had cancer.

The next morning, Twain hurried over to East Sixty-Sixth Street where Grant confirmed Gilder's terms and added that he was about to sign a contract. When Fred read the proposed terms aloud, with the 10 percent royalty, Twain silently grunted in disbelief. He pitied Grant as a simple, tenderhearted babe in the woods. "I didn't know whether to cry or laugh," he explained.[30] As he later wrote, the *Century* had the barefaced cheek to offer Grant the same royalty it would have given "to any unknown Comanche Indian whose book they had reason to believe might sell 3,000 or 4,000 or 5,000 copies."[31] Twain knew Grant's memoirs would sell hundreds of thousands of copies and assured him the *Century* terms were "simply absurd and should not be considered for an instant."[32] Insisting that Grant was selling himself much too cheaply, he said he should up the stakes and demand a 20 percent royalty or 70 percent of net profits.

Twain knew he was muscling in on the *Century*'s cozy deal with Grant and could be accused of sharp practice as well. So he concocted a story about walking home in the rain from a lecture when he fleetingly overheard two shadowy figures mention Grant's decision to publish his memoirs. If Twain had no scruples about stealing Grant from the *Century*, Grant was more honorable. When he told Twain that demanding such exorbitant royalties would place him in the position of a robber, the famous author was ready with a witticism: "I said that if he regarded that as a crime it was because his education had been neglected. I said it was not a crime, and was always rewarded in heaven with two halos."[33] When Grant asked what publisher would possibly accede to such conditions, Twain said any reputable publisher in America. Still Grant balked at deserting the *Century*. "To his military mind and training it seemed disloyalty," recalled Twain.[34] The next day, the author returned with a novel proposition: "Sell *me* the Memoirs, General."[35] He proposed a 20 percent royalty or 70 percent of net profits and offered to write a $50,000 check on the spot.

It took Grant time to fathom the wisdom and morality of Twain's superior offer. Sweetening the terms, Twain offered to give Grant living expenses as he composed the book and even offered Jesse a place on the publishing house staff—no trifling incentive for Grant as he fretted about his family. As he mulled over Twain's offer, Grant must have recalled how many times he had been fleeced in his life. For once he would not allow himself to be shortchanged. "On reexamining the Contract prepared by the Century people," he told George Childs, "I see that it is all in favor of the publisher, with nothing left for the Author."[36] Grant leaned toward the 70 percent profit plan in which he would make money only if Twain did too, but the latter tried to convince him that the 20 percent royalty was a better deal for him. In the end, the honorable Grant insisted on the 70 percent profit arrangement.

By January, Grant's condition had deteriorated and he required daily visits from Drs. Douglas and Shrady. When he meditated a therapeutic trip to Hot Springs, Arkansas, the doctors told him he was too weak to make the journey. Formerly robust and brawny, Grant began to lose flesh rapidly, shedding thirty pounds. At one point, Julia was told the "dreadful truth" by the doctors, but could not accept it: "I could not believe that God . . . would take this great, wise, good man from us, to whom he was so necessary and so beloved."[37] Her whole life had revolved around her husband and she tried to face the stark truth as bravely as she could. "Genl Grant is very, very ill," she told a friend on February 28. "I cannot write how ill—my tears blind me."[38]

With Julia having sold her property in Washington, the Grants lived in passable comfort again. Both Twain and Charles Webster visited constantly, preaching the virtues of their publishing house. They brought a leather-bound edition of *Huckleberry Finn,* inscribed to Fred's daughter, Julia, who remembered Twain "with his shaggy mane of long white hair, waving or carelessly tossed about his low brow, and his protruding eyebrows, which almost hid the deep-set eyes shining beneath them." She thought him a "crazy man, and I would draw close to one or another of the grown-ups when he was around."[39] Soon Fred Grant was paging through *Huckleberry Finn* by candlelight.

Behind closed doors, Twain and Webster went wild with excitement at the prospect of landing Grant's memoirs. "There's big money for us both in that book," Webster told Twain, "and on the terms indicated in my note to the General we can make it pay *big*."[40] Returning from a lecture tour in late February, Twain was taken aback by how gray and haggard Grant had grown. "I mean you shall have the book—I have about made up my mind to that," Grant reassured him, but he wanted to write first to Roswell Smith of the Century Company "and tell him I have so decided. I think this is due him."[41] Once again, Grant instinctively did the decent thing. As Twain was leaving, Fred pulled him aside and divulged that doctors thought his father might have only a few weeks to live—news that didn't deter Twain from the deal.

On February 27, 1885, Grant signed a contract with Charles L. Webster and Company and Twain rushed a much-needed thousand-dollar check into his hands. "It was a shameful thing," recalled Twain, "that a man who had saved his country and its government from destruction should still be in a position where so small a sum—$1000—could be looked upon as a godsend."[42] The news, announced a few days later, created a hubbub in the press. The memoirs would be sold by subscription in two-volume boxed sets, lessening reliance on reviews, and Twain mapped out a sales campaign worthy of Grant's military efficiency. He divided the country into sixteen sections with as many general agents, who would oversee an army of ten thousand door-to-door canvassers. They would follow a sales manual that sounded like Twain shouting through a megaphone. They were told to eschew "the Bull Run voice" and "keep pouring *hot shot*" into the hapless customer until he signed on the dotted line. Not missing a trick, Twain would have retired veterans knocking on doors, asking people to help out their old general. Twain hailed this campaign as "the vastest book enterprise the world has ever seen."[43]

On March 1, 1885, *The New York Times* ran a headline that robbed Ulysses and Julia Grant of any remaining hope: "Grant Is Dying." The subhead continued: "Dying Slowly from Cancer; Gravely Ill; Sinking into the Grave; Gen. Grant's Friends Give up Hope."[44] The article, not mincing words, quoted Grant's doctors as saying that he had only a few months to live "and that his death may occur in a short time."[45] It pointed out that Grant had been advised by Dr. Da Costa to see his physician but had dangerously deferred the visit. By the next day, the national press corps had camped outside the East Sixty-Sixth Street residence. The extraordinary outpouring of bipartisan concern blotted out the scandals of Grant's presidency and restored him to his rightful niche in the American pantheon. Hundreds of sympathetic messages piled up at the Grant residence, including telegrams from Jefferson Davis and the sons of Robert E. Lee and Albert Sidney Johnston. A black man from Washington, George M. Arnold, told Fred Grant "to let Gen Grant know how the Colored people of this country feel towards him, how they love honir [sic] and pray for him."[46]

Grant was stunned by the grim prognosis of the newspapers. "That his days were numbered was an intimation for which he was not prepared," wrote Badeau.[47] At times, he hobbled over to the window and gazed at the correspondents keeping a constant vigil outside his windows, offering them a wan smile. The power of the new mass media made Grant's illness a national spectacle, with his doctors offering twice-daily updates on his condition. Grant had always been at his best when dealing with the hard realities of life and he accepted his plight with majestic fortitude.

Grant's illness gave fresh impetus to efforts to relieve his financial distress. He still hoped to be placed on the army retired list with the rank and full pay of general, which would endow him with $13,500 per annum. When President Arthur proposed a special pension for him, he hotly resisted, believing this would tag him as an object of charity. William Tecumseh Sherman opposed Grant's restoration to the army retired list, preferring an outright pension, telling Senator John Logan that "to give the president the right to place General Grant on duty as a full General on our small Peace Establishment, will lead to intrigues damaging to the Army, and making the situation of both Genl Sheridan & myself most uncomfortable."[48] Sherman's view soon found its way into the press, and when Logan transmitted it to Grant, he grew indignant. "He is not looking after the interests of the Army," Grant snapped, "nor do I believe he represents their feeling in regard to the bill you champion."[49] It was yet another proof of the private war Sherman had waged against Grant, usually without the latter's knowledge. Perhaps embarrassed by the disclosure, Sherman began to lobby to restore Grant to the army list.

On February 16, the anniversary of Fort Donelson's fall, the retirement bill was voted down, leaving Grant sorely disappointed. Then the *New York Times* story on his illness altered the political atmosphere in Washington, resuscitating the bill's prospects. Time, however, was short: the new Democratic president, Grover Cleveland, would be sworn in at noon on March 4. When Congress adjourned on the night of March 3 without passing the bill, Grant despaired. "You know during the last day of a session everything is in turmoil," he reflected. "Such a thing cannot possibly be passed."[50] On the morning of March 4, in an extraordinary sequence of events, the House approved the bill right before the noon deadline. Senators had already adjourned to the Capitol for the inauguration. They were abruptly rounded up and herded back into the Senate chamber, the hands of the clock were turned back twenty minutes, and, to tempestuous applause, they approved Grant's bill. Chester Arthur hurried to the Capitol to sign it. As his last presidential act, he nominated Grant, and President Cleveland renewed his commission as general of the army. Chester Arthur instructed the president pro tempore of the Senate to send Grant a congratulatory telegram.

Mark Twain was with Grant when it arrived and witnessed the tremendous tonic it administered to his spirits, likening it to "raising the dead."[51] All those present knew it was Grant's fervent wish to die a full general and they stood there brimming with emotion. Only Grant could contain his emotions. "He read the telegram, but not a shade or suggestion of a change exhibited itself in his iron countenance," Twain said. "The volume of his emotion was greater than all the other emotions there present combined, but he was able to suppress all expression of it and make no sign."[52] Typically laconic, Grant said, "I am grateful the thing has passed." Julia was ebullient: "Hurrah, they have brought us back our old commander."[53] That same day, the army's adjutant general officially notified Grant of his reappointment and, in his own hand, Grant slowly scrawled his reply. "I accept the position of General of the Army on the retired list."[54]

EVEN AS HIS ENERGY EBBED, and despite gruesome pain, Grant applied himself to his manuscript with steady dedication, his memory unfailingly retentive. Sometimes he napped and returned to writing when he awoke and often lengthened his working day by writing after dinner. Observing his ardor, Edwards Pierrepont speculated that Grant "wanted to take advantage of every moment to hasten the work that will probably be the last labor of his life."[55] Now a regular visitor at Grant's house, Twain prevailed upon him to hire the stenographer Noble E. Dawson, who set to work and admired how Grant "made very few changes and never hemmed and hawed." As he dealt with sharp mouth pain, Grant tried to master a new but laborious way of speaking without moving his tongue. The day Dawson showed Twain the manuscript of the first volume, the writer was "astonished . . . and said there was not one literary man in one hundred who furnished as clear a copy as Grant."[56] As a result, Twain's editing was mostly restricted to trivial matters of grammar and punctuation.

Grant took time out to settle one score. Elihu Root, the U.S. attorney for the Southern District of New York, was prosecuting Grant & Ward partner James D. Fish for violating national banking laws and Grant was eager to give a deposition. When lawyers arrived at East Sixty-Sixth Street on March 26, they found Grant in an armchair, ensconced before a hickory wood fire, wearing a skullcap and dressing gown. He testified for three-quarters of an hour, sometimes flinching with pain. If harsh in denouncing Fish and Ward, Grant was toughest on himself, admitting he had never perused the firm's monthly statements. Asked whether he had ever mistrusted Ferdinand Ward, he replied, "I had no mistrust of Mr. Ward the night before the failure, not the slightest . . . It took me a day or two to believe it was possible that Ward had committed the act he had."[57]

At the close of the deposition, the lawyers lingered to chat with Grant. "You're certainly looking remarkably well," one said, but Grant disagreed, ruefully shaking his head. "I am conscious of the fact that I am a very sick man."[58] His testimony, read aloud in court, made a huge impression. Fish was sentenced to ten years in Auburn Prison, later commuted to four years; Ferdinand Ward would serve six years in Sing Sing. By forcing Grant to relive the Grant & Ward nightmare, the deposition exacted a terrible bodily toll and within hours he experienced a wrenching cough and had to be doused with cocaine and morphine.

On March 29, Grant awoke gasping from a restless sleep, couldn't clear his throat secretions, and succumbed to violent coughs. It took two hours before the doctors arrived and Grant's family thought he might expire in the interim. Doctors plied him with injections of brandy and ammonia—national temperance groups objected to the brandy—and dislodged objects wedged in his throat, but he underwent another terrifying episode two hours later, crying out in a strangled voice, "I can't stand it! I am going to die!"[59] Doctors applied chloroform to quiet him and mitigate the pain. Dr. Fordyce Barker blamed the deposition for weakening Grant, whose deeply lined face showed complete exhaustion. Dr. Shrady gloomily informed the press, "It is doubtful if the General's health could stand another choking attack."[60] By April 4, Grant had bounced back unexpectedly and Dr. Douglas teased him, "General, we propose to keep to this line if it takes all summer," which elicited a smile from Grant.[61]

Around this time he performed a ceremony that he had contemplated for some time. He asked Fred to compose a letter requesting a future president of the United States to appoint his grandson Ulysses (Fred's son) as a West Point cadet. Grant summoned family members and doctors as witnesses before he affixed his signature to the document. It was such a solemn gesture for him that as he folded the paper, a hush gripped the room. In 1898 President William McKinley would honor the request by appointing Ulysses S. Grant III, later a major general, to the academy.

Easter Day that year dawned bright and clear, and large crowds promenaded along Fifth Avenue, many pausing at the corner of East Sixty-Sixth Street to gaze concernedly at Grant's town house. From the bay window, Dr. Shrady observed the swelling crowd mingling on the sidewalk below. The scene abounded with reporters, but ordinary citizens also gathered there, often weeping. Grant took his cane, shuffled to the window, and, screened by curtains, pondered the multitude. "I am very grateful to them," he told the doctor, who suggested, "Why not tell them so, General?"[62] Shrady pointed out that newspaper readers might appreciate a direct message from him. "Very well," said Grant. As Shrady grabbed a yellow paper, Grant dictated: "General Grant wishes it stated that he is very much touched by, and very grateful for, the sympathy and interest manifested for him by his friends and by those"—here he momentarily wavered—"who have not been regarded as such."[63] Adam Badeau cheered, "Splendid! Splendid! Stop right there, General Grant! I would not say another word." After minor edits, the statement went out to newspapers across America.

As cancerous sores spread in Grant's mouth, Dr. Shrady studied his courteous, gentlemanly patient, the "far-off look" in his eyes and his meditative mood.[64] "He had the gentlest disposition, like that of an unspoiled young girl."[65] Shrady said Grant knew his disease was terminal and that he could only look forward to more grisly pain. Nonetheless, he discussed his symptoms clinically, even taking his own pulse, a scientific detachment that had served him well in battle. "Brave though he had been on the battlefield, his courage in facing death from an incurable disease was not only a revelation but an inspiration," Shrady wrote.[66]

A couple of days after Easter, Grant was "seized with a severe fit of coughing . . . followed by a hemorrhage of arterial blood," reported one newspaper, which didn't think he would survive the night.[67] Grant awoke to a telegram from Queen Victoria, inquiring anxiously after his health, followed two weeks later by one from Prime Minister William Gladstone. As Grant approached the twentieth anniversary of Appomattox, he suffered no illusions. "My chances, I think, of pulling through this are one in a hundred."[68] Privately, Fred Dent sounded even more dubious, writing that his brother-in-law was "going to die soon unless a miracle saves him."[69]

Neither morbid nor mournful, Grant faced his mortality in clear-eyed fashion and his sensible nature never deserted him. A lifelong Methodist, he had always viewed religious excess with a certain irony, having once told a clutch of ministers that America boasted three parties: Democrats, Republicans, and Methodists. The Reverend John P. Newman now became a familiar face at East

Sixty-Sixth Street. When he led the family in evening prayers, Grant found the experience a bit trying. Fred said his father was a good Christian but "*not* a praying man," yet Grant allowed Newman to pray for him to soothe Julia. Grant had never been baptized. On the night of April 1, when he had a terrible ordeal that required morphine, Julia asked Dr. Newman to baptize him. When Grant awoke, Newman informed him that he was about to baptize him—"Thank you, Doctor," the patient replied, "I intended to take that step myself"—and applied water to Grant's brow from a silver bowl. Jesse Grant insisted his father was unconscious when baptized and grew "annoyed and indignant" when he found out what had happened, but said nothing for fear of upsetting Julia.[70]

Dr. Newman became a controversial figure as he issued grandiose pronouncements on the state of Grant's soul, crediting his recovery from the April 1 crisis to the power of prayer. A foe of cant, Mark Twain was aghast at Newman's statements and wrote him off as a mountebank: "It is fair to presume that most of Newman's daily reports originated in his own imagination."[71] Buck's father-in-law, former senator Chaffee, also condemned Newman's shameless efforts to distort Grant's religiosity: "General Grant does not believe that Doctor Newman's prayers will save him. He allows the doctor to pray simply because he does not want to hurt his feelings."[72] When Newman told Grant that God wanted to employ him for "a great spiritual mission," Grant deflated his rhetoric by inquiring, "Can he cure cancer?"[73]

Twain admired the even-tempered humility of the withered general. As world luminaries inundated him with telegrams, Twain was struck by his "perennial surprise that he should be the object of so much fine attention."[74] He pondered Grant's kindness and "aggravatingly trustful nature" and couldn't fathom how the man who had negotiated tough terms at Fort Donelson and Vicksburg was such a ready mark for Ferdinand Ward.[75] Grant was still ashamed of having been fooled by Ward's blatant deception, but refused to submit to vengeance. Twain, by contrast, said he himself was "inwardly boiling all the time. I was scalping Ward, flaying him alive, breaking him on the wheel, pounding him to jelly, and cursing him with all the profanity known to the one language I am acquainted with."[76]

Grant was fated to have one final disappointment in a trusted figure. Ever since joining Grant's staff in 1864, Adam Badeau had relied on Grant for advancement at every turn. Thanks to Grant he had retired from the army as a brevet brigadier general, worked in the White House, and served as U.S. consul in London. The bearded, bespectacled Badeau fancied himself a literary man, becoming Grant's authorized wordsmith, and lectured on his military campaigns. His career was shadowed by drinking allegations. When he shared a Washington boardinghouse with Henry Adams, the latter said he "resorted more or less to whiskey for encouragement."[77] Grant retained him as London consul even after Hamilton Fish reported that Badeau had engaged in extended drinking bouts, some lasting for days. One Grant intimate remembered Badeau "in the vicinity of the White House, so drunk, that he walked in a circle two or three time[s] round before he straightened out."[78] It was yet another case of Grant loving not wisely but too well.

Grant had spelled out clearly the terms upon which Badeau would assist him with his memoirs. Knowing his memoirs would compete with Badeau's history, he promised to pay him $5,000 from the first $20,000 in royalties and $5,000 from the next $10,000. Badeau seemed content with the arrangement. But, like many sycophants, Badeau nursed secret resentments of the man upon whom he had relied, hidden grievances that boiled over in April as work on the memoirs dragged on longer than expected and Grant's illness made working conditions arduous. Grant would give pages to Badeau, who corrected spelling and grammar or assisted with the narrative flow—standard copyediting tasks. Although Badeau helped to polish the book and knit together random passages, the essential content and style came from Grant and were fully consistent with his earlier writings. Badeau, however, feared history would honor the wrong man, the inferior writer and historian U. S. Grant, and his version of events found its way into print on April 29 when the *New York World* ran a gossipy item denying that Grant could possibly author his own reminiscences. "The work upon his new book, about which so much has been said, is the work of Gen. Adam Badeau," it declared.[79] Mark Twain erupted in fury, branding the *World* "that daily issue of unmedicated closet paper." Instead of settling for an apology or a retraction, he implored Grant to bring a lawsuit whose punitive damages would "cripple—yes, *disable*—that paper financially."[80] When no other papers dignified the charge, Twain relented and advised against legal action.

On May 2, Badeau composed an insulting letter to Grant that protested the arrangement under which he worked. He didn't bother to mask his rage or show respect for his longtime patron. Because Grant now had to dictate his memoir, Badeau claimed his job would be to "connect the disjointed fragments into a connected narrative. This work is the merest literary drudgery—*such as I would never consent to do for any one but you* . . . I desire the fame of my own book, not of yours. Yours is not, and will not be, the work of a literary man, but the simple story of a man of affairs and of a great general; proper for you, but not such as would add to my credit at all."[81] Incensed that Grant's book would "supplant and stamp out mine," he demanded payment of $1,000 monthly in advance and, more shockingly, 10 percent of all profits from Grant's book.[82] A pallid Badeau melodramatically handed Grant the letter that morning, after which Fred found his father pacing moodily. Grant had always taken pride in his writing style and was deeply wounded by Badeau's letter. Removing it from a drawer, he gave it to Fred. "Read this & tell me what you think of it," he said.[83] According to Julia, the Badeau letter represented "the most cruel blow" her husband had ever received.[84]

During the next few days, a weakened Grant wrote an impassioned reply that covered eleven foolscap pages and is unique in his annals. Seldom, if ever, did he deliver such blunt, unsparing criticism. He started out by saying that he and Badeau must now part, since he could find many people to perform the task of editing who would find it neither drudgery nor degrading. Then came a devastating critique of Badeau that showed Grant's powers of psychological penetration: "You are petulant, your anger is easily aroused and you are overbearing even to me at times, and always with those for whom you have done or are doing, literary work."[85] He reviewed Badeau's history of quarrels with publishers and politicians and how he grew enraged if his advice went unheeded. Grant blamed the poor sales of Badeau's *Military History* on his interminable delays and long-winded style. Then turning to Badeau's charge that he needed help writing his book, Grant offered a stirring defense of his own style:

> I have only to say that for the last twenty-four years I have been very much employed in writing. As a soldier I wrote my own orders, directions and reports. They were not edited nor assistance rendered. As President I wrote every official document, I believe, bearing my name . . . All these have been published and widely circulated. The public has become accustomed to them and [know] my style of writing. They know that it is not even an attempt to imitate either a literary [or classical style] and that it is just what it is pure and simple and nothing else.[86]

Badeau's reply was bitterly ungracious: "You look upon my assistance as that of an ordinary clerk or literary hack; I thought I was aiding you as no one else could in doing a great work."[87] He promised to remove his belongings from East Sixty-Sixth Street and secure new lodgings. The feud left Badeau in an awkward position: he had been excommunicated by the dying Grant even as he traded on his intimacy with him. In a letter published years later, Badeau pretended that Grant hadn't been in his right mind when he wrote the angry dismissal: "This letter . . . could never have received Gen. Grant's sanction had he been well in body and mind; drugged, diseased, and under the influence of his son, he put his name to a paper unworthy of his fame, full of petty spite and vulgar malice, such as he never displayed, and worse yet, of positive and palpable falsehood."[88]

Grant was not through cutting Badeau down to proper size. Two months later, he sent him a taunting letter, saying Fred had been forced to redo Badeau's work on the memoirs, having found too many errors. "To be frank with you you are helpless, and filled with a false pride . . . You, a literary man, cannot sharpen a lead pencil, open a box or pack up your books." He let Badeau know he had long overlooked his drinking history. "On one occasion you were sent from London to Madrid with very important dispatches, got overcome with liquor and switched off by the wayside and did not turn up in Madrid for some days after you should have been there . . . your nature is not of that unselfish kind I had supposed."[89]

Luckily, Grant was surrounded by loving family members who didn't disappoint him. Nellie came from England and moved into the house. Grant grew even more doting with his children. He had always inspired loyalty in people who worked for him, especially his butler and valet—and more recently nurse— Harrison Terrell, who was born into slavery and had been with him for four years. While some family members seemed to dislike Terrell, Grant always defended him and refused to allow him to be mistreated. Twain remembered Grant's referring to the discrimination visited upon Terrell as a black man by saying, "We are responsible for these things in his face—it is not fair to visit our fault upon them—let him *alone*."[90]

In his final months, Grant showed exceptional kindness to Terrell, furnishing him with a glowing recommendation letter for use after his death so he could find employment as a War Department messenger. Terrell's son Robert had just graduated cum laude from Harvard. While he was there, Grant had provided him with a beautiful letter to obtain summer work in the Boston Custom House:

"My special interest in him is from the fact that his father—a most estimable man—is my butler, beside I should feel an interest in any young man, white or colored, who had the courage and ability to graduate himself at Harvard without other pecuniary aid than what he could earn."[91] Robert Terrell was to befriend Booker T. Washington and become the first black municipal judge in Washington.

Harrison Terrell had unusual opportunities to observe Grant's drinking habits. Like earlier commentators, he acknowledged that even "a couple of small swallows" caused Grant to slur his speech and noted that he invariably abstained from alcohol at stressful moments.[92] "It is not true that Gen. Grant was a whiskey guzzler," he insisted. "Like many another man, he liked an occasional nip very well, but, after all, he was no more than a moderate drinker."[93] Andrew Carnegie, who had dined frequently with Grant in New York, recalled how he would turn his wineglass upside down at dinners: "That indomitable will of his enabled him to remain steadfast to his resolve, a rare case as far as my experience goes."[94] All available evidence suggests Grant had abstained from alcohol and largely vanquished the problem through sheer willpower and perseverance—his stock in trade—and the protective vigilance of his loving wife. It was one of the supreme triumphs of a life loaded with major accomplishments.

Mark Twain had struggled with similar cravings for alcohol and tobacco. When they discussed the subject, Grant mentioned that although doctors had urged him to sip whiskey or champagne, he could no longer abide the taste of liquor. Twain pondered this statement long and hard. "Had he made a conquest so complete that even the *taste* of liquor was become an offense?" he wondered. "Or was he so sore over what had been said about his habit that he wanted to persuade others & likewise himself that he hadn't ever even *had* any taste for it."[95] Similarly, when Grant told Twain that, at the doctors' behest, he had been restricted to one cigar daily, he claimed to have lost the desire to smoke it. "I could understand that feeling," Twain later proclaimed. "He had set out to conquer not the *habit* but the *inclination—the desire*. He had gone at the root, not the trunk."[96] Although Twain hated puritanical killjoys who robbed life of its small pleasurable vices, he respected abstinence based on an absence of desire.

Nothing riled Twain more than assertions that he had secretly ghostwritten Grant's memoirs—a canard that has echoed down the years. Twain was the first to admit that Grant's lean, ironic prose was unique and paid homage to Grant's

"flawless" style.[97] He could no more imitate Grant than vice versa. A close inspection of Grant's manuscript in the Library of Congress shows the writing in
his own hand, starting with the clear, flowing penmanship of the early months
down to the cramped, slanted fragments of the later period when pain and nar-
cotics fogged his mind. Some final sections appear to be in the handwriting of
Noble E. Dawson or Fred Grant, but never of Twain.

With Badeau gone, Grant experienced a remarkable burst of productivity
and wrote with keen relish. As in wartime, he was at his best when death lurked
around the corner. Alone in his library, he subordinated everything to writing,
and newspapers meticulously chronicled his literary progress. "So absorbed did
he become in the business at hand," one paper reported, "that he voluntarily gave
up his noonday drive and afternoon walk."[98] Amid this astonishing output,
Twain was nonplussed to learn from Fred that his father needed an encouraging
editorial word: "I was as much surprised as Columbus's cook could have been to
learn that Columbus wanted his opinion as to how Columbus was doing his
navigating."[99] Grant was overjoyed when Twain told him his memoirs would
stand alongside Caesar's *Commentaries* for purity, simplicity, and fairness and
qualify as "the best purely narrative literature in the language."[100] On May 23,
Grant realized he had to pen a dedication for his narrative. "These volumes are
dedicated to the American soldier and sailor," he wrote simply.[101] When Fred
questioned whether the dedication alluded only to those who had fought for the
North, he replied that it was for "those we fought against as well as those we
fought with. It may serve a purpose in restoring harmony."[102]

On April 27, when Grant celebrated his sixty-third birthday, Andrew Carnegie rushed over sixty-three roses and Julia illuminated the dinner table with
sixty-three candles. Grant calmly faced the prospect of his own death and refused to skirt the issue. In mid-May, he dictated a message for a reunion of the
Grand Army of the Republic that had a touching, patriarchal tone: "Tell the
boys that they probably will never look into my face again, nor hear my voice,
but they are engraved on my heart, and I love them as my children."[103] On Memorial Day, four hundred veterans trudged past his window as he stared down
at them. Afterward, he slumped in his armchair and yielded to dreamy reflections as their martial music faded away down the block.

Despite Grant's grave situation, Twain was galvanized by the projected sales
for his book and hovered over every aspect of publication. By late May, he

boasted that he and Charley Webster had collected 100,000 orders for the two-volume boxed sets. To cater to this robust demand, they had lined up twenty presses and seven binderies to crank out the books. Twain now predicted staggering sales: 300,000 sets, or 600,000 individual volumes.

In mid-May, when Grant's physicians wondered how to spare him the fierce heat of a Manhattan summer, his friend Joseph W. Drexel made an offer he could not resist. Saratoga Springs, a stylish resort in upstate New York known for fine summer weather, mineral waters, and a Thoroughbred racetrack, had become a favorite haunt of Wall Street financiers. Drexel was a minor partner in the Hotel Balmoral, recently opened at the peak of Mount McGregor, 1,100 feet above sea level; just down the road he had built a charming, roomy cottage that he placed at Grant's disposal. His associate W. J. Arkell later confessed he had hoped that if Grant "should die there, it might make the place a national shrine—and incidentally a success."[104] The doctors loved the idea of Grant breathing in pine-scented mountain air, free from summer heat, mosquitoes, and noxious city vapors. Excited by escaping from East Sixty-Sixth Street, Grant told a reporter that he walked around his room after breakfast "getting himself in condition for long tramps through the woods after he got in the country."[105] After Grant suffered a bad day and postponing the trip was reluctantly broached to him, he exclaimed, "Now or never!"[106]

Early on the morning of June 16, 1885, a shrunken man with white hair and a gray-flecked beard—Grant had now dropped sixty pounds—shuffled from 3 East Sixty-Sixth Street and stepped into bright sunlight. Despite a sweltering day, he stood bundled in a black coat and black beaver hat, a white scarf concealing a neck tumor "as big as a man's two fists put together," wrote a journalist.[107] Grant was accompanied by Julia, Fred and Ida, Nellie, and five grandchildren, plus Dawson, Terrell, and Dr. Douglas. A carriage bore them to Grand Central Depot, where Grant disembarked and moved slowly toward the train, leaning on his cane, his slippers scraping the pavement. He traveled aboard a private car owned by William H. Vanderbilt, which was emptied to make room for two bulky leather armchairs that enabled Grant to sit on one and rest his legs on the other. As the train chugged upstate, small crowds gathered at stations and crossings and waved as he sped by. Once at Mount McGregor, he boarded a narrow-gauge railroad that lifted him to the summit. With customary grit, he tried to totter up the last stretch of dirt path alone, aided by his cane, under a welcoming arch that proclaimed, "Our Hero."[108] When his strength failed, two husky police officers deposited him in a wicker chair and carried him the remaining distance to the cottage.

The house was painted a rich gold color, trimmed in brown and faced with dark green shutters. Joseph Drexel had furnished it expressly for Grant's stay, knowing he would be largely restricted to the first floor. Grant's two black leather armchairs faced each other in a corner bedroom, right off the porch, so he could sleep sitting up and write with a board across the armrests. For pain relief, he took a cocaine-and-water solution and received periodic injections of brandy and morphine to pump up his heart rate. Doctors had to keep scouring dead matter and debris from his mouth. Grant immediately scratched away at his manuscript. "I have worked faster than if I had been well," he told Twain. "I have used my three boys and a stenographer."[109] Even when Julia coaxed him onto the verandah for rest, he yearned to get back to work. The work sustained him, giving him a reason to soldier on. "It is very pleasant to be here," he told her, "but I must go to my writing or I fear my book will not be finished."[110] When he sat on the porch, often in a silk top hat, hundreds of onlookers sauntered by to steal glimpses of him from the pathway leading up to the hotel. Frail, emaciated, starving to death from his inability to eat, he wore warm clothing in the early summer heat. His wit never abandoned him. Sneaking peeks at news headlines, he told Dr. Shrady that *The New York Times* has been "killing me off for a year. If it does not change, it will get it right in time."[111]

Racing against the Grim Reaper, Grant put in several hours of work per day, often pausing, short of breath, after an hour. Unable to talk any longer, he kept a pad and pencil at his side, scribbling tiny notes to family and doctors. "About an hour ago," he wrote to Dr. Douglas, "I coughed up a piece of stringy matter about the size of a small lizard."[112] In another message he wrote, "I am a verb instead of a personal pronoun. A verb is anything that signifies to be; to do; or to suffer. I signify all three."[113] One day, when he seemed to drift off into the twilight of death, he suddenly awoke. "I was passing away peacefully and soon all would have been over," he wrote. "It was like falling asleep." There was something poignant about Grant as he mutely raised his eyes, searching the faces of interlocutors. As Buck said, "His eyes were always expressive and it hurt me to look at him and see his suffering . . . Watching him suffer was the hardest thing I have ever been through."[114]

Analyzing his own symptoms with clinical detachment, he told Dr. Douglas that he would die from a hemorrhage, strangulation, or exhaustion. All physicians could do was "to make my burden of pain as light as possible."[115] He went through terrifying sensations of being strangled by thick ropes of phlegm. "I have no desire to live," he scribbled to Reverend Newman. "But I do not want you to let my family know this."[116] Despite the relief morphine brought, Grant had a horror of addiction and swallowed only three drops per day. Even though he sipped old port and drank some wine to relieve symptoms, they didn't help, making him forswear alcohol one last time. "I do not think alcoholic drinks agree with me," he wrote. "They seem to heat me up and have no other effect."[117]

On June 29, Grant composed a private letter to Julia that discussed his burial place for the first time. He was in a quandary since they were "comparative strangers" in New York City. He preferred West Point as his resting place, except that Julia would be excluded there. "I therefore leave you free to select what you think the most appropriate place for depositing my earthly remains."[118] He bid her "a final farewell until we meet in another, and I trust better, world."[119]

Grant had never been especially reflective about the improbable course of his life. Now the whole pattern stood wondrously revealed to him, as he described to Dr. Douglas:

> It seems that one man's destiny in this world is quite as much a mystery as it is likely to be in the next. I never thought of acquiring rank in the profession I was educated for; yet it came with two grades higher prefixed to the rank of General officers for me. I certainly never had either ambition or taste for a political life; yet I was twice president of the United States. If anyone had suggested the idea of my becoming an author, as they frequently did I was not sure whether they were making sport of me or not. I have now written a book which is in the hands of the manufacturers.[120]

Perhaps reflecting on his grievous disappointments with people, he wrote philosophically, "I am glad to say that while there is much unblushing wickedness in this world, yet there is a compensating goodness of the soul."[121]

At the end of June, with the first volume of Grant's memoirs in page proofs, Twain went to Mount McGregor to supervise the final portion. One afternoon, with the voiceless Grant sitting in his porch wicker chair, Twain bantered with Buck and Jesse when the talk turned to James Fish, who had been sentenced the day before. Twain let loose a string of expletives, Jesse condemned his sentence as too light, and Buck engaged in angry oaths. Calmly taking up pad and pencil,

Grant wrote, *"He was not as bad as the other,"* referring to Ferdinand Ward.[122] Twain was amazed at Grant's forbearance, writing that "he never uttered a phrase concerning Ward which an outraged adult might not have uttered concerning an offending child."[123]

The dying Grant exerted a powerful symbolic influence upon the American imagination, his illness becoming a grand pageant of North-South reconciliation. Nothing pleased him more than Confederate and Union soldiers alike expressing concern for his condition. On July 10, he received a surprise visit from his old friend Simon Buckner, who had unconditionally surrendered to him at Fort Donelson and wanted Grant to meet his new young wife. Now a Kentucky newspaper editor and soon to be governor, Buckner wished to convey the gratitude of Confederate soldiers who appreciated Grant's magnanimity at Appomattox. In his written response, Grant attempted to find meaning in the war's mass suffering: "I have witnessed since my sickness just what I have wished to see ever since the war: harmony and good feeling between the sections . . . I believe myself that the war was worth all it cost us, fearful as it was."[124] Grant emphasized his soldierly bond with Buckner. "The trouble is now made by men who did not go into the war at all, or who did not get mad till the war was over."[125] Although Buckner came as a private citizen, Grant urged him to publicize the visit and retire any residual rancor from the conflict.

In this forgiving spirit, Grant summoned Benjamin Bristow, the crusading treasury secretary who had proven his scourge during the Whiskey Ring investigations. So embittered had Grant been toward Bristow that when he later ran into him in New York, he cut him dead, turning on his heels and walking away in silence. Nevertheless, Bristow set aside his hurt feelings and heeded Grant's invitation. As soon as he arrived, Grant unburdened himself with a forthright apology. "I want to tell you that I misjudged you," he murmured. "I thought you were after Babcock to get me, and my administration. I was wrong, and you were right."[126] Bristow was flabbergasted by this contrition from a dying man. Years later he said Grant "never had a more loyal friend or one who labored more zealously to serve him personally & officially."[127] The one person Grant didn't summon to his bedside was Elihu Washburne, who he believed had betrayed him during the 1880 nomination battle in Chicago.

In his final days, Grant extended an especially warm welcome to Colonel John Eaton, who had been charged with relief and resettlement of blacks during the war. Grant's face was shrouded by a cloth and Eaton could see little of his features. Grant beckoned him closer with wiggling fingers, then scrawled a message. "I am very glad to see you . . . I should like to have you say something about our . . . utilizing the negroes down about Grand Junction, Tennessee. In writing on that subject for my book I had to rely on memory."[128] Eaton found it infinitely touching that Grant had devoted space to that story alongside the epic chronicle of his own military victories.

Grant believed a special providence kept him alive to complete his book. He was so intent on finishing it that he instructed Fred, if he died and the manuscript wasn't ready for the printer, he should embalm his body and delay the funeral to wrap it up. "This is now my great interest in life," he wrote, "to see my work done."[129] On July 16, he put down his pen, his mighty labor over, and informed Dr. Douglas that he was "not likely to be more ready to go than at this moment."[130] Somehow, in agony, he had produced 336,000 splendid words in the span of a year. He had made a career of comebacks and this one was arguably his most impressive as he battled against mortality to preserve his legacy and protect Julia. Once again he had thoroughly conquered adversity. For Grant, the end of writing now meant the end of life. He took the farewell letter he addressed to his wife on June 29 and placed it in his coat pocket along with a lock of Jesse's hair and the ring Julia had given him, knowing she would discover these items after his death.

The *Personal Memoirs of U. S. Grant,* widely viewed as a masterpiece, is probably the foremost military memoir in the English language, written in a clear, supple style that transcends the torment of its composition. Grant recognized the implausible course of his life, beginning his preface with the humble words "Man proposes and God disposes."[131] He focused on his childhood, West Point, the Mexican War, and the Civil War, omitting his marriage, family life, presidency, Reconstruction, round-the-world trip, and post–White House political involvement. There was not a word about Ferdinand Ward. Grant projected the unassuming modesty, veined with irony, of a man confident of his own worth who didn't need to bluster to other people. There was no posing, no striking of heroic attitudes, no pretense of being infallible. Scrupulously honest, Grant confessed to doubts and fears on the battlefield and presented the extraordinary spectacle of a self-effacing military man, a hero in spite of himself. An ambivalent message lay at the heart of the narrative. Grant was frankly insistent that the northern cause had been just, the southern misguided. Instead of settling scores, however, he stepped forth one last time as a gracious figure of national harmony.

It never occurred to Grant to delve into embarrassing parts of his story, leading to some breathtaking evasions. He unashamedly skipped over the bleak St. Louis years in the 1850s and didn't deal with his drinking problem. One of the most striking omissions was any mention of John Rawlins's vital wartime role in keeping him sober. Perhaps it would be churlish to expect somebody gritting his teeth with pain to excavate such a painful past. Some Grant intimates thought he shrank from discussing Rawlins's role because it would have entailed an admission of his own weakness. But it may also have been the case, as Twain argued, that Grant originally intended to include portraits of other generals, "but he got so many letters from colonels and such, asking to be added that he resolved to put none in and thus avoid the creation of jealousies."[132]

Praise for the *Personal Memoirs* was at first ambivalent. Henry James complained that Grant's style was "hard and dry as sandpaper."[133] Matthew Arnold found the two volumes full of "sterling good-sense" and praised their prose for "saying clearly in the fewest possible words what had to be said, and saying it, frequently, with shrewd and unexpected turns of expression."[134] In a less charitable moment, he faulted Grant for writing "an English without charm and high breeding."[135] But William Dean Howells found the book a revelation. "I am reading Grant's book with the delight I fail to find in novels," he told Mark Twain, who commended the work as "a great, unique and unapproachable literary masterpiece."[136] Twain had more than literary reasons to celebrate the book, which sold in excess of 300,000 two-volume sets. Seven months after Grant's death, Julia received a whopping $200,000 check from Twain and $450,000 in the end—an astonishing sum for book royalties at the time. No previous book had ever sold so many copies in such a short period of time, and it rivaled that other literary sensation of the nineteenth century, *Uncle Tom's Cabin*. Clearly Grant had emerged victorious in his last uphill battle.

ON JULY 20, Ulysses S. Grant asked to be rolled over to a scenic spot on the mountaintop that offered a wide-angled vista of the Adirondack foothills to the north, the Green Mountains of Vermont to the east, and the Catskills dimly visible to the south. Bundled up with a blanket over his lap, he was wheeled in a bath wagon that had two large wheels in the rear, a smaller one up front, which Harrison Terrell pushed from behind with a metal bar. A few weeks earlier, Terrell had pulled Grant up to the Hotel Balmoral, facetiously complaining he had been reduced to a draft horse, to which Grant scribbled: "For a man who has been accustomed to drive fast horses this is a considerable comedown in point of speed."[137] But this new outing lacked humor and left Grant gasping for air. "He was carried into the drawing room & death seemed to seize him," said Reverend Newman. "We gathered around him & I prayed for him."[138]

As his life neared its end, Grant rested in a circle of family affection and his nine-year-old granddaughter Julia later sketched the scene:

> Grandmama was crying quietly and was seated by his side. She had in her hands a handkerchief and a small bottle, perhaps of cologne, and was dampening my grandfather's brow. His hair was longer and seemed to me more curled, while his eyes were closed in a face more drawn than usual and much whiter. Beads of perspiration stood on the broad forehead, and as I came forward, old Harrison gently wiped similar drops from the back of the hand which was lying quietly on the chair arm. My father [Fred] sat at the opposite side from Grandmama, and the doctor and nurse stood at the head, behind the invalid.[139]

Characteristically the dying Grant was stoically concerned with his family's well-being after he was gone, saying, "I hope no one will be distressed on my account."[140] He had already told pastor John Heyl Vincent, "I am ready to go. No Grant ever feared death. I am not afraid to die."[141] At 8:08 a.m. on July 23, 1885, Grant died so gently that nobody was quite certain at first that his spirit had stolen away. His death reflected words he had once written to a bereaved widow during the Mexican War, saying that her husband had "died as a soldier dies, without fear and without a murmur."[142] Grant's corpse weighed ninety pounds and lay under an oval picture of Abraham Lincoln. It was hard to believe this wizened form represented the earthly remains of the stouthearted general. "I think his book kept him alive several months," Twain wrote upon hearing the news. "He was a very great man and superlatively good."[143] An undertaker rushed to preserve the body with ice before it decayed in the summer heat, embalming Grant under a George Washington portrait. The cadaver was attired in an outfit befitting a president—black suit, patent leather slippers, a little black bow tie—before being sealed under glass in a temporary coffin and covered with an American flag.

For Julia, the desire to rest beside her husband for eternity became her paramount concern in choosing a burial spot. They had spent only a small portion of their lives in New York City, but had become assimilated residents. Grant had praised the town, stating that "through the generosity of [its] citizens I have been enabled to pass my last days without experiencing the pains of pinching want."[144] Many people wanted Grant interred at Arlington National Cemetery or the Soldiers' Home in Washington and Galena even staked a claim. In opting for a New York tomb, Julia cited four factors: she believed it had been her husband's preference; she could visit his tomb often; many Americans would be able to come; and—most important—she would be allowed a final resting place by his side. When local opposition arose to a pair of Central Park sites, Mayor William R. Grace suggested the "prominent height" and leafy tranquillity of the comparatively new Riverside Park, designed by Frederick Law Olmsted and Calvert Vaux, overlooking the Hudson River.[145]

With flags lowered to half-mast across America and mourning symbols swathing the White House, the Grant family conducted a private funeral at Mount McGregor on August 4. Two days later Grant's casket began a journey southward from Albany to New York City, where three hundred thousand people filed past the open coffin as it lay in state at City Hall. People descended on Manhattan in record numbers for the public funeral on August 8. They poured on foot across the Brooklyn Bridge, descended from elevated railroad stations, and slipped into the city through Grand Central Depot. The 1.5 million people flooding the city would make it the grandest funeral in New York history.

At 8:30 a.m. on August 8, Civil War veterans hoisted Grant's coffin to a waiting catafalque that had black plumes sprouting at each corner. Twenty-four black stallions, arranged in twelve pairs and attended by black grooms, stood ready to pull the hearse. Twenty generals preceded the horses, led by Winfield Scott Hancock, whose vanity Grant had mocked and who now sat astride a noble black steed. Every protocol for a military funeral was followed, including the riderless horse with boots facing backward in the stirrups. The funeral was a vast, elaborate affair, befitting a monarch or head of state, in marked contrast to the essential simplicity of the man honored. The grandeur emphasized the central place that Grant had occupied in the Civil War and its aftermath. "Out of all the hubbub of the war," wrote Walt Whitman, "Lincoln and Grant emerge, the towering majestic figures."[146] He thought they had lived exemplary lives that vindicated the American spirit, showing how people lifted from the lower ranks of society could attain greatness. "I think this the greatest lesson of our national existence so far."[147]

The procession streamed up Broadway until it reached the Fifth Avenue Hotel on Madison Square, where it took on a veritable army of dignitaries, including all the members of the Grant family except for Julia, who remained secluded at Mount McGregor. President Cleveland headed an eminent escort that included Vice President Thomas Hendricks, the entire cabinet, and Supreme Court justices. Both surviving ex-presidents, Rutherford B. Hayes and Chester A. Arthur, attended. Congress and statehouses across the country emptied out to pay homage, sending fifteen U.S. senators, twelve congressmen, eighteen governors, and ten mayors to pay their respects. From city halls across America eight thousand civil and municipal officers converged to participate in the march.

Nobody doubted that William Tecumseh Sherman and Philip H. Sheridan would serve as honorary pallbearers, but Julia Grant knew her husband would have wanted two Confederate generals to balance their northern counterparts, so Joseph Johnston and Simon Buckner represented the South. Predictably, northern military units predominated, but the presence of Confederate soldiers touched onlookers. "It was quite a sight to see the Stonewall Brigade [march] up Fifth Avenue with their drums marked Staunton, Va.," one said. "They wore the grey, with a black and brass helmet. There were several companies of Virginia and Southern troops."[148] Contingents of black veterans were liberally represented among the sixty thousand soldiers, supplemented by eighteen thousand veterans of the Grand Army of the Republic. Rabbi E. B. M. Browne acted as an honorary pallbearer, a reminder of how thoroughly Grant had atoned for his wartime action against the Jews. At Grant's death, Philadelphia's *Jewish Record* observed, "None will mourn his loss more sincerely than the Hebrew, and . . . in every Jewish synagogue and temple in the land the sad event will be solemnly commemorated with fitting eulogy and prayer."[149]

Southern reaction to Grant's death signified a posthumous triumph. His onetime image as a fierce warrior of the Civil War had been replaced by that of a more pacific figure. As the *News and Courier* of South Carolina editorialized, "Had his life ended but a few years since, the mourning for the great leader would have been more or less sectional in its manifestation. Dying as he now dies, the grief is as widespread as the Union."[150] Grant had won over unlikely southern converts. When John Singleton Mosby learned of his death, he was bereft: "I felt I had lost my best friend."[151] In Gainesville, Georgia, a white-bewhiskered James Longstreet emerged in a dressing gown to tell a reporter emotionally that Grant "was the truest as well as the bravest man that ever lived."[152] In southern towns and border states, veterans from North and South linked arms as they paid tribute to Grant's passage. Black churches held "meetings of sorrow" that eulogized Grant as a champion of the Fifteenth Amendment and the fight to dismantle the Ku Klux Klan. Summing up Grant's career, Frederick Douglass wrote: "In him the Negro found a protector, the Indian a friend, a vanquished foe a brother, an imperiled nation a savior."[153]

Church bells tolled and muffled drums resounded as the funeral procession glided past buildings shrouded in black, *The New York Times* likening the uninterrupted flow of humanity to a giant "river into which many tributaries were poured."[154] The honor guard of mourners stretched for miles, taking five hours to reach the burial site. Like a wraith haunting the crowd, a slim, pale young man, his identity masked by smoked glasses, watched as the canopied hearse rolled by. He was, by his own description, America's most hated man. It was Ferdinand Ward, still awaiting trial, who had bribed his way out of the Ludlow Street Jail for several hours to attend the funeral. Ward remained unrepentant, preferring to see himself as a victim rather than a perpetrator of the Grant & Ward scandal. He remained totally delusional about his relationship with Grant. "Our friendship never changed through all the period of stress and trouble," he told the press years later, "but remained until the time of his death."[155] The anger of Grant's family and friends toward Ward and Fish had never abated. "Wall Street killed him," Sherman stated baldly. "There isn't any doubt about it. He would have been alive to-day, if he hadn't fallen into the hands of Ward and those fellows."[156]

By midafternoon, in bright sunshine, the funeral cortege reached the small temporary brick tomb at Riverside Drive and 122nd Street. Warships floating in the Hudson River let loose a cannonade in tribute to Grant. A lone bugler blew taps at the vault—the same tune that had floated over Grant's army camps during the war. As the notes drifted over the crowd, Sherman stood ramrod straight, his body shaking with tears. It was a memorable sight: the bête noire of the South, seemingly impervious to softer feelings, overcome with profound emotion.

A dozen years later, on a cool spring day, with more than a million people in attendance, President William McKinley presided over the dedication of the General Grant National Memorial—"Grant's Tomb" in popular parlance—financed by public contributions. Leading the fund-raising drive had been the lawyer Richard T. Greener, the first black graduate of Harvard College, which would have pleased Grant. An opulent domed affair of granite and marble, Grant's Tomb was the largest mausoleum in North America. When Julia Grant died of heart failure in 1902 at age seventy-six—in later years she befriended Varina Davis, the widow of Jefferson Davis, and supported the suffragette movement—she and Ulysses were entombed together. They lay encased in red granite sarcophagi housed in an open structure much too monumental for these two simple midwestern souls. The mausoleum's spectacular scale testified to Grant's exalted place in the nineteenth-century American mind, perhaps rivaling that of Lincoln, and the site soon evolved into New York's number one tourist destination, drawing half a million people annually.

Perhaps nobody had watched the funeral procession on August 8, 1885, with a wider range of emotions than Mark Twain, who stared down for five hours on the somber pageantry from the windows of his publishing office at Union Square. He would always be indescribably proud to have published Grant's *Personal Memoirs,* even though its commercial success distracted him from his own writing career. At the end of the funeral, when the crowds had dispersed, he and William Tecumseh Sherman retreated to the Lotos Club, where they sat down over liquor and cigars to wrestle anew with the mystery of Grant's personality—a source of never-ending wonder to both men. Sherman always insisted that Grant was a mystery even to himself, a unique intermingling of strength and weakness such as he had never encountered before.

Now he said categorically to Twain that Grant had no peer as a military genius: "Never anything like it before."[157] Perhaps sensing that the man would soon harden into a monument, with the rich flavor of his personality lost to posterity, Sherman laughed at the chaste image of Grant purveyed by the newspapers. "The idea of all this nonsense about Grant not being able to stand rude language & indelicate stories!" he thundered in disbelief. "Why Grant was *full* of humor, & full of the appreciation of it." He recalled how Grant would roar with mirth at the salty, off-color stories peddled by Senator James W. Nye of Nevada. "It makes me sick—that newspaper nonsense. Grant was no namby-pamby fool; he was a *man*—all over—rounded & complete."[158] The comment made Twain realize that in supervising the *Memoirs,* he had failed to press Grant on one key point that would have completed the human portrait and now he kicked himself for this critical omission: Grant had not addressed his struggle with alcohol. It was a contest, Twain reckoned, as huge as any of the titanic battles he had fought and won. "I wish I had thought of it!" Twain exclaimed with frustration. "I would have said to General Grant, 'Put the drunkenness in the Memoirs—& the repentance & reform. Trust the people.'"[159] But he knew that no hint of that existed in the narrative, that it had been too sore a point with Grant, who, in his quiet, inscrutable way, carried his private thoughts on the subject to the grave.

ACKNOWLEDGMENTS

The first person I must thank is someone who is no longer alive and whom I never met: John Y. Simon, the editorial genius behind the *The Papers of Ulysses S. Grant,* published by Southern Illinois University Press. Over the span of more than four decades, starting in 1967, he published thirty-one of the thirty-two thick volumes of Grant's papers. There had never been any edition of Grant's papers before this magnum opus of sustained scholarship. Packed with fifty thousand documents, this splendid edition has transformed our understanding of the man, making Grant biographies from earlier generations seem dated. Blessed with this abundant trove of papers, historians can no longer caricature Grant as an empty-headed dunce, a stereotype that has particularly damaged assessments of his presidency. The Grant who emerges from these papers is articulate and thoughtful, with a firm grasp of many issues.

Once the Grant publication project was completed, the massive store of materials accumulated by John Y. Simon was transferred to Mitchell Memorial Library at Mississippi State University in Starkville, Mississippi. There, under the able leadership of John F. Marszalek, the Grant papers have found a new home under the rubric of The Ulysses S. Grant Presidential Library. In addition to the fifty thousand documents from the published papers, the library contains another two hundred thousand documents that never made it into print—a scholarly feast for anyone even remotely curious about Grant. I especially profited from the numerous oral histories, profiles, newspaper interviews, letters, and diaries that conjure up Grant's life with extraordinary vividness. With his invaluable insights and suggestions, nobody contributed more to this book than John Marszalek, and he and his wife, Jeanne, were exemplary hosts into the bargain. The first-rate team of archivists and assistants at the library provided help with unfailing courtesy and efficiency. I will thank them in alphabetical order: Amanda Carlock, Aaron Crawford, Meg Henderson, Bob Karachuk, David Nolen, and Ryan P. Semmes. I also enjoyed many stimulating discussions with the historians Doug Forrest and L. B. Wilson, who accompanied me to the library each day.

I am extremely grateful to the good folks at the Library of Congress—especially Michelle A. Krowl, its Civil War and Reconstruction specialist, and Jeffrey M. Flannery, head of the Reference and Reader Services Section at the Manuscript Division—for permission to examine the original manuscript of Grant's *Personal Memoirs,* bound in nine volumes and ordinarily kept under lock and key. To see Grant's slanted, wobbly handwriting in his final days was indescribably moving. I also salute the staff at the Newberry Library in Chicago, which houses the revealing Orville E. Babcock Papers. Nelson D. Lankford, vice president for programs at the Virginia Historical Society, guided me through their collections. I also wish to thank Steve Laise, chief of cultural resources at Manhattan sites of the National Park Service, and Stephen Keane, for providing access to the archives of the General Grant National Memorial, stored at Fort Wadsworth on Staten Island. Frank J. Scaturro and the Grant Monument Association added welcome encouragement. At the New-York Historical Society, Marilyn Satin Kushner directed me to the riches of the Steven K. Yasinow Collection of Thomas Nast Cartoons. I also wish to thank Louise Mirrer, the society president; Michael Ryan, the vice president; and Ted O'Reilly, head of the manuscript department. At The Players Foundation for Theatre Education in Manhattan, Raymond Wemmlinger provided access to Adam Badeau's evocative letters to Edwin Booth, a hitherto overlooked source of information. These papers form part of the Hampden-Booth Theatre Library.

One reward of Grant research was that it lured me to many corners of the country that had been terra incognita for me. Anyone who has made the rounds of Civil War battlefields must admire the professionalism and encyclopedic knowledge of the guides and park rangers. I want to thank James H. Ogden III, chief historian at the Chickamauga and Chattanooga National Military Park; A. Wilson Greene, president and CEO of Pamplin Historical Park in Petersburg; Susan Hawkins at the Fort Donelson Visitor Center; Peter Maugle, a park ranger and historian at the Fredericksburg and Spotsylvania National Military Park and his colleague Steve Connelly; and Park Ranger Ben Anderson at the Cold Harbor Unit of the Richmond National Battlefield Park. Bob Swift offered superb commentary at the Appomattox Court House National Historical Park.

I was impressed by the deeply informed battlefield tours given by John W. Schildt at the Antietam National Battlefield and Joel Busenitz at the Gettysburg National Military Park. I was fortunate to receive a private tour of the Shiloh battlefield from two excellent historians from the University of Mississippi: Joseph P. Ward, then the chairman of the history department, and John R. Neff, director of its Center for Civil War Research. I would also like to thank Morgan Gates and the staff of the Vicksburg National Military Park.

Ulysses S. Grant led a vagabond life, leaving behind a string of residences. I learned much about his boyhood from Greg Roberts at the U. S. Grant Birthplace in Point Pleasant, Ohio, and Ellen McCaughey at the U. S. Grant Boyhood Home & Schoolhouse in Georgetown, Ohio. The scenes of Ulysses and Julia Grant's courtship at White Haven are easy to imagine at the beautifully kept Ulysses S. Grant National Historic Site in St. Louis, where superintendent Timothy S. Good and historian Pamela K. Sanfilippo brought that era to life. In Galena, the staff at the Ulysses S. Grant Home offered a comprehensive tour. I found the visit to Grant's final residence on Mount McGregor especially moving. I am indebted to site manager David Hubbard and to William Underhill of the Friends of Ulysses S. Grant Cottage for opening up the house before the official summer season while William Meyer kindly furnished photos. Special thanks to Laura Cohen Apelbaum, former executive director of the Jewish Historical Society of Greater Washington, for taking me to Adas Israel, the small synagogue whose dedication Grant attended in June 1876.

Many friends have accompanied me on these historical adventures and their questions and company have always been invigorating. My stalwart friend Bruce McCall steered me through six straight battlefields, from the Wilderness to Cold Harbor, as we re-created the Overland Campaign. I also want to thank John and Ronna Schneider for driving me around Grant's boyhood haunts; Theresa and Denise Melroy for a freezing but memorable trip to Galena; John Tosi, who escorted me to Fort Donelson and the former site of Fort Henry along with a side trip to Fort Pillow; Martha Stearn and Nancy Norton, who were delightful companions on the visit to the Fort Vancouver National Historic Site; and Courtney Lobel, who joined me on informative trips to Antietam and Gettysburg.

I enjoyed the aid of two fine research assistants: Nick Lehr, who dredged up many useful articles for me, and Michelle Long, who showed special diligence in researching some tough assignments. Many friends alerted me to Grant-related materials that I might have missed. Philip Kunhardt advised me on

Abraham Lincoln books and photographs. Adam Goodheart gave me an over-view of nineteenth-century newspapers. Walter Stahr apprised me of Grant mentions in Edwin M. Stanton's papers at the Library of Congress as he pursued his own Stanton biography. Lynn Sherr generously shared her extensive research files on Susan B. Anthony and her 1872 vote for Grant, a subject largely ignored by earlier biographers. Leon Friedman provided information about Grant's selection of Supreme Court justices. David Michaelis told me of papers related to Ulysses S. Grant III. Karenna Gore pointed me to books and blogs on the Civil War. Liz Robbins provided me with a rare first edition of an 1868 campaign biography of Grant. Hans Binnendijk jogged my imagination with probing questions about Grant. Douglas Schwalbe unearthed a packet of faded newspaper clips about the Grant Cottage in Long Branch, New Jersey. Otis and Nancy Pearsall and Marcia Ely brought to my attention a forgotten reminiscence of Julia Grant in the memoirs of Mrs. Roger A. Pryor. Mercer Warriner and Elizabeth Diggs alerted me to the unpublished memoir of Alexander Murray Ferrier with its recollections of Galena. Michael Evenson steered me to Ian Hope's important work on West Point during Grant's tenure there. A host of Grant descendants, including Ulysses Grant Dietz, Claire Telecki, Miriam Sellgren, John Griffiths, and Julia Castleton, passed along impressions about their famous forebear. I also wish to thank Judy Goldstein, who allowed me to use her lovely apartment as I recuperated from ankle surgery one summer, giving me time to pore over the Civil War trilogies of Shelby Foote and Bruce Catton. Finally I would like to thank Harriet Simon, the widow and able colleague of John Y. Simon, for her encouragement and support.

Research on alcoholism formed an important part of the project. My brother, Dr. Bart Chernow, plied me with vital information and journal articles. Polly McCall, an addiction specialist with long experience with alcoholism, was a fountain of useful ideas. Dr. Henry D. Abraham was generous with his views on the subject of Grant and drinking. Judy Collins helped to educate me about the history of the temperance movement and the early influence of the Washingtonian movement. Many friends and acquaintances, who shall remain nameless here, discussed with me their struggles with alcoholism and I am especially grateful for their candor.

Five readers vetted the manuscript and they have enriched the book throughout. As one of our leading authorities on both Grant and William Tecumseh Sherman, John F. Marszalek was exceedingly generous in providing copious, insightful commentary, even when he differed with some of my conclusions. Harold Holzer, former chairman of the Abraham Lincoln Bicentennial Foundation and a renowned and prolific Lincoln authority, was especially helpful on that and many other dimensions of the story. With great patience, he allowed me to pester him with questions at frequent intervals. Frank Williams, retired chief justice of the Supreme Court of Rhode Island, founding chairman of the Lincoln Forum, and president of the Ulysses S. Grant Association, brought his wide knowledge to bear on many topics. Brenda Wineapple, author of *Ecstatic Nation,* a superb history of the Civil War and Reconstruction era, proved especially perceptive about Grant's psychology. Oskar Eustis, head of the Public Theater in New York and a great history buff, gave the book a warmly appreciative reading amid many demands on his time. These five readers saved me from many errors of fact and interpretation and I am deeply grateful for the time they took to wade through my long manuscript.

At Penguin Press, I must thank Casey Denis for her adept editorial assistance, Sarah Hutson for her energetic publicity work, and copy editor Maureen Clark and senior production editor Bruce Giffords for their scrupulous attention to my text. Evan Gaffney created the beautiful jacket, Lucia Bernard the handsome interior design, and Jeffrey L. Ward the terrific maps. At this point in the acknowledgments, I usually thank my editor, Ann Godoff, and my agent, Melanie Jackson, for their sterling contributions to the book in question and I must do so here again. Melanie had many profound reflections on Grant, and Ann had a particularly fine sense of the complex architecture of the story. But with this book—my seventh with Melanie, my sixth with Ann—I must also thank them for the loving encouragement and expert guidance they have given me throughout my career. They have enabled me to enjoy a life as a biographer far more interesting and rewarding than I had any right to expect when I quit my ambition to be a novelist thirty years ago. Quite simply, I am the luckiest writer in town to have these two exceptional ladies so solidly in my corner. When they are on my side, I feel as if I can never go too far wrong.

NOTES

ABBREVIATIONS

EBC. Edwin Booth Collection, Hampden-Booth Theatre Library, The Players Foundation for Theatre Education, Players Club, New York City

EBWP. Elihu B. Washburne Papers

EMSP. Edwin M. Stanton Papers

FL. Raymond H. Fogler Library, University of Maine

GFP. Grant Family Papers

GMA. Grant Monument Association

GPL. Ulysses S. Grant Presidential Library, Mississippi State University, Starkville, Mississippi (S = Series; B = Box; F = Folder)

Grant, *Memoirs.* Ulysses S. Grant. *Memoirs and Selected Letters.* New York: Library of America, 1990.

HGP. Hamlin Garland Papers. Copies used for this book at Ulysses S. Grant Presidential Library. Originals at Special Collections, Collection no. 0200, USC Libraries, University of Southern California

JHWP. James H. Wilson Papers

JSPP. James S. Pike Papers

Julia Grant, *Memoirs.* Julia Dent Grant. *The Personal Memoirs of Julia Dent Grant.* Edited by John Y. Simon. Carbondale: Southern Illinois University Press, 1975. Reprint.

LLP. Lloyd Lewis Papers

LoC. Library of Congress

LRGP. Lucretia Rudolph Garfield Papers

NL. Newberry Library

NYHS. New-York Historical Society

OEBP. Orville E. Babcock Papers

OR. *War of the Rebellion . . . Official Records of the Union and Confederate Armies.* 128 vols. Washington, D.C.: Government Printing Office, 1880–1901.

PUSG. *The Papers of Ulysses S. Grant.* Edited by John Y. Simon et al. Carbondale: Southern Illinois University Press, 1967–2012.

Richardson, *A Personal History.* Albert D. Richardson. *A Personal History of Ulysses S. Grant.* Washington, D.C.: National Tribune, 1868.

SCP. Sylvanus Cadwallader Papers

Sheridan, *Memoirs.* Philip Henry Sheridan. *Personal Memoirs of P. H. Sheridan, General, United States Army.* 2 vols. New York: Charles L. Webster, 1888.

Sherman, *Memoirs.* William Tecumseh Sherman. *Memoirs of General W. T. Sherman.* New York: Library of America, 1990.

TNC. Thomas Nast Cartoons, Steven K. Yasinow Collection

USGA. Ulysses S. Grant Association

USGH. Ulysses S. Grant Homepage. Interviews. www.granthomepage.com/interviews.htm.

USGP. Ulysses S. Grant Papers

Washburne, *Biography.* Mark Washburne. *A Biography of Elihu Benjamin Washburne: Congressman, Secretary of State, Envoy Extraordinary.* Vol. 2, *Illinois Republican During the Civil War and the Rise of Ulysses S. Grant.* N.p.: Xlibris Corporation, 2001.

WCCP. William Conant Church Papers

WFSP. William Farrar Smith Papers

Wilson, *Rawlins.* James Harrison Wilson. *The Life of John A. Rawlins: Lawyer, Assistant Adjutant General, Chief of Staff, Major General of Volunteers, and Secretary of War.* New York: Neale Publishing, 1916.

Young, *Around the World.* John Russell Young. *Around the World with General Grant.* Baltimore and London: Johns Hopkins University Press, 2002. Reprint.

INTRODUCTION: THE SPHINX TALKS

1. Ward, *A Disposition to Be Rich,* 236.
2. Ibid., 235.
3. Grant, *Memoirs,* 1:5.
4. Flood, *Grant's Final Victory,* 73.
5. *The Saturday Evening Post,* September 9, 1901.
6. Flood, *Grant's Final Victory,* 165.
7. Green, "Civil War Public Opinion of General Grant."
8. Kaplan, *Mr. Clemens and Mark Twain,* 276; Flood, *Grant's Final Victory,* 140.
9. Twain, *The Letters of Mark Twain,* 3:261.
10. Flood, *Grant's Final Victory,* 130-31.
11. Paine, "Mark Twain's Letters." Letter to Henry Ward Beecher, September 11, 1885.

12. Fowler, *Patriotic Orations,* 164–65.
13. *USGA Newsletter,* April 1964.
14. Wilentz, "The Return of Ulysses."
15. Young, *Around the World,* 378.
16. Simpson, *Ulysses S. Grant,* 464.
17. Keegan, *The American Civil War,* 124.
18. Ibid., 328.
19. Wilentz, "The Return of Ulysses."
20. Woodward, "The Enigma of U. S. Grant."
21. Douglass, "U. S. Grant and the Colored People."
22. Ibid.
23. Wilentz, "The Return of Ulysses."
24. Murthy, "Facing Addiction in the United States."

CHAPTER ONE: COUNTRY BUMPKIN

1. *USGA Newsletter,* January 1971.
2. GPL. S2 B54 F36. Letter from Henry K. Hannah to Hamlin Garland, September 9, 1896.
3. Simon, "Ulysses S. Grant and the Jews."
4. Grant, *Memoirs,* 1:17.
5. Grant, "The Early Life of Gen. Grant."
6. Grant, *Memoirs,* 1:17.
7. Grant, "The Early Life of Gen. Grant."
8. Dorsett, "The Problem of Ulysses S. Grant's Drinking During the Civil War."
9. Grant, *Memoirs,* 1:18.
10. Corum, *Ulysses Underground,* 41.
11. Simpson, *Ulysses S. Grant,* 7.
12. Ibid., 1.
13. Grant, *Memoirs,* 1:19.
14. *USGA Newsletter,* October 1970.
15. White, *American Ulysses,* 20.
16. Cramer, *Ulysses S. Grant,* 128–29.
17. Richardson, *A Personal History,* 58.
18. Cramer, *Ulysses S. Grant,* 59–60.
19. Smith, *Grant,* 22.
20. *New York Graphic,* September 16, 1879.
21. *Troy Intelligencer,* April 17, 1892.
22. GPL. S2 B54 F9. "Interview with W. E. Wade." HGP.
23. *The Castigator,* February 27, 1827.
24. Ibid., January 15, 1828.
25. Grant, *Memoirs,* 1:30.
26. *USGA Newsletter,* October 1970.
27. *The Castigator,* September 25, 1832.
28. Donald, *Lincoln,* 129.
29. Stevens, *Grant in St. Louis,* 86.
30. GPL. S2 B54 F39. Letter from G. N. Merrymasher to Hamlin Garland. HGP.
31. Ibid. S2 B54 F9. "Interview with W. E. Wade." HGP.
32. Perret, *Ulysses S. Grant,* 10.
33. *USGA Newsletter,* October 1970 & January 1971.
34. *New York Graphic,* September 16, 1879.
35. *The Philadelphia Press,* December 20, 1879.
36. Simpson, *Ulysses S. Grant,* 9.

37. Smith, *Autobiography of Mark Twain,* 1:476.
38. *Chicago Daily Tribune,* November 1, 1879.
39. *Burlington Free Press,* July 29, 1885.
40. *The St. Louis Globe-Democrat,* April 27, 1897.
41. Richardson, *A Personal History,* 48.
42. Corum, *Ulysses Underground,* 78.
43. *The Philadelphia Press,* December 20, 1879.
44. *PUSG,* 12:332. Letter to Julia Dent Grant, October 20, 1864.
45. Grant, *Memoirs,* 1:27.
46. *PUSG,* 15:329.
47. Simpson, *Ulysses S. Grant,* 9.
48. Grant, *Memoirs,* 1:19.
49. *USGA Newsletter,* October 1970 & January 1971.
50. GPL. S2 B54 F35. Letter from Nathan Fenn to Julia Dent Grant. HGP.
51. Porter, "Personal Traits of General Grant."
52. Simpson, "Butcher? Racist?"
53. Perret, *Ulysses S. Grant,* 14.
54. Porter, *Campaigning with Grant,* 166.
55. Grant, "The Early Life of Gen. Grant."
56. *The Philadelphia Press,* December 20, 1879.
57. *USGA Newsletter,* January 1971.
58. Grant, *Memoirs,* 1:26.
59. LoC. USGP. Series 4, Vol. 1. Original manuscript of Grant's *Memoirs.*
60. Grant, *Memoirs,* 1:26–27.
61. *USGA Newsletter,* January 1971.
62. Porter, *Campaigning with Grant,* 214.
63. Richardson, *A Personal History,* 60.
64. GPL. S2 B54 F12. Letter from Richard Dawson to Hamlin Garland, July 17, 1896. HGP.
65. White, *American Ulysses,* 22.
66. GPL. S2 B54 F3. "Interview with Jane Howard Chapman." HGP.
67. Grant, *Memoirs,* 1:28.
68. *PUSG,* 1:3.
69. Ibid., 36. Letter to Julia Dent, August 31, 1844.
70. *New York Herald,* July 24, 1878.
71. Richardson, *A Personal History,* 60.

CHAPTER TWO: THE DARLING YOUNG LIEUTENANT

1. Richardson, *A Personal History*, 66.
2. Grant, *Memoirs*, 1:29.
3. Simpson, *Ulysses S. Grant*, 11.
4. Grant, *Memoirs*, 1:33.
5. *PUSG*, l:5. Letter to R. McKinstry Griffith, September 22, 1839.
6. Ibid.
7. Ibid., 1:6.
8. Ibid., 6.
9. Foote, *The Civil War*, 1:701.
10. *The New York Times,* July 24, 1885.
11. GPL. S2 B54 F12. "Interview with Fred Dent." HGP.
12. Snell, *From First to Last*, 8.
13. White, *American Ulysses*, 41–42.
14. "Grant Reminiscences." *Chicago Daily Tribune*, September 1, 1885.
15. Eaton, *Grant, Lincoln and the Freedmen*, 256.
16. Porter, *Campaigning with Grant*, 342.
17. Young, *Around the World*, 378.
18. *The New York Times*, July 24, 1885.
19. Simpson, *Ulysses S. Grant*, 16.
20. Young, *Around the World*, 261.
21. Ibid., 433.
22. Ibid., 304.
23. Grant, *Memoirs*, 1:32.
24. GPL. S2 B54 F23. Letter from M. T. Burke to Hamlin Garland, September 26, 1896. HGP.
25. Perret, *Ulysses S. Grant*, 28.
26. Ibid., 31.
27. Grant, *Memoirs*, 1:33.
28. Ibid., 33–34.
29. Ibid., 34.
30. Catton, *Grant Takes Command*, 24.
31. Fry, "An Acquaintance with Grant."
32. Ibid.
33. Ibid.
34. McFeely, *Grant*, 16.
35. Badeau, *Grant in Peace*, 401.
36. Grant, *Memoirs*, 1:35.
37. GPL. S2 B54 F23. Letter from M. T. Burke to Hamlin Garland, September 26, 1896. HGP.
38. Grant, *Memoirs*, 1:39.
39. Longstreet, *From Manassas to Appomattox*, 5.
40. GPL. S2 B54 F13. "Interview with Julia Dent Grant." HGP.
41. Casey, "When Grant Went a-Courtin'."
42. Stevens, *Grant in St. Louis*, 17–18.
43. Julia Grant, *Memoirs*, 33.
44. Casey, "When Grant Went a-Courtin'."
45. Julia Grant, *Memoirs*, 39.
46. Farmer, *National Exposition Souvenir*, 58.
47. Julia Grant, *Memoirs*, 37.
48. Ibid., 35–36.
49. Ibid., 34–35.
50. Casey, "When Grant Went a-Courtin'."
51. "Longstreet's Reminiscences." *The New York Times*, July 24, 1885.
52. Farmer, *National Exposition Souvenir*, 59.
53. Pryor, *My Day*, 379.
54. Farmer, *National Exposition Souvenir*, 59.
55. *Saratoga Daily Advertiser*, April 27, 1893.
56. USGH. "Interview with Julia Dent Grant."
57. McFeely, *Grant*, 24.
58. *Los Angeles Times*, February 23, 1896, and Julia Grant, *Memoirs*, 42.
59. GPL. S2 B5 F20. *Los Angeles Times*, February 23, 1896, and Julia Grant, *Memoirs*, 34.
60. Taussig, "Personal Recollections of General Grant."
61. USGH. "Interview with Eliza Shaw."
62. Casey, "When Grant Went a-Courtin'."
63. Ibid.
64. GPL. S2 B5 F20. "Interview with Julia Grant." HGP.
65. *St. Louis Republican*, July 24, 1885.
66. Casey, "When Grant Went a-Courtin'."
67. Ibid.
68. Julia Grant, *Memoirs*, 50.
69. Ibid., 49.

CHAPTER THREE: ROUGH AND READY

1. Stahr, *Seward*, 96.
2. Grant, *Memoirs*, 1:41.
3. Perret, *Ulysses S. Grant*, 51.
4. GPL. S2 B54 F29. "Conversations with Grant" by John Russell Young. HGP.
5. *PUSG*, 1:28. Letter to Mrs. George B. Bailey, June 6, 1844.
6. Ibid., 40. Letter to Julia Dent, January 12, 1845.
7. Casey, "When Grant Went a-Courtin'."
8. Berkin, *Civil War Wives*, 232.
9. *PUSG*, 1:44. Letter to Julia Dent, May 6, 1845.
10. Grant, *Memoirs*, 1:50.
11. *PUSG*, 1:48. Letter to Julia Dent, July 6, 1845.
12. Ibid., 50. Letter to Julia Dent, July 11, 1845.
13. Ibid., 53. Letter to Julia Dent, September 14, 1845.
14. Ibid., 57. Letter to Julia Dent, October 10, 1845.
15. Sherman, *Memoirs*, 105.
16. Greenberg, *A Wicked War*, 99.
17. Grant, *Memoirs*, 1:95.
18. Girardi, *Civil War Generals*, 68.
19. *PUSG*, 31:65. Letter to Thomas H. Taylor, September 19, 1883.
20. "General Grant and the South." *The New York Times*, July 24, 1885.
21. Ibid.
22. USGH. "Interview with J. D. Elderkin." HGP.
23. GPL. S2 B54 F27. Letter from Jesse R. Grant to Thomas L. Hamer, April 20, 1846. HGP.
24. Shapiro, *Shakespeare in America*, xix.
25. Perret, *Ulysses S. Grant*, 49.
26. Shapiro, *Shakespeare in America*, xix.
27. Young, *Around the World*, 376–77.
28. *PUSG*, 1:71. Letter to Julia Dent, February 5, 1846.

29. Ibid., 81. Letter to Julia Dent, April 20, 1846.
30. Grant, *Memoirs,* 1:66.
31. Smith, *Grant,* 48.
32. *PUSG,* 1:96. Letter to John W. Lowe, June 26, 1846.
33. Ibid., 85. Letter to Julia Dent, May 11, 1846.
34. Smith, *Grant,* 339.
35. Garland, "Grant's Quiet Years at Northern Posts."
36. Grant, *Memoirs,* 1:68.
37. Ibid., 69.
38. *PUSG,* 1:87. Letter to Julia Dent, May 11, 1846.
39. Young, *Around the World,* 246.
40. *PUSG,* 1:91. Letter to Julia Dent, June 5, 1846.
41. Ibid., 102. Letter to Julia Dent, July 25, 1846.
42. Ibid., 97. Letter to John W. Lowe, June 26, 1846.
43. Ibid., 106–7. Letter to Bvt. Col. John Garland, August 1846. [n.d.]
44. USGH. "Interview with J. D. Elderkin." HGP.
45. *PUSG,* 1:121. Letter from Brig. Gen. Thomas L. Hamer to a friend [Dec. 1846].
46. Ibid., 105. Letter to Julia Dent, August 14, 1846.
47. Grant, *Memoirs,* 1:76.
48. Smith, *Grant,* 55.
49. Simpson, "Butcher? Racist?"
50. Smith, *Grant,* 55.
51. Grant, *Memoirs,* 1:78.
52. Ibid., 81–82.
53. Ibid., 82.
54. *PUSG,* 1:117. Letter to Julia Dent, November 7, 1846.
55. Ibid.
56. GPL. S2 B54 F43. "Interview with Chilton A. White." HGP.
57. Grant, *Memoirs,* 1:83.
58. Smith, *Grant,* 59.
59. Grant, *Memoirs,* 1:83.
60. Porter, *Campaigning with Grant,* 193.
61. Grant, *Memoirs,* 1:94.
62. *PUSG,* 1:128. Letter to Julia Dent, February 25, 1847.
63. Korda, *Clouds of Glory,* 117.
64. Grant, *Memoirs,* 1:87.
65. *PUSG,* 1:129. Letter to Julia Dent, April 3, 1847.
66. Greenberg, *A Wicked War,* 208.
67. *USGA Newsletter,* January 1971.
68. Grant, *Report of the First Reunion,* 41.
69. *PUSG,* 1:131. Letter to Julia Dent, April 24, 1847.

70. Ibid., 132.
71. Ibid., 145. Letter to Addressee Unknown, September 12, 1847.
72. Ibid., 144. Letter to Addressee Unknown, August 22, 1847.
73. Korda, *Clouds of Glory,* 141.
74. *PUSG,* 1:143. Letter to Addressee Unknown, August 22, 1847.
75. Julia Grant, *Memoirs,* 315.
76. "Longstreet's Reminiscences." *The New York Times,* July 24, 1885.
77. Grant, *Memoirs,* 1:104.
78. USGH. "Interview with J. D. Elderkin." HGP.
79. GPL. S2 B54 F41. Letter from Major Edwin A. Sherman to Edward J. Wheeler, October 6, 1908. HGP.
80. *PUSG,* 11:298. Letter from Bvt. Lt. Gen. Winfield Scott to Elihu B. Washburne, July 2, 1864.
81. Grant, *Memoirs,* 1:106.
82. Ibid., 109.
83. *PUSG,* 1:183. Letter from Bvt. Maj. Gen. Roger Jones, January 14, 1850.
84. Young, *Men and Memories,* 2:474.
85. Korda, *Clouds of Glory,* 155.
86. Pryor, *Reading the Man,* 167.
87. *New York World,* July 5, 1881.
88. Grant, *Memoirs,* 1:111.
89. *PUSG,* 1:146. Letter to Julia Dent, September 1847.
90. Ibid., 147.
91. Grant, *Memoirs,* 1:112.
92. *PUSG,* 1:149. Letter to Julia Dent, January 9, 1848.
93. Grant, *Memoirs,* 1:119.
94. Ibid., 120.
95. *PUSG,* 1:157. Letter to Julia Dent, May 7, 1848.
96. GPL. S2 B54 F13. "Interview with J. D. Elderkin." HGP.
97. Simpson, *Ulysses S. Grant,* 44–45.
98. GPL. S2 B4 F10. Letter from Tekones Rowe [John Rowe?] to his wife, May 12, 1848.
99. Ibid., S2 B24 F12. Letter from Richard Dawson to Hamlin Garland, July 17, 1896. HGP.
100. Grant, *Memoirs, 1*:129.
101. Foner, *Fiery Trial,* 52.
102. Grant, *Memoirs,* 1:42.
103. Foner, *Fiery Trial,* 53.

CHAPTER FOUR: THE SON OF TEMPERANCE

1. Perret, *Ulysses S. Grant,* 80.
2. GPL. S2 B5 F20. "Interview with Julia Grant." HGP.
3. Casey, "When Grant Went a-Courtin.'"
4. Ross, *The General's Wife,* 45.
5. Waugh, *U. S. Grant,* 33.
6. GPL. S2 B54 F9. "Interview with Samuel Simpson." HGP.
7. *Troy Intelligencer,* April 17, 1892.
8. USGH. "Interview with Louisa Boggs." HGP.

9. GPL. S2 B21 F8. LLP.
10. USGH. "Interview with Louisa Boggs." HGP.
11. Ross, *The General's Wife,* 48.
12. Julia Grant, *Memoirs,* 56.
13. Ibid., 57.
14. Ibid.
15. Ibid., 58.
16. Ibid.
17. Ibid.
18. Richardson, *A Personal History,* 110.
19. *The New York Times Book Review,* July 1, 2012.

20. Smith, *Grant,* 75.
21. Garland, "Grant's Quiet Years at Northern Posts."
22. Perret, *Ulysses S. Grant,* 85.
23. USGH. "Interview with Colonel James E. Pitman." WCCP.
24. GPL. S2 B5 F20. "Interview with Julia Grant." HGP.
25. Ibid.
26. Julia Grant, *Memoirs,* 68.
27. USGH. "Interview with Colonel James E. Pitman." WCCP.
28. Simpson, *Ulysses S. Grant,* 51.
29. USGH. "Interview with Colonel James E. Pitman." WCCP.
30. GPL. S2 B54 F8. "Interview with Silas Farmer." HGP.
31. *PUSG,* 1:194. Letter to Bvt. Maj. Oscar F. Winship, June 14, 1850.
32. Simpson, *Ulysses S. Grant,* 52.
33. USGH. "Interview with Colonel James E. Pitman." WCCP.
34. Ibid.
35. Richardson, *A Personal History,* 119.
36. *PUSG,* 1:206–7. Letter to Julia Dent Grant, June 7, 1851.
37. Ibid., 212. Letter to Julia Dent Grant, June 22, 1851.
38. Ibid., 223. Letter to Julia Dent Grant, August 3, 1851.
39. Ibid., 215. Letter to Julia Dent Grant, June 29, 1851.
40. Simpson, *Ulysses S. Grant,* 53.
41. Garland, "Grant's Quiet Years at Northern Posts."
42. Okrent, *Last Call,* 9.
43. Perret, *Ulysses S. Grant,* 87.
44. Garland, "Grant's Quiet Years at Northern Posts."
45. Ross, *The General's Wife,* 68.
46. Julia Grant, *Memoirs,* 69.
47. Ibid., 71.
48. Ibid.
49. *PUSG,* 1:243. Letter to Julia Dent Grant, July 1, 1852.
50. LoC. WCCP. Box 2. "Interview with H. C. Hodges."
51. Perret, *Ulysses S. Grant,* 93.
52. *PUSG,* 1:248. Letter to Julia Dent Grant, July 15, 1852.
53. GPL. S2 B5 F27–28. Undated obituary of Ulysses S. Grant Jr.
54. McFeely, *Grant,* 47.
55. Garland, "Grant's Quiet Years at Northern Posts."
56. *Ohio Daily Journal,* January 27, 1880.
57. Grant, *Memoirs,* 1:131.
58. Garland, "Grant's Quiet Years at Northern Posts."
59. Grant, *Memoirs,* 1:131.
60. Ibid., 132.
61. Lewis, "Reminiscences of Delia B. Sheffield."

62. Garland, "Grant's Quiet Years at Northern Posts."
63. *PUSG,* 1:253. Letter to Julia Dent Grant, August 9, 1852.
64. Ibid., 252.
65. Ibid., 288. Letter to Julia Dent Grant, February 15, 1853.
66. *San Francisco Chronicle,* October 6, 1879.
67. *PUSG,* 1:257. Letter to Julia Dent Grant, August 20, 1852.
68. Ibid., 257–58.
69. Grant, *Memoirs,* 1:135.
70. *PUSG,* 1:267. Letter to Julia Dent Grant, September 19, 1852.
71. Ibid., 279. Letter to Julia Dent Grant, January 3, 1853.
72. Allen and Boskey, "The Aftereffects of Alcoholism."
73. GPL. S2 B54 F10. "Interview with General A. G. Smith." HGP.
74. Ibid. S2 B24 F13. "Interview with Julia Dent Grant." HGP.
75. *PUSG,* 1:268. Letter to Julia Dent Grant, October 7, 1852.
76. Stahr, *Seward,* 138.
77. *PUSG,* 1:270. Letter to Julia Dent Grant, October 26, 1852.
78. Ibid., 286. Letter to Julia Dent Grant, January 29, 1853.
79. USGH. "Interview with J. D. Elderkin." HGP.
80. Lewis, "Reminiscences of Delia B. Sheffield."
81. Garland, "Grant's Quiet Years at Northern Posts."
82. *PUSG,* 1:307. Letter to Julia Dent Grant, July 13, 1853.
83. GPL. S2 B54 F30. Letter from Thomas M. Anderson, November 25, 1897. HGP.
84. *PUSG,* 1:296. Letter to Julia Dent Grant, March 19, 1853.
85. GPL. S2 B54 F41. Letter from Major Edwin A. Sherman to Edward J. Wheeler, October 6, 1908. HGP.
86. *PUSG,* 1:300. Letter to Julia Dent Grant, May 20, 1853.
87. Lewis, "Reminiscences of Delia B. Sheffield."
88. Ellington, *The Trial of U. S. Grant,* 122.
89. Smith, *Grant,* 638.
90. GPL. S2 B4 F10. Letter from Henry C. Hodges to William C. Church, January 5, 1876. WCCP.
91. Simpson, *Ulysses S. Grant,* 58.
92. Lewis, "Reminiscences of Delia B. Sheffield."
93. GPL. S2 B24 F15. "Interview with General Robert Macfeely." HGP.
94. Ellington, *The Trial of U. S. Grant,* 168.
95. Perret, *Ulysses S. Grant,* 101.
96. *PUSG,* 1:288. Letter to Julia Dent Grant, February 15, 1853.

CHAPTER FIVE: PAYDAY

1. *PUSG,* 1:315. Letter to Julia Dent Grant, January 18, 1854.
2. Ibid.

3. Ibid., 316. Letter to Julia Dent Grant, February 2, 1854.
4. Ibid., 317.

5. Ibid., 316.

6. Ibid., 320. Letter to Julia Dent Grant, February 6, 1854.

7. Ibid., 321.

8. Ellington, *The Trial of U. S. Grant,* 151.

9. Shields, "General Grant at Fort Humboldt in the Early Days."

10. Ibid.

11. GPL. S2 B54 F39. Letter from Stephen L. Merchant to Hamlin Garland, December 27, 1896. HGP.

12. Shields, "General Grant at Fort Humboldt in the Early Days."

13. Ellington, *The Trial of U. S. Grant,* 133.

14. Shields, "General Grant at Fort Humboldt in the Early Days."

15. GPL. S2 B24 F14. "Interview with General Henry Heth." HGP.

16. LoC. WCCP. Box 2. "Interview with W. I. Reed."

17. Grant, *Memoirs,* 1:141.

18. *PUSG,* 1:323. Letter to Julia Dent Grant, March 6, 1854.

19. Ibid.

20. Smith, *Grant,* 88.

21. GPL. S2 B54 F7. "Interview with General Augustus Chetlain." HGP.

22. LoC. WCCP. Box 2. Letter from Col. Granville O. Haller to William Conant Church. [n.d.]

23. GPL. S2 B54 F9. Letter from Ben Perley Poore to Hamlin Garland, August 1, 1885. HGP.

24. Ibid. S2 B4 F9–11. Letter from Thomas M. Anderson to Gen. Charles King, January 20, 1915.

25. Ibid. S2 B4 F10. Letter from Henry C. Hodges to William C. Church, January 5, 1876. WCCP.

26. Ibid. S2 B54 F30. Letter from Thomas M. Anderson to Hamlin Garland. August 15, 1896. HGP.

27. Ibid.

28. Morgan, "From City Point to Appomattox with General Grant."

29. Wilson, *Rawlins,* 18.

30. Woodward, *Mary Chesnut's Civil War,* 520. Diary entry for January 1, 1864.

31. *PUSG,* 1:330–31. Letter from Jesse Grant to Jefferson Davis, June 21, 1854.

32. McFeely, *Grant,* 56.

33. Ross, *The General's Wife,* 75.

34. Ibid.

35. "Mrs. U. S. Grant Sinking." *Chicago Sunday Tribune,* December 14, 1902.

36. Young, *Around the World,* 378.

37. *The New York Times,* July 24, 1885.

38. Richardson, *A Personal History,* 135.

39. Ellington, *The Trial of U. S. Grant,* 163.

40. Shields, "General Grant at Fort Humboldt in the Early Days."

41. *PUSG,* 1:332. Letter to Julia Dent Grant, May 2, 1854.

42. Grant, *Memoirs,* 1:139.

43. GPL. S2 B24 F13. "Interview with Julia Dent Grant." HGP.

44. Ibid.

45. Ibid. S2 B25 F13. "Interview with Major Elderkin." HGP.

46. Garland, "Grant's Quiet Years at Northern Posts."

47. "New Story of Grant." *The St. Louis Globe-Democrat,* December 13, 1896.

48. Stahr, *Seward,* 144.

49. *PUSG,* 32:11–12. Letter to Thomas H. Stevens, June 13, 1854.

50. Ibid., 1:305. Letter to Julia Dent Grant, June 28, 1853.

51. GPL. S2 B54 F33. Letter from Walter B. Camp to Hamlin Garland, October 17, 1896. HGP.

52. USGH. "Interview with Simon Bolivar Buckner." HGP.

53. Ranney, *The Papers of Frederick Law Olmsted,* 346.

54. Corum, *Ulysses Underground,* 240.

55. Waugh, *U. S. Grant,* 41.

56. Stevens, *Grant in St. Louis,* 36.

57. GPL. S2 B5 F20. "Interview with Julia Dent Grant." HGP.

58. McFeely, *Grant,* 56–57.

59. Ibid., 57.

60. Julia Grant, *Memoirs,* 76.

61. Ibid.

62. USGH. "Interview with Louisa Boggs." HGP.

63. GPL. S2 B54 F34. Letter from G. W. Fishback to Hamlin Garland, March 7, 1895. HGP.

64. Julia Grant, *Memoirs,* 78.

65. Garland, "Grant's Life in Missouri."

66. *USGA Newsletter,* January 21, 1971.

67. Richardson, *A Personal History,* 140.

68. Taussig, "Personal Recollections of General Grant."

69. Ibid.

70. Julia Grant, *Memoirs,* 78.

71. Grant, *Memoirs,* 1:141.

72. Julia Grant, *Memoirs,* 79.

73. USGH. "Interview with Julia Grant."

74. Julia Grant, *Memoirs,* 75.

75. *St. Louis Republican,* July 24, 1885.

76. Grant, "General Grant's Son Speaks of His Father."

77. GPL. S2 B5 F20. "Interview with Julia Grant." HGP.

78. Grant, "General Grant's Son Speaks of His Father."

79. *St. Louis Republican,* July 24, 1885.

80. Grant, "My Father as I Knew Him."

81. GPL. S2 B54 F23. Letter from M. T. Burke to Hamlin Garland, September 26, 1896. HGP.

82. Watrous, "Grant as His Son Saw Him."

83. Julia Grant, *Memoirs,* 162.

84. "Grant Reminiscences." *Chicago Daily Tribune,* September 1, 1885.

85. Julia Grant, *Memoirs,* 162.

86. GPL. S2 B5 F27–28. Undated obituary for Ulysses S. Grant, Jr.

87. Ross, *The General's Wife,* 139.

88. Smith, *Grant,* 92.
89. Stevens, *Grant in St. Louis,* 44.
90. GPL. S2 B54 F37. Letter from Jesse A. Jones to Hamlin Garland, March 16, 1896.
91. *St. Louis Republican,* July 24, 1885.
92. Smith, *Grant,* 91.
93. Stevens, *Grant in St. Louis,* 43.
94. USGH. "Interview with James Longstreet."
95. Ibid.
96. *PUSG,* 1:335. Letter to Jesse Root Grant, December 28, 1856.
97. Simpson, *Ulysses S. Grant,* 68.
98. Julia Grant, *Memoirs,* 91.
99. Grant, *Memoirs,* 1:150.
100. Young, *Around the World,* 284.
101. Fish, "General Grant."
102. McFeely, *Grant,* 68.
103. Grant, *Memoirs,* 1:143.
104. Goodheart, *1861,* 65.
105. Julia Grant, *Memoirs,* 181.
106. Simpson, *Ulysses S. Grant,* 71.
107. Ibid., 67.
108. Ross, *The General's Wife,* 96.
109. Perret, *Ulysses S. Grant,* 107.
110. Garland, "Grant's Life in Missouri."
111. GPL. S2 B54 F12. "Interview with Louisa Boggs." HGP.
112. Simpson, "Butcher? Racist?"
113. GPL. S2 B54 F23. Letter from M. T. Burke to Hamlin Garland, September 26, 1896. HGP.
114. *PUSG,* 1:337. Letter to Jesse Root Grant, February 7, 1857.
115. Julia Grant, *Memoirs,* 162.
116. Ross, *The General's Wife,* 93.
117. Julia Grant, *Memoirs,* 80.
118. GPL. S2 B54 F12. "Interview with Louisa Boggs." HGP.
119. Grant, *Memoirs,* 2:473.
120. "How Grant Got to Know Rawlins." *Army and Navy Journal,* September 12, 1868.
121. GPL. S2 B24 F12. "Interview with Mrs. Baker." HGP.
122. Julia Grant, *Memoirs,* 80.

123. USGH. "Interview with Louisa Boggs."
124. Garland, "Grant's Life in Missouri"; USGH. "Interview with Louisa Boggs."
125. GPL. S2 B54 F12. "Interview with Louisa Boggs." HGP.
126. Ibid.
127. Wickenden, "Union Man."
128. Garland, "Grant's Life in Missouri."
129. McFeely, *Grant,* 68–69.
130. Young, *Around the World,* 375.
131. Richardson, *A Personal History,* 155.
132. *The Macon* [Missouri], January 24, 1917.
133. Ross, *The General's Wife,* 96.
134. USGH. "Interview with Louisa Boggs."
135. *PUSG,* 1:346. Letter to Jesse Root Grant, March 12, 1859.
136. Ibid., 347. "Manumission of Slave," March 29, 1859.
137. Stevens, *Grant in St. Louis,* 52.
138. USGH. "Interview with Mary Robinson."
139. Taussig, "Personal Recollections of General Grant."
140. "Chat in Public Resorts." *New York Tribune,* August 2, 1885.
141. Julia Grant, *Memoirs,* 326.
142. Grant, *Memoirs,* 1:142.
143. Julia Grant, *Memoirs,* 482.
144. Stevens, *Grant in St. Louis,* 58.
145. Donald, *Lincoln,* 169.
146. Grant, *Memoirs,* 1:142.
147. Foote, *The Civil War,* 1:31.
148. Grant, *Memoirs,* 1:19.
149. Garland, "Grant's Life in Missouri."
150. Julia Grant, *Memoirs,* 82.
151. GPL. S2 B54 F25. "Interview with George W. Fishback."
152. Julia Grant, *Memoirs,* 82.
153. *PUSG,* 1:355. Letter to Julia Dent Grant, March 14, 1860.
154. GPL. S2 B5 F13. Letter from Jesse Root Grant to James G. Wilson, March 20, 1869.
155. Ibid. S2 B54 F9. "Interview with Andrew M. Haines." HGP.

CHAPTER SIX: THE STORE CLERK

1. Julia Grant, *Memoirs,* 83.
2. *The Revolution,* March 3, 1869.
3. *Chicago Inter-Ocean,* November 4, 1879.
4. Julia Grant, *Memoirs,* 84.
5. GPL. S2 B54 F23. Letter from M. T. Burke to Hamlin Garland, September 26, 1896. HGP.
6. Grant, "My Father as I Knew Him."
7. USGH. "Interview with Melancthon T. Burke."
8. *Troy Intelligencer,* April 17, 1892.
9. GPL. S2 B5 F20. "Interview with Julia Grant." HGP.
10. Cramer, *Ulysses S. Grant,* 31.
11. Flood, *Grant's Final Victory,* 217.
12. *PUSG,* 1:359. Letter to Addressee Unknown, December 1860.
13. GPL. S2 B54 F9. "Interview with Andrew M. Haines." HGP.

14. Garland, "Grant at the Outbreak of the War."
15. *Troy Intelligencer,* April 17, 1892.
16. GPL. S2 B21 F5. Letter from Lawrence E. Blair to Lloyd Lewis, May 27, 1945. LLP.
17. *Troy Intelligencer,* April 17, 1892.
18. Ibid.
19. Ibid.
20. Grant, *In the Days of My Father,* 10–11.
21. GPL. S2 B54 F9. "Interview with Melancthon T. Burke." HGP.
22. Ibid. S2 B21 F5. Letter from Lawrence E. Blair to Lloyd Lewis, May 21, 1945. LLP.
23. Armstrong, *Warrior in Two Camps,* 84.
24. Ibid., 73–74.
25. Simpson, *Ulysses S. Grant,* 74.
26. Armstrong, *Warrior in Two Camps,* 204.
27. USGH. "Interview with Melancthon T. Burke."

28. Washburne, *Biography*, 491.
29. Goodheart, *1861*, 39.
30. *USGA Newsletter*, July 1964.
31. Grant, *Memoirs*, 1:144.
32. Richardson, *A Personal History*, 166.
33. *PUSG*, 1:357. Letter to Mr. Davis, August 7, 1860.
34. Grant, *Memoirs*, 1:144.
35. GPL. S2 B54 F23. Letter from M. T. Burke to Hamlin Garland, September 26, 1896. HGP.
36. Ibid. S2 B54 F9. "Interview with M. T. Burke." HGP.
37. Julia Grant, *Memoirs*, 86.
38. Perret, *Ulysses S. Grant*, 115.
39. Garland, "Grant at the Outbreak of the War."
40. "How Grant Got to Know Rawlins." *Army and Navy Journal*, September 12, 1868.
41. Grant, *Memoirs*, 1:145.
42. Stahr, *Seward*, 211.
43. Grant, *Memoirs*, 1:146.
44. *PUSG*, 32:17. Letter to Charles W. Ford, December 10, 1860.
45. Vincent, "The Inner Life of Ulysses S. Grant."
46. Catton, *The Coming Fury*, 314.
47. GPL. S2 B54 F10. "Interview with M. T. Johnson." HGP.
48. *PUSG*, 32:145. Letter from Jesse Root Grant to Salmon P. Chase, February 28, 1861.
49. Foner, *Fiery Trial*, 155.
50. Catton, *The Coming Fury*, 260.
51. *New York Herald*, July 2, 1878.
52. Goodheart, *1861*, 177.
53. Armstrong, *Warrior in Two Camps*, 76.
54. McFeely, *Grant*, 73.
55. Young, *Around the World*, 375.
56. GPL. S2 B5 F20. "Interview with Julia Grant." HGP.
57. Farmer, *National Exposition Souvenir*, 59.
58. Catton, *Grant Moves South*, 487–88.
59. Garland, "Grant at the Outbreak of the War."

60. Wilson, *Rawlins*, 46.
61. Richardson, *A Personal History*, 170.
62. Ibid.
63. Ferrier, "Memoir," 23.
64. Garland, "Grant at the Outbreak of the War."
65. Richardson, *A Personal History*, 171.
66. Simpson, *Ulysses S. Grant*, 68; Garland, "Grant at the Outbreak of the War."
67. Garland, "Grant at the Outbreak of the War."
68. USGH. "Interview with Augustus Chetlain."
69. *PUSG*, 2:3–4. Letter to Frederick Dent, April 19, 1861.
70. Ibid., 7. Letter to Jesse Root Grant, April 21, 1861.
71. Richardson, *A Personal History*, 173.
72. Ferrier, "Memoir," 23.
73. Chetlain, "Reminiscences of General Grant."
74. "How Grant Got to Know Rawlins." *Army and Navy Journal*, September 12, 1868.
75. Vincent, "The Inner Life of Ulysses S. Grant."
76. *PUSG*, 2:9. Letter to Julia Dent Grant, April 27, 1861.
77. Ibid., 13–14. Letter to Mary Grant, April 29, 1861.
78. GPL. S2 B54 F23. Letter from M. T. Burke to Hamlin Garland, September 26, 1896. HGP.
79. McCullough, *Greater Journey*, 278.
80. Foner, *Fiery Trial*, 6.
81. GPL. S2 B54 F7. "Talk by General Augustus Chetlain." HGP.
82. Washburne, *Biography*, 27.
83. Simpson, *Ulysses S. Grant*, 82.
84. USGH. "Interview with John Russell Young."
85. *PUSG*, 2:21. Letter to Jesse Root Grant, May 6, 1861.
86. Grant, *Memoirs*, 1:157.
87. Garland, "Grant at the Outbreak of the War."
88. McFeely, *Grant*, 74.
89. *PUSG*, 2:24. Letter to Julia Dent Grant, May 6, 1861.

CHAPTER SEVEN: THE QUIET MAN

1. USGH. "Interview with Mary Robinson."
2. *PUSG*, 2:31. Letter to Julia Dent Grant, May 15, 1861.
3. Stevens, *Grant in St. Louis*, 67.
4. USGH. "Interview with Louisa Boggs."
5. Julia Grant, *Memoirs*, 87.
6. Young, *Around the World*, 388–89.
7. Ibid., 390.
8. Smith, *Grant*, 105.
9. Garland, "Grant at the Outbreak of the War."
10. *The St. Louis Times*, August 5, 1874.
11. *Galena Daily Advertiser*, May 31, 1861.
12. *PUSG*, 2:37. Letter to Jesse Root Grant, May 30, 1861.
13. Ibid., 35. Letter to Bvt. Brig. Gen. Lorenzo Thomas, May 24, 1861.
14. Julia Grant, *Memoirs*, 92.
15. "Grant's Only War Speech." *New York Tribune*, September 27, 1885.

16. Ibid.
17. GPL. S2 B54 F10. "Interview with S. S. Boggs." HGP.
18. Richardson, *A Personal History*, 178.
19. Simpson, *Ulysses S. Grant*, 84.
20. Garland, "Grant at the Outbreak of the War."
21. GPL. S2 B54 F10. "Interview with S. S. Boggs." HGP.
22. "Grant's Only War Speech." *New York Tribune*, September 27, 1885.
23. Garland, "Grant at the Outbreak of the War."
24. Smith, *Grant*, 111.
25. Moore, "Grant's First March."
26. *PUSG*, 2:59. Letter to Julia Dent Grant, July 7, 1861.
27. Ibid., 62. "General Orders No. 24," July 9, 1861.
28. Ibid., 60. Letter to Julia Dent Grant, July 7, 1861.
29. Crane, "Grant as a Colonel."
30. Ibid.
31. Ibid.

32. GPL. S2 B24 F14. "Interview with Captain Ed Garland."
33. Grant, *Memoirs*, 1:163.
34. Ibid., 164.
35. Paine, *Mark Twain's Notebook*, 182.
36. Stahr, *Seward*, 300.
37. *New York Herald*, July 6, 1878.
38. *PUSG*, 2:83. Letter to Julia Dent Grant, August 3, 1861.
39. Crane, "Grant as a Colonel."
40. Ibid.
41. *PUSG*, 2:81. Letter to Jesse Root Grant, August 3, 1861.
42. *Troy Intelligencer*, April 17, 1892.
43. Catton, *Grant Moves South*, 20.
44. *PUSG*, 2:105. Letter to Mary Grant, August 12, 1861.
45. Ibid.
46. Thayer, "Grant at Pilot Knob."
47. Young, *Around the World*, 264.
48. Thayer, "Grant at Pilot Knob."
49. *PUSG*, 2:97. Letter to Julia Dent Grant, August 10, 1861.
50. Ibid., 128. Letter to Capt. Speed Butler, August 22, 1861.
51. Grant, *Memoirs*, 1:170.
52. Ibid., 171.
53. Smith, *Grant*, 117.
54. Thayer, "Grant at Pilot Knob."
55. *PUSG*, 2:149. Letter to Julia Dent Grant, August 29, 1861.
56. Young, *Around the World*, 376.
57. Richardson, *A Personal History*, 183.
58. Grant, *Memoirs*, 1:173.
59. Stevens, *Grant in St. Louis*, 85.
60. Grant, *Memoirs*, 1:174.
61. Catton, *Grant Moves South*, 52.
62. Ibid., 4.
63. Wilson, *Rawlins*, 428–29.
64. Crane, "Grant as a Colonel."
65. LoC. JHWP. Letter from John A. Rawlins to Mary Rawlins, August 22, 1861.
66. Ibid. Letter from John A. Rawlins to Mary Emma Rawlins, February 13, 1864.
67. Armstrong, *Warrior in Two Worlds*, 74.
68. GPL. S2 B21 F18. "Statement of Edward Rawlins." LLP.
69. Wilson, *Rawlins*, 24–25.
70. *PUSG*, 2:207. "General Orders No. 5," September 8, 1861.
71. GPL. S2 B10 F66. "John A. Rawlins." Pledge signed October 14, 1862.
72. Simpson, *Ulysses S. Grant*, 279.
73. "Gen. Grant's Morality." *Chicago Daily Tribune*, January 27, 1887.
74. Wilson and Simon, *Ulysses S. Grant*, 119–120.
75. *Chicago Daily Tribune*, September 1, 1885.
76. GPL. S2 B24 F16. "Interview with Lieutenant Frank Parker." HGP.
77. "How Grant Got to Know Rawlins." *Army and Navy Journal*, September 12, 1868.
78. Washburne, *Biography*, 63.

CHAPTER EIGHT: TWIN FORTS

1. Foner, *Fiery Trial*, 169.
2. Foote, *The Civil War*, 1:53.
3. Perret, *Ulysses S. Grant*, 138.
4. Grant, *Memoirs*, 1:175.
5. *PUSG*, 2:194. "Proclamation, to the Citizens of Paducah!," September 6, 1861.
6. GPL. S2 B54 F9. "Interview with A. H. Markland." HGP.
7. *PUSG*, 3:23. Letter to Julia Dent Grant, October 6, 1861.
8. Ibid., 2:214. Letter to Julia Dent Grant, September 8, 1861.
9. Ibid.
10. Julia Grant, *Memoirs*, 95.
11. *PUSG*, 5:8. Letter to Julia Dent Grant, April 3, 1862.
12. Ibid., 3:64. Letter to Julia Dent Grant, October 20, 1861.
13. Smith, *Grant*, 127.
14. *PUSG*, 3:137. Letter to Jesse Root Grant, November 8, 1861.
15. Richardson, *A Personal History*, 191.
16. Ibid.
17. Grant, *Memoirs*, 1:180.
18. Ibid., 82–83.
19. GPL. S2 B54 F5. "Interview with William Lonergan." HGP.
20. Grant, *Memoirs*, 1:185.
21. Ibid., 184.
22. Catton, *Grant Moves South*, 79–80.
23. *PUSG*, 3:130. "Orders," November 8, 1861.
24. McFeely, *Grant*, 93.
25. Wilson, *Rawlins*, 66.
26. Smith, *Grant*, 130.
27. McFeely, *Grant*, 95.
28. Richardson, *A Personal History*, 200.
29. Young, *Around the World*, 391.
30. Catton, *Terrible Swift Sword*, 68.
31. Julia Grant, *Memoirs*, 93.
32. Ibid.
33. Ibid.
34. Ibid.
35. *PUSG*, 3:212. Letter to Capt. John C. Kelton, November 22, 1861.
36. Ibid., 4:47. Letter to Brig. Gen. Montgomery C. Meigs, January 13, 1862.
37. Simpson, *Ulysses S. Grant*, 106.
38. *PUSG*, 3:76. Letter to Mary Grant, October 25, 1861.
39. Ibid., 226–27. Letter to Jesse Root Grant, November 27, 1861.
40. Ibid., 238–39. Letter to Jesse Root Grant, November 29, 1861.
41. Marszalek, *Commander of All Lincoln's Armies*, 132–33.
42. Ibid., 133.

43. McPherson, *Tried by War*, 27.
44. *PUSG*, 3:228. Letter to Jesse Root Grant, November 27, 1861.
45. Ibid., 209. Letter to Capt. John C. Kelton, November 21, 1861.
46. Ibid., 4:111. Dispatch from Cairo, January 12, 1862.
47. Ibid., 110. Letter to Capt. William J. Kountz, January 29, 1862.
48. Ibid., 112.
49. Ibid., 113.
50. GPL. S2 B54 F5. "Interview with Charles Galligher." HGP.
51. LoC. EBWP. Box 20. Letter from William Bross to Secretary of War Simon Cameron, December 30, 1861.
52. *Chicago Sunday Tribune Magazine*, January 14, 1962.
53. Ibid.
54. Ibid.
55. Washburne, *Biography*, 94.
56. Ibid.
57. *PUSG*, 4:116. Letter from John A. Rawlins to Elihu B. Washburne, December 30, 1861.
58. Ibid., 117.
59. Ibid., 118.
60. Richardson, *A Personal History*, 188.
61. *PUSG*, 4:277. Letter from William R. Rowley to Elihu B. Washburne, January 30, 1862.
62. Julia Grant, *Memoirs*, 96.
63. Berner, *Mrs. Leland Stanford*, 35.
64. *PUSG*, 4:96. Letter to Mary Grant, January 23, 1862.
65. Ibid., 91. Letter from Brig. Gen. Charles F. Smith to Capt. John A. Rawlins, January 22, 1862.
66. "General Rawlins' Address." *Report of the Proceedings of the Society of the Army of the Tennessee*, 1877.
67. Marszalek, *Commander of All Lincoln's Armies*, 192.
68. Catton, *Grant Moves South*, 124.
69. Grant, *Memoirs*, 1:190.
70. *PUSG*, 27:17. Letter to Gen. William T. Sherman, January 29, 1876.
71. Marszalek, *Commander of All Lincoln's Armies*, 116.

72. *PUSG*, 4:99. Telegram to Maj. Gen. Henry W. Halleck, January 28, 1862.
73. Ibid., 104. Letter from Maj. Gen. Henry W. Halleck, January 30, 1862.
74. McPherson, *Tried by War*, 63.
75. Ibid.
76. Ibid., 69.
77. Bunting, *Ulysses S. Grant*, 43.
78. McPherson, *Tried by War*, 69.
79. *PUSG*, 4:122. Letter to Maj. Gen. Henry W. Halleck, January 31, 1862.
80. Porter, *Campaigning with Grant*, 245.
81. Catton, *Grant Moves South*, 138.
82. Simpson, *Ulysses S. Grant*, 111.
83. Smith, *Grant*, 144.
84. Grant, *Memoirs*, 1:191.
85. *PUSG*, 4:149. Letter to Julia Dent Grant, February 4, 1862.
86. Bunting, *Ulysses S. Grant*, 43.
87. Smith, *Grant*, 121.
88. Richardson, *A Personal History*, 201.
89. Chetlain, "Reminiscences of General Grant."
90. *PUSG*, 32:160. Letter from Brig. Gen. Charles F. Smith to his wife, March 1863. [n.d.]
91. Ibid., 4:151. "Field Orders No. 1," February 5, 1862.
92. White, "Civil War Diary of Patrick H. White."
93. Catton, *Terrible Swift Sword*, 151.
94. Ibid.
95. Smith, *Grant*, 147.
96. McClellan, *The Civil War Papers of George B. McClellan*, 172.
97. Smith, *Grant*, 148.
98. McPherson, *War on the Waters*, 75–76.
99. Smith, *Grant*, 149.
100. McFeely, *Grant*, 98.
101. *PUSG*, 4:193–94. Letter from Maj. Gen. Henry W. Halleck, February 8, 1862.
102. Ibid., 193. Letter to Maj. Gen. Henry W. Halleck, February 11, 1862.
103. Ibid., 179. Letter to Mary Grant, February 9, 1862.
104. Grant, *Memoirs*, 1:197.

CHAPTER NINE: DYNAMO

1. *PUSG*, 4:273. Letter to Orvil L. Grant, February 22, 1862.
2. Grant, *Memoirs*, 1:196.
3. *PUSG*, 4:180. Letter to Mary Grant, February 9, 1862.
4. Ibid., 182. Letter from Flag Officer Andrew H. Foote, February 11, 1862.
5. McFeely, *Grant*, 99.
6. Simpson, *Ulysses S. Grant*, 113.
7. *PUSG*, 4:195. Telegram to Maj. Gen. Henry W. Halleck, February 12, 1862.
8. Ibid., 203. Letter to Julia Dent Grant, February 13, 1862.

9. White, "Civil War Diary of Patrick H. White."
10. Foote, *The Civil War*, 1:195.
11. Ibid., 203.
12. Grant, *Memoirs*, 1:203.
13. Ibid., 206.
14. *New York Herald*, July 24, 1878.
15. Grant, *Memoirs*, 1:204.
16. Catton, *Grant Moves South*, 165.
17. McFeely, *Grant*, 100.
18. Catton, *Grant Moves South*, 166.
19. Simpson, *Ulysses S. Grant*, 115.
20. Girardi, *The Civil War Generals*, 65.
21. *The New York Times*, July 24, 1885.

22. Catton, *Grant Moves South*, 167.
23. Grant, *Memoirs*, 1:205.
24. Ibid., 206.
25. Catton, *Grant Moves South*, 173.
26. Simpson, "Butcher? Racist?"
27. McFeely, *Grant*, 104.
28. Smith, *Grant*, 161.
29. Foote, *The Civil War*, 1:211.
30. Catton, *Grant Moves South*, 174–75.
31. *PUSG*, 4:218. Letter to Brig. Gen. Simon B. Buckner, February 16, 1862.
32. "General Rawlins' Address." *Report of the Proceedings of the Society of the Army of the Tennessee*, 1877.
33. *PUSG*, 4:218. Letter from Brig. Gen. Simon B. Buckner, February 16, 1862.
34. USGH. "Interview with Simon Bolivar Buckner." HGP.
35. Simon, "Grant at Belmont."
36. Grant, *Memoirs*, 1:212.
37. USGH. "Interview with Simon Bolivar Buckner." HGP.
38. Catton, *Grant Moves South*, 182.
39. *New York Tribune*, February 22, 1862.
40. Ibid., 229. Letter to Julia Dent Grant, February 16, 1862.
41. Ibid., 264. Letter to Elihu B. Washburne, February 21, 1862.
42. Young, *Around the World*, 6
43. Waugh, *U. S. Grant*, 55.
44. Catton, *Grant Moves South*, 179–80.
45. *The New York Times*, February 25, 1862.
46. Foote, *The Civil War*, 1:214.
47. Ibid.
48. Porter, *Campaigning with Grant*, 381.
49. Parker, *The Life of General Ely S. Parker*, 136–37.
50. Taussig, "Personal Recollections of General Grant."
51. *PUSG*, 4:222. Letter from Col. James B. McPherson, February 21, 1862.
52. Washburne, *Biography*, 101.
53. Simpson, *Ulysses S. Grant*, 119.
54. Burlingame, *With Lincoln in the White House*, 69.
55. .Goodwin, *Team of Rivals*, 427.
56. *PUSG*, 4:271. Letter to Julia Dent Grant, February 22, 1862.
57. Ibid., 284. Letter to Julia Dent Grant, February 24, 1862.
58. Keegan, *The American Civil War*, 161.
59. Grant, *Memoirs*, 1:214.

60. Girardi, *The Civil War Generals*, 68.
61. Stevens, *Grant in St. Louis*, 93.
62. *PUSG*, 4:257. Letter to Brig. Gen. George W. Cullum, February 21, 1862.
63. Ibid., 320. Letter from Maj. Gen. Henry W. Halleck to Maj. Gen. George B. McClellan, March 3, 1862.
64. Ibid. Letter from Maj. Gen. Henry W. Halleck to Maj. Gen. George B. McClellan, March 4, 1862.
65. Ibid. Telegram from Gen. George B. McClellan to Maj. Gen. Henry W. Halleck, March 3, 1862.
66. Simpson, *Ulysses S. Grant*, 123.
67. *PUSG*, 11:231. Letter from Charles A. Dana to John A. Rawlins, July 13, 1864.
68. GPL. S2 B6 F14. From *Personal Memoirs of John H. Brinton*.
69. Marszalek, *Commander of All Lincoln's Armies*, 150.
70. *PUSG*, 4:319. Telegram from Maj. Gen. Henry W. Halleck, March 4, 1862; Smith, *Grant*, 178.
71. Ibid., 331. Letter to Maj. Gen. Henry W. Halleck, March 7, 1862.
72. GPL. S2 B54 F18. "Interview with John M. Thayer." HGP.
73. *New York Herald*, July 24, 1878.
74. Grant, *Memoirs*, 1:221.
75. *PUSG*, 4:338. Letter from Brig. Gen. John A. McClernand et al., March 9, 1862.
76. GPL. S2 B24 F15. "Interview with Mr. McDonald." HGP.
77. Sherman, *Memoirs*, 966.
78. Porter, *Campaigning with Grant*, 375.
79. Sherman, "General Sherman's Opinion of General Grant."
80. GPL. S2 B4 F10. Letter from William T. Sherman to Col. John Eaton Tourtellotte, February 4, 1887.
81. McPherson, "The Bloody Partnership."
82. Simpson, *Ulysses S. Grant*, 462.
83. Ibid., 460.
84. Smith, *Grant*, 15.
85. *New York Herald*, July 24, 1878.
86. Cramer, *Ulysses S. Grant*, 193–94.
87. *PUSG*, 4:355. Telegram from Maj. Gen. Henry W. Halleck, March 13, 1862.
88. Ibid., 306. Letter to Julia Dent Grant, March 1, 1862.

CHAPTER TEN: A GLITTERING LIE

1. Grant, *Memoirs*, 1:222.
2. *PUSG*, 4:348–49. Letter to Julia Dent Grant, March 11, 1862.
3. Ibid., 375. Letter to Julia Dent Grant, March 15, 1862.
4. Grant, *Memoirs*, 1:221.
5. Wilson, *Rawlins*, 80.
6. Green, "Civil War Public Opinion of General Grant."
7. Grant, *Memoirs*, 1:239.

8. *PUSG*, 4:400. Letter to Maj. Gen. Henry W. Halleck, March 21, 1862.
9. Foote, *The Civil War*, 1:325.
10. *PUSG*, 5:7. Letter to Julia Dent Grant, April 3, 1862.
11. Ibid., 9. Letter to Brig. Gen. William T. Sherman, April 4, 1862.
12. Grant, *Memoirs*, 1:224.
13. *PUSG*, 5:14. Letter to Maj. Gen. Henry W. Halleck, April 5, 1862.

14. Perret, *Ulysses S. Grant,* 187.
15. *PUSG,* 5:14. Letter from Brig. Gen. William T. Sherman, April 5, 1862.
16. Catton, *Grant Moves South,* 220–21.
17. Foote, *The Civil War,* 1:169.
18. Perret, *Ulysses S. Grant,* 187.
19. "General Rawlins' Address." *Report of the Proceedings of the Society of the Army of the Tennessee,* 1877.
20. Young, *Around the World,* 390.
21. Wilson, *Rawlins,* 90.
22. McPherson, *Battle Cry of Freedom,* 409.
23. GPL. S2 B4 F9. Letter from W. R. Rowley to E. Hempstead, April 19, 1862.
24. White, "Civil War Diary of Patrick H. White."
25. Ibid.
26. GPL. S2 B4 F10. Letter from Mrs. W. H. Cherry to T. M. Hurst, December 6, 1892.
27. *USGA Newsletter,* January 1964.
28. *PUSG,* 6:275. Letter to Elihu B. Washburne, November 7, 1862.
29. *USGA Newsletter,* January 1964.
30. Ibid.
31. Simpson, *Ulysses S. Grant,* 131.
32. Catton, *Grant Moves South,* 230.
33. Grant, *Memoirs,* 1:228.
34. Sherman, *Memoirs,* 917.
35. *PUSG,* 7:29. Letter to Maj. Gen. Henry W. Halleck, December 14, 1862.
36. Wilson, *Rawlins,* 87.
37. *PUSG,* 18:193. Letter from Brig. Gen. Lewis Wallace, February 28, 1868.
38. Grant, *Memoirs,* 1:241.
39. Chetlain, "Reminiscences of General Grant."
40. White, "Civil War Diary of Patrick H. White."
41. Wilson, *Rawlins,* 88.
42. Simpson, *Ulysses S. Grant,* 133.
43. "New York: High Honors Paid to Gen. Grant by the Lotos Club." *Chicago Daily Tribune,* November 21, 1880.
44. McPherson, *Battle Cry of Freedom,* 412.
45. *PUSG,* 5:111. Letter to Julia Dent Grant, May 4, 1862.
46. Foreman, *A World on Fire,* 245.
47. Grant, *Memoirs,* 1:234.
48. Grant, "My Father as I Knew Him."
49. Smith, *Grant,* 201.
50. Richardson, *A Personal History,* 243.
51. Sherman, *Memoirs,* 259–60.
52. Grant, *Memoirs,* 1:235.
53. Waugh, *U. S. Grant,* 58.
54. Foote, *The Civil War,* 1:350.
55. LoC. USGP. Container 10.2, Reel 3. Letter from William S. Hillyer to his wife, April 11, 1862.
56. Grant, *Memoirs,* 1:238.
57. McPherson, *Battle Cry of Freedom,* 413.
58. Faust, *This Republic of Suffering,* 36.
59. *PUSG,* 5:119–20. Letter to Elihu B. Washburne, May 14, 1862.
60. Curtis, *The Correspondence of John Lothrop Motley,* 2:210. Letter from Dr. O. W. Holmes to John Lothrop Motley, October 10, 1865.
61. Young, *Around the World,* 393.
62. Foreman, *A World on Fire,* 247.
63. Foote, *The Civil War,* 1:372.
64. Ibid.
65. *PUSG,* 5:103. Letter to Julia Dent Grant, April 30, 1862.
66. GPL. S2 B4 F9. Letter from L. S. Felt to Elihu B. Washburne, April 12, 1862.
67. Catton, *Grant Moves South,* 259.
68. Stevens, *Grant in St. Louis,* 89.
69. GPL. S2 B21 F17. Letter from William R. Rowley to Elihu B. Washburne, April 19, 1862. LLP.
70. Ibid. S2 B10 F66. Letter from John A. Rawlins to his aunt, June 15, 1862.
71. Ibid. S2 B24 F18. "Interview with Gen. James Harrison Wilson." HGP.
72. Ibid. S2 B54 F10. "Interview with Benjamin Johnson." HGP.
73. Ibid. S2 B54 F3. "Interview with R. C. Rankin." HGP.
74. Simon, "From Galena to Appomattox."
75. Washburne, *Memoirs,* 132.
76. Catton, *Grant Moves South,* 260.
77. GPL. S2 B4 F11. Letter from Col. Clark B. Lagow to E. B. Washburne.
78. Julia Grant, *Memoirs,* 99; Catton, *Grant Moves South,* 260.
79. McPherson, *Tried by War,* 84–85.
80. Richardson, *A Personal History,* 336.
81. *PUSG,* 9:522. Letter from Elihu B. Washburne, January 24, 1864.
82. Green, "Civil War Public Opinion of General Grant."
83. Nevins and Thomas, *The Diary of George Templeton Strong,* 3:216. Diary entry for April 9, 1862.
84. Catton, *Grant Moves South,* 272.
85. *PUSG,* 4:413. Letter to Julia Dent Grant, March 23, 1862.
86. *PUSG,* 5:119. Letter to Elihu B. Washburne, May 14, 1862.
87. USGH. "Interview with W. W. Smith." HGP.
88. Richardson, *A Personal History,* 254.
89. *PUSG,* 5:79. Letter from William S. Hillyer to Jesse Root Grant, April 21, 1862.
90. Ibid., 82. Letter from Jesse Root Grant to Gov. David Tod, July 11, 1862.
91. Ibid., 264. Letter to Jesse Root Grant, August 3, 1862.
92. Ibid., 6:61–62. Letter to Jesse Root Grant, September 17, 1862.
93. Marszalek, *Commander of All Lincoln's Armies,* 122–23.
94. Ibid., 83. Letter to Mrs. Charles F. Smith, April 26, 1862.
95. Fry, "An Acquaintance with Grant."
96. Marszalek, *Commander of All Lincoln's Armies,* 97. Simpson, *Ulysses S. Grant,* 136.
98. Catton, *Grant Moves South,* 272.
99. Borchgrave and Cullen, *Villard,* 194.

100. Simpson, *Ulysses S. Grant,* 142.
101. Marszalek, *Commander of All Lincoln's Armies,* 124.
102. *PUSG,* 5:134. Letter to Julia Dent Grant, May 31, 1862.
103. Ibid., 118. Letter to Julia Dent Grant, May 13, 1862.
104. Grant, *Memoirs,* 1:251.
105. *PUSG,* 5:114. Letter to Maj. Gen. Henry W. Halleck, May 11, 1862.
106. Ibid., 130. Letter to Julia Dent Grant, May 24, 1862.
107. Sherman, *Memoirs,* 275.
108. Ibid., 276.
109. Newsham, "The Turning Point of the War."
110. Sherman, *Memoirs,* 276.
111. Newsham, "The Turning Point of the War."
112. Chetlain, "Reminiscences of General Grant."
113. Marszalek, *Commander of All Lincoln's Armies,* 126.
114. McFeely, *Grant,* 117.

115. *PUSG,* 5:138. Letter to Julia Dent Grant, June 3, 1862.
116. USGH. "Interview with W. W. Smith."
117. Washburne, *Biography,* 148.
118. Ibid.
119. Green, "Civil War Public Opinion of General Grant."
120. Grant, *Memoirs,* 1:259.
121. Ibid., 261.
122. *PUSG,* 5:165. Letter to Maj. Gen. Henry W. Halleck, June 27, 1862.
123. Ibid., 207. Telegram from Maj. Gen. Henry W. Halleck, July 11, 1862.
124. Donald, *Lincoln,* 369.
125. McPherson, *Tried by War,* 101.
126. *PUSG,* 5:226. Letter to Elihu B. Washburne, July 22, 1862.
127. Sheridan, *Memoirs,* 1:181.
128. McPherson, *Tried by War,* 121.
129. Ibid., 119.
130. GPL. S2 B6 F14. Diary entry of Gideon Welles, November 4, 1862.

CHAPTER ELEVEN: EXODUS

1. *PUSG,* 5:226. Letter from Elihu Washburne, July 25, 1862.
2. Ibid., 244. Letter from Maj. Gen. Henry W. Halleck, August 2, 1862.
3. Grant, *Memoirs,* 1:265.
4. Porter, *Campaigning with Grant,* 165.
5. *PUSG,* 5:310. Letter to Mary Grant, August 19, 1862.
6. Ibid., 124. Letter to Julia Dent Grant, May 16, 1862.
7. Catton, *Never Call Retreat,* 115.
8. *PUSG,* 5:272. Letter from Maj. Gen. William T. Sherman to Maj. John A. Rawlins, August 14, 1862.
9. Ibid., 226. Letter from Elihu Washburne, July 25, 1862.
10. Ibid., 311. Letter to Mary Grant, August 19, 1862.
11. Simpson, *Ulysses S. Grant,* 153.
12. *PUSG,* 6:67. Telegram to Maj. Gen. Henry W. Halleck, September 19, 1862.
13. Ibid., 71. Telegram to Maj. Gen. Henry W. Halleck, September 20, 1862.
14. *The New York Times,* October 5, 1862.
15. *PUSG,* 6:87. Letter from Franklin A. Dick to Attorney General Edward Bates, September 28, 1862.
16. Julia Grant, *Memoirs,* 104.
17. *PUSG,* 6:143. Telegram from President Abraham Lincoln, October 8, 1862.
18. Ibid., 155. Letter to Mary Grant, October 16, 1862.
19. Foote, *The Civil War,* 1:725.
20. Cadwallader, *Three Years with Grant,* 20.
21. *PUSG,* 6:266. "Special Field Orders No. 1," November 7, 1862.
22. Young, *Around the World,* 312-13.
23. *Baltimore American,* September 12, 1862.

24. Foote, *The Civil War,* 1:704.
25. McPherson, *Battle Cry of Freedom,* 559.
26. Eaton, *Grant, Lincoln and the Freedmen,* 2.
27. *PUSG,* 6:315. Telegram to Maj. Gen. Henry W. Halleck, November 15, 1862.
28. Eaton, *Grant, Lincoln and the Freedmen,* 2 and 5.
29. Ibid., 6.
30. Ibid., 12.
31. Ibid., 15.
32. Grant, *Memoirs,* 1:285.
33. Ibid.
34. Douglass, "U. S. Grant and the Colored People."
35. Foner, *Fiery Trial,* 234.
36. Young, *Around the World,* 299.
37. LoC. USGP. Series 4, Vol. 9. "Memoirs," 291. Original manuscript of Grant's *Memoirs.*
38. Stahr, *Seward,* 356.
39. Foote, *The Civil War,* 2:116.
40. GPL. S2 B10 F66. Letter from John A. Rawlins to "Enos," December 20, 1862.
41. LoC. JHWP. Box 50. Letter from John A. Rawlins to Mary Sheean, December 14, 1862.
42. *PUSG,* 5:244. Letter from Maj. Gen. Henry W. Halleck, August 2, 1862.
43. Sarna, *When General Grant Expelled the Jews,* 43–44.
44. Cadwallader, *Three Years with Grant,* 22.
45. *PUSG,* 5:240. Letter from Maj. Gen. William T. Sherman to John A. Rawlins, July 30, 1862.
46. Ibid., 6:394. Letter to Maj. Gen. William T. Sherman, December 5, 1862.
47. Ibid., 7:50. "General Orders No. 11," December 17, 1862.
48. Ibid., 56–57. Letter to Christopher P. Wolcott, December 17, 1862.
49. Ibid., 4:326–27. Letter to Julia Dent Grant, March 5, 1862.

50. Ibid., 412. Letter to Julia Dent Grant, March 23, 1862.
51. Ibid., 6:344. Letter to Jesse Root Grant, November 23, 1862.
52. *Milwaukee Sunday Telegraph*, December 26, 1886.
53. *PUSG*, 19:21. Letter from William S. Hillyer to the editor of the *New York World*, January 29, 1869.
54. Wilson, *Rawlins*, 96.
55. *The Cincinnati Enquirer*, May 17, 1864.
56. Ash, "Civil War Exodus."
57. *PUSG*, 7:54. Letter from Maj. Gen. Henry W. Halleck, January 21, 1863.
58. Ash, "Civil War Exodus."
59. *PUSG*, 7:55–56. Letter from Elihu B. Washburne, January 6, 1863.
60. Sarna, *When General Grant Expelled the Jews*, 25.
61. *PUSG*, 7:54. Telegram from Paducah merchants to President Lincoln, December 29, 1862.
62. Sarna, *When General Grant Expelled the Jews*, 30.
63. Julia Grant, *Memoirs*, 107.
64. Sarna, *When General Grant Expelled the Jews*, 48.
65. Ibid., 141.
66. Green, "Civil War Public Opinion of General Grant."
67. GPL. S2 B24 F16. "Interview with J. P. Riordan." HGP.
68. Ibid. S2 B24 F18. "Interview with General James Harrison Wilson." HGP.
69. Ibid. S2 B18 F69. "Abraham Lincoln."
70. Foote, *The Civil War*, 2:60; White, *American Ulysses*, 245.
71. White, *American Ulysses*, 245.
72. McPherson, *Tried by War*, 153.
73. *PUSG*, 9:82. Diary entry of Gideon Welles, July 31, 1863.
74. White, *American Ulysses*, 246.
75. Grant, *Memoirs*, 1:285.
76. McPherson, *Tried by War*, 153.
77. *PUSG*, 6:30. Letter to Maj. Gen. William T. Sherman, November 14, 1862.
78. Foote, *The Civil War*, 2:73.
79. Ibid., 1:570.
80. Eaton, *Grant, Lincoln and the Freedmen*, 26.
81. *PUSG*, 7:225. Letter to Silas Hudson, January 14, 1863.
82. Grant, *Memoirs*, 1:290.
83. Catton, *Never Call Retreat*, 34.
84. Foreman, *A World on Fire*, 360.
85. Smith, *Grant*, 224.
86. *PUSG*, 7:171. Telegram to Maj. Gen. Henry W. Halleck, January 5, 1863.
87. Foote, *The Civil War*, 2:133.
88. *PUSG*, 7:209. Telegram to Maj. Gen. Henry W. Halleck, January 11, 1863.
89. Ibid., 210. Telegram from Maj. Gen. Henry W. Halleck, January 12, 1863.
90. McPherson, *Tried by War*, 153–54.

CHAPTER TWELVE: MAN OF IRON

1. Wineapple, *Ecstatic Nation*, 245.
2. Crane, "Grant as a Colonel."
3. Cramer, *Ulysses S. Grant*, 106.
4. *PUSG*, 9:218. Letter to Elihu B. Washburne, August 30, 1863.
5. Young, *Around the World*, 157.
6. Julia Grant, *Memoirs*, 83.
7. Ibid., 126.
8. *USGA Newsletter*, January 1971.
9. Ross, *The General's Wife*, 138.
10. Ibid.
11. *PUSG*, 7:24. Letter to Julia Dent Grant, December 13, 1862.
12. Ibid., 308. Letter from Brig. Gen. Charles S. Hamilton to U.S. Senator James R. Doolittle, February 11, 1863.
13. Ibid., 468. Letter to Maj. Gen. Henry W. Halleck, March 24, 1863.
14. Ibid., 225. Letter to Silas Hudson, January 14, 1863.
15. Waugh, *U. S. Grant*, 61.
16. Catton, *Grant Moves South*, 368.
17. Foote, *The Civil War*, 2:186.
18. Foreman, *A World on Fire*, 366.
19. Catton, *Grant Moves South*, 368.
20. *PUSG*, 7:413. Letter to Brig. Gen. William A. Hammond, March 12, 1863.
21. Simpson, *Ulysses S. Grant*, 175.
22. *PUSG*, 32:43. Letter to William S. Hillyer, February 5, 1863.
23. Foote, *The Civil War*, 2:145.
24. Eaton, *Grant, Lincoln and the Freedmen*, 44.
25. Foote, *The Civil War*, 2:202; Cadwallader, *Three Years with Grant*, 48.
26. *PUSG*, 7:287. Letter from 1st Lt. James H. Wilson to Lt. Col. John A. Rawlins, February 4, 1863.
27. Foote, *The Civil War*, 2:202.
28. *PUSG*, 7:455–56. Letter to Maj. Gen. William T. Sherman, March 22, 1863.
29. Cadwallader, *Three Years with Grant*, 51.
30. Maihafer, "Mr. Grant and Mr. Dana."
31. Waugh, *U. S. Grant*, 62.
32. McPherson, *Battle Cry of Freedom*, 590.
33. McPherson, *Tried by War*, 168.
34. *PUSG*, 7:386. Letter from Col. Lewis B. Parsons, March 9, 1863.
35. Grant, *Memoirs*, 1:295.
36. Smith, *Grant*, 230.
37. Washburne, *Biography*, 242.
38. Catton, *Grant Moves South*, 209.
39. *PUSG*, 7:275. Letter from Capt. William J. Kountz to Abraham Lincoln, circa March 15, 1863.
40. Cadwallader, *Three Years with Grant*, 114.
41. Smith, *Grant*, 231.
42. McPherson, *Battle Cry of Freedom*, 588.
43. McPherson, *Tried by War*, 168.
44. Dana, *Recollections of the Civil War*, 28.
45. Maihafer, "Mr. Grant and Mr. Dana."
46. *The New York Times*, May 31, 1914.

47. Maihafer, "Mr. Grant and Mr. Dana."
48. Dana, *Recollections of the Civil War*, 61.
49. Washburne, *Biography*, 258.
50. Maihafer, "Mr. Grant and Mr. Dana."
51. Wilson, *Rawlins*, 124.
52. Simpson, *Ulysses S. Grant*, 279.
53. *PUSG*, 7:479–80. Letter to Julia Dent Grant, March 27, 1863.
54. Foote, *The Civil War*, 2:219.
55. Richardson, *A Personal History*, 293.
56. McPherson, *Tried by War*, 169.
57. *PUSG*, 7:478. Letter to Maj. Gen. Henry W. Halleck, March 27, 1863.
58. Catton, *Grant Moves South*, 387.
59. Foote, *The Civil War*, 2:326.
60. Young, *Around the World*, 426.
61. McPherson, *War on the Waters*, 165.
62. Foote, *The Civil War*, 2:324.
63. Simpson, *Ulysses S. Grant*, 160.
64. Dana, *Recollections of the Civil War*, 37.
65. Grant, *Memoirs*, 1:307.
66. *PUSG*, 8:86. Letter from Maj. Gen. William T. Sherman to John A. Rawlins, April 17, 1863.
67. McPherson, *Battle Cry of Freedom*, 626.
68. Foote, *The Civil War*, 2:330.
69. *PUSG*, 8:109. Letter to Jesse Root Grant, April 21, 1863.
70. Catton, *Grant Moves South*, 419.
71. Ibid., 420.
72. Ibid.
73. *PUSG*, 8:144. Telegram to Maj. Gen. Henry W. Halleck, May 3, 1863.
74. McPherson, *Battle Cry of Freedom*, 628.
75. White, *American Ulysses*, 265.
76. Grant, *Memoirs*, 1:317.
77. Young, *Around the World*, 429.
78. Grant, *Memoirs*, 1:318.
79. Dana, *Recollections of the Civil War*, 43.
80. Grant, *Memoirs*, 1:318.
81. Ibid., 321.
82. Washburne, *Biography*, 249.
83. White, *American Ulysses*, 269.

84. *PUSG*, 8:143. Telegram to Maj. Gen. Henry W. Halleck, May 3, 1863.
85. Catton, *Grant Moves South*, 438.
86. *PUSG*, 29:328. Letter to Mrs. E. B. Moore, May 1863. [n.d.]
87. McPherson, *Tried by War*, 170.
88. Perret, *Ulysses S. Grant*, 254.
89. Grant, *Memoirs*, 1:325.
90. Ibid.
91. *PUSG*, 8:155. Letter to Julia Dent Grant, May 3, 1863.
92. Foote, *The Civil War*, 2:351.
93. *PUSG*, 8:160. Letter to Maj. Gen. Stephen A. Hurlbut, May 5, 1863.
94. Ibid., 171. General Orders No. 32, May 7, 1863.
95. Smith, *Grant*, 244–45.
96. *PUSG*, 8:200. Letter to Maj. Gen. James B. McPherson, May 11, 1863.
97. Foote, *The Civil War*, 2:363.
98. Catton, *Grant Moves South*, 441.
99. Foreman, *A World on Fire*, 438.
100. *Pittsburgh Times*, June 17, 1881.
101. Young, *Around the World*, 312.
102. Grant, *Memoirs*, 1:339.
103. Cadwallader, *Three Years with Grant*, 80.
104. GPL. S2 B13 F38. "James H. Wilson Journal." Entry for July 12, 1863.
105. Catton, *Grant Moves South*, 443.
106. Smith, *Grant*, 249.
107. Foote, *The Civil War*, 2:372.
108. Catton, *Grant Moves South*, 445.
109. Grant, *Memoirs*, 1:348.
110. Cadwallader, *Three Years with Grant*, 83.
111. Simpson, *Ulysses S. Grant*, 201.
112. Catton, *Grant Moves South*, 447.
113. Burlingame, *With Lincoln in the White House*, 114.
114. Green, "Civil War Public Opinion of General Grant."
115. Cadwallader, *Three Years with Grant*, 87.
116. Catton, *Grant Moves South*, 456.
117. Cadwallader, *Three Years with Grant*, 86.
118. Smith, *Grant*, 251.

CHAPTER THIRTEEN: CITADEL

1. Grant, *Memoirs*, 1:354.
2. Simpson, *Ulysses S. Grant*, 202.
3. Foote, *The Civil War*, 2:382.
4. Grant, *Memoirs*, 2:589.
5. Foote, *The Civil War*, 2:384.
6. Cadwallader, *Three Years with Grant*, 92.
7. *PUSG*, 8:261. Letter to Maj. Gen. Henry W. Halleck, May 24, 1863.
8. Cadwallader, *Three Years with Grant*.
9. Sherman, *Memoirs*, 354.
10. Young, *Around the World*, 302.
11. Catton, *Grant Moves South*, 455.
12. McPherson, *Tried by War*, 170.
13. Ibid., 177.
14. Taliaferro, *All the Great Prizes*, 69.
15. McPherson, *Tried by War*, 181.
16. Maihafer, "Mr. Grant and Mr. Dana."

17. *PUSG*, 8:322–23. Letter from John A. Rawlins, June 6, 1863.
18. Ibid., 323. Endorsement of letter by John A. Rawlins. [n.d.]
19. *New York Sun*, January 28, 1887.
20. Wilson, *Rawlins*, 139.
21. Cadwallader, *Three Years with Grant*, 62.
22. *PUSG*, 12:199. Letter to Sylvanus Cadwallader, September 23, 1864.
23. GPL. S2 B13 F43. "Sylvanus Cadwallader."
24. Quoted on the back cover of the University of Nebraska reprint of Cadwallader, *Three Years with Grant*.
25. Cadwallader, *Three Years with Grant*, 353.
26. GPL. S2 B13 F43. "Sylvanus Cadwallader."
27. Dana, *Recollections of the Civil War*, 83.
28. *New York Sun*, January 28, 1887.

29. Cadwallader, *Three Years with Grant*, 103.
30. Ibid., 104.
31. Ibid., 108.
32. Ibid., 109.
33. Ibid., 116.
34. Ibid., ix.
35. Ibid.
36. Ibid.
37. Ibid.
38. McFeely, *Grant*, 135; *New York Sun*, January 28, 1887.
39. *The Macon* [Missouri], January 24, 1917.
40. *New York World Sunday Magazine*, April 25, 1897.
41. Grant, *In the Days of My Father General Grant*, 15.
42. USGH. "Interview with General Grenville Dodge."
43. *Missouri Democrat*, May 31, 1866.
44. Foreman, *A World on Fire*, 443.
45. Simpson, *Ulysses S. Grant*, 209.
46. Foote, *The Civil War*, 2:407.
47. Catton, *Grant Moves South*, 460.
48. Foote, *The Civil War*, 3:333.
49. Ibid., 2:425.
50. Ibid.
51. Ibid., 408.
52. Foreman, *A World on Fire*, 443.
53. Holzer, *The Civil War in 50 Objects*, 475.
54. Foreman, *A World on Fire*, 358.
55. Wineapple, *Ecstatic Nation*, 282.
56. Holzer, *The Civil War in 50 Objects*, 198.
57. *PUSG*, 8:370. Letter from Col. John E. Whiting to Maj. Gen. John A. McClernand, June 15, 1863. Endorsed by McClernand and sent to Grant.
58. Ibid., 93. Letter from Maj. Gen. Henry W. Halleck, March 30, 1863.
59. Ibid., 91–92. Letter to Maj. Gen. Henry W. Halleck, April 19, 1863.
60. Simpson, *Ulysses S. Grant*, 187.
61. Catton, *Grant Moves South*, 403.
62. Eaton, *Grant, Lincoln and the Freedmen*, 64.
63. Ibid.
64. *PUSG*, 8:342. Letter to Abraham Lincoln, June 11, 1863.
65. Douglass, "U. S. Grant and the Colored People."
66. Eaton, *Grant, Lincoln and the Freedmen*, 102–3.
67. Ibid., 86.
68. Ballard, *Grant at Vicksburg*, 67.
69. Dana, *Recollections of the Civil War*, 86.
70. Ibid.
71. Keegan, *The American Civil War*, 294.
72. Grant, *Memoirs*, 1:366.
73. *PUSG*, 8:328. Letter to Brig. Gen. Lorenzo Thomas, June 16, 1863.
74. Ibid., 9:219. Letter from Senator Henry Wilson to Cong. Elihu B. Washburne, July 25, 1863.
75. Goodwin, *Team of Rivals*, 549.
76. Holzer, *The Civil War in 50 Objects*, 179.
77. *PUSG*, 9:196–97. Letter to Abraham Lincoln, August 23, 1863.
78. Niven, *The Salmon P. Chase Papers*, 428. Diary entry for August 29, 1863.
79. Egerton, *The Wars of Reconstruction*, 36.
80. Grant, *Memoirs*, 1:373.
81. Smith, *Grant*, 221.
82. Catton, *Never Call Retreat*, 7.
83. *OR*, I, xxiv, part 1, 285.
84. Grant, *Memoirs*, 1:374.
85. *PUSG*, 8:455. Letter from Lt. Gen. John C. Pemberton, July 3, 1863.
86. Young, *Around the World*, 433.
87. *PUSG*, 8:455. Letter to Lt. Gen. John C. Pemberton, July 3, 1863.
88. Foote, *The Civil War*, 2:609.
89. Simpson, *Ulysses S. Grant*, 213.
90. Grant, *Memoirs*, 1:376.
91. *PUSG*, 31:240. Letter to Marcus J. Wright, November 30, 1884.
92. Ibid., 8:457. Letter to Lt. Gen. John C. Pemberton, July 3, 1863.
93. Ibid., 458. Letter from Lt. Gen. John C. Pemberton, July 3, 1863.
94. Watrous, "Grant as His Son Saw Him."

CHAPTER FOURTEEN: DELIVERANCE

1. Grant, *Memoirs*, 1:383.
2. Wilson and Simon, *Ulysses S. Grant*, 82.
3. Porter, *Campaigning with Grant*, 103.
4. Catton, *Grant Moves South*, 479.
5. Armstrong, *Warrior in Two Camps*, 86.
6. Smith, *Grant*, 256.
7. Catton, *Grant Moves South*, 483.
8. Grant, *Memoirs*, 1:379.
9. Wilson and Simon, *Ulysses S. Grant*, 82.
10. Ibid., 83.
11. Dana, *Recollections of the Civil War*, 99.
12. GPL. S2 B24 F16. "Interview with Lieutenant Frank Parker." HGP.
13. Korda, *Ulysses S. Grant*, 89.
14. Catton, *Never Call Retreat*, 207.
15. McPherson, *Battle Cry of Freedom*, 665.
16. Foote, *The Civil War*, 2:623.
17. Beale, *Diary of Gideon Welles*, 1:364. Diary entry for July 7, 1863.
18. Stahr, *Seward*, 369.
19. Smith, *Grant*, 259.
20. Simpson, *Ulysses S. Grant*, 215.
21. *PUSG*, 9:197. Letter from President Abraham Lincoln, July 13, 1863.
22. "General Rawlins' Address." *Report of the Proceedings of the Society of the Army of the Tennessee*, April 1929.
23. Eaton, *Grant, Lincoln and the Freedmen*, 90.
24. *New York Tribune*, June 17, 1906.
25. GPL. S2 B18 F69. "Alcohol."
26. Richardson, *A Personal History*, 337.
27. Wineapple, *Ecstatic Nation*, 283.
28. Adams, "The Session."
29. Young, *Around the World*, 375–76.

30. *PUSG,* 9:130. Letter to Charles W. Ford, July 28, 1863.

31. Marszalek, *Sherman,* 229.

32. Donald, *Lincoln,* 446.

33. Foote, *The Civil War,* 2:593.

34. Young, *Around the World,* 307.

35. *PUSG,* 9:146. Letter to Charles A. Dana, August 5, 1863.

36. Young, *Around the World,* 387.

37. *PUSG,* 4:444. Letter to Julia Dent Grant, March 29, 1862.

38. Green, "Civil War Public Opinion of General Grant."

39. Simon, "From Galena to Appomattox."

40. Beale, *Diary of Gideon Welles,* 1:386. Diary entry for July 31, 1863.

41. GPL. S2 B24 F15. "Interview with Mr. McDonald." HGP.

42. *PUSG,* 9:124–25. Letter to Brig. Gen. Lorenzo Thomas, July 27, 1863.

43. GPL. S2 B13. "Rawlins Letters." Letter from John Rawlins, September 15, 1863. JHWP.

44. Young, *Around the World,* 625.

45. *PUSG,* 9:45–46. Letter from Maj. Gen. William T. Sherman, July 14, 1863.

46. Marszalek, *Sherman,* 229.

47. Grant, *Memoirs,* 1:387–88.

48. *PUSG,* 9:92. Letter to Brig. Gen. Charles P. Stone, July 21, 1863; Cadwallader, *Three Years with Grant,* 126.

49. *PUSG,* 9:110. Letter to Maj. Gen. William Henry Halleck, July 24, 1863.

50. Ibid., 9:23. Letter to Brig. Gen. Lorenzo Thomas, July 11, 1863.

51. Ibid., 197. Letter from Abraham Lincoln, August 9, 1863.

52. Ibid., 196. Letter to Abraham Lincoln, August 23, 1863.

53. Ibid., 8:483. Letter to Maj. Gen. James B. McPherson, July 5, 1863.

54. Ibid., 9:3. Letter to Maj. Gen. James B. McPherson, July 7, 1863.

55. Wittenmyer, *Under the Guns,* 176, 178–79.

56. Grant, *Memoirs,* 1:388.

57. *PUSG,* 9:200. Letter to Maj. Frederick T. Dent, August 23, 1863.

58. Catton, *Grant Takes Command,* 20.

59. Eaton, *Grant, Lincoln and the Freedmen,* 98.

60. *Missouri Democrat,* September 2, 1863.

61. *PUSG,* 9:190. Letter from Jesse R. Grant to Maj. Gen. Nathaniel P. Banks, August 19, 1863.

62. *New Orleans Era,* September 4, 1863.

63. Catton, *Grant Takes Command,* 22.

64. Ibid., 24.

65. Ibid., 23; Grant, *Memoirs,* 1:390.

66. *PUSG,* 9:223. Lawrence Van Alstyne diary entry for September 4, 1863.

67. Catton, *Grant Takes Command,* 25.

68. GPL. S2 B24 F16. "Interview with Lieutenant Frank Parker." HGP.

69. LoC. USGP. Series 4, Vol. 6. Original manuscript of Grant's *Memoirs.*

70. Grant, *Memoirs,* 1:390.

71. GPL. S2 B4 F10. Letter from N. P. Banks to his wife, September 5, 1863.

72. Ibid. Letter from W. B. Franklin to George B. McClellan, February 4, 1864.

73. Ibid. S2 B12 F22. "Mark Twain." Letter from Samuel Clemens to Henry Ward Beecher, September 11, 1885.

74. Ibid. S2 B4 F10. Letter from Gen. William B. Franklin to William F. Smith, December 28, 1863. WFSP.

75. Cadwallader, *Three Years with Grant,* 117.

76. *PUSG,* 9:475. Letter from John A. Rawlins to Mary E. Hurlbut, November 17, 1863.

77. Eaton, *Grant, Lincoln and the Freedmen,* 107.

78. Catton, *Never Call Retreat,* 246.

79. GPL. S2 B13 F38. "James H. Wilson Journal." Letter from Charles A. Dana to Edwin Stanton, September 20, 1863.

80. Richardson, *A Personal History,* 262.

81. *PUSG,* 9:298. Letter from Brig. Gen. John A. Rawlins to Mary E. Hurlbut, November 23, 1863.

82. McPherson, *Tried by War,* 196.

83. Foote, *The Civil War,* 2:747.

84. *PUSG,* 9:274. Letter from Maj. Gen. William T. Sherman, October 4, 1863.

85. Foote, *The Civil War,* 2:782.

86. Stahr, *Seward,* 379.

87. Ibid.

88. Grant, *Memoirs,* 1:391.

89. Eaton, *Grant, Lincoln and the Freedmen,* 115.

90. GPL. S2 B13 F38. "James H. Wilson Journal." Letter from Charles A. Dana to Edwin Stanton, September 27, 1863.

91. Foote, *The Civil War,* 2:767.

92. *PUSG,* 9:298. Letter from Brig. Gen. John A. Rawlins to Mary E. Hurlbut, November 23, 1863.

93. Simpson, *Ulysses S. Grant,* 226.

94. Carnegie, *Autobiography,* 106.

95. Donald, *Lincoln,* 186.

96. Foote, *The Civil War,* 1:244.

97. Ibid., 2:630.

98. "Grant Reminiscences." *Chicago Daily Tribune,* September 1, 1885.

99. *PUSG,* 15:46. "Testimony," May 18, 1865. Before the Committee on the Conduct of the War.

100. Grant, *Memoirs,* 2:749.

101. Young, *Around the World,* 334.

102. Grant, *Memoirs,* 2:404.

103. Catton, *Grant Takes Command,* 34.

104. Ibid.

105. Grant, *Memoirs,* 2:409.

106. Ibid.

107. GPL. S2 B21 F16. Letter from Brig. Gen. John A. Rawlins to Mary E. Hurlbut, October 18, 1863.

108. Nevins and Thomas, *The Diary of George Templeton Strong,* 3:366. Diary entry for October 22, 1863.

109. Brooks, *Lincoln Observed,* 72.

110. *PUSG,* 12:329. Telegram to Maj. Gen. Henry W. Halleck, October 20, 1864, and 11:125–26,

telegram from Assistant Secretary of War Charles A. Dana to Abraham Lincoln, July 1, 1864.
111. Grant, *Memoirs*, 2:410.
112. *Missouri Democrat*, November 3, 1863.
113. McFeely, *Grant*, 143.
114. Perret, *Ulysses S. Grant*, 274.
115. Young, *Around the World*, 298.
116. Grant, *Memoirs*, 2:410.

CHAPTER FIFTEEN: ABOVE THE CLOUDS

1. Porter, *Campaigning with Grant*, 6.
2. Wilson, *Rawlins*, 166.
3. Porter, *Campaigning with Grant*, 14–15.
4. Ibid., 5.
5. Dana, *Recollections of the Civil War*, 124.
6. *PUSG*, 13:291. Letter to Maj. Gen. William T. Sherman, January 21, 1865; Young, *Around the World*, 303.
7. Young, *Around the World*, 304.
8. Smith, *From Chattanooga to Petersburg*, 8.
9. Foote, *The Civil War*, 2:804.
10. Porter, *Campaigning with Grant*, 7.
11. Wilson and Simon, *Ulysses S. Grant*, 100.
12. *The St. Louis Globe-Democrat*, April 27, 1897.
13. Foote, *The Civil War*, 2:811.
14. *PUSG*, 9:335. Telegram to Maj. Gen. Henry W. Halleck, October 28, 1863.
15. Catton, *Never Call Retreat*, 259.
16. Grant, *Memoirs*, 2:449.
17. Foote, *The Civil War*, 1:567.
18. *PUSG*, 9:396. Letter to Julia Dent Grant, November 14, 1863.
19. Catton, *Grant Takes Command*, 63.
20. Sherman, *Memoirs*, 387.
21. Smith, "Holocaust Holiday."
22. Smith, *Grant*, 269.
23. GPL. S2 B14 F5. "James H. Wilson–Adam Badeau." Letter from James H. Wilson to Adam Badeau, November 21, 1863.
24. Dana, *Recollections of the Civil War*, 74.
25. Smith, "Holocaust Holiday."
26. USGH. "Interview with W. W. Smith." HGP.
27. *PUSG*, 9:218. Letter to Elihu B. Washburne, August 30, 1863.
28. Ibid., 475–76. Letter from Brig. Gen. John A. Rawlins, November 17, 1863.
29. GPL. S2 B21 F16. Letter from John A. Rawlins to Mary Emma Hurlbut, November 10, 1863. LLP.
30. Ibid.
31. Ibid.
32. *PUSG*, 9:476. Telegram from Maj. Gen. David Hunter to Edwin M. Stanton, December 14, 1863.
33. Ibid., 413. Letter to Col. John Riggin Jr., November 18, 1863.
34. Ibid., 428. Telegram to Maj. Gen. Henry W. Halleck, November 21, 1863.
35. Ibid.
36. Foreman, *A World on Fire*, 562.
37. *PUSG*, 9:443. Letter to Maj. Gen. George H. Thomas, November 24, 1863.
38. Catton, *Never Call Retreat*, 67.

117. McFeely, *Grant*, 144.
118. USGH. "Interview with Oliver Otis Howard."
119. Simpson, *Ulysses S. Grant*, 228.
120. Catton, *Grant Takes Command*, 38.
121. White, *American Ulysses*, 297.
122. *PUSG*, 9:317. Letter from Surgeon Edward D. Kittoe to Julia Dent Grant, October 24, 1863.
123. Ibid., 317–18.

39. Marszalek, *Commander of All Lincoln's Armies*, 165.
40. Grant, *Memoirs*, 2:771.
41. Ibid., 441.
42. Foreman, *A World on Fire*, 56.
43. *PUSG*, 9:491. Letter to Elihu B. Washburne, December 2, 1863.
44. *New York Herald*, July 24, 1878.
45. *New York Tribune*, August 22, 1878.
46. Foote, *The Civil War*, 2:850.
47. *PUSG*, 29:262. Grenville M. Dodge, conversation with Grant, October 27, 1882.
48. Ibid., 9:434. Telegram to Maj. Gen. Henry W. Halleck, November 23, 1863.
49. Foreman, *A World on Fire*, 563.
50. *PUSG*, 9:561. Letter to Col. John C. Kelton, December 23, 1863.
51. Smith, "Holocaust Holiday."
52. McPherson, *Battle Cry of Freedom*, 680.
53. Catton, *Grant Takes Command*, 83.
54. Foote, *The Civil War*, 2:854.
55. Cadwallader, *Three Years with Grant*, 151.
56. Simpson, *Ulysses S. Grant*, 242.
57. *PUSG*, 9:563. Letter to Col. John C. Kelton, December 23, 1863.
58. Dana, *Recollections of the Civil War*, 150; Waugh, *U. S. Grant*, 67.
59. *PUSG*, 9:496. Letter to J. Russell Jones, December 5, 1863.
60. GPL. S2 B13 F38. "James H. Wilson Journals." Letter from Charles A. Dana to Edwin M. Stanton, November 26, 1863.
61. Smith, *Grant*, 280.
62. Foreman, *A World on Fire*, 566.
63. Armstrong, *Warrior in Two Camps*, 90–91.
64. Smith, *Grant*, 281.
65. Wilson and Simon, *Ulysses S. Grant*, 76.
66. Nevins and Thomas, *The Diary of George Templeton Strong*, 3:374. Diary entry for November 27, 1863.
67. *PUSG*, 32:61. Letter to John J. Speed, November 30, 1863.
68. Curtis, *The Correspondence of John Lothrop Motley*, 2:146. Letter to his mother, December 29, 1863.
69. Catton, *Grant Takes Command*, 91.
70. White, *American Ulysses*, 311–12.
71. *PUSG*, 9:465. Letter to Maj. Gen. Ambrose E. Burnside, November 29, 1863.
72. Sherman, *Memoirs*, 394.
73. Washburne, *Biography*, 294.
74. Foote, *The Civil War*, 2:918.
75. Simpson, *Ulysses S. Grant*, 246.
76. Ibid., 247.

77. *PUSG,* 9:541. Letter to Barnabas Burns, December 17, 1863.
78. Wilson, *Rawlins,* 434.
79. USGH, "Interview with Sarah Hill."
80. Catton, *Grant Takes Command,* 111.
81. GPL. S2 B24 F14. "Interview with J. Russell Jones." HGP.
82. *PUSG,* 9:554. Letter from William T. Sherman, December 29, 1863.
83. Ibid., 555.
84. Ambrose, *Halleck,* 157.
85. Foote, *The Civil War,* 2:918.
86. *PUSG,* 9:522. Letter to Elihu B. Washburne, December 12, 1863.
87. LoC. EMSP. Reel 7. Letter from Ulysses S. Grant to Henry W. Halleck, January 15, 1864.
88. Catton, *Grant Takes Command,* 104–5.
89. Ibid., 105.
90. Grant, *Memoirs,* 2:459.

91. Ibid., 459–60.
92. Foote, *The Civil War,* 2:917.
93. GPL. S2 B5 F20. "Julia Grant Interview." HGP.
94. LoC. JHWP. Box 50. Letter from John A. Rawlins to unnamed recipient, January 16, 1864.
95. Julia Grant, *Memoirs,* 125.
96. Washburne, *Biography,* 290.
97. Ibid., 291.
98. Julia Grant, *Memoirs,* 126–27.
99. *Missouri Democrat,* January 30, 1864.
100. Catton, *Grant Takes Command,* 115.
101. "Gen. Grant's Morality." *Chicago Daily Tribune,* January 27, 1887.
102. Wilson, *Rawlins,* 395.
103. Catton, *Grant Takes Command,* 126.
104. LoC. JHWP. Box 50. Letter from John A. Rawlins to Mary E. (Hurlbut) Rawlins, February 14, 1864.

CHAPTER SIXTEEN: IDOL OF THE HOUR

1. *PUSG,* 10:121–22. Letter to Julia Dent Grant, February 14, 1864.
2. Washburne, *Biography,* 299.
3. Ibid., 304.
4. Ibid., 301.
5. Ibid.
6. Morgan, "From City Point to Appomattox with General Grant."
7. Wilson, *Rawlins,* 396.
8. *PUSG,* 29:38. Letter to Elihu B. Washburne, December 24, 1878.
9. Ibid., 10:187. Letter to Maj. Gen. William T. Sherman, March 4, 1864.
10. Ibid., 187–88. Letter from Maj. Gen. William T. Sherman, March 10, 1864.
11. Ibid., 188.
12. LoC. JHWP. Box 50. Letter from John A. Rawlins to Mary E. Rawlins, March 5, 1864.
13. Ibid. Letter from John A. Rawlins to Mary E. Rawlins, March 8, 1864.
14. Ibid. Letter from John A. Rawlins to Mary E. Rawlins, March 5, 1864.
15. *PUSG,* 10:259. Letter to Henry Wilson, April 4, 1864.
16. GPL. S2 B21 F17. Letter from Ely Parker to Elihu B. Washburne, April 12, 1864. LLP.
17. *PUSG,* 10:260. Letter from Lt. Col. William R. Rowley to Elihu B. Washburne, April 10, 1864.
18. Summer, *The Diary of Cyrus B. Comstock,* 260. Diary entry for March 7, 1864.
19. *PUSG,* 10:187. Letter to Maj. Gen. William T. Sherman, March 4, 1864.
20. GPL. S2 B13 F66. "Rawlins Letters." Letter from John A. Rawlins to Mary E. Rawlins, March 8, 1864. JHWP.
21. Wilson, *Rawlins,* 400.
22. Taliaferro, *All the Great Prizes,* 45.
23. Foote, *The Civil War,* 2:52.
24. Porter, *Campaigning with Grant,* 22.
25. Richardson, *A Personal History,* 387.
26. Foote, *The Civil War,* 3:5.

27. Simpson, *Ulysses S. Grant,* 287.
28. Titone, *My Thoughts Be Bloody,* 312.
29. Simpson, *Ulysses S. Grant,* 259.
30. Porter, *Campaigning with Grant,* 19.
31. Ibid.
32. Catton, *Grant Takes Command,* 126.
33. Porter, *Campaigning with Grant,* 20.
34. Catton, *Grant Takes Command,* 126.
35. Julia Grant, *Memoirs,* 128.
36. *New York Herald,* March 12, 1864.
37. Badeau, *Grant in Peace,* 171.
38. Burlingame, *With Lincoln in the White House,* 130.
39. *PUSG,* 10:195. "Speech," Abraham Lincoln, March 9, 1864.
40. Ibid.
41. Grant, *Memoirs,* 2:473.
42. *New York Herald,* May 27, 1878.
43. "Grant Reminiscences." *Chicago Daily Tribune,* September 1, 1885.
44. *New York Herald,* May 27, 1878.
45. Grant, *Memoirs,* 2:474.
46. *New York Herald,* May 27, 1878.
47. Porter, *Campaigning with Grant,* 26.
48. Wilson, *Rawlins,* 403.
49. Woodward, *Mary Chesnut's Civil War,* 585. Diary entry for March 12, 1864.
50. Waugh, *U. S. Grant,* 78.
51. Catton, *Grant Takes Command,* 131.
52. Dana, *Recollections of the Civil War,* 227.
53. Simpson, *Ulysses S. Grant,* 334.
54. Morris, *Sheridan,* 544.
55. Grant, *Memoirs,* 2:770.
56. Porter, *Campaigning with Grant,* 115.
57. Smith, *Grant,* 292.
58. Porter, *Campaigning with Grant,* 29.
59. Young, *Around the World,* 305–6.
60. Girardi, *The Civil War Generals,* 65.
61. Foote, *The Civil War,* 3:11.
62. Catton, *Grant Takes Command,* 410.
63. Foote, *The Civil War,* 3:12.

64. Catton, *Grant Takes Command*, 120.
65. Young, *Around the World*, 264.
66. Badeau, *Military History of Ulysses S. Grant*, 2:19.
67. Ibid., 19–20.
68. Catton, *Grant Takes Command*, 137.
69. USGH. "Interview with General Grenville Dodge."
70. Catton, *Grant Takes Command*, 137.
71. Sherman, *Memoirs*, 430.
72. Foote, *The Civil War*, 3:13.
73. Ibid., 2:966.
74. Grant, "The Early Life of Gen. Grant."
75. Simpson, *Ulysses S. Grant*, 267.
76. GPL. S2 B4 F11. "Grant and Drinking."

CHAPTER SEVENTEEN: ULYSSES THE SILENT

1. Badeau, *Military History of Ulysses S. Grant*, 2:32.
2. *PUSG*, 15:165. Letter to Edwin M. Stanton, June 20, 1865.
3. Ibid., 10:253. Telegram from William T. Sherman, April 9, 1864.
4. Ibid., 15:175. Letter to Edwin M. Stanton, June 20, 1865.
5. Ibid., 10:201. Letter to Maj. Gen. Nathaniel P. Banks, March 15, 1864.
6. GPL. S2 B13. "Rawlins Letters." Letter from John A. Rawlins to Mary Emma Rawlins, April 13, 1865. JHWP.
7. Grant, *Memoirs*, 2:485.
8. Goodwin, *Team of Rivals*, 618.
9. Stahr, *Seward*, 396.
10. Young, *Around the World*, 375.
11. Ambrose, *Halleck*, 168.
12. Young, *Around the World*, 375.
13. Ibid.
14. GPL. S2 B13. "Rawlins Letters." Letter from John A. Rawlins to Mary E. Rawlins, April 22, 1864. JHWP.
15. Wilson, *Patriotic Gore*, 313.
16. *PUSG*, 10:315. Letter to Julia Dent Grant, April 17, 1864.
17. Ibid., 316.
18. Armstrong, *Warrior in Two Camps*, 96.
19. Badeau, *Military History of Ulysses S. Grant*, 38.
20. Wilson, *Rawlins*, 421–22.
21. Simpson, *Ulysses S. Grant*, 284.
22. Ibid.
23. Foreman, *A World on Fire*, 605.
24. Girardi, *The Civil War Generals*, 73.
25. Simpson, *Ulysses S. Grant*, 284.
26. Ibid., 284–85.
27. Girardi, *The Civil War Generals*, 67.
28. GPL. S2 B4 F11. "Grant and Drinking." Letter from Maj. Henry L. Abbott to his mother, March 13, 1864.
29. Young, *Around the World*, 387.
30. Waugh, *U. S. Grant*, 82.
31. Young, *Around the World*, 388.
32. *New York Herald*, July 24, 1878.
33. Porter, *Campaigning with Grant*, 24.
34. Sheridan, *Memoirs*, 1:346.
35. Porter, *Campaigning with Grant*, 24.
36. GPL. S2 B13. "Rawlins Letters." Letter from John A. Rawlins to Mary E. Rawlins, March 8, 1864. JHWP.
37. Ibid.
38. Ibid. Letter from John A. Rawlins to Mary E. Rawlins, April 12, 1864.
39. Ibid. Letter from John A. Rawlins to Mary E. Rawlins, April 17, 1864.
40. Ibid. S2 B54 F18. "Interview with General Harry Wilson." HGP.
41. Genetin-Pilawa, "The Indian at Appomattox."
42. Ibid.
43. USGH. "Interview with Ely S. Parker."
44. Ibid.
45. Ibid.
46. Porter, *Campaigning with Grant*, 196.
47. Ibid., 133.
48. Ibid., 250.
49. Ibid., 242.
50. Ibid., 251.
51. *The New York Times*, March 25, 1885.
52. Porter, *Campaigning with Grant*, 66.
53. Ibid., 81.
54. Ibid., 214.
55. Ibid.
56. Ibid., 213–14.
57. Ibid., 215.
58. Armstrong, *Warrior in Two Camps*, 87.
59. Badeau, *Military History of Ulysses S. Grant*, 20.
60. Ibid.
61. Ibid., 21.
62. *PUSG*, 13:299. Letter to Elihu B. Washburne, January 23, 1865.
63. Ibid., 10:274. Letter to Maj. Gen. George G. Meade, April 9, 1864.
64. Ibid.
65. Waugh, *U. S. Grant*, 78.
66. Nevins and Thomas, *The Diary of George Templeton Strong*, 3:416. Diary entry for March 18, 1864.
67. Girardi, *The Civil War Generals*, 67.
68. Foote, *The Civil War*, 3:123.
69. Porter, *Campaigning with Grant*, 47.
70. Grant, *Memoirs*, 2:476.
71. Young, *Around the World*, 384.

72. Korda, *Clouds of Glory,* 345.
73. Foote, *The Civil War,* 3:547.
74. Korda, *Clouds of Glory,* 67–68.
75. Wineapple, *Ecstatic Nation,* 251.
76. Pryor, *Reading the Man,* 320.
77. Foote, *The Civil War,* 1:478.
78. GPL. S2 B24 F15. "Interview with James Longstreet." HGP.
79. Grant, *Memoirs,* 2:748.
80. Foote, *The Civil War,* 2:37.
81. Korda, *Clouds of Glory,* 320.
82. Waugh, *U. S. Grant,* 188.
83. Pryor, *Reading the Man,* 416.
84. Jones, *A Rebel War Clerk's Diary,* 370. Diary entry for February 1, 1865.
85. Ibid., 401.
86. Ibid., 409.
87. Paine, *Mark Twain's Notebook,* 116.
88. Foreman, *A World on Fire,* 606.
89. Wineapple, *Ecstatic Nation,* 224.
90. *New York Herald,* July 24, 1878.
91. Catton, *Grant Takes Command,* 147.
92. Simpson, *Ulysses S. Grant,* 270.
93. GPL. S2 B13. "Rawlins Papers." Letter from John A. Rawlins to Mary E. Rawlins, April 23, 1864. JHWP.
94. Badeau, *Military History of Ulysses S. Grant,* 55.
95. Grant, *Memoirs,* 2:463.
96. *PUSG,* 10:302. Letter to Maj. Gen. Benjamin F. Butler, April 17, 1864.
97. Ibid., 306. Letter to Maj. Gen. David Hunter, April 17, 1864.

CHAPTER EIGHTEEN: RAGING STORM

1. *PUSG,* 10:377. Letter to Julia Dent Grant, April 30, 1864.
2. Ibid., 380. Letter from Abraham Lincoln, April 30, 1864.
3. Ibid. Letter to Abraham Lincoln, May 1, 1864.
4. Ammen, "Recollections and Letters of Grant. Part 1."
5. *PUSG,* 10:394. Letter to Julia Dent Grant, May 2, 1864.
6. Ibid.
7. Porter, *Campaigning with Grant,* 37.
8. Washburne, *Biography,* 327.
9. Perret, *Ulysses S. Grant,* 307.
10. Cadwallader, *Three Years with Grant,* 175.
11. Grant, *Memoirs,* 2:524.
12. Porter, *Campaigning with Grant,* 42.
13. *PUSG,* 15:169. Letter to Edwin M. Stanton, June 20, 1865.
14. Foote, *The Civil War,* 3:148.
15. Badeau, *Military History of Ulysses S. Grant,* 99.
16. Pryor, *Reading the Man,* 417.
17. *PUSG,* 10:397. Telegram to Maj. Gen. Henry W. Halleck, May 4, 1864.
18. Badeau, *Military History of Ulysses S. Grant,* 100.
19. Porter, *Campaigning with Grant,* 46.
20. Ibid., 63.
21. Catton, *Grant Takes Command,* 185.
22. Ibid., 189.
23. Ibid., 192.
24. Grant, *Memoirs,* 2:527.
25. Washburne, *Biography,* 332.
26. Catton, *Grant Takes Command,* 195.
27. Smith, *Grant,* 327.
28. Foreman, *A World on Fire,* 609.
29. Ibid., 612.
30. Grant, *Memoirs,* 2:531.
31. Simpson, *Ulysses S. Grant,* 297.
32. Badeau, *Military History of Ulysses S. Grant,* 120.
33. Porter, *Campaigning with Grant,* 72.
34. Curtis, *The Correspondence of John Lothrop Motley,* 2:211. Letter from Dr. O. W. Holmes, October 10, 1865.
35. Simpson, *Ulysses S. Grant,* 298.
36. Grant, *Memoirs,* 2:534.
37. Foote, *The Civil War,* 3:185–86.
38. Porter, *Campaigning with Grant,* 71.
39. Beckwith, "With Grant in the Wilderness, by His 'Shadow.'"
40. Foote, *The Civil War,* 3:187.
41. Ibid., 186.
42. Holzer, *Lincoln and the Power of the Press,* 47.
43. Wilson, *Rawlins,* 218.
44. Grant, *Memoirs,* 2:534.
45. Donald, *Lincoln,* 501.
46. Dorsett, "The Problem of Ulysses S. Grant's Drinking During the Civil War."
47. GPL. S2 B13 F26. "Walt Whitman."
48. *New York Herald,* September 12, 1876.
49. Porter, *Campaigning with Grant,* 66.
50. Badeau, *Military History of Ulysses S. Grant,* 134.
51. Smith, *Grant,* 338.
52. Porter, *Campaigning with Grant,* 79.
53. Foote, *The Civil War,* 3:190.
54. Porter, *Campaigning with Grant,* 78.
55. GPL. S2 B13 F38. "James H. Wilson Journal." Letter from Charles A. Dana to Edwin Stanton, May 8, 1864. JHWP.
56. Porter, *Campaigning with Grant,* 291.
57. Wilson, *Rawlins,* 217.
58. Burlingame, *Lincoln Observed,* 108.
59. Foote, *The Civil War,* 3:375.
60. McPherson, *Tried by War,* 219.
61. Foote, *The Civil War,* 3:191.
62. Washburne, *Biography,* 341.
63. Foote, *The Civil War,* 3:204.
64. Porter, *Campaigning with Grant,* 84.
65. Ibid.
66. Sheridan, *Memoirs,* 1:370.
67. Grant, *Memoirs,* 2:497.
68. Sheridan, *Memoirs,* 1:387.
69. Foote, *The Civil War,* 3:198.
70. *PUSG,* 10:415. Letter to Maj. Gen. Henry W. Halleck, May 9, 1864.
71. Porter, *Campaigning with Grant,* 89.
72. Catton, *Grant Takes Command,* 217.
73. Porter, *Campaigning with Grant,* 90.
74. *PUSG,* 10:418–19. Telegram to Maj. Gen. Henry W. Halleck, May 10, 1864.

75. USGH. "Interview with M. Harrison Strong."
76. Smith, *Grant*, 348.
77. Badeau, *Military History of Ulysses S. Grant*, 163.
78. *The New York Times*, March 17, 1881.
79. Washburne, *Biography*, 343.
80. *PUSG*, 10:434. Letter to Edwin M. Stanton, May 13, 1864.
81. Simpson, *Ulysses S. Grant*, 307.
82. Wilson, *Rawlins*, 219.
83. *PUSG*, 10:422. Letter to Maj. Gen. Henry W. Halleck, May 11, 1864.
84. Waugh, *U. S. Grant*, 86.
85. Catton, *Grant Takes Command*, 295.
86. McPherson, *Battle Cry of Freedom*, 731.
87. Porter, *Campaigning with Grant*, 57.
88. McFeely, *Grant*, 166.
89. Sheridan, *Memoirs*, 1:452.
90. *Cincinnati Gazette*, October 5, 1880.
91. *PUSG*, 10:427. Telegram to Maj. Gen. George G. Meade, May 11, 1864.

92. Porter, *Campaigning with Grant*, 101.
93. Smith, *Grant*, 350.
94. Porter, *Campaigning with Grant*, 101.
95. Ibid., 104.
96. Foote, *The Civil War*, 3:217.
97. McPherson, *Battle Cry of Freedom*, 730.
98. Campi, *Civil War Battlefields*, 99.
99. Porter, *Campaigning with Grant*, 110.
100. Dana, *Recollections of the Civil War*, 197.
101. Holmes, *Touched with Fire*, 117.
102. *PUSG*, 10:444. Letter to Julia Dent Grant, May 13, 1864.
103. Catton, *Grant Takes Command*, 235–36.
104. GPL. S2 B54 F14. "Interview with General Henry Heth." HGP.
105. Porter, *Campaigning with Grant*, 119.
106. *PUSG*, 10:443–44. Letter to Julia Dent Grant, May 13, 1864.

CHAPTER NINETEEN: HEAVENS HUNG IN BLACK

1. Bunting, *Ulysses S. Grant*, 220.
2. *PUSG*, 10:477. Telegram to Maj. Gen. Henry W. Halleck, May 22, 1864.
3. Foreman, *A World on Fire*, 615.
4. *PUSG*, 10:460. Telegram from Maj. Gen. Henry W. Halleck, May 17, 1864.
5. Burlingame, *Lincoln Observed*, 109.
6. Holmes, *Touched with Fire*, 122.
7. Wilson, *Rawlins*, 198–99.
8. Donald, *Lincoln*, 500.
9. Porter, *Campaigning with Grant*, 127.
10. Badeau, *Military History of Ulysses S. Grant*, 208.
11. *PUSG*, 10:464. Letter to Maj. Gen. George G. Meade, May 18, 1864.
12. Smith, *Grant*, 359.
13. Catton, *Grant Takes Command*, 249.
14. Simpson, *Ulysses S. Grant*, 320.
15. *PUSG*, 10:480. Telegram to Maj. Gen. Henry W. Halleck, May 23, 1864.
16. Foote, *The Civil War*, 3:273–74.
17. McPherson, "Our Monstrous War."
18. Foote, *The Civil War*, 3:275.
19. Badeau, *Military History of Ulysses S. Grant*, 262.
20. *PUSG*, 10:491. Letter to Maj. Gen. Henry W. Halleck, May 26, 1864.
21. Foote, *The Civil War*, 3:279.
22. Porter, *Campaigning with Grant*, 164.
23. GPL. S2 B13. "Rawlins Letters." Letter from John A. Rawlins to Mary E. Rawlins, May 30, 1864. JHWP.
24. Badeau, *Military History of Ulysses S. Grant*, 279.
25. Holmes, *Touched with Fire*, 138.
26. Simpson, *Ulysses S. Grant*, 323.
27. McFeely, *Grant*, 159.
28. *PUSG*, 11:5. Letter to Julia Dent Grant, June 1, 1864.

29. McPherson, *Battle Cry of Freedom*, 735.
30. Foote, *The Civil War*, 3:290.
31. Keegan, *The American Civil War*, 247.
32. Foote, *The Civil War*, 3:292.
33. McFeely, *Grant*, 171.
34. McPherson, *Battle Cry of Freedom*, 735.
35. *PUSG*, 11:9. Telegram to Maj. Gen. Henry W. Halleck, June 3, 1864.
36. GPL. S2 B13 F38. "James H. Wilson Journal." Letter from Charles A. Dana to Edwin Stanton, June 3, 1864. JHWP.
37. Ibid. S2 B13. "Rawlins Letters." Letter from John A. Rawlins to Mary E. Rawlins, June 4, 1864. JHWP.
38. *PUSG*, 15:176. Letter to Edwin M. Stanton, June 20, 1865.
39. Bean, "Memoranda of Conversations Between General Robert E. Lee and William Preston Johnston."
40. Grant, *Memoirs*, 2:588.
41. LoC. USGP. Series 4, Vol. 8. Original manuscript of Grant's *Memoirs*.
42. Young, *Around the World*, 310.
43. USGH. "Interview with W. W. Smith." HGP.
44. Beckwith, "With Grant in the Wilderness, by His 'Shadow.'"
45. Porter, *Campaigning with Grant*, 184.
46. *PUSG*, 11:17. Letter to Gen. Robert E. Lee, June 5, 1864.
47. Ibid., 22. Letter to Gen. Robert E. Lee, June 6, 1864.
48. Ibid., 26–27. Letter to Gen. Robert E. Lee, June 7, 1864.
49. McPherson, "Grant: A Biography."
50. *New York Herald*, July 24, 1878.
51. *Missouri Democrat*, May 31, 1866.
52. Catton, *Grant Takes Command*, 301.
53. *Pittsburgh Times*, June 17, 1881.
54. *PUSG*, 15:175. Letter to Edwin M. Stanton, June 20, 1865.

55. McPherson, *Battle Cry of Freedom*, 742.

56. Foote, *The Civil War*, 3:295.

57. Beale, *Diary of Gideon Welles*, 3:275. Diary entry for February 8, 1868.

58. Foner, *Fiery Trial*, 303.

59. Waugh, *U. S. Grant*, 94.

60. "Stories of Grant." *Chicago Daily Tribune*, April 12, 1885.

61. Donald, *Lincoln*, 513.

62. Ibid., 515.

63. Ibid., 513.

64. McPherson, *Battle Cry of Freedom*, 742.

65. Taliaferro, *All the Great Prizes*, 84.

66. Stevens, *Grant in St. Louis*, 82.

67. Smith, *Grant*, 366.

68. Washburne, *Biography*, 351.

69. Catton, *Grant Takes Command*, 282.

70. *PUSG*, 11:55. Letter to Julia Dent Grant, June 15, 1864.

71. Simpson, *Ulysses S. Grant*, 344.

72. *PUSG*, 11:45. Telegram from President Abraham Lincoln, June 15, 1864.

73. Kazin, "The Generals in the Labyrinth."

74. *Missouri Democrat*, May 31, 1866.

75. McPherson, *Battle Cry of Freedom*, 740.

CHAPTER TWENTY: CALDRON OF HELL

1. Nevins and Thomas, *The Diary of George Templeton Strong*, 3:464. Diary entry for July 1, 1864.

2. FL. JSPP. Box 273, letter 173. Letter from Charles A. Dana to James S. Pike, July 10, 1864.

3. *PUSG*, 11:141. Telegram to Maj. Gen. Henry W. Halleck, June 28, 1864.

4. Ibid., 32:65. Letter to Jesse Root Grant, July 5, 1864.

5. Ibid., 11:176. Letter to J. Russell Jones, July 5, 1864.

6. Korda, *Clouds of Glory*, 564.

7. *PUSG*, 11:170. Telegram to Maj. Gen. Henry W. Halleck, July 5, 1864.

8. Marszalek, *Commander of All Lincoln's Armies*, 206.

9. Grant, *Memoirs*, 2:606.

10. *PUSG*, 11:199. Telegram from President Abraham Lincoln, July 10, 1864.

11. Catton, *Grant Takes Command*, 313.

12. GPL. S2 B13. "Rawlins Letters." Letter from John A. Rawlins to Mary E. Rawlins, July 11, 1864. JHWP.

13. McPherson, *Tried by War*, 226.

14. Korda, *Clouds of Glory*, 405.

15. Donald, *Lincoln*, 518.

16. *PUSG*, 11:242–43. Letter to Maj. Gen. Henry W. Halleck, July 14, 1864.

17. Ibid., 253. Telegram from Charles A. Dana to Brig. Gen. John A. Rawlins, July 15, 1864.

18. Ibid., 280. Telegram to President Abraham Lincoln, July 19, 1864.

19. Ibid. Telegram from President Abraham Lincoln, July 20, 1864.

76. Simpson, *Ulysses S. Grant*, 339.

77. Foreman, *A World on Fire*, 634.

78. McPherson, *Battle Cry of Freedom*, 741.

79. *PUSG*, 32:70. Letter to Henry Wilson, December 8, 1864.

80. Stahr, *Seward*, 403.

81. Julia Grant, *Memoirs*, 131.

82. Porter, *Campaigning with Grant*, 217.

83. Foote, *The Civil War*, 3:443.

84. Porter, *Campaigning with Grant*, 217.

85. Ibid.

86. Ibid., 218.

87. Ibid., 218–19.

88. Ibid., 219–20.

89. EBC. Letter from Adam Badeau to Edwin Booth, June 27, 1864.

90. Porter, *Campaigning with Grant*, 220.

91. Ibid.

92. Ibid., 223.

93. EBC. Letter from Adam Badeau to Edwin Booth, June 27, 1864.

94. Porter, *Campaigning with Grant*, 223.

95. Donald, *Lincoln*, 516.

96. Ibid.

20. Ibid., 9:477. Letter to Secretary of War Edwin M. Stanton, November 12, 1863.

21. Longacre, *Army of Amateurs*, 176.

22. Snell, *From First to Last*, 325.

23. Smith, *From Chattanooga to Petersburg*, 9.

24. *PUSG*, 11:208. Letter from Gen. William F. Smith to Senator Solomon Foot, July 30, 1864.

25. Smith, *From Chattanooga to Petersburg*, 174–75.

26. Longacre, *Army of Amateurs*, 177.

27. GPL. S2 B10 F66. Letter from John A. Rawlins to Mary E. Rawlins, June 29, 1864.

28. Longacre, *Army of Amateurs*, 177.

29. *PUSG*, 11:156. Letter from Maj. Gen. Henry W. Halleck, July 3, 1864.

30. Longacre, *Army of Amateurs*, 181.

31. Smith, *From Chattanooga to Petersburg*, 52.

32. Ibid., 131–32.

33. Catton, *Grant Takes Command*, 256.

34. *Chicago Daily Tribune*, January 22, 1887.

35. *PUSG*, 11:210. Letter from John A. Rawlins to Mary E. Rawlins, July 19, 1864.

36. Ibid. Letter from Assistant Secretary of War Charles A. Dana to John A. Rawlins, July 11, 1864.

37. Grant, *Memoirs*, 2:503.

38. Foote, *The Civil War*, 3:323.

39. Ibid., 400.

40. Keegan, *The American Civil War*, 330.

41. Sherman, *Memoirs*, 573.

42. Foote, *The Civil War*, 3:415.

43. Julia Grant, *Memoirs*, 326.

44. Ibid.

45. Porter, *Campaigning with Grant*, 244.

46. Grant, *Memoirs*, 2:506.

47. Beckwith, "With Grant in the Wilderness, by His 'Shadow.'"
48. *PUSG*, 11:397. Letter to Lydia Slocum, August 10, 1864.
49. McPherson, *Battle Cry of Freedom*, 758.
50. Grant, *Memoirs*, 2:607.
51. Foreman, *A World on Fire*, 641.
52. Grant, *Memoirs*, 2:771.
53. McPherson, *Battle Cry of Freedom*, 759.
54. *PUSG*, 13:142. "Testimony," December 20, 1864.
55. Catton, *Grant Takes Command*, 321.
56. Wilson, *Rawlins*, 249.
57. Foote, *The Civil War*, 3:535.
58. Catton, *Grant Takes Command*, 322.
59. Grant, *Memoirs*, 2:612.
60. Porter, *Campaigning with Grant*, 264.
61. Ibid., 267.
62. Faust, *This Republic of Suffering*, 46.
63. Porter, *Campaigning with Grant*, 269.
64. Young, *Around the World*, 300.
65. *PUSG*, 13:140. "Testimony," December 20, 1864.
66. Ibid., 11:363. Letter from Lt. Col. Theodore S. Bowers to Brig. Gen. James H. Wilson, August 1, 1864.
67. Ibid. Letter from Lt. Col. Theodore S. Bowers to Brig. Gen. James H. Wilson, August 2, 1864.
68. Foote, *The Civil War*, 3:538.
69. Waugh, *U. S. Grant*, 92.
70. Beale, *Diary of Gideon Welles*, 2:92. Diary entry for August 2, 1864.
71. GPL. S2 B18 F69. "Abraham Lincoln."
72. Sheridan, *Memoirs*, 1:461.
73. *PUSG*, 11:358. Telegram to Maj. Gen. Henry W. Halleck, August 1, 1864.
74. Ibid., 360. Telegram from Abraham Lincoln, August 3, 1864.
75. Morris, *Sheridan*, 1.
76. Foote, *The Civil War*, 3:866.
77. Cadwallader, *Three Years with Grant*, 305.
78. Morris, *Sheridan*, 258.
79. *New York Herald*, July 24, 1878.
80. Young, *Around the World*, 305.
81. USGH. "Interview with Augustus Chetlain." HGP.
82. Simpson, *Ulysses S. Grant*, 461.
83. Morris, *Sheridan*, 179.
84. Ibid., 184.
85. Foreman, *A World on Fire*, 644.
86. Porter, *Campaigning with Grant*, 236.
87. *PUSG*, 11:378. Letter to Maj. Gen. David Hunter, August 5, 1864.
88. Ibid., 381. Letter to Maj. Gen. William T. Sherman, August 7, 1864.
89. Ibid. Telegram from Maj. Gen. William T. Sherman, August 7, 1864.
90. Catton, *Grant Takes Command*, 348.
91. Ibid., 353.
92. Ibid.
93. Morgan, "From City Point to Appomattox with General Grant."
94. Simpson, *Ulysses S. Grant*, 370.
95. Porter, *Campaigning with Grant*, 275.
96. *PUSG*, 12:16. Letter to Elihu B. Washburne, August 16, 1864.
97. Porter, *Campaigning with Grant*, 234.
98. GPL. S2 B21 F15. Letter from Ely Parker to Col. William R. Rowley, July 11, 1864.
99. Porter, *Campaigning with Grant*, 273.
100. GPL. S2 B14 F5. "James H. Wilson–Adam Badeau." Letter from James H. Wilson to Adam Badeau, August 1, 1864.
101. Wilson, *Rawlins*, 237.
102. Ibid., 261.
103. GPL. S2 B4 F4. From "Inside Lincoln's Army: The Diary of Marsena Rudolph Patrick, Provost Marshal General, Army of the Potomac." Edited by Davis S. Sparks. Diary entry for August 18, 1864.
104. Simpson, *Ulysses S. Grant*, 376.
105. Wilson, *Rawlins*, 258.
106. Porter, *Campaigning with Grant*, 283.
107. Ibid., 284.
108. Smith, *Grant*, 384.
109. Jones, *A Rebel War Clerk's Diary*, 466. Diary entry for August 26, 1864.
110. Woodward, *Mary Chesnut's Civil War*, 637. Diary entry for August 19, 1864.

CHAPTER TWENTY-ONE: CHEW & CHOKE

1. GPL. S2 B21. Letter from George K. Leet to Col. William R. Rowley, August 23, 1864. LLP.
2. *PUSG*, 11:425. Telegram from Abraham Lincoln, August 17, 1864.
3. Porter, *Campaigning with Grant*, 279.
4. Nevins and Thomas, *The Diary of George Templeton Strong*, 3:467. Diary entry for July 23, 1864.
5. Catton, *Never Call Retreat*, 381.
6. Wineapple, *Ecstatic Nation*, 322.
7. Burlingame, *Lincoln Observed*, 114.
8. *PUSG*, 11:396–97. Letter to Isaac N. Morris, August 10, 1864.
9. GPL. S2 B14 F5. "James H. Wilson–Adam Badeau." Letter from James H. Wilson to Adam Badeau, August 19, 1864.
10. Eaton, *Grant, Lincoln and the Freedmen*, 186.
11. Ibid., 190.
12. Ibid., 191.
13. Ibid.
14. *PUSG*, 12:17. Letter to Elihu B. Washburne, August 16, 1864.
15. Ibid., 36. Letter to Commander Daniel Ammen, August 18, 1864.
16. Stahr, *Seward*, 406.
17. Foner, *Fiery Trial*, 306.
18. Grant, *Memoirs*, 2:625.
19. *Cincinnati Gazette*, October 5, 1880.
20. *PUSG*, 11:383. Telegram from Maj. Gen. William T. Sherman to Maj. Gen. Henry W. Halleck, August 7, 1864.
21. Keegan, *The American Civil War*, 267.

22. Catton, *Never Call Retreat,* 398.

23. McPherson, *Battle Cry of Freedom,* 751.

24. Foner, *Fiery Trial,* 308.

25. Wilson and Simon, *Ulysses S. Grant,* 113.

26. *PUSG,* 12:155. Letter to Maj. Gen. William T. Sherman, September 12, 1864.

27. Ibid., 128. Telegram from Maj. Gen. William T. Sherman, September 6, 1864.

28. Sherman, *Memoirs,* 889.

29. Guelzo, "The Civil War's Unlikely Genius."

30. Grant, *Memoirs,* 2:634.

31. Porter, *Campaigning with Grant,* 288.

32. Catton, *Grant Takes Command,* 363.

33. Morris, *Sheridan,* 194.

34. Porter, *Campaigning with Grant,* 298.

35. Julia Grant, *Memoirs,* 132.

36. *New York Tribune,* September 19, 1864.

37. *PUSG,* 12:179–80. Letter to Julia Dent Grant, September 20, 1864.

38. Simpson, *Ulysses S. Grant,* 379.

39. McPherson, *Tried by War,* 245.

40. *PUSG,* 12:177. Telegram to Maj. Gen. Philip H. Sheridan, September 20, 1864.

41. Ibid., 193. Telegram to Maj. Gen. Philip H. Sheridan, September 22, 1864.

42. Ibid. Telegram from Secretary of War Edwin M. Stanton to Julia Dent Grant, September 23, 1864.

43. Sheridan, *Memoirs,* 2:82.

44. *PUSG,* 12:328. Telegram from Maj. Gen. Philip Sheridan, October 19, 1864.

45. Porter, *Campaigning with Grant,* 307–8.

46. Ibid., 301.

47. EBC. Letter from Adam Badeau to Edwin Booth, October 1, 1864.

48. Smith, *Grant,* 387.

49. EBC. Letter from Adam Badeau to Edwin Booth, October 1, 1864.

50. Porter, *Campaigning with Grant,* 294.

51. Ibid., 313.

52. *PUSG,* 12:291. Telegram from Maj. Gen. William T. Sherman, October 9, 1864.

53. Ibid., 290. Telegram from Maj. Gen. William T. Sherman, October 11, 1864.

54. Ibid., 375. Letter from Maj. Gen. William T. Sherman, November 6, 1864.

55. Young, *Around the World,* 302.

56. *PUSG,* 12:303. Telegram from Secretary of War Edwin M. Stanton, October 12, 1864.

57. Ibid., 302–3. Telegram to Secretary of War Edwin M. Stanton, October 13, 1864.

58. Ibid., 318. Telegram from Maj. Gen. William T. Sherman, October 16, 1864; telegram to Maj. Gen. William T. Sherman, October 17, 1864.

59. Sherman, *Memoirs,* 634.

60. *PUSG,* 12:372. Telegram from Maj. Gen. William T. Sherman, November 2, 1864.

61. Sherman, *Memoirs,* 655.

62. Grant, *Memoirs,* 2:647.

63. Simpson, *Ulysses S. Grant,* 391.

64. Grant, *Memoirs,* 2:638.

65. Beale, *Diary of Gideon Welles,* 2:214. Diary entry for December 29, 1864.

66. Simpson, *Ulysses S. Grant,* 385.

67. Porter, *Campaigning with Grant,* 314.

68. *PUSG,* 11:281. Telegram to Maj. Gen. Henry W. Halleck, July 19, 1864.

69. Ibid., 12:298. Telegram to Maj. Gen. William T. Sherman, October 12, 1864.

70. Ibid., 27. Telegram to Maj. Gen. Benjamin F. Butler, August 18, 1864.

71. Ibid., 263. Letter from Gen. Robert E. Lee, October 3, 1864.

72. Ibid. Letter to Gen. Robert E. Lee, October 3, 1864.

73. Ibid., 325. Letter from Gen. Robert E. Lee, October 19, 1864.

74. Ibid., 345. Letter to Julia Dent Grant, October 24, 1864.

75. Ibid., 262. Letter to Julia Dent Grant, October 2, 1864.

76. Ibid., 24. Letter to Frederick Dent, August 17, 1864.

77. Ibid., 166. Letter to Julia Dent Grant, September 14, 1864.

78. Ibid., 212–13. Letter to Edwin M. Stanton, September 27, 1864.

79. Donald, *Lincoln,* 542.

80. McPherson, *Battle Cry of Freedom,* 804.

81. Donald, *Lincoln,* 544.

82. *PUSG,* 12:398. Telegram to Edwin M. Stanton, November 10, 1864.

83. Egerton, *The Wars of Reconstruction,* 86.

84. Taliaferro, *All the Great Prizes,* 97.

85. Ross, *The General's Wife,* 173.

86. EBC. Letter from Adam Badeau to Edwin Booth, November 28, 1864.

87. GPL. S2 B13. "Rawlins Papers." Letter from John A. Rawlins to Mary E. Rawlins, November 23, 1864. JHWP.

88. Porter, *Campaigning with Grant,* 328.

89. Ibid.

90. *PUSG,* 13:67. Telegram to Maj. Gen. George H. Thomas, December 5, 1864.

91. Grant, *Memoirs,* 2:655–56.

92. Young, *Around the World,* 303.

93. *PUSG,* 13:83. Telegram to Maj. Gen. Henry W. Halleck, December 8, 1864.

94. Ibid., 88. Telegram to Maj. Gen. George H. Thomas, December 8, 1864.

95. Ibid. Telegram from Maj. Gen. George H. Thomas, December 9, 1864.

96. Young, *Around the World,* 303; Porter, *Campaigning with Grant,* 347.

97. Wilson and Simon, *Ulysses S. Grant,* 117.

98. Ibid.

99. Ibid., 118.

100. McPherson, *Tried by War,* 253.

101. *PUSG,* 13:124. Telegram to Maj. Gen. George H. Thomas, December 15, 1864.

102. Keegan, *The American Civil War,* 277.

103. *PUSG,* 13:151. Telegram to Maj. Gen. George H. Thomas, December 22, 1864.

104. Ibid., 130. Letter to Maj. Gen. William T. Sherman, December 18, 1864.
105. Ibid., 129.
106. Ibid., 21–24. Telegram to Maj. Gen. George H. Thomas, November 24, 1864.
107. Sherman, *Memoirs,* 657.
108. Egerton, *The Wars of Reconstruction,* 65.
109. *PUSG,* 13:74. Letter from Maj. Gen. William T. Sherman, December 16, 1864.
110. Foner, *Fiery Trial,* 321.

CHAPTER TWENTY-TWO: HER SATANIC MAJESTY

1. Grant, *Memoirs,* 2:662.
2. Simpson, *Ulysses S. Grant,* 393.
3. Porter, *Campaigning with Grant,* 337.
4. Ibid.
5. McPherson, *War on the Waters,* 215–17.
6. *PUSG,* 13:223. Letter to Edwin M. Stanton, January 4, 1865.
7. Ibid., 224. Telegram from Maj. Gen. Edward O. C. Ord, January 11, 1865.
8. Ibid., 22:234. Letter from John B. Alley to Senator Henry Wilson, November 30, 1871.
9. Ibid., 13:185. Telegram from Secretary of the Navy Gideon Welles, December 28, 1864.
10. Ibid., 219. Letter to Bvt. Maj. Gen. Alfred H. Terry, January 3, 1865.
11. McPherson, *Battle Cry of Freedom,* 820–21.
12. GPL. S2 B1 F38. Letter from Adam Badeau to James H. Wilson, January 26, 1865.
13. "Admiral Porter's Letter to Ex-Secretary Welles." *New York Tribune,* December 5, 1870.
14. Julia Grant, *Memoirs,* 179.
15. *PUSG,* 21:68. Letter from Vice Admiral David D. Porter, December 3, 1870.
16. Porter, *Campaigning with Grant,* 329–30.
17. *PUSG,* 13:163. Letter to Julia Dent Grant, December 24, 1864.
18. Ibid., 204. Letter to William W. Smith, January 1, 1865.
19. Simpson, *Ulysses S. Grant,* 404.
20. Nevins and Thomas, *The Diary of George Templeton Strong,* 533. Diary entry for December 27, 1864.
21. Beale, *Diary of Gideon Welles,* 1:214. Diary entry for December 29, 1864.
22. Wilson, *Rawlins,* 297.
23. *PUSG,* 32:73. Letter to James L. Crane, January 2, 1865.
24. Pryor, *Reading the Man,* 421.
25. Wineapple, *Ecstatic Nation,* 351.
26. Foote, *The Civil War,* 3:761.
27. McPherson, *Battle Cry of Freedom,* 822.
28. Goodwin, *Team of Rivals,* 691; Foote, *The Civil War,* 3:773.
29. Westwood, "Lincoln and the Hampton Roads Peace Conference."
30. McFeely, *Grant,* 200.
31. Grant, *Memoirs,* 2:685.
32. *USGA Newsletter,* July 1964.

111. *PUSG,* 13:75. Letter from Maj. Gen. William T. Sherman, December 16, 1864.
112. Ibid., 170. Letter from Maj. Gen. William T. Sherman, December 22, 1864.
113. Sherman, *Memoirs,* 705.
114. Egerton, *The Wars of Reconstruction,* 109.
115. Sherman, *Memoirs,* 711.
116. Donald, *Lincoln,* 553.
117. Foote, *The Civil War,* 3:713.

33. Ibid.
34. Ibid.
35. Ibid.
36. Foote, *The Civil War,* 3:774.
37. *PUSG,* 13:345. Telegram to Edwin M. Stanton, February 1, 1865.
38. Westwood, "Lincoln and the Hampton Roads Peace Conference."
39. Ibid.
40. Badeau, *Grant in Peace,* 18.
41. Wilson, *Patriotic Gore,* 429.
42. Foote, *The Civil War,* 3:777.
43. Donald, *Lincoln,* 560.
44. Grant, *Memoirs,* 2:686.
45. Porter, "Lincoln and Grant."
46. *PUSG,* 13:281. Letter from President Abraham Lincoln, January 19, 1865.
47. Catton, *Grant Takes Command,* 419.
48. Smith, *Grant,* 390.
49. *PUSG,* 13:391. Telegram to Edwin M. Stanton, February 8, 1865.
50. Grant, *Memoirs,* 2:688.
51. *PUSG,* 13:429. Letter to Isaac N. Morris, February 15, 1865.
52. Jones, *A Rebel War Clerk's Diary,* 571.
53. Ibid., 583.
54. Wineapple, *Ecstatic Nation,* 359.
55. Jones, *A Rebel War Clerk's Diary,* 573. Diary entry for February 11, 1865.
56. *PUSG,* 13:131. Letter from Maj. Gen. William T. Sherman, December 24, 1864.
57. McPherson, *Tried by War,* 244.
58. *PUSG,* 13:201. Telegram from Maj. Gen. Henry W. Halleck, December 31, 1864.
59. Foote, *The Civil War,* 3:751.
60. Ibid.
61. Grant, *Memoirs,* 2:765.
62. *PUSG,* 13:295. Letter from Maj. Gen. William T. Sherman, January 29, 1865.
63. Simpson, *Ulysses S. Grant,* 408.
64. Grant, *Memoirs,* 2:681.
65. Foote, *The Civil War,* 3:794.
66. Mayer, *All on Fire,* 577.
67. *PUSG,* 14:31. Letter to Elihu B. Washburne, February 23, 1865.
68. Jones, *A Rebel War Clerk's Diary,* 585. Diary entry for February 25, 1865.
69. *PUSG,* 13:458. Telegram to Maj. Gen. Philip H. Sheridan, February 20, 1865.

70. Julia Grant, *Memoirs*, 136.
71. Porter, *Campaigning with Grant*, 387.
72. *PUSG*, 14:63–64. Memo from Maj. Gen. Edward O. C. Ord, February 27, 1865.
73. Julia Grant, *Memoirs*, 141.
74. *PUSG*, 14:99. Letter from Gen. Robert E. Lee, March 2, 1865.
75. Ibid., 91. Telegram from Edwin M. Stanton, March 3, 1865.
76. *PUSG*, 14:100. Telegram to Edwin M. Stanton, March 4, 1865.
77. Wineapple, *Ecstatic Nation*, 346.
78. Donald, *Lincoln*, 567–68.
79. Stahr, *Seward*, 428.
80. Donald, *Lincoln*, 565.
81. Gordon-Reed, *Andrew Johnson*, 2.
82. Grant, *Memoirs*, 2:690.
83. Porter, *Campaigning with Grant*, 396.
84. *PUSG*, 14:186. Letter to Jesse Root Grant, March 19, 1865.
85. Ibid., 175. Letter from Maj. Gen. William T. Sherman, March 12, 1865.
86. Ibid. Letter to Maj. Gen. William T. Sherman, March 16, 1865.
87. Foote, *The Civil War*, 3:836.
88. Ibid., 815.
89. Ibid., 816.
90. Ibid., 817.
91. Young, *Around the World*, 333.
92. Goodwin, *Team of Rivals*, 709.
93. Ibid.
94. Porter, *Campaigning with Grant*, 404.
95. Goodwin, *Team of Rivals*, 710.
96. Ibid.
97. Catton, *Never Call Retreat*, 38.
98. Young, *Around the World*, 332.
99. Ibid., 331.
100. Donald, *Lincoln*, 572.
101. Ibid.
102. Porter, "Lincoln and Grant."
103. Ibid.
104. "Grant Reminiscences." *Chicago Daily Tribune*, September 1, 1885.
105. Young, *Around the World*, 331.
106. Porter, "Lincoln and Grant."
107. Donald, *Lincoln*, 275.
108. Ibid., 160.
109. Ibid., 324.
110. Ibid., 475.
111. Burlingame, *Lincoln Observed*, 248.
112. Foote, *The Civil War*, 3:845.
113. Ross, *The General's Wife*, 184.
114. Badeau, *Grant in Peace*, 360.
115. Donald, *Lincoln*, 427.
116. Ross, *The General's Wife*, 178.
117. Ibid.
118. *PUSG*, 11:192. Letter to Maj. Gen. Henry W. Halleck, July 8, 1864.
119. Badeau, *Grant in Peace*, 358–59.
120. Ibid., 359.
121. Ibid.
122. Ibid., 360.
123. Foote, *The Civil War*, 3:837.
124. Porter, *Campaigning with Grant*, 417.
125. Foote, *The Civil War*, 3:838.
126. Sherman, *Memoirs*, 813.
127. Ibid., 810.
128. Porter, *Campaigning with Grant*, 420.
129. Sherman, *Memoirs*, 15.
130. Holzer, *Lincoln on War*, 283.
131. Donald, *Lincoln*, 574.
132. Goodwin, *Team of Rivals*, 713.
133. Sherman, *Memoirs*, 813.
134. Foote, *The Civil War*, 3:856.
135. Ibid., 857.
136. Porter, *Campaigning with Grant*, 425.
137. Ibid., 426.

CHAPTER TWENTY-THREE: DIRTY BOOTS

1. Foote, *The Civil War*, 3:853.
2. Grant, *Memoirs*, 2:695.
3. Ibid., 696.
4. Sheridan, *Memoirs*, 2:116.
5. Simpson, *Ulysses S. Grant*, 419.
6. Catton, *Never Call Retreat*, 441.
7. Ibid.
8. Badeau, *Grant in Peace*, 98.
9. GPL. S2 B13. "Rawlins Letters." Letter from John A. Rawlins to Mary E. Rawlins, March 29, 1865. JHWP.
10. *PUSG*, 14:253. Letter to Maj. Gen. Philip H. Sheridan, March 29, 1865.
11. Ibid., 273. Telegram to Julia Dent Grant, March 30, 1865.
12. Morris, *Sheridan*, 244.
13. Badeau, *Grant in Peace*, 98.
14. *PUSG*, 14:273. Telegram to Abraham Lincoln, March 31, 1865.
15. Porter, *Campaigning with Grant*, 441.
16. Morris, *Sheridan*, 247.
17. Cadwallader, *Three Years with Grant*, 305.
18. Porter, *Campaigning with Grant*, 437.
19. Foote, *The Civil War*, 3:873.
20. Ibid., 875.
21. Grant, *Memoirs*, 2:704.
22. *PUSG*, 14:330. Letter to Julia Dent Grant, April 2, 1865.
23. Korda, *Clouds of Glory*, 647.
24. Julia Grant, *Memoirs*, 149.
25. *PUSG*, 14:327. Telegram from Abraham Lincoln, April 2, 1865.
26. McPherson, *Battle Cry of Freedom*, 846.
27. Foreman, *A World on Fire*, 759.
28. Woodward, *Mary Chesnut's Civil War*, 782. Diary entry for April 7, 1865.
29. Young, *Around the World*, 434.
30. Nevins and Thomas, *The Diary of George Templeton Strong*, 575. Diary entry for April 3, 1865.
31. Cadwallader, *Three Years with Grant*, 310.
32. Grant, *Memoirs*, 2:707.

33. Donald, *Lincoln*, 576.
34. Goodwin, *Team of Rivals*, 716.
35. Foote, *The Civil War*, 3:894.
36. GPL. S2 B11 F57. Letter of April 1900 [n.d.] from Charles A. Clark to Ida Tarbell.
37. Porter, *Campaigning with Grant*, 452.
38. Catton, *Grant Takes Command*, 450.
39. Porter, *Campaigning with Grant*, 452.
40. McPherson, *Battle Cry of Freedom*, 846.
41. Curtis, *The Correspondence of John Lothrop Motley*, 2:202. Letter to the Duchess of Argyll, May 27, 1865.
42. Jones, *A Rebel War Clerk's Diary*, 612. Diary entry for April 5, 1865.
43. Holzer, *Lincoln on War*, 285.
44. Foote, *The Civil War*, 3:898.
45. Julia Grant, *Memoirs*, 150.
46. Ibid.
47. Foote, *The Civil War*, 3:901.
48. GPL. S2 B13. "Rawlins Letters." Letter from John A. Rawlins to Mary E. Rawlins, April 4, 1865. JHWP.
49. *PUSG*, 14:342. Telegram to Edwin M. Stanton, April 4, 1865.
50. Ibid., 348. Letter from Maj. Gen. Philip H. Sheridan, April 5, 1865.
51. Young, *Around the World*, 308.
52. Cadwallader, *Three Years with Grant*, 312.
53. Richardson, *A Personal History*, 480.
54. Young, *Around the World*, 309.
55. Ibid.
56. Grant, *Memoirs*, 2:717.
57. Young, *Around the World*, 309.
58. Sheridan, *Memoirs*, 2:182.
59. Foreman, *A World on Fire*, 763–64.
60. McPherson, *Battle Cry of Freedom*, 848.
61. Goodwin, *Team of Rivals*, 721.
62. *PUSG*, 14:358. Letter from Maj. Gen. Philip H. Sheridan, April 6, 1865. Telegram from Abraham Lincoln, April 7, 1865.
63. Young, *Around the World*, 309.
64. Grant, *Memoirs*, 2:724.
65. *PUSG*, 14:362. Telegram to Maj. Gen. George G. Meade, April 7, 1865.
66. Grant, *Memoirs*, 2:728.
67. Smith, *Grant*, 399.
68. *PUSG*, 14:361. Letter to Gen. Robert E. Lee, April 7, 1865.
69. Porter, *Campaigning with Grant*, 458.
70. Foote, *The Civil War*, 3:929.
71. Wilson, *Patriotic Gore*, 333.
72. *PUSG*, 14:361. Letter from Gen. Robert E. Lee, April 7, 1865.
73. Ibid., 367. Letter to Gen. Robert E. Lee, April 8, 1865.
74. Green, "Civil War Public Opinion of General Grant."
75. Foote, *The Civil War*, 3:932–33.
76. *PUSG*, 14:367. Letter from Gen. Robert E. Lee, April 8, 1865.
77. *New York Herald*, July 6, 1878.
78. Porter, *Campaigning with Grant*, 463.
79. Foote, *The Civil War*, 3:936.
80. Wilson, *Rawlins*, 320.
81. Porter, *Campaigning with Grant*, 463.
82. *PUSG*, 14:371. Letter to Gen. Robert E. Lee, April 9, 1865.
83. McPherson, *Battle Cry of Freedom*, 848.
84. Simpson, *Ulysses S. Grant*, 432.
85. *PUSG*, 14:373. Letter from Gen. Robert E. Lee, April 9, 1865.
86. Richardson, *A Personal History*, 490.
87. Morris, *Sheridan*, 256.
88. Young, *Around the World*, 382.
89. *New York Herald*, July 24, 1878.
90. USGH. "Interview with John Russell Young."
91. GPL. S2 B24 F18. "Interview with Amos Webster." HGP.
92. Chamberlain, *The Passing of the Armies*, 180.
93. Foote, *The Civil War*, 3:939.
94. Ibid.
95. Longstreet, *From Manassas to Appomattox*, 537.
96. Holzer, *The Civil War in 50 Objects*, 307.
97. Korda, *Clouds of Glory*, 665.
98. Smith, *Grant*, 404.
99. Foote, *The Civil War*, 3:946.
100. Porter, *Campaigning with Grant*, 475.
101. Grant, *Memoirs*, 2:735.
102. Korda, *Ulysses S. Grant*, 157.
103. Grant, *Memoirs*, 2:736.
104. Porter, *Campaigning with Grant*, 475.
105. Ibid., 476.
106. *PUSG*, 14:374. Letter to Gen. Robert E. Lee, April 9, 1865.
107. Young, *Around the World*, 383.
108. Catton, *Grant Takes Command*, 465.
109. Porter, *Campaigning with Grant*, 482.
110. Armstrong, *Warrior in Two Camps*, 109.
111. Ibid.
112. Holzer, *The Civil War in 50 Objects*, 315.
113. Grant, *Memoirs*, 2:741.
114. Porter, *Campaigning with Grant*, 482.
115. Morgan, "From City Point to Appomattox with General Grant."
116. Porter, *Campaigning with Grant*, 479–80.
117. Ibid., 485.
118. Foreman, *A World on Fire*, 767.
119. Waugh, *U. S. Grant*, 100.
120. Catton, *Grant Takes Command*, 469.
121. Foote, *The Civil War*, 2:32.
122. "Longstreet's Reminiscences." *The New York Times*, July 24, 1885.
123. *PUSG*, 15:204. Letter to Edwin M. Stanton, June 20, 1865.
124. Cadwallader, *Three Years with Grant*, 329.
125. *PUSG*, 14:375. Telegram to Edwin M. Stanton, April 9, 1865.
126. Ibid. Telegram from Edwin M. Stanton, April 9, 1865.
127. Donald, *Lincoln*, 580.
128. Ibid.
129. Sherman, *Memoirs*, 815.

130. Goodwin, *Team of Rivals*, 725.
131. Burlingame, *Lincoln Observed*, 182.
132. McPherson, *Tried by War*, 262.
133. Foner, *Fiery Trial*, 331.
134. McPherson, *Tried by War*, 262.
135. Julia Grant, *Memoirs*, 152.
136. USGH. "Interview with John Sergeant Wise."
137. Armstrong, *Warrior in Two Camps*, 111.
138. *New York Herald*, July 24, 1878.
139. Ibid.
140. Julia Grant, *Memoirs*, 153.
141. USGH. "Interview with M. Harrison Strong."
142. "Grant's Drinking Habits." *New York Sun*, January 28, 1887.
143. *PUSG*, 14:31. Letter to Elihu B. Washburne, February 23, 1865.

144. *The New York Times*, July 24, 1885.
145. McPherson, "America's Wicked War."
146. Ibid., "Our Monstrous War."
147. *PUSG*, 20:143. Letter to Henry C. Bowen, April 21, 1870.
148. *New York Herald*, May 28, 1878.
149. Ibid.
150. Pepper, *Under Three Flags*, 328.
151. Wilson, *General Grant*, 366–67.
152. Fuller, *Grant & Lee*, 245.
153. Pepper, *Under Three Flags*, 327.
154. *New York Herald*, July 24, 1878.
155. Young, *Around the World*, 385.
156. Grant, *Memoirs*, 2:774.
157. *PUSG*, 29:318. "Speech," Chicago, December 4, 1879.
158. Grant, *Memoirs*, 2:774.

CHAPTER TWENTY-FOUR: A SINGULAR, INDESCRIBABLE VESSEL

1. Julia Grant, *Memoirs*, 153.
2. Ibid., 154.
3. Porter, "Lincoln and Grant."
4. Holzer, *The Lincoln Assassination*, 181.
5. Kauffman, *American Brutus*, 215.
6. Ibid., 215–16.
7. Holzer, *The Lincoln Assassination*, 185.
8. Kauffman, *American Brutus*, 216.
9. *PUSG*, 14:384. Telegram from Maj. Gen. John Gibbon, April 13, 1865.
10. Donald, *Lincoln*, 591.
11. Ibid., 591–92.
12. Ibid., 582–83.
13. Beale, *Diary of Gideon Welles*, 2:282–83. Diary entry for April 14, 1865.
14. Ibid., 2:283. Diary entry for April 14, 1865.
15. Ibid.
16. Wilson and Simon, *Ulysses S. Grant*, 133.
17. Holzer, *Lincoln on War*, 246.
18. Young, *Around the World*, 332.
19. "Grant Reminiscences." *Chicago Daily Tribune*, September 1, 1885.
20. Porter, *Campaigning with Grant*, 497.
21. Donald, *Lincoln*, 593.
22. Goodwin, *Team of Rivals*, 734.
23. Burlingame, *Lincoln Observed*, 275.
24. Badeau, *Grant in Peace*, 362.
25. Julia Grant, *Memoirs*, 155.
26. Ibid.
27. Grant, *In the Days of My Father General Grant*, 35.
28. Julia Grant, *Memoirs*, 156.
29. Ibid.
30. Young, *Around the World*, 332.
31. Ibid.
32. Kauffman, *American Brutus*, 283.
33. Holzer, *The Civil War in 50 Objects*, 320.
34. Wilson and Simon, *Ulysses S. Grant*, 134.
35. Bolles, "General Grant and the News of Mr. Lincoln's Death."
36. Porter, *Campaigning with Grant*, 499–500.
37. *PUSG*, 14:390. Telegram from Maj. Thomas T. Eckert, April 14, 1865.
38. Ibid., 25:259. "Speech," October 15, 1874.

39. Ammen, "Recollections and Letters of Grant. Part 1."
40. Young, *Around the World*, 331.
41. Julia Grant, *Memoirs*, 156.
42. Grant, *Memoirs*, 2:751.
43. Wilson and Simon, *Ulysses S. Grant*, 110.
44. Egerton, *The Wars of Reconstruction*, 91.
45. *PUSG*, 14:396. Letter to Julia Dent Grant, April 16, 1865.
46. Ibid., 390. Letter from Edwin M. Stanton, April 15, 1865.
47. Kauffman, *American Brutus*, 248.
48. *PUSG*, 14:391. Telegram to Maj. Gen. Edward O. C. Ord, April 15, 1865.
49. Ibid., 397. Telegram to Edwin M. Stanton, April 17, 1865.
50. Julia Grant, *Memoirs*, 157.
51. LoC. USGP. Container 102, Reel 3. Grant tribute to Lincoln, October 1874.
52. Wineapple, *Ecstatic Nation*, 374.
53. Ibid., 384.
54. Truman, "Anecdotes of Andrew Johnson."
55. Foner, *Fiery Trial*, 176.
56. Gordon-Reed, *Andrew Johnson*, 43.
57. Foner, *Fiery Trial*, 176.
58. Gordon-Reed, *Andrew Johnson*, 55.
59. *Memphis Bulletin*, October 30, 1863.
60. Borchgrave and Cullen, *Villard*, 178.
61. Foner, *Reconstruction*, 44.
62. Ibid., *Fiery Trial*, 44.
63. *PUSG*, 14:405. Letter to Charles W. Ford, April 17, 1865.
64. Ibid., 429. Letter to Silas A. Hudson, April 21, 1865.
65. Catton, *Grant Takes Command*, 482.
66. *PUSG*, 14:419. Telegram from Maj. Gen. William T. Sherman, April 17, 1865.
67. Foote, *The Civil War*, 3:968.
68. *PUSG*, 14:375. Letter from Maj. Gen. William T. Sherman, April 12, 1865.
69. Foote, *The Civil War*, 3:993.
70. *PUSG*, 14:422. Letter to Julia Dent Grant, April 20, 1865.

71. Beale, *Diary of Gideon Welles,* 2:295. Diary entry for April 21, 1865.
72. Grant, *Memoirs,* 2:755.
73. Palmer, *The Selected Letters of Charles Sumner,* 297. Letter to John Bright, April 24, 1865.
74. Foote, *The Civil War,* 3:995.
75. *PUSG,* 28:42. Letter from Adam Badeau to Gen. William T. Sherman, February 28, 1877.
76. Young, *Around the World,* 425.
77. Simpson, *Ulysses S. Grant,* 446.
78. Ibid.
79. Foote, *The Civil War,* 3:994.
80. Catton, *Grant Takes Command,* 487.
81. *PUSG,* 14:433. Letter to Julia Dent Grant, April 25, 1865.
82. Badeau, *Grant in Peace,* 150.
83. Ibid., 120.
84. Sherman, *Memoirs,* 852.
85. *PUSG,* 15:14. Letter from Maj. Gen. William T. Sherman, April 28, 1865.
86. Ibid., 74. Telegram from Maj. Gen. William T. Sherman, May 10, 1865.
87. Ibid.
88. Ibid.
89. Ibid., 74–75.
90. Wilson, *Patriotic Gore,* 186.
91. *PUSG,* 15:15. Letter from Maj. Gen. William T. Sherman to Brig. Gen. John A. Rawlins, April 29, 1865.
92. Ibid., 73. Letter to Maj. Gen. William T. Sherman, May 19, 1865.
93. Sherman, *Memoirs,* 864.
94. Grant, *Memoirs,* 2:761.
95. Waugh, *U. S. Grant,* 112.
96. Sarna, *When General Grant Expelled the Jews,* 53.
97. Julia Grant, *Memoirs,* 101.
98. Chamberlain, *The Passing of the Armies,* 244.
99. Porter, *Campaigning with Grant,* 507.
100. Sherman, *Memoirs,* 865.
101. Julia Grant, *Memoirs,* 159.
102. Foote, *The Civil War,* 3:1017.
103. Grant, *Memoirs,* 2:768.
104. Sherman, *Memoirs,* 866.
105. Porter, *Campaigning with Grant,* 512.
106. Buinicki, "'Average-Representing Grant': Whitman's General."

CHAPTER TWENTY-FIVE: SOLDIERLY GOOD FAITH

1. Grant, *In the Days of My Father General Grant,* 47.
2. *PUSG,* 12:90. Letter to Julia Dent Grant, August 25, 1864.
3. Catton, *Grant Takes Command,* 413.
4. Cadwallader, *Three Years with Grant,* 120.
5. Julia Grant, *Memoirs,* 158.
6. Ibid., 135.
7. Eaton, *Grant, Lincoln and the Freedmen,* 247.
8. "Chat in Public Resorts." *New York Tribune,* August 2, 1885.
9. Julia Grant, *Memoirs,* 164.
10. Summer, *The Diary of Cyrus B. Comstock,* 341. Diary entry for January 23, 1867.
11. Greely, *Reminiscences of Adventure and Service,* 232.
12. Williams, *Diary and Letters of Rutherford Birchard Hayes,* 13. Letter to S. Birchard, January 10, 1866.
13. Summer, *The Diary of Cyrus B. Comstock,* 339. Diary entry for December 8, 1866.
14. *PUSG,* 14:428–29. Letter to Julia Dent Grant, April 21, 1865.
15. Badeau, *Grant in Peace,* 18.
16. Morgan, "From City Point to Appomattox with General Grant."
17. Simpson, *Ulysses S. Grant,* 448.
18. Cramer, *Ulysses S. Grant,* 100.
19. Truman, "Anecdotes of Andrew Johnson."
20. Young, *Around the World,* 336; Grant, *Memoirs,* 2:761.
21. Foner, *Fiery Trial,* 177.
22. Grant, *Memoirs,* 2:751.
23. Young, *Around the World,* 336.
24. Grant, *Memoirs,* 2:752.
25. Gordon-Reed, *Andrew Johnson,* 112.
26. Smith, *Grant,* 443.
27. Gordon-Reed, *Andrew Johnson,* 11.
28. Ibid., 124.
29. Simpson, *Ulysses S. Grant,* 441.
30. Smith, *Grant,* 417.
31. *The Daily Inter Ocean,* October 21, 1885.
32. *PUSG,* 15:7. Telegram from Maj. Gen. Henry W. Halleck, May 5, 1865.
33. Ibid., 11. Telegram to Maj. Gen. Henry W. Halleck, May 6, 1865.
34. *Philadelphia Inquirer,* June 8, 1865.
35. *PUSG,* 15:150. Letter from Robert E. Lee, June 13, 1865.
36. Ibid. Endorsed letter to Edwin M. Stanton, June 16, 1865.
37. Ibid., 149. Letter to Edwin M. Stanton, June 16, 1865.
38. Simpson, *Ulysses S. Grant,* 453.
39. Young, *Around the World,* 385–86.
40. White, *American Ulysses,* 418.
41. "A Grant Party in the South." *The New York Times,* May 24, 1866.
42. Korda, *Clouds of Glory,* 688.
43. Pryor, *Reading the Man,* 449.
44. Korda, *Clouds of Glory,* 680.
45. Ibid.
46. Pryor, *Reading the Man,* 470.
47. Bean, "Memoranda of Conversations Between General Robert E. Lee and William Preston Johnston."
48. Korda, *Clouds of Glory,* 69.
49. Pryor, *Reading the Man,* 451.
50. *New York Herald,* July 24, 1878.
51. Grant, *Memoirs,* 2:775.
52. Young, *Around the World,* 247.

53. USGH. "Interview with M. Harrison Strong."
54. Stahr, *Seward,* 442.
55. Sheridan, *Memoirs,* 2:206.
56. Catton, *Terrible Swift Sword,* 3.
57. Young, *Around the World,* 248.
58. *PUSG,* 15:163. Telegram from Maj. Gen. Philip H. Sheridan, June 28, 1865.
59. Stahr, *Seward,* 443.
60. Beale, *Diary of Gideon Welles,* 2:317. Diary entry for June 16, 1865.
61. Ibid., 322. Diary entry for June 23, 1865.
62. Stahr, *Seward,* 443.
63. Beale, *Diary of Gideon Welles,* 2:333. Diary entry for July 14, 1865.
64. Morris, *Sheridan,* 266.
65. *The New York Times,* August 10, 1865.
66. Perret, *Ulysses S. Grant,* 366.
67. Wilson and Simon, *Ulysses S. Grant,* 133.
68. *PUSG,* 16:84. Letter to Edward C. Boynton, February 17, 1866.
69. *The St. Louis Globe-Democrat,* April 27, 1897.
70. *PUSG,* 30:19. Letter to Edward F. Beale, October 22, 1880.
71. *New York Herald,* September 25, 1877.
72. Perret, *Ulysses S. Grant,* 366.
73. Vincent, "The Inner Life of Ulysses S. Grant."
74. *PUSG,* 15:86. Letter from Rep. Elihu B. Washburne, May 18, 1865.
75. Ibid., 85. Letter to Elihu B. Washburne, May 21, 1865.
76. Richardson, *A Personal History,* 514.
77. Ross, *The General's Wife,* 194.
78. *PUSG,* 15:300. Letter to Brig. Gen. John A. Rawlins, August 20, 1865.
79. Cadwallader, *Three Years with Grant,* 351.
80. McFeely, *Grant,* 237.
81. *Troy Intelligencer,* April 17, 1892.

82. Ross, *The General's Wife,* 194.
83. *PUSG,* 15:358. Letter to Edwin M. Stanton, October 20, 1865.
84. Ibid., 390. Telegram to Maj. Gen. George H. Thomas, November 4, 1865.
85. Ibid., 301. Letter to Brig. Gen. John A. Rawlins, August 20, 1865.
86. Nevins and Thomas, *The Diary of George Templeton Strong,* 4:51. Diary entry for November 18, 1865.
87. *PUSG,* 15:403. Letter from Rep. Elihu B. Washburne to Bvt. Col. Adam Badeau, October 25, 1865.
88. Egerton, *The Wars of Reconstruction,* 106.
89. *PUSG,* 15:400. Letter from Maj. Gen. George G. Meade, November 8, 1863; ibid., 16:53. Letter from Maj. Gen. Peter J. Osterhaus to Brig. Gen. John A. Rawlins, November 11, 1865.
90. Summer, *The Diary of Cyrus B. Comstock,* 323. Diary entry for November 22, 1865.
91. Grant, *Memoirs,* 1:419.
92. *PUSG,* 15:423. Letter to Julia Dent Grant, November 29, 1865.
93. Badeau, *Grant in Peace,* 30.
94. Summer, *The Diary of Cyrus Comstock,* 324. Diary entry for December 1, 1865.
95. Ibid.
96. Ibid.
97. Wineapple, *Ecstatic Nation,* 383.
98. *PUSG,* 15:434. Letter to Andrew Johnson, December 18, 1865.
99. Ibid., 435.
100. Ibid.
101. Simpson, "Butcher? Racist?"
102. Schafer, *Intimate Letters of Carl Schurz,* 356. Letter to his wife, January 12, 1866.
103. Ibid., 457. Letter to his wife, December 20, 1868.

CHAPTER TWENTY-SIX: SWING AROUND THE CIRCLE

1. Egerton, *The Wars of Reconstruction,* 177.
2. Wineapple, *Ecstatic Nation,* 398.
3. *PUSG,* 16:7–8. "General Orders No. 3," January 12, 1866.
4. Summer, *The Diary of Cyrus B. Comstock,* 331. Diary entry for January 30, 1866.
5. Egerton, *The Wars of Reconstruction,* 193–94.
6. Smith, *Grant,* 426.
7. *PUSG,* 16:72. Letter from Bvt. Col. Theodore S. Bowers to southern commanding officers, February 17, 1866.
8. Ibid., 69. Letter to Andrew Johnson, February 17, 1866.
9. Stiles, *Custer's Trials,* 238.
10. Egerton, *The Wars of Reconstruction,* 149.
11. Nevins and Thomas, *The Diary of George Templeton Strong,* 4:71. Diary entry for February 23, 1866.
12. *PUSG,* 16:101. Letter to Maj. Gen. William T. Sherman, March 10, 1866.
13. Foner, *Reconstruction,* 243.
14. Egerton, *The Wars of Reconstruction,* 200–201.
15. Foner, *Reconstruction,* 250.

16. Nevins and Thomas, *The Diary of George Templeton Strong,* 4:129. Diary entry for August 7, 1866.
17. Foner, *Reconstruction,* 209.
18. *PUSG,* 16:114. Letter to Andrew Johnson, March 14, 1866.
19. Ibid., 235. Letter from Maj. Gen. George Stoneman, May 12, 1866.
20. Egerton, *The Wars of Reconstruction,* 207.
21. Ibid.
22. *PUSG,* 16:233. Letter to Edwin M. Stanton, July 7, 1866.
23. Ibid., 230. Letter to Maj. Gen. George H. Thomas, July 6, 1866.
24. Ibid., 228. "General Orders No. 44," July 6, 1866.
25. *Missouri Democrat,* May 31, 1866.
26. Ibid.
27. Ibid.
28. *PUSG,* 16:199. Letter to Edwin M. Stanton, May 16, 1866.
29. Ibid., 234–35. Letter from Attorney General James Speed to President Andrew Johnson, July 13, 1866.

30. Egerton, *The Wars of Reconstruction*, 215.
31. Griffin and Smith, *Autobiography of Mark Twain*, 2:70.
32. McFeely, *Grant*, 263.
33. *PUSG*, 16:246. Letter to Maj. Gen. William T. Sherman, July 21, 1866.
34. *The New York Times*, September 24, 1866.
35. Egerton, *The Wars of Reconstruction*, 208.
36. Wineapple, *Ecstatic Nation*, 414.
37. Egerton, *The Wars of Reconstruction*, 208.
38. *PUSG*, 16:288. Telegram from Maj. Gen. Philip H. Sheridan, August 1, 1866.
39. Ibid.
40. Ibid., 289. Telegram from Maj. Gen. Philip H. Sheridan, August 2, 1866.
41. Ibid., 290. Telegram from Maj. Gen. Philip H. Sheridan, August 13, 1866.
42. Ibid., 289. Telegram to Edwin M. Stanton, August 3, 1866.
43. Ibid., 294. Telegram from Edwin M. Stanton to Maj. Gen. Philip H. Sheridan, August 7, 1866.
44. Hesseltine, *Ulysses S. Grant: Politician*, 70.
45. *PUSG*, 16:294. Letter from Maj. Gen. Philip H. Sheridan to President Andrew Johnson, August 6, 1866.
46. Egerton, *The Wars of Reconstruction*, 208.
47. McFeely, *Grant*, 249.
48. Badeau, *Grant in Peace*, 38.
49. Ibid.
50. Ibid., 47.
51. GPL. S2 B13. "Rawlins Letters." Letter from John A. Rawlins to Mary E. Rawlins, August 30, 1866. JHWP.
52. Ibid. S2 B10. "Swing Around the Circle."
53. *PUSG*, 16:306. Letter to Julia Dent Grant, August 31, 1866.
54. Ibid., 32:92. Letter to Clarence W. Richardson, September 16, 1866.
55. McFeely, *Grant*, 253.
56. Ibid., 252.
57. Waugh, *U. S. Grant*, 115.
58. *New York Herald*, September 6, 1866.
59. Cadwallader, *Three Years with Grant*, 340.
60. Randall, *The Diary of Orville Hickman Browning*, 2:115. Diary entry for December 3, 1866.
61. Beale, *Diary of Gideon Welles*, 2:593. Diary entry for September 17, 1866.
62. Foner, *Reconstruction*, 26.
63. Stiles, *Custer's Trials*, 250.
64. Beale, *Diary of Gideon Welles*, 2:591. Diary entry for September 17, 1866; *The New York Times*, September 5, 1866.
65. Beale, *Diary of Gideon Welles*, 2:593. Diary entry for September 17, 1866.
66. *PUSG*, 16:307. Letter to Julia Dent Grant, September 4, 1866.
67. Stahr, *Seward*, 473.
68. Foner, *Reconstruction*, 265.
69. *PUSG*, 16:308. Letter to Julia Dent Grant, September 9, 1866.
70. Stiles, *Custer's Trials*, 251.
71. McFeely, *Grant*, 252.

72. *Chicago Daily Tribune*, September 14, 1866.
73. Beale, *Diary of Gideon Welles*, 2:591. Diary entry for September 17, 1866.
74. GPL. S2 B1 F38. "Adam Badeau Letters." Letter from Adam Badeau to James H. Wilson, September 13, 1866.
75. Randall, *The Diary of Orville Hickman Browning*, 2:94. Diary entry for September 20, 1866.
76. Hesseltine, *Ulysses S. Grant: Politician*, 76.
77. *PUSG*, 17:14. Letter to Lt. Gen. William T. Sherman, January 13, 1867.
78. Ibid., 16:302. Letter to Andrew Johnson, August 22, 1866.
79. Ibid., 330–31. Letter to Maj. Gen. Philip H. Sheridan, October 12, 1866.
80. Beale, *Diary of Gideon Welles*, 3:175. Diary entry for August 20, 1867.
81. Nevins and Thomas, *The Diary of George Templeton Strong*, 4:123. Diary entry for January 30, 1867.
82. Randall, *The Diary of Orville Hickman Browning*, 2:103–4. Diary entry for October 25, 1866.
83. *PUSG*, 15:426. Letter from Maj. Gen. Philip H. Sheridan, February 7, 1866.
84. *Missouri Democrat*, May 31, 1866.
85. *PUSG*, 16:347. Letter to Andrew Johnson, October 21, 1866.
86. Sherman, *Memoirs*, 904.
87. Ibid.
88. Ibid.
89. *PUSG*, 16:340. Letter from Lt. Gen. William T. Sherman to Ellen Sherman, October 26, 1866.
90. Sherman, *Memoirs*, 906.
91. Badeau, *Grant in Peace*, 52.
92. Julia Grant, *Memoirs*, 169.
93. Badeau, *Grant in Peace*, 53–54.
94. Ibid., 51.
95. *PUSG*, 17:50. Letter to Maj. Gen. Oliver O. Howard, January 18, 1867.
96. Beale, *Diary of Gideon Welles*, 3:42. Diary entry for February 15, 1867.
97. Ibid., 44.
98. Foner, *Reconstruction*, 276.
99. Hesseltine, *Ulysses S. Grant: Politician*, 114.
100. Beale, *Diary of Gideon Welles*, 3:27. Diary entry for January 19, 1867.
101. *PUSG*, 17:38. Letter to Edwin M. Stanton, January 29, 1867.
102. *The New York Times*, February 20, 1867.
103. Ibid.
104. Egerton, *The Wars of Reconstruction*, 222.
105. *PUSG*, 17:76. Letter to Elihu B. Washburne, March 4, 1867.
106. Beale, *Diary of Gideon Welles*, 3:65. Diary entry for March 13, 1867.
107. Wineapple, *Ecstatic Nation*, 438.
108. Berg, *Wilson*, 41.
109. *PUSG*, 17:76. Letter to Elihu B. Washburne, March 4, 1867.

110. Summer, *The Diary of Cyrus B. Comstock,* 344. Diary entry for February 28, 1867.
111. Beale, *Diary of Gideon Welles,* 3:63. Diary entry for March 11, 1867.
112. *PUSG,* 17:39. Letter from Maj. Gen. Philip H. Sheridan, January 25, 1867.
113. Ibid., 91. Letter to Maj. Gen. Philip H. Sheridan, March 29, 1867.
114. Ibid., 122. Letter to Maj. Gen. Philip H. Sheridan, April 21, 1867.
115. Ibid.
116. *PUSG,* 17:95. Letter to Maj. Gen. Philip H. Sheridan, April 5, 1867.
117. Ibid., 127. Letter from Bvt. Brig. Gen. Orville E. Babcock to Col. Adam Badeau, May 10, 1867.
118. Ibid.
119. Ibid., 128. Letter from Bvt. Brig. Gen. Horace Porter to Adam Badeau, May 1867 [n.d.].
120. Egerton, *The Wars of Reconstruction,* 289.
121. *PUSG,* 17:126. Letter from Maj. Gen. Philip H. Sheridan, May 10, 1867.

122. Sheridan, *Memoirs,* 2:267.
123. Morris, *Sheridan,* 291.
124. *PUSG,* 17:185. Letter to Maj. Gen. Philip H. Sheridan, June 7, 1867.
125. Beale, *Diary of Gideon Welles,* 3:121. Diary entry for June 27, 1867.
126. *PUSG,* 32:104. Letter to Elihu B. Washburne, May 3, 1867.
127. Ibid., 17:212, 214. "Testimony." July 18, 1867.
128. Ibid., 214.
129. White, *American Ulysses,* 443.
130. *PUSG,* 17:236. Telegram from Secretary of War Edwin M. Stanton, July 22, 1867.
131. Ibid. Telegram to Edwin M. Stanton, July 23, 1867.
132. *PUSG,* 17:239–40. Letter to Edwin M. Stanton, July 24, 1867.
133. Truman, "Anecdotes of Andrew Johnson."
134. Cramer, *Ulysses S. Grant,* 68–70.
135. "Speech of General Rawlins." *Army & Navy Journal,* July 13, 1867.

CHAPTER TWENTY-SEVEN: VOLCANIC PASSION

1. Young, *Around the World,* 333–34.
2. Ibid., 333.
3. Beale, *Diary of Gideon Welles,* 3:154. Diary entry for August 3, 1867.
4. *PUSG,* 17:252. Letter to Andrew Johnson, August 1, 1867.
5. Ibid., 269. Letter from Andrew Johnson to Edwin M. Stanton, August 5, 1867.
6. Ibid. Letter from Edwin M. Stanton to Andrew Johnson, August 5, 1867.
7. Badeau, *Grant in Peace,* 112.
8. Julia Grant, *Memoirs,* 165.
9. Wilson, *Rawlins,* 344.
10. *PUSG,* 17:268. Letter to Edwin M. Stanton, August 12, 1867.
11. Ibid., 269. Letter from Secretary of War Edwin M. Stanton, August 12, 1867.
12. Beale, *Diary of Gideon Welles,* 3:169. Diary entry for August 13, 1867.
13. Randall, *The Diary of Orville Hickman Browning,* 2:158. Diary entry for August 16, 1867.
14. *PUSG,* 17:277–78. Letter to Andrew Johnson, August 17, 1867.
15. Ibid., 280. Letter from Andrew Johnson, August 19, 1867.
16. Ibid., 343. Letter to Lt. Gen. William T. Sherman, September 18, 1867.
17. White, *American Ulysses,* 450.
18. Randall, *The Diary of Orville Hickman Browning,* 2:161. Diary entry for October 8, 1867.
19. Beale, *Diary of Gideon Welles,* 3:234. Diary entry for October 19, 1867.
20. Schafer, *Intimate Letters of Carl Schurz,* 408. Letter to his wife, October 12, 1867.
21. *PUSG,* 18:331–32. Letter from Henry J. Raymond, October 13, 1867.
22. GPL. S2 B10. "Presidential Campaigns."
23. Ibid.
24. Stahr, *Seward,* 496.

25. *PUSG,* 18:58–59. Letter from Andrew Johnson, November 30, 1867.
26. Ibid., 59.
27. Stahr, *Seward,* 497.
28. *PUSG,* 17:291. Letter from Bvt. Brig. Gen. Orville E. Babcock to Rep. Elihu B. Washburne, August 13, 1867.
29. GPL. S2 B6 F65. Letter from President Andrew Johnson to the Senate, December 12, 1867.
30. Beale, *Diary of Gideon Welles,* 3:240. Diary entry for December 12, 1867.
31. Ibid., 180. Diary entry for August 22, 1867.
32. Ibid., 197. Diary entry for September 5, 1867.
33. Ibid., 483. Diary entry for December 12, 1868.
34. Ibid., 556. Diary entry for March 17, 1869.
35. Ibid., 246. Diary entry for December 24, 1867.
36. Ibid., 180. Diary entry for August 22, 1867.
37. Egerton, *The Wars of Reconstruction,* 255.
38. Ibid., 254.
39. Ibid., 256.
40. *PUSG,* 17:260–61. Letter from Bvt. Maj. Gen. John Pope, July 24, 1867.
41. Ibid., 18:95–96. Letter from Bvt. Maj. Gen. John Pope, December 31, 1867.
42. Ibid., 17:354. Letter to Bvt. Maj. Gen. Edward O. C. Ord, September 22, 1867.
43. Ibid., 18:34. Letter to Lt. Gen. William T. Sherman, November 21, 1867.
44. Badeau, *Grant in Peace,* 110.
45. Palmer, *The Selected Letters of Charles Sumner,* 415–16. Letter to John Bright, January 18, 1868.
46. *PUSG,* 18:117. Letter to Andrew Johnson, January 28, 1868.
47. Ibid., 107. Letter from Lt. Gen. William T. Sherman, January 27, 1868.
48. Julia Grant, *Memoirs,* 166.
49. Randall, *The Diary of Orville Hickman Browning,* 2:173. Diary entry for January 14, 1868.
50. Badeau, *Grant in Peace,* 111.

51. *PUSG,* 18:108. Letter from Lt. Gen. William T. Sherman, January 14, 1868.

52. Grant, *In the Days of My Father General Grant,* 47.

53. Niven, *Gideon Welles,* 558.

54. Randall, *The Diary of Orville Hickman Browning,* 2:174. Diary entry for January 14, 1868.

55. *PUSG,* 18:118. Letter to Andrew Johnson, January 28, 1868.

56. Beale, *Diary of Gideon Welles,* 3:261. Diary entry for January 14, 1868.

57. Ibid.

58. Randall, *The Diary of Orville Hickman Browning,* 2:180. Diary entry for February 6, 1868.

59. Beale, *Diary of Gideon Welles,* 3:267, 273–74. Diary entry for February 8, 1868.

60. Hesseltine, *Ulysses S. Grant: Politician,* 107.

61. *PUSG,* 18:118. Letter to Andrew Johnson, January 28, 1868.

62. Hesseltine, *Ulysses S. Grant: Politician,* 111.

63. *PUSG,* 18:126. Letter to Andrew Johnson, February 3, 1868.

64. Badeau, *Grant in Peace,* 115.

65. *PUSG,* 18:146. Letter from Andrew Johnson, February 10, 1868.

66. Ibid., 22:297. George H. Williams, Eulogy for Grant, August 8, 1885.

67. Ibid., 18:139–40. Letter from Lt. Gen. William T. Sherman, February 14, 1868.

68. Ibid., 141. Letter from Lt. Gen. William T. Sherman to Andrew Johnson, February 14, 1868.

69. Sherman, *Memoirs,* 917.

70. Badeau, *Grant in Peace,* 142.

71. Julia Grant, *Memoirs,* 171.

72. Ibid.

73. *PUSG,* 18:170. Letter from Robert Bonner to Jesse Root Grant, February 26, 1868.

74. Nevins and Thomas, *The Diary of George Templeton Strong,* 4:187. Diary entry for February 7, 1868.

75. GPL. S2 B4 F9. Letter from Helen Griffing to Theodore Tilton, January 17, 1868.

76. Ibid. Letter from Rufus P. Stebbins to Elihu B. Washburne, March 10, 1868.

77. Smith, *Grant,* 453.

78. Egerton, *The Wars of Reconstruction,* 233.

79. Badeau, *Grant in Peace,* 134.

80. Hesseltine, *Ulysses S. Grant: Politician,* 115.

81. Kennedy, *Profiles in Courage,* 120.

82. Egerton, *The Wars of Reconstruction,* 233.

83. Ibid., 234.

84. *PUSG,* 18:89. Letter from Bvt. Maj. Gen. Edward O. C. Ord, February 29, 1868.

85. Jordan, *Roscoe Conkling,* 101.

86. Badeau, *Grant in Peace,* 136.

87. Palmer, *The Selected Letters of Charles Sumner,* 425–26. Letter to Francis Lieber, May 2, 1868.

88. *PUSG,* 18:190. Letter from Edwards Pierrepont, March 16, 1868.

89. Ibid., 212. Letter to Maj. Gen. Philip H. Sheridan, March 31, 1868.

90. Ibid., 257. Letter to Charles W. Ford, May 15, 1868.

91. Kennedy, *Profiles in Courage,* 126.

92. Julia Grant, *Memoirs,* 170.

93. Randall, *The Diary of Orville Hickman Browning,* 211. Letter from Andrew Johnson to Edmund Cooper, July 6, 1868.

CHAPTER TWENTY-EIGHT: TRADING PLACES

1. *PUSG,* 18:196. Letter to Andrew Johnson, March 13, 1868.

2. Ibid., 255. Telegram from Stephen B. Packard, May 14, 1868.

3. Ibid. Letter to Bvt. Maj. Gen. Robert C. Buchanan, May 15, 1868.

4. *New York Herald,* June 5, 1871.

5. Ibid.

6. Julia Grant, *Memoirs,* 171.

7. Hesseltine, *Ulysses S. Grant: Politician,* 119.

8. *New York Herald,* May 22, 1868.

9. Bunting, *Ulysses S. Grant,* 82.

10. Beale, *Diary of Gideon Welles,* 1:481. Diary entry for December 1863 [n.d.].

11. Donald, *Lincoln,* 265.

12. Badeau, *Grant in Peace,* 144.

13. Young, *Around the World,* 379.

14. *PUSG,* 18:266. Letter from Maj. Gen. Philip H. Sheridan, May 22, 1868.

15. Ibid., 264. Letter to Joseph R. Hawley, May 29, 1868.

16. Wineapple, *Ecstatic Nation,* 445.

17. Sarna, *When General Grant Expelled the Jews,* 66.

18. Bunting, *Ulysses S. Grant,* 83.

19. Egerton, *The Wars of Reconstruction,* 236.

20. *The New York Times,* July 22, 1868.

21. Sarna, *When General Grant Expelled the Jews,* 66.

22. Buinicki, "'Average-Representing Grant': Whitman's General."

23. *PUSG,* 19:9. Letter to Julia Dent Grant, July 17, 1868.

24. Ibid., 43. Letter to John M. Schofield, September 25, 1868.

25. Ibid., 12–13. "Speech," August 7, 1868.

26. Ibid., 12. "Speech," August 15, 1868.

27. Palmer, *The Selected Letters of Charles Sumner,* 438. Letter to Henry W. Longfellow, August 4, 1868.

28. Nevins and Thomas, *The Diary of George Templeton Strong,* 4:230. Diary entry for October 31, 1868.

29. McFeely, *Grant,* 283.

30. Julia Grant, *Memoirs,* 172.

31. Foner, *Reconstruction,* 340.

32. Buinicki, "'Average-Representing Grant': Whitman's General."

33. *PUSG,* 19:70. Letter to Capt. Daniel Ammen, November 23, 1868.

34. GPL. S2 B4 F52. "Grant and Jews." Letter from Schuyler Colfax to John Russell Young, August 12, 1867.

35. *PUSG,* 19:20. Letter from Joseph Medill to Rep. Elihu B. Washburne, June 16, 1868.

36. Ibid., 37. Letter to Isaac N. Morris, September 14, 1868.

37. White, *American Ulysses,* 467.

38. Egerton, *The Wars of Reconstruction,* 235.

39. Wineapple, *Ecstatic Nation,* 448.

40. Foner, *The Life and Writings of Frederick Douglass,* 36.

41. Egerton, *The Wars of Reconstruction,* 241.

42. *PUSG,* 26:3. "To Senate," January 13, 1875.

43. Ibid., 19:42. Letter to Elihu B. Washburne, September 23, 1868.

44. Ibid., 57. Letter to Isaac N. Morris, October 22, 1868.

45. Ibid., 32:118. Letter to J. Russell Jones, October 22, 1868.

46. Badeau, *Grant in Peace,* 150.

47. *PUSG,* 18:293. Letter from Lt. Gen. William T. Sherman, June 7, 1868.

48. Randall, *The Diary of Orville Hickman Browning,* 2:220. Diary entry for October 14, 1868.

49. Badeau, *Grant in Peace,* 149.

50. *PUSG,* 19:64–65. "Speech," November 4, 1868.

51. Ibid., 68–69. Letter to Matías Romero, November 11, 1868.

52. Waugh, *U. S. Grant,* 123.

53. *PUSG,* 19:130. "Speech," February 13, 1869.

54. McFeely, *Grant,* 290.

55. Ibid., 289–90.

56. *PUSG,* 28:457–58. Recollection of John A. Kasson, 1885 [n.d.].

57. Williams, *Diary and Letters of Rutherford Birchard Hayes,* 56–57. Letter from Rutherford B. Hayes to his uncle, December 19, 1868.

58. *PUSG,* 22:41. James McCosh, "Speech," June 27, 1871.

59. Ibid., 21:188. Letter from Bvt. Maj. Gen. James H. Wilson to Hiram Barney, December 29, 1868.

60. Ibid., 19:94. "Speech," December 15, 1868.

61. Ibid. Letter to Julia Dent Grant, December 14, 1868.

62. McFeely, *Grant,* 285.

63. GPL. S2 B13. "Rawlins Letters." Letter to Mary E. Rawlins, December 10, 1868. JHWP.

64. *PUSG,* 16:187. Letter to Edwin M. Stanton, May 8, 1866.

65. Wilson, *Rawlins,* 352.

66. "'This Thankless Office.'" *American History Illustrated,* January 1977.

67. *PUSG,* 19:103. Letter to Lt. Gen. William T. Sherman, January 5, 1869.

68. Sumner, *Republicanism vs. Grantism,* 14.

69. GPL. S2 B10. "Presidential Campaigns." Letter from C. Washburn to William Drew Washburn, February 26, 1870.

70. Nevins, *Hamilton Fish,* 1:138.

71. Adams, *The Education of Henry Adams,* 250.

72. Young, *Around the World,* 290.

73. *The Philadelphia Times,* December 17, 1879.

74. Beale, *Diary of Gideon Welles,* 3:559–60. Diary entry for March 24, 1869.

75. *PUSG,* 20:231. Letter from John Russell Young to Elihu B. Washburne, January 5, 1869.

76. Ibid., 30:172. "Speech," March 11, 1881.

77. Beale, *Diary of Gideon Welles,* 3:500. Diary entry for January 5, 1869.

78. Ibid., 498. Diary entry for January 2, 1869.

79. Singleton, *The Story of the White House,* 2:123.

80. Gordon-Reed, *Andrew Johnson,* 142.

81. Badeau, *Grant in Peace,* 60.

82. *PUSG,* 19:160. Letter to Mary Grant Cramer, March 31, 1869.

83. Richardson, *A Personal History,* 58.

84. *PUSG,* 19:122. Letter from Jesse Grant to Bvt. Brig. Gen. Frederick Dent, February 17, 1869.

85. GPL. S2 B21 F7. "Howe's Historical Collections of Ohio." LLP.

86. *PUSG,* 19:139. "Inaugural Address," March 4, 1869.

87. Ibid., 140.

88. Ibid.

89. Ibid., 142.

90. Ibid.

91. Foner, *The Life and Writings of Frederick Douglass,* 40.

92. Foner, *Reconstruction,* 448.

93. Egerton, *The Wars of Reconstruction,* 265.

94. Boutwell, *Reminiscences of Sixty Years,* 2:229–30.

95. Ross, *The General's Wife,* 204.

96. *PUSG,* 21:188. Letter from Bvt. Maj. Gen. James H. Wilson to Hiram Barney, March 5, 1869.

CHAPTER TWENTY-NINE: SPOILS OF WAR

1. Jordan, *Roscoe Conkling,* 122.

2. Nevins, *Hamilton Fish,* 1:371.

3. Williams, *Diary and Letters of Rutherford Birchard Hayes,* 59. Letter to S. Birchard, March 7, 1869.

4. Jordan, *Roscoe Conkling,* 119–20.

5. Beale, *Diary of Gideon Welles,* 3:565. Diary entry for March 27, 1869.

6. *PUSG,* 21:148. Letter from Ebenezer R. Hoar to Jacob D. Cox, February 9, 1871.

7. Fish, "General Grant."

8. USGH. "Interview with Ely S. Parker."

9. Sumner, *Republicanism vs. Grantism,* 16.

10. Summer, *The Diary of Cyrus B. Comstock,* 378. Diary entry for March 6, 1869.

11. Nevins, *Hamilton Fish,* 1:281.

12. Smith, *Grant,* 472.

13. Flood, *Grant's Final Victory,* 233.

14. Foner, *The Fiery Trial,* 13.

15. Hesseltine, *Ulysses S. Grant: Politician*, 154.
16. Julia Grant, *Memoirs*, 177.
17. Grant, *In the Days of My Father General Grant*, 73.
18. Ibid., 97.
19. Ibid.
20. Summer, *The Diary of Cyrus B. Comstock*, 383. Diary entry for January 20, 1870.
21. GPL. B24 F16. "Interview with Eliza M. Shaw." HGP.
22. Ross, *The General's Wife*, 216.
23. Schafer, *Intimate Letters of Carl Schurz*, 475. Letter to his wife, March 20, 1869.
24. Smith, *Grant*, 554.
25. Sarna, *When General Grant Expelled the Jews*, 85.
26. *Harper's Weekly*, January 9, 1869.
27. Foote, *The Civil War*, 1:166.
28. Donald, *Lincoln*, 570.
29. Scaturro, *President Grant Reconsidered*, 45.
30. *PUSG*, 19:160. Letter to Mary Grant Cramer, March 31, 1869.
31. Beale, *Diary of Gideon Welles*, 3:576. Diary entry for April 12, 1869.
32. *PUSG*, 19:109. Letter from Orville E. Babcock to George T. Downing, January 1870 [n.d.].
33. Ibid., 108. Letter from George T. Downing et al., May 13, 1869.
34. Ibid., 20:11. Letter from Ebenezer D. Bassett, March 17, 1869.
35. Foner, *The Life and Writings of Frederick Douglass*, 36.
36. *PUSG*, 19:108. Letter from George T. Downing et al., May 13, 1869.
37. Scaturro, *President Grant Reconsidered*, 102.
38. Douglass, "U. S. Grant and the Colored People."
39. Sarna, *When General Grant Expelled the Jews*, 88.
40. Ibid., 101.
41. Ibid., 102.
42. Ibid., 104.
43. Ibid., 111.
44. Ibid., 112.
45. McPherson, *Battle Cry of Freedom*, 859.
46. Cramer, *Ulysses S. Grant*, 149.
47. Hesseltine, *Ulysses S. Grant: Politician*, 292.
48. *PUSG*, 24:272. "Draft Annual Message," December 1, 1873.
49. Ibid.
50. Grant, *In the Days of My Father General Grant*, 57.
51. Julia Grant, *Memoirs*, 174.

52. Ibid.
53. Ibid.
54. Ibid., 175.
55. Singleton, *The Story of the White House*, 131.
56. Greely, *Reminiscences of Adventure and Service*, 235.
57. Hamilton, *Amos T. Akerman*, 93.
58. Nevins, *Hamilton Fish*, 1:135.
59. Badeau, *Grant in Peace*, 177.
60. Ibid., 174.
61. Fish, "General Grant."
62. *PUSG*, 20:73. Letter to John P. Newman, circa December 1869 [n.d.].
63. Ibid. Letter to John P. Newman, December 24, 1869.
64. Hesseltine, *Ulysses S. Grant: Politician*, 191.
65. Randall, *The Diary of Orville Hickman Browning*, 2:429. Diary entry for October 28, 1875.
66. Ammen, "Recollections and Letters of Grant. Part 1."
67. Sherman, *Memoirs*, 928–29.
68. *USGA Newsletter*, April 1964.
69. Ibid.
70. GPL. S2 B13 F26. "Walt Whitman."
71. *Philadelphia Public Ledger*, July 9, 1872.
72. *PUSG*, 19:189. "Proclamation," May 19, 1869.
73. USGH. "Interview with Colonel James E. Pitman."
74. Email of July 21, 2017, from George McCarter, author of an unpublished biography of George W. Childs.
75. Ross, *The General's Wife*, 229.
76. *PUSG*, 27:167. Letter to Rutherford B. Hayes, July 4, 1876.
77. USGH. "Interview with William H. Crook."
78. Ibid.
79. Julia Grant, *Memoirs*, 178.
80. GPL. S2 B5 F28. Undated reminiscence of Jesse Root Grant Jr.
81. Truman, *The President's House*, 160.
82. Badeau, *Grant in Peace*, 411.
83. McFeely, *Grant*, 404.
84. "Mrs. U. S. Grant Sinking." *Chicago Sunday Tribune*, December 14, 1902.
85. Hesseltine, *Ulysses S. Grant: Politician*, 294.
86. USGH. "Interview with Eliza Shaw."
87. GPL. S2 B24 F15. "Interview with Olive Logan." HGP.
88. Julia Grant, *Memoirs*, 192.

CHAPTER THIRTY: WE ARE ALL AMERICANS

1. *USGA Newsletter*, April 1964.
2. Foner, *Reconstruction*, 311.
3. Smith, *Grant*, 480.
4. *PUSG*, 19:163. "To Congress," April 7, 1869.
5. Morris, *Fraud of the Century*, 41.
6. Lemann, *Redemption*, 55.
7. *PUSG*, 19:222. Letter from Lewis Dent, August 14, 1869
8. Ibid. Letter to Lewis Dent, August 1, 1869.
9. Eaton, *Grant, Lincoln and the Freedmen*, 258.
10. Ibid., 259.
11. Hesseltine, *Ulysses S. Grant: Politician*, 181.

12. Badeau, *Grant in Peace*, 27.
13. Ibid., 26.
14. Hesseltine, *Ulysses S. Grant: Politician*, 181.
15. Morris, *Sheridan*, 324.
16. Wineapple, *Ecstatic Nation*, 539.
17. Stiles, *Custer's Trials*, 312.
18. Bunting, *Ulysses S. Grant*, 119.
19. Wineapple, *Ecstatic Nation*, 549.
20. *New York Herald*, June 8, 1871.
21. *PUSG*, 15:40–41. Telegram to Maj. Gen. John Pope, May 17, 1865.
22. *Philadelphia Public Ledger*, October 12, 1872.

23. Cozzens, *The Earth Is Weeping*, 118.
24. *PUSG*, 18:257–58. Letter to Lt. Gen. William T. Sherman, May 19, 1868.
25. Armstrong, *Warrior in Two Camps*, 137.
26. *PUSG*, 20:39. "Speech," December 6, 1869.
27. Armstrong, *Warrior in Two Camps*, 147; Cozzens, *The Earth Is Weeping*, 115.
28. *Cincinnati Gazette*, November 31, 1870.
29. *PUSG*, 21:41. "Draft Annual Message," December 5, 1870.
30. Nevins, *Hamilton Fish*, 1:260.
31. Cox, "How Judge Hoar Ceased to Be Attorney-General."
32. Nevins, *Hamilton Fish*, 1:259.
33. *PUSG*, 24:62. "Second Inaugural Address," March 4, 1873.
34. Ibid., 20:74. "Memorandum," 1869–70 [n.d.].
35. Ibid., 75.
36. Ibid., 74.
37. Ibid.
38. Ibid.
39. *New York Herald*, July 24, 1878.
40. Grant, *Memoirs*, 2:778.
41. Nevins, *Hamilton Fish*, 1:261.
42. Ibid.
43. Cox, "How Judge Hoar Ceased to Be Attorney-General."
44. *PUSG*, 19:209. Letter to Buenaventura Báez, July 13, 1869.
45. GPL. SX BL. "Orville Babcock Papers." Diary entry for July 24, 1869.
46. Cox, "How Judge Hoar Ceased to Be Attorney-General."
47. Ibid.
48. Ibid.

49. Nevins, *Hamilton Fish*, 1:246. Letter from Hamilton Fish to George Bancroft, September 4, 1869.
50. *PUSG*, 20:169. Hamilton Fish diary entry for July 10, 1870.
51. Smith, *Grant*, 496.
52. Nevins, *Hamilton Fish*, 1:244.
53. Smith, *Grant*, 497.
54. *PUSG*, 20:26. "Annual Message," December 6, 1869.
55. Ibid., 19:260. Letter from John A. Rawlins to Gen. Grenville M. Dodge, August 19, 1869.
56. Parker, "General Rawlins."
57. Nevins, *Hamilton Fish*, 1:246. Letter from Hamilton Fish to George Bancroft, September 4, 1869.
58. *Washington Evening Star*, September 7, 1869.
59. Armstrong, *Warrior in Two Camps*, 145.
60. McFeely, *Grant*, 330.
61. *PUSG*, 19:240. Letter to Roscoe Conkling, September 5, 1869.
62. Nevins, *Hamilton Fish*, 1:247.
63. Eaton, *Grant, Lincoln and the Freedmen*, 305.
64. *PUSG*, 19:240. Letter to Mary E. Rawlins, September 6, 1869.
65. Ibid., 260. Letter from Senator George E. Spencer to Gen. Grenville M. Dodge, September 9, 1869.
66. Ibid., 220. Letter from Adolph E. Borie to Adam Badeau, October 3, 1869.
67. Ibid., 257. Letter from Lt. Col. James H. Wilson to Orville E. Babcock, October 13, 1869.
68. LoC. SCP. Box 1. Letter from Gen. John E. Smith to Sylvanus Cadwallader, February 4, 1896.
69. GPL. S2 B13 F43. Letter from James H. Wilson to Sylvanus Cadwallader, October 12, 1904.
70. Catton, *Grant Takes Command*, 137.

CHAPTER THIRTY-ONE: SIN AGAINST HUMANITY

1. Kaplan, *Mr. Clemens and Mark Twain*, 157.
2. Nevins and Thomas, *The Diary of George Templeton Strong*, 4:409. Diary entry for January 8, 1872.
3. Klein, *The Life and Legend of Jay Gould*, 102.
4. *PUSG*, 20:234. Letter from Julia Dent Grant to Katherine Felt, April 25, 1869.
5. *New York Herald*, October 8, 1869.
6. *PUSG*, 15:220. Letter to Andrew Johnson, June 26, 1865.
7. Boutwell, *Reminiscences of Sixty Years*, 171.
8. Adams, "The New York Gold Conspiracy."
9. *PUSG*, 19:244. Letter to George S. Boutwell, September 12, 1869.
10. *New York Tribune*, September 13, 1869.
11. *PUSG*, 19:244–45. Letter from Jay Gould to Horace Porter, September 16, 1869; telegram from Horace Porter to Jay Gould, September 19, 1869.
12. Adams, "The New York Gold Conspiracy."
13. Klein, *The Life and Legend of Jay Gould*, 106.
14. *PUSG*, 19:245. Letter from Julia Dent Grant to Virginia Grant Corbin, September 18 or 19, 1869.

15. Julia Grant, *Memoirs*, 182.
16. Adams, "The New York Gold Conspiracy."
17. Boutwell, *Reminiscences of Sixty Years*, 175.
18. Ibid., 168–69.
19. McFeely, *Grant*, 321.
20. Ibid.
21. *PUSG*, 19:257. Letter from Lt. Col. James H. Wilson to Horace Porter, October 12, 1869.
22. Ibid., 256. Letter from Robert Bonner, October 11, 1869.
23. Ibid., 255. Letter to Robert Bonner, October 13, 1869.
24. Ibid., 256. Telegram from Robert Bonner, October 16, 1869.
25. Adams, *The Education of Henry Adams*, 254.
26. Ibid., 248.
27. Taliaferro, *All the Great Prizes*, 177.
28. *PUSG*, 22:79. Letter to Hamilton Fish, July 21, 1871; ibid., 20:318, letter to Adam Badeau, October 23, 1870.
29. Simpson, "Henry Adams and the Age of Grant."
30. GPL. S2 B5 F19. "Letters of Henry Adams."
31. Waugh, *U. S. Grant*, 104.

32. Adams, *The Education of Henry Adams,* 249.
33. Ibid., 248.
34. Ibid., 247.
35. Ibid.
36. Adams, "The Session."
37. Adams, *The Education of Henry Adams,* 34.
38. Grant, *In the Days of My Father General Grant,* 105–6.
39. Young, *Around the World,* 281.
40. *PUSG,* 28:306. Letter to Hamilton Fish, November 14, 1877.
41. Badeau, *Grant in Peace,* 153.
42. Adams, *The Education of Henry Adams,* 258.
43. Badeau, *Grant in Peace,* 212.
44. Wineapple, *Ecstatic Nation,* 481; Palmer, *The Selected Letters of Charles Sumner,* 465.
45. Grant, *Memoirs,* 2:777.
46. Nevins, *Hamilton Fish,* 1:160.
47. *The Times* (London), June 3, 1869.
48. *PUSG,* 20:50. "Speech," December 11, 1869.
49. *The Nation,* January 20, 1870.
50. Badeau, *Grant in Peace,* 58.
51. *PUSG,* 20:91. Letter to Elihu B. Washburne, January 28, 1870.
52. Ibid., 130–31. "To Congress," March 30, 1870.

CHAPTER THIRTY-TWO: THE DARKEST BLOT

1. Scaturro, *President Grant Reconsidered,* 11.
2. *PUSG,* 20:20. "Speech," December 6, 1869.
3. Ibid., 60. Letter to Elihu B. Washburne, December 17, 1869.
4. Sumner, *Naboth's Vineyard,* 14.
5. *PUSG,* 28:307. Letter to Hamilton Fish, November 14, 1877.
6. Nevins, *Hamilton Fish,* 1:322. Letter from Senator Timothy O. Howe to Hamilton Fish, November 8, 1877.
7. *PUSG,* 28:307. Letter to Hamilton Fish, November 14, 1877.
8. Palmer, *The Selected Letters of Charles Sumner,* 558. Letter from John W. Forney to Orville E. Babcock, June 6, 1870.
9. *PUSG,* 28:308. Memorandum of George S. Boutwell, November 12, 1877.
10. McFeely, *Grant,* 341.
11. Smith, *Grant,* 502.
12. Nevins, *Hamilton Fish,* 1:312.
13. McFeely, *Grant,* 356.
14. Palmer, *The Selected Letters of Charles Sumner,* 631. Letter to William Washburn, March 9, 1874.
15. Nevins, *Hamilton Fish,* 1:317.
16. Sumner, *Republicanism vs. Grantism,* 20.
17. Nevins, *Hamilton Fish,* 1:317.
18. McFeely, *Grant,* 342.
19. Nevins, *Hamilton Fish,* 1:318.
20. Jones, *John A. Logan,* 42.
21. *PUSG,* 20:135. Hamilton Fish diary entry for April 4, 1870.
22. Ibid., 154–55. "To the Senate," May 31, 1870.
23. Nevins, *Hamilton Fish,* 1:330. Diary entry for June 1, 1870.

53. Ibid., 137. "Speech," April 1, 1870.
54. Cramer, *Ulysses S. Grant,* 65–66.
55. Berg, *Wilson,* 41.
56. Foner, *Reconstruction,* 417.
57. Ibid., 238.
58. Young, *Around the World,* 336.
59. *PUSG,* 20:55. Hamilton Fish diary entry for January 7, 1870.
60. Julia Grant, *Memoirs,* 198.
61. *PUSG,* 20:78. Letter from Edwin M. Stanton to Bishop Matthew Simpson, October 26, 1869.
62. Ibid., 80. Letter from Edwin M. Stanton, December 21, 1869; Young, *Around the World,* 334.
63. Ibid. Letter to Department Heads, December 24, 1869.
64. Young, *Around the World,* 334.
65. *PUSG,* 20:56. Letter from Robert C. Grier, March 31, 1869.
66. *New York Tribune,* February 14, 1870.
67. Friedman and Israel, *Justices of the United States Supreme Court,* 1181.
68. *PUSG,* 20:92. Letter from Elihu Washburne, January 7, 1870.

24. *PUSG,* 20:162. Hamilton Fish diary entry for June 4, 1870.
25. NL. OEBP. Box 3, F149. Letter from J. W. Fabens to Orville E. Babcock, June 6, 1870.
26. Nevins, *Hamilton Fish,* 1:331.
27. McFeely, *Grant,* 343.
28. Nevins, *Hamilton Fish,* 1:364. Diary entry for June 13, 1870.
29. Ibid. Diary entry for June 14, 1870.
30. *PUSG,* 20:180. Rutherford B. Hayes diary entry for June 27, 1870.
31. Perret, *Ulysses S. Grant,* 399.
32. Badeau, *Grant in Peace,* 205.
33. Nevins, *Hamilton Fish,* 1:204.
34. Badeau, *Grant in Peace,* 206.
35. *PUSG,* 20:185. Hamilton Fish diary entry for June 25, 1870.
36. Ibid. Hamilton Fish diary entry for July 1, 1870.
37. Ibid. Cable from Hamilton Fish to John Lothrop Motley, July 1, 1870.
38. Ibid., 186. Letter from John Lothrop Motley to Hamilton Fish, July 14, 1870
39. Badeau, *Grant in Peace,* 207.
40. Palmer, *The Selected Letters of Charles Sumner,* 516. Letter to Timothy O. Howe, August 28, 1870.
41. Nevins, *Hamilton Fish,* 1:380. Letter from Bancroft Davis, August 3, 1870.
42. Palmer, *The Selected Letters of Charles Sumner,* 522. Letter to Hamilton Fish, September 14, 1870.
43. Ibid., 515. Letter from John Bigelow, July 23, 1870.
44. *New York Herald,* February 22, 1878.
45. *PUSG,* 28:307. Letter to Hamilton Fish, November 14, 1877.

46. Boutwell, *Reminiscences of Sixty Years,* 214.
47. Smith, *Grant,* 502.
48. *PUSG,* 20:171. Hamilton Fish diary entry for June 17, 1870.
49. Hesseltine, *Ulysses S. Grant: Politician,* 210.
50. *PUSG,* 22:351. Letter from Jacob D. Cox to Willard Warner, January 30, 1872.
51. Nevins, *Hamilton Fish,* 1:379. Benjamin Moran diary entry for July 15, 1870.
52. McFeely, *Grant,* 367.
53. Webb, "Benjamin H. Bristow."
54. Ibid.
55. *PUSG,* 23:66. "To House of Representatives," April 19, 1872.
56. Ibid., 20:211. Letter from Gov. William W. Holden, March 10, 1870.
57. Ibid., 210. Letter to Gov. William W. Holden, July 22, 1870.
58. Swinney, "Enforcing the Fifteenth Amendment, 1870–1877."
59. *PUSG,* 20:249. Letter from Gov. Robert K. Scott, October 22, 1870.
60. Ibid., 250.
61. Ibid., 21:19. Letter from Gov. William H. Smith, November 18, 1870.
62. Egerton, *The Wars of Reconstruction,* 298.
63. Ibid., 299.
64. *PUSG,* 21:263. Letter from Mrs. S. E. Lane, April 19, 1871.
65. Egerton, *The Wars of Reconstruction,* 278.
66. Foner, *Reconstruction,* 442.
67. Ibid., 428.
68. *PUSG,* 21:151. Letter from Gov. William W. Holden, January 1, 1871.
69. Ibid., 259. Letter from Gov. Robert K. Scott to Brig. Gen. Alfred H. Terry, January 17, 1871.
70. Ibid., 262. Letter from Reps. Warren D. Wilkes and Samuel Nuckles, March 2, 1871.
71. *Philadelphia Public Ledger,* March 22, 1871.
72. Kousser and McPherson, *Region, Race, and Reconstruction,* 407.
73. Stiles, *Custer's Trials,* 357.
74. *PUSG,* 21:218–19. Letter to James. G. Blaine, March 9, 1871.
75. Ibid., 247. Letter from Rep. James A. Garfield to Jacob D. Cox, March 23, 1871.
76. Ibid.
77. Ibid., 249. Rep. James B. Beck, "Speech," March 30, 1871.
78. Ibid., 250. Rep. John B. Hawley, "Speech," April 1, 1871.
79. Parsons, *Ku-Klux,* 166.
80. Marszalek, *Sherman: A Soldier's Passion for Order,* 426.
81. Foner, *The Life and Writings of Frederick Douglass,* 63.
82. Kousser and McPherson, *Region, Race, and Reconstruction,* 406.
83. *PUSG,* 21:337. General Orders No. 48, issued by Adjutant General Edward D. Townsend, May 15, 1871.
84. Egerton, *The Wars of Reconstruction,* 300.
85. Foner, *Reconstruction,* 457.
86. Wineapple, *Ecstatic Nation,* 560.
87. *PUSG,* 21:336. "Proclamation," May 3, 1871.
88. Ibid., 336–37.
89. Ibid., 355. Letter from Adjutant General Edward D. Townsend to Brig. Gen. Alfred H. Terry, May 13, 1871.
90. Ibid., 22:164. Quoted in letter from Senator John Scott, September 1, 1871.
91. Ibid., 167. Letter from Javan Bryant, September 8, 1871.
92. Ibid., 23:65. Letter from Amos T. Akerman, October 16, 1871.
93. Ibid., 22:161. "Proclamation," October 12, 1871.
94. Webb, "Benjamin H. Bristow."
95. Gillette, *Retreat from Reconstruction, 1869–1879,* 42.
96. Hamilton, *Amos T. Akerman,* 70.
97. Foner, *Reconstruction,* 458.
98. Hamilton, *Amos T. Akerman,* 79.
99. Ibid.
100. *PUSG,* 22:201. Hamilton Fish diary entry for October 31, 1871.
101. Egerton, *The Wars of Reconstruction,* 301.
102. *PUSG,* 21:345. Letter from Senator Adelbert Ames to Blanche Butler Ames, October 26, 1871.
103. Hamilton, *Amos T. Akerman,* 94.
104. Palmer, *The Selected Letters of Charles Sumner,* 570. Letter to Gerrit Smith, August 20, 1871.
105. Hamilton, *Amos T. Akerman,* 85.
106. Parsons, *Ku-Klux,* 174.
107. *PUSG,* 22:288. Letter to Amos T. Akerman, December 12, 1871.
108. Ibid., 296. Letter from Amos T. Akerman, December 13, 1871.
109. Ibid., 297. George H. Williams, August 8, 1885, eulogy for Grant.
110. Scaturro, *President Grant Reconsidered,* 72.

CHAPTER THIRTY-THREE: A DANCE OF BLOOD

1. *PUSG,* 21:39. "Draft Annual Message," December 5, 1870.
2. Williams, *Diary and Letters of Rutherford Birchard Hayes,* 122. Letter to S. Birchard, December 11, 1870.
3. *The New York Times,* December 8, 1870.
4. Sumner, *Naboth's Vineyard,* 3.
5. Ibid.
6. Ibid., 5.
7. Ibid., 7.
8. *PUSG,* 21:81, December 21, 1870; Sumner, *Naboth's Vineyard,* 14.
9. Palmer, *The Selected Letters of Charles Sumner,* 533. Senator Zachariah Chandler, "Speech," December 21, 1870.
10. Jordan, *Roscoe Conkling,* 161.
11. *PUSG,* 21:82. *Congressional Globe,* 41–43, speech by Senator Oliver P. Morton, December 21, 1870.
12. McFeely, *Grant,* 351.
13. Ibid.

14. Nevins, *Hamilton Fish*, 2:450.
15. *PUSG*, 21:135. Letter from Frederick Douglass to Senator Charles Sumner, January 6, 1871.
16. Palmer, *The Selected Letters of Charles Sumner*, 547. Letter from Hamilton Fish to Benjamin Morgan, December 30, 1870.
17. Wineapple, *Ecstatic Nation*, 486.
18. Palmer, *The Selected Letters of Charles Sumner*, 540. Letter from Charles Sumner to Gerrit Smith, January 17, 1871.
19. McFeely, *Frederick Douglass*, 77.
20. Foner, *The Life and Writings of Frederick Douglass*, 67.
21. *PUSG*, 21:149. Letter from Ebenezer R. Hoar to Jacob D. Cox, February 9, 1871.
22. *PUSG*, 21:290. Letter from Benjamin F. Wade to Caroline Wade, February 1, 1871.
23. Ibid., 367. Hamilton Fish diary entry for March 19, 1871.
24. Nevins, *Hamilton Fish*, 2:451 and 461. Letter to Elihu Washburne, February 20, 1871.
25. Boutwell, *Reminiscences of Sixty Years*, 214.
26. *New York Herald*, September 25, 1877.
27. Hesseltine, *Ulysses S. Grant: Politician*, 237.
28. Palmer, *The Selected Letters of Charles Sumner*, 546. Letter to Edward Eggleston, March 10, 1871.
29. *PUSG*, 21:369. Senator Charles Sumner, "Speech," March 27, 1871.
30. Sumner, *Republicanism vs. Grantism*, 44.
31. McFeely, *Frederick Douglass*, 277.
32. Douglass, "U. S. Grant and the Colored People."
33. Foner, *The Life and Writings of Frederick Douglass*, 83.
34. Ibid., 70.
35. *The New York Times*, March 30, 1871.
36. *PUSG*, 21:294. "To Congress," April 5, 1871.
37. Ibid., 238. Letter to Alexander G. Cattell, March 21 [23?], 1871.
38. Jordan, *Roscoe Conkling*, 167.
39. *PUSG*, 21:295. "To Congress," April 5, 1871.
40. Ibid., 370. Letter from Senator Carl Schurz to Jacob D. Cox, April 4, 1871.
41. Palmer, *The Selected Letters of Charles Sumner*, 570. Letter from Senator Charles Sumner to Gerrit Smith, August 20, 1871.

42. *PUSG*, 22:232. Letter to Henry Wilson, November 15, 1871.
43. Jordan, *Roscoe Conkling*, 174–75.
44. GPL. S2 B5 F20. "Hamlin Garland."
45. Palmer, *The Selected Letters of Charles Sumner*, 556. Letter to John Sherman, May 1, 1871.
46. LoC. USGP. Series 4, Vol. 6. "Memoirs."
47. *PUSG*, 22:248. Letter to George W. Childs, November 28, 1871.
48. Nevins, *Hamilton Fish*, 1:438.
49. *PUSG*, 21:55. "Annual Message," December 5, 1870.
50. Foreman, *A World on Fire*, 802.
51. McFeely, *Grant*, 354.
52. Ibid.
53. *PUSG*, 21:63. Letter from Hamilton Fish to Senator Simon Cameron, May 30, 1871.
54. Ibid., 22:54. Hamilton Fish diary entry for May 29, 1871.
55. Ibid., 107. Letter to Schuyler Colfax, August 4, 1871.
56. Nevins, *Hamilton Fish*, 2:495. Diary entry for April 22, 1871.
57. *PUSG*, 22:53–54. Letter from Hamilton Fish, July 10, 1871.
58. *New York Herald*, June 3, 1871.
59. *PUSG*, 22:79. Letter to Hamilton Fish, July 21, 1871.
60. Fish, "General Grant."
61. *PUSG*, 22:320. Hamilton Fish diary entry for December 5, 1871.
62. Ibid. Hamilton Fish diary entry for December 20, 1871.
63. Nevins, *Hamilton Fish*, 2:527. Letter from Prime Minister Gladstone to Queen Victoria, January 30, 1872.
64. Foreman, *A World on Fire*, 803.
65. *PUSG*, 23:14. Benjamin Moran diary entry for February 28, 1872.
66. Nevins, *Hamilton Fish*, 2:531.
67. *PUSG*, 23:14. Letter from Orville E. Babcock to Adam Badeau, March 10, 1872.
68. Ibid., 122. Hamilton Fish diary entry for May 18, 1872.
69. NYHS. TNC. Cartoon of July 6, 1872.
70. Nevins, *Hamilton Fish*, 2:564. Letter to ElihuWashburne, October 7, 1872.
71. Badeau, *Grant in Peace*, 230.

CHAPTER THIRTY-FOUR: VINDICATION

1. Fowler, *Patriotic Orations*, 161.
2. USGH. "Interview with Eliza Shaw."
3. "Longstreet's Reminiscences." *The New York Times*, July 24, 1885.
4. *PUSG*, 28:448. Letter to Daniel Ammen, August 13, 1878.
5. Badeau, *Grant in Peace*, 405.
6. USGH. "Interview with James B. Fry."
7. Flood, *Grant's Final Victory*, 20.
8. Grant, "My Father as I Knew Him."
9. Boutwell, *Reminiscences of Sixty Years*, 251.

10. *PUSG*, 20:91. Letter to Elihu B. Washburne, January 28, 1870.
11. Hamilton, *Amos T. Akerman*, 87.
12. Cox, "How Judge Hoar Ceased to Be Attorney-General."
13. *PUSG*, 20: 242–43. Letter from Jacob D. Cox, August 22, 1870.
14. Nevins, *Hamilton Fish*, 2:466. Diary entry for October 4, 1870.
15. *PUSG*, 20:292. Letter from Jacob D. Cox, October 3, 1870.

16. Ibid. Letter to Jacob D. Cox, October 5, 1870.

17. Scaturro, *President Grant Reconsidered*, 58.

18. Palmer, *The Selected Letters of Charles Sumner*, 605. Letter from Jacob D. Cox, August 3, 1872.

19. Hesseltine, *Ulysses S. Grant: Politician*, 218.

20. *PUSG*, 21:40–41. "Draft Annual Message," December 5, 1870.

21. *The New York Times*, July 24, 1885.

22. *PUSG*, 22:359. Letter from Rep. James A. Garfield to Jacob D. Cox, January 16, 1872.

23. Ibid., 23:3. Letter to Joseph Medill, February 1, 1872.

24. Ibid., 62. "Order," April 16, 1872.

25. Ibid., 293. Letter from Charles W. Eliot, November 26, 1872.

26. Ibid., 28:265. Letter to Edward F. Beale, September 9, 1877.

27. Young, *Around the World*, 281.

28. Hesseltine, *Ulysses S. Grant: Politician*, 254.

29. Taliaferro, *All the Great Prizes*, 202.

30. *Cincinnati Gazette*, October 5, 1880.

31. Nevins, *Hamilton Fish*, 2:589.

32. "Grant Reminiscences." *Chicago Daily Tribune*, September 1, 1885.

33. Watrous, "Grant as His Son Saw Him."

34. *The Southern Illinoisan*, January 7, 2007.

35. Jordan, *Roscoe Conkling*, 174.

36. Ibid., 134.

37. Ibid., 136.

38. Ibid., 137.

39. Ibid.

40. *PUSG*, 20:142. Letter from Orville E. Babcock to Thomas Murphy, July 14, 1870.

41. Jordan, *Roscoe Conkling*, 138.

42. *New York Tribune*, November 21, 1870.

43. *PUSG*, 22:240. Letter to Thomas Murphy, November 20, 1871.

44. Hesseltine, *Ulysses S. Grant: Politician*, 256.

45. Jordan, *Roscoe Conkling*, 174.

46. *PUSG*, 23:56. Hamilton Fish diary entry for February 13, 1872.

47. Nevins and Thomas, *The Diary of George Templeton Strong*, 411. Diary entry for January 25, 1872.

48. Levine, "Indian Fighters and Indian Reformers."

49. *PUSG*, 22:72. Report of the House Committee on Appropriations, February 25, 1871.

50. Ibid., 71. Letter to Ely S. Parker, July 13, 1871.

51. Ibid., 84. Letter from William Welsh to Jacob D. Cox, September 13, 1871.

52. *Philadelphia Evening Telegram*, August 12, 1875.

53. *New York Herald*, June 8, 1871.

54. *PUSG*, 23:270. Letter to George H. Stuart, October 26, 1872.

55. Ibid., 22:72. Letter from Ely S. Parker to Columbus Delano, January 12, 1871.

56. Ibid., 23:40. Letter to Maj. Gen. John M. Schofield, March 6, 1872.

57. Ibid., 22:77–78. Letter from Samuel F. Tappan, May 25, 1871.

58. Ibid., 23:145. "Speech," May 28, 1872.

59. *New York Herald*, August 6, 1872.

60. *PUSG*, 22:230. Letter to Schuyler Colfax, November 14, 1871.

61. Badeau, *Grant in Peace*, 14.

62. McFeely, *Grant*, 381.

63. Scaturro, *President Grant Reconsidered*, 77.

64. Hesseltine, *Ulysses S. Grant: Politician*, 262.

65. Jordan, *Roscoe Conkling*, 179.

66. McPherson, "Grant or Greeley?"

67. Wineapple, *Ecstatic Nation*, 500.

68. Foner, *Reconstruction*, 503.

69. *PUSG*, 21:8. Letter to John Russell Young, November 15, 1870.

70. Young, *Around the World*, 291.

71. *PUSG*, 22:232. Letter to Henry Wilson, November 15, 1871.

72. Hesseltine, *Ulysses S. Grant: Politician*, 274.

73. Wineapple, *Ecstatic Nation*, 318.

74. Truman, "Anecdotes of Andrew Jackson."

75. Parsons, *Ku-Klux*, 192; *Daily Arkansas Gazette*, June 4, 1871.

76. Wineapple, *Ecstatic Nation*, 493.

77. Foner, *Reconstruction*, 503.

78. Wineapple, *Ecstatic Nation*, 494.

79. Sumner, *Republicanism vs. Grantism*, 4.

80. Ibid., 27.

81. Williams, *Diary and Letters of Rutherford Birchard Hayes*, 204. Letter to S. Birchard, June 10, 1872.

82. Jordan, *Roscoe Conkling*, 180.

83. *New York Herald*, June 14, 1872.

84. Jordan, *Roscoe Conkling*, 180.

85. Ibid.

86. Foner, *Reconstruction*, 505.

87. Foner, *The Life and Writings of Frederick Douglass*, 81.

88. *PUSG*, 24:169. Letter from Elihu B. Washburne to Adam Badeau, July 19, 1872.

89. Ibid., 20:313. Letter to Oliver P. Morton, October 20, 1870.

90. *PUSG*, 21:350. Letter to Charles W. Ford, May 3, 1871.

91. Ibid., 22:273. "Annual Message," December 5, 1871.

92. Egerton, *The Wars of Reconstruction*, 282.

93. Ibid., 280.

94. *Washington Evening Star*, April 17, 1872.

95. Corum, *Ulysses Underground*, 257.

96. *PUSG*, 23:100–101. Letter from Charles Lenox Remond and Charles E. Pindell, September 5, 1872.

97. Smith, *Grant*, 550.

98. McPherson, "Grant or Greeley?"

99. Ibid.

100. Ibid.

101. *PUSG*, 23:214. Gerrit Smith, "Speech," June 22, 1872.

102. McPherson, "Grant or Greeley?"

103. Palmer, *The Selected Letters of Charles Sumner*, 603. Letter from Frederick Douglass, July 19, 1872.

104. Foner, *The Life and Writings of Frederick Douglass,* 75.
105. Bunting, *Ulysses S. Grant,* 115.
106. Douglass, "U. S. Grant and the Colored People."
107. Ibid.
108. *PUSG,* 23:211. Letter to Gerrit Smith, July 28, 1872.
109. Ibid., 200. Letter to Roscoe Conkling, July 15, 1872.
110. McFeely, *Grant,* 384.
111. Fish, "General Grant."
112. *PUSG,* 23:242. Letter to J. Russell Jones, September 5, 1872.
113. Hesseltine, *Ulysses S. Grant: Politician,* 287.
114. Foner, *Reconstruction,* 508.
115. Williams, *Diary and Letters of Rutherford Birchard Hayes,* 213. Letter to S. Birchard, September 22, 1872.
116. Wineapple, *Ecstatic Nation,* 503.
117. Jordan, *Roscoe Conkling,* 181.
118. Clews, *Fifty Years in Wall Street,* 189.
119. Wineapple, *Ecstatic Nation,* 552.
120. *PUSG,* 23:237. Letter to Elihu B. Washburne, August 26, 1872.
121. Waugh, *U. S. Grant,* 142.
122. Ibid., 143.
123. Nevins and Thomas, *The Diary of George Templeton Strong,* 4:434. Diary entry for August 28, 1872.
124. Nevins, *Hamilton Fish,* 2:609. Letter to C. C. Amsden, October 25, 1872.
125. *PUSG,* 24:66. Letter from Elizabeth Cady Stanton, March 10, 1873.
126. *Philadelphia Evening Telegraph,* June 11, 1871.
127. Gordon, *The Selected Papers of Elizabeth Cady Stanton and Susan B. Anthony,* 199. Letter from Susan B. Anthony to Elizabeth Cady Stanton, July 10, 1872.
128. *New York Herald,* October 8, 1872.
129. Sherr, *Failure Is Impossible,* 109.
130. *St. Louis Democrat,* March 3, 1873.
131. Sherr, *Failure Is Impossible,* 267.
132. Egerton, *The Wars of Reconstruction,* 296.
133. Grant, *In the Days of My Father General Grant,* 150.
134. Foner, *Reconstruction,* 510.
135. Young, *Around the World,* 379.
136. Waugh, *U. S. Grant,* 145.
137. Egerton, *The Wars of Reconstruction,* 269.
138. Taliaferro, *All the Great Prizes,* 158.
139. *New York Tribune,* December 5, 1872.
140. Wineapple, *Ecstatic Nation,* 503.
141. *PUSG,* 24:68. Letter to Schuyler Colfax, March 4, 1873.
142. Webb, *Benjamin Helm Bristow,* 120.
143. Jordan, *Roscoe Conkling,* 190.
144. Scaturro, *President Grant Reconsidered,* 61.
145. *The New York Times,* March 5, 1873.
146. *PUSG,* 24:61. "Second Inaugural Address," March 4, 1873.
147. Ibid., 62.
148. Ibid., 63.
149. Ibid., 62.
150. Ibid., 64.
151. Gillette, *Retreat from Reconstruction, 1869–1879,* 74.

CHAPTER THIRTY-FIVE: A BUTCHERY OF CITIZENS

1. Wineapple, *Ecstatic Nation,* 495.
2. Ammen, "Recollections and Letters of Grant. Part 1."
3. *PUSG,* 24:3. Letter to William W. Belknap, January 5, 1873.
4. Ibid., 52. "To Congress," February 25, 1873.
5. Ibid., 57. Hamilton Fish diary entry for February 21, 1873.
6. Ibid. Letter to Elisha Baxter, February 26, 1873.
7. Ibid., 53. Letter from Joseph T. Hatch, January 21, 1873.
8. Ibid., 54. Endorsement of telegram from William P. Kellogg, March 5, 1873.
9. Lemann, *Redemption,* 21.
10. *PUSG,* 26:6. "To Senate," January 13, 1875.
11. Ibid., 7.
12. Ibid., 24:123. Letter from Gov. William P. Kellogg, May 8, 1873.
13. Ibid., 122. "Proclamation," May 22, 1873.
14. Lemann, *Redemption,* 25.
15. Foner, *Reconstruction,* 550.
16. *Harper's Weekly,* March 6, 1875.
17. *PUSG,* 25:215–16. Letter from Gov. William P. Kellogg, August 19, 1874.
18. Ibid., 26:8. "To Senate," January 13, 1875.
19. Ibid.
20. Ibid., 25:187. Letter to William W. Belknap, September 2, 1874.
21. Ibid., 224. Letter from Gen. William H. Emory, September 17, 1874.
22. Ibid., 26:9. "To Senate," January 13, 1875; ibid., 25:213. "Proclamation," September 15, 1874.
23. Nevins, *Hamilton Fish,* 2:741.
24. Hesseltine, *Ulysses S. Grant: Politician,* 358.
25. *PUSG,* 25:222. Hamilton Fish diary entry for September 16, 1874.
26. Hesseltine, *Ulysses S. Grant: Politician,* 348.
27. *PUSG,* 25:226. Letter from Marshall Jewell to Elihu B. Washburne, September 19, 1874.
28. Ibid., 223. Hamilton Fish diary entry for September 16, 1874.
29. Ibid., 224.
30. Ibid., 234. Letter from "a Lover of Justice" to Julia Grant, September 23, 1874.
31. Ibid. Anonymous letter to Julia Grant, September 17, 1874.
32. Ibid., 235. Letter from "We the Colored people of New Orleans," September 25, 1874.
33. McFeely, *Grant,* 386.

34. *PUSG,* 23:308. Hamilton Fish diary entry for December 3, 1872.

35. Ibid., 24:253. Letter to Roscoe Conkling, November 8, 1873.

36. Jordan, *Roscoe Conkling,* 199.

37. Ibid., 201.

38. *PUSG,* 24:254. Letter from Hamilton Fish, November 30, 1873.

39. Ibid., 285. Hamilton Fish diary entry for December 1, 1873.

40. Hesseltine, *Ulysses S. Grant: Politician,* 361.

41. *PUSG,* 24:285. Letter from Horace Porter to Benjamin H. Bristow, December 18, 1873.

42. Ibid., 287. Letter from Noah H. Swayne to Benjamin H. Bristow, December 21, 1873.

43. Ibid., 286. Hamilton Fish diary entry for December 30, 1873.

44. Webb, *Benjamin Helm Bristow,* 132.

45. Smith, *Grant,* 562.

46. Hesseltine, *Ulysses S. Grant: Politician,* 363.

47. *Harper's Weekly,* February 7, 1874.

48. *PUSG,* 23:329. Letter to Isaac H. Bailey, December 16, 1872.

49. Ibid., 197. Letter from Julia Dent Grant to Margaretta Pierrepont, December 6, 1872.

50. Ibid., 24:161. Letter to Adolph E. Borie, July 3, 1873.

51. USGH. "Eliza Shaw Interview."

52. *PUSG,* 24:161. Letter from Aaron F. Perry, July 5, 1873.

53. Hesseltine, *Ulysses S. Grant: Politician,* 301.

54. *PUSG,* 24:293. Letter to Abel R. Corbin, December 16, 1873.

55. Ibid., 21:33. Letter from David Clark to Sayles J. Bowen, July 22, 1872.

56. *The New National Era,* July 30, 1874.

57. *PUSG,* 21:31. Letter from James Smith to David Clark, June 30, 1870.

58. Ibid., 30. Letter from David Clark, July 8, 1870.

59. *The New National Era,* August 25, 1874.

60. Ibid.

61. Ibid.

62. Ibid., August 7, 1874.

63. Ibid., August 25, 1874.

64. *PUSG,* 21:32. Letter from David Clark to Sayles J. Bowen, July 22, 1872.

65. McFeely, *Grant,* 378.

66. *PUSG,* 21:73. Letter to Ulysses S. Grant Jr., December 8, 1870.

67. Ibid., 27:78. Letter from Gen. William T. Sherman to U.S. Senator John Sherman, March 10, 1876.

68. Ibid., 23:83. Letter from Gen. William T. Sherman to Ellen Sherman, June 13, 1872.

69. Ibid., 249. Letter to Abel R. Corbin, September 13, 1872.

70. Ross, *The General's Wife,* 219.

71. *PUSG,* 25:260. Letter to Adam Badeau, October 25, 1874.

72. Ibid., 21:28. Letter to Ulysses S. Grant Jr., October 9, probably 1870.

73. Ross, *The General's Wife,* 240.

74. *PUSG,* 25:261. Letter to Adam Badeau, October 25, 1874.

75. Ibid.

76. Ibid., 23:221. Letter from Julia Grant to Maj. Cyrus B. Comstock, August 12, 1874.

77. Grant, "My Father as I Knew Him."

78. Ross, *The General's Wife,* 219.

79. *PUSG,* 23:121. Letter to Robert C. Schenck, May 17, 1872.

80. Badeau, *Grant in Peace,* 413.

81. Ross, *The General's Wife,* 237.

82. Julia Grant, *Memoirs,* 181.

83. *PUSG,* 24:163. Letter to Edward J. Sartoris, July 7, 1873.

84. Ibid.

85. GPL. S2 B13 F26. "Walt Whitman."

86. Ross, *The General's Wife,* 239.

87. Grant, "General Grant's Son Speaks of His Father."

88. GPL. S2 B6 F59. "Henry James Letters." Letter of May 19, 1879.

CHAPTER THIRTY-SIX: THE BRAVEST BATTLE

1. *PUSG,* 24:214. Letter from William A. Richardson, August 28, 1873.

2. Ibid., 213. Telegram from Oliver P. Morton, September 19, 1873; ibid., 24:214. Telegram from Thomas Murphy, September 19, 1873.

3. *Harper's Weekly,* October 11, 1873.

4. *PUSG,* 24:219. Letter to Horace B. Claflin and Charles L. Anthony, September 27, 1873.

5. Nevins, *Hamilton Fish,* 2:703. Diary entry for October 3, 1873.

6. *PUSG,* 24:226. Letter to Anthony J. Drexel, October 10, 1873.

7. Hesseltine, *Ulysses S. Grant: Politician,* 331.

8. Nevins, *Hamilton Fish,* 2:701.

9. Schlesinger, *The Cycles of American History,* 35.

10. Donald, *Lincoln,* 395.

11. *PUSG,* 20:21. "Annual Message," December 6, 1869.

12. Jordan, *Roscoe Conkling,* 207.

13. *PUSG,* 25:172. Letter from Vice President Henry Wilson, April 5, 1874.

14. Jordan, *Roscoe Conkling,* 208.

15. *New York Tribune,* April 18, 1874.

16. *Washington National Republican,* April 18, 1874.

17. Young, *Around the World,* 239.

18. Ibid., 240.

19. *PUSG,* 26:310. Letter from Hamilton Fish, September 24, 1875.

20. Nevins, *Hamilton Fish,* 2:713. Diary entry for April 21, 1874.

21. *PUSG,* 25:77. Telegram from Edwards Pierrepont, April 22, 1874.
22. Hesseltine, *Ulysses S. Grant: Politician,* 336.
23. Williams, *Diary and Letters of Rutherford Birchard Hayes,* 255. Letter to Gen. M. F. Force, April 27, 1875.
24. Nevins, *Hamilton Fish,* 2:714. Letter to Gen. L. Schuyler, April 25, 1874.
25. *PUSG,* 25:80. Letter from Henry C. Guffin, April 27, 1874.
26. Ibid., 172. Letter from Vice President Henry Wilson, April 5, 1874.
27. Hesseltine, *Ulysses S. Grant: Politician,* 338.
28. Webb, *Benjamin Helm Bristow,* 136.
29. Ibid., 137.
30. *PUSG,* 25:140. Resolution of the Union League of America, October 21, 1874.
31. Ibid., 122. Hamilton Fish diary entry for June 7, 1874.
32. Ibid., 26:37. "To Senate," January 14, 1875.
33. Ibid., 23:118. Hamilton Fish diary entry for October 27, 1874.
34. Morris, *Fraud of the Century,* 25.
35. Marszalek, *Sherman: A Soldier's Passion for Order,* 387.
36. *PUSG,* 25:249. Letter from Gen. William T. Sherman to Col. Joseph C. Audenried, November 6, 1874.
37. Ibid., 145–46. Letter from Hamilton Fish, July 13, 1874.
38. Wineapple, *Ecstatic Nation,* 567.
39. Lemann, *Redemption,* 80.
40. Nevins, *Hamilton Fish,* 2:746.
41. Hesseltine, *Ulysses S. Grant: Politician,* 373.
42. Ibid; Webb, *Benjamin Helm Bristow,* 154.
43. *PUSG,* 25:284. "Draft Annual Message," December 7, 1874.
44. Young, *Around the World,* 244.
45. *PUSG,* 25:281. "Draft Annual Message," December 7, 1874.
46. Ibid.
47. Ibid., 230. Letter from the Reverend H. W. Harris, September 25, 1874.
48. Ibid., 13. Letter from L. F. Pannell, February 20, 1875.
49. Swinney, "Enforcing the Fifteenth Amendment, 1870–1877."
50. Ibid.
51. Nevins, *Hamilton Fish,* 2:771. Diary entry for March 12, 1875.
52. Ibid., 772. Diary entry for April 12, 1875.
53. *PUSG,* 26:105. Letter to George H. Williams, April 28, 1875.
54. *Harper's Weekly,* June 5 and June 10, 1875.
55. *PUSG,* 25:157. Letter from Alexander K. Davis, July 20, 1874.
56. Lemann, *Redemption,* 74.
57. *PUSG,* 25:159. Telegram from Senator Charles E. Furlong, August 4, 1874.
58. Lemann, *Redemption,* 74.
59. *PUSG,* 25:191. Letter from H. H. Montgomery, September 23, 1874.
60. Ibid., 192. Letter from Isaac Loveless, November 9, 1874.
61. Lemann, *Redemption,* 88.
62. Ibid.
63. Ibid., 91.
64. Ibid.
65. Ibid.
66. *PUSG,* 25:307. Letter to Capt. Arthur W. Allyn, December 19, 1874, sent via Secretary of War William W. Belknap.
67. Ibid., 305–6. "Proclamation," December 21, 1874.
68. Ibid., 307. Telegram from Adjutant General Edward D. Townsend to Lt. Gen. Philip H. Sheridan, January 4, 1875.
69. Lemann, *Redemption,* 99.
70. Ibid., 98.
71. *PUSG,* 26:16. Letter from A. P. Williams, December 17, 1874.
72. Morris, *Sheridan,* 351.
73. Nevins, *Hamilton Fish,* 2:751.
74. Webb, *Benjamin Helm Bristow,* 158.
75. Morris, *Sheridan,* 352.
76. Ibid.
77. Ibid.
78. *The Nation,* January 7, 1875.
79. Nevins and Thomas, *The Diary of George Templeton Strong,* 4:547. Diary entry for January 7, 1875.
80. Ibid., diary entry for January 11, 1875.
81. *PUSG,* 26:21. Letter from Wendell Phillips to Secretary of War William Belknap, January 9, 1875.
82. Ibid., 21. Hamilton Fish diary entry for January 9, 1875.
83. Ibid.
84. Ibid., 22. Pennsylvania House of Representatives Resolution, January 11, 1875.
85. Ibid., 23. Hamilton Fish diary entry for January 11, 1875.
86. Ibid.
87. Ibid., 8–9. "To Senate," January 13, 1875.
88. Ibid., 9.
89. Ibid., 12.
90. Ibid., 13–14.
91. Ibid., 25. Letter from Frederick Dent Grant to Lt. Gen. Philip H. Sheridan, January 14, 1875.
92. Ibid., 25. Letter from House Speaker James G. Blaine, January 14, 1875.
93. Ibid., 29. Letter from John S. Mosby, January 23, 1875.
94. Morris, *Sheridan,* 535.
95. Hoar, *Autobiography of Seventy Years,* 1:209.
96. *PUSG,* 26:30. Letter from Lt. Gen. Philip H. Sheridan to Orville E. Babcock, January 25, 1875.
97. Ibid., 20. Letter from Rufus B. Bullock to Orville E. Babcock, February 4, 1875.
98. Ibid., 34. Letter from Roland T. Bull et al., May 1, 1875.
99. Ibid., 579–80. Letter from Charles Sumner to Henry W. Longfellow, February 25, 1872.

100. Egerton, *The Wars of Reconstruction*, 311.
101. *Harper's Weekly*, June 13, 1874.

102. *PUSG*, 26:132. Anonymous letter, March 2, 1875.

CHAPTER THIRTY-SEVEN: LET NO GUILTY MAN ESCAPE

1. *PUSG*, 18:267. Letter from Maj. James S. Brisbin, May 25, 1868.
2. Ibid., 21:350. Letter to Charles W. Ford, May 3, 1871.
3. *The American*, August 5, 1885.
4. Stevens, *Grant in St. Louis*, 112.
5. Morris, *Fraud of the Century*, 25.
6. Stevens, *Grant in St. Louis*, 121.
7. Webb, *Benjamin Helm Bristow*, 185.
8. *St. Louis Post-Dispatch*, October 7, 1973.
9. Smith, *Grant*, 591.
10. Webb, *Benjamin Helm Bristow*, 155
11. White, *American Ulysses*, 557.
12. *PUSG*, 26:285. Bluford Wilson testimony, July 27, 1876.
13. Webb, *Benjamin Helm Bristow*, 193.
14. Ibid., 194.
15. Nevins, *Hamilton Fish*, 2:769. Diary entry for May 22, 1875.
16. *PUSG*, 26:238. Hamilton Fish diary entry for May 22, 1875.
17. Ibid., 240. Letter from Orville E. Babcock to John McDonald, July 14, 1875.
18. NL. OEBP. Box 1. Letter to Thomas C. Fletcher, October 1, 1877.
19. Grant, *In the Days of My Father General Grant*, 119–20.
20. Nevins, *Hamilton Fish*, 2:788.
21. *PUSG*, 26:233. Letter from William D. W. Barnard, July 19, 1875.
22. Ibid., 232. "Endorsement," July 29, 1875.
23. Ibid., 233. Letter from Secretary of the Treasury Benjamin H. Bristow, July 30, 1875.
24. Nevins, *Hamilton Fish*, 2:789. Diary entry for September 17, 1875.
25. *PUSG*, 26:284. Letter from Secretary of the Treasury Benjamin H. Bristow to Bluford Wilson, August 9, 1875.
26. Webb, *Benjamin Helm Bristow*, 198.
27. *PUSG*, 26:374. Letter from William L. Burt, October 21, 1875.
28. Hesseltine, *Ulysses S. Grant: Politician*, 385.
29. *PUSG*, 26:377. Letter from David P. Dyer to Edwards Pierrepont, November 29, 1875.
30. *The St. Louis Globe-Democrat*, November 30, 1875.
31. *PUSG*, 26:379. John B. Henderson, Closing Arguments, December 3, 1875.
32. Ibid., 384. Hamilton Fish diary entry for December 10, 1875.
33. Ibid., 380. Hamilton Fish diary entry for December 7, 1875.
34. Ibid., 378. Hamilton Fish diary entry for December 3, 1875.
35. Ibid., 430. Letter to Annie Campbell Babcock, December 17, 1875.

36. U.S. Congress, *House Testimony Before the Select Committee Concerning the Whiskey Frauds*, 44th Congress, 1st session, House Miscellaneous Document 186, 366.
37. *Chicago Inter-Ocean*, February 8, 1876.
38. McFeely, *Grant*, 413.
39. Webb, *Benjamin Helm Bristow*, 219.
40. *PUSG*, 27:139. Hamilton Fish diary entry for February 6, 1876.
41. Ibid.
42. Nevins, *Hamilton Fish*, 2:802. Diary entry for February 6, 1876.
43. *PUSG*, 27:23. Letter from Horace Porter, February 4, 1876.
44. Ibid., 45. Hamilton Fish diary entry for February 8, 1876.
45. Ibid., 46.
46. Ibid., 27–28. "Deposition," February 12, 1876.
47. Ibid., 35.
48. Ibid., 223. "Testimony," Edwards Pierrepont, March 23, 1876.
49. Ibid., 139. Hamilton Fish diary entry for February 14, 1876.
50. Badeau, *Grant in Peace*, 247.
51. Webb, *Benjamin Helm Bristow*, 11.
52. U.S. Congress, *House Testimony Before the Select Committee Concerning the Whiskey Frauds*, 44th Congress, 1st session, House Miscellaneous Document 186, 369.
53. GPL. S2 B24 F13. "Interview with Ulysses S. Grant, Jr." HGP.
54. *PUSG*, 28:164. "Order," March 1, 1877.
55. Ibid., 27:142. Hamilton Fish diary entry for May 15, 1876.
56. Ibid., 137. Letter from Benjamin H. Bristow, June 17, 1876.
57. Ibid., 136–37. Letter to Benjamin H. Bristow, June 19, 1876.
58. Ibid., 185. Letter to Benjamin H. Bristow, July 12, 1876.
59. Ibid., 146. Hamilton Fish diary entry for October 12, 1876.
60. Scaturro, *President Grant Reconsidered*, 36.
61. Jordan, *Roscoe Conkling*, 192.
62. Stevens, *Grant in St. Louis*, 133–34.
63. "Stories of Grant." *Chicago Daily Tribune*, April 12, 1885.
64. Randall, *The Diary of Orville Hickman Browning*, 2:417. Diary entry for July 5, 1875.
65. Young, *Around the World*, 379.
66. Grant, *In the Days of My Father General Grant*, 182.
67. *PUSG*, 26:133–34. Letter to Harry White, May 29, 1875.
68. Ibid., 129. Letter to Edwin Cowles, May 29, 1875.
69. Julia Grant, *Memoirs*, 186.
70. Ibid.

71. McFeely, *Grant*, 426.
72. *PUSG*, 27:124. To the Editor, *Sunday School Times*, June 6, 1876.
73. Eaton, *Grant, Lincoln and the Freedmen*, 270.
74. Ibid.
75. *PUSG*, 26:343. "Speech," September 29, 1875.
76. Ibid., 344.
77. "A Presidential Reformer." *The Catholic Record*, April 1876.
78. Cramer, *Ulysses S. Grant*, 151.
79. *PUSG*, 26:387. "Annual Message," December 7, 1875.
80. Ibid., 388.
81. Ibid., 293. Letter from William H. Harney to Gov. Adelbert Ames, September 6, 1875.
82. Ibid., 295. Telegram to Adjutant General Edward D. Townsend, September 8, 1875.
83. Ibid., 296. Telegram from James Z. George to Edwards Pierrepont, September 9, 1875.
84. Ibid., 297. Telegram from Attorney General Edwards Pierrepont, September 11, 1875.
85. Ibid. Telegram from Gov. Adelbert Ames to Attorney General Edwards Pierrepont, September 11, 1875.
86. Ibid., 312. Letter to Attorney General Edwards Pierrepont, September 13, 1875.

87. Ibid.
88. McFeely, *Grant*, 421.
89. *PUSG*, 26:314. Telegram from Attorney General Edwards Pierrepont to Gov. Adelbert Ames, September 14, 1875.
90. Ibid. Telegram from Attorney General Edwards Pierrepont, September 16, 1875.
91. Lemann, *Redemption*, 125.
92. *PUSG*, 26:315. Letter from Gov. Adelbert Ames, September 30, 1875.
93. Lemann, *Redemption*, 140.
94. Ibid., 132.
95. Ibid.
96. Ibid., 133.
97. Ibid., 137.
98. Ibid., 146.
99. Ibid., 148.
100. *PUSG*, 26:320. Letter from Hiram R. Revels, November 6, 1875.
101. Lemann, *Redemption*, 166.
102. McFeely, *Grant*, 424.
103. Lemann, *Redemption*, 167.
104. Ibid., 136.
105. Ibid., 137.

CHAPTER THIRTY-EIGHT: SADDEST OF THE FALLS

1. Nevins, *Hamilton Fish*, 2:775. Diary entry for April 29, 1865.
2. McFeely, *Grant*, 433.
3. *Baltimore American and Commercial Advertiser*, July 27, 1875.
4. Nevins, *Hamilton Fish*, 2:806.
5. *PUSG*, 27:68. Testimony by Orvil Grant before a House committee examining expenditures in the War Department, March 9, 1876.
6. "The Week." *The Nation*, March 16, 1876.
7. "A Trait of Grantism." *New York Tribune*, March 10, 1876.
8. Stiles, *Custer's Trials*, 432.
9. Ibid.
10. Julia Grant, *Memoirs*, 190.
11. Smith, *Grant*, 594.
12. Grant, *In the Days of My Father General Grant*, 125.
13. *PUSG*, 27:53. Letter to William W. Belknap, March 2, 1876.
14. Julia Grant, *Memoirs*, 191.
15. *New York Herald*, March 3, 1876.
16. *PUSG*, 27:55. Hamilton Fish diary entry for March 3, 1876.
17. Eaton, *Grant, Lincoln and the Freedmen*, 293.
18. *PUSG*, 27:77. Hamilton Fish diary entry for March 5, 1876.
19. Randall, *The Diary of Orville Hickman Browning*, 2:443. Diary entry for March 2, 1876.
20. Hamilton, *Amos T. Akerman*, 96.
21. *PUSG*, 27:56. Letter from Gen. William T. Sherman to U.S. Senator John Sherman, March 4, 1876.

22. Ibid., 57. Hamilton Fish diary entry for March 7, 1876.
23. Ibid., 59. Hamilton Fish diary entry for March 21, 1876.
24. Ibid.
25. Ibid.
26. Nevins, *Hamilton Fish*, 2:808. Diary entry for March 31, 1876.
27. *PUSG*, 27:61. Jeremiah Black, Closing Argument, July 24, 1876.
28. *The New York Times*, July 12, 1876.
29. *PUSG*, 27:183. Hamilton Fish diary entry for July 10, 1876.
30. Nevins, *Hamilton Fish*, 2:829.
31. Young, *Around the World*, 288.
32. Webb, *Benjamin Helm Bristow*, 229.
33. Ibid., 238.
34. *PUSG*, 26:131. Letter from Robert T. Kent, April 30, 1875.
35. Morris, *Fraud of the Century*, 113.
36. *PUSG*, 28:265. Letter to Edward F. Beale, September 9, 1877.
37. Ibid., 27:133. Telegram to Gov. Rutherford B. Hayes, June 16, 1876.
38. Ibid. "Speech," June 19, 1876.
39. Ibid., 167. Letter to Rutherford B. Hayes, July 4, 1876.
40. Jordan, *Roscoe Conkling*, 243.
41. Kousser and McPherson, *Region, Race, and Reconstruction*, 434.
42. *New York Tribune*, July 15, 1876.
43. Egerton, *The Wars of Reconstruction*, 312.
44. Morris, *Fraud of the Century*, 73.

45. *PUSG*, 25:35. "To Congress," February 25, 1874.
46. Ibid., 27:108. "Address," May 10, 1876.
47. *New York Tribune*, May 11, 1876.
48. Julia Grant, *Memoirs*, 88.
49. Stiles, *Custer's Trials*, 409.
50. *PUSG*, 26:84. Letter from Secretary of the Interior Columbus Delano, March 17, 1875.
51. Ibid., 139. "Council with Sioux Delegation," June 2, 1875.
52. Ibid., 140.
53. Ibid., 209. Letter from Othniel C. Marsh, July 10, 1875.
54. Ibid., 208. Letter to Othniel C. Marsh, July 16, 1875.
55. Ibid., 203. Letter to Columbus Delano, July 16, 1875.
56. Ibid., 225. Speech by Thomas C. Fletcher, August 10, 1875.
57. Ibid., 226. Response by Red Cloud, August 10, 1875.
58. *The New York Times*, November 2, 1875.
59. *PUSG*, 26:363. Letter from George H. Stuart, December 2, 1875.
60. Ibid.
61. McFeely, *Grant*, 437.
62. *Chicago Inter-Ocean*, April 3, 1880.
63. *PUSG*, 16:202. Letter to Matías Romero, May 16, 1866.
64. Ibid., 15:431. Letter from Cadwallader C. Washburn, October 17, 1865.
65. Stiles, *Custer's Trials*, 297.
66. *New York World*, May 2, 1876.
67. *PUSG*, 27:60. Letter from William W. Belknap to his sister, May 2, 1876.
68. *New York World*, May 2, 1876.
69. Cozzens, *The Earth Is Weeping*, 229.
70. *PUSG*: 27:74. Telegram from Gen. William T. Sherman to Brig. Gen. Alfred Terry, May 8, 1876.
71. Ibid., 170. Letter from Gen. William T. Sherman, July 8, 1876.
72. Morris, *Sheridan*, 363.
73. *New York Herald*, September 2, 1876.
74. Smith, *Grant*, 539.
75. *PUSG*, 27:178. Telegram from Gen. William T. Sherman to Gen. Philip H. Sheridan, July 22, 1876.
76. *New York Herald*, September 12, 1876.
77. Ibid.
78. *PUSG*, 28:64. "Draft Annual Message," December 5, 1876.
79. Ibid., 65.
80. Smith, *Grant*, 541.
81. *The New York Times*, October 4, 2012.
82. *PUSG*, 27:161. Letter from Morris Cohen, June 30, 1876.
83. Sarna, *When General Grant Expelled the Jews*, 123.

CHAPTER THIRTY-NINE: REDEEMERS

1. Lemann, *Redemption*, 199.
2. *Pittsburgh Telegraph*, October 3, 1876.
3. Ibid.
4. Jordan, *Roscoe Conkling*, 244.
5. Kousser and McPherson, *Region, Race, and Reconstruction*, 435.
6. *New York Herald*, September 12, 1876.
7. *PUSG*, 27:321. Letter from Secretary of War James D. Cameron to Gen. William T. Sherman, August 15, 1876.
8. Ibid., 203. Letter from Gov. Daniel H. Chamberlain to Secretary of War James D. Cameron, July 12, 1876.
9. Ibid., 234. Letter from Gov. Daniel H. Chamberlain to Senator Thomas J. Robertson, July 13, 1876.
10. Ibid., 201. Letter from Gov. Daniel H. Chamberlain, July 22, 1876.
11. Ibid., 199. Letter to Daniel H. Chamberlain, July 26, 1876.
12. Ibid., 200.
13. Ibid., 231. "To Senate," July 31, 1876.
14. Ibid., 205. Letter from L. Cass Carpenter, August 19, 1876.
15. Ibid., 206. Letter from David T. Corbin to Alphonso Taft, August 21, 1876.
16. Ibid., 332. Letter from James Majar et al., September 25, 1876.
17. Ibid., 330. Letter from Gov. Daniel H. Chamberlain, October 11, 1876.
18. Ibid., 329. "Proclamation," October 17, 1876.
19. Hesseltine, *Ulysses S. Grant: Politician*, 411.
20. *PUSG*, 28:85. Letter from W. W. Heath, December 15, 1876.
21. Lemann, *Redemption*, 163.
22. *PUSG*, 27:320. Letter from James H. Pierce to Attorney General Alphonso Taft, September 22, 1876.
23. Ibid., 299. Letter from Senator Joseph R. West, October 3, 1866.
24. Lemann, *Redemption*, 177–78.
25. Eaton, *Grant, Lincoln and the Freedmen*, 283.
26. Hesseltine, *Ulysses S. Grant: Politician*, 413.
27. Morris, *Fraud of the Century*, 171.
28. *PUSG*, 28:26. Telegram from Secretary of the Interior Zachariah Chandler, November 9, 1876.
29. Morris, *Fraud of the Century*, 173.
30. *PUSG*, 28:19–20. Telegram to Gen. William T. Sherman, November 10, 1876.
31. Ibid., 24. Hamilton Fish diary entry for November 14, 1876.
32. Ibid.
33. Ibid., 34. Letter from "An Outlaw of the west," November 18, 1876.
34. Ibid., 24. Letter from "United Order of Bush Rangers," November 22, 1876.
35. Ibid., 51. Letter from John C. Winsmith, November 17, 1876.
36. Ibid., 49. Telegram from Gov. Daniel H. Chamberlain, November 25, 1876.

37. Ibid. Letter to James D. Cameron, November 26, 1876.
38. Ibid., 86. Letter from Henry L. Newfville [*sic*], December 18, 1876.
39. Ibid., 56. Hamilton Fish diary entry for November 30, 1876.
40. Ibid., 58. Letter to Col. Thomas H. Ruger, December 3, 1876.
41. *The New York Times,* December 8, 1876.
42. Morris, *Fraud of the Century,* 202.
43. *PUSG,* 28:77. Letter from Senator John Sherman et al., December 6, 1876.
44. Ibid., 114. Letter to Brig. Gen. Christopher C. Augur, January 14, 1877.
45. Ibid., 116. Hamilton Fish diary entry for January 17, 1877.
46. Scaturro, *President Grant Reconsidered,* 112.
47. *PUSG,* 28:149. Hamilton Fish diary entry for January 17, 1877.
48. Jordan, *Roscoe Conkling,* 255.
49. *PUSG,* 28:143. "To Senate," January 29, 1877.
50. Ibid., 158–59. Letter to Edwards Pierrepont, February 11, 1877.
51. Williams, *Diary and Letters of Rutherford Birchard Hayes,* 416. Diary entry for February 17, 1877.
52. Young, *Around the World,* 286.
53. Foner, *Reconstruction,* 579.
54. *The New York Times,* July 21, 1878.
55. Young, *Around the World,* 286.
56. Nevins, *Hamilton Fish,* 2:855.
57. Grant, *In the Days of My Father General Grant,* 205.
58. Webb, *Benjamin Helm Bristow,* 213.
59. *PUSG,* 28:62. "Draft Annual Message," December 5, 1876.
60. Ibid., 63.
61. Ibid., 69.
62. Ibid.
63. Hesseltine, *Ulysses S. Grant: Politician,* 418.
64. *PUSG,* 28:79. "Memorandum," Rep. Abram S. Hewitt, December 3, 1876.
65. Grant, *In the Days of My Father General Grant,* 197.
66. Perret, *Ulysses S. Grant,* 444.
67. "Mrs. U. S. Grant Sinking." *Chicago Sunday Tribune,* December 14, 1902.
68. Greely, *Reminiscences of Adventure and Service,* 233.
69. *New York Herald,* March 3, 1877.
70. McFeely, *Grant,* 449.
71. Badeau, *Grant in Peace,* 259.
72. *New York Herald,* July 24, 1878.
73. Waugh, *U. S. Grant,* 156.
74. Smith, *Grant,* 605.
75. McFeely, *Grant,* 449.
76. *PUSG,* 28:142. Letter to John F. Long, January 28, 1877.
77. *PUSG,* 28:456. Letter from Hamilton Fish, July 12, 1878.
78. Wineapple, *Ecstatic Nation,* 586.
79. Foner, *Reconstruction,* 582.
80. Waugh, *U. S. Grant,* 104.
81. "'This Thankless Office.'" *American History Illustrated,* January 1977.
82. Waugh, *U. S. Grant,* 105.
83. "Overrated and Underrated Americans." *American Heritage,* July–August 1988.
84. *PUSG,* 28:168. Statement by Peter P. Pitchlynn, Choctaw delegate, et al., February 26, 1877.
85. Egerton, *The Wars of Reconstruction,* 348.
86. Young, *Around the World,* 335.
87. Egerton, *The Wars of Reconstruction,* 326.
88. Ibid.
89. *PUSG,* 28:252. Letter to Commodore Daniel Ammen, August 26, 1877.
90. "Overrated and Underrated Americans." *American Heritage,* July–August 1988.
91. GPL. S2 B4 F8. "Frederick Douglass Papers." Speech of October 21, 1890.
92. *PUSG,* 28:168–69. Letter from T. Jefferson Martin, March 12, 1877.

CHAPTER FORTY: THE WANDERER

1. *Cincinnati Enquirer,* March 27, 1877.
2. Ibid., March 28, 1877.
3. *PUSG,* 28:181. Letter to Hamilton Fish, April 1, 1877.
4. Badeau, *Grant in Peace,* 297.
5. *PUSG,* 28:199. Letter to Jesse Root Grant Jr., May 9, 1877.
6. Young, *Around the World,* 5.
7. *PUSG,* 28:203. "Speech," May 17, 1877.
8. Ammen, "Recollections and Letters of Grant, Part 2."
9. Grant, *In the Days of My Father General Grant,* 211.
10. Buinicki, "'Average-Representing Grant': Whitman's General."
11. *PUSG,* 21:11. Letter from John Russell Young, November 5, 1870.
12. Young, *Around the World,* 9.
13. *New York Herald,* July 24, 1878.
14. "Grant Reminiscences." *Chicago Daily Tribune,* September 1, 1885.
15. USGH. "Interview with John Russell Young."
16. *PUSG,* 28:205. "Testimonial," May 26, 1877.
17. Grant, *In the Days of My Father General Grant,* 212.
18. *PUSG,* 28:207. "Speech," May 30, 1877.
19. Young, *Around the World,* 13.
20. Waugh, *U. S. Grant,* 158.
21. *The Times* (London), May 23, 1877.
22. McFeely, *Grant,* 457.
23. Julia Grant, *Memoirs,* 203.
24. *PUSG,* 28:213. William E. Gladstone diary entry for June 5, 1877.
25. *Chicago Inter-Ocean,* June 2, 1883.

26. GPL. S2 B2 F6. Letter from Benjamin Disraeli to Anne Lady Chesterfield, June 22, 1877.

27. *The Times* (London), June 16, 1877.

28. Simon, *General Grant by Matthew Arnold,* 12.

29. Young, *Around the World,* 378.

30. Grant, *In the Days of My Father General Grant,* 227.

31. Badeau, *Grant in Peace,* 282.

32. Julia Grant, *Memoirs,* 207.

33. McFeely, *Grant,* 459.

34. *PUSG,* 28:232. Edward Henry Stanley diary entry for June 26, 1877.

35. Badeau, *Grant in Peace,* 288.

36. Ibid., 179.

37. Young, *Around the World,* 27.

38. Ibid., 246.

39. Grant, *In the Days of My Father General Grant,* 218.

40. *PUSG,* 28:xxvi. "Chronology," August 1877 [n.d.].

41. Ibid., 249. Letter to Ulysses S. Grant Jr., August 25, 1877.

42. Ibid., 253–54. Letter to Abel R. Corbin, August 26, 1877.

43. Ibid., 275. "Speech," September 22, 1877.

44. McFeely, *Grant,* 463.

45. Ibid., 462.

46. *PUSG,* 28:219. Letter to Elihu B. Washburne, June 18, 1877.

47. Young, *Around the World,* 45.

48. Ibid., 249.

49. Grant, *Memoirs,* 2:776.

50. Young, *Around the World,* 374.

51. Julia Grant, *Memoirs,* 217.

52. Ibid., 262.

53. Ibid.

54. *PUSG,* 28:318. Letter to Ulysses S. Grant Jr., November 21, 1877.

55. Campbell, *Citizen of a Wider Commonwealth,* xii.

56. Grant, *In the Days of My Father General Grant,* 257.

57. Young, *Around the World,* 83.

58. *PUSG,* 28:327. Letter from Lt. Commander Albert G. Caldwell to his family, December 20, 1877.

59. Ibid.

60. Perret, *Ulysses S. Grant,* 454.

61. *PUSG,* 28:343. Letter to Frederick Dent Grant, January 25, 1878.

62. *New York Herald,* May 30, 1878.

63. Julia Grant, *Memoirs,* 236.

64. *PUSG,* 28:356. Letter from Lt. Commander Albert G. Caldwell to his mother, March 5, 1878.

65. Ibid., 368. Letter from Lt. Commander Albert G. Caldwell to his mother, March 19, 1878.

66. Grant, *In the Days of My Father General Grant,* 299.

67. Badeau, *Grant in Peace,* 305.

68. *New York Herald,* June 14, 1878.

69. *The Philadelphia Times,* October 20, 1879.

70. Young, *Around the World,* 155.

71. *New York Herald,* July 2, 1878.

72. Young, *Around the World,* 158.

73. Ibid., 160.

74. Cramer, *Ulysses S. Grant,* 15.

75. Julia Grant, *Memoirs,* 252.

76. Ibid., 253.

77. *PUSG,* 28:466. Letter to William W. Smith, September 1, 1878.

78. Ibid., 29:20. Letter to Edward F. Beale, December 6, 1878.

79. McFeely, *Grant,* 468.

80. Smith, *Grant,* 607.

81. McFeely, *Grant,* 468.

82. *PUSG,* 28:361. Letter to Adam Badeau, March 22, 1878.

83. McFeely, *Grant,* 479.

84. *PUSG,* 28:367. Letter to Rear Admiral Daniel Ammen, March 25, 1878.

85. *The New York Times,* December 7, 1878.

86. *PUSG,* 29:15. Letter from Secretary of the Navy Richard W. Thompson, October 23, 1878.

87. Ibid., 14. Letter to Richard W. Thompson, November 14, 1878.

88. Ibid., 65. "Travel Diary," February 20, 1879.

89. Julia Grant, *Memoirs,* 268.

90. Cramer, *Ulysses S. Grant,* 165.

91. McFeely, *Grant,* 472–73.

92. Campbell, *Citizen of a Wider Commonwealth,* 223.

93. Young, *Around the World,* 238.

94. *PUSG,* 29:124. Letter to Elihu B. Washburne, May 4, 1879.

95. Ibid., 125. John Russell Young diary entry for May 6, 1879.

96. Ibid., 84. "Travel Diary," May 23, 1879.

97. Ibid., 86. "Travel Diary," June 4, 1879.

98. Ibid., 152. "Conversation with Prince Kung," June 8, 1879.

99. Ibid., 156.

100. Julia Grant, *Memoirs,* 294.

101. *PUSG,* 29:193. Letter to Adam Badeau, August 1, 1879.

102. Ibid., 183. Letter to Daniel Ammen, July 16, 1879.

103. Ibid., 176. Address from the Tokyo Reception Committee, July 3, 1879.

104. Campbell, *Citizen of a Wider Commonwealth,* 1.

105. Young, *Around the World,* 414.

106. *PUSG,* 29:204. "Conversation with Emperor Meiji," August 10, 1879.

107. *The New York Times,* January 6, 1880.

108. Waugh, *U. S. Grant,* 161.

109. Julia Grant, *Memoirs,* 306.

110. "Grant Reminiscences." *Chicago Daily Tribune,* September 1, 1885.

111. Ibid.

112. Ibid.

113. Ibid.

114. *The Philadelphia Times,* October 20, 1879.

115. *PUSG,* 29:93. Letter from John Russell Young to Thomas Nast, February 6, 1879.

116. *Chicago Daily Tribune,* September 23, 1879.

117. *PUSG,* 29:140. Letter from Adam Badeau to Gen. William T. Sherman, May 16, 1879.

118. Badeau, *Grant in Peace,* 317.
119. Julia Grant, *Memoirs,* 307.
120. *San Francisco Chronicle,* September 21, 1879.
121. Ibid.
122. GPL. S2 B54 F18. "Interview with Amos Webster." HGP.
123. Ibid. S2 B4 F9–11. "Drinking Folders." Letter from Thomas M. Anderson to General Charles King, January 20, 1915.
124. Leitman, "The Revival of an Image."
125. Waugh, *U. S. Grant,* 162.
126. *PUSG,* 29:356. Letter from James M. Comly to President Rutherford B. Hayes, October 27, 1879.
127. Ibid., 248. Letter to Adolph E. Borie, September 28, 1879.
128. Julia Grant, *Memoirs,* 311.
129. Ibid.
130. *Chicago Inter-Ocean,* October 29, 1879.
131. Ibid., October 31, 1879.
132. *Chicago Daily Tribune,* November 2, 1879.
133. *Chicago Inter-Ocean,* November 5, 1879.
134. Ibid., November 4, 1879.
135. Kaplan, *Mr. Clemens and Mark Twain,* 224.
136. GPL. S2 B24 F14. "Interview with Russell Jones." HGP.
137. Gold, "Grant and Twain in Chicago."
138. Ibid.
139. Ibid.
140. Griffin and Smith, *Autobiography of Mark Twain,* 2:181.
141. Kaplan, *Mr. Clemens and Mark Twain,* 225.
142. Griffin and Smith, *Autobiography of Mark Twain,* 2:75.
143. *PUSG,* 29:297. "Speech," November 13, 1879.
144. Ibid., 293. "Speech," November 12, 1879.
145. Griffin and Smith, *Autobiography of Mark Twain,* 2:71.
146. Kaplan, *Mr. Clemens and Mark Twain,* 226.
147. Ibid.
148. Ibid.
149. Ibid., 227.
150. Ibid.
151. Smith, *Autobiography of Mark Twain,* 1:475.
152. Gold, "Grant and Twain in Chicago."
153. *Pittsburgh Commercial Gazette,* December 16, 1879.
154. *PUSG,* 29:341. Letter to Adam Badeau, December 27, 1879.
155. *Louisville Courier-Journal,* December 11, 1879.
156. *PUSG,* 29:314. Letter from President Rutherford B. Hayes to Lucy Webb Hayes, December 27, 1879.
157. Ibid., 340. "Speech," December 26, 1879.
158. *The Philadelphia Press,* December 19, 1879.

CHAPTER FORTY-ONE: MASTER SPIRIT

1. *PUSG,* 28:370. Letter to Abel R. Corbin, March 29, 1878.
2. Young, *Around the World,* 285.
3. *The Times* (London), July 11, 1878.
4. Grant, *In the Days of My Father General Grant,* 208.
5. *The Times* (London), February 27, 1925.
6. *PUSG,* 28:480. Letter from Gen. Philip H. Sheridan to Gen. William T. Sherman, October 29, 1878.
7. Ibid., 480. Letter from Gen. William T. Sherman to Gen. Philip H. Sheridan, October 13, 1878.
8. Ibid., 29:138. Letter from Gen. William T. Sherman, July 17, 1879.
9. Ibid., 139.
10. Ibid., 344. Letter from John Russell Young to Gen. William T. Sherman, February 14, 1880.
11. Ibid., 305. Letter to Adam Badeau, November 21, 1879.
12. GPL. S2 B24 F13. "Interview with Ulysses S. Grant, Jr." HGP.
13. *PUSG,* 29:356. Letter from Elihu B. Washburne to John A. Logan, December 29, 1879.
14. Godkin, "General Grant's Political Education Abroad."
15. *Chicago Inter-Ocean,* January 6, 1880.
16. *PUSG,* 29:347. Letter to Ellen Grant Sartoris, January 18, 1880.
17. Ibid., 364. Letter to George W. Childs, February 26, 1880.
18. *Washington National Republican,* January 23, 1883.
19. *PUSG,* 29:365. Letter to George W. Childs, February 26, 1880.
20. *Chicago Inter-Ocean,* April 3, 1880.
21. "With Grant in Mexico." *The Philadelphia Times,* March 14, 1880.
22. *PUSG,* 29:354. Letter from Elihu B. Washburne, February 11, 1880.
23. Jordan, *Roscoe Conkling,* 322.
24. *PUSG,* 29:371. Letter to Elihu B. Washburne, March 25, 1880.
25. Ibid., 369. "Speech," Galveston, Texas, March 24, 1880.
26. *Galveston News,* March 26, 1880.
27. McFeely, *Grant,* 481.
28. *New Orleans Picayune,* April 6, 1880.
29. *Chicago Inter-Ocean,* February 20, 1880.
30. *The New York Times,* March 29, 1880.
31. *Memphis Appeal,* April 13, 1880.
32. *Mobile Register,* April 22, 1880.
33. *Chicago Inter-Ocean,* April 4, 1880.
34. *PUSG,* 29:380. "Speech," April 12, 1880.
35. Ibid., 388. "Speech," April 16, 1880.
36. Ibid.
37. Egerton, *The Wars of Reconstruction,* 318.
38. Jordan, *Roscoe Conkling,* 326.
39. *PUSG,* 29:411. Letter from John Russell Young to John Hay, June 4, 1880.
40. Badeau, *Grant in Peace,* 319.
41. Ibid., 320.
42. Leitman, "The Revival of an Image."
43. GPL. S2 B5 F26. Letter from Edmund Smith to Mr. Chandler, April 29, 1880.
44. *Troy Intelligencer,* April 17, 1892.

45. *PUSG,* 23:4. Letter to James E. McLean, February 4, 1872.
46. *New York Sun,* September 5, 1878.
47. Ibid.
48. "Mr. Orville [*sic*] D. Grant Insane." *The New York Times,* September 5, 1878.
49. Ibid.
50. *PUSG,* 29:29. Letter to Michael John Cramer, December 10, 1878.
51. *The New York Times,* January 28, 1879.
52. GPL. S2 B5 F26. Letter from Edmund Smith to Mr. Chandler, April 29, 1880.
53. *PUSG,* 29:374. Letter from Elihu B. Washburne to Senator John A. Logan, April 30, 1880.
54. Jordan, *Roscoe Conkling,* 329.
55. Julia Grant, *Memoirs,* 321.
56. Ibid.
57. Jordan, *Roscoe Conkling,* 332.
58. Ibid., 331.
59. Ibid., 333–34.
60. Ibid., 334.
61. Ibid., 335.
62. Ibid.
63. Ibid., 336.
64. Millard, *Destiny of the Republic,* 38.
65. Young, *Around the World,* 288.
66. *Chicago Inter-Ocean,* June 15, 1881.
67. *PUSG,* 29:373. Letter from Treasury Secretary John Sherman to William H. Smith, April 19, 1880.
68. *Chicago Inter-Ocean,* May 6, 1880.
69. Smith, *Grant,* 617.
70. Ross, *The General's Wife,* 276.
71. *PUSG,* 29:416. Letter to Roscoe Conkling, June 10, 1880.
72. GPL. S2 B24 F13. "Interview with Ulysses S. Grant, Jr." HGP.
73. USGH. "Interview with Augustus Chetlain."
74. GPL. S2 B5 F19. William H. Wilson diary entry for July 5, 1880.
75. Pryor, *My Day,* 375.
76. Williams, *Diary and Letters of Rutherford Birchard Hayes,* 3:600. Diary entry for June 5, 1880.
77. *Milwaukee Sentinel,* June 10, 1880.
78. *Chicago Inter-Ocean,* October 6, 1880.
79. Millard, *Destiny of the Republic,* 59.
80. *Leavenworth Times,* July 4, 1860.
81. *PUSG,* 29:445. Letter to Adam Badeau, August 12, 1880.
82. *Denver Tribune,* July 18, 1880.
83. *PUSG,* 29:441. Letter from James A. Garfield, July 26, 1880.
84. Julia Grant, *Memoirs,* 322.
85. *Cincinnati Gazette,* October 5, 1880.
86. Smith, *Autobiography of Mark Twain,* 1:75.
87. Ibid.
88. Ibid., 483.
89. *PUSG,* 30:14. "Speech," October 20, 1880.
90. *New York Tribune,* October 22, 1880.
91. Ibid., October 24, 1880.
92. *PUSG,* 30:15. "Speech," October 21, 1880.
93. *New York Herald,* October 27, 1880.
94. *PUSG,* 30:63. Letter to Ellen Grant Sartoris, November 4, 1880.
95. *New York Tribune,* November 4, 1880.

CHAPTER FORTY-TWO: A MISERABLE DIRTY REPTILE

1. *PUSG,* 30:75. Letter to James A. Garfield, November 11, 1880.
2. Ibid., 127. Letter to James A. Garfield, January 26, 1881.
3. Ibid., 209. Letter to Senator John P. Jones, April 24, 1881.
4. Ibid., 204. Letter to James A. Garfield, April 24, 1881.
5. Ibid., 215. Letter to Adam Badeau, May 7, 1881.
6. Ibid., 205. Letter from President James A. Garfield, May 15, 1881.
7. Ibid., 206.
8. *Pittsburg Times,* June 16, 1881.
9. *New York Evening Post,* June 13, 1881.
10. Millard, *Destiny of the Republic,* 144.
11. Ibid.
12. LoC. LRGP. Letter to Julia Dent Grant, July 26, 1885.
13. *PUSG,* 30:249. Telegram to Secretary of War Robert T. Lincoln, July 2, 1881.
14. Ibid.
15. *New York World,* July 5, 1881.
16. Ibid.
17. Ibid.
18. *PUSG,* 30:248. Letter to Adam Badeau, July 27, 1881.
19. Ibid.
20. *Chicago Inter-Ocean,* September 7, 1881.
21. *The New York Times,* September 20, 1881.
22. Ibid.
23. *New York World,* July 5, 1881.
24. Badeau, *Grant in Peace,* 337.
25. Julia Grant, *Memoirs,* 322.
26. *The Two Republics,* April 24, 1881.
27. *Chicago Morning News,* June 13, 1881.
28. *PUSG,* 30:63. Letter to Ellen Grant Sartoris, November 4, 1880.
29. Julia Grant, *Memoirs,* 323.
30. Ibid.
31. *PUSG,* 30:282. Letter to William R. Rowley, October 30, 1881.
32. Julia Grant, *Memoirs,* 324.
33. *PUSG,* 30:130. Letter to Elizabeth King, January 27, 1881.
34. Ibid., 464. *Congressional Record,* 47-1, 1289.
35. Ward, *A Disposition to Be Rich,* 152.
36. *Pittsburg Times,* June 17, 1881.
37. Ward, *A Disposition to Be Rich,* 196.
38. Ibid., 143–44.
39. Ward, "General Grant as I Knew Him."
40. Ibid.
41. Ibid.
42. Ibid.

43. Griffin and Smith, *Autobiography of Mark Twain*, 2:67.
44. *PUSG*, 31:153. "Memorandum," May 1884 [n.d.].
45. Ward, *A Disposition to Be Rich*, 193.
46. Ibid.
47. *The New York Times*, April 9, 1885.
48. Ward, *A Disposition to Be Rich*, 163.
49. Ibid., 194.
50. Ibid., 201.
51. Griffin and Smith, *Autobiography of Mark Twain*, 2:66.
52. Vincent, "The Inner Life of Ulysses S. Grant."
53. *PUSG*, 31:67. Letter to Ellen Grant Sartoris, October 2, 1883.
54. *Burlington Free Press*, July 29, 1885.
55. Badeau, *Grant in Peace*, 418.
56. *St. Louis Post-Dispatch*, May 7, 1884.
57. "Stories of Grant." *Chicago Daily Tribune*, April 12, 1885.
58. Ward, *A Disposition to Be Rich*, 211.
59. Fry, "An Acquaintance with Grant."
60. *PUSG*, 31:139. Letter from Ferdinand Ward to Ulysses Grant Jr., May 5, 1884.
61. Ward, *A Disposition to Be Rich*, 217.
62. Badeau, *Grant in Peace*, 419.
63. Ibid.
64. *The New York Times*, May 9, 1884.

CHAPTER FORTY-THREE: TAPS

1. *The St. Louis Globe-Democrat*, April 3, 1877.
2. *PUSG*, 31:100. Letter to Adam Badeau, January 21, 1884.
3. *Kentucky Stock Farm*, October 8, 1885.
4. Julia Grant, *Memoirs*, 329.
5. Flood, *Grant's Final Victory*, 57.
6. Ibid., 57–58.
7. Ibid., 58.
8. Ibid., 60.
9. Waugh, *U. S. Grant*, 171.
10. Perry, *Grant and Twain*, 63.
11. *PUSG*, 31:205. Letter from Roswell Smith to Richard Watson Gilder, September 9, 1884.
12. Perry, *Grant and Twain*, 65.
13. Badeau, "The Last Days of General Grant."
14. Perry, *Grant and Twain*, 69.
15. Flood, *Grant's Final Victory*, 110.
16. Julia Grant, *Memoirs*, 189.
17. *The Philadelphia Press*, July 29, 1884.
18. *PUSG*, 31:211. Letter to Cornelius B. V. Ward, October 4, 1884.
19. Perret, *Ulysses S. Grant*, 471.
20. Perry, *Grant and Twain*, 71.
21. Badeau, "The Last Days of General Grant."
22. Perry, *Grant and Twain*, 81, 121.
23. Badeau, *Grant in Peace*, 428.
24. Ross, *The General's Wife*, 293.
25. Perry, *Grant and Twain*, 80.
26. Waugh, *U. S. Grant*, 175.
27. Kaplan, *Mr. Clemens and Mark Twain*, 258.
28. Paine, *Mark Twain's Notebook*, 175.
29. Kaplan, *Mr. Clemens and Mark Twain*, 261.

65. Flood, *Grant's Final Victory*, 20.
66. Ibid., 35.
67. *New York Graphic*, May 6, 1884.
68. *PUSG*, 31:332. "Deposition," March 26, 1885.
69. Fry, "An Acquaintance with Grant."
70. Flood, *Grant's Final Victory*, 35.
71. Ibid., 37.
72. Ward, *A Disposition to Be Rich*, 222.
73. *The New York Times*, October 28, 1885.
74. Ward, *A Disposition to Be Rich*, 235.
75. Julia Grant, *Memoirs*, 327.
76. Ward, *A Disposition to Be Rich*, 234.
77. *PUSG*, 31:146–47. Letter from Charles Wood, May 10, 1884.
78. Cantacuzène, *Revolutionary Days*, 11.
79. *The Washington Post*, July 19, 1886.
80. *New York Herald*, May 10, 1884.
81. *The Washington Post*, May 24, 1884.
82. Ward, *A Disposition to Be Rich*, 235.
83. *New York Evening Post*, May 6, 1884.
84. *PUSG*, 31:142. Letter from William T. Sherman to Senator John Sherman, May 7, 1884.
85. *The Washington Post*, December 30, 1884.
86. *The New York Times*, May 15, 1884.
87. Ward, *A Disposition to Be Rich*, 231.
88. Ibid.
89. Ward, "General Grant as I Knew Him."

30. Smith, *Autobiography of Mark Twain*, 1:78.
31. Ibid.
32. Ibid.
33. Griffin and Smith, *Autobiography of Mark Twain*, 2:61.
34. Ibid., 61–62.
35. Ibid., 63.
36. *PUSG*, 31:237. Letter to George W. Childs, November 23, 1884.
37. Julia Grant, *Memoirs*, 329.
38. *PUSG*, 31:294. Letter from Julia Dent Grant to Anna R. Hillyer, February 28, 1885.
39. Cantacuzène, *Revolutionary Days*, 18.
40. Kaplan, *Mr. Clemens and Mark Twain*, 271.
41. Paine, *Mark Twain's Notebook*, 174.
42. Perry, *Grant and Twain*, 119.
43. Kaplan, *Mr. Clemens and Mark Twain*, 272.
44. *The New York Times*, March 1, 1885.
45. Ibid.
46. *PUSG*, 31:364. Letter from George M. Arnold to Frederick Dent Grant, March 17, 1885.
47. Badeau, *Grant in Peace*, 437.
48. *PUSG*, 30:136. Letter from Gen. William T. Sherman to Senator John A. Logan, February 5, 1881.
49. Ibid. Letter to John A. Logan, February 9, 1881.
50. Flood, *Grant's Final Victory*, 135.
51. GPL. S2 B12 F22. "Mark Twain." Telegram from Mark Twain to his wife, March 14, 1885.
52. Griffin and Smith, *Autobiography of Mark Twain*, 2:70.

53. Flood, *Grant's Last Victory,* 136; Ross, *The General's Wife,* 294.
54. *PUSG,* 31:321. Letter to Attorney General Richard C. Drum, March 4, 1885.
55. *New York Tribune,* March 20, 1885.
56. Perry, *Grant and Twain,* 162.
57. Flood, *Grant's Final Victory,* 143.
58. *The New York Times,* March 27, 1885.
59. Ibid., March 30, 1885.
60. Perry, *Grant and Twain,* 170.
61. Ibid., 172.
62. Shrady, "The Last Days of Our Great General."
63. Ibid.
64. Ibid.
65. Ibid.
66. Ibid.
67. *New York Tribune,* April 8, 1885.
68. Ibid., April 7, 1885.
69. *PUSG,* 31:337. Letter from Frederick T. Dent to Capt. Lafayette E. Campbell, April 15, 1885.
70. GPL. S2 B24 F13. "Interview with Ulysses S. Grant, Jr." HGP.
71. Smith, *Autobiography of Mark Twain,* 1:99.
72. Flood, *Grant's Final Victory,* 142.
73. Perry, *Grant and Twain,* 183.
74. GPL. S2 B12 F22. "Mark Twain." Letter from Samuel Clemens to Henry Ward Beecher, September 11, 1885.
75. Ibid.
76. Ward, *A Disposition to Be Rich,* 240.
77. McFeely, *Grant,* 497.
78. *PUSG,* 31:280. Letter from William B. Moore to Frederick Dent Grant, March 27, 1888.
79. *New York World,* April 29, 1885.
80. Kaplan, *Mr. Clemens and Mark Twain,* 273.
81. *PUSG,* 31:358. Letter from Adam Badeau, May 2, 1885.
82. Ibid.
83. Ibid., 359. Endorsement by Frederick Dent Grant of Adam Badeau's letter of May 2, 1885.
84. Ibid., 286. Letter from Julia Dent Grant to Clarence A. Seward, May 23, 1888.
85. Ibid., 354. Letter to Adam Badeau, May 2–5, 1885.
86. Ibid., 355–56.
87. Ibid., 359. Letter from Adam Badeau, May 9, 1885.
88. *New York Sun,* March 21, 1888.
89. *PUSG,* 31:430–31. Letter to Adam Badeau, July 12, 1885.
90. GPL. S2 B12 F22. "Mark Twain." Letter from Samuel Clemens to Henry Ward Beecher, September 11, 1885.
91. *PUSG,* 31:52. Letter to Roland Worthington, July 3, 1883.
92. *New York Sun,* May 3, 1903.
93. Ibid.
94. Carnegie, *Autobiography,* 79.
95. GPL. S2 B12 F22. "Mark Twain." Letter from Samuel Clemens to Henry Ward Beecher, September 11, 1885.
96. Ibid.
97. Simon, *General Grant by Matthew Arnold,* 57.
98. *New York Tribune,* May 1, 1885.
99. Griffin and Smith, *Autobiography of Mark Twain,* 2:71.
100. Kaplan, *Mr. Clemens and Mark Twain,* 274.
101. *PUSG,* 31:410.
102. Ibid. Letter to Frederick Dent Grant, July 6, 1885.
103. Ibid., 363–64. "Message," May 14, 1885.
104. Perry, *Grant and Twain,* 208.
105. *New York Tribune,* June 14, 1885.
106. Ibid., June 15, 1885.
107. Flood, *Grant's Final Victory,* 188.
108. Ibid., 191.
109. *PUSG,* 31:391. Letter to Samuel Clemens, probably June 29–30, 1885.
110. Julia Grant, *Memoirs,* 331.
111. USGH. "Interview with Dr. George F. Shrady."
112. Flood, *Grant's Final Victory,* 204.
113. *PUSG,* 31:441. Letter to John H. Douglas, circa July 1885 [n.d.].
114. Grant, "General Grant's Son Speaks of His Father."
115. *PUSG,* 31:375. Letter to John H. Douglas, June 17, 1885.
116. Ibid., 377. Letter to John P. Newman, circa June 20, 1885.
117. Ibid., 400. Letter to John H. Douglas, July 1, 1885.
118. Ibid., 387. Letter to Julia Dent Grant, June 29, 1885.
119. Ibid., 388.
120. Ibid., 414–15. Letter to John H. Douglas, July 8, 1885.
121. Perry, *Grant and Twain,* 221.
122. Smith, *Autobiography of Mark Twain,* 1:83.
123. Ibid., 82.
124. Procter, "A Blue and Gray Friendship."
125. Ibid.
126. Webb, *Benjamin Helm Bristow,* 294.
127. Ibid., 295.
128. Eaton, *Grant, Lincoln and the Freedmen,* 296–97.
129. *PUSG,* 31:410. Letter to Frederick Dent Grant, circa late June/early July 1885.
130. Ibid., 437. Letter to John H. Douglas, July 16, 1885.
131. Grant, *Memoirs,* 1:5.
132. Paine, *Mark Twain's Notebook,* 183.
133. Kazin, "The Generals in the Labyrinth."
134. Simon, *General Grant by Matthew Arnold,* 13.
135. Kaplan, *Mr. Clemens and Mark Twain,* 274.
136. Catton, "U. S. Grant: Man of Letters."
137. *New York World,* June 27, 1885.
138. *PUSG,* 31:440. John P. Newman journal entry for July 21, 1885.
139. Cantacuzène, *Revolutionary Days,* 20.
140. *PUSG,* 31:441. John P. Newman journal entry for July 22, 1885.
141. Vincent, "The Inner Life of Ulysses S. Grant."
142. *PUSG,* 1:121. Letter to Mrs. Thomas L. Hamer, December 1846 [n.d.].
143. Flood, *Grant's Final Victory,* 232.

144. Waugh, *U. S. Grant*, 199.
145. GMA. GFP. Box 1. Letter from Mayor W. R. Grace to Julia Dent Grant, July 23, 1885.
146. Buinicki, "'Average-Representing Grant': Whitman's General."
147. *USGA Newsletter*, April 1964.
148. Waugh, *U. S. Grant*, 241.
149. Sarna, *When General Grant Expelled the Jews*, 135.
150. Waugh, *U. S. Grant*, 252.
151. USGH. "Interview with John Singleton Mosby."
152. "Longstreet's Reminiscences." *The New York Times*, July 24, 1885.
153. Achenbach, "U.S. Grant Was the Great Hero of the Civil War but Lost Favor with Historians."
154. Ross, *The General's Wife*, 313.
155. Ward. "General Grant as I Knew Him."
156. "Chat in Public Resorts." *New York Tribune*, August 2, 1885.
157. Paine, *Mark Twain's Notebook*, 185.
158. GPL. S2 B12 F22. "Mark Twain." Letter from Samuel Clemens to Henry Ward Beecher, September 11, 1885.
159. Ibid.

BIBLIOGRAPHY

BOOKS

Adams, Henry. *The Education of Henry Adams.* New York: Library of America Paperback Classics, 1983.

Ambrose, Stephen E. *Halleck: Lincoln's Chief of Staff.* Baton Rouge: Louisiana State University Press, 1962.

Armstrong, William H. *Warrior in Two Camps: Ely S. Parker, Union General and Seneca Chief.* Syracuse, N.Y.: Syracuse University Press, 1978.

Arnold, Matthew. *General Grant by Matthew Arnold with a Rejoinder by Mark Twain.* Edited by John Y. Simon. Carbondale: Southern Illinois University Press, 1966.

Badeau, Adam. *Grant in Peace: From Appomattox to Mount McGregor.* Hartford, Conn.: S. S. Scranton, 1887.

———. *Military History of Ulysses S. Grant.* Bedford, Mass.: Applewood Books, 1881. Reprint, n.d.

Ballard, Michael B. *Grant at Vicksburg: The General and the Siege.* Carbondale: Southern Illinois University Press, 2013.

Berg, A. Scott. *Wilson.* New York: G. P. Putnam's Sons, 2013.

Berkin, Carol. *Civil War Wives: The Lives and Times of Angelina Grimké Weld, Varina Howell Davis, and Julia Dent Grant.* New York: Alfred A. Knopf, 2009.

Berner, Bertha. *Mrs. Leland Stanford: An Intimate Account.* Stanford, Calif.: Stanford University Press, 1935.

Blair, Henry William. *The Temperance Movement; or, The Conflict Between Man and Alcohol.* Boston: William E. Smythe, 1888.

Borchgrave, Alexandra Villard de, and John Cullen. *Villard: The Life and Times of an American Titan.* New York: Doubleday, 2001.

Boutwell, George S. *Reminiscences of Sixty Years in Public Affairs.* 2 vols. New York: Greenwood Press, 1968. Reprint.

Brands, H. W. *The Man Who Saved the Union: Ulysses Grant in War and Peace.* New York: Doubleday, 2012.

Brooks, Noah. *Lincoln Observed: Civil War Dispatches of Noah Brooks.* Edited by Michael Burlingame. Baltimore: Johns Hopkins University Press, 1998.

Browning, Orville Hickman. *The Diary of Orville Hickman Browning.* Vol. 2, *1865–1881.* Edited by James G. Randall. Springfield: Illinois State Historical Library, 1933.

Bunting, Josiah, III. *Ulysses S. Grant.* New York: Times Books/Henry Holt, 2004.

Cadwallader, Sylvanus. *Three Years with Grant: As Recalled by War Correspondent Sylvanus Cadwallader.* Lincoln: University of Nebraska Press, 1996. Reprint.

Campbell, Edwina S. *Citizen of a Wider Commonwealth: Ulysses S. Grant's Postpresidential Diplomacy.* Carbondale: Southern Illinois University Press, 2016.

Campi, James, Jr. *Civil War Battlefields Then and Now.* San Diego: Thunder Bay Press, 2012.

Cantacuzène, Princess Julia. *Revolutionary Days: Including Passages from My Life Here and There, 1876–1917.* Chicago: R. R. Donnelley & Sons, 1999.

Carnegie, Andrew. *The Autobiography of Andrew Carnegie and His Essay "The Gospel of Wealth."* Mineola, N.Y.: Dover, 2014. Reprint.

Catton, Bruce. *The Coming Fury.* Vol. 1 of *The Centennial History of the Civil War.* Garden City, N.Y.: Doubleday, 1961.

———. *Terrible Swift Sword.* Vol. 2 of *The Centennial History of the Civil War.* Garden City, N.Y.: Doubleday, 1963.

———. *Never Call Retreat.* Vol. 3 of *The Centennial History of the Civil War.* Garden City, N.Y.: Doubleday, 1965.

———. *Grant Moves South.* New York: Back Bay Books/Little, Brown, 1988.

———. *Grant Takes Command.* Boston: Back Bay Books/Little, Brown, 1969. Reprint.

Chamberlain, Joshua Lawrence. *The Passing of the Armies.* New York: Barnes & Noble, 2004. Reprint.

Chase, Salmon P. *The Salmon P. Chase Papers.* Vol. 1, *Journals, 1829–1872.* Edited by John Niven. Kent, Ohio: Kent State University Press, 1993.

Chesnut, Mary. *Mary Chesnut's Civil War.* Edited by C. Vann Woodward. New Haven, Conn., and London: Yale University Press, 1981. Reprint.

Clews, Henry. *Fifty Years in Wall Street.* Hoboken, N.J.: John Wiley & Sons, 2006. Reprint.

Colman, Edna M. *White House Gossip: From Andrew Johnson to Calvin Coolidge.* Garden City, N.Y.: Doubleday Page, 1927.

Comstock, Cyrus B. *The Diary of Cyrus B. Comstock.* Edited by Merlin E. Summer. Dayton, Ohio: Morningside House, 1987.

Corum, G. L. *Ulysses Underground: The Unexplored Roots of U. S. Grant and the Underground Railroad.* West Union, Ohio: Riveting History, 2015.

Cozzens, Peter. *The Earth Is Weeping: The Epic Story of the Indian Wars for the American West.* New York: Alfred A. Knopf, 2016.

Cramer, M. J. *Ulysses S. Grant: Conversations and Unpublished Letters.* New York: Eaton & Mains, 1897.

Dana, Charles A. *Recollections of the Civil War.* New York: D. Appleton, 1898.

Dietz, Ulysses Grant, and Sam Watters. *Dream House: The White House as an American Home.* New York: Acanthus Press, 2009.

Donald, David Herbert. *Lincoln.* New York: Simon & Schuster, 1995. Reprint.

Downs, Gregory P. *After Appomattox: Military Occupation and the Ends of War.* Cambridge, Mass.: Harvard University Press, 2015.

Duncan, Bingham. *Whitelaw Reid: Journalist, Politician, Diplomat.* Athens: University of Georgia Press, 1975.

Eaton, John. *Grant, Lincoln and the Freedmen: Reminiscences of the Civil War.* New York: Negro Universities Press, 1969. Reprint.

Egerton, Douglas R. *The Wars of Reconstruction: The Brief, Violent History of America's Most Progressive Era.* New York: Bloomsbury Press, 2014.

Ellington, Charles G. *The Trial of U. S. Grant: The Pacific Coast Years, 1852–1854.* Glendale, Calif.: Arthur H. Clark, 1987.

Farmer, Lydia Hoyt. *The National Exposition Souvenir: What America Owes to Women.* Buffalo, N.Y.: Charles Wells Moulton, 1893.

Faust, Drew Gilpin. *This Republic of Suffering: Death and the American Civil War.* New York: Alfred A. Knopf, 2012.

Ferrier, Alexander Murray. "Memoir." Unpublished typescript written 1879. Courtesy of Mercer Warriner.

Flood, Charles Bracelen. *Grant's Final Victory: Ulysses S. Grant's Heroic Last Year.* Cambridge, Mass.: Da Capo Press, 2011.

Foner, Eric. *The Fiery Trial: Abraham Lincoln and American Slavery.* New York: W. W. Norton, 2010.

———. *Reconstruction: America's Unfinished Revolution, 1863–1877.* New York: Harper & Row, 1989. Reprint.

Foner, Philip S. *The Life and Writings of Frederick Douglass.* Vol. 4, *Reconstruction and After.* New York: International Publishers, 1955.

Foote, Shelby. *The Civil War: A Narrative.* Vol. 1, *Fort Sumter to Perryville.* New York: Vintage Books, 1986. Reprint.

———. *The Civil War: A Narrative.* Vol. 2, *Fredericksburg to Meridian.* New York: Vintage Books, 1986. Reprint.

———. *The Civil War: A Narrative.* Vol. 3, *Red River to Appomattox.* New York: Vintage Books, 1986. Reprint.

Foreman, Amanda. *A World on Fire: Britain's Crucial Role in the American Civil War.* New York: Random House, 2010.

Fowler, Charles Henry. *Patriotic Orations.* New York: Eaton & Mains, 1910.

Friedman, Leon, and Fred L. Israel, eds. *The Justices of the United States Supreme Court, 1789–1969.* New York: R. R. Bowker, 1969.

Fuller, Major General J. F. C. *Grant & Lee: A Study in Personality and Generalship.* Bloomington: Indiana University Press, 1957.

Gillette, William. *Retreat from Reconstruction, 1869–1879.* Baton Rouge: Louisiana State University Press, 1982. Reprint.

Girardi, Robert. *The Civil War Generals: Comrades, Peers, Rivals in Their Own Words.* Minneapolis: Zenith Press, 2013.

Goodheart, Adam. *1861: The Civil War Awakening.* New York: Alfred A. Knopf, 2011.

Goodwin, Doris Kearns. *The Bully Pulpit: Theodore Roosevelt, William Howard Taft, and the Golden Age of Journalism.* New York: Simon & Schuster, 2013.

———. *Team of Rivals: The Political Genius of Abraham Lincoln.* New York: Simon & Schuster, 2006. Reprint.

Gordon, Ann D., ed. *The Selected Papers of Elizabeth Cady Stanton and Susan B. Anthony.* Vol. 2, *Against an Aristocracy of Sex, 1866 to 1873.* New Brunswick, N.J.: Rutgers University Press, 2000.

Gordon-Reed, Annette. *Andrew Johnson.* New York: Times Books/Henry Holt, 2011.

Grant, Arthur Hastings, ed. *Report of the First Reunion of the Grant Family Association at Windsor and Hartford, Conn. on October 27, 1899.* Poughkeepsie, N.Y.: Press of A. V. Haight, 1899.

Grant, Jesse R. *In the Days of My Father General Grant.* New York: Harper & Brothers, 1925.

Grant, Julia Dent. *The Personal Memoirs of Julia Dent Grant.* Edited by John Y. Simon. Carbondale: Southern Illinois University Press, 1975. Reprint.

Grant, Ulysses S. *The Best Writings of Ulysses S. Grant.* Edited by John F. Marszalek. Carbondale: Southern Illinois University Press, 2015.

———. *Memoirs and Selected Letters.* New York: Library of America, 1990.

———. *Ulysses S. Grant: Essays and Documents.* Edited by David L. Wilson and John Y. Simon. Carbondale: Southern Illinois University Press, 1981.

Greely, Major-General A. W. *Reminiscences of Adventure and Service: A Record of Sixty-Five Years.* New York: Charles Scribner's Sons, 1927.

Greenberg, Amy S. *A Wicked War: Polk, Clay, Lincoln, and the 1846 U.S. Invasion of Mexico.* New York: Alfred A. Knopf, 2012.

Hamilton, Lois Neal. *Amos T. Akerman and His Role in American Politics.* Master's thesis for the Faculty of Political Science, Columbia University, May 9, 1939. Copy at Grant Presidential Library.

Haskell, William G. *Memorial Sermon on the Life and Death of Gen. John Aaron Rawlins.* Danbury, Conn.: Times Job Printing Establishment, 1869.

Hayes, Rutherford Birchard. *Diary and Letters of Rutherford Birchard Hayes.* Vol. 3, *1865–1881.* Edited by Charles Richard Williams. Columbus: Ohio State Archæological and Historical Society, 1924.

Hesseltine, William B. *Ulysses S. Grant: Politician.* New York: Frederick Ungar, 1957. Reprint.

Hoar, George F. *Autobiography of Seventy Years.* Vol. 1. New York: Charles Scribner's Sons, 1906.

Holloway, Laura C. *The Ladies of the White House; or, In the House of the Presidents.* Cincinnati: Forshee McMakin, 1881.

Holmes, Oliver Wendell, Jr. *Touched with Fire: Civil War Letters and Diary of Oliver Wendell Holmes, Jr., 1861–1864.* New York: Fordham University Press, 2000.

Holzer, Harold. *The Civil War in 50 Objects.* With the New-York Historical Society. New York: Viking, 2013.

———. *Lincoln and the Power of the Press: The War for Public Opinion.* New York: Simon & Schuster, 2014.

———, ed. *The Lincoln Assassination: Crime and Punishment, Myth and Memory.* Edited with Craig L. Symonds and Frank J. Williams. New York: Fordham University Press, 2010.

———, ed. *Lincoln on War.* Chapel Hill, N.C.: Algonquin Books, 2011.

Hope, Ian Clarence. *A Scientific Way of War: Antebellum Military Science, West Point, and the Origins of American Military Thought.* Lincoln: University of Nebraska Press, 2015.

Jones, James Pickett. *John A. Logan: Stalwart Republican from Illinois.* Tallahassee: Florida State University/University Presses of Florida, 1982.

Jones, John B. *A Rebel War Clerk's Diary at the Confederate States Capital.* 2 vols. N.p.: Civil War Classic Library [n.d.]. Reprint.

Jordan, David M. *Roscoe Conkling of New York: Voice in the Senate.* Ithaca, N.Y.: Cornell University Press, 1971.

Kaplan, Justin. *Mr. Clemens and Mark Twain: A Biography.* New York: Simon & Schuster Paperbacks, 1966. Reprint.

Kauffman, Michael W. *American Brutus: John Wilkes Booth and the Lincoln Conspiracies.* New York: Random House, 2005. Reprint.

Keegan, John. *The American Civil War.* New York: Alfred A. Knopf, 2009.

Kennedy, John F. *Profiles in Courage.* New York: Harper Perennial Modern Classics, 2006. Reprint.

Klein, Maury. *The Life and Legend of Jay Gould.* Baltimore: Johns Hopkins University Press, 1986.

Korda, Michael. *Clouds of Glory: The Life and Legend of Robert E. Lee.* New York: HarperCollins, 2014.

———. *Ulysses S. Grant: The Unlikely Hero.* New York: Harper Perennial, 2009. Reprint.

Kousser, J. Morgan, and James M. McPherson, eds. *Region, Race, and Reconstruction: Essays in Honor of C. Vann Woodward.* New York: Oxford University Press, 1982.

Lemann, Nicholas. *Redemption: The Last Battle of the Civil War.* New York: Farrar, Straus and Giroux, 2006.

Life and Services of General U.S. Grant, Conqueror of the Rebellion and Eighteenth President of the United States. Washington, D.C.: Philp & Solomons, 1868.

Light, F. W. *A Short History of Warsash.* Southampton, U.K.: Warsash Nautical Bookshop, 1992. Reprint.

Long, A. L. *Memoirs of Robert E. Lee: His Military and Personal History.* Edited by Marcus J. Wright. Secaucus, N.J.: Blue and Grey Press, 1983.

Longacre, Edward G. *Army of Amateurs: General Benjamin F. Butler and the Army of the James, 1863–1865.* Mechanicsburg, Pa.: Stackpole Books, 1997.

Longstreet, James. *From Manassas to Appomattox: Memoirs of the Civil War in America.* New York: Barnes & Noble, 2004. Reprint.

McClellan, George B. *The Civil War Papers of George B. McClellan: Selected Correspondence, 1860–1865.* Edited by Stephen W. Sears. N.p.: Da Capo Press, 1992. Reprint.

McCullough, David. *The Greater Journey: Americans in Paris.* New York: Simon & Schuster Paperbacks, 2011. Reprint.

McFeely, William S. *Frederick Douglass.* New York: W. W. Norton, 1991. Reprint.

———. *Grant: A Biography.* New York: W. W. Norton, 1981.

McKitrick, Eric L. *Andrew Johnson and Reconstruction.* Chicago: University of Chicago Press, 1960.

McPherson, James M. *Battle Cry of Freedom: The Civil War Era.* New York: Oxford University Press, 2003. Reprint.

———. *Tried by War: Abraham Lincoln as Commander in Chief.* New York: Penguin Books, 2009. Reprint.

———. *War on the Waters: The Union and Confederate Navies, 1861–1865.* Chapel Hill: University of North Carolina Press, 2012.

Marszalek, John F. *Commander of All Lincoln's Armies: A Life of General Henry W. Halleck.* Cambridge, Mass.: Belknap Press of Harvard University Press, 2004.

———. *Sherman: A Soldier's Passion for Order.* New York: Free Press, 1993.

———. *Sherman's Other War: The General and the Civil War Press.* Kent, Ohio: Kent State University Press, 1999. Reprint.

Mayer, Henry. *All on Fire: William Lloyd Garrison and the Abolition of Slavery.* New York: W. W. Norton, 1998. Reprint.

Millard, Candice. *Destiny of the Republic: A Tale of Madness, Medicine, and the Murder of a President.* New York: Doubleday, 2011.

Morris, Roy, Jr. *Fraud of the Century: Rutherford B. Hayes, Samuel Tilden, and the Stolen Election of 1876.* New York: Simon & Schuster, 2004. Reprint.

———. *Sheridan: The Life and Wars of General Phil Sheridan.* New York: Crown, 1992.

Mosby, John Singleton. *The Memoirs of Colonel John S. Mosby.* Boston: Little, Brown, 1917.

Moskin, J. Robert. *American Statecraft: The Story of the U.S. Foreign Service.* New York: Thomas Dunne Books/St. Martin's Press, 2013.

Motley, John Lothrop. *The Correspondence of John Lothrop Motley.* Vol. 2. Edited by George William Curtis. London: John Murray, 1889.

Nevins, Allan. *Hamilton Fish: The Inner History of the Grant Administration.* 2 vols. New York: Frederick Ungar, 1957.

Nicolay, John G. *With Lincoln in the White House: Letters, Memoranda, and Other Writings of John G. Nicolay, 1860–1865.* Edited by Michael Burlingame. Carbondale: Southern Illinois University Press, 2000.

Niven, John. *Gideon Welles: Lincoln's Secretary of the Navy.* New York: Oxford University Press, 1973.

Okrent, Daniel. *Last Call: The Rise and Fall of Prohibition.* New York: Scribner, 2010.

Olmsted, Frederick Law. *The Papers of Frederick Law Olmsted.* Vol. 5, *The California Frontier, 1863–1865.* Edited by Victoria Post Ranney. Baltimore: Johns Hopkins University Press, 1990.

Parker, Arthur C. *The Life of General Ely S. Parker: Last Grand Sachem of the Iroquois and General Grant's Military Secretary.* Lynchburg, Va.: Schroeder, 2005. Reprint.

Parsons, Elaine Frantz. *Ku-Klux: The Birth of the Klan During Reconstruction.* Chapel Hill: University of North Carolina Press, 2015.

Pendel, Thomas F. *Thirty-Six Years in the White House.* Washington, D.C.: Neale Publishing Company, 1902.

Pepper, George W. *Under Three Flags; or the Story of My Life.* Cincinnati: Curts & Jennings, 1899.

Perret, Geoffrey. *Ulysses S. Grant: Soldier & President.* New York: Random House, 1997.

Perry, Mark. *Grant and Twain: The Story of an American Friendship.* New York: Random House Trade Paperbacks, 2005. Reprint.

Porter, Horace. *Campaigning with Grant.* New York: Mallard Press, 1991. Reprint.

Pryor, Elizabeth Brown, ed. *Reading the Man: A Portrait of Robert E. Lee Through His Private Letters.* New York: Penguin Books, 2007.

Pryor, Mrs. Roger A. *My Day: Reminiscences of a Long Life.* New York: Macmillan, 1909.

Randall, J. G. *Midstream: Lincoln the President.* New York: Dodd, Mead, 1952.

Richardson, Albert D. *A Personal History of Ulysses S. Grant.* Washington, D.C.: National Tribune, 1868.

Rosenheim, Jeff L. *Photography and the American Civil War. The Metropolitan Museum of Art, New York.* New Haven, Conn.: Yale University Press, 2013.

Ross, Ishbel. *The General's Wife: The Life of Mrs. Ulysses S. Grant.* New York: Dodd, Mead, 1959.

Rusk, Ralph L. *The Life of Ralph Waldo Emerson.* New York: Charles Scribner's Sons, 1949.

Sarna, Jonathan D. *When General Grant Expelled the Jews.* New York: Nextbook/Schocken, 2012.

Scaturro, Frank J. *President Grant Reconsidered.* Lanham, Md.: Madison Books, 1999.

Schlesinger, Arthur M., Jr. *The Cycles of American History.* Boston: Houghton Mifflin, 1986.

Schurz, Carl. *Intimate Letters of Carl Schurz.* Edited by Joseph Schafer. Madison: State Historical Society of Wisconsin, 1928.

Shapiro, James, ed. *Shakespeare in America: An Anthology from the Revolution to Now.* New York: Library of America, 2014.

Sheridan, Philip Henry. *Personal Memoirs of P. H. Sheridan, General, United States Army.* 2 vols. New York: Charles L. Webster, 1888.

Sherman, William Tecumseh. *Memoirs of General W. T. Sherman.* New York: Library of America, 1990.

Sherr, Lynn. *Failure Is Impossible: Susan B. Anthony in Her Own Words.* New York: Times Books/Random House, 1995.

Simpson, Brooks D. *Ulysses S. Grant: Triumph over Adversity, 1822–1865.* Boston: Houghton Mifflin, 2000.

Singleton, Esther. *The Story of the White House.* Vol. 2. New York: McClure, 1907.

Smith, Dr. Bob, and Bill Wilson. *Alcoholics Anonymous Big Book.* N.p.: Alcoholics Anonymous World Services, Inc., 2007. Reprint.

Smith, Jean Edward. *Grant.* New York: Simon & Schuster Paperbacks, 2001.

Smith, William Farrar. *From Chattanooga to Petersburg Under Generals Grant and Butler.* Boston: Houghton, Mifflin, 1893.

Snell, Mark. *From First to Last: The Life of General William B. Franklin.* New York: Fordham University Press, 2002.

Stahr, Walter. *Seward: Lincoln's Indispensable Man.* New York: Simon & Schuster, 2012.

———. *Stanton: Lincoln's War Secretary.* New York: Simon & Schuster, 2017.

Stevens, Walter B. *Grant in St. Louis.* St. Louis: Franklin Club of Saint Louis, 1916.

Stiles, T. J. *Custer's Trials: A Life on the Frontier of a New America.* New York: Alfred A. Knopf, 2015.

———. *The First Tycoon: The Epic Life of Cornelius Vanderbilt.* New York: Alfred A. Knopf, 2009.

Stoddard, William O. *Lincoln's Third Secretary: The Memoirs of William O. Stoddard.* Edited by William O. Stoddard Jr. New York: Exposition Press, 1955. Reprint.

Strong, George Templeton. *The Diary of George Templeton Strong.* Vol. 3, *Civil War, 1860–1865.* Edited by Allan Nevins and Milton Halsey Thomas. New York: Macmillan, 1952.

————. *The Diary of George Templeton Strong.* Vol. 4, *Post-War Years, 1865–1875.* Edited by Allan Nevins and Milton Halsey Thomas. New York: Macmillan, 1952.

Sumner, Charles. *Naboth's Vineyard.* Speech in the Senate of the United States, December 21, 1870. Washington, D.C.: F. & J. Rives & Geo. A. Bailey, 1870.

————. *Republicanism vs. Grantism.* Speech in the Senate of the United States, May 31, 1872. Washington, D.C.: F. & J. Rives & Geo. A. Bailey, 1872.

————. *The Selected Letters of Charles Sumner.* Vol. 2. Edited by Beverly Wilson Palmer. Boston: Northeastern University Press, 1990.

Taliaferro, John. *All the Great Prizes: The Life of John Hay, from Lincoln to Roosevelt.* New York: Simon & Schuster, 2013.

Titone, Nora. *My Thoughts Be Bloody: The Bitter Rivalry That Led to the Assassination of Abraham Lincoln.* New York: Free Press, 2010.

Tripler, Eunice. *Some Notes of Her Personal Recollections.* New York: Grafton Press, 1910.

Truman, Margaret. *The President's House: 1800 to the Present.* New York: Ballantine Books, 2005.

Twain, Mark. *The Autobiography of Mark Twain.* Vol. 1. Edited by Harriet Elinor Smith. Berkeley: University of California Press, 2010.

————. *The Autobiography of Mark Twain.* Vol. 2. Edited by Benjamin Griffin and Harriet Elinor Smith. Berkeley: University of California Press, 2013.

————. *The Autobiography of Mark Twain.* Vol. 3. Edited by Benjamin Griffin and Harriet Elinor Smith. Oakland: University of California Press, 2015.

————. *The Letters of Mark Twain.* Fairfield, Iowa: 1st World Library–Literary Society, 2004.

————. *Mark Twain's Notebook.* Edited by Albert Bigelow Paine. New York: Cooper Square Publishers, 1972.

————. *The Selected Letters of Mark Twain.* Edited by Charles Neider. New York: Harper & Row, 1982.

U.S. Congress, *House Testimony Before the Select Committee Concerning the Whiskey Frauds.* 44th Congress, 1st session, House Miscellaneous Document 186.

Vaillant, George E. *The Natural History of Alcoholism.* Cambridge, Mass.: Harvard University Press, 1983.

Varon, Elizabeth R. *Appomattox: Victory, Defeat, and Freedom at the End of the Civil War.* New York: Oxford University Press, 2014.

Vidal, Gore. *1876: A Novel.* New York: Random House, 1976.

————. *United States: Essays 1952–1992.* New York: Random House, 1993.

Ward, Geoffrey C. *A Disposition to Be Rich: How a Small-Town Pastor's Son Ruined an American President, Brought on a Wall Street Crash, and Made Himself the Best-Hated Man in the United States.* New York: Alfred A. Knopf, 2012.

Washburne, Mark. *A Biography of Elihu Benjamin Washburne: Congressman, Secretary of State, Envoy Extraordinary.* Vol. 2, *Illinois Republican During the Civil War and the Rise of Ulysses S. Grant.* N.p.: Xlibris Corporation, 2001.

Waugh, Joan. *U. S. Grant: American Hero, American Myth.* Chapel Hill: University of North Carolina Press, 2009.

Webb, Ross A. *Benjamin Helm Bristow: Border State Politician.* N.p.: University Press of Kentucky, 1969.

Welles, Gideon. *Diary of Gideon Welles, Secretary of the Navy Under Lincoln and Johnson.* 3 vols. Edited by Howard K. Beale. New York: W. W. Norton, 1960.

White, Ronald C. *American Ulysses: A Life of Ulysses S. Grant.* New York: Random House, 2016.

Whitman, Walt. *Prose Works 1892.* Vol. 1, *Specimen Days.* Edited by Floyd Stovall. New York: New York University Press, 1963. Reprint.

————. *Walt Whitman in Camden.* Vol. 6, *September 15, 1889–July 6, 1890.* Edited by Gertrude Traubel and William White. Carbondale: Southern Illinois University Press, 1982.

Wilkerson, Isabel. *The Warmth of Other Suns: The Epic Story of America's Great Migration.* New York: Vintage Books, 2011. Reprint.

Wilson, Edmund. *Patriotic Gore: Studies in the Literature of the American Civil War.* New York: Oxford University Press, 1962.

Wilson, James Grant. *General Grant.* New York: D. Appleton, 1897.

Wilson, James Harrison. *The Life of John A. Rawlins: Lawyer, Assistant Adjutant General, Chief of Staff, Major General of Volunteers, and Secretary of War.* New York: Neale Publishing, 1916.

Wineapple, Brenda. *Ecstatic Nation: Confidence, Crisis, and Compromise, 1848–1877.* New York: HarperCollins, 2013.

Winik, Jay. *April 1865: The Month That Saved America*. New York: Harper Perennial, 2006. Reprint.

Wittenmyer, Annie. *Under the Guns: A Woman's Reminiscences of the Civil War*. Boston: E. B. Stillings, 1895.

Young, John Russell. *Around the World with General Grant*. Baltimore and London: Johns Hopkins University Press, 2002. Reprint.

———. *Men and Memories: Personal Reminiscences*. Vol. 2. New York: F. Tennyson Neely, 1901.

ARTICLES

Achenbach, Joel. "U.S. Grant Was the Great Hero of the Civil War but Lost Favor with Historians." *The Washington Post*, April 24, 2014.

Adams, Henry Brooks. "The New York Gold Conspiracy." *The Westminster Review* 38 (July and October 1870).

———. "The Session." *The North American Review* 111, no. 228 (July 1870).

"Admiral Porter's Letter to Ex-Secretary Welles." *New York Tribune*, December 5, 1870.

"A Grant Party in the South." *The New York Times*, May 24, 1866.

Allen, Suzanne, and Elizabeth Boskey. "The Aftereffects of Alcoholism: Alcoholic Neuropathy." www.healthline.com/health /alcoholism/alcoholic-neuropathy.

Ammen, Daniel. "Recollections and Letters of Grant. Part 1." *The North American Review* 141, no. 347 (October 1885).

———. "Recollections and Letters of Grant. Part 2." *The North American Review* 141, no. 348 (November 1885).

Anderson, Robert. "A New Lincoln Letter." *Chicago Sunday Tribune Magazine*, January 14, 1962.

"An Hour with Gen. Grant." *The New York Times*, May 24, 1866.

"A Presidential Reformer." *The Catholic Record* 10, no. 60 (April 1876).

Ash, Stephen V. "Civil War Exodus: The Jews and Grant's General Orders No. 11." *The Historian* 44 (1982).

"A Trait of Grantism." *New York Tribune,* March 10, 1876.

Badeau, Adam. "The Last Days of General Grant." *Century Illustrated Magazine* 30, no. 6 (October 1885).

Bean, W. G. "Memoranda of Conversations Between General Robert E. Lee and William Preston Johnston." *Virginia Magazine of History and Biography* 73, no. 4 (October 1965).

Beard, Rick. "General Grant Takes a Spill." *Opinionator* (blog), *The New York Times,* September 4, 2013. https://opinionator .blogs.nytimes.com.

Beckwith, Samuel H. "With Grant in the Wilderness, by His 'Shadow.'" *The New York Times*, May 31, 1914.

Berman, Laura. "Finding a Home for Grant House." *The Detroit News*, October 10, 2013.

Bolles, Charles E. "General Grant and the News of Mr. Lincoln's Death." *Century Illustrated Magazine* 40, no. 2 (June 1890).

Boynton, Henry V. "Grant's Liquor Drinking." *New York Sun*, January 23, 1887.

Buinicki, Martin T. "'Average-Representing Grant': Whitman's General." *Walt Whitman Quarterly Review* 26, no. 2 (Fall 2008).

Cadwallader, Sylvanus. "Grant and Rawlins." *The St. Louis Daily Globe-Democrat,* February 11, 1887.

Casey, Emma Dent. "When Grant Went a-Courtin'." Typescript memoir. Missouri History Museum Library, Missouri Historical Society.

Catton, Bruce. "U. S. Grant: Man of Letters." *American Heritage* 19, no. 4 (June 1968).

"Chat in Public Resorts." *New York Tribune,* August 2, 1885.

Chetlain, Augustus L. "Reminiscences of General Grant." *The Magazine of History* 5, no. 4 (April 1907).

Cox, Jacob Dolson. "How Judge Hoar Ceased to Be Attorney-General." *The Atlantic Monthly* 76, no. 455 (July 1895).

Crane, James L. "Grant as a Colonel." *McClure's Magazine* 7, no. 1 (June 1896).

Davis, David Brion. "How They Stopped Slavery: A New Perspective." *The New York Review of Books*, June 6, 2013.

Delbanco, Andrew. "'The Central Event of Our Past': Still Murky." *The New York Review of Books*, February 9, 2012.

———. "The Civil War Convulsion." *The New York Review of Books*, March 19, 2015.

———. "His Own Best Straight Man." *The New York Review of Books*, February 24, 2011.

Deutsch, Abigail. "Lincoln's Legacy." *Carnegie Reporter*, Winter 2012.

Dorsett, Lyle W. "The Problem of Ulysses S. Grant's Drinking During the Civil War." *The Hayes Historical Journal* 4, no. 2 (Fall 1983).

Douglass, Frederick. "U. S. Grant and the Colored People." *Elevator* 8, no. 20 (August 24, 1872).

"English Tributes to General Grant." *The Literary Digest* 15, no. 6 (June 5, 1897).

Fish, Hamilton. "General Grant." *Independent* 37, no. 1913 (July 30, 1885).

Foner, Eric. "The Emancipation of Abe Lincoln." *The New York Times*, January 1, 2013.

———. "'*The Man Who Saved the Union: Ulysses Grant in War and Peace*' by H. W. Brands." *The Washington Post*, November 2, 2012.

Fry, James B. "An Acquaintance with Grant." *The North American Review* 141, no. 349 (December 1885).

Garland, Hamlin. "Grant at the Outbreak of the War." *McClure's Magazine* 9, no. 1 (May 1897).

———. "Grant's Life in Missouri." *McClure's Magazine* 8, no. 6 (April 1897).

———. "Grant's Quiet Years at Northern Posts." *McClure's Magazine* 8, no. 5 (March 1897).

"General Grant and the South." *The New York Times*, July 24, 1885.

Genetin-Pilawa, C. Joseph. "The Indian at Appomattox." *Opinionator* (blog). *The New York Times*, October 17, 2013. https://opinionator.blogs.nytimes.com.

"Gen. Grant's Morality." *Chicago Daily Tribune*, January 27, 1887.

"Gen. Grant's Occasional Intoxication." *New York Sun*, January 28, 1887.

Godkin, E. L. "General Grant's Political Education Abroad." *The Nation* 30, no. 764 (February 19, 1880).

Gold, Charles H. "Grant and Twain in Chicago: The 1879 Reunion of the Army of the Tennessee." *Chicago History* 7, no. 3 (Fall 1978).

"The Gold Ring." *The New York Times*, October 18, 1869.

Grant, Frederick D. "My Father as I Knew Him." *New York World Sunday Magazine*, April 25, 1897.

Grant, Jesse Root. "The Early Life of Gen. Grant." *New York Ledger*, March 7, 1868.

Grant, Ulysses S., Jr. "General Grant's Son Speaks of His Father." *San Diego Daily*, April 24, 1922.

———. "President Grant, My Father, as I Remember Him." *The Bismarck Tribune*, April 27, 1922.

Grant, Ulysses S., III. "Civil War: Fact and Fiction." *Civil War History* 2, no. 2 (June 1956).

"The Grant Family's Cotton Speculations." *New York Tribune*, September 19, 1872.

"Grant Reminiscences." *Chicago Daily Tribune*, September 1, 1885.

"Grant's Drinking Habits." *New York Sun*, January 28, 1887.

"Grant's Only War Speech." *New York Tribune*, September 27, 1885.

"Grant Was Not 'Slouchy' Nor a Drinker, Affirms General's War-Time Secretary." *The Christian Science Monitor*, May 2, 1929.

Green, Anna Maclay. "Civil War Public Opinion of General Grant." *Journal of the Illinois State Historical Society* 22, no. 1 (April 1929).

Greenbaum, Mark. "Lincoln's Do-Nothing Generals." *Disunion* (blog). *The New York Times*, November 27, 2011. https://opinionator.blogs.nytimes.com.

Grinder, Brian, and Dan Cooper. "John Sherman: The Finance General." *Financial History* (Summer 2012).

Groom, Winston. "How Shiloh Changed the Civil War." *The New York Times*, April 8, 2012.

Guelzo, Allen C. "The Civil War's Unlikely Genius." *The Wall Street Journal*, November 2, 2016.

Holzer, Harold. "Lincoln's 'Flat Failure': The Gettysburg Myth Revisited." *History Now* 37 (Fall 2013).

"How Grant Got to Know Rawlins." *Army and Navy Journal* 6, no. 4 (September 12, 1868).

Kazin, Alfred. "The Generals in the Labyrinth." *The New Republic* 204, no. 7 (February 18, 1991).

Kirkpatrick, R. Z. "General Grant in Panama." *The Military Engineer* 26, no. 146 (March–April 1934).

Leitman, Spencer L. "The Revival of an Image: Grant and the 1880 Republican Nominating Campaign." *Missouri Historical Society Bulletin* 30, no. 3 (April 1974).

Levine, Richard R. "Indian Fighters and Indian Reformers: Grant's Indian Peace Policy and the Conservative Consensus." *Civil War History* 31, no. 4 (December 1985).

Lewis, William S. "Reminiscences of Delia B. Sheffield." *Washington Historical Quarterly* 15, no. 1 (January 1924).

"Longstreet's Reminiscences." *The New York Times,* July 24, 1885.

McGhee, James E. "The Neophyte General: U.S. Grant and the Belmont Campaign." *The Missouri Historical Review* 67, no. 4 (July 1973).

McPherson, James M. "America's Wicked War." *The New York Review of Books,* February 7, 2013.

———. "The Bloody Partnership." *The New York Review of Books,* December 15, 2005.

———. "A Bombshell on the American Public." *The New York Review of Books,* November 22, 2012.

———. "Grant: A Biography." *Civil War History* 27, no. 4 (December 1981).

——— "Grant or Greeley? The Abolitionist Dilemma in the Election of 1872." *The American Historical Review* 71, no. 1 (October 1965).

———. "The Great Betrayal." *The New York Review of Books,* November 30, 2006.

———. "Our Monstrous War." *The New York Review of Books,* July 10, 2014.

———. "Specimen Days." *The New York Review of Books,* December 16, 2004.

Maihafer, Harry J. "Mr. Grant and Mr. Dana." *American History* 35, no. 5 (December 2000).

Marszalek, John F. "The Anti-Semite Who Wasn't." *Moment* (March/April 2012).

Montagna, Dennis. "A Different Kind of Civil War Memorial." *The Wall Street Journal,* March 30–31, 2013.

Moore, Ensley. "Grant's First March." *Transactions of the Illinois State Historical Society for the Year 1910,* vol. 15, 1912.

Morgan, Brigadier-General M. R. "From City Point to Appomattox with General Grant." *Journal of the Military Service Institution of the United States* 41, no. 148 (September–October 1907).

"Mr. Orville [*sic*] D. Grant Insane." *The New York Times,* September 5, 1878.

"Mrs. U. S. Grant Sinking." *Chicago Sunday Tribune,* December 14, 1902.

Murthy, Vivek H. "Facing Addiction in the United States: The Surgeon General's Report of Alcohol, Drugs and Health." *Journal of the American Medical Association* 317, no. 2 (January 20, 2017).

Newsham, Major Thomas J. "The Turning Point of the War." *The New York Times,* September 1, 1889.

"New Story of Grant." *The St. Louis Globe-Democrat,* December 13, 1896.

"New York: High Honors Paid to Gen. Grant by the Lotos Club." *Chicago Daily Tribune,* November 21, 1880.

Norman, Geoffrey. "Grant Takes Charge." *The Weekly Standard* 19, no. 28 (March 31–April 7, 2014).

Oakes, James. "A Different Lincoln." *The New York Review of Books,* April 9, 2009.

Olmsted, Frederick Law. "The Genesis of a Rumor." *The Nation* 6, no. 147 (April 23, 1868).

"Overrated and Underrated Americans." *American Heritage* 39, no. 5 (July–August 1988).

Paine, Albert Bigelow. "Mark Twain's Letters." *Harper's Magazine* 135, no. 807 (August 1917).

Parker, Ely S. "General Rawlins." *Report of the Proceedings of the Society of the Army of the Tennessee,* November 17, 1869.

Phifer, Mike. "Wrecking on the Railroad." *Civil War Quarterly* (Early Winter 2016).

Porter, David D. "Secret Missions to San Domingo." *The North American Review* 128, no. 271 (June 1879).

Porter, General Horace. "Lincoln and Grant." *Century Illustrated Magazine* 30, no. 6 (October 1885).

———. "Personal Traits of General Grant." *McClure's Magazine* 2, no. 6 (May 1894).

———. "Reminiscences of General Grant." *Harper's Magazine* 71, no. 424 (September 1885).

Procter, John R. "A Blue and Gray Friendship." *Century Illustrated Magazine* 53, no. 6 (April 1897).

Rawlins, John A. "General Rawlins' Address." *Report of the Proceedings of the Society of the Army of the Tennessee,* Cincinnati, 1877.

Rich, Michael W. "Henry Mack: An Important Figure in Nineteenth-Century American Jewish History." *American Jewish Archives Journal* 47, no. 2 (1995).

Schmitz, Neil. "Doing the Fathers: Gertrude Stein on U. S. Grant in *Four in America.*" *American Literature* 65, no. 4 (December 1993).

Schwartz, Sanford. "The Art of Our Terrible War." *The New York Review of Books,* April 25, 2013.

Sears, Stephen W. "High Stakes at Antietam." *American Heritage* (Summer 2012).

Sherman, William T. "General Sherman's Opinion of General Grant." *Century Illustrated Magazine* 53, no. 6 (April 1897).

Shields, Clara McGeorge. "General Grant at Fort Humboldt in the Early Days." *Humboldt Times* (Eureka, Calif.), November 10, 1912.

Shrady, George F. "The Last Days of Our Great General." *The Saturday Evening Post* 173, no. 33 (February 16, 1901).

Shugerman, Jed Handelsman. "The Creation of the Department of Justice: Professionalization Without Civil Rights or Civil Service." *Stanford Law Review* 66, no. 1 (January 2014).

Simon, John Y. "From Galena to Appomattox: Grant and Washburne." *Journal of the Illinois State Historical Society* 58, no. 2 (1965).

———. "Grant at Belmont." *Military Affairs* 45, no. 4 (December 1981).

———. "Ulysses S. Grant and the Jews: An Unsolved Mystery." *The Record* 21 (1955).

Simpson, Brooks D. "Alexander McClure on Lincoln and Grant." *Lincoln Herald* 95, no. 3 (Fall 1993).

———. "Butcher? Racist? An Examination of William S. McFeely's 'Grant: A Biography.'" *Civil War History* 33, no. 1 (March 1987).

———. "Henry Adams and the Age of Grant." *The Hayes Historical Journal* 8, no. 3 (Spring 1989).

Smith, Scott S. "Gen. William Sherman's Total War Produced Victory." *Investor's Business Daily,* April 23, 2013.

Smith, William Wrenshall. "Holocaust Holiday." *Civil War Times Illustrated* 18, no. 6 (October 1979).

"Speech of General Rawlins." *Army and Navy Journal,* July 13, 1867.

Stevens, John Paul. "The Court & the Right to Vote: A Dissent." *The New York Review of Books,* August 15, 2013.

Stevens, Walter B. "Joseph P. McCullagh . . . Third Article." *The Missouri Historical Review* 25, no. 4 (April 1931).

Stiles, T. J. "A Man of Moral Courage." *The New York Times Book Review,* October 23, 2016.

"Stories of Grant." *Chicago Daily Tribune,* April 12, 1885.

Summers, Mark W. "'To Make the Wheels Revolve We Must Have Grease': Barrel Politics in the Gilded Age." *Journal of Policy History* 14, no. 1 (2002).

Swaim, Barton. "On Being a Southerner." *The New Criterion* (November 2011).

Swinney, Everette. "Enforcing the Fifteenth Amendment, 1870–1877." *The Journal of Southern History* 28, no. 2 (May 1962).

Taussig, William. "Personal Recollections of General Grant." *Missouri Historical Society Publications* 2, no. 3 (1903).

Thayer, John M. "Grant at Pilot Knob." *McClure's Magazine* 5, no. 5 (October 1895).

"The Week." *The Nation* 22, no. 559 (March 16, 1876).

"'This Thankless Office.'" *American History Illustrated* 11, no. 7 (January 1977).

Trombley, Leah. "Grant Cottage: A Treasure Almost Lost." Typescript. Courtesy of The Friends of Grant Cottage.

Truman, Benjamin C. "Anecdotes of Andrew Johnson." *The Century Illustrated Monthly Magazine* 85 (January 1913).

Vincent, John H. "The Inner Life of Ulysses S. Grant." *The Chautauquan* 30, no. 6 (March 1900).

Ward, Ferdinand. "General Grant as I Knew Him." *New York Herald,* December 19 and 26, 1909, and January 2, 9, and 16, 1910.

"Washington." *The New York Times,* October 24, 1869.

"Washington Letter." *The American Israelite* 26, no. 1151 (June 23, 1876); letter signed "Sopher."

Watrous, A. E. "Grant as His Son Saw Him." *McClure's Magazine* 2, no. 6 (May 1894).

Webb, Ross A. "Benjamin H. Bristow: Civil Rights Champion, 1866–1872." *Civil War History* 15, no. 1 (March 1969).

Westwood, Howard C. "Lincoln and the Hampton Roads Peace Conference." *Lincoln Herald* 81 (Winter 1979).

White, Patrick H. "Civil War Diary of Patrick H. White." *Journal of the Illinois State Historical Society* 15, nos. 3–4 (October 1922–January 1923).

Wickenden, Dorothy. "Union Man." *The New Yorker*, October 1, 2012.

Wilentz, Sean. "The Return of Ulysses." *The New Republic*, January 25, 2010.

———. "Who's Buried in the History Books." *The New York Times*, March 14, 2010.

Wills, Garry. "How Lincoln Played the Press." *The New York Review of Books*, November 6, 2014.

"With Grant in Mexico." *The Philadelphia Times*, March 9, 13, and 14, 1880.

Woodward, C. Vann. "The Enigma of U. S. Grant." *The New York Review of Books*, March 19, 1981.

ILLUSTRATION CREDITS

INDEX

Page numbers in *italics* refer to illustrations.

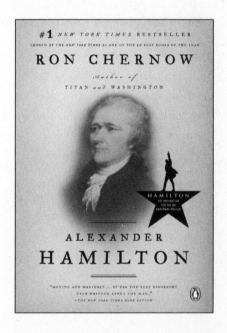

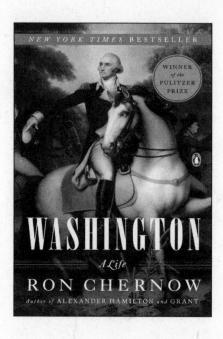